THE END OF THE OLD ORDER

Napoleon and Europe

THE END OF THE OLD ORDER

Napoleon and Europe, 1801–1805

Frederick W. Kagan

Da Capo Press
A Member of the Perseus Books Group

Interior design by Lisa Kreinbrink
Set in 10.5-point AGaramond

Cataloging-in-Publication data for this book is available from the Library of Congress.
10 ISBN 0–306–81137–5
13 ISBN 0–306–81137–1
Published by Da Capo Press
A Member of the Perseus Books Group
http://www.dacapopress.com

Da Capo Press books are available at special discounts for bulk purchases in the U.S. by
corporations, institutions, and other organizations. For more information, please contact
the Special Markets Department at the Perseus Books Group, 11 Cambridge Center,
Cambridge, MA 02142, or call (800)255–1514 or (617) 252–5298, or email
special.markets@perseusbooks.com

1   2   3   4   5   6   7   8   9/08   07   06   05   04

For my father,
*who taught me everything I know about being
a good historian and a good man.*

Contents

Abbreviations

VPR	Vneshniaia Politika Rossii, Series I
SIRIO	Sbornik Imperatorskago Russkago Istoricheskago Obshchestva
AKV	Arkhiv Kniazia Vorontsova
Corr. de Nap	Correspondance de Napoléon ler
SVM	Stolietie voennago ministerstva, 1802–1902
RGVIA	Russkii Gosudarstvennyi Voenno-Istoricheskii Arkhiv (Moscow)
GARF	Glavnyi Arkhiv Russkoi Federatsii (Moscow)
SHAT	Service Historique de l'Armée de Terre (Vincennes)
AN	Archive Nationale (Paris)
KA	Kriegsarchiv (Vienna)
HHSt	Haus-, Hof-, und Staatsarchiv (Vienna)
GStA	Geheime Staatsarchiv (Berlin)
HKR	Hofkriegsrat (in Austrian Kriegsarchiv)
AFA	Alte Feldakten (in Austrian Kriegsarchiv)
FML	Feldmarshal-Leutnant (Austrian military rank equivalent to full general, just below Field Marshal)

Maps

Key to Military Map Symbols

Unit Sizes

⊠ Platoon

⊠ Company/Troop/Battery

⊠ Battalion/Squadron

⊠ Regiment

⊠ Brigade

⊠ Division

⊠ Corps

⊠ Army

Unit Types

⊠ Infantry

◻ Cavalry

⊡ Artillery

▦ Light Infantry/Skirmishers

◩ Horse Artillery

Nationalities

⊠ French

◣ Russian

◿ Prussian

◤ Austrian

◪ Spanish

▥ British

⊠ Other French allies

◩ Other coalition allies

Acknowledgments

This volume is the result of more than seven years of effort, and in all that time there has hardly been a moment when it did not bring me joy. The pleasure it has given me came partly from the subject matter and partly from the support, encouragement, and assistance of innumerable mentors, colleagues, friends, and helpers. I could not possibly have completed it without them.

Dennis Showalter, Linda Frey, and Marsha Frey have been invaluable friends and advisers for many years. Discussions with them helped refine my approach to the topic, understanding of the period, grasp of the sources, and intellectual growth. Their support and encouragement, including their willingness to read large portions of the manuscript, were essential, and I am grateful for their help and friendship.

Most of this work was prepared (on my own time) while I was teaching military history at the U.S. Military Academy at West Point. I could never have undertaken this project without the intellectual preparation I received from that experience, both from the generations of cadets I had the privilege of teaching and from the many colleagues from whom I had the privilege of learning. I am particularly grateful to the leaders of the History Department for their support of my endeavors over the years: Brigadier Generals (Retired) Robert A. Doughty and Casey Brower, Colonels Lance Betros, Cole Kingseed, and Matthew Moten, and Lieutenant Colonel Steve Arata.

I was also blessed to teach alongside of some of the sharpest intellects in the military, especially Colonel H. R. McMaster; Lieutenant Colonels Ty Seidule, Chris Kolenda, and Gunner Sepp; and my fellow *napoléonien*, Major Jim Haynsworth. From them I learned more about the nature and art of war than any amount of study could have taught me. It was my particular good fortune to be able to lead the officers and warrant officers of the 1st Squadron of the 4th U.S. Cavalry Regiment, under the command of H. R. McMaster, on a staff ride of the Austerlitz battlefield, and to accompany the officers of the Rear Detachment of the 1st Infantry Division, under the command of Chris Kolenda, on a staff ride to Jena and Auerstedt. I was also thrilled to be able to examine the various battlefields around Ulm with three of my former cadets, Andrea Twitchell, Matt Caldwell, and Wynne Beers. The experience of reviewing these marvelously well-preserved battlefields with such experienced, educated, and professional soldiers was unforgettable, and played no small part in my developing understanding of those battles.

I am also grateful to General (Retired) Christian Delanghe, of the French Armée de Terre, his wife, Arlette, and his lovely family. The Delanghes made me welcome in France and offered invaluable advice and support, along with their own brilliant hospitality. Francziska Thiery, the delightful proprietress of the Hotel Richard Löwenherz in Dürnstein, provided not only a lovely place to stay in the beautiful Wachau region of Austria, but valuable advice about sources and local history relating to the Battle of Dürnstein. Her nephew, Dr. Gottfried Thiery, was kind enough to send a narrative of the battle held by the Dürnstein Parish.

The extensive archival research this project required could have been a nightmare, but was not because of the extraordinarily helpful staff of the Österreichisches Kriegsarchiv in Vienna and the Service Historique de l'Armée de Terre in Vincennes. In Vienna, I was particularly fortunate to have the assistance of Dr. Rainer Egger, the former director of the archive, and Karl Rossa, who cheerfully brought me invaluable materials I would never have found on my own. I am especially grateful to Mr. Rossa for his help in locating the account of the Austrian exercises of 1804, held on what would become the Austerlitz battlefield a year later.

The work of compiling the necessary resources would nevertheless have been insurmountable but for the assistance of several research assistants: Alexandra Grigorieva and Andrey Ganin in Russia, Dave Beffert and Eleanora Sharef in Germany, and Sylvain Dray in Paris. All were indefatigable in navigating the complex bureaucracies of French, Russian, and German archives, and in locating critical materials and sending copies to me. I cannot express sufficient gratitude for their efforts on my behalf.

That this project took only seven years is the result of generous financial support from the Earhardt Foundation, the John M. Olin Foundation, and the U.S. Military Academy's Faculty Development Research Fund, all of which paid for extensive travel, photocopying, and, in the case of the Olin Foundation, a year's leave of absence to devote myself to this project.

I must also thank John Radziewicz and Bob Pigeon of Da Capo for their patience and support. All authors conclude their acknowledgments by noting that any flaws remaining are their own, and that is more true of this work than of most. I am inexpressibly grateful that John and Bob and their colleagues have been flexible and creative in their approach to this project, always encouraging me not to make any sacrifices that would diminish the quality of the work, even as the manuscript grew large and numerous deadlines passed. Any remaining flaws in this work have persisted despite their best efforts.

Finally, I must thank my family for their continued support, encouragement, and assistance. A lengthy manuscript inevitably means long disquisitions on the most obscure details of history, and my family has borne many such hours with grace and insight. My wife, Kim, accompanied me on many a dreary archival venture, to countless minor battlefields, and through every step of the intellectual voyage. I will always be glad, above all, that she suggested I undertake this project in the first place. My father, Donald, read every word of the manuscript, frequently more than once, and helped me as always to develop my understanding and my approach. Whatever is meaningful in that approach came from him. My mother, Myrna, watched another member of her family struggle through a massive historical study without flinching, and with constant support and encouragement. And I have enjoyed and benefited from the camaraderie of fighting through my own multivolume history as my brother, Bob, did the same.

I can only conclude by hoping that this work brings the reader as much pleasure in the exploring as it gave me in the writing.

Introduction
to Napoleon
and Europe

Carl von Clausewitz offered several definitions of war in his masterful treatise. War is a duel. It is the use of force to compel the enemy to do one's bidding. It is like a wrestling match in which the position of each side depends on the position of the other. It is a trinity composed of primordial violence, hatred, and enmity; reason; and chance. It is an extension of politics by other means. Considering the brilliance of Clausewitz's work, the ambiguity and diversity of his definition is remarkable—and appropriate. For war is the most complex human undertaking, involving all the activities of peaceful human society and the ever-present danger of death and destruction as well.

The Napoleonic Wars shaped much of Clausewitz's thought. They were the library he mined most frequently for historical examples to illustrate his theories of strategy, tactics, and the art of command. To Clausewitz, the Napoleonic Wars revealed not simply the genius of Napoleon but also the complexity of war and the interrelationships between war and politics.

Yet the Napoleonic Wars have largely gone into history in a more simplistic fashion. Military historians, following Clausewitz's contemporary, Baron Antoine Henri de Jomini, focus primarily on the military operations. They attempt to explain Napoleon's early victories and ultimate defeat primarily in terms of the numerous battlefields of the day. Social, political, diplomatic, and economic historians, on the other hand, normally make only the most basic references to the military events of the time.

But Clausewitz had the keener insight. The study of war cannot be divorced from the study of politics, diplomacy, society, and economics. All are interrelated in the minds of the decisionmakers, and all interact in the physical world as well. Any attempt to study one aspect of human activity in isolation from the others will ensure a partial and distorted understanding of that area. It is not enough simply to say that war is an extension of politics. Understanding war also requires understanding the politics of which it is an extension. Clausewitz even took this principle so far as to recommend that senior generals be allowed to sit in on policy discussions, not so that they could influence the discussion but so that it could influence their decisions.[1]

Clausewitz's insight was nothing revolutionary in the Napoleonic age. The distinction between politics and war did not seem so clear in a time when many political leaders took the field with their armies on the day of battle. Many generals were high nobles with powerful voices in the domestic affairs of their states, and it would have seemed foolish to imagine that they would put political matters aside when going to war. The real separation of war and politics was a product of a later age. It came with the rise of a sense of military professionalism driven by the growth of general staffs that attempted to exclude the influence of amateurs in military decisions. The struggle between Otto von Bismarck and Helmuth von Moltke the Elder was the apotheosis of this tendency in the nineteenth century, and the effects of that duel are felt around the world to this day.

To read a civil–military dichotomy back into the pre-Moltkean world is inappropriate, whether it is done explicitly or by default, when war and politics are considered in isolation from each other. It strips the Napoleonic experience of some of its most profound lessons about how war actually works—lessons that the Bismarck–Moltke struggle and its aftermath have largely obscured.

What is the relationship among domestic politics, international relations, and war? What role do individuals and their personalities play in driving the course of events? How do states come together in coalitions? What makes those alliances strong or weak? What makes them succeed or fail? How important are the "great men" of history compared to their numberless subjects, fellow citizens, and subordinates? How can there be so little correlation between military victory and political success? These questions, so important in the world today, belong at the heart of the study of the Napoleonic Wars, which offer many valuable insights into them.

In his efforts to learn from the great wars of his epoch Clausewitz had another advantage—he was not French and did not idolize Napoleon. Although he called the emperor "the god of war," he did not study the wars to discern the keys to Napoleon's genius that he and others might imitate them. He cited Napoleon's mistakes and the mistakes of his enemies as often as Napoleon's brilliance; and if he distilled from Napoleonic practice certain key concepts, he did not thereby imagine that Napoleon always executed those concepts in the best possible way.

This detachment from the greatest hero of the age was critical in allowing Clausewitz to evaluate the events of the wars more objectively and establish his own valuable insights based on that evaluation. No figure in history has distorted his own era as much as Napoleon did. No other great wars of the modern world bear the name of the leader of a single belligerent. Despite his small physical stature, the image of Napoleon bestrides the first fifteen years of the nineteenth century like a colossus, compelling all who would look at that epoch to chart their course by reference to him.

This hero worship is not an accidental development. Napoleon deliberately sowed it and nurtured it throughout his life. Napoleon was even more successful as a propagandist than as a general. On the battlefield, he lost almost as many fights as he won. In the pages of history, however, he lost only one: Waterloo. Exiled to St. Helena after that battle, Napoleon was hardly able to influence how contemporaries perceived the story of that fight. Had he been permitted to do so, there can be little doubt that it would now be celebrated in France as yet another great military victory followed by an inexplicable political disaster. Even the catastrophe of 1812 is commonly and erroneously presented as a campaign Napoleon lost without ever losing a battle.

For Napoleon brilliantly divorced his military victories from their political contexts in public, even as he carefully wove the two together in his own thoughts and actions. To the people of France and Europe Napoleon portrayed his wars as an endless search for the glory France rightly deserved. This theme of glory, which he used to replace the French revolutionary calls to liberty, equality, and brotherhood, seemed to make war a good in its own right. His military successes justified themselves; his setbacks demanded vengeance to efface the slur on France's honor and his own. According to his propaganda, the wars of his era were started by hostile, suspicious, and jealous enemies or by weak-willed and perfidious allies, seduced into fighting him by those implacable foes.

Napoleon invoked the rhetorical traditions of the French Revolution, which he terminated and partly reversed when he seized power, to explain the hostility of the rest of the continent. He perpetuated the myth of "reactionary" Europe, unwilling to accept the "new order" in France and fearful that he would destroy the tyrannical hold Europe's feudal lords still held over their subjects. Napoleon's propaganda was so skillful (and his opponents' so inept) that echoes of this myth are still heard today. Many think that Europe's fearful, resentful monarchs attacked Napoleon in efforts to destroy the French Revolution, which they detested, and restore the Bourbon monarchy, which had long been their cherished dream. Only Napoleon's brilliance on the battlefield— and their own military incompetence bred from their hidebound conservatism—kept this nightmare from descending on France for fifteen years. So the popular version goes.

Napoleon's success in perpetrating these myths is neither surprising nor unusual. From earliest times, historians and their readers have often identified too closely with their subjects. Thucydides' excessive veneration of the flawed Pericles was the first such distortion in histories, and countless others followed. Napoleon was at once so attractive and repellant, so successful and such a failure, that his ambiguity is endlessly intriguing.

It is a mistake, however, to succumb to Napoleon's charms without giving his adversaries their fair chance at seduction, even if they do not initially elicit our sympathy. The grim visage of Austria's Emperor Francis reflects the disillusionment of a man who has presided over the collapse of the position his empire held in the world for more than a decade. King Frederick William III of Prussia is less off-putting in physiognomy but more so in personality, steeped in a Pietist tradition that kept him continually focused on his own failings. King George III of Britain, half mad, attracts few admirers, particularly in this era, and his even more unstable son, the future Prince Regent and then George IV, is almost repulsive. Only Tsar Alexander I of Russia is both attractive and engaging, but his youth, inexperience, and callowness at times strike jarring notes even so.

A closer examination reveals a more engaging picture. Each monarch reigned at the time of greatest crisis in his realm. All, apart from George III, were educated in the traditions of the Enlightenment and had a deeper sense of obligation to their subjects than almost any of their predecessors had. They contemplated the suffering that followed the internal and external wars, coups d'état, and cataclysms of the 1790s with real pain, and they found nothing to celebrate in the prospect of war with Napoleon. There have been few coalitions of states initially less willing to fight than the Third and Fourth Coalitions that attacked Napoleon in 1805 and 1806.

To look through the eyes of Europe's monarchs at the beginning of the nineteenth century is to see a world of fear, danger, responsibility, and limited opportunities. We are familiar with Napoleon's struggle to gain power and his struggle to remake Europe to his liking. For too long, however, his towering figure has obscured his adversaries' desperate and tormented struggle to fulfill their obligations to their subjects, preserve their states and their power, and seek to implement the high ideals inculcated into them as young men. The tragedy of their failure to do so is no less engaging than Napoleon's fall—and considerably more important for the subsequent history of Europe and the world as it actually developed.

Napoleon's shadow has also covered the opponents who fought him on the battlefield. We are more than familiar with Arthur Wellesley, Duke of Wellington. But for too many, Mikhail Kutuzov remains the ponderous, dim-witted, slow-moving, elemental representation of the Russian peasant evoked so movingly and inaccurately by Leo Tolstoy. The hapless Austrian Field Marshal Lieutenant Karl von Mack has passed into history as a stupid blunderer whose character, background, and personality merit no attention. That he was virtually the only senior general in any army of the time who was born a commoner and rose from the enlisted ranks to effective overall command of an army escapes notice. The effects of his background on his personality and performance in the critical days of 1805 are, therefore, also largely unknown.

Austrian historians have long lionized Archduke Charles, Francis's younger brother, as the only authentic military genius of the Habsburg army of the day, attempting to set him up as an anti-Napoleon who would have brought victory to Austria much sooner if only he had been heeded. These efforts to counter one great man with another have generated distortions of their own, however, concealing the blemishes of this manic-depressive, epileptic archduke behind the still greater flaws of his contemporaries.

The colorless depiction that most of Napoleon's adversaries receive in the histories of this period creates a curious problem: if they were all so weak and incompetent, how is it that Napoleon ultimately lost? The customary answer is a throwback to the tragic heroes of the ancients. Napoleon's hubris and arrogance, qualities essential to his early success, ultimately got the better of him and led him to a series of mistakes that caused his downfall. Some are unwilling to go even that far, attributing his failure to the ailments that affected him at the battles of Borodino and Waterloo or even to "General Winter": Russia's wretched climate.

The focus on the great man imposes its highest price at this point. If Napoleon lost his wars because of physical infirmity or intractable climes, then the modern student of war or politics has little to learn. One would like to find more meaning in the campaign of 1812 than the advice that invading Russia is unwise or that the physical condition of leaders is important.

But Napoleon did not lose his wars by himself or with the help of the weather alone; his adversaries won them. The allies developed new methods of organizing and using their armies, largely in response to Napoleon's exploits. His continental foes aped what they saw as key aspects of Napoleon's military system in order to defeat him. Massive reform programs in Prussia and Russia were supposed to make their armies more French while the Austrians incorporated Frenchness in a lesser degree and more gradually. Perhaps the allies defeated Napoleon by becoming Napoleon.

This simple explanation is also inadequate, however. The allied armies of 1813–1815 were not that different from those of 1805–1807. They were marginally restructured and reorganized, but the advantages of those "new" organizations were far fewer than is generally supposed. For the armies of 1805–1807 were not badly organized to begin with. Myth has it that in 1805 the allies fought Napoleon with eighteenth-century armies that were far behind the Grande Armée in virtually every important technique and characteristic. They relied, it is said, on closed-rank formations where the French relied on skirmishers. They marched in shapeless masses where the French marched in independent corps. They relied on cumbersome supply systems while the French lived off the land. They were thus slower, less flexible, and less effective on the battlefield than the "modernized" French troops.

None of these myths has serious grounding in reality. Beginning in 1805, Napoleon's enemies organized their armies into all-arms corps. Except for the

Prussians, they used skirmishers as extensively as the French did—because the French army of Napoleon's day used skirmishers far less than the armies of the French Revolution had. And in 1805, as we shall see, the Austrian army that met Napoleon in southern Germany did so without magazines and with plans to live off the land—as the French did. Napoleon made every effort in that campaign to establish a sophisticated supply system, and his army ended up living off the land only because he failed to do so. Once again, structural explanations of improvements in the allied armies will not suffice.

The real story of the coalitions that fought Napoleon lies not in their increasing military prowess but in their growing skills as members of a coalition. It was a political improvement. Ultimately the translation of that political growth into military power at the higher levels of war led to allied successes in 1813, 1814, and 1815. British troops at the battle of Waterloo fought no better than they had fought for years before in Spain. And the same General Blücher who led the Prussian troops onto that bloody field at just the right moment had made some of the disastrous decisions leading to Prussia's 1806 defeat at Auerstedt. How the Prussians fought at Waterloo mattered less than the fact that they were present at all—a fact that resulted from a decade of painful lessons about how allies should and should not behave in the face of danger.

The greatest value in studying the Napoleonic Wars today lies in the objective evaluation of the major players, the interactions among key figures within states, and the interactions of states and armies. Clausewitz identified the complexity of war and its inextricable interrelationship with politics, but he was a warrior and military theorist who had no time to explore the politics in any detail. The goal of this and subsequent volumes is to present an integrated diplomatic, military, and political history of the Napoleonic period worthy of Clausewitz's insight. The reader must judge its success.

THE END OF THE
OLD ORDER

Introduction to
The End of the Old Order

The roots of the Napoleonic Wars are entangled with the fundamental political and philosophical transformations of the eighteen century, including the French Revolution as well as an array of events and ideas unconnected with it. Shifting relationships among the powers, including the advent of Prussia as a great power, dramatically changed European politics in midcentury. The complicated development and spread of Enlightenment ideas throughout Europe changed the way people and rulers thought about politics. The political causes of the Napoleonic Wars date from the first years of the nineteenth century, and the spark that ignited the first conflict in 1805 predated hostilities by months. Yet the origins of these wars and the wars themselves cannot be understood outside of their longer historical context.

Accounts of the Napoleonic Wars customarily begin in 1805 with the outbreak of the first war or sometime in the late 1790s, when Napoleon made his name during the campaigns in Italy. These starting points make sense only from Napoleon's perspective. He and his many admirers take an interest only when he comes on the scene, describing the history that preceded his arrival in cursory fashion. But the world did not begin anew when Napoleon seized power in France. His coup d'état occurred in the middle of a war he did not begin, and he found himself embroiled in not only military operations he had not designed but political situations with histories stretching back for decades. To his adversaries, Napoleon's coup was one in a long line of French domestic political upheavals whose significance was not immediately apparent.

Several historical accidents combined to make France seem more central to the development of European history in the eighteenth century than it actually was. Americans are familiar with the French from this period as adversaries in the French and Indian War and as essential allies in the American Revolutionary War. The political significance and emotional appeal of the French Revolution for democratically minded Americans also makes that event seem seem like the focal point of European politics in the 1790s.

In the great struggles beyond Europe in the eighteenth century, France was one pole opposing the aspiring naval hegemony of Great Britain. Within Europe, however, the Franco–British rivalry was peripheral to a more important struggle between Austria and Prussia for the mastery of Germany and central Europe in the second part of the century.

This struggle began in 1740, when the Habsburg Emperor Charles V died and left his throne to his daughter, Maria Theresa. At nearly the same time, Frederick II, soon to be known as Frederick the Great, succeeded to the Prussian throne and attacked the Habsburg province of Silesia. Frederick hoped to expand his kingdom and place it among the great powers of Europe. Misogynist that he was, he believed that despoiling Maria Theresa would be easy. His attack plunged Europe into the eight-year War of the Austrian Succession and then, following another eight years of peace, into the Seven Years War (which extended into America as the French and Indian War). Although both Austria and Prussia emerged from this cataclysm exhausted, Prussia made a significant long-term gain because Frederick carried off Silesia in the end. Henceforth, Berlin and Vienna saw each other as mortal foes.

The Habsburgs were more or less comfortable in their position as leaders of Germany before 1740, even if their partial defeat during the War of the Spanish Succession (1701–1714) ended their hopes of a more expansive European empire. The peace and stability of central Europe had rested on their comfortable leadership, since the conservative Habsburgs had largely worked to defend the myriad smaller states of the Holy Roman Empire (which they ruled throughout this period, apart from a lapse between 1740 and 1745) against larger predators such as Prussia. The loss of Silesia destroyed that equilibrium. Maria Theresa and especially her son and coruler, Joseph II, felt that the monarchy had been seriously weakened and sought ways of strengthening it. Joseph cast his gaze on Bavaria, the largest of the remaining second-tier states in Germany that ran along Austria's western border. An abortive effort to exchange Bavaria for the Austrian Netherlands (what is now Belgium), cut off from the body of the Habsburg lands and exposed to French attack, led to a renewal of war with Prussia in 1778–1779 (the War of the Bavarian Succession). For the first time in decades, the other states of Europe saw Austria as a predator and found in the archpredator, Frederick, the upholder of the status quo and the rights of small states. This odd turnabout further weakened the Austrians by alienating some of their former friends in the empire and strengthening Frederick still more.

Upon his accession to sole rule in 1780, Joseph embarked on a misguided attempt to repair the damage to Austria from the inside out. He launched a series of reforms designed to centralize Habsburg control over the diverse and semiautonomous lands of the Habsburg Empire (Austria, Hungary, much of the Balkans, northern Italy, and Belgium—as distinct from the Holy Roman

Empire, which encompassed all of Germany but none of the non-German lands) and to homogenize the government of all of those lands. The attempt naturally backfired, as nobles throughout the empire resisted and even brought out their subjects in defense of the old order. When Joseph died in 1790, significant portions of the empire were in open revolt, and his successor, Leopold II, spent the two years of his brief reign quelling the insurgency and restoring the older ways in an effort to placate his rebellious subjects. Joseph's efforts had led only to the further erosion of Austria's power and position within Europe.

Despite the territorial gains of the Silesian Wars and the gains in prestige occasioned by the War of the Bavarian Succession, Prussia entered the last decade of the eighteenth century as a weak state. Frederick had emptied the treasury and exhausted the state in his struggles against France, Austria, and Russia. The continued maintenance of an army large enough to be taken seriously on the basis of the smallest population in Europe was a heavy burden on a poor state. Prussia's geostrategic position also remained parlous. The core territories were in the middle of Europe (centered on Berlin and Danzig) near both Austria and Russia. The kingdom's population and resources were to a significant extent scattered across western Germany piecemeal, isolated from one another and vulnerable to predation. The westernmost bordered France. The monarchy's position in Europe was so poor that discussions about Prussian policy in Berlin usually began, "One has only to look at the map . . . "

Worse still, Frederick had adopted a deliberate policy of bluff after 1763 in an effort to reduce the expense of being a first-class power on a second-class base. He returned the conscripted Prussian soldiers to their homes after the war and hired mercenaries instead. He retired the various nonnoble generals who had demonstrated so much talent and gained so much experience in his wars and replaced them with inexperienced noblemen. He focused his army on spit-and-polish parade ground drills less because he thought such exercises would improve their fighting skills than because the parades provided opportunities to impress visiting dignitaries with the simulacrum of Prussian military strength. Frederick's successors, more cautious and timid than he, thus reigned fully conscious of their own weakness, the fragility of their state, and the dangers besetting it. The Austro-Prussian struggles left both states drained, resentful, suspicious, and fearful.

No state suffered more between 1740 and 1790 than France. The start of the eighteenth century had seen Louis XIV's kingdom engaged in a struggle for control of the continent. Exhausted by the War of the Spanish Succession, Louis XV settled down to consolidate and rebuild. Sensing opportunity in Frederick's predation of 1740, Louis XV joined the Prussian king in attacking Austria. But once Frederick gained control of Silesia, he left the fight and abandoned Louis to the struggle against Austria and Great Britain. In so doing, he created a reputation of perfidiousness and treachery that haunted

Prussian kings for decades. In the renewed struggle of the Seven Years War, France and Britain changed sides. Now Louis supported Austria and Russia against Prussia and Great Britain. The result was again a disaster for France. French armies were humiliated on the continent, and British fleets and small armies swept away most of France's overseas colonies. The British emerged from the struggle well on the road toward maritime supremacy and extra-European hegemony; France was exhausted.

The American Revolution occasioned the beginning of the final collapse of the French monarchy. Louis thought he saw an opportunity to weaken Britain by supporting her rebellious colonies. Although French help allowed the colonies to break away, Britain was not as weakened as expected. On the other hand, the effort bankrupted France and led to the series of abortive economic and political reforms that created the preconditions for the French Revolution. By 1790, in the early days of that revolution, France had slipped into irrelevance on the continent and abroad. Other European powers initially responded to this development with pleasure—a weakened France, they thought, created new opportunities to recover from their own weakness and recoup recent losses.

Apart from Britain, only Russia fared well in the decades between the Seven Years War and the revolution in France. Tsaritsa Elizabeth, the implacable foe of Frederick the Great, died in 1762 and her son, the Prussophile Peter III, acceded to the throne and left the war before the Romanov empire became exhausted. Soon Peter was assassinated and was succeeded by his wife, Catherine II, who dramatically expanded Russian power. In a series of struggles against Russia's traditional enemies—Sweden, Poland, and the Ottoman Empire—Catherine expanded Russia's borders, resources, and prestige. She also brought Russia into the circle of European great powers and out of its centuries-long semi-isolation on the eastern fringe of Europe. The apotheosis of this Europeanization of Russia came when Catherine signed the Treaty of Teschen, which ended the War of the Bavarian Succession, as a guarantor. She thereby became a coguarantor of the Holy Roman Empire and earned a seat at virtually any conference called among the great powers to discuss European affairs. Between 1763 and 1790, therefore, power in Europe began to shift toward the periphery and away from the exhausted center. Virtually all observers thought that the outbreak of revolution in France would intensify this trend.

The French Revolution and European Reaction

The French Revolution is a complex phenomenon with manifold roots. The social injustice popularized in histories and novels played a role, to be sure. But the archaic economic and political structures of France combined with the financial crisis resulting from the series of failed wars described above set the stage for the crisis that brought down the monarchy. The significance of the revolution for Europe was primarily twofold. The further weakening of French power shifted the focus of European politics eastward, while the ideals espoused with increasing vigor and radicalism by the revolutionaries seemed to threaten the more conservative regimes of the continent.

The emotional impact of the French Revolution and the propaganda skills of the revolutionaries affected the historiography of this period just as Napoleon influenced his own age. The popular view has accepted the idea that other monarchs viewed the French Revolution as the most important event in Europe and that those "reactionary" rulers were innately hostile to the Enlightenment concepts espoused by the revolutionaries. Neither idea is true.

The issue that preoccupied the rulers of Prussia, Austria, and Russia between 1791 and 1796 was not France but Poland.[1] The Russian and Austrian victory over the Ottoman Empire in 1792, combined with the collapse of French power after the Revolution, deprived Poland of its two staunchest defenders. The Polish kingdom was internally riven and poorly organized to defend itself, so the loss of outside sponsors spelled its final doom. In 1793, therefore, Frederick William II of Prussia and Catherine the Great of Russia agreed to the Second Partition of Poland (the first had come in 1772, at the end of a Russo–Turkish War begun four years earlier), which greatly truncated the Polish monarchy.

Emperor Francis II of Austria, who took the throne in 1792 following the death of his father, Leopold, had opposed the partition on principle and for sound reasons of state. Conscious of the weakness of his empire, Francis was content to maintain a weak buffer state on his frontiers and prevent Austria's archenemy, Prussia, and potential foe, Russia, from gaining power at his expense. But the French revolutionaries had declared war on Austria, as the nearest and most accessible of their potential enemies (and also because Francis was the brother of the hated French queen, Marie Antoinette), and Francis could spare no troops to fight Catherine and Frederick William even had he wanted to. As a result, the partition went ahead and Austria gained nothing from it.

Attempts by Polish nationalists to revive their land in the two years following that partition provided the pretext for the elimination of the Polish state in the Third Partition of 1795. Once more Catherine and Frederick William agreed on their goals and means, but this time Francis decided that he could not afford to lose out again. He therefore joined the coalition to destroy the vestiges of the hapless Polish monarchy and was rewarded with the largest share of the remaining territory.

With so much potential wealth at stake in the partitions and nothing of value at stake in the fight against revolutionary France (no one imagined that victory would lead to meaningful annexations), the rulers of the continent paid more attention to the east than the west, even if that decision seems odd to us in retrospect. When Frederick William sent the Duke of Brunswick marching with an army against the French in 1792, therefore, his heart and his effort were not in that fight. His decision after the French victory that year at Valmy—to abandon the struggle against France—implicitly recognized that, compared to Poland, the game in the west was not worth the candle.

Francis could not abandon that fight so lightly, however, because French revolutionary armies overran the Austrian Netherlands (Belgium) in 1793 and held on to that Habsburg province despite efforts by Francis to recover it. The Prussian abandonment of the First Coalition against France seemed another act of opportunistic betrayal similar to Frederick's withdrawal from his alliance with France in 1742. The Prussian treaty with France of 1795 thus reinforced the predominant view that Prussia's rulers could not be trusted. It also committed Frederick William II and his successor, Frederick William III, to a policy of neutrality in the wars against France that they had pursued for a decade.

It also emphasized Austria's predicament. Consistently weakened over the course of the previous half century, Austria was on the front lines in any struggle against France because of the geographic proximity of her western-most provinces; also, the French revolutionaries believed the Habsburgs to be their most determined continental foes. In the 1790s, as in the wars against Napoleon, Francis generally suffered from the fact that he needed his allies more than they needed him. They could choose to fight France or not; he had no such luxury. This fact of European geopolitics shaped the course of the next twenty years of history.

But if the French revolutionaries (or subsequent students of the period) thought that Francis was ideologically committed against them because of their Enlightenment convictions, they were wrong. His reaction to the Enlightenment and the French Revolution, like that of other monarchs, was more complicated than that.

To understand that reaction, we must recall that the Enlightenment itself displayed great variety. The British Enlightenment, the French *Eclairissement*, and the German *Aufklärung* were separate but related phenomena. In addition, individual thinkers emphasized different aspects of Enlightenment thought. Some focused on political economy, others on individual liberties, still others on the role of reason or the relationship between individuals and societies. These different emphases allowed rulers (and others) to choose selectively and synthetically among them to support desired arguments.

Although the Enlightenment seemed hostile to the concepts and practices of autocracy and divine-right kingship, clever rulers such as Frederick the Great, Catherine the Great, and Joseph II recognized that they could accommodate elements of the Enlightenment without compromising their autocratic powers. These "enlightened despots" were no less omnipotent than their divine-right predecessors had been, but they cloaked their despotism in the guise of Enlightenment principles that would preserve order and prosperity within their states.

The children and grandchildren of the enlightened despots—especially the generation of monarchs that included Francis I, Frederick William III, and Alexander I—took an even more complex view. These rulers were powerfully molded by tutors who believed in certain Enlightenment ideals. The three monarchs in training were taught that the sovereign is the servant of his people, that he must judge according to their needs and not his own, and that all subjects of the state, even the ruler, must obey the law. Alexander's tutor taught him to respect, value, and seek constitutionalism; Frederick William and Francis were persuaded that a social contract bound them to their subjects.

These men were not predisposed to look kindly on the ruthless, boundless autocracy Louis XVI attempted to defend in old-regime France, which was among the most politically backward states on the continent in 1789. Nor were they conditioned to view harshly the early efforts of the French nobility, or even of the nonnoble elements of the Estates General that Louis had convened, to persuade the king to accept restrictions on his power that their upbringing had taught them were appropriate for any monarch.

The real opposition of Europe's rulers to the French Revolution sprang from the lawlessness and violence into which it descended in 1791, epitomized by the seizure, trial, and execution of the king and queen, and the revolutionaries' declaration of war on the crowned heads of Europe starting with Austria in 1792.

The implacability Francis showed in the decade-long struggle against Revolutionary France rested on even more pragmatic grounds: the war effectively began with the French seizing Austrian territory and continued as Francis tried vainly to get it back. Although Catherine the Great attempted to justify both her gains in Poland and her refusal to send troops against France by claiming to be fighting Jacobism in eastern Europe, no one was deceived. And if Francis permitted his subordinates to arrest and try suspected Jacobins in Austria, he also insisted on allowing normal legal processes to work, often to their advantage. He was determined not to violate his own Enlightenment principles while attempting to stamp out the violent revolutionary radicalism that he deplored. Catherine and Frederick William II were the most vocal enemies of the radical revolution's ideology among Europe's leaders, finally. But if Frederick William made a halfhearted attack on the revolution before making peace, Catherine never sent troops against France at all. So much for the notion that antirevolutionary ideology lay at the core of the French revolutionary wars.

The War of the First Coalition settled into a series of desultory campaigns following the major combats of 1792–1794 until Napoleon took command of the French army in Italy in 1796. In the campaigns of 1796–1797, Napoleon not only made his name as a brilliant general but inflicted a series of stunning defeats on Austrian arms. Faced with the prospect of a French victory, the other European monarchs offered Austria no aid. Frederick William II and his son, who succeeded him in 1797, and Paul I of Russia, who took power in 1796, continued to revile the Revolution and its leaders but did not join the struggle. The British, who had made common cause with Austria in 1793 following the French invasion of Belgium, continued their belligerent status but offered Francis no material assistance. Faced with defeat in a theater that bordered directly on the core territories of the Habsburg Empire and no prospect of reinforcement, Francis reluctantly agreed to the Treaty of Campo Formio in 1797, which formally ended hostilities on the continent (Britain continued to maintain its belligerent status toward France and was not a party to that treaty).

If the Treaty of Campo Formio ended the war in Europe, however, it did not establish a permanent or stable peace. French victories had brought large areas under French control that had previously been independent states or had belonged to Austria or Prussia. Much of that territory was inside the boundaries of the Holy Roman Empire, of which Francis was the titular head. The treaty therefore provided for a European congress, ultimately held at Rastadt, to determine appropriate compensation for the major powers that had lost territory to France. The complete resolution of the upheavals in Europe thus required continued negotiation and tension among the great powers.

All of the major powers except Austria gained in the War of the First Coalition. Apart from the territories seized during the two Polish partitions, Prussian negotiators secured compensation that exceeded their actual losses. The British benefited by seizing French colonies overseas, and Hanover, King George's possession on the continent, remained securely in the Prussian neutrality zone. Russia realized substantial gains in the Polish partitions. The fact that both Catherine and Paul had held aloof from the wars against France left Russia untested and unstrained compared to the other powers. The French, of course, gained enormously, seizing Belgium and large territories along the Rhine, among other things.

Austria was further weakened by the loss of Belgium, although some of her statesmen argued that the gains of Polish territories, which were adjacent to the core Habsburg lands and out of the reach of France, offset that loss and made the monarchy more secure. The war had imposed a severe financial burden, however, which was exacerbated by the disorders of the 1780s and early 1790s. Prussia's betrayal of Austria in 1795 convinced Francis that he faced perfidious allies and predators throughout Europe, and the compensation negotiations begun at Rastadt contained ominous overtones for the Holy Roman Empire.

For these reasons and others, the peace of Campo Formio was not destined to last long. Within two years, a new coalition challenged France, and war exploded on the continent once more. The details of the formation of that coalition, its collapse, and the resulting peace treaty are essential to understanding the origins of the first war against Napoleon in 1805 and will be the subject of the following chapter.

Conclusion

This review of the half century preceding Napoleon's rise to power has been cursory. Statesmen have long memories, however, and they make decisions in the context of not only their own experiences but what they understand of the history of the international system decades before their rise to power. Napoleon was no exception to this principle. He had imbibed not only the Enlightenment principles championed by the French revolutionaries but also the visceral hatred the French held for the British. But Napoleon was also an upstart. He rose to national prominence in France in 1796, and three years later he took power with no formal training or practice in the tasks of governing and functioning as a state leader. His continental adversaries, however, had at least a decade of such training and experience behind them. Neither did they adhere to the French revolutionary conviction that a new era had dawned with the proclamation of the republic, a conviction epitomized by the adoption of a new revolutionary calendar. In France, and for many students and readers of Napoleonic history, the past was dead. For the crowned heads of Europe, their statesmen, and their generals, however, it was alive. This was only one difficulty the new French monarch faced in trying to communicate with his enemies.

Thus it would be easy to see the Napoleonic Wars as resulting from failures to communicate; certainly the gap between Napoleon's worldview and his opponents' played a prominent role in causing and protracting hostilities. But perfect communication would not have led to perfect peace. As Napoleon solidified his power in France and his enemies sought to recover from the damage of the eighteenth century in various ways, all of these efforts interacted to bring about a series of devastating conflicts. The purpose of this volume is to trace those political interactions and their extensions in the first such conflict, the War of the Third Coalition in 1805.

1

The Peace

Lunéville, Paris, Amiens, 1801–1802

The treaties ending the revolutionary wars in 1801 favored France strongly. The signatories yielded to France because they felt great pressure to make peace. Many sources of that pressure, however, were transitory. The treaties did not reflect a permanent set of power relationships on the continent, but a perception of those relationships skewed by ephemeral policies and fleeting fears. As Napoleon's aggression continued in the years following the signing of these treaties, the transitory pressure for peace in Vienna, St. Petersburg, and London began to evaporate. A desire to revise those treaties developed, especially in London. This growing tension created the essential preconditions for the renewal of war. To understand why war broke out in 1803 and then in 1805, it is essential to explore why peace broke out in 1801 and 1802.

The War of the Second Coalition, 1799–1801

The Second Coalition against Revolutionary France suffered from many of the problems that doomed the first. The allies did not share common goals, and their fear of France was not strong enough to convince them to set their differences aside in the interest of ultimate victory. Divergent political objectives translated into military blunders that opened the way for the coalition's defeat. Since later coalitions replicated many of these same flaws, the War of the Second Coalition deserves a brief consideration, even apart from the importance of the peace treaties that ended it.

The Second Coalition consisted of Austria, Russia, England, and Turkey. It coalesced in 1799 in response to a series of French provocations following the

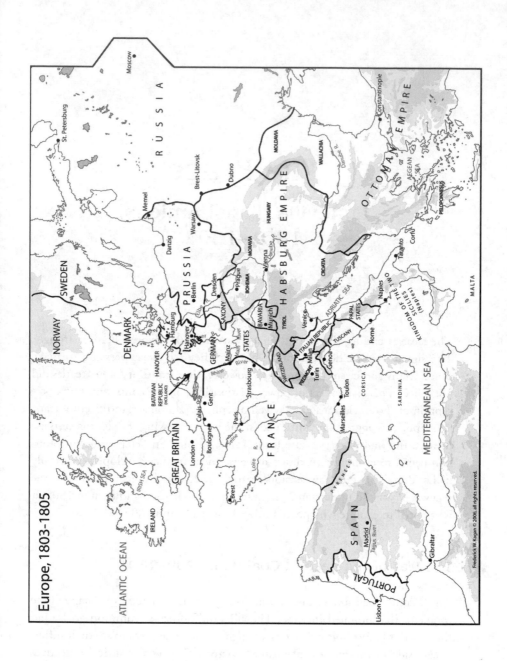

Europe, 1803–1805

ATLANTIC OCEAN

IRELAND

GREAT BRITAIN
London
Boulogne
Brest

NORWAY

SWEDEN

DENMARK
Hamburg
HANOVER
BATAVIAN
REPUBLIC
(HOLLAND)
Gent
Calais
Paris
Seine R.
Loire
FRANCE
Strasbourg
Marseilles
Toulon

St. Petersburg

Memel
Danzig
Warsaw

R U S S I A

Moscow

Brest-Litovsk
Dubno

P R U S S I A
Berlin
Dresden
SAXONY
GERMAN
STATES
Mainz
Rhine   River
SWITZERLAND

Prague
BOHEMIA
MORAVIA
Vienna
Danube R.
BAVARIA
Munich
TYROL

H A B S B U R G   E M P I R E

HUNGARY

MOLDAVIA

WALLACHIA

CROATIA

O T T O M A N   E M P I R E

Constantinople

AEGEAN
SEA

PELOPONNESUS

Venice
ADRIATIC SEA
ITALIAN REPUBLIC
Milan
PIEDMONT
Turin
Genoa
TUSCANY
PAPAL
STATES
Rome

Naples
KINGDOM OF THE TWO
SICILIES
(Naples)

Tarento
Corfu

MALTA

CORSICA
SARDINIA

MEDITERRANEAN SEA

SPAIN
Madrid
Tagus River
PYRENEES

PORTUGAL
Lisbon

Gibraltar

Peace of Campo Formio, beginning with Napoleon's expedition to Egypt in 1798.[1] This adventure was born of Napoleon's dreams of conquest, romantic involvement with the east, and hatred of Britain; in addition, his jealous superiors desired to remove their most successful general—and potential rival—from France.

Russia's participation in this coalition was epochal, although it did not seem so at the time. Russia had crossed swords with France briefly in the War of the Polish Succession in the 1730s, but otherwise had been a peripheral if powerful force on Europe's eastern marches. Tsaritsa Elizabeth's war against Frederick the Great had been an extension of Russia's traditional concern with her western border, and Catherine the Great had focused exclusively on conflicts with Russia's neighbors. When Tsar Paul sent a Russian expeditionary force to fight Revolutionary France in Italy and Switzerland, he was accelerating the process of integrating Russia into the European states system and making his empire a truly continental force. The results of the war obscured this fact for some time.

One of the reasons for the turnabout in Russian foreign policy in this period was economic. Tsar Paul rejected French control of Egypt because it would threaten the stability of Russia's economy.* Between 1787 and 1792 Russia wrested control of the northern coast of the Black Sea from Turkey, realizing vast economic rewards. Grain from Ukraine and Poland and iron from the Urals now flowed through Black Sea ports and the Mediterranean to markets in western Europe and elsewhere. During Paul's reign (1796–1801), over half of the grain Russia exported went through the Black Sea ports.[2] As Russia's economic interests shifted toward the Mediterranean, security concerns began to shift as well.

The free flow of Black Sea exports was vital to Russia. Catherine's heavy spending on wars and other interests had brought large debts and depreciated Russia's currency. Only increased revenue from indirect taxes, especially import and export duties, promised to relieve the fiscal crisis.† Anything that endangered the shipment of trade goods from the burgeoning ports of the Black Sea coast threatened Russia's security. Although Napoleon and the Directory then governing France intended the invasion of Egypt to harm Britain, they

---

*At the time Paul was regarded as insane, but most of his abrupt and apparently irrational policy changes can be explained by changes in the international situation, especially in regard to Russia's security. Napoleon's invasion of Egypt is an important example. See the excellent collection of essays in Hugh Ragsdale, ed., *Paul I: A Reassessment of His Life and Reign* (Pittsburgh, Pa.: University of Pittsburgh Press, 1979), some of which call his "insanity" into question.

†Russia could raise revenue only by raising direct taxes on the peasantry, borrowing, issuing new paper currency, or from indirect taxes in the form of import and export duties. Increasing direct taxes might lead to economic collapse or peasant revolt. Borrowing, if it was possible, would place Russia at the mercy of foreign bankers and increase the debt. Issuing additional currency would bring inflation that threatened economic collapse.

inadvertently struck Russia an even more unnerving blow. The invasion might allow the French to establish a powerful base in the eastern Mediterranean from which to close the Turkish Straits, through which Russia's Black Sea trade had to pass.[3] This danger would become real if hostility ever broke out between France and Russia.

Paul was also provoked by his exclusion from the Conference of Rastadt, which was reconstructing the Holy Roman Empire.* As a signatory of the Treaty of Teschen of 1779, Catherine became a guarantor of the constitution of the Holy Roman Empire, entitled to a seat at the table of any conference deliberating its future. Paul's exclusion was humiliating and dangerous. German interests affected Russia, since they directly affected her nearest neighbors, Austria and Prussia. The Russian ruling family had extensive family ties throughout Germany—Catherine had been a German princess before she became a Russian tsaritsa, and the wife of the heir apparent, Alexander, was a princess of Baden. The Romanovs could not look on with unconcern as their relatives were dispossessed.

Finally, Paul was furious that Napoleon had seized the island of Malta on his way to Egypt, dispersing the Knights of St. John of Jerusalem who had ruled that island for ages. Paul had become the protector of the Order of the Knights of St. John in 1797, and grand master in late 1798 (after Malta fell to the French). What Paul desired in accepting these positions is unclear, but Malta was another French advance in the Mediterranean, and it added to the list of grievances.[4] Paul's opposition to Napoleon's Egyptian expedition, like Alexander's later opposition to French expansion in Italy (which promised French Mediterranean hegemony in another way), was based on security concerns. If Napoleon had not struck at Britain through Egypt, Paul might not have gone to war against France.

French aggression in Italy and Germany drove Austria back to war. The French used the instability that followed the Treaty of Campo Formio to undo the treaty and make further gains.† In 1798 French troops seized Rome and brought the pope back to France as a prisoner, setting the stage for a complete French takeover of the peninsula. In the same year, French armies invaded and subdued Switzerland and consolidated their hold over Holland. At Rastadt the French undermined the imperial constitution by insisting that the major powers that had lost land to France be compensated by "secularizing" the independent

---

*In a certain sense Paul should have been just as mad at the Austrians and Prussians, who also participated in this conference, as the French, since all of them failed to consult him. But the French, who were clearly in control of the proceedings, were also the biggest winners in the negotiations. Paul was already hostile to the revolutionary government, so his anger was mainly directed at Paris. T. C. W. Blanning, *The French Revolutionary Wars* (New York: Arnold, 1996), pp. 228–229.

†The Conference of Rastadt fulfilled one of the terms of Campo Formio, which required such a conference to regulate various affairs touching the German states.

church principalities in the empire—giving them to those states. This policy, which suited the radically anticlerical French revolutionary government, discomfited Austria by depriving her of loyal allies within the empire. It also became increasingly clear to Emperor Francis of Austria that both Italy and Germany could become French satellites. Accordingly, Francis moved closer to Russia and Britain.

The increasingly threatened Directory in Paris declared war on this nascent coalition in March 1799, with disastrous results for France. A combined Austro–Russian army under the command of Russian Field Marshal A. A. Suvorov drove the French back over the Rhine and almost out of Italy. But Archduke Charles, commanding Austria's armies in Germany, failed to follow up on his victories and repeatedly allowed the French to regroup. The allies fell out, and Emperor Francis, in overall charge of coalition military operations, ordered Suvorov and his army over the Alps into Switzerland, nominally to support Charles's German army in further attacks into France. The real motives for this decision emphasized the serious divergences between Russia's war aims and Austria's.[5]

Although Tsar Paul entered the war for practical reasons, he also pursued the ideological goal of restoring the prerevolutionary order. When Suvorov cleared northern Italy of French forces, he announced to the people of Piedmont that the old order would be restored. Francis and his advisers, however, wanted to improve their strategic position in Italy. They resented the Russians' determination to return them to the situation of 1789, at the end of a half century of Austrian defeats and retreats. As Francis had revisionist aims and Paul sought the status quo ante bellum, conflict between the two allies was unavoidable. Francis had ordered Suvorov out of Italy largely to prevent him from restoring the prerevolutionary order. The military consequences of that decision shattered the coalition.

Charles had withdrawn his forces from Switzerland before Suvorov completed crossing the Alps, exposing the Russian commander to defeat. With nothing to be gained from further operations in that theater, the coalition no longer served Paul in Germany. With Suvorov expelled from Italy, Paul realized that the alliance would not serve his objectives there either. Around the same time, Napoleon's Egyptian expedition was collapsing, his ultimate defeat was certain, and the potential French threat to Russia's free passage to the Mediterranean therefore disappeared. The destruction of the French fleet, moreover, meant that Britain, not France, was the arbiter of Malta's fate. Thus Paul had achieved his most important objectives by 1800, and he was not likely to achieve his other goals by continued operations with his present alliance partners. The tsar therefore recalled Suvorov and his army in January 1800 and left Austria in the lurch. Although Russia's withdrawal has been called irrational, it was actually a calculated response to real changes in the situation.

Napoleon abandoned his army in Egypt and seized power in France in the coup d'état of 18 Brumaire (November 9), 1799. He hurried to Italy, soundly thrashed the Austrians at Marengo, and drove them out of the peninsula entirely.[6] Francis was, nevertheless, slow to make peace. His francophobic foreign minister, Baron Franz Maria von Thugut, remained a powerful voice for the continuation of the war. Francis himself was reluctant to make a separate peace with France, which would violate the terms of his treaty with Britain. On the other hand, Archduke Charles, the emperor's talented but difficult younger brother, was determined to have peace at any price, and resistance in the foreign office fell away when the advocate and architect of the war retired in the face of Charles's opposition.

Austrian foreign policy consequently spiraled into confusion, alternating between optimism and despair in a pattern familiar to those who knew Francis. Ludwig Cobenzl, who had taken charge of part of the foreign affairs portfolio, went to Lunéville to negotiate for peace, trying to get at least a moderately defensible line in Italy. Events on the battlefield, however, decided the outcome of the negotiations. The last of a series of armistices expired on November 13, 1800, and on December 2 General Jean-Victor Moreau, commanding the Army of the Rhine while Napoleon remained in Paris, outmaneuvered the Austrians and defeated them at the battle of Hohenlinden. With his negotiating position thus destroyed, Francis was forced to accept the Treaty of Lunéville on February 9, 1801.

Francis did not make peace merely because France had once again beaten his armies on the battlefield. The issues at stake were important enough to risk and suffer military defeats as long as hope of a turnaround remained. But by January 1801 Austria's position both internally and externally had deteriorated so severely that future recalcitrance was likely to accelerate disaster. Shortly after the signing of the Treaty of Lunéville, Francis wrote to Cobenzl, "I have exhausted my monarchy in people and in money to such an extent that it is beyond the position in which it can take its designated place in the European balance; I have lost all of my political relations at once and can count in this debilitated condition on not a single true ally."[7]

Internally, Austria's position was becoming untenable. Her economy had been seriously damaged by the taxes, debts, and inflation needed to keep her forces in the field for almost a decade of continuous warfare against France. Neither increased taxes nor British subsidies were enough to offset the costs of these wars, and Austria, like Russia and France before her, had been forced to resort to the inflationary practices of issuing unbacked paper currency and increasing her debt.[8] Military expenditures comprised the overwhelming proportion of this spending.[9] With no means of increasing actual revenues, the state was forced to make peace.

Even so, Francis might not have accepted the harsh terms Napoleon was determined to impose on him had Austria's international situation not been collapsing apace. After withdrawing from the Second Coalition in January 1800,

Paul became increasingly hostile toward Britain. He resented the Royal Navy's dominance of the seas and interference with Russian trade. Efforts to resurrect the League of Armed Neutrality that had opposed British maritime policies during the last part of the American revolutionary war created a situation of such tension between Russia and Britain that both states seriously contemplated war.

Paul's hostility to Britain was less rational than his decision to leave the war in 1800, but reason was not entirely absent. As Russia turned from an ally to a neutral, Britain made it clear that Russia's trade moved at her sufferance. The Royal Navy undertook to prevent trade between France and any other state, a policy that Paul, dependent as he was on foreign trade, hotly resented. Once again, Russian poverty dictated conflict with any who might disrupt her trade. Thus Paul armed a body of troops to invade India and raise an insurrection against British rule there, and he ordered his subordinates to consider how best to meet a British attack on Russia's Baltic coast.

Napoleon saw in Paul's policies against Britain a move toward alliance with France. On January 21, 1801, in a message sent to guide his brother Joseph in his negotiations with Cobenzl, he wrote, "Russia is in a very hostile disposition toward England. You will easily see what an interest we have in not rushing anything, since peace with the Emperor [Francis] is nothing in comparison with an alliance that would master England and preserve Egypt for us." Summing up, he added, "Continue the protocol, discuss the basic questions, even the redaction of a definitive treaty; but do not sign anything for ten days, after which we will be in accord with Paul I."[10]

Napoleon clearly believed that he had Paul in his power and that a Franco–Russian entente, if not alliance, would shortly follow. What seemed natural in Paris seemed just as natural in Vienna, and Francis had every reason to fear that Napoleon would gain a powerful ally in his quest to subdue Britain as well as crush Austria. Worse still, the intermediary in Paul's discussions with Napoleon was Prussia, and a Russo–Prussian alliance suited Austria almost as badly as a Franco–Russian agreement. It seemed likely that Francis, who had lacked a representative in St. Petersburg since April 1800, would be isolated in Europe if he did not end the war quickly.

The Treaty of Lunéville resulted from a combination of domestic and international circumstances, not just Austria's battlefield defeats. Some factors, like Russia's attitudes, were changeable and unpredictable; others, like Austria's internal weakness, were difficult to alter and all too obvious. Francis would not have signed the treaty if he could have refused, and it was harsh enough to justify attempts to revise it.

Lunéville bound Austria to respect the Rhine frontier for France on her own behalf and on behalf of the empire, accept the Adige frontier in Italy, and recognize the "independence" of the Swiss, Dutch, and Italian satellites that France established on her borders. The most important provisions, however, concerned compensation. Both Austria and Prussia had lost territory during the revolutionary wars, and Napoleon was ready to compensate them in accord with eighteenth-century tradition by giving them formerly independent territories. Thus when Napoleon insisted on removing the Habsburg archduke Ferdinand from his hereditary holding in Tuscany, he offered him Salzburg in exchange. The principle of "secularizing" independent clerical principalities by handing them out to major powers as compensation, adopted during the negotiations at Campo Formio in 1797, was further extended at Lunéville.

During the negotiations at Campo Formio, Francis had ensured that Prussian territory on the left bank of the Rhine would be safeguarded. By keeping Prussia intact, Austria also kept Prussia from demanding compensation. When Francis was forced to grant France the Prussian territories on the left bank of the Rhine in 1801, however, the treaty ensured that Prussia had an opportunity to participate in the destruction of the empire in the name of securing her own compensation (and Prussia always demanded compensation in excess of what her losses had been). Lunéville therefore sounded the death knell of the Holy Roman Empire as it had been for centuries, since the principles of compensation and secularization would destroy the independence of scores of small principalities and augment the power of the larger German states at the same time.

Lunéville was a one-sided treaty. It destroyed the Catholic princes of the empire, who had traditionally supported the House of Habsburg. It promised to reorganize the empire for the benefit of Prussia and the other anti-Austrian German states. It permanently displaced Austria from northwestern Italy and solidly established France there. It created a series of nominally independent French vassals throughout Italy. In contrast, it provided few favorable terms to Austria, although it preserved the Habsburg lands and gave Austria peace when she needed it most.

The treaty's long-term viability depended on Napoleon's conduct. Francis might have accepted the loss of secure buffer zones in Italy and Germany if Napoleon had refrained from encroaching further on areas of vital interest to Austria. He was weary of war and eager to find a way to make the peace work, and the buffer zones would only be important if there was a likelihood of Austro–French hostilities. Had Napoleon shown any inclination to keep the peace, there is every reason to imagine that Francis would have accepted his losses and focused his energies on the internal reconstruction of his state. Napoleon's continued attempts to expand his control in Italy and Germany, however, helped convince Francis to resume war to prevent his position from deteriorating further.

The treaty also confirmed Napoleon's contempt for Austria. Immediately after concluding the negotiations, Napoleon wrote Joseph to warn him against being too friendly with Cobenzl and to inform him that he himself would not write Cobenzl or make any special display for his benefit. He concluded, "It would not be at all inappropriate to tell him, moreover, that if he had not had the good sense to remain at Lunéville [rather than breaking off the negotiations during a crisis in them] we would have imposed harsher conditions on the House of Austria."[11] Napoleon's contempt for Austria, together with Francis's growing conviction that his state could risk no further assaults on its influence and power, helped unravel the peace.

Paul's Negotiations with France and Prussia

In January 1801 Napoleon believed himself on the verge of a Franco–Russian alliance. But Paul insisted on a number of preconditions for peace that Napoleon would find hard to accept: (1) the return of Malta to the Order of the Knights of St. John; (2) the reestablishment of the king of Sardinia in his estates, including Piedmont, now occupied by the French; (3) the integrity of the Kingdom of the Two Sicilies (Naples); (4) the integrity of the Electorate of Bavaria; and (5) the integrity of the Duchy of Württemberg.[12] Napoleon was willing to work with Paul to take Malta from Britain but refused to leave it in the tsar's hands. He had no intention of restoring Piedmont to the king of Sardinia or guaranteeing the integrity of Bavaria and Württemberg, which might prejudice his plans for compensations within the empire. Naples proved the worst sticking point, however. Napoleon was eager to resume the war against Britain. He was determined to make no peace with the Kingdom of the Two Sicilies until it had closed its ports to British ships. Even then, he insisted on the French right to hold the critical ports on the Gulf of Taranto until Britain had made peace with France.[13] He also placed mounting pressure on Portugal to sever relations with Britain and close her ports to British trade in support of this policy. He worked to induce Spain to cooperate with him to enforce this decree in Lisbon by invading Portugal.

Napoleon unsuccessfully tried to convince Paul to make a joint declaration of peace and friendship without reference to Paul's conditions, promising to consider his conditions following the declaration. In the end, Napoleon's hopes for a Russian alliance perished with Russia's tsar, who was assassinated, with the halfhearted participation of his son and heir, Alexander, on March 23, 1801. On learning of his death, Napoleon "loosed a cry of despair and at once was convinced that his death was not natural and that the blow had come from England." He was (justly) certain that he would not find the same degree of accommodation in Alexander that he thought he had found in Paul.[14]

Paul's death also put Prussian king Frederick William III in an awkward position. The War of the Second Coalition had raised the possibility that France or Russia might force Prussia to participate in it. Paul's turn against

Britain and turn toward France had saved Frederick William from this danger. When Paul withdrew from the Second Coalition and then made moves against Britain, Frederick William attempted to mediate a reconciliation between France and Russia. It could be just as disastrous for Prussia if France and Russia came to an agreement without her as it would be for them to come to blows, since they might try to regulate the affairs of northern Germany without his input.[15] Frederick William, accordingly, bent every effort to facilitating the reconciliation on his terms. Since it was precisely the turn toward France and against Britain that had stirred up the plot against Paul in 1801, the accession of Alexander I in March of that year was as unfortunate for Frederick William as for Napoleon. Russia was now very unlikely to offer terms that would suit the French leader, and the prospects for a Prussian-brokered Franco–Russian agreement were significantly dimmed.

Paul's death created a serious dilemma for Frederick William in Hanover. Since the mid–1790s, French had schemed to strike at Britain by seizing Hanover, George III's patrimony.* Napoleon's coconspirator, Emmanuel Joseph Sieyès, suggested once again in January 1799 that this was the only way to drive Britain from the war.[16] French revolutionary governments recognized Hanover's neutrality in return for Prussia's neutrality, but Napoleon would have none of it. He refused to accept the principle that George III could be at war with him as king of England and at peace with him as elector of Hanover. When Napoleon seized power, therefore, he pressed Frederick William to take the electorate himself. As Paul moved toward war with Britain, Russia increasingly supported this French pressure in Berlin.

Despite the obvious geopolitical advantages of such a move, the king could not bring himself to countenance it. He knew that taking Hanover would lead to open war with Britain, which would send warships to block the Elbe and Weser rivers. He also objected to the seizure of "hereditary lands" (but not the secularization of Church lands) on principled grounds.[17] Frederick William's upbringing, with its emphasis on duty and right behavior, as well as identifying and correcting personal failure, introduced elements of seeming irrationality into his decisionmaking.†

---

*The ruling house of Britain at this time was the Hanoverian dynasty (its designation was changed during World War I to the House of Windsor, for obvious reasons), and George was elector of Hanover at the same time as he was king of Great Britain. The Electorate maintained its own government separate from that of Britain, and was represented in London by its own ministers. It had been the practice from the founding of the Hanoverian house for Britain's rulers to separate the interests of their German lands from their decisions as British sovereigns, although some observed this principle more closely than others.

†See Thomas Stamm-Kuhlmann, *König in Preussens grosser Zeit: Friedrich Wilhelm III, der Melancholiker auf dem Thron* (Berlin: Siedler Verlag, 1992), for the best and most recent biography of the Prussian king, with particular emphasis on his upbringing and its effect on his personality and decisionmaking at critical moments.

By March 1801, however, the pressure was becoming unbearable. Paul himself, now preparing for war against Britain, pressed Frederick William to act. By the end of 1800 Napoleon made it clear that if Prussia did not occupy Hanover, then he would do so.[18] The Prussian ambassador in Paris, Girolamo Lucchesini, believed that the French and Russians would try to force Prussia to take direct action against Britain either by seizing Hanover or by closing the Elbe and the Weser to British traffic.[19] By February 1801, foreign minister Christian August Heinrich Curt von Haugwitz had come to the conclusion that Prussia had no choice but to occupy Hanover or else watch as France occupied not only the electorate but the mouths of the Elbe and the Weser as well.[20] The degree to which Prussia was forced to seize Hanover in 1801 is the subject of some debate, but clearly "while the Prussian decision was freely and rationally taken, the broader context was unmistakably coercive. Prussia may not have been literally forced to invade Hanover, but the imperative to forestall a French operation amounted to the same thing."[21]

When Napoleon had earlier offered Hanover to the Prussians as compensation for her losses on the Rhine, Frederick William refused because accepting would guarantee hostilities with Great Britain. Napoleon then began to contemplate taking Hanover for himself. This idea rightly horrified Haugwitz. This action would not only put French armies in the electorate but also alienate Britain by transferring George's territory directly to her enemy.[22] The change of regime in Russia also spelled danger, since the Anglophile Alexander was likely to resent this tacit Prussian support for France. Frederick William therefore decided that he must act. His troops occupied the electorate in April 1801 and met little military opposition, but he found himself dangerously exposed. He knew that Alexander was more strongly inclined toward Britain than Paul had been and realized that the Prussian occupation was likely to displease him even more than Prussian complaisance before a French occupation would have done.[23] Only when peace negotiations were opened between Britain and France was Prussia saved from this perilous position, and Frederick William withdrew his forces from the electorate in November 1801 with relief.

This incident had a powerful effect on the Prussian king. The Franco–Russian accord had forced him to depart from his policy of strict neutrality in Germany and subsequently expose himself to Britain's wrath for no gain: he could neither take the electorate himself nor trade it for anything more useful. His fickle Russian allies soon deserted him, and France seemingly was the only state on which he could rely. Even Napoleon proved unreliable, however, first demanding Hanover for himself and then beginning to make peace separately with Great Britain. If the great powers had planned and conspired to reinforce in Frederick William's mind the need to maintain the policy of strict neutrality that he favored, they would hardly have acted differently. This crisis brought home to Berlin yet again the weakness of Prussia's position and the need for a policy of balancing dangers without compromising Prussia, a policy that Frederick William would pursue to his misfortune for another five years.

Alexander

A significant part of Prussia's and Napoleon's discomfiture in 1801 resulted from Paul's untimely death. The manner of Paul's death had a profound effect on the new tsar and merits a brief digression. Alexander's childhood had been defined by the tension between the autocratic, militaristic, and somewhat imbalanced Paul and the much more liberal, intellectual, and moderate Catherine. His education had been based heavily on Enlightenment principles, as we have seen, but he was also drawn to the military parades and discipline that delighted his father.[24]

Russian court society was far from pleased with Paul's rule, which was erratic and harsh. When the tsar turned on his erstwhile allies in 1800 and began preparing an army to march against British possessions in India, his Anglophile courtiers began plotting to remove him in earnest. Alexander held aloof from this planning, but Paul apparently learned something about the plot, or perhaps he simply grew nervous on his own account. He suspected that Alexander was involved in the plotting and made a number of comments suggesting that he might either exile or kill his son to protect himself against assassination.

Alexander finally allowed himself to be drawn into the gathering conspiracy, apparently hoping that the plotters would seize Paul and force him to abdicate. In the event, Paul (naturally) refused to give up the throne, and the conspirators killed him. Alexander was shattered by this horrible event. The conspirators had not come well-armed to the confrontation, for fear of setting off the alarm prematurely, and so they apparently bludgeoned and strangled the tsar to death, mutilating his body in the process. Alexander doubted his own fitness to rule and had never hated his father to the extent of wishing to participate in his assassination. His mother, the empress, screamed that she must be placed on the throne in Paul's stead, and the conspirators had to lock her in her chambers to silence her outcries. Alexander initially refused to take the throne, but senior conspirator Count Petr Pahlen impatiently ordered the young man to do his duty. Alexander never forgave Pahlen or trusted him or his coconspirators.

Although very young when he took the throne, Alexander was not an unknown quantity in Europe. He and his immediate advisers were generally thought to be pro-British and anti-French, and there were concerns that he would change Russia's policy dramatically and unpredictably. These views were not without foundation, but they were exaggerated.

Alexander took power at the age of twenty-three. He lacked a clear understanding of Russia's position in the world and had no plan of his own. He had to rely on his senior advisers, even Pahlen, who had engineered the coup d'état that placed him in power, and N. P. Panin, a coconspirator Paul had banished shortly before his death. The new tsar began by pursuing the same foreign policy objectives as Paul—with some important changes.

Since Paul's war against Britain helped spark his assassination, Alexander immediately recalled the Cossacks from the road to India, restored amicable relations with London, and for the moment abandoned Malta. At first he maintained all the conditions Paul had insisted on in negotiating with France. Gradually he developed his own voice in foreign affairs.

In July 1801 Alexander sent A. I. Morkov to replace his ambassador to France S. A. Kolychev, and sent his new envoy an instruction that laid out his worldview and objectives.[25] Alexander above all wanted a period of peace in order to enact measures reforming the government and administration, from providing Russia with a written constitution to emancipating the serfs. These large tasks were inconceivable without a secure peace. Alexander also wanted to be the man who brought peace to Europe and established a stable order in the world. The religious rhetoric that surrounds similar pronouncements at the end of his reign is not present here, but the underlying ambition is the same.

Alexander, nonetheless, tried to drive a hard bargain with Napoleon, and his obstinacy was based in both idealism and realpolitik. Alexander proclaimed that he was determined to honor the agreements his predecessors had made with the numerous states of Europe, great and small. In particular, he meant to honor Paul's treaties with the Kingdom of Naples, Bavaria, and the king of Sardinia. He may sincerely have believed it essential to maintain his commitments, for good or ill. Yet practical considerations, which he noted separately, argued powerfully for maintaining specifically these, and not other, previous commitments.*

Alexander identified two overriding goals of Russian foreign policy in Europe: maintaining a balance between Prussia and Austria to keep both from expanding and limiting French aggrandizement. The three specific agreements he sought to uphold all tended to secure one or the other of these two objectives. The demand to restore his holdings to the king of Sardinia required France to abandon Piedmont, thus seriously hampering Napoleon's efforts to dominate and control Italy. His insistence on the evacuation of Naples supported the same objective. It was in Russia's interest, Alexander

---

*Alexander found other reasons strong enough, for example, to break the treaties that bound him not to make a separate peace with England before she recognized the principle of the rights of neutrals and indemnified Sweden for damage done to Swedish shipping. His was a very pragmatic, if sincere, idealism. See F. Martens, *Recueil des Traités et Conventions conclus par la Russie avec les Puissances Etrangères* (St. Petersburg: A. Böhnke, 1902), 11:1–28, for a discussion of the rapprochement with England.

felt, to maintain an equilibrium among Prussia, Austria, and France. This would be impossible without the continued existence of the independent German states guaranteed by the Holy Roman Empire. Alexander believed that any attack on Bavaria's integrity would lead to Bavarian demands for compensation, with Frederick William and Francis eagerly adding their own, thus precipitating the destruction of the independent German states and inviting French participation in dividing the spoils. The demand to preserve Bavaria's integrity thus foreclosed the possibility of Austrian, Prussian, and French expansion at that state's expense and reduced the risk of a general attack on the constitution of the Holy Roman Empire.

Alexander did not yet understand two critical facts of European international relations at this time: Napoleon's implacable ambition and Austria's growing weakness. Despite warnings from his envoys regarding Napoleon's plans to take over all of Europe, he was not convinced that Napoleon was uncontrollable.[26] He hoped that Napoleon would see the advantages of coming to terms with him. He made peace believing that his partner was as genuine as he was and would abide by the terms agreed on, especially since, in his mind, they favored Napoleon so heavily. Resentment and a desire for vengeance naturally followed Alexander's realization that this was not so.

Alexander remembered Austria's attempts in the last war to aggrandize herself in Italy but did not seem to recognize the desperation and weakness that motivated Francis. This is not surprising. Francis did not make the state of his treasury or army widely known, and Alexander had no personal knowledge of Austria or its rulers. He saw Austria through the eyes of a young man listening to the slanted reports of ministers angered by Austria's behavior during the last war. In that view, Austria was a predator ready to recast the international situation in her own interest unless checked by some outside force, and was eager to inveigle Russia into supporting that international transformation. Alexander believed that Russia, on the contrary, should exploit Austria's rivalry with Prussia to check Austrian expansionism. Neither side, however, should be allowed to make gains at anyone's expense, and a firm balance between the two powers should be maintained at all times.[27]

These opinions were at odds with reality. Frederick William was too timid to check Austria or serve the other role that Alexander saw him playing—helping restrain France. Austria, on the other hand, was the European state most dedicated to imposing reasonable limits on France, which Alexander also sought, and most willing to do so at the least benefit to herself. Alexander's fear of Austria's supposed rapaciousness would poison his relationship with Vienna for the rest of his reign, despite the fact that Russian foreign policy increasingly relied on Austrian support and active participation.

Implicit in Alexander's writings was the notion that Russia could take Europe or leave it. All the objectives he identified were desirable but not vital.

Only the goals of maintaining an Austro–Prussian balance and consequently checking attempts by both powers to increase their strength were important for Russia's security, and the accomplishment of that objective was not in doubt. Alexander saw no vital interests that would force Russia to go to war against his will or for longer or at greater cost than he desired.

Yet Alexander signed a treaty of peace and friendship with Napoleon in October 1801 that failed to secure virtually any of his objectives. Despite Alexander's demands, it contained no details of the settlement.[28] The secret protocols committed both parties to act in concert with regard to compensation to the German states that had lost territory during the revolutionary wars and to adopt "as an invariable principle the maintenance of a just equilibrium between the houses of Austria and of Brandenburg [Prussia]."[29] The two states also promised to "establish an intimate concert and communicate their views" to resolve outstanding issues in Italy. Napoleon pledged to respect the integrity of the Kingdom of Naples, but was allowed to occupy the ports of Bari and the Bay of Otranto "until the fate of Egypt is decided." Both parties agreed to "concern themselves in a friendly manner and gradually with the interests of H[is] M[ajesty] the King of Sardinia, and to respect the current state of affairs there." Napoleon also swore to work with Russia to obtain appropriate compensation for the Duke of Württemberg, and to respect the territorial integrity of the electorate of Bavaria.

Alexander had therefore obtained only the guarantees for Württemberg and Bavaria among the conditions he had previously set as sine qua non for any treaty. The king of Sardinia, it was clear, would never see Piedmont again, while French troops would remain in Naples until Napoleon felt it convenient to withdraw them. Alexander also dropped his earlier desire to order the French out of Egypt. In return, the tsar had Napoleon's promise that his views would be taken into consideration in Italy and Germany, and that Russia and France would act together to restore a basis of peace and stability to Europe.

Alexander's diplomatic defeat can be partially attributed to the fact that Napoleon outmaneuvered him. As the negotiations dragged on, Napoleon changed the situation so that Alexander's various demands became irrelevant or irretrievable. As Piedmont was incorporated into France proper during the summer of 1801, Alexander recognized that Napoleon had no intention of abandoning that critical province and that it was useless to insist on it in the treaty. Since he was not willing to go to war over the issue, his only hope was that Britain would demand the restoration of Piedmont to the king of Sardinia as part of her peace with France. He was to be disappointed in this hope as well.[30]

At the same time, Napoleon was negotiating with the king of Naples (if this term can be used for such proceedings) in Italy, not Paris. The location was chosen to ensure that the Russians could neither follow nor participate in the negotiations. Consequently Napoleon produced a treaty with Naples in

March 1801 that gave him the right, among other things, to maintain French troops on Neapolitan soil.[31] How could Alexander insist that Napoleon make a treaty with Russia more favorable to Naples than the one he had made with the king of Naples himself? Napoleon's initiative repeatedly presented Alexander with a series of faits accomplis to which he could only agree if he wanted a peace treaty with France.

Apart from Napoleon's actions, Alexander had a very bad hand to play. Because Russia was not actively involved in the war against France, Napoleon had no urgent need to make peace with St. Petersburg. The major impetus driving Napoleon's urge for peace was his desire to drag Russia openly into his war against Britain. He was even satisfied, for a time, simply to publicize the fact of his negotiations with Russia, in hopes that the British would be scared into a suitable peace. When Alexander made peace with London in July 1801, however, his value as a potential French partner disappeared. Having nothing to offer Napoleon and posing no viable threat to France, the tsar's bargaining position was terrible, and he was forced to accept a bad treaty in order to get any accommodation from Napoleon at all.

It is important to remember why Alexander ruled out continued war against France. Domestic considerations—Russia's economic problems and Alexander's desire to focus on reform—overwhelmed the relatively minor defeats the Treaty of Paris imposed on him, balanced as they were against the relatively minor gains in that agreement. It will be our task subsequently to understand how other nonvital issues between 1803 and 1805 would convince Alexander to choose war instead.

Alexander did not think his treaty with France would settle the conflicts of Europe. He knew that the "final pacification of Europe," as he referred to it, would require the settlement of all outstanding issues in Italy and Germany. In a sense he was testing Napoleon to see how well he behaved in the execution of the treaties he had signed; in another sense he was just overly optimistic. But in a more profound sense, Alexander was right not to worry too much about the terms of the treaty he had signed.

The situations that had forced both Austria and Russia to accept poor peace agreements were transitory. In Austria's case, the isolation the Vienna cabinet suffered following Russia's abdication from the coalition, combined with its troubled domestic situation, induced Francis to sign the treaty. Although the latter factor hindered Austria's movements throughout this period and kept even the hawks in Vienna sincerely dovish well into 1804, Austria's international isolation would become paramount for Francis and his advisers. In 1805 Austria had the option of cleaving to a powerful coalition or becoming even more isolated than she had been in 1801. The desire to escape her isolation would become predominant. In other words, Austria's willingness to continue to accept Napoleon's bad deals and bad faith depended on an international situation that might change dramatically in a relatively short period of time.

Russia's situation was even more changeable. Russia was not militarily exhausted in 1801, nor was the state so seriously "disrupted" by Paul's "madness" as to be incapable of offering a serious threat to Napoleon. France was both exhausted and disorganized, first by the confused actions of a succession of revolutionary governments and then by Napoleon's recent accession to supreme power, which he had not yet wielded except in wartime. But Alexander felt insecure on his throne, unready to cope with the responsibilities of ruling and guiding his state in troubled times, and convinced that his mad father had pushed the state to the brink of collapse. Conversations with elder advisers and contemporary friends strengthened these convictions. The Russian "weakness" that drove Alexander to accept losing almost all of his foreign policy objectives in 1801 was largely illusory. The new tsar became more self-confident as disorders in the government were righted. He also became more confident that his reforms were taking firm root (or were impossible). It was natural that he would resent the treaty he had signed and Napoleon's continued assaults on the fragile peace. The stability of the treaty depended not so much on its terms as on Alexander's sentiments and Napoleon's future behavior.

The Treaty of Amiens, completed by France and Britain in March 1802, was very similar in this regard to the Franco–Russian Treaty. It stipulated, among other things, that Britain give up nearly all of the extra-European lands gained during a decade of conflict, including the strategic island of Malta and positions in India. Britain was far from being completely defeated, and had certainly not been defeated enough to be satisfied with such a one-sided peace. The drive for peace had resulted from momentary disillusionment with the war and a feeling, not entirely justified, of exhaustion. Once again, when Napoleon made it clear that he had no serious intention of honoring the treaties he had signed, at least not in the way the British and others read them, Britain decided to return to war.*

It is not entirely fair to say that the seeds of the war of 1805 were sown in the peace treaties of 1801–1802, however. Those treaties were all one-sided and, with the possible exception of Lunéville, gave France more than she had earned from her battlefield victories. Certainly they were all as harsh as they could be while still being accepted by the defeated powers. None of this means that they were doomed to failure at an early date. In Austria the desire for peace was deep and broad; Alexander would certainly have preferred to continue to focus on his various domestic projects. Perhaps war between Britain and France was bound to resume not long after the Treaty of Amiens, but there was no pressing reason why that war should spread quickly to the continent if Britain

---

*We will consider this treaty in greater detail in a subsequent chapter.

and France did not choose to do so. As a Russian foreign minister would note in 1803, since neither Britain nor France could destroy the other and thus upset the balance of power, their war was no concern of the continental powers unless they took unacceptable steps on the continent.[32] The peace, though harsh and in some sense unjust, was stable, at least for a time, *if Napoleon had worked to maintain the stability instead of undermining it.* In the end Napoleon did the opposite; hostility was renewed in months and war shortly thereafter. The Peace of 1801–1802 put the powder in the bomb; Napoleon lit the fuse. The transitory nature of the conditions that had enabled the peace in the first place, which none of the principals recognized, was at least as important as Napoleon's actions in renewing war. When those conditions changed, Austria, Russia, and Britain began to seek new ways to achieve the objectives that Napoleon had obstructed in 1801–1802.

2

War Renewed,
1801–1803

The first treaty to collapse was the weakest: the Peace of Amiens between Britain and France. This treaty least reflected the military outcomes of the war it ended and depended on a despondent mood in Britain that proved fleeting. Above all, this peace imposed immediate and tangible tests of both sides' commitment to sustaining it—tests that both countries failed. In mid-May 1803, fourteen months after its completion, Britain renounced the treaty and renewed the war with France.

British and French ships and soldiers then clashed worldwide. Yet the renewed war need not have had immediate consequences for the war-weary European continent. The war broadened because of the specific way in which Amiens disintegrated, coupled with the way in which the Peace of Lunéville and the Peace of Paris (the treaty between Russia and France) worked out on the continent. As Alexander watched Napoleon's and Addington's tergiversations and listened to their increasingly bellicose rhetoric, he did not remain the neutral observer that both sides expected. For complex reasons, he began to incline sharply toward the British side of the argument, despite his agreements with Napoleon. When the Anglo-French war resumed, Alexander had ceased to be either impartial or detached.

Finishing the Peace

One weakness of the treaties of 1801–1802 was that they required continued negotiations to establish the peace. The Treaty of Lunéville specifically called for the powers to develop a plan to compensate the German states for the lands they lost on the left bank of the Rhine. That negotiation involved Austria, Prussia,

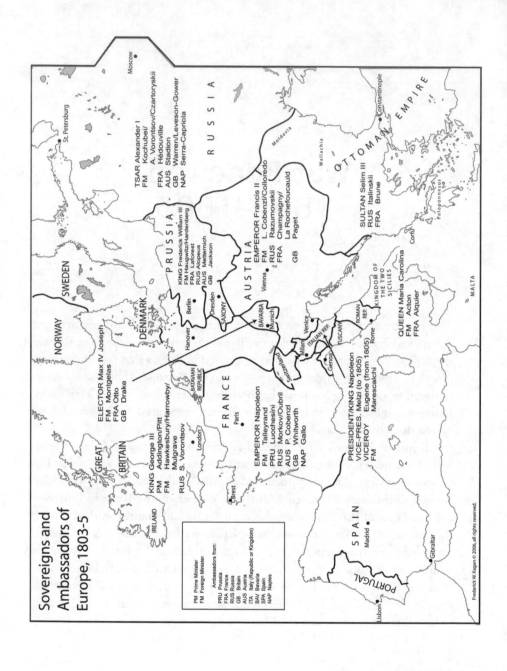

Sovereigns and Ambassadors of Europe, 1803-5

NORWAY

SWEDEN

RUSSIA

Moscow

St. Petersburg

TSAR Alexander I
FM Kochubei/
    A. Vorontsov/Czartoryskii
FRA Hédouville
AUS Stadion
GB   Warren/Leveson-Gower
NAP Serra-Capriola

OTTOMAN EMPIRE

Constantinople

Moldavia

Wallachia

SULTAN Selim III
RUS Italinskii
FRA Brune

PRUSSIA

KING Frederick William III
FM Haugwitz/Hardenberg
FRA Laforest
RUS Alopeus
AUS Metternich
GB   Jackson

Berlin

Hanover

Dresden

SAXONY

DENMARK

ELECTOR Max IV Joseph
FM Montgelas
FRA Otto
GB   Drake

AUSTRIA

Vienna

EMPEROR Francis II
FM L. Cobenzl/Colloredo
RUS Razumovskii
FRA Champagny/
     La Rochefoucauld
GB   Paget

BAVARIA

Munich

Venice

Milan

ITALIAN REP.

Switzerland

BATAVIAN
REPUBLIC

Genoa

TUSCANY

ROMAN
REP.

Rome

Corfù

Peloponnesus

KINGDOM OF THE TWO SICILIES

QUEEN Maria Carolina
FM Acton
FRA Alquier

MALTA

FRANCE

Paris

EMPEROR Napoleon
FM Talleyrand
PRU Lucchesini
RUS Morkov/Oubril
AUS P. Cobenzl
GB   Whitworth
NAP Gallo

PRESIDENT/KING Napoleon
VICE-PRES. Melzi (to 1805)
VICEROY Eugene (from 1805)
FM Marescalchi

GREAT BRITAIN

KING George III
PM Addington/Pitt
FM Hawkesbury/Harrowby/
    Mulgrave
RUS S. Vorontsov

London

Brest

IRELAND

SPAIN

Madrid

Gibraltar

PORTUGAL

Lisbon

PM Prime Minister
FM Foreign Minister

Ambassadors from:
PRU Prussia
FRA France
RUS Russia
GB   Britain
AUS Austria
ITA Italy (Republic or Kingdom)
BAV Bavaria
SPA Spain
NAP Naples

and all the German states; France and Russia played important roles because of their status as guarantors of the imperial constitution. Francis sought to use the negotiations to revise the treaty in Austria's favor. Although the treaty specifically promised the Habsburg Duke of Tuscany the territories of Berchtesgaden and Salzburg in compensation for his losses in Italy, Francis hoped to substitute other areas on the peninsula for those lands. In addition, Francis needed to find a way out of diplomatic isolation, which also required difficult, lengthy negotiations. Continuing peace rested on these negotiations.

Alexander was well aware of his own relative military power and his effective invulnerability. He thus attempted at first to pursue a detached, altruistic policy, playing the role of honest broker in the negotiations over the future of Germany. He inclined toward friendship with Napoleon at the expense of Francis, whose weakness he did not understand. He also suspected him of harboring plans for domination in Germany and Italy. He hoped to entrammel France in a restraining alliance to keep Napoleon from further mischief and use that alliance in turn to hold Francis in check.

At the same time, he kept a wary eye on Napoleon's expansion and set a number of tests, which Napoleon always failed. Alexander kept waiting for evidence that Napoleon would recognize his limits, adhere to his commitments, and strive to keep the peace. It did not take that long to convince Alexander that such hopes were vain and that Napoleonic France was the most dangerous potential foe and disturber of the peace that he faced. Throughout this period, however, Alexander sought to avoid war for as long as possible so that he could focus on the internal reforms he felt Russia desperately needed.

Frederick William hoped for peace. He knew that he was likely to be the first victim in any large-scale war between France and Russia. Alexander was not an attractive ally. Russia, although powerful, was so far from Prussia's western frontier that Prussian arms would have to withstand the full force of any Napoleonic onslaught for too long. As the international environment deteriorated throughout 1803, however, Frederick William came to fear that an open alliance with Napoleon ran the risk of provoking a Russian attack. The king therefore clung to neutrality and saw a threat to Prussia's survival in the prospect of renewed war.

The Settlement of Germany

The international situation after the signing of the Peace of Amiens was thus highly atomized: no two powers were close enough to coordinate their policies, let alone impose a common vision of order on the continent. Alexander contemplated stepping into the void. V. P. Kochubei, the new foreign minister selected from among Alexander's group of like-minded young friends, had advocated and pursued a policy of avoiding entangling alliances and isolation from European affairs. He wanted the tsar to focus on domestic reforms and saw little benefit for Russia from direct involvement in the sordid politics of Europe. His view still dominated in the spring of 1802, but its hold on Alexander's mind was weakening and Kochubei's influence was waning.

Alexander's intervention in European affairs could not have the beneficent effect he desired, however, because his perceptions of the situation were skewed during the process of negotiating compensation for the German states. He was determined to establish peace throughout the continent at the earliest moment, but he feared that Austro–Prussian jealousy and the ambitions of the German powers would protract the process of pacification indefinitely.[1] As a result, he was initially prepared to cooperate with Napoleon in working out an arrangement and more or less forcing its acceptance in Vienna and Berlin.

He was also prepared to reject an Austrian proposal, offered in March 1802, for a quadruple alliance of Austria, Prussia, Russia, and Britain against Napoleon. Count Franz Joseph Saurau, the Austrian ambassador in St. Petersburg, warned that the "ambition" and the "boldest undertakings" of France could not be contained except by such an alliance. A. B. Kurakin, a senior official in the Russian Foreign Ministry, responded that the time was not yet right; Britain was preoccupied with domestic and overseas concerns, and Prussia opposed such alliances. Saurau rejoined that it was up to Alexander to take the lead. If the tsar would "be the first and propose this quadruple alliance," he declared, "Austria would hasten to defer completely to his will." Saurau was also convinced that Britain and Prussia would be forced to follow suit.[2] But the ears of both the Francophile Kurakin and of the tsar were deaf to such pleas. They still mistrusted Austria more than France, and Alexander sought security through balancing potential foes rather than forging alliances.*

Alexander sought an understanding with Frederick William, however, when he met with him in June 1802 at Memel. He did so contrary to the desires of both Vienna and his own foreign minister, Kochubei, who learned of the meeting only a few weeks before it occurred. He was incensed. Not only

---

*Alexander discussed the possibility of establishing an alliance between Russia, France, and Prussia in a March meeting of the unofficial committee, the group of young friends who advised him in the early years of his reign, but it is not likely that he was serious. First, the question was raised in a challenging manner by Foreign Minister Kochubei. Second, no effort was made to act on this apparent resolution, either in Paris or when the tsar met with the king of Prussia at Memel a month later. Third, this meeting is reminiscent of a similar meeting in 1801 at which Alexander declaimed against signing treaties with any states—shortly before signing one with France. Although the high-spirited meetings of this group offer insight into Alexander's mind, what he actually said at those meetings may not have represented his actual thoughts and beliefs, especially when, as in this case, the member who challenged him was one who was losing his confidence, as Kochubei was. See Grand Prince Nikolai Mihailovich, *Le Comte Paul Stroganov,* trans. F. Billecocq (Paris: Imprimerie Nationale, 1905), vol. 2, doc. 139, journal of 5 April 1802. Also partially reproduced in Protocol of a Meeting of the Unofficial Committee, 5 April 1802, VPR, vol. I, doc. 67.

had his prerogatives as foreign minister been violated, but he opposed the no-tion of a Russian alliance with any state. He feared that Alexander would fall under the spell of Frederick William or his beautiful queen, Louise.[3] By all ac-counts, Alexander was pleased with the flattery offered to him by both the Prussian royalty and the local people and army units (whose review was the nominal reason for Frederick William's presence there). The Prussian royal couple was delighted and considered the visit a tremendous success.[4]

The true significance of the encounter is hard to fathom. Little came of the personal relationships Alexander supposedly established there, for Frederick William remained neutral in 1805 and Alexander's policies leading up to the conflict were not notably pro-Prussian; indeed the tsar, as we shall see, nearly went to war against Frederick William. The meeting aroused fear in Vienna, however, and may have helped persuade Napoleon that an approach through Prussia might bear fruit in St. Petersburg again as it had in 1801.[5]

There may have been a more profound effect, although it is harder to gauge. Although the two monarchs came to know and like each other at Memel, no clear agreements were struck. They undertook to work in concert and keep each other's needs and aims always in mind. With terms so vague, it is likely that each ruler mistook the other's goodwill as support for particular programs. Thus Frederick William probably imagined that Alexander would sanction Prussia's neutrality and guarantee the aggrandizement of his state, then being arranged in Paris in the name of compensation. Alexander probably believed that the ties he had established with Frederick William would hold firm through the trials to come, even in a conflict with Napoleonic France, al-though he did not foresee such an eventuality at that point. Memel may well have sown the seeds of a disastrous miscalculation in 1805—Alexander's con-viction that Prussia could be brought into the war against France.[5]

As the tsar cautiously felt his way toward a commitment to European af-fairs, Napoleon worked rapidly and aggressively to expand his domination of western Europe. He sought to revolutionize the organization of Germany and Italy, and he was ruthless in accomplishing this goal. He used familiar methods: dividing his foes by separate negotiations and preventing the critical issues from being decided in a congress:

> I wish to conduct three negotiations separately: one with Russi a . . . to try to discover as much as possible what arrangements will suit her; the second with the court of Berlin, and to agree with this court on the arrangements that relate to it, as well as those of the Prince of Orange, the Elector of Bavaria, and the Elector of Baden; the third with Austria, to agree with that power on arrangements relating to the Grand Duke of Tuscany and to one or, at most, two ecclesiastical electors, and to the Elector of Bavaria.

In this brief list, Napoleon clarified his intention to exclude Austria from the German reorganization. All he was willing to discuss with Vienna was compensation for the Habsburg Grand Duke of Tuscany. Napoleon intended to satisfy Frederick William (and to a lesser extent Alexander) and thereby persuade him to commit to a de facto alliance with France in defense of the new order. This method of negotiation was more likely to lead to the specific rearrangement of Germany and Italy that Napoleon desired, as well as perpetuate the diplomatic isolation of Vienna.

Napoleon did not aim merely at securing the agreement of the various powers separately to a better peace than he could have gotten as the result of a general and joint negotiation, however. He also wanted to destroy the real significance of the Holy Roman Empire and break Germany into two hostile camps, one ranged around Vienna and one around Berlin, where he could hold the balance:

> In this way, the German Empire will find itself actually divided into two empires, because the matters relating to it will have been arranged at two different centers. Once these arrangements have been completed, will the German constitution still exist? Yes and no; yes, because it will not have been destroyed; no because its affairs will not have been arranged all together and because, more than ever, there will be opposition on various issues between Berlin and Vienna.[6]

It is important to note here that Napoleon's vision of a Germany divided between Austria and Prussia differed sharply from Alexander's. Whereas the tsar desired a balance between the two German states, Napoleon did not work for such an end. To him, Germany was stable if Prussia, backed by France and at least the benevolent neutrality of Russia, was predominant and Austria isolated, dispossessed, and helpless. The reason was simple. Napoleon did not fear that an overly powerful Prussia would be tempted to aggrandize herself at the expense of a weakened Austria because he never doubted his ability to cajole Prussia into passivity by threats or promises. Once again, this organization of the European states could have been stable as long as Napoleon sought peace and stability. Since he did not, however, its instability was manifest almost immediately.

In Memel, Alexander learned of the methods Napoleon proposed to resolve the issue of compensation. He was informed that the Prussians had just signed a convention with Napoleon on that issue. In addition, Bavaria signed a similar convention with France at nearly the same moment.[7] These agreements spelled out the compensation to be granted to Bavaria and Prussia before Russia had agreed, let alone the Holy Roman Empire or Europe generally.

Napoleon was concerned with Alexander's possible reaction to this news, but he felt that he had prepared the ground by bribing the tsar. He promised extensive gains for Baden and Württemberg, whose princes were closely linked to Alexander by blood and marriage, even proposing an electorate for the Margrave of Baden, Alexander's father-in-law.[8] This bribe was indiscreet, for Alexander maintained throughout the negotiations that he was seeking a stable and secure peace for Europe and not gains for himself or Russia. Although Alexander did in fact insist on such gains, Napoleon's ham-handedness was unfortunate and insulting—especially when he later tried to claim payment for services so obviously rendered.

In the meantime, however, Alexander decided to come to terms with Napoleon. Discussions about the shape of compensation in Europe had been going on for some time between the Russian ambassador in Paris, A. I. Morkov, and Napoleon's foreign minister, Charles Maurice de Talleyrand-Périgord. They determined the basic terms of compensation during the spring of 1802. In June a Russo–French agreement on compensation was ready for signature. Morkov was bitterly hostile to the negotiation and to the idea of such an agreement, although he carried out his master's will more or less faithfully. But on the eve of the signing of the agreement, he warned Alexander of the folly he was about to commit:

> In fact, Sire, if the plan in question is adopted and executed, Germany will undergo a complete upheaval. The princes who will have gained power through the favor of France will be attached to her forever, and in serving her ambitious views will always think that they are serving their own. The only formidable power, Austria, who could still raise a barrier against the torrent of French ambition, by losing all consideration and all influence, will necessarily lose a great part of her means of sustaining a struggle already unequal.[9]

These words were half wise and half foolish. Morkov put his finger precisely on the damage that the compensation would do to Austria's position in Europe and therefore to the prospects for stability on the continent. He was also right that the states bought by Napoleon in 1802 would largely stay bought, hoping for continued benefits resulting from loyalty to their new master. He was wrong, however, in imagining that there was much Russia could do about it. Napoleon would not have settled for anything less than he demanded except as the result of a defeat in a war that Alexander could not fight at that time. The only real alternative Alexander had was to withdraw from European affairs, as Kochubei advised him to do. But he was not willing to withdraw and so found himself forced to participate in the further erosion of Austria's security and Europe's stability.

Alexander, aware of his predicament, responded to Morkov that he was cognizant of the distastefulness of the step he was about to take. But he felt that the alternative course of removing himself from European affairs was unwise and would prove more harmful in the end. He pointed out that Russia was the only state in Europe that would even try to stand up for Austria's rights, such as they were. There was no certainty that Austria would get even the promised compensation. He began to see the necessity of defending Austria against Napoleon's depredations, but he felt that he could only accomplish that aim in concert with Napoleon rather than conflict.

The agreement signed on June 3, 1802 signaled Alexander's determination to take an active role in the conduct of European affairs, as well as his rejection of Kochubei's policy of Russian isolation.[10] It also reflected Alexander's growing conviction that Napoleon posed a danger that had to be checked, although for the moment he opted for a loose restraining alliance rather than conflict. But it also represented a response based on weakness and did great harm to any notion of stability in Europe at that time.

Had Alexander been stronger or willing to ally himself with other states against France, he might have been able to insist on the discussion of compensations openly at a conference. All of the major players clearly had this in mind after the Treaty of Lunéville. Such negotiations would probably not have produced a radically different result, since Napoleon was determined to have what he wanted. But it would have lessened the atomization of Europe and the every-state-for-itself mind-set that characterized most of 1802. Instead, Napoleon again divided his foes among themselves diplomatically, sowing distrust and resentment. Even as his excessive demands and open ambitions were leading to the formation of the coalition against him, Napoleon was also weakening that coalition and confusing its future members about their real needs and concerns.

Alexander imagined that he had gained a voice in the future organization of Europe by consenting to Napoleon's destruction of the Holy Roman Empire and continued punishment of Austria. He tested that assumption by pressing the case of the king of Piedmont-Sardinia more forcefully than ever. He was reluctant to leave France in possession of Piedmont, which Napoleon had annexed in September 1802, and he sought compensation for the dispossessed king somewhere on the mainland of Italy. There seem to have been equal parts monarchical solidarity and realpolitik in this policy. On the one hand, Alexander was sincerely distressed at the plight of the Sardinian king, who found the climate of Sardinia so unhealthy that he could not live there. On the other hand, Alexander wanted to restore the independence of Piedmont, which would have stabilized the newly established states of northern and central Italy and secured them from French domination. Failing that aim, he hoped to grant the king compensation elsewhere in northern Italy that would serve the same purpose.[11] But Napoleon would have none of it, and by the end of the year, the negotiations concerned merely which few hectares of land along the western

Italian coastline the king could have. In no sense did Alexander succeed in establishing a buffer between Piedmont and the rest of Italy.

Alexander was willing to swallow even that failure in the interest of general peace. After all, if Napoleon's intentions were peaceful, then it mattered relatively little what exactly he possessed in Italy, and the well-being of the king of Sardinia was a small price to pay for a stable European order. This tense but benevolent attitude could not survive the outbreak of a new Anglo–French war.

The Turn to War, 1803

The crucial event along the path from peace to war on the continent was the renewal of war between Britain and France. That conflict did not have to lead inevitably to war on the continent. The question depended largely on how each side conducted hostilities against the other, as the Russians recognized. Given that one of the belligerents was Napoleon, however, the likelihood that war would spread to the continent was high, for Napoleon lashed out at any targets he could hit rather than confining his efforts to his actual enemy. As usual, in seeking to hit Britain everywhere in Europe, he did her very little harm but struck Russia and Austria in a way that drove them toward an alliance against France.

One of the reasons it is difficult to explain the turn from peace to war between 1801 and 1805 is that the context in which events occurred was at least as important as the events themselves. As we shall see, Napoleon's exploits in Italy in 1805 were not markedly more "aggressive" than what he had gotten away with in 1802 or 1803. Nor were his arguments for maintaining French troops in other states less valid later when they were rejected than they had been earlier when they were accepted. It is easy to point to the relative triviality of the issues that served as casus belli, to argue either that Alexander, Francis, and Pitt were determined to go to war no matter what, or that their policies were driven by such inanities as the execution of a single French exile. In truth, no such matter led to war.

As we have seen, Alexander was genuinely interested in peace, but not at the expense of Russia's security and interests in Europe. He would accept certain Napoleonic actions only if he could be convinced that Napoleon was equally sincere in his pacific professions. Napoleon, however, convinced him otherwise in a series of actions that seemed to be provocations to Alexander, who was now hostile and suspicious following the renewal of war with Britain.

It was a mark of Alexander's shift of focus that he replace his isolationist foreign minister, Kochubei, with Alexander Vorontsov. Elder brother of the Russian ambassador to Britain, Anglophile Simon Vorontsov, Alexander Vorontsov leaned generally in Britain's direction, but he was not willing to place Russia's policy at Britain's disposal. He advocated a strong Russian presence in Europe in pursuit both of peace and the status quo and of Russia's particular interests. He was not committed to making an alliance with any particular state, but he was far more willing to contemplate any alliance than Kochubei had been.

It is not true that Tsar Alexander was the pawn of his advisers and that his policy changed as he changed those who nominally served him. Alexander had already rejected Kochubei's notions of isolationism before replacing him, first by going to Memel and then by signing the June compensation agreement with Napoleon. As the most authoritative historian of this issue argues strongly, Alexander chose advisers to suit his changing moods, but he did not change his moods to suit his new advisers.[12]

Replacing Kochubei with Vorontsov was odd, however, on another level. Alexander was a young ruler surrounded by the aged remainders of two previous monarchs. Hostile to his father and uncomfortable with his grandmother, Alexander was never at ease with the elders around him. He surrounded himself, instead, with confidants of approximately his own age, some, including Kochubei, members of the "unofficial committee,"* others in a less formal pattern. In his early years, Alexander found it difficult to work with the senior statesmen who had served his father and his grandmother, a fact that would greatly complicate his relationship with General M. I. Kutuzov, among others. Although Vorontsov was sixty years old, nearly forty years older than the tsar, Alexander felt comfortable with him because the new foreign minister took the side of the young men rather than of the elders in many of the disputes of the day. He was, in a sense, young in policies if old in years. His presence at the helm of Russia's foreign policy was important, however, because it lent weight and seriousness to the tsar's decisions. Bewigged aristocrat though he was, Vorontsov skillfully blended the two worlds in which Alexander had to live.[13] His appointment, moreover, clearly signaled Alexander's intention to play an active role in Europe, his preference for Britain as a potential partner, and his distrust of France.[14]

The Outbreak of War Between France and Britain

The view from Paris in the fall and winter of 1802 was very different from the outlook from London, Vienna, or St. Petersburg. As the compensation issue

---

*The unofficial committee *(neglasnyi komitet)* was a group of Alexander's young friends and confidants. Almost all of them were given at least one and frequently several senior positions in the government after Alexander took the throne. The group met more or less regularly with Alexander for the first few years of his reign. The group was "unofficial" in the sense that it was not a regularly constituted state body and had no rights or duties other than those assigned by the tsar at any given moment.

began to look settled and the isolation of Austria complete, Napoleon began to focus on what he regarded as the domestic business of a peaceful France. It was unfortunate for the peace of Europe that what Napoleon regarded as France's own business appeared to the other European states to be a series of threats to their security and provocations that they could not ignore.

During the last third of 1802, Napoleon addressed a number of strictly internal issues. He worked to rationalize the functions of his government, improve its financial condition and stability, and normalize the position of the Catholic Church following the Concordat of July 1801 with the pope. He also undertook a reform of the French army and navy to stabilize their position in the aftermath of the revolution and its wars.[15]

Napoleon also occupied himself with a number of issues that transcended France's boundaries. He worked both politically and militarily to consolidate his position in Italy. He spent a great deal of effort to acquire and establish normal government over a number of colonies, old and new.[16] He began hounding the refugees of the ancien régime from their prominent positions in the countries that had taken them in.[17] And he found himself drawn into the affairs of neighboring Switzerland when the postrevolutionary disorder in that country reached a stage he would no longer tolerate.

Napoleon probably had no desire to intervene in Switzerland and never gave any thought to the international repercussions of his actions. He took France's ascendancy in the Helvetian Republic for granted and assumed that the other great powers did also. He had withdrawn French troops from Switzerland earlier in the year, as he had promised to do, but it did not occur to him that he was thereby pledging never to send them back. When he did so in October 1802, he generated fear in London and St. Petersburg that his appetite for conquest was insatiable and his word worthless.[18]

The changed atmosphere in the other European courts largely produced the reaction to Napoleon's reoccupation of Switzerland, which in itself posed no real threat. The occupation violated the Treaty of Lunéville, but none of the states concerned would have challenged Napoleon's contention that Switzerland was part of France's sphere of influence—and its disorders therefore his problem. And the reform of the Swiss government imposed by Napoleon's "act of mediation" was so acceptable to the Swiss that it serves as the basis of Swiss government to this day.

Alexander nevertheless received word of the reoccupation of Switzerland with dismay. Napoleon announced somewhat apologetically that the situation in Switzerland compelled him to send French troops back into that country, but he assured the tsar that "the independence and the territory of that part of the republic [into which French troops were sent] would be maintained in their entirety."[19] This note crossed one sent by Alexander the next day, informing Napoleon that "the evacuation by French troops of the Kingdom of

Naples, of the Papal states, and of Switzerland, being a new step toward the independence of those states, has given me a real pleasure."[20] Not surprisingly, Alexander and Vorontsov saw the reoccupation of Switzerland as further evidence that Napoleon would not be bound by his own treaties, would not take the interests of other states into consideration sufficiently, and, above all, was not concerned about maintaining the peace. Alexander made no move to resist the invasion and did not even consider issuing a forceful rebuke.[21] But his confidence in his ability to work with Napoleon or even seek an alliance with Napoleon that might restrain him was further eroded. His desire to find allies to help him check France likewise increased.

The reaction in London was stronger because Britain was the apparent target of other Napoleonic ventures and because the language he used to explain and justify his actions to the Court of St. James was bellicose and insulting. In dealing with Alexander, whom he hoped to keep sweet, Napoleon was diplomatic and respectful. On the one hand, he implicitly acknowledged the tsar's right to concern himself in such matters and, on the other, he offered reassurances of his peaceful intentions. In contrast, he met British protests aggressively. Napoleon ordered his envoys to London to state that Britain, which was not a signatory to the Treaty of Lunéville, had no valid interest in the affairs of the continent and no legal basis for protest. In response to British demands that he withdraw his troops from Switzerland on the grounds that their presence violated the agreements of Amiens and Lunéville, Napoleon replied that since France had thousands of troops in Switzerland, Piedmont, and the Italian Republic at the time of the signing of the Treaty of Amiens, the British could hardly use that treaty to object to their continued presence in smaller numbers. Since the king of England did not formally recognize Napoleon's satellites in Italy and along the Rhine, moreover, he had no right to involve himself in matters that did not concern him by demanding changes in a situation he did not recognize. Napoleon added, challengingly, that the Treaty of Amiens did not address the situation on the continent at all and that the British king, who was not a party to the Treaty of Lunéville, had no right to make any demands on the continent. The first consul refused, finally, to "allow England to interfere [in Switzerland] because she would only busy herself in sowing disorder there; it would be a new Jersey from which troubles against France would be fomented."[22]

Napoleon was outraged that the British harbored émigrés of the ancien régime and allowed them to wear the decorations and orders of a French government that, he pointed out, Britain no longer recognized.[23] He saw the virulent attacks on France in British newspapers as a deliberate provocation. He thus rejected the British protests with scorn.

The British notes themselves had been far from friendly, and London reacted to Napoleon's rebuff very strongly. The reasons for British hostility were easily found. First, by the end of 1802 it was becoming increasingly clear that the Treaty of Amiens established a very bad peace for Britain. Second, Napoleon's aggressive efforts to acquire a colonial empire were seen as a clear and present danger to Britain's security and prosperity. And third, Napoleon's demands that Britain censor her press to suit him and expel the émigrés insulted the sovereignty of the British state.

From the British perspective, Napoleon's efforts to recover an overseas French empire in peacetime were the most upsetting of his actions. It was bad enough that he had ordered General Victor Emmanuel Leclerc to put down the uprising of Toussaint l'Ouverture in Haiti and sent General Claude Victor Perrin with several battalions to take possession of Louisiana in late 1802.* Worse still, he showed that he seriously intended to take possession of the portions of India promised him in the Treaty of Amiens and build up a rival Indian empire around them.† These efforts, moreover, generated constant naval and military activity around France's seaports, as troopships filled with soldiers and convoys escorted them out to sea.

The British correctly perceived these moves as threats. Napoleon intended to engage in a global commercial and military rivalry with Britain that he hoped someday to win. The British were also right to see danger in the intervention in Switzerland and, above all, in Napoleon's high-handed replies to their protests. Although France controlled Switzerland, northern Italy, and the Netherlands, when the peace was concluded, Britain, Russia, and Austria all hoped that these states would come to function as independent buffers over time. Indeed, such a development was essential to the long-term stability of the peace, for if those countries remained French puppets, then French hegemony in Italy at least was assured. The Act of Mediation that Napoleon imposed on the Swiss at bayonet point was only the most obvious and visible demonstration of the vassalage of the supposed buffer states.

Nor could the British accept the principle that the Treaty of Amiens excluded them from any role in continental affairs, as Napoleon claimed. That the prime minister, Henry Addington, had been willing to sign a peace effectively ceding the Netherlands to France was remarkable enough. But he could not then accept Napoleon's fiat that the affairs of western Europe were not Britain's concern. For one thing, the fact that George III was elector of

---

*The initial order to concentrate a force for Victor to take to North America was given in August 1802; by December of that year Napoleon was growing frantic about getting him off on his mission (presumably before hostilities with England made it impossible). See Napoleon to General Berthier, 24 August 1802, *Corr. de Nap.*, doc. 6268, and Napoleon to Rear Admiral Decrès, 19 December 1802, *Corr. de Nap.*, doc. 6497.

†Among the other terms of the Treaty of Amiens mentioned in the preceding chapter, it restored to France most of her colonial possessions around the world, including those in India, that the British had conquered during the war.

Hanover as well as king of England gave him (and, by extension, Britain) a voice in the affairs of the Holy Roman Empire. Neither the king nor his ministers could watch calmly as France built up an impregnable glacis of client states, making herself invulnerable to attack in Europe even as she reached out to secure colonies overseas.

The intervention in Switzerland was thus an important turning point, stoking Anglo–French hostility and pointing to war. A series of further provocations cemented the turn. In October Napoleon sent a harsh warning to the Batavian Republic that he would not tolerate any changes in the government there or its policies, and that he was prepared to defend his interests through the use of force.[24] He failed to evacuate French forces from Dutch territory as he had pledged to do in the Treaty of Lunéville.

The British continued to maintain forces in Malta and Egypt, two countries they had pledged to evacuate within six months of the ratification of the Treaty of Amiens. Napoleon protested these violations of the treaty, but Lord Hawkesbury, the British foreign minister, met these protests with evasions. On January 30, 1803, no doubt in retaliation, Napoleon published the report of Colonel Horace Sébastiani concerning his travels throughout Egypt and the Ottoman Empire, in his official government organ, the *Moniteur*. This report included claims that the British army in Egypt was exhausted and useless and that a French force of 6,000 men could easily retake that land.[25] Napoleon had prepared Sébastiani's mission at the beginning of September.[26] His instructions emphasized the need to learn all there was to know about the state of British forces in the region and of the crucial fortresses in Egypt and the Middle East generally.

It seems unlikely that Napoleon intended to do anything with the information Sébastiani collected. The threat implicit in the *Moniteur* report was, in all likelihood, a bluff. Napoleon was in the process of building up a fleet that could challenge Britain, but it was not ready in early 1803. As late as mid-January 1803, Napoleon did not think that he would go to war with Britain before the fall of 1804.[27] Napoleon was probably convinced that the Addington government was weak and could be cowed by threats and intimidations—his preferred diplomatic tools. This impression is strengthened not only by the tone of Napoleon's written correspondence with various diplomats but by two conversations he had with Lord Whitworth, the British ambassador to France.

The first took place in mid-February when Napoleon called in Whitworth to discuss British protests over the Sébastiani report. According to Whitworth, the conversation was largely a two-hour monologue in which the First Consul delivered an ultimatum: Britain must evacuate Malta or face war. In addition, Napoleon complained once again about articles in the British press antagonistic to France and prominent émigrés in England and their activities. He also asserted that "if he had felt the smallest Inclination to take Possession of [Egypt] by Force, he might have done it a Month ago, by sending Twenty-five thousand Men to Aboukir, who would have possessed themselves of the whole Country in Defiance of the Four thousand British in Alexandria."[28] He added that he had 480,000 soldiers "ready for the most desperate Enterprizes," and that he was prepared, if necessary, to assault England. He warned that "to preserve Peace, the Treaty of Amiens must be fulfilled; the Abuse in the public Prints, if not totally suppressed, at least kept within Bounds, and confined to English papers; and the Protection so openly given to his bitterest Enemies . . . must be withdrawn. If [England wanted] war, it was necessary only to say so, and to refuse to fulfill the Treaty." Whitworth felt he had received an ultimatum.

Napoleon soon strengthened that impression. During a reception at the Tuileries in mid-March attended by the entire diplomatic corps, Napoleon engaged in a bizarre harangue against Whitworth. He began by asking if Whitworth had any news from London about the most recent proposals. When Whitworth said that he did not, Napoleon replied, "So you are determined to go to War." Whitworth assured the First Consul that England was not, but Napoleon went to a small group of diplomats nearby, including the Russian ambassador, Morkov, and said, "The English want war, but if they are the first to unsheathe the sword, I shall be the last to replace it." He continued a little later, "You can perhaps kill France, but you can never intimidate her." In response to Whitworth's repetition that his country did not want war, Napoleon concluded, "You must then respect Treaties; Woe to those who do not respect Treaties; they will be responsible for it to all of Europe."*

The importance of these incidents lies less in the fact that they led to war between Britain and France than in the impact they made in St. Petersburg. By this point in 1803 the imminent renewal of conflict between France and Britain was as certain as any event can be, and these conversations were simply sparks thrown off by the fuse as it burned down to the powder. The way Morkov reported them to Alexander and the way the Russian court received them were actually important.

Morkov's Francophobia was well-known, and he made the most of the bellicosity in Napoleon's expostulations. His reports are worth quoting at length as an example of the exploitation, worthy of a Bismarck, of foolish belligerence:

> [Napoleon] insisted upon the evacuation of Malta as a certain measure
> on which depended the maintenance of the peace or the renewal of war.

---

*Whitworth to Hawkesbury, 14 March 1803, *Papers Relative to the Discussion with France*, doc. 43, pp. 133–134. Napoleon's version of the conversation is somewhat different, although the essentials are the same. The fullest account is in Napoleon to General Hédouville, the French ambassador to St. Petersburg, 16 March 1803, *Corr. de Nap.*, doc. 6636. A briefer version is in Napoleon to General Andréossy, Ambassador to Great Britain, 13 March 1803, *Corr. de Nap.*, doc. 6630.

He told [Whitworth] that England had tried to establish as complaints what had been done in Italy, in Switzerland, and in Holland; that all of what had been done was in the natural order of affairs and could easily have been foreseen during the negotiations at Amiens, that they should either not have concluded peace then or that they should hold to everything they had promised to do and especially with regard to Malta; that he did not hide his plans for Egypt; that he had the firm resolution to acquire it and very soon, either through conquest or through an arrangement with the Ottoman Porte; that this was also the desire of the inhabitants of that country, among whom he had a great number of intelligencers, and to find and encourage them he had sent Sébastiani not long ago. Since the English Ambassador had wished to cite all these avowals to strengthen the alleged motivations of his court not to restore Malta, as the only port in the Mediterranean from which she could counteract these aims so harmful to her interests, Bonaparte told him with anger, "that if that court persisted in its resolution, he would declare war immediately, that he already had an army of 400,000 combatants which he could augment with another 50,000; that he would try to make a landing in England and that he would put himself at the head of that expedition; that this would be a war of extermination in which he expected to have a great deal of success."[29]

Morkov had demonstrated repeatedly his hatred of the French alliance and his determination to undo it, and it is no surprise to find Napoleon's words, bellicose enough to begin with, transformed into specific threats in his reports.

Morkov even made the scene at the Tuileries seem more dramatic than perhaps it was. After the opening exchange, in which Napoleon told Whitworth that it seemed that France and Britain were due to fight for another fifteen years even as they had just completed fifteen years of war, Morkov attempted to throw oil on troubled waters, suggesting that it would be better to find an accommodation for the good of humanity. Napoleon replied that he wanted nothing more than peace,

"but Malta or war," and he added with an indignant movement, "We will have to throw black crepe over treaties and the statue of good faith after this." [After circulating] he rejoined the English Ambassador again and after having asked after his wife, when the latter answered that she had stayed at home to take care of one of their children who was sick, he said, "You have spent a bad season here; I hope that you will remain for the good one; but that does not seem likely after what has just occurred. France has not acted to intimidate England; but England will not intimidate France either. You can, he added, *kill* her, but you will not make her bend over the rights her treaties give her, and we are ready to come right to your land to reclaim them." He left the circle and while withdrawing he cried aloud, "*Malta or war, and woe to those who violate the treaties!*"[30]

Flamboyant in everything, Napoleon outdid himself in this exchange. In the hearing of at least fifty people (Whitworth claimed that 200 could hear), Napoleon issued an ultimatum to Britain even as he sought to blame her for the war's outbreak. He certainly eased Morkov's task of painting him as a belligerent bully unsuited to the role of head of state, helping to ensure that, despite his best efforts, this view of him as the aggressor and Britain as the victim would endure in St. Petersburg and Europe, despite the fact that it was Britain that formally broke her treaties and started the war.

Fear of French intentions toward Turkey largely conditioned Russia's reaction to the news of the impending collapse of the Peace of Amiens. Russian and Turkish forces had fought a common enemy for the first time in history as members of the Second Coalition, and Russia had been courting the Porte in hopes of making Turkey a more or less reliable and stable ally. Alexander firmly believed that a partition of Turkey did not suit Russia, at least as long as Constantinople was kindly disposed toward St. Petersburg. He saw that his best role was posing as the defender of the integrity of the Turkish empire against foreign depredation. Although he could have seen the continued British occupation of Egypt as one such threat, Alexander was far more concerned about Napoleon.

Russia was deeply committed to various projects in and around the Ottoman Empire at this time. In 1799 a Russo–Turkish fleet had seized the Ionian Islands from France (which had previously taken them from Venice), and Russia had been deeply involved in their fate ever since. By mid-1802 the Russian minister in the islands, Count G. D. Mocenigo, was attempting to reestablish peace and stable government there, with the assistance of a small Russian garrison. Projects for a constitution for the Republic of the Seven United Islands, as it was called, flew back and forth between Corfu and St. Petersburg. Across the Balkans the Russians had acquired rights of protection over the principalities of Moldavia and Wallachia, and they compelled the Porte to select pro-Russian and pro-Greek rulers for these regions. Confusion in Constantinople and disorder in the principalities kept this matter alive throughout 1803, and there was even a short debate over whether to send Russian troops to the area. (They decided not to do so.) Farther east, the Russians had begun annexing Georgia, at the request of certain Georgian families who feared that disorder in their Christian land would leave them at the mercy of the neighboring Muslims. Needless to say, the Ottomans were not enthusiastic about these Russian activities and, without an external threat, it is likely that Russian–Turkish relations would have been considerably more hostile than they were.[31]

But Napoleon's repeated declarations that he intended to retake Egypt and could easily do so, as well as his ceaseless intrigues in Corfu, Constantinople, and the Danubian principalities, convinced the Turks no less than the Russians that France was a serious menace to the continued existence of the Ottoman Empire and kept alive one of the strangest alliances in modern history. The Russians learned that Napoleon had sent agents, including Colonel Sébastiani, to the principalities to stir up trouble.[32] Their ambassador to the Porte reported that the French were working assiduously to turn the Turks back toward France and against both the Russians and the British.[33] From Corfu Mocenigo wrote that the French were placing the "Latin church" in those islands under their special protection as a way of intervening in the area.[34] Napoleon's threats and intrigues thus helped the Russians see the British side of the Anglo–French quarrel. Alexander ordered his ambassador in Constantinople to reassure the Turks on the subject of continued British occupation of Egypt.[35] He took this step out of his conviction that Napoleon intended to retake Egypt in short order.[36] Napoleon's adventures in the eastern Mediterranean were thus the second strong impetus driving the Russians away from France and toward an entente, at least, with Britain.

The real problem, however, was in Germany. In the same dispatch in which he described Napoleon's public interviews with Whitworth, Morkov related rumors of Napoleon's plans should hostilities be renewed. He noted, to begin with, the weakness of Napoleon's position: "There are few vessels in the ports, the largest and best part of the fleet is in the [Caribbean] islands and will be the first prey of the English. His armament along the coast of Holland is very weak and will be exposed to the same fate as his squadron in the islands." All the more reason, Morkov noted presciently, to foresee that Napoleon's actions would come on the continent, rather than at sea. Napoleon had already decided, he said, to reoccupy a large portion of the Kingdom of Naples, especially around the port of Otranto. Talleyrand, he reported, had relayed to a mutual acquaintance the possibility that the French might then seize the Peloponnesus as well. But the most troubling news was that it appeared that Napoleon's messenger to Berlin, General Géraud Christophe Michel Duroc, was charged with informing Frederick William that Napoleon intended to occupy not merely Hanover but Hamburg as well in order to cut off all of north Germany from England.[37]

Alexander reacted dramatically to this news. On March 29, 1803, he ordered a large-scale mobilization. Over 60,000 soldiers were sent to positions along the Baltic coastline, ready to move out on twenty-four hours' notice. Two weeks later another 12,000 soldiers were added.[38] This army was broken into four corps and was a balanced force of nine cavalry regiments, thirty-six infantry regiments, field, siege, and horse artillery batteries, and various supporting arms.

The location of the concentration areas makes it appear that Alexander intended to use it in northern Germany; forces designated for operations in the Mediterranean would have concentrated at Black Sea ports or on the Turkish frontier.

This action was a sharp break with Alexander's previous military policy. Upon taking the throne in March 1801, Alexander immediately embarked on rationalizing the chaos that his father Paul had spread throughout the armed forces and reducing military expenditures that he felt harmed the welfare and future development of the Russian state. In June 1801 he established a military commission under the chairmanship of his brother, Constantine, and including, among others, Kutuzov, Prince Petr Mikhailovich Volkonskii, and Dolgorukii. The commission worked steadily through 1805 producing new tables of organization and equipment for all of the formations in the Russian army with an eye toward rationalizing them and saving money. Some of the changes, such as reducing the number of companies per battalion from six to four, were aimed at implementing lessons learned in the previous campaigns against France.[39] Russian strategists, however, did not consider the possibility of war with France in 1802 and even into 1803. A detailed strategic evaluation of Russia's position in June 1803 studied prospects for war against Sweden, Prussia, Austria, and Turkey, but not against France.[40]

Although the Military Commission continued to work through 1805 reorganizing Russia's army, Alexander's focus had clearly shifted. With renewed war imminent between Britain and France, he believed he had to be ready to respond militarily in northern Europe, and he was prepared to sacrifice the demands of economy to do so.

Despite his preparations, Alexander was reluctant to take sides in the exploding Anglo–French crisis, having refused a proffered British alliance against France in November 1802, albeit very politely.[41] Alexander's hesitancy arose from several sources. First, he sincerely continued to hope for the preservation of peace in order to allow him to complete the process of putting Russia's house in order. Second, he did not think that Napoleon was ready for war and feared taking steps that would force the nations of Europe to choose sides. Third, he mistrusted the British cabinet, which he believed to be weak and confused and not a good prospect for an alliance. And, fourth, in the dispute as it was framed up until the middle of 1803, there was little that he could actually do.

Alexander's turn to war did not result from frustration with Russia's internal reforms and a hope that foreign adventures would provide a suitable outlet for his energies.[42] There seems to be considerable evidence, rather, that he embraced war reluctantly, realizing that even contemplating armed conflict endangered his desired internal reforms. By the beginning of 1803, however, Alexander was not entirely the master of his own fate. Foreign minister Alexander Vorontsov noted, "Of course, the abandonment of these principles [of external peace and internal reform] may not depend entirely upon the will of our sovereign, for it is necessary that other powers also follow these same principles." He added, "In the event of a visible danger of some sort of new upheaval in the political nature of the current order of the European powers or an intention to disturb the political existence of the Ottoman Porte . . . then the Emperor will find it necessary for the sake of Russia's own security to take active measures and abandon the peaceful system, so desirable for the well-being and reform of Russia."* These are not the words of a bellicose minister or tsar, and the restraint with which Russia conducted her policy over the next year highlighted the reluctance to abandon the path of more or less impartial mediation that Alexander preferred. But the storm clouds that would blow away that impartiality were visible, and Vorontsov and Alexander both realized that Napoleon was on the road to forcing them to declare themselves. They had already decided that in the event, they would not declare for France.

Alexander continued in the hope that the moment of decision could be delayed for a long time because he did not believe that Napoleon was ready for war. Vorontsov noted that despite the "passionate views of the First Consul, which often create dangers for other cabinets, I tell you that I am not entirely sure that he is as ready as many believe for breaking the peace and for new undertakings. It seems that there is more instability and boasting in that head than systematic views."[43] This evaluation seems valid. Napoleon's behavior throughout this crisis seems inconsistent with his preparations for war, as we have seen. Although the outbursts directed against Lord Whitworth both publicly and privately were probably calculated expressions of anger and instability, they do not seem to have been motivated by any clear policy. The only possibility is that Napoleon seriously contemplated retaking Egypt by force, in which case the continued British presence there and in Malta would have been a serious problem for him. But it is hard to imagine what he thought he would gain by such a strategy. The Russians' confidence that Napoleon was not ready for war mistook the situation in another respect. Both the Russians and Napoleon, it seems, underestimated the Addington government's will to resist him or perhaps overestimated its capacity to hold its ground in Parliament and with the king if it did not resist him. Alexander's miscalculation was almost certainly the child of Napoleon's own.

Alexander's mistrust of the Addington cabinet was both well founded and irrelevant. The Addington government had made one mistake after another, with the negotiation and signature of the Treaty of Amiens easily being the worst.† Its determined efforts to maintain the peace with France while making

---

*A. R. Vorontsov to S. R. Vorontsov, 1 February 1803, VPR, vol. I, doc. 153. This letter, like most of the formal letters sent out by the Russian foreign minister, was read and approved by Alexander.

†See Charles John Fedorak, *Henry Addington, Prime Minister, 1801–1804: Peace, War, and Parliamentary Politics* (Akron, Ohio: University of Akron Press, 2002), for a counterargument that attempts to put the Addington government in a much more sympathetic light.

up some of the ground given away at Amiens made it seem both more bellicose toward France than it actually was and weaker than it turned out to be.
Like all governments in even partially democratic states that are perceived to
be weak, the Addington government felt increasing pressure to seem strong.
By the spring of 1803, the warhawks were getting the upper hand in London,
but Addington and Hawkesbury were not of that party. The pressure on their
apparently weak government to act aggressively became overwhelming and, as
the Russians and Napoleon expected, they took the easy way out. They found
to everyone's surprise that the easy way was the way of war. The Russians' and
Napoleon's confusion about the true strength of that government was therefore understandable. But if Napoleon proved wrong in his belief that the
British could be browbeaten with threats and troop movements in 1803, the
Russians were equally wrong to mistrust the British who proved, over the long
term, the most consistent and durable of Napoleon's opponents. The aberra-
tion of the Addington regime, however, helped paralyze Alexander during the
crisis by reducing London's attractiveness as an ally.[44]

The final problem holding the tsar back during the war crisis was that
there was nothing he could do, since the crisis centered around a dispute over
Malta and, to a lesser extent, Egypt. Absent an ally in Prussia or Austria, the
Russians could not readily attack France even if that had been on anyone's
mind. The mobilization of an army on the Baltic coast seems to have presupposed that some combination of German states would have either resisted a
French invasion of Hanover or would have invited the Russians in to resist on
their behalf, although there is no record of diplomatic efforts in March to secure such an invitation. More difficult still were the issues of the Mediterranean. How was Russia to defend Malta, whatever interests she might or might
not have had there? Egypt? British trade at sea? Vorontsov went even further:
"If, on the collapse of peace with England, France confined herself in the use
of her power to an attack on her hostile neighbor, Russia would not have any
reason to concern herself with the combat of these equally powerful states."[45]
An attack by France against England could only be an invasion of England or
an attack on her colonies, and, in either case, France would have to find a way
to overcome the tremendous advantage of the Royal Navy, which seemed unlikely. Nor was England's puny army likely to be of much value against
Napoleon's vast force. Russia had little to fear from the struggle of shark
against lion—as long as it remained such a fruitless, hopeless exercise.

Vorontsov realized, however, that Napoleon's declared strategy would
make it impossible for Russia to sit idly by: "The intention already expressed
by the First Consul of striking blows against England wherever he can, and
under this pretext of sending his troops into Hanover, Northern Germany,
and the Kingdom of Naples, entirely transforms the nature of this war as it relates to our interests and obligations." Russia could not stand by as Napoleon

seized Hamburg as he was sure to do, having taken Hanover. In the case of Naples, Russia was bound by treaty to defend the territorial integrity of that state. Thus for all the desirability of simply letting France and Britain go at it, Russia would be forced into the quarrel. What is more, it had become certain that Russian intervention would be on the side of Britain.

Still, Alexander was undecided about what action to take in the summer of 1803. It appears that the French request for his arbitration of April of that year momentarily disarmed his fears—and he momentarily disarmed his forces. On May 8 he issued an order to the troops he had mobilized in March and April to stand down and return to their normal peacetime positions.[46] The poor soldiers who had formed up and marched for several weeks, only to be told to march back again, were no doubt aggrieved, but they would have been much more angry had they known that this march and countermarch was just the beginning of a series of alarms leading up to the final crisis of August 1805.

3

Alexander's Turn Against Napoleon, 1803–1804

The renewal of hostilities between France and Britain was the pivotal event in the origin of the War of the Third Coalition. The actions Napoleon took alienated Alexander, whose search for allies led straight to the formation of the Third Coalition. The rise of this Franco–Russian antagonism came in one sense from mutual misunderstanding—Alexander and Napoleon could not see the world from each other's viewpoints and constantly misread each other's intentions. The conflicting atmospheres in Paris and St. Petersburg rendered communication between Alexander and Napoleon virtually impossible. Measures that seemed to Napoleon to be natural, necessary, and in no way threatening seemed to Alexander to be aggressive and dangerous. Alexander thought his actions throughout the crisis to be restrained, judicious, and evenhanded, yet Napoleon saw them as hostile, offensive, and lacking the ordinary decency that must prevail among friendly states. In such a climate of mutual incomprehension, nearly every action either side took raised the other's ire.

In another sense, however, there was no misunderstanding: Alexander became overtly hostile because he believed that Napoleon recognized no limits except those imposed by superior force. The tsar was right. A personality clash and growing tension were thus inevitable, but the expansion of the war was not. Although the six months following the collapse of the Treaty of Amiens cemented Alexander's determination to oppose Napoleon, it did not provide the tsar with the German allies necessary to act on that determination. Absent such allies, Alexander's wrath could have few practical consequences. For the time being, anger and rage grew in St. Petersburg and Paris like a voltage differential between two wires, but there was as yet no medium to conduct the spark.

Paris, 1803

The war with Britain preoccupied Napoleon in 1803, the more so because the outbreak of conflict caught him unprepared. Uncharacteristically, the Addington government attacked at just the right moment for Britain, when the Royal Navy was poised to sweep the French fleet from the seas at virtually no risk to itself. When Addington declared war on May 18, 1803, France had at sea approximately 25 ships of the line, 25 frigates, and 107 corvettes and smaller craft. This force was spread across the seas: the bulk, including 12 ships of the line, at Santo Domingo; 3 ships of the line and a moderate force at Toulon; 3 ships of the line and a small force at Brest; and the rest scattered from Holland to India, Martinique, Senegal, and elsewhere.[1] Against this force the Royal Navy could send at once 34 ships of the line and 86 frigates. In addition, following the outbreak of war, the Admiralty steadily put into commission 77 ships of the line and 49 frigates from its reserve.[2]

The day before the declaration of war, Admiral Cornwallis with ten ships of the line began moving toward Brest, France's main Atlantic port, which had at that moment only two ships of the line in commission and three that had just been completed.[3] Worse still, Napoleon had ordered ten French ships of the line and one frigate of those stationed at Santo Domingo to sail to Toulon in March. One was captured in the West Indies almost immediately, but the others altered course and sailed for safe harbors in France and Spain, several taking shelter at Corunna and Cadiz.[4] Nowhere did Napoleon have sufficient power to challenge the Royal Navy's blockading forces long enough to concentrate his fleet. He had lost the war at sea before it began.

Addington also prepared the British army. The king called out the militia in March, and by year's end the army included more than 94,000 regulars (counting those in Ireland), 85,000 militiamen, and 400,000 volunteers.[5] British statesmen suggested bombarding French ports and making landings on the French (or Dutch) coast. In the meantime, they hastened to blockade all the principal French ports, as well as the remainder of the French forces in Santo Domingo, and they seized the islands of St. Pierre and Miquelon off the Canadian coast and St. Lucia and Tobago in the Caribbean.

Napoleon had not prepared his fleet or his army for a war and could only respond to the British attacks defensively. In the days following the declaration of war Napoleon sent a flurry of orders to General Alexandre Berthier, his chief of staff, to man and equip coastal strongpoints and critical fortifications in an effort to defend the French coast and harbors from British assault.[6] He began to issue letters of marque to French corsairs on May 21, authorizing them to attack British shipping, and ordered a vast augmentation of his fleet, both large vessels and small, on June 3.[7] He ordered his admirals to conduct training cruises in their harbors or slightly beyond them, if the blockading forces were temporarily absent, but these orders were meaningless—there is no way to train a fleet to battle readiness without putting to sea.

The defensive nature of these measures made Napoleon look foolish. The despised Addington had stolen a march on him and had won the initial skirmishes. Worse still, the Royal Navy had achieved such an advantage that Napoleon could not reverse it. The situation was unbearable, and Napoleon naturally turned toward aggressive measures on the continent in the summer and fall of 1803.

Part of the First Consul's determination to strike where he could came from insecurity. In 1803 Napoleon's hold on power was not as firm as it would be later. He had ruled in France for only three and a half years in an epoch when French governments changed frequently—the Directory he had unseated had not lasted much longer than that. He also knew that a significant number of people in France and beyond resented his sole rule. A new leader who had seized power in a coup d'état with a promise to restore France to her ancient glory could ill afford the embarrassment he suffered at the hands of the Royal Navy.

Napoleon felt it necessary to address the initial defeats publicly. Two days after the declaration of war, he told the Senate, "Whatever injuries the enemy might have been able to cause us in places where we could neither anticipate nor reach, the result of this combat will be such as we have the right to expect from the justice of our cause and the courage of our warriors." He even addressed the supposed internal weaknesses of France that her enemies would try to play upon. Asserting that the British were supporting the "vile scoundrels" who had previously fomented insurrection against the Revolution and were prepared to do so again, Napoleon declared,

> Vain calculations of hatred! France is divided by factions and tormented
> by storms no more: France is restored to internal tranquility, regenerated
> in her administrations and in her laws, ready to fall with all of her weight
> on the stranger who dares to attack her and to unite against the brigands
> whom an atrocious policy would throw back again onto her soil to orga-
> nize pillage and assassinations there.[8]

Rhetoric aside, these addresses are uncharacteristically moderate. They do not promise an immediate response and refer only briefly to ultimate victory. The second even concludes, "Whatever the circumstances might be we will always cede to England the initiative in violent proceedings against peace and the independence of nations, and she will receive from us the example of moderation that alone can maintain social order."[9] How extraordinary it is to read a Napoleonic address announcing a war that concludes with a promise of moderation!

This care and caution in speech resulted in part from the fact that Napoleon himself did not know exactly when and how he would be able to strike back. He was loath to promise too much too quickly, when he had no plans ready to hand and when the prospect of rapid, decisive action was so remote, owing to the terrible balance of naval forces against him. He feared the domestic consequences of having his response to the British attack appear to hang fire, especially since he was certain that the British would spare no effort to arm hostile émigrés and send them clandestinely into France and neighboring states to cause trouble. Napoleon's overt dismissal of this danger in his first address to the Senate is evidence that it was a danger not to be dismissed lightly.

In the summer of 1803, Napoleon felt tremendous pressure to act as dramatically, decisively, and rapidly as possible. He hastened to attack the British wherever he could. On May 22 he ordered the arrest of all British subjects in France between the ages of eighteen and sixty who were enrolled in the militia or held a commission from His Britannic Majesty; they would be held as prisoners of war. He instructed the Italian Republic to issue a similar edict on the same day.[10] These orders were partly motivated by the fact that the British had already taken French seamen prisoner and would certainly take more, whereas Napoleon would have very few opportunities to seize British soldiers or sailors to exchange for them. They were also, however, among the first quick blows Napoleon could strike against Britain.

The First Consul had prepared the next two blows even before the British declared war.* On May 13 he ordered General Edouard Mortier to prepare a force to occupy Hanover. On the same day Talleyrand instructed his envoy in Naples to inform the King of the Two Sicilies that a French force would occupy the port of Tarento and other key positions should the Peace of Amiens fail.[11] Mortier defeated the small Hanoverian force and signed a convention with its leader effectively ceding him the electorate by 3 June; General Gouvion Saint-Cyr occupied the designated points in Naples later that month.†

These measures were natural in the context. George III of Britain was also the elector of Hanover. Seizing that small German state struck Britain directly and provided a bargaining chip and the prospect of more British prisoners of war. Naples was another natural target. For one thing, Napoleon thought that

---

*Although Napoleon prepared elements of his army to strike back at Britain even before hostilities had formally recommenced, he did nothing to prepare his navy for such an eventuality. This failure probably reflects Napoleon's weakness as a naval strategist; he did not think clearly about what the British might do to the unprepared French fleet with a sudden attack. The inevitable delays involved in naval maneuvers and the danger to which ships caught during such maneuvers were exposed, however, might also have militated against efforts to concentrate his fleet in advance of hostilities.

†The invasion of Naples was ordered on 23 May 1803; Napoleon to General Murat, 23 May 1803 (*Corr. de Nap.*, 6763). The positions that Saint Cyr "reoccupied" were those to which Napoleon referred when telling the British that the situation at the time of the negotiating Treaty of Amiens was less favorable to them than the one they were complaining about in 1802. See above, Chapter 2.

the court of the Kingdom of the Two Sicilies was a wholly owned subsidiary of the Court of St. James because an Englishman, Lord Acton, served as prime minister. For another thing, Naples contained the best harbors in southern Italy, including Naples itself, Tarento, and Brindisi. Napoleon was determined not to allow these ports to fall into British hands but, on the contrary, to retain and preserve them for his own use.

The pretext for the invasions was that since Britain had violated the Treaty of Amiens by refusing to evacuate Malta, France was obliged in self-defense to retake the territories she had held prior to the ratification of that treaty. (This included ports in Naples.)[12] Most likely Napoleon was desperate to take some offensive action at the outbreak of war to demonstrate that he could harm Britain and to compensate for the damage the Royal Navy had done so rapidly to the French fleet and colonies.

In truth, the seizure of Hanover and of Naples did not hurt Britain that much. British strategy did not revolve around either of those states, especially since there was no significant British land force ready in mid-1803 to undertake operations on the continent. The June invasions might have wounded British prestige, but everyone in Britain and Europe had expected the British response to come by sea and in the colonies, which it did. Although the blow aimed at Britain missed its intended target, it affrighted and affronted a number of bystanders, especially Austria and Russia, as we shall see.

Napoleon did not abandon his attempts to strike Britain after these first steps. On June 20 he forbade the importation of British or colonial goods into France by British or neutral vessels.[13] This declaration began the economic war that Napoleon would pursue against Britain to the end of his reign. It would ultimately lead to the imposition of the continental system in 1806 and to everything that flowed from that policy.

In addition, Napoleon began to root out those he suspected of plotting to overthrow him or cause mischief. On May 25 he issued 12,000 francs to the prefect of Morbihan, on the southeastern coast of the Brittany peninsula, "either for the search for hidden brigands or to give 12 francs for each musket that is turned in."[14] He ordered the minister of justice to compile information on all mayors and priests of the region, as well as "on the situation of public opinion in these communities and those of the inhabitants who could be suspected of being the heads of correspondence with" Georges Cadoudal, the former leader of the *chouan* resistance movement that had flared throughout Brittany and the Vendée region for much of the revolutionary period.[15] Napoleon ordered Berthier to establish garrisons of gendarmes in a number of communities in Brittany and the Vendée "by which people correspond with England and the Morbihan."[16] In June, Napoleon first ordered the arrest of individuals whom he believed were agitating against him, and he designated questions to be put to individual suspects subjected to interrogations.[17] He also began to focus his attention on the coverage French journals and pamphleteers accorded to the renewal of hostilities, ordering the minister of justice to reprimand some and to censor others.[18]

This concern for the internal stability of his regime was not unfounded. Napoleon was about to increase conscription to fill out his armies, and such increases traditionally led to insurrections and disturbances in rural France throughout the revolution. Napoleon was also convinced that the British were supporting disaffected French émigrés, as we have seen, and that some of those émigrés, most notably the devoted rebel Georges Cadoudal (known simply as Georges), maintained contacts throughout France ready to act when the time was right.

Once again, the First Consul's actions, although high-handed and occasionally draconian, were understandable in the context. Napoleon was convinced that Addington was nurturing a fifth column against him. He thought it essential to destroy the basis for domestic opposition to his actions and attack the external conspiracy that was attempting to create and sustain it. The actions that he took to pursue this objective, however, had ramifications far beyond the pursuit of a few brigands and would-be revolutionaries.

The Formation of the Army of England

In June, Napoleon also began to prepare a strike against Britain in response to the provocations, attacks, and defeats he had suffered since mid-May at the hands of the Royal Navy. He formed a large army on the Channel coast and a flotilla of small ships to transport it to the shores of perfidious Albion. He intended to resolve the problem of Britain once and for all.

There is considerable controversy over Napoleon's plans for the invasion of England. Some argue that Napoleon never seriously intended to invade England and undertook these plans and preparations to cover his real preparations for attacking Europe.* The chief support for this view, however, "is based ultimately on the theory that he never made mistakes."[19]

The evidence that Napoleon intended, at least in 1803 and 1804, to invade Britain is in fact overwhelming, however, and even his most assiduous defender accepts this conclusion.[20] The magnitude of the effort and expense

---

*This argument is strengthened by Napoleon's own statements subsequent to the war of the Third Coalition. In 1810, for example, he told Count Clemens von Metternich, "I would never have been stupid enough to undertake an assault on England . . . The army assembled at Boulogne was always an army aimed at Austria." Prince Richard Metternich-Winneburg, ed., *Aus Metternich's nachgelassenen Papieren* (Vienna: Wilhelm Braumüller, 1880), 1:42, note; also cited in August Fournier, *Gentz und Cobenzl: Geschichte der österreichischen Diplomatie in den Jahren 1801–1805, nach neuen Quellen* (Vienna: Wilhelm Braumüller, 1880), pp. 92–93.

involved in constructing the various flotillas and their armaments exceeded what Napoleon could reasonably have undertaken as a diversion. The surest argument, however, is that when the scheme was first put into action in June 1803 there was not the slightest prospect of a war on the continent in which the army of England might have been used. Prussia was a more or less staunch French ally; Austria was weak and cowed; Russia was still trying to mediate the Anglo–French conflict, as we shall see. Napoleon remained unaware of Alexander's abortive mobilization, moreover. One would have to credit Napoleon not merely with extraordinary foresight, but with nearly divine omniscience to suppose that he foresaw in June 1803 that he would need a large land army to fight Austria and Russia in September 1805. The truth is that Napoleon seriously intended to invade Britain in the winter of 1803, and he bent every effort to make the invasion succeed.[21]

The preparations for the invasion of England comprised three major undertakings: (1) naval preparations for the crossing, (2) the creation of the Army of England to do the fighting once the crossing had been effected, and (3) the reorganization of state finances to fund the first two tasks. Although the naval preparations were costly and complicated, they proved largely irrelevant to the war that was actually fought. The formation, organization, and training of the Army of England, however, as well as the development of the financial underpinnings to support it, would have dramatic consequences for the course of European and military history.

The order to form the Army of England was issued on June 14, 1803.[22] Napoleon decreed that six camps be established at Gand, Saint-Omer, Compiègne, Saint-Malo, Bayonne, and in Holland. He specified that the forces in these separate camps, each commanded by a lieutenant general and supplied with artillery and engineer assets of its own, would ultimately fight as a single army. Over the next several months, the troops trickled into their camps, built barracks and exercise grounds, and settled into camp life. Napoleon first visited the area in early July, although he was most concerned with securing the defense of the coasts and with the minor actions of French and British frigates off Calais and Dunkirk.[23]

The camps were organized and reorganized with the usual Napoleonic energy, and by the end of August four camps were coalescing into corps that would make themselves immortal in the campaigns that began in 1805. By an order issued on August 28, Napoleon placed General Nicolas Jean-de-Dieu Soult in command of the camp of Saint-Omer, also gave him overall command of the other camps, and granted him the right to correspond directly with Napoleon.[24] Generals Louis Nicolas Davout, Michel Ney, and Pierre François Charles Augereau commanded the other camps. All had extensive experience commanding brigades and divisions in the revolutionary wars, and most were respected as drillmasters and trainers. Their division commanders were likewise seasoned combat officers. In time they would forge a formidable military force.

In September 1803, however, they were not ready to go to war: "Nothing was ready to start a campaign; the regiments were far from being complete, the cavalry lacked horses, and one had just seen how the artillery was not in a satisfactory state."[25] There were delays as troops and commanders continued to arrive until late October. In some cases the movement to the coast had to be slowed while tents were procured or barracks constructed; brigades were ordered first to one place, then to another, reflecting Napoleon's constant changes of mind in small matters.

Napoleon was not deterred by these setbacks. He worked feverishly to circumvent his naval inferiority. He reasoned that a large fleet of small armed craft could transport an army of 100,000 men across the Channel in one night or, at most, two. However assiduous the Royal Navy might have been in patrolling the Channel, he figured, it should be possible to find a moment of weakness and force the passage. He therefore ordered that thousands of small transports and gunships be constructed by November 1803, when he hoped to cross under cover of long winter nights. The construction of the flotilla took longer than expected, however, and Napoleon, who never understood the sea, continually discovered new and unexpected problems. By September he realized that he would not be ready to invade on his original date, so he postponed it to January 1804. In December he changed the plan considerably, deciding that he needed the main fleet to protect the crossing, if only for twelve hours. The plan that would lead to the Battle of Trafalgar was born.[26]

Subsequent events led the invasion to be postponed until September 1804, and then even later. The critical fact, however, is that the Army of England was supposed to be ready for action by the winter of 1803. It stayed together encamped in fighting formations for the following two years. Its commanders expected to be hurled across the English Channel within a few months. As a result, this force spent the two years between September 1803 and its advance into Germany in August 1805 training realistically and striving to retain constant battle readiness.[27] The same formations went to war under the same commanders. It is nearly impossible to think of another military force in modern times that has ever had such an advantage of being able to conduct prolonged training at the highest level of readiness in peacetime.* This fact helps explain Napoleon's stunning success in 1805–1807. It also gave Napoleon an extraordinary political advantage, since he had an army ready to go to war and most of his enemies did not—a threat that he never hesitated to use.

*France was at war from March 1803 on, but not with a continental enemy until September 1805. The training of the Army of England was not interrupted by deployments to meet current operations or imminent threats to which it had to divert its energies.

Napoleon's adversaries did not maintain their armies on such a footing. Neither Russia nor Austria, to say nothing of Prussia, intended to go to war in the near future. All three states suffered from financial weakness, and maintaining an army on a war footing for a long time is expensive. The steps Napoleon took to rectify France's finances were the last crucial element of his grand project of retribution against Britain.

Napoleon had the advantage of being able to draw on resources beyond France's own to support his armies and his wars. When war with Britain prevented France from maintaining her acquisitions in Louisiana, Napoleon sold that vast territory to the United States for a large sum. By maintaining Augereau's camp at Bayonne in position to attack Spain, Napoleon pressed the court of Madrid to buy its neutrality with a large subsidy.[28] Threats to Portugal produced an agreement for a one-time payment of a similar variety. The First Consul mercilessly extracted resources from Holland and Italy and plundered Hanover. He also worked hard to ensure that French business would recover from the blows dealt by the Royal Navy at the start of hostilities.[29]

The massive influx of cash in 1803 from Napoleon's various extortions was far more important than British gold. Napoleon could tell his subordinates to go about their business without worrying about the cost. He could afford to expand both the army and the navy at the same time. He could afford to maintain his army on a war footing continuously from September 1803. Although Napoleon's war against Britain did not achieve its objectives, his preparations for that war created ideal conditions for the campaigns he waged in 1805–1807.

From May 1803 onward, Napoleon prepared for war against Britain, frenetically working to build up the fleet and invasion force, destroy potential domestic enemies, and set his finances on a sound footing. He also exploited ways that came to hand to retaliate against Britain. From his perspective, all of these actions were rational and appropriate, considering that Britain had declared war and begun the conflict with such notable successes. Napoleon did not at this time harbor ill intentions toward any continental state. He did not mean to threaten Austria, Russia, or Prussia, and he did not understand why, since the British had so clearly placed themselves in the wrong by violating the Treaty of Amiens, those states should not see the appropriateness and necessity of the actions he took.

The renewal of hostilities with Britain also provided Napoleon with a touchstone he could use to measure other states: did they or did they not take his part in the struggle? Napoleon regarded with suspicion any states that did not join him and supposed that their leaders had been suborned by British gold. He was convinced that the kings of Spain, Portugal, and Naples were the dupes of Anglophile ministers, and he made peace with those states conditional on the dismissal of those ministers. Portugal and Naples resisted this demand, but in Spain a nervous monarch dismissed Prime Minister Godoy, known as the Prince of Peace.

Neutrality commonly elicits suspicion and hostility when a state at war or facing imminent danger must interact with other states not similarly threatened. The leaders of a beleaguered state often find it difficult to understand how the world appears to those who are still safe, and still more difficult to see how their own defensive reactions can appear to be offensive and aggressive to those who need not fear. So it was in this case, for virtually every one of the moves Napoleon undertook to defend himself or to attack Britain appeared to the other European states to be dangerous acts of aggression on his part calling for a response on theirs.

Hanover

Alexander watched Napoleon's adventures in Switzerland and Holland, as well as Colonel Sébastiani's expedition to the Near East, with growing anxiety. These actions, which predated Britain's refusal to evacuate Malta, convinced Alexander that Napoleon was untrustworthy and sought to aggrandize France beyond what she had won in her victories during the Revolution. Even before the renewal of war, the tsar had decided to side with Britain in the contest. Although Alexander distrusted both the intentions and the capability of the Addington government, Napoleon was the greater threat to the continental peace the tsar was determined to maintain.

News of the invasion of Hanover arrived in St. Petersburg followed by news of the invasion of Naples. To Napoleon, these actions were appropriate responses to the British violation of the Treaty of Amiens, since he had withdrawn from Naples after the ratification of that treaty. Furthermore, he refused to recognize that George III could be at war with him as king of England and at peace with him as elector of Hanover.

Alexander saw these invasions in an entirely different light. Napoleon had violated treaties that he and Alexander had signed guaranteeing the neutrality of Naples and the status quo in Germany.* When Napoleon represented his invasions of Naples and Hanover as responses to the British breach of Amiens, he conveniently ignored the fact that they violated his agreements with the tsar.[30]

---

*The peace treaty between France and Russia of October 1801 specifically guaranteed the neutrality of Naples (articles 4–5), while Russia's adherence to the Austro–French treaty regulating the compensation in Germany of December 1802 (Russia ratified the agreement in February 1803) could be seen as guaranteeing the status quo there, including George III's possession of Hanover. See F. Martens, *Recueil des traités et conventions conclus par la Russie avec les puissances etrangères* (St. Petersburg: A. Böhnke, 1902), 13:266ff. for the Franco–Russian Treaty, 2:378ff. for the Austro–French agreement.

The legalities of the situation bothered Alexander less than the strategic problems they posed. Napoleon's occupation of Naples gave him an excellent jumping-off point for an invasion of the Balkans or for causing trouble in the Ionian Islands. Although the Franco–Russian peace treaty guaranteed Russia's preponderant influence in the Ionian Islands, Napoleon had already violated other terms of that agreement. The seizure of Hanover, moreover, threatened to destabilize northern Germany completely, and Alexander was determined to prevent that.

In the summer of 1803, therefore, Alexander first turned away from his policy of attempting to manage Napoleon's aggressiveness through the peaceful means of a grouping alliance. He now believed that Russia might have to go to war against France to defend the peace of Europe. Alexander's conception of such a conflict was entirely defensive and reactive. He sought to keep continental Europe, and especially northern Germany (which was the most threatened region), out of the renewed Anglo–French conflict. He probably hoped that a simple declaration of his determination to protect the neutrality of northern Germany backed by a show of force would suffice, but he apparently was willing to fight if necessary.

At the end of May 1803 the tsar began to pressure Frederick William to defend Hamburg if Hanover was lost. The Russian ambassador in Berlin, M. M. Alopeus, offered assistance to Count Haugwitz, Prussia's minister of foreign affairs. Alopeus warned, "It is of the first importance, Count, not to confine oneself to words and simple diplomatic representations. One must prepare one's arms not for offensive purposes, but as measures of security that alone can make an impact."[31]

Frederick William made no meaningful response, and the continued Prussian inaction angered Alexander and Vorontsov. As a result, the next dispatch was more threatening. Vorontsov ordered Alopeus to demand a meeting with Haugwitz and insist on a clear answer from him about whether Frederick William intended to oppose French advances in Germany, "as the true interests of the court of Berlin require, assuring that minister that H[is] I[mperial] M[ajesty] will be ready to assist with them." The tsar wanted to know, accordingly,

1. What is the number of troops that [Frederick William] believes it will be possible to send and how many he will need from us, both in order to oppose the occupation of northern Germany by the French and to drive them out of it if the invasion is already complete.

2. If H[is] Prussian M[ajesty] is disposed to these measures, and if he finds it appropriate to regulate the affair through a convention between us and the court of Berlin and to bring into this common measure for the security of Germany the other states that have the same interest, such as the King of Denmark, the Elector of Saxony, the

Elector of Hesse, the Duke of Brunswick, and the Hanseatic Cities, you are authorized, sir, to receive a proposal of such an act or convention from the court of Berlin.[32]

Vorontsov concluded by instructing Alopeus to point out that a Prussian failure to agree would leave the Russians with no other recourse than to remain "spectators" in an affair that concerned Berlin more than it did St. Petersburg.

Alexander had been mobilizing an army on the Baltic coast to intervene in Hanover since the end of March.[33] He ordered it to stand down on May 8, several weeks before he sent the first note to Berlin. The reasons for this decision are not clear. As Alexander took up the mantle of arbitrator between Britain and France, he probably hoped that the outbreak of war could be delayed. Mobilizing his army was expensive, and it would cost even more to maintain the force on the Baltic coast indefinitely. Alexander may also have expected Frederick William to refuse his offer (as he ultimately did) and thus chose not to pay the cost of maintaining an army that probably would not be used. The timing is curious all the same.

The Prussians remained obstinately silent, and so Alexander himself took up the charge two weeks later. Impatient for action in a fluid situation, Alexander sent Frederick William a concrete proposal for establishing a Russo–Prussian "concert" to defend northern Germany from French aggression. This proposal committed Alexander to put an army of 25,000 men on a war footing immediately and to be ready to augment it to 50,000 or 60,000 if necessary. Prussia would commit to maintaining a force of equal size. Saxony would be asked to contribute up to 20,000, Hesse up to 18,000, and so forth. The goal of this armament would be to drive the French out of Hanover, either through diplomacy or by force, and to take joint possession of Hanover until a final peace was made.[34]

Alexander emphasized his impartiality and the altruism of his actions in the accompanying note to Alopeus:

> Although by the position of my empire I find myself almost beyond the reach of the dangers that I see hanging over the rest of Europe, I will nevertheless not hesitate, as you will see in the project of the convention, to offer a number of troops equal to that I wish Prussia to put in place for her own defense. The less my particular interest is in play in what I propose, the more my advice can have weight, having no principal aim but the advantages of H[is] Prussian M[ajesty] himself as well as of the security and independence of Germany.[35]

Russia had some direct interest in maintaining trade with northern Germany, but the motive Alexander was hiding behind his altruism was his conviction that Russia needed continental peace above all. He was willing, as Vorontsov had earlier advised, to watch idly as Britain and Napoleon fought, secure in the conviction that Britain would end up defending Russia's Near Eastern interests as she defended her own and that neither belligerent was likely to destroy the other. The peremptory demand for Prussian cooperation was part of an effort to ensure that the conflict did not spill over by ensuring the neutrality of northern Germany. If the conflict did spread, Alexander feared he would be drawn into it on worse terms. Two points should not be lost: Alexander was willing to contemplate a limited war against France in order to achieve this aim, and his goals at this point were entirely defensive. Napoleon had, in effect, crossed a line in the sand and Alexander no longer thought he could restrain Napoleon by working with him. Instead, he began to believe that he could restrain Napoleon better by finding allies to oppose his actions.

In the end, Alexander's policy shift had no immediate consequences, for Frederick William was determined to remain neutral at all costs. In March he had seen the danger Alexander reacted to in June, and he had made his decision almost immediately. As the prospect of war with Britain grew, Napoleon bestirred himself to obtain at least Prussia's tacit consent to the first belligerent measure he planned to take, the seizure of Hanover. Accordingly, he sent General Géraud Christophe Michel Duroc to Berlin at the end of March to inform Haugwitz and Frederick William of his intentions and to gauge their reactions. The Prussian response was very mild. Although Haugwitz pointed out that the British were certain to blockade the Hanseatic ports of Hamburg and Bremen following the French occupation of Hanover, he gave no indication that Prussia would oppose the occupation in any meaningful way. He also encouraged Duroc to believe that the relationship established between Frederick William and Alexander at Memel could be used to keep Russia neutral in such a dispute.[36]

In truth, the news of Napoleon's plans triggered a feverish reassessment of Prussia's policies. Frederick William's advisers split. Haugwitz and others advocated the defense of Hanover, while cabinet secretary Johann Wilhelm Lombard and a few colleagues argued for strict adherence to the policy of neutrality that had become Prussia's hallmark.* Frederick William's memories of his last encounter with Hanover fueled his timidity, for the Russians had persuaded him to occupy the electorate in 1801 as a way of striking at Britain but then, following Paul's death, had reversed course and made peace with Britain, leaving him in a highly awkward position.[37]

---

*Although Lombard was only a cabinet secretary, his real influence went far beyond what would be expected from someone in that position. See Brendan Simms, *The Impact of Napoleon: Prussian High Politics, Foreign Policy, and the Crisis of the Executive, 1797–1806* (New York: Cambridge University Press, 1997), pp. 133–135, for a discussion of Lombard's real role.

The king's first response was to draw up a number of plans for keeping the French out of Hanover or getting them out once they had invaded, transferring Hanover to Prussia for the duration of the war (with the agreement of the major powers, however, rather than as the result of a unilateral Prussian action).[38] Napoleon vaguely offered Hanover to Prussia in return for her support, even in neutrality.[39] It is unlikely that this offer played a large role in Frederick William's thinking. He was almost as fearful of Russia as of France, and he must have been aware that Napoleon's promises were not necessarily binding on the rest of Europe, even if the French ruler actually kept them.

Napoleon threatened to ally himself with Austria if Prussia proved difficult, which probably influenced Frederick William much more.[40] In his effort to scare Frederick William, Napoleon claimed mendaciously that Austria was trying to emerge from her isolation by allying with France. He emphasized that if Prussia did not prove to be a reliable ally, he would have to consider a return to the alliance system of 1756, of which the cornerstone was the Franco–Austrian alliance, however distasteful it might be. It was bad enough to have the French in Hanover—in the center of the kingdom, as Haugwitz moaned—but it would have been twenty times worse if, in addition, Prussia found France aligned with Austria. The threats and, to a lesser extent, the veiled promises kept Frederick William haplessly neutral. Haugwitz made a last effort on June 4 to persuade the king to work with Russia in the face of the clear and present danger posed by France. It failed. Haugwitz's rival, Lombard, drafted the note sent on June 6 to the Prussian ambassador in Paris, Lucchesini, capitulating to the seizure of Hanover.[41]

In this context, the Russian notes of June and July were doomed before they were presented. Frederick William rejected the Russian approaches politely but firmly. He claimed that he was ready to defend Hanover, but the Hanoverians opposed Prussian intervention and capitulated rapidly when they might have made a determined resistance. This claim was a half truth: although the Hanoverians did oppose Prussian intervention and did capitulate quickly, Frederick William had never seriously contemplated defending the electorate against French attack, even if he hoped at various times that the French would allow him to occupy and hold it for them for the duration of the conflict. Above all, however, he told Alexander that he was determined to avoid war; he was convinced that Napoleon would stop at Hanover and not threaten Hamburg or Bremen, and he feared that measures taken to oppose Napoleon would only facilitate the war he was dedicated to preventing. Thus the Prussian king attempted to remain on good terms with both powerful neighbors while staying out of conflict with either; he achieved this by relying on communication delays between Berlin and St. Petersburg and Napoleon's quick actions, which made it possible for Frederick William always to claim with some truth that the Russians were out of date.

The consequences of this decision were serious. First, it ended any prospect of opposing Napoleon at this point, when such opposition would have been relatively easier to manage than it proved two years later, and, second, it committed Frederick William to a way of thinking that would prove insurmountable during the actual crisis leading to war. As he considered his options in 1803, Prussia's king became convinced that neutrality was the only safe course to follow; he would not abandon that belief even when the situation changed dramatically.

From Alexander's perspective, it was a frustrating decision that prevented him from meaningfully opposing Napoleon's aggression. When the news reached St. Petersburg that Napoleon had invaded Hanover after all, Alexander responded with another mobilization, although this one was much smaller—six regular infantry and one jaeger regiments with no cavalry and a small complement of artillery.* He hoped, no doubt, to send this small force to support a Prussian move in defense of Hanover, but Frederick William's obstinacy made that impossible. This time, however, it does not appear that Alexander had this force stand down, despite the impossibility of its immediate use. The demands of economics and international politics were giving way to the concerns of military expediency and action.

In the long run, Frederick William's refusal to join Alexander in the defense of northern Germany indicated that Prussia would not be a reliable partner in the struggle to contain France. As subsequent events shifted the focus of attention to Italy, Austria's natural sphere of interest, Prussia's apparent pusillanimity contributed to Alexander's increasing preference for an alliance based on Vienna rather than Berlin.

Above all, the events of mid-1803 cemented Alexander's turn away from France and confirmed his conviction that Napoleon had to be opposed. The tsar still imagined war only as a defensive operation in which Napoleon's aggressive moves would be stopped and reversed, and he hoped that preparation for war would make war itself unnecessary. The mobilizations he ordered in March and June 1803, however, show that he was willing to spend money, and possibly Russian soldiers, in resisting Napoleon.

The Russian army received no benefits from these initial alarms, in contrast to the benefits France received from creating the camps at Boulogne. The large force mobilized in March did nothing more than form up and march around. The much smaller force mobilized in June may have trained when it arrived in its concentration areas, but that would have had little significance. First, the force was too small (not more than 12,000 infantry and a few guns) to train effectively in the large, realistic maneuvers that the French forces were

---

*SVM, vol. 4, pt. 1, bk. 2, sec. 2, p. 280. Jaeger regiments were light infantry used primarily as skirmishers to cover the movements of regular infantry.

conducting on the Channel coast. Second, without cavalry, the Russian force could not practice combined arms operations. Third, this force, which ultimately remained in northern Germany, did not end up fighting in a decisive theater. Fourth, there is no evidence that Alexander was willing to relax the financial and bureaucratic limitations on peacetime training for the benefit of this force. Thus, while the renewal of war in May 1803 sparked a full-scale mobilization and training of the French army, Russia's mobilization did nothing but spend money.

The Collapse of Franco-Russian Relations

It is not clear how well Napoleon was informed of Alexander's overtures to Frederick William. He probably was not aware of the depth of the tsar's opposition to him, since on June 10 he offered to submit the causes of conflict between England and France to Alexander's arbitration.[42] Napoleon's motivation for this move is also unclear. He made the proposal less than a week after publicly accusing Alexander of playing a "double game" and not working hard enough to avoid the war; he stopped just short of accusing the tsar of taking Britain's part. Even on that occasion, Napoleon admitted that the "intentions of the Emperor" might be "good," but "if so . . . they are badly supported by his ministers."[43]

This theme, which appeared in Napoleon's dealings with Spain, Portugal, and Naples, would continue to befuddle his relations with Alexander. Napoleon seems to have been convinced that Alexander meant him well or could be a useful tool but that he was surrounded by Anglophile ministers who thwarted his good intentions. This charge was not utterly baseless. Alexander Vorontsov, the foreign minister, respected his Anglophile brother Simon, the ambassador to the Court of St. James. The foreign minister himself mistrusted Napoleon, Morkov, the Russian ambassador in Paris, hated Napoleon, and all three continually advised Alexander to take Britain's part against France. Napoleon erred, rather, in supposing that Alexander himself did not share this view. On the contrary, Alexander repeatedly affirmed his support for both Vorontsovs' and for Morkov's policies, and his own rescripts show no important divergence from the policies they advocated. It may be, nevertheless, that Napoleon sincerely believed that when Alexander faced the issue directly, the decision would suit him.

It is equally possible that Napoleon expected Britain or Alexander to refuse his offer, as both eventually did. In this case, Napoleon might have been attempting to paint himself in the most positive and peace-loving light, hoping to persuade Alexander and the other continental monarchs of his benign intentions. However that may be, the effort backfired in a way that stoked the growing antagonism between Paris and St. Petersburg.

Napoleon's proposal briefly swayed even the fiercely Francophobic Morkov. In a letter to Simon Vorontsov, Morkov described a private interview with Napoleon and concluded, "The result of this interview seems to me not to leave any doubt about the sincerity of the peaceful intentions which the 1st Consul has just shown."[44] Napoleon even offered a plan to serve as the basis for Alexander's decision: Alexander would take charge of Malta, Napoleon would evacuate Holland and Switzerland immediately, Britain would be given the island of Lampedusa, the fate of the king of Sardinia would be determined to Alexander's satisfaction, and Napoleon would agree to any discussion aimed at establishing the "security and independence of Europe in general" as long as the territorial status quo of France before the war was retained.

Shortly thereafter, Napoleon took Morkov aside at another event and spoke with him for three hours. The conversation was a clear example of the inability of Napoleon and Alexander's court to communicate in the context of the situation of 1803. Napoleon began by emphasizing to Morkov the "grandeur" of the role he was inviting Alexander to play by arbitrating the dispute between England and France. Morkov responded that the tsar understood the honor but was disturbed "to see that [Napoleon] would not fulfill the engagements he had undertaken with him, by refusing to do justice to the king of Sardinia and by violating the neutrality of Naples, Germany, and above all the Hanseatic cities."[45]

Napoleon gave a lot of ground in response to this charge. The king of Sardinia, he declared, would not lose by waiting, and Napoleon "knew very well that what he was doing with regard to the king of Naples was entirely unjust, but that he had an interest in doing the English as much harm as possible, directly or indirectly; and that it was from this same consideration that he acted with regard to the Hanseatic cities." This was quite an admission. Face-to-face with Morkov and alone, Napoleon dropped the pose he had presented to the rest of Europe. He did not claim the right to occupy Naples and Hanover because the British had violated their treaty but put the conversation on a realpolitik footing. No doubt he expected Morkov to recognize his candor and reciprocate by dropping what Napoleon believed to be a pose on Alexander's part. But Alexander was not posing, nor was Morkov.

Instead, Morkov replied with a thrust:

"You admit then," I said to him, "that you do not wish to recognize any other right than that of your convenience and force, and if that is the case, then where is the security of Europe? Where is the confidence that [Europe] could put in the treaties that states make with you?" Napoleon, unable to continue to hold his temper in check, replied that Britain gave a beautiful example of respect for treaties and asked, "Why is it that all of the powers do not unite to force [England] to observe that of Amiens?"

Here lay the crux of the misunderstanding between France and Russia in 1803. Napoleon felt that Britain had clearly violated the treaty and knew that Alexander staunchly defended treaties. He could not imagine that the tsar would fail to be repelled by Britain's perfidy. He was willing to recognize that his own actions were, in a sense, unjust, expecting the Russians to recognize the higher justice—surely they would not deny him the right to respond to an unprovoked attack that contravened international norms? Yet to the Russians, the British attack was not unprovoked and violated international norms less than Napoleon's invasions did. The British occupation of Malta had little strategic significance for Russia, whereas the invasion of Hanover and Naples seemed to threaten Russian interests in the increasingly Francophobic atmosphere of St. Petersburg. The circle could not be squared, and neither side could understand the other's viewpoint.

This conversation, however, did not degenerate into the First Consul's usual tirade. Although Napoleon repeated that he could easily destroy Britain, he tried to explain to Morkov how he could desire peace on the one hand and aggressively prepare for war on the other. When Morkov asked point-blank, "But if the E[mpero]r . . . should grant Malta to the English?" Napoleon replied thoughtfully. "I flatter myself," he said, "that he will be too just for that, but I would submit to it, because I have given him my word." This astonishing statement suggests that Napoleon was confident either that Alexander would not let him down or that the issue would never come to the test—or perhaps even that Napoleon would consider giving up Malta to secure the tsar's friendship.

Napoleon's belief was made even more explicit by Talleyrand in a note to Hédouville, the French ambassador in St. Petersburg:

> [The tsar] is too enlightened not to recognize how significant it is to the tranquillity of Europe that a government, whose interests all conflict with those of the continent, should retain the means to trouble at its desire the powers that alone can oppose the maritime and commercial despotism that England wishes to exercise. What is more, H[is] M[ajesty], who guaranteed the article concerning Malta, will assuredly not wish to leave this island in the hands of England . . . We have desired, proposed, asked for his mediation; but that has been with the just and plain confidence that this mediation would have as its basis a perfect feeling for the needs of Europe and for its principle the sincere and reciprocal esteem that has been expressed between the 1st Consul and H[is] M[ajesty] the E[mpero]r of Russia.[46]

Napoleon was disappointed when he realized that Alexander was not well disposed toward France and suspicious of Britain, as he had supposed, and when he recognized that the tsar did not see the world as he saw it.

There was considerable justice in Napoleon's lament. The British were just as arbitrary and violated international norms just as thoroughly in their own actions as he did. Apart from the fact that the British violations were mostly reactions to Napoleon's, the major difference was that Britain's actions came mostly on the sea, and the Royal Navy had already been establishing a maritime hegemony for several decades that the other major powers were increasingly willing to accept. Napoleon's actions took place on land, however, and in places where the other European states were not willing to accept *his* hegemony. Napoleon's complaint was really the anger of a would-be hegemon against an increasingly established one.

The British refused to allow the discussion to focus solely on Malta—a case that, put by itself, they were certain to lose. Rather, they insisted that Alexander resolve all of the issues in dispute between Britain and France, and they refused Napoleon's demand to suspend military operations until Alexander had made his decision. Above all, the British spoke of Russian mediation, rather than arbitration, something that suggested a moderated negotiation between Britain and France rather than a simple decision by the tsar. Napoleon was unwilling to accept these conditions, as Talleyrand noted, but Alexander Vorontsov nevertheless hastened to put together a basis for mediation largely in accord with the British proposal.[47]

Vorontsov began by rejecting Napoleon's demand for a cease-fire on the grounds that no British ministry could possibly accept such a condition. He then proposed that Alexander agree to take Malta, which would eliminate "the most important subject of discord between the two warring sides." The "main stumbling block" having been removed, France would then withdraw its forces from Hanover, Holland, Switzerland, and Italy, "and would undertake henceforth not to send them again into those lands." Vorontsov noted that the Italian Republic was explicitly included in this list, for "although it was under the supreme leadership of Bonaparte, it must nevertheless exist independently from France and defend itself with its own proper forces." The king of Sardinia would be properly compensated, and both powers would guarantee the integrity of the Ottoman Empire. In return, Britain would recognize the new order in Italy and return to France all the prizes taken at sea and whatever lands might have been acquired since the outbreak of the war. Above all, Vorontsov emphasized that Russia would mediate but not arbitrate the conflict.[48]

Even as the tsar was reviewing this proposal, an interview between Hédouville and Alexander Vorontsov demonstrated the reception it was likely to receive in Paris. Vorontsov began by suggesting that no British minister could submit such a wide range of issues to arbitration. Hédouville responded that Malta was the "real apple of discord."[49] To his surprise, Vorontsov demurred, stating that Britain, and indeed all of Europe, had a wide range of causes to fear and distrust France, including the French occupation of Holland, Switzerland, and Italy. Once again, an opportunity for clearing the air went unrecognized, for Hédouville concluded that "the number of [Vorontsov's] objections will convince you that he leans toward England, although he assures one that he is only Russian." In the wide-ranging discussion that ensued, it became clear that the conflict between France and Russia was irreducible. The Russians did not see British actions as a threat because they believed Britain meant them no harm. They were not at all convinced, however, that the same could be said of Napoleon, and so they distrusted him. It was surely for that reason among others that Vorontsov proposed a basis for mediation that ensured not only Britain's interests but Russia's as well.

The break came quickly. On July 23 Talleyrand wrote to Morkov to tell him how upset Napoleon was with the Russian proposal.[50] On July 28 he wrote again, categorically rejecting the Russian proposal point by point and refusing further communication on that topic.[51] The next day, Napoleon himself wrote to Alexander, thanking him for his efforts on behalf of continental peace, which had now failed, and asking him to recall Morkov, "a minister who is so personally disagreeable to me."[52]

It is difficult to understand why Napoleon would take such a step at this time, unless we accept the idea that he sincerely believed that Alexander was being misled by his advisers. In a note to Hédouville dated July 18, Talleyrand had offered no objections to Morkov other than his British sympathies and haughty attitude.[53] Napoleon would subsequently accuse Morkov of taking part in the plots swirling around Paris, but his accusations postdate his request for Morkov's recall. It is also possible, as Morkov himself suggested, that Napoleon resented the fact that the Russian ambassador attempted to preserve the tsar's dignity and aura at the expense of Napoleon's. Still another possibility is that Napoleon was signaling his displeasure with Alexander's final offer of mediation terms.

However that may be, tensions between St. Petersburg and Paris were seriously exacerbated. Alexander was incensed that Napoleon would presume to dictate his choice of representative to Paris. He naturally recalled Morkov but then refused to appoint another ambassador in his place, working instead through the chargé d'affaires, Oubril. This decision in turn outraged Napoleon, who made it clear to Oubril that he resented the gesture and would refuse to accord the chargé any dignity whatsoever.

The Turn to Austria

As the fall of 1803 approached, Alexander found himself in an increasingly uncomfortable position. Relations with France had been nearly broken off and were becoming overtly hostile. He was deeply concerned that Napoleon would take advantage of Prussia's cowardice to extend his control in northern Germany or Naples's weakness to strengthen his grip on Italy or even attack the Ottoman Empire. He wanted to prevent the Anglo–French conflict from spreading even farther into Europe, but Prussia's fecklessness had deprived him of an ally. Because of Russia's geographic position, however, there was little Alexander could do without a central European partner. In October, therefore, Alexander accepted the inevitable and approached Vienna.

This approach required a certain delicacy because it was clear to the Austrians that Alexander had turned to them as a last resort. Throughout 1802, Alexander had worked with Napoleon to decide the affairs of Germany jointly and then force that decision on Vienna. He had approached Prussia on several occasions, including the visible visit to Memel, in a way that made it clear that he preferred to work with Berlin. Alexander had no reason to suppose that his approaches to Francis now would be received warmly.

In a long message to Vienna on October 18 Alexander Vorontsov recapitulated Russia's policies throughout the period of rising tensions that preceded the renewal of war between France and Britain, and then discussed his efforts to join with Prussia in defending north Germany. He excused the delay in approaching Vienna with a gentle slap at Austria's passivity: "If our august master has delayed in [making such an approach] to this point, it was because of the fear of uselessly compromising the court of Vienna and because he wished to respect the wise and pacific system that it has adopted."[54] In other words, Alexander delayed because he expected that Francis would be even more pusillanimous than Frederick William.

This belief was well founded. Austria in 1803 was deeply conscious of her own weakness. The struggle against France between 1792 and 1801 had exhausted Austria's will and finances. To support the struggle, Francis had been forced to print money, raise taxes, and borrow heavily. In 1801 some Austrian advisers had even recommended partial bankruptcy to alleviate the crisis.[55] Francis had emerged from the War of the Second Coalition determined to maintain peace long enough to put Austria's house in order both financially and militarily. He appointed his brother, Archduke Charles, president of the Hofkriegsrat, the body that controlled the Austrian military, with orders to "submit a detailed plan for the regulation of the military establishment of the entire Monarchy."[56]

Charles was an excellent choice. Although he was just thirty years old in 1801, Charles had commanded the Austrian armies in Germany in 1796 and 1799–1800 and had won a number of notable victories. Five feet tall and subject to epileptic fits, Charles was nevertheless an inspirational leader on the battlefield and a moderately skilled tactician. His great and enduring faults, however, were excessive caution and a certain moodiness when things were not going well. He was generally apt to overstate difficulties and to fall prey to self-pity.

Charles was a serious military thinker who wrote a number of treatises on campaigns and on the nature of war itself. He recognized that the French Revolution was transforming war, but he was too socially conservative and too focused on tactical minutiae to appreciate the changes. Worse still, he never had his brother's full confidence. Francis feared that his charismatic and militarily successful brother might challenge him, and he was always quick to heed ill-intentioned rumors that Charles's enemies whispered into his ears. Nevertheless, as a thinking soldier who had fought and, unusually, defeated the French on a number of occasions, Charles was clearly the man to turn the Austrian army around. For a time, Francis gave him his opportunity.[57]

Charles was profoundly impressed by the weakness of Austria's finances. His reforms of the Austrian military system focused primarily on saving money. He presided over a dramatic reduction in the military budget, from 87 million florins in 1801 to 34.5 million in 1804.[58] He focused his main efforts, however, on reorganizing the Austrian military administration in order to make it more efficient. He subordinated the Hofkriegsrat, which had directed Austria's military affairs for centuries, to the War Ministry (he was the minister) and dramatically streamlined its bureaucratic procedures. He also got Francis to reorganize the higher echelons of the state administration. In the past, a large number of agencies had reported directly to Francis, inundating him with information and preventing proper coordination of policies. On Charles's advice, Francis replaced that system with a single Staats und Konferenz Ministerium in which the Ministries of the Interior, Foreign Affairs, and the military (the Kriegs und Marine Ministerium) were represented.[59] Although Charles examined questions of tactics and organization and worked to improve the position of the general staff, nothing that he did between 1801 and 1805 aimed primarily at improving the fighting abilities of the Austrian army in the short term. Of all the senior leaders in Austria at this time, Charles was the most committed to maintaining a long period of peace to give his reforms time to take effect.

Charles's reform efforts paralleled Alexander's: the major political issue in Russia in 1802 and 1803 was the establishment of several ministries and the ensuing reorganization of the Russian government.[60] Neither accident nor collusion led Russia and Austria along similar lines at this time, but rather the recognition dawning in Europe that states had to adapt themselves to the new conditions of war. The major wars of the eighteenth century had ended with the financial exhaustion of most of the major powers. That exhaustion played a powerful role in bringing France, Spain, and Austria to the peace table following the War of the Spanish Succession, and bringing France, Austria, and Prussia to the bargaining table after the Seven Years War. In each case, a prolonged period of peace had followed as the exhausted states worked to restore their finances and military means. The French revolutionary wars had been no less exhausting, but even optimists in 1801 could not delude themselves that the peace could be made to last for decades. Restructuring state organizations to make them less expensive and more efficient in the administration of funds seemed more urgent than it had been in 1714 or 1763. Administrative reform would be a constant leitmotif throughout the Napoleonic Wars as France's enemies located and mobilized more resources and used them as efficiently as possible.

This focus on the limited resources available for war had an important impact on the development of the foreign and military policies of the continental powers. Austria, Russia, and Prussia were almost continuously on the brink of financial collapse during their conflict with France. After 1805, Francis, Alexander, and Frederick William believed they had mobilized all of the resources available to them and further mobilization was impossible. The fact that further resources were invariably found when needed did not detract from the pervading sense of helplessness and hopelessness that enervated policies directed at opposing Napoleon. Napoleon avoided this trap until approximately 1809 for a number of reasons, including his ability to wage war at the expense of already conquered peoples and mobilize a greater proportion of France's resources than had ever before been possible, thanks to the changes wrought by the Revolution. Napoleon's relative wealth was a terrific advantage to him in the early years of conflict.

These considerations consequently made Vienna nervous about its response to Alexander's overtures in October 1803. Escaping from the isolation into which the Franco–Russo–Prussian collaboration of 1802 had sunk it was a priority, but avoiding a war with France any sooner than necessary was essential.* The Austrians had been aware of the cooling relations between France and Russia since August, Alexander's efforts to entice Prussia into aggressive action, and the failure of both. In August Prince P. P. Dolgorukii, on a mission to Vienna on behalf of the Russian army, asked Ludwig Cobenzl when the two imperial courts would combine to put an end to the French "robberies."† Cobenzl's reply indicated the line Austria would prefer to take:

---

*Adolf Beer, *Österreich und Russland in den Jahren 1804 und 1805. Archiv for österreichische Geschichte*, 1875, 35:136, esp. n. 2, letter (of Francis?) to Archduke Charles, 17 October 1803: "We have experienced the inconveniences of the union between France and Russia too much not to see the benefits of that which drives them apart, but we must not wage war in order to achieve that unless we are unavoidably forced to it."

†August Fournier, *Gentz und Cobenzl: Geschichte der österreichischen Diplomatie in den Jahren 1801–1805, nach neuen Quellen* (Vienna: Wilhelm Braumüller, 1880), p. 81. It is not clear which Dolgorukii this was, as it might conceivably have been M. P. Dolgorukii, Petr's younger brother. It was probably the elder Petr himself, however, whom Alexander had already entrusted on missions of similar delicacy. See Grand Prince Nikolai Mikhailovich, *Kniazia Dolgorukie, spodvizhniki Imperatora Aleksandra I v pervye gody ego tsarstvovaniia: Biograficheskie ocherki* (St. Petersburg: Ekspeditsiia zagotovleniia gosudarstvennykh bumag, 1902).

I observed for my part that our object was not in any way to involve Russia in a war against the French [!], that we needed peace, and that my master shared in this regard the views and the philanthropic system of Emperor Alexander. But I repeated to him that I did not at all think that a war was necessary to prevent Bonaparte from going further than he seemed to wish to go, but that I thought that if Bonaparte saw the two principal courts of the continent, meaning the two imperial courts, as tightly unified as they needed to be for their mutual advantage, that alone would stop him from doing a large number of things.[61]

Thus Cobenzl outlined Austria's position with perfect clarity before formal negotiations had begun. What Austria desired most was an alliance with Russia; least was a war against France. The trick was to negotiate with Alexander to achieve both objectives; the catch was that Alexander might want war.

The initial reaction in Vienna to the Russian approaches was hopeful if cautious:

If the Russian rapprochement with us had for its object involving us in a war with France, it would not suit our interests at all, because the continuation of peace for as long as possible must always be the essential aim of our policy. But Vorontsov said himself that he wishes for the continuation of peace, and with the Emperor Alexander's character, this momentary anger against Prussia and France will no more involve him in a war than what he said and did against the Swedes whom he could have devoured. If it is possible without compromising us with France, it is good that Bonaparte is no longer in good with Alexander, it is good that the Prussian perfidy is known at Petersburg; a rapprochement between Russia and us that does not entail war would put the French in the position of having to treat us better, as well as [putting in the same position] Prussia, Bavaria, etc. etc. We must therefore take what comes from Russia and respond to it with friendship, but with measure, so as not to be drawn further than we want.[62]

The initial Russian approaches thus triggered a reassessment of Austrian policy, and the memorandum containing instructions for Count Clemens von Metternich, dispatched to Berlin in early November 1803, provided the opportunity for a thoughtful evaluation of Austria's position, needs, and goals.[63]

In one sense, the memorandum noted, Austria had done very well in settlements following the revolutionary wars. By "exchanging" the Netherlands and Lombardy for part of Poland and Venice, Vienna had greatly strengthened its position. The Netherlands and Lombardy had been almost indefensible, as well as a source of constant tension with France. Venice and Poland, on the contrary, were contiguous with the main body of the empire and thus defensible, and they did not interest France at all. Therefore the basis of Austria's previous conflicts with France was finally resolved.*

The Austrians recognized, however, that Napoleon's aggressiveness posed a long-term danger to them and to Europe as a whole, and that some response was necessary. They saw the same alternatives Alexander had originally seen: to work with Napoleon, trying to lead him to a more peaceful approach to international relations, or to ally themselves with Russia and thereby impress Napoleon with the strength of the potential opposition, forcing him to control himself and his ambitions.

By this point, however, the latter course of action was fraught with danger. The British, it was thought, wished to involve other continental powers in a war with France to force Napoleon to move the Army of England from the Channel and use it elsewhere. Although the Russians might have had better intentions, they were far away from any potential theater. If the Russians made some gesture against France, they themselves would suffer no consequences, but the French forces in Italy and Germany might descend on helpless Austria long before any Russian assistance could arrive.[64]

The goal of Austrian policy should be to form an alliance with Russia to impress Napoleon, while maintaining a neutrality that would allow Vienna to act as a mediator between Napoleon and Alexander and in this way maintain the peace of Europe by ensuring that Napoleon did not convert his fruitless war at sea into a productive war on land.

This feckless policy had no chance of success. Alexander was increasingly determined to take action of some sort and became impatient with Austrian temporizing and Vienna's efforts to remain on good terms with Bonaparte. Napoleon, for his part, had already demonstrated his "with me or against me" principle of foreign policy; as Alexander and Napoleon drifted apart, the latter was certain to demand that Vienna make a clear choice.

Austria's options were bad: too exhausted to contemplate war but unable to view Napoleon's continual aggressions with equanimity, Austria desperately needed an ally in Russia but did not want to fight Russia's war. In the end, there was only one possible response—ally herself with Russia lest Alexander withdraw from European affairs and leave Austria to Napoleon's (and Prussia's) not so tender mercies. This fact meant that once Alexander approached Francis, the latter would be forced to do Russia's bidding. The Russian (and British) perception that Austria could be made to bear the burden of the coalition was accurate. All Vienna could do was to delay the inevitable treaty with

---

*The exchange of the Netherlands and Lombardy for Venice and Poland was, for the most part, informal. Austria lost the Netherlands in 1794 to French invasion and gained part of Poland during the Third Partition in 1795—events that were largely unrelated. Even at the time, however, Vienna claimed a right to a share of Poland on the grounds that it deserved compensation for the loss of Belgium.

Russia for as long as possible without finally alienating Alexander, and this Cobenzl set out to do.[65]

The Raising of Shields

Unfortunately for Cobenzl and his plans, Alexander had other ideas. In late November 1803, following troubling indications that Napoleon intended to expand his control over northern Germany, Vorontsov wrote Alexander proposing the mobilization of a large army composed of several corps. One corps, comprising about 40,000 men, would be deployed along the Prussian border and the Baltic coast, ready to intervene in northern Germany should Napoleon commit further aggressions. Another corps of about 30,000 men would be deployed around Brest-Litovsk, ready to cooperate with Austria should Francis finally realize that the time had come to take a stand. Still another corps, this one of 20,000, would be kept in readiness in southern Ukraine to repel a French attack on Greece or the Balkans. A large army of 80,000 would be kept in reserve, ready to assist any of the first three forces.[66]

Alexander's hopes for an alliance strengthened a few days after Vorontsov's report, when he received a dispatch from his chargé d'affaires in Vienna, I. O. Anstett, describing a conversation he had with Cobenzl about Alexander's offer of an Austro–Russian alliance.[67] Although Anstett was frustrated with Cobenzl's vague replies to direct questions, he thought the Austrians wished to join with Russia in some way and might be persuaded to undertake a meaningful alliance if both carrot and stick were large enough. This was certainly the conclusion that Alexander and Vorontsov drew. Alexander wrote to Count Johann Philipp Stadion, the Austrian ambassador in St. Petersburg, that the most recent messages from the Viennese court "give rise to the hope that an agreement between the two Imperial courts will not be difficult to obtain and that to this end it was only necessary to come to an understanding and to continue to explain oneself with unreserved frankness."[68]

Vorontsov went even further, promising:

> Russia will be able immediately to put into action up to 90 thousand men supported by a reserve corps of 80 thousand. H[is] Imperial] M[ajesty] proposes simultaneously to stop the progress of the French in the North, at which point he will be obliged to concentrate all necessary means to face the enemy and at the same time to fight on the coast of Greece.*

---

*Vorontsov originally noted that Russia could put into action 180,000 men, but Alexander crossed that out and replaced it with the phrases here translated (VPR, vol. 1, p. 597 n.).

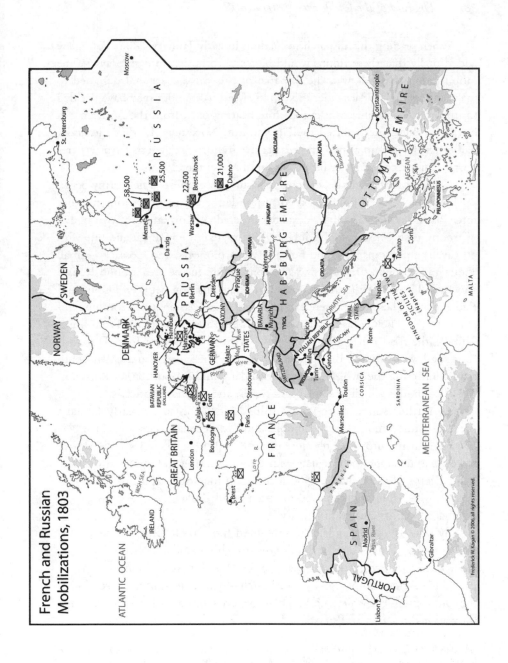

French and Russian
Mobilizations, 1803

When reading this dispatch to Stadion in early January 1804, Vorontsov added orally that these troops would be ready to march in eight days.[69] The mobilization that followed the dispatch of this missive seemed designed to make it possible for Alexander to keep his word. Alexander may have decided to undertake a mobilization even before hearing back from the Austrians, in fact, for Hédouville reported to Talleyrand on November 13 that Alexander had ordered a call-up of two draftees per five hundred male serfs.* Anstett's report was not received in St. Petersburg until November 29.

However that might be, concrete measures to mobilize a field army began on December 26, 1803, with a correspondence about provisions for that force.[70] On January 6, 1804, Alexander ordered the formation of two bodies of troops, each consisting of 7 infantry regiments, one with 20 and one with 30 cavalry squadrons, foot and horse artillery, pioneers, and Cossacks—in all about 43,500 men. One body was to concentrate in the area around Kobrin and Brest-Litovsk, while the second was to take position between Dubno and Radzivilov.[71] These forces were explicitly organized "as an army composed of two corps."[72] Their concentration areas gave Alexander flexibility. From Brest-Litovsk, the road runs west through Warsaw toward Berlin; from Dubno it runs southwest through Brody toward Vienna. There was also a north–south road connecting the two positions. Alexander could support either Prussia or Austria or both with all or some of his forces, and on short notice.

To further support the plan outlined by Vorontsov in early January, Alexander undertook a second mobilization in February, creating three new combined arms corps totaling more than 58,500 men. These formations were to concentrate along the Prussian frontier near Taurrogen, Olita, and Grodno. A final corps of more than 25,500 men (again including all arms) was mobilized in May 1804 and deployed in and around Zaslavl', to the south of the original two corps created in January.[73]

By May 1804 Alexander had mobilized more than 127,500 men, organized into two armies each of three corps stretching along the Russian frontier from the Baltic Sea to the Austrian border.[74] The first concentrations were probably nearing completion by mid-March—before news of the execution of the Duc d'Enghien (which most scholars believe triggered Alexander's decision for war) had reached St. Petersburg.†

---

*Hédouville to Talleyrand, 13 November 1803, SIRIO, vol. 77, doc. 164, pp. 406–409. Vorontsov himself announced this call-up to Stadion in early December 1803 (Beer, *Österreich und Russland in den Jahren 1804 und 1805*, p. 137). Russian troop call-ups were based on a certain number drafted out of every five hundred male serfs. They varied from one or two per five hundred for a normal annual levy to as high as eight per five hundred during a national military emergency, in which case there might be multiple levies in a single year, even within a few months of each other.

†See below. Some analyses of the outbreak of the war point to the execution of the Duc d'Enghien as the key event that turned Alexander against Napoleon. This mobilization makes it clear that Alexander had turned long before then.

This Russian mobilization had a great deal in common with Napoleon's camps along the French coast. In each case an army of more than 100,000 men was formed, organized into corps of about 20,000 men each comprising infantry, artillery, cavalry, and supporting branches. These armies remained in their positions throughout 1804 and into 1805, and formed the core elements of the forces that clashed decisively on the road from Ulm to Austerlitz.

The quality of those two forces was different, however, and this difference bears examination. Not much is knowable about the Russian forces and what they did between January 1804 and September 1805, owing to lacunae in available archival resources.[75] It seems clear, however, that they, like those involved in the previous smaller mobilization, could not have been training as aggressively, extensively, and realistically as their French counterparts. Alexander, unlike Napoleon, still did not put his country on a war footing in early 1804 (for the excellent reason that he was not at war), and so he did not suspend normal budgetary considerations that restricted training in European armies during peacetime. They may even have acquired greater stringency owing to the extraordinary sums Alexander had to allot to provision his mobilized troops. In addition, whereas Napoleon's troops trained to prepare for an invasion set at a specific date, normally months ahead, Alexander's troops were supposed to be ready to move with twenty-four hours' notice—something that normally hinders large-scale training.

Finally, Alexander's corps did not move out in 1805 with anything like the organization they had in 1804. The diplomatic and strategic situation shifted constantly between January 1804 and September 1805, with the result that a highly improvisational Russian force structure actually went to war. Napoleon's troops, on the contrary, moved and fought at the outset of the campaign in the same corps, serving the same corps and divisional commanders with whom they had trained for the preceding two years with few exceptions.

The tactical conduct of individual Russian regiments was generally very good, however, thanks no doubt to the prolonged period of anxious mobilization. In addition, the fact that the Russian forces were organized and deployed in all-arms formations called corps was significant. There is a great deal of truth to the notion that Napoleon's introduction of the corps system during the Marengo campaign was a significant advantage to the French and helped achieve his subsequent stunning victories.[76] The issue, however, is complicated by the fact that the Russians also recognized the value of the corps system early on and by 1804 had incorporated changes aimed at improving it.

The Russians had organized one of their armies into corps already in the campaign of 1800. In 1804 both armies were organized in that fashion. The corps of 1804, furthermore, were almost twice as large as the corps of 1800 and included not only infantry and cavalry regiments but also horse artillery and engineer troops. In addition, the corps of 1804 were explicitly organized to meet specific tasks, shown by the significant variation in the size of cavalry in each, presumably determined by mission and location.[77]

The problem the Russians faced was that the corps they created in early 1804 did not march into battle as units. Unlike Napoleon's corps, they lacked the advantage of familiarity with superior commanders and with the commanders of other units at the same level. The idea of creating corps-size forces of all arms, even if they were improvised structures, had nonetheless deeply permeated the Russian army by 1805, with notable results for that and subsequent campaigns.

Conclusion

The Franco–Russian rift resulted from Napoleon's unwillingness to accept any limitations on his actions, coupled with the breakdown of communications between Paris and St. Petersburg. The interventions in Italy, Switzerland, and Holland in 1802 had already raised Alexander's suspicions of his supposed ally, while the invasion of Hanover and Naples made him resentful and afraid. Napoleon's request for Morkov's recall, an unnecessary provocation that led to a dramatic deterioration of formal relations between France and Russia, together with the activities of French agents in Corfu and the Balkans, created an atmosphere of near panic in St. Petersburg and convinced Alexander that his own interests required that he seek allies with whom to oppose Napoleon, even to the point of waging war if necessary.*

Alexander's alarm was excessive. He did not recognize that Napoleon's invasion of Naples and Hanover was a more or less rational effort to strike back in a war that was going badly for France. It was by no means inevitable that Napoleon would attempt to extend his European dominion beyond those territories; a French invasion of the Ottoman Empire would have been insane.

Alexander, however, read Napoleon perfectly in several crucial respects. He had seen rightly that Napoleon's determination to strike back at Britain in any available way was certain to harm Russia's vital interests. He was also right to believe that declarations and diplomatic maneuvering would not prevent Napoleon from acting on that determination. His conclusion that if nothing

---

*The idea that British gold "purchased" Russian participation in the coalition is untenable in light of the Russian mobilizations of 1803 and 1804 and Alexander's approaches to Prussia and Austria in those years. Alexander had largely rebuffed British approaches in the spring and summer of 1803 and focused instead on securing an ally in either Prussia or Austria with whom to work to prevent further Napoleonic expansion after the renewal of war between Britain and France. Before he entered into any discussions with Britain about the possibility of an alliance at all, Alexander had already plunged into negotiations with Austria and had spent millions of rubles to mobilize and maintain a large army on a war footing. British gold had nothing to do with Alexander's turn away from France, his initial approaches to Prussia and Austria, or his vast mobilization for the possibility of war with France.

was done to raise resistance to Napoleon then further French "aggressions" would take place was sound, even if his belief in the imminence of those aggressions was overdrawn. His conviction that only he, allied with one of the other two continental powers, could raise such resistance was correct.

All of Alexander's efforts in 1803 and through the fall of 1804 were defensive—he aimed to have forces and agreements in place with which to resist (or deter) further Napoleonic attacks. We must now turn our attention to the complicated problem of understanding why Alexander decided, beginning in late 1804, that he would have to prepare an offensive and preemptive war against France, and how the coalition that would wage that war was formed.

4

The Seeds of War

Alexander's turn toward Austria in late 1803 had no more immediate consequences than his turn to Prussia earlier that year. Francis put the tsar off with
delays and prevarications whereas Frederick William had simply refused.
Alexander saw that drawing Francis into an alliance against Napoleon would be
a slow and laborious business. The tsar could have reacted to this realization by
abandoning all hope of opposing Napoleon and leaving the German powers to
their fate, except for two things. First, Napoleon took a series of actions in
spring 1804 that Alexander saw as new provocations. Second, the Addington
government fell in the same period, and the legendary William Pitt (the
Younger) took up the reins of state in London once more.* These events led
Alexander to reevaluate his grand strategy. He determined once again to oppose
Napoleon and turn for help, this time, to Britain. He also decided that he must
do more than defend Germany and Italy—he must attack and defeat Napoleon
in France.

Schemes and Schemers

The wars of the revolutionary period in France had been accompanied by significant internal insurrections against the various revolutionary governments. The
most dramatic occurred in the Vendée region and Brittany, although significant
counterrevolutionary movements developed in the occupied areas of Germany,
Italy, and Switzerland, and elsewhere in France as well.[1] The rebels, called
vendéens (or, more generally, *chouans*), opposed the deposition and execution of
the king, conscription, and the revolutionary governments' assault on the

---

*Pitt was prime minister from 1783 to 1801, when he resigned over the issue of Catholic emancipation
and was replaced by Addington.

Catholic Church. Those in northwestern France received money, weapons, and sanctuary from Britain, the closest and most determined foreign foe of the Revolution. Georges Cadoudal, a miller's son, was an effective *chouan* leader who led a large-scale insurgency in the Vendée and elsewhere before leaving for Britain in 1800.

Georges, as he was known, was in contact with the exiled Bourbon princes, and he hoped one day to restore them to the throne. His activities between 1800 and 1803 were circumscribed by the fact that Louis XVIII hoped that Bonaparte, having finally crushed the revolution, would restore the Bourbons himself.[2] While the Bourbons waited and hoped, and other would-be rivals of the new First Consul looked to see how he would behave in power (and whether he would last), the *chouannerie* practically vanished. Many former *chouans* renounced their hostility to the new regime and were amnestied. Others simply melted back into the countryside.

In February 1803, however, Louis XVIII realized that the only king Napoleon would restore to the French throne was himself. His disillusionment with Bonaparte, followed immediately by the renewal of war between Britain and France, reenergized the *chouans*. By August 1803, Georges and a number of picked comrades had infiltrated into France and were hiding in Paris. From there, they prepared for a direct strike against Napoleon, whom they saw as the center of opposition to their plans for the restoration of the Bourbons. They imagined that they would assassinate Napoleon on the road to Paris from Saint-Cloud, his sometime residence. Generals Charles Pichegru and Jean Victor Marie Moreau, who formed part of the plot, would then take power and declare their support for the Bourbon dynasty. The Comte d'Artois (the future King Charles X) would cross over from Britain to claim the throne on behalf of his brother, Louis XVIII, who would arrive subsequently from his exile in Poland.[3] The revolution would finally be reversed.

The émigré princes and the British supported this conspiracy with an extensive network of agents throughout France and the neighboring countries. One of the critical go-betweens was the British ambassador to Bavaria, Sir Francis Drake, assisted by the émigré Duc d'Antraigues, who now claimed Russian citizenship and resided in Saxony. Through agents in France, Drake and d'Antraigues collected intelligence that they passed on to both London and St. Petersburg, and they also worked to foment insurrection against Bonaparte's rule.[4]

As soon as the war with Britain resumed, Napoleon became nervous about the presence of French émigrés near France's frontiers, suspecting them of complicity in some plot against him. He demanded that the neighboring states arrest, expel, or transport these émigrés to more distant lands.[5] By August 1803 Napoleon was hunting and arresting supposed rebels within France, even before he learned of Georges's arrival in Paris.

As summer turned to fall, Napoleon's efforts to root out the conspiracy within France became more peremptory and brutal. He ordered the minister of justice, Claude Ambroise Régnier, to arrest, try, and even summarily execute individuals he specified, making a mockery of the judicial system he was laboriously constructing.[6] In one case he noted that "someone had seen signals sent from the land to which there was a response from the sea," and he ordered the minister of justice to send a secret agent into the village to identify who was conspiring with the British and inflict severe and exemplary punishment on them.[7]

The dramatic break came in early 1804 when one of the conspirators who had accompanied Georges into Paris was arrested, tried, and condemned to death. In an effort to save his life, he revealed that Georges was hiding in Paris and leading a plot that aimed to kill Napoleon during the first half of February.[8] The investigation expanded, and soon Napoleon's agents and police were on the hunt for Georges, Pichegru, who was known to have accompanied him, Moreau, accused of being in the plot, and a Bourbon prince who had been mentioned in the papers and plans taken from the schemers.

At the same time, Napoleon struck back at the émigré–British espionage net. He found that he could not easily eliminate Drake with the evidence readily at hand, so he developed an elaborate plan to blow his cover while feeding disinformation to his enemies at the same time. Napoleon ordered Régnier to send a former *chouan* named Méhée to Drake to offer to sell him papers that a disloyal chamberlain offered to take from Napoleon's own portfolios. He meticulously (and mendaciously) explained that Napoleon always kept these portfolios with him and that they contained the plans for the proposed invasion of England. In return, the "disloyal chamberlain" who promised to procure those papers would require a considerable sum of money and the names of royalist agents in Paris with whom he could hide once the thefts were discovered.* Drake took the bait enthusiastically, and letters began to come back to Méhée that compromised many royalist and British agents in France.

Napoleon took the opportunity to feed Drake disinformation. He had Méhée write that the supposed preparations for a landing in England were really a feint, that all of the ships being built could be used as fishing boats instead, and that the real aim was the invasion of Ireland. He added that another major operation would be the invasion of the Peloponnesus, "which has definitely been decided upon," and that Napoleon was preparing 40,000 troops at Tarento and a fleet at Toulon for that expedition.[9] To give some verisimilitude to this last bit of nonsense, Napoleon ordered a concentration of French forces

---

*Napoleon to Régnier, 1 November 1803, *Corr. de Nap.*, 7240 and the annex, document 7241. Napoleon amused himself by going into great detail about what this chamberlain would need in order to escape the police.

from Italy and Elba at Tarento and French ships at Livorno,[10] although he never seriously intended to launch such an undertaking.

Napoleon pulled the trigger in early March 1804, ordering the publication of a compromising letter that Drake had sent to Méhée, along with evidence that Napoleon had invented the entire affair, that there never was any dishonest chamberlain, that the supposed French turncoats were in fact working for Napoleon under orders—in short, that he had not only compromised Drake but made a fool of him.[11] The plan worked perfectly, and Drake and his agents were recalled. This elegant bit of counterespionage had unforeseen consequences, however. Among other things, it strengthened the conviction of Alexander and his advisers that Napoleon intended to invade Greece, something the tsar was determined to prevent.

In the meantime, Napoleon had begun to turn France upside down in his search for Georges, Pichegru, and the other conspirators and spies. As the hunt advanced, Napoleon ordered the gates of Paris to be closed at night. The police discovered many conspirators, and Napoleon came to believe that France was honeycombed with traitors. He wrote to General Marmont in Holland, "If you find any spies, bring them before a military tribunal and have them shot; you must have some, these miserable English are inundating us with them."[12] He wrote to General Soult that "the English are sending agents everywhere. . . . You are inundated with spies at Boulogne."[13] To General Jean-Joseph-Paul-Augustin Dessole, who had temporarily taken command of the Army of Hanover from General Mortier, he said, "I want you to exercise the greatest possible surveillance in order to arrest the spies and English agents with whom you must be inundated."[14]

As the hunt intensified and the panic increased, denunciations multiplied, some of them valid. Before long, Napoleon had zeroed in on Georges's hiding place, and the police closed in on March 9. As they moved to take him, however, Georges escaped, killing a policeman and running toward the Odéon. He was finally seized and cast into prison, shortly to be executed. Moreau and Pichegru had already been taken into custody. By mid-March, all of the principal leaders of the conspiracy were in Napoleon's hands, except one.

The papers and confessions of the conspirators repeated that one of the Bourbon princes was to come to France, yet the police had found no such prince. Napoleon considered the problem. Louis XVIII was in Poland and had made no move. The Comte d'Artois was in Britain, and Napoleon believed that he would not risk himself in such a dangerous action. He was right in his understanding of the count's character, but wrong in his overall evaluation: the Comte d'Artois was the "prince of the blood" who had informally promised Georges to come to Paris, but he did not budge from his exile. Napoleon dismissed the other princes in Britain and Poland as well for a variety of reasons.[15] That left only the Duc d'Enghien, son of the last prince of Condé, who was then living with his mistress on a manor in Ettenheim, a small village in the electorate of Baden, not fifteen kilometers from the French border. Napoleon decided that he was the one destined to enter France and raise the Bourbon banner on behalf of Louis XVIII.[16]

On March 10 Napoleon uncharacteristically called together a council of state. Charles-François Lebrun and Jean-Jacques-Régis Cambacérès, the other two consuls, were present, as was Talleyrand, minister of justice Régnier, and the once and future minister of police, Joseph Fouché. Talleyrand argued that extreme measures against this émigré prince were necessary, while Cambacérès argued for a more moderate approach. Napoleon seemingly wanted to act boldly to prove to all that "any rapprochement between him and the Bourbons was henceforth impossible."[17] Fouché claims that Napoleon told him later, "Have not you and yours [i.e., the Jacobin opposition] said a hundred times that I would end up being the Monk of France and re-establishing the Bourbons? Very well, there will be no going back. What stronger guarantee could I give the revolution that you cemented with the blood of a king? It is necessary to finish it, moreover: I am surrounded by conspiracies; I must instill terror or perish."*

Napoleon accordingly issued the orders for a dramatic expedition. He sent Generals Michel Ordener and Armand Augustin Louis Caulaincourt with three hundred dragoons into Baden. They were to surround Ettenheim, seize the Duc d'Enghien and General Charles François Dumouriez (another revolutionary war hero turned traitor and émigré whom Napoleon erroneously thought was there), and bring them back to France.[18] They were to take provisions with them and not harm the inhabitants in any way, but they were to seize the émigrés by force and prohibit their escape.

The plan went off smoothly. The horsemen crossed the Rhine during the night of March 14–15, surrounded the mansion of the Duc d'Enghien on the morning of March 15, and led him away to France without any opposition. Within a few days, he had been taken by Napoleon's orders to the Chateau de Vincennes. In that castle on the outskirts of Paris, surrounded by beautiful woods, the Duc d'Enghien was held in such secrecy that even the castellan did not know who he was.[19]

Since the duke had never been a part of the conspiracy, his arrest took him completely by surprise, and he apparently did not believe at first that any harm would come to him. He thought that if he could meet with Napoleon to explain himself, all would be set right.[20] He was soon disabused of this hope. His

---

*Michel Vovelle, ed., *Mémoires de Joseph Fouché, duc d'Otrante* (Paris: Imprimerie Nationale, 1992), p. 212. Fouché's evidence is suspect, since he also claims that he opposed the execution of d'Enghien and foresaw the reaction to it in Europe. A recent biographer takes for granted Fouché's complicity in the decision to seize and kill the duke. (See Tulard, *Joseph Fouché*, p. 170.) The sentiments he ascribes to Napoleon at this juncture do seem, however, to be a just reflection of the First Consul's thought processes. (See Godechot, *La contre-révolution*, p. 401; Tulard, *Joseph Fouché*, p. 169.)

request to see the First Consul was refused. Napoleon read the papers seized along with the duke and found nothing interesting in them.[21] He nevertheless arraigned the duke on charges of having borne arms against France and participating in conspiracies against his native land.[22] He personally drew up the list of questions to be put to the duke by the military tribunal he had assembled—questions designed to ensure that he would be found guilty.[23] The duke admitted to the tribunal that he had borne arms against France years before. According to the law amnestying the émigrés, such an admission merited the death penalty, but only for émigrés arrested on French soil, which the duke was not. The tribunal nonetheless condemned the duke, and he was shot that night in the moat of the Chateau de Vincennes.

It has become a commonplace among historians that the execution of the Duc d'Enghien was a crucial turning point on the road to war, and indeed it was, although not in the sense normally ascribed to it. This event, it is said, turned Alexander against Napoleon and drove him to seek continental allies, build up his armed forces, and prepare the final break with France.[24] In truth the execution generated very little change in Russia's course, although Alexander reacted quickly and heatedly. This event by itself could not have led to the formation of a new coalition, although it was part of a chain of events that led to war.

Fear and Loathing in St. Petersburg

Alexander was unable to comprehend the atmosphere of fear and suspicion that reigned in France at this time. He apparently did not believe his advisers' repeated assurances that Napoleon's hold was weak and could be broken by decisive action. As Napoleon promulgated throughout Europe reports—many of them true—of the spectacular plots and intrigues ranged against him, Alexander suspected him of laying a groundwork of spurious justification for further acts of aggression. The seeds of disharmony planted by the invasion of Hanover and Naples had already grown into a hedge that prevented Alexander from believing Napoleon, even when he was telling the truth.

Part of the problem was that Napoleon's way of defending himself against the plotters was characteristically offensive and generated irritants in St. Petersburg. It began with the collapse of the negotiations over Alexander's mediation of the Anglo–French conflict and Napoleon's demand that he recall his Anglophile ambassador, Morkov, whom Napoleon accused after the fact of participating in the plots against him.[25] Shortly thereafter, Napoleon ordered a member of the Russian delegation in Paris to be arrested and held on the charge of involving himself in a number of "intrigues."[26] He next ordered the pope to arrest an émigré named Vernègues, a Russian subject in Rome, for taking part in conspiracies against France.[27] He then took aim at the Duc d'Antraigues in Dresden, demanding that the elector of Saxony exile him from the electorate.[28] When the elector refused to do so, Napoleon considered sending troops to seize d'Antraigues, but his agent, sent to examine the possibilities for such an action, concluded that the duke was too secure in an isolated mansion, and that the attempt would probably fail.[29] Napoleon returned to the diplomatic offensive instead, demanding repeatedly that Alexander recall d'Antraigues.[30]

Not only did Alexander refuse to recall d'Antraigues, who was enormously valuable to him as a spy (as Napoleon rightly suspected), but he attempted to support the other French émigrés now claiming, as Russian subjects, to be unfairly persecuted by Napoleon. Alexander's opposition to Napoleon's attacks against the émigrés had two foundations. First, he believed that once the French government had banished these people from France, confiscated their goods, and decreed that they could not reenter their homeland on pain of death, it lost all right to control their behavior. They became subjects of whatever lands were willing to take them in, with all the rights, immunities, and obligations that such residence might entail. Alexander saw in Napoleon's continued persecution of these former French citizens a plain contravention of the law of nations, an act of aggression against the states that harbored them.[31]

On the other hand, Alexander was incensed that Napoleon would presume to dictate the choice of his agents in foreign courts—and not even in France! To Alexander this matter became a point of honor. He knew that Napoleon had attempted to dictate in Spain, Portugal, and Naples the appointments even of prime ministers, and he resented being numbered among such weak and trivial powers. Even in the maneuverings to get Morkov recalled, Alexander made plain his distaste for allowing Napoleon to dictate the choice of his ministers, although he did not deny that the First Consul had the right to ask for the recall of ambassadors to himself whom he found displeasing. The tsar thus saw Napoleon's actions with regard to the émigrés as violations of international law and protocol and insults to his honor. It is hardly surprising, therefore, that he defended d'Antraigues, who survived Drake's humiliation and stayed at his post (continuing to provide valuable intelligence to the allies as time went on). He also attempted to protect Vernègues in Rome, only to be thwarted by the pope's capitulation to Napoleon's increasingly exigent demands for the émigré's arrest.

Alexander correctly believed that Napoleon's actions belied a lack of respect for Russia's power and prerogatives in Europe. When the pope finally had Vernègues taken into custody and handed over to the French, Napoleon noted regarding the inevitable Russian protest, "One must not attach any importance at all to the demarche that has been made by the Russians. . . . Russia is outside of the sphere of Europe and, even apart from the fact that Vernègues is French [i.e., not simply a Russian subject beyond Napoleon's power], this matter can not in the least concern her."[32] He and Talleyrand returned to this theme repeatedly and had the indelicacy to communicate it directly to the Russians in the wake of the d'Enghien affair.

Word of the seizure and execution of the duke did not reach St. Petersburg until mid-April 1804, and it occasioned a serious reconsideration of Russian policy, if little immediate action. The invasion of German territory and the seizure of the duke, to whom he was very distantly related, outraged Alexander. The event by itself would have been bad enough, but in the context it was unbearable. Napoleon had already offended Alexander's dignity by demanding the recall of Morkov and d'Antraigues. He had violated Alexander's notions of correct behavior by invading Hanover and Naples and by persecuting the émigrés throughout Europe. Now he had invaded the territory held by Alexander's own father-in-law in a flagrant violation of international norms. Alexander felt it was time to make a public stand.

He assembled the State Council, a group consisting of the principal ministers of state and Alexander's senior advisers, including Kochubei, Czartoryskii, and Morkov, and presented a question: Should the tsar not seize this opportunity to break all contact with France?[33] Alexander absented himself from the discussion (an excellent technique for getting advice rather than agreement) and had Czartoryskii, who had become acting foreign minister upon Alexander Vorontsov's semiretirement in February 1804, begin the session by reading a lengthy letter setting forth the tsar's views.* Not confining himself to the d'Enghien affair, Alexander asked rhetorically what gain Russia had realized from reestablishing diplomatic relations with France, since Napoleon had violated every treaty or protocol between the two states? He recognized that the other courts of Europe seemed bent on preserving a meaningful but cowed silence, but wondered if this was not the time for Russia to take the lead. He hoped, more pragmatically, that modeling defiance would embolden others (especially Francis, as well as Frederick William) to join with him in opposing Napoleon's apparently boundless ambition.

Alexander implicitly accepted Napoleon's evaluation of Russia's peripheral position, but he saw it as an advantage and not a hindrance. He considered the possibility that Russia, having broken relations with France, might not able to make an alliance with any other continental power and asked, "What would she risk by that? Suspending all relations is not yet starting a war, and France cannot attack us directly. To get to us she would have to cut into other powers that would then be forced to defend themselves while giving us the occasion to

---

*Vorontsov had abdicated day-to-day control over foreign affairs voluntarily because of old age and illness rather than a desire by Alexander to replace him. We will consider Czartoryskii and his stewardship of Russia's foreign policy in more detail below.

fly to their defense." What is more, the tsar "could not have any doubt of finding, when it became necessary, in England a sure ally always ready to unite and concert actions with him."

Alexander felt that he had complete freedom of action. If Napoleon chose to attack him, he would stimulate the formation of the very coalition that Alexander was trying to form by diplomacy. Alexander's belief in Russia's independence from Europe and Europe's need for Russia are clear once again. Britain would be there whenever Russia wanted her, for Britain would always support would-be allies against France. And since Napoleon could not possibly harm Russia without harming Austria and Prussia first and more seriously, Alexander could choose his moment and his terms to ally with them.

Alexander recognized some possible dangers and problems with his recommended course of action, however. Once Napoleon had realized that reconciliation with Russia was not possible, he would not hesitate to avenge himself on the neighboring states that Alexander had taken under his protection. Naples would become the first victim, and the Russian troops on Corfu would be endangered. The French might also choose to strike Denmark, which would not be able to defend herself.

Alexander disdained these considerations, however, fearing that if no significant opposition was raised, Napoleon would conclude that he could do anything he liked in Europe without consequences. He noted that it was possible to try to gain time—to go into mourning and demand a formal explanation from Napoleon, while preparing to assist Denmark, strengthening the garrison in Corfu, and so forth. He feared, however, that such a course would give Napoleon the opportunity to expel Oubril and the Russian mission, thereby offending Alexander before Alexander had the chance to offend him.

Interestingly, and so unlike Napoleon's council, the committee came to a conclusion that was the opposite of the one the tsar had recommended. Although all agreed that Alexander should place the court in mourning, opinions were divided about the wisdom of breaking off relations at once. Several were swayed by the logic of delay—Russia should gain time to make her own preparations before taking a step that could very well precipitate a French attack. Morkov agreed and added that, in addition to a note to France demanding an explanation, Alexander should send a note to the Diet of the German Empire at Ratisbonne formally protesting the violation of German territory. He pointed out that Alexander had a sound legal footing for taking such an action, since Russia was a comediator of the Holy Roman Empire by virtue of her participation in the Treaty of Teschen. He warned, however, that it was essential that Oubril, the chargé he had left behind, be furnished with notes and instructions that would allow him to leave the minute he sensed that he was about to be expelled.

Traditional Russian isolationism resurfaced at this council, with several members of the committee arguing against any action at all. Opposing

Napoleon over such a trivial issue, they said, might draw Russia into a war that would benefit the other European powers but not Russia. Count Zavadovskii "regarded Russia as sufficiently secure with her own forces and her geographical position, even if the French succeeded in overthrowing all of the neighboring countries." His ally in that argument, Count Nicolas Romantsoff, declared that however tragic the execution of the duke might have been, it did not touch Russia directly. Russian policy, he said, should not be influenced by emotion. On the other hand, he continued, if His Majesty was determined to let Napoleon know of his displeasure, then he should recall Oubril at once. He based this inconsequential argument on the fear that, should Napoleon expel Oubril, such an insult might force Alexander to war, whereas Alexander's decision to recall Oubril would not run such a risk. In the end, the committee made no clear recommendation.

This debate emphasized once more the Russian conviction that the initiative was in Alexander's hands as long as he acted decisively. If Alexander recalled Oubril, that would not lead to war; if Napoleon expelled him, it would. Alexander might lodge a formal protest against French actions at Ratisbonne, which Napoleon was certain to see as a mortal insult. But it would not necessarily goad Napoleon into aggressive action. Any Napoleonic insult directed at St. Petersburg, however, would be unacceptable. Above all, Russia could go to war if, when, where, and how she chose. If she did, Britain, for one, would certainly have to fall in line, and the other states of Europe would probably have to do so as well. The sense of Russia's power, isolation, and importance was still decisive in Russian councils.

Alexander accepted the committee's wavering recommendations. He immediately ordered the Russian court into mourning. He sent a vehement note to Ratisbonne and to the other capitals of Europe protesting Napoleon's violation of German sovereignty.[34] He also instructed Oubril to inform Napoleon directly of his dissatisfaction and to call on him "to employ the most effective means in order to calm all governments about the fears to which he had just given rise, and to put an end in Europe to a state of affairs too alarming for their security and their independence."[35] At the same time, Czartoryskii sent Oubril a note of recall and orders to use it if there was any indication that Napoleon might expel him or that he might recall Hédouville from St. Petersburg.[36]

The military preparations also continued. Alexander already had 50,000 men on the Prussian border between Libau and Grodno and another 40,000 at Brest-Litovsk. He sent 6,000 more to reinforce the garrison of Corfu and was already considering who would command these various forces. Alexander also increased the pressure on Vienna and Berlin to come to terms with him, promising military support to each against France (and to Austria against Prussia).

Yet Dmitrii P. Tatishchev, a younger relative of the Vorontsovs working at the Foreign Ministry, doubted that war would come unless Napoleon took the first move. "Once the struggle has been engaged," he wrote to Simon Vorontsov in London, "I hope that it will be pursued vigorously; but one will not decide upon it willingly; the first step will be costly to take." He contrasted this evaluation with Alexander's initial determination to expel Hédouville but noted, "Unfortunately that is our humor: we can be strongly affected, but not for long. In a moment of exasperation, one will choose the most extreme measures; but once the first moment has passed we are scared of everything and will even consent, if we are allowed, to several sacrifices in order to preserve our inactivity." Tatishchev, for one, recognized that the initiative still lay with Napoleon, whatever Alexander and his council might think, and was convinced that if Napoleon could overcome his nature and bend his neck, then "our armaments will finish with parades."[37]

Tatischev's insightful remarks recognized that a state or ruler who does not desire war for his own purposes is generally reluctant to be drawn into one. Angered and wounded by perceived insults and threats, he may lash out violently to those around him, proposing to undertake aggressive, even rash actions to salve his *amour propre*. That Alexander had spoken openly against the French made Hédouville worry for the safety and dignity of the French legation.[38] But Alexander still wanted to avoid war. He hoped that an open alliance with Austria and at least a secret convention with Prussia would deter Napoleon from further action, and he hoped that the troops he was assembling would ultimately finish with parades. It was no accident that he called the State Council together to deliberate on his next move and accepted, perhaps with some relief, its recommendation to pursue a more moderate course. After all, committees, especially large ones meeting in the absence of the ruler, usually recommend compromises, not dramatic action. Alexander was willing to fight and he was coming to hate Napoleon. But would he not have preferred an indefinite state of cold war in which Napoleon was hostile, but confined? It seems that even after the execution of the Duc d'Enghien, such was his inclination.

His relations with Prussia, Austria, and Britain bear out this view. Although he wasted no time in approaching the German courts with the aim of finalizing treaties with them, both the approach and the proposed terms of the treaties were entirely defensive and laid all of the onus for starting the war on Napoleon. Alexander reassured both the Austrians and the Prussians that he did not want war; he demanded only that they agree to fight the French if Napoleon's troops in Germany were increased or crossed the lines they already occupied: "I am very far from desiring war; I even hope to delay it for as long as possible, and at any event I would not wish to commence it until I was absolutely forced to it by a French aggression, or by seeing [the French] encroach upon countries whose existence must interest Russia more or less."[39]

The problem with this approach highlights a common failing in efforts at deterrence. Alexander was willing to fight but wished to avoid fighting. He hoped to convince Napoleon that his aggressiveness was not worthwhile by sending signals of strength. The problem was that Napoleon's worldview diverged sharply from the tsar's. Convinced that Alexander was both weak and strategically irrelevant, confident that he had bought Prussia and cowed Austria, Napoleon saw in Alexander's actions not the quiet strength that Alexander wished to portray but a pusillanimous petulance. He was outraged by the double standard applied to him. The British (and Russians) could spy on him openly and maintain networks aimed at killing him and toppling his government, but he could not defend himself or engage in legitimate counterespionage? Alexander's response strengthened the First Consul in his belief that if the tsar himself was not openly hostile to France, his advisers were ensuring that his policies were so.

Alexander had taken enough action to anger and offend Napoleon but not enough to deter him. The tsar had apparently forgotten that he had ordered his military preparations to be conducted in deep secret or did not realize how effectively the Russians kept that secret: Hédouville did not know that the Russians had mobilized 100,000 troops on the borders, and Napoleon does not seem to have been aware of it through 1804. They could hardly be intimidated by what they did not know.

Napoleon's Turn

If Napoleon was not scared by the things he did not know about, he was furious at the things he did. Oubril had a stormy meeting with Talleyrand at which he read Alexander's note of protest over the execution of the duke. As he listened to the recitation, Talleyrand mumbled under his breath, "This does not concern the Emperor of Russia at all. It is for the Emperor of Germany, at the [Imperial] Diet, for the Elector of Baden to complain, but no one there dreamed of such a thing, and how can the Emperor [of Russia] know whether or not we made a preliminary approach" to the elector of Baden? When Oubril had finished, Talleyrand repeated, "But by what right does the Emperor occupy himself with such a subject? . . . And moreover, how does the Emperor know that the French government had not asked for the agreement of the Elector of Baden for this action?" Oubril did not trouble to explain why Alexander was convinced that Napoleon's advance into German territory had not had the prior approval of the Elector (as, indeed, it did not), but focused instead on Russia's rights to concern herself with German affairs based on the Treaty of Teschen. Talleyrand became angry and said "that he saw everywhere in this action Morkov's spirit and manner of acting." Oubril made a last effort to convince Talleyrand that there was no division between Alexander and his advisers, but Talleyrand was not persuaded.[40]

Napoleon seemed more willing than before to believe that Alexander really was the problem. He ordered Hédouville recalled and determined not to replace him with another ambassador, leaving in Russia only a chargé d'affaires, as Alexander had left only Oubril in Paris.[41] He also vented his frustration on the Prussian ambassador, telling Talleyrand to tell Lucchesini

> that my intention is not to suffer the tone and the arrogance of the Russian court; that I cannot see without indignation that, from the depths of Russia, they wish to interfere in the internal affairs of France; that the Pope has returned Vernègues to us, but that it is nonetheless insulting that Vernègues and d'Entraigues [sic], who were both ministers of the Count of Lille [Louis XVIII], under the pretext of being attached to the Russian legation at Venice and Genoa during the coalition, remain accredited in foreign countries as Russian agents; that I am no less shocked to see that they have sent Mr. Bestrof here, known for his inconsiderate conduct in Paris; that I would already, if the Russian threats had inspired any fears in me, have ordered the two regiments that were ordered to leave Hanover to return there, and that I have not done any such thing; that I have no fear of Russia whatsoever.[42]

Talleyrand declared to Oubril that Napoleon was sad to see that the "influence of the enemies of France had prevailed in the cabinet of Petersburg." He stated that Alexander had no right to complain of France's actions, seeing that neither Prussia nor Austria had protested. Worst of all, he added that Russia's behavior raised the question, "if, when England meditated the assassination of Paul I, one had learned that the others of that conspiracy were one league from the frontiers, one would not have hastened to seize them."[43] The not so veiled reference to Alexander's participation in the plot to kill his father did not go unnoticed in St. Petersburg, needless to say.

For all that, Napoleon's bark was worse than his bite, at least in the short term. He did not allow his fury with Alexander to distract him from the plans for the invasion of England or from the object that had displaced the conspiracies against him as his second preoccupation: his impending coronation.

Emperor of the French

It is not clear why Napoleon decided to crown himself emperor. He seems to have felt that the attempts on his life would lose steam if he held a hereditary position and had a named successor. He may also have believed that he could put an end to royalist machinations designed to convince or force him to restore the Bourbons. The logical fallacies in both of these arguments are clear and it is hard to believe that Napoleon did not see them: he had no son at that time, and any "hereditary" successor he might name would be unlikely to survive the jealousies and counterattacks of his peers. No one with any sense at all, including the princes of the blood, could imagine after the execution of the Duc d'Enghien that Napoleon might restore the Bourbons to their throne. Nevertheless, the timing is telling: Napoleon's elevation, about which there was no word before the explosion of the Cadoudal conspiracy, must have been tied more or less directly to that and subsequent events.

Napoleon's elevation to the status of emperor of the French had dramatic diplomatic consequences. On hearing of Napoleon's intentions, Czartoryskii wrote to Alexander that he should be pleased. First, he noted that it would cool the ardor of those (meaning the princes and some British) who wanted to overthrow Napoleon in order to bring back the monarchy, since Napoleon would already have done that, just with a different dynasty. Second, perhaps contradictorily, he pointed out that the coronation would heighten tensions within France, possibly promoting rebellions that Napoleon would make himself very unpopular putting down. In any event, he reasoned, Napoleon would be distracted from foreign adventures for a time.[44]

Czartoryskii was pleased about the coronation for another reason. The changed designation of the French head of state would require every other nation to issue new credentials to its representatives; in Russia's case, Oubril would need new letters of accreditation. Czartoryskii saw two happy options. First, Napoleon might approach the other European powers prior to declaring himself emperor, in which case the Russians should insist on the withdrawal of French troops from Germany and Italy as a condition of recognizing him in this new capacity. Second, Napoleon might simply crown himself without any prior approach, in which case Alexander should simply refuse to reaccredit Oubril, thereby refusing to recognize Napoleon in his new dignity. Needless to say, Napoleon chose the second option.

Alexander wasted little time in trying to benefit from Napoleon's decision. In mid-June Czartoryskii wrote the Russian ambassador in Vienna, Razumovskii, describing Napoleon's elevation as a "new usurpation" and noting that, "although this title adds nothing to the power Bonaparte exercises in France, it may serve as a pretext for his unbounded ambition to extend his domination still further beyond its current limits."[45] The aim of this note was clearly to use Napoleon's proposed coronation to drive Francis toward an alliance. Francis, however, had already considered the problem and come to a different conclusion.

Napoleon's decision to promote himself created a brief diplomatic crisis in Europe. The Austrians were well aware that Alexander would be displeased if they recognized Napoleon's new title, and Francis even promised not to do so prior to consulting with Alexander. The emperor then reversed his decision, however, informing Napoleon that he would recognize his new title if Napoleon agreed to recognize Francis as hereditary emperor of Austria.[46] It seems clear that he made this decision in fear. Ludwig Cobenzl wrote to d'Antraigues (still in Dresden and relaying information to the tsar) that it was insane to imagine that Francis would risk a war over the French head of state's title, especially when that head of state could send "three to four hundred thousand soldiers into the heart of southern Germany and Italy."[47] Nor was this fear baseless, for in July Napoleon noted to Oubril "the delay which Austria is interposing in recognizing him, that if that power continued to prevaricate he would fix a term for her to make a decision and then, if she let that term pass without sending new letters of accreditation to her ambassador, he would change the face of Europe."[48]

The demand that Napoleon recognize Francis as emperor of Austria was probably intended to allow the Habsburg Empire to survive the collapse of the Holy Roman Empire. It had already become clear during the negotiations concerning compensation that the Holy Roman Empire continued to exist and function, to the limited extent it did, only at Napoleon's discretion. Francis had obviously been forced to consider the possibility that he, or at least his heir, would cease to hold the position of emperor. He would then have to revert to his own hereditary titles, King of Bohemia, King of Hungary, and, worst of all, Grand Duke of Austria. The imminent collapse of the Holy Roman throne forced Francis to face what Habsburgs had been ignoring for more than three and a half centuries—that the Habsburg Empire absent the Holy Roman throne had no recognizable and independent central dignity. Consequently Francis sought to invent an independent central dignity on which to fall back if necessary. It was also a way for him to claim that he had demanded something from Napoleon in return for recognizing *his* imperium and had not simply caved in to Napoleon's demand.

Napoleon was delighted to make this exchange, although he noted that it would be necessary for Francis actually to declare himself emperor of Austria before Napoleon could recognize him as such.[49] He was delighted because it meant that Francis would recognize him as emperor and also because it was certain to sow discord between Austria and Russia, and even within the Austrian court, as indeed it did.* One of the fiercest Francophobes in Vienna, the itinerant publicist Friedrich von Gentz, noted acidly that "Emperor of Austria" was so ridiculous that one might as well have chosen "Emperor of Salzburg, of Frankfurt, or of Passau."[50] Nevertheless, even the war party in Austria, still coalescing around Cobenzl and Colloredo, feared to provoke Napoleon's wrath prematurely.

---

*Napoleon to Talleyrand, 25 August 1804, *Corr. de Nap.*, doc. 7960: "It's actually the Court of Vienna that needs my recognition, since it is very likely that it will encounter difficulties throughout Europe. Russia's vanity will be wounded, that of Prussia even more."

The Austrian decision to recognize Napoleon's new title dashed in Alexander's mind any hope of an alliance. Czartoryskii wrote that it seemed to eliminate any chance that the Austrians would respond positively to the new proposals for restraining France, and he intimated that the tsar would abandon Europe to its fate in that case. Alexander, "perfectly calm about the security of his empire and having fulfilled the demands of his dignity . . . will readily leave to those who believe themselves able to deal with the storm by following a system other than his own the problem of warding it off."[51] The execution of the Duc d'Enghien, together with Napoleon's declaration of his intention to make himself emperor, seemed to drive Alexander away from war rather than toward it.

These events, however, solidified an open state of cold war between France and Russia, even if neither side expected it to heat up in the near future. Although furious at Alexander's reactions, Napoleon did not believe that the crisis with Russia would expand into a full-blown war. To Soult, commanding the invasion army preparing on the shores of the Channel, he wrote,

> I imagine that rumors of a continental war are circulating in the camp as they are in Paris. That would be annoying from the single point of view that it could distract our attention from England, for those who look for trouble from us will find it! . . . [I] have 60,000 men more than in [December-January 1800–1801], the moment when our armies were at the height of their prosperity and strength. But all these forces, which I plan to augment still further with the conscription of last year, will not be necessary at all. The German states, Austria, and Prussia get along very well with us.[52]

Explaining his actions and the situation to General Guillaume-Marie-Anne Brune, his ambassador to the Ottoman sultan, he noted,

> I have recalled Hédouville following the indiscretion of the court of Petersburg, which had the ineptitude to go into mourning for the Duc d'Enghien without having any ties of blood with him and despite the fact that no other family with ties to the Bourbons imitated it. I could not but withdraw my ambassador from Petersburg; but I think that affairs will not go further and that they will continue to rest in this state of coolness, since the cabinet of Saint Petersburg is so extremely inconsequent that one cannot attach any faith to its demarches, almost all made at random.[53]

The eventual withdrawal of both Oubril and the French chargé in St. Petersburg did little to change this situation. Napoleon had come to view Russia with dislike and contempt; Alexander had openly propounded his hatred for and opposition to Napoleon. Both were ready to resist further "aggressions" by the other, but neither side was ready or able to move militarily against the other.

Nevertheless, in late September 1804 Alexander sent his trusted confidant, N. N. Novosil'tsev, to London with secret and open instructions to begin negotiations with Great Britain about the formation of a coalition aimed at removing Napoleon from power in France.

The Turn to Britain

Alexander's approach to Britain in September 1804 takes some explaining. The British had let the Russians know for some time that they would be happy to help resist Napoleon, but Alexander had always been cool to their overtures. He had steadfastly maintained that his aim was purely defensive, yet he initially proposed an offensive coalition to Britain. It is not enough to point to the execution of the Duc d'Enghien, for a full six months elapsed between that event and Novosil'tsev's mission (in the course of which Alexander turned down another British offer of alliance). It is no more appropriate to identify the formal cessation of relations between France and Russia, which occurred in the first few days of September 1804, since both Napoleon and Alexander repeatedly explained that it was not in any way tantamount to a declaration of war. The traditional emphasis on the limitless gold of perfidious Albion does not explain why Alexander rebuffed British approaches in July 1803 but made his own direct approach in September 1804.

The real causes of Alexander's change of heart were threefold. First, the fall of the Addington ministry and the rise of Pitt in May 1804 transformed Britain in Alexander's mind from a weak, unreliable, and selfish partner into a vibrant, trustworthy, and competent ally against the common foe. Second, by late summer 1804, it had become painfully clear that the Austrians would not sign even a defensive treaty without the promise of financial subsidies that could come only from Britain and, furthermore, that any direct Austrian approach to Britain was likely to fail. Third, Napoleon's activities in the eastern Mediterranean became steadily more alarming and helped convince Alexander and his advisers that Russia's vital interests were, indeed, involved in the effort to contain France.

Alexander refrained from negotiating meaningfully with the Addington government for several reasons. Although Alexander might have sympathized with London in 1803, Britain bore the onus for restarting the war by violating the terms of the Treaty of Amiens and then refusing Russian mediation. In addition, the British policy for conducting the war at sea was, as Napoleon repeatedly stated, not really in Russia's interests. Russian ships and trade were affected by the blockades of the French coast, and by the inevitable French reprisals. Britain's absolute refusal to consider abandoning Malta for whatever compensations might be offered also concerned the tsar. These problems would reemerge in 1805 as the final details of the coalition treaty were being hammered out.

A more serious hindrance to negotiations, however, was the Addington government's attitude toward the composition of the coalition and the sort of support the British would give it. As late as April 1804, Sir J. B. Warren, the British ambassador in St. Petersburg, persisted in demanding that the coalition include both Prussia and Austria and that the objective of the coalition be the reestablishment of the status quo ante bellum, meaning specifically the withdrawal of French troops from Hanover, Naples, and elsewhere beyond the boundaries established by the Treaties of Amiens and Lunéville. It was clear, in addition, that Addington was not prepared to offer enough money in subsidies soon enough to offset the expense of the Austrian mobilization that would be necessary before any war could begin.[54]

Czartoryskii quickly pointed out that these conditions were unacceptable. Although it might be possible to drive Austria to an alliance before too long, it would be extremely difficult to bring Prussia to heel in any reasonable span of time. Neither state, moreover, would contemplate an offensive war against France, since both feared French power. No coalition with Austria, finally, would be possible unless the British agreed to subsidize Austria with a significant grant—not a loan—for the purpose of putting her army on a war footing and supporting the costs of the campaign.[55] This discussion had been dragging on in a desultory fashion since the first British approach to Russia in late 1802, and there was little likelihood that Addington's government would have moved it along.

Scholars debate the wisdom and even the content of Addington's strategy. Although some see in his passivity a kind of fecklessness and lethargy, others emphasize his efforts to form a coalition and Britain's difficult situation in 1803 and early 1804.[56] Whether wise or foolish in retrospect, however, Addington's government was perceived at the time to be weak and passive, a feeling that led to Russia's estrangement and the government's ultimate fall. Simon Vorontsov confided in British friends that Alexander distrusted Addington's regime, "marked as they are throughout Europe for their utter imbecility; which, the Count said, occasioned no surprise to him, as he knew from all the foreign Ministers here, and from his correspondence with different parts of Europe, that they are held in universal contempt."[57] At another point, Vorontsov opined that "if this Ministry lasts, Britain will not survive." This view probably arose in considerable degree from attacks by Pitt and his partisans, which acquired a serious scale and urgency in the early months of 1804, although some of Pitt's partisans had been attacking the Addington government from its inception.[58] This contempt, combined with the impracticability of the British proposals for a coalition, ruled out serious negotiations for an alliance.

Addington's resignation in April 1804 thus revolutionized the situation. Although the Russians rejoiced at Pitt's return and British policy received a brief lift, even this new ministry soon revealed the weakness of British policy in the Napoleonic wars. Napoleonic propaganda portrayed Britain as a determined, aggressive, and implacable foe between 1800 and 1815, regularly spinning webs of gold to trap the European states in wars against France. This explanation overstates the determination and cohesiveness, not to say stability, of British governments in this time. In contrast to the relatively stable British governments that fought World War I and World War II, which had one change of administration in each conflict, six different prime ministers, nine different foreign secretaries, six different secretaries for war, and eight different first lords of the admiralty held office during the Napoleonic wars. Few of these figures were powerful leaders, and the prime minister rarely enjoyed the full support of parliament and king. Even the elevation of Pitt, by far the strongest British leader of the time, was marred by the king's refusal to allow Charles James Fox, the leader of the opposition to the war, to enter the cabinet. The king's hostility resulted more from Fox's attitudes toward Catholic emancipation than from his attitudes toward the war, but then there was little about Fox that George III liked at all. This refusal to form a "ministry of all the talents" embracing the leaders of the major factions ensured the continuance of factional strife and infighting even as a war for Britain's safety was being waged. The growth of real hostility between Pitt and Addington, and especially between their respective supporters, also helped fragment the parliament and add to this factionalism and discord.[59] Britain's success in war against Napoleon had more to do with Napoleon's actions and the fortunes of war on the continent, as well as with Britain's inherent strategic advantages, than it did with any skill, steadfastness, or determination of British governments.

The Russians in 1804 did not identify British limitations but simply rejoiced that Pitt would bring Britain to her senses. Simon Vorontsov's note providing the details of Pitt's cabinet was a paean to the great man. He pointed out that the cabinet appointments in themselves were irrelevant

> [b]ecause all of the individuals who compose the current administration are animated and directed by a man of great force of will and a genius with which there is nothing to compare in our days,—a man who to the widest talents joins a disinterestedness and a zeal for his sovereign and his country that one can only admire the more one comes to perceive it.[60]

Here, then, was a man Alexander could do business with.

Pitt wasted little time letting Alexander know that he was prepared to deal seriously and in good faith. In June, after he had a chance to form his cabinet and gain an understanding of the state of play in the European diplomatic scene, Pitt sent word that he was willing to accept a coalition that included either Austria or Prussia (but not necessarily both), that he might be willing to assist financially with the mobilization of the coalition states, and that he would, in any event, furnish up to £5 million in subsidies for actual military operations.[61] At last Britain made a definite offer of a meaningful sum to support a realistic coalition!

Pitt stubbornly hung on to a last remaining demand, however. The purpose of the alliance was not simply to prevent France from making any new gains (although Britain would come to the support of any country that found itself at war with France). The allies would have to fight, instead, to provide "some permanent security to the Continent." What is more, the British warned that it would take some three to four months to get Britain's defenses in order, and no meaningful action could be undertaken before October.[62] The Russians tried to extort additional subsidies from Britain but abandoned the effort; they did insist on a clear definition of the goals and objectives of the alliance.[63] There, however, the matter stood for two months.

Alexander Vorontsov had withdrawn from active control over the Russian foreign ministry in February 1804 for reasons of health, as we have seen.* At this point, however, he briefly emerged from semiretirement to give his formidable support to a fundamental change in Russia's course. Czartoryskii had dutifully kept him informed of the kaleidoscopic changes in the European scene over the past half year, sending copies of documents and occasional notes, summaries, and requests for advice to the aged luminary. On the whole, Vorontsov's interventions in response to this material had been limited in scope and effect. By the time he received word of what was afoot and responded, decisions had often been taken and acted on.[64] In early August 1804, however, Vorontsov intervened with a powerful thunderbolt.

In a lengthy memorandum, he noted that agreements by Denmark, Sweden, and Prussia to oppose further French aggression in northern Germany had secured the part of Europe that was both vital to Russia's interests and threatened by French aggression.[65] He continued, "Now the question emerges: is securing ourselves in this area sufficient for perfect security from the aggressions of the French government and from any new upheaval in the conditions and existences of the several powers comprising the association of Europe?" The answer, of course, was no.

Noting the pusillanimity of Austria, customary by now in Russian memorandums, Vorontsov then changed course. He pointed out how critical Britain

---

*Patricia Kennedy Grimsted, *The Foreign Ministers of Alexander I: Political Attitudes and the Conduct of Russian Diplomacy, 1801–1825* (Los Angeles: University of California Press, 1969), pp. 98–99. Vorontsov remained the nominal foreign minister throughout the War of the Third Coalition, although active control over the ministry reverted to his deputy, Czartoryskii.

was to the defense of European stability: "one cannot fail to recognize that England is the wall that maintains the security and independence of Europe and on which all those who still think of their own independence can lean." He wondered, however, how long Britain would be willing to bear such a burden alone. Improvements in the Royal Navy and Britain's land defenses, he argued, had made it nearly impossible for Napoleon to invade the island. Britain, furthermore, had gained so many French and Dutch colonies around the world that she might well decide to withdraw from the continent in order to secure those new acquisitions overseas. In such a situation, Vorontsov wondered, what would prevent Britain from making peace with France?*

Vorontsov then proceeded to consider the consequences of such a Franco–British peace. Napoleon would have some 200,000 troops on the Channel coast, suddenly without a mission. He might well decide, in the absence of a war with Britain, to use those troops to pursue new conquests or punish recalcitrant neighboring states. In sum, "nothing would be as harmful for the independence of Europe" as such a peace.

What was to be done? Vorontsov concluded that Russia and the other continental powers that desired independence and peace must conclude a meaningful alliance with Great Britain to forestall any feeling in London that peace should be on the agenda. He continued,

> If it is desired (as it must undoubtedly be) that by this war the center of Europe will in the future be secure from French domination, that Italy be liberated from her hands, that Holland and Switzerland [be freed] from their dependence on France, and that Germany be restored to her previous borders, then there is no way to act in order to achieve this other than in combination with the greatest force. With good fortune and unanimity among cabinets, it seems that this expectation might not be vain.

This paragraph shifted the entire ground of the Russian strategic discussion in 1804, following Pitt's earlier lead in this direction. Hitherto the focus had been on defending Europe from further French encroachments, with the occasional footnote that a defensive war would ultimately roll back earlier French gains. Now Vorontsov took it for granted that the goal of Russian policy was the liberation of Europe from the French yoke.

There is more to this change of heart than the assassination of the Duc d'Enghien (to which no reference is made) or even the rise of Pitt, although these events and their consequences helped Vorontsov develop his new conclusions. Vorontsov likely sat down and thought the problem of Russia's security

---

*Odd though these reflections seem in the context of 1803–1804, they were not wildly unrealistic, as we shall see in the aftermath of the War of 1805.

through to the end, something that neither he nor anyone else had really done before in the rush of events. He realized that simply restraining Napoleon was not good enough. French gains by mid-1804 were so great that Europe trembled before a new master. It was clear to Vorontsov that Russia would not be secure as long as that situation persisted, because Napoleon's gains precluded the possibility of restoring a stable balance to the continent. That obvious conclusion led to another: Russia's security was tightly connected to the quest to restore France to her previous borders. Russia needed to fight an offensive war.

Vorontsov's memorandum did not mention Russia's isolation from Europe, the security she possessed by being far from France, or the fact that France could not attack Russia without simultaneously creating allies eager for her help. On the contrary, the focus was not on Russia at all but on the perceived vulnerability of Europe. Vorontsov assumed that Russia's security was inextricably bound up with Europe's security and stability. He did not lose sight of Russia's special interests, as we shall see in the details of his proposal, but he did recognize Russia's obligation in her own interest to protect the interests of others. His thinking shifted away from high-minded idealism to realpolitik. Vorontsov had lost interest in the prospect of "defending Europe" from French depredations and was concerned with defending Russia's vital interests by helping other European states defend themselves against a powerful France.

If Vorontsov's proposal reflected a high degree of political realism, however, it also contained a great deal of military and strategic naïveté. He proposed to use British subsidies to place large Austrian armies in Italy and on the Rhine, the latter preferably commanded by Archduke Charles and supported by the armies of Bavaria, Württemberg, and Hesse-Cassel. With the assistance of other British subsidies, Sweden and Denmark would cooperate with a Russian force to drive the French from Hanover and liberate Holland. He recognized, however, that the only real prospect for success was to convince the king of Prussia and the elector of Saxony to participate.

A negative note in the memorandum was continuing distrust of Austria. Vorontsov recommended that an auxiliary corps of 30,000 troops be sent to Italy, not so much to help the Austrians as "to restrain the Austrian ministry so that in the event of success it does not cut Italy up according to its desires and its own local views, as happened under [Paul] and which led, so to speak, to the undoing of all of the amazing successes of Prince Suvorov." Vorontsov designated another 30,000–40,000 Russians to support the Austrians on the Rhine (always assuming that the British would pay for it). But in addition to the 110,000 or so Russian troops that Vorontsov proposed to use in active operations, he advocated the creation of another corps of 50,000–60,000 men deployed on the Austrian and Prussian borders "in order to restrain the Berlin court from the ambivalence of its views and relations with France, and no less also the Viennese court, if, in the case of its successes in Italy, it begins to act in accord with its own particular views away from the conditions agreed upon about the fate of Italy." For all of Austria's efforts, her gains in Italy were to be modest, however, for Vorontsov was determined to reestablish the king of Sardinia in his old territories, with the addition of much of Genoa, so that he could serve as a buffer to future French aggression on the peninsula.

This proposal thus encapsulated everything that was good and bad about the Third Coalition. On the one hand, there was an element of enlightened self-interest in Vorontsov's recognition that Russia needed to defend the stability and security of Europe beyond her own borders. On the other hand, the proposal demonstrated Russia's distrust of her potential allies and incorporated measures into the planning of operations designed as much for their effect on allies as for their effect on the enemy.

From a military perspective, the plan contained a fatal flaw. It was written as though allied forces would operate against an inert, lifeless enemy who would do exactly what was expected of him and make no effort to seize the initiative. There was no consideration of what the actual objectives of each force would be, how they would communicate with and support one another, and what Napoleon might do to disrupt the attack. Vorontsov ignored the Alps as a barrier to lateral communication between the armies in Italy and on the Rhine. He also overlooked the difficulties of landing and supplying a Russian force in northern Germany without Prussian support.

None of these omissions are surprising. Vorontsov was a diplomat and not a general, and he was more interested in the political issues he was raising and solving than in the practical military considerations that emerged from his plan. Nor was such an approach necessarily problematic, as long as the preliminary plan was subsequently presented to senior military officers able to identify and correct its military and strategic deficiencies. Unfortunately for the allies, the actual development of war plans remained the province of diplomats and political advisers for far too long, and critical, objective military advice was never really sought or heeded. The enormous difficulties of actually forming a coalition and agreeing on the basic outlines of its military operations ended up precluding the employment of military experts and methods in the development of these military plans. There can be no doubt of the baleful consequences of this manner of doing business.

There is no direct evidence that Vorontsov's memorandum influenced Alexander's thinking, but the indirect evidence is considerable. There is no trace of the basic objectives and programs outlined in Vorontsov's memorandum in Russian policy before he wrote this document. Afterward, beginning with the documents written to support Novosil'tsev's mission, those objectives and programs became the basis of Russian policy. This is not surprising, as Alexander held Vorontsov in the highest esteem, even in retirement. This document played an important role in focusing Alexander's attention on the real problems he faced and possible, if flawed, solutions to them.

Vorontsov's Russian realpolitik, however, was only one input into Alexander's strategic decisionmaking. Although Czartoryskii also concluded that French power must be rolled back, not merely checked, he approached the problem from a different direction.

Idealism and Realpolitik in Russian Strategy

Adam Czartoryskii was the son of a Polish family of high nobility that had long fought for the independence of their homeland. Born in 1770, he was close enough in age to Alexander (only seven years older) to have been molded by the same events. Czartoryskii was at once a child of the Enlightenment, having studied with and befriended *philosophes* during extensive travels, and a patriotic Pole. After the last partition of Poland in 1795 extinguished that country's independence, Czartoryskii reconciled himself to the belief that Poland would be resurrected only through Russian power, and he became a loyal servant of the Russian throne. He became attached to Alexander after serving as an aide-de-camp to the young grand prince in 1796, and they maintained a warm, confidential friendship marked with mutual esteem for many years, despite growing differences over policy. Their friendship even survived an affair between Czartoryskii and Alexander's wife, Grand Princess Elizabeth, in the last years of the eighteenth century that led Paul to banish Czartoryskii temporarily from St. Petersburg. When Alexander took the throne, Czartoryskii's star rose rapidly, like those of the other members of the "unofficial committee." As soon as the tsar created the Foreign Ministry in 1802, he appointed Czartoryskii to the post of assistant minister of foreign affairs.[66] Despite their friendship and shared views, however, Alexander never felt it wise to promote Czartoryskii to the position of foreign minister, fearing a backlash against the Polish and Roman Catholic "foreigner" who was nevertheless more devoted to Alexander than many Russians.[67]

Czartoryskii's political program was a blend of realism and naïveté. In 1803 he presented Alexander with a voluminous memorandum proposing a political system for Russia.[68] Beginning from traditional Enlightenment thought, Czartoryskii argued for the establishment of a permanent "political system" based on an immutable set of principles, starting with the conviction that the purpose of the state was to preserve the security and prosperity of its people, both internally and externally. He spoke of the science of international relations and the law of nations. He identified the establishment of "perpetual peace" as his aim, although he did not really expect to achieve it.

Czartoryskii fell somewhere in the middle in the debate between Russian national isolationists and Russian internationalists. He relied on Russia's geographic isolation to give Russia greater power and leverage in Europe and to preserve Russia's freedom of action, but he believed that Russia must involve herself in the affairs of Europe in order to pursue the idealistic system he proposed she adopt. He saw Napoleon as an enemy to his cherished international order, but when the memorandum was presented in 1803 (the exact date is unclear), he foresaw a cold war in which Napoleon was checked but not destroyed. On the other hand, Czartoryskii imbued his proposals for Russian foreign policy with a program for Polish independence. He wanted Russia to reacquire the Polish territories that Austria and Prussia had taken in 1793 and 1795 and integrate them into a united Poland, although he was willing to see a reunited Poland ruled over by a Russian prince and formally incorporated into the Russian empire. Czartoryskii presented a bizarre blend of Russian and Polish nationalism, of Enlightenment idealism and hardcore realpolitik.

All of these traits emerged in the instructions Czartoryskii drafted for Alexander to send to Novosil'tsev to guide him in his mission to England in September 1804. In a preliminary note sent to Simon Vorontsov, Alexander acknowledged that he had satisfied all the demands of his honor, integrity, and security by breaking off relations with France and arranging with the other European powers to resist further French encroachments. He continued that however calm he might be under such a system about Russia's security, he could not deny that "even supposing that Bonaparte advances no farther in his usurpations, he will nevertheless continue to control arbitrarily the part of Europe that he holds under his domination, and will not allow the other [part] to be free of disquiet about his ultimate aims." Alexander preferred to find a way to "contribute actively to the reestablishment of order and happiness in Europe, if I could have the hope of really succeeding in this desirable goal." He concluded,

> The goal that one would propose in igniting a general war can only be to put an end to the dangers by which Europe is threatened by the excessive aggrandizement of France, to restore the independence of the States who are suffering under the yoke of Bonaparte and to assure the general tranquility of Europe on solid bases for the future.[69]

This was a call to roll back all French conquests and depose Napoleon from his throne, for Alexander believed that there could be no meaningful peace with him.

Czartoryskii's idealism emerged even more clearly in the lengthy instruction he drafted for Alexander to send to Novosil'tsev.[70] It was devoted to a consideration of the desired state of Europe after the successful outcome of the war, addressing not so much the particular territorial settlements to be made as the general tenor of international relations and the overall structure of the European system.

The final goal was a restructuring of Europe no less dramatic than that completed at Westphalia in 1648. "Nothing would prevent [the states of Europe] when the peace had been concluded from concerning themselves with a treaty that would become the basis for the reciprocal relations of the European States." The disingenuous avowal followed: "We are not trying to realize the dream of perpetual peace here at all." But the treaty should nevertheless aim "to fix, on clear and precise principles, the prescriptions of the law of nations." The idealism continued:

> Why not submit [to the treaty] the positive law of nations, assure the privileges of neutrality, insert the obligation never to start a war without having exhausted the means that a third-party mediation might offer, in order to have aired states' respective grievances and tried to resolve them? It is on such principles that one could proceed to a general period of peace and give rise to a league whose stipulations would form, so to speak, a new code of the law of nations that, sanctioned by the greater part of the States of Europe, would become, without difficulty, the immutable rule of the conduct of cabinets inasmuch as those who sought to ignore it would risk drawing on themselves the forces of the new union.

After so many alarms, "after having experienced the inconveniences of a precarious or illusory independence," most states would happily sign such an agreement. The smaller states would attach themselves to it "heart and soul."

The practical bases of the agreement would be, on the one hand, the indissoluble tie between Britain and Russia and, on the other, the rectification of European borders. To the greatest extent possible, states should be given borders according with the natural boundaries offered by rivers, mountains, and other natural features. Each state should also be formed in accord with ethnic boundaries. Small states should either be increased in size so as to present real obstacles to the larger states' aggressions, or they should be formed into federations so that their combined power could achieve the same purpose.

Napoleon could not be left in power in such a system, and the instructions proposed replacing him with a monarchy. Czartoryskii eschewed the notion of imposing a form of government, let alone a particular individual as king, on the French people. He hoped, instead, to use propaganda and gentle coercion to lead the French to desire the restoration of the previous system—to propose it themselves and choose the person (subject to the approval of the victorious allies) to rule over it.

The specific territorial gains of the allies were not named. But the proviso that Russia must receive equivalent gains if Austria, Prussia, and Sweden received gains for their participation sounded a jarring note. The issue, according to the idealism of the rest of the document, should simply have been the preservation and restoration of natural boundaries, not the expansion of Russian territory, which could only take place at the expense of her neighbors. Alexander probably supported this aim because of his sense of Russia's dignity and honor; Czartoryskii probably had a specific and practical goal. If Russia were to receive gains to compensate her for the gains of Austria, Prussia, and Sweden, those gains could only come at the expense of the Ottoman Empire or the Polish territories that the German states had seized during the partitions. Here and elsewhere, however, the Russians repeatedly stated that their desire was the preservation, not the destruction, of the Ottoman Empire. This codicil seems a clever attempt by Czartoryskii to ensure that one outcome of the war would be the unification of Poland under Russian rule.

Despite the statements that Russia and Britain had no interests in conflict, a significant bone of contention appeared toward the end of the document. Czartoryskii must have noticed that the British manner of arbitrarily ruling the seas had nothing in common with his notions of the law of nations. Alexander, whether or not he cared about the law of nations, certainly saw that British blockades and the British definition of neutrality were harmful to Russian shipping and trade. The instructions therefore ordered Novosil'tsev to insist that the British agree to the regulation of the law of the sea, accepting certain "modifications" that the Russians would propose. This attempt at controlling her ally significantly delayed the alliance, for the British fought such a proposal tooth and nail and the Russians eventually had to give way.[71]

The lack of specific details about gains and contingencies was countered by a set of additional instructions dealing more carefully with Switzerland and Holland, addressing the possibility that a Russian grand princess might take over the role of leading aristocrat in the latter country. They specified that any alliance with Britain for an offensive war must be predicated on Austria's participation. "If Austria obstinately remained on the defensive and Bonaparte did not provoke her, this [neutrality] would necessitate other combinations."[72]

Some see ominous overtones in the provision that concerned Russia's possible gains: "In addressing the advantages that the two powers might obtain at the end of the struggle, we have not designated more specifically any acquisition for Russia, since the conduct of her neighbors and the operations that one might find it necessary to undertake against them would produce possibilities and free us in this regard." Clearly the thought behind this provision was that either Prussia would refuse to play and Russia would go to war with her, or that Austria would participate in the coalition, but then misbehave, perhaps in Italy, justifying Russian retaliation—or both. Once again, this provision seems to hearken back to Czartoryskii's dream of uniting Poland under Russian rule.

The instructions envisioned two possible treaties with Turkey, one establishing pseudo-independent republics of Slavs and Greeks under the joint control of Russia and Turkey, rather like the Ionian Islands, the other fundamentally preserving the status quo with Turkey so as to keep Russia's hands free to deal with Prussia. Two other provisions considered the actions of Russian forces in the event that Prussia decided to oppose the alliance and in the event that Prussia remained neutral.

One historian of the period characterized these instructions as follows:

> The Russian programme contained three kinds of discourse: first, a Wilsonian internationalist idealism; second, a Rooseveltian, fake-realist, liberal-paternalist new order, intended to concentrate real power and decision in the hands of Two Policemen who would police Europe for peace, concealing this arrangement behind a façade of internationalism; and finally, a fairly naked version of Russian imperialism (Stalinist or Catherninian, as you will). It is tempting and natural to suppose that the first two sets were only fig-leaves for the third, the real Russian programme. The temptation must be resisted. It makes Czartorsykii and Alexander into cynics and Machiavellians, when in fact they were the kind of idealists common in international politics, genuinely convinced of the nobility of their own aims and the selfishness of everyone else's. All three sets of instructions were genuine—and therefore all the more dangerous.[73]

States that incorporate any degree of idealism in their policies always experience an unresolved tension between idealism and realism. But this tension does not mean that the idealism is a cynical cover for realpolitik motives. The politics of the formation of foreign policy in any state, even an absolute monarchy, are complicated. Even Alexander, even Napoleon felt it necessary to woo particular interest groups or support their particular causes. Czartoryskii made a sound argument that the Poles, the Slavs, and the Greeks would be powerful allies if they were courted, and would help Russia win the war, which, in turn, would help Russia establish the new world order he desired. It can be argued that Napoleon believed that only by crowning himself emperor of the French could he secure the Revolution from the Jacobin and royalist opposition. The real danger in history and politics is to imagine that people must be either realists or idealists, each using the other's arguments as a cloak. Most people are a little of both.

Alexander's instructions to Novosil'tsev bore the germ of the Treaty of Vienna and the subsequent "Congress period," a long peace lasting from 1815 to about 1848. Many of the same claims for the elevation of the law of nations and a peaceful world order maintained benevolently by a concert of powers led by Russia and Britain can be found in these documents of 1804 and others in the later period. The seeds of disharmony among the post-1815 states that introduced tension and conflict into that system can also be seen here: Russia's designs on Prussia, distrust of Austria, and disagreements with Britain.

The idealistic elements of this policy never really changed, although the degree to which they influenced Alexander's actions varied during the struggle with Napoleon. The largest single change would be the loss of Russia's innocence—the belief that Russia could stand aside from Europe's struggles if she chose, the conviction that her participation in Europe's wars was more or less altruistic. By 1815 that notion would be gone for good, but in 1804 it was still a powerful motivation.

This sense of aloofness was another powerful factor that bound the Russians to the British. Vorontsov had relied on the possibility that Britain might decide to make a separate peace as the cornerstone of his argument for approaching them at that moment for an alliance. The one thing that Britain and Russia could really agree on, after the need to eliminate Napoleon, was that Austria and if possible Prussia should bear the brunt of the war. Russia would help with auxiliary corps, Britain with subsidies and ships, but the main body of the coalition armies would be drawn from German troops. To the Russians this approach was only fair. After all, it was the Germans who stood to benefit the most from the war by having the threats to their vital interests eliminated once and for all. It was German territory that would be liberated, German rivers that would be reopened, German armies that could be stood down. The sense that the Austrians and the Prussians desperately needed Russia (and Britain), while Russia (and Britain) could readily withdraw and leave Europe to its own devices permeated the Third Coalition, poisoned relations among the powers, and hampered the effective coordination of its actions. It was one of the principal reasons for the failure of the alliance.*

Conclusion

Napoleon also maintained a complex balance of realism and idealism, and his fight with Russia had idealistic overtones. He really believed that Alexander's support for the émigrés was immoral and violated the law of nations, that his own actions in attacking Hanover and Naples were justified by Britain's failure to adhere to the terms of the Treaty of Amiens, and so forth. He never complained that the British were spying on him or trying to support insurrections against his rule once the war had started again in 1803. He expected nothing less from his enemy and acknowledged that he would do exactly the same

---

*Paul W. Schroeder makes this point clearly in *The Transformation of European Politics, 1763–1848* (New York: Oxford University Press, 1994), p. 260, but then goes too far in pointing to the hegemonic objective of British and Russian policy that Austria and Prussia were to subserve. The element of aloofness and perceived altruism was still very strong in 1804. Alexander had not yet come to see himself as a hegemon, even if his policies would have led to the establishment of his hegemony.

when he had the opportunity. He distinguished between behavior proper to a belligerent and behavior proper to a neutral state.

Napoleon's balance between idealism and realism, however, tilted much more toward the latter than Alexander's did. Napoleon's idealism was bound up with his own personal honor and dignity, which he identified with the honor and dignity of France herself. When he felt that he had been offended or insulted, he believed that his security and survival depended on his avenging the offense. Dismissing this trait as the result of his "Corsican blood" is merely flippant.

The real motivating factor behind Napoleon's actions was a deep conviction that the perception of power drives the world. His struggle with Alexander turned around objections that Alexander wounded his honor and insulted his dignity. He believed that such wounds hurt his ability to conduct his policies. Napoleon perceived that Austria and Prussia feared his power and saw his ability to pursue his policies successfully as depending on that fear. He could not allow Alexander's temerity to undermine it.

But Napoleon believed strongly in certain aspects of the Revolution. He believed in the ideal of the rule of law; that men should rise to power based on merit, not birth; that the ruler should be freely accepted and acknowledged by the people and not a tyrant set over them; that the ruler's first duty was the welfare of the state. When he violated the principle of the rule of law by ordering people suspected of espionage to be tried and executed, he believed that he was doing it for the higher purpose of defending the state that enshrined the principle. When he established his own hereditary tyranny, he believed that he did so with the consent of the French people. There is considerable evidence that such was really the case. Above all, when he acted to preserve his own honor and dignity abroad, he did so in the conviction that he was thereby safeguarding the well-being of France.

The most fundamental difference between Napoleon and Alexander was that Napoleon saw the world in terms of power relationships, while Alexander sought natural law and right. The conflict between the two, however, ended up turning largely on power relationships, and here Napoleon initially had the advantage. This was a realm where he saw clearly but Alexander tended to be confused.

The conflict between Russia and France resulted largely from this clash of worldviews. Alexander saw Napoleon's reckless disregard of international laws and norms as a serious threat to the stability of Europe and eventually to his own security. He took each new indication of Napoleon's unwillingness to be checked by the law of nations as evidence of the danger he posed and the need to resist him. There was a great deal of truth in this view, although Alexander found that translating it into effective action was beyond his ability.

Napoleon never understood the criteria by which Alexander evaluated him. He could not understand Alexander's increasing hostility and explained it in the only way that made sense to him: Alexander must be under the influence of the British. For the next several years Napoleon would make a consistent and coherent effort to convince Alexander that the correlation of forces favored France, and that Britain was ill intentioned and unreliable. Since Napoleon and Alexander did not speak in shared diplomatic concepts, it is not surprising that this effort failed, but it is impossible to understand the policies of either side without understanding these fundamental motivations.

By September 1804 this clash of worldviews, together with the practical considerations resulting from the change in British leadership, led Alexander to the conviction that he must go to war with Napoleon. He set about first wooing Britain to the struggle and then converting the defensive arrangements he had made with Austria, Prussia, and other states into a coalition for an offensive war against France.*

Napoleon had not yet come to a similar conclusion. He remained focused on the war against Britain and continued to bend every effort to preparing his invasion fleet and army for the coming landing. Even for Napoleon, however, the balance had shifted. He no longer believed that he had friendship with Alexander but recognized the existence of a cold war between France and Russia. He continued to believe that he could prevent the emergence of a general European war by pressing Austria and Prussia with threats and bribes, but he no longer expected Alexander to help him in that endeavor.

The key was Austria. Both Russia and, to a lesser extent, Britain had given up on Prussia as a potential ally, but both still believed that Austria could be won over to the idea of an offensive war against France. Both acknowledged that if Austria remained recalcitrantly neutral, there could be no general war. The year between Novosil'tsev's mission to London and the outbreak of hostilities would contain the decisive negotiations that shaped the course of not only the War of 1805 but the next decades of European history.

---

*See the next chapter for a discussion of the Austro–Russian Agreement of 1804.

5

Austria's Turn

However hostile Alexander might have become toward France, continental war was not possible without the participation of either Austria or Prussia. In the end, Frederick William refused to join the coalition but Francis did so. Why did Austria, just as determined to maintain peace and neutrality as Prussia, ultimately opt for war? Why did Frederick William not feel the same threats as Francis and respond similarly?

The answer lies partly in idiosyncrasies of Prussian politics (to be examined later) but mostly in the nature of the events that drove Austria into the coalition. The locus of those events was not Germany, as it had previously been, but Italy. Napoleon's encroachments on the Italian peninsula, particularly his determination to make of the Italian Republic a kingdom with a Bonaparte on its throne, posed such a deadly danger to Austria that even Cobenzl and Francis felt it necessary to consider taking up arms to prevent it. Developments in Italy hardly touched Prussia at all. For Prussia, the dangers continued to be largely abstract, and fears of France were balanced by fears of Russia and Austria. As will become clear in subsequent chapters, this shift of focus from northern to southern Europe also had a dramatic effect on the development and execution of the allied war plans, creating the essential preconditions for Napoleon's spectacular success at Ulm.

Austria

Austria's policymakers faced so many constraints and challenges between the fall of 1803 and the outbreak of war in September 1805 that they were unable to formulate a consistent, coherent, or realistic policy. Austria was not entirely the plaything of chance and the other powers, but neither did her statesmen have much control over her course. Their correspondence, heavily laden with a sense of inevitability, reflects their desperation. All of the major players in Austria's leading circles agreed that Austria must attempt to avoid war at almost any cost. As time went on, however, the contradictions inherent in Austria's policies became blatant, ultimately driving the empire to war more or less against its leaders' will.

Two related internal factors severely constrained Austria's options at this juncture: poverty and military weakness. We have already seen these factors at work in the period following the signing of the Treaty of Lunéville, but they became worse as time went on. Although Archduke Charles worked hard to bring order to the War Department, to increase its efficiency and reduce its crushing expense, he was unable to reduce costs dramatically.[1] Inflation was a significant factor in the overall financial situation and in the military's failure to reduce its budget significantly. At the same time, Charles's reorganizations and economies hurt war readiness, judged by the number of soldiers actually with the colors (as opposed to those "on the books"), the number of horses maintained to transport supplies and munitions, the quantities of supplies in warehouses, and so on.* The limits of Austria's preparedness were visible in maneuvers conducted in 1803 and 1804, which were embarrassing because of the poor performance of the officer corps.† Although Austria continued to spend far too much on the military from the standpoint of pure economics, therefore, she generated less and less real military power as time went on.

This military weakness was well known to Charles, Cobenzl, Colloredo, and Francis. They were aware that a massive infusion of cash and effort would be required to produce an army that could defend the monarchy, let alone undertake offensive actions. The conflict came to a head over the reply to the Russian proposal for an alliance of late 1803.[2] Charles opposed any alliance with Russia in a long memorandum on Austria's ability to carry out the terms of the proposed treaty. Cobenzl, on the other hand, recognized the foreign political imperatives that required Austria to sign the treaty and opposed Charles's memorandum with one of his own. The resulting schism, which ultimately led

---

*Cobenzl noted that 100,000 men would have to be found to put the army on a war footing; the cavalry would have to be remounted as well. He estimated the cost of preparing Austria for war at 40 million florins, with each actual campaign costing at least 110 million florins thereafter. [Cobenzl] to Stadion, 1 April 1804, in Adolf Beer, "Österreich und Russland in den Jahren 1804 und 1805," *Archiv für österreichische Geschichte* 53 (1875): 205. Archduke Charles reported in March 1804 that a levy of 108,598 men would be required to put the army on a war footing. From Charles's memorandum to Francis II in response to the Russian proposal of 20 December 1803, written on 3 March 1804, Archdukes Albrecht and Wilhelm, eds., *Ausgewahlte Schriften weiland seiner kaiserlichen Hoheit Erzerzogs Carl von Oesterreich* (Vienna: Wilhelm Braumüller, 1894), 5:615.

†Colloredo to Thugut, 25 October 1803, in Fournier, *Gentz und Cobenzl*, p. 110 n. 1. The detailed evaluation of at least one of these maneuvers has survived (Archduke Charles to Baillet de La Tour, 7 September 1804, Kriegsarchiv Memoiren, 6 Abteilung, 188), and it is more balanced than Colloredo's letter. This evaluation is of interest because the maneuvers it considers were held on the battlefield of Austerlitz. We shall consider its implications for that battle below.

to Charles's demotion and the elevation of Baron Karl von Mack, would have the most baleful conceivable consequences.

On March 5, 1804, Charles sent a lengthy memorandum to Francis, advising him under no circumstances to make an alliance with Russia.[3] He noted that Russia was an unreliable ally that might well withdraw her forces from the coalition on some trivial pretext, leaving Austria alone on the field of battle. Even if the Russians were true to their word, however, Charles strongly doubted that they could arrive in the theater of war in a timely fashion. Napoleon, he argued, would not sit and watch while Austria and Russia united their forces and prepared for war, but would drop preparations for an invasion of England and swing south and east with all of his forces—directly at Austria. Noting that Napoleon's movement would take weeks while the Russians' would take months, Charles had no doubt of who would arrive first.

He also dismissed the notion that Britain would offer any meaningful assistance. Even with the best intentions in the world, he noted, Britain would have to retain a significant land force at home to protect against the possibility of French invasion. The continent would likely see few or no British troops. Britain, Charles argued, was much more likely to use her forces to devour vulnerable Dutch colonies than to attack France on the continent, for "other than Marlborough there has never been an Englishman who thought that England could win the mastery of the sea on the Danube."[4]

Pointing to the changes in the European situation since the beginning of the revolutionary wars, Charles noted that Austria had no need of a war with France and did not stand to benefit from it in any way. He concluded that, in these circumstances, "It should not be hard . . . with such arguments to show the French ministry the importance of Austrian neutrality and to take advantage of that position of Austria's for the maintenance of peace."[5]

Charles overestimated French forces while underestimating allied forces, and his belief in the certainty of Russian perfidy ignored the change in leadership in St. Petersburg between 1800 and 1804, as well as the new course of Russian policy. His conviction that the war was not in Austria's interest was sensible, however, as was his fear that Russian troops would not arrive in time to provide assistance. But Charles ignored the international situation completely, and this was his undoing. By failing to recognize that the cardinal task of Austrian policy was to escape from international isolation, rather than avoid war, he made his comments irrelevant and provided grist to the mill of those such as Cobenzl who disagreed with him.

Cobenzl wasted little time in responding to Charles's note. The crux of his response revolved around the question, "Does it depend on us not to be attacked and forced into war, and would it not be desirable, in case such a misfortune should arrive, that we had already come to an understanding with Russia on the mode and the method of her cooperation?"[6] This was a keen political insight. Charles was right that Austria needed to avoid war, and Cobenzl did not disagree with him. But a state can only be sure to avoid war if it is willing to sacrifice every interest, even survival. No great power can do so. When another state's actions become intolerable or mortally dangerous, some sort of resistance is necessary. But resistance of any sort (especially against Napoleon) entails significant risk of war. A desire to avoid war is an appropriate grand strategic approach to the world; to fail to prepare for the possibility that war might come nonetheless is the height of irresponsibility. Cobenzl indicted Charles for taking precisely such an irresponsible approach.

In the first place, Cobenzl recognized the danger that Napoleon would pose to Austria if his aggressions were allowed to proceed unchecked:

> The invasion of Sicily, the incorporation of Parma and Plaisance, an even greater dependence of the Italian Republic, of Liguria, perhaps of Tuscany, Naples, Switzerland and above all Holland, will add so much more to his means that it will remain only to offer our throat to the knife.[7]

Britain, he was sure, would ultimately give up the struggle if it became clear that she would have to carry it on alone, and Austria would face the full force and enmity of a strengthened France by herself.

Cobenzl was keenly aware of the delicacy of the policy he wished to pursue toward Russia. Even if everything Charles said about the impossibility of war were true, Cobenzl argued, "it is essential that we use language with Russia that does not too much reduce either her confidence in our zeal for the good cause or that élan of courage and energy that she is showing at this moment, and which it is in our interest to maintain up to a certain point." If Austria made it clear that she would only join Russia if she herself were attacked, "that would make [Russia] perceive that she cannot count on us any more than on Prussia, and that there is nothing better for her to do than to reconcile herself with France" and find other ways to secure Russia's essential interests in the north and in the Ottoman Empire.

Cobenzl hoped, however, that a careful approach could both solidify the Austro–Russian relationship and at the same time cool Alexander's ardor for war:

> It seems . . . that the best means of avoiding a war, which we must undoubtedly expect if our state of weakness and isolation is noticed, lies in taking advantage of Russia's current disposition toward the reestablishment of our former union, in accompanying the exposition of the circumstances and the motives that prevent us from accepting for the moment the projects of the court of St. Petersburg not only with a plan for political measures necessary to influence general affairs usefully, but also with a plan of active cooperation for the hypothetical case in which a

war becomes inevitable. This plan itself, in detailing the difficulties to be overcome, the magnitude of the means necessary for success, and above all the necessity for Russia to join the totality of her forces to ours, will sufficiently reduce the ardor of our ally and will inspire in her enough restraint as not to expose us to a contretemps, without, however, entirely discouraging her and driving her back into her former apathy.[8]

He concluded by repeating his hope that a simple alliance between Russia and Austria, even without concrete or meaningful plans or preparations for war, would suffice to turn Napoleon away from further ambitious projects.

These comments combined political realism with naïveté. Cobenzl shrewdly recognized the dangers of Charles's outright distrust and dismissal of the Russians and of his conviction that Austria's military and financial weakness should overcome all other considerations. His belief that Alexander would be easily put off from his desire to use force to oppose Napoleon was ill founded, however, and his conviction that Napoleon would be easily deterred by a simple alliance between Austria and Russia was delusional. Still, the policy he proposed was probably the best one: string the Russians along for as long as possible, make military operations look hard but not impossible, and finally give in before the Russians became fed up with the delays. If the memorandum had stopped there, and if Charles could have been compelled to support this policy line, then events might have turned out better. Unfortunately Cobenzl moved from the sphere of politics, in which he was well versed, to that of war, in which he was not.

Cobenzl began by questioning Charles's assertions as to the impossibility of waging war. Would a battle lost on the Adige really put Vienna in danger? Was it really impossible to conduct operations in northern Italy without taking Mantua? Or to support operations in Switzerland and Germany without controlling Italy? Was it true that 150,000 Russians combined with 200,000 Austrians could not hold out against Napoleon? Would it really cost 53 million florins to prepare for war and 150 million for a single campaign? Cobenzl held off from offering answers to these questions and proposed instead to seek a second opinion. He asked permission to refer these questions to General Strauch, since Cobenzl knew no one else in Vienna at that time who had a right to an opinion, and to send an answer to the Russians deferring the discussion of military plans in detail until a later date.

Cobenzl also argued, however, that it would be necessary to develop those detailed plans, and although he was too politic to say so explicitly, he did not trust Charles to come up with them. He proposed, accordingly,

to address myself for this purpose to a General among the most distinguished by reputation, by expertise, and by experience. There are only two on whom the choice could fall: Bellegarde and Mack. Since the former is the more circumspect, the latter more determined and ardent, I admit that the first would seem to me preferable to consult if the Minister of War's report was not so discouraging, but that for this reason Mack's opinion seems to me more appropriate to clarify the doubtful points by the opposition of arguments, and as a result it would be to this latter that I would desire to be allowed to address myself.

This decision marked a fateful passage in European history, for the subsequent campaign of 1805 owed a great deal to the fact that Mack replaced Charles as Francis's principal military adviser; the events leading up to the surrender of the Austrian army at Ulm resulted in large part from Mack's personality.

Baron Karl von Mack had a checkered career. Born to a Protestant civil servant in 1752, he rose quickly through the ranks and gained considerable military experience. He served as adjutant to Feldmarshal-leutnant (FML) Kinsky in the War of the Bavarian Succession (1778–1779), on the general staff during the Turkish War of 1788–1790, and as quartermaster general of the Austrian Rhine army of Prince Coburg against the French revolutionary armies in 1793–1794. He was at one time the military tutor of Archduke Charles, under whom he subsequently served in Germany, and was awarded the Order of Maria Theresa in 1789 for his part in the capture of Belgrade from the Turks. On the other hand, he developed the operational plan for the Austrian campaign in the Netherlands in 1794, which failed completely. Worse still, he commanded the Neapolitan army that was soundly defeated in 1799. Forced to flee his own troops, he was captured by the French and managed to escape only in 1800.[9]

Mack's personality was well suited to the task Cobenzl set him, although perhaps less suited to the needs of the Habsburg empire:

> General Mack was not the type to be content with early retirement. Full of energetic initiative and hasty bustle, excessively self-confident and ambitious, he eagerly pressed himself into the foreground. On the other hand he could be submissive and dutiful and open to intrigues if it suited his advantage. With his much-vaunted eloquence, with a lively imagination, ingenious ideas and often convincing minimization of opposing forces he won himself committed followers in the highest circles. His "Instructions for Generals" published in 1794 breathed impetuous aggressiveness, strongly recalled Napoleon's "activité-activité-vitesse!" and warned not to be deterred even by a superior enemy.[10]

It was precisely this spirit that Cobenzl desperately wanted to offset Charles's gloomy prophecies. Mack was the sort of person who saw solutions to every problem and found no task too daunting, and Cobenzl found him a congenial coworker. Although Mack's recent career did not bode well for either his war plans or his prospects as a commander, Cobenzl had no intention of fighting in March 1804. He simply wanted someone to draw up a set of proposed war plans that were not so hopeless as to convince Alexander of Austria's complete pusillanimity, and Mack was just the man for the job. The real significance of this decision only became clear later.

Cobenzl wanted more than someone to draw up war plans, however. He wanted to find a way to institutionalize a counterbalance to the counsels of impossibility and despair emanating from Charles and seconded by his immediate supporters. Unwilling, however, to proceed openly against Archduke Charles, Cobenzl worked instead to replace the quartermaster general (the head of the nascent general staff), Duka (Charles's favorite), with Mack. Cobenzl hoped that Mack would get along with Charles and that his enthusiasm and energy would help overcome Charles's pessimism and apathy.[11] It took almost a year, however, for Cobenzl's plan to succeed.

Cobenzl's opposition to Charles and his favorites does not mean that he was willing to contemplate war. On the contrary, Cobenzl was hostile to any kind of war, especially offensive war. During the debate over the Russian proposal for an alliance, Charles and his friends accused Cobenzl of running the risk of entangling the monarchy in a war against France. Cobenzl responded, "No, without doubt, I do not want to involve the Monarchy in a war—one would have to be crazy to do such a thing. But I want to ensure that, if it is attacked, it will not still be without the means of defense, as it positively is at this moment."[12] Cobenzl, like the others, was mesmerized by the first and most powerful external constraint on Austrian policy in 1804 and the first half of 1805—the Army of England.

Napoleon had formed the Army of England along the French coast while preparing for his invasion of Great Britain. Although Napoleon clearly intended to use this force for its original purpose as late as the summer of 1805, the Austrians realized at once that it could serve another purpose. The existence of a large French force, fully mobilized on a war footing and training incessantly, put the Austrians at a tremendous disadvantage politically and militarily. They believed that Napoleon could cross the Rhine and march on their territories, fully ready for war, at any moment. They had no force that could stop him, nor could they create one quickly (several months was the most optimistic estimate).*

Cobenzl noted that the Austrian army was not ready to fight because of lack of funding and manpower, and it was deployed in the wrong areas. In order to

---

*"Bonaparte can attack us from one moment to the next, for his personal interest, without our having given him the least grounds," Cobenzl to Colloredo, 27 March 1804, cited in Fournier, *Gentz und Cobenzl*, p. 220.

save money, most of the forces had been moved to cantonments in Hungary, Galicia, and Bohemia, where sustaining them was less expensive than in the exhausted and poorer provinces along the western borders. The French, on the other hand, maintained nearly 100,000 soldiers "in a perfect state of mobility" in Italy and could overrun Austrian Venice and the Tyrol "with a decisive superiority" before Austrian reinforcements could arrive. What is more, "the armies that Bonaparte would send from France to support his troops in Italy could arrive in less time than proportional assistance could cross the space between the frontiers of Russia and those of Tyrol and of Italy." He concluded, "It is easy to see that in provoking France to a struggle that the circumstances render so unequal, Austria would expose herself to the probable danger of seeing her states in Italy and the Tyrol succumb under the initial efforts of an enemy who knows very well how to profit from all of his advantages and his superiority."[13]

Francis's initial response to the Russian proposal for a defensive alliance, therefore, demanded "that in the proposed concert there will be due concern for the obstacles that result as much from the current state of the forces and of the frontiers of my monarchy as from the immense dangers to which it would be exposed in this state by demonstrations and armaments that would provoke an immediate invasion by France before I would be able to put myself in a state of defense or the help of Y[our] I[mperial] M[ajesty] could reach me."[14]

Cobenzl drew the natural conclusions from these facts. Any Austrian move that Napoleon construed as a provocation could bring the entire French army crashing down on a helpless Austria: "Therefore it is clear that the least military movement aiming to remedy the vices of this dislocation by augmenting the number of troops in the most exposed provinces, would give umbrage to the First Consul . . . and that sooner than giving us the time to assemble enough forces to render them imposing, he would spare nothing to preempt us in order not to be himself preempted."[15] He adduced in support of this conclusion a recent Napoleonic ultimatum in response to a minor movement of Austrian forces toward the western frontiers.

As a result, every time a point of discord arose in French–Austrian relations, Cobenzl automatically assumed that an Austrian failure to placate Napoleon could lead to a French attack, even if Napoleon made no threat. When Napoleon did make such a threat, after he crowned himself emperor of the French and then demanded that Austria recognize his new title, the Austrian collapse was virtually instantaneous.[16] Austria's failure to maintain a war-ready army, combined with Napoleon's deployment of such a force, even preparing for war against another foe, eviscerated Austria's foreign policy and led to a nearly perfect example of self-deterrence.

The self-deterrence would have been complete but for a second external factor constraining Austria's policy: the need to remain on friendly terms with Russia. Austrian leaders all agreed that Austria could not fight France alone.

Charles, who distrusted the Russians more than the French, concluded that Austria simply should not fight. Cobenzl was not sure that Austria would be allowed the choice. Since Napoleon could fall upon Austria with a massive force instantly, he reasoned, what was to prevent him from doing that if not the fear of creating a coalition of major European states against him? Over time Cobenzl convinced himself that the minute Napoleon found that Austria was indeed alone and without allies, he would attack. Cobenzl thus believed that it was vital for Austria to retain a strong link with Russia.

But Alexander, as we have seen, was becoming more hostile to Napoleon every day. Although he had initially asked Austria for a defensive alliance, Cobenzl suspected that the tsar would use any method to transform that bond into an offensive alliance as soon as he could. Nor was this fear misplaced; even as the final agreements between Austria and Russia were being negotiated and signed, Alexander had sent Novosil'tsev to London with a proposal for an offensive alliance against France into which Austria and Prussia were to be drawn. Cobenzl, who was unaware of the exact purpose of Novosil'tsev's trip, was desperate to find a way to restrain Alexander without alienating him. He was forced to walk a fine line, trying not to do anything that would bring Napoleon's army down on his head while at the same time trying not to look so weak and Francophile that Alexander would write off Austria as a lost cause.

Cobenzl's fears that Alexander might abandon Austria were exaggerated. An Austrian refusal to join the nascent coalition would have infuriated the tsar and resulted in an immediate cooling of relations between St. Petersburg and Vienna. If Napoleon had attacked Austria, however, Alexander would likely have come to her aid nevertheless. His reaction to the outbreak of the Franco–Prussian war of 1806, following Prussia's betrayal of the coalition the previous year, supports this supposition.

Cobenzl's fears of driving Russia away were not based solely on the tsar's supposedly mercurial temper, but also on hard geopolitical concerns. It is much farther from the Austro–Russian border in southwestern Poland to, say, Salzburg than it is from the English Channel. Unless Russia had made prior arrangements with Austria and thereby gotten the jump on the French, Austria would have to fight against the whole weight of the French army until Russian help arrived. There were two major problems with this approach. First, Cobenzl, Charles, and Francis doubted their army's ability to hold off the full force of a French attack for very long (or, indeed, at all). Second, even if the army did hold, the war would be fought in the core Austrian territories. The economic price of such a war, it was believed, would be devastating, and the relatively minor border adjustments that the Austrians perceived as the most they could expect in compensation even from a victorious war would not remotely pay for the damage they would have suffered. Fighting the French before the Russians arrived was unacceptable.

At this point the crisis of Austrian grand strategy becomes starkest. Austria cannot afford to wait for the Russians to arrive after the war has begun. Therefore, the Russians must start marching before the French. Therefore, Austria must have not only a clear alliance with Russia but a carefully drawn up plan of operations. As soon as the Russians crossed the Austrian border, however, Napoleon would learn of it and take it as an intolerable provocation. He would then put his own army in motion and, since he was much closer than the Russians, arrive at the theater of war first and force the Austrians to fight alone. Therefore, whether or not Austria had an alliance with the Russians, she would bear the full brunt of the initial French attack and fight on her own territory, which was unacceptable.

There was no way out of the conundrum created by the existence of a large French army maintained indefinitely on a war footing. If Napoleon had actually invaded England with his army, the Austrians would have had an opportunity to mobilize and strike if they chose, without fear of immediate retaliation. In order to invade England, however, Napoleon had to gain control of the Channel, which no one in Vienna or anywhere else thought he could do.

That reflection led Cobenzl to another. Would Napoleon not at some point become embarrassed that his preparations to invade England had come to nothing? Would he not then seek to put the vast army he had maintained for so long at such expense to some more profitable use? Might he not, in other words, strike Austria simply to feed his army at someone else's expense and gain what glory he could on the continent, having been denied the glory he sought? War might come to Austria even if Austria did nothing wrong.

Charles, looking at this terrible situation (and believing that the Russians would not show up), argued for making whatever concessions Napoleon demanded and hoping for the best. Francis was inclined to accept this advice. A more radical party organized around the German publicist Friedrich von Gentz, the Russian ambassador, Razumovskii, and the other Russians in Vienna demanded an immediate alliance with Russia and war with France (and the replacement of Cobenzl with a more warlike minister—if one could be found!). Cobenzl sought another way.

In the language of today, Cobenzl attempted a policy of containment based on deterrence. He rejected the notion that Austria should fight to undo the gains Napoleon had made since the Treaty of Lunéville or overthrow Napoleon. But he believed that Napoleon should not be allowed to make further significant gains. Aware that diplomacy alone would not contain Bonaparte, Cobenzl sought to create an alliance of all major powers, including Prussia, aimed at resisting continued French expansion. The overwhelming military power of such a coalition, he believed, would force Napoleon to rethink any plans he might have for aggression, while its openly defensive nature would avoid provoking him. The negotiations founding the coalition had to remain secret, of course, lest Napoleon attack Austria to preempt its formation. But once completed the coalition had to declare the willingness of all of Europe to resist further French depredations.

As a way out of Austria's impasse, this idea was highly imaginative. But it was unrealistic for two reasons: it was unacceptable to Austria's putative allies and it misread Napoleon's personality and intentions. To begin with, Pitt and the British government would never have accepted such an alliance. They were at war with France, and the Austrian proposal would have had the effect of neutralizing the continent—thereby depriving Britain of any hope of finding continental allies in her struggle against France and confining the war to the sea, the colonies, and, if Napoleon could ever manage it, the coast of England. No British prime minister would ever have signed on to such an alliance, let alone bankrolled it as the Austrians, because of their poverty, were compelled to demand.

The Prussians would have found the idea equally unacceptable. Frederick William saw Vienna as only slightly behind France on the list of threats he faced. He and his ministers repeatedly asked why Prussia should agree to fight wars that would have the effect of strengthening their archrival, Austria. But above all, Frederick William was determined to cling to the policy of neutrality to the last possible moment. Joining a coalition with the avowed purpose of resisting Napoleon, even if it was a purely defensive coalition, would have broken that neutrality and invited a French attack, which he feared at least as much as Cobenzl, Francis, and Charles did.

Alexander would have been similarly unwilling to accept such an alliance. For one thing, he understood perfectly well that Britain would never join a coalition with such a purpose. He feared that if Britain despaired of finding a continental ally, then she would make a separate peace with Napoleon and thereby eliminate any possibility of further resistance. By this point, however, another factor had entered the equation in St. Petersburg. Alexander had conceived a deep distrust of Francis's intentions and suspected him of seeking to accommodate and appease Napoleon. Since this suspicion was by no means without foundation, it was difficult to convince the Russians of its baseness. In the end, Cobenzl would find it impossible to match direct Russian proposals for war with his own proposals for a defensive coalition precisely because any such action would lead to the collapse of Alexander's trust in Austria.

None of the states on whom Cobenzl was counting to join this putative coalition could have been expected to agree to the terms of the pure containment policy he was advocating. Even if he could have induced all of them to join, however, the policy was virtually certain to fail.

Cobenzl's approach rested on the assumption that Napoleon could be deterred simply by the size of the potential aggregate forces that would eventually be brought to bear against him. It would not matter, Cobenzl believed, that Austria could not resist a French attack long enough for the Russians to arrive, for the Russians—and the Prussians and the British—would eventually arrive and overwhelm Napoleon, nullifying any successes he might have achieved to that point. Since, Cobenzl believed, French defeat in such a war was obvious, Napoleon would never start it and so Austria would never have to face the consequences of her inability to defend herself.

There is ample evidence, however, to suggest that Napoleon did not work that way. He did not reckon the aggregate force of a coalition arrayed against him. If he had done so, he would never have gone to war, since the coalitions of 1805, 1806, 1809, and 1813–1815 all outnumbered the forces he could readily bring to bear, sometimes dramatically. Napoleon relied on the technique of dividing his enemies and defeating them in detail. As long as he saw the possibility of doing that, he cared nothing for how many times he might have to repeat the process. In order to deter Napoleon it would have been necessary to amass an enormous coalition army somewhere near the French border and keep it there on a war footing indefinitely—which was out of the question.

It probably would not have worked anyway. Napoleon never accepted limitations on his power or his actions and never believed that any situation he was in was hopeless. That personality trait—the inability to recognize impossibility—was an important component of his success. It meant that he continued to see opportunities long after his enemies had convinced themselves that he was defeated, and so he was able to surprise his foes with his determination. The negative side of this character trait cost him dearly on those occasions when his situation was in fact hopeless.

Above all, this personality trait meant that Napoleon was not deterrable. How can someone be deterred who never believes that he has no chance to win? For Napoleon, winning was the only thing that mattered—the cost to France, his soldiers, or himself was immaterial as long as he triumphed in the end. There was no policy of containment or deterrence that might have succeeded against such a leader.

This fact was far less evident in 1805 than it was subsequently. Napoleon had faced desperate situations on many occasions such as during the Battle of Marengo, at the bridge at Arcola, Lodi, in Egypt, and so on, and he had behaved with great determination and self-confidence in most of those crises. We can now see from his actions during and after the Russian campaign, in the campaign of 1814, the escape from Elba, and the Hundred Days, the full depth of this character trait; Cobenzl can perhaps be excused for failing to recognize it perfectly in 1804 and for failing to see the hopelessness of his desire to bring the other continental powers and England to agree to a deterrence treaty. Given the careful evaluations that he and others had made of the situation, with all concluding that Austria faced a hopeless situation and there was no reasonable course of action for her to pursue, it seems petty to blame him for deluding himself into believing that he had found a way out. The man who knows that he has no water will die just the same as the one who believes he has found an oasis.

Cobenzl worked hard in June 1804 to convince himself and others that he had found a true oasis. He argued that the threat of further French encroachments was greatly overstated by the Russians and the British (and by the Austrian opposition party). People had been warning about "imminent" French invasions of all sorts of territories for months and nothing had happened. He argued that the fact that nothing had happened proved that Napoleon had no ill intentions because Napoleon "was not in the custom of placing such long intervals between the conception and the execution of his true designs." What is more, Napoleon would be distracted by the need to consolidate support inside and outside of France for his new position as emperor, which Cobenzl was sure would increase internal opposition in France.[17]

Desperate to avoid giving the Russians any ground to start a war or forcing Austria to take action that might promote one, Cobenzl tried to convince himself that it would be all right for Napoleon to make himself king of Italy. He pointed out that Napoleon already effectively controlled northern Italy from his position as "temporary" president and that a change in his status hardly represented enough of a change in the situation to go to war.[18] This was whistling in the dark, as we shall see, made possible by Cobenzl's hope that nothing would come of the rumors that Napoleon intended to crown himself king of Italy. As soon as it became clear that such an event was all but decided on, and indeed imminent, Cobenzl changed his tune.

Italy

Napoleon's actions in Italy in 1804 and 1805 played a pivotal role in bringing Austria into the coalition against France and in shaping the strategy that the coalition would pursue. It is not easy, unfortunately, to understand exactly what Napoleon's motivations were. Although that problem is common to most of Napoleon's major decisions, it is worse in the case of Italy because of the complexity and the contradictory nature of the policies he pursued in the peninsula. Then too Napoleon's overall strategy and policy in Italy has received relatively little attention from scholars.[19]

It is possible to portray Napoleon as a power-mad criminal whose policies were driven by indications that someone might oppose him, and the facts do not contradict this view.* This interpretation is unhelpful in understanding why the European situation developed as it did in 1804 and 1805, however. It is easy to condemn Napoleon for his aggressiveness, his contempt for international order and the concerns of other states, his megalomania, and his willingness to use force, as well as other behaviors that, from an ethical standpoint, seem criminal. But condemnation is not explanation, and it is still important to try to understand why Napoleon behaved as he did, because his goals and his intentions and the ways in which they were interpreted by various interested parties played a critical role in driving the events of the day.

It is possible, as one historian has argued, that Napoleon's policy in Italy was internally inconsistent.[20] Napoleon may have desired philosophically and perhaps emotionally to unify the Italian peninsula and develop it into an independent state at some distant time. He reportedly made numerous statements to this effect from his exile on St. Helena, and some of his proclamations and rhetoric in the first years of the nineteenth century seem to support this notion. It is clear, nevertheless, that any time the interests of an Italian state came into potential conflict with those of France, Napoleon favored France. He thus failed on several occasions to join small territories bordering the nascent republic or kingdom of Italy to that state, sometimes even preferring to annex those territories directly to France instead.†

It is not necessary to conclude from these contradictions that his statements were simply hypocritical cover for an overtly hegemonic design. He may sincerely have believed at an intellectual level in the importance of developing an independent Italian state while also believing that, at a practical level, more immediate considerations of strategy and politics must predominate. We must never forget that Napoleon had the autocrat's sincere conviction that whatever served his interest served the interest of his people—in this case the people of Italy. He may well have felt that, once France had secured herself and cowed the other European states into obedience, then it would be possible to turn to the proper affairs of Italy. In that line of thinking, reminiscent of

---

*This is the view offered most dramatically by Paul Schroeder in "Napoleon's Foreign Policy: A Criminal Enterprise," *Journal of Military History,* April 1990, pp. 147–162, and carried over into his magisterial study of the international relations of this time, *The Transformation of European Politics, 1763–1848* (New York: Oxford University Press, 1994). In neither work does Schroeder consider in any detail the goals or motivations behind Napoleon's actions in Italy.

†As was the case with Parma and Plaisance, which Melzi asked Napoleon to join to the Italian Republic in late 1803. Instead, Napoleon annexed them to France in 1805. See Edouard Driault, *Napoléon en Italie (1800–1812)* (Paris: Librairie Félix Alcan, 1906), pp. 224–226; Albert Pingaud, *Bonaparte, Président de la République Italienne* (Paris: Librairie académique, Perrin et Cie., 1914), 2:440.

Stalin's attitude toward the international communist movement, French hegemony in Italy truly was in Italy's own best interest.

Another explanation focuses on Napoleon's imperial ambitions.[21] In this view, Napoleon intended to set himself up as the new "Emperor of the West," the new Charlemagne, virtually from the moment he ascended to supreme power in France. An excellent student of history, Napoleon was well aware that what distinguished this illustrious predecessor was that he ruled France, Germany, and Italy. He set out to acquire predominance in Germany and Italy to justify his claim to be Charlemagne's heir. When he made himself president of the Italian Republic in 1802 and then king of Italy in 1805, therefore, it was part of a coherent plan to justify his bid for universal monarchy.

There is much to support this view. Napoleon took every opportunity to highlight the parallels between himself and Charlemagne. He placed the Ottonian crown on his head in December 1804, and did the same with the Iron Crown of Lombardy in May 1805. The formal coronation ceremony in Paris was heavily laden with Carolingian imagery, and the presence of the pope at that sacrament was clearly aimed as much at highlighting the parallel as at appeasing the religious sentiments of French Catholics. Napoleon received the new letters of accreditation of the Austrian ambassador at Aix-la-Chapelle, the ancient capital of Charlemagne's empire, and he recognized Francis's accession as emperor of Austria from the second imperial city, Mainz. None of this was accidental. Napoleon was deliberately establishing the relationship between his new empire and that of the Carolingians.

Napoleon's writings and sayings, always calculated to achieve some specific political goal, cannot be trusted even to provide an accurate assessment of his aims. We should be careful, however, not to seek too much simplicity. Napoleon's was a personality and a genius complex enough to be inconsistent. He had many ideas and projects in his head at any given moment. That facet of his personality gave him great intellectual flexibility in difficult situations. He may have believed simultaneously in all three aims: the pure glory and hegemony of France, the establishment of an independent Italy, the formation of a new Carolingian empire.

Although these goals were mutually contradictory when laid out, the contradictions were less obvious and less clearly systematic when it came to the implementation of actual policies. Like most people who pursue incompatible aims, Napoleon chose among them when they conflicted and otherwise ignored the contradictions. This is the essential fact that emerges from the consideration of his strategy in Italy.

Now consider the problem of his opponents, trying to make logical sense of this illogical and sometimes senseless hodgepodge. The great limitation of intelligence is the impossibility of having a clearer idea of the enemy's intentions than the enemy has. Napoleon's confusion and internal contradiction about his goals for Italy in turn confused not only his international opponents in Vienna but also his allies and servants inside Italy.

Napoleon's basic relationship to Italy was one of conqueror to conquered. He first became involved in the peninsula as commander of the Army of Italy during the campaign of 1796–1797 and he returned as First Consul commanding the same army during the Marengo campaign of 1800. As French armies and coalition armies chased each other across northern Italy during these campaigns, rival political structures rose or fell accordingly. With the French conquest of the area in 1796–1797 arose the Cisalpine Republic, which would become the core of the Republic of Italy and later the Kingdom of Italy. Centered around its capital city of Milan, this area had belonged directly to the Habsburg Crown, and many of its citizens were initially ecstatic at the thought of replacing Habsburg tutelage with republican liberty. They were soon undeceived, however, as French armies came and stayed, and as the French government, perpetually starved for cash, demanded that the Italians feed and pay those armies.

When the Austrians and Russians temporarily drove off the French in 1799, they abolished the republic's government and began the process of reestablishing their own rule. The inhabitants were generally mixed about this process but increasingly weary of war. Napoleon's crushing victory at Marengo put paid to Austrian efforts at regaining Italy, however, and the Cisalpine Republic was speedily restored.

To the surprise of many Italians, Napoleon then dithered about putting the republic's government on a permanent basis. He claimed that he was awaiting the final peace settlement and the final end of hostilities, and many Italians feared that he was prepared to give up his gains in northern Italy in return for preferred prizes elsewhere. These fears proved to be groundless. The Treaty of Lunéville with Austria recognized and guaranteed the existence *and independence* of the Cisalpine, Ligurian, and other satellite republics in Italy and along the Rhine frontier.

The Austrians apparently took Napoleon at his word. They were aware that all of northern Italy was within Napoleon's sphere of influence. Exhausted by their exertions and demoralized by their defeat, they did not protest his annexation of Piedmont in 1802 or his "election" as president of the newly formed Italian Republic that same year. They were aware that at the "Consulte de Lyon" Napoleon dictated to the assembled Italian deputies both the constitution of the new republic and the choice of all of the principal ministers and legislators. Viennese statesmen generally recognized that Napoleon's victory had given him the clear ability, if not the right, to arrange matters in northern Italy pretty much to his liking, however displeased they felt. On the other hand, they seem to have believed his repeated assertions that active French control over the region was only temporary and that the new republics would eventually emerge from French tutelage to become independent states.

This belief was a central part of any notion that Austria could accept the Peace of Lunéville. Before the French revolutionary wars, northern Italy was broken up into a number of moderate-size regions that offered a general Austrian control of the area and, most importantly, significant buffer zones separating the core Austrian territories from France. The large independent states of Venice, Switzerland, and Piedmont-Savoy effectively neutralized northern Italy, while Austrian control over Milan and Tuscany permitted forward defense or intervention as necessary.

The Treaty of Lunéville confirmed the collapse of this system. Austria gained the Venetian mainland, while France took effective possession of Piedmont-Savoy (soon to be annexed, as we have seen). Only the Cisalpine Republic and Switzerland now stood between the Austrian and French frontiers. The loss of Tuscany secured the flank of any French advance and precluded any real hope of a forward defense, except, perhaps, in Venice. In this context, it was one thing for Napoleon to establish regimes friendly to France in the Cisalpine Republic; it was another thing entirely for him to seize permanent control over that region, thus establishing himself and his army directly on the Austrian frontier.

It may be reasonably objected that once Napoleon made himself president of the Italian Republic, the game was up—he had permanent control. Several factors, however, mitigated that conclusion. For one thing, Napoleon had been "elected" president of the Italian Republic for a term of ten years (indefinitely renewable, to be sure). Even after he had himself proclaimed First Consul for Life in France, he made no move to make his leadership of the Italian Republic more permanent. For another thing, Napoleon did not administer the Italian Republic directly. He left the actual day-to-day running of affairs to his vice president—an Italian named Francesco Melzi, Count of Eril.

Melzi was a Milanese nobleman born in 1753 to an old aristocratic family related on his mother's side to José de Palafox y Melzi, the Spanish general who would become famous defending Saragossa against the French in 1808.[22] Melzi was marked out by his intelligence and skill early on as a future leader of his country, but a strange combination of circumstances actually led him to that position. His first taste of meaningful public service came when he was named to the delegation sent to pay homage to Napoleon following the Battle of Lodi in 1796. He impressed Napoleon at that meeting, but as Napoleon pursued his campaign farther east, revolutionary affairs in Milan turned against Melzi. Proscribed, jailed, and released again in 1797, he was called on to serve his state once more but refused. He relented enough to travel to Rastadt hoping to serve as the Milanese (now Cisalpine Republic) representative at the congress attempting to settle the fate of Germany and Italy there. Following that mission, he retired to his estates near Saragossa for two years, not involving himself in the troubles of his native land. It was Napoleon who ended his *secessio* by calling him to Paris in 1801 to take part in the discussions that ultimately led to the formation of the Italian Republic and his selection as its vice president.

Melzi was a fascinating choice as the effective local ruler of the Italian Republic. His talents and intellect, together with his limited involvement in the unpleasant early days of the Cisalpine Republic, caused his countrymen to respect him as a natural leader and protector of the new state. Napoleon selected Melzi and kept him in his post despite his repeated requests to retire because he felt that only Melzi could give legitimacy to his regime.

But Melzi was committed to the independence of Italy—something that Napoleon, in the end, could not allow. He made his position plain to Napoleon whenever the subject arose. What is more, he acted on this sentiment. While nominally representing the French satellite Cisalpine Republic at Rastadt, Melzi independently sought out the Austrian representative, Ludwig Cobenzl, and presented him with the plans for the reorganization of northern Italy, hoping to secure Austria's acquiescence and friendship.[23] As vice president of the Italian Republic, Melzi received the clandestine Austrian envoy sent to him, Baron Moll, and continued to trade information with him into 1805.[24] Napoleon was aware of some of these activities but found Melzi too effective, too honest, and too popular to sacrifice or even discipline. Melzi's longevity in power despite his avowed determination to maintain as much independence as possible seemed to confirm Napoleon's ambivalence toward Italy.

Relying on a native to run the vassal state under Napoleon's authority was common Napoleonic practice at this time. The Ligurian, Batavian, and Helvetian Republics all had similar relationships with France, although Napoleon was not the formal head of state of any of them, as he was in Milan. The British and the Russians, predisposed to read ill into Napoleon's every action, saw through this facade and concluded that the satellite republics were vassal states in Napoleon's thrall. The Austrians did not doubt Napoleon's degree of control over those states, nor did they misunderstand the dire implications for them of such control. They also saw, however, the hopeful signs already mentioned that Napoleon might over time be inclined to moderate his control and allow his satellite states to function more properly as buffers. Only such a hope, however ill founded, could have made the situation after Lunéville tolerable to the weary Austrian leadership.

The indication in mid-1804 that Napoleon might transform the Republic of Italy into a kingdom under his own rule came as a thunderbolt. Not only did it represent yet another instance of a clear violation of the letter and spirit of Lunéville and yet another example of Napoleon's "boundless ambition," but it meant, more practically, the permanent and eternal subjugation of all of northern Italy right up to the Austrian frontier to Napoleon and his heirs. Austria, having extricated herself from a dangerous frontier with France in the Austrian Netherlands, now had to contemplate a permanent mutual border in

Italy. This situation was even less tolerable than the previous one; when the French overran Belgium, it meant the unfortunate loss of a distant province; when the French overran northern Italy, it placed the French army irresistibly on a short road to Vienna.

The Kingdom of Italy

Napoleon Bonaparte became Napoleon the First, Emperor of the French, on May 18, 1804. The leaders of the Italian Republic were not unaware that this revolution in international affairs would have important ramifications for their polity. On May 7 Napoleon met with Ferdinando Marescalchi, the nominal minister of foreign affairs of the Italian Republic, and made it clear to him that the status of the Italian Republic would have to change, that its independence was not an option, and that he could not imagine one of his brothers on its throne. He also made it clear that he desired a proposal to come from Italy resolving this apparent dilemma.[25]

In his note to Melzi reporting this conversation, Marescalchi added that he believed that if the proposal came swiftly and was satisfactory, then the Consulta (effectively the ruling body of the nominal republic) could ask in return for several concessions: the separation of the two states after Napoleon's death, the reduction and perhaps even the final elimination of the military tribute that the republic was forced to pay to France, maybe even the annexation of Parma and Plaisance to the territory of the new kingdom. Marescalchi was convinced that Napoleon would never consent to granting meaningful independence to the Italian state he had created and that "neither war nor peace could lead Bonaparte to relinquish our country."[26]

Surprisingly, Melzi and his colleagues did not restrict themselves to the concessions Marescalchi had advised them to seek in return for prompt action. Eleven days after the announcement of Napoleon's elevation, Melzi sent the new emperor a proposal for turning the Italian Republic into the Kingdom of Italy—and granting it considerable autonomy, possibly independence.[27]

Although Article 1 of this proposal transformed the Italian Republic into a kingdom and Article 2 named Napoleon the first king, most of the rest of the proposal imposed a series of restrictions on Napoleon's own power and still more on that of his successors. The future kings of Italy would descend from Napoleon's own heirs, but the succession would be by secundogeniture with the proviso that no subsequent king of Italy could be at the same time emperor of France. Subsequent rulers were also obliged to live permanently within the Kingdom of Italy. These measures were an attempt to ensure that the Kingdom of Italy would in fact be independent from France after Napoleon's death. The proposal also demanded that the bases of the new constitution guarantee, among other things, the integrity of the territory of the new kingdom and "its political independence." Melzi justified these restrictions of Napoleon's power in his cover letter by asserting "that all of the conditions that accompany the principal idea are strictly required by the respect that is due either to public opinion or to the rights of the nation."[28]

It goes without saying that the final organization of the new Italian state bore little resemblance to this proposal. The significance of this episode lies, rather, in the direct attempt of Melzi and his colleagues to establish a truly independent state under the nominal but not really effective suzerainty of Napoleon and his heirs. The instructions sent to Marescalchi on this point are telling: "The second condition, concerning the residence [of kings after Napoleon within the territory of the kingdom] consolidates the sovereignty and the national independence . . . and finally reassures and satisfies all of the Italians who hope to see their country restored to its ancient glory and freed of the always disagreeable influence of foreigners."[29] And the significance of that attempt is twofold—first, it shows that Melzi and his colleagues were not simply Italian quislings but actually sought a reasonably independent Italian state and, second, it reveals that they thought it possible to persuade Napoleon to accept such a development.

If this belief was simply wishful thinking, it was directly supported by Napoleon himself. He received the proposals of the Consulta with surprising equanimity and grace, although he put off consideration of them until a later time. But he did make an important categorical statement: "The Italian Republic will remain one and independent. We will establish there, as the Consulta desires, an order of affairs more conformable to the spirit of the century in which we live, and to the degree the society has achieved."[30] Napoleon even went so far as to state that he intended to have his successor (almost certainly the son that his brother Louis expected shortly) educated in Italy: "I want him to be raised in Italy and that from his childhood he know the language and the habits; that he be entirely Italian."[31] Melzi and his colleagues can be forgiven, in the face of such private rhetoric, for imagining a greater prospect for independence than actually existed.

Although Melzi and Napoleon used the word "independence," they meant entirely different things. Melzi meant to establish a truly independent state in which there were no foreign troops, no subsidies were paid to foreign states, and internal affairs were largely regulated by the natives. He hoped to create a buffer state, neutral between Austria and France but under Napoleon's protection, and thereby preserve the Italian peninsula from further participation in the wars of Europe.[32] Napoleon meant by independence a state that was under its own government but would of its own accord adopt the policies most suitable for France.

This divergence of views became evident in the next exchange of letters. Melzi attempted in July 1804 to convince Napoleon of the necessity to end, or at least dramatically reduce, the amount of tribute the Italian Republic was forced to pay to France. He pointed out that the amount paid by just one of its departments in 1804 was greater than what the entire region had paid to Austria before the wars. The result was that extremely high taxes undermined the legitimacy and popularity of the government. He also insisted on obtaining Austria's sanction for the new order of affairs in order to ensure that war would not result when the the republic was transformed into a kingdom.[33]

This time, Napoleon got angry. In a note aimed at Melzi but sent to Marescalchi, he declared that he would not reply to Melzi's letter "because I believe that it was written without reflection. It would give me a very bad opinion of the Italian lands and of Lombardy in particular if I thought of them that they desired to return to Austria for the sole reason that they paid less. Melzi had an attack of gout when he wrote this."[34] Independence was not independence but depravity when it produced demands at odds with the needs of French security.

Melzi did not keep the conflict between himself and Napoleon a secret. He was determined to obtain Austrian blessing for the proposed changes in northern Italy, thereby averting any danger of war resulting from them. At the same time, he also seems to have hoped that Austria could act in such a way as to deflect Napoleon from his apparent intention to take the crown of Italy for himself. This desperate and contradictory policy had the effect of making Austria privy to Napoleon's real plans months before he was prepared to inform Vienna.

The relations between Melzi and the Austrian agent, Moll (and through Moll to Cobenzl), became more intimate during the negotiations over Austria's recognition of Napoleon's title and Napoleon's recognition of the new imperial dignity of the Austrian house in June and July. Cobenzl, through Moll, kept Melzi abreast of these discussions. Melzi responded with the following astonishing confidence:

> If you wish to know what result [of the discussions over the fate of the Italian Republic] seems to me the most probable, according to the limited information of which I am cognizant, I will give you my personal opinion quite frankly. Here it is: I believe that Napoleon has not yet decided, that he is still listening, but that he is leaning toward having himself declared hereditary king of our country . . . If he is given the time to take a decision and to publish it, he will not want to go back on it. Everything depends, I think, on not giving him the time to decide the above. I am therefore of the opinion that one should not delay in explaining oneself confidentially with Champagny [the French ambassador in Vienna].[35]

Here is the vice president of one of Napoleon's vassal states calling for Austria to intervene in the decision about the future fate of his government and country! For the Austrians, that interesting fact was less important than the news that Napoleon intended to make himself hereditary king of Italy. That news came as a thunderbolt and occasioned a fundamental change in Cobenzl's thinking about the current crisis.

A few weeks before the dispatch of this message, Cobenzl had, as we have seen, been trying to convince himself and others that Napoleon's fangs had been drawn and that he harbored no offensive designs. In that frame of mind, Cobenzl even tried to argue that it would not matter if Napoleon transformed his presidency into a kingship. When presented with the imminent reality, however, he changed his mind completely.* In a resounding note he declared:

> The future fate of the Italian Republic seems to us to be . . . the touch-stone of what Europe will have to fear or to hope for from the ulterior views of the Emperor of the French. If he succeeds in uniting the lands that compose this Republic to the domain of his Empire, already so vast, despite the treaties, if he subjects them to one of the members of his family, which would have nearly the same effect, one could be sure that all of Italy would not be long in being subjugated, as well as Switzerland and Holland; thence there would be no lack of occasions and pretexts for establishing a French dictatorship over the North and the South of Germany, and the ground will have been laid, as well, for the invasion of Greece and Egypt.[36]

Cobenzl had seen the problems of a permanent Napoleonic domination of northern Italy all along. Once he had seen its reality and imminence, he could no longer delude himself about the danger it posed to his state. Cobenzl went so far as to act on Melzi's recommendation, as Colloredo said to Champagny that "he would not like to believe that France would give all of the powers of Europe the basis of a justified mistrust by making new encroachments in Italy."[37] Nothing of value, however, was forthcoming from Paris.

The news from Italy was joined by rumors of an alliance between France and Bavaria that would give the latter Salzburg and the Innviertel. Shortly thereafter, Cobenzl learned that Napoleon apparently had given orders to prepare the fortress of Mainz to support an army of 100,000 men across the Rhine. These rumors together convinced Cobenzl that he had to find further reinforcements for his state, increasingly under siege and in danger. Surprisingly, he turned to Prussia first, but in the end he had to rely on Russia.[38]

The negotiations for an Austro–Russian treaty had been hanging fire for some time—on Cobenzl's deliberate orders, as we have seen. In September

---

*Cobenzl apparently learned of Napoleon's initial discussions with Marescalchi about transforming the Italian Republic into a kingdom in early July. See Fournier, *Gentz und Cobenzl*, p. 140 n. 1.

1804, however, Stadion reported from St. Petersburg that the game was up. The tsar would not agree to Cobenzl's demands for 150,000 Russian troops and would not back away from his demand that the *casus foederis* include an attack on Naples. Stadion had become convinced that urgent action was required lest Austria lose any prospect of Russian support.[39]

The crisis in Italy played a definite role in the denouement of this negotiation, although it was not openly acknowledged. Cobenzl knew that he was no longer securing for Austria protection against an abstract French threat that might materialize at some distant point. He had come to believe, rather, that the French threat was near and getting ever nearer and that he could not risk losing Russian support at this crucial juncture.

The result was a purely defensive treaty between Austria and Russia.[40] The *casus foederis* were as follows: an attack by Napoleon on either Austria or Russia, specifically including the Russian troops deployed in the Ionian Islands; an unprovoked attack by Napoleon against the part of the Kingdom of Naples that he did not already occupy; or a move by Napoleon to extend his control in northern Germany beyond Hanover. If one or more of those cases befell, Austria would be obliged to put 230,000 troops in the field and Russia 120,000, ensuring that the coalition forces in the main theater of war (which was not and could not be specified) would not be inferior to French forces there. Russia and Austria also guaranteed each other against Prussia, should Frederick William launch an attack during a war between the allies and France. A detailed list of Austria's potential gains in the case of successful conflict included the recovery of Tuscany and other parts of northern Italy. But it specifically excluded gains in Germany and even foresaw the possibility of Austria ceding German territory to Bavaria or Baden, always assuming that those states joined the coalition. Finally, Alexander undertook to use his best efforts to convince the British to subsidize Austria handsomely, but Francis agreed that he would be bound by the treaty even if Alexander failed in that endeavor.

This treaty was not really in Austria's interest, and Cobenzl signed it *faute de mieux*. It bound Austria to fight a war against France if Napoleon attacked Russia, the Ottoman Empire, or any of a number of minor German states that were more or less hostile to Vienna. It required her to assume the lion's share of the military burden in that war, and it did not assure her that she would receive any remotely adequate financial support from her allies. The only positive benefit was that it formally destroyed the isolation in which Austria had found herself following the Peace of Lunéville, and it assured her of having allies in case of further Napoleonic aggressions, which Cobenzl had come to believe were likely. Most importantly, signing this treaty meant that Austria had finally chosen her side. It would not be possible, henceforth, for Vienna to straddle between St. Petersburg and Paris—she had cast her lot with the nascent coalition.

Conclusion

Just as the French invasion of Hanover turned Alexander against Napoleon, the reports of Napoleon's intentions to make himself king of Italy had the same effect on Cobenzl. In the spring of 1805 Cobenzl convinced himself and others that Austria had to undertake an offensive war against Napoleon, but he had already recognized that possibility in late 1804. Attempting to persuade his wavering ruler to ratify the Austro–Russian convention and feel good about it, Cobenzl said that although he was as eager as Francis to avoid war, it might not be possible. He added, "I know of only two possibilities for a war: 1. If Napoleon attacks us and we must defend ourselves, and 2. if he, without attacking us directly, makes important conquests that increase his already extravagant strength still more." To allow Napoleon to make such conquests without fighting would be to deprive the monarchy henceforth of the means of resisting France.[41] This assertion was a dramatic departure from his previous position that Austria would not go to war against France except in her own immediate self-defense. Cobenzl remained remarkably consistent, furthermore, in his subsequent willingness to go to war over Napoleon's Italian coronation.

Once again, Napoleon had antagonized a state that he should have been able to keep neutral and had driven its leaders into outright hostility and mistrust. It was not intentional. Napoleon's actions in Italy, from his perspective, had nothing to do with Austria. The decision to crown himself emperor of the French was the result of purely internal circumstances. The subsequent conviction that he had to change his status as ruler of Italy flowed naturally from the previous decision and also, perhaps, from his determination to take up Charlemagne's mythical mantle.

It is easy to see in this Carolingian revival an attack on Francis—the actual successor, distant and unworthy though he might have been, to the founder of the Holy Roman Empire. It is unlikely that Napoleon thought of Francis in this regard at all. If he desired to make himself the new Charlemagne, it was because he felt that his skills and energy, which placed him so far above any of the other rulers of Europe, should be matched by titles and respect far above them as well.

Napoleon also had a problem in Italy. The Italian Republic was not doing very well at consolidating itself and integrating its various populations—the people of the former papal legations were particularly problematic in this regard. Melzi, though temporarily indispensable, was neither loyal nor sufficiently subservient. Napoleon would likely have been forced to make significant changes in the structure and personnel of the Italian Republic at any event, and his elevation to emperorship merely provided the excuse.

Under this focus on internal political and psychological issues lay an assumption that was devastating for Austria. Napoleon saw Italy as his land, and his repeated statements that he would "leave Austria not a foot of land in Italy" were no more accidental than Ronald Reagan's famous malapropisms regarding the Soviet Union. Although they did not reflect an immediate policy or plan, they did represent an intention. Whether or not Napoleon meant to create a unified or independent Italy, he certainly meant to establish his hegemony in the peninsula to the absolute exclusion of Austria. This intention reflected, again, not a fear of Austria (which he did not fear even in combination with Russia and Britain), but simply his determination to have things exactly as he wanted them in his "sphere of influence" without any outside interference. It was a purely hegemonic policy.

Would Napoleon have stopped with attaining hegemony in Italy? It is impossible to say. Some argue that his fixation on Italy simply reflected his fixation on the Orient; over time, he would have used Italy as a springboard for adventures in Egypt or the Balkans. Such a possibility cannot be ruled out entirely. Napoleon's appetite tended to grow with the eating and there would always have been pretexts for further aggressive efforts to "defend" himself against England or Russia. It is also possible that he would have become satisfied with his expanded empire and come to a modus vivendi with his neighbors.

Whatever the possibilities, Cobenzl rightly felt that Austria could not take the chance. Napoleonic control over Italy, together with the preponderant influence he now exercised in Switzerland and southern Germany, posed a mortal threat to the Habsburg empire. By the end of 1804, Cobenzl had concluded that he could not accept that danger, even if the alternative was war.

One of the factors driving Cobenzl to that conclusion was the fear of Austria losing any hope of allies in case of further Napoleonic encroachments or attack. The fear of losing Russian support, as always, helped push Austria to take steps that she found distasteful. This terrible situation resulted primarily from Austria's military weakness and her hyperconsciousness of that weakness before a France that many Austrians saw as invincible. They turned out to be right in that fear, at least in the short run, as we shall see. We must first consider, however, the final round of diplomacy that actually led to the formation of the Third Coalition against France.

6

The Formation of
the Third Coalition

Despite initial vacillations and delays, the Third Coalition came into being rapidly. Russia and Britain began negotiations in December 1804, concluded a draft treaty in April 1805, and ratified it in July. Austria, whose leaders knew nothing about the Anglo–Russian treaty until it had been signed, adhered to it in August 1805. Since it took approximately a month for a courier to make the trip from St. Petersburg to London and three weeks to travel from Vienna to the Russian capital, the final negotiations occurred quickly.

The coalition took shape speedily, for two reasons. The momentum building for war by the end of 1804 had become almost irresistible, and fundamental issues of disagreement among the allies were papered over in the interest of responding to changes in the international situation. This speed led to basic weaknesses in the coalition, however. The powers of the Third Coalition went to war in September 1805 because they felt they had to, not because they earnestly wanted to, and the alliances that bound them could not overcome fundamental mistrust and divergent aims.

Britain and Russia

Tsar Alexander had approached William Pitt with a combination of enthusiasm and suspicion. Simon Vorontsov's reports were nothing short of hymns to the great man. He even wrote a brief biography of Pitt for Alexander's edification.[1] Vorontsov's repeated statements that Russia and Britain had no interest in conflict and were natural allies were based on emotion, not calculations of interest. Although they had no common border yet (Russian penetration deep into central Asia was still several decades away), two fundamental issues drove

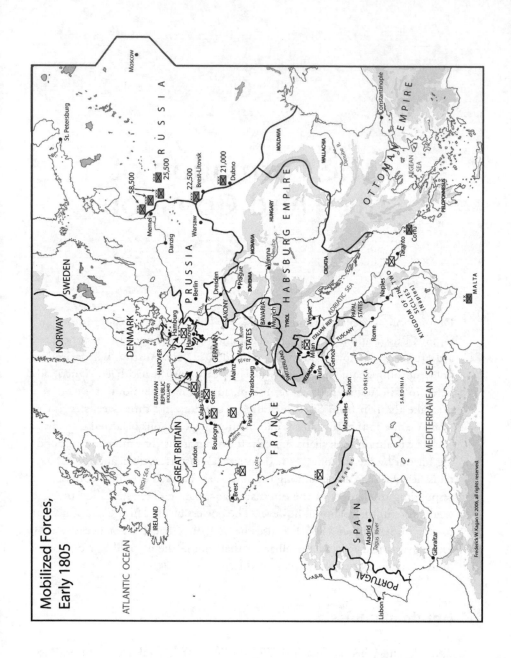

Mobilized Forces,
Early 1805

ATLANTIC OCEAN

IRELAND

GREAT BRITAIN

London

Brest

NORWAY

SWEDEN

St. Petersburg

DENMARK

Hamburg
Hanover
HANOVER
BATAVIAN
REPUBLIC
(HOLLAND)

Calais
Gent
Boulogne
Paris

Seine R.

FRANCE

Loire R.

Marseilles
Toulon

CORSICA

SARDINIA

Madrid

SPAIN

Tagus River

PORTUGAL

Lisbon

Gibraltar

MEDITERRANEAN SEA

Memel
58,500

Danzig

Berlin
PRUSSIA

Dresden
Elbe

SAXONY

GERMANY
STATES

Mainz

Main River

Rhine

Strasbourg

SWITZERLAND

PIEDMONT
Turin
Genoa

MILAN
ITALIAN REP.

TUSCANY

Warsaw

25,500

22,500
Brest-Litovsk

21,000
Dubno

RUSSIA

Moscow

BOHEMIA
Prague

BAVARIA
Munich

TYROL

Vienna
Danube

HUNGARY

MORAVIA

HABSBURG EMPIRE

CROATIA

Venice

ADRIATIC SEA

Rome

PAPAL
STATES

Naples

KINGDOM OF THE TWO
SICILIES (Naples)

Taranto

Corfu

PELOPONNESUS

AEGEAN
SEA

Constantinople

OTTOMAN EMPIRE

WALLACHIA

MOLDAVIA

Danube R.

MALTA

IRISH SEA

PYRENEES

a wedge into the Anglo–Russian friendship: Britain's interpretation of the law of the sea and Russia's relationship with Turkey.

During the American Revolutionary War Great Britain had imposed an embargo on her rebellious colonies that excluded neutral as well as belligerent shipping. The plan was to cripple the American economy and force the rebels to see reason. This failed, as efforts to place embargoes on autarkic continents usually do. British actions antagonized Catherine the Great so much, however, that she formed the League of Armed Neutrality to defend the rights of neutral shipping. Similar British actions against France during the revolutionary wars prompted Paul to revive the League of Armed Neutrality and played a role in driving him to decide to go to war with Britain. The continuation of this British policy throughout the Napoleonic struggle plagued Anglo–Russian relations. It also led to the War of 1812 between Britain and America.

Alexander disliked British maritime policy because it hurt Russian trade whenever Russia chose to be neutral in a continental war involving Britain. It was a policy based purely on military power and not on generally accepted international law. Britain stopped neutral shipping, closed rivers, and impressed sailors because the Royal Navy was unchallenged on the high seas. British admiralty courts regularly ruled in favor of Britain because they could and there was nothing any other state could do about it. That way of doing business was incompatible with Alexander's vision of a perpetual alliance between Britain and Russia that would support and enforce a new Westphalian system committed to the preservation of international law. The tsar wanted the British to see reason on this point as part of the price for an alliance treaty.

The British suspected Alexander of harboring designs on the Ottoman Empire. The shibboleth of Russian desires to take Constantinople and the straits is now ineradicably embedded in Anglo–American histories. For many historians it is an article of faith that the Russians aimed to destroy Turkey and seize the straits from the time of Peter the Great, if not before. The British, who saw in Turkey a buffer protecting their growing Indian empire, seized on any evidence of Russian expansionism as proof of the theorem.

But Russia's relationship with the Ottoman Empire was more complicated than that. During the reign of Catherine the Great, for instance, the Russians were pursuing the complete destruction of the Ottoman state and the seizure of European Turkey at least. At other times, Russian tsars explicitly recognized that a weak Ottoman state was preferable to direct Russian control over part of it. In 1833 Nicholas I landed an expedition south of Constantinople to preserve the Ottoman sultanate from an internal rebellion that threatened to destroy it.*

---

*True Russophobes see this action as evidence of Russia's predatory designs, something that secret discussions between the tsar and his leading advisers reveal to be nonsense. See Frederick W. Kagan, *The Military Reforms of Nicholas I: The Origins of the Modern Russian Army* (New York: St. Martin's, 1999), for a consideration of Russia's "Turkey problem" in the 1820s and 1830s (and beyond).

Alexander repeatedly exclaimed both publicly and privately that he had no intention of harming Turkey but preferred to prop up the state that was already being called the "sick man of Europe." The British can be forgiven for not trusting him, however. He was named, after all, for Alexander the Great while his younger brother Constantine was named for the founder of Constantinople. Catherine had given the boys those names intentionally—Alexander was to rule Russia and Constantine a revived Greco–Byzantine state centered on the Bosphorus. Decades of Russian expansion at Ottoman expense during her reign underlined the seriousness of her purpose, something that Alexander's pacific statements could not erase from British memory.

These two bones of contention hampered the formation of the Anglo–Russian alliance (and would lead to its collapse after the end of the Napoleonic Wars). The British would have been willing to shelve them in favor of an immediate alliance against France, but Alexander was determined to do more than simply defeat France. He wanted to form an intimate union between Britain and Russia, thereby ensuring support for the idealistic new international system that he hoped, however much he denied it, would end war forever.

It is tempting to see Adam Czartoryskii's influence behind Alexander's determination to form a new "international system," and he indeed played a critical role in formulating the actual program. But the idealistic worldview was Alexander's; his determination to form a new world order outlasted Czartoryskii's dismissal by decades. Even in 1805 Alexander showed that he was willing to push this principle far beyond the point at which Czartoryskii would have abandoned it to practical realities. Alexander was a confused child of the Enlightenment, and the idea of forming a new basis for international law and the relations among states, once presented to him, became his own goal and dream.

He determined, accordingly, to test the British against this new measure before he allied himself with them, just as he had tested Napoleon following the conclusion of the Franco–Russian peace treaty. A major element of weakness in the Third Coalition resulted from this test. It antagonized the British, who, by Alexander's lights, failed badly.

The initial signs were all positive. Alexander sent one of his most trusted friends, N. N. Novosil'tsev, to London to lay the basis for a treaty. He adopted this approach because he knew that Simon Vorontsov worshiped Pitt, and he did not completely trust his ambassador to follow his orders and pursue Russia's interests if they led to conflict with Pitt. He wanted as his negotiator a younger man who was his personal friend and shared his outlook on the world, someone he could indoctrinate with a detailed program before the negotiations. Simon was an aged diplomat, set in his ways, and was living in London. Consequently he did not meet the requirements for being Alexander's personal and trusted agent. Finally, as Alexander wanted to test Britain before committing to the alliance, it seemed better to send a less official envoy.

Novosil'tsev could discuss matters with Pitt and simply return home if they turned out badly. If Simon made a formal proposal that was rejected or had to be withdrawn, however, the consequences for both Britain and Russia would have been much more dramatic (or so Alexander thought).

Novosil'tsev met with Pitt on December 25, 1804, propounding Alexander's view of the world in great detail.[2] All of the goals of the proposed coalition could, he said, "be reduced to one alone: that of *reestablishing the equilibrium of Europe and placing its security and its tranquility on the most solid bases.*"[3] This objective, he continued, could be broken down into three different parts or periods, to be pursued successively. First, France must be returned "to its former borders or to any others that seem to conduce the better to the general tranquility of Europe." Second, "natural barriers to the ambition of Bonaparte" must be erected that would keep France in check and prevent future French expansion. Finally, the new order must be consolidated "by the most intimate and perpetual alliance between Russia and Great Britain and by a treaty that will be made between these two powers, the countries that they will have delivered from the French yoke, and all others that wish to join with them to maintain this order of affairs, which the conservation of the balance renders so indispensable."[4]

Novosil'tsev then went on to consider ways and means. Russia and Britain could not act alone. It would be necessary to assemble a large coalition including both Austria and Prussia if possible, but at least one of those two powers, so that allied troops could actually reach France. The coalition should bring overwhelming force to bear against France, and the powers should settle on a detailed plan for the war before hostilities commenced.

Novosil'tsev pointed out, however, that it was also important to reduce the support available to Napoleon. To this end it was essential that the smaller states of Europe had "no doubts that the two powers that are at the head of the coalition will have nothing personal in view and will only concern themselves with the task of recovering and consolidating the political independence" of the states then enslaved to France. Holland, Switzerland, and Italy would form governments of their choosing as soon as they were able. Novosil'tsev concluded,

> The conduct, the language, and the proclamations of Russia and England, always in accord with these principles, will not only produce the desired effect on those nations, but, according to all the calculations of probability, will also serve as a means of preparing France herself for salutary changes in her government, will reduce resistance and lessen the difficulties that the coalition might encounter in pursuing its objective.[5]

Pitt expressed complete agreement with the principles stated by Novosil'tsev. He proposed, however, that the allies make the greatest possible efforts to secure the adherence of both Austria and Prussia, and he argued that it would be necessary to that end to consider the "indemnities" that each state would receive. Novosil'tsev gently refused to consider those proposals in any detail, only noting that the "indemnities" offered to Austria and Prussia should be as small as possible "in order to avoid making the same mistake of the first time [during the Second Coalition], when all of the efforts that were made were attributed uniquely to the desire to profit from a general dismemberment" of the weak states of Europe.*

The discussion then turned to the question of British subsidies. Pitt replied by repeating the offer made earlier of £5 million to be divided among the allies according to the amount of force each was able to put into the field. In the interests of aiding those that needed to mobilize, he was willing to date the beginning of the subvention to January 1, 1805. But he was not able to offer more money.

Novosil'tsev then turned to a more detailed discussion of the postwar situation. The states bordering France, he said, must be made strong enough to be able to resist future French encroachments. Holland, Switzerland, and Italy should all be augmented, and the German empire must be reorganized so that all could offer meaningful resistance to France. The real guarantee of the peace of Europe, however, would lie in the permanent pact between Britain and Russia in defense of the new order, which must become "an alliance that nothing will be able to break except a complete change of system and of principles on one part or the other."

Pitt replied that the principles of the Russian court "were in every respect as analogous to the sentiments of H[is] Britannic M[ajesty] and of his ministry as it was possible to desire and at the same time so strongly to the taste of the nation and so conformable to the character and the sentiments of the individuals who composed it that the government had no other way of maintaining its popularity than by following them to the letter." All the economic interests of the country required that every effort be made "that might *lead to, solidly establish and conserve the general tranquility.*" The government of Britain, Pitt added, had always in war and in peace "given proofs of its disinterestedness and of its ardent desire to see the reestablishment of general tranquility in Europe through any sacrifices that it was in its power to make."[6]

The conversation did not end on that happy note, however. Novosil'tsev complained of the tenor and tone of Britain's communications to Russia. Specifically, he referred to an exchange of messages relating to proposals for a new Russian treaty with Turkey. In April 1804, as part of the series of mes-

---

*This line of argument tends to vitiate Czartoryskii's earlier hopes of gaining Poland for Russia in exchange for gains made by Austria and Prussia to the west. It may reflect Alexander's turning away from that position and prospect, or it may be that the tsar, like Czartoryskii, expected to take advantage of Prussian or Austrian misbehavior in order to attain that goal.

sages Alexander sent to foreign courts announcing his intention to remonstrate with France about the seizure of the Duc d'Enghien, Czartoryskii sent a note to the ambassador in Turkey instructing him to reassure the Turks about Russia's amity toward them and also to seek reassurance that in the event of a war between Russia and France, Turkey would renew her alliance with Russia.[7] Much to everyone's surprise, the Turks eagerly seized on this opening to request that the current Russo–Turkish treaty be renewed at once, well before the end of its term.[8]

The Turkish request and the Russian response to it reflected the rapidly changing situation within the Ottoman Empire in 1804. A serious Serbian revolt against Ottoman rule was developing at this time in response to dynamics within the Ottoman Empire as well as to the effects of the French invasion of Egypt in 1798.* The Russian response was complicated and aimed primarily at restoring the peace and maintaining good relations with Istanbul. Czartoryskii considered establishing autonomous Serbian and other minority states within the Ottoman Empire but under Russian protection, like the Septinsular Republic. At various times in 1804–1805 the Russians considered even more extreme solutions to this problem, including partitioning the Ottoman Empire in various ways, according to the changing situation in the Balkans and the changing relationship between St. Petersburg and the Porte.

The Russians therefore found the Turkish request for a premature renewal of the Russo–Turkish treaty awkward.[9] The current treaty was not sufficiently favorable to Russia (Czartoryskii thought it was not favorable at all), but mid-1804 was not a time when Alexander or his ministers wanted to be negotiating with Turkey. On the other hand, the British government had apparently made a reference to the possible need to occupy territory in Turkey and Greece, suggesting to the Russians that a partition of the country might be acceptable under certain circumstances.[10] Czartoryskii, accordingly, pursued a two-track program. He instructed his ambassador in Constantinople to delay and explain that Russia needed to consult with Britain before negotiating a treaty.[11] He immediately sent a proposal to Britain with several topics for discussion, one of which was the possible partitioning of Turkey. He implied that the idea had originated in comments by the British minister.[12]

---

*I shall treat this complicated history in greater detail in subsequent volumes of this work. See Roger V. Paxton, "Russian Foreign Policy and the First Serbian Uprising: Alliances, Apprehensions, and Autonomy, 1804–1807," in Wayne S. Vucinich, ed., *The First Serbian Uprising, 1804–1813* (New York: Columbia University Press, 1982), pp. 41–71; Stanford J. Shaw, "The Ottoman Empire and the Serbian Uprising, 1804–1807," in Vucinich, ed., *First Serbian Uprising*, pp. 71–94; and Stanford J. Shaw, *Between Old and New: The Ottoman Empire Under Sultan Selim III, 1789–1807* (Cambridge: Harvard University Press, 1971). All of these works state or imply that it was the Russians who pressed the sultan to renegotiate the treaty, and it may indeed have appeared so to the sultan. The Russian documents make it fairly clear, however, that such was not the initial intention of Czartoryskii or Alexander, however adroitly they may have seized on the opportunity once it was presented to them.

It appears that neither Pitt nor foreign minister Lord Harrowby had thought about partitioning Turkey, and they were surprised and taken aback by this apparently aggressive Russian proposal. The message they sent back to the Russians effectively questioned their integrity. Alexander always said that Austria had proposed a partition, which he resisted. Yet Czartoryskii's overtures seemed to be "far from indicating a decided disinclination to a plan of that description."[13] The message continued, "The views of Russia are so indistinctly expressed in the dispatch of Prince Czartorisky, that it is impossible to form a judgment how far they may be consistent either with the views, or the good faith of his Majesty."

Novosil'tsev (and presumably Alexander and Czartoryskii, who must have instructed him to discuss it) evidently found it impossible to pass this controversy by. The British, he said, seemed to suspect Russia of having ulterior designs on the Ottoman Empire and were questioning Alexander's bona fides. Pitt was not immediately conciliatory. Judging from the contents of Czartoryskii's proposal, he said, it seemed possible that the Russians actually had such ulterior motives. Novosil'tsev responded curiously. He assured Pitt that Russia had no such designs, that Alexander wanted to defend and support Turkey against France and under no circumstances would he "consent . . . to make himself master of Constantinople."

So far, so good, but Novosil'tsev went on. Why, he asked, should Britain object to Russia seizing parts of Turkey? Did Pitt think that Britain's trade or security would be harmed? Why should Britain fear the expansion of a power so friendly to her? Finally Pitt was thrown on the defensive. He assured Novosil'tsev that it was not a question of whether or not Russian occupation of Turkey was in Britain's interests, but whether the moment was propitious for such a transaction. Both countries had to direct their efforts at liberating the states enslaved by France and throwing the iniquities of Napoleon's invasions into stark relief by the purity of their own actions—something that negotiations over the partition of Turkey would not do. "Well," said Novosil'tsev, "that's all I wanted." Such language would have been suitable for remonstrating with the tsar, but the tone Harrowby used implied that Alexander was not entirely above board.

This exchange was a tempest in a teapot. Alexander had no intention of partitioning Turkey or even occupying large parts of Ottoman territory, and it is not clear that Pitt or Harrowby suspected him of such a design. Yet the mistrust was patent and not easily resolvable. The British had already come to see Russia as a rival in the eastern Mediterranean and feared Russia's apparent ascendancy at the Porte. The suspicion that resulted from those feelings hung like a cloud over the Anglo–Russian alliance even during friendly exchanges.

One reason why the exchanges were so friendly was that Novosil'tsev did not raise two fundamental points of discord: maritime law and the return of

Malta. In his report to Alexander, Novosil'tsev explicitly defended his failure to raise the issue of Russia's proposed changes to maritime law, explaining that the time had not yet come for such a discussion. He was convinced, however, that the British could be led, little by little, to accept the necessary changes. He did not raise the issue of Malta because he had not been asked to—the issue was not mentioned in any of the instructions he or Simon Vorontsov were given, and he made no mention of it in his note apologizing for his failure to discuss the Maritime Code.[14] Although Czartoryskii commended Novosil'tsev for his judgment in not bringing up this issue prematurely, Novosil'tsev's silence in retrospect was probably a mistake, since it led both sides to an unreasonably optimistic view of their relationship.[15]

Pitt was as satisfied and optimistic as the Russians. He wrote to foreign minister Lord Harrowby that "the principles" on which the two powers could build were "so completely our own" that they need not hesitate to contract a "provisional engagement" in advance of a treaty. The aim of confining France to her "ancient limits" but not forcing an explicit Bourbon restoration was "very satisfactory."[16]

Another colleague wrote of Pitt at this time, "His schemes, large and deep. His hopes sanguine."[17] The mutual satisfaction resulting from Novosil'tsev's initial conversations with Pitt soon broke down, however. The stumbling block was Malta.

Czartoryskii had raised the question of Britain's possession of Malta in the summer of 1804 for the first time since the abortive arbitration–mediation plan of mid-1803. At first he simply noted that "he understood that our [British] Government was not averse to relax [its position] upon the Article of Malta, since we had enlarged our territory in the East Indies and secured it by such brilliant conquests." British ambassador to Russia J. B. Warren replied that Britain's possessions in India, commerce in the Mediterranean, and need to defend Egypt made it impossible for Britain to give up the island.[18] Czartoryskii returned to the charge two weeks later, noting that if Napoleon evacuated Naples, Holland, and part of the Netherlands, then "he supposed Great Britain might be induced to give up Malta." Warren replied that abandoning the island "seemed to me a very unlikely and unwise measure," since Napoleon could easily and swiftly reoccupy those territories, whereas Britain could only retake Malta with difficulty. This time, Czartoryskii pressed harder. He claimed that "it was not the desire of this Court [of St. Petersburg] but that of others to whom the presence of so many British ships in those seas might not be equally agreeable." Warren replied more forcefully that "it would be an impolitic measure in this country to assist in any plan that might occasion the British force to retire from the Mediterranean." There the matter rested.[19]

The basis for Czartoryskii's queries was a rumor that France had made a peace offer to Great Britain that London was seriously considering and that negotiations were under way.[20] Although this was not the case at that time, it set a pattern for the issue of Malta in which rumors or proposals for peace negotiations led the Russians to seek British concessions about the fate of the island.

In the first weeks of 1805, Napoleon launched a large-scale diplomatic offensive probably designed to smooth over the announcement of his transformation of the Italian Republic into a kingdom. To Emperor Francis he simply announced the change of government. To King George he proposed the start of peace negotiations without mentioning Italy. His letter to the king of Spain, on the other hand, pressed that unhappy monarch to mobilize to defend himself against British depredations.*

Napoleon's notes to the king of Naples and Alexander are more interesting, however. To the former he simply stated that French troops were in Naples purely "because the affairs of the Levant are not finished," and that they would be withdrawn "when Malta is evacuated by England and Corfu by Russia." To Alexander he wrote, first, that he intended to make one of his relatives king of Italy and, second, that he "would accede with all my heart" to the "project that I am assured Your Majesty has of procuring Corfu and Malta for the King of Sardinia." He included in this last letter copies of his notes to the kings of England and Naples.[21] Napoleon strengthened his emphasis on Malta in his proclamation of March 17 declaring himself king of Italy, in which he stated that he would pass the crown to one of his "legitimate male children" when Naples, Corfu, and Malta were evacuated.[22]

The purpose of this barrage of royal correspondence was to obfuscate the creation of the kingdom of Italy. It did not really succeed in that goal, but it succeeded indirectly in sowing serious discord between Alexander and Pitt—almost certainly part of Napoleon's plan. The British decided that ignoring Napoleon's peace overture was not possible, and the cabinet drafted a response with the purpose of maintaining the British people's support for the war.[23] Czartoryskii also believed that a response to Napoleon's notes was essential, although his audience was different—he wanted to use the opportunity to advance the cause of winning Prussia and Austria to the coalition.† It became necessary for both sides to decide what terms to offer Napoleon, in addition to what sacrifices to demand of him.

---

*The most notorious was the seizure and partial destruction of a small Spanish treasure fleet bound from the New World by the Royal Navy in October 1804. See W. M. James, *The Naval History of Great Britain During the French Revolutionary and Napoleonic Wars* (Mechanicsburg, Pa.: Stackpole, 2002), 3:280–283.

†Czartoryskii to Novosil'tsev, 16 February 1805, VPR, vol. II, doc. 103. The ideas Czartoryskii developed were independent of those laid out by Pitt, whose memoranda were not received in St. Petersburg until 27 February and were presented to Czartoryskii on 2 March (Leveson Gower to Mulgrave, 6 March 1805, in Holland Rose, *Select Despatches*, doc. 65).

The British government determined to make no approach to Napoleon except in tandem with Russia. Pitt felt it essential, furthermore, to come to agreement with Alexander about the basis for the Anglo–Russian alliance before proposing peace terms to Napoleon. Subsequently Pitt sent three lengthy documents to St. Petersburg. One proposed a draft alliance treaty, one proposed the basis of a reply to Napoleon's peace offer, and the third explained Pitt's view of the alliance's ultimate goals.[24]

All three strengthened the Russian belief that the British government wholeheartedly shared their "principles" and "system." In his general review of the aims of the alliance, Pitt accepted the three objectives Novosil'tsev had suggested: rescuing the states "subjugated" by France, creating strong neighbors on the French frontier that could withstand future attempts at expansion, and establishing a general peace treaty that would define and uphold the new order. He even agreed that Britain and Russia should commit themselves jointly to guarantee this treaty.[25] The demands Pitt wanted to make of Napoleon in return for peace were also unremarkable: restoring the king of Sardinia's former possessions (presumably including Piedmont); evacuating Naples, Hanover, Switzerland, and the Netherlands and guaranteeing their future independence and security; and reestablishing German fortresses on the Rhine.[26] Although Pitt did not detail what Britain might be prepared to give up in order to secure this peace, he noted that Britain "would be readily disposed to make any sacrifice for the attainment of that desirable object, which might be compatible with its solid and permanent existence."

The only really jarring notes in these documents, from the Russian perspective, were Pitt's efforts to gain Austrian and Prussian adherence to the nascent coalition through bribes. Since Britain's primary strategic concerns in Europe centered on Belgium and the Netherlands, Pitt's determination to lure Prussia into the alliance on almost any terms was perfectly understandable. He was prepared to offer Frederick William a great deal of territory on the Rhine, in the Netherlands, even to the Baltic coast if necessary. In order to offset the jealousy such Prussian gains would inflame in Vienna, as well as to induce Austria to join the coalition, he also proposed substantial gains for the Habsburgs in Italy, including the restoration of Tuscany to the Habsburg grand duke who had formerly held it.

Clearly Pitt did not expect peace to come from the allies' offer to France. He was concerned primarily to satisfy the British populace of the justness of the war, although he also seized on the opportunity to move closer to Russia.[27] It is not clear if Czartoryskii and Alexander were as realistic about prospects for peace, but they were certainly determined to make their offer appear genuine. To this end, Czartoryskii was determined to induce Pitt to offer to abandon Malta. He instructed Novosil'tsev, accordingly, to find out definitively if Britain "absolutely wanted to keep Malta."[28]

The issue was not simply the desirability of looking good on the European stage, although that was important: "It is indispensable that at least at the start [Britain] consent to having the mediators propose to return Malta to the Order of St. John with the necessary guarantees that it would not ever fall back into the power of the French." Czartoryskii continued,

> The Treaty of Amiens decided the question, and to keep the appearance of impartiality it is necessary to hold to that; this would be an honorable proof of moderation on the part of England; besides, this would not be too much to pay for the total evacuation of the French from Italy and all the other conditions that one would impose on them. The Emperor desires that even at the true peace Malta be restored to the order.[29]

He concluded overoptimistically by noting that he did not believe that the British government would raise much of a fuss over the issue.

The posturing before Europe was important. Pitt had effectively subcontracted the negotiations for an alliance with Austria and Prussia to St. Petersburg, and the Russians found themselves in a difficult spot. Britain was determined to drive the whole continent into an offensive war at the first moment, Prussia adamantly opposed such a war, and Austria was continually wavering on the issue. Czartoryskii and Alexander believed that if the British were "obstinate" over the issue of Malta, it would sabotage the efforts made in their own interests.

There was more than realpolitik here, however. Alexander believed that the British had a moral obligation to give up Malta. They had consented to abandon the island in 1802, and he believed that any future peace should take the Treaties of Amiens and Lunéville as a point of departure. The British argument that French violations had voided the former and relieved Britain of the obligation to abandon Malta apparently held little weight with him. The Malta issue turned out to be for Alexander a test of Britain's bona fides and goodwill—a test Pitt failed spectacularly.

The request for Britain to evacuate Malta was not intended as part of the test Alexander originally set for Pitt, however. The tsar was concerned at first that the British might not share his general view of the world; when he discovered that they did, he and Czartoryskii believed that no obstacles remained to agreement. It apparently did not occur to Czartoryskii or Alexander that the British would refuse to abandon Malta. At first this issue was a minor point to be settled on the road to bigger things. It became important only because of the specific way in which negotiations and world events developed.

Secure in the misperception that all was well, however, the obvious next step was to negotiate a final treaty. Czartoryskii decided to conduct the negotiations in St. Petersburg rather than London because he did not trust Simon

Vorontsov to pursue Russia's interests at the expense of Britain's. He also feared that the British government would leak details of the negotiations to the public and the international world, either intentionally or through incompetence. The treaty was therefore hammered out between Granville Leveson Gower, who had replaced Warren as ambassador, and Czartoryskii.

Czartoryskii did not receive Pitt's initial proposed treaty warmly.[30] He was dissatisfied with the amount, distribution, and timing of the proposed subsidies, but even more with the large indemnifications offered to Austria and Prussia. Relating to the proposals for enlarging Prussia, he warned Leveson Gower that "the Court of St. Petersburgh could not so entirely lose sight of the interests of Russia, as to contribute to, or consent to any very great augmentation of the power and resources of a neighbouring state, already powerful from the largeness of its military establishment."[31] Concerning the proposed expansion of Austria's lands in Italy, Czartoryskii noted that he could not "see the advantage of gratuitously thus aggrandizing the possessions of another powerful neighbour upon the Russian frontier [!], [and] that it was not to be expected that his Imperial Majesty should exhaust his own resources in rendering over-powerful the only two great States whose frontiers were in contact with his own empire." Leveson Gower unsuccessfully urged the importance of offering sufficient bribes to Austria and Prussia to bring them into the coalition while also creating in those states powerful buffers to prevent future French aggressions.[32]

This disagreement highlights the transformative effect of the partitions of Poland. Just as Austria, having been made neighbor to Prussia and Russia, felt increased pressure from the east, so Russia increasingly felt the relative strength of her two neighbors to the west, a matter that in previous decades had been viewed with greater equanimity.* But it also highlights a fundamental disagreement about the nature of the postwar world as seen in London and St. Petersburg.

Alexander wanted to create a series of relatively powerful middle states and confederations of smaller states that would check French aggression and serve as a buffer between France and the other great powers. He believed that the system of international law, guaranteed jointly by Russia and Britain, would secure those middle states against possible French depredations. He implicitly placed no reliance on Austria and Prussia because he mistrusted them—he feared that they would continue to act in their own interests either as predators or passive observers.

---

*Frederick the Great's campaigns roused Tsaritsa Elizabeth to opposition and drove her to seek his destruction. Catherine the Great, on the other hand, found nothing to fear in adding enormous territories to both Prussia and Austria not only during the Polish partitions but also, in the case of Austria, during the wars against Turkey. Although Russia was amply compensated, Czartoryskii's complaint to Leveson Gower here is not that Russia would not be compensated, but simply that Austria and Prussia would gain strength.

Pitt, on the other hand, was engaged in traditional realpolitik. He felt that a strengthened Austria and Prussia would be willing to stand up to a reviving or aggressive France, and that their opposition would be the best defense. Although he also supported the idea of buffer states, he clearly imagined that they would be effective only with the support of their immediate Germanic neighbors. Despite his principled endorsement of a Russo–British guarantee of the new system, he did not share Alexander's utopian notions about the likely effectiveness of such an arrangement. Consequently he sought to develop power centers independent of Britain and Russia that would serve as bulwarks against France. These views were incompatible because of Russian attitudes toward continental power, which played a small role in creating friction between Russia and Britain in 1805. Its longer-term consequences, however, especially following the peace of 1815, were much more dramatic.

The negotiations began in St. Petersburg at the end of March with a relatively informal discussion between Czartoryskii and Leveson Gower.[33] Czartoryskii asked, among other things, if Britain would offer Napoleon part of France's former possessions in India. This would "afford [Napoleon] at least the semblance of treating, upon a footing of equality" in return for the sacrifices being demanded of him. Leveson Gower replied that such an offer was out of the question, "that it was not to be expected that we should pay, by the cession of any part of our own territory, for the deliverance of those countries which had been acquired not only in defiance of the laws of nations, but in direct violation of positive stipulations." The most that Britain would be prepared to offer, Leveson Gower added, was the restoration of conquests Britain had made since 1803. The meeting nevertheless ended on a positive note, and Leveson Gower concluded in his report to London, "From the assurances I now receive, I have reason to hope that no insurmountable difficulty will occur in the conclusion of a treaty founded upon the basis of your lordship's *projet*. The Russian cabinet adopt entirely the principles of that *projet*, and the modifications regard, I am assured, points of detail, to which there can be no objection to accede."

A draft treaty was prepared swiftly—sixteen days later Leveson Gower had signed it and sent it to London for ratification.[34] He was concerned, however, for he had been obliged to insert an article about Malta. This subject had come up abruptly; no mention was made of Malta in the March 22 meeting. Leveson Gower reported fighting tenaciously to exclude it altogether, as he had with great difficulty succeeded in excluding an article concerning changes in the maritime law. He added, however, that the tsar was "determined not to conclude a treaty of offensive operation against France, if I refused to agree to the proposition of" terms relating to Malta and a number of other more minor stipulations. Until the last moment Czartoryskii had insisted on including the clauses on both Malta and the Maritime Code as conditions sine qua non, and had threatened to break off the negotiations if Leveson Gower proved obstinate. But the Englishman finally prevailed:

> Both these propositions have (notwithstanding repeated threats of breaking up the negotiation) been given up, the former [concerning the Maritime Code] by totally expunging the article, the second [on Malta] by the addition of a restriction, which in fact renders the provision itself quite null, for it is left perfectly open to His Majesty's ministers to assent or to refuse such authority being given to M[r]. Novosilzow, according as in their judgment they shall think fit.

He was right; the restrictions on the article concerning Malta left so much discretion in Britain's hands as to make the article nearly meaningless.

Czartoryskii and the tsar were disappointed in this outcome. They desired to make the peace offer to Napoleon as tempting as possible (which was the main reason for inserting the article concerning Malta) and wanted to place the allies, especially Britain, on the highest possible moral ground. Czartoryskii did not believe that Leveson Gower's opposition to the article concerning Malta actually reflected the view of the government in London, and he instructed Simon Vorontsov to attempt to get the restrictions removed when he submitted the treaty for ratification.[35]

Czartoryskii explained to Simon that the negotiations were undermining Alexander's faith in Pitt. "It is the persuasion that England wanted only what is just and moderate," he wrote, "that has led the Emperor to act. It is to this idea that he returns and he analyzes it continually." If the British "refused to sacrifice Malta for peace, the Emperor will not ratify the convention." Although Leveson Gower had negotiated very skillfully ("one would not want to have to negotiate with him frequently"), Czartoryskii added, he had antagonized the tsar over the question of Malta, and it would be best if he were recalled and replaced, despite his qualities.

Alexander was shocked at the idea that Britain might actually demand to keep Malta, and he wrote to Simon Vorontsov that "I would have broken off all further discussion myself if I had been able to believe that the English government shared in this regard the sentiments of its ambassador." Furthermore, "I had the restriction [to the article on Malta] signed, but in the expectation that it would not have any significance and that H[is] Britannic M[ajesty] would hasten to inform me and my plenipotentiary that he would adhere to the article as it was originally conceived."[36] He went on to explain his feelings in some detail:

> It is not that I attach, for my part, the least importance to whether or not Malta remains in the hands of the English; quite the contrary, Russia

would find its commercial and political interest in letting it stay there, and I would very much like not to have the extravagant and onerous expense of being the guardian of that rock; but Malta was considered the cause of the current war: England, nevertheless, never declared that she wanted to keep that island after having once ceded it. She has constantly declared that she wanted uniquely to have sufficient guarantees that Malta would not fall into the power of the French; as for guarantees I propose the best ones possible, and if I found some other mode of procuring them, I would hastily adopt it. It was absolutely necessary to have recourse to an expedient of this type: the English government cannot at this moment, without an obvious contradiction, assert the sincere desire for peace and declare at the same time that it wants to keep Malta at any price, because it is clear in advance that this condition will render the peace from this moment on absolutely impossible; opinion about that is unanimous throughout Europe and is founded on arguments too obvious for me to have to enumerate them. The demarche that we wish to make to Bonaparte has as its goal proving to all of Europe that there is no way to make peace with him. Only this conviction will make Austria act and will procure for us, possibly, the cooperation of Prussia. But what will these powers believe if, in charging me with such a negotiation, I did not anticipate the impossibility of making peace in wanting to maintain Malta in its present state? I would find myself compromised before them, before all of Europe, and, what is more, I would lose the hope of directing their policy and their action . . . In place of proving that we sincerely wanted peace, our propositions would demonstrate the contrary; in place of gaining opinion for our side, we would render it opposed. One would be able to reproach me with reason for discarding myself the principles of moderation and justice that I have proclaimed, and I am determined not to merit this reproach.[37]

How should we interpret this emotional outburst? Part of it was sincere. Although there is no evidence that Prussia or Austria cared whether or not Britain kept Malta in determining whether to adhere to the coalition, Alexander may have believed that they did. The British determination to keep Malta, however justified in strategic logic, did nothing to convince continental powers of British disinterestedness. The arguments that a turnaround on Malta at that point would humiliate Alexander were probably closer to the truth. Even though the negotiations were secret and he had made no public pronouncement about Malta, the fact that he had made plans based on offering Malta to Napoleon was galling and embarrassing. There is more to the matter than that, however.

Czartoryskii had been subjected to enmity and criticism within St. Petersburg court circles since his elevation to vice chancellor. The fact that he was a

Pole alienated some; others disliked his grandiose, aggressive, and anti-French policies. As Alexander moved increasingly toward conflict with Napoleon, ably and enthusiastically supported by Czartoryskii, a small conspiracy arose that aimed to remove the latter from office and prevent war. The conspirators included A. I. Morkov, the Francophobe former ambassador to France, and Prince Panin, among others.[38]

The conspirators had chosen their time well. Czartoryskii's principal allies (both for keeping himself in power and supporting his program of war with France) were state chancellor Alexander Vorontsov and Novosil'tsev, along with a few other members of the "unofficial committee." Vorontsov's retirement to Moscow in 1804 was a political blow to Czartoryskii even as it elevated him to de facto control of Russia's foreign policy. Novosil'tsev's mission to London in late 1804 and early 1805 was nearly a disaster, since it removed one of Prince Adam's main allies from the capital at a critical time. The conspiracy worked hard to turn Alexander against Czartoryskii but not succeed, and against the idea of war with France, which it nearly did.

Unimpressed by the attacks on his de facto foreign minister, Alexander worked to break up the conspiracy by permanently banishing Panin from St. Petersburg and ordering Morkov to leave the city temporarily. He also made Czartoryskii a senator and a full member of the State Council.[39] But support for Czartoryskii was not necessarily support for his policies, and Prince Adam and his allies soon came to fear that Alexander's commitment, even willingness, to go to war with Napoleon was evaporating.

Czartoryskii had tried in February to convince Alexander to send Novosil'tsev to Paris with an offer of mediation between Britain and France that would also serve as an ultimatum.[40] He was surprised to find the emperor hostile to the idea. "I cannot unravel his motives" in opposing the concept, he wrote the following day. He had tried to phrase the idea in a way suited to gain Alexander's favor but feared that Alexander was resisting making a final decision. Czartoryskii continued grimly, "The idea of a war oppresses and torments him." He then added that Novosil'tsev's absence had "greatly weakened the good party, and the gossips have gained traction with the Emperor."[41]

When Novosil'tsev returned to St. Petersburg, he found that Prince Adam had not been exaggerating. He wrote to Simon Vorontsov that the ambassador's fears about the success of the hostile cabal were "not without foundations." He continued, "All those who have been in Paris seem to have been ensorcelled by Bonaparte; they speak only of his great military talents, of the formidable force of which he disposes and of the danger that one runs in fighting him." He concluded, though, that "however much the Emperor exaggerates . . . the dangers that Europe will have to run in a war with France . . . he is nevertheless well-disposed and one might say resigned to act with all of the firmness that the present circumstances demand, *as long as he is well persuaded that the cause that he is embracing is just in all respects."*[42] Leveson Gower's resistance to the articles on Malta and the Maritime Code, Novosil'tsev added dolefully, did nothing to strengthen the tsar's confidence in the virtue of the cause.

The situation was still manageable at that point. Alexander was willing to settle, albeit reluctantly, for a British offer to return Malta only to be used as a propaganda tool in bargaining with Napoleon, and even then he would probably have accepted conditions on the use of that tool. Since no one really imagined that Napoleon would agree to the terms being offered him, even if they included Malta, the Russians could not understand why the British should make such heavy weather over the issue. No one was really asking them to give Malta up, and even discussions about their final cession of the island always presupposed guarantees for its security and even utility. Alexander was beside himself with rage when he learned in June that Pitt not only refused to drop the restrictions on the Malta article that Leveson Gower had insisted on but also refused to ratify the treaty unless the Malta article was removed altogether.

Czartoryskii compared these events to being splashed with cold water, and he wrote to Simon Vorontsov that he had even toyed with the idea of trying to keep the news from the tsar for a while.[43] His fears of Alexander's reaction were well founded. The tsar was furious: "I have never seen our Master more discontent and more beside himself," he wrote. "Although by nature calm, this time he showed such a fit of anger that I feared that we would take some precipitate resolution that would be more the fruit of a moment of resentment than of reasonable reflection. Nothing," he noted, "wounds more than an injustice." Not only were the British compromising Alexander and themselves before Europe, but they had no idea of the difficulties in which the tsar found himself. An Austrian note refusing to accede to an offensive alliance had been received at nearly the same time as Vorontsov's note from London, and so the tsar found himself criticized by the British for being too "soft on France" and at the same time by the Austrians for being a warmonger. For a moment he seems to have toyed with the idea of simply throwing up his hands and abandoning Europe to her fate.[44]

Alexander's anger at Britain was also fueled by his weakened resolve to go to war. Two days after writing to Simon Vorontsov, Czartoryskii warned his elder brother, "The Emperor himself is not at all decided nor inclined toward war; from a good motive no doubt, since it would spill the blood of his subjects. Only the belief that everything has been done to avoid it might make him take that decision."[45] And here was Britain holding out on an issue that Alexander and Czartoryskii believed, again with no apparent evidence, meant a great deal to European opinion.

There are a number of reasons why Alexander may have begun to waver on the desirability of war in mid-1805, apart from the anti-Czartoryskii cabal. He seems to have felt a revulsion against Pitt and Britain for what he perceived to be excessive self-interestedness and desire for aggrandizement. He had long been disgusted with Austria for her pusillanimity, and even more so with Berlin. It must have been very difficult for him to be excited about the prospect of going to war with such allies and, from his perspective, on behalf of them.

Was he also scared? As time went by, preparations for conflict continued. War became ever more likely and ever more real. Alexander was a young twenty-seven. Unlike the other continental rulers, he had never seen combat. Frederick William had participated in the campaigns against revolutionary France, and Francis saw action in the Turkish War. Now Alexander was thinking about pitting his army against a man whom some of his own ministers and advisers assured him was the greatest military genius of the time.

His fear may have been reinforced by confused ideology. His early years had alternated between the enlightened court of Catherine the Great (as distinct from the tough realpolitik of her cabinet, from which he had been excluded) and the martinettism of his father's palace at Gatchina. He was confused by that experience and left somewhat divided in his mind about what was right. He made numerous statements before assuming the throne about his unfitness to rule. He had probably never felt more unfit than in the testing and turbulent days of mid-1805 as he prepared to lead the world into a war against the man whom Clausewitz would later dub "the god of war."

If Alexander's vacillation and angry outbursts are explicable in part by this small detour into the realm of psychohistory, Pitt's position is harder to explain. Why would he risk the collapse of a coalition that offered Britain hope of continental allies against France simply to avoid offering Malta to Napoleon in a document drafted purely for political propaganda purposes? Whatever the strategic importance of the island to Britain, the article that Leveson Gower accepted bound Britain to nothing whatsoever. Even in the worst-case, it gave Britain every legal right to refuse to surrender the island even in the unlikely event that Napoleon accepted the offer. At the very least, to accept Leveson Gower's article would have put off the disagreement, probably until after the war had begun. Why did Pitt dig in his heels?

Part of the answer can be put simply: "The news of the Anglo–Russian agreement reached London on 9 May. By that time Pitt was in serious, and worsening, political trouble."[46] The period between April 8 and July 2, 1805, marked the height of opposition attacks on Pitt's ministry. The first strikes were directed against First Lord of the Admiralty, Lord Melville, for peculations he and his subordinates had committed during the previous Pitt administration. Although Pitt struggled valiantly to defend the man who was at that time overseeing the ongoing naval campaign against Napoleon, he failed. Melville was forced to resign his post and end his career as a public servant, although he was subsequently acquitted of the charges brought against him.

Shortly thereafter, Pitt came under attack. On May 23 an opposition member brought forward a bill charging the prime minister with financial improprieties during the first years of the revolutionary wars. Pitt managed to beat off this attack, accepting a mild censure from the House of Commons on July 2.[47]

This crisis harmed Pitt and delayed his response to Russian overtures and concerns. Melville had to be replaced immediately in order to ensure continuous control and direction over the naval war against France. The struggle over Melville's replacement led to another cabinet loss. Addington, now a peer as Lord Sidmouth, had been persuaded earlier in the year to rejoin the government in order to weaken the opposition and strengthen Pitt's hand. Angered over a variety of issues relating to the assignment of posts and his own treatment, however, Sidmouth resigned again on July 4.[48] These crises and intrigues reduced Pitt's effective control over Parliament and tarnished his image; it is even claimed that his health was harmed.

> In May 1804 Pitt had returned with widespread expectation to the place which was his, it seemed, almost by right. Since then his command of the Commons, still potent, had been shaken at important points; his opening Cabinet had failed to settle down; and its enforced reshapement, to accommodate safer Parliamentary majorities, produced an outcome worse in some respects perhaps than if the experiment had never been made.[49]

These difficulties probably help explain Pitt's intransigence over Malta. Agreeing to give up Malta would have caused him to be attacked in Commons.* The note Pitt sent to Voronstov explaining his reasons for failing to ratify the convention stressed this, as well as the strategic desirability of Britain's retaining the island. It would be impossible, he wrote, "to reconcile the opinion either of the Parliament or of the people of this country to such a concession under such circumstances," the more so in that Malta was "an important British station in the Mediterranean, the most popular and prominent object, as well as, in some degree, the point of honour of the war."[50] Pitt could ill afford an apparent diplomatic defeat at that time.

That fact, however, cut both ways. Although it drove Pitt to try his best to force the Russians to remove the issue of Malta from the table, it would not in the end have driven him to abandon the treaty despite his threats.† The

---

*Simon Vorontsov had no doubt about the strength of support throughout the government for the retention of Malta, as he explained in a furious letter to Czartoryskii on receiving the latter's query about Britain's willingness to give up the island. Voronstov to Czatroyski, 18 May 1805, AKV, vol. 15, pp. 303ff.

†Paul Schroeder overstates the argument that only Napoleon's seizure of Genoa saved the Anglo–Russian alliance from an otherwise inevitable collapse.

erosion of Pitt's control over Parliament made the conclusion of the Anglo-Russian treaty essential even if it became clear that "in the last resort Malta would have to be abandoned for the sake of a general agreement." For "a diplomatic success was highly desirable with which to face Parliament as soon as possible, or at the least after the summer recess." If, as it was becoming increasingly clear in June, Sidmouth might bolt from the ministry, then a new approach to the opposition would have to be made. "In such an attempt a new European Coalition could provide an important inducement."[51] Thus there is little likelihood that Pitt would have refused to ratify the treaty simply over the question of Malta.

Nor is it likely that Alexander would have scuttled the alliance over that rock. By June 1805, things had gone too far for Alexander to pull back. He had broken off diplomatic relations with France, and Napoleon now saw Russia as his enemy. The tsar had signed a defensive treaty with Austria in which he promised to use his "best offices" to secure for Vienna subsidies from London. He was ensnared not only in diplomatic efforts to bring the Austrian court to support an offensive war, but also in negotiations over the precise military plan to be followed; and the Austrians had already begun to mobilize their army and move their forces toward the frontier. Alexander had already mobilized more than 100,000 Russians and was keeping them on his borders. But he could not proceed to war without Great Britain. He could not abandon the project without enduring total humiliation that would have annihilated his influence on the European scene. In the end, the dispute over Malta could never have been more than a bump in the road leading to the formation of the Third Coalition.

It was an important bump, nevertheless. It highlighted real disagreements between Britain and Russia even if they materialized over less important issues. Alexander was driven in 1805 by a weird combination of idealism and realpolitik, both equally important to him. His loss of confidence in Pitt and Britain weakened the nascent coalition in important ways and set the conditions for further weakening down the road. It kept alive the sense of mistrust and suspicion that had dogged Anglo–Russian relations in the War of the Second Coalition. It was in every way harmful to the cause of those who wanted to oppose Napoleon.

The entire debate over Malta was rendered irrelevant in early July, when the news arrived in St. Petersburg that Napoleon had annexed Genoa and the Ligurian Republic to France in the process of reorganizing and consolidating his hold on northern Italy. The relative insignificance of the Malta dispute became immediately apparent as Alexander dropped his insistence on the article and recalled Novosil'tsev, who had made it as far as Berlin on his mission to deliver the controversial peace offer cum ultimatum to Napoleon. Napoleon had not saved the Anglo–Russian treaty negotiations from failure because neither side could have allowed them to fail. He did, however, provide Alexander with the easiest possible face-saving escape from an embarrassing position, and the tsar leaped on the opportunity. Final ratification of the alliance treaty was exchanged on July 28. The Third Coalition had finally begun to take shape.

7

The Road to War

The Anglo–Russian treaty laid the foundations for the Third Coalition, but the decision for war came from Vienna. Whatever threats Napoleon might make, whatever inducements the British and the Russians might offer, only Austria or Prussia could make war possible. Frederick William had already refused to do so and he stuck by that decision despite Alexander's threats even after the war had begun. Francis, however, chose the road of war. This decision was the inevitable denouement of Austria's predicament—forced to choose between war and the loss of the Russian alliance, Francis's decision was never in doubt. He might have delayed making it for much longer, however, but for Napoleon's final provocations.

The complexity of decisionmaking processes in Europe varied dramatically in the early eighteenth century. The simplest structure was in France, where Napoleon's will was law as absolutely as that of any European monarch since Louis XIV. In Russia, although Alexander's will was also law, policy was made through an interaction between the tsar and his principal advisers, especially the ministers of foreign affairs, Alexander Vorontsov and then Adam Czartoryskii. In Frederick William's Prussia that process was more complex still, as rival factions surrounding Foreign Minister Haugwitz and his rival, Hardenberg, also competed with cabinet secretaries such as Johann Wilhelm Lombard for access to the king and influence on his policies.[1] But Austria's was the most complex of all.*

---

*Historians have been inclined to mitigate this complexity by viewing the events of this period primarily through the eyes of one or another of the participants. By far the most common perspective is that of Archduke Charles (see Gunther Rothenberg, *Napoleon's Great Adversary: Archduke Charles and the Austrian Army, 1792–1814* [New York: Sarpedon, 1982] and Oskar Criste, *Erzherzog Carl von Oesterreich: Ein Lebensbild im auftrage seiner Enkel, der Herren Erzherzoge Friedrich und Eugen* [Vienna: Wilhelm Braumüller, 1912], 2:261ff). From this perspective, Charles fought against a "war party" led by Ludwig Cobenzl that unseated his advisers through intrigues and then drove him effectively from power. This view was shared by some contemporaries as well (see Sir A. Paget to Lord Mulgrave, 19 March 1805, in Augustus B. Paget, ed., *The Paget Papers: Diplomatic and Other Correspondence of the*

Emperor Francis was no cipher. The critical decisions about war and peace, changes in personnel and organization, foreign policy and finance, were all his to make absolutely. The first complexity arose, however, from the presence and stature of Archduke Charles, Francis's younger brother. Charles established a name for himself as the only Austrian general to defeat the French revolutionary armies or even avoid being humiliated by them. In the years to come, he would establish himself as a serious military thinker. Francis, who was no general, could not match these accomplishments. He put Charles in charge of reorganizing the Austrian army after the War of the Second Coalition (and after the War of the Third Coalition as well), investing him with nearly supreme powers over the armed forces—for a time.

The trouble was that Francis was also suspicious and perhaps jealous of Charles. He seemed to fear being upstaged by his popular, successful younger brother. Francis's mistrust of his brother, which had no foundation in Charles's intentions and actions, weakened the latter's position greatly and offered opportunities to his enemies. But Charles's success made it difficult for Francis to fire him or even circumvent him. Through the campaign of 1809, Charles was thought to be irreplaceable, and Francis had to work with him whether he liked his policies or not.

The next complexity arose from the structure of government and the way Francis ran it. Although vice chancellor Ludwig Cobenzl effectively directed Austria's foreign policy, his relationship with Francis was unclear. His close friendship with Franz Colloredo, the Kabinettsminister and Francis's former tutor, played an important role. But uncharacteristically for European monarchs at this time, Francis continued to employ and rely on Cobenzl even when he did not like the advice he was getting, and Cobenzl succeeded in the unusual feat of convincing the emperor to pursue a path he had initially despised. This arrangement created a situation in which Austria's emperor, prime minister, and military director were all working at

---

Right Hon. Sir Arthur Paget, G.C.B., 1794–1807 [New York: Longmans, Green, 1896], pp. 163–168). Paget, the British ambassador in Vienna, regarded Cobenzl and the supposed "war-party" with contempt as well, an emotion he directed at almost all the Austrian ministers or officials he encountered. Fournier presents a more complex view, recognizing that Ludwig Cobenzl was the target of the war party that had formed around Friedrich Gentz, until he turned around in late 1804 and began to struggle openly with Charles (August Fournier, *Gentz und Cobenzl: Geschichte der österreichischen Diplomatie in den Jahren 1801–1805, nach neuen Quellen* [Vienna: Wilhelm Braumüller, 1880]). In the first view, Francis is a largely antipathetic figure whose mistrust of Charles and favor for the incompetent war party leads to disaster. In the second view, Francis is largely lost from sight in the focus on the high politics among the various parties. Fournier comes closest to presenting a balanced picture, but his focus on Cobenzl is subtly distorting. Amazingly, there is no substantial modern biography of Francis, and the only detailed biographies that cover the period of his emperorship were written immediately after his death and are brief and exculpatory. See *Kaiser Francis I*, 1846; B. Puchler, *Francis I*, 1841; Cölestin Wolfsgruber, *Franz I: Kaiser von Oesterreich* (Vienna: Wilhelm Braumüller, 1899); Walter Consuelo Langsam, *Francis the Good: The Education of an Emperor, 1768–1792* (New York: Macmillan, 1949).

cross-purposes—one reason why would-be allies found Austria confusing and frustrating to work with.

Austria's road to war had three major turning points. First, Cobenzl became convinced that Austria might have to go to war, even take the offensive, to protect herself against further Napoleonic depredations in crucial areas. That bridge was crossed when Cobenzl learned of Napoleon's intention to make himself king of Italy in the autumn of 1804. Cobenzl's change of heart on the question of war put him at odds with Archduke Charles, who was unwilling to consider going to war against France under any circumstances. Because preparations and plans for war had to be undertaken by someone who earnestly believed in them if there was to be any prospect of an alliance with Russia, let alone success in a future war, Cobenzl could go no farther as long as Charles retained control of the Austrian military. The second turning point came, then, when Cobenzl succeeded in an intrigue that deprived Charles of that control in the spring of 1805. Even when Francis clipped his brother's wings and Cobenzl installed the hawkish Baron Karl von Mack and the pliant Count Maximillian Baillet de Latour as head of the military, however, Francis's objections to war remained an insuperable obstacle. The third and final turning point came in early July 1805, when Cobenzl finally convinced Francis that he must go to war.

It is easy to see the causes of an inevitable Austrian reaction in Napoleon's aggression in Italy in the spring and summer of 1805, or see in Austria's supposed lust for conquest a greed that had driven her policies for years. Both approaches stumble on a paradox, however: Napoleon's depredations of March–June 1805 occurred too late to have *caused* Austria's participation in the war, since efforts to improve the strength and position of the Austrian army, including expensive drafts and movements of troops, had been under way since the end of 1804—which was also the time of the first Austro–Russian alliance. But Austria's supposed greed for territorial gain is also inadequate as an explanation, because as late as June 1805 Francis was unwilling to join a new offensive coalition against Napoleon. The complexity of Austrian policy also caused important problems for the nascent coalition, especially by convincing Alexander of Vienna's hopeless timidity and the British of Austria's incompetence and rapacity. For all of these reasons, we must delay the consideration of battle plans and battles in order to consider how it happened that Austria opted for war.

The Fall of Archduke Charles

Archduke Charles was not timid by nature. In one of his early works of military theory he laid down a principle Napoleon could have loved: "Above all one must make it a rule in this war . . . always to be on the enemy's neck whenever possible, always to follow his footsteps, to attack him whenever one can with advantage, especially if he is found, even with only part of his army, in open terrain."[2] Yet by 1804 he was digging in his heels against any notion of going to war with France, and the following year he conducted a campaign marked by desultory maneuvering, slowness, and a determination to avoid battle. His military writings also changed, becoming more conservative, battle averse, and geometrical.[3] Why did Charles change his mind?

Part of the answer lies in his royalty. It was all very well for the famous military theorists of the time—Bülow, Lloyd, Jomini, even Clausewitz—to theorize about offensive or defensive actions, lines of maneuver, the wisdom or unwisdom of seeking battle, and so forth. But Charles, alone among them, had commanded a large army in the field, as very few military theorists have ever done, and had been responsible for the entire military establishment of his country. He led the reorganization of the Habsburg government in the first years of the nineteenth century and participated in discussions relating to Austria's internal and external policies. As the emperor's brother, moreover, Charles felt an obligation to consider the well-being of the monarchy from all perspectives, not simply that of the military administration that he happened to head. As a result, Charles integrated an understanding of Austria's finances and internal organization into his notions about fighting. He came to the conclusion that Austria could not afford battles. This conviction was strong in 1804 and 1805 because of the parlous state of Austria's finances, still suffering from the last unsuccessful war.

Charles's experience as a commander in the last war also influenced his thought. Although he fared well, defeating the French more often than they defeated him, he watched as Napoleon's successes in other theaters undid whatever advantages his own victories obtained. He also participated in the event that triggered the political collapse of the Second Coalition. His premature withdrawal from Switzerland led to the defeat of Suvorov's army there, which led in turn to Tsar Paul's angry decision to pull out of the war altogether. From this event Charles acquired a fixed belief in Russia's perfidy that subsequent events did nothing to shake.

In his role as head of the combined military administration, moreover, Charles had presided over the reduction in the combat power of the Austrian army in an attempt to save badly needed money. Soldiers were put on semipermanent leave, horses were not purchased or replaced, supplies were not maintained, weapons were not readied. At the end of April 1805 the Habsburg army was nearly 160,000 troops below its authorized strength of 367,000.[4] Quartermaster General Duka estimated that it would take six months to put the army on anything like a war footing.[5] Charles's pessimism in this circumstance was quite understandable.

It led him, however, into the realm of complete political unreality. He came to believe that Austria's interests were best served exclusively by forming an alliance with France, and he would not relinquish that belief, no matter what happened. He argued that, whereas Russia and Austria had interests in conflict in the Balkans and with regard to the Ottoman Empire, a Franco–Austrian alliance would secure the interests of both powers and ensure the tranquillity of Europe. He implicitly recognized that this would only be true if Napoleon behaved rationally (according to Charles's notions of rationality, at any event), and he does not seem to have noticed the evidence that Napoleon did not see the world from that perspective at all.[6] When Napoleon declared himself Emperor of the French, Charles repeated the naïve argument that Austria could have no real interest in what the leader of France chose to call himself.[7]

This steady opposition to the alliance with Russia (of which Charles was not informed until after it had been signed) convinced Cobenzl that the Archduke must be removed as an effective obstacle to his plans. Among other things, the Austro–Russian treaty called both for a significant Austrian rearmament and the negotiation of contingency warplans—for neither of which activities was Charles an appropriate leader. Cobenzl frankly shuddered at the thought of having to send the Russians memoranda on Austria's military status drafted by Charles or his advisers—it would have been the end of the alliance! Cobenzl was quite right: in mid-January 1805 Charles objected to a dispatch sent to Count Stadion in which the movement of Austrian troops into her western provinces was held up as proof of Austria's adherence to the commitments of the Austro–Russian treaty on the grounds that it might give the Russians the wrong idea—they might think Austria would actually be ready for war one day.[8]

Cobenzl, accordingly, launched a three-pronged attack. He worked to convince the emperor that he must remove Charles from control of the entire military administration. He worked to suborn and then to dismiss Mathias von Fassbender, Charles's principal civilian adviser. He began maneuvering to have Mack replace Duka as quartermaster general. Within four months he had achieved all three objectives.

Cobenzl found it relatively easy to convince Francis to strip Charles of control. The emperor was always suspicious of his famous and successful brother, and Charles was not the most astute family politician. But Francis found an even more obvious and, in principle, objective argument for reducing Charles's power. If, he noted, war began despite his best efforts to avoid it, Charles and Archduke John (who had been assisting him in the military administration) would both leave Vienna to take command of the emperor's armies. "What," he asked, "would then happen to the War Department and the Hofkriegsrat?" Noting that he could issue orders if necessary, he asked Charles of his own accord to make the appropriate dispositions to limit his own power.[9]

Although Francis used this argument mainly as political cover to reduce Charles's power, it nevertheless had validity. The development of a prominent and important military administration and military staff system was a relatively new phenomenon throughout Europe at this time. Leaders in various states found it difficult to balance the desirability of uniting the military administration and staff under the control of some talented general with the need to have the best generals take the field with the armies. Tension also existed between the desire to have the chief of staff who had developed the war plan command the army that would execute it, and the fact that such an action decapitated the staff necessary to prosecute the war successfully. Such tensions would be visible in Austria in 1809, in Russia in 1812 and subsequently, and even as late as 1828 when the chief of the Russian main staff took the field, together with the tsar, in the Russo–Turkish War of that year. This tension, in a slightly different form, was also important in the development of the German general staff during the Wars of German Unification and even World War I. In both cases the chief of the general staff remained in the rear, coordinating the war effort, but at the expense of having his orders questioned and sometimes ignored by field commanders who did not wish to see their control of their forces shackled by a mere staff officer. Over the course of the century, however, it became clear that if control of the military administration and staff was united in a single individual and that individual took the field with the armies, the war effort suffered badly.* Most states had not learned these lessons by 1805, however.

Sensing either the justice in Francis's request or the inevitability of the outcome, Charles did not attempt to fight changes in the military organization, but he explained that proposals to remedy the situation that he had been preparing for some time were not quite ready.[10] Francis took the problem out of his hands. He informed Charles that he was going to reestablish the Hofkriegsrat as an independent agency, separate from the War Ministry. When Charles presumed to suggest that Francis make their brother John president of the newly reestablished body, Francis rebuked Charles and emphasized the complete independence of the new body from the archduke. Charles would remain war minister, but that was all. Francis named General Baillet de Latour president of the Hofkriegsrat and FML Prince Schwarzenberg its vice president. No longer did Charles control Austria's military establishment.[11]

With Charles largely out of the way, his subordinates fell quickly. Fassbender had compromised himself by giving state secrets to foreign diplomats,

---

*The problems resulting from this situation in 1809 and 1812 are apparent in most histories of those wars and will be considered in greater detail in subsequent works. The problems of 1828 are explored in Frederick W. Kagan, *The Military Reforms of Nicholas I: The Origins of the Modern Russian Army* (New York: St. Martin's, 1999). For the Wars of German Unification, see Gordon A. Craig, *The Politics of the Prussian Army, 1640–1945* (New York: Oxford, 1964); Sir Michael Howard, *The Franco–Prussian War: The German Invasion of France, 1870–1871* (London: R. Hart-Davis, 1961). For World War I, almost any operational history describes the tension between Helmut von Moltke the Younger and the army commanders.

allowing Cobenzl to have him removed. Deprived of the archduke's support, Duka fared no better. At the end of April, Mack replaced him as quartermaster general, and Duka was relegated to a meaningless command.[12] In Mack, Cobenzl finally had a military counterpart willing to work with him. Instead of the six months that Duka believed would be necessary to put the Austrian army on a war footing, Mack promised to do it in two.* Mack energetically set about reorganizing and filling out the Austrian army with the emperor's approval. By making these personnel moves, Francis implicitly rejected Charles's assertion that Austria must avoid war at all costs. The emperor continued to fear war and preferred peace even at a high price, but as he supported Mack's mobilization efforts and removed the last obstacle other than himself to Cobenzl's more belligerent policies, he tacitly accepted the possibility that he would have to lead his state into war.

The Final Crisis

The events that completed the process of driving Austria to war in 1805 took place in Italy, which played a significant role in determining the course the war ultimately followed. Francis was unmoved by the rumors in late 1804 that Napoleon intended to make himself king of Italy, despite Cobenzl's change of heart. But the Austrian emperor found it difficult to remain insouciant when Napoleon actually claimed the Iron Crown of Lombardy. Napoleon's subsequent actions finally convinced Francis to take up the cudgel in his own defense.

Once again, Napoleon's motives remain unclear. Ostensibly, having decided that he could not remain president of an Italian Republic while being emperor of the French, Napoleon first offered the crown of Italy to his brother Joseph. Since he wanted to avoid provoking the other European powers by uniting the newly created kingdom with France, Napoleon stipulated that Joseph renounce his right of succession to the French throne before ascending that of Italy. To Napoleon's surprise and dismay (supposedly), Joseph refused to renounce his claim and thereby refused the throne of Italy. Nonplussed (seemingly), Napoleon then declared that he would adopt the eldest son of his brother Louis as Napoleon II, make him king of Italy, and govern as regent in his name until he reached his majority. Once more, apparently to his surprise, Napoleon's plan was wrecked when brother Louis angrily announced that he would keep his wife and children and refused to allow the adoption. Without wasting time on recriminations against his recalcitrant brothers, Napoleon

---

*Duka's pessimistic presentation of Austria's capabilities may have been the final nail in his coffin. His memorandum, outlining all of the obstacles in the path of rearmament, was dated 20 April 1805, and he issued an order replacing himself with Mack on 26 April 1805. KA AFA 1805 Deutschland, IV/6 and IV/8 respectively.

then turned to Josephine's son Eugene Beauharnais, whom he named viceroy of Italy, to govern the territory of which Napoleon himself, reluctantly and against his will, had been forced to become king.[13]

Making sense of this sequence of events is hard. Possibly it all happened exactly as Napoleon claimed and for the reasons given—his brothers would not accept the need to renounce their claims to the French throne and so Napoleon was forced to take the throne himself. That explanation is hard to believe, however, because of the speed with which these negotiations occurred and failed, the fact that his brothers' refusals did not anger Napoleon (which would have been extremely uncharacteristic), and the fact that Joseph subsequently accepted the thrones of Naples and then of Spain with many of the same restrictions that he refused to accept in Italy. As one of the premier historians of Franco–Italian relations in this period noted, "In truth only [Napoleon] himself, being Emperor, could be King of Italy; master of the crown of Charlemagne, the Iron Crown of the Lombard Kings could only belong to him; to give it to another would have been nonsense such as he would not commit."[14] There is considerable validity in this line of reasoning.

Why, then, did Napoleon go to the trouble of playing out this comedy, especially considering that his role in it was somewhat embarrassing? Napoleon hoped in this way to reduce the anxiety that this latest acquisition would cause in Vienna. Thus he wrote to Francis on New Year's Day 1805 that he had renounced his claims to Italy in favor of Joseph, who in turn had renounced his claims to the throne of France—the tense of the verbs in the message is interesting since, whatever else was true, neither event had happened yet. Napoleon explained that by this decision he was sacrificing his "personal grandeur" and "weakening [his] power" but concluded, "I will be amply compensated for that if I can have done something agreeable for Your Majesty."[15] The rest of the letter contained a threat more veiled and implicit than usual in Napoleon's correspondence with Vienna—Napoleon clearly intended this communication to pacify Francis.

Amazingly, it did not. To this point, Francis had given Napoleon every reason to believe that a combination of threat and conciliation would be enough to keep him passive. Francis had watched helplessly and inactively as Napoleon reordered first Germany and then Italy to his liking. He even recognized a number of Napoleon's conquests in northern Italy, including the incorporation of Piedmont into France, without a demur. When Napoleon proclaimed himself emperor of the French, Francis tamely submitted and seemed to support Napoleon's action by making himself hereditary emperor of Austria. Although rumors that the Republic of Italy had been transformed into a kingdom stirred Cobenzl, they had elicited no response from Francis. Napoleon had every right to be surprised that this latest expansion actually met some resistance.

Napoleon suffered from a blindness common to aggressive dictators. He could not recognize that there was a point at which even the most timid leader would feel it necessary to resist him in defense of his own independence. After defeating the Austrians soundly and exercising emotional and moral supremacy over them in the years of pseudopeace, Napoleon imagined that Francis would never oppose him, certainly not unless he attacked Austrian territory directly—something he had no intention of doing. Napoleon did not understand that as states continue to behave weakly and timidly, a resistance begins to build up against further weak and timid actions. The passive ruler begins to fear that he has lost his independence, that he is entirely at the mercy of the state he is attempting to appease, that there will be no end of the demands made of him unless he takes a stand somewhere. An aggressive dictator, like a successful blackmailer, recognizes that point and does not pass it, but few have ever mastered that art. Napoleon certainly misread Francis in 1805.

One reason was that Napoleon could not see the world from Francis's viewpoint. He knew that he controlled Italy, that the Italian Republic was a puppet, and that he could do whatever he would with the rest of the peninsula, including Naples. He believed that Francis's previous passivity showed that the Austrians also recognized that fact. Why, then, should they raise a fuss when Napoleon made a few, from his perspective, minor adjustments in territories that he saw, and believed they saw, as already belonging to him?

He did not realize that Austrian passivity rested on self-delusion. Cobenzl, still less Francis, could not have accepted any of the changes Napoleon had made in Italy since Lunéville except by believing that they were temporary (as Napoleon had claimed). Cobenzl came to realize that Napoleon must be resisted when he learned of the French emperor's intention to transform the Italian Republic into a kingdom. It took Francis a little more time and a few more pieces of evidence to reach the same conclusion.

At that, the transformation of the Italian Republic was not enough. Francis replied in the mildest possible terms to Napoleon's letter of January 1, 1805, announcing Joseph's accession to the Italian throne.[16] The reply was so mild that Napoleon and Talleyrand used it in the Italian Republic to prove that the Austrians supported Napoleon's actions.[17] Even the sequel was not enough to change the course of Austrian policy at once, however. "The blow has landed," Cobenzl declared when he read Napoleon's letter of March 17 announcing his own accession, "and it found Austria in the middle of an internal crisis," a historian adds.[18] Cobenzl had just succeeded in removing Charles from a position of supreme control over the Austrian military but was still scheming to eliminate Fassbender and Duka and to bring in Mack. He was not ready for the confrontation that he believed Napoleon's actions should have caused.

Cobenzl saw in Napoleon's declaration proof of his ambition to found a universal monarchy, and he saw that Austria was in a terrible position: "Finally the prediction that Napoleon wishes to make himself King of the Romans, etc., etc. seems unfortunately only too probable.* It is without doubt a difficult task to place any obstacle in the way of his projects, but if we do not place any obstacles we will cease to exist. There is at its root the cruel alternative in which we find ourselves."[19] He wanted Francis's response at least to hint at the Austro–Russian alliance in order to show Napoleon that Austria had the power to oppose him if it chose, but Francis would not go that far. His response to the news that Napoleon would take the crown himself was even meeker and milder than his response to the news of Joseph's supposed elevation. The second letter demonstrates how little progress Cobenzl had made in bringing Francis over to his way of thinking.

Francis may still have hoped to draw Prussia into a defensive triple alliance with Austria and Russia that could check Napoleon without the need for a war. The Austrians were not aware of the terms of the Anglo–Russian negotiations until March 1805, and even then Czartoryskii told Stadion only that an envoy would be sent to Paris on behalf of both the London and St. Petersburg courts with terms of peace that would be "made as moderate as possible and such as to leave one not without hope of seeing them accepted by France."[20] In this context, given his known aversion to going to war, Francis probably greeted with enthusiasm the word that Alexander had sent a former Austrian general now in Russian service, Baron Ferdinand Wintzingerode, to Berlin to negotiate with the Prussians. The tsar had decided, Metternich reported, "not to suffer the neutrality of Prussia in the event of a war, of which the chances increased daily."[21] If Alexander could force Frederick William to join the coalition quickly, then the news might deter Napoleon and help Europe avoid war.

The hope of drawing Prussia into the coalition proved illusory, however.† By the end of March, Wintzingerode concluded that Frederick William was unshakeable. Although Prussia might join a coalition once the war started, especially if pressed by the Russians, there was no prospect of drawing the court of Berlin into a preemptive treaty. The foreign minister was even arguing that the Russo–Prussian treaty of the previous year, far from committing Prussia to oppose France, served rather to debar the Russians from taking any action that might compromise the neutrality of northern Germany.[22] Metternich did not finally give up hope until Wintzingerode actually left Berlin in mid-May, but then he abandoned all thought of drawing Prussia into an alliance.[23]

This comedy probably served to focus Francis's attention on the problem. Austria could look only to Russia for support; Napoleon had a fairly reliable ally in Prussia. The effect of Wintzingerode's mission to Berlin was to foreclose the hope that an alliance of the three continental powers might peacefully

---

*The title "King of the Romans" was the traditional term used to designate the successor to the sitting Holy Roman Emperor.

†This topic will be considered in greater detail in the following chapter.

check further Napoleonic encroachments. The fact that Wintzingerode went from Berlin to Vienna to discuss specific contingency plans in the event of war against France emphasizes the turn events were already taking. When he arrived, he negotiated with Mack, and the result of that negotiation would be the basis for the allied war plan actually executed later that year.* One final set of events was needed, however, to drive Francis over the edge and convince him to commit to an alliance for an offensive war, and Napoleon was not slow to provide the first part of that set, almost certainly without realizing it.

The development of political institutions in the "republics" of northern Italy after Lunéville was not, on the whole, felicitous. Problems in the integration and political organization of the Italian Republic had convinced Napoleon of the necessity to transform that state into a kingdom in the first place (thereby giving him the opportunity to alter its constitution fundamentally). Similar problems also arose in the territories of Lucca and the Ligurian Republic.[24] The leaders of the former seemed to have concluded that something must be done, and they took advantage of Napoleon's presence in Milan for his coronation to request that Lucca be given a new constitution with a prince of Napoleon's family as its leader. Napoleon readily complied at the end of June 1805.[25]

The situation of the Ligurian Republic was rather different. It appears that Napoleon decided in May that he wanted to annex Genoa and the republic of which it was the capital to France. In an order of May 24, he declared, "Before going to Genoa and having the intention, between us, to join Genoa to France, I would be more comfortable to find another frigate there."[26] Napoleon wrote and dispatched this letter before any Genoese had mentioned the possibility of French annexation.[27] The following day, Napoleon's representative in Genoa, Saliceti, presented the Genoese senate with a draft decree of annexation. In the absence of the Doge and a number of senators (who had gone to pay their respects to Napoleon in Milan), the decree was approved. Napoleon kept the Genoese delegation cooling its heels until news of the decree had arrived, and then graciously acceded to the request of the people of the Ligurian Republic.[28]

There is little evidence that the Genoese were hostile to the annexation (Saliceti described the prevailing mood as one of "resignation"), so the degree to which this action was an aggression is limited. It was, however, a clear violation of the Treaty of Lunéville (as Napoleon's acceptance of the Iron Crown of Lombardy had also been), and it was the final straw for Francis.

Why did Napoleon take this action? The annexation of Genoa to France, like the establishment of Napoleon's sister and brother-in law in Lucca, seems to destroy the idea that Napoleon intended to unify Italy. If that had been his aim, why not annex those lands to the Kingdom of Italy, which shared a border with both of them? Nor is it clear that any need to facilitate the war against

---

*See below, Chapters 10–11, for the details of the formation of the war plans.

Britain played a large part in his decision, for the Genoese had been forthcoming in their support for that war, even arresting the British consul and other British subjects and seizing what British ships they could.[29] Napoleon may have resented the fact that Francis had accredited a chargé d'affaires in Genoa in fall 1803 for the first time in eighty years, but it is hard to explain why he should have waited so long to react to that offense.[30]

The likeliest explanation is twofold. First, Napoleon took the opportunity while in northern Italy for his coronation to focus his attention once more on that region (which he considered his own). He saw at once that the political arrangements made prior to 1801 were not working and, with characteristic energy, set out to fix them. In doing so he did not simply repair the deficiencies of governments established at a time when republicanism was the byword, but adjusted those governments to the new situation in which France was once again the bastion of monarchism. There was, in this view, nothing aggressive or even noteworthy about his actions. They were simply part of a general rationalization of the situation in a disturbed and dysfunctional area of which Napoleon happened to be the hegemon.

The second part of the explanation is an even deeper level of realpolitik. Genoa is by nature the port of Piedmont—as Talleyrand hastened to point out in explaining Napoleon's decision to the Austrian representative.[31] From the standpoint of Napoleon's mercantilist economic policies, it made a great deal of sense for the port to be under the control of the same power that controlled Piedmont; otherwise the theoretical excise revenues of Piedmontese exports would be going to a foreign state. Finally, Genoa's harbor was an important naval station, and Napoleon was increasingly determined to occupy all such harbors and control them directly.

Napoleon apparently did not understand what the consequences of his actions would be. Although he told Cambacérès that the annexation should not upset any great power except for Britain, he resorted to a diplomatic ruse to soften the blow to Austria.[32] Talleyrand instructed François Alexandre Frédéric de la Rochefoucauld, Napoleon's ambassador in Vienna, to explain that the Genoese had requested annexation. Although inclined to grant their request, Napoleon was mulling it over.[33] His statements to other ambassadors, written on the same day, reveal the lie in this maneuver.[34] This time, however, the diplomatic dance had no effect on Austria. The annexation of Genoa would prove to be the last argument Cobenzl needed to convince Francis to go to war.

One of the reasons that Napoleon's diplomacy failed to undo the damage caused by his unilateralism was the fear he generated in Austria by the concentration of forces in northern Italy that accompanied his coronation in Milan in May. In late March Napoleon had ordered minister of war Berthier to assemble an army on the plain of Marengo for him to review on his way to Milan.[35] That army, which came to number about 30,000 men, caused extreme alarm in Vienna.* In April the Austrian court considered the problem of reinforcing its troops in Italy under the heading, "Most Urgent Orders."[36] This document proposed to send additional forces to Italy under the pretext of establishing a camp for field exercises there.

That proposal in turn evoked a detailed reconsideration of Austria's position from Archduke Charles.[37] Although he recognized that Austrian forces in Italy could not withstand a French attack if Napoleon were so minded, he also feared that the provocative act of reinforcing Habsburg troops there would trigger the very attack it was designed to withstand. He tied all military measures, as usual, to the deceptively simple question: Was Francis confident that Napoleon wanted war or not? If so, then Charles agreed that Austria must hasten to prepare her defenses. If not, then the monarchy must take all steps possible to avoid war, including needless and probably ineffective measures such as sending reinforcements to the one common border with France.

Charles's fear was compounded by a moderate overestimation of French strength in northern Italy, which he put at 40,000 men.† But fear now worked for war rather than against it. Francis had already rejected Charles's determination to avoid war at all costs by stripping him of his power and supporting Mack's more aggressive rearmament program in the spring, and he stood by that decision at this difficult time. He ordered Charles to execute the plan of sending reinforcements to Italy under the cover of establishing an exercise camp—at once.[38]

Napoleon's pressure in Italy combined with a dramatic increase in pressure from Russia at nearly the same time. As soon as Czartoryskii pressured Leveson Gower into signing the draft Anglo–Russian treaty in April *sub spe rati,* Alexander sent word to Razumovskii instructing him to gain Austria's accession to the treaty.‡ The revelation of the terms of the treaty fell on Vienna like a thunderbolt. As late as March 22, Cobenzl had been reassuring a nervous Francis that, whatever Britain and Russia decided, they could not force Austria to go to war.

---

*Napoleon to Berthier, 27 March 1805, *Corr. de Nap.*, doc. 8491, identifies fifteen regiments to be assembled in northern Italy for Napoleon to review. Figuring four battalions for every regiment (and some had only three) and an average of 560 men per battalion (the average strength when Masséna took command in early September; see Général Koch, ed., *Mémoirs de Masséna* [Paris: Paulin et Lechevalier, 1850], p. 49), the maximum infantry strength could not have exceeded 33,600 and was almost certainly less than that.

†Charles to Francis, 25 May 1805, KA AFA 1805 Italien, V/12. Charles was probably off by about 33 percent, since he claimed that Napoleon had 40,000 troops available for offensive operations instead of the fewer than 30,000 making up the mobile army.

‡The term *sub spe rati* is a technical diplomatic term that requires explanation. An ambassador negotiating a treaty is normally provided with explicit instructions identifying the maximum and minimum terms he should demand and can accept. He is generally authorized to sign any treaty that meets the minimum terms. Because of the delays in communications in this era, however, ambassadors were sometimes forced to accept terms that were not authorized by their instructions. In such a case, they generally did so *sub spe rati*—in the hope that their court would accept the terms. A sovereign's repudiation of a treaty condition submitted *sub spe rati* was considered less serious than repudiation of a treaty that his ambassador signed in accord with his instructions and with no such stipulation.

Even the revelation of the Austro–Russian convention of 1804 would not affect things, since that convention had foreseen a purely defensive conflict. But on April 14, Stadion reported the terms of the Anglo–Russian treaty, and the Austrians were aghast. Even Cobenzl seems to have recoiled from the imminence of a war he himself had come to recognize was necessary.[39]

In early May, Razumovskii tightened the screws: Alexander could not continue to keep his army idle on the Austrian border, and if war did not come in 1805, Britain would probably end up making a separate peace with France anyway, depriving the Austrians of any hope for a subsidy. When Wintzingerode arrived in Vienna, he reiterated these points. A dispatch from Czartoryskii to Razumovskii sent on June 14, 1805, emphasized the fact that Alexander was losing all patience with Vienna's delays.[40]

Cobenzl had had enough. On July 2 he presented Francis with a lengthy memorandum that amounted to a declaration for war.[41] The Russians, he began, demanded a final answer to their proposals to adhere to the Anglo–Russian alliance. The answer must be yes. "The most recent events in Italy," he wrote, "confirm completely that Emperor Napoleon is dominated by his insatiable desire for conquests, which finds no barrier either in treaties or in his own most solemn declarations, and which is only strengthened and spurred on to new aggrandizing undertakings by the indulgence and the moderation of other powers."

Only by arming and resisting could Austria find any safety. "It may yet be possible to achieve this aim through a peaceful arrangement," he admitted, "which would be the most desirable of all," but it was also possible that only through the "force of arms" could the Austrian state find any security. With the necessary modifications, the Anglo–Russian proposals offered the hope of achieving this goal. Cobenzl identified several of those modifications, focusing on the need for the Russian army to advance into Austrian territory not when Napoleon had rejected the peace proposals to be offered to him, but when those proposals were first sent. In this way alone, he believed, could Austria avoid the danger of being attacked with the full weight of the French army before her own was ready and long before the Russian reinforcements could appear. Francis was finally convinced of the danger, and he approved Cobenzl's proposals with some minor modifications.[42] On August 9, 1805, Czartoryskii and Stadion exchanged declarations binding Austria to the coalition and committing Europe to war.[43]

The Third Coalition had taken its final form, but in the war plans and capitals of the new allies, all still hoped that it would be possible, in the end, to cajole or coerce Prussia into acceding to the coalition. As we shall soon see, Prussia's failure to do so seriously, perhaps fatally, unhinged the plans of the allies and gave Napoleon an enormous advantage over them that he would not have had if they had simply accepted Prussian neutrality from the outset. Consequently we must turn our attention to Berlin to search for an understanding of why the allies were so confident that they could suborn Frederick William and why they were wrong.

8

Prussia Opts Out

Frederick William III's decision to ally himself with neither Napoleon nor the Third Coalition was a crucial turning point in European history. It transformed the military and diplomatic situation of the continent and played an important role in determining the outcome of the war that followed. It also planted the seeds of the Fourth Coalition and the war it fought in 1806–1807. There have been few times when a single decision made by a single leader has shaped the future development of an international system so profoundly. Explaining this decision and exploring its consequences are two of the foremost tasks facing the historian of this period.[1]

Frederick William III's reaction to the crisis that followed the renewal of war between France and Britain resulted from a complex interaction of his own personality, the "high politics" of the court (the intrigues and relations of the king with his senior ministers and advisers), and Prussia's geostrategic situation. He was by nature indecisive and preferred inaction to action. He saw inaction as a safer course that promised to keep his state out of war—always one of his major objectives. He hoped that Prussia's neutrality would also help keep Europe from plunging into another devastating war. In addition, like many people who doubt their own capabilities, he saw in action only danger and risk, and was rarely drawn to the benefits that his advisers argued could be obtained by acting decisively. This focus on risks and dangers and the conviction that no good result was likely to outweigh the damage done by war, combined with his natural indecisiveness, made it virtually impossible for him to decide to fight.

His conviction of his own inadequacy had another important consequence. He did not trust his own decisionmaking abilities or even his capacity to make sound judgments about the advice his senior officials gave him. As a result, he constantly sought opinions from many different advisers with conflicting viewpoints. Although he hoped to gain a fuller and more detailed understanding of the matter at hand, the result was usually to make it possible to accept a position

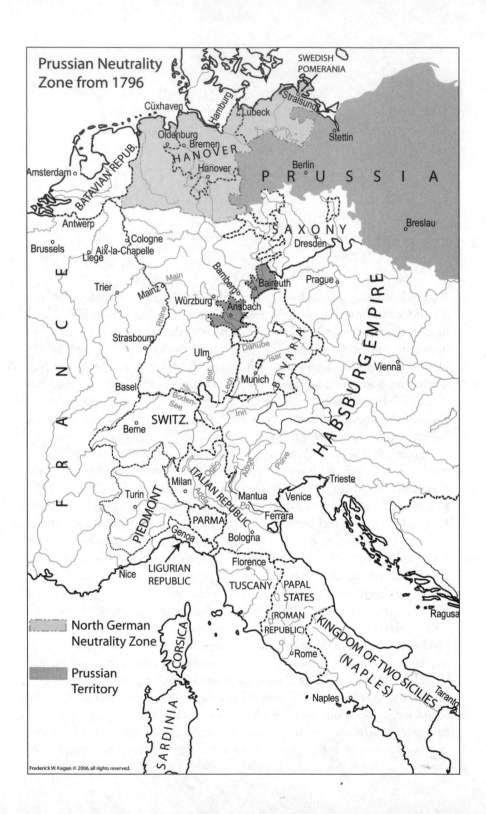

Prussian Neutrality
Zone from 1796

SWEDISH
POMERANIA

Cüxhaven
Hamburg
Lübeck
Stralsund

Oldenburg
Bremen
HANOVER
Hanover

Stettin

Amsterdam

BATAVIAN REPUB.

Berlin

P R U S S I A

Antwerp

Breslau

Brussels
Cologne
Aix-la-Chapelle
Liège

S A X O N Y

Dresden

Trier
Mainz
Main

Bamberg
Baireuth
Prague

Würzburg
Ansbach

Strasbourg
Rhine

Ulm
Danube
Isar

Vienna

BAVARIA

H A B S B U R G   E M P I R E

Basel
Iller
Lech
Munich

Boden
See

Berne
SWITZ.
Inn

Oglio
Adige
Plave

Trieste

Milan
ITALIAN REPUBLIC
Mantua
Venice

Turin
Adda
Po

PIEDMONT
Genoa
PARMA
Ferrara

Nice
Bologna

LIGURIAN
REPUBLIC
Florence

TUSCANY
PAPAL
STATES

(ROMAN
REPUBLIC)

Ragusa

CORSICA

KINGDOM OF TWO SICILIES
(N A P L E S)

Rome

North German
Neutrality Zone

Prussian
Territory

SARDINIA

Naples

Taranto

that reflected a compromise among all of the opinions he had heard. That compromise position, naturally enough, was generally one of inaction.

The high politics of the Prussian court reinforced this trend. Frederick William's determination to hear all sides of an argument led him to encourage his advisers to compete with one another on an issue. This problem was especially acute for Haugwitz and Hardenberg, who alternately held the formal responsibility for conducting Prussia's foreign affairs, and for Lombard, the king's secretary who handled external matters. It became common for these three men, all of whom had the king's ear, to ensure that their views conflicted. Each hoped that by staking out his own position and drawing the king to it he might also thereby gain the ascendancy over his rivals. The nature of the Prussian governmental system thus ensured that Frederick William would receive not merely conflicting but intentionally contradictory advice from his principal advisers.[2]

Prussia's geostrategic situation also militated toward passivity. Each time the prospect of war with one side or the other became apparent, the dangers of action seemed immense, since Frederick William and his advisers believed that either France or Russia could destroy Prussia singlehandedly. As Alexander became more estranged from Napoleon, however, demands for alliance with one came increasingly to imply war with the other, which was unacceptable. Each time Napoleon pressed his suit, Frederick William and his ministers saw only the dangers of an angry Russia. But whenever Alexander tried to force Frederick William to join the coalition, they could see only the risks of a war with France. Gone were the days when Frederick the Great might have attempted to resolve such a dilemma by bold and aggressive action. The general awareness in Berlin of Prussia's financial and military weakness ensured that the result of this balance of fears would be passivity.

But in the end Frederick William could not simply follow a passive policy. One of the legacies Frederick the Great bequeathed to his successors was a determination to assert Prussia's great power status. The preservation of at least the fiction of an independent Prussian policy was therefore a primary consideration for Frederick William. The ever-present fear of becoming a French or Russian satellite repelled him from numerous overtures. It would become a dominating force in Prussian policy in 1805 and 1806.

Finally, the king was unwilling to behave "badly." He had always applied a moral test to foreign policy that was unique in Prussian history to that time. This tendency can be seen in his insistence that Prussian compensation for losses in the revolutionary wars come at the expense of secularized church lands, not other princes' hereditary lands. It was also visible in his revulsion at the thought of seizing Hanover as a reward for services rendered to France even as he recognized the political and geostrategic desirability of such an action.

Prussian policy between 1803 and 1806 was a curious blend of rationality, irrationality, idealism, and realpolitik. The king was the center of that policy and, as many contemporaries noted, it was uniquely his, although the nature of Prussian high politics complicated his own decisionmaking process and added an element of irrationality to the result. But Frederick William thought himself the most rational of monarchs and would have denied the accusation that emotionalism, still less fear, drove his policies to any significant extent.[3]

Hanover Revisited

The crisis resulting from Napoleon's invasion of Hanover in 1803 clearly illuminates the tensions and contradictions of Prussia's policy. As we have seen, Napoleon informed Frederick William that he intended to seize the electorate before he began operations against it and attempted to gain the king's consent. Frederick William gave him tacit permission to seize the land, having offered a number of compromises in a vain effort to convince Napoleon to abandon his plans. Alexander attempted to persuade Frederick William to fight Napoleon to defend the Prussian neutrality zone, into which Hanover fell, but to no avail. Both Russia and France offered Prussia alliances that Frederick William politely refused.*

Frederick William's decision not to oppose Napoleon's seizure of the electorate in 1803 was a landmark in Prussian policy. Hardenberg said later that it was the last time Prussia had a chance to choose her course of action freely.[4] Although this statement is an exaggeration, it holds a kernel of truth. In the spring of 1803, Frederick William had a series of options. He could grant Napoleon's request for permission to take the electorate, with or without accepting Napoleon's proffered alliance. He could oppose Napoleon's notification of his intention to move into Hanover. If he chose that course of action, he could announce his disapproval of the action, mobilize his own forces to resist, or reach for the proffered Russian alliance. Finally, he could have seized the electorate preemptively, either in his own name or in order to "protect" it on behalf of King George III of Britain. In subsequent years, Prussia rarely faced such a wide array of options. As the international situation grew increasingly polarized and the likelihood of war grew daily, Prussia's options were rapidly constrained to choosing between war and peace and, if the choice was war, whether to ally with France or Russia. Yet Frederick William did not relish choosing among so many options.

Napoleon informed the king in mid-May 1803 that he intended to seize Hanover and that he preferred to ally himself with Prussia rather than Austria, but he would approach Vienna if Frederick William proved obstinate.[5] Haug-

---

*See Chapter 3 for a discussion of these events in the context of the development of Franco–Russian relations. The discussion that follows will focus on their significance for Prussian policy.

witz recognized that a crisis had come, and he pressed Frederick William to oppose the French move. He attempted to convince the king to mobilize some of his forces and announce that fact to Napoleon. The king, instead, called a conference to consider the matter, telling Haugwitz that however much he might value his advice, "the duty of my office demands that I not take a position based exclusively on the opinion of any single one of my ministers, and I have therefore in this crisis called together several of my old generals to a council."[6] The Duke of Brunswick, the most respected soldier in the realm, was one of the critical voices at this council. Much to Haugwitz's surprise (for he had previously supported Haugwitz's more activist recommendation), he counseled caution: "It would not be wise to provoke such a dangerous power as France."[7]

When Frederick William responded to Napoleon's message on May 28 his tone was surprisingly mild. Haugwitz had included in his draft of the note a passage alluding to the partial mobilization of the Prussian army, but the king deleted that passage before dispatching the letter. He also decided not to mobilize that corps. As a result, Frederick William's response to Napoleon's warning of the impending French invasion was merely an offer to guarantee to France financial subsidies drawn from the hapless electorate.[8] The king contented himself with establishing a militarily insignificant cordon along his frontier with Hanover that Napoleon did not find objectionable.[9]

Napoleon's approach to Prussia was the opposite of his approach toward Austria. Whereas he saw in Francis primarily an enemy to be cowed with threats or ignored, he genuinely courted Frederick William, although not without the occasional threat. The reasons for this disparity are not entirely clear. Perhaps Napoleon favored Prussia because he had never fought her and because Frederick William's policies were passive while Francis's were obstinate. Perhaps he believed that Prussia's obvious weakness would induce Frederick William to become the satellite that Francis stubbornly refused to be. Perhaps he genuinely believed that France and Prussia could work together for a common purpose, at least as regards Hanover, whereas France and Austria were fated always to have interests in conflict. Or perhaps he saw that he could get what he wanted from Frederick William in this way, whereas he believed that only threats and hostility would yield benefits with Francis. He certainly wanted different sorts of things from each monarch. Whatever the reason, Napoleon's treatment of Prussia between his ascent to power and 1806 was unusual in his foreign relations.*

Even before he received the king's response, Napoleon tried to drive Frederick William into an alliance with him. On May 27, Talleyrand spoke to the Prussian ambassador in Paris, Girolamo Lucchesini, repeatedly referring

---

*Napoleon's policy toward Bavaria was the closest comparison to his policies toward Prussia. The major difference was that the elector of Bavaria threw in his lot with Napoleon more or less wholeheartedly, something that Frederick William never did. See below for further consideration of Napoleon's relationship with the court of Munich.

to the "danger" that Napoleon might be "forced" into renewing the unpopular system of 1756 based on an alliance with Austria if the Prussians did not speedily ally themselves with France. He even delivered a formal note pressing once again for an immediate treaty.[10] Frederick William found himself in a difficult position, and he left this note unanswered for more than a month. Although Talleyrand had assured him that Russia was simply a "mountain of snow" that held no danger for Prussia, especially if Berlin were allied with Paris, the Prussians were not so sure. As Lombard wrote, "The mountain of snow has terrible avalanches, and they can run for years without in any way diminishing the mass of the mountain, and they can engulf a great deal."[11] He also noted that it was folly to speak of a "defensive" alliance between Prussia and a France that was already at war with Britain—surely any such alliance would automatically make Frederick William a cobelligerent.

Lombard was generally pro-French throughout this discussion, and so his cautionary advice rested primarily on fear of Russia and to a lesser extent Britain. Count Haugwitz, who was generally anti-French at this time, relied on fear of France to advocate forming a close relationship with Russia. He claimed (with no visible evidence or indeed veracity) that 60,000 French troops were marching toward Hanover with other corps forming in Holland and on the lower Rhine (those "other corps" were some of the Channel camps preparing to receive the Army of England Napoleon was assembling). Was it possible, he asked on June 4, "to remain calm about their approach toward the center of the monarchy and to wait, without considering any means of defense, [to see] if Bonaparte's aims extended beyond the simple occupation of the German possessions belonging to His Britannic Majesty?"[12] The king had chastised Haugwitz for seeing things too darkly.[13] Haugwitz noted that Frederick William had "opposed the lively representations that my zeal led me to submit to his profound judgment with the opinion of others of his servitors whose counsels led to complete passivity."[14] But the time for that passivity had passed, he argued, because French troops were already on the march. On May 31, the Russian ambassador in Berlin, M. M. Alopeus, had offered an effective alliance to preserve the neutrality of north Germany, and Haugwitz believed that this overture should be accepted, at least as the basis for negotiations.[15]

The effect of Alexander's overture on Prussian policy was strange. He intended, as we have seen, to convince Frederick William openly to oppose Napoleon's seizure of Hanover, and he was ready to send his own troops to north Germany to support Prussia. There was no chance that this approach would succeed, but it did embolden Frederick William to resist Napoleon's efforts at seduction.

Haugwitz seized on the Russian offer to counterbalance the danger of a Franco–Prussian alliance or entente. On June 8 he wrote, "I have had occasion to perceive that the court of Russia . . . is occupied with ideas very different from a concert with France. They are starting to open their eyes in Petersburg to the danger with which all of Northern Europe finds itself menaced by the French invasion of Hanover."[16] The king recognized the validity of this point: "The Russian overtures are precious. They assure me, at the moment when the choice between evils could not be more doubtful, of all of the means of my powerful ally."[17] It is interesting, considering that there was no alliance between Prussia and Russia at that time, that Frederick William described Alexander in that way. Perhaps the effect of the meeting at Memel in 1802 was still lingering in his mind despite the fact that neither state had contracted formal obligations to the other.

Frederick William was, nevertheless, unwilling to accept Alexander's offer, even if he used it to embolden himself to reject Napoleon's. He noted that "before coming to an understanding with [Alexander], I have had to reflect, to determine strictly for myself what I would want," and that he would have to avoid repeating recent mistakes in the future by adopting "a policy that awaits events to judge its duty and allows itself to be surprised by them."[18] This statement is deeply ironical, considering that the king concluded a few sentences later that he would not mobilize any forces against contingencies that might arise, nor would he oppose the French occupation of Hanover. What did he mean by it?

Frederick William resigned himself to the changed situation that resulted from Napoleon's conquest of Hanover. Furthermore, he was convinced that Napoleon would not go beyond what he had already taken. Consequently the king declared to Haugwitz that at that moment only direct French attacks on Prussian territory could persuade him to take up arms. Short of that, he refused to countenance "any means other than those of diplomacy against the small usurpations that these unquiet neighbors may permit themselves in the North."[19]

This policy effectively jettisoned the idea of a neutral zone in north Germany defended by Prussian arms. The neutrality of north Germany had been established by the Treaty of Basel between France and Prussia that ended the latter's participation in the War of the First Coalition in 1795. When the Prussians found the original grandiose demarcation line of the neutrality zone to be indefensible (both sides violated it repeatedly), a smaller, more reasonable zone was established, this one also guaranteed by a Franco–Prussian treaty of August 1796. The Prussians maintained the neutrality of this smaller zone until the end of the war in 1801.[20]

The neutrality zone with Hanover at its core was central to Prussia's security. It provided the state with an extensive defensive glacis and ensured that the first blows directed against Prussia could be met on foreign soil. It also gave Prussia ascendancy over her smaller neighbors. Napoleon's seizure of Hanover, however,

shattered the last balance of the much-praised North German neutrality. Prussia could then fall back only on the neutrality of its own state territory.

[The effectiveness of this approach] was highly questionable strategically. Hitherto Prussia had been the leading power and defender of all of the states of the Protestant north, and in return the weaker neighbors had formed a valuable glacis. Hanover was indispensable in this. It bordered in the East the core lands of Brandenburg and was bounded in the West by the Prussian possessions on the Rhine, Weser, and Ems. Without Hanover these scattered territories could not be defended.[21]

For Frederick William to accept the disastrous collapse of his geostrategic situation was foolhardy. This acceptance was based, as we have seen, to a large degree on fear of the consequences of a war with France. As he wrote Alexander when rejecting the Russian alliance offers in early July, "My position is extremely painful." However seriously he might take the problems to which the tsar called his attention, the king declared, "I find infinitely repugnant any measure that might provoke war . . . Even the most successful war would entail the ruin of my provinces and of the prosperity of the North more surely than a few temporary usurpations."[22]

But Frederick William's passivity in this crisis was also based on hope. At the end of May, after all, Napoleon had accompanied word of his intentions to seize the electorate with an offer of an alliance and the promise that neither Prussia's possessions nor the Hanseatic towns of Hamburg and Bremen, so crucial to Prussia's economy, would be harmed. The king eagerly seized on early evidence that Napoleon had kept his promises, writing on June 6, "The direction that the French troops have taken, the orders that were given to them, everything in the note of the [French] minister of foreign relations exudes the same principles and justifies my confidence."[23] To Haugwitz, whom he had rebuked for excessive pessimism, he wrote nine days later of Napoleon's various dispatches, "One cannot deny that they are completely satisfactory concerning the most essential elements of our demands. If the French confine themselves exactly to the occupation of the electorate, as I must finally believe that they will after such solemn promises, then the most important considerations have been saved, Russia will no longer be able to demand a change in [Napoleon's] tone, and the collision so greatly feared is for the moment suspended."[24] To his ambassador in Paris, Lucchesini, he wrote, "I cannot deny France the right to seek out her enemy wherever she can reach her . . . I do not for the moment see in the position of the French anything but the proximity of friendly troops, the engagements of the First Consul, and a new security in our relations."[25] Frederick William's attempt to avoid choosing sides in the summer of 1803 rested on the illusory expectation that Napoleon's restraint would deny Alexander any cause to demand further action from Prussia.

Like Alexander after the signing of the Franco–Russian convention of 1801, Frederick William looked to see if Napoleon would keep his word. In the meantime, he preferred a policy of neutrality and passivity, even as he ordered war plans developed in the event of a break with France.[26]

To Arm or Not to Arm

The summer and fall of 1803 saw the development and collapse of efforts at a Franco–Prussian alliance and a Russo–Prussian alliance before Frederick William finally negotiated a defensive treaty with Alexander in early 1804. The fact that the Prussian king was negotiating for two mutually exclusive alliances at the same time reflected the pressures on Prussian policy, but not confusion. Frederick William knew perfectly well what he wanted to do and he pursued a coherent program to achieve it: he wanted peace above all and to secure north Germany's neutrality at almost any price up to, but not including, the risk of war. His initial inclination was to deal with Napoleon directly, since it was Napoleon who most threatened that neutrality on the one hand, and could most readily guarantee it if he were so minded on the other. Constantly pressed both by Haugwitz and the obvious geostrategic considerations, however, Frederick William was determined not to alienate Alexander in the process.

Although Frederick William had convinced himself that the French occupation of Hanover was not really a problem for his state, he knew that he could not continue to hold that view if Napoleon took advantage of his position in the electorate to cut off Prussia's trade. Hanover controls most of the Elbe and the Weser, two of Prussia's most important trade outlets. Moreover, the electorate borders on the Hanseatic towns of Bremen and Hamburg and their coastal possessions—all critical depots for Prussian commerce. The closure of the Elbe and the Weser to British shipping would inevitably provoke a British retaliation that would close those rivers to *all* shipping.

Napoleon initially took care to assure Frederick William that he would respect the neutrality of the Hanseatic towns, even promising in mid-June to revoke orders to General Mortier, who commanded the French army in Hanover, to sequester British shipping in Bremen.[27] Not two weeks later, however, Napoleon was already shifting his ground. Using a variety of sophistries, Talleyrand asked Lucchesini not to press for a formal response to his note asking for assurances of French intentions toward Hamburg, Bremen, and the rivers. Lucchesini concluded from this conversation, "[First], that the First Consul not only was not disposed for the moment to abandon the conquest of Hanover, but that he was not even willing to engage not to take up military positions on neutral territory, and [second], that he had above all decided to exclude from the Elbe and the Weser English vessels of every variety."[28] The Prussians' initial hope of reaching a formal agreement with Napoleon about the neutral cities and rivers had to be cast aside, and Frederick William felt obliged to send Napoleon a protest over his occupation of Hanseatic territories and the closure of the rivers at the end of June.[29]

Rising tensions drove Haugwitz to the fore with another aggressive proposal on June 30.[30] It was clear, he noted, that Napoleon did not intend to abide by his promises to confine himself and his armies to the territory of Hanover. Frederick William, however, had already established that only an attack on Prussian territory would drive him to undertake active measures to resist France. Haugwitz therefore proposed a series of measures short of hostilities that he hoped would bring France to heel and provide Prussia with the necessary security.

Haugwitz began insightfully by recognizing the advantage Napoleon was gaining by massing troops in and around Hanover. Because of those concentrations, Napoleon "is the master of [whether or not] to advance those new troops either into Holstein, or into Hesse and Saxony." He noted that "without seeming to have inimical intentions, without attacking Prussian territory, he could bend all to his will. He could obtain by these easy conquests [of Saxony and Holstein] the double goal of encircling Prussia from several sides and depriving her of the states that have and might again ally with her to defend the independence of North Germany and of Prussia."[31]

In this vision Haugwitz showed a great deal more sense than the contemporary Austrian leaders when confronted with the mobilizing French army. Napoleon's mobilized troops gave him an unanswerable advantage both militarily and diplomatically against states that refused to maintain combat-ready forces. Haugwitz absolutely did not want to go to war or provoke a conflict, but he rightly sensed that only by a Prussian mobilization could he give Prussia's peace policies any reasonable chance of success. As he put it most succinctly, "It is essential not to confuse Bonaparte in peacetime and [acting as a statesman], using delicacies . . . and paying heed to political or administrative considerations, with that same man at the head of his army."[32] This was a most profound observation.

Haugwitz proposed to concentrate a Prussian army of 40,000–50,000 men. He sought to accompany that mobilization with a declaration to Napoleon that Prussia did *not* object to the French occupation of Hanover, *providing* Napoleon limited his depredations to the electorate, that he not maintain more than 16,000 troops there, and that he not increase his armaments on the western frontiers of Germany. Once this mobilization began, Haugwitz continued, Prussia had two options. She could either remain belligerently neutral, opposing French aggression with threats, at least, or she could attempt to negotiate an agreement with Napoleon from a position of relative strength. In either case, Haugwitz felt it essential to secure Alexander's support.

Frederick William did not take Haugwitz's advice. Instead, he temporized by sending his cabinet secretary, Lombard, to meet with Napoleon in Brussels at the end of July. He gave Lombard no written instructions but ordered him to obtain either the withdrawal of the measures Napoleon had already undertaken against neutral territory or the promise that "at least these would be the last transgressions." But Lombard did not believe that he could achieve either goal and only hoped to accomplish the third of his missions: to obtain "more light on the future and as a result on the duties of the King."[33] In a private note he put his task even more succinctly: "Should Prussia arm or not? That is essentially the question that the King wants to have clarified."[34]

Unfortunately for Prussia, Napoleon used his charm to seduce Lombard completely.[35] Driven by the war with Britain to take a step that he knew would displease Frederick William, Napoleon said that he had seized Hanover in a way that minimized the harm to Prussia's interests. He even apologized for not giving Frederick William fair warning of the impending invasion, noting, on the one hand, that he wished to avoid giving Prussia the opportunity to express its anger to him and, on the other, the necessity to maintain military secrecy. After all, General Edward Mortier had only 16,000 French troops to suppress "a brave and desperate army" (that made no serious effort to defend itself).

At a time when reports of French armaments were consistently exaggerated, Napoleon added, he would not have been surprised if the Prussians armed themselves, "although I sincerely appreciate the sentiment that turned you away from" such a course. But Frederick William should not listen to rumors or reports that Napoleon intended to close the Danish straits to British shipping: "Without doubt I would be charmed if it were done, without doubt I am convinced that the union of the four Northern Powers for a great and vigorous measure would be the only means of crushing the despotism of England, but that is their affair and not mine." He concluded, "I have no right to demand it and I will never ask for something for which I do not have the right to ask."[36]

Napoleon did not give Lombard time to consider this sophistry but went on to discuss his occupation of Cüxhaven, a neutral territory bordering on Hanover. He first dismissed it merely as a "miserable dump where the English execute their vexations with impunity . . . which was necessary to secure my left flank against the attacks of their marine." It was not "worth raising one's voice over." He then considered what was, for him, the more important principle: the injustice of the international arena. "I find everywhere an unfortunate tendency to interpret badly everything that emanates from me that I never find when it comes to England. She oppresses everyone's commerce, and everyone is silent. I occupy a village and everyone cries out."[37]

Napoleon next considered the problem of his closing the rivers Elbe and Weser to British goods. That was not something that he had chosen to do, he said, but the "essential result of the occupation of their banks." After all, "I cannot conceive how one could imagine for a moment that the British flag might float under the range of French cannon without them having to attack it. This is an affair of honor from which it is impossible to withdraw." Even if he wanted to, "it would not even be in my power to act differently. The troops will never see this hated flag under their eyes tranquilly, and despite my orders the French soldiers and the sailors of England would have bloodied the bank in a few days." Why, he concluded, was this important to Prussia? After all, Prussia had other ports and other rivers.

The reason for this careful and sophistic wooing emerged at the end of the discussion: Napoleon wanted a treaty with Prussia. Lombard, taken by surprise and without instructions, told the First Consul that, whereas France had only Austria and Prussia to "fear," France alone was not enough for Prussia. Touching "three colossuses [Prussia] eminently needs Russia, and an isolated system that does not harmonize her interests with those of the two neighbors that she can fear and that she wishes to love, would be an imperfect or dangerous construction."[38]

Napoleon made it clear that his desire for an alliance was based on immediate geostrategic considerations. It was only a question, as Lombard wrote in his report, "of ensuring that during the course of this war France would not be attacked by another power; that if Austria could once again sell herself to England, we would believe ourselves obligated by our current relations to embrace the cause of France."[39] Napoleon wanted to cement that commitment through an alliance, in return for which he would recompense Prussia appropriately.

Lombard recognized that the First Consul had no intention of satisfying any of Frederick William's claims against him for the violation of neutral territory or the closing of the rivers to British shipping. He was, nevertheless, swept away by his impressions of the great man. He guaranteed the accuracy of the words reproduced in his report, he wrote, "but what I cannot render you, Sire, is the tone of kindness and noble frankness with which he always returned to his respect for your rights and for those of your neighbors."

Lombard even took the opportunity to write a subsequent report exclusively about his impressions of Napoleon as a man. He began by declaring, "Bonaparte wanted peace. Full of military glory he aspired to that of administrator." He would have been good at it too, since the general impression of the "violence of his character and the precipitation of his judgments" was quite wrong. "In discussion he is calm, attentive, always has the air of wishing to understand, and is not irritated by being contradicted." Lombard did not understand the full implications of the disclaimer he added: "That, at least, Sire, is how he has constantly been with me."[40]

Now Napoleon was concentrating his energy on the war with Britain and its difficulties. Prussia was very important to him. "He has a pronounced respect, Sire, for your military power and would never, unless I have been duped in my observations, risk drawing on himself the weight of your arms in an unjust cause." Napoleon therefore "attaches a great price to the fact that we were not arming, and they lavished caresses on me here only because I had let the minister know . . . that this question [of Prussia's armament], debated at my departure and unfortunately almost decided, had principally motivated my mission."

Having come to that wise and well-founded conclusion, Lombard and Frederick William nevertheless missed the greatest significance of these events. Napoleon reached out to Prussia in July 1803 with uncharacteristic humility and delicacy in the hopes of winning her over to a defensive alliance. He was willing to flatter Frederick William and his representative in a most un-Napoleonic way and hold out vague promises of great gains for Prussia if she would promise to protect him against an Austrian attack. This was by far the best deal that Prussia would get because it was motivated by Napoleon's perception of his own weakness and needs.

Napoleon's initial plan for the invasion of England envisaged a crossing in November 1803.[41] His first approaches to Prussia for an alliance in July coincided with frantic activity to bring his army and fleet to readiness for a decisive battle within a few months. At the time of the discussions with Lombard, Napoleon's forces were only just beginning to trickle into their camps along the English Channel, and his fleet was only just under construction. He clearly did not feel that he was the master of the continental situation.

That feeling was surely heightened by growing tensions with Russia that would lead to the demand for Morkov's recall in September. Napoleon was not certain what position Austria would adopt, as it took some time for Francis to make it clear that he would remain completely docile. The First Consul could not be sure, finally, that his seizure of Hanover and other provocations in north Germany would not persuade Frederick William to put at least an observation army on foot—something Napoleon would not have failed to do had the situations been reversed. The combination of Napoleon's manifest unpreparedness for the war that had just begun and the manifold uncertainties about how the continental powers would react made him as desperate as he was capable of being to lure Prussia into an immediate defensive alliance. Such an alliance at that time would have secured his eastern borders and allowed him to concentrate fully on the imminent invasion of England.

If Prussia wanted to negotiate with Napoleon, then the best time was in early August 1803, when Napoleon was most cognizant of his need for help from Berlin. For Frederick William to gain the maximum benefit, he would have to come speedily to terms on a public treaty that promised France direct support in the event of an Austrian attack. For such a guarantee in August, Napoleon would have been willing, it seems, to pay a considerable price.

Such an agreement, however, would have made Prussia a French satellite. The Prussians were aware that Alexander would resent Frederick William's decision and would become hostile to Prussia. The Austrians, of course, would also be hostile. Consequently Prussia would be entirely dependent on

Napoleon's support and goodwill and would have lost the ability to pursue any sort of independent policy. Frederick William was, as it turned out, unwilling to incur the anger of Alexander by binding himself to Napoleon, so he could not hope to reap the benefits of Napoleon's urgent needs. He was unwilling to make a simple defensive alliance with Napoleon.

The impression Napoleon made on Lombard and the king (to whom he sent a letter during the course of his conversations with Lombard) completely undermined Haugwitz's proposal to form an army of observation.[42] This was unfortunate for Prussia. In July 1803 Frederick William had an opportunity to maintain the basis for an equal discussion with Napoleon by partially matching his mobilization. Even the corps of 40,000–50,000 troops that Haugwitz advocated would have been sufficient to preserve Prussia from the risk of a sudden invasion and consequently would have secured greater freedom of action for Prussian diplomacy. By allowing himself to be seduced by Napoleon's soft and gentle language, however, Frederick William voluntarily placed himself in the same position Francis would soon occupy. A mobilized and war-ready French army could be inside the core Prussian territories long before the Prussian army could mobilize in response to a sense of danger. This situation, which deteriorated steadily for Prussia as time went on and French preparations became complete, would help emasculate Prussian foreign policy. The decision not to arm in July 1803 perpetuated the neutrality policy.

Frederick William did not see it that way, since he cherished the neutrality policy and saw only that his interactions with Napoleon might strengthen it. Even Haugwitz allowed himself to be deceived into believing that the situation was what he wanted it to be. He thus helped launch Prussia on a foolhardy policy of attempting to bring France and Russia together into a triple alliance. The pursuit of this policy in the end did nothing more than squander precious time.

What did Bonaparte want, Haugwitz asked rhetorically in mid-August.[43] He wanted guarantees that Austria would not attack France while he was invading Britain. "He only wishes, therefore, to be sure that the peace of the continent will not be troubled by a hostile enterprise of the court of Vienna against him, or, in other words, he asks for a guarantee for the maintenance of peace on the continent." What does Russia want? Russia "has no other object . . . than to guarantee the North of Europe from the dangers by which she supposes it is menaced [by France]. . . . She also therefore aspires only to the maintenance of peace on the continent." The resolution was obvious: Russia and Prussia would guarantee jointly that Austria would not attack France during the current war. Napoleon would promise to send no more than 16,000–20,000 troops into Hanover, "cease all concentrations or military preparations on the frontiers of Germany that might give umbrage," refrain from using the Elbe and the Weser as bases for an attack on Britain, and stop all efforts to hinder the free flow of commerce on those rivers. Haugwitz was willing to abandon the last two points if necessary.

The notion that Napoleon and Alexander could be brought together by a logical process was foolish. Alexander, as we have seen, saw Napoleon as the only meaningful threat to north Germany precisely because he did not believe that Napoleon would keep his word. Since the only benefit the proposed treaty offered Russia was Napoleon's promise to observe such neutrality as he had not already violated, Alexander was not likely to be attracted to it. Napoleon was coming to the conclusion that Alexander's court was highly Anglophile and untrustworthy, despite Alexander's personal feelings.[44] He was not likely to value the intervention of this "mountain of snow" in a simple agreement with Prussia.

Nevertheless, Frederick William was determined to try, and the offers were sent out on August 15.[45] They were rejected almost immediately. Talleyrand treated Lucchesini to a violent assault on September 8 about the Anglophilia of the Russian ministers and refused to consider a tripartite treaty. In addition, he warned Prussia away from dealing with the Russians as well.[46] Alexander rejected the proposals on September 24, although more politely. He noted that by Frederick William's proposal "France would be still further certain to give the rein to her ambitious views, being entirely free of disquiet from the side of the continent and able to bring all of her forces to bear against England."[47] This objection was odd, since Frederick William's whole idea was to ensure that France focused her efforts against Britain and not Germany. It manifested the degree to which Alexander had already decided to side with Britain against Napoleon in September 1803.

Frederick William was horrified by this new proof of the collapse of Franco–Russian relations, which he regarded as a calamity for Prussia and Europe.[48] He was determined not to make a treaty with France that would antagonize Alexander, but he was equally determined not to give up trying to neutralize north Germany. When word arrived in late October that Alexander had rejected the Prussian offer, Haugwitz proposed a new course of action.[49] Although an alliance with France that excluded Russia "would be a political monster and could only lead to unfortunate results," an agreement between Berlin and Paris might be reached that was short of an alliance. The goal would be to get Napoleon to agree to withdraw from Hanover and neutralize all of northern Germany, but Prussia should be prepared to accept only the withdrawal from Hamburg and its territories as well as the banks of the Elbe and the Weser. Haugwitz had abandoned the notion of a Prussian mobilization and now sought to obtain what he could by negotiating from a position of weakness. The king readily approved this plan on November 10.[50]

Times, however, had changed in Paris. In September, Napoleon had abandoned his original target date for the invasion of Britain and now was aiming for January 1804. By December, however, he had to abandon even that date, pushing the invasion back into the late spring and then the fall of 1804.[51] The formation of the camps of the Army of England along the English Channel was approaching completion by November. Napoleon now had nearly 200,000 troops ready to hand. Relations with Russia had been effectively broken off, with no very harmful result. Austria remained completely quiescent. The need for the Prussian alliance had diminished dramatically, as Talleyrand noted in February 1804:

> At the beginning of the summer, not having entirely prepared the means of defense and not knowing so perfectly the forces and the dispositions of the continental powers, the First Consul could have feared and had to avoid carefully a double war. Today when he has 500 thousand men under orders and money to pay their salaries, today when he has proofs in hand that far from desiring war, the two imperial courts will even make sacrifices to keep the peace, General Bonaparte, concerning himself only with the present, could pass by alliances.[52]

He sought an alliance with Prussia simply to "establish with her a conservative system for old Europe." The First Consul had less need for Prussia's friendship in November than he had felt in July, and he adjusted his terms accordingly.

On November 30, Lucchesini reported that Napoleon refused to evacuate Hanover, although he conceded that he might significantly reduce the number of troops in the electorate if Prussia "guaranteed [Napoleon] against attacks from England, quarrels with Russia, and imprudences from Denmark."[53] He also insisted that Prussia sign a defensive treaty with France against Austrian or Russian attack in Germany, Italy, or elsewhere. In addition, he now intimated that Prussia should guarantee the territories of the Ottoman Empire jointly with France. In return, he promised Frederick William that he would support a substantial, if vague, extension of Prussian territory and power.

Frederick William sent a formal draft of a proposed convention back to Napoleon on December 15 in which he tried to compromise.[54] Prussia would agree to a defensive alliance against Austria and Russia, although the terms of that alliance were hedged. In return, Napoleon would withdraw his troops from all of north Germany except Hanover and would not keep more than 6,000 troops in the electorate. In secret articles, Napoleon would not try to keep the electorate, or any territory beyond the Rhine, after the war, and would promise to consult with Frederick William over the fate of Hanover in any event.

Napoleon's demands only became more exorbitant after this Prussian effort at compromise. On December 30, Talleyrand hinted that the result of a French success in the war against Britain might be the permanent transfer of Hanover to Prussia. He also suggested that France would work together with Prussia to ensure that the Holy Roman crown fell to Frederick William when it next became vacant (which Talleyrand hoped might be soon, as Francis was thought to be sickly). With these bribes in view, he then insisted that (1) the agreement be a formal treaty and not simply a convention; (2) it guarantee the results of the Congress of Ratisbonne that had doled out compensations for German losses in the French Revolutionary wars; (3) it guarantee the independence and territories of the Ottoman Empire; and (4) it guarantee the existing state of affairs in Italy.[55]

The shift in the balance of Franco–Prussian relations was made clear in a dispatch Talleyrand sent on the same day to the French ambassador in Berlin, Antoine René Charles Mathurin de Laforest, following his conversation with Lucchesini:

> This alliance is more important for Prussia at the moment than it is for France. In the circumstances in which Europe finds itself, Prussia has everything to fear from being isolated, and in joining intimately with the [French] Republic she has, on the contrary, only great advantages to hope for.[56]

The First Consul found it convenient to establish an alliance system, but if Prussia chose not to participate, there were other ways to do that. Frederick William had clearly missed his chance. In July he could either have joined with Napoleon on highly favorable terms (supposing, of course, that Napoleon would have abided by them as the situation changed) or he could have mobilized and attempted to negotiate (or not) from a position of equality.

By the end of 1803, however, Napoleon was not disposed to compromise at all. "With 500,000 soldiers whose salary was regularly paid," he reemphasized to Lucchesini, "with a disposable revenue of 600 million francs and extraordinary resources for three years to come, France alone and without allies had nothing to fear from attacks on the continent."[57] He increased the size of the bribes he was offering, but actually they would have cost him nothing. It was in his interest to see Frederick William and not Francis's successor on the Holy Roman throne, and Hanover was in principle British territory—giving it to the Prussians in theory was easy. Napoleon would have been willing to make these trivial "sacrifices" in order to own a Prussian satellite, which was now required to guarantee territorial arrangements hundreds of miles from its borders, as well as from any important Prussian interest.

The notion of Prussia going to war with Austria or Russia—or both— over the fate of the Ottoman Empire in 1804 was beyond absurd, as was the idea of Prussian troops marching south to avenge an Austrian attack on French possessions in Italy. Frederick William could not possibly have agreed to such terms, and he rejected them in mid-January 1804.[58] Did Napoleon mean to break up the negotiations? Surely not—he had been pursuing the idea of a convention with Prussia assiduously for months. It seems likely, rather, that he had decided by the end of 1803 that he was only willing to have Prussia at all if he could own her completely.

Frederick William's rejection of this proposed treaty was not simply the result of his distaste for its impossible terms. He recognized that it was a highly unequal agreement that imposed far more obligations on Prussia than on France, and offered more significant advantages to Napoleon than to himself.[59] He did not feel that he could sign such an unequal treaty. Even the pseudo-promise of Hanover did not sway him when he recognized that he would be exchanging his independence and nominal great power status for the electorate.

It is interesting that the traditional fear of the Russian reaction does not enter into his discussions of Napoleon's new terms. He did not reject this proposal because of Prussia's geostrategic situation, but because he could not accept it without demeaning his state fatally. Napoleon's remarks as the talks failed continued to emphasize how demeaning it would be. The aim of an alliance with Prussia in 1804, Talleyrand told Lucchesini in early February 1804, was not to avoid a continental war but to establish the basis for a durable peace, and "to aid the Prussian monarchy in closing the last gap that separated it still from the ranks of first-order powers."[60] The need to assert Prussia's independence became the primary basis for the decision to abandon a French alliance.

The Russian Alliance

Two unrelated events came together to produce a Russo–Prussian alliance. First, the collapse of the Franco–Prussian negotiations drove Frederick William to seek Alexander's support by proposing a new treaty in February 1804, lest he become completely isolated in Europe. Second, the tsar's reaction to Napoleon's seizure and execution of the Duc d'Enghien in mid-March 1804 convinced him to receive Frederick William's proposal with more enthusiasm than he had previously felt for dealing with Prussia. Neither side understood the other's motives, and neither realized how the other perceived the treaty that was signed in May.

Haugwitz believed that the failure of the negotiations with France, which had become clear by the beginning of 1804, created a dangerous dilemma: "The acceptance and the refusal of these peremptory [French] demands offer equally dangerous chances."[61] He concluded that only one course of action promised any security, assuming it could be pursued with sufficient secrecy: "to continue the negotiation [with France] and, while waiting, to assure ourselves of the positive intentions of Russia and of her effective assistance in case something happens." He therefore counseled Frederick William to explain fully to

Alexander the goal of the negotiations he had been pursuing with Napoleon, the course of those negotiations, their failure, and Napoleon's current demands. He should then ask Alexander for his "friendly advice about the acceptance or refusal of the French proposals and for a positive declaration about the nature and extent of the effective assistance that one could expect from him in case something happened, and even in order to preempt possible French enterprises."[62] Frederick William accepted this proposal completely[63] and dispatched a letter to Alexander on February 21 in which he included a lengthy memorandum outlining the state of Franco–Prussian negotiations to date.[64]

Haugwitz failed, however, to secure the king's approval of his next initiative—renewed consideration of a Prussian mobilization.[65] "Military measures," he wrote at the end of February, "are too closely tied to those of politics and they influence the issue and the results of the latter too decisively" not to consider them carefully. The French troops maintained in and around Germany had created a dangerous situation: "it depends on the will of a single man, and it would require only a rapid movement that could be completed in ten days to realize a project against Holstein, Mecklemburg, Saxony, but above all Hesse, and to cause alarm in the capital of Prussia." Haugwitz recognized the danger of provoking Napoleon by raising troops on Prussia's western borders, so he confined himself to calling for the mobilization of the garrisons of Berlin and Potsdam and of the troops stationed in the east of the country, especially Silesia.

Frederick William rejected this idea completely. "You know," he wrote on March 13, the eve of the seizure of the Duc d'Enghien, "what decided me in general on the question of whether or not to arm. It is that since the French already have an army in readiness in my neighborhood, each demonstration of mine could be for them a motive or at least a pretext to augment it, and so in protecting myself against future dangers I would in fact have added to present dangers."[66] As we have seen, by failing to arm as soon as Napoleon invaded Hanover, when Napoleon would not have been as readily able to take offense (let alone action) against such a movement, Frederick William chose a path of permanent helplessness. He was right: Napoleon would have taken offense at a Prussian armament in March 1804, since it could only signal overt Prussian hostility toward him. In June 1803 such a mobilization could have been justified as a simple precaution, but there could be no such justification after the collapse of nine months of negotiations. Hoping to expand his options by delaying decisions, Frederick William had reduced them.

His unwillingness to arm dramatically reduced Prussia's utility to Russia in her quest for securing the neutrality of northern Germany. Alexander had already been impressed by Frederick William's apparent pusillanimity in the face of Napoleonic provocations. The king's request for "friendly advice," therefore, was not greeted with overwhelming joy when it arrived in mid-March in St. Petersburg. Czartoryskii was especially dubious. The news of

Prussia's new policy, he wrote on March 17, "would have caused us here a great satisfaction, if we could have allowed ourselves to expect that it would be possible to count on these dispositions; but a similar expectation was too forcefully deceived last summer for one to allow oneself easily to adopt the flattering hope of seeing Prussia enter with us into a concert of measures to guarantee the North of Germany from a certain loss."[67] He was willing to resume discussions with Prussia but concluded that "we have become incredulous and we must see and touch before believing."

Alexander's response to Frederick William's approach was also cool. In a letter of March 15 he repeated several times that "it is not for me to advise Y[our] M[ajesty]," and gently rebuked Frederick William for following such a passive policy for so long. He held out considerable hope, however, to the embattled Prussian king: "If I see Y[our] M[ajesty] engaged for the defense of the independence and the well-being of all of Europe, I assure you that you will find me by your side in an instant and that Prussia will need have no fear that Russia will leave her alone in such a noble struggle."[68]

It is by no means clear that a Russo–Prussian formal convention was imminent in mid-March 1804, despite the Prussian king's renewed efforts to forge such an alliance. In the course of the negotiations in 1803, Frederick William had done himself a great deal of harm in the eyes of Alexander and his advisers, who had evaluated his policies correctly. They rightly saw even in this fresh approach to them evidence of timidity and the desire to continue to pursue a passive policy, and they required fresh proofs that Prussia had really "turned around" before committing directly to her support.

The event that changed the mood in St. Petersburg did not occur in Berlin but in Baden. When Napoleon's troops seized the Duc d'Enghien from Ettenheim on March 15, took him back prisoner to the Château de Vincennes, and interrogated, tried, and shot him, Alexander and many of his advisers flew into a fury.[69] Although the execution of the duke did not fundamentally alter Alexander's feelings or intentions toward Napoleon, it did inaugurate a Russian diplomatic offensive aimed at energizing the other continental states to oppose further French encroachments. Prussia was the primary beneficiary of that offensive.

Alexander wrote to Frederick William on April 21 to congratulate him on his rejection of the most recent French proposals (which proposals and rejections were basically identical to several that had gone before). He then went on to declare, "You wish to stop [Napoleon] if he undertakes to march forward; I am ready to support you with all my means." This is surely the part of the sentence that Frederick William happily seized on—the second part must have caused him much more concern: "But, Sire, I would hope that we could clearly agree on our actions and establish between us a union that would become the center of a general system of opposition against the declared enemy of the rights and proprieties of others."[70] After Russo–Prussian negotiations failed in 1803, Alexander had been inclined to dismiss Frederick William as hopelessly weak. His need to find allies to support the firm stance he wished to take in response to the seizure of the Duc d'Enghien, however, drove him to see the Prussian king in a new light. Whereas before he had looked for signs of weakness in every apparently strong statement the king had made, now he looked desperately for signs of strength.

This changed Russian attitude highlighted the ambivalence of Prussia's position. Even before Alexander had drafted his note, Haugwitz had identified the manifold contradictions of Frederick William's policies in a memorandum of March 30:

> Y[our] M[ajesty] . . . does not want to make war on France, nor to permit her usurpations to continue further, nor to have recourse, in order to ensure that, to armaments, nor to put Russia off from the help that one could expect from her in danger, nor, however, to tie your hands about the application of the principle by entering into too determined a concert with the Emperor.

He concluded unnervingly, "It is no longer the moment to examine if so many delicate conditions can be met at the same time."[71] Alexander may have hoped that the Prussians would resolve to oppose Napoleon's "boundless ambition" (and even Frederick William had begun to use this phrase), but he was deluding himself.[72] Frederick William desired only peace and passivity, and if he approached Russia for a convention, it was only to secure himself in his passive pose. He was convinced that he could not even arm against France, let alone oppose Napoleon openly, and he approached Russia out of fear of French hostility or further Napoleonic encroachments rather than from a desire to do anything positive. But Alexander now saw Prussia through glasses as rose-colored as his earlier vision had been dark.

Thus a Russo–Prussian convention was rapidly concluded on a basis of mutual self-deception. The Russian declaration of May 4 specified that if the French troops in Hanover crossed the border, Prussia and Russia would immediately resist the encroachment with significant force. The Prussian forces would move at once without waiting for the Russians to arrive, whereas the Russian troops, already on the border, would advance to their support at the first request.[73]

The Prussian counterdeclaration of May 26 hedged on the question of the *casus foederis*, noting that "to determine the moment when the *casus foederis* will exist, one must look at things largely and in their spirit." Minor attacks against the small neighboring states of Hanover should not lead to full-scale war between Russia, Prussia, and France. Only French attacks against states along the Weser, especially Mecklemburg, Denmark, and the Hanseatic cities, should occasion the outbreak of hostilities. Russian ambassador Alopeus convinced Hardenburg, who had replaced Haugwitz as foreign minister, that attacks against the Duchy of Oldenburg and the Manor of Yever would also be included in the *casus foederis*, which remained both broad and vague.[74]

Alexander accepted the Prussian counterdeclaration in June and pronounced himself satisfied with Hardenburg's verbal commitments about Oldenburg and Yever, but he still had misgivings.[75] He was displeased with the tone of the Prussian note, which seemed too submissive to Napoleon and sounded almost like an apology for taking action rather than a declaration of opposition. He was also disturbed that the king would not try to hold the line of current French occupation exactly. He recognized, he wrote, the inherently trivial importance of the small territories beyond the Weser, but even they could give advantages to the French troops in Hanover that he would have preferred to deny them. He recognized, in short, the continued determination of the Prussian court to avoid provoking Napoleon and even defer to him. He was determined, however, to see Prussia, his new ally, in the best light now, and expressed his confidence that Frederick William would abide by his new obligations.

This confidence was misplaced. Frederick William failed the two crucial tests of this period spectacularly, from Alexander's perspective. Apprised of Napoleon's intention to make himself emperor, Frederick William instructed Lucchesini in late April to

> seize (as soon as possible) an occasion for expressing to Talleyrand that, after having seen with pleasure the supreme power granted for life to the First Consul, I would see with still more interest the order of affairs effected by his wisdom and his great actions consolidated by the establishment of the heredity of this power in his family, and I will make no difficulty about recognizing it.[76]

He held firm to that promise by sending Napoleon formal congratulations (and recognition) for his new title directly on June 28.[77] Napoleon was highly satisfied with the Prussian course in this regard.[78]

Frederick William had also reacted tamely to the seizure and execution of the Duc d'Enghien. This matter, however, had caused a stir in Berlin and demanded a more careful and detailed consideration than had the recognition of Napoleon's imperial title. In early May the Count of Lille (Louis XVIII) had sent Frederick William a formal note informing him of the death and complaining of the circumstances surrounding it.[79] Queen Louise wanted to send the court into mourning, as Alexander had done. Lombard was horrified and begged Hardenberg to intervene: "To go into mourning in imitation of Russia at a moment when we are suspected of having had secret reasons for breaking off the negotiation in Paris [at the beginning of 1804] will not reestablish our relations." He concluded, "The best that we could do . . . is to give no sign of life concerning this event." He then launched into a series of sophistries to the effect that since the king did not formally recognize Louis XVIII as the head of the Bourbon family, there was no one alive who could formally notify him of the death (and thereby force him to go into mourning) except the king of Spain, who could be relied on to do no such thing, since he was already under Napoleon's thrall.

Hardenberg agreed, citing geopolitical reasons as usual: "Our vexed position does not seem to permit us to adopt the example of Russia alone, which is in a very different situation in which it costs nothing to express this sentiment, as long as we serve as the boulevard" for any potential future conflict. He concluded, "Let us add that this demonstration, while satisfying a very honorable sentiment, would without contradiction expose us at least as much, with a man as sensitive as Bonaparte, as the assembling of a corps of troops, without imposing upon him at the same time as much as such a measure would do."[80] The matter was quietly shelved, although not before Napoleon got wind of it and indicated to his ambassador, at least, his displeasure with the fact that the idea had come up at all.[81]

Alexander had pressed many of the courts of Europe to oppose Napoleon's violation of German neutrality forcefully, and had put his own court into mourning as a way of leading the other European states toward opposition. He naturally sought to bring Frederick William along with him as a leader of this opposition. He wrote the king in late April that he was determined to take a strong stand with "energetic demarches," and added, "I hope that Y[our] M[ajesty] will not let me act alone in favor of the outraged honor and destroyed security of the German Empire, and that [you] will join your demarches with mine to prevent henceforth any so manifest injury of the law of nations."[82] This opposition could take the form "either of a common negotiation at Paris conducted in a tone of firmness and dignity unknown thus far to the French government, or by opposing a vigorous resistance to its fatal enterprises."

Frederick William, however, had no notion of using firmness toward Napoleon or opposing any vigorous resistance to his actions. When Talleyrand made it clear to Lucchesini at the end of May that the only hope for maintaining the peace of Europe was to suppress any response by the German Imperial Diet to the inflammatory Russian notes, the Prussian minister happily fell in with the French desires—the response was suppressed.[83] Oddly enough, Alexander thanked Frederick William in early June for the "language that your minister at Ratisbonne used at the Diet" when his letter was presented, even as he complained that the king had not responded to his first note seeking cooperation over the Enghien affair.[84]

Frederick William finally replied in mid-July, with the usual sad references to Prussia's "geographic position" that made "delicacy indispensable."[85] He proclaimed, "The principles expressed in your letter are mine," adding, "you share with me the desire to maintain the peace and to see it restored to Europe." Any such step as Alexander proposed to take, however, would inevitably lead to war with France. He granted that the Russo–Prussian alliance was an "essential step toward the system" that Alexander had wanted to create, but that union should not be consummated by war at that time. "The war with France that we wish to avoid would be the result as guaranteed as it would be prompt." The allies would do better to await more propitious times. There the matter rested for nearly three months.

This correspondence had made it clear to Alexander that Frederick William did not share his vision for political action. Alexander did not know of a more important way in which Frederick William betrayed the principles that he believed undergirded the Russo–Prussian alliance. In a conversation between Talleyrand and Lucchesini in mid-May, the French foreign minister had warned that if a Franco–Russian war broke out, the French garrison in Hanover would have to be augmented, unless Napoleon could trust Frederick William completely.[86]

He also passed on a demand from Napoleon: "In the case that Russia asked for the passage through your states of Russian troops destined against France, would you engage to refuse it?" The matter seemed urgent to Lucchesini because he believed, in light of the imminent termination of diplomatic relations between France and Russia, that a continental war was inevitable. "A continental war, I cannot repeat enough," he wrote, "is in the current circumstances the secret wish of the First Consul." It would salve his honor wounded by the failure to invade England, would employ his restless generals, and would "resolve by battles a question that negotiations will decide with difficulty, that is the fate of the Italian Republic after the re-establishment of the monarchy in favor of the man who is its president."[87]

Frederick William's response of May 24 showed with absolute clarity the meaning and significance he gave to his alliance with Alexander.[88] He proclaimed that he would definitely refuse to grant Alexander permission to send Russian troops across Prussian territory, a decision that was the "simple and natural consequence" of the neutrality policy. He saw his alliance with Russia as supporting Prussian neutrality, rather than opposing French expansionism. He added, however, that he regarded himself as bound to this policy only on the basis of two assumptions: (1) France would not augment the troops it maintained in Hanover and (2) "the neutral states of this part of the Empire would not be made to bear the burden of the current war." In this way, Frederick William believed that he had squared the circle: he promised to protect Napoleon from Russia as long as Napoleon himself abided by the (much revised) terms of Prussian neutrality. If Napoleon did violate those terms, however, (thereby bringing into play the *casus foederis* of the Russo–Prussian treaty), then Frederick William could permit, and indeed, demand by right, Russian assistance in perfect conscience.

If Frederick William had any doubts of the wisdom of this policy, he buried them under the conviction that the discussion was irrelevant. "None of Russia's declarations either at Ratisbonne or at Paris itself indicates any imminent [Russian] aggression, nor even an offensive intention." The king was repeating the calming words of Hardenberg, who assured him that Lucchesini's belief about the imminence of a continental war was completely unjustified.[89] There was a great deal of truth to Hardenberg's view. In the summer of 1804 Alexander was still pursuing an entirely defensive policy, and although he would certainly have been irked by Frederick William's promise to prevent him from sending troops across Prussian territory, he nevertheless had no intention of doing so except in response to a new Napoleonic provocation (that would theoretically have activated the Russo–Prussian treaty in any case).

The trouble with the Prussian conviction that Alexander intended to play a passive role was not that it was wrong in May 1804, but that the king and his advisers were slow to update it, partly because of the limitations of what they could know of Alexander's changing way of thinking. Even in May, Hardenberg's belief that the "paths are still open to reconciling Emperor Alexander and the future Emperor Napoleon" was wrong.[90] His belief that Napoleon was actively working to avoid war and especially continental war was off the mark, and the notion that Pitt's advent to power in London made a Franco–British peace more likely was delusional and showed an astonishing ignorance of the British politics of the time.[91] His beliefs that the British could be induced to give back Malta and that any Russo–British alliance would be purely defensive and relate only to Italy or the Levant were likewise without any foundation. The king's positive repetition of this notion in September 1804 was less excusable and more dangerous than it had been in May: "I know from the source that [Alexander] has refused all liaisons that have an offensive goal against France."[92]

A subsequent reiteration of this conviction reveals part of the problem. "I have always been convinced," Frederick William wrote in October, "that Emperor Alexander is perfectly of the same sentiments and aspires . . . only to assuring peace on bases that are solid and conformable to the independence of Europe."[93] The problem with this statement was less the fact that it was now false, since Alexander had sent Novosil'tsev to Britain in September with a proposal for an offensive alliance, but that it revealed the degree of misunderstanding that existed between Berlin and St. Petersburg. Taken on its own terms, Frederick William's pronouncement was perfectly accurate. By October 1804, however, Alexander had come to believe that it was impossible to find "solid bases conformable to the independence of Europe" as long as Napoleon had the force and territories he held at that time. Frederick William still believed that Alexander was pursuing a policy of pure containment long after the tsar had determined to roll back the gains of an empire he had come to see as evil. The misunderstandings were cleared up shortly in a crisis that badly undermined the Russo–Prussian relationship.

The Russians ignored Prussia completely for the better part of two months after receiving Frederick William's last note of July 11 refusing to oppose Napoleon openly over the Enghien affair.[94] The marriage of an archduchess, the army maneuvers at Peterhof, and the "conflict of affairs and work that followed that period" supposedly prevented Czartoryskii from learning the tsar's will in regard to Berlin. They had not prevented the Russian court from conducting voluminous correspondence with other states and ministers, however, including the dispatch of Novosil'tsev with two lengthy sets of instructions to London.[95] It seems likely that the silence was a way of showing gentle displeasure. However that may be, Alexander resumed the offensive in October 1804 in less dulcet tones.

"I regret infinitely," he wrote, "that our manner of envisaging recent events, although uniform in principle, has not been able to be so in its application." The tsar could "not but be pained to see that secondary motives will continue to the end to prevent the German powers from adopting in current affairs a course more conformable to their dignity as well as to justice."[96] Czartoryskii's note to Alopeus covering this tsarist missive was more direct.[97] He blamed the collapse of Russian efforts to oppose Napoleon over the Enghien affair directly on Lucchesini, even implying that the Austrians would have held firm if their ambassador had not allowed himself to be led astray by his Prussian counterpart.

Czartoryskii then enunciated the usual Russian line that if the German powers had no care for protecting themselves, then Russia could hardly be expected to put herself out on their behalf. On the other hand, he explicitly rejected Hardenberg's notion (offered at the time of the Enghien affair) that Russian support could only come after it had been asked for.[98] What Czartoryskii had in mind is not clear. Hardenberg's statement had pertained to the failure of the Margrave of Baden to seek assistance from the Imperial Diet, which the Prussians claimed meant that they could not oppose the French on behalf of Baden, an independent state within the Holy Roman Empire. Czartoryskii may simply have meant that it was not necessary to wait for a small state overrun by French forces to seek outside help before Russia came to its assistance. He may also have meant, however, that the Russo–Prussian guarantee obligated Prussia to go to war with France whether or not the court of Berlin received such a request from an injured minor state. Events would shortly show that such was precisely the interpretation that the Russians placed on their treaty with Prussia.

Czartoryskii then continued that, although the Russians desired to maintain the peace and reestablish it on the firmest basis, they would not do so at the cost of "suffering the least humiliation" or of allowing Napoleon to run free by giving him the hope that he might succeed in "all the excesses that his ambitions inspire in him."[99] This statement of the differences between Berlin and St. Petersburg over the meaning of "maintaining the peace" would go unrecognized, as had all other such indications.

Part of the reason for this continued miscommunication was the determination on both sides to see hope for their mutual commitments. Although Czartoryskii noted that "if one only considered the respective courts in their diplomatic relations, one would necessarily conclude from that that between them reigns coolness and little concert," the situation was actually much better than that. The tsar, he wrote, "is no less intimately convinced that on any *essential and decisive* occasion the King of Prussia would be in accord with him."[100] Disappointed though he was with Frederick William's tergiversations, Alexander still hoped that when the chips were down, the Prussian king would come through. This conviction made the shock caused in St. Petersburg by the Prussian reaction to the Rumbold affair even more profound than it would otherwise have been.

The Rumbold Affair

On October 24, 1804, Napoleon repeated the Enghien operation by sending troops into Hamburg to seize the British envoy, Sir George Rumbold, with all his papers. Napoleon's motive is somewhat obscure. In early 1804 he had trapped the British emissary in Munich, Sir Francis Drake, into participating in a manufactured spy conspiracy. Following that, foreign minister Hawkesbury apparently attempted to defend the conduct of British ministers abroad. Napoleon was determined to demonstrate to Europe that British ministers were running extensive spy rings, and to that end he ordered Marshal Jean Baptiste Jules Bernadotte, then commander of his forces in Hanover, to seize Rumbold and his papers in October. He intended to announce the seizure to Europe along with proof of Rumbold's complicity in spying.[101] The result was a diplomatic uproar.

Napoleon did not envisage such a result from a minor undertaking. This miscalculation was partly the result of his usual inability to see his actions from the perspective of others. He never could understand why other European states were not outraged by the British abuse of diplomatic immunity when their ministers abroad spied. But the miscalculation had another cause. Napoleon's previous actions had dealt a series of blows to Prussia's international prestige and honor. He had pressed Frederick William so hard that he refused to submit to further insults. As a result, the Prussian king turned briefly against Napoleon, much to the latter's surprise.

The increasing mention of Prussia's dignity in official correspondence (always a sure sign that leaders feel it to be under siege) was clear as early as

May 1804. On May 24 Lombard wrote to Lucchesini of "the system that you designate by three words, *otium cum dignitate* [repose with dignity], to which I would substitute only these, *cum dignitate pax* [peace with dignity]."[102] In the course of a stinging rebuke to Lucchesini (mostly on other grounds), Frederick William reemphasized the point in July. Although he wanted to live in peace, "I will never, be very certain, purchase it at the price of my dignity."[103] He enjoined Lucchesini to maintain his dignity firmly at Napoleon's court.

We have already seen the role that injured honor played in the collapse of the Franco–Prussian negotiations in early 1804. The more Napoleon treated Frederick William as a junior partner, the more unwilling the king was to continue negotiating with him. Lucchesini professed not to understand why the negotiations had been broken off, since a Franco–Prussian alliance, he believed, would have rendered a continental war impossible. That was the king's goal, was it not?[104] Absent an understanding of the central importance of Frederick William's honor and his determination to maintain Prussia's status as an independent great power, Prussia's behavior in this period is inexplicable.

The Rumbold affair highlights this fact. In October, Frederick William was in the middle of another effort to mediate between France and Russia. He had sought Alexander's permission to re-open negotiations, which the tsar gave grudgingly,[105] and he had sent General Knobelsdorff to Paris with a similar offer.[106] To preserve Prussian dignity, Hardenberg insisted that Napoleon meet Knobelsdorff in private, just as Frederick William had met Napoleon's previous envoy. When word of Rumbold's seizure came, during Knobelsdorff's voyage at the end of October, Hardenberg immediately ordered the envoy to stop where he was and await further orders.[107] "This major matter," he wrote to the Prussian ambassador in London, "holds all others in suspense." There could be no mediation effort while the Rumbold affair was in train.[108]

The Prussian court found itself in the midst of a crisis. Not only had Napoleon violated the neutrality of a Hanseatic town, but Rumbold himself was personally accredited to Frederick William.* In the grand tradition of Frederick William's court, a conference was called immediately. The normally pro-French Lombard had suddenly become hostile to Napoleon, and he ensured that the Francophobe former minister Count Schulenburg was invited to participate, along with himself and Hardenberg.[109] The conference decided to send a firm letter to Napoleon and recall the Duke of Brunswick to advise on military preparations.

The letter was drafted that very day, October 30.[110] Frederick William made it clear that this was a matter of honor. He urged no issue of Prussian

---

*The Holy Roman Empire was broken into *Kreisen* or "circles" for administrative purposes. Frederick William was the head of the Lower-Saxon *Kreis*, of which Hamburg was a part. The British minister was accredited therefore both to the Hamburg senate and to Frederick William as head of the *Kreis*.

security or interest other than that of his own injured dignity. Napoleon, he wrote, was powerful enough to back down. He himself, however, "will have lost it for good, if on this occasion I cannot prove to Europe that my policy rested on a just appreciation of our relations and on the fact that I had understood your principles better than others." Even Laforest discerned from gossip at the Prussian court (since Lombard uncharacteristically had broken off relations with him temporarily) that Prussia's honor was badly bruised. "No one," he was told, "dares at Potsdam to doubt that the honor of the monarchy will have been compromised in the eyes of Europe and Prussia brought to the last degree of degradation if she does not act with energy on this occasion." He noted that the appearance of Schulenburg in the discussions was ominous for France, since Schulenburg feared that Frederick William might "allow himself to fall into a complete dependence on France" and was determined to oppose such an outcome.[111] Lombard himself, Laforest wrote, was angry that Napoleon had deceived him in their conversations in Brussels.[112] The king sent a separate message to Lucchesini to instruct him that his discussions with Talleyrand should be characterized by "the balance of moderation, dignity, and calm."[113]

It is not clear that Frederick William would not have gone to war over this matter had Napoleon proved recalcitrant. Certainly Hardenberg did not find such an idea inconceivable.[114] It is perfectly clear that Frederick William did not want to go to war, and he worked to ensure that he got his way in his usual manner. Since he could not force Napoleon to release Rumbold (he asked for nothing more even in his stern letter), he could at least find counselors to advise him against taking the step he did not want to take. Accordingly, he wrote to Haugwitz, now in retirement, "What must Prussia do to keep her dignity and to fulfill her obligations . . . ? There are many people who vote in favor of war; *not me*. It seems to me that there is a way to get out of this without coming to such a radical solution."[115] This note gave Haugwitz the opening to reenter Prussian foreign policymaking, which he did, now on the side of cooperation with the French. Hardenberg had felt it necessary to advocate more dramatic efforts against Napoleon (short of war if at all possible). It is likely that these two advisers, with Schulenburg and Lombard in the wings as well, would have served once again to paralyze Frederick William with contradictory advice—at the king's own desire.[116]

To the surprise of almost everyone on the continent and in Britain, however, Napoleon for once relented. Hardly more than a week after Frederick William's angry letter had been dispatched, Lucchesini met with Talleyrand to discuss the matter.[117] Talleyrand promised to seek redress for Prussia from Napoleon at once. The next day, Frederick William's note was read to Napoleon. He apologized through Talleyrand and ordered that Rumbold be released and sent to the Island of Jersey (British territory off the coast of France). He sent a letter back to Frederick William that very night, apologizing for seizing Rumbold and promising to explain himself fully.[118] Frederick William, as Lombard wrote to Hardenberg, was "in the clouds" with joy.[119]

Why did Napoleon give way so quickly? Because he was not giving way at all, except in tone. His initial orders made it clear that what he was interested in was Rumbold's papers. He hoped to use them to prove that the British minister, like all other British ministers, was maintaining a spy ring. Although Minister of Police Fouché claimed that he interceded to prevent Rumbold from suffering the Duc d'Enghien's fate, this is clearly nonsense.[120] There was no reason for Napoleon to harm the British ambassador to Hamburg, and no evidence whatsoever that he ever contemplated doing anything other than seizing the minister's papers and letting him go. At worst he might have held him hostage, hoping to exchange him for a French officer or spy captured by the British.

By presenting the release of his "captive" to Frederick William as a mark of special favor, however, he revolutionized the dangerous situation he had created. The British tried to press Frederick William to demand more recompense than the simple release of their ambassador, but Hardenberg ridiculed that notion with the good humor of a man just released from the gallows: one does not go to war for "a box of papers."[121] By mid-November the crisis was over, as far as the Prussians were concerned.

The Russian court, however, following events four weeks behind (the time it took a courier to travel from St. Petersburg to Berlin), was horrified by this turn of events. Without even consulting with his own court, Alopeus told Hardenberg on October 28 that Prussia must mobilize in response to the kidnapping. He even quoted to him the relevant article of the Russo–Prussian treaty of May that stipulated that "the *casus foederis* . . . will take place at the first enterprise of the French against a State situated on the right of the Weser."[122] Frederick William did not take this threat lightly, although his reaction was silly. He tried to cast doubt on the validity of the agreement by refusing the exchange of presents between the ministers signatory, customary upon the ratification of a treaty.[123]

Hardenberg mollified Alopeus by telling him that if Napoleon did not respond to the king's protest within three weeks, Prussia would mobilize an army of 94,000 men.[124] This may have been a device to put the Russians off for a while, or it may have been an earnest of the panicky atmosphere in Berlin in the immediate wake of the kidnapping. When Alopeus's report reached St. Petersburg in mid-November, Czartoryskii and Alexander seized on it as evidence that Frederick William would keep his word after all, at least when it really mattered.[125] Czartoryskii's only fear was that the Prussian court would accept the release of Rumbold when so much more was clearly called for. At a minimum, Napoleon should be made to apologize and explain himself publicly to all of Europe—which, if insisted on, would have led to war.

The mood in St. Petersburg was grim when word arrived in late December that Frederick William had settled for the release of Rumbold and a private apology.[126] All tones of friendliness and comradeship had disappeared. Alexander declared that he could not agree with the course of action Frederick William had adopted. His tone even became menacing. Czartoryskii warned that if Prussia sided with France on the question of the ultimate disposition of Hanover, and "does not turn a favorable ear to our representations, that court [of Berlin] will have ceased to be neutral, and far from maintaining equal regard and the same impartiality toward the two belligerent powers, will seem to have made common cause with the French" by freeing up French troops to be used elsewhere.

Once again the main problems involved perspective and communication. The Russians saw the Rumbold affair as an act of aggression triggering their alliance with Prussia. Therefore Frederick William's failure to act was a violation of that alliance and brought into question the worth of his given word to Russia. For Frederick William, the kidnapping of Rumbold was simply an affair of honor, resolved amicably once Napoleon uncharacteristically made reparation and apologized. Since the primary and indispensable goal of Prussian policy was the avoidance of war, Napoleon's backtracking was more than good enough. But since Novosil'tsev was deep in conversations with Pitt about an offensive alliance against France (about which the Prussians knew nothing), Napoleon's actions were intolerable. Whereas before miscommunication had brought the courts of Berlin and St. Petersburg together by concealing the extent of disagreements that had been papered over, now they drove them apart. Alexander gave up almost all hope of bringing Frederick William around to the "right" policy of openly opposing Napoleon, and the idea began to circulate in London and St. Petersburg of compelling Prussia to fight by stationing a Russian army on her frontier. The Russo–Prussian alliance had lasted barely six months.

Austrian and Russian Alliance Overtures

Despite his resentment toward Frederick William, Alexander could not simply dismiss him. Among other things, the Austrians would not permit it. The Austrian court had to reconsider its position after the conclusion of the Austro–Russian defensive alliance in November 1804 and as the international situation deteriorated over the course of 1805. This reconsideration intensified as rumors of Napoleon's impending decisions about Italy and supposed preparations for an offensive war on the continent surfaced. The result was that Francis, at Cobenzl's urging, decided to make a sincere and determined effort to form a defensive alliance with Prussia.[127] Although the idea had been mooted in Vienna at least since April 1804, the replacement of the hated Haugwitz by Hardenberg in August seemed to offer some hope of promising results. But the Austrians strongly suspected that Lombard was in the pay of the French and would work devotedly to thwart any such development.[128]

The new Austrian ambassador in Berlin, thirty-two-year-old Count Clement von Metternich-Winneburg, also held out no hope for the success of a direct Austro–Prussian negotiation. "It seems sure that it is only in Saint Petersburg that the Court of Prussia can be conquered, and the most perfect joining of our views, the most intimate combination of our means with those of Russia to arrive at this goal seems to offer all probabilities of success."[129] This conviction, seconded by the Russians, launched a bizarre three-way negotiation between Berlin, Vienna, and St. Petersburg.

The Rumbold affair, which seemed to promise a conflict of some sort between France and Prussia, emboldened the Austrians to open negotiations with Prussia at the end of November.[130] Consequently Metternich first coordinated his activities with Alopeus, as he had been instructed to do, and then approached Hardenberg with his offer. Apparently by accident, Alopeus was announced in Hardenberg's antechamber in the middle of this conversation and, with the approval of both parties, admitted to the conversation.*

The result of the discussion was unspectacular. Hardenberg asserted that he was enchanted by the Austrian overtures and would try to convince the king to accept them, although he was sure that Frederick William would not agree to any convention that resembled a coalition. When the king returned to Berlin a few days later, Hardenberg approached him and attempted to persuade him to accept the Austrian proposal for a negotiation. But he received only a prevarication: the matter was too important to be decided at once. In the meantime, both the king and his minister pressed Metternich and Alopeus to maintain the utmost secrecy, asking that even the Prussian ministers in Vienna and St. Petersburg not be informed of the course of the negotiations, or even of their existence. The king declared that "if Bonaparte . . . learned of [the negotiation], he would fall on [Austria or Prussia] to prevent their junction."[131] Metternich and Alopeus perforce agreed to these terms.

Although Frederick William and his ministers were certainly determined to prevent any word of the negotiations from reaching Napoleon's ears, the precautions Hardenberg prescribed seem excessive for that purpose. The French, in particular, got nothing whatever out of St. Petersburg, where they did not even have any diplomatic representation at the time. Perhaps Hardenberg wanted to prevent Haugwitz and Lombard from finding out what he was doing and attacking it before he had had a chance to press the king in the right direction. In that case it would have been essential to prevent the Prussian

---

*This "accident" is hard to accept, although both Metternich and Alopeus told their courts that the event was fortuitous (Metternich to Colloredo, 4 December 1804, in Oncken, *Österreich und Preußen*, doc. 7; Alopeus to Czartoryskii, 16 December 1804, VPR, vol. II, doc. 76). It seems more likely that Metternich told Alopeus when he was going to meet Hardenberg and the latter showed up, possibly without prearrangement, knowing that Hardenberg and Metternich could choose to include or exclude him, as seemed appropriate. If so, it was a delicate way of offering support to the Austrian effort.

ministers abroad from learning of the negotiations, since their reports invariably crossed Lombard's desk before even Hardenberg saw them. Such an interpretation would argue that Hardenberg was indeed committed to the success of the negotiations, something that Metternich, for one, certainly believed.[132]

However that may be, Hardenberg managed to persuade the king to accept the principle of negotiating with Austria, and he read Metternich a verbal note to that effect on the day after Christmas.[133] The Austrian response was dramatic. Colloredo sent Metternich two long memoranda in early January 1805, one for Hardenberg and the other for Metternich explaining the line to take in his negotiations.[134] In the first, Colloredo attempted to explain Austria's policy in Germany for the past half century in a nearly apologetic tone. He argued that as long as Austria had held Lombardy and the Netherlands, she had been obliged to dominate German affairs in order to defend those two far-flung provinces. Since the revolutionary wars had deprived her of both of those liabilities, substituting for them the easily defensible Polish and Venetian territories, she was no longer obliged to follow a policy line in Germany to which Prussia would have reason to object. From the Austrian perspective nothing now stood in the way of a true Austro–Prussian rapprochement. Nor was this argument mere window dressing to support an alliance bid: Austrian statesmen had been making it to each other for some time.[135]

If the open message to Hardenberg was meant to calm Prussian fears about Austria, the private message to Metternich sought to stoke Berlin's fears of France. Napoleon, Colloredo warned, was attempting to destroy the German constitution by forming a league of the new electorates he had created during the negotiations over compensations. He sought to become a new Charlemagne and aspired to "universal Monarchy." "The fate of Europe," he intoned, "depends on the determination of the sovereigns of Austria, Russia, and Prussia, and the sincerity and energy that they put into their union, on the elevated viewpoint that they give their concert."

He also argued that Prussia could no longer afford to ignore events outside of North Germany. If the great powers allowed Napoleon to gain control over Italy, Spain, Portugal, and the minor German states, then the time might come when "even the combination of the weakened Powers would no longer suffice to stem the tide." Metternich summarized this message succinctly but powerfully in the note he sent back to Hardenberg in mid-January.[136]

At this point, Alexander decided to intervene by sending a trusted envoy, Baron Ferdinand Wintzingerode, to Berlin at the end of January to speak directly with the king.* Advancing the Austro–Prussian negotiations was only

---

*Colloredo, at least, seems to have believed that the delay in a Prussian response was one of the factors that motivated the dispatch of Wintzingerode. If so, then Alexander was very impatient, for the timing of the various notes and his decision to send an envoy would have required Frederick William to respond almost immediately. See Colloredo to Metternich, 4 February 1805, in Oncken, *Österreich und Preußen*, doc. 13.

one of the goals Alexander assigned Wintzingerode, whose mission was motivated at least as much by Alexander's growing mistrust of Alopeus.[137] The ostensible purpose of Wintzingerode's mission was to resolve the crisis that had been brewing over Swedish Pomerania.

For some time, Gustavus IV of Sweden had been building up his armed forces in Pomerania and negotiating, through the Russians, for a British subvention to support his participation in the projected new coalition. Frederick William feared that either Napoleon would seize on this armament as a provocation and invade Pomerania, which lay within the Prussian neutrality zone, or that the Swedes would make an offensive move of their own, thus giving Napoleon an even better pretext for invasion. Therefore he threatened to invade Pomerania if Gustavus did not stop. Alexander, however, had just signed a defensive alliance with Gustavus, which would have committed him to go to war against Prussia in such a circumstance. Wintzingerode's first order of business was to lay this fact before Frederick William and convince him to abandon a fruitless and self-destructive policy.

The Prussians' arguments for seizing Pomerania bothered Alexander. After all, he pointed out, by the terms of the Russo–Prussian convention, if Napoleon attacked Pomerania, Berlin would be obligated to come to Gustavus's defense. Of course Alexander would hasten to help defeat Napoleon as promised. Frederick William's only interest in the Russo–Prussian convention was to ensure that it was never executed, however, as Alexander well knew. This incident strengthened Alexander's conviction that there was no hope of bringing Prussia to join an active coalition.

. The tsar resented the way the Prussians had treated him during previous negotiations and their failure to execute agreements they had already made. Czartoryskii reported on January 28 that he had to "combat a marked reluctance on the Emperor's part to making the least demarche" to Berlin.[138] The importance of helping Austria secure the Prussian alliance, however, convinced him to try anyway. Thus Wintzingerode's mission was supplemented by a dispatch to Alopeus ordering him to negotiate for such a coalition. A draft of the letter that Alexander hoped all three sovereigns would exchange was enclosed.[139] The Austro–Prussian negotiation thereby became a Russo–Prussian discussion.

The terms of the actual agreement were simple: each state would come to the assistance of any of the others that Napoleon might attack, with a specified number of troops (Alexander promised 100,000). The actual *casus foederis* that Alexander had in mind, which Czartoryskii expounded in the covering memorandum to Alopeus, was infinitely broader. The allies would go to war in any of the following circumstances: (1) The French army crosses the Rhine or the Weser anywhere along its entire length; (2) Napoleon occupies Switzerland; (3) Napoleon occupies the capital of Naples, Calabria, and the fortresses of Capua and Gaeta; (4) the French attack Turkey or the Ionian Isles; (5) Napoleon establishes the rule of the Batavian Republic as hereditary in his family or the "states his troops occupy in Italy or in Germany, and if he announces in an undeniable manner the intention to have himself crowned Emperor of Germany."*

The discussion of each case included a lengthy explanation of how it was really in Prussia's interest to subscribe to the requirement to go to war for interests far removed from Prussia herself. In addition to the customary exhortation to consider the well-being of Europe and prevent Napoleon from becoming unbeatable through distant acquisitions, a new refrain entered the discussion. If Prussia wanted Austria's help, then Prussia would have to serve Austria's interests. With the loss of the Netherlands, Austria no longer had any active concern for the events of northern Germany, as Prussia was not directly involved in those of Italy. The coalition could only be based on the mutual, reciprocal, and equal commitment of the two powers to defend each other's interests. Russia's similar position explained the strictures regarding Naples, with which Alexander had a defensive alliance, and the Ionian Isles and the Ottoman Empire.

This was an enlightened and valid exposition of the basis of alliances among equals—they only work if the powers involved are prepared to help serve the interests of the others. Arrangements in which some powers seek their own interests and others help them without gain are not really alliances but hegemonies or quasi-empires. They usually do not last long unless the dominant power is willing to use force to keep its satellites in line.

Despite the coercive tone of his messages (which threatened Frederick William directly with war if he took any of several proscribed actions), Alexander sincerely believed that he was trying to serve Prussia's interests. Was it not in Prussia's interest to keep Napoleon in check? To prevent him from dominating the entire continent? To keep strategically critical lands out of his control? To secure the free trade of Germany's cities and rivers? The problem was not with Alexander's selfishness, but with the divergence between his perceptions of Prussia's interests and those of Prussia's king. Frederick William had rejected a more attractive alliance offer from Napoleon on the grounds that it would embroil him in territories far removed from his own sphere of concern. He had the same objections to this much less attractive Russian offer. At least Napoleon had offered him Hanover, the one prize that Prussian statesmen had come to care about, and the one prize that Russia, negotiating for an alliance with Britain at the same time, could not promise.

Wintzingerode therefore found the negotiations hard when he arrived in Berlin in March. In a lengthy interview with Hardenberg (conducted jointly with Alopeus), he tried to resolve the matters of discord between Russia and Prussia and probe the foreign minister about prospects for an alliance.[140]

---

*It is not clear from the language of the note whether any one of these events would be sufficient, or if all were required to trigger the *casus foederis*.

Those prospects seemed dim. To Wintzingerode's charges that Prussia had not lived up to her previous commitments and was at that moment arming a force on Russia's border (which was untrue), Hardenberg retorted that Russia herself had played Prussia false on previous occasions and was seeking causes of disaffection and distrust. Hardenberg did promise that Prussia would abandon her designs on Swedish Pomerania, but his statements on more important matters were both better and worse than the Russians had hoped for.[141]

On the one hand, Hardenberg took the opportunity to fulfill his commitment to Napoleon. He announced the view that the Russo–Prussian alliance precluded Russia from sending forces through the neutrality zone even in a war with France; the zone included not merely Prussian territory but all of north Germany. This was a critical piece of information, since Alexander had told Wintzingerode that he was willing to accept Prussian neutrality but was not willing to allow Frederick William to keep him out of north Germany entirely. Such a decision, he believed, would make Prussia a de facto auxiliary of France and would destroy the supposed neutrality on that basis.[142] On the other hand, Hardenberg, pressed hard, stated that if Prussia were forced to choose sides, she would choose Russia, although he refused to make a formal or official statement to that effect.

Hardenberg's fears that Lombard and Haugwitz might prevent him from persuading the king to consider the alliance offers seriously proved well founded. At the end of February, Haugwitz sent a memorandum to the king that provided Frederick William with the balancing viewpoint he had surely desired. The theme was the excessively broad commitment Alexander desired as the *casus foederis* of the proposed convention. Although "no event which takes place in Europe," he wrote, "is in the last analysis irrelevant to Prussia . . . the interest which she takes in it differs according to the amount of influence which it has on [Prussia's] own existence."[143] This was exactly what Frederick William wanted to hear, and it probably motivated the negative response that Hardenberg gave to Wintzingerode and Alopeus.[144]

Afraid to reject the Russian alliance offer outright, Frederick William decided to send his own emissary, Adjutant General Friedrich Wilhelm Zastrow, to Alexander to explain his motives and attempt to palliate the tsar and his court in April.[145] Zastrow was to repeat the same tired arguments that Frederick William's ministers and ambassadors had already offered. Although Russia was strong and remote enough to declare against Napoleon openly, Prussia's terrible geostrategic position made such policies suicidal. Russia could afford to take a grand view of the continent, but weak Prussia had to confine her concerns to her own immediate interests. Zastrow was to repeat, moreover, the injunction that Frederick William would defend the Prussian neutrality zone even against Russia, if necessary. The attempts to defend Prussia's actions over Pomerania and the wounded, petulant tone in which the king refuted Alexander's accusations of Prussian armaments were not calculated to soothe an offended tsar.

Was Frederick William's decision to reject this alliance offer a mistake? His concerns for Prussia's fragile geostrategic situation were valid, as was his fear that Napoleon might preempt the formation of a new coalition against him. Considering that his primary objective was to avoid a war, it would have been an error to join, even on strictly defensive terms, a power that he rightly be-. lieved was preparing to start one. The question is not so much whether Frederick William should have negotiated a tripartite agreement, but if he should have jettisoned his determination to avoid war at all costs in the spring of 1805.

A bold monarch would certainly have done so. The gathering war clouds suggested that war between France and Russia was highly likely. Frederick William could have guessed that a Franco–Russian war would have dramatic consequences throughout the continent; one side would win and the other would lose, since Napoleon had never yet shown an inclination to accept a draw. In such an event, a bold ruler calculates the odds and tries to ensure that he ends up supporting the winning side actively enough to receive the benefits of victory.

But only Napoleon could offer Frederick William what he wanted most— Hanover. Frederick William, moreover, was as far from being a bold ruler as it is possible to be. He refused to consider what Europe might look like after a Franco–Russian war, and only concocted sophistries to justify clinging to an increasingly outdated neutrality policy. Having decided that he would maintain Prussian neutrality until he was forced to abandon it, he then missed, in mid-1805, the point at which he should have made that decision.

He paid a high price for this mistake. Alexander was disgusted by the pusillanimity of Prussia's policy and insulted, once again, by having an alliance proposal rejected in Berlin. He gave up once and for all on the notion of trying to woo or lure Frederick William and embraced an idea that had been floated months earlier of using force to compel the timorous Prussian king to adhere to the rising coalition. When war approached for certain in late July Frederick William saw with alarm that the large Russian army on his frontier was mobilizing to attack him.*

Napoleon's Final Alliance Bid

The end of July 1805 saw the beginning of a tragicomedy in which Napoleon repeated down to the smallest details Alexander's experience of attempting to negotiate an alliance with Prussia. As word of Austrian preparations for war reached

---

*Simms overstates the degree to which Alexander accepted the policy of forcing Prussia to fight prior to Wintzingerode's mission. Although Czartoryskii certainly accepted that idea (and perhaps helped originate it), the tsar's statement to Wintzingerode that he would tolerate Prussia's neutrality but not the neutrality of all of north Germany suggests that he was still of two minds about what course of action to pursue, as he continued to be even after war broke out.

Paris, Napoleon began considering his military options and requirements. He decided to free up his forces in Hanover, both to use them against Austria and so as not to not have to defend the electorate against seaborne coalition attacks.* He accordingly offered Prussia the electorate in return for a guarantee of his possessions in Italy, for the security of the Ottoman state, and so forth.[146]

This French offer was more attractive than the Russian overtures. It promised Frederick William Hanover, the only territory that Prussia's statesmen then coveted. It bound the Prussians only to a defensive alliance. They rightly believed that Napoleon was not really interested in inveigling them into attacking their neighbors, whereas they were correctly worried that the Russians were. The times had changed even since April. The storm clouds at the end of July were so dark that even Frederick William could not ignore them, and his ministers had concluded that the time had come to choose sides. Lucchesini, for one, sounded the alarm in grim tones: "I see with sadness the moment approaching that we have only perceived from afar hitherto, when these two terrible rivals, France and Russia, seeking points of contact to reach one another, will only allow Prussia . . . the liberty to choose which of their sides to take." He concluded, "I cannot convince myself or give Y[our] M[ajesty] hope that Napoleon will allow Prussia the liberty of remaining neutral."[147] At the same time, he thought that the offer of Hanover was so significant that it should overcome the king's reluctance to ally himself with France.[148]

Hardenberg was even more encouraging to the French ambassador than he had been to Metternich and Alopeus.[149] The king had authorized him to discuss a Prussian occupation of Hanover, he told Laforest, and he even went further. He recognized the importance of seizing the moment when Napoleon needed Prussia and was prepared to make her a good offer, and he wished "to distinguish his ministry by an operation that would redress the most monstrous defect of Prussia's geographic position." Hardenberg was now personally committed to the idea of an agreement with France, possibly even to the extent of an alliance.

The reasons for the wild variations in the positions individual ministers held at the Prussian court, even over relatively short spans of time, are important. As late as April Hardenberg was pressing for a Russian alliance against France, and barely three months later he was pressing even harder for an alliance with France against Russia. This shift is representative of the changes in not only Hardenberg's position but also those of Haugwitz, Lombard, and the other chief foreign policy advisers. It reveals the folly of attempting to identify

---

*The former motive is clear from his actual use of the army in Hanover in his operations against Austria; the latter from his discussions with Frederick William over the king's unwillingness to defend the coast of Hanover should the allies attack it. See, e.g., Lucchesini to Hardenberg, 29–30 July 1805, in Bailleu, *Preußen und Frankreich*, vol. 2, doc. 259; and Talleyrand to Laforest, 30 July 1805, in Bailleu, *Preußen und Frankreich*, doc. 261.

Haugwitz or Hardenberg as the head of a "pro-French" or "pro-Russian" faction except at a given moment.

There were two main reasons for this variation. The king's conscious and deliberate policy of playing Hardenberg and Haugwitz off against one another virtually ensured that their positions would shift, since each had to make sure that his position nullified that of the other. Second, like all diplomats both ministers were constrained to operate within the system of their master. When Frederick William foreclosed one option, they had to seek alternatives. There is no reason to imagine that if the king had accepted Hardenberg's advice to begin negotiating with the Russians in April, the minister would have changed his mind and started to support the French in July. But since Frederick William rejected the Russian proposal, Hardenberg was obliged to make the best policy he could under those circumstances. There was more at work here, in other words, than sheer personal opportunism, although there was certainly more than enough of that characteristic as well.

Laforest put his finger on the problem of any foreign state attempting to negotiate with Prussia: "But it is not Mr. Hardenberg who must be persuaded." The minister told the French envoy that he feared the king's reaction. "He is sure of a disgrace," Laforest reported, "if he insists on doing violence to the tenacious ideas of the king."[150] Hardenberg even outlined for Laforest the steps that he would need to take to persuade the king. He had to mollify his hypertrophied conscience, soothe him about seizing territory with rights of reversion that fell to the junior branch of the House of Brunswick (which was closely allied to the king's family and to Prussia), and convince him to emerge from the shell of his neutrality. Surprisingly, the initial omens were positive.

The king's other cabinet secretary, Beyme, advised him in mid-August to accept the French offers as Hardenberg had.[151] An advisory council composed of Hardenberg, Schulenburg, and the Duke of Brunswick also advised him to accept even the risk of war with Russia in return for Hanover.[152] The guarantees of French possessions in Italy were disturbing and unpleasant, but by August 1805, virtually all of the senior diplomatic and military advisers in Berlin had come to believe that such disadvantages should be accepted considering the great gains to be made.

Those gains were not limited to the possession of Hanover, moreover. Napoleon and numerous Prussians repeatedly declared their hope that Prussia's adherence to France would derail the formation of the coalition. Austria could hardly be pleased with the prospect of facing a Prussian attack from the north while she fought against France, especially since Francis was reluctant to go to war in the first place. Prussia's declaration might tip the balance in Vienna back in favor of peace. Such an event might even induce Pitt to seek peace following the final loss of Britain's only continental possessions, it was hoped somewhat illogically. The Franco–Prussian alliance was thus portrayed and accepted as a measure best calculated to preserve and even restore peace to Europe and the world—as well as a way to end once and for all the worst of the geostrategic nightmares that Prussia faced.

Frederick William consented. On August 17, he instructed Lucchesini to pursue the alliance negotiations aggressively and with only minor counterdemands.[153] Hardenberg told Laforest that he had brought the king around.[154] Then the normal ebb and flow of Prussian high politics intervened, together with Frederick William's customary horror at taking any meaningful decision. Haugwitz, who was excluded from the conference that had recommended accepting the alliance, submitted a lengthy memorandum arguing against it.[155]

He made the usual arguments about the virtues of the Prussian neutrality system and the undesirability of involving Prussia in the defense of French interests in Italy. He emphasized the fear of a war with Russia, adverting to the large, combat-ready Russian forces already deployed along the Prussian border. Would the French really help Prussia against the "mountain of snow" as Napoleon promised? He found such assurance no more valuable than Hardenberg had found Russian promises to help against France. Hanover was important, but it was not worth a disastrous war. The other supposed advantages of the alliance, he noted, including the permanent pacification of Europe, were probably delusions. There was no reason to be confident that the other powers would lay down their arms the moment the Prussians made a declaration. The Russo–Prussian treaty, however, bound Russia to defend the neutrality of northern Germany, something Prussia *had already done successfully* during the last coalition war. Frederick William was evidently swayed by these arguments. Despite Napoleon's dispatch of a trusted adjutant on a mission identical to Wintzingerode's, the king rejected the proposed treaty on September 9 because it would "tend only to enchain me feet and fingers tied to the cause and interests of France and would have involved me in an offensive war, incalculable in its effects and its limits."[156] The only difference between this failed negotiation and the previous one was that Frederick William had finally decided that he had to mobilize his army—and not a moment too soon.

The Last Hand Is Played

The allies had not been idle as Frederick William first agreed to and then rejected Napoleon's final proposals. Austrian, Russian, British, Swedish, and Neapolitan armies had been mobilizing to execute a coalition war plan since July. It called for forcing Prussia to join the coalition by invading her territory. An army of 150,000 Russians was to be prepared on the Prussian border by September 28, and if the Prussians had not agreed to join the coalition by that date, that army would march.[157] Alopeus was told to prolong negotiations with Prussia until that date, mostly to lull the Prussian court into a false sense of security, since it was believed that negotiations would not persuade Frederick William.

It is not clear why the allies believed that invading Prussia would force her to join them (a similar line of reasoning was also applied to Bavaria, as we shall see). They seemed to think that fear drove Frederick William's policy, so that it was necessary to make him more scared of the coalition than he was of Napoleon.[158] This logic does not explain, however, why in August the Russians had decided simply to invade without trying to intimidate Prussia, and why they believed that such an action would lead to the desired result.

Personality may have played as important a role on the Russian side as it had on the Prussian. Czartoryskii was a Polish nobleman who had fought against the Russians during the partitions of his country. He had not abandoned his patriotism for his destroyed fatherland, and he believed that Russia alone could restore Poland to even a shadowy existence. He hoped that Alexander would seize the Polish territories held by Prussia (and perhaps Austria) and unite them with those under Russian control to form a semi-autonomous Kingdom of Poland. He appears to have deliberately courted a conflict with Prussia in order to make this dream a reality.[159]

Although Alexander generally subscribed to Czartoryskii's schemes for the reconstruction of Europe, which included a revived Poland under Russian suzerainty, it is by no means clear that he actually sanctioned the program of courting conflict with Prussia in order to achieve it. On the contrary, his actions during the denouement of the crisis with Berlin show that he never fully shared his foreign minister's enthusiasm for the project.

The Prussians held another series of meetings and councils in light of the Russian mobilizations. Frederick William played Hardenberg and Haugwitz off against each other and deliberately sought conflicting opinions, and the result was typical. Frederick William decided to remain neutral, even if it meant going to war with Russia. He hoped, encouraged by Hardenberg, that he would not have to do so, but he ordered a full-scale mobilization just in case.[160]

The king was relying in part on Alexander's personal goodwill toward him and the tsar's reluctance to go to war against a friend, even though Alexander had explicitly told Wintzingerode to disabuse the king of that notion.[161] Frederick William's estimate of the situation was correct. In late September, Hardenberg begged for a direct meeting between the two monarchs to settle the matter and asked the Russians to take no action beforehand. At the last minute, Alexander agreed. On September 27, the day before the Russian troops were to cross the Prussian border, a courier arrived in Berlin with the word that those troops had been halted and would await the outcome of a direct meeting of the two heads of state.[162] Frederick William had been spared the decision after all.

French action, moreover, intervened to make it irrelevant. In early October word arrived in Berlin that Marshal Bernadotte had marched from

Hanover through the Prussian territory of Ansbach on his way to fight the Austrians. This clear violation of Prussian neutrality, without so much as a by-your-leave from Napoleon, transformed the situation in Berlin and rendered the Russo–Prussian dispute irrelevant. When Alexander and Frederick William finally met in late October the agenda was completely different from the one originally agreed on. Napoleon may well have saved the two monarchs in Europe who felt most warmly toward each other from going to war as the rest of Europe exploded in flames.

The damage, however, had been done to the coalition even without Russo–Prussian combat. Prussia did not join the coalition before the war broke out and did not begin full-scale mobilization until mid-September, months after the other coalition states. Initially the mobilization was directed against Russia, not France. Prussia had not participated in the coalition war planning. Even if she had joined the coalition in September, it is unclear what her contribution would have been. The truth was that Frederick William's policy of delay and prevarication had made his state incapable of contributing positively to any alliance, and had denied him the goodwill of the major powers of Europe.

He pursued this policy for many reasons, but ultimately because it suited his personality and views. The Prussian high politics of this time revolved around an effort to bend the king away from his cherished neutrality—and every such effort failed. Appearances to the contrary notwithstanding, the king was not a weak person. He skillfully manipulated his advisers to ensure that he could adhere to his preferred policy. For all of the noise and effort those advisers made, the policy was always his. One man helped shape the destiny of the continent by his determined inaction. In the summer of 1805, the full significance of these events for the Prussian state could not yet be imagined. In the meantime, Frederick William had ensured for good or ill what had always been his aim—Prussia would take no direct part in the War of the Third Coalition.

9

The Opposing Alliances

The Napoleonic Wars did not arise simply from Napoleon's insatiable ambition, Pitt's gold, or hyperconservative European monarchs eager to undo the results of the French Revolution. Still less were they the result of a Napoleonic grand plan to conquer Europe. Above all, they were not inevitable. If a few personalities had been a little different, if a few events had not coincided so closely in time, there need not have been continental war in 1805, and perhaps not for years after that.

Napoleon would have insisted on organizing Italy to suit himself and would likely have begun to interfere more actively in the affairs of the minor western German states. As it happened, the Russians and the Austrians chose to resist him at a reasonably early stage of those activities, when he controlled only a portion of Italy and very little of Germany. Their actions were probably wise, perhaps even belated, from the standpoint of their own policies and interests, but they were not inevitable.

In 1801 both Austria and Russia were determined to maintain peace for a long time in order to facilitate internal reforms. The notion that Alexander began looking for European adventures when his internal reforms began to encounter obstacles is foolish. He started preparing to resist Napoleon before many of those reforms had even been put into effect, let alone begun to fail. His attempts to form coalitions to defend against and then attack Napoleon encountered far more serious obstacles than his internal reform program ever did. Alexander persevered remarkably in the uphill and seemingly hopeless task of finding the allies he needed to fight France. This determination casts grave doubt on the idea he would abandon a task as soon as it proved to be hard. Nevertheless, it is more than reasonable to imagine an alternative history in which he decided to abandon Europe to its fate and refocus his efforts on internal matters. If that had happened, there would have been no war on the continent.

In Austria, the likelihood of war was remote until the last moment. As the Austrian reforms encountered difficulties, Francis and many of his advisers became even more determined to avoid a war that could only complicate their efforts further and perhaps compromise them completely. He resisted enormous Russian and British pressures and rejected numerous attractive territorial offers designed to cajole or woo him into an alliance. Even when Napoleon crowned himself king of Italy in a ceremony designed to emphasize the similarities between France's new emperor and Charlemagne, Francis still resisted Cobenzl's increasingly frantic efforts to get him to join with the Russians. When Napoleon seized Genoa, Francis reacted typically for a monarch who has been pursuing a timid policy until he is pushed too far. But he need not have seen that particular action as the last straw. Any significant Austrian delay in the summer of 1805 could have made war that year impossible, and the possible effects of postponing the struggle until 1806 are incalculable.

The actions of Europe's leaders preceding the outbreak of the War of the Third Coalition were not inevitable, although they were natural and even likely. This war, like any historical event, was contingent on a specific chain of causality, and neither its outbreak nor its outcome was more predetermined than those of any other conflict.

The specific course of events that led to the renewal of war on the continent also shaped the war that was to come. The coalition that fought against Napoleon, as well as the coalition that Napoleon himself led in 1805, were both the products of the particular events that brought them into existence. The diplomatic crisis that formed them shaped the goals they fought for. Those goals in turn shaped the war plans and the conduct of the campaigns that followed.

The Goals of the Third Coalition

The objectives of the Third Coalition were confused from the outset. The coalition treaty contains numerous vague references to restoring the "peace," "independence," "tranquillity," and "security" of the states of Europe, creating a "federative system" of the great powers to guarantee that peace indefinitely, and calling a conference to adjust various territorial problems that had arisen during the revolutionary wars and Napoleon's early reign.[1] The only concrete objectives identified, however, were (1) the French evacuation of Hanover and northern Germany, (2) the reestablishment of Swiss and Dutch independence, (3) the recreation of an independent and enlarged state of Piedmont-Sardinia to serve as a buffer between France and Italy, (4) "the security of the Kingdom of Naples and the complete evacuation of Italy, including the Island of Elba, by French forces," and (5) "the establishment of an order of things in Europe that effectively guarantees the security and independence of the different

States and presents a solid barrier against future usurpations."[2] Plans for war had to be constructed around these objectives, despite the thoughts, hopes, or goals the various coalition partners might have had.

The aim of overthrowing Napoleon is conspicuously absent from this list. That absence resulted from Alexander's ambivalence. Although he believed, along with Pitt and later Cobenzl, that Napoleonic France could not be a stable element of a peaceful Europe, he was reluctant to avow the goal of precipitating another revolution. This reluctance was explicitly manifested in the treaty. The allies did not want "to interfere in any way with the national wish in France relative to the form of [her] Government."[3] A secret article emphasized this reluctance: "The Principles of the two Sovereigns [do not permit] Them in any case to seek to constrain the free wish of the French Nation."[4] They clearly hoped, nevertheless, that the French people would voluntarily choose to replace Napoleon with another monarch, and they proclaimed their intention (secretly) to use propaganda to attempt to convince the French people to see things their way.

The question of whether or not the allies intended to depose Napoleon forcibly in 1805 is in many respects moot. It is inconceivable that Napoleon would have accepted the peace terms established by the coalition treaty. They would have been compelled to continue fighting until he was completely defeated, which would almost certainly have entailed his removal from power. It is likely that Alexander, Pitt, and Francis understood that, which explains the oblique references to France's "form of government" in a treaty that does not explicitly identify the removal of the current government as an objective.

The question is, however, important from the perspective of war planning. Whatever they may have hoped and even expected, the allies did not plan to conquer France. Instead, they aimed to deprive Napoleon of the territories he had seized in Italy and Germany and reorganize them along certain preconceived lines that they believed would prevent future French "usurpations." These objectives necessarily produced a centrifugal and dispersed strategy. The coalition powers would have to operate along a front that stretched from the North Sea to Calabria. Their goals required them to seize and hold Holland, Hanover, Switzerland, the Kingdom of Italy, Piedmont, Tuscany, Genoa, and Naples at a minimum. These were daunting tasks even for the 500,000 troops the allies pledged to put into the field, and they left little force to spare for invading and occupying France. The individual armies had to calculate specific objectives on the basis of the territories those armies were supposed to seize, more than on the location of the main French body.

It can be argued that this preoccupation with seizing relatively small individual territories instead of finding and destroying the enemy's main body, as Napoleon preferred to do, reflected the typical eighteenth-century limited war mentality. Monarchs of that time, it is said, fought for small territorial gains for their dynasties, and these limited objectives produced limited wars of maneuver with little direct fighting between large armies. The French Revolution is supposed to have ended these limited dynastic wars in favor of total, people's wars. The monarchs of Europe, some argue, lost so often to the French revolutionary armies and to Napoleon because they did not understand this change in warfare and continued to fight in the eighteenth-century style long after the French had rendered that style obsolete.[5]

Like most historical myths, there is not much validity to this one. Even in the eighteenth century, war was not actually "limited" and focused on maneuver to the exclusion of battles, considering the fierce and deadly fights that proliferated in the War of the Spanish Succession, the War of the Austrian Succession, and the Seven Years War (nearly 28 years of fighting that included numerous bloody battles such as Blenheim, Malplaquet, Zorndorf, Rossbach, and Leuthen). But the allied focus on territorial objectives in 1805 had little to do with a desire to avoid battle or a belief that the war would be thus "limited." It resulted, rather, from the nature of the negotiations that had led to the formation of the coalition in the first place.

If Alexander had ever announced that he intended to destroy the French army and depose Napoleon, Francis would have bolted from the coalition at once. However delusional Alexander might have been about coercing or cajoling Frederick William into the alliance, even he knew that such an announcement would make the Prussian king his determined foe and might even have pushed Prussia overtly into the French camp. There were two reasons for this.

First, Austria and Prussia were so reluctant to go to war that Alexander's only hope of winning over either was to pose as the defender of Europe against French depredations. Moreover, he had to show that he was moderate. He repeatedly attempted to prove that he had exhausted all possibility of negotiating with Napoleon and that force was the only way to undo Napoleon's unjust seizures of territory and treaty violations. Such diplomacy left no room to state any clear policy favoring regime change in France.

Second, despite their fears of Napoleon, it was not in the interests of Francis or Frederick William for France to be destroyed or even severely weakened. As the advisers of both rulers repeatedly noted, it was no more desirable for Europe to be dominated by Russian power than by French. Both sovereigns were determined to avoid becoming satellites of Paris or St. Petersburg. France must serve as a counterweight to Russia and vice versa; on no account should Austria or Prussia use their forces to support a Russian program for the destruction of France. An openly avowed policy of regime change in France, however, could only look like such a program to the fearful German states. Their mistrust of their powerful ally would have deepened and the coalition would probably have fractured.

The weakness of the coalition militated powerfully against an honest evaluation and statement of its goals. The resulting vagueness and confusion about all but the most immediate (and least important) territorial objectives hindered the development of an effective war plan. This confusion would also have hindered the conduct of the diplomacy necessary to end the struggle had combat gone more favorably for the allies. Alexander (and Pitt) had thus been able to bring together a coalition only at the expense of its clarity of purpose and effectiveness. As states in more modern times have discovered, efforts to make a coalition broader can sometimes compromise the likelihood of its success.

Russian and British attitudes toward the coalition also augured badly for its stability, especially in the face of adversity. Until the outbreak of the war (and beyond) the Russians saw their participation in the struggle as optional, even altruistic. Napoleon threatened no direct Russian interests except their general concern for the welfare of Europe, Alexander and Czartoryskii repeatedly asserted. This assertion was in fact untrue, as we have seen. Russian trade suffered from the blockade of German rivers caused by Napoleon's occupation of Hanover. Alexander was also convinced that Napoleon was considering plans against (or with) the Ottoman Empire that might put the Turkish Straits in French hands—a deadly threat to Russia's economic health. Finally, Alexander had his honor to think about in regard to agreements Napoleon had publicly made with him and then violated and defensive treaties with Naples and subsequently with other states. Russia's interests played a role in both diplomacy and war planning, but they were not strong enough to convince the tsar or his advisers that Russia *had* to fight. *If* the Austrians would agree to participate, *if* the British would provide subsidies, *if* everyone would promise to be moderate in the subsequent territorial settlements, even *if* Britain promised to give up Malta, then Russia would fight. If not, as Russian diplomats repeatedly told foreign ministers, Russia could always withdraw behind her invulnerable ramparts and let Europe settle its problems with its own resources.

The British were no better. Addington's government behaved as though it was not serious about forming a coalition, whatever its actual intentions were, while Pitt's negotiations read more like a merchant bargaining for hired help than a statesman who feels that he must bring a coalition together at all costs. After the initial maritime and colonial successes, the British government did not, on the whole, feel that Napoleon threatened it, or that it would emerge from the war without great gains. A continental alliance that might put a permanent end to the French threat was welcome, if it could be obtained on reasonable terms. But the British were highly skeptical that anything meaningful would result from any coalition, and past history supported them in this suspicion. Pitt bargained hard in part to ensure that the coalition would be both strong and determined enough to succeed where previous alliances had failed.

The result of the aloofness and supposed altruism of Russian and British policy was the creation of a fatal fault line in the coalition. The Austrians knew that the war was a matter of life and death—once committed they could not withdraw. They also knew, however, that Britain or Russia could withdraw at any time (as the Russians had done in 1800). Suspicion was inevitable. Would the Russians stay and fight in difficult circumstances? Would the Austrians try to negotiate with Napoleon when they had achieved their initial aims? Would the British pay the subsidies they had promised? Declarations in the various alliance documents that no state would make a separate peace are remarkable for their frequency and vehemence, indicating the concern all sides felt for the fragility of the coalition.

In 1805 Alexander, Francis, Pitt, Gustavus IV, and a number of other minor rulers began a war because they believed that fighting was safer and wiser than waiting. With the exception of the British, who were already at war with Napoleon, all of these leaders decided to fight out of a calculated balance of fear: they feared waiting more than they feared fighting. They did not agree on a clear, straightforward political program, and they did not even agree that it was *necessary* to fight—only that it was more desirable than to wait. This is not the stuff of which stable and powerful coalitions are made. It remained to be seen how it would fare in the massive struggle its leaders had chosen to begin.

Napoleon and His Allies

Napoleon did not face the Third Coalition with French resources alone. Such a fight would, indeed, have been hopelessly unequal. His coalition was also riven with conflicting objectives, especially with regard to a continental war. His own objectives were hardly clearer than those of the coalition facing him. The nature of both his alliance system and his objectives, however, gave him significant advantages over his enemies.

The central aspect of Napoleon's preparation for the War of 1805 is that he never intended to fight it. He had been bending his military efforts entirely to defeating Britain. His diplomatic efforts diverged from that goal only to arrange matters in his sphere of influence in Italy and Germany to his liking. He had no intention of attacking Austria or Russia, still less Prussia, and he had done everything he could to Britain short of invading the islands—a task for which he was earnestly preparing.

The coalition that he had assembled was thus designed to help him against Britain and, secondarily, provide him with defensive security against the possibility (which he considered remote) that Austria or Prussia might be induced to attack him. Spain was the largest and most powerful French ally in 1805. Initially the Spanish government had been reluctant to join Napoleon in a fight that seemed not to concern them. Over the course of 1804, however, the Royal Navy took Spanish ships under fire with increasing regularity, and in October the British seized part of the Spanish treasure fleet and scattered the rest. Spain declared war on Britain in December. Thereafter the Spanish contributions to Napoleon were made more willingly, although never with any real enthusiasm. Napoleon had simply coerced the Portuguese, on the other hand, with the threat of occupation. Their contributions were paid even more grudgingly and with the sense that there was nothing else to do—for now.

In Italy the situation was more complicated. The high contributions Napoleon had imposed on the Republic of Italy rankled badly and undermined the regard that many Italians once had for the French. The formation and dispatch of a body of troops from the republic was greeted ambivalently. Many were proud to see an Italian flag flying over a formation of troops and hoped that it presaged greater things; others resented the deployment of those troops to the English Channel.

If the Italians were ambivalent, however, the Dutch were downright hostile. Napoleon commandeered all he could of the Dutch fleet and set the Dutch shipyards to work churning out small boats to ferry his invasion army across the Channel. The contributions he imposed on Holland to pay for those boats and the sailors to man them undermined the government Napoleon had imposed on the country so badly that by 1805 he concluded that he must reorganize it completely. Switzerland posed perhaps the least problem for Napoleon in terms of popular resentment, but it also offered the least in terms of resources.

None of these "allies" joined him voluntarily. In Holland and Italy, support for the French cause in the war was largely confined to the upper circles of the government who knew that their continued power and well-being depended on Napoleon's continued support. The Spanish resented British depredations, but they also resented the satellite status Napoleon had imposed on them, to say nothing of the heavy contributions he demanded. The Portuguese were overtly hostile. As long as Napoleon had military force and appeared successful, however, none of these dubious allies would dare oppose him. The balance of fear for them was clear, and until Napoleon's ability to keep himself secure and in power was brought into question, he could be sure of their grudging support.

The advantage that Napoleon gained from this hegemony was enormous. The Dutch bore an important proportion of the costs of building and manning the Channel fleet. The Italian Republic underwrote a large part of the expense of defending northern Italy. Spanish, Portuguese, and Italian contributions defrayed the costs of maintaining a large French army on a war footing for two years. Those contributions were complemented by the sale of Louisiana to the United States in 1803 and by forced levies and loans imposed on Hanover and some of the surrounding areas. In a year in which French expenditures were over 800 million livres, these extraordinary contributions brought in more than 91 million or, including the sale of Louisiana, 141 million—17 percent of the budget.[6] This figure excludes the support to French units within Italy and Holland mentioned above. Since money was one of the most important factors constraining the development and use of military power in the first decades of the nineteenth century, Napoleon's ability to extort vast sums from reluctant allies allowed him to face a theoretically much larger and richer coalition with equanimity. Napoleon effectively subordinated the economy of a considerable part of western Europe to the cause of French military power, thereby allowing him to maintain a higher degree of military power at a much lower cost to France than he would otherwise have been able to do, a factor crucial to understanding his successes in the first years of renewed continental warfare.

Bavaria

Napoleon had one willing ally in his continental war: Bavaria. The elector of Bavaria would play a critical role in a war between France and Austria after the settlement of Lunéville. The loss of Austria's possessions in the Netherlands meant that France and Austria could only attack each other in Germany through Bavarian territory. The elector, moreover, maintained a sizable and reputable military establishment. Although it could not hope to withstand an attack by either of its great power neighbors, this military could provide a respectable auxiliary force to whichever side succeeded in wooing or cajoling the elector. It was a prize worth taking pains to win.

Bavaria's position, both politically and geographically, was similar in many important respects to Prussia's: a relatively weak state with great power neighbors to the east and west. Bavarian politicians were sorely tempted to throw in their lot with one side or the other, but they were fearful of reprisals. The elector himself would have preferred a strategy of neutrality, armed if necessary, and was reluctant to commit himself wholeheartedly to an alliance with either side.[7] Unlike Frederick William, however, Elector Maximilian IV Joseph could not reasonably hope to sustain such a strategy. He had neither sufficient force to intimidate would-be attackers nor sufficient advantages to offer them in return for his neutrality. He would have to choose sides.

The choice was not, in principle, difficult. Only France was in a position to offer Bavaria (like Prussia) her most important desiderata: the suppression of the legacies of the Holy Roman Empire within the electorate and the adjustment of her eastern and southern borders at Austria's expense. The Austrians and Bavarians, moreover, had been engaged in a series of minor conflicts since the Treaty of Lunéville, conflicts that led on several occasions to military mobilizations. Vienna had little or no hope of wooing Bavaria successfully, although Francis hoped to coerce the elector to join with him through the threat of (and use of) force, a policy nearly identical to the one Alexander pursued toward Prussia.

As was the case with Prussia, however, French negotiators found discussions in Munich unexpectedly hard. The problem was the same one that led to the collapse of the Franco–Prussian negotiations: Napoleon insisted on a Bavarian guarantee of his possessions in Italy, but the elector preferred not to commit himself to the defense of French interests far from his borders. Both were making reasonable demands.

Max Joseph's desire to avoid being drawn into the burgeoning conflict in Italy was as understandable as Frederick William's similar wish. If there was to be a war over Italy, the German states (other than Austria) would always prefer to have that conflict confined to Italy itself. If the Austrians attacked French-controlled Italy, however, Napoleon would want the freedom to counterattack not only in the peninsula but also in Germany. Napoleon needed Bavaria to side with France if the Austrians attacked him in Italy. The campaigns of 1796–1797 and 1800–1801 demonstrated the importance of facing Austria with two simultaneous threats in the two main theaters. The geography of southern Germany, moreover, was more favorable to a rapid and decisive French advance than was northern Italy.

The elector's objections to this course of action were overcome partially because of the staunch advocacy of his leading minister, Maximilian Karl Joseph Montgelas, and partly because of the deteriorating situation. Montgelas actively supported a French alliance because he believed that only France could liberate Bavaria from the legacies of the Holy Roman Empire, including the continued control of territories within the electorate by the "immediate nobility" and by other German princes.* He saw the French alliance as a positive good and worked hard to swing his prince over to this viewpoint.

Montgelas was opposed by the electress, as well as other court factions. The most serious obstacle to his program, though, came from the elector himself. Max Joseph simply did not wish to take a stand. He feared that the Austrians would ravage his state before the French could intervene, and he also feared provoking a conflict that he might otherwise have been able to avoid. By August 1805, however, Montgelas was able to point to the large-scale Austrian mobilization and to Napoleon's own declarations that he would not leave Bavaria neutral. The imminence of war led to reflections on the war's likely outcome. A policy of neutrality could hardly preserve the electorate from invasion and occupation, although it would almost certainly deprive the elector of any meaningful compensation. The prudent decision was to side with Bavaria's natural ally, France. Montgelas was finally able to obtain the elector's consent to this policy in the form of a secret offensive–defensive treaty ratified in Munich on August 23, 1805.†

---

*The "immediate" nobles were those who held their lands directly from the Holy Roman Emperor, not the political head of whatever territory they found themselves in. They were thus exempt from taxation, conscription, and the application of local law.

†See Gmeinwiser, "Die bayerische Politik," pp. 25–45, for the course of the negotiations and his appendices for the crucial documents. The dates and locations of the treaty documents were subsequently altered to make it appear as though the alliance had resulted from the Austrian attack on Bavaria, instead of predating it, as was really the case. See Gmeinwiser, "Die bayerische Politik," pp. 74–75 n. 122.

By this treaty Napoleon secured a valuable and willing ally. Napoleon guaranteed Bavaria's territorial integrity (including territories in dispute with Austria) and promised expansion for the electorate and a royal crown for the elector. In return, Max Joseph promised Napoleon to fight if Austria attacked France anywhere and to place 20,000 Bavarians alongside Napoleon's troops. The elector also promised to defray the cost of maintaining French troops in his territory and concert his military operations with Napoleon. By this signal triumph of French diplomacy, Napoleon won himself an open road into the heart of Habsburg territory—all unknown to the Austrians themselves.

Napoleon's Objectives

Like the allies, Napoleon did not have clear objectives in the war he was about to fight. He had been preparing to fight Britain to the death. The continental war was nothing but a distraction for him. Initially he had no goal but to end it as quickly as possible and return to the business at hand—defeating Britain in some way. It is by no means clear, however, that he would have continued preparations for an invasion after the end of the War of the Third Coalition even absent the debacle of Trafalgar. There was nothing he particularly wanted from Austria or Russia other than to be left alone, and he had no notion that he could harm Britain through a continental war other than psychologically, by depriving her of allies.

Despite its vagueness, however, the objective of ending the war as quickly as possible was easier to pursue than the complicated and confused ends the coalition sought. It was simply a matter of examining the coalition and identifying a weak but critical spot that could be hit hard enough to fracture the fragile alliance. The challenge for Napoleon would lie in executing a plan aiming for that goal and, even more, in creating conditions at the peace conducive to obtaining his larger objective, the defeat of Britain. The success of that endeavor, however, rested on having a clear program for defeating his island nemesis, something that turned out to be highly problematic.

The balance of objectives and intentions between Napoleon and the allies gave the emperor of the French significant advantages. The correlation of military forces favored the coalition. We have already seen how the nature of the coalition's objectives militated toward frittering away that advantage in small operations dispersed over a wide periphery, whereas the nature of Napoleon's objectives gave him a freer hand to develop his strategy. Only in the test of war would it be seen which side would meet the challenge better.

10

The Austrian
War Plan

The significance of a plan in determining the outcome of a war depends to a great extent on the war's length. In briefer conflicts the conditions that shape the prewar planning change less, and it is less likely that events will move beyond the ideas and possibilities that the prewar planners perceived. Since the War of 1805 lasted little more than three months, the prewar plans are important indeed.

This war nonetheless highlights the unpredictability and volatility of military actions. The events that followed the initial engagements accorded with the presuppositions of neither side, and both Napoleon and the coalition leaders found themselves scrambling to respond to unforeseen changes in the situation. Although the prewar plans did not determine the outcome of the conflict, they provided its basic shape and structure. They also rendered the outcome of the *initial* operations of the war nearly inevitable.

The coalition took the initiative in this conflict, igniting it politically and making the first military moves. The development of the allies' war plan reflected the tortuous path of the diplomacy that went into the coalition's formation. War planning occurred even as the diplomatic efforts were under way that finally brought the war about. This fact was the first critical element that constrained coalition war planning. At no time did allied political or military leaders lose sight of the diplomacy that they were simultaneously conducting, with the result that they never focused on the purely military considerations of the conflict. The "war plan" that emerged from innumerable conferences, notes, and counterdeclarations was as much a plan for diplomatic as for military action.

There is nothing inherently wrong with such an approach to war planning. It is as dangerous to allow political considerations to play too small a role in war planning as it is to allow them to become too prominent. The leader's skill lies in balancing the requirements of both political and military considerations and in ensuring that the plan is reasonable and technically appropriate in both fields. Neither Napoleon nor the coalition succeeded in that endeavor in 1805.

The personalities and leadership styles of the different European rulers played a profound role in that failure. Napoleon could be an excellent military leader and a successful political actor, but not generally both at the same time, as we shall see. On the coalition side the problem lay in the way the Russian and Austrian states functioned in developing military strategy, although that problem flowed in part from the personalities of the leaders as well.

Significantly, before 1813 Alexander did not have any single trusted advisor about military affairs or even a small trusted group. He was more comfortable with the political advisers who surrounded him, mostly because they were younger. As we have seen, the tsar mistrusted the older generation of Russian statesmen, with the exception of Alexander Vorontsov. Alexander was able to bring younger men like Czartoryskii and Novosil'tsev into high and trusted positions within the political hierarchy of the state, but doing so in the army was more difficult.

A responsible ruler does not simply appoint some junior colonel to be a field marshal because he is more comfortable with him, and Alexander was well enough versed in the nature of military systems to understand that fact. Diplomats at that time, on the other hand, could see dramatic promotions in their careers, since there was no bureaucratic foreign service personnel system to insist that everyone go through similar career stages.

As a result of these conditions, Alexander's war plans flowed from the pens of diplomats, not generals. There is no evidence that the senior officers in the Russian army at the time were involved in drafting those plans. Czartoryskii developed them, sometimes aided by Alexander Vorontsov, and these plans paralleled his efforts to draw both Austria and Prussia into the coalition. Neither statesman had any experience with the military.[1] When war actually broke out, Czartoryskii and Alexander seemed more concerned about what was going on in Berlin than what was happening in Bavaria, where the initial operations were unfolding.

In Austria a different situation led to a similar result. The Austrian military system was more sophisticated than the Russian at that time. In addition to the war minister and the president of the Hofkriegsrat, who were both ex officio important military players in the development and conduct of Austria's war plans and wars, the Austrian army had one of the most highly developed general staff systems in Europe. Whereas Alexander had to turn for military advice primarily either to old former commanders or to young adjutants (a situation very similar to that in Prussia), Francis could choose from a selection of talented and experienced staff officers when he wanted advice about war planning.

The presence of Archduke Charles complicated this system. Between 1801 and early 1805 he dominated Austria's defense policy to the exclusion of the staff and other advisers. After he was demoted and Baron Karl von Mack was elevated, he sulked Achilles-like in the wings, periodically attempting to derail the new policy. Since the emperor could not fire or banish him at that time, there was no easy way to prevent the disturbances he caused.

Francis had not selected Mack to bring military reason and technical skill to coalition war planning, but to uphold a particular political line, as we have seen.[2] Mack was not the most talented Austrian general, and his personality problems tended to diminish such competence as he had, as contemporaries frequently noted.[3] His most important problem, however, was that he owed his position to Cobenzl's belief that he would support the war effort. He had repeatedly promised the foreign minister that he could get the army ready quickly and that Austria could win the war. Having taken the job on those terms, he could hardly conduct an honest evaluation of those very assumptions. Even when Austria had a professional military officer at the head of its war effort, therefore, the political and diplomatic issues of the time continued to override technical military concerns.

These problems were important, but they were secondary to one overriding issue in allied war planning. Until well into 1805, coalition plans for war envisioned a defensive struggle against France aimed at preventing further Napoleonic incursions. As the allies made the transition to an offensive war plan in mid-1805, the conceptions and commitments entailed in their previous program had developed considerable momentum. When they decided to launch a preventive war instead of waiting for Napoleon to strike first, the allies did not rework their plans and objectives from the ground up but simply modified their original ideas. The result was a war plan that could have succeeded but opened promising opportunities to an aggressive enemy commander.

The Defensive Coalition (through March 1805)

Alexander's initial response to the deterioration of Franco–Russian relations was to fashion alliances with the states most immediately affected by Napoleon's aggression. As we have seen, he turned to Frederick William as soon as he was sure that Napoleon would seize Hanover. When that effort initially failed, he turned next to Austria. He did not restrict his coalition-building activities to Europe's major powers, however, but also courted the minor states that he had a chance of winning over, including Sweden, Denmark, and Naples.

He was brilliantly successful in this endeavor, considering that central Europeans feared Napoleon and believed that Russia was too far away to assist them in the face of French hostility. Despite these concerns, the Danish court agreed to make a defensive alliance with Alexander in March 1804.* Alexander promised to provide a corps of 40,000 troops to be supported by 20,000 to 25,000 Danish soldiers in the defense of Mecklemburg and Holstein, Denmark's two most threatened continental possessions. The Danes attempted to refuse Alexander's requirement that the *casus foederis* include any foray of French troops beyond "the line behind which they are currently" deployed, a term included in the Russian counterdeclaration. In the end, a compromise was achieved: Denmark would acknowledge that the *casus foederis* had come into play if Russia found herself forced by French aggression to undertake military actions for the defense of northern Germany.[4]

Swedish Pomerania, Stockholm's last outpost on the European mainland, held a strategic position in north Germany and an excellent port, Stralsund, where Russian or British troops could be sent. Alexander and Pitt both thought it a prize worth winning. Sweden's half-mad king, Gustavus Adolphus IV, was easy to bring into an alliance, although he was a demanding negotiator and partner. He was extremely hostile to Napoleon, as to all manifestations of the French Revolution, and actually seemed to court conflict with France. He made the first overtures to Russia, asking Alexander to send troops to defend Swedish Pomerania in April 1804.[5] Alexander responded favorably and negotiations began. They soon bogged down, however, over the question of the *casus foederis*. Gustavus also preferred not to be obliged to fight simply because Napoleon crossed the Weser anywhere along its course. Other points of disagreement were the destination of the Russian relief forces, the command of the joint Russo–Swedish army, and British subsidies. In the end, compromises were reached on all major questions and Alexander promised to work hard to obtain the necessary subsidies for Sweden. The agreement finally concluded in January 1805 obliged Alexander to dispatch to Stralsund between 40,000 and 50,000 men, while Gustavus would send 20,000 to 25,000 troops—virtually the same numbers specified in the agreement with Denmark. The *casus foederis* was expansive and committed the Swedes to fight if Napoleon crossed the line he currently held.[6]

Alexander's efforts to defend Naples were easier than those he made to protect the Scandinavian courts. In 1798 Tsar Paul had made a defensive treaty with the king of the Two Sicilies guaranteeing the integrity of his possessions, and Alexander regarded that treaty still binding in 1805.[7] It would have been simple for the tsar to coordinate his efforts to defend the last remaining independent Italian state but for two problems.

The first was that Napoleon's troops had reoccupied a number of critical Neapolitan ports following the renewal of war with Britain, so the court of

---

*The alliance was in the form of mutual declarations; the Russian declaration is "Counterdeclaration of Russia about combined actions with Denmark for the defense of northern Germany from French aggression," 29 March 1804, VPR, vol. I, doc. 270.

Naples had to tread carefully. The moment Napoleon decided that the continued independence of Naples was no longer useful to him, he could march his forces from their outposts in Calabria to the capital to end it. There was little Alexander could do immediately in such an event.

The second problem was the queen of Naples, Maria Carolina, one of the last Bourbon monarchs still on a throne in Europe. (The king of Spain was the other.) She hated the French Revolution and Napoleon and was devoted to anti-French schemes. For years she had even retained an Englishman, Lord Acton, as prime minister, a fact that outraged Napoleon. The Russians believed she might provoke a conflict with the hated French before the conditions necessary for success had been established; Alexander and Czartoryskii were almost as concerned with restraining her as with defending her.*

For the two years following the French reinvasion of Naples, Alexander had contented himself with giving moral support to the king of the Two Sicilies, making the evacuation of Naples a nonnegotiable element in every peace overture that went to Paris, and building up Russian forces at Corfu. By October 1804, however, the Neapolitans wanted more. Their ambassador in St. Petersburg, Serra Capriola, asked for a promise that Russia would send a powerful corps into Naples if war broke out.[8]

Czartoryskii was cool to the idea. In November he noted that Napoleon was more likely to start a war on the continent in southern Italy than in Germany, and that Russian forces in Corfu might be sent to defend the king of Naples. But he thought the contingency unlikely and recommended that the Austrians work to deter the French.[9] The tsar, however, was determined to honor his commitments and protect Naples. He accordingly ordered an aged Russian general, B. P. Lacy, to travel to Naples incognito. Lacy was to examine the defensive requirements and capabilities of the country, develop appropriate plans, and take command of Russian troops sent to Naples in the event of hostilities. Before the outbreak of hostilities, Lacy pretended to be a retiree taking his ease in sunny southern Italy for his health.[10]

Most importantly, Alexander undertook to work the defense of Naples into his overall plan. He insisted that the British promise to send 15,000 men to Malta to be ready to join the 15,000 Russians at Corfu in the defense of Naples.[11] He also ordered Razumovskii to ensure that Lacy was coordinating his plans with Mack and the Austrians.[12] Although the British refused to commit 15,000 troops to the defense of Maria Carolina's crown, Pitt ordered Nelson to cooperate with the Russians in the event of war and designated a smaller number of British troops stationed at Malta to defend Sicily and, if necessary, southern Italy.[13]

---

*Naples had a reigning king, Ferdinand, but his influence was meager compared to that of his Bourbon wife.

As we have seen, Alexander's efforts to fashion defensive alliances with Austria and Prussia also bore fruit. In May he concluded an alliance with Frederick William in which he promised to send 40,000 to 50,000 Russian soldiers to the Prussian king's assistance in support of an equal number of Prussian troops. The *casus foederis* was nominally any further Napoleonic encroachment into the Prussian neutrality zone.[14] And in November he persuaded Francis to agree to concrete terms in an exchange of letters. Alexander promised to send 115,000 men to the assistance of the Austrians, who would supply 235,000. In addition, Alexander promised to contribute another large body of troops to ensure that Prussia "remained passive."[15]

There was a certain illogic to these agreements, taken together. In the worst case, Alexander had committed himself to sending 50,000 troops to Mecklemburg (to defend either Denmark or Sweden or both), 50,000 to assist Prussia, 115,000 to Austria, and 15,000 to Naples—230,000 Russian troops, more than twice the number Alexander had mobilized when these agreements were signed, would have been dispersed in an arc from the North Sea to the southernmost tip of Italy, fighting separately in at least four distinct theaters with five allies bound only by bilateral agreements with Russia.

Alexander and Czartoryskii noted subsequently that the coalition they had created would put into the field 235,000 Austrians, 50,000 Prussians, 25,000 Swedes and the same number of Danes, 15,000 British, and a considerable number of Neapolitans and Balkan allies for a grand total of more than 580,000 troops. This statistic might have been reassuring to nervous politicians, but it should have made the generals nervous.

As late as November 1804, when all the treaties except for the Russo–Swedish convention had been concluded, there was no plan to put this massive army in motion for a simultaneous attack (or defense) on all fronts. Despite the enormous complexity and danger of such an offensive plan, it might have succeeded in pinning down numerous small French forces in various theaters and allowed the allies to crush Napoleon. But that was not the idea. Instead, each contingent would come into play only as Napoleon crossed a predetermined line. Consequently the French would have the initiative and the ability to mass a large proportion of their forces against a relatively smaller, isolated contingent of allies. On the other hand, the allies would have crushing superiority in numbers overall and might hope to make good initial losses over time.

This consideration, however, was entirely beside the point. Alexander, still less Czartoryskii, was not trying to develop a coherent war plan against France prior to November 1804 and even for some time after that. Rather, he was executing a program first outlined by Alexander Vorontsov in November 1803 aimed simply at securing areas of concern to Russia from Napoleonic depredations.[16]

Vorontsov's memorandum, which played an important role in convincing the tsar to oppose Napoleon, laid out the dangers Napoleon's encroachments in northern Germany posed to Russia.[17] It also described the prospects of a French invasion of the Balkans launched from southern Italy, which promised to destroy the Ottoman Empire and the Septinsular Republic then under the protection (and control) of Russian troops.* Alexander executed the military components of this proposal immediately, ordering the mobilization of a large army broken into several corps along Russia's western frontier. He also began to execute the political portion of the program, as we have seen.

Vorontsov's plan was explicitly defensive and included no program for an attack on France. He aimed "not to allow [Napoleon] to establish himself . . . in places from which he will be able to harm us." For economic purposes it was crucial to keep Napoleon out of northern Germany, especially the Hanseatic cities; hence the need for agreements with Denmark (which Vorontsov explicitly advocated), Sweden, and Prussia. For reasons of imperial security it was essential to maintain the integrity of the Ottoman Empire (against French attack at least). Corfu would be maintained as a base of operations for spoiling the feared French invasion of Albania. The desirability of preventing any augmentation of the French army in Naples also increased. In 1803 Italy was not considered likely to be a major theater of either political or military activity. But that situation changed in late 1804 and early 1805; when Napoleon transformed the Italian Republic into the Kingdom of Italy, the need to guarantee the last likely ally on the peninsula, Naples, also grew.

The bilateral agreements Alexander concluded through early 1805 can be explained as the elaboration and execution of a plan to secure areas of vital interest to the Russian empire. Considering the unwillingness of the two major German powers to contemplate an offensive war at that time, this approach was not absurd. Alexander had only two choices. He could either stand back and watch as Napoleon undertook whatever operations he pleased against areas Alexander regarded as essential to Russia's security, or the tsar could make such deals as allies offered to guard those areas as best he could.

His actions in 1803 make it clear that Alexander would have preferred to work with one of the major German powers and develop a coherent plan. When both Prussia and Austria refused to come to terms with him rapidly, however, he sought the support of smaller states that felt directly threatened by Napoleon and were therefore reluctant to turn down Russian assistance. The Russian alliance system was thus an arrangement *faute de mieux* and from the standpoint of achieving Alexander's initial objectives under the prevailing conditions, it is

---

*The Septinsular Republic was a collection of small islands off the western Balkan coast. It had been held by Venice through the end of the eighteenth century and became semiautonomous under joint Russian and Ottoman suzerainty at the end of the War of the Second Coalition. Its capital was on Corfu.

hard to see how it could have been improved. The question was, How would that alliance system and the thought process behind it affect the development of a new system and war plan when both the objectives and the conditions that underlay it changed?

This problem was exacerbated by the fact that a similar situation prevailed in Vienna. Through spring 1805 the Austrians believed that they had committed to a strictly defensive alliance with Russia, and their war plans reflected that belief.[18] Their beliefs were supported by a succession of proposed Russian war plans that were explicitly defensive in nature.

The initial Russian request of October 1803 for discussions aimed at securing Europe from further Napoleonic encroachments was followed by a concrete proposal for action in the event of a French attack.[19] The proposal directly addressed the possibility of a French attack in north Germany combined with an attack against the Adriatic coast of the Ottoman Empire, although it indirectly acknowledged the possibility of a French attack against Austria in Italy. Napoleon might, Alexander noted, attack first in one area and only subsequently in others, hoping to draw allied forces away from his real targets. The solution proposed was to be ready to respond in all theaters.

Alexander offered to put 90,000 men in the field at once supported by a reserve army of 80,000. He directly participated in drafting the note, if not the warplan. He personally changed the initial wording of the draft to clarify this deployment—the original had simply stated that he would put 180,000 men in the field.[20] Of this large force the bulk was clearly (although not explicitly) intended to resist French invasions of northern Germany, but Alexander promised to send 30,000 soldiers "by the shortest road" to Italy, to support the Austrians there. He hoped that by fighting in both north Germany and the Balkans he would alleviate the burden on the Austrians to defend their own territory. The plan rightly recognized that Napoleon's dispositions were important: "The enemy cannot concentrate numerous armies everywhere, and it is the turn that he will give his operations that will allow us to modify ours and let us employ more or fewer forces at the different points at which we must be ready to operate."

Military practicality played little role in the development of this plan. How did Alexander propose to shift forces in a timely manner from northern Germany to the Balkans or to northern Italy in response to Napoleon's concentrations? Furthermore, it was not clear that Prussia would be anything other than neutral. A professional staff officer would have considered what the line of march for such troops would have looked like—that is what professional staff officers spent most of their time doing in those days. The lighthearted notion that troops could magically be shifted hundreds of miles (through possibly neutral territory) in response to a perception of French deployments that would probably give at most a few weeks' worth of warning (considering the time it takes for a courier to travel from the French frontier to a Russian army headquarters in Poland, let alone St. Petersburg) shows that no professional staff officer participated in the drafting of this program in any meaningful way.

Alexander did not confine himself to proposing a deployment and action plan for Russian forces, however. He also suggested that the Austrians parcel out their own soldiers into three distinct theaters hundreds of miles apart. He recognized that Francis would have to maintain significant forces in Italy and opposite Switzerland. He hoped, however, that the Austrians would maintain an army on the Turkish frontier ready to intervene there in case the French attacked. Alexander requested, furthermore, that Francis maintain a "reserve corps" in Bohemia. That force would primarily "impose" on Frederick William and on the elector of Bavaria to support the tsar's efforts to bring them into the alliance or, at worst, keep both of them strictly neutral.*

The use of the term "reserve" in this plan is interesting. Alexander noted that the "reserve army" of 80,000 men he had promised to maintain would "border our frontier [and] will be designated to feed and support the *corps d'armée* that will need it, and at the same time keep the Court of Berlin in check in case it does not wish to make common cause with us."† There are several problems with this concept. First, an army stationed along Russia's western borders is not in a position to support forces operating in Hanover, or in the Balkans or Italy. The marching times for such journeys are measured in weeks and months—not periods that would allow reserve forces to affect the outcome of a decisive clash involving endangered armies. Second, if the purpose of the "reserve" army was to "impose" on Prussia, then the forces that composed it could hardly be dispersed as reinforcements across all of Europe. In reality, this plan was likely to waste significant potential combat power in the Russian and Austrian reserve armies stationed in Poland and Bohemia respectively in exchange for dubious political gains.

On the other hand, the plan was devised under the assumption that Napoleon would not concentrate his army for a single decisive blow but would divide it among the various theaters of most concern *to the allies* (for Alexander did not attempt to consider what Napoleon's political or strategic objectives might be). In that case, the dispersal of the allied forces, although perhaps regrettable, was understandable. The tsar wanted to prevent Napoleon from seizing

---

*This appears to be one of the first concrete proposals to use the threat of force to bring Prussia into the coalition, and the idea seems to have originated in St. Petersburg, since there had not yet been any discussion with the British on this subject. See W. H. Zawadzki, *A Man of Honour: Adam Czartoryski as a Statesman of Russia and Poland, 1795–1831* (Oxford: Clarendon, 1993), for a dissenting view.

†The use of the term *corps d'armée* here is interesting. It reflects the fact that this concept of military organization, which Napoleon originated during the Marengo campaign of 1800 and to which so much of his success is commonly ascribed, had penetrated into the minds even of the civilian leadership in Russia so much that Alexander and Vorontsov felt that the Russian army was now organized similarly.

key territory by a *coup de main* that might destroy the Ottoman Empire irretrievably or drive Prussia into an open alliance with him. The notion that it was
necessary to have forces everywhere to oppose an initial French advance, to be
supported subsequently by larger concentrations of allied forces coming to their
aid, was not absurd—as long as Napoleon did what was expected of him.*

The Russian proposal started a fierce debate in Vienna over the proper political strategy to pursue, as we have seen, but it also occasioned a serious reconsideration of Austria's military position and what sort of military plan would
make sense in a war with France.[21] Cobenzl laid out a series of criticisms of
Alexander's military proposals in an evaluation of the Russian plan, probably
prepared in February 1804 and focusing primarily on its political aspects.[22]

The crux of Cobenzl's criticism rested on two beliefs. He argued that a
sound military strategy concentrated maximum force against the enemy in a
few decisive spots, rather than scattering soldiers around in small groups. He
also thought that Napoleon would not be lured into dispersing his own soldiers piecemeal hoping to meet the allied advances across the breadth of Europe. The Austrians were certain, rather, that the moment Napoleon saw them
arming for war against him, he would concentrate all of his forces with the aim
of destroying the Habsburg Empire. Cobenzl's conclusion was obvious:

> . . . the plan of respective operations must aim only at a single goal, that of
> opposing to France great masses of forces acting in concert and mutually
> supporting one another so as to force the French troops to evacuate Ger-
> many, [retreat] behind the Rhine, which does not offer them the support
> of any fortress, and likewise the better part of Lombardy, weakly covered
> by Mantua, in order to deprive the French of the only resources that can
> put them in a condition to support so formidable a continental war.

The 30,000 Russian troops Alexander offered as support for Austrian operations in Italy were inadequate. Although Cobenzl did not go into details, clearly
he believed that the bulk of the "200,000" troops the tsar was proposing to send
into battle should be allocated to support Austrian armies in Germany and Italy.
This approach would satisfy both the military requirement of massing the greatest number of allied forces against Napoleon in two spots and the political "fact"
that Napoleon was certain to attack Austria with everything he had.

Cobenzl's plan still had a conservative and defensive aim. He did not consider the possibility of advancing into France, or even the problem of ending
the war. The only goal of the massive concentration of forces he proposed was

---

*It was also a strategic approach commonly used by the allies against the French revolutionary state and
its armies. Archduke Charles and the Prussian reformer Gerhard von Scharnhorst, among others, railed
repeatedly against this sort of "cordon" defense that allowed the French to seize and hold the initiative
throughout the early campaigns of the revolutionary wars.

to deprive Napoleon of the resources of Germany and northern Italy—the same restricted goal Alexander sought. The Austrian vice chancellor did not appear to consider that 400,000 troops was a large force to use to achieve such a limited objective, or that the military strength remaining to Napoleon even after he had been deprived of his most recent conquests was nevertheless considerable. On the other hand, Cobenzl had no intention of fighting. He wanted to make certain that if Austria agreed to a war plan, it would be militarily reasonable and serve her interests. His primary goal, however, was to reestablish the alliance with Russia and ensure that the tsar would guarantee Vienna's security without having Austria's relations with France harmed, to say nothing of starting a war. For Cobenzl the war plan was a sideshow.

Archduke Charles took it more seriously. At the beginning of March 1804 he submitted to Francis a long memorandum considering the Russian proposal in detail, taking account of Cobenzl's initial comments, and evaluating Austria's overall position in the event of war. His conclusion was very clear: Austria should under no circumstances fight or accept any treaty that might lead to war.[23]

Charles began with a detailed exploration of the military situation and the options open to Austria and France, as well as the likely outcomes of various courses of action. He proceeded, as Cobenzl did, from the notion that the decisive event in the war would be the clash between Austria and France in either Italy or Germany or both. This assumption implicitly rejected the premise that had motivated Alexander's plan, namely, that the war was a coalition effort in which all theaters were equally important (or vulnerable).

Charles was convinced that the Russians and the British would provide no significant assistance to Austria. Section 2 of his memorandum was devoted to an exposition of all the torts, felonies, and misdemeanors the Russians and British had committed against Austria in all previous conflicts in which they had been allied.[24] Repeatedly, Charles asserted, Europe's great peripheral powers had left Vienna turning slowly in the wind either because they had attained their objectives or they were nursing some imaginary wrong done them by the Austrians. The British, he added, did not have enough useful force to stage a significant landing on the French coast anyway, while the Russians were so far away from the likely theaters of war that the conflict was certain to be over before the first Russian troops even arrived.

He concluded that Austria would therefore have to face the prospect of single combat with Napoleon. This underlay his evaluation of the respective military positions of Austria and France, presented in section 1 of his proposal.[25] Charles meticulously totted up the number of battalions available to both states, including the Italian, Swiss, and Dutch republics allied to France, but excluding Austria's own potential allies. He concluded that France would have almost 160 battalions more than Austria available for immediate operations in the decisive theaters of war (399 to 240.5). Even to bring this hopelessly weak force into the field, he added, Austria would have to resort to drafts that would destroy her economy and wreck her finances, while Napoleon could conscript a virtually infinite number of troops. Charles did not neglect to point out that the French mobilization base, including as it did all of the territories that Napoleon had seized since taking power, was much larger than the Austrian, especially since the confused laws of the Habsburg Empire effectively prevented Vienna from drafting recruits from half of the population.

From this basis of grand strategic hopelessness, Charles proceeded to consider likely courses of action that the Austrians and the French might take. The decisive theater, he stated, would be Italy. Because of the importance of this belief for the development of the allied war plans, Charles's reasoning is worth quoting at length:

> It can be taken as certain that by far the greater part of the forces mentioned will be sent to Italy. On the Austrian side, this is because only here—assuming that one has and could have adequate strength at the necessary time—would there be an acquisition worth consideration, because here the danger for the Austrian monarchy is the greatest and most imminent and because only through the advance into Italy, or at least by holding there, can our state be saved from an immediate enemy invasion. On the French side, it is because the French government has the greatest personal interest in holding the Italian Republic; because here with the first step the severest injury will be inflicted on Austria; because after one victorious battle [the French] will have penetrated into unfortified Austrian provinces, into the heart and even to the capital of the monarchy itself; and because the French army right on the Italian and Swiss borders will have its military resources immediately to its rear when it enters the Austrian monarchy. On the other hand, the French army in Germany will be relatively much farther from its reinforcements before it reaches the Austrian border. Even by the shortest line through Swabia and Bavaria [the French] will not be able to strike against Austria until later [than] the decisive blow that the French superiority in Italy will allow [France] to strike in the first days after the outbreak, [attacking] directly into Austrian territory with the probability of favorable results. All of this [will occur] long before it would be physically possible for any Russian reinforcements to be received.
>
> The Adige must therefore be accepted as the first and best theater of war; if the war is to have any purpose, one must operate offensively here.[26]

Three basic assumptions undergirded this exposition and argument. First, that Austria was only fighting to seize whatever territories she would be promised as compensation for participating in the coalition. Second, that Napoleon would proceed cautiously and in accord with one of the theories of warfare

then prevalent. Third, that Napoleon's aim would be the unlimited destruction of the Habsburg monarchy. Of these, the second assumption proved the
most important.

As we have seen, by 1804 Charles had changed dramatically as a military
leader from the young man who had crossed swords successfully with revolutionary France in the previous decade. He had become more openly cautious
and conservative, and he had been seduced by a certain strand of eighteenth-
century military thought that would see its epitome in the nineteenth-century
works of Baron Antoine Henri de Jomini. This line of argument, put forth
most notably by Heinrich von Bülow but expounded by others, focused on
the geometry of operations and on the relationship between the field army and
its logistical base.[27]

Charles's attempts to consider the relationship between the French army
and its base, from which it would draw reinforcements as well as supplies at the
moment of decisive combat, convinced him that Italy would be much more suitable for Napoleon's struggle than Germany. Ignoring the complexities of Bavarian politics (of which Charles may not have been aware), the French in Germany
would have to operate from hastily assembled forward bases when they hit the
main Austrian army, whereas in Italy the French would be operating from their
own well-stocked permanent bases. There was nothing wrong with this line of
thought—everything Charles wrote was true. From this perspective, Italy was a
better base for Napoleon to operate from than Germany. The question was: Did
Napoleon rate such considerations as highly as Charles and Bülow?

Another unspoken assumption about Napoleon's likely actions underlay
Charles's identification of Italy as the decisive theater. Charles implicitly assumed that the war would come after a period of rising hostility during which
Napoleon would redeploy his army to the positions from which he intended to
attack Austria. Only this assumption can explain why Charles paid no attention
to the fact that the great bulk of the French army was currently deployed along
the English Channel, and therefore much more likely to strike in Germany
than Italy, whatever the relative merits of the latter theater as a base of offensive
operations against Austria. It seems not to have occurred to Charles that
Napoleon would redeploy and attack in a single movement without first concentrating his armies for an appropriately balanced and well-conceived attack.

A final assumption emerges from Charles's attempt to destroy the notion
that the Austrians could hope for any meaningful success in the German theater. He writes,

> In order to second the offensive and defensive efforts of the Italian Impe-
> rial-Royal [Austrian] Army [and] to prevent an invasion of the Tyrol, a
> second, although not so considerable army, must oppose the French
> army that will probably be advancing from Strasburg by the shortest line

through Swabia against Austria. With this army, one must strive to reach
the Iller [in western Bavaria] before the enemy.

He continues by arguing that even if this second Austrian army should defeat the French forces in front of it, such a victory would only throw the
French back over the Rhine—and onto one of their strongest fortification
belts through which the Austrians could not hope to advance. The real significance of this passage, however, is elsewhere.

The Iller is a small river that runs from just east of the Bodensee (Lake
Constance) through Bavaria west of Munich and into the Danube near Ulm.
Charles's insistence on seizing it made perfect sense for a plan that identified
Italy as the main theater of war. If the Austrians held the line of the Bodensee,
the Iller, and either the Danube or some northward extension of the Iller line,
then they would have secured the passes over the Tyrolean Alps into northern
Italy, thereby protecting the flank and rear of the main army operating there.
Holding any line east of the Iller would have exposed the Tyrol and the passes.
If the Austrians merely stood on the Austro–Bavarian frontier, then the rear of
the army in Italy would have been completely vulnerable.

These considerations all assume that Napoleon's main purpose in moving
on the Danube would be to strike at the Austrian army in Italy. The proposed
invasion of Bavaria, however, also made sense in the event that Napoleon decided to drive toward Vienna through Germany. By moving forward, the Austrians would secure a more rational and defensible line than their own border
and would ensure that the first battles would be fought in Bavarian territory.
This was an important consideration for two reasons. First, Charles was extremely concerned with the state of Austria's finances. Fighting the war at the
expense of the Bavarians was a good way to mitigate its economic consequences
for the Habsburgs. Second, the Tyrol is not a rich province and Charles was
worried about supplying a strong army there. Bavaria was a much wealthier region and would have been quite capable of supporting an Austrian force.

One drawback to the plan of advancing the "Iller army" deep into Bavaria
was that it would be harder for the two main Austrian armies to reinforce each
other than it would have been had the Austrians tried only to hold the Tyrol.
This problem did not concern Charles because he insisted that the Iller army
must not be weakened by sending reinforcements to Italy. In the event of
disaster in the latter theater (which Charles believed was virtually certain),
Austria's only hope would be the (possibly victorious) Iller army. If both armies
were beaten, it would be the end of the Habsburg monarchy.[28]

In outline, Charles proposed the following war plan. The main Austrian
army would concentrate on the border of Italy and invade and seize northern
Italy when the war broke out. A secondary and smaller Austrian army would
advance as soon as hostilities began to the line of the Iller in Bavaria. It would

defeat the oncoming French army, which he assumed would be moderately sized, but would not attempt to follow up its victories. Instead, it would remain on the defensive in Bavaria until such time as (miraculously) the Italian army had driven the French from northern Italy. Charles did not make it clear what would happen at that point, probably because he thought it inconceivable that either army would be successful.

Although Charles considered the military issues and options more carefully than Cobenzl had, his evaluations and judgments were less objective than those of the vice chancellor. He was convinced of two things from the outset: that the French armies would defeat anything Austria could put into the field, and that any war, even a successful one, would ruin the monarchy. The entire purpose of his memorandum was to demonstrate those two points and thereby persuade his brother not to accept the Russian overtures. This was not Prussian-style court politics—Charles felt no obligation to take a stance opposed to Cobenzl or anyone else simply to benefit politically. On the contrary, he held firm to his beliefs and arguments, as we have seen, long after they began to cost him political power and influence. He strongly held the two core opinions identified above, and he was convinced that he had to do everything in his power to dissuade Francis from adopting a fatal policy. This approach was not ignoble; it may even have been praiseworthy, considering what it cost Charles at the time and subsequently. Unfortunately it reduced military planning even by the military professionals to the status of an appendix to a political program, and it ensured that the meticulous and professional aspects of Charles's memoranda would never be considered separately from the political program that motivated them.

Cobenzl's response to Charles's memorandum, which we have already considered from the perspective of its importance for Austria's domestic politics and foreign policies, focused exclusively on the political program that motivated it.[29] Cobenzl even asserted that Charles had offered no alternative to the Russian plan, and that the military details he provided demonstrated the folly of Alexander's ideas. In this note he suggested for the first time that Mack be brought onboard to develop the war plans that Charles refused to consider seriously.

Cobenzl's slanderous quip makes it easy to believe that Charles's ideas of March 1804 were irrelevant and that Mack was the one who developed the ultimate Austrian (and allied) war plan. This was not the case. Cobenzl did not challenge Charles's notions about where the decisive theater should be, how the Austrian armies should be deployed, or the need to advance to the Iller. These core elements of the ultimate allied war plan were repeated throughout the internal Austrian discussions and formed the basic elements of the plan that Mack inherited but did not originate. Mack's subsequent history and Charles's heroism in the campaign of 1809, as well as the personalities of the two men, have led to a tendency to blame Mack for all of the faults of the allied war plan. As we shall see, in this matter as in others Mack was unfortunate and perhaps wronged.

Cobenzl's reaction to Charles's memorandum conditioned its immediate impact. The Austrian response to the Russian proposals included many of the outlines of Charles's war plan but mitigated their tone because Cobenzl feared that Charles's defeatism would destroy any prospect of future Russian support.[30] The formal Austrian counterproposal of April 1, 1804, focused primarily on the politics of the negotiation and addressed the military problems only obliquely.[31]

In this counterproposal Francis tried to restrict the terms of the alliance to a simple renewal of the Austro–Russian agreements of 1792 and 1795: mutual guarantees of military support if either state was attacked. The second contained the basic provisions of the Third Partition of Poland—its renewal in the circumstances of 1804 would reinforce both the clauses about mutual defense and the territorial arrangements that resulted from that transaction.[32] Francis was also eager to insert the statement that the coalition's goal would never be "to bring about a counter-revolution in France, but only to remediate the common dangers of Europe."

On the military side, vagueness reigned. Francis promised to contribute at least 200,000 soldiers and demanded of Alexander no fewer than 150,000 beyond the "observation corps" that both states would maintain to keep Prussia quiet. Since the *casus foederis* was to be an attack by France on the territory of either Austria or Russia, the consideration of operations in northern Germany or the Balkans became irrelevant. Francis was concerned, however, with the realities of military movements. He noted that Austria was close to France, whereas the Russians were far from the likely theaters of war. Without proposing a specific plan for addressing this problem, he insisted that war plans must pay "the greatest attention" to ensure that the movement of allied forces allowed the "time and the chance to make my forces and my frontiers able to open the campaign with the energy necessary to attain the goal of the war." Francis did not elaborate further on this vague statement in the formal counterproposal.

In the accompanying notes sent to Johann Philipp Stadion, the Austrian ambassador in St. Petersburg, Cobenzl included more detail. He first rejected the notion that Napoleon had any serious designs on Greece or the Balkans in general, and he disputed the idea that northern Europe should be the focus of allied operations because there "even reverses would not force [Napoleon] to a peace such as must be desired."[33] The main blows would have to be struck in northern Italy and southern Germany.

In a second, lengthier note, Cobenzl further elaborated both the difficulties Austria faced in accepting Alexander's offer and the plans he would like to pursue in the event of war.[34] Here he asserted that Napoleon had 500,000 men under arms, and that he could move 350,000 to 400,000 against the allies. The Austrians insisted that the coalition meet the French with equal numbers in the theaters of concern to Vienna—northern Italy and southern Germany. It was not enough, Cobenzl declared, simply to hold the Austrian frontiers in these areas. Italy would have to be invaded and the fortresses protecting it reduced one by one. Bavaria would also have to bear the weight of Austrian arms to reduce the economic burden on the badly depleted Habsburg lands. These two operations were not sufficient, however. It would also be necessary to invade Switzerland, presumably to secure the Alpine passes that would facilitate communications between the two Austrian armies.

The purpose of all this was clear: Cobenzl's stated aim was to convince the tsar that the conflict against France would be hard and thereby cool his ardor for war, while avoiding the danger of persuading him that Austria was useless, thereby turning him away from the Austrian alliance.[35] The responses he crafted nearly failed to attain either objective but did insert the essential parts of the Austrian war plan into the coalition negotiations.

In his first response on May 7, Alexander attempted to straddle the issue. He promised Francis that 100,000 Russian troops would move against France, in addition to the large "reserve" army he intended to maintain on the Prussian frontier. The Austrians could have 40,000–50,000 at their immediate disposal to send where they would, but "the destination of the remaining 50,000 cannot be designated in advance, since it will depend on the point where the enemy directs his efforts, either to the north or to the south." He attempted (vainly) to convince Francis that the "reserve" army was necessary both to "impose" on Prussia and serve as a pool of replacements to keep the other armies up to strength. He continued to cite the importance of the 10,000 men he had already stationed at Corfu and promised that the Russian fleet would be active as well.[36]

At this point the negotiations began to focus on the number of troops the Russians would commit to Austria. In June, the Austrians demanded 150,000 and would not be moved from that figure, which they based on the assumptions that Napoleon would have 350,000–400,000 troops to throw against Vienna and that he must be met with equal force in each theater.[37] Cobenzl would modify this number only if Prussia could be persuaded to join the coalition. In that case, Austria would accept only 100,000 troops; otherwise, he told an exasperated Razumovskii, he intended to hold firm to his demand.[38]

Alexander refused to commit more than 100,000 troops to the operating field armies, although in September he ordered Novosil'tsev to tell Pitt that he would commit 110,000.[39] He also indicated in that note that he planned to send a Russian army of 40,000 men to free Hanover, either through Prussian territory or through Austrian territory just south of Prussia. When Hanover had been cleared, the Russians would join with Hanoverian and British troops to throw the French forces back into the south of Holland.

This was the real crux of the dispute over the number of Russian troops stipulated in the Austro–Russian convention. Alexander did not want to have his hands tied to committing all or most of his available forces to the Austrian theaters of northern Italy and southern Germany. He wanted to be able to drive Napoleon from his conquests all along the line from Denmark to Sicily. The Austrians wanted to ensure that they would receive Russia's full support in the event of a war and prevent Alexander from frittering away his army in small detachments spread out over an enormous area. The end was a compromise in Alexander's favor. The final treaty of November 1804 specified a total allied force of 350,000 troops, of which the Austrians would provide 235,000 and the Russians 115,000.[40] The Austro–Russian convention offered no further details about the war plan, only committing the two sides to work out such a plan "immediately."

This first effort at coalition war planning was irrelevant in the sense that the Austro–Russian convention foresaw a defensive war that aimed to drive the French from their ill-gotten conquests. The war of 1805, however, was an offensive operation launched by the allies in hopes of restoring the balance of power in Europe (and, implicitly, removing Napoleon from the throne of France). The Austro–Russian war plan, moreover, concerned only Austrian and Russian troops, whereas the actual war involved the British and Neapolitans as well, and everyone had high hopes that the Prussians would join too. The period after November 1804 should have seen a thorough reexamination of the allied war plans in light of rapidly changing circumstances—the Anglo–Russian negotiations, Napoleon's activities in Italy, Austrian rearmament, Prussia's continued refusal to participate in negotiations for an alliance, and so forth. We must now consider why there was no thorough reconsideration and the consequences of that failure of coalition planning.

Britain and Allied War Planning

The Anglo–Russian Convention of April 1805 (ratified at the end of July) formally committed the Russians and, when they adhered to it in early August, the Austrians to an offensive war against France for the first time. Surprisingly, this fundamental transformation of the nature of the coalition occasioned little change in the details of the coalition war plans. The Russians communicated to London the plans they were developing with the Austrians (described in detail below), and the Court of St. James indicated its general approval of those plans. Otherwise, the negotiations for the coalition treaty with Great Britain did not address war plans in detail.[41]

Britain's relative unimportance in allied war planning resulted partly from the timing of affairs and partly from Britain's perceived role in the war. From the standpoint of British participation in developing the campaign plan, it was unfortunate that Alexander's courier forwarding the tentative plans arrived at the beginning of June—in the middle of the crisis over the ratification of the Anglo–Russian convention.[42] The diplomatic efforts of both courts were directed to healing the breach caused by Alexander's insistence that Pitt offer to evacuate Malta in return for a satisfactory settlement from Napoleon, and Pitt's refusal to do so even though no one thought Napoleon would accept the offer anyway. Not only did no one have time to peruse war plans, but it would have been impolitic to do so, since the formal position of both sides was that the treaty might not be ratified. In such a circumstance how could either side enter into a detailed negotiation about how to execute the agreement? By the time the diplomatic crisis ended in late July, the Austro–Russian war plan had been more or less finalized and troops were beginning to move.

It is unclear whether Pitt would have played an active role in the development of the war plan even in the absence of a major diplomatic crisis. The Austrians saw in Britain only a paymaster, and a parsimonious one at that. Although Alexander appreciated the importance of the Royal Navy and sought to obtain its assistance in moving his troops, and although he periodically endeavored to draw a larger portion of British troops or Hanoverian exiles into the continental war, he too saw the British armed forces as largely irrelevant to the larger struggle.

The British did little to dispel the notion that their primary contribution to the coalition was financial. The miserliness of their subsidies (at least from the Russian and Austrian perspectives) was exceeded only by Pitt's parsimony when it came to contributing troops to the fight. There was never any prospect of a major British army landing on or near the French coast, and Alexander's efforts to persuade Pitt to increase the size of the British force destined to operate in Naples came to little. British gold was not the cause of the formation of the Third Coalition, but the behavior of British statesmen at this time strengthened Napoleon's contemporary and subsequent propaganda to that effect.

Nevertheless, Pitt worked hard to strengthen Alexander's determination to send armies to Naples and northern Germany as well as liberate Hanover.[43] He thereby hardened the tsar's resolve to force Prussia into the coalition peacefully or by arms, since only with the cooperation of Berlin could the allies expel Napoleon from Hanover and Holland. Since Alexander had already decided what he was going to do, the only effect of Pitt's pressure was to make the commitment of substantial Russian forces to northern Germany and southern Italy nonnegotiable elements of the allied war plan.

It also highlighted the interaction between the weakness of the coalition and allied war planning. Britain had no important interests in southern Germany and Switzerland and very limited interests in northern Italy. Her interests were concentrated in Naples, Sicily, and Malta; Hanover, Sweden, and Denmark; and the Dutch coast, since those areas were significant to the control of the Mediterranean and the North and Baltic Seas and their trade. Austria had no real interest in northern Germany, Holland, or Scandinavia; very limited interest in Naples; and none at all in Malta. To the extent that Russia had direct interests involved in the war, they matched Britain's more closely than Austria's, with an even greater emphasis on northern Germany.

The intersection of the direct interests of the allied powers was therefore a null set. No single area or combination of areas in Europe drew the powers together into a natural coalition. The range of their interests, however, approached the breadth of the continent, unless they transcended their consideration of direct interests and moved toward solving the deeper problem posed by Napoleon's power in France. None of the allied rulers were really willing to do so, however, and the coalition plans consequently aimed at attaining the direct interests of all of the powers.

In a coalition of states strongly bound to one another, it might have been possible to persuade one or more to delay the pursuit of their direct interests in order to concentrate forces and pursue a better military plan. Such a coalition might have been able to forswear the immediate defense of Naples, which was bound to be free of French control following allied victories in northern Italy, or the immediate liberation of northern Germany and Holland, which was equally certain to follow the success of allied arms in southern Germany and France. The Third Coalition, however, was no such strong alliance.

Previous wars against revolutionary France had conditioned the powers to mistrust one another and seek to gain their ultimate objectives at the outset. Frank discussion of this issue was impossible because all of the alliances remained tenuous until August 1805. The final Austrian adherence to the Anglo–Russian convention remained in doubt even after Russian and Austrian troops had begun moving, until Leveson Gower agreed to a series of (in his opinion) exorbitant Austrian demands for British financial assistance.[44] States threatening to withhold their agreement to vital alliances over issues of financial and territorial compensation are unlikely to sacrifice the immediate pursuit of those compensations in the war plans. The conflicting interests of the allied powers, along with the inherent weaknesses in the coalition, led to the development of a war plan that pursued every objective simultaneously. The allied leaders agreed to that war plan, almost as an afterthought to the conclusion of the coalition treaties.

The Austro–Russian War Plan

The conclusion of the Austro–Russian defensive alliance in November 1804 made the development of a joint war plan urgent, since the treaty specified that the two empires would agree on a plan of action immediately. When Francis had ratified the treaty, he told Cobenzl that he still wanted peace above all and wished to avoid actions that might lead to war.[45] Francis thus took the initiative in producing war plans either for this reason or perhaps because he feared that Alexander would develop plans to send his army all over the continent to support every ally except Austria. He therefore ordered Charles, then war minister and president of the Hofkriegsrat, to draft a plan as rapidly as possible in secrecy, lest Napoleon learn what was afoot in Vienna.[46]

Charles had been kept ignorant of the impending alliance and reacted with anger and hostility when Cobenzl informed him of it in early December.[47] The plan he drafted in response to Francis's note exuded even more despondency and hopelessness than his previous efforts. He clearly implied that any plan for war against France was a mindless undertaking.[48]

He began by presenting a lengthy and misleading assessment of the relative power of France and the coalition. Charles grossly overestimated the strength of the French army at 598,084 Frenchmen, and 651,964 troops if Napoleon's allies were included in the tally.[49] This estimate was off by almost 50 percent: the French army as late as mid-August 1805 numbered only 446,745 men, including many of the allied contingents.[50] A large part of the error emerged because Charles estimated the size of a French line regiment at about 3,600, whereas in reality the average was approximately 2,300. The discrepancy arose because the Austrians believed that Napoleon could conscript an endless supply of Frenchmen and foreigners and that his regiments would be at full strength. In reality, Napoleon could do no such thing.

Charles also pointed to the financial problems Austria faced, the inadequate subsidies that Britain might provide to offset the costs of the new war, and the enormous distances the Russian troops would have to cover to arrive anywhere near the theater of operations. Even the Austrian troops, he wrote, would be hard-pressed to move from their cantonments in the eastern part of the monarchy to their concentration areas along the western borders in less than three months. He believed that it would take another three months to draft the recruits and buy the horses needed to fill out the war establishment of the army. It did not occur to him that these actions could take place simultaneously, so he insisted that Austria could not be ready for war in less than six months.

In the war plan he proposed, Charles followed his ideas of the previous March with a few minor changes. He insisted on dividing the Austrian troops into three armies. The main one, in Italy, would have 134 infantry and 12 cavalry regiments, the army in Germany would have 55 infantry and 21 cavalry regiments, while an army in the Tyrol would have 42 infantry and 2 cavalry regiments.[51] Charles declared again that the main blow must come in Italy, but his reasoning in this memorandum was somewhat different. Once again he pointed out that the French Rhine frontier was too strongly fortified to give any hope of a rapid victory. A blow through Switzerland against Franche-Comté would be best, but Switzerland could not be taken until Italy had been cleared of French troops.

The Italian army, accordingly, should begin offensive operations as soon as war broke out. It would cross the Adige, drive the French from the Mincio,

Mantua, and Peschiera, and advance to the Adda at least. In the meantime, the army in Germany would advance immediately into Bavaria, but Charles hedged on its initial destination. Whereas previously he had insisted that it march as far as the Iller, now he suggested that it might not go beyond the Lech.[52] Charles offered no explanation for this change or for his selection of the Lech, which offers a less useful defensive line if the aim is to secure the rear of the army in Italy. Perhaps it was not necessary for the army in Germany to expose itself by moving so far to the west, since this revised plan included a reasonably strong army to hold the Tyrol. Perhaps his pessimism got the better of him and he had decided that the initial plan was too bold. In any event, he still believed that the army in Germany would go over to the defensive as soon as it reached the river line. There it would wait for the Russian armies to catch up and for the army in Italy to succeed before beginning the assault into Switzerland.

Charles was not the only one drafting war plans, however. In November 1804, Mack wrote up his own notions of what the allied army should do in the event of conflict. He presented the plan to the emperor later that year or in early January 1805.[53] Whereas Charles disdained the contributions of Austria's allies and ignored their armies (except to point out reasons why they could never really help Austria), Mack's memorandum spent more time on the allies than on his own forces.

The Russians, Mack wrote, would need to take special pains to keep their armies up to strength far from their frontiers, and he recommended that two smaller forces follow the main Russian army in order to make replacements readily available. He also noted the importance of lightening the load of the Russian forces so that they could cross Austria and arrive in the theater of operations as rapidly as possible.

The bulk of the memorandum addressed the problem of Prussia. Mack considered two possible scenarios: that Prussia joined the coalition and Prussia refused to join. In the first case, an allied army supported by Prussian forces could march directly through Hanover and into Holland, thereby achieving the coalition's objectives in northern Germany. If Prussia actively supported the coalition, then the success of the allies was "infallible" (in a copy of the memorandum sent to Charles this was changed to "highly probable").[54] If Prussia did not join the coalition, then Mack thought that the alliance might not achieve its objectives in north Germany, even if the Russians sent a moderate force there to cooperate with the Swedes and the British. He concluded that buying Prussia's participation was worthwhile, even at the expense of substantial territorial gain for Berlin.

When Mack considered the actions of the Austrian army, however, he added little to Charles's initial plans of March 1804, except perhaps optimism.[55] Austrian forces should be broken into three armies—one in Germany, one in Italy, and one in the Tyrol. The army in Germany should advance to the

Bodensee (Lake Constance) and then prepare for operations in Switzerland. The army in Italy should lay siege to Mantua and Peschiera and advance as far as Milan (just beyond the Adda) if it could. The army in the Tyrol should advance into Switzerland and begin to seize the key passes to facilitate further operations.

Mack thought that the politicians had to be responsible for preventing Napoleon from attacking Austria before she was ready. The cabinet (by which he meant Cobenzl and Colloredo) should deceive the French about Austria's adherence to the coalition and keep Napoleon in doubt for so long that "if the mask is lifted, he will no longer be able to reach the outermost Austrian frontiers with overwhelming force before they can be strengthened." Beyond recommending that the cabinet use "cleverness," "circumspection," and "secrecy," Mack had no good idea of how Cobenzl should keep Napoleon ignorant of the movement of hundreds of thousands of Austrian and Russian troops, tens of thousands of horses, and enormous quantities of supplies.

Charles disagreed with Mack in the matter of optimism rather than planning details. In response to Russian objections in regard to putting their army under an Austrian commander in chief and fighting in Switzerland, Charles defended both Austrian tenets aggressively. Since Austria would put her main force in Italy and since the forces left in Germany and the Tyrol would be inadequate to force their way through Switzerland, the Russians had to support those armies. The importance of unity of command led Charles into a lengthy historical digression to prove that failure to achieve such unity nearly always led to defeat.[56] Charles noted that Mack's suggestion of having a reserve of recruits follow the Russian army was unworkable, and that Mack vastly underestimated the difficulties allied armies would face in trying to reduce Holland's excellent fortresses, even if the Prussians joined the coalition.[57]

Mack disagreed completely. He argued that Russian reinforcements were not needed for the army in Germany, and that the Russians should send their troops to north Germany instead, seizing Hanover and then advancing into Holland.[58] The allies would gain several advantages from such a plan. It would induce the British to commit a larger force to the continent in hopes of retaking Hanover and liberating Holland. It would force Napoleon to divert substantial troops from fighting Austria to fighting the allies in north Germany. And it would eliminate the problems of coalition command-and-control relationships by keeping the Russian and Austrian armies separate.

The last point is perhaps the most important. In previous wars the separateness of coalition armies had been a weakness of alliance warfare. The independence of Prussian and Russian forces had allowed those countries to withdraw from the wars against France in 1795 and 1800 without much difficulty. Had their forces been intermingled with Austrian and British troops, withdrawal would have been considerably more complicated and dangerous, which might have given pause to Frederick William II and Paul.

Mack even considered that Russian forces based in Corfu might divert French forces away from fighting the main Austrian army in northern Italy. He identified the failure to coordinate the actions of allied forces in Naples and northern Italy as one of the main causes of the allies' defeat in the War of the Second Coalition. His experiences in that war no doubt played a role in this evaluation: he was taken prisoner by the French while commanding a Neapolitan army in 1799.[59]

Charles responded to Mack's arguments with his usual depressing vigor.[60] With the exception of Eugene and Marlborough, he wrote, no coalition armies have flourished except under a unified command. Keeping the Austrian and Russian forces separate invited disaster. Charles doubted that the Russians would be able to take Holland. He did not believe that the British would send more than a token force to the continent whatever the war plan, since the large army they had raised consisted mainly of militia recruited solely for the purpose of defending their homeland. He was naturally dubious that the Prussians would join.

Charles also presented an argument that would be very harmful to the coalition. Francis, he wrote, had a solemn obligation to defend the Austrian monarchy first and foremost. Since Austria had the most to lose and was at the greatest risk of all the allies, Francis should insist on a plan of action that best defended his own territory. Only when that unlikely goal had been secured could Francis and his allies consider operations designed to acquire new conquests for any of them. The Russian army should hasten to defend Austria's western frontier along with the Austrian army in southern Germany. The full force of the combined Austro–Russian force there would not be too large for the purpose.

Charles and Mack agreed on many of the details of the Austrian war plan. The army would be divided into three parts, the main blow would be struck in Italy, the German army would advance into Bavaria and then go over to the defensive, the final attack would be through Switzerland into Franche-Comté. They both imagined that Napoleon would redeploy the bulk of his forces from the English Channel to meet the major Austrian attack in Italy. Neither considered what to do about the exposed right flank of the Austrian army in southern Germany. Mack's plan dealt with this problem only implicitly. A large Russian, British, Swedish, and maybe even Prussian force invading Hanover and Holland would effectively cover the Austrian army in Germany. Charles did not address this issue at all.

Inexplicably, neither Charles nor Mack considered the possibility that Napoleon would direct his main force against the Austrian army in Germany, not in Italy, and attempt to drive rapidly on Vienna. In the absence of any evidence that might explain this lapse in imagination, we can only consider several factors that might have played a role.

The problem of mirror imaging probably contributed to this failure. The coalition war plans presupposed that states apportion their armies to separate theaters in direct relation to the importance of their interests in those theaters. Because the Austrians had the most to gain and the most to lose in Italy, they planned to send the bulk of their army there. The British, interested primarily in Holland and southern Italy, dispatched their limited ground contingents accordingly. Alexander, whose interests in northern Germany and southern Italy were much greater than those in southern Germany, likewise proposed to divide his forces in accord with his interests.

Charles and Mack both reasoned that Napoleon would behave in a similar fashion. As the war plans were being written, word of Napoleon's intention to crown himself king of Italy was circulating throughout Vienna. France bordered Austria directly only in Italy. Surely, the Austrians reasoned, Napoleon would feel obliged to defend his newest and most vulnerable conquest if they threatened to attack it. After all, that is what they would have done in his place.

Past events may also have given momentum to a certain mind-set from which the Austrian leaders found it hard to escape. In both previous contests with Napoleon, Italy had been the decisive theater. Both Mack and Charles had participated in those fights. Perhaps they were unable to imagine that Napoleon might behave otherwise.

There is an important geopolitical consideration, however, that reinforced their notion that Napoleon would be ill-advised to focus his efforts on southern Germany, although neither Charles nor Mack adverted to it prior to the war.* The line of the Iller or even the Lech could be extended to reach the isolated Prussian territory of Ansbach. Then the Austrian army in southern Germany would have a flank secured by Prussia's armed neutrality or active participation on the side of the coalition. In that case, Napoleon would have been forced to attack the Austrian positions along the river line frontally, a process that could take considerable time. All the while, the Austrian army in Italy would be driving toward the Adda. Eventually Napoleon would find himself unable to win quickly in Germany and unable to prevent his expulsion from Italy. Austrian seizures of the Alpine passes (which both Mack and Charles called for) would ensure that he could not transfer troops from one theater to the other, whereas the Austrians could.

This assumption suffered from two glaring problems. First, it requires the conviction that Napoleon would not violate Prussian neutrality and that the Prussians, if they joined the coalition, could prevent him from marching through Ansbach. Second, it ignores the possibility that the Prussians might join the French. Such an eventuality would have made nonsense of the entire plan, since it would have exposed the Austrians to an attack not only from the north by the French but also by Prussian forces into Bohemia or southern Germany.

---

*Mack used this line of argument in his ex post facto defense of the operation, however. See below, Chapter 15.

Charles and Mack both referred to the possibility that Frederick William might join France, but neither considered its military consequences in any detail. Both discussed Prussia's allegiance only in terms of its effect on coalition offensive operations in northern Germany. The assertion that the Russians would take care of the Prussians should the latter join the French simply covered their unwillingness to consider a real worst case.

Why did neither Mack nor Charles consider this and other likely worst cases? Probably because they could not develop a plan for them that offered a chance of success. Austria did not have the troops to mount a major offensive in Italy, prepare for another in Germany, and keep a reserve army in Bohemia (although Alexander had asked the Austrians to do precisely that). Only the Russians could deal with the defensive problems posed by Prussia; if they failed, then all was lost.

It is easy to see why Mack, pledged to develop a plan that would work, did not detail contingencies that might make that plan unworkable. But Charles did not want to go to war. Why did he not present this crushing argument about the hopelessness of the task? The politics of the court probably ruled that out. Francis had asked Charles to develop a plan. By February 1805 Charles knew that Mack was developing competing plans. Francis had promised to send a plan to his new ally, and Charles must have sensed that he was losing his struggle to keep control of the Austrian army and Austrian policy. To refuse to produce a plan on the grounds that all plans were hopeless would have been political suicide and would have accomplished nothing. In February 2005 Francis was unwilling to reconsider the wisdom of his new Russian alliance. Charles's only hope was to produce a plan that was risky and might fail but could be sold as the only possible program.

Whatever the reason for the Austrian failure to consider the possibility that Napoleon would not act according to their preconceptions, two things stand out. First, Charles deserves at least as much blame as Mack. It became a consensus of opinion in Austria, and there is no record of anyone challenging it prior to the outbreak of hostilities. Second, it left a dangerous weakness in the allied war plan. Since Alexander, as we shall see, did not presume to dictate to the Austrians what to do with their armies, the consensus of February became the operations plan of August. We shall plumb the depths of its significance in subsequent chapters.

11

The Coalition
War Plan

The basic outlines of the Austrian war plan were established by March 1805. The intense arguments between Charles and Mack ended in compromises, and Charles lost his position as predominant influence over the military. The problem of how Austria's war plans fit into coalition operations as a whole, however, remained unsolved. There was still considerable ambiguity about what exactly the Russian armies would do while the Austrians advanced into Bavaria and northern Italy. The resolution of these questions had an explosive effect on the initial operations of the war. Unfortunately for the coalition, the discussion of coalition war plans became subordinated to the major political and diplomatic issues of the day after Austria settled on her own plan of operation. It was equally unfortunate that the impetus behind the discussions, which lasted from April until September 1805, came primarily from the diplomats in St. Petersburg rather than from professional officers in either capital.

Proposals and Counterproposals

The resolution of the military–political crisis in Vienna (through the promotion of Mack and the demotion of Charles) cleared the way for Austria to send Russia the long-awaited war plan.[1] This plan reflected a combination of Mack's and Charles's proposals. The French frontier was weakest, it argued, behind Switzerland, and only there could the allies attack with any hope of a rapid success. But the Tyrol could not support the large army that would be needed to make such an attack, so Swabia would have to be seized first. Any attack in Switzerland would be paralyzed by a French advance from northern Italy, however, since such an advance would threaten the security of the Alpine passes and, therefore, the rear of the armies operating in southern Germany. Thus emerge the same general outlines of the plan that both Mack and Charles had accepted all along: the Austrian main army would deploy in Italy and attack at once, trying to reach the Adda. The army in Germany would advance to the Lech and await the success of the Italian army—and the arrival of Russian reinforcements.

This last consideration reflected Charles's final triumph over Mack in an essential issue. Mack had insisted that the entire Russian army attack into northern Germany in order to avoid having mixed Austro–Russian forces. Charles, however, had argued that the Austrian army in Germany could not hold out alone against the forces Napoleon could throw at it. Charles won: the Austrian war plan now called for a Russian army to join the Austrian force in southern Germany as rapidly as possible.

The Russian response did not focus on any of these issues, as we shall see. Alexander fixated on the first part of the memorandum, in which the Austrians laid out Charles's exaggerated calculations of French strength and came to a worrisome (for the Russians) conclusion: "Considering this calculation and the advantages of terrain that France has . . . the maintenance of peace remains infinitely to be desired until more favorable circumstance" arrives.[2]

This part of the Austrian proposal set in motion a dramatic chain of events in St. Petersburg that reverberated across the continent. Alexander readily accepted the Austrians' arguments about focusing on Italy first and then Switzerland, and on the distribution and initial operations of the Austrian armies.[3] He suggested that a Russian army might be stationed on the left bank of the Danube near Donauwörth, and that the second promised contingent would move into Bohemia and from there into Franconia, "or wherever else the situation demands."

Austria's continued passivity bothered Alexander. The Russian response thus focused mainly on combating Vienna's pessimism. The tsar argued that the French army was not as large as the Austrians thought (which was true), that the British would be able to make a useful diversion even if they did not land, and, above all, that there was no reason to believe that circumstances would improve if the allies delayed the attack. On the contrary, Napoleon's control over France and the newly conquered lands would strengthen every day he was left undisturbed. If the allies attacked quickly, Alexander suggested, they might well find support among those dissatisfied with the current regime but not yet crushed into submission both in France and in the occupied lands.[4]

What is more, Napoleon would continue to use the interval of peace as he always had—sowing confusion, dissension, and discord among the allies to destroy the coalition before it had been formed. "There is nothing more dangerous than the politics of the French government," Alexander declared, "which has always been able to win more through negotiations than through battles." The fear of the weakness of the coalition drove Alexander to press for rapid action.

The tsar did more than simply press for speedy decisions in Vienna, though; he upped the ante. In reply to the Austrian proposal he promised to send 180,000 troops to aid Francis, rather than the 115,000 troops stipulated by the treaty of November 1804.[5] He accompanied this promise with a new plan that did not discuss the operations of the Austrian armies but encompassed all of Europe in its breadth and ambition.[6]

The scale of Alexander's new plan was breathtaking. The allies aimed, he declared, to force France back to its prerevolutionary frontiers by driving Napoleon from Italy, Switzerland, the right bank of the Rhine, Holland, Hanover, and even Belgium. The coalition could not achieve this goal through an "ordinary war in which the forces are calculated only to balance those of the enemy." The allies must instead "overwhelm the enemy with so great a superiority that he will not be able to defend himself on any front." Opposition to Napoleon in France might then grow large enough to compel him to hold back troops to suppress it.

Alexander's belief that Napoleon's political fortunes were tied to his military situation was not without historical foundation. Throughout the revolutionary wars, the political stability of French generals and governments hinged on battlefield success. Generals who failed, especially early in the revolutionary period, were frequently not only cashiered, but executed. Several French émigré officers now dotted Alexander's court, no doubt reminding him of this fact. This passage actually reflects the Russian view that Napoleon was just another French revolutionary general, head of yet another French revolutionary government. They clearly did not understand the degree to which Napoleon's ascent to power in Paris had fundamentally changed the rules in France and therefore in Europe. Considering that Napoleon had ruled for only a few years, this error is understandable but no less dangerous for being so.

The body of the plan envisaged three "phases," although it did not specify how long the phases would take or what the temporal connection was between them. In the first phase, the Austrian armies would advance as Charles and Mack had proposed, and Alexander would send two armies of 50,000 men each to support them. One would race by forced marches toward the Danube and the Lech to join the Austrian armies there as soon as possible. The other would march through Bohemia, presumably toward middle Germany, with the explicit aim of further assisting the Austrian army in Germany. At the same time, 16,000 Russians would disembark at Stralsund in Swedish Pomerania to join with a Swedish army there. By then 25,000 Russians would have entered Naples to defend the Kingdom of the Two Sicilies and act in conjunction with its armies in southern Italy.

Alexander now turned to the real purpose of all these maneuvers: "It is at this point that one must negotiate with Prussia." These Russian maneuvers would put Frederick William in an untenable position. There would be 80,000 Russian troops along Prussia's eastern border, 16,000 in Pomerania,

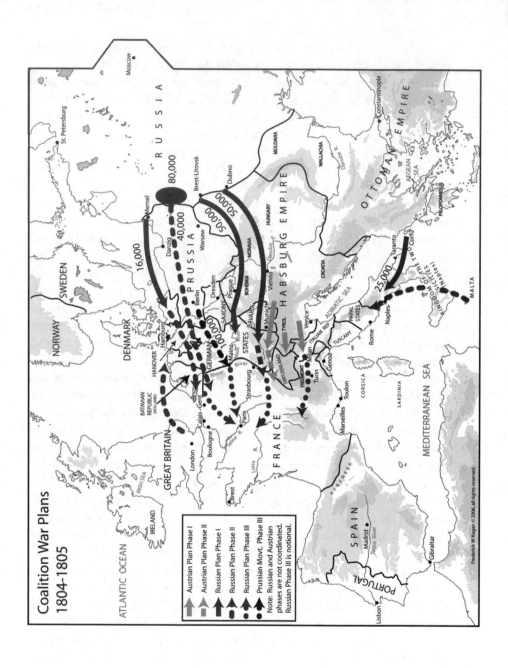

Coalition War Plans
1804-1805

Austrian Plan Phase I
Austrian Plan Phase II
Russian Plan Phase I
Russian Plan Phase II
Russian Plan Phase III
Prussian Movt. Phase III

Note: Russian and Austrian
phases are not coordinated.
Russian Phase III is notional.

and 50,000 marching through Bohemia, whose ultimate destination would be unknown in Berlin. Frederick William would be forced to join the allies at once, and with him "we will acquire Sweden, Denmark, Saxony, Hesse, [and] the Dukes of Mecklembourg and of Brunswick," all effectively vassals of the Hohenzollern house. The British would support the entire operation with landings on the Elbe and the Weser.

The second phase of the operation would open with the adherence of Prussia and her satellites to the coalition, as the allies mustered 557,000 troops, not counting the British forces and those of the minor European states. With Prussia a member of the coalition, the Russian army of 80,000 on her eastern frontier would become superfluous, and Alexander would set 40,000 troops marching from that army toward the Elbe, which would bring the total allied strength up to 597,000 men.

"With such a force we will finally be able to attack the French from Naples to the mouth of the Elbe." Austria will operate in Italy and the Tyrol, Russia in Swabia and then beyond the Rhine. Success in Italy would restore the king of Sardinia to his continental holdings, adding some 25,000 troops to the allied cause. When the Russian armies entered Swabia, 12,000 Bavarians, 8,000 Württembergers, and 5,000 Badeners would also join the coalition forces. By this time 20,000 Neapolitans and 30,000 British troops would be fighting in southern Italy and making landings all along the French Channel coast.

Prussia's adherence to the coalition would bring some 100,000 excellent troops to bear in central and northern Germany. Alexander's plan directed them to the fortress of Mainz. These operations would surely have driven the French out of Hanover, leaving the way clear for the Russo–Swedish force in Pomerania, supported by the contingents of the minor German states, to invade Holland with 51,000 men. The Russian contingent of 40,000 released from the Prussian eastern frontier would join with the Saxons, Hessians, and Brunswickers to drive on the Meuse and cut communications between France and Holland. If they succeeded in that task, they would then drive on Flanders. The liberation of Holland would bring 15,000 more troops over to the allied cause.

The third phase would thus begin with coalition forces totaling over 732,000 men, "not counting what Spain, Portugal, Switzerland, and the minor German princes might be able to furnish." The plan ends at this point, however, offering no clue of what Alexander thought the coalition would do with this massive army stationed along the French frontiers. Presumably he imagined that either Napoleon's regime would have collapsed by then, or that the allies would simply march into France from all directions until it fell.

This plan suffered from a number of obvious problems; most importantly, the author's failure to understand time–space relationships in war. It is said that "amateurs talk about strategy while professionals talk about logistics," but the truth is that the mistake armchair strategists make most frequently is failing to understand what a military unit can and cannot do in a given period of time: the time–space relationship. At a given epoch in history, this relationship is tightly bounded. Men and horses can only march so far in a day; they must rest, eat, drink, and sleep for a certain number of hours if they are to survive the journey in fighting condition. Today tanks, trucks, helicopters, and aircraft can only travel so far in a given period of time, and they must be refueled and repaired at regular intervals. This is an issue that goes beyond mere logistics— supplying forces with material they need to survive and function. The skilled professional commander has an intuitive understanding of what his forces can accomplish in a given time period, and a solid grasp of what is impossible. The amateur rarely is able to take such considerations into account. The Russian war plan was clearly drafted by amateurs.

In the first phase, the Austrians were to wait in Germany until the Russian armies reached them, which would take something like two months since they had to cover a distance of about 665 miles. At the same time, 16,000 Russians would land in Stralsund—a bold claim considering the difficulties of ensuring a precise arrival date for sailing ships in the Baltic (or any other sea, for that matter). This landing of Russian troops in Stralsund would have to occur some six weeks or so after the campaign had begun, since that is how long it would take the second Russian army to arrive in Bohemia. At that point, the Prussians would be "surrounded" by 16,000 Russians and 25,000 Swedes to the north (150 miles from Berlin), 50,000 Russians to the south (180 miles from Berlin), and 80,000 Russians to the east (about 475 miles from Berlin). The problem of coordinating these three Russian armies against the Prussian forces, which could be expected to number between 150,000 and 200,000 men operating on interior lines in defense of their capital, would be enormous; it would take weeks to get a message from one to the other and back again even by fast courier.

It is not impossible that Frederick William would have joined the coalition when faced with a Russian deployment of this variety, but it would surely have taken several weeks more to convince him to do so and to iron out the terms of his adherence. Phase two of the plan, thus, could not possibly begin earlier than about three months after the campaign had begun.

In the second phase, Alexander imagined that 100,000 Prussians would attack Mainz, while 40,000 Russians would have marched from the eastern Prussian border to the Meuse, and the Russo–Swedish force in Pomerania would have marched to Holland. Mainz is 350 miles from Berlin—about a one-month march. The Prussian border is closer, but Frederick William would not have concentrated his army on his western border while preparing to repulse a Russian attack from the east, even if he gave in and joined the coalition at the last moment. In all likelihood, he would have concentrated it either in Berlin or on his eastern frontier, hundreds of miles farther from Mainz. If the campaign began on July 1 (and considering the fact that Alexander's note did not reach Vienna until the end of June, this would have been a very optimistic date), then the second phase could not start until about October 1. The Prussian army could not be expected to reach Mainz until early November.

It would take about that long for the Russo–Swedish army at Stralsund to march to Holland (a distance of about 375 miles), so that operations against Napoleon's easternmost satellite would also have to begin in early November, not a very propitious time to be starting a campaign. The Russian army of 40,000 released from the Prussian eastern frontier, however, would have to travel over 875 miles to get to its intended target on the Meuse. It could not be expected to accomplish this feat in less than three months. This operation, which Alexander clearly intended to support the operations of the Russo–Swedish force in Holland, could not have started until January 1, 1806, at the earliest, two months after the Russo–Swedish force arrived at the Dutch frontier.

Ideas of coordinating the Neapolitan army with the main Austrian forces in Italy or elsewhere likewise ignored the fact that it is 400 miles from Naples to the designated southern boundary of the Austrian operations in the north, the Po River. The plan also assumed that the armed forces of each liberated state would magically appear at the allies' side instantly. The presupposition that these armed forces would not have been either coopted or destroyed by Napoleon was unfounded.

Apparently Alexander and Czartoryskii did not imagine that these events would take place in a single year or campaigning season. They argued that their objectives might take three campaign seasons to accomplish, although the new plan produced such overwhelming force that the allies might hope to succeed in two. The main purpose of this argument was not to address the problem of coordinating the phases in time but to prove that fighting a shorter but more vigorous war was less expensive for the allies than a slower but more careful campaign; 200,000 men fighting in two campaigns cost less than 150,000 men fighting in three.[7]

It is possible to imagine, then, that the invasion of Holland and even the siege of Mainz would not begin until the spring of 1806, and that 1805 would see only the first phase of operations in which the Austrians cleared northern and southern Italy, the Austro–Russian army established itself in Swabia, and the Prussians were forced to join the coalition. Frederick William's appearance in spring 1806 at the head of 100,000 men in front of Mainz is perfectly reasonable from a military point of view, and the apparently sudden deployment of tens of thousands of Hessians, Saxons, Württembergers, Sardinians, and Neapolitans is also explicable if those forces are only supposed to undertake action in early 1806.

The Russian plan, therefore, clearly envisioned several phases in which echelons of troops would advance at different times. The Austrians would move first. Then the Russian reinforcing armies would arrive in southern

Germany and the Russian contingent would land in Stralsund. By this point in the campaign, more than two months after the first movements had begun, the allies would optimally have cleared northern Italy and taken up position in eastern Bavaria. None of these actions would have materially reduced Napoleon's military power or hurt him badly. They were merely steps preparatory to a subsequent massive invasion aimed at north Germany and likely to begin in the spring of 1806. A major flaw in the Russian plan is that it takes no account of the Austrian notion of driving through Switzerland into Franche-Comté beyond the fact that Alexander supported the idea. Therefore it is impossible to tell in which phase of the campaign Alexander wanted that operation to take place. The plan's most important flaw, however, is that Napoleon would have at least six months to take his own actions and launch his own attacks while the allies finished their mobilization in the north before the final assault on France.

Failing to take the enemy's likely actions into account is another besetting sin of the amateur strategist, exacerbated in this case by the enormous complexity of the plan. Alexander might have resolved this dilemma in one of two mutually exclusive ways. By the more conservative Russian estimates, Napoleon had about 500,000 troops with which to confront the allies.[8] Alexander argued that the threat of British landings along the entire coast of France and Italy, together with Napoleon's need to retain a considerable force in France to maintain order (and his own power), would require the commitment of at least one-third of this French force, leaving about 330,000 French troops available for the initial operations. Those troops would face 250,000 Austrians supported by 115,000 Russians—hardly a terrifying ratio.

By this line of argument, the initial allied deployments in Germany and Italy should have been sufficient to contain and even defeat the French army, assuming that Napoleon dispersed his available forces between Italy and Germany in a manner similar to what the allies had done. If he chose to concentrate in one theater or the other, however, he could probably destroy the allied army before help could arrive; Alexander imagined that in this case the victory would be temporary, considering the massive reinforcements the coalition expected to receive.

This notion, however, ignores important complexities. What if Napoleon concentrated in Germany and destroyed the allied armies there? Prussia would not only be freed of the threat of Russian encirclement, but would have a large and victorious French army on her western frontier—a powerful inducement to resist Alexander's blandishments. The balance of political calculations that rested on the carefully echeloned movement of Russian forces might collapse if the Austrians could not hold in Germany.

The precision timing required by the Russian plan was worrying from many perspectives. In order to achieve the desired effect on Prussia, Russian armies separated from each other by hundreds of miles of potentially hostile territory would have to synchronize their actions without being able to communicate with one another in a timely fashion. A similar problem held in Italy, mitigated there only by the possibility of communicating by ship through the Adriatic Sea.

The notion that large armies could be tightly coordinated with one another across vast land distances was not new. The first two coalitions had attempted similar operations against Revolutionary France, occasionally on a scale close to what Alexander had in mind for the final offensive of his third phase (although never on a scale as large as that contained in his first phase). The hope of such coordination was fed by the occasional success of having independent armies work together, and it encouraged the more feverish brains among European military leaders, Mack's chief among them, with the promise of future operations synchronized on an enormous scale. Repeated failures were chalked up not to the inherent impossibility of executing this concept, but to particular failures of individual armies and commanders. It would be years before Europe's military leaders came to recognize the real limitations that horse- and foot-carried communications imposed on their efforts to synchronize the movements of vast armies over great distances. In the meantime, Alexander and Czartoryskii had developed an elaborate war plan that rested on a degree of coordination their forces could not achieve and took inadequate account of their ability to move forces long distances in short periods of time.[9]

The Austrian Response

The Russian plan caused a flurry of debate in Vienna when it arrived in June. Charles, Mack, and Cobenzl all drafted responses to it.[10] As usual, Mack and Cobenzl accepted the Russian plan with some enthusiasm and focused on criticizing certain important technical problems. Charles did not fail to highlight technical problems, but he continued his campaign to lure Francis away from the impending war. All three responses emphasized the widening gap between the war plan the Austrians intended to execute and the grandiose vision that Alexander was pursuing.

Mack's Response

In contrast with his earlier war plan, which focused heavily on coalition operations in northern Germany and southern Italy, Mack's reply to the new Russian war plan centered on a series of coordination issues between the accepted Austrian plans and the proposed Russian operations.[11] Mack began by producing his own calculus of forces available to Napoleon and concluded that they numbered about 476,000—far fewer than the numbers Charles had insisted on and lower even than those proposed by Alexander, although still somewhat higher than the actual number. Mack believed that the war was feasible based on the ratios of available forces.

He did not believe, however, that the plan for a British landing at the mouths of the Elbe and Weser was sound. For one thing, he feared that the British could not make a success of such landings unless they were supported by the Prussians. And he clearly did not accept Alexander's happy confidence that the Prussians would join the coalition at an early date. He pointed out that British landings in north Germany were not helpful as a diversion because they would draw French reinforcements into an area that the allies wanted to invade. It would be much better for the coalition, and safer for the British, if they confined themselves to landings or even demonstrations on the Atlantic and Mediterranean coasts of France, hoping to draw French troops to regions far removed from the allied offensives.

Mack did not, however, consider the difficulty of timing such demonstrations. It takes weeks to march an army across France. To have any effect, the British landings would have to occur at a precise moment in time prior to the arrival of the allied main armies. If they arrived too soon, the French might drive them off and return to the main theater in time. If they arrived too late, Napoleon might ignore a relatively minor threat in favor of the more immediate one. Considering that there was no way for the armies in northern Germany to communicate with the British fleet on the Atlantic or Mediterranean coasts in any timely fashion, the likelihood that any British demonstration or landing could be meaningful was close to nil. Mack may have understood that fact and offered this compromise as a way to ensure that the British did not end up drawing French reinforcements to precisely where they should not be drawn, while politicly offering the Royal Navy a way to continue to play a supposedly valuable role.

Mack's next two criticisms were intertwined. He began by rejecting the idea put forth by Alexander that the Austrians need not maintain an observation army on the Prussian frontier. He argued that 80,000 Russians on Prussia's eastern border would not be enough to guarantee Austria against Prussian attack. He also pointed out quite shrewdly that the Russian "second army" that was supposed to march through Bohemia could not at the same time race to support the Austrians in southern Germany and delay its advance to intimidate, let alone fight, the Prussians.

He was convinced, however, that the Austrians needed the immediate support of both Russian armies to achieve their objectives in Swabia, Switzerland, and subsequently in France. He insisted that the second army must cooperate in the "conquest of Switzerland, *pivot of all our movements, the only direction from which France is vulnerable*; [a] movement that alone could consolidate our successes and, without the success of which it is completely impossible to hope for a successful war."*

His solution was simple and obvious: Alexander must commit more troops. The 40,000-strong army he proposed to release after Prussia had joined the coalition should be sent much sooner. In this way, the Austrians could have the support of the first two armies while this third army could help intimidate the Prussians. It could be replaced on the eastern Prussian frontier with a large force of Cossacks, who would be perfectly suited to range over the open terrain of Poland and eastern Prussia. Alexander had raised his offer from 115,000 to 180,000 troops; Mack now demanded 231,000.

Mack also complained about Alexander's plans in Italy. It was foolish, he wrote, to send Russian troops to southern Italy to cooperate directly with the Neapolitans. As the Austrians advanced in the north, the French would be forced to withdraw from Naples anyway. Their failure to do so in 1799, he argued, would serve as a lesson for them and help ensure that they would not make the same mistake again. He was concerned, on the other hand, that the Austrian army advancing in Italy would have to weaken itself seriously to protect its southern flank (along the Po River) against the French troops moving up from the south. He suggested, therefore, that the Russians land their troops at the Po and help secure that flank, thereby allowing the Austrian army to move more rapidly and securely to the west.

Finally Mack addressed the deployment of the Russian armies to be sent to Germany. He argued once again that it was unwise to intermingle forces from different states in a single army. The Russians should relieve the Austrians in Bavaria while the latter would join their comrades in the Tyrol in preparation for the major push through Switzerland. It was not necessary to have a large force on the left (north) bank of the Danube as Alexander had proposed, he argued. Only a small observation corps directed toward Stuttgart would be necessary.

Mack finished by casting doubt on the utility of drawing the minor German states into the coalition—they were perfidious and cowardly and would bolt at the worst possible moment. He also complained that Alexander's plan had no uncommitted armies to act as reserves, and he expounded on the importance of reserve armies to meet unexpected dangers and replace losses in the advancing armies. In this way he resurrected his attempt to get Alexander to send smaller groups of recruits behind each of his major forces to help keep them up to strength throughout the campaign.

Mack's comments were reasonably shrewd. The folly of detaching Russian forces to southern Italy should have been obvious, but for Alexander's and Pitt's determination to secure their direct interests as soon as the war broke out. Mack's

---

*Emphasis in the original.

effort to draw as many forces as possible to the decisive point in Switzerland also made more sense than Alexander's vision of scattering his armies across Germany.

It is interesting, however, that his remarks about the need to secure the flank of the army operating in Italy were not matched by any similar fear for the flank of the army in Germany. That latter force was just as exposed on its right flank as the Italian army was on its left, and Mack's call for a small "observation corps" directed at Stuttgart would have mitigated but not solved that problem. This lacuna may have resulted from the fact that there was a French army already in southern Italy against which the Austrian army would have to defend itself, whereas Mack and Charles did not believe that Napoleon would put an army in central or northern Germany. If there was some other reason why Mack did not consider this obvious problem, no record of it has survived.

Most importantly, Mack, like Alexander, failed to integrate Austrian operations into the Russian "phases." When would the Austrians attack Swabia? When would they drive into Switzerland? When would they invade Franche-Comté? Mack's complaints about Alexander's plans for the second Russian army suggest that Mack saw the Austrian offensive opening in what Alexander would consider the first phase. In that case, the Austrians would be driving into Switzerland and beyond while *nothing significant* was happening to the north on their right flank. They would be driving into France unsupported and lacking reinforcements for months. This would disrupt the vision Alexander presented of an attack on France only in phase three with coordinated assaults from all directions.

If, on the other hand, Mack believed that the assault into Switzerland and beyond would take place during phase two, after Prussia had joined the coalition, then his complaints about the program for the second Russian army were spurious. It would have plenty of time to intimidate Prussia and still arrive in time to participate in the assault on Switzerland. Clearly Mack did not consider this issue any more than Alexander did. The Austrians and the Russians were developing two separate war plans and coordinating them only where they actually touched—with the first Russian army directed toward southern Germany.

Charles's Response

Charles's memorandum, like his previous notes, began with a plea to consider peace. "Must one renounce all possibility of remaining on good terms with France?" he asked. "Has it been proven pointless or dangerous to seek this? Can one therefore have hope of avoiding war, or not?"* After a brief exhortation that

---

*Remarks about the Russian Negotiations Communicated to Me on the 20th of This Month, 23 June 1805, in Albrecht and William, eds., *Ausgewählte Schriften*, 6:153–162. This memorandum is only part of a barrage of similar efforts to force Francis to decide whether or not war with France was "inevitable." See also Charles to Francis, 25 May 1805 and 26 May 1805, KA AFA 1805 Italien, V/12 and V/7½ respectively.

states should avoid war if possible, however, Charles accepted the necessity to fight and noted that the war should be prosecuted with all possible vigor.

He considered measures for bringing the Austrian army to its full war footing and addressed the important question of when the Russian armies should be put in motion. He recognized that the French armies were not concentrated for a continental war, and were as far from the theater of operations as the Austrians and even some of the Russian troops. He warned, however, that the French soldiers were already on a mobilized war footing with horses, equipment, and personnel, and might be able to move faster than the Austrians and the Russians. Napoleon would certainly put his army in motion the moment he learned that the Russians had crossed the Austrian frontier.

Charles argued that the moment the crossing had been decided on, the Austrians should mobilize fully. They should bring all units up to full strength, form the light infantry, pioneers, and other last-minute additions, form the artillery train, find mounts for artillery and supplies, fill up magazines, and so forth. They must be ready to meet a French attack almost at once.

Charles then focused on the details of the Russian reinforcing armies and laid out a series of questions for Alexander's envoy, Baron Wintzingerode, who had recently arrived in Vienna to hammer out the details of allied cooperation. Charles was concerned with the line of march, transportation, logistics, and combat support services (artillery, engineers, etc.) for the Russian army as it passed through Austrian territory, as well as command relationships.

Reiterating the point he had made in earlier memoranda, Charles insisted that the Russian armies cooperating with the Austrians be directly subordinated to Austrian commanders. He feared that this arrangement would be difficult to work out in Germany, where the Austrians did not intend to station a large army and where the Russians would therefore have a claim to share command. Francis would have to be firm, he insisted; the Russians would have to accept an Austrian commander.

It was only in this context that Charles considered the deployment of allied armies in Germany. In order to prevent the risk of serious setbacks in Germany, he argued, the Russian army would have to cooperate closely with the Austrian forces in the area between the Bodensee and the Danube. The support he offers for this assertion gives some clue to the Austrian thought process that led to their failure to support or anchor the right wing of their army in Germany: "Any operation on the left [northern] bank* of the Danube and from there to the Lower Rhine is impractical because it will lead to nothing and because he

---

*River banks are designated left or right when facing in the direction the river flows. The Danube flows roughly west to east, so the left bank is the northern bank for most of its stretch. The Rhine flows from south to north, so its left bank is the western shore. The "upper" portion of a river is near its source; the "lower" portion near its mouth. The "lower Rhine" is the part stretching from about Mainz to the English Channel.

who has concentrated his army between the Danube and the Bodensee is the master of Swabia and Franconia."[12] He concluded that two armies operating independently in that region risked being defeated in detail; the Russians therefore had to be directly subordinated to the Austrian commander.

It is unclear how Charles thought the right flank of this army would be secured, but he may not have considered the problem carefully; like Mack, he thought of the deployment in southern Germany as a brief stop preparatory to the invasion of Switzerland. For a commander who was so concerned with the security of his lines of communication and his flanks, however, this lacuna remains as inexplicable as it was important at the time.

Charles found another reason for serious discontent with the Russian plan: he completely mistrusted Prussia. He was dubious, to begin with, that the Russians would be able to force the Prussians to join the coalition at all. To compel a small state like Saxony to join an alliance as Frederick the Great did is one thing, he argued; to compel a great power with 230,000 men under arms and a nation of "born soldiers" is quite another. The likeliest outcome, he believed, would be a "double war" in which Austria alone would be threatened on all sides.

Even if the Prussians did join the coalition, however, the danger would not disappear. What was to prevent Frederick William from making a secret pact with Napoleon and going over to the French at some allied reverse or some other opportune moment? Here Charles revealed his ignorance of Frederick William's character. Frederick the Great might well have done such a bolt, as his actions during the First Silesian War indicate only too clearly. His grandnephew, however, was no such bold and unscrupulous politician and would at worst have withdrawn from an alliance no longer to his liking. Austro–Prussian suspicion, however, had run very deep from the wounds Frederick the Great had inflicted on the relationship, and Charles could not escape from the permanent hostility that suspicion had engendered in many hearts at both courts.

For all Charles's apparent willingness to find the best ways and means for supporting the war effort, however, he ended the memorandum on a pessimistic note. Had Francis fully considered, he wondered, the cost to the Austrian people of the forthcoming war? They would not only have to supply men and materials for their own armies, but would have to support the rapacious Russians as well. Charles drew no sharp conclusion and made no specific recommendation, but the meaning was clear enough: Was Francis certain that he had to fight a war that would harm Austria?

Like Mack's memorandum, Charles's made a number of shrewd observations about the strategy and operations of the coalition. It did not, however, recognize the problem of sequencing operations properly in time any better than Mack's had, and it failed to consider adequately the exposure of the right flank of the Austrian armies. Above all, it did not recognize the fact that the Russians and the Austrians were developing two distinct war plans not clearly related to each other, and so it neither highlighted nor remedied that important problem.

Cobenzl's Response

Cobenzl's examination of the Russian war plan depended on the political context in which he was operating. For some months, as we have seen, Cobenzl had believed that Austria should join Russia in opposing Napoleon. He had been unable to win Francis over to this view, however. In early June 1805, word reached Vienna that Napoleon had annexed Genoa, and Cobenzl seized on that news to try to sway Francis. His reaction to the Russian note was written amid his efforts to persuade the emperor to go to war, and this memorandum therefore was aimed to assist that persuasion.[13]

Cobenzl's task in this regard was easy, since Alexander had designed his war plan explicitly to accomplish the same goal. The first part of the memorandum is thus a long and detailed summary of the Russian notes and comments presented in a positive and persuasive light. Cobenzl placed heavy emphasis on the possibility that Britain would make peace with Napoleon if the Austrians did not act soon, thereby eliminating not only a helpful ally but needed financial subsidies.

He placed even greater emphasis on the consequences for the Austro–Russian relationship if Francis did not commit to war at that point. Cobenzl wrote quite perceptively that initially Alexander had been drawn to both Napoleon and Frederick William and that he had only turned to Austria because of the provocations of the former and the spinelessness of the latter. He cited evidence from a number of diplomatic sources that Alexander was prepared to abandon the continent to its fate if Francis did not commit to him at that moment. Further vagueness or prevarication in the Austrian response would restore Vienna to the position of isolation from which Cobenzl had with the greatest difficulty and good fortune extricated it.*

But joining the coalition was not a course to be feared, he argued. Ignoring the complexities of time and phasing, Cobenzl seized on the overall numbers that Alexander promised to bring into the field, as Alexander and Czartoryskii had surely intended him to. Those numbers promised a nearly 2-to-1 advantage over French forces in the field. Cobenzl also tried to convince Francis that Alexander's plan would invariably win Prussia over. Not only was the Russian plan the only game in town, Cobenzl argued, but it would almost infallibly work. One conclusion was obvious: when Wintzingerode sat down

---

*See, for example, Czartoryskii to Razumovskii, 14 June 1805, VPR, vol. II, docs. 135, 137. Fears of Alexander's bolting the coalition may have been exaggerated, but Alexander certainly stoked Vienna's fears that Britain might make peace assiduously.

with the Austrian military leadership, the Austrians should commit to the alliance and to offensive war.

Another conclusion was less obvious, however. Alexander had not yet decided to recall Novosil'tsev from his mission to Napoleon, and Cobenzl and the Austrians believed that that mission was extremely important. No one (except perhaps Charles, although he did not comment on it) seriously believed that Alexander's negotiator would have any success in Paris, but it was a way to buy time for military preparations and put the coalition even more firmly in the right when the war did begin. Cobenzl therefore proposed to ask Alexander to moderate his terms still more so that Napoleon would not reject them out of hand, but would begin a negotiation.

He also seems to have imagined, however (the language is somewhat confused), that Alexander's troops would begin their march through Austrian territory as a "demonstration" to support the negotiations in Paris (and also to intimidate the Prussians), and that the Austrians should not publicly commit themselves to war until the Russian armies had arrived within supporting distance of Austria's own forces. This program was nonsense—Austria's military leaders understood Napoleon much better than Cobenzl did in this regard, since they believed that he would take the Russian army's crossing of Austria's frontiers as a de facto declaration of war.[14]

Once again, Cobenzl's memorandum contains sound analysis. His understanding of the precariousness of the Austro–Russian relationship was exaggerated but fundamentally right. It is hard to say whether Russian and Austrian fears that Britain would make peace if war did not begin in 1805 were reasonable, although Pitt occasionally encouraged them as a way to spur dragging negotiations. There is some evidence that Frederick William would have bought into the coalition had Alexander's armies acted as proposed in this Russian war plan.

But for all that, Cobenzl's comments addressed only the question of whether or not to go to war, not how to do it. He once again unfairly dismissed Alexander's proposal as not a real war plan. To be sure, a foreign minister should concern himself more with the former question than with the latter. But Cobenzl did not deal honestly with his master. Without examining the war plans in any detail, he accepted them uncritically, not only the allies' proposed actions but Alexander's promises for the outcomes of those actions. Therefore Cobenzl recommended that Francis accept Alexander's proposal on the grounds that it would work, without ever considering how solid those grounds actually were.

The reason was simple. Cobenzl desperately wanted Francis to commit himself to war, and he seized on anything that might strengthen his hand in that regard. He thus used Napoleon's seizure of Genoa to support his argument just as he accepted Alexander's promises to achieve the same end. The fact that Austria was teetering on the brink of the coalition and that Cobenzl was desperate to push her over meant that consideration of the Russian war plans was cursory rather than careful. War plans are best developed by allies who have already decided to fight rather than by those who are still considering the question of war.

The Austrian counterproposal given to Razumovskii on July 7, 1805, was a curious blend of these three different reactions, but adhered most closely to Cobenzl's proposals.[15] It focused heavily on political and diplomatic issues at the expense of purely military considerations. Most importantly, however, it tried to reconcile the different phasing of the Austrian and Russian plans, although not carefully and not explicitly. Above all, it was a political document that intervened in military planning primarily for political purposes, but also because of inherent flaws in the military planning process.

The counterproposal began with an insistence on doing everything possible to prove that war was unavoidable. And so, as Cobenzl had suggested, the Austrians insisted on reducing the harshness of the terms Novosil'tsev would propose to Napoleon. The document then turned to the question of timing: when were the forces to begin moving relative to the conduct of negotiations in Paris?

The Austrians identified the problem clearly: it would still take them four months to finish mobilizing and deploying (this statement shows Charles's hand in the document), while the French could arrive in the theater of war in two months. To avoid this problem, the Russian troops would begin to move across the Austrian frontier as soon as the peace proposals were made to Napoleon, around August 10–12. The Austrians calculated that in this way the Russian forces would arrive at Braunau sixteen days before the French could get to the Lech.

Six days after the Russian forces had crossed the frontier, Frederick William would have heard of that event.* The Russians should immediately demand that he at least allow their armies to cross Prussian territory and should support this demand with the full weight of the 80,000 troops stationed on the eastern Prussian frontier (Mack had lost the struggle to demand more troops from Russia), and with the second army of 50,000 destined to support the Austrians in Germany. Whether the Prussians agreed to permit the crossing or not, the large Russian army would enter Prussian territory "a few days" after the first Russian army had entered Austrian territory. The second Russian army would move at the same time into either Prussian territory or Austrian, depending on the Prussian reply to Alexander's ultimatum.

---

*The concern with tying the movement of armies to the dates at which others would have learned of those movements pervaded allied war planning. It even drove Austrian mobilization plans; see "Main Concept" from Charles to Francis, 23 July 1805, KA AFA 1805 Italien, VII/12.

This second army would follow a route through the northern Habsburg lands that would threaten Prussia and get it to the theater of war almost as quickly as if it had taken a more direct route. The landing of Russian and Swedish forces in Pomerania would be carefully timed to coordinate with the other movements. In this way, the allies would bring between 500,000 and 600,000 troops into operation against the French (including Prussians, British, and others), almost at once and in direct support of the Austrian offensives in Switzerland and southern Germany.

This counterproposal focused on solving the Prussia problem. In Alexander's original plan, Prussia could not have been expected to enter the war until after the Russian armies had arrived in Germany and, presumably (although this was never discussed), the Austro–Russian offensive there had begun. The Austrians in this note attempted to move forward both the Prussian adherence to the coalition and the benefit they expected to derive from it through earlier and more peremptory action. This plan clearly envisioned all of the operations in the first two phases of Alexander's plan taking place in 1805 and almost simultaneously.

The counterproposal suffered from two large flaws. First, the time–space relationship implicit in it was even worse than that in Alexander's plan. Things simply could not have moved as fast as this Austrian plan demanded. The Prussians, who had not yet mobilized, could not have had the 60,000 or 100,000 troops the Austrians demanded of them ready until far too late, and it is highly questionable whether the Russian armies on the eastern Prussian frontier could have arrived at their designated targets in time to take any meaningful part in operations. This plan, attempting implicitly to resolve problems of phasing, destroyed what rationality there had been in the phasing of Alexander's original plan.

Oddly enough, the second problem was political. Although Cobenzl had argued carefully in his memorandum evaluating Alexander's war plan that Prussia would be coerced if she were surrounded by Russian armies, the Austrian counterproposal called for issuing an ultimatum to Berlin before the Russian armies had even moved. When Alexander insisted, according to this plan, on free passage for his troops, there would be no Russian forces in Stralsund and no forces on Prussia's southwestern border. Frederick William would have no greater incentive to accede to the coalition than he had before operations had begun, and the whole point of the plan for moving Russia's armies Alexander had forwarded would be destroyed.

The Austrians probably developed this plan for several reasons. First and foremost, it was designed to ensure conditions that would enable Cobenzl to press Francis to go to war. The discussion concerning negotiating terms as well as the plan to bring 600,000 troops on line almost at once were clearly aimed at quieting Francis's fears. Second, it attempted to solve the problem that the

Russian plan left Austria's armies to bear the burden of the war not briefly but for months, possibly even for the entire first campaigning season. Third, it tried to resolve a problem that Alexander's plan had created by reconciling the Austrian plan of operations with the timetable Alexander's plan vaguely included. It is unclear why the Austrians did not mention this last problem explicitly in their writings to each other, but their failure to consider the problem openly led to a failure to solve it. The Austrian counterproposal aimed more at resolving the political issues connected with the opening of hostilities than developing the best possible plan for fighting.

Conference in Vienna

The effects of these various plans and counterplans were felt when Russian and Austrian generals sat down together for the first time to work out the details of their joint operations. Alexander had decided to facilitate Razumovskii's negotiations in May by sending a trusted adjutant (and former Austrian officer), Baron F. F. Wintzingerode to Vienna.[16] Wintzingerode had been in the Austrian capital since early June. On July 16 he met with Mack, Schwarzenberg, and a representative of the state chancellor (Cobenzl), Collenbach.[17]

The conference spent a great deal of time on questions of military minutiae prepared by Archduke Charles: how many regiments there were in the Russian army, how many soldiers in each regiment, how many cannons, how many horses, how many carts, how much food would be needed, and so forth. The allied generals also developed a march route for the first Russian army (concentrating near Brody), according to which it would cross the Austrian frontier on August 16 and arrive on the banks of the Inn at Braunau on October 16 (these dates were subsequently changed to August 20 and October 20). The army would travel in six roughly equal columns that would be two days' march apart; the last column would arrive on the Inn ten days after the first one did. These details would become extremely significant in the campaign that followed.

Even more significant, however, was the plan developed for the second Russian army, then concentrating near Brest in Russian Poland. Mack had been right: Wintzingerode declared that this army's march would be dictated by the need to force Prussia into the coalition, and its arrival in southern Germany might well be delayed as a result of that operation. Its route of march depended entirely on whether Prussia joined the coalition and even on the attitude of Saxony. If Prussia proved obstinate, then its march would be delayed, although Wintzingerode assured his no doubt nervous listeners that Alexander would make every effort to get this second army to Germany as rapidly as possible.

Once in southern Germany, this army would join with the first Russian army and would cooperate in the invasion of Switzerland. *Only after the arrival of this second army* would observation detachments be sent out toward the Rhine to watch for enemy "diversions" from that direction. The allied generals decided not to deploy this second army along the lower or middle Rhine because they were convinced that this force, even reinforced by the first Russian army, could undertake no meaningful attack against the French Rhine fortifications. The concentration on offensive operations and the failure to consider possible enemy countermeasures led the allied generals to ignore the danger to their unsupported and undefended right flank.

Turning to the operations of the Russian army destined for Naples, Wintzingerode did not give way at all to the Austrians' efforts to coordinate those operations better with their own in northern Italy. Wintzingerode agreed to ask Alexander to order General Lacy, the Russian army commander, to pursue the retreating French forces as vigorously as possible. But the Russians were determined to land their force in the boot of Italy and march north, doing little or nothing to protect the southern flank of the Austrian army on the Po.

Wintzingerode gave way gracefully, however, to the Austrian demand that the Russian armies in Germany be subordinated to Austrian command. He insisted that those armies would take orders only from Francis himself or Charles. But in case of necessity he believed that Alexander would allow his commander to take orders from another of the Austrian archdukes. When the second Russian army arrived, it would fall under the orders of the commander of the first and would thereby be under Austrian overall command as well.

The agreements reached at this conference represented important compromises in the Russian war plan and important defeats for the Austrians. Alexander had effectively agreed to the Austrians' demand to undertake his first and second phases conjointly and simultaneously. The absurd notion that Russian forces would instantly coerce Prussia to join the coalition without advancing from their concentration areas, and would then immediately proceed on their way to support the Austrians, was accepted as a central part of the plan. In reality, however, there was no chance that events would follow this happy time frame; the second Russian army would certainly not arrive in Germany until weeks after the first, far too late to support an attack on Switzerland in 1805, as the Austrians seemed to intend.

The Austrian attempt to find a way to bring power rapidly to their aid seemed certain to backfire, since it would delay the arrival of 50,000 Russians urgently needed in southern Germany in return for the hope that the Prussians would intervene to aid the allies earlier than they otherwise would have, but certainly not instantly. This mistaken Austrian demand apparently resulted from Cobenzl's efforts to convince Francis to join the war effort, as well as from the allies' failure to consider carefully the timing of the plans they were developing separately for their armies intended to act together.

Mack had been right all along about this key point: the Russians could co-erce the Prussians at once or race to the aid of the Austrians with substantial forces. But they could not do both at the same time. His proposal to request more troops from Alexander had obviously been overruled, probably by Cobenzl. The result was what Mack had anticipated—a defeat for Austria in the war planning. He could count on the support of 50,000 Russians in south-ern Germany, but no more. With that aid alone, the Austrian armies would have to bear the full brunt of the French attack for weeks, perhaps months, be-fore significant reinforcements arrived.

The Austrians suffered a similar defeat over Russian operations in Italy. It is not clear what they asked for in the conference with Wintzingerode, but it is certain that they received only a vague promise of limited help. Even in this critical theater, Alexander's determination to pursue his own direct interests first and before considering the needs of the overall allied war plan robbed the Austrians of vital assistance for their main army.

Why did the Austrians not demand more or refuse to accept these terms, so much lower than those Alexander had promised them? Mack's optimism and aggressiveness no doubt played a role, but only a minor one. The real reason was that Cobenzl, not Mack, was setting Austria's political and military policy at this time. And Cobenzl cared only about securing the Russian alliance by go-ing to war with France. It is hard to imagine a deal that he would have refused or conditions he would not have abandoned to secure that goal. Austria's in-creasingly frantic attempts to escape from isolation and find a secure alliance led her to accept a war plan that maximized the danger her statesmen had feared all along—the need to sustain the blows of a French army unsupported in the ini-tial period of the war. Cobenzl had done the best he could in bargaining with a very bad hand, but the weakness of his position compromised him in the end. Austria had become enslaved to the grandiose plans of Alexander and Czarto-ryskii. Cobenzl's efforts to mitigate his servitude only increased Austria's danger.

Last-Minute Changes

Alexander speedily accepted the plan sent by Cobenzl on July 7 and the results of Wintzingerode's conference with Mack, Schwarzenberg, and Collenbach on July 16.[18] Francis finally joined the coalition on August 9, 1805.[19] A new problem, however, soon emerged. Czartoryskii wrote to Razumovskii less than a week later to say that since the Austrians had taken so long to commit them-selves to fighting and then demanded that the operations against Prussia be started immediately, the Russian army along the eastern Prussian border was not ready. It would not be able to cross the frontier until September 28.[20] That was bad news enough, but worse followed.

Because the first goal of the Russian army assembling at Brest was to co-operate with its neighbor to the north in bringing Frederick William to heel, its departure would be delayed to September 16 to allow it to coordinate with the other force. The army at Brody, however, had orders to begin its march not later than August 22. According to the plan agreed on in mid-July, the Brest army should have marched on August 26. There would now be a twenty-six-day gap between the two armies, rather than the five days originally agreed on. By the time this message reached Vienna, there was nothing to do; the first Russian army had already begun its march, while the second had not even prepared to do so.

This momentous decision revealed Alexander's preoccupations. He was not primarily concerned with the fate of the Austrian armies in Italy or Germany, probably because he believed them secure. On the other hand, operations in Italy and Germany were not his problem. His immediate concern had to be with the operations designed to bring Prussia into the war, which were entirely his responsibility. It was natural for him to concentrate his forces on the missions that he had to perform himself, even if it was unfortunate from the standpoint of the overall coalition plan. Alexander thus focused on the Prussian problem, and Czartoryskii sent Alopeus detailed descriptions of the proposed military operations and the means of coordinating his diplomatic efforts with those operations.[21]

In the end, as we have seen, even this revised Russian plan fell down as Alexander agreed at the end of September to meet with Frederick William rather than launch an immediate invasion. That decision was almost irrelevant, however, in light of the earlier decision to delay the march of the Brest army.

The Austrian war plan was finalized on August 29 in a meeting attended by Charles, Archduke John and Archduke Ferdinand, Count Baillet de Latour, Mack, Schwarzenberg, Zach, Count Grünne, Major General von Mayer, Colloredo, Cobenzl, and Collenbach.[22] The discussion was based on a memorandum Charles had prepared describing the various options open to the armies in Germany and Italy and making recommendations.*

---

*General Bases on Which the Combined Military Operations of the Imperial-Royal Armies in Germany, Italy, and the Tyrol Should Be Conducted, 29 August 1805, in Albrecht and Wilhelm, *Ausgewählte Schriften*, 6:163–168. The document is also reprinted in Alfred Krauss, *1805: Der Feldzug von Ulm* (Vienna: L. W. Seidel, 1912), as appendix 5. Krauss argues, on no very convincing evidence, that Mack actually wrote this memorandum and Charles simply signed it, but it is not far from the tone and content Charles's memoranda had for some time; one must either believe that he wrote none of those or that he wrote this one as well (Krauss makes no reference to Charles's many earlier interventions in the debate over Austrian strategy). It seems more likely that Krauss is simply furthering his efforts to exculpate Charles from the disaster at Ulm and, in the tradition of imperial Austrian scholarship, to lay all the blame at the feet of Mack and Cobenzl. The editors of the *Ausgewählte Schriften* raise no questions about the authorship of the document, nor does Oskar Criste, *Erzherzog Carl von Osterreich* (Vienna: Wilhelm Braumüller, 1912), 2:317–318.

This memorandum is noteworthy because it contains the only written consideration of the dangers confronting the Austrian army in Germany and the options open to its commander. Charles writes that the German army must advance into Swabia as rapidly as possible and anchor itself there to await the success of the army in Italy. He had reverted to the plan of charging out to the Iller and now proposed to anchor the left flank of this army on the western edge of the Bodensee near Stockach.

The French, he argued, would try to destroy the Austrian army in Germany before the Russians arrived. They could come by one of two paths. The first led from Strasbourg to Stockach and then in a drive between the Danube and the Bodensee, while the second ran from Mainz or Mannheim to Ulm. He believed that Napoleon would take the first route (to Stockach) because it was shorter and would bring his forces into the theater more rapidly.

It was possible, he wrote, that the French would arrive before the Russians in such force that the Austrian army would be unable to face them. In this case the Austrians had to withdraw south to the foot of the Tyrolean Alps to await reinforcements. It might be necessary, however, for the Austrians to fall back on Salzburg; if so, they would have to defend the city without fail. In case the French advanced from Mannheim toward Ulm or Regensburg, Charles wrote,

> the initial direction of our march through Bavaria as along the shortest line would suffer no change, and only after we had moved out from Munich must we turn ourselves toward the Danube in order to halt [the French] either through a stand behind this river or through an advance across it and a movement against the rear and the communications of the advancing enemy army, thereby gaining time until we can accept battle.

Charles did not fear that the French would turn the right flank of the Austrian army in Germany because he believed that its lines of communications ran east toward Salzburg or south to the Tyrol, and were therefore secure from a French attack. This belief was not unfounded, as long as the commander of that army identified the French movements and responded to them in a timely fashion.

Although this was the first time these problems were considered in writing, it is unlikely that it was the first time they were considered. The Austrians had always seen the army in southern Germany as being closely tied to the Tyrol, and it had probably not been necessary before to lay out exactly why its open right flank was not a problem. In this final memorandum, written as the armies had begun their march, Charles clearly felt that it was time to cover all

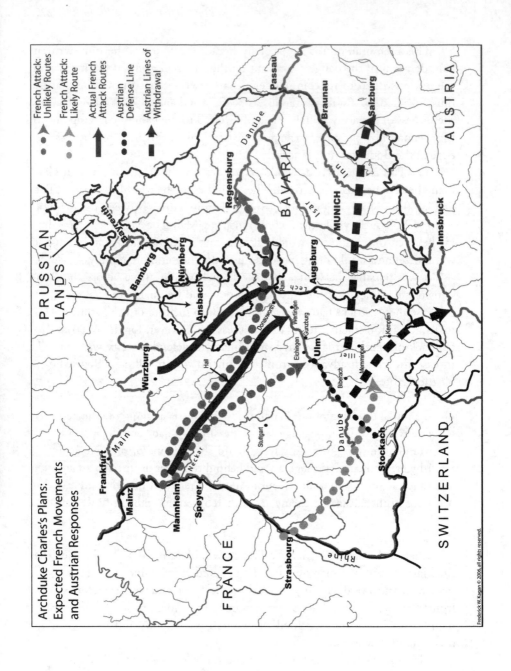

Archduke Charles's Plans:
Expected French Movements
and Austrian Responses

Legend:

French Attack: Unlikely Routes

French Attack: Likely Route

Actual French Attack Routes

Austrian Defense Line

Austrian Lines of Withdrawal

PRUSSIAN LANDS

FRANCE

BAVARIA

AUSTRIA

SWITZERLAND

Frankfurt
Mainz
Mannheim
Speyer
Strasbourg
Würzburg
Bamberg
Nürnberg
Ansbach
Bayreuth
Hall
Stuttgart
Regensburg
Donauwörth
Rain
Nördlingen
Günzburg
Eichingen
Ulm
Biberach
Memmingen
Kempten
Augsburg
MUNICH
Passau
Braunau
Salzburg
Innsbruck
Stockach

Rivers: Main, Neckar, Danube, Rhine, Lech, Isar, Inn, Iller

bases and consider all possibilities carefully. But it is unlikely that there was much in his discussion that was news to those assembled to hear it.

Charles also considered the forthcoming operations in Italy in some detail. The Austrian army there, he argued, must attempt to force a decisive battle from the outset. Assuming that it was victorious, it must then advance as rapidly as possible to the Adda. Its further operations depended on the outcome of initial operations in Germany. If the German army established itself in Swabia and linked up with the two Russian auxiliary corps (the memorandum was evidently drafted before word arrived of Alexander's last change of plans), then the Italian army could continue its advance to the west. If the German army ran into trouble, however, then the Italian army could send reinforcements through the Tyrolean passes to assist it. Charles also specified what to do in case the initial "decisive" battle went against Austria.

This is the first detailed written consideration of the interaction of the two main Austrian armies, and it is possible that it is the first detailed consideration of that problem at all. As an evaluation of contingencies and possible responses to them, it is sound in a general way but lacks the essential consideration of precise timing. By August 29 the dates of the beginning of operations in both theaters were known, and it should have been possible to establish parallel time lines for initial and then expected movements. In this way it would have been possible to find critical decision points created by the time–space relationships in and between the theaters: if help is to arrive in Germany by a given date, it must leave Italy by a certain time. Charles's consideration of contingencies was helpful but too vague to form the basis of a solid war plan.

The weakness in this memorandum was symptomatic of the weakness of the entire allied war planning effort. Although operations in particular theaters were developed in detail, coordination among theaters was sketchy. Russian and Austrian operations were never carefully coordinated, and even the operations of the various Austrian armies were not well coordinated until the end of August. It does not appear that the activities of the various Russian armies were ever well coordinated.

This failure of coordination was not the result of incompetent military and political leadership; the war plan was too grandiose and complicated for the command and staff structures of the time. This war plan was the most ambitious attempt to coordinate the movements of vast armies over the entire European continent that had yet been undertaken. No similar effort was made to coordinate the coalition forces during the Silesian Wars, still less during the War of the Spanish Succession or in earlier conflicts.

Allied leaders made some efforts toward all-encompassing plans during the French revolutionary wars (Mack had been involved in drafting one for the 1794 campaign), but they did not approach the scale of the war plan developed in 1805.[23] Even the smaller but still complex plans the allies attempted in 1794 and in Italy in 1796–1797 did not succeed on the whole. Their outcomes did not inspire confidence that a bolder, larger, even more complex plan involving as many as 732,000 troops would do better.

Part of the problem was that the command structure of the various allied armies was not equal to the task of planning and coordinating such a large-scale offensive. The same men who developed the grand strategy for the war were also responsible for developing detailed war plans for each individual theater. It was as though, to put the problem in modern terms, George C. Marshall and Franklin D. Roosevelt had to set priorities between Japan and Germany, develop the basic concept for how to defeat both enemies, and coordinate the allocation of resources to the different theaters, as well as develop the specific plans within each theater for operations such as the D-Day landings and the attack on Okinawa.

In World War II, these tasks were divided. Roosevelt and Marshall set overall priorities and allocated resources, while Eisenhower in Europe and MacArthur and Nimitz in the Pacific developed the detailed war plans in each theater. Alexander, Francis, Mack, and Charles had to be Roosevelt, Marshall, Eisenhower, MacArthur, Nimitz—and sometimes Bradley and Patton too—all at the same time. They needed powerful theater commanders who could lift the burden of operational planning from their shoulders and allow them to concentrate on strategic and grand strategic coordination, but the command structures of the time did not permit such an organization.

Even if they had named theater commanders and charged them with developing plans for the troops in their theaters, however, they would not have solved the problem. There were no adequate staff organizations capable of doing such planning and coordination. The Austrian armies in Italy, Germany, and the Tyrol, as well as the Russian armies marching toward Germany and those on the Prussian frontier, would have needed large, highly developed staffs to do the planning and coordination for their troops. Although in 1805 those armies did have rudimentary staffs that established detailed march routes, worried about supplies, and monitored the muster rolls, they were unequal to the challenge of planning operations in addition to these other essential tasks, still less to coordinating their operations with those of other armies.

Even had all of these staffs and command structures been in place, however, the allies would still have found the execution of their grandiose plans highly problematic because of the limitations of the communications technology at the time. Since many of the allied armies were weeks of hard riding from one another, it was impossible to coordinate their activities once operations had begun. In the age of radios or even telegraphs this problem would have been easily resolved, but when all messages had to go by courier, it was insoluble. Careful planning by well-organized staffs might have been able to overcome this problem by determining in advance the precise actions each army would take. But such planning rarely survives the initial contact with the enemy, and the staffs of that time were not up to the challenge of trying it.

Why did the allies attempt such a large, complex plan when the experiences of the French revolutionary wars highlighted the problems with attempting grandiose war plans? The answer is probably twofold. First, many leaders at this time, such as Mack, saw the possibility for changing warfare in the development of independent formations at the operational level. Multiple independent corps (or armies) made possible operations over a much larger area and offered the prospect of more decisive victories—and therefore shorter wars. This was a goal worth striving for. Each failure of such a plan, moreover, could be attributed to multiple causes: this commander made a mistake, that ally was perfidious, the enemy was lucky, and so forth. For those determined to see a revolution in warfare, it was always possible then (as it is today) to ignore failure and focus on possibility.

Another possible reason why the lessons of the previous decade remained unlearned in 1805 is that most of the people doing the war planning had not participated in the earlier conflicts. Alexander and Czartoryskii had played no role in the limited Russian participation in the revolutionary wars. Mack had done so on several occasions, but mostly on a much smaller scale; his direct command experience was at the head of a few tens of thousands of Italian and Austrian troops, whose defeat he explained away, interestingly, as a failure of coordination between armies. Cobenzl had spent most of the revolutionary wars in St. Petersburg as the Austrian ambassador to Russia, and had not finally taken control of Austrian foreign policy until 1801. Even Charles's military activities during the revolutionary wars were primarily confined to his own theater; his rise to control of the entire military apparatus of Austria also postdated the Treaty of Amiens. These men would have been aware of the large-scale plans developed against France and their failure, but they did not participate actively in the development of those plans (apart from Mack's effort in 1794). Those who could have told them the lessons of those years, assuming that they had learned them, were dead or in retirement by 1805—not to mention being discredited by their failures.

Thus the first war against Emperor Napoleon was designed on an expansive scale, far beyond what the armies of that time could have been expected to achieve. It was not a hopeless plan, nor was it doomed from the start. Despite its many failings, it was not a foolish undertaking. Considering the constraints on allied actions and the stresses induced by the political situation of the time, it is not clear that there were better options. It was a plan, however, that relied for success on a great deal of good fortune, on skillful and resolute generals to execute it, and on a cooperative enemy. The allies, as it happened, had none of those advantages in the event—a problem that might well have destroyed a far better war plan than this one.

12

Napoleon's War Plans

Decision

The War of 1805 was a makeshift affair for Napoleon. Throughout the spring and summer of 1805 he had concentrated on the invasion of England and especially the naval maneuvers that would make it possible. Events in Italy also occupied his attention, as he worked on a political order that suited him and trained his new viceroy of the Kingdom of Italy, his stepson Prince Eugène Beauharnais. But on August 23, 1805, Napoleon abandoned his project for an immediate cross-Channel invasion and committed himself instead to a continental war.

The coalition planning process had begun in earnest in February 1805 with Charles's careful consideration of Mack's proposed war plans. Napoleon should have been at a disadvantage, since his enemies had a six-month headstart in serious war planning. He turned this situation to his advantage, however, through flexibility in his thinking and planning. Even as he bent every effort to preparing for the invasion of Britain in July and August, he simultaneously began to consider how he would face a continental coalition. Once he decided to commit to fighting a continental war, moreover, he continued to adjust his plans according to his developing understanding of the changing situation. The initial campaign of the War of 1805 for Napoleon was a masterpiece not of skillful planning, but of flexible reaction to an uncertain and fast-changing strategic environment.

The War at Sea, December 1804–July 1805

Napoleon missed the early signs that a new coalition including Austria was forming. This intelligence failure was a crucial element as events developed in 1805, and it flowed from a misreading of Austria and of Francis. At the turn of the year Napoleon had become concerned about Francis's intentions. Word of Austrian encroachments in Germany, the Habsburgs' abuse of traditional feudal powers, and the growth of the Austrian garrisons along the Italian frontier all reached Napoleon tinted by the fevered imaginations of his agents in Bavaria and Austria.[1]

Napoleon responded aggressively. He reinforced his garrisons in Piedmont and Italy and recalled officers who were on leave. He also concentrated a division on the Adige, the border between Austria and France.[2] "I have no idea that Austria would wish to make war," he told General Domenico Pino, the war minister in Milan, "but the military system is to oppose force with force and sound policy demands that one puts oneself on guard the moment a force seems to menace you."[3] Napoleon also sent stern warnings to Francis through the ambassadors in Paris and Vienna.[4]

The warnings had their effect: Francis wrote Napoleon a lengthy note aimed at pacifying him.[5] Amazingly, Napoleon revoked the orders for military movements and told his leading ministers and advisers that his mind was at ease now regarding Austria's dispositions.[6] He remained unwilling to contemplate war with Austria as a serious possibility for nearly six months.

Napoleon's initial alarm was as inappropriate as his subsequent belief that Francis was permanently docile. In January 1805 Francis accepted the need to develop a defensive war plan to submit to the Russians in support of the Austro–Russian alliance (of which Napoleon was completely unaware). As late as June 1805, however, he remained determined not to begin offensive operations against France. Serious Austrian efforts at rearmament and redeployment did not begin until March or April. Napoleon's fear of an imminent Austrian attack in January 1805 was unfounded.

Napoleon's belief that Francis was slipping into the hostile camp, however, was thoroughly justified. Francis replaced Charles because of his opposition to hostilities with France and then began rearming and redeploying his forces to support a possible war against Napoleon. Napoleon rightly recognized that the constellations in Vienna were moving against him, but he initially exaggerated how far. His reaction to Francis's conciliatory letter was equally exaggerated.

Francis devoted most of his note to explaining that Austrian troops deployed as a cordon against malaria (which had broken out in Italy) were not aimed against France. He made much of his efforts to seek reconciliation with France and called on God several times to witness his determination to avoid another conflict. He also accepted Napoleon's first note to him, apprising him of his intention to place one of the Bonaparte brothers on the newly created Italian throne. He only called on Napoleon to abide by his own promises to keep the Kingdom of Italy distinct and independent of France.[7]

Perhaps this apparent acceptance of Napoleon's revisions in northern Italy convinced Bonaparte of Francis's good intentions. The Austrian emperor had, after all, previously made no difficulty about recognizing Napoleon's elevation to imperial rank, and had raised no meaningful opposition to the assassination of the Duc d'Enghien or during the Rumbold affair. Whatever minor games Francis was playing in Germany, according to Napoleon's anti-Austrian agents, Bonaparte had good reason to believe Francis cowed.

It is hard to believe that Napoleon thought his military movements in Italy in January 1805 had affected the German emperor's attitude, since he must have known that Francis's letter was written before news of those movements could have reached his ears. Shows of French military power previously had deterred Austria from imposing on Bavaria, and Napoleon may have seen greater weakness in the fact that this time Francis capitulated before learning of Napoleon's plans to intimidate him. Be that as it may, however, Napoleon wrongly concluded that the Austrians would reject Russian and British overtures for a new coalition, and he clung to this delusion throughout the first half of 1805.

Putting Austria and threats of a continental coalition completely from his mind, Napoleon turned back to the twin problems of invading England and reorganizing Italy to his taste. There was never any question of conflict between these two activities because Napoleon saw his activities in Italy as facilitating his plans to destroy England. For one thing, Italy was to provide resources essential to the naval and colonial war with Britain. This was one of his reasons for annexing Genoa: Napoleon hoped to draw sailors and ships from this seafaring area and make use of its excellent port.[8] Napoleon's continued presence in the peninsula was also intended to serve as a diversion. The British, he believed, would not think an invasion imminent if he himself was hundreds of miles from his Channel armies.[9] Although Napoleon was pursuing an independent objective in reorganizing Italy to his taste, he made that objective serve the larger goal of defeating England.

His plan to destroy Great Britain was the most grandiose project Napoleon ever developed, including the Russian campaign of 1812. It involved maneuvering scores of ships and hundreds of thousands of troops across the globe. Napoleon planned operations not only along the English Channel but against Portugal, in the Caribbean, in the Mediterranean, in Ireland, and in and around the Indian subcontinent. His objective was not merely to invade and subjugate the British Isles but to seize Britain's worldwide colonial empire at the same time. In scale and complexity it was a plan unparalleled in history to that point and for decades thereafter.

This plan came into being gradually and piecemeal. The most dramatic shift in Napoleon's thinking about his war against Britain came between October and December 1804, when he temporarily abandoned the idea of invading England. Up to that point he had been planning to send his fleets from Toulon, Brest, and elsewhere racing into the English Channel to clear the way for the invasion flotilla. Throughout 1804 difficulties had continued to mount, including the fact that the invasion flotilla was not ready and preparations to ready it involved considerable risk.[10]

The international situation changed dramatically with the British attack on the Spanish treasure fleet in October 1804. That event caused the hitherto timid Spanish court to declare war on Great Britain and join with Napoleon in an anti-British alliance (signed in early January 1805).[11] Napoleon now had the Spanish fleet theoretically at his disposal to assist with clearing the English Channel and supporting the invasion flotilla. The Spanish fleet, however, would not be ready for action before mid-1805 at the earliest, since Spain, being neutral and poor, had not maintained her ships or sailors on a war footing.

Napoleon may have recognized the advantages in putting off the invasion until later in 1805, when he had readied the invasion flotilla and the Spanish fleet was prepared to lend meaningful assistance. That recognition may explain his decision to abandon the invasion plan for the time being. It has been suggested that Napoleon's fears of a new coalition being formed against him dissuaded him from pursuing an invasion plan that would leave him exposed to defeat on the continent even if he won in Britain.[12] This notion deserves careful examination.

What did Napoleon know about the coalition forming in December 1804? He was certainly not aware of the Austro–Russian convention of November 1804, since as late as July and August 1805 he was still writing that he thought the Austrians might join the coalition later that year.* If he had known of that treaty, he surely would not have allowed himself to be pacified by Francis's letter to him of February 1, 1805. The Anglo–Russian negotiations conducted by Novosil'tsev began in mid-December 1804, and the Anglo–Russian convention was not finalized until April 1805. Since Novosil'tsev traveled to London officially as a commercial representative while negotiating the Anglo–Russian convention, a ruse that even the British ambassador in St. Petersburg did not immediately penetrate, it is unlikely that Napoleon was aware of the content of those discussions.[13] He was aware of Alexander's hostility, since the Russian chargé d'affaires, Pierre d'Oubril, asked for his passport to leave France in August 1804. Napoleon dismissed tensions with Russia, however, writing to Berthier that "we are on cold terms with Russia, but not at war," and advised his war minister not to go overboard in preparing for a possible continental war.[14]

---

*"[Austria] will respond with lovely phrases and will gain time so that I will not be able to do anything this winter; her subsidy treaty and her adherence to the coalition will be signed this winter, under the pretext of an armed neutrality." Napoleon to Talleyrand, 23 August 1805, *Corr. de Nap.*, doc. 9117; also in Alombert-Goset and Colin, *La campagne de 1805*, 1:140. Napoleon was certainly aware of Austria's armaments and growing hostility, but he ascribed Francis's actions mostly to fear and clearly did not see the coalition forming against him as rapidly as it did.

It is difficult to conclude, therefore, that Napoleon saw the coalition forming in December 1804 and abandoned his plans for invading England in order to prepare to meet it. This conclusion is even more difficult to sustain in light of the fact that, as we shall see, in August 1805, when he was very well aware of the imminence of continental war, he nevertheless continued to press for the invasion up until the last possible moment, and abandoned it only when fleet maneuvers made it impossible.

The only explanation for his decision that is supported by evidence is that he sought to give himself time to correct deficiencies in the invasion flotilla and await the mobilization of the Spanish fleet. This explanation is rational and comprehensible, but it may not be complete.

The plan Napoleon ordered his admirals to execute in December 1804 called for a large-scale raid on British and Dutch colonies in the Caribbean.[15] Admiral Pierre Charles de Villeneuve's fleet at Toulon would carry nearly 7,000 soldiers and tons of powder and supplies to take and garrison the Dutch colonies along the South American coast, including Cayenne, Surinam, and Demerara.[16] Napoleon ordered another fleet, under the command of Edouard Thomas Missiessy at Rochefort, to carry approximately 3,000 troops, powder, and weapons to reinforce the garrisons of Martinique and Guadeloupe and to take Dominica and St. Lucia.[17] He commanded these two squadrons to join up at Martinique and then return to France.

None of these orders mention invading Britain or taking control of the English Channel. In addition to the explanations for Napoleon's decision offered above, though, there are two other possibilities. Napoleon may have been examining the idea of drawing the Royal Navy away from the Channel by testing it. In that event, the maneuvers of Villeneuve and Missiessy would have been primarily a ruse intended to allow the emperor to observe the British reaction.

Forced to consider the possibility that he would not be able to invade Britain, moreover, Napoleon may have sought other ways of striking at his nemesis. In this case, the test would have been: Could he seize and hold colonial possessions in the Caribbean? If he had decided to cancel the invasion once and for all and if these initial ventures had turned out well, the next move might have been to launch more such expeditions in an attempt to gain a truly global footing for France and hurt Britain where none of her previous adversaries had succeeded in striking her.

The real likelihood is that all of these ideas coexisted in Napoleon's mind at the same time. He may or may not have seriously considered canceling the invasion of Britain, but he almost certainly sought to test the Royal Navy's reaction to colonial expeditions, see if he could make and hold gains overseas, take positive action during the delay imposed by the need to await Spanish preparations and the development of his own flotilla, and make colonial gains while he was about it.

It is unlikely that Napoleon had a clear idea of what he intended to do after he completed these expeditions. His subsequent orders, as we shall see, relied on contingency and adaptation to circumstances rather than an attempt to adhere to a preconceived plan. Remarkably, Napoleon does not seem to have made a definite commitment to any particular goal. One possible development of his plans led to the invasion of Britain, another eschewed that action in favor of a colonial war. It is even possible that Napoleon ordered these naval maneuvers in the hope of attaining a still more unlikely goal: peace.

On January 2, 1805, Napoleon wrote directly to King George III imploring him to begin negotiations for peace.[18] The letter is difficult to parse. Those who wish to argue that Napoleon canceled the invasion of England for fear of a continental coalition point to the passage in this letter warning George that the continent will remain passive.[19] But Napoleon also warns the British monarch of a danger to his colonies. Why would George wish to continue the war, he asks rhetorically. "To take her colonies away from France? Colonies are a matter of secondary importance for France; *and does Your Majesty not already possess more of them than he can keep?*"[20] If all had gone according to plan, this not so veiled threat would have reached George at about the same time as word arrived that Villeneuve had put to sea for points unknown; perhaps the British would have learned of Missiessy's departure as well. Those expeditions were very well timed to intimidate George and persuade him to call off the war, which may have been one of their primary purposes.

If this is the case, then it follows that Napoleon had lost confidence in the invasion plan. Once again, though, it would be a mistake to simplify his thinking. Seizing British colonies was an absolute good in Napoleon's mind, with no bad consequences. If the expeditions helped persuade George to the peace table, well and good. If not, then Napoleon had gained an advantage overseas and could move toward the next steps depending on the new circumstances.

All in all, it seems likely that the expeditions launched in December were simply intended to change the prevailing situation and move it in a generally positive direction. Napoleon had planned no clear course of action beyond these moves. It seems certain that he was simultaneously preparing for a number of mutually contradictory courses of action. When the time came, he would choose the most appropriate one and never regret resources expended on preparing for contingencies that did not arise. As ever, the great mistake in studying this decision is to look for simplicity and consistency, since Napoleon was above all a complex and contingent thinker.

The expeditions of December did not live up to Napoleon's expectations, however modest. Villeneuve delayed putting to sea for a month, primarily because of poor weather and unhelpful winds. He did not leave Toulon until

January 18, 1805, and then, infuriatingly, he returned almost immediately. He sailed out of the harbor on the winds of a gale, and the storm intensified once his fleet was at sea. The inexperienced sailors, hindered by hordes of confused and seasick soldiers milling about the decks, could not maneuver effectively. Masts were snapped, sails ripped off, rigging destroyed. Several boats began shipping water badly; some were blown off course completely. Looking rather as though he had just been through a lost fleet action, Villeneuve brought his bedraggled fleet limping home.[21]

Missiessy was more fortunate. He sailed out of harbor without incident on January 11. Although calm winds delayed the fleet for two weeks, he arrived in the Caribbean on February 20 and proceeded to carry out his initial instructions with regard to Martinique, Dominica, Guadeloupe, and several other small islands.[22] On March 12, he received word that Villeneuve would not be going to the Caribbean and he was on his own in independent command.[23] He continued his cruise through the Caribbean, and on March 28 he set sail for France. This rapid departure prevented him from receiving new orders that Napoleon sent at the end of February ordering Missiessy to remain in the Antilles until the end of June in order to await new dispositions.[24] Napoleon had changed his mind again—and again.

On January 16, 1805, after Missiessy left Rochefort but before Villeneuve departed from Toulon, Napoleon issued orders for a new expedition in a different direction. The fleet of Brest under Admiral Ganteaume was to set sail at once for India carrying 20,000 French troops and 3,000 Spanish. The emperor was not at all sure that even this large force would prevail against the most important British overseas possession, but "20,000 Frenchmen, 3,000 Spaniards, and 3,000 other French from the Isles of France of Réunion will undoubtedly wage a terrible war against England, whatever might be the final result of it."[25] It is possible that when Napoleon learned of Villeneuve's embarrassing return to port he decided to send his fleet to support this Indian expedition as well.[26]

The plans for the Indian expedition were short-lived, however. In early February 1805 Napoleon learned that the Spanish had put their fleet in order much faster than he ever anticipated. Thirty-one ships of the line would be prepared, instead of the 20 that Napoleon had expected. They might be ready as early as April.[27] By the beginning of March Napoleon had settled on an entirely new plan—one that led directly to the invasion of England.[28]

The availability of sizable Spanish reinforcements apparently convinced the emperor that if he could concentrate his forces they could hope to outface any British fleets they encountered. Ganteaume, Villeneuve, and Missiessy, accordingly, all received orders to rendezvous at Martinique, having dropped off supplies and reinforcements at various Caribbean outposts, and then race back to France. Napoleon hoped that his combined fleets would arrive before Boulogne between June 11 and July 11, and that the invasion would begin at once. He would be on the English Channel at that time, in preparation for the greatest (if shortest) expedition of his career.

It is difficult to resist the notion that his change of heart reflected the surprising efficiency of the Spanish naval ministry, especially since more than a month elapsed between his decision to contravene his preparations for possible war against Austria and the preparation of this new naval plan.[29] This synchronism supports the notion that he had originally delayed the invasion of England primarily to await Spanish support. It is also possible, however, that in March 1805 as in December 1804 he was simply following the most attractive of numerous possible and occasionally contradictory options. Since Villeneuve had not left Toulon and Ganteaume had not yet sailed from Brest on his way to India, and since Missiessy was already ranging free in the Caribbean, Napoleon may have seen an opportunity when offered such prompt and significant Spanish support. Such opportunism, seized on so dramatically, was part of his nature.

A leading historian of Napoleon's plans to invade England has seized on the flaws in his naval plan and on the fact that Napoleon left the outcome of this venture up to someone else as evidence that he was preparing to abandon the British invasion without losing his reputation. If Ganteaume was defeated at sea, which, he asserts, was likely, then Napoleon could turn his attention to the continent without dishonor. If, on the other hand, Ganteaume succeeded by some miracle in arriving on the Channel coast, then Napoleon would happily put the invasion fleet in motion.[30]

This argument would dovetail nicely with the understanding of Napoleon's thought processes described above, but for two major problems. First, there is no evidence that Napoleon made plans or preparations for a continental war between February and July 1805. Second, it assumes that Napoleon was infallible in making dispositions at sea—against a veritable mountain of contrary evidence.

Since Napoleon was unaware of the seriousness and scale of the coalition forming against him and continued to trust the good intentions of Francis until the end of July, he could only be displeased by Ganteaume's defeat. He considered the possibility that Ganteaume would not be able to depart from Brest, in which case Villeneuve would be at liberty to raid British commerce—although always with an eye toward subsequently uniting with Ganteaume.[31] There can be no doubt from his orders and his tone that he had no happy fallback plan should this complex naval maneuver fail.

Whatever Napoleon's ultimate thoughts, the great expedition was put in train in March 1805. It was to culminate with the invasion of Britain in June or early July. After ordering renewed efforts to concentrate the invasion flotilla and prepare its ports of embarkation, there was little Napoleon could do to affect the outcome until the fleet arrived in front of Boulogne—or failed to do so. Consequently he turned his attention elsewhere.

As usual, inactivity in one realm of Napoleon's endeavors meant a feverish focus in another. The delegates of the Italian Republic had been cooling their heels in Paris since Napoleon's coronation as emperor of the French in December 1804. Napoleon had circulated a number of rumors about placing one of his brothers on a newly created Italian throne, but nothing came of it. In mid-March 1805 Napoleon began to address the problem of Italy—two weeks after dispatching the orders that sent the French fleet to Martinique.

A council of state had "approved" Napoleon's plan to make himself king of Italy on February 5. About a week before, the Italian delegates had given Napoleon a proposal for a constitution for the new Italian kingdom. Nothing happened for six weeks. Then on March 15 Napoleon sent back a revision of the proposed constitution, and on March 17 the assembled Italian delegates received the emperor's decree making himself king of Italy.[32] Clearly Napoleon had decided to focus on Italy—not Germany—while his fleets laid the basis for the invasion of England.

Napoleon's undertaking in Italy between March and July served three major purposes. First, having turned his attention back to the peninsula, he determined, as he usually did when he focused on an issue, to solve all the problems at once and achieve all his goals. The violence and speed of his actions, which looked like unequivocal aggression to the other states of Europe, resulted from his need to accomplish his objectives before his naval maneuvers were complete and he had to abandon Italy to invade Britain. Since he had convinced himself that Francis was truly pacified, and since he was completely focused on Italy and his invasion project, it is no wonder that Napoleon did not consider the effects his actions would have on his likely adversaries.

Napoleon could consider, plan, and conduct a greater number of major activities at one time than most people could, but he was still mortal. That he ignored the foreign political consequences of his Italian undertakings makes sense when we reflect on the other activities that were occupying his mental energies at the time. Failing to recognize his limits would bedevil the emperor on numerous other occasions in his later career as well.

Napoleon exacerbated this problem by centralizing all decisionmaking in his own person. He did not trust his minister of the navy and colonies, Vice Admiral Denis Decrès, to oversee the naval campaign. He did entrust General Nicolas Jean-de-Dieu Soult, in overall command of his forces mustered on the English Channel, with preparing the troops for the task ahead. In both cases, however, he continued to interfere in low-level tasks and undertakings; in the case of the navy he kept track of the movements of every ship of the line, frigate, sloop, and transport. This micromanaging did not necessarily harm the conduct of either operation; Napoleon had created a centralized system and his subordinates expected him to micromanage them. Even his prodigious mental powers were soon exhausted, however, and consequently he ignored other aspects of high policy.

This centralization ensured that all of Napoleon's undertakings supported one another, and his activities in Italy were no exception. One of the major aims of the annexation of Genoa, which eased the path of the formation of the Third Coalition, was to augment French naval capabilities. Genoa was an excellent port inhabited by a maritime people. Despite the concerns of his subordinates on the ground, Napoleon was determined to exploit those resources to support his naval undertakings.[33]

Another purpose of the Italian maneuvers developed over time. Napoleon hoped that his continued presence in Italy would convince the British that no invasion was imminent. He believed that the more he was visibly entangled in the affairs of Italy, the more the British would believe that he would not abandon those affairs to get on a boat bound for Dover.[34] His several goals for staying in Italy coexisted in Napoleon's mind, and he pursued each as long as he felt appropriate.

Napoleon may have had still another goal in mind. As a seemingly endless series of letters in the *Correspondance de Napoléon* indicates, Napoleon bent every effort to instructing his young stepson, Eugène Beauharnais, in the art of governing as viceroy of Italy.[35] One of the purposes of this pedantic discourse was certainly to enable Napoleon to devolve the day-to-day responsibilities for governing Italy on Eugène. It may also be that Napoleon had dynastic objectives in mind as well, depending on what future role he envisioned Eugène playing in his empire.

In the meantime this naval expedition did not go according to plan anymore than the previous one had. Villeneuve sailed promptly from Toulon on March 30 and arrived shortly at Cartagena, where a Spanish flotilla awaited him. For reasons that remain unclear, he did not manage to join with that flotilla, which stayed instead in port. He then sailed to Cadiz, where another Spanish flotilla under the redoubtable Admiral Ferdinando Carlos, Duke of Gravina, awaited him. A more concerted effort to link those two fleets failed, and Gravina was forced to follow Villeneuve as best he could.[36] The two fleets finally converged in the Caribbean.

As Ganteaume attempted to leave Brest, however, he was blockaded by a strong British fleet he could not escape without facing a battle that Napoleon feared he might lose—and therefore prohibited.[37] By mid-April Napoleon was already developing new plans for his grand expedition that took into account the possibility that Ganteaume would not be able to set sail at all. At the same time, however, he continued to exhort his admiral to make his way to the open sea as rapidly as possible, and his orders to both Ganteaume and Villeneuve became increasingly complex and contingent.

Napoleon's first thought was to divert the British blockading fleets to Brest and its vicinity by keeping Ganteaume there and sending Missiessy to join him after returning from the Caribbean. Villeneuve could then sail around Ireland to Dunkirk and Boulogne.[38] This complex plan was replaced two days later by another. Ganteaume would remain in Brest; Missiessy was once again forgotten. This time Villeneuve would sail back to Ferrol, release the Spanish flotilla there and combine it with his own, and then sail on to Brest. With this augmented fleet, Villeneuve would scatter the British blockading force and join with Ganteaume. A massive French fleet of more than fifty ships of the line would then clear the Channel and support the invasion.[39]

This plan shows that Napoleon had failed to learn several obvious lessons from his previous efforts at playing admiral. Sailing ships cannot be ordered to sail from port on a given day. If the winds are not right, they must wait. At Brest the winds had proven capricious and uncooperative already. Villeneuve's abortive efforts to link up with the Spanish fleets at Cadiz and Cartagena emphasized the difficulty of such maneuvers. Napoleon persisted, however, in imagining that he could order Villeneuve to make two such rendezvous in short succession and still arrive in the English Channel in time to support the invasion. This stubborn unwillingness to learn lessons concerning his own limitations bedeviled Napoleon throughout his career.

The complexities and contingencies of Napoleon's plans caused great confusion in a time when communications took a long time to reach their destination, if ever. By the end of April Napoleon seems to have become confused about what he expected and intended. In the same letter to Decrès he wrote, "At all events my intention is that Villeneuve arrive before Ferrol" and "I still place hope in the departure of Ganteaume."[40] In another note Decrès emphasized to Villeneuve that it was vitally important for him to seize as many British colonies in the Caribbean as he could and crucial for him to support the overall invasion of Britain. Napoleon apparently was not aware of the inconsistencies and tensions within and between his various different orders.[41]

The problem lay in the extreme complexity of Napoleon's thought processes. He was constantly juggling contingencies and attempting to prepare for mutually contradictory cases simultaneously. If Ganteaume escaped from Brest, Napoleon wanted to prepare for him to link up with Villeneuve at Martinique and then race back to clear the Channel. If Ganteaume did not manage to set forth, then Napoleon wanted Villeneuve to proceed to Ferrol and then unblock Brest, join Ganteaume, and clear the Channel through force majeure. In the meantime, he wanted Villeneuve to damage British interests in the Caribbean as much as possible, thus achieving a number of objectives. He would deprive Britain of a source of wealth and might convince the British to sue for peace. He might succeed in establishing a new French power base overseas. At least he would divert significant British reinforcements away from Europe to undo the damage Villeneuve and Missiessy had caused. All of these goals were perfectly consistent with both of the (mutually contradictory) plans for clearing the Channel and securing the invasion route.

Communicating these complexities to his subordinates, however, was a challenge Napoleon could not always meet. Part of the problem lay in the need for secrecy—every message to one of his admirals might fall into the hands of the British and reveal the details of a plan that relied on deception for success. Another part of the problem was a characteristic of Napoleon's personality. Convinced of his own superiority, Napoleon nevertheless chafed at his subordinates' inability to divine his thoughts. Finally there was the problem of time. Napoleon worked incredibly hard and had remarkable powers of concentration and endurance. There is only so much time in the day, however, and he was simultaneously micromanaging events at sea and around the world, as well as reorganizing Italy. His orders, even the longer explicatory missives, always have an air of breathless haste about them. It is not surprising that he did not take time he really did not have, violating rules of secrecy he constantly commended to his admirals, to lay out the backgrounds and preconceptions that shaped his thoughts and plans. The consequences, however, were baleful—his subordinates repeatedly failed to penetrate his thought and discern what he would want them to do when unexpected situations appeared.

The result of this miscommunication was that Villeneuve accomplished far less in the Caribbean than Napoleon had hoped. Although eager to seize British colonies on his arrival, Villeneuve held to the letter of his initial orders. By the time Napoleon's new orders arrived a month later, instructing him to do all possible damage to British possessions, the French admiral found the British too well prepared for him to undertake meaningful action. His failure to read Napoleon's mind cost France an important opportunity.[42]

Tracing Napoleon's subsequent thinking and French naval movements lies beyond the scope of this work. He briefly flirted with the idea of an Indian expedition in the event that Villeneuve failed to return to Europe in a timely fashion and developed various ideas and orders for raiding the Irish coast, as well as plans for another expedition to the Caribbean by the recently returned Missiessy. For our purposes, the next critical moment in the naval struggle came in mid-July. Paradoxically, Napoleon first became seriously alarmed about Austrian intentions at the same time.[43] From mid-July until August 23 Napoleon was obliged to keep one eye on the continent and the other on the sea.

War Plans in Conflict

Napoleon's plans for the war against the Third Coalition arose from his ability to consider two contradictory contingencies at the same time. He continued to prepare for the invasion of Britain, but in July he began a diplomatic offensive designed to deter the Austrians from attacking him, and in August he began to make preparations for turning the Army of England toward the heart of Europe and away from the sea.

Napoleon refused to countenance the possibility of going to war with Austria throughout the spring and summer of 1805. In April he wrote to the war minister of the Italian Kingdom, Domenico Pino, "there is not the least probability of a war (the new assurances that I have received from the Emperor of Germany lead me to believe that)."[44] The discovery of the Austrian secret agent Baron Moll, who had been passing information from Melzi to Cobenzl as Napoleon was considering declaring himself king of Italy, led Napoleon to snarl a threat in the direction of Vienna, but four days later he ordered Marshal Jourdan to inform the Austrian commander in Venetia of the maneuvers Napoleon intended to hold at Alexandria.[45] He instructed Jourdan to select someone to observe the Austrians' reactions; apparently he meant to convey to them that the camp of review would not be dissolved if they mobilized in response. Still, these are not actions Napoleon would have taken had he intended to overawe or deter a hostile Austria—he would never go out of his way to reassure the Austrian garrison commander that he had no hostile intentions![46]

Napoleon's credulity went even further. When Marshal Joachim Murat warned him in May that the Russians and the British had concluded a treaty, which they had, in fact, done in April, Napoleon rebuked him: "What you write me about the conclusion of an alliance treaty between England and Russia is absurd; it is entirely false. These rumors, which the English spread to distract us momentarily, are fabricated."[47] He assured Decrès that these rumors were a diversion meant to gain fifteen or twenty days by distracting Napoleon from his naval endeavors. He also began a spirited counterpropaganda campaign. If Pitt announced the treaty in Parliament, then Decrès was to declare publicly that all efforts to draw Russia into the war would fail.[48] Cambacérès was instructed to insinuate at the exchange and elsewhere that the Russians had refused to listen to Pitt's overtures and to make much of Alexander's request of a passport for Novosil'tsev.[49] Napoleon even instructed Fouché to fabricate letters from St. Petersburg to show that the French were treated well there now, that the British were generally disliked, and that the Russians would under no circumstances involve themselves in the present conflict.[50] A few days later he wrote again to Decrès, "I do not know what this present English salvo [the rumor of the treaty] means; it is possible that it has a frivolous aim. It is a ruse that they frequently employ when there is discouragement and ferment in the crews" of their ships.[51]

Napoleon's words should never be taken at face value, of course, and these notes, even to his senior ministers, even to the naval minister overseeing the complex and dangerous worldwide fleet maneuvers, might have been aimed at deceiving them and the French public about the threat of a new coalition. Presumably the purpose would have been to permit Napoleon to retain his focus on the Royal Navy and the Dover coast. This may have been Napoleon's goal in denying the existence of the new coalition. There is considerable room for doubt, however.

First, there is no record of a threat or hostile demarche, however secret, directed at Alexander in hopes of deterring him. Napoleon accorded Novosil'tsev his passport cheerfully, although not expecting a positive result.[52] He may have meant to use the negotiations to delay the formation of the coalition to buy time for his fleet assembling off the Dover coast.

Second, if Napoleon believed that the coalition was forming yet pretended to his closest ministers as well as the public that it was not, his goal could only have been to induce the coalition to attack. Napoleon was capable of trusting Decrès, to say nothing of Talleyrand and Fouché, with secrets that required public dissembling. The naval minister was one of only three or four men who knew the whole plan for the fleet and the invasion. It is absurd to imagine that Napoleon felt it necessary to lie to Decrès merely to ensure that the latter convincingly denied rumors of an impending continental war.

But if Napoleon was deliberately luring the coalition to attack, he was going far beyond his demonstrated ability to prepare simultaneously for mutually exclusive contingencies—he was attempting to bring about a contingency that would wreck his own cherished plans. The only army that could meet an attack in Germany was the one he needed to invade England. If he brought the coalition to attack him, he would have to delay the invasion far beyond the point at which the naval maneuvers he was working on would be relevant.

Some would present this line of reasoning as proof that Napoleon had given up hope of invading England, and that the orders and money he lavished on the invasion project throughout July and August were intended to deceive the allies. Despite the fact that there is no evidence to support this notion, it is not beyond the conceivable. Throughout his career Napoleon showed more than enough sophistication and duplicity to carry through such a plan. Nevertheless, this idea does not make sense in light of any rational overarching goal he might have been pursuing.

The only consistent goal Napoleon ever enunciated or adhered to was the destruction of England. From 1801 to 1807 the only aims he defined with regard to Austria and Prussia, to say nothing of Russia, were defensive and reactive. The treaties he made with both states after defeating them were punitive and designed to eliminate those states as threats in the future. Then he returned to the task of dealing with Britain. Napoleon's thoughts and actions make sense if we understand that the war with Britain was first and foremost among his concerns and plans; continental affairs were a distraction or a sidelight. If we try to see long-range plans and programs for the reorganization of Europe, we always come up against the blank wall that there is no evidence or only contradictory evidence to support such an interpretation. If Napoleon's primary aims did involve continental Europe, then they were inconsistent and contradictory.

If Napoleon really did believe that Austria was cowed, Alexander was seeking to appease him, and Britain remained isolated, then his failure to make preparations for a continental war in May, June, and July 1805 makes perfect sense. On June 20 he reassured Cambacérès once more, "I have no uncertainty at all about continental peace; you can be assured of that; and if I have let it appear that I have any doubts, it is because I believed that it is more prudent to make it known that I do not fear it [war]."[53] Napoleon did not begin to change his mind until the end of July.

What caused Napoleon to consider seriously the possibility that a new coalition was forming is not clear. A series of trivial and unpredictable events apparently led him to recognize the impending danger, and then he acted faster than the allies had anticipated.

Napoleon united a large body of troops in his Kingdom of Italy in April-May 1805. He reviewed the troops on the plains of the Battle of Marengo, and they remained to witness his coronation in Milan. They then dispersed.[54] The Austrians responded by mobilizing a sizable force in Venice and the Tyrol for the purpose of observing this French concentration. When the French forces dispersed, however, the Austrians did not. They remained in their positions and dug in. Mack had been working hard to bring the Austrian army up to its full normal *peacetime* level, repairing damage done to the force by parsimonious budgets based on optimistic expectations of protracted peace. To Napoleon, this may have looked like a mobilization.[55]

These mobilizations occurred in April and May 1805, but Napoleon did not recognize or react to them at that time. He did not become concerned until the end of July, when little was taking place. The meeting between Schwarzenberg, Mack, and Wintzingerode occurred on July 16, and their decisions were not ratified for some time thereafter. Austria formally joined the coalition on August 9, and orders to place the army on a war footing did not come until August 27.[56]

Heads of state react not to real events but to their perceptions of those events, filtered through the eyes of their subordinates. In this case, it may be that Eugène's inexperience helped trigger Napoleon's premature (from the Austrian perspective) decision to contemplate continental war. Napoleon left Italy in haste for the Channel coast in early July. For the first time, twenty-four-year-old Eugène found himself alone and in charge of a kingdom. He took his responsibilities seriously, especially those relating to obtaining information about threats to his new territory.

Napoleon's departure to France, he reported, did more than merely make his new Italian subjects sad; it led to talk of war. "They are always talking a little about war, they are gossiping about your hasty departure."[57] A few days later he added, "The rumors of war continue, all of the reports of the delegates on the Adige are full of them. Your Majesty will know better than us the truth, and I would only make account of these reports to the extent that they are worthy of being presented to you."[58] Napoleon responded, "I am well founded in my hope that there will be no war; nevertheless, the preparations that the Austrians are making require me to put prepare myself."[59]

Things worsened rapidly, at least in Eugène's opinion: "All of the reports coming from the other side of the Adige are about war. The works at Brescia and Chiogga continue actively. One talks of cannons, magazines, munitions, etc. What is certain is that the Austrians either wish to do something or have a terrible fear of Your Majesty's army; what is very certain is that our poor Italians are dying of fear." Eugène went on to explain that the continual war alarms were hindering his efforts to consolidate French rule in Italy. Austrian partisans, and apparently there were many of them, resisted more strongly as they came to believe that a war was imminent.[60]

On July 24 Napoleon sent Austrian ambassador in Paris Philip Cobenzl a note complaining about the treatment of several prominent Frenchmen at the hands of Austrian authorities, and also about the "sanitary cordon" the Austrians had maintained along the banks of the Adige since late 1804, ostensibly to prevent the spread of malaria. This note was markedly balanced, contained no threat beyond the warning that Napoleon would set up a countercordon if the Austrians did not remove theirs, and stated that Napoleon wanted to live in peace with Austria. It noted, however, that Austrian armaments were beginning to look like preparations for a coalition, something that would not be tolerated.[61]

Napoleon's responses to Eugène became less reassuring but were far from bellicose: "You say that all the rumors are of war. You must not combat those rumors. What Austria does she probably does from fear. Besides, I could well prevent her from preparing and fall upon her." He went on to order Eugène to keep Austrian officers out of his forts.[62]

Other factors probably entered into Napoleon's situation assessment. He certainly knew of Wintzingerode's mission and its general purpose, although he may not have been aware of the July 16 conference between Wintzingerode, Mack, and Schwarzenberg.[63] He had learned for sure of Novosil'tsev's recall following his seizure of Genoa, but it is difficult to tell what he made of it. Talleyrand wrote to a French agent in Russia that the recall of Novosil'tsev was evidence that Alexander had recognized the degree to which Pitt was making a fool of him and had decided not to interfere between France and Britain. There was no trace of the notion that Alexander was contemplating an alliance with Britain.[64] Of course this letter may have been intended to deceive Alexander about the extent of Napoleon's ignorance and play for time, although there is no corroborating evidence for such an interpretation.

Napoleon most likely believed that the Austrians were mobilizing on their own through fear or for some project he did not understand or particularly care about. He seems to have believed that they were considering joining a coalition but had not yet done so. It would not be the first time; Francis had mobilized on at least two previous occasions during disputes with Bavaria over the settlement of German issues, and there had been numerous warnings of a newly forming coalition. French threats had been enough to disperse gathering Austrian regiments before. Napoleon had no reason to suppose that the present occasion, triggered possibly by Austrian resentment over Genoa or even Napoleon's recent coronation, would be any different. His initial threats to Vienna probably did not reflect a conviction that war was imminent, and they were certainly not written with an eye toward goading Francis into war. Napoleon was bending all diplomatic efforts to pacifying Austria once again.

Accordingly, he instructed Talleyrand to prepare a note that he described as "long, sugary, and reasoned" for delivery to Austrian ambassador Philip Cobenzl as soon as possible.[65] The note met Napoleon's requirements for length, reasonableness, and sweetness. In it Talleyrand considered evidence that a new coalition was forming, noting Wintzingerode's presence in Vienna following his hostile visit to Berlin and the recent "lapses" of the Russians, probably including the recall of Novosil'tsev, and British pronouncements. He then discussed reasons Austria might have for fearing or wanting to wage war against France and found them specious. Russia, he argued, was infinitely more dangerous to Austria than France would ever be, and he invited Cobenzl to consider the consequences of the Greek cross standing over Constantinople in place of the crescent.

The ultimatum, when it came, was buried in sweetness and delivered more in sorrow than in anger. Austria's actions, Talleyrand wrote, were distracting Napoleon from his focus on defeating the British. Already the emperor had spent a fortune rebuilding and provisioning fortresses in Italy to prepare for a possible Austrian attack. If the Austrian buildup continued, then Napoleon, who had no corps to spare, would have to march an army from the Channel coast into Germany and Italy. In that event, forced by Austrian misdeeds to abandon the invasion of England, Napoleon would choose an honorable war on the continent over a dishonorable and meaningless peace. The way to prevent this chain of events was simple: Francis had to withdraw his excessive forces from the French frontiers.

As a bid to persuade Francis not to join a coalition, this was not a bad try. The tone of the letter was reasonable and the threats were couched in a gentle way that was not immediately obvious. It had no chance to succeed, of course, since Francis had already committed himself to the coalition and his officers were hard at work concerting war plans with the Russians. Napoleon's effort at conciliation (and gentle intimidation) arrived too late.

The emperor was initially optimistic, however. Talleyrand reported on a meeting with Philip Cobenzl in which the latter offered Austria's mediation in the Anglo–French war in place of Novosil'tsev's canceled mission. He admitted that Austria had 72,000 troops in Italy, while insisting that Napoleon had in his portion of the peninsula more than the 50,000 that Talleyrand was prepared to admit. If Napoleon wished to negotiate a convention that would reduce troops on both sides equitably, Philip Cobenzl believed that his court might accept such a treaty.[66] Napoleon seemed mollified: "Austria fears for herself," he wrote back. "I think that this note is a pacific protestation that means that she does not share the folly of Russia. What Austria must gather from my response is that this declaration is not sufficient; that there must be actions; that the route of preparations is the route of war."[67] By August 10, Napoleon had turned back to considering the minor problems of Austria's treatment of French and Belgian citizens and public establishments—surely an indication that he expected Francis to fold.[68]

Two days later, Napoleon's tone changed completely. The change appears to have been started by a note from his ambassador in Munich, Louis Guillaume Otto, reporting on Austrian military preparations in Germany.[69] In addition, the Austrian response to his demand for disarmament could not have pleased him.[70] The first two paragraphs, declaring Francis's intention to answer Napoleon's query about his armaments fully and his desire to remain at peace with France, were sound enough. Napoleon's eyebrows must have risen as he heard the "but" that began the next paragraph. Far from being cowed, Francis was inflamed. He described in detail Napoleon's systematic violations of the Treaty of Lunéville and obliquely but clearly demanded that independence be returned to Italy, Holland, and Switzerland. He also demanded that the king of Sardinia receive the compensation Napoleon had promised. Francis did not deny the presence of large Austrian armies in Venice and the Tyrol but claimed he had sent them in response to Napoleon's armaments in the Kingdom of Italy. The Austrian emperor made no promise to disarm or remove his troops from the frontiers of his realm. He repeated his offer to mediate or support Russian mediation of the Anglo–French war.

Worst of all, the note revealed that a coalition was brewing. Francis made it clear that he was in close contact with both Alexander and Pitt and was operating in accord with them, at least to some extent. This note seemed designed to outrage Napoleon and goad him to war, but that was surely not its purpose. The main aim of this inflammatory missive was likely to convince Alexander that Francis was sincerely committed to the coalition.

Relations between tsar and emperor had become strained as Alexander grew increasingly mistrustful of Francis's intentions. Wintzingerode's meetings in Vienna did not entirely allay the Russian suspicions, and this note was drafted before Francis had formally adhered to the coalition treaty. Cobenzl constructed this response with an eye on St. Petersburg hoping to cement a relationship he regarded as essential to Austria's security. If he thought about its likely effect on Napoleon, that probably seemed less important to him than its effect on Alexander.

From the standpoint of coalition diplomacy, this decision was sound; from the standpoint of coalition war planning it was unfortunate. The war plan calculated that the Russians would arrive in Bavaria before the French did, assuming that Napoleon would not move his forces until he learned of the Russian move into Austrian territory.[71] That move would begin during the last week of August. The Austrians expected Napoleon to need at least a week to learn of the Russians' movement, meaning that he would start moving his troops at the beginning of September.

When Napoleon sent a note demanding that the Austrian court explain its armaments in early August, the right thing to do from a military perspective was to stall and straddle with a conciliatory reply. It might have been wise to order a few regiments to move back from the frontier, if only to confuse things. The blunt counterultimatum Cobenzl sent had the opposite effect. It clarified for Napoleon a situation that could have been kept murky for some time. Once again tension and mistrust among the allies seriously hampered coalition war making.

Napoleon's language changed after he received Cobenzl's note. He ordered Talleyrand to show evidence of Austria's armaments to Philip Cobenzl and then declared, "I await his response without which I shall march troops into Switzerland and I will raise my camps on the ocean; that I can no more be conciliated with words; that I do not want any army in the Tyrol; that the Austrian troops must return to their garrisons; without that I will start the war."[72] To Cambacérès he wrote even more bluntly: "The fact is that [Austria] is arming; I want her to disarm; if she does not, I will go to make her a good visit with 200,000 men that she will remember for a long time."[73]

Historians of the war see Napoleon's flurry of messages on August 13 as evidence that he had decided to attack Austria; they even attempt to see the outline of his campaign plan in threats sent to the court of Vienna.[74] The truth is more complex. Between August 13 and August 23 Napoleon began to conceptualize a war against the continental powers, but only as one of two mutually contradictory alternatives. His correspondence and his actions, moreover, make it clear that he worked to preserve his invasion of Britain and adopted the second option of continental war only when the first became impracticable. As usual, however, he kept both options open and worked actively on each right up to the moment of choosing one.

He wrote to Talleyrand, "I am committed; I want to attack Austria and be in Vienna before next November in order to face the Russians if they should appear; or I very much want, and that is the word, that there be only one Austrian regiment in the Tyrol and eight in Styria, Carinthia, Carniola, Friuli, and the Italian Tyrol."75 Explaining his method in sending increasingly harsh notes to Vienna, Napoleon declared, "If the note that I am sending [now] had been sent at first to Austria, she would have thought that I want war, when in fact I want it only in a single alternative. *I prefer above all that Austria adopt a peaceful posture.*"76

Napoleon then instructed Talleyrand about the tenor of the conversation he was to have with Philip Cobenzl. The critical element of that conversation was an ultimatum: either Napoleon would learn by the return of his courier in fifteen days (by August 28) that orders had been sent out to start Austrian units back to their garrisons, or Francis would not spend Christmas in Vienna. The wild and contradictory threats in this note do not express even the broadest outlines of a military campaign plan, and Napoleon would hardly broadcast such a plan to his intended victim!

Only one passage is revealing in that regard: "France, menaced on the side of Italy, can hardly arrive there in time to preempt the enemy; but she will send troops over the Rhine to seek out the enemy in the heart of his own states." This passage emphasizes a fatal flaw of the coalition war plan. The allies assumed that because they were making Italy the main theater initially, Napoleon would oblige by sending a major portion of his army there. That he might well have done, if his reaction to his first war scare of 1805 is any indication, for in January he gave orders to send several regiments racing toward Italy at once. By August 1805, however, Napoleon had fallen far behind the coalition in large part because the allies kept the coalition's existence and plans secret for so long. It no longer made sense for Napoleon to take the time to fight in Italy. The allies' diplomatic deception worked to the undoing of their war plan in this regard and helped drive Napoleon to choose the one course of action most destructive of allied operations.

It is easy to draw too strong a conclusion from Napoleon's declaration to Talleyrand that "I am committed." He continued to work hard to bring about his preferred alternative, the invasion of England, ignoring the paradoxical situation he was creating. Even as he worked hard to transport the Army of England to England, he was sending ultimatums to Austria that could only be made good by the same army.

Villeneuve had found his way back to Europe by late July and headed toward Ferrol to raise the blockade there and gather in the reinforcements waiting for him at that port. He encountered a British squadron under the command of Admiral Sir Robert Calder on July 22, but the battle was indecisive and Villeneuve proceeded on his way. By the end of the month he reached Ferrol and linked up with the large squadron there. By this time, his orders had become confused, but he believed that he had to sail out of Ferrol and either free the Brest squadron or, if he could manage it, charge into the English

Channel and support the invasion. If both of those courses of action seemed impracticable, then he believed that he was to sail south to Cadiz and await reinforcements and further orders.[77]

The outlook was not brilliant for Napoleon's naval plans. Villeneuve was becoming increasingly dispirited. Contrary winds had delayed the fleet's return to France, his ships had suffered much in their sails and rigging, he was running out of food and water, and he had hundreds of men sick with scurvy and dysentery. The battle of July 22 was desultory, and Napoleon's complicated plans were confusing. Above all, Villeneuve's efforts to find and link up with a French flotilla that he expected to be waiting at Vigo failed when the ship he sent to find that flotilla was captured by a British cruiser.[78]

Napoleon became disgusted with Villeneuve, declaring at one point that the admiral "is a poor man who sees double and has more perception than character"; and "Villeneuve is one of those men who need the spur more than the bridle."[79] Perhaps for that reason, Napoleon appears to have concealed from Villeneuve persuasive (and accurate) evidence that Nelson had returned to the waters of Spain and was searching for him. He consistently understated the size the British fleet would reach if Nelson and Calder managed to effect a junction.[80] He left his admiral poorly prepared for a meeting between the two fleets.

Napoleon's decision to issue an ultimatum to Vienna on August 13 had an odd consequence for his naval maneuvers: he tried to speed them up. In a series of orders issued on that day and the next, Napoleon commanded Villeneuve to sail at once from Ferrol with the combined fleet and batter his way through to Brest and into the Channel, even if it meant fighting a general fleet action, something the emperor had hitherto ordered Villeneuve to avoid.[81]

The emperor did everything in his power to encourage Villeneuve: "If you can appear here [Boulogne] for three days, even if you only appear for 24 hours, your mission will be fulfilled." He continued, "Never has a squadron run a few risks for such a great aim, and never have my soldiers on land and sea been able to spill their blood for a greater and nobler result. For the great object of making possible a landing on that power that, for six centuries, has oppressed France, we could all die without regretting our lives."[82] To Lauriston he was more succinct: "We are ready throughout. An appearance of twenty-four hours will suffice."[83]

Napoleon's orders to Villeneuve make no sense unless he hoped to land in England within a few weeks. If he had already decided to abandon the invasion and turn against Austria, then it was madness to risk his fleet in a general engagement that could serve no purpose. The ultimatum he had sent to Vienna would have served to put the Austrians on their guard. If he was attempting to lull Francis, then promising to drive him from his capital before Christmas was an odd way of going about it. As for maintaining a fiction that he still intended to launch the invasion, his own continued presence at

Boulogne combined with any combination of safer naval maneuvers would have done as well.

There is no evidence to suggest that Napoleon in August 1805 saw a continental war as anything other than a delay before the intended invasion. He badly needed the fleet that he was so callously hazarding for such an endeavor, and if he had decided to shelve the naval project temporarily, then the well-being of that fleet should have been his first concern. The fact that he ordered Villeneuve to charge forth from Ferrol and blast into the Channel, through the entire British fleet if necessary, indicates that he had something else in mind.

We have already seen that Napoleon underestimated preparations for the coalition offensive. In August he did not believe that the Austrians had yet joined the coalition or that the allies would undertake serious activity in 1805.[84] He concluded, accordingly, that he would have time to invade Britain during the fall and be back on the continent to face the coalition—if the destruction of Britain did not lead to its collapse. That is why he increased the pressure on Villeneuve to race into the Channel at virtually the same moment he was sending an ultimatum to Austria.

While waiting for Villeneuve to present himself before Boulogne, however, Napoleon also scrambled to assemble a coalition that would prevent or support a war against Austria. He quickly accepted the most recent alliance proposal from the elector of Bavaria, instructing his ambassador in Munich to hasten the signature of that treaty.[85] He tried once more to entice Frederick William into an alliance, offering him Hanover as a reward for mobilizing on the Bohemian frontier, thereby pinning the Austrians or placing them in a very bad position. Not only did he instruct Talleyrand to make this offer, but he wrote directly to Frederick William as well, and he sent a special envoy, General Géraud Christophe Michel Duroc, to Berlin to conduct the negotiations.[86] As we have seen, Napoleon induced the Bavarians to ally themselves with him, but not the Prussians. He also worked to rally the minor German princes to his side.[87]

The emperor now began undertaking military preparations for the first time during this crisis. On August 15 Berthier ordered three dragoon regiments to concentrate at Strasbourg. Three days later Napoleon ordered an infantry regiment and a regiment of hussars from Paris and Versailles to Strasbourg. He told Talleyrand to make much noise of this movement but deny that he was raising his camps on the ocean.[88] He also ordered an Italian division to the borders of Naples.[89]

The bad news kept streaming in. Napoleon's ambassadors in Munich and Vienna reported a massive Austrian mobilization and the formation of camps near the western borders of the Habsburg Empire. Forts were being provisioned, supplies were being purchased. Senior officers had been recalled and some sent to their units; others were called to Vienna for high-level conferences.

It is not clear when these letters reached Napoleon, but starting on about August 20 he would have begun to read descriptions of Austria's preparations for imminent war.[90]

The news from the sea was no better. Villeneuve finally sailed from Ferrol on August 13. He had not received Napoleon's orders commanding him to charge into the Channel come what may, and believed that he was still supposed to avoid battle. He had also become completely discouraged and despondent. When he thought he sighted enemy ships on August 15, he adhered to the old orders and turned south to Cadiz, thereby destroying all hopes of a cross-Channel invasion before mid-September at the earliest.[91]

Napoleon learned of Villeneuve's departure on August 22—the date by which the admiral could reasonably have arrived at Brest. He wrote at once by telegraph to Ganteaume at Brest, telling him to make ready to sail at once and keep Villeneuve from entering Brest at all costs. The fleets were to join up outside of the harbor and proceed at once to the Channel. To Villeneuve he wrote (at Brest), "I hope that you have arrived at Brest. Set forth and do not lose a moment and, with my combined squadrons, enter the Channel. England is ours. We are all ready, all is embarked. Appear for 24 hours and all is finished."[92]

But the emperor was beginning to have his doubts. He mistrusted Villeneuve, as we have seen, and he began to chafe that he had not heard of the admiral's arrival at Brest yet via the telegraph. He wrote to Decrès asking what should be done if Villeneuve had gone to Cadiz instead of Brest.[93] In another note of the same day, however, he told Decrès that if Villeneuve had gone to Cadiz, then he was to be sent racing back into the Channel.[94] Decrès, however, plucked up his courage and demurred strongly. If Villeneuve's fleet was at Cadiz, he wrote, "I beg you to consider this event as the decision of destiny, which is preserving it [the fleet] for other operations. I beg you not to have it return from Cadiz to the Channel because such an attempt at this time could only be met with misfortunes." Perhaps even more boldly, Decrès condemned Napoleon for failing to heed the advice of his professional sailors: "It is unfortunate for me to understand the profession of the sea, since this understanding does not obtain any confidence and does not produce any result in the combinations of Your Majesty."[95]

It appears that this time, Decrès had the effect he desired. On August 23 Napoleon wrote Talleyrand the note that is generally taken to indicate that he had decided for war on the continent.[96] In truth, he had come to no such decision. He began by declaring, "The more I reflect on the situation of Europe, the more I see that it is urgent to commit myself decisively." The rest of the note presented two alternatives. Napoleon did not yet feel that he had to choose between them because he continued to misread the pace of coalition preparations. "I do not, in reality, expect anything from the Austrian explanation," he wrote. "She will respond with nice phrases and gain time in order to prevent me from doing anything this winter; her subsidy treaty and her act of coalition will be signed this winter, under the pretext of an armed neutrality, and in April I will find 100,000 Russians in Poland, supplied by England, with their horses, artillery, etc., and 15,000 to 20,000 English at Malta, and 15,000 Russians at Corfu. I will find myself thus in a critical situation. I am committed."

But was he? "My squadron left Ferrol on 26 Thermidor [August 14], with 34 ships of the line [actually 29]; it had no enemies in view. If it follows its instructions, joins with the squadron from Brest and enters the Channel, there is still time, I am the master of England. If, on the contrary, my admirals hesitate, maneuver badly and do not accomplish their objective, I have no other recourse than to await the winter to cross with the flotilla." He continued, "The operation is hazardous; it will become the more so if, pressed by time, political events oblige me to leave here in April. In this state of affairs, I run to the most pressing [problem]: I raise my camps . . . and by 1 Vendémiaire [September 23] I will be in Germany with 200,000 men and in Naples with 25,000. I will march on Vienna and not put down my arms until I have Naples and Venice and have so increased the states of the elector of Bavaria that I will have nothing more to fear from Austria."

Even after Decrès's plea, Napoleon was still wavering. He had probably come to realize that he had no alternative, that he had to turn against the coalition. The invasion of England, however, was his dearest ambition. He would not have been human if he had not clung to it a little beyond reason. Although orders to move, to transform the Army of England into the Grande Armée, and to send it marching toward Germany went out in the next couple of days, Napoleon did not give orders to wind up the invasion flotilla until August 30, and did not send new orders to Villeneuve until September 1.

One can imagine Napoleon pacing about the camps at Boulogne as the troops pack up and prepare to march southeast, knowing that he must abandon the invasion but hoping against hope that a courier will arrive telling him that Villeneuve is in the Channel. "There is still time," he must have been muttering to himself, "give him a chance." But in his heart he knew that Villeneuve would not come, and he gradually turned his full attention to the war he knew he had to fight.

13

Napoleon's War Plans

Concept and Action

The war plans Napoleon developed to fight the coalition in 1805 reflected the contingent nature of his decision to go to war against Austria instead of Britain. It is a mistake to look for a Napoleonic system of war or for a plan developed at the beginning of the campaign and then followed. Nor was Napoleon simply a scrambler who kept getting himself into bad situations and then ingeniously finding his way out. Napoleon developed a concept of a campaign—an idea of how he intended to win. He created an initial plan to support that idea, but he did not expect to follow that plan. He adhered to the general concept and continually shifted his actual plans in accord with changes in the circumstances of the war. His war plan was always in motion and developed over time in tune with his perception of the changing situation. This was true even for so complex and far-reaching a plan as the naval campaign against Great Britain. It was even more true when Napoleon could place himself at the head of his army, no more than a day's hard riding from any of his subordinates, as in the War of 1805.

Concept and Initial Plans

There is no single document or set of documents that clearly lays out Napoleon's concept for the campaign of 1805. We must deduce his idea partially from his correspondence and partially from his actions. He clearly identified Austria as the center of gravity of the coalition and Vienna as Austria's center of gravity.* The prospect of British landings in France or Holland, with or without Russian troops, did not trouble him. He was more concerned with the prospect of coalition activities in the southern Italian peninsula, but he hoped that the forces of the Kingdom of Italy, together with the French troops already in Naples, would suffice to deal with those threats. He seems from the outset to have decided to deal with the Austrian threats to northern Italy by marching to Vienna rather than by attempting to confront the Austrians on the Adige.

Napoleon thus intended to race southeast with the Army of England, now rechristened the Grande Armée, destroy any Austrian armies he encountered in Bavaria or near the Austrian frontier, and drive rapidly on Vienna. There is no evidence that he knew what he would do at that point. He mentioned on some occasions "facing" the Russians after seizing Vienna but offered no details. Perhaps he believed that when he seized Vienna, Austria would surrender. With one brief exception, after all, no major European capital had fallen in war since the Treaty of Westphalia.† Napoleon had every reason to expect that his capture of Vienna would send a resounding shock through the Habsburg monarchy that would bring Francis to his knees. He may, on the other hand, have been overwhelmed by the task of turning the Army of England into the Grande Armée and deciding how to confront the imminent Austrian threat.

Napoleon's war aims were also unclear. At first he seems to have intended to smash the coalition and ensure that Austria would not again take up arms against him. The real aim behind that program may have been to facilitate another attempt to invade England in 1806, this time without fear for events on the continent.[1] As Berthier wrote to Marmont, "This is only . . . a quick movement; there is reason to think that we will soon be free of the House of Austria and we will return to the Ocean."[2] Just as Napoleon had no constructive aims in the diplomacy he conducted with the major continental powers between 1802 and 1805, he continued to have primarily negative aims as he went to war. He offered no positive vision for what Europe should look like when the war was over, nor did he clarify what demands he intended to make of his enemies once he defeated them. Contingency was all.

---

*Center of gravity is a complicated and controversial concept. Carl von Clausewitz, who brought the term into common use among military analysts and officers, offered several definitions, but the thrust of all of them is that the center of gravity is the point at which the enemy should be attacked to achieve the maximum effect. He made it clear on several occasions that this would usually be the major concentration of the enemy's armed forces. The concept has changed in the context of the debates over military transformation in the 1990s and early 2000s in ways that need not concern us here. Readers interested in this concept will find a more detailed discussion, along with references to the modern controversy over this topic, in Frederick W. Kagan, *Finding the Target: The Transformation of the U. S. Military* (New York: Encounter, 2006).

†The exception was the short-lived Russian occupation of Berlin during a raid in the Seven Years War.

Napoleon's actual concept for the initial operations did not spring fully formed from his head on August 23 or in the days immediately following. He had been developing those concepts throughout August even as he awaited the outcome of developments at sea and in the realm of diplomacy. He ordered Berthier, accordingly, to have the army of Hanover assemble at the southernmost point of the electorate, Göttingen.[3] He ordered Marmont's corps in Holland, already embarked for the invasion, to be ready on twenty-four hours' notice to disembark and march as rapidly as possible to Mainz.[4] He ordered the preparation of 500,000 biscuits at Strasbourg and 200,000 at Mainz, indicating the initial concentration areas he intended for his army.[5]

He did not expect the Austrians to mobilize and move with as much speed and determination as they did. Their efficiency caught him off guard and forced him to change his initial plans. At first, he had intended to race into Bavaria before the Austrians could cross the Inn, thereby protecting his new ally in Munich.[6] The concentration he ordered to support that plan placed his cavalry in a line along the Rhine from Sélestat to Speyer. Ney's corps would march to Sélestat; Soult's and Lannes's corps to Strasbourg; Davout's to Haguenau; and Marmont's and Bernadotte's to Würzburg. The Grenadiers Division under the command of Oudinot would march to Strasbourg. There it would prepare to cross the river and continue along the Danube valley toward Vienna.[7]

This deployment would have left more than 120 miles between the left flank of the army (Bernadotte and Marmont) and the left-most corps of the center (Davout). Natural points for these forces to link up were at Stuttgart, Ulm, Augsburg, or even Munich. Since Napoleon had instructed the elector of Bavaria to prepare 500,000 biscuits both at Würzburg and at Ulm, it is likely that he saw the latter town as the hub of his future movement and expected to join the left wing to the center of his army in its vicinity.[8]

Napoleon's initial concept of this operation thus entailed a major push from west to east across the Rhine, Baden, Württemberg, and Bavaria, linking up with forces marching south from Hanover and Holland somewhere in central Bavaria. Presumably he then expected to be facing Austrian forces across the Inn and possibly Russian or Austrian forces in Bohemia, since he sent scouts out to explore the terrain leading into Bavaria from that Habsburg province.[9] Having concentrated his army in this forward and central position, he would have protected his ally and placed himself in a good location from which to attack northeast into Bohemia, east-southeast into Austria, or south toward the Tyrol. He made it clear to the elector that he intended to attack rapidly and not remain long in Bavaria, a declaration that pleased a sovereign who feared for the prosperity of his lands under the weight of 200,000 French troops. Napoleon probably intended to decide in what direction to march only after he had ascertained the dispositions and intentions of the coalition forces arrayed against him.

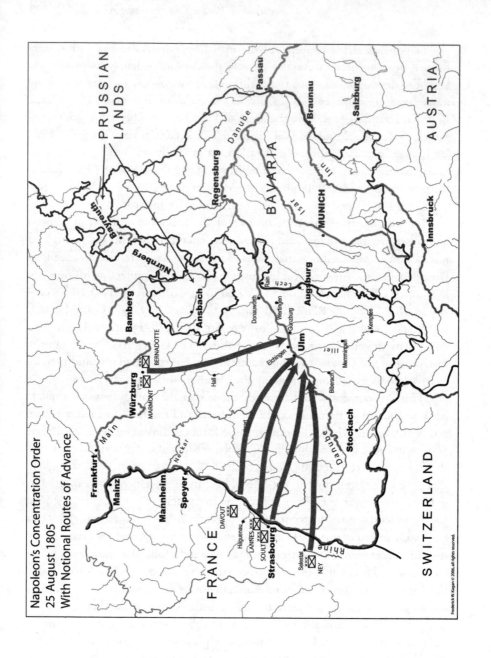

Napoleon's Concentration Order
25 August 1805
With Notional Routes of Advance

PRUSSIAN LANDS

AUSTRIA

Passau
Braunau
Salzburg

Danube

Regensburg

BAVARIA

Inn

MUNICH

Isar

Innsbruck

Bayreuth

Nürnberg

Bamberg

Ansbach

Rain
Lech

Augsburg

Donauwörth
Wertingen
Günzburg

Ulm
Elchingen
Kempten

BERNADOTTE

Iller

Würzburg

Hall

MARMONT

Memmingen

Biberach

Main

Danube

Stockach

Frankfurt

Neckar

Mainz

Mannheim

Speyer

DAVOUT

Haguenau
LANNES
SOULT
Strasbourg

Sélestat
NEY

Rhine

FRANCE

SWITZERLAND

This plan only made sense if Napoleon expected the Austrians to allow him the time to effect a junction of his armies in the middle of Bavaria. He certainly would not have run the risk of trying to join his forces in the face of an Austrian army advancing rapidly across the Inn and through Munich.[10] Napoleon obviously thought it possible that he would have to face not only an Austrian army to his southeast but also a Russian army coming out of Bohemia; he would have been exposing Marmont and Bernadotte to attack from two directions by overwhelming forces without hope of reinforcement. As soon as he understood how advanced the coalition preparations were and how rapidly his enemies intended to move, Napoleon changed his plans.[11]

Even as he was giving the orders for this initial disposition, Napoleon recognized that he had underestimated the Austrians. He wrote to Talleyrand, "I would not have believed the Austrians so determined; but I have been fooled so many times in my life that I do not blush about it."[12] Accordingly, he began thinking about shifting the junction point of the two armies to the north, which meant moving the concentration areas for the five corps of the right wing farther down the Rhine. Napoleon could not have been thinking in late August about encircling the Austrian army at or near Ulm, or anywhere in Bavaria for that matter, since he clearly had no idea of what the Austrian plans actually were. If he had intended to draw the enemy onto the territory of his ally, moreover, he would not have ordered the elector to prepare 500,000 biscuits at Ulm. He must have changed his plan when he understood that the Austrians had stolen a march on him and he could not count on uniting his forces in central Bavaria.*

At the beginning of September, Napoleon ordered a new set of concentration areas for his corps on the Rhine. Bernadotte and Marmont would still concentrate at Würzburg, and there is an indication that Napoleon intended Bernadotte to link up with the Bavarian forces on the Danube at Donauwörth.[13] Davout's corps would now concentrate at Speyer, however; Soult between Landau and Wissembourg; Ney at Haguenau; Lannes at Brumath; and the guard and grenadiers at Strasbourg, where the imperial headquarters was to be established. Murat, now designated Napoleon's lieutenant, empowered to take command in the emperor's absence, also took command of the Cavalry Corps, spread out from Sélestat to Strasbourg.

---

*Alombert-Goget and Colin, *La campagne de 1805,* 1:166–170. We know that Napoleon intended to unite the two wings of his army from Berthier to Bernadotte, 28 August 1805, in Alombert-Goget and Colin, *La campagne de 1805,* pp. 367–369, among others. Against this interpretation must be set Berthier's assurance to Bernadotte on 5 September that the Austrians were not ready to advance. Perhaps Napoleon did not communicate his change of mind concerning the Austrian danger to Berthier. There was no need for him to do so while simply laying out the new plans for initial dispositions. Berthier was far too busy drafting routes of march for 200,000 men to think about what the change in orders might mean. Berthier to Bernadotte, 5 September 1805, in Alombert-Goget and Colin, *La campagne de 1805,* 1:436.

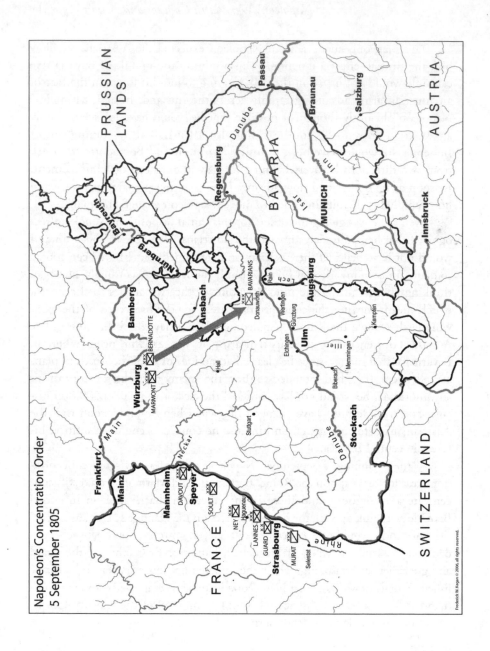

Napoleon's Concentration Order
5 September 1805

PRUSSIAN LANDS

AUSTRIA

BAVARIA

Passau

Braunau

Salzburg

Danube

Inn

MUNICH

Innsbruck

Regensburg

Isar

Bayreuth

Nürnberg

Bamberg

Ansbach

BAVARANS

Donauwörth

Rain

Lech

Augsburg

Wertingen

Günzburg

Ulm

Elchingen

Kempten

BERNADOTTE

Würzburg

MARMONT

Hall

Memmingen

Iller

Biberach

Main

Stuttgart

Danube

Stockach

Neckar

Frankfurt

Mainz

Mannheim

DAVOUT

Speyer

SOULT

NEY

Haguenau

LANNES

GUARD

Strasbourg

MURAT

Selestat

Rhine

FRANCE

SWITZERLAND

This new deployment reduced the gap between the left wing and the center to about ninety miles. It also allowed the Grande Armée to use the roads leading from Mannheim and Karlsruhe into northern Bavaria, whereas the previous plan would have constrained three corps (Davout, Soult, and Lannes) and the guards and grenadiers all to take the roads that led from Strasbourg into central Bavaria. This consideration may have been paramount. Napoleon may have realized the traffic jam in Baden he would have created with his initial deployment and sought to allow the different corps to use different lines of march, which this new plan permitted. Since this aim was fully compatible with the aim of moving the left wing of the army closer to the forces of the center, it is likely that Napoleon had both goals in mind—and it is possible that the change of plan had nothing to do with his perception of the Austrian movements.

However that may be, Napoleon had positioned himself superbly to react to any of a series of Austrian and Russian moves. When they had concentrated, his forces would cover an arc from Sélestat to Würzburg. If the Austrians advanced toward the south in order to threaten Swabia and Switzerland, Napoleon was ideally positioned to concentrate on their northern flank. If they advanced toward Strasbourg and Heidelberg, Napoleon could attack them on three sides. If Russian troops advanced out of Bohemia while the Austrians advanced into Bavaria, Napoleon could detach two and maybe three corps to deal with the Russians while concentrating three or more corps against the Austrians. And if, as Napoleon initially hoped, the Austrians were slow to advance, this formation would have allowed Napoleon to concentrate all of his forces against them at any of a large number of points inside Bavaria or on her frontiers. This was a concentration plan that kept all of Napoleon's options open and allowed him the greatest possible flexibility to respond to the enemy's movements. Moreover, it left him in a superb position to take advantage of any mistakes his enemy might make.

Italy

Napoleon always intended Italy to be a subsidiary theater during the war of 1805. For some time he feared that the Austrians might make a rapid attack in great force and sweep his troops all the way back to Piedmont. He was also concerned that the queen of Naples would allow the Russians and British to make a large landing in her domains, which might place the armies of Italy between two fires. Once again he made his initial dispositions to deal with these worst-case scenarios, but he rapidly modified those plans as he came to understand the intentions and capabilities of his enemies.

Whereas Napoleon had clearly begun developing plans for the contingency of a war in Germany in late July, he does not seem to have carefully considered the situation in Italy until nearly a month later. The main reason for this delay probably lay in Napoleon's understanding of the relationship between the two theaters. The emperor believed that his successes in Germany would first force the Austrians to strip their army in Italy of a considerable number of troops in order to defend Vienna and then force them to withdraw altogether from any successes they might have obtained on the peninsula. The only problem he saw at first was how to ensure that his armies held as far east as possible and were not destroyed before his forces in Germany came to their rescue.

Napoleon's initial plan in Italy consisted of three parts. Marshal Masséna, whom he sent to the Kingdom of Italy to replace Marshal Jourdan as overall commander in the north, would seize the Austrian part of Verona and then take up a defensive position on the Adige. He would try to hold the main Austrian army there until Napoleon had defeated the allies in Germany.[14] General Gouvion Saint Cyr, who commanded the French forces in Naples, was to stage a lightning strike against the court of Naples, depose the current rulers, disarm the army, and establish a French regency there. When he had accomplished that mission, Saint Cyr was to assume a defensive posture against any subsequent Anglo–Russian landing.[15] To support these movements Napoleon sent the French forces in Piedmont, Genoa, Corsica, and the Kingdom of Italy to the Adige, and all of the forces of the Kingdom of Italy itself to Saint Cyr's army at Pescara.[16]

Napoleon contemplated the possibility that his armies in Italy would be beaten and driven back. He ordered Berthier and Eugène to provision and arm fortresses far to the west, including Turin and Alessandria.[17] He told Saint Cyr that he did not necessarily expect him to be able to hold off a Russo-British force but wanted him to delay it for as long as possible in order to "give time to the armies of Germany and Italy to send you numerous and powerful reinforcements."[18] He admitted that Saint Cyr's activities in dethroning the rulers of Naples were "of little utility for the general operations." By holding off an Anglo–Russian expedition, however, he "would prevent or considerably delay their junction with the Austrian army on the Adige."

The emperor continued to outline his general concept of the overall plan to Saint Cyr, presumably to reassure him, since his army was in the most precarious position of any of the forces detached from Napoleon's main body in Germany. "The great blows will be struck in Germany," he wrote,

> where the Emperor will go in person, and the operations of the Army of Italy, even if they have no success, should not influence yours at all. The enemy could be at Milan and you should nevertheless remain in Naples; because his success, if he obtains any, will be only of short duration and an ephemeral chimera. If the Emperor's operations are crowned with the success that one has the right to expect, their first result will be to release

Italy, 1803-1805

HABSBURG EMPIRE

FRANCE

Rhone

Trient

Udine
Gorz

Vicenza
Verona
Mantua Legnago
Trieste

Milan

KINGDOM OF ITALY

Turin

Po

Venice

Alessandria

Par

Pa

Genoa

Nice

Arno

Florence

TUSCANY

PAPAL

STATES

CORSICA
(FRANCE)

Tiber

Rome

NAPLES
(KINGDOM OF
THE TWO SICILIES)

Naples

Taranto

SARDINIA

KINGDOM OF THE TWO SICILIES

the Army of Italy and to send you the help you will need to throw the allied forces into the sea, retake all the lands that you will have lost, and
even threaten Sicily.

He reiterated a similar reassurance to Eugène: "I will occupy the enemy in
Germany so that he will not have the time to lose fussing with you in Italy."[19]
Success in Germany, for Napoleon, was the key to success in Italy, and he believed that nothing the Austrians could achieve in Italy would affect the outcome of the war, or even his operations in Germany, in the least.

Consequently Napoleon had little to fear in Italy. His commander in
charge of the main army there, Marshal Masséna, had fought under Napoleon
in northern Italy in 1796–1797 and had defeated a combined Austro–Russian
army under Field Marshal Suvorov at Zurich in 1799. The emperor selected
him because of his skills and achievements and his knowledge of the geography of northern Italy.[20] He ordered the major forts to be prepared for a long
siege and reinforced the troops defending the area. Above all, he did not fear a
reverse in that area.

It is all the more revealing, therefore, that Napoleon himself determined
the initial deployments of the Army of Italy and designated its first operations
in detail, writing from Paris days before his armies finished their assembly on
the Rhine for the advance into Germany.[21] Napoleon knew the terrain and situation as well or better than his marshal did, and there is no reason to suppose
that Masséna would have developed a plan any better or worse than the one
Napoleon came up with. The emperor, however, had personal command of a
vast and complex movement of forces, and he had to run a large empire and
conduct various diplomatic initiatives designed to support the war at the same
time. From the standpoint of focusing his energies on the most important
tasks, it was a mistake for him to micromanage a campaign hundreds of miles
away. It reflected his commitment to that style of command and Italy's continuing importance to him.

The plan that Napoleon developed in mid-September took advantage of
the fact that there were relatively few possible routes for an Austrian advance
into French Italy from the borders of that time. He dismissed the idea that the
Austrians would attempt to march through the rough terrain of the Trentino
to the north of Lake Garda. Their advance was bounded by the southern tip of
that lake on the right and by the Adriatic on the left, which formed a maneuver corridor only seventy-five miles wide.

Napoleon ordered Masséna to prepare to cut holes in the Adige dikes near
Legnago and flood the lower Adige region. Legnago had a large garrison with
provisions to last for a yearlong siege. When Masséna took the Austrian portion of Verona, the Austrians would have to move through the twenty-five-
mile gap between Verona and Legnago, while the French would be able to

attack them on both flanks. Napoleon was confident that Masséna's forces, although initially outnumbered, would be able to hold off the Austrian advance. He wrote to his marshal that the Austrians had already begun marching their forces in the Trentino north toward Innsbruck. He was sure that they would begin pulling other troops from Italy when they learned of his movements in Germany. "Win me some victories," he concluded.[22]

Naples and Hanover: Calculated Risk

Napoleon's strategy with regard to Naples and Hanover seems foolish at first glance. In both cases he relied on treaties that had not been ratified or were meaningless, but he pulled his troops out nevertheless. The result, not surprisingly, was that Prussian troops occupied Hanover in October 1805 and an Anglo–Russian army landed in Naples in late November.

In reality, Napoleon's strategy in northern Germany and southern Italy was sound. He firmly believed that success in war required concentrating the greatest possible force at the decisive point. Such an approach requires accepting risks elsewhere, and Napoleon excelled at balancing those risks with the expected benefits of success in the main theaters. We have already seen how Napoleon explicitly accepted the risk that the Army of Italy would be driven back into Piedmont. He did so in the conviction that the success of the Grande Armée in Germany and on the Danube would render any such Austrian successes ephemeral and meaningless. The same sound belief undergirded his policy in Hanover and Naples. Whatever the British, Russians, Neapolitans, or Prussians did in those two areas, he rightly reasoned, would be irrelevant in the situation that prevailed after he destroyed the Third Coalition's main forces. The apparent risks he accepted in Naples and Hanover were neither more nor less than the risks he took in commanding the Grande Armée along the Danube.

Naples

Napoleon's plans for dealing with Naples evolved with his changing perception of a changing situation. Initially he intended for Saint Cyr to seize the fortresses and court of Naples in a lightning raid/coup-d'état. Napoleon hoped that Saint Cyr would forestall the expected Anglo–Russian landings in southern Italy or delay the advance of those armies up the Italian peninsula.[23] He subsequently ordered Villeneuve to take the united Franco–Spanish fleets from Cadiz and Cartagena to Naples to deliver reinforcements to Saint Cyr, seize British and Russian ships in that port, and raid allied shipping, especially in and around Malta.[24] Napoleon clearly aimed to secure southern Italy and thereby protect the right flank of Masséna's army operating to the north.

Napoleon changed his mind in response to a problem and an opportunity. The problem arose from the fact that Saint Cyr was far from sanguine about his ability to carry out Napoleon's orders. The Neapolitans, he wrote, had surrounded his force with spies so that there was no hope of moving undetected. In fact, he wrote, the government of Naples "has employed all means to prevent that which one wishes to undertake today." It had armed the civilian population and strongly garrisoned its fortresses. He also feared that the Russian troops at Corfu and the British at Malta, the size of which he greatly exaggerated, would fall on him before he completed his operations against Naples. He hoped to convince Napoleon to change his plan, although he promised, if so ordered, to undertake the operation even with little confidence in its success.[25]

The opportunity to abandon such a doubtful plan emerged as the result of the confused diplomacy of the Neapolitan court. Although Queen Maria Carolina did everything in her power to bring Naples into an alliance with Russia and Britain, she was constrained by the presence of 20,000 French soldiers in her realm. For months, she had been pressing the Neapolitan ambassador to France, the Marquis de Gallo, to persuade Napoleon to withdraw his troops. The Neapolitan pleas became more urgent following the earthquake of July 26, 1805, which killed several thousand people and caused enormous property damage.

Napoleon had instructed his ambassador in Naples, Alquier, to make a treaty that would keep Naples neutral and thereby secure southern Italy without fighting. Alquier, watching the bellicose preparations and receiving a constant stream of intelligence about the Neapolitans' intentions to welcome the British and Russian troops and ships, found these instructions almost silly. There was no way, he believed, that the Neapolitans would sign a neutrality treaty, or any sort of treaty, with France.[26] He would have made his prediction with even greater confidence had he known that the Neapolitans signed a treaty with Russia on September 10 in which the Russians promised to come to their assistance if the French troops in Naples moved beyond their current cantonments, and the Neapolitans promised to support a subsequent Anglo–Russian move toward northern Italy.[27] Alquier was surely astounded to learn in early October that the Neapolitans had signed a neutrality treaty with France.

It seems certain that part of the reason for this turnabout was Neapolitan underhandedness. Having repulsed Alquier's offers to negotiate a neutrality treaty in mid-September, the Neapolitans approached the French ambassador less than a week later asking to begin precisely such negotiations.[28] The French ambassador believed that the reason for the change of heart was news that the combined Franco–Spanish fleet was to leave Cadiz for the Mediterranean. Maria Carolina and her court were bargaining for time.

That desire to bargain for time may have led the queen to write Gallo on September 15, begging him once again to find a way to get the French out of her realm. If so, her note had an unintended consequence. The Marquis of Gallo was an ambassador of the overly dramatic, self-important variety. When he received Maria Carolina's letter, he threw himself into a negotiation with Talleyrand that resulted in the signing of a Franco–Neapolitan treaty on September 22.[29]

According to that treaty, Naples promised to maintain the strictest neutrality, barring all foreign troops from her soil and all foreign warships from her ports. Additionally, Napoleon insisted that the Neapolitans promise not to place their armies under command of a foreigner, not to recognize the British possession of Malta except with his permission, and not to return the former prime minister, Lord Acton, back to power. Gallo was wise enough to know that he had greatly exceeded his instructions and signed the treaty merely *sub spe rati*. He had nevertheless placed his own court in an untenable position.

Napoleon seized on Gallo's overtures as a way to escape from the problem Saint Cyr described. He wanted to neutralize southern Italy but did not want to risk his army there. His messenger carrying the signed treaty to Naples for ratification also carried instructions to Alquier and Saint Cyr that ensured a rapid end to the game. If the Neapolitan court did not ratify the treaty within forty-eight hours of receiving it, then Saint Cyr was to stage his coup d'état immediately. If the Neapolitans ratified it promptly, then Saint Cyr was to set off immediately to join Masséna.[30] The Neapolitans were to be informed more or less directly of the consequences of failing to ratify the treaty.

The Neapolitan royal couple was less than thrilled with this treaty. Its terms trampled on their sovereignty by restricting their ability to appoint commanders and political leaders. It did not actually contradict the Russo–Neapolitan treaty of September 10, which would only come into force if the French troops in Naples moved beyond their current boundaries. Maria Carolina, however, had clearly intended to go beyond the stated terms of that treaty and actively promote an Anglo–Russian landing in her country. The French neutrality treaty vitiated that intention and left the Neapolitans potentially compromised in the eyes of their allies.[31]

They therefore attempted to drag out the ratification process, hoping to delay until the Anglo–Russian force was ready to assist them. Alquier would have none of it, as he had been instructed, and demanded his passport when the deadline had come and gone. The Neapolitans refused, and he threatened to complain to Napoleon (and presumably also to Saint Cyr, who was better positioned to render immediate assistance).[32] Maria Carolina was forced to concede, and the ratifications were duly exchanged on October 8.[33]

The Neapolitans wasted no time in making clear their intention to violate the treaty they had just signed. On the same day ratifications were exchanged, the Neapolitan court addressed to the Russian ambassador a formal note annulling the neutrality treaty.[34] It claimed, not entirely without justice, that Napoleon's threat to seize Naples if they refused to sign constituted duress and invalidated the treaty. The real reason, however, was also made clear: "His Sicilian Majesty awaits with impatience the arrival in his Estates of the Russian and English troops, with the support of which he hopes, with God's aid, not only to free his Estates from the French troops that are there now, but to bar the entry to them for the future." This statement went beyond the treaty of September 10, which foresaw a landing only if the French moved beyond their current bounds. It revealed the depth of the Neapolitan commitment to the allied cause. Planning for the landing and subsequent operations continued without abatement, even as the neutrality treaty was negotiated and ratified. The Neapolitans did not disclose their annulment of the treaty to Napoleon.

The French emperor implemented his commitments under the treaty at once. He had ordered Saint Cyr to leave Naples as soon as the treaty was ratified, and his general obeyed. Saint Cyr began making preparations to leave as soon as he had heard of the ratification, and by the end of October French troops were out of Naples and on their way north.[35] This fact played an important role in the decisions of Archduke Charles when he learned of it, as we shall see. It also meant that the Russo–British landing could take place in mid-November without facing resistance or risk.

Was Napoleon duped by the Neapolitans? It seems unlikely. He hated Maria Carolina and saw in her an implacable foe determined to assist his enemies. It had to occur to him that her signature on a neutrality treaty might not bind her actions against him. In truth, he was probably setting up another complicated set of contingencies, all of which could suit him. If the Neapolitans adhered to the treaty against all odds and expectations, so much the better. If they did not and an Anglo–Russian force landed in Naples, Saint Cyr could still move south and fight a delaying action covering the Army of Italy's right flank. In the worst case, that landing would force the Army of Italy to withdraw to the west, but even that withdrawal would be temporary and would be erased as soon as Napoleon was in a position to dictate peace from Vienna.

In the meantime, the treaty gave diplomatic cover to the withdrawal of Saint Cyr's corps and extricated Napoleon from a potentially tricky situation. Saint Cyr had convinced him that the coup d'état he had planned was unwise and dangerous. In that case, the continued presence of French troops in Naples only exposed those troops to potential disaster. Removing them became an important positive goal.

In the end, Napoleon was balancing risks. Saint Cyr might have been able to take down the Neapolitan government and seize the fortresses, thereby preventing a successful Anglo–Russian landing. He also might have failed to accomplish that goal and taken significant losses while trying. By withdrawing his force, Napoleon increased the likelihood of a landing but ensured that Saint Cyr would be able to fight (if it became necessary) on terms of his choosing amid a population that was not already armed and hostile.

Napoleon may finally have come to the conclusion that the goal of preventing an Anglo–Russian landing in Naples was not worth any risk at all. It is a long march from Naples to the Adige or to Piedmont, for that matter. Napoleon could be in Vienna long before any Anglo–Russian force might make its way to anywhere important, let alone defeat the French armies it found there. The danger of the success of that expedition was simply not great enough to justify risking Saint Cyr's army. The neutrality treaty was probably cover for a withdrawal that Napoleon had already decided to order.

The notion that the neutrality treaty was little more than cover for extricating Saint Cyr's army from a difficult position is strengthened by the fact that Napoleon apparently did not inform either Masséna or Eugène of the treaty or of Saint Cyr's movements. Saint Cyr's force did not take part in Masséna's struggle with Charles nor does it appear that Napoleon intended it to. It remained deployed along the southern border of the Kingdom of Italy, effectively covering the flank of Masséna's army from that more secure position but doing little else. Napoleon abandoned his original intention of securing southern Italy and left it to a more propitious moment—after he defeated the Third Coalition.

Hanover

If Napoleon's policy in Naples was based on a sophisticated understanding of his enemies, his policy in Hanover was based on confusion. Napoleon completely misunderstood Prussia's king and his policies throughout 1805 and consequently made two potentially costly mistakes. In August he ordered Bernadotte to abandon the electorate of Hanover before obtaining Frederick William's adherence to a Franco–Prussian treaty, and he sent Bernadotte marching through the Prussian territory of Ansbach without so much as a by-your-leave from the Prussian king. These political errors not only led to a potentially dangerous situation in 1805 but sowed the seeds of the war of 1806 as well.

Napoleon had good reason to be confused about Frederick William's aims and intentions. The emperor's August 23 decision to go to war against Austria came just before the climax of the negotiations in Berlin. As we have seen, Frederick William had been inclined to adhere to the proposed French treaty, supported by all of his advisers except for Haugwitz, who had been excluded from the discussions of this matter.[36] Laforest had duly noted the positive leanings of the Prussian court in a note of August 14, which Talleyrand received not later than August 25.[37] On August 22, however, Haugwitz finally weighed in with a lengthy memorandum assaulting the proposed alliance and firmly recommending that the king continue to abide by his previous neutrality policy. As Napoleon was deciding how to proceed in his war against Austria, he had every reason to believe that Frederick William had been persuaded to become allied with him, even though the bureaucratic wheels had been set in motion that would lead the Prussian king to make the opposite decision.

Why did Napoleon order Bernadotte to march out of Hanover, through Ansbach, and into Bavaria? It was certainly not to outflank an Austrian army that had not yet crossed the Inn. Napoleon did not even have a clear idea of its plans, as we have seen. One reason was his desire to concentrate the maximum available combat power at the decisive place and time. But another likely reason for this fateful decision was political: Napoleon felt it necessary to get tangible support to the elector of Bavaria as rapidly as possible.

The protracted negotiations for a Franco–Bavarian treaty, described above, were marked by the enthusiasm of the elector's minister, Montgelas, and the reluctance of the elector himself.[38] The final form of the treaty had been established on July 28, but ratifications were not exchanged until August 24, owing in part to the elector's hesitancy. As the date approached when he would have to commit himself formally to the alliance, the elector became even more fearful. The French ambassador in Munich, Otto, reported shortly after the exchange of ratifications that the elector had nearly decided to break off the negotiation entirely:

> He told me "that his Country was open on all sides, that the troops of Bohemia would invade the Upper Palatinate and Franconia, those of Austria and the Tyrol Bavaria, those of Vorarlberg Swabia, that his army would be made prisoners of war before the French Army could arrive on the Rhine, that if we had only 20,000 men at Strasbourg and as many at Mainz, that he could still have the hope of saving at least part of his forces, but that he saw with the greatest chagrin that he would be completely ruined before we could set foot in Swabia, that he owed it to his people and his family not to play such a dangerous game, and that he was persuaded that His Majesty the Emperor would render justice to his intentions."[39]

Otto managed to overcome these fears, pointing out mainly that Bavaria would hardly be in a better position if she alienated France and had no friend in the world at all. He also found it necessary to soothe the elector's fears over Prussia's attitude: "I know ... that nothing in the world could engage the Elector of Bavaria to arm against Prussia and that he would sooner renounce his relations with France than his devotion for a Prince whom he regards with reason as the chief of his party in Germany." Otto induced the elector to ratify the treaty, but the French ambassador remained concerned about what Bavaria might do if there seemed to be a Franco–Prussian rift or if things did not go well militarily.

This was not the first time the Bavarians had emphasized their concerns for the safety of their electorate. The final treaty included an article the elector had insisted on binding Napoleon to support his army if the Austrians "temporarily" dispossessed him.[40] Bernadotte's corps (and to a lesser extent Marmont's) represented the only military force at Napoleon's disposal that could intervene rapidly in Bavaria. Napoleon did not believe that Austrian preparations for invasion were as far advanced as they proved to be, but he could not in any case have believed that Bernadotte, Marmont, and the Bavarian army could stop the Austrian army from crossing the Inn. They could have received a retreating Bavarian army, though, and protected it while the main body of the Grande Armée arrived.

Napoleon had already ordered Bernadotte and Marmont to concentrate their corps at Würzburg, which the elector of Bavaria held, as part of his original plan to meet the Austrians as far east as possible. His initial orders did not specify an objective for those corps after they had reached Würzburg. Shortly after receiving word of the ratification of the Franco–Bavarian treaty, however, Napoleon sent Bernadotte new instructions. The elector, he wrote, had just decided to put 25,000 troops at Napoleon's disposal. If the Austrians attacked, he would withdraw that force through Donauwörth to link up with Bernadotte's corps.[41] The Army of Hanover had become a receiving force to cover the withdrawal of the Bavarians in the face of an Austrian attack.

It surely did not escape Napoleon that having a powerful force of two French corps, strengthened by the addition of the Bavarian army, so far to the east created all sorts of strategic opportunities, depending on what the Austrians and the Russians did. But since his initial plan called for a rapid advance across the Palatinate ending in an arc from Ulm to Wießenburg, in which the Hanoverian and Bavarian armies constituted the left wing of a relatively concentrated force fronting Munich, it does not appear that he initially intended to take much advantage of the eastward deployment of those forces.

It seems most likely that Napoleon ordered Bernadotte to abandon Hanover partly to support his wavering but critical ally in Munich and partly in order to concentrate the maximum possible combat power against his main enemy in what he conceived to be the decisive theater. The result of that decision was to leave Hanover at the mercy of the Prussians if they did not end up allying with France, but Napoleon did not fear that outcome.

In the first place, when he gave the initial orders he believed that the signing of a Franco–Prussian treaty was imminent. Even when the Prussians seemed to be wavering, it did not occur to Napoleon that they would go over to the allies wholeheartedly. He wrote to Talleyrand on September 12 that Frederick William might not have the courage to stand by his earlier determination to sign the proposed treaty. In that case Napoleon wished to revert to an earlier form of the treaty whereby Prussia would take Hanover *en dépôt* during the war in return for an annual payment of 6 million francs.[42] He did not imagine that he might find himself confronted with a Prussia joined to the coalition against him that might then seize Hanover with the intention of holding it or even restoring it to Britain.

Napoleon did, however, consider the possibility that Prussia might refuse the treaty and that the British might take the opportunity to reconquer their lost territory. He intended to leave only 3,000 men in the fortress of Hameln, so that "Prussia's refusal can only cost me 3,000 men." And "if 30 or 40,000 English come to besiege it, you know how fortunate that would be. Frederick went well and rapidly from Prague to Rosbach [sic]."[43]

This statement, recalling the extremely rapid operational movements that characterized Frederick the Great's fighting in the Seven Years War, reflects yet another contingency that Napoleon apparently was willing to consider. If the British put a large land force on the continent, the emperor might have been willing to abandon the march to Vienna, still more the subsequent drive to support his armies in Italy, in order to defeat the land forces of his main enemy. Whether he would actually have done so in a given concrete situation is another question entirely, but this statement shows the extraordinary flexibility of Napoleon's mind—as well as his unremitting fixation on Britain as his principal foe.

If the decision to abandon Hanover reflected a calculated risk, the decision to send Bernadotte's corps through the Prussian territory of Ansbach without Frederick William's permission resulted from a political error. This march, ordered first on September 22, primarily reflected the fact that Napoleon was deceived about Frederick William's intentions toward him. Ansbach was a territory of moderate size that straddled the roads from Würzburg and Mannheim/Heidelberg toward Munich. It might have been possible to devise routes of march that skirted this outlying Prussian territory, sending the forces from Würzburg through Nürnberg and those from Mannheim/Heidelberg through Stuttgart. Such routes would have forced too many corps onto too few roads, and would also have maintained a wide gap between the left flank of the army and the center even as the army attempted to concentrate in the face of an anticipated Austrian advance. Those were the military reasons to march through Ansbach.

Could Napoleon have anticipated the reaction to the march in Berlin? Certainly not at the beginning of September, when he imagined that he was on the verge of signing an alliance with Prussia. By September 19, however, three days before he ordered Bernadotte to cross Ansbach, Napoleon had already begun considering the necessity of allowing Prussia to remain neutral, and he began to make dispositions with Talleyrand to that end.[44]

This decision reflected the news Napoleon was receiving from Duroc in Berlin. On September 3, Napoleon's envoy reported that the going was hard but he hoped to persuade the king to make a real treaty. By September 8, he wrote that he would likely have to return to France without accomplishing his objective. The Prussian army, he wrote, would be delighted to fight the Austrians, happy to fight the French, but miserable to fight the Russians. On September 19 he reported that "we have the assurance that for the moment one cannot hope to lead the King to a treaty of offensive and defensive alliance that might require him to wage war." Prussian neutrality was the best they could hope for.[45] The leitmotif of these reports was Frederick William's fear of war, especially war against Russia.

Duroc feared the consequences of Bernadotte's march through Ansbach as he was reporting the likely failure of his mission, and he attempted to offer Napoleon an alternative. At the end of August, Napoleon had informed him of his intention to concentrate Bernadotte's corps at Würzburg, although he gave no hint of its ultimate destination.[46] Duroc then considered its possible future movements. If Bernadotte's army moved from Hanover through Würzburg, Schweinfurt, and Bamberg, then *between* Ansbach and Bayreuth to Sulzbach and Amberg, it would be in upper Bavaria "facing Bohemia and closer to the Inn and the threatened frontiers." If it remained at Würzburg, however, "it would be obliged in order to arrive [at those frontiers] to cross Ansbach or, if not, to move into Swabia and behind Bavaria."[47] Duroc, knowing his master well, was trying to persuade him not to make an important political error.

Napoleon rejected Duroc's advice and drafted an order to Bernadotte to cross Ansbach within hours of receiving Duroc's message.[48] Perhaps Napoleon was infuriated by the Prussian king's refusal to make an alliance with him, which was the main news conveyed by Duroc's letter. In his usual black-and-white view of the world, it did not occur to Napoleon that Frederick William might remain neutral. In transports of anger, Napoleon and those around him must have hinted darkly around this time that Frederick William was surely preparing to go over to the other side.[49] Some even argue that Napoleon intentionally traversed Prussian territory in order to force Frederick William to make a decision, trusting in the clear benefits France had to offer to tip the scales in Napoleon's favor even though he was the one to violate Prussia's neutrality.[50]

These calculations reflected a fundamental failure to understand Frederick William and his position. Napoleon knew that the king feared war and feared the Russians above all. He knew that the Russians had mobilized an army on Prussia's eastern frontier. As September went on, he learned that Frederick

William was determined to maintain a policy of strict neutrality and was running risks with the Russians in order to do so. His march through Prussian territory in those circumstances could not fail to compromise Frederick William badly in the eyes of the Russians. His failure to seek permission for the march insulted and humiliated a monarch who was desperately trying to preserve the dignity of his state. Napoleon's belief that Frederick William was a cowardly worm was incorrect, and it led him to make ill-advised decisions.

Even had he understood Frederick William perfectly, of course, Napoleon might still have ordered Bernadotte across Ansbach. The military exigencies of that movement were pressing, and Napoleon learned so late of Frederick William's change of heart that he would have found it difficult to disrupt the plans he was developing, which had been based initially on the assumption of Prussia's support. There is no evidence, however, that Napoleon went through this thought process or anything like it. He does not seem to have attempted to see the world from Frederick William's perspective, contenting himself with the conviction that the Prussian king was simply a timid rabbit that shied away from any danger real or fancied. It did not occur to him that Frederick William was as concerned with the honor of his kingdom as with its security—indeed that he saw the two issues as inseparably intertwined—and that, dishonored by Napoleon's brusque destruction of his neutrality system, he would find it necessary to ally himself with Napoleon's enemies. Napoleon might reasonably have come to the same decision even had he contemplated the situation carefully, but it was astonishing that he allowed himself to run risks without considering their magnitude. After all, one might well ask if the military advantages of taking the road through Ansbach were really worth bringing the 200,000-strong Prussian army into the field against France.

This decision, as well as the prior determination to abandon Hanover before signing a treaty with Prussia, reflected a certain shortsightedness in Napoleon's thought process. He recognized that he might lose Hanover temporarily but decided to leave that problem to another day in order to pursue his immediate goals. Perhaps emboldened by the fact that the Prussian army was only being mobilized in September and would not be ready to fight for some time, Napoleon did not trouble to consider the possible effects of crossing Ansbach. He would have plenty of time to deal with any repercussions that might emerge from that decision. In the short run, Napoleon's belief that he would be able to deal with the long-term consequences of his actions only when those bills were presented later would prove well founded, as we shall see. Eventually those long-term consequences built up to a level beyond what even Napoleon could handle.

For now, however, Napoleon's plans on the continent were set. He would pull out of Naples and cease to concern himself with the danger of an Anglo–Russian landing there. He would pull out of Hanover and trust to his skill and success to ensure that he could retake it if the Prussians seized it in his absence.

He justified those risks in the name of concentrating his forces against the main enemy in Italy but especially in Germany, where Napoleon hoped to strike the decisive blow that would shatter the coalition once and for all. As late as mid-September Napoleon still did not know what that blow would look like, exactly. He had given orders to concentrate his army in an advantageous position from which he would strike as the enemy's movements and the circumstances suggested. Even after the armies were well in motion, Napoleon's plans remained fluid while his intention remained fixed. That combination of fluidity and fixedness gave Napoleon a great advantage throughout the subsequent war.

The War at Sea

Napoleon's thoughts did not stop at the coastline, even as he prepared plans for his armies across the continent. Since the dispositions he made for his fleets in September 1805 led directly to the Battle of Trafalgar, with all its world-changing consequences, the history of the wars of this period cannot stop at the coastline either.

Napoleon recognized a grand strategic dead end when he saw one. Villeneuve's movement to Cadiz, combined with Napoleon's turning of the Grande Armée to the east, put paid to any notion of a rapid invasion of England. Napoleon did not waste time trying to convince himself that it was otherwise (although he did waste a fair amount of time inveighing against Villeneuve's timidity and perfidy to Decrès). Neither did he immediately develop a coherent new plan using his fleet to strike at his archenemy. Instead, he developed a scheme that was entirely contingent on events that he hoped would generate unforeseen opportunities for him to exploit as they emerged.

In a lengthy memorandum to Decrès of September 13, Napoleon explained the purpose of his original maneuvers. He wanted to amass an army of 150,000 men at Boulogne, he wrote, and transport it to Britain under the cover of his fleet. Since such a plan could not be kept completely secret, he had developed a ruse. By building a vast fleet of small gunships at Boulogne and its environs, he hoped to persuade the British that he intended to cross *without* the assistance of his ships of the line, so that they would be surprised when the fleet showed up in the Channel to support the crossing.* This plan miscarried, he wrote, because Villeneuve entered Ferrol instead of moving briskly to join the fleet waiting there to his and sailing at once for the Channel. At the same

---

*Napoleon to Decrès, 13 September 1805, *Corr. de Nap.*, doc. 9209. This description of the earlier plan is a distortion. Napoleon had clearly intended to use the flotilla initially to cover a crossing without the participation of the battle fleet. He had changed his mind when he realized the futility of that endeavor. It is interesting that Napoleon would try to rewrite the history of his own decisions privately and to the one man who could know for sure that he was being deceived.

time, the failure of this maneuver revealed the plan that had been behind it. Now the British knew that Napoleon had intended to amass a battle fleet in the Channel to cover the crossing of his invading army.

The emperor believed that he could use the revelation of his earlier plan to effect a diversion. By forming an army of 60,000–80,000 men at Boulogne and activating numerous naval, merchant, and sailing ships around that area at the moment the main battle fleet left Cadiz, Napoleon hoped to persuade the British that his original plan was still operative. In this way, he counted on forcing the British to maintain a large army ready to repel his invasion force, and to keep a large part of their fleet in reserve in the Thames or the Dunes to combat his battle line that would come to cover that invasion force.

At the same time, he ordered Villeneuve to sail from Cadiz into the Mediterranean.[51] The French battle fleet was to link up with a smaller flotilla at Cartagena and then sail to Naples, where it would disembark reinforcements for Saint Cyr's army, seize British and Russian ships in the harbor, and stage raids on a British convoy Napoleon believed was headed for Malta. Then Villeneuve was ordered to sail to Toulon. He wrote to Decrès, "The existence of so considerable a squadron at Toulon will have incalculable results; it will make an invaluable diversion for me. This is the most useful role this squadron can play for me in the present circumstances."[52]

Napoleon never specified what he expected to come of these diversions: he identified no main effort from which they would be distracting the attention of the British. Possibly he sought to keep the British from sending reinforcements to her allies on the continent, but this explanation is unlikely. His message to Duroc concerning his feelings about the possibility of a British landing in Hanover reveals the almost irrational degree to which he desired a head-to-head confrontation with a large British army.[53] It seems more likely that he was as usual setting up a chain of mutually contradictory possible courses of action.

He clearly identified one such possible course of action to Decrès: by forming a supposed "invasion" army at Boulogne, he was also forming a large reserve for operations in Germany if necessary.[54] This statement implies that Napoleon was ready, at least under some circumstances, to abandon all pretense of preparing to invade Britain in order to support his armies on the Rhine, the Inn, or farther north. It is even possible, although he makes no mention of this possibility, that Napoleon intended that reserve to meet the contingency of Prussian hostility.

Another possibility was that the presence of a new army at Boulogne would terrify the British, who finally understood the danger so narrowly averted by Villeneuve's error in judgment. The Admiralty might then concentrate so much of its forces in the home waters as to permit Napoleon's fleet in the Mediterranean, which he intended to entrust to Vice Admiral Rosily as soon as Villeneuve had landed at Toulon, to undertake more significant operations in Italy, perhaps against Malta, perhaps even against Egypt or the Balkan peninsula. If Napoleon envisaged this possibility, it was only very remotely, for he made no effort whatsoever to ready the ground forces that would be necessary for any of those operations.

He did, however, speak of landing an army in Ireland, reverting to French revolutionary schemes nearly a decade old.[55] Such a landing, he wrote, would also terrify the British, who would be compelled to mass even greater land and naval forces in England in order to forestall the subsequent movement of French troops from Ireland. It is unclear whether he seriously contemplated such a landing or whether he hoped to scare the British with the very hint of it.

It is possible, finally, that Napoleon hoped that a possibility would arise that would permit him to send the 80,000-man reserve army at Boulogne across to Dover, thereby accomplishing his original intention. He certainly discussed this possibility in greater detail than necessary while considering the fear it would throw into the British people. On the other hand, he told Decrès that it was necessary to have crews only for one-quarter of the ships of the supposed invasion fleet, in order to create the necessary verisimilitude. Nor did he issue even the most preparatory orders to Villeneuve or Decrès for the main fleet to try again to enter the Channel. If an opportunity had arisen, however faint, though, Napoleon might have sought to seize it.

Whatever his ultimate goals, the result of these orders was to send Villeneuve racing out of Cadiz to his final rendezvous with Admiral Horatio Nelson. The Battle of Trafalgar, which took place on October 21, crushed whatever possibility Napoleon had seen in naval maneuvering. His attempts to gain ground and discomfit the British, revived once again in mid-September, could have no important impact on the overall war without the support of the main battle fleet.[56] Unless and until Napoleon undertook yet again to rebuild the French navy, France had permanently lost the war at sea. The full significance of this event would not become visible until the summer of 1806, after a number of even more dramatic events had intervened.

Conclusion

Napoleon had no plan of war in 1805. He developed a number of clear objectives, a series of conceptions of how he intended to go about achieving them, and a succession of plans for individual operations that changed from day to day and even hour to hour. He did generally adhere to the principle of concentrating the greatest possible number of forces at what he hoped would be the decisive place and time. That principle, however, was far from providing a clear-cut specific program of operations.

Napoleon's preparations for war reveal a remarkable mental agility and flexibility, and an almost infinite willingness to adapt plans to changing circumstances. They also reveal a corresponding unwillingness to think the likely course of operations through to its conclusion. The initial plan for the invasion of Britain is the exception that proves the rule. Napoleon had attempted to order his admirals to crush intervening contingencies in order to make a highly complex plan work. When it failed, he reverted even in his naval operations to the most contingent plans, seeking only to create some opportunity that even he could not foresee. Pressed on this issue, Napoleon would surely have responded that he planned as far as it was reasonable to plan and relied on the superior capabilities of his brain, his staff, and his army to do better than the enemy at meeting whatever situations arose beyond that point. The subsequent course of the campaign will reveal the soundness and the weakness of this enormous self-confidence.

14

Race to the Iller

Personality can have an overwhelming impact on history. Leaders make decisions not based on a rational evaluation of precisely established data, but on their perceptions, skewed by their experiences and emotions, of data that is frequently only partly accurate. The Ulm campaign of 1805 is one of the best examples of this phenomenon. We have already seen the importance of rulers' personalities in bringing the various states of Europe to the crisis of war in August. The outcome of the opening phases of that war depended on the personalities of those rulers and their leading subordinates. Napoleon's initial offensive operation against the Austrian army, in particular, could not have had the outcome it did if the Austrian army had not been commanded, to all intents and purposes, by Mack.

Mack was not responsible for the details of the Austrian war plan or even its main outlines, since Charles had established those long before Mack was recalled to active service, as we have seen. Nor can Mack's supposed insanity alone explain the outcome of the Ulm campaign, as Habsburg historians have argued in an attempt to exonerate the monarchy and the charismatic Archduke Charles.[1] The critical decisions in this campaign, however, were peculiarly Mack's. They were the products of his distorted perspective of the world and himself.

Mack Seizes Command

Mack was not born noble.[2] His father was a civil servant in Nennslingen, a small town between Ansbach and Ingolstadt, roughly sixty miles north of Munich. He entered Austrian service at the age of eighteen as an enlisted soldier. Seven years later he was promoted to the rank of *Unterleutnant*, and in the War of the Bavarian Succession he served as adjutant to FML Kinsky. He attracted the attention of Emperor Joseph and FML Lacy through hard work and intelligence, and was promoted to the rank of captain in 1783 with an assignment to the general staff.

The turning point in Mack's career came during the Turkish War of 1788–1792. In 1789, as a lieutenant colonel attached to Field Marshal Loudon's staff, Mack planned the storming of Belgrade. Loudon had been hostile to the idea and grew even more so when he learned that a Turkish relief army was on the way. Mack begged for two days to reconnoiter this oncoming army, and Loudon consented. Accompanied by six hussars, Mack rode to the Turkish army and raced back with the report that Loudon need not concern himself with it. The field marshal was persuaded and seized Belgrade.[3]

This action won Mack the emperor's attention and great rewards. He was made colonel almost at once (eight months after being promoted to lieutenant colonel) and was awarded the Knight's Cross of the Order of Maria Theresia. In 1793 he served as quartermaster general of Prince Coburg's army during its successful attack against revolutionary France, for which he received command of a Cuirassiers Regiment. The following year he was promoted to the rank of major general in the general staff and participated, with less success, in planning the operations of 1794. Wounded in that campaign, he went into retirement for three years.

Historians frequently describe the failure of Mack's plan of 1794 and his ignominious surrender to the French following the collapse of his command over the Neapolitan army in 1798 as forerunners of the events of 1805. But Mack's earlier experiences played a greater role in shaping the character and the mind that made the pivotal decisions during the Ulm campaign.

Mack was an autodidact and a self-made man. In an era when only the most senior and established nobles could hope to rise to high rank in Austrian service, let alone command forces or influence the course of campaigns, Mack rose from common soldier to quartermaster general of the main Austrian army through his own intelligence, self-confidence, and determination. The pivotal event of his career surely reinforced his belief in his own capabilities. Loudon had opposed the storming of Belgrade and panicked at the approach of a relief force. Mack held firm in his belief and convinced his chief not to take counsel of his fears. Consequently he won not only the day but also a place for himself in the emperor's favor. This was not a man who would easily or readily consider the possibility that his evaluation of a situation was inaccurate, or that he was incapable of accomplishing any task he set for himself.

It has been suggested that Mack did not understand the limitations of the Austrian soldiers of his day because he had held a field command only briefly (the 22 months he spent as a colonel in the 3rd Light Cavalry Regiment in 1791–1792).[4] This explanation seems unlikely. We must recall that Mack spent seven years as a soldier—more than enough time to gain an appreciation for the life of soldiers and their capability on the march.

It is more likely that Mack, driven by an insatiable desire for power and recognition that he could achieve only with the greatest difficulty in the Austrian army of his day, refused to recognize limitations. He clung to illusory hopes of success and refused to consider the possibility of failure. Because of his low birth and humble standing in the glittering aristocratic ranks of the senior officers of the Austrian army, Mack must have sensed that any failure would mean the end of his influence, power, and ambition. He had already suffered failure and consequent oblivion following the failed Italian campaign of 1798. He must have clung even more desperately to his hopes of victory and vindication in the campaign of 1805, direction of which fell into his hands quite unexpectedly.

Mack's background was humbler than Napoleon's, but he rose through the ranks of a conservative army rapidly and without the assistance of a revolution. His rise had been marked by an episode similar to Napoleon's Toulon, in which he had demonstrated courage, creativity, and intelligence before a skeptical leadership that fawned on him in the wake of his success. He had Napoleon's drive for power and influence, and something of his ruthlessness. He had the same frenetic energy and frustration with obstacles in his way. He did not have Napoleon's charisma however, and so made more enemies than allies. Above all, he did not have Napoleon's coup d'oeil, intelligence, or skill.

Mack's position in 1805 was complicated by the fact that he was not actually in command of any troops. Francis had appointed him quartermaster general attached to his own imperial person, which carried no independent command authority. In principle, his role was the same as it had been in 1793 and 1794—the drafter of plans and coordinator of movements. That was not how things turned out.

Francis did not immediately take the field to command his armies in person, despite the fact that he held the nominal overall command from the outset of the campaign. Mack went forward to oversee preparations for the invasion of Bavaria in advance of his imperial master, creating a complicated situation. In principle, Mack had no authority to order a single soldier to move one foot. He should have forwarded recommendations for orders back to Francis in Vienna and awaited orders from the emperor to effect the desired movements. In practice, such a system would have been absurd, and it was not followed. Mack issued orders in his own name as if he were in command, and the Austrian generals preparing for the invasion largely followed them, especially since Archduke Ferdinand, the actual commander of the army in Germany, did not arrive to take up his command until September 20, twelve days after the Austrian armies had crossed the Inn.[5]

When Ferdinand arrived, a power struggle began. The young archduke knew his prerogatives and was not inclined to take orders from Mack, whom he disliked and distrusted. The situation became so tense that Ferdinand at one point commanded his army to stop an advance ordered by Mack. The archduke appealed to Francis, who supported Mack.*

Situations like this are not uncommon. Whenever the ruler claims to be the effective supreme military commander and allows the chief of his general staff to operate independently from him in the theater of war, tensions may arise between that chief of staff and the senior commanders, who see themselves as reporting directly to the monarch. Such a problem plagued the Russian armies operating against the Turks in 1828, the Prussian armies operating against the French in 1870, and the German armies on the Rhine in 1914.[6] This problem is endemic to military systems in which the most senior military official below the sovereign is a chief of staff rather than a commander or minister and is not merely a function of personality clashes.

Mack's personality, however, did exacerbate this situation. Mack wanted to command the army . He would probably have liked to command all of the armies, but that was clearly out of the question. So he set about establishing de facto control over the army in Germany, hoping to brush Ferdinand aside.†

His personal campaign began in earnest in mid-August. He wrote to Francis on August 15 to suggest that the emperor assume active charge of the military preparations and assign Charles the command of the army in Italy, Ferdinand the army in Germany, and John the various corps in the Tyrol and Vorarlberg. He suggested that Francis replace Charles temporarily as war minister with Colloredo (Mack's ally through his sponsor, Cobenzl), and that the emperor designate Mack as "Quartermaster General with Your Supreme Person and subordinate the other Quartermaster-Generals to me."[7] Two weeks later, Mack wrote that he "must ask to be given the authority to do everything that must be done for our defense on the Inn, at Salzburg or elsewhere."[8] Mack may even have arranged to have Ferdinand held back in Vienna until September 17, while he launched the campaign and maneuvered the armies to his liking.[9] The crisis that led to Ferdinand's appeal to Francis was primarily the result of Mack's determined effort to take advantage of the confusion in the Austrian command structure to gain an independent command for himself.

Why did Francis put up with this borderline insubordination from his aggressive, insecure quartermaster general? The emperor must have known Mack reasonably well, since they served together on Loudon's staff during the 1789 campaign against the Turks. Francis had been present during the storm

---

*That support may have been temporary and intended to alleviate the tension until Francis himself arrived to take up the reins. See below.

†Moriz Edlen von Angeli, *Erzherzog Carl von Osterreich als Feldherr und Heeresorganisator* (Vienna: Wilhelm Braumüller, 1897), pp. 442–443, sees Mack as conspiring to gain control over Austria's military from the moment Cobenzl first consulted him about war plans. There is no evidence against this thesis, although it probably credits Mack with excessive forethought and clarity of purpose.

of Belgrade that made Mack's career, and must have been aware of the attention showered on the young officer by his uncle, Emperor Joseph. There is no record, however, of how Francis felt about Mack as a person or an officer.

Whatever he felt about Mack, Francis clearly could not do without him in the fall of 1805. When the other senior military leaders had said no to war against France, Mack alone had said yes. Charles was the wrong person to be put in charge of military operations, since he had fought against the war steadfastly for more than a year. Mack was the only other senior officer deeply involved in planning for the war, and his energy had been vital to moving events forward. Any replacement other than Charles would need time to understand the situation and the context, and would probably not be as enthusiastic as Mack, who had everything to gain by success and everything to lose by failure. There was no time to change chiefs of staff, and Francis apparently did not consider it. This was the situation created by Cobenzl's ill-advised decision to reach out to Mack for guidance simply because he supported the war, without considering his actual qualifications. Mack, with his virtues and his faults, would run Austria's war effort in Germany.

The Austrian Invasion of Bavaria

Bavaria posed a complicated problem for Austria and the coalition, as we have seen. The Austrians needed to cross the electorate to get to defensive positions that would secure the Tyrolean passes, and they wished to fight on the elector's soil in order to reduce their own war costs. The Austrians would have preferred to bring the elector over to the coalition, together with his 20,000-strong army, and some versions of the coalition war plan counted Bavarian troops on the side of the allies.

But the Austrian generals were not Bavaria's dupes. Although hoping to bring the elector over, they were prepared to fight against him and were not especially dismayed by the prospect. By the end of August, Francis had set in motion a two-part plan for dealing with Bavaria. He sent the vice president of the Hofkriegsrat, Prince Karl zu Schwarzenberg, to Munich with orders to negotiate an alliance treaty with Bavaria. From the first, however, his mission was as much to find out whether the elector had yet chosen sides, and if so, how firm his decision was as to negotiate and sign an alliance treaty.[10]

The elector had just allied himself with Napoleon when Schwarzenberg arrived. Yet Schwarzenberg had a strong hand and played it well. Escorted by a hundred hussars, he sealed off the Electoral Palace in Nymphenburg from the outside for his negotiations.[11] Schwarzenberg's hand was stronger since word had reached Munich before his arrival of the movement of Austrian armies at the Inn.[12]

Elector Max Joseph was petrified. He wrote to Montgelas and other advisers trying to find a way out of the impasse. He told Schwarzenberg that he would agree to open negotiations about joining the Bavarian army to Austria's, but first he had to speak to Montgelas, who was away from Munich at the moment. The purpose of this deception apparently was to gain time, perhaps for the French army to move closer, perhaps to receive renewed promises of support from Napoleon. His efforts went so far that Schwarzenberg reported to Mack and Francis that he had succeeded, and that Max Joseph would put the Bavarian army at the disposal of the allies.[13]

The end was never in doubt. Although the Austrian menace was more immediate than any danger from France, the Austrians could not match the inducements that Napoleon had already promised. And the generations of resentment between Bavaria and Austria were too strong to be overcome in a moment. Max Joseph rejected the Austrian ultimatum, ordered his army to march north toward Würzburg and Bamberg, and set off with his family and court.[14]

The Austrians were unfazed by this development, although Max Joseph's apparent duplicity lent enthusiasm to their invasion of the electorate.[15] Even before Schwarzenberg arrived in Munich, Mack developed a plan for seizing the Bavarian capital and preparing for the advance to the Iller. On September 3, he "proposed" his plan to the emperor and began to implement it.

The Austrian army had been concentrating the forces earmarked for operations in Germany in a camp at Wels. Mack now proposed breaking the troops already in that camp into two columns. One, under the command of FML Klenau (who also had overall command of this expedition), would march to Braunau; the other, commanded by FML Gottesheim, to Schärding. On September 8, these two columns would cross the Inn. Klenau would march west toward Munich, while Gottesheim followed a more northerly road through Landshut to Freising. Both columns were to arrive at their destination by September 13.* Another body of troops was to march from Vorarlberg into western Bavaria to seize Pfullendorf and Biberach, thus cutting Munich off from the west and France.[16] Two more columns, commanded by FML Riesch, were to take the place of Klenau's departing columns at Schärding and Braunau, while still another advanced from Salzburg.[17]

Mack hoped to achieve a number of different objectives with these movements. The faster the Austrian armies moved onto Bavarian territory, he reasoned, the faster the Bavarians, and not the Austrians, would be paying to supply them. In addition, as Austrian forces continued to concentrate toward the Inn, it was important to free up space for their quarters. The invasion of Bavaria, Mack noted, was an extension of the concentration of the Austrian army. Mack was

---

*Mack to Francis, 3 September 1805, KA AFA 1805 Deutschland, IX/1. The northern column would have marched about 16.5 miles per day.

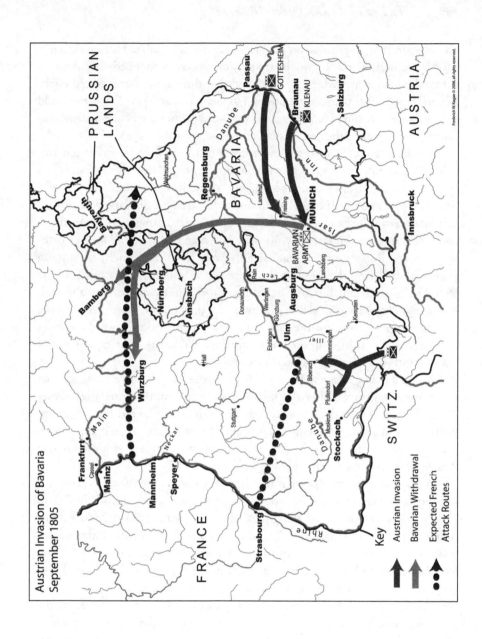

Austrian Invasion of Bavaria
September 1805

Key

Austrian Invasion

Bavarian Withdrawal

Expected French
Attack Routes

PRUSSIAN LANDS

AUSTRIA

FRANCE

SWITZ.

BAVARIA

Bayreuth

Passau

GOTTESHEIM

Braunau

KLENAU

Salzburg

Danube

Regensburg

Weidmunchen

Landshut

Freising

MUNICH

Isar

Inn

Innsbruck

BAVARIAN ARMY

Landsberg

Nürnberg

Ansbach

Bamberg

Rain

Donauwörth

Werlingen

Günzburg

Augsburg

Lech

Kempten

Würzburg

Eichingen

Ulm

Iller

Memmingen

Hall

Biberach

Pfullendorf

Main

Stuttgart

Neckar

Danube

Moskirch

Stockach

Frankfurt

Cassel

Mainz

Mannheim

Speyer

Strasbourg

Rhine

also eager to take up position on the Iller as rapidly as possible. He hoped to fortify his position there and give the troops time to rest in that defensive position before the French arrived.[18] Mack believed that these movements would establish an imposing army in a good position in Germany, and that Napoleon could not bring decisive forces to bear against that army before the final Austrian reinforcements, as well as the first Russian army, had arrived.[19]

Mack's unconcern with the movements of the Bavarian army is remarkable. That the Austrians did not fear Max Joseph's allying himself with the French was understandable. The elector's army, however, was the size of a French corps, and a substantial addition to the strength of Napoleon's forces. His mobilization of that army in his capital, Munich, presented the Austrians with an unforeseen opportunity. If Mack had marched Klenau's forces northwest toward Regensburg instead of southwest toward Munich, he stood a chance of capturing the Bavarian army, forcing it to fight, or scattering it. He would still have been able to march those forces rapidly to the Iller, although not as rapidly as he originally envisioned. As the columns were crossing the Inn, Mack gave orders for them to send detachments north toward Neuburg and Straubing, but his purpose was to drive the Bavarians more rapidly out of their country—and into Napoleon's hands.[20]

Mack did not adequately consider this issue (nor is there evidence that other Austrian generals did either). He was so fixated on the imperative of executing his plan as rapidly and decisively as possible that he did not see an opportunity to deprive the enemy of an accretion of strength when it arose. Both the Austrian occupation of Bavaria and the Bavarian linkup with the Grande Armée, therefore, took place without incident.

A final point worth noting is that from the outset, the Austrian army was broken into a number of independent combined arms units, similar to French corps, that marched along parallel roads in order to reach their destinations more rapidly and ease the burden of supplying them. This practice was not new to the Austrian army in 1805. Austrian campaigns since 1788 at least had used multiple independent all-arms forces. One of the main differences between the Austrian and French use of independent corps in 1805 was that whereas Napoleon separated his corps in order to march faster to the point where they would concentrate for a single battle, the Austrians assigned different objectives to the various corps. Although Mack saw the movements of the pieces of his army as supporting a single operational goal, he did not imagine that those pieces would necessarily concentrate at any point to fight together. This difference in the conception of the use of independent corps would play an important role in driving Mack's perceptions of the forthcoming campaign.

Although the use of independent corps was not new in the Austrian army in 1805, Mack had introduced a number of reforms immediately before it set out on this campaign, including an order to reduce the amount of baggage that accompanied the force. He even ordered Klenau's forces to leave behind a great deal of the baggage they had brought with them to Wels, stationing elderly and unfit soldiers there to guard it.[21] He aimed to increase the marching speed of the Austrian army, and he did. During the movement to the Iller line, Austrian units marched as many as twenty-five miles a day without rest days.[22]

Mack was likely seeking to replicate some of the advantages the French revolutionary armies were thought to gain from their reduced supply trains, but there was certainly more to it than that. Mack was impatient. He wanted everything done yesterday. Speed of execution was all-important to him. It was only natural that he would do everything in his power, once he had taken effective command, to forge a military instrument that could move rapidly to support his vision of rapid war. Whether he would be able to control that instrument in the face of an army even more perfectly formed for such warfare was another question entirely.

Coup d'Oeil

Carl von Clausewitz immortalized the term "coup d'oeil" in *On War*, but it had been in use among military theorists for at least fifty years before. A French phrase that literally means "glance," by the Napoleonic period it meant a general's ability to perceive the shape of a battle and see what action to take in order to change that shape to his advantage. It means not merely perception, but the ability to sense opportunity and know how to take advantage of it. Clausewitz and others rightly identified coup d'oeil as one of the most important qualities that made Napoleon successful. It was a quality Mack did not have.

Mack's lack of coup d'oeil was as critical to his failure as Napoleon's possession of it was to his success. There was good reason, however, for Mack to have a difficult time recognizing the shape of the campaign that was developing around him, in light of the intelligence he was receiving and what he knew about the allies' plans and intentions. Mack's failure must also be explained by reasons rooted in his personality and in experiences that prevented him from accepting interpretations of Napoleon's movements that would have led to the collapse of Mack's plans.

Mack sought to make a number of important changes to the war plan based on his perceptions of Napoleon's intentions and capabilities. Although it was originally Charles, not Mack, who argued that Napoleon would make his main effort in Italy rather than Germany, Mack accepted that conviction and made it his own. By late August rumors had begun to reach the Austrian high command that Napoleon had broken camp at Boulogne and was racing with his whole force toward Germany. Mack was initially reluctant to accept this fact and even more reluctant to believe that it would require him to change his plans dramatically. "I do not yet believe this news," he wrote to Francis, "although I think that it is possible, without in the least losing heart, for he [Napoleon] cannot be stronger overall than we are and if he sent his main body toward Germany, then it would only be necessary to send some of the troops now marching to Italy . . . to Germany instead." He also thought that the Austrians might have to fortify positions along the Inn and the Salza to prepare for an attack on the French army.[23]

This evaluation of the situation mixed intelligence and folly. Mack was right not to believe that Napoleon had broken camp on August 21, since the emperor did not decide to do so until two days later. He was also right to accept the possibility that Napoleon would break camp soon, and that he would send his main forces to Germany rather than Italy. Mack was also correct that if the Austrians diverted forces from Italy to Germany, they would be able to hold off the French army, at least until Russian reinforcements arrived. This was especially true if the Austrians fortified Salzburg, Braunau, and other points along the Inn and Salza. These judgments were sound.

Mack's understanding of the relationship between space and time, however, was problematic. It actually took Napoleon nearly six weeks to concentrate his army on the Danube. If Mack had requested reinforcements from the Army of Italy at once (on August 21), and if Francis had received and approved the request instantly, and if orders had been drafted, sent to, and received by the troops affected at once, and if those troops had rushed by forced marches to Germany, they could have arrived in time. If orders had been sent at once to make all haste to prepare reasonable field fortifications along the Inn and Salza, if there had been workers already mobilized in those places, and if those workers had set to their task with feverish haste, then Mack might have had a primitive defensive line to fall back on.

The problem with these calculations is less that Mack underestimated how rapidly Napoleon could move than that he overestimated how responsive his own army could be. We will encounter this problem repeatedly during Mack's command. He did not account for the inevitable inefficiencies in the transmission and execution of orders, let alone the peculiar inefficiencies of an army and state whose leaders, apart from himself and the Cobenzl clique, had never wanted to fight in the first place. He did not understand, finally, that his own frenzy—and Mack was constantly in a swirl of motion and activity—did not transmit itself to the rest of the apparatus. Had Mack been in Napoleon's position for as long as the French emperor, he might have created an organization responsive enough to suit him. But Mack was simply a cog in a vast, rusty machine, and he could not, despite his frantic efforts, remake that machine into something it was not. Nor did he ever recognize that failure and its significance.

Three days after rejecting the possibility that Napoleon would bring the whole Grande Armée to Germany, Mack reconsidered the probable shape of the campaign. He wrote to Francis, "It is not only possible, but very likely that Napoleon will direct his main force toward Germany in order to strike a decisive blow before the arrival of the Russians, because he can rely on his fortresses in Italy for the time being." Consequently Mack asked that Francis order five regiments to march from Klagenfurth, where they had been destined for the Army of Italy, to Salzburg, and two regiments in Vienna to march to Bavaria.*

It is difficult to tell what caused Mack to reconsider the original assumption that Napoleon would send his main forces to Italy. He cannot have heard of Napoleon's decision to break camp and march against him, since Napoleon made that decision only the day before Mack wrote to Francis that he thought it nearly certain that the Boulogne army would march to Germany. He may have picked up reports of some of Napoleon's preliminary cavalry concentrations along the Rhine, although those concentrations should not have been enough in themselves to reveal the emperor's intentions; they could just as well have been screening the movement of the Grande Armée to the south. It is most likely that the rumors of French movements toward the Rhine caused him to reflect on the situation and realize that he had no news of any large-scale French movements toward Italy. Whatever the cause, Mack's belief that Napoleon would come for him with his main army rapidly turned into a conviction, and the quartermaster general worked frenetically to respond.

He tried hard to avoid giving the appearance of panic. In early September he wrote to Francis that the army already assembled for the invasion of Bavaria was quite considerable, that however fast Napoleon moved he could not arrive before the Austrians linked up with the Russians, and that the situation could be improved further if Francis recognized the neutrality of Switzerland. In that case, Mack argued, Austrian troops in the Tyrol and Vorarlberg would no longer be needed to defend against a French attack out of Switzerland, and could be redirected to his army in Germany instead.[24]

This happy conclusion apparently rested on two false assumptions: that Napoleon would not bring more than about half of the Army of England with

*Mack to Francis, 24 August 1805, KA AFA 1805 Deutschland, VIII/31. This request had no immediate result, but on September 16, Francis ordered three regiments from Auffenberg's corps to join Ferdinand's army, along with two (the ones Mack had requested) from the Italian army. Francis to Latour, 16 September 1805, KA AFA 1805 Italien, IX/195.

him into Germany, and that the Austrian regiments were at anything like full strength.* Mack supposedly told the war council held on August 29 that he believed Napoleon would send only 70,000 men into Germany. He would have to leave 30,000–40,000 men on the English Channel and 20,000 in Paris. Mack did not believe that the forces in Holland and Hanover would abandon those conquests, and he thought Napoleon had about 20,000 sick soldiers on his rolls.†

These arguments were plausible and had some justification in intelligence reports, although they were wrong.‡ Napoleon did feel it necessary to leave a sizable force on the English Channel, as we have seen. It did not occur to Mack that he would leave relatively untrained and unseasoned troops there, however, as he chose to do. Nor was Mack foolish to doubt that Napoleon would abandon Hanover. We have already seen the great risks Napoleon ran in doing so. Those risks would have seemed even greater to an Austrian general who knew of the Russian plan to force Prussia to fight with the allies. The abandonment of Holland in such a situation would have seemed similarly dangerous, especially in light of the allied plans, of which Mack was well aware, to land an army somewhere on the Channel coast. Mack's conviction that Napoleon would retain a large force in Paris was the least well founded of these assumptions, although it may have reflected the allied conviction that Napoleon's hold on power was tenuous and supported mainly by military force.

In other words, Mack saw Napoleon's options only within the context of what Mack himself knew. He did not attempt to consider how the world looked

---

*This issue brings the problems of the historiography of this campaign into sharpest relief. The only historians who have examined the Ulm campaign carefully, in detail, and with reference to archival sources were Austrians writing before the fall of the Habsburg monarchy: Alfred Krauss, *1805: Der Feldzug von Ulm* (Vienna: L. W. Seidel, 1912); Alois Moriggl, *Der Feldzug von Ulm und seine Folgen für Oesterreich überhaupt und für Tirol insbesonders* (Innsbruck: Verlag der Wagner'schen Buchhandlung, 1861); Angeli, *Erzherzog Carl*. Their primary purpose was to blame Mack for the Austrians' failures and exonerate the imperial family, including Francis, Charles, and Ferdinand. As a result, they tended to use evidence about Mack's incompetence and insanity uncritically. In particular, they treated Ferdinand's account of the campaign, written in 1806, as a completely accurate rendering of Mack's thoughts and intentions, while they generally dismissed Mack's own explanations for his actions. The discussion of Mack's arguments about Napoleon's likely actions that follows accepts Ferdinand's account as the only firsthand evidence available on this point. We must recognize the ex parte nature of this evidence, however, and accept the possibility that it distorts Mack's thoughts and perhaps even his statements. Ferdinand was as eager to exonerate himself in the aftermath of the Ulm debacle as subsequent Austrian historians might have been.

†Ferdinand's memorandum, KA AFA 1805 Deutschland, XIII/106, cited in Krauss, *Der Feldzug von Ulm*, p. 167. Krauss notes that the protocols of this conference are lacking. He does not note that Ferdinand's assertion that Mack fought off the idea of sending reinforcements from Italy to Germany is demonstrably untrue, since Mack asked for such reinforcements repeatedly starting on August 24 (in documents Krauss himself cites).

‡A report sent from Mainz on 7 September announced that the French would have 60,000 troops on the Rhine by the end of the month. Other reports indicated the units that were moving toward the Rhine, but not generally reliable strength figures for them. See Collected Intelligence Reports, KA AFA 1805 Deutschland, XIII/124.

to Napoleon. Mack knew (or thought he knew) that the Russians and the British would shortly pose a major threat to Napoleon's northern flank and to France's Channel coast by driving the Prussians to fight and making amphibious landings. He assumed that Napoleon would not open himself up to such attacks and that the emperor would therefore retain large bodies of troops to protect against them.

Far from sharing Mack's conviction that Prussia would join the coalition, Napoleon believed Frederick William to be on the verge of signing a treaty with France! And Napoleon was so little concerned with his own hold on power that he feared neither denuding Paris of troops nor permitting a British landing near French soil. There is even evidence that he courted such a landing as an opportunity to smash a large British army, as we have seen.

Finally, there is reason to believe that the allies had not learned one of Napoleon's secrets to success. Mack was well aware that the emperor moved rapidly and decisively. He did not realize that Napoleon always sought to concentrate the greatest possible force at the decisive point. There was good reason for Mack (and the other allied leaders) not to have learned this point from Napoleon's previous campaigns. Only once before had the allies fought a Napoleon who was also the head of the French state—during the 1800 Marengo campaign. Napoleon had moved rapidly and kept his own army concentrated and the allied armies separated. But he had not drawn the other French armies with him to Italy. The final battle of the campaign in fact had been won not by Napoleon with the main body in Italy, but by Moreau with another main body at Hohenlinden, a half hour's car ride from Munich.

The allies had never yet seen Napoleon set out from the beginning to plan a war and deploy his forces in accord with his desires. They had seen him as an operational and tactical commander, but never as a strategic or grand strategic commander. They imagined that they understood his principles of war in battle and campaign, but they did not understand how those principles were altered (or not) at the higher levels. Lacking that understanding, Mack can be forgiven for not seeing that Napoleon would ignore all perils in order to concentrate the great bulk of his army in Germany.

Mack's overestimation of his own forces is less forgivable. In a report to Francis in mid-September, Mack calculated the strength of the forces available to him on the assumption that each battalion had 800 men and each squadron 140.[25] This estimate was wildly optimistic. Strength figures sent from the Hofkriegsrat to Charles eight days later show that the overall average strength for Austrian infantry battalions was 532 men and for cavalry squadrons, 90, although the armies in Germany were somewhat better manned than those in Italy or elsewhere.[26]

Why did Mack, who as quartermaster general should have known the actual strength of the forces he was moving about, make such a mistake? Austrian historians would have us believe that it resulted from his usual divorce from reality and his conviction that an order once given is instantly and perfectly executed. Francis had only decided to place the Austrian army on a war footing on August 27.[27] Mack may simply have seized on that order and proceeded to operate from the assumption that it had been executed.

There is another possible psychological explanation, however. Having decided that Napoleon was coming for him with all the forces at his disposal, Mack may simply have been unwilling to recognize the true danger he faced. Such a recognition would have required him to abandon the race to the Iller line and instead try to hold the line of the Lech, the Isar, or possibly even the Inn, while awaiting the arrival of the Russians (of course, the farther east Mack had waited, the sooner the Russians would have been able to join with him). But such a decision would have been an admission of error. Mack's personality may have rebelled at such an admission and led him to take refuge in self-delusional justifications such as this one.

Of course it is possible that Mack honestly did not know the size of the forces available to him. Although he was the emperor's quartermaster general, he was not with the emperor in Vienna and had not taken a staff with him. Reports from the Hofkriegsrat continued to go to Charles, as war minister, and do not appear to have gone through Mack. Since Mack was not the chief of staff of Ferdinand's army any more than he was its commander, it is possible that he never saw the strength returns for that army. In other words, Mack's efforts to seize control of the military operations in Germany may have cut him off from the ordinary sources of information he would need to conduct those operations. This is not to say that Mack could not have insisted on having strength reports sent to him from the Austrian armies, had he thought of it. To explain that failure, we must probably turn back to his personality and venture that he did not ask for information that he probably suspected would disturb him and his plans.

However that may be, Mack's self-delusion led him to accept the fight in Germany on Napoleon's terms. He knew before the first Austrian soldier crossed the border that Napoleon was coming after him with the whole Grande Armée. That knowledge did not persuade him to change his own plans. It led him to begin to ask for reinforcements from the other Austrian armies and hasten his movements toward the Iller. But it did not lead him to an honest reevaluation of a situation that had changed completely when one of its critical assumptions collapsed.

From the outset, then, Mack's personality increased the danger facing the Austrian armies and their allies. Coup d'oeil means that the commander must read the developing situation accurately and then must see the best course of action to pursue. In the first phase of the campaign, Mack correctly evaluated Napoleon's intentions but failed to choose the right course of action. From that point, the problem of understanding what the French were actually doing became only harder.

Race to the Iller

The first critical decision in the campaign came in mid-September. As Napoleon's troops prepared to cross the Rhine, Mack had to decide how to respond to the indications that they were about to do so. On September 5, the Austrian ambassador to Electoral Hesse, Baron Wessenberg, sent the first clear report that the Grande Armée was moving southeast.* Marmont's corps, he wrote, had disembarked under orders to march at once to Mainz. Another large corps was marching through Lorraine toward upper Alsace. Bernadotte's corps had begun to concentrate on the frontiers of Hesse, and the elector, who had no idea what was going on, had concentrated his meager forces in response. Wessenberg's interpretation was that Bernadotte was awaiting the formal commencement of hostilities before driving south to the Danube as rapidly as possible.†

Since this report probably went to Colloredo in Vienna, it is not clear when it would have reached Mack. But by September 14 the quartermaster general was convinced that Napoleon was moving rapidly. In response, he accelerated the movement of his army to the Iller line. He ordered FML Riesch (and probably also FML Klenau) to eliminate rest days from his march plan until he reached his final destination. He also gave orders to reduce the baggage and excess horses in order to facilitate this acceleration and lighten the army's logistical burden.[28] Mack took no apparent action to respond to the news that Bernadotte might be marching from the north against his right flank. Electoral Hesse is far north of the Iller position and a French corps marching from Hanover through Hesse could be going almost anywhere.

The situation rapidly grew more complicated. A further report from Hesse sent on September 11 noted that the exact destination of Bernadotte's corps was not yet known, but he apparently had orders to march to the Rhine to rejoin the main body of the French army.[29] This report adds that although the French troops seemed to be pretty good, they were not animated by the spirit the French had exhibited in 1794 and 1795.

Mack was not interested in Bernadotte's corps for the moment. Believing that Napoleon was hastening on his way and facing opposition from leading Austrian generals to his plan to advance to the Iller, Mack paused to provide Francis with a detailed consideration of the situation and a careful justification for his proposed plan of action.[30]

---

*Look for the town of Cassel on the map of the Austrian invasion routes to see the approximate location of Electoral Hesse (as opposed to the larger territory of Hesse-Darmstadt to the south).

†Wessenberg to Anon., 5 September 1805, KA AFA 1805 Deutschland, IX/78. This letter was probably sent to Colloredo, to whom correspondence from ambassadors was directed. Wessenberg also asked that future instructions to him be sent to Ratisbonne (Regensburg) in case he was forced out of Hesse—Colloredo would have been the one sending him such instructions.

Mack first described the confused situation. Earlier reports of a French crossing of the Rhine had proven false. He now had word that the French would cross the river between September 15 and September 18. In truth, he wrote, it did not much matter. Clearly the French were ready to move and their crossing could begin any day. Mack did not seem surprised at the speed of the French advance. Earlier he had assured Francis that the French would not be able to move quickly because they needed to mobilize and concentrate. But here he did not worry about the failure of his calculations, as well as those of the coalition war planners. He simply accepted the French advance and considered how to adjust his own dispositions accordingly.

In response to Napoleon's concentration on the Rhine, Mack defended his efforts to accelerate the army's movement to the Iller line—the only one that could defend the Tyrolean passes, he wrote. Failure to hold it would allow Napoleon to swing through the Tyrol and take Charles's Italian army in the rear. The Austrians could split their army in Germany, he noted. Part could withdraw to the east (he did not specify which position they should attempt to hold) while another part could try to hold the Tyrol. But he ruled out such a plan as dangerous and unwise. It would allow Napoleon to fall on either part of the divided army and defeat it separately. If he destroyed the army guarding the Tyrol, then his way would be clear into the rear of the Italian army. If he destroyed an Austrian army along, say, the Inn, then the road to Vienna would be wide open. Only the Iller line allowed the German army to remain concentrated and still accomplish the defensive tasks required of it both to facilitate the overall plan and defend the monarchy. The Austrian army must "try to reach the Iller with all effort humanly possible and must decide to win or die there."

Clearly Mack had in mind the twin admonitions of his master. He reminded Francis that the emperor had warned him against allowing himself to be surprised by the enemy's main body or being forced into retreats that would discourage and exhaust the army. Adhering to those mandates, he wrote, was the goal of his dispositions. He felt it necessary therefore to explain in some detail why he thought the German army could hold out against the forces Napoleon was about to bring to bear.

He began by accepting the highest estimates of Napoleon's strength on the Rhine that had appeared in French reports and newspapers—40,000. He believed that another 70,000 men were on their way from the Channel army. Bernadotte's corps was also on the move, he wrote, adding another 20,000 to the total, for a grand total of 130,000 troops. This estimate of the forces he was facing was low but not wildly off the mark. He set against it, however, an inaccurate evaluation of the strength of his own forces, which we have already considered, and asserted that he would be able to match Napoleon's army with a force of equal strength, at least as long as the emperor gave orders at once for a corps under the command of Auffenberg to march from the Tyrol to Germany.

Mack knew that the strength of the Austrian army fell short of the figure he claimed but dismissed the problem in a curious way: "One can not object that our battalions and squadrons are not at full strength, because the French are also" incomplete. This remark seems at first irrelevant, since Mack had offered a breakdown by battalion and squadron for the Austrian army and had given total troop strengths for the French.[31] This criticism is unfair. Most of the intelligence reports that Mack was receiving estimated the size of French formations based on the number of battalions and squadrons in them, assuming those units to be at full strength.[32] He offered Francis the result of those calculations without troubling him with the calculations themselves, but here pointed out that those calculations were as likely to be inaccurate for the French as they were for the Austrians. It is also true that the French intelligence estimates made an even more dramatic error in assuming that Austrian units were at full strength, as we shall see in the next chapter.

Mack's point was valid—many French formations were under strength. The Austrian formations were, on the whole, even more understrength. The reason was that Napoleon had been straining for two years to bring his Channel army up to its full peacetime complement and then, for part of that time, to a full wartime complement. For a variety of reasons he had not succeeded in that task, but the Austrians had not even begun trying until the spring of 1805. Mack did not recognize the benefits that Napoleon had received from preparing for war against Britain. As the comment about the quality of the French soldiers cited above shows, none of the other Austrian leaders recognized those benefits either.

Mack also made overoptimistic calculations, as usual, believing that units he wanted diverted to his army would arrive in time to take part in operations. Interestingly, he left the Russian armies out of his calculations in the note of September 16. He had clearly concluded that the Austrian army would have to hold off the initial French onslaught by itself. He believed that the reinforcement he desired from Italy and the Tyrol would arrive in a timely fashion, however. That belief proved to be unfounded too.

By now Mack had used up most of his credit with the emperor. By mid-September Francis was no longer willing to accept Mack's judgment but decided instead to take an active role. He was spurred in this direction by the growing hostility of Archduke Charles, and possibly Archduke Ferdinand as well, to his flighty quartermaster general.*

When Francis had received Mack's initial request for the movement of troops from the Tyrol to Germany, he turned it over to Charles for his consideration.

---

*Ferdinand's conflict with Mack emerged openly only after the decisions of Emperor Francis that we are about to consider. It is likely, however, that that conflict had been simmering for some time, and Ferdinand was in Vienna with Francis while Mack was moving the Austrian armies about in Germany. The young archduke had plenty of opportunity to work on the doubts that had probably already been growing in Francis's mind, considering how hostile the emperor had been to the war in the first place.

Charles responded with a blistering assault on Mack as a person and as a military leader and on Mack's proposed plans as well.[33] The quartermaster general, Charles wrote, was constantly overstepping the bounds of his authority. He was interfering in the tactical deployments of the corps commanders, corresponding directly with commanders of units in other armies, improperly interfering in the logistical and economic arrangements of the forces, appointing people to posts in contradiction with the orders of those who actually had the right to do so, and "taking command over all military, political, and civil subjects with the protecting words: 'Supreme Order.'"

These accusations would lead to a court-martial in most armies, but Charles continued his attack. Mack's dispositions for the invasion of Bavaria exposed the Austrian army to great danger, the archduke wrote, because the forces were excessively divided and operating at great distances from one another. Mack had totally denuded the northern Tyrol of troops, Charles noted, before he had taken up positions that would defend it. Charles thereby added military incompetence to the charges of misuse of authority and malfeasance.

Francis did not fire his quartermaster general or investigate Charles's allegations. He recognized that the military situation was too exigent to concern himself with such matters. He did, however, decide to defer consideration of Mack's request for reinforcements by submitting it to the Hofkriegsrat not for execution, as Mack had asked, but for deliberation.* More importantly, he decided to go to Munich to meet Mack and work out an overall plan of action. He asked Mack to acquire all the information they would need, but his note clearly implied that decisions and actions should await his arrival.[34]

Francis's note crossed another report from Mack, written on the same day.[35] The quartermaster general had become concerned about the weakness of his army relative to Napoleon's, whatever he might have written in his previous report. He begged Francis to send him Auffenberg's corps, dramatizing his plea with his usual "I throw myself at the feet of Your Majesty." Clearly Napoleon was sending no reinforcements to his armies in Italy and therefore the Austrian army there was in no danger. Nor could it help the army in Germany, since Napoleon would force Charles to fight a war of protracted sieges. The French and Austrian armies were equal in strength, Mack insisted, but if Napoleon "has 200,000 men in Germany and only 100,000 in Italy; and we have only 130,000 in Germany and 180,000 in Italy, then we will obviously

---

*The documents cause some confusion. Apparently Francis ordered three regiments of Auffenberg's corps and two from Charles's army to join Ferdinand's army on 16 September (KA AFA 1805 Italien, IX/195). This movement was apparently executed; the two Italian regiments dropped off the roles of the Italian army—compare dispositions of 12 September 1805 (IX/134) with those of 23 September (IX/265). But neither Mack nor Francis refers to this movement, which is odd considering that such transfers were the subject of these critical and heated discussions. Mack's continued requests for troops, however, are consistent. He was asking for more, and more were eventually sent.

be in danger in Germany while our Italian superiority cannot save us in any way." "How horrible it would be," he continued, to allow Napoleon to defeat the army in Germany before the Russians arrived simply because of a faulty disposition.

Mack asked not only that Auffenberg's corps be set marching at once for Germany, but that an additional corps of twenty to thirty battalions (probably about 20,000 men) be concentrated at Innsbruck and put at the disposal of the commander of the army of Germany. He asked Francis to raise another reserve army of 30,000 men by early 1806 in order to participate in offensive operations in cooperation with the Russians. This army should be stationed in the Tyrol, ready to assist in Germany or Italy as necessary.

The flaw in this argument lies in its incompleteness. Mack was right— when Napoleon did not transfer reinforcements to Italy, the allied war plan was destroyed and the army of Germany, and with it the hereditary Habsburg lands, was placed in imminent danger. He was right that part of the response should have been to transfer forces to Germany to help meet this new threat. Such a transfer would derail Charles's proposed invasion of Italy and the subsequent planned invasion of Switzerland, of course, but Mack was right to accept the collapse of that plan in order to meet the more urgent contingency.

Mack did not think the situation through to its logical conclusion, however. If the invasion of northern Italy was to be severely truncated, then the protection of the Tyrolean passes became less important. With the diversion of significant forces from Charles's army, it became unlikely that he would advance far enough to the west for the passes to be of importance in his campaign. Consequently there was no reason to insist on holding the Iller line. It would have made sense, in the course of this reevaluation of Austrian strategy, to have abandoned that line in favor of the Lech or the Inn and awaited Napoleon's blow closer to the Russian reinforcements.

Why did Mack not see through to this conclusion? Part of the problem may have been an unwillingness to abandon the plan he had set out to execute. It is a common enough problem in military history that when generals recognize an important change in the situation, they alter some of their preconceptions but not others. The need to get to the Iller rapidly may have been so ingrained in Mack's psyche by this point that he did not recognize its irrelevance in the changed circumstances.

Another part of the problem may have been a reluctance to defend the monarchy on its frontiers. Mack had written in his first reconsideration that it was important to defend Austria as far away from Vienna as possible; that was one of the reasons he gave for the importance of seizing the Iller line.[36] Falling back to the Inn meant giving up ground that Mack would have preferred to make Napoleon fight for. A defeat at the Inn, he rightly recognized, was in principle much more dangerous than a defeat on the Iller.

A final part of Mack's refusal to reconsider his advance may have been his precarious position with Francis. His notes in this period exude self-justification and defensiveness. His first reconsideration had revealed how much he had taken to heart Francis's instruction not to expose the army to a surprise defeat but also not to retreat from advanced positions, thereby discouraging and exhausting the troops. Abandoning the advance to the Iller in mid-September would have meant ordering a retreat and a variety of countermarches. It would have meant abandoning the plan Mack had made his own. Would his "command" have survived violating the emperor's instructions and admitting that the whole premise of his campaign had been faulty? Mack might not have been willing to take the risk.

Two days later, Mack finally recognized that the allied assumptions about Napoleon's actions were completely wrong and that the whole allied plan was misconceived.[37] He stated somewhat disingenuously that he had never participated in the decision to place the Austrians' main force in Italy rather than Germany and went on to provide a devastating critique of that decision. It might have made sense, he argued, if it was thought that Napoleon would quickly learn of the Austro–Russian alliance and the Russians' march across the Austrian border. Then it would have been reasonable to suppose that the emperor would send his main forces into Italy, the better to strike a decisive blow against Austria. It was clear, however, that Napoleon had not penetrated that secret and had no time to divert significant forces to Italy. The success of allied secrecy had forced Napoleon to do what the allies did not want him to do: send his main army to Germany.

In this context, the present division of the Austrian armies made no sense. Mack demanded, with an exigency unusual for him in dealing with Francis, that the emperor give him control over all the Austrian troops in western Tyrol and the Vorarlberg, and that he send substantial reinforcements from Italy at once. The basis for the urgency of this request was an invented pretext: Mack had received information that reports of Napoleon sending 70,000 men to Italy were fabricated rumors. This was nonsense. Mack had never mentioned any such movement of French forces and had been writing for days now that Napoleon was sending his main body to Germany. Intelligence reports from the beginning of September had confirmed this repeatedly.[38] The urgency came from elsewhere.

During the allied planning process, coalition generals paid little attention to Napoleon's possible actions, probably because their task of coming to grips with a plan on such a gigantic scale involving the armed forces of three major and many minor powers occupied the full attention of their limited staffs. Serious consideration of the enemy's options, however important such a task might have been, was simply a bridge too far for planners and diplomats struggling to bring together a continent-spanning coalition and its war plan.

When Mack found himself at the head of the army in Germany, however, the situation changed completely, and discerning Napoleon's possible courses of action became the single most important task he faced. Mack turned his full attention to that task in early September. By the time of the memoranda considered above, Mack had amassed a substantial amount of intelligence about what Napoleon was actually doing and also tried to see the world a little from Napoleon's perspective. As a result, he came to the shocking realization that the allied plans were nonsensical.

Failure to consider the enemy's possible actions or focus on one's own actions to the exclusion of the enemy's is not unusual, even on modern military staffs. War plans are not created by isolated individuals working in a political vacuum. They are generated by overworked staffs functioning in a complex bureaucratic and political environment. Planners' perceptions of the world and the enemy are colored not only by their own preconceptions and prejudices, but also by their understanding of how their masters want the world to be. Allied war planning in 1805 was an extreme case of the problems this sort of process can lead to, but one that is by no means unique in the annals of military history.

Having begun to reconsider the allied grand strategic plans in light of his new understanding of Napoleon, Mack looked at other parts of plans that might be relevant to the endangered Austrian army in Germany. What was going on in Prussia? Would the Prussians enter the war? Would they defend the neutrality of the minor German states? Would the Russian armies be able to traverse Prussian territory? These questions had suddenly become urgent for Mack as he considered the actual disposition of Napoleon's troops and contemplated their likely final destinations.

Mack had picked up the major French troop concentrations along the Rhine with fair accuracy. He understood that a large French force was concentrated around Strasbourg and Hunningue (which consisted in reality of the corps of Lannes, Ney, and Murat), and saw another one concentrated around Mannheim and Mainz (Davout, Marmont, and possibly Soult). He believed that these forces comprised two distinct armies, each having its own objective. The force at Strasbourg, he believed, was intended to attack his own army in Germany. He did not trouble, for the moment, to consider how, when, or where that attack would come. The force at Mannheim and Mainz, he thought, would march through Würzburg toward Bohemia, although he admitted that this second force might be intended to support the attack against him if he received significant reinforcements from Italy in a timely fashion.

Why Mack believed that the northern wing of the Grande Armée was heading to Bohemia is not clear. Probably he thought that Napoleon knew of the approaching Russian armies and wanted to interdict them before they linked up with the Austrians. This assumption was not entirely foolish, considering that the Austrians had not yet discovered Napoleon's mania for concentrating his forces and that their own war plans tended to assign distinct objectives to different forces. A commander who develops complex plans looks for complexity in his enemy. It is likely that Mack fell into that trap.

Since Mack did not see the left wing of the Grande Armée as being directed against him, he looked for strategic solutions to the problem of reacting to it. His preoccupation with Prussia in this note is clearly a response to his recognition of the danger to his north. If the Prussians entered the war or allowed the Russians to traverse their territory, then large forces coming from the east would meet this prong of the French army and overwhelm it. Those forces could then continue on to Hanover and Holland, thus opening up the northern front that the allied war plan had foreseen and taking the pressure off Mack. It may be objected that neither the Prussian nor the Russian armies could have arrived in time to affect the outcome of the struggle on the Iller, but Mack did not know the state of negotiations or mobilization in Berlin. The tone of his note indicates that he hoped for a specific response from Francis: things were taken care of and a Russo–Prussian army was already on the march.

Mack did not confine himself to hoping that the Prussians would solve his problems, however. He also asked Francis to divert the Russians' route of march. Instead of taking the road south from Brunn toward Krems and the road to Braunau, Mack asked that the first Russian army march due west from Brunn through Jihlava and Tabor to Waldmünchen on the eastern Bavarian border with Bohemia. From there, he wrote, the Russians could be sent to Straubing or to Amberg and Nurnberg, depending on the situation.[39] He focused on the advantage of this movement for speeding up the arrival of the Russians in the theater, since this was a more direct route. Such a movement, however, would also have put the Russians on a collision course with the northern wing of the French army, thus relieving Mack of the burden of worrying about that force.

The problem with this memorandum was not its content but its timing.* Mack evaluated the grand strategic situation perfectly. The allied war plan had foolishly imagined that Napoleon would react to a development the allies had been desperately (and successfully) trying to keep secret. Worse still, the war

---

*Krauss, *Der Feldzug von Ulm*, is completely misled in his consideration of this memorandum by Mack's assertion that he had not been involved in the original plans to divide the Austrian army between Germany, Italy, and the Tyrol (pp. 200–201). Although Mack had no right to make such a claim, since he had participated in the discussions of the overall war plan and had never complained about the disposition, Krauss's attack is actually part of an important distortion in Austrian history. The grain of truth in Mack's claim is that it was originally Charles, not he, who proposed to divide the Austrian armies in this way and to make the main theater initially Italy. Krauss (and other Austrian historians) have ignored the evidence of this fact in order to exonerate Charles, and the violence with which Krauss assails Mack at this juncture on this point is unwarranted. Furthermore, the issue was moot by September 19. The very focus on this argument, rather than on Mack's perception of the situation and his proposed responses, highlights the determination of Austrian scholars to blame Mack for Austria's failures.

plan had not even considered the possibility that Napoleon would not fall in with the allies' expectations. When Mack realized the extent of the war plan's bankruptcy, however, it was too late to do much about it. The proposal to shift the movement of the Russian army was folly. The Austrians had prepared supplies along the original line of march in order to allow the Russians to move quickly; no such supplies existed along the roads Mack proposed to shift the Russians onto. Attempting to make the change in late September would only delay the arrival of the Russians.

The proposals to send troops from the Tyrol, Vorarlberg, and Italy made more sense, assuming that everything happened instantly. But Mack did not consider what he intended to do with those reinforcements. The other major problem with this memorandum is that Mack did not consider the operational implications for his army of the grand strategic problems he identified. He continued to believe that the Austrian army must race to the Iller and hold its ground there. He even began to discuss the qualities of the various fortress towns, including Ulm, that dotted that line. He maintained the plans for his own army while attempting to change the movements of the other allied armies. He identified and reacted to more distant threats while an immediate danger developed virtually undetected.

During the next few days Mack did not reexamine the alterations he was imposing on Austrian strategy because he became involved in a major skirmish with Ferdinand.

Ferdinand had every reason to hate Mack. Apart from the fact that Mack did not have good relations with those around him, he had systematically excluded Ferdinand from controlling the army he was nominally commanding, having schemed to displace Charles, Ferdinand's uncle, from control of the Austrian military establishment. From the beginning of the campaign, therefore, Ferdinand had joined his uncle in opposing everything that Mack suggested and did.

He opposed the advance to the Iller from the outset. In the second week of September he sent memoranda to Charles and Francis arguing that the army should be retained between the Inn and the Lech, with the heavy cavalry on the Austrian side of the Inn. If Napoleon crossed the Iller, then the Austrians should attempt to fight him on the Lech. If not, then they should await the full concentration of the Russian army on the Inn, which would not be complete before November 9.[40]

Ferdinand's complaints elicited a compromise from Francis. On September 16 he wrote that he would permit a vanguard of thirty battalions and thirty squadrons of cavalry to hold the Iller line, with only small detachments in advance of that river, while the rest of the army would remain concentrated in such a fashion that it would not be attacked by the entire French army prior to the arrival of the Russians. At the same time, however, he instructed Ferdinand to abide by the advice given him by Mack and by the quartermaster general of the army in Germany, FML Mayer.[41]

Tense as his personal situation was, Mack made it worse. His note of September 17 began by explaining to Francis that although Mack had sent Ferdinand "proposals" for the disposition of forces he thought necessary, Ferdinand had not yet responded. The military situation, Mack continued, would not admit of delay. He had been forced, in the absence of word from the army's actual commander, to set the troops in motion according to his own plans.

Whatever the military wisdom of this procedure, it was a political catastrophe. When Ferdinand arrived near Munich on September 20, he found that Mack had gathered the staff of the army in the Bavarian capital while he himself was somewhere around Ulm and Memmingen, despite the fact that Ferdinand had summoned him to a meeting. Worse still, the nominal commander of the army in Germany learned that Mack had sent the vanguard of the army beyond the Iller, with detachments as far as Stockach and Moskirch, and that the main body was moving by forced marches to positions on the Lech and the Iller.[42]

Ferdinand was furious that Mack would violate the emperor's orders by advancing the army farther than Francis had permitted. Mack had also disobeyed Ferdinand's order to be present for a meeting, although it is not clear that Ferdinand had any right to order Mack around, since they both reported directly to the emperor. He also disapproved of the forced marches that Mack had ordered, believing that they exhausted the army and prevented the establishment of stable logistical arrangements. Indeed, he complained that the economic side of the army was in complete disarray.

Accordingly, Ferdinand called off the forced marches. The main body would take position between the Isar and the Lech. When Mack returned, Ferdinand intended to insist that this body return to a position between the Lech and the heights of Munich. He would gradually withdraw the vanguard from beyond the Iller, leaving only cavalry detachments on that line.

Clearly Ferdinand did not foresee the danger of the impending French envelopment from the north at this point. He does not mention it in his notes to Francis, and his disposition is not especially calculated to meet that threat—a position between the Lech and the heights of Munich can still be vulnerable to an attack from the direction of Ansbach, depending on the precise orientation of the defensive lines, something Ferdinand did not write about at all. It is not clear from these memoranda how well Ferdinand understood the French movements, since he did not refer to them.

The primary motivation behind Ferdinand's recommendations and orders was fear bred by the conviction that Napoleon was bringing a larger army to Germany than the Austrians had been expecting. Apparently he accepted Mack's belief that the main blow would come from Strasbourg across the Iller line and down the Danube. He complained that Mack's disposition exposed the Austrian army to a battle too far west, and therefore too far away from supplies and reinforcements, as well as from the support of the advancing Russian army. He paid no attention to Mack's arguments about the importance of holding the Iller line (it is not clear whether or not he was aware of those arguments). He did not even consider the strategic and grand strategic situation at all.

His recommendations, therefore, were only half sound. He was right that the Austrian army in Germany stood a better chance of success if it deployed farther east, but Mack had never disputed that. By ignoring the strategic and grand strategic arguments for holding the Iller line, Ferdinand greatly weakened his case. This recommendation was fundamentally the proposal of an army commander trying to take care of his own force with no regard for the impact of his decisions on the overall situation. Mack, on the other hand, had made the wrong decision (as it turned out), based on a much more sophisticated and responsible (if still flawed) understanding of the overall requirements of Austria and the coalition. Possibly for this reason Ferdinand's recommendations had a more limited effect than he desired, although his youth and relative inexperience, as well as Francis's unwillingness to replace his mercurial quartermaster general, surely told against him as well.

When Mack heard of Ferdinand's decision, he was aghast. He had already written a note back to the archduke apologizing in a backhanded way for not coming to the meeting. He was too busy, he wrote, supervising the fortification of Memmingen and other critical spots along the Iller line, and he was sure that the archduke would understand how a moment's delay could have disastrous consequences. He had already signed this note when Ferdinand's message arrived, announcing that the archduke had halted the forward march of Riesch's three columns. "I throw myself at your feet," the quartermaster general wrote, begging Ferdinand to change his mind. He offered no clear explanation of why it was crucial to take up the positions he had ordered, but simply reiterated that any time lost could lead to catastrophe. If the archduke did not reverse himself, Mack concluded, there would be nothing left for him to do but leave the army and go back to Vienna to offer his head to the emperor in judgment for his actions.[43]

This note was extremely impolitic. It began by intimating that Ferdinand had nothing to do but snipe at Mack's plans, whereas the quartermaster general was engaged in serious and urgent business. Could Ferdinand not meet Mack closer toward the Iller line, Mack wondered, thus saving him the need to travel to the rear at such a critical time? Even the tenor of the postscript was unwise. It combined transparent blandishments with ultimata and repeated the hackneyed expressions of emergency that Mack used so often. One of the problems with a military leader who lives in a continual state of emergency is that those who interact with him find it difficult to recognize a real crisis when it arises.

Needless to say, Mack's arrogant ultimatum did not succeed. On the contrary, it appears to have put the young archduke very much on his dignity and mettle. He wrote back chastising Mack, in effect, because Ferdinand's couriers could not find him the day before. The implication was that if Mack would stop racing around like a maniac and start acting like a commander, it would be easier to deal with him. Ferdinand then flatly refused to rescind his halt order. He had issued that order, he said, not from his own beliefs but as a result of the instructions Francis had given him just before he left Vienna. The emperor did not want the army stationed on the Iller, he wrote, and the archduke would not violate the emperor's wishes. Furthermore, Ferdinand informed Mack that Francis was already in Bavaria; indeed, he would be in Landsberg (about halfway between Munich and Memmingen) that night. The emperor wanted to meet with both Mack and Ferdinand, but the archduke wanted to meet Mack beforehand. He all but instructed Mack to come to Landsberg and see him prior to the meeting with the emperor.[44]

For all that, the meetings did not go well for Ferdinand. Mack presented his report (which apparently has not been preserved), and Francis accepted his judgment. The emperor rescinded Ferdinand's halt order, and Riesch's troops began marching again. Mack returned to the Iller line and busied himself with its hasty fortification. Shortly thereafter, Francis finally decided, in the face of mounting intelligence, to transfer troops from Italy to Germany. On September 23 he ordered Charles to send five infantry regiments to Innsbruck by forced march. He also organized a new formation under FML Kienmayer around Neuburg and Ingolstadt (almost due north of Munich). This corps had the mission, among other things, of observing Bernadotte's corps and the Bavarian troops.[45] Mack had won his argument. The Austrian army would concentrate on the Iller and forces would be transferred from Italy to Germany. His relationship with the emperor, however, had been compromised by his struggle with Ferdinand, making a precarious position even more tenuous.

Conclusion

The Austrian decision to occupy the Iller line was one of the most crucial of the entire war. It created an opportunity for Napoleon to transform the campaign, as we shall see. The traditional explanations for this decision do not stand up. It was not made because the Austrians expected the Russians to arrive sooner than they did, nor because they did not understand how quickly Napoleon could move his army. It was not made because Napoleon's feint lured the Austrians into a trap or because the Austrians were unaware of the movements of the French army. The decision resulted, rather, from a complex interaction of personalities, from grand strategic, strategic, and operational realities, and from the difficulty of evaluating an enemy's intentions. There was nothing foreordained about this contingent event.

This decision was clearly wrong. It ignored the problem of the army's right flank even though the decisionmakers were aware of the movements of Bernadotte's corps and the Bavarian troops. Napoleon's disinformation about the ultimate destination of those forces led to understandable confusion, but it should not have prevented Austria's leaders from considering the possibility that French forces would fall on their right flank.

In his ex post facto self-justification, Mack wrote that he never considered this problem because it did not occur to him that the French would violate Prussian neutrality by marching through Ansbach. He believed that the mobilization of the Prussian army and Frederick William's strong declarations about his neutrality would be enough to secure his right flank.[46] Since none of the Austrian leaders openly considered this problem in any of the documents that survive from September 1805, it is not possible to evaluate the validity of this assertion. In light of Mack's obvious belief that Francis's recognition of Swiss neutrality would protect the western flank of the Tyrol, he may also have believed that Prussian neutrality would protect the northern flank of his own army. He knew that the Prussians were contemplating fighting the Russians to protect their own neutrality, and consequently it was reasonable for him to infer that Napoleon would not risk compromising Frederick William since the Prussian king was rendering him such a signal service. Apparently Mack did not know that the Prusso–Russian tensions were a well-kept secret from Napoleon, or that the French emperor thought himself on the verge of an alliance with Prussia throughout this period. Therefore his conviction that Ansbach would protect his flank was not unsound. His belief that Bernadotte's corps was aiming at Bohemia was also, as we have seen, not unreasonable, when looked at from Mack's viewpoint. The problem with occupying the Iller position did not lie in the Austrians' failure to see what Napoleon actually did.

It lay, rather, in the fact that Mack clung to it inflexibly even after it had lost its strategic justification. The Iller line had been meaningful primarily because it protected the rear of the Austrian army in Italy. Reconstructing the Austrian war plan from what the Austrians actually did, rather than what they said or wrote beforehand, it seems clear that the timing of the plan was meant to be as follows. The army in Germany would leap out to the Iller to forestall any French *coup de main* into Bavaria and secure itself with fortifications along that critical defensive line. Sometime later, the Austrian army in Italy would advance through the northern part of the peninsula and head for Piedmont. By that time, the Russian armies would have linked up with the Austrians in Bavaria, and it would be possible to invade Switzerland and march into Franche-Comté. At some point in this sequence, the Prussians would begin their march through Hanover toward Holland. The French would then face concentric attacks all along their eastern borders, probably sometime in early 1806.

The urgency about seizing Bavaria came from the need to secure the rear of the army in Italy, the desirability of sustaining as many Austrian troops as possible at someone else's expense, and the need to fortify a defensive position before the French could attack it. Since the Austrians initially imagined that Napoleon would send most of his troops to Italy, the risks entailed in this early invasion seemed reasonable.

Napoleon's failure to send troops to Italy, combined with his speedy decision to attack in Germany (rather than the speed with which his forces moved), undid all these calculations. It should have been instantly apparent that the main battle in this war would take place in Germany, not Italy. That fact should have triggered two decisions. First, holding the Iller line had become meaningless and dangerous. It was meaningless because the army in Italy had not even begun its advance, and the loss of the Tyrolean passes at that juncture would have had little significance. It was dangerous because Napoleon was directing such overwhelming force against the Austrians in Germany that even had he attacked the Iller line directly, he would almost certainly have smashed its defenders and driven right through it. The Austrians should have abandoned that line for one farther east as soon as it became clear that Napoleon was not sending large reinforcements to Italy.

The second decision should have been to send all available reinforcements from Italy and elsewhere to the German army at once. Whatever was going to happen, Napoleon's decision to send his main force to Germany meant that the original war plan was not going to be executed. If Napoleon ensured that the main fight was in Germany, then the Austrians had to send as many troops there as possible. Since the original war plan was now dead, there was no reason to keep those troops in Italy for an invasion that had become meaningless. The Austrian leadership had to recognize quickly that its original war plan had gone by the boards and develop a completely new war plan, independent of the old one, suited to the changed circumstances. The Austrians remained inflexibly committed to their original plan, however, and attempted to modify it rather than jettison it.

Why were these two crucial decisions not made? The decision to hold the Iller line despite the changing circumstances was primarily Mack's responsibility. The insecurity of his position with Francis was an important part of this decision. His personality was another important part. Abandoning this plan would have meant admitting that he had made mistakes. It would also have meant giving in to the criticism of those around him, such as Archduke Charles and Archduke Ferdinand. Since his first major military success, however, Mack had learned to trust his own instincts and mistrust those of others. His self-confidence and unwillingness to admit error played an important part in this decision.

The conflict between Mack and Ferdinand also played an important part. It turned the discussion of Austria's strategic options into a battle of wills. Mack felt that more than his ego and dignity were at stake—if he gave in to Ferdinand, he would lose effective control over the army, his standing with the emperor, and any chance of benefiting from a successful campaign. Ferdinand's direct and personal attacks on Mack surely intensified this feeling. This clash of personalities distracted Austria's leaders from the realities of the campaign at a crucial time, moreover. Between September 16 and September 28, as the Austrians were bickering about who was really in charge in Germany, Napoleon was deciding on a bold new plan to seize the opportunity they had presented him, as we shall see. Personality dysfunction in higher headquarters can have dreadful consequences for a military organization.

This bickering over whether or not to hold the Iller line, however, need not have carried over into Francis's decision about sending reinforcements to Germany. That it did was probably the result of efforts by Ferdinand and Charles to undermine Mack's standing with the emperor. Francis could not see his way to replacing the troublesome quartermaster general, but he did lose enough confidence in him to defer this critical decision just long enough to ensure that the reinforcements could not arrive in Germany in time. For this mistake, Francis must bear most of the responsibility. It was clear enough by the second week of September that the French were not going to fight in Italy. Further intelligence that accumulated between then and September 23, when he finally made the decision, should not have been necessary. Personalities once again played the crucial role in leading the Austrian leadership to make the wrong decisions.

Even though the Austrians made these mistakes, the outcome of the campaign, still less the war, was not predetermined. By trying to hold the Iller line with an inadequate force, the Austrians presented Napoleon with an opportunity. The way he seized that opportunity, together with the way the Austrians reacted to his action, led to the crucially important resolution of this phase of the conflict.

15

Napoleon Seizes
an Opportunity

Napoleon's initial plans for war against Austria focused on getting into
Bavaria as rapidly as possible in order to soothe the rattled elector and presumably meet and defeat the Austrians before the Russians arrived. His initial
dispositions indicated that he intended to sweep across the Rhine from west
to east, meeting the Austrians somewhere in Bavaria or on the Inn. Shifting
his deployment to the north seems to have had more to do with logistics and
a desire to facilitate the concentration of the army than with concrete plans
for dealing with the enemy.*

When the campaign began, Napoleon had no idea what the allies were going
to do. As his armies approached the Rhine, he and his subordinates struggled
to make sense of the mass of information they had received—much of it false—to
understand the Austrians' intentions. Napoleon wisely did not rush into making a
plan before he understood those intentions. He therefore made a series of partial

---

*Standard accounts of this campaign compress Napoleon's planning process and read the intentions of
late September into the initial orders issued at the end of August. They imply that Napoleon foresaw
the Austrian movement forward to the Iller line, intended from the outset to encircle Mack's army, and
deliberately laid a trap to facilitate that plan. David Chandler, *The Campaigns of Napoleon* (New York:
Macmillan, 1966), pp. 384–385; Christopher Duffy, *Austerlitz, 1805* (London: Seeley Service, 1977),
40–41; David Gates, *The Napoleonic Wars, 1803–1815* (New York: Arnold, 1997), 21–22; Scott
Bowden, *Napoleon and Austerlitz: An Unprecedentedly Detailed Combat Study of Napoleon's Epic Ulm-
Austerlitz Campaigns of 1805* (Chicago: Emperor's, 1997), 164–166. Bowden, for example, cites
Napoleon's correspondence with Murat about troop movements along the Rhine frontier as evidence
that Napoleon was deliberately baiting the Austrians. When these orders are examined in their context,
however, as we shall see below, it becomes clear that they could not and did not spring from any such
intention. It is worth noting in this connection as well that Chandler continually speaks of the Aulic
Council as the Austrian decisionmaking body and the group at which Napoleon's deception was aimed.
This is incorrect. The Aulic Council was a body pertaining to the Holy Roman Empire. Since the War
of 1805 was not an empire war, this body had no significance for it. The decisionmaking body in
Vienna was the Hofkriegsrat, and this is surely what Chandler had in mind.

and even cautious dispositions while waiting for the enemy's plans to become apparent. When he had satisfied himself that he understood what the Austrians were doing, he recognized that he had an opportunity to obtain a more significant victory than he had originally hoped for. The Austrians' occupation of the Iller line, together with Napoleon's own unrelated decision to adopt a more northerly initial disposition for his army, gave him a chance not just to defeat the enemy but encircle and annihilate him. He saw the opportunity and seized it adroitly.

In Search of Understanding

Napoleon had significant advantages over his Austrian counterparts in his efforts to understand his enemy's intentions. Napoleon's movements during the first month of the campaign were confined to French-controlled territory. It was possible for the Austrians to guess the concentration areas of the various corps in France, and they could track the movements of Bernadotte and Marmont on their way to Würzburg. From those facts, which Austrian spies and officers gathered with relative efficiency, it was possible to guess vaguely at Napoleon's ultimate intentions, but there was not a lot of information to go on.

Most of the Austrians' moves during this period, by contrast, took place in Bavaria. Since many Bavarians resented the Austrian invasion, it was easier for French agents to learn of the Austrians' movements than it was for Austrians to figure out what was going on in France. More importantly, however, while the French troops were simply moving into their initial concentration areas for the invasion to follow, the Austrians were marching toward their final destinations. The hard intelligence that reached Mack concerned only French preparations for the campaign, whereas the hard intelligence that reached Napoleon told him exactly what the Austrians were doing.*

Even so, Napoleon and his subordinates faced a significant challenge in understanding the Austrians' intentions. Despite the fact that the Austrian army consistently followed a plan that had been laid out by September 1, it was not until September 27 that Napoleon put enough confidence in his understanding of that plan to develop and execute one of his own.

Grand Strategic and Strategic Intelligence

Napoleon's first task was to discern the allies' capabilities and resources and to understand their overall plan. He started off with a set of serious handicaps in

---

*This fact is evident from the Austrian reports of early September, which are useful only in that they confirm repeatedly that Napoleon was sending the Army of England, and Marmont's and Bernadotte's Corps, to Germany. See KA AFA 1805 Deutschland, XIII/124.

both areas. The deep ignorance of the military capabilities of the various allied states manifested by French agents in early September 1805 emphasizes the absurdity of the notion that Napoleon had been planning a war with Austria all along. Initial reports of Austrian strength assumed that Austrian infantry battalions had 1,100 men each—nearly twice the actual figure.[1] Working, presumably, from this false assumption, other reports suggested that the Austrian army numbered over 400,000 men—again, a figure nearly double the right one.[2] By the end of September, these estimates had settled down toward reality. One French agent guessed that the Austrian army did not number more than 242,642 effective troops.[3] The total number of troops the Austrians actually had available for this war (subtracting garrisons and border troops that they did not intend to use) was 193,147.[4] It is impressive that French agents took only three weeks to correct their wildly wrong estimates but surprising that this effort began shortly before the Austrians crossed the Inn. This fact alone shows that in mid-August 1805 Napoleon did not anticipate fighting a war with Austria in September.

Estimates of the Russian forces available for this campaign were also inaccurate, although for this the French can be more readily forgiven. The actual strength of the Russian army in January 1805 was 341,287 regular troops with another 110,215 in Cossack and other irregular formations.[5] The French never tried to calculate that figure, which was of little importance to them, since Alexander would never send his entire army to western Europe. Their concern was with the size of the Russian auxiliary corps sent to help the Austrians and operate elsewhere on the European continent. In attempting to ascertain the size of these corps, French agents were hampered by Russian secrecy. Alexander had closed off the concentration areas of his armies to foreigners and had forbidden his senior officers in St. Petersburg to speak with foreigners. The French failed to penetrate this cloak of secrecy.

They had to rely instead on what they could pick up in Austria, where French agents could operate more freely. In addition, Austria did not have a history of successful deception or counterespionage. However, French agents could only extract from the Austrians what the Austrians themselves believed to be true—that the Russians were sending two separate corps of 50,000 men each to their aid. Through much of September French agents asserted that 100,000 Russians were marching to Austria's assistance.* Occasionally they reported that 200,000 Russians were on the way.[6] Murat's estimate of the Russian forces was closer to reality. He told Napoleon that 80,000 Russian troops were concentrated on the border of Austrian Galicia.[7] By the end of the month

---

*Report from Hamburg, 4 September 1805, in Alombert-Goget and Colin, *La campagne de 1805*, vol. 2, pt. 1, p. 208; Durand to Talleyrand, 15 September 1805, p. 254. An exception was a report at the end of August suggesting that 60,000 Russians were ready to cross into Austrian Galicia while another 100,000 observed the Prussian frontier. Otto to Talleyrand, 28 August 1805, p. 191.

it was becoming clear that the French had only one Russian army to worry about in the immediate future, numbering around 40,000 men.[8]

What did Napoleon make of these reports? He certainly received word that large Russian armies were advancing on him with considerable phlegm. It seems that he never accepted the highest estimates of the strength of the Russian auxiliary corps. He wrote to Duroc that "the Austrians say" that two columns of 25,000 each were coming to their aid.[9] In a draft address to the French people he announced that "it is said" that 100,000 Russians were in the pay of the English to help the Austrians.[10]

He definitely thought the Russians had been slower to move into Austria than they actually were. He wrote to Eugène Beauharnais on September 16 that the Russians had not yet entered Galicia, when in reality the lead elements of the first Russian army were near Tarnow, several hundred kilometers into Austrian territory.* His initial calm about the approaching Russian corps may have resulted from an erroneous belief that they were much farther off than they actually were. By the time the Russians had come close enough to be a real threat, Napoleon was receiving accurate intelligence about the small size of their columns. Once again, the fact that Napoleon could wait until the end of September before deciding on a detailed plan of operations in Germany meant that he could wait until his image of the enemy's movements had clarified before committing himself to a single course of action.

Understanding the size of the enemy forces facing him was only part of Napoleon's task. He also had to understand how the enemy intended to deploy his forces and what he intended to do with them. In the first instance, he had to understand how the coalition intended to divide its forces among the various potential theaters of war. The protracted nature of the Austrian mobilization made it relatively easy to figure out their deployments and plans.

French agents were able to ascertain the main concentration points of the Austrian army early on. By the first days of September they knew that there were large camps at Wels and Laibach, whose troops were probably intended to operate in Germany and Italy respectively. They were also aware of camps at Budweis, Bregenz, Klettau, and Minkendorf, and they rightly understood that most of the troops in the camp at Budweis had been sent to Wels.[11] When Mack ordered the troops at Wels to advance to Braunau in preparation for the invasion of Bavaria, the French agents picked it up quickly.[12]

The French had a harder time understanding how the Austrians had divided their forces among the different theaters. Early reports tended to underes-

---

*Note to Kutuzov with a march plan for the Russian troops, KA AFA 1805 Deutschland, IX/70. By September 21, Kutuzov was in Kalvaria, a small town just southwest of Krakow: Kutuzov to Bagration, 9 (21) September 1805, in Beskrovnyi, *M. I. Kutuzov: Sbornik dokumentov* (Moscow: Voennoe Izdatel'stvo, 1951), vol. 2, doc. 28, p. 49.

timate the weight of troops the Austrians were sending to Italy and overestimate their forces in the Tyrol and Vorarlberg. In fact tens of thousands of Austrian troops were in motion throughout the Habsburg lands, and French agents were not generally successful at identifying the destinations of those troops.[13] These early reports could not clarify whether the Austrians would make their main effort in Italy, Switzerland, or Germany.

The French were slow to recognize the errors in their estimates of Austrian troop strength in Germany. As late as September 17, Murat was reporting 85,000 Austrian troops in and around Bavaria, whereas the actual total was closer to half that figure.[14] The error probably arose from the overestimation of the average strength of the Austrian battalions, since a report sent in a few days later identified sixty-three battalions and seventy-six squadrons in Ferdinand's army, which actually had fifty-nine battalions and around seventy squadrons.[15]

By September 21, French estimates finally began to approach reality. A letter to Murat of that date, which he forwarded to Napoleon on the same day noting that most of its information had been independently confirmed, reported that there were no more than 42,000 Austrian troops in Bavaria, not counting the army of Bregenz.[16] Other reports soon confirmed these estimates.[17]

The delay in establishing the overall strength of the Austrian army was not terribly important since the original estimates were obviously inflated, and Napoleon would have cared more about reports of units marching west than about the theoretical total strength of the enemy's army. The delay in correcting the original overestimations of Austrian strength in Germany, however, may have been more meaningful. It meant that Napoleon probably believed he faced a more significant enemy than he actually did, and that the destruction of that force would do greater damage to the Austrian army overall than was in fact the case.

Whether Napoleon would have changed his approach to the war had he known the actual strength of the Austrian forces in Germany is unclear, but when he ordered the Grande Armée to concentrate entirely on the Rhine and when he developed his initial dispositions for its march into Bavaria, he thought he was facing an enemy twice as large as it actually was. It is hard to imagine that the corollary is not also true: that the Austrian army in Italy was larger than he originally expected it to be. At all events, the French were not noticeably better than the Austrians in evaluating the strengths and grand strategic deployments of their enemies.

Operational Intelligence

The failure of French intelligence at the highest levels of war was irrelevant in a sense. There is no evidence that Napoleon ever considered doing anything other than directing the concentrated might of the Army of England against whatever Austrian force happened to be in Germany. Given his conviction that Prussia would not join the allies and that he could undo any damage in Italy with a victory in Germany, this determination seems appropriate. Napoleon's plans at the highest level do not seem to have resulted from any clear interaction with the enemy.

The opposite is true at the operational level. Napoleon's agents had a difficult time evaluating the Austrians' intentions or even understanding their movements as Ferdinand's army marched into Bavaria. Yet Napoleon remained determined to respond flexibly to whatever the Austrians did, and to some extent he saw his movements as resulting from theirs.* Napoleon, Berthier wrote the elector of Bavaria at the end of September, makes it a principle to keep his entire army mobile and ready to hand so that he can "send it alternately wherever the mistakes of the enemy call for it."[18] But first he had to see the mistakes.

The overestimation of the size of the Austrian armies in the Tyrol and Vorarlberg, coupled perhaps with excessive eagerness for the coming fight, led a number of French agents and officers to exaggerate both the scale and the speed of the Austrian movement to the west. From the beginning, French agents believed that the Austrians would advance to the Iller line and even beyond it. At the end of August, Otto reported that the Bavarians believed that an Austrian army was designated for Günzburg, roughly thirteen miles down the Danube from Ulm.[19]

Bacher, the French chargé at Ratisbonne who provided much of the more reliable intelligence to the French leadership in this period, first reported the Austrians' crossing of the Inn on September 11, three days after it had happened.[20] Bacher rightly identified the three Austrian columns moving across Bavaria and their initial destinations of Landshut, Freising, and Munich. He immediately jumped to the conclusion that the Austrians would take up the positions they had held prior to the resumption of hostilities in 1799, which ran from Stockach on the western end of Lake Constance to Biberach and then northeast toward Ulm.

This news caused a small flurry in Napoleon's headquarters. The emperor apparently feared that the Austrians had stolen a march on him and would shortly be attacking his positions on the Rhine. He therefore ordered Murat to fortify key towns along the upper Rhine, including Huningue, Belfort, Neuf-Brisach, and Sélestat.[21] He ordered Murat to be ready to cross the river at once if Napoleon received news from Otto that persuaded him to order such a movement. When Napoleon concluded a treaty with the elector of Baden,

---

*See, for example, Berthier to Ney, 20 September 1805, in Alombert-Goget and Colin, *La campagne de 1805*, vol. 2, pt. 1, p. 287: "The dispositions ordered here are always subordinated to the movements of the enemy."

Murat received further orders to be ready to help defend that electorate if the Austrians attacked it.[22]

Murat then panicked and forwarded to Napoleon unconfirmed intelligence reports that the Austrians had seized Laufenburg, a mere twenty-two miles east of Basel, driving off the French troops stationed there. Deserters were reporting that the two Austrian cavalry regiments that had accomplished this feat were followed by many other Austrian troops.[23] Murat went on to report that he was on the point of seizing the bridge over the Rhine at Basel in order to preempt any Austrian attack. After all, he noted, the Austrians had already violated neutrality by crossing the Inn, had they not?

This brief panic lasted only a day and had the salutary effect of forcing Murat to settle down. The next day he reported that there were no Austrian troops at Laufenburg and only about 2,000 at Ravensburg. Francis had not yet come to Munich, as had been reported previously.[24] The day after that, Murat sent a long message to Napoleon apologizing for the bad intelligence and promising not to send forward any information that had not been confirmed. He recapitulated the situation as he was aware of it. The Austrians had crossed the Inn on September 8 and taken Landshut and Munich. A small force of 2,000 troops had marched from Bregenz to Ravensburg. It was being said that the Austrians would continue across the Lech and take position in the Black Forest, but Murat did not believe it.[25] In a detailed exposition of his understanding of the Austrian position, Murat argued that it would be folly for Mack to pass the easily defensible Lech line and leave his right flank completely open and resting on the unfortified cities of Ulm and Ingolstadt. The French perspective and understanding of their situation made this an obvious observation, while the Austrian perspective made it an irrelevant consideration.

Murat's reasoning was proven faulty that very day by two detailed, accurate dispatches, including one from the clearsighted Bacher.[26] These reports made it plain that the Austrians would take up positions within days at Stockach, Biberach, Ulm, Memmingen, and Günzburg—in other words, along the line not of the Iller, but of the Danube stretching from the western edge of Lake Constance in an arc back to Ulm. Bacher also reported that Austrian forces were at Straubing and Abensburg, perhaps indicating that they intended to extend the line north of the Danube as well.

After the brief panic about the security of the Rhine frontier, Napoleon had absorbed intelligence from Murat and others more or less passively. Now he demanded to know if the Austrians had actually reached Ulm and Donauwörth or if the Bavarians still held those positions.[27] That day Murat telegraphed Napoleon that the Austrians had definitely crossed the Lech and were moving by forced marches to the west. He attributed the increased speed of the Austrian advance to the likelihood that word of the raising of the camp at Boulogne had just reached Vienna and was being transmitted back as orders to the Austrian army. Since he regarded the movement to the Iller as militarily senseless in the face of the French dispositions, it never occurred to him that Mack's perception of those dispositions led him to drive his army forward as rapidly as possible.[28] The next day, Murat reported that the Austrians had definitely taken Biberach and Riedlingen.[29]

Napoleon had begun sketching out his plans for the forthcoming movement to the Danube before he received these messages. A brief undated note among his papers (which must have been written between September 15 and 17) sketched out an advance toward the positions the Grand Armée would actually take up in mid-October. He did not execute the plan at this time, however, perhaps because the situation was not yet clear. It is another evidence of his tendency to develop alternative concepts in his mind simultaneously.[30]

At about the same time, Napoleon drafted a different plan that would have produced an entirely different final concentration for his army. Lannes's and Ney's corps would both follow routes leading to Ulm. Soult would march to Aalen, Davout to Nördlingen, and Marmont and Bernadotte to Weißenburg.[31] The French army would thus concentrate in an arc swinging from Ulm to the northeast, a position admirably suited to attack the flank of an Austrian position based on the River Lech and Augsburg. It was a poor position to try to take up, however, if the Austrians already held Ulm, since it would mean that two French corps would have to fight the main enemy army to take up their final concentration areas. Consequently Napoleon's concern to understand whether the Austrians had or had not taken Ulm was understandable.

Informed that they were about to take the city and were moving even farther west, Napoleon developed yet another plan.[32] First, Lannes would cross the Rhine with his corps and march north toward a position between Rastatt and Esslingen. It is apparent from the instructions to Lannes, Murat, and Ney that Napoleon still feared that his lead troops might encounter significant Austrian resistance as they approached the Black Forest, for he made detailed preparations to ensure that Murat and Ney would support Lannes if necessary during this maneuver.[33] The main purpose of the maneuver, however, was probably to get Lannes to a position from which he could advance along a different route from Murat's corps, which was also concentrated near Strasbourg. This would have been the completion of Napoleon's efforts to undo his initial error in concentrating too much force around that city.

When Lannes's movement was complete, Murat would march along the route originally assigned to Lannes in the plan of September 17. When he reached Tübingen, however, he was to march northeast to his final destination of Göppingen northwest of Ulm instead of due east to Ulm itself. Ney's orders would bring him to Giengin, northeast of Ulm (he had originally been ordered to Ulm itself as well). Soult's final destination of Aalen did not change from the order of September 17 to that of September 20, although the route Napoleon traced for him in this second order was much farther north. Davout's route was similarly shifted to the north, although it led him to the same destination—Nördlingen. The plan of September 20 did not mention Marmont and Bernadotte; it is likely that Napoleon intended to leave their route of march and final destination unchanged. Lannes received no orders for movement beyond Rastatt.

The new plan differed from the old by replacing Lannes's infantry corps with Murat's cavalry. It shifted both that corps and Ney's north in order to avoid Ulm, which Napoleon now believed would soon be occupied by the Austrians. Assuming that Marmont and Bernadotte pursued the same route to the same destination (Weißenburg), this plan would bring the Grande Armée down firmly on the flank and rear of the Austrian army arrayed along the Iller.

Since Napoleon rarely explains the intentions that lie behind his plans, we can only guess at them. It seems clear that as late as September 20 Napoleon did not intend to encircle the Austrian army on the Iller. This plan concentrated the bulk of the French army along an east–west line that overlapped the Austrian position but would not necessarily trap the Austrians. A rapid Austrian decision to withdraw would have allowed Mack to race eastward along the Ulm–Augsburg road while his forces to the south rushed along the route Biberach-Memmingen-Landsberg-Munich. Napoleon's troops would have been hard-pressed to cut off either movement.

The purpose of this plan clearly was to establish favorable conditions for a decisive battle, not to obtain an operational envelopment. Napoleon would have turned the flank of the Austrian line and would have had forces moving into the rear of that line. Although Napoleon's easternmost troops probably would not have been able to take position astride the Austrians' lines of retreat, they would have been able to fall on fleeing Austrian columns and take them in the flank. This plan foresaw a great deal of combat, all of it on Napoleon's terms.

Napoleon, however, did not execute the plan of September 20. Shortly after Berthier had dispatched the orders for it, Napoleon began to receive more detailed and accurate intelligence about the Austrians' positions and intentions. As we have seen, it was only in the period immediately following September 21 that Napoleon began to receive reports accurately describing the size of the Austrian army in Germany. This fact may have played a role in the revision of his plans.

An Austrian army of 80,000 men in Germany was large enough to hold its own along the Danube and threaten Napoleon's lines of communications along the Rhine, especially if Russian reinforcements were due to arrive imminently; Napoleon was receiving a stream of contradictory reports about that question. This fact explains otherwise inexplicable orders to Lannes, Ney, and Murat implying that a strong Austrian force might attack the French vanguard

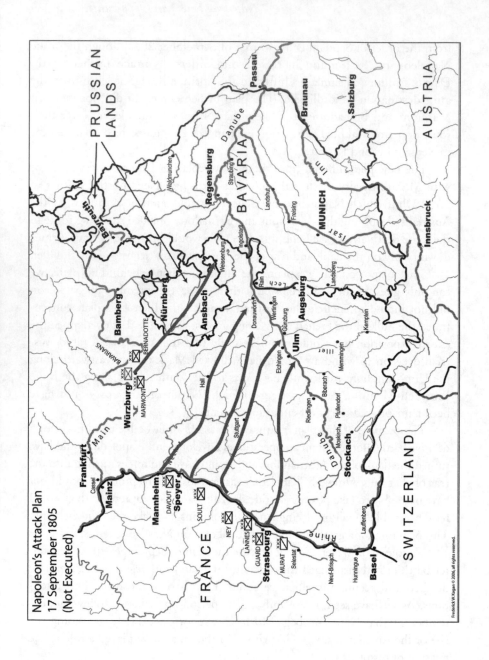

Napoleon's Attack Plan
17 September 1805
(Not Executed)

PRUSSIAN LANDS

AUSTRIA

Passau

Braunau

Salzburg

Danube

Regensburg

Straubing

BAVARIA

Innsbruck

Landshut

Freising

MUNICH

Isar

Inn

Bayreuth

Weidmunchen

Bamberg

Nürnberg

Ansbach

Weissenburg

Ingolstadt

Rain

Lech

Donauwörth

Augsburg

Wertingen

Günzburg

Ulm

Landsberg

Kempten

BAVARIANS

BERNADOTTE

Würzburg

MARMONT

Hall

Stuttgart

Eichingen

Iller

Memmingen

Frankfurt

Main

Cassel

Mainz

Mannheim

DAVOUT

Speyer

SOULT

Biberach

Riedlingen

Moskirch

Pfullendorf

Danube

Stockach

FRANCE

NEY

LANNES

Strasbourg

GUARD

MURAT

Selestat

Rhine

Lauffenberg

SWITZERLAND

Neuf-Brisach

Hunningue

Basel

Frederick W. Kagan © 2006, all rights reserved.

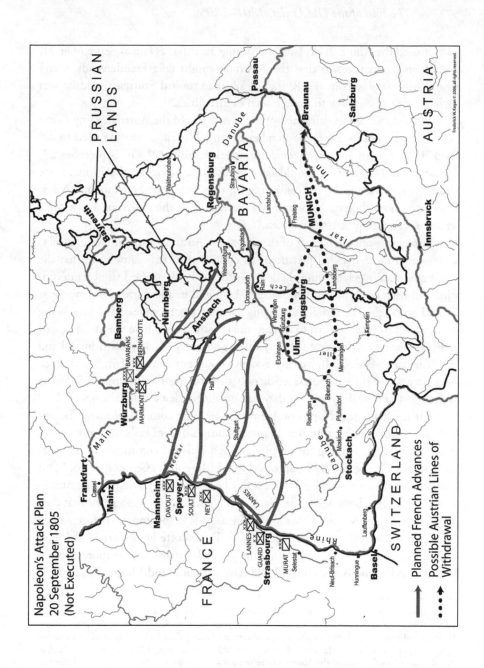

Napoleon's Attack Plan
20 September 1805
(Not Executed)

PRUSSIAN LANDS

AUSTRIA

Passau

Salzburg

Braunau

Danube

BAVARIA

Regensburg

Straubing

Waldmünchen

Landshut

MUNICH

Freising

Innsbruck

Isar

Inn

Nürnberg

Bamberg

Ansbach

Weissenburg

Ingolstadt

Donauwörth

Rain

Lech

Augsburg

Landsberg

BAVARIANS

BERNADOTTE

Würzburg

MARMONT

Wertingen

Günzburg

Eichingen

Ulm

Augsburg

Iller

Kempten

Hall

Stuttgart

Biberach

Memmingen

Neckar

Riedlingen

Moskirch

Pfullendorf

Danube

Stockach

Frankfurt

Cassel

Mainz

Main

Mannheim

DAVOUT

Speyer

SOULT

NEY

LANNES

Strasbourg

LANNES

GUARD

MURAT

Selestat

Lauffenberg

Neuf-Brisach

Hunningue

Basel

SWITZERLAND

Rhine

FRANCE

Bayreuth

⟶ Planned French Advances

⋯⟶ Possible Austrian Lines of Withdrawal

Frederick W. Kagan © 2006, all rights reserved.

as it crossed the Rhine. It explains the strange fact that as late as September 21, Napoleon was concerned that the Austrians might take Freudenstadt, a city twenty-eight miles from the Rhine, or advance toward Stuttgart, and he was giving orders about how to handle such eventualities.[34]

As soon as Napoleon learned of the actual size of the Austrian army (from three separate observers) on September 21 and 24, talk about the need to defend the vanguard against preemptive attack vanished.[35] On September 23, Murat wrote Ney that he should have no difficulty crossing the Rhine, since the enemy seemed to be concentrating on the Lech and the Munda.[36] A few days later, nonetheless, Napoleon was referring to the Austrian army, once again, as consisting of 100,000 men.*

The more accurate reports of the size of the Austrian army in Germany also contained a more detailed picture of its deployment. It became clear that the Austrians were largely leaving the left (northern) bank of the Danube unoccupied and had concentrated their forces at Ulm and in a line stretching southeast toward Stockach. The rapidly advancing Austrian troops appeared to be slowing as they reached what seemed to be their final destination. These reports of slowed marches unwittingly reflected the arguments between Mack and Ferdinand and the latter's halt order, followed by Francis's countermanding of it. The French were unaware of these disputes, seeing only that the Austrian troops seemed to be stopping at or near the positions they had imagined they would take up.

For the first time, Napoleon seemed to become comfortable with his understanding of the situation. He stopped issuing insistent calls for more intelligence and started making the cryptic and self-satisfied comments to his close collaborators for which he is famous. He told Joseph on September 26, "Our maneuvers will soon start."[37] The next day he wrote Talleyrand that the Austrians were at the debouches of the Black Forest and added, "God grant that they stay there. My only fear is that we will scare them too much. Before fifteen days are out, we will see a great deal."[38] To Bernadotte he declared, "if I have the good fortune that the Austrian army sleeps for three or four more days on the Iller and in the Black Forest, I will have turned it and I hope that nothing

---

*Napoleon to Augereau, 30 September 1805, *Corr. de Nap.*, 9299. Napoleon noted that this figure of 100,000 men included those around Lake Constance, presumably meaning those in the Tyrol as well. Since he had previously noted that the Austrians were reinforcing their army in Germany with troops from the Tyrol (Napoleon to Masséna, 29 September 1805, *Corr. de Nap.*, 9286), it is not entirely clear that this estimate of the size of the Austrian force from September 30 was the same as the one that had convinced Napoleon to order the change in operational plans. He certainly did not imagine that the Austrians had sent 60,000 troops from the Tyrol to Germany in three days, which suggests that he had not actually accepted the accurate evaluations of Austrian strength that had been sent to him. It is possible, however, that Napoleon was including the Austrian troops in the Tyrol, whose strength he apparently exaggerated, in the total (Napoleon to Bernadotte, 2 October 1805, *Corr. de Nap.* 9312). He may have deliberately accepted the higher figure in order to magnify the importance of his own success. Certainly he did not use this figure in his correspondence in a way that had any effect on the conduct of operations.

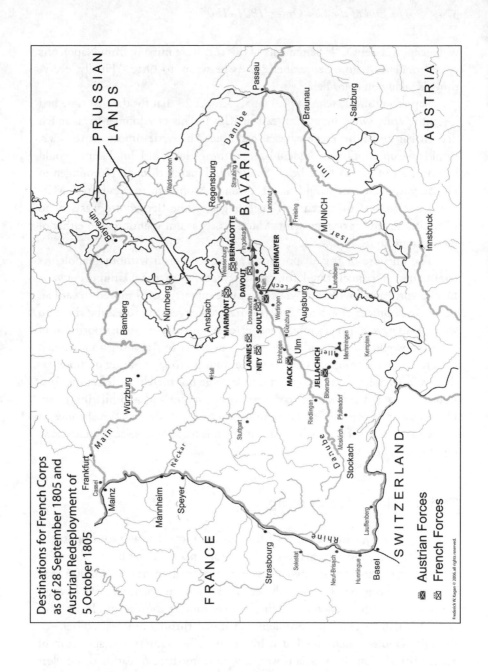

Destinations for French Corps
as of 28 September 1805 and
Austrian Redeployment of
5 October 1805

PRUSSIAN LANDS

AUSTRIA

Passau

Braunau

Salzburg

Danube

Bayreuth

Waldmünchen

Regensburg

Straubing

BAVARIA

Inn

Landshut

MUNICH

Freising

Isar

Innsbruck

Bamberg

Nürnberg

Ansbach

BERNADOTTE

Weissenburg

Ingolstadt

KIENMAYER

DAVOUT

Rain

Lech

MARMONT

Donauwörth

Landsberg

Würzburg

SOULT

Wertingen

Augsburg

Günzburg

LANNES

Eichingen

NEY

Ulm

MACK

JELLACHICH

Iller

Memmingen

Kempten

Hall

Stuttgart

Biberach

Neckar

Riedlingen

Pfullendorf

Moskirch

Main

Frankfurt

Cassel

Mainz

Danube

Stockach

Mannheim

Speyer

Lauffenberg

SWITZERLAND

FRANCE

Strasbourg

Rhine

Selestat

Neuf-Brisach

Huningue

Basel

⊠ Austrian Forces

⊠ French Forces

Frederick W. Kagan © 2006, all rights reserved.

will escape but debris."[39] Statements of this sort were missing from Napoleon's correspondence before September 26. As he wrote to Otto, "Finally, everything is taking on color here."[40]

Napoleon thus sketched a plan on September 28 that for the first time had his entire army swinging around east of Ulm.[41] This envelopment was much deeper than any of his previous plans had been. The westernmost corps, Ney's, would take up position at Heidenheim, north-northeast of Ulm. Lannes would be northeast of him at Neresheim. Soult would march through Nördlingen to Donauwörth. Davout would march through Monheim to Neuburg.* Marmont was ordered to march to Treuchtlingen, while Bernadotte was sent to Eichstatt, northwest of Ingolstadt. Murat's corps is not mentioned in either of these dispositions.

The purpose of this disposition can be seen even without Napoleon's comments. It concentrated four infantry corps on the Danube between Donauwörth and Ingolstadt, while two more infantry corps moved toward an inner envelopment closer to Ulm. Austrian forces seeking to escape this trap would thus have to run a gauntlet that extended seventy-five miles northeast of Ulm and would put the leading French corps closer to Augsburg and Munich than the Austrian troops at Ulm and Memmingen, to say nothing of those farther west. Napoleon saw an opportunity emerge not merely to defeat the Austrians but to win a spectacular victory by encircling and annihilating them. His flexibility in planning and determination to adapt his operational concepts to the movements of the enemy made it possible for him to seize this chance so rapidly and effectively.

The Russians Are Coming

The date of arrival and strength of the Russian forces coming to support the Austrians were important matters to Napoleon's plans in Germany. According to the original allied plan, two Russian armies totaling nearly 100,000 men should have been marching rapidly for Bavaria and the Palatinate. We have already seen that the French had difficulty determining the size and location of these Russian forces. This problem continued throughout September. Although Napoleon had concluded by the time he wrote the disposition of September 28 that the Russians were not an immediate threat, it is not clear what basis he used to come to that conclusion.

---

*The general order cited above has Soult moving only to Nördlingen, but a note Berthier sent to Bernadotte on the same day, clearly for the purpose of coordinating his movements with those of the main body, indicates that Soult was to go on to Donauwörth. A similar situation held for Davout's corps, which was to stop, according to the general order, at Monheim, but which Berthier told Bernadotte would continue to Neuburg.

French agents did not agree on when the Russians began to march through Austrian territory. Initial reports from late August and early September indicated (correctly) that the march was imminent or had just begun.[42] Then for some reason an erroneous corrective began. On September 7 a report came in that the Russians had not yet crossed the border.[43] On September 10, Murat reported that 80,000 Russians were still on the frontiers of Austrian Galicia.[44]

These conflicting reports prompted Napoleon to try to learn the truth. He ordered Duroc in Berlin to find out definitively whether or not the Russians had entered Austrian territory.[45] Laforest was to spare no expense and use every spy at his disposal to get this information. Talleyrand had already sent out a circular to the French representatives in Dresden, Berlin, Copenhagen, and Constantinople seeking the most detailed and accurate statement of the location, name, and strength of all Russian regiments. "His Majesty attaches a great deal of importance to this information," he concluded, "and I invite you to assemble it and transmit it to me with care."[46]

It is interesting that Napoleon assigned urgency to this task so late in the maneuver. He clearly had no idea in late August where exactly the Russians were or what they were going to do (once again demonstrating that he could not possibly have intended to fight a war against Austria and Russia before late August). When he started the Grande Armée marching toward the Rhine, however, he made no effort to fill this intelligence gap. Only in the second week of September did he decide that the issue warranted his attention. By then it was late to send for this information, considering how long it takes messengers to travel from France to the Austro–Russian border and back again.

Nonetheless Talleyrand's circular got a rapid response from Durand, the French minister in Dresden. On September 15, Durand reported that the Russian troops had entered Austrian territory at Brody and were probably near Troppau with about 50,000 men. He thought that another force of about the same strength was following closely behind the first.[47] This report exaggerated the speed of the Russians' movements, for on September 15 the leading Russian column was probably in the vicinity of Tarnow, twelve marches away from a position level with Troppau (the Russian line of march was actually more southerly than the route through Troppau).[48] Most importantly, however, Durand reported that the second Russian army was not racing toward Bavaria, as one might have expected, but was stationary on the borders of Prussian Silesia. He guessed that the position of this army was connected with an ongoing Austro–Prussian negotiation, and reported that the Austrian envoy in Berlin was said to be using the Russian presence as a lever in his conversations. This guess was perfectly accurate.

This news should have been disturbing to Napoleon, since it indicated that the Russians could arrive in Bavaria early in October—in time to affect whatever plans he might have been developing there. This news was confirmed by a report from the normally reliable Bacher.[49] He wrote that the Russians were crossing

Moravia headed for Bohemia and would arrive in the Upper Palatinate in ten or fifteen days—by September 27 or October 2. Didelot's report of the same day was more reassuring, however. It indicated that the lead Russian column would be in Linz by October 6, followed shortly by five others.[50] This report would have given Napoleon substantially more time to finish off the Austrians before he had to worry about the arrival of Kutuzov's army. Bertrand offered an unconfirmed report that contradicted this reassurance, however: the Russians had been at Brünn on September 14 and were marching through Bohemia.[51]

French agents attributed widely diverging objectives to the Russians. Most of them assumed that the Russian forces would march through Bohemia into the Upper Palatinate to operate there and in Franconia. Only a few argued that they would march through Linz toward Braunau and southeastern Bavaria. The difference was important. The road to the Upper Palatinate was shorter than the one toward Munich, while a Russian army emerging from Braunau could be easily contained by French forces enveloping the Austrian Iller line. If the Russians advanced into the Upper Palatinate, however, they could readily march into the rear of the Grande Armée as it executed that maneuver. The consensus of intelligence seemed to suggest that that danger was a real possibility.

Murat initially accepted it. He reported that the Russians were expected in Prague on September 28 and would march from there into the Upper Palatinate and Franconia.[52] Two days later, however, he changed his mind. Now he wrote that the Russians were expected shortly in Vienna.[53] A report from the following day suggested that the Russians would be in Bavaria by October 2.[54]

Napoleon was not able to sort through this tangle of contradictory intelligence, certainly not before he selected his course of action in Germany. All he could say to comfort Bernadotte, surely worried about the possibility of a Russian army crashing into his exposed left flank, was that "the Russians have not arrived. I am ready for anything."[55] He even told Otto that "if it is true that the Russians are advancing [!], then perhaps it would be appropriate for the Elector [of Bavaria] to move to Kalckreuth."[56] What advantage Napoleon saw in such a move is not clear, but it shows that he did not dismiss the possibility of the Russians arriving in the Upper Palatinate in the near future.

Napoleon did not decide to ignore the possible Russian threat to his operations in Bavaria based on an accurate understanding of the location and strength of the Russian force. He did so because of his enormous self-confidence and willingness to take risks. Certain that he could handle any possible contingency, Napoleon seemingly lost interest in trying to see through the tangle of misinformation he was receiving about where the Russians were and what they were doing. We have already seen how he dismissed the possibility that the British would land a force in undefended Hanover with a blithe reference to Frederick the Great's rapid marches and counter-marches. He appears to have dismissed the Russian threat with a similar blitheness based on a similar self-confidence. The envelopment and destruction of Mack's army would go on, whatever the Russians might do.

The Long, Fast March

In the last days of September French soldiers who had been on the march since leaving the English Channel wearily set out on the roads of southern Germany. Historians portray this march as a "triumph of careful planning and staff work" with "few hitches." The routes of march were well stocked and the soldiers well supplied.[57] Much is made of Napoleon's efforts to have logistics officers prepare supplies along the projected march routes ahead of the troops' arrival and of his work to divide the area into distinct districts in which each corps could forage. The false supposition that in September and October Napoleon executed a plan that leaped fully formed from his head in late August leads to the notion that the French army executed that plan flawlessly and easily. This was not the case.

Although the plan for moving toward Bavaria had been gestating in Napoleon's mind for some time before he issued the order that implemented it, concrete preparations to support that maneuver began when the troops started to break camp. Napoleon hoped to use a combination of foraging and prepositioning to feed his armies, but most of the orders to prepare supplies ahead of the arrival of French forces went unexecuted. The notes of Napoleon's officers are filled with complaints about the failure of local authorities to meet the quotas assigned them by Berthier and Napoleon or even permit foraging by French troops.[58]

Particular problems arose in the Prussian territories and in the territories of German princes who preferred to remain neutral in the conflict. The elector of Hesse, for example, attempted to prevent Bernadotte from marching across his land, even though he had signed an agreement with Napoleon to permit and even support that crossing.[59] For a time it seemed that Bernadotte's corps might be cut off from its communications line back to Hanover by the recalcitrant elector.[60] The elector of Württemberg tried to prevent the French from marching through or cantoning in his capital of Stuttgart or his residence at Ludwigsburg, just north of that pivotal city.[61] The Prussian authorities in Ansbach and small neighboring enclaves even drew up their troops in combat formations and forbade the inhabitants from acceding to French requisitions demands.[62]

These minor problems were speedily resolved. The Württembergers and Hessians gave way to superior French force and a desire to stay on the right side of Napoleon. The Prussians dropped their pro forma opposition, which had established their attempt to preserve the neutrality line Frederick William had declared. These political issues, however, delayed French marches and distracted the attention of various marshals, Berthier, and Napoleon himself at a critical junction in the campaign, although they did not in the end hinder French success.

Napoleon's efforts to assign separate march routes to each corps to permit foraging were not entirely successful. Clearly he had not considered this issue in his initial orders of late August and early September, since those orders projected the movement of multiple corps along a few roads, which would have vitiated any attempt to assign different foraging sectors to them. We have already seen how concern for this issue probably played an important role in shifting the overall French deployment to the north to begin with.

Once the campaign was under way, the execution of this plan was far from smooth. The corps commanders and their subordinates repeatedly complained that other units were poaching on their assigned territories. Occasionally some soldiers were forced to bivouac in open fields because other units had taken their assigned lodgings. Sometimes they found it difficult to secure the requisite supplies.[63]

The sum total of these problems, which resulted from inadequate preparatory work and the inevitable friction created when 200,000 men move in a confined space, did not prevent Napoleon from accomplishing his aims. It did add to the physical and psychological toll the campaign took on his soldiers, however, and it occupied the attention of French senior leaders at a time when they could least afford to be distracted from their efforts to understand the enemy. The important as well as subtle problems that arose from this supply method would become clear in subsequent campaigns.

Napoleon's forces also suffered from a serious problem during the war of 1805: weakness at the highest levels of the French command structure. Napoleon's establishment of the marshalate in 1804 crucially affected the development of command relationships in the French army in the nineteenth century. Its effects were still felt sixty-six years later, when Napoleon's nephew deliberately adopted the same command relationships in the Franco–Prussian War.[64]

The establishment of a permanent group of corps commanders with reasonably stable divisional structures underneath them helped give the Grande Armée the flexibility and agility it needed to overcome adversaries that frequently outnumbered it. The value of the corps system, fully developed by Napoleon himself only in the Marengo campaign of 1800, was so obvious that by 1809 it had been adopted by all of the other continental armies.*

The problem with the corps system as Napoleon developed it, however, was that it required him to control (through Berthier, of course) ten separate large military units, including eight concentrated in a single theater operating under

---

*We shall consider the reforms of the other continental armies, including the incorporation of corps systems modeled on the French, in subsequent volumes of this series.

his immediate command.* Assigning a discrete march route to each corps in an arc extending over a distance of nearly 100 miles meant that Napoleon could not make all crucial decisions. That fact would not have been so important if it had not been essential for small groups of those corps to cooperate intimately with one another. Since all of the marshals reported directly to Napoleon, however, he was in principle the only one who could coordinate the units.

What was needed was an intermediate command level between Napoleon and the marshals, a sort of army commander who could control the activities of several corps. But the marshals were jealous of their prerogative of reporting directly to and receiving orders directly from the emperor. They did not take well to receiving orders from each other, and Napoleon could not have established a real "army commander" without mortally offending some of the others.†

Consequently he tried a compromise. He had initially faced the problem that the Grande Armée had started concentrating on the Rhine long before he arrived there; he had deliberately delayed his arrival to obscure his intention to attack the allies on the continent. He adopted the expedient of naming Murat his "lieutenant" and authorizing him to issue orders to the other marshals as necessary for the security of the army in Napoleon's absence.[65]

He faced a similar problem on the left flank of his army, however. Bernadotte and Marmont were to unite and then join with the fleeing Bavarians near Würtzburg by the end of September. At that point, their forces would total more than 40,000 troops, separated from the main body of the Grande Armée by more than sixty miles. Napoleon placed Bernadotte in overall command to ensure the effective coordination of these forces.[66]

Since Napoleon did not rescind Murat's position as his lieutenant or his nominal power over the corps of the right wing of the army after his own arrival, the Grande Armée advanced into Germany in what was, technically, a traditional organization. Murat commanded the right wing, Bernadotte the left wing, and Napoleon himself commanded the center and the reserve. Napoleon thus recreated, at this level of command, a structure that dated back to Alexander the Great.

Napoleon's system suffered from two important problems, however. First, he did not actually designate wing (or army) commanders, but rather assigned corps commanders the additional role of coordinating the movements of other

---

*The Grande Armée consisted of seven numbered infantry corps (Bernadotte, Marmont, Davout, Soult, Lannes, Ney, and Augereau) and Murat's reserve cavalry corps. In addition, Napoleon directly controlled Masséna's army of Italy and Saint Cyr's force in and around Naples.

†David Chandler, ed., *Napoleon's Marshals* (1987; London: Cassell, 2000), pp. xlvii–xlviii. Some marshals operated more or less willingly under the de facto command of others during the 1805 and subsequent campaigns. Napoleon could conceivably have molded at least some of them into more willing and effective subordinates of one another, had he tried. We shall consider individual examples of conflict among marshals throughout the rest of the series. The controversy around Bernadotte's behavior during the Battles of Jena and Auerstedt, in particular, will be discussed in volume 2.

corps. This technique of "dual-hatting" commanders has the defect of forcing those commanders to divide their attention between controlling their own units and coordinating the movements of others. In the heat of a campaign or battle, however, "dual-hatted" commanders tend to focus on their own soldiers and allow coordination with other units to break down. We will see the problems this tendency caused for the French later on in the campaign.

The second problem sprang from the marshals' jealousy of one another. The selection of Murat and Bernadotte as wing commanders was rational. Murat's stature was greater than that of any other marshal because he was married to Napoleon's sister, Caroline, making him a member of the imperial family. He was also senior to the other marshals in point of nobility, since he had been created a prince. Bernadotte's claim to priority over Marmont resulted from his seniority in the service and his political importance in France, which had played a role in convincing Napoleon to make him a marshal in the first place.[67]

This arrangement worked well on the left wing of the army, where Marmont seemed content to follow Bernadotte's orders, and surviving documents reflect relatively little tension between the two marshals. Murat, however, found the going harder on the right flank.

Napoleon designated Murat as his lieutenant on August 26, calling him the "commander in chief of the army in the absence of His Majesty."[68] In addition, he wrote to Murat, "I have sent to [the other marshals] direct orders in accord with the [attached] dispositions; but, if unexpected enemy movements obstruct their execution, they [the other marshals] must inform you and take your orders."[69] Berthier used nearly identical language in notes to Ney, Soult, and Lannes of the same date.[70] The order sent to Davout was somewhat different, for Davout was the farthest away (apart from Bernadotte and Marmont), and Napoleon expected him to come under Murat's control only "in extraordinary circumstances."[71] The next day, Napoleon ordered Murat to work with Lannes to drive Austrian pickets out of advanced positions in the Black Forest.[72] He clearly meant for Murat to have at least a coordinating role as long as Napoleon was far from the theater of war (he was still at Saint-Cloud when these orders were issued).

Murat attempted to fill the role he supposed Napoleon had assigned him. He worked to coordinate the actions, administration, and logistics of the corps nearest his, those of Ney, Lannes, and Soult, and he received initial cooperation from those marshals.[73] Murat remained confused about his position in the chain of command and his role in the operational maneuver, however. He wrote to Napoleon,

> Sire, the marshals commanding the various corps received the order to cross the Rhine directly from the minister of war; I received it myself as commander of the reserve cavalry [corps] and not as commander of the army in your absence. By this disposition it seems that each must await new orders

to act separately and that there will not be any more central authority of any variety. Nevertheless, I beg Your Majesty to be perfectly reassured, because, if you do not arrive today, I will not forget that I have the honor to be your lieutenant and I am certain that each will execute my orders assiduously.[74]

This was an astute observation. If Napoleon really intended Murat to be the wing commander, then all of his orders to the other marshals composing that wing should have been passed through Murat. Given their reaction to Murat's initial efforts to coordinate the movements of the army, it is by no means clear that the marshals would have rejected this organization, whatever their jealousy.

But Napoleon was unwilling to take such a step. He continued to direct the movement of each corps, and sometimes even individual regiments. He clearly expected Murat to take charge only if unforeseen circumstances required a sudden change of plan. Thus he undercut Murat's small authority with his brother marshals and made Murat self-conscious and uncomfortable in his role as Napoleon's lieutenant. He also failed to create a new level in his command hierarchy that would have facilitated the coordination of large-scale operations by multiple corps detached from the main body. This failure generated a limited number of problems in the first phase of the campaign, but it loomed larger as the war unfolded across central Europe.

The French problems in logistics and command organization were largely mirrored in the Austrian army. It is a popular myth that the French had an advantage over their adversaries after 1805 because they lived off the land, foraging as the armies advanced into enemy territory. As a result, it is said, they were able to move faster than their enemies, who were still tied to the antiquated magazine system of supply thought to characterize eighteenth-century armies. There is very little truth to this belief in general, but it specifically did not apply to the army Mack led into Bavaria.

Determined to increase the army's rate of march, Mack had taken drastic steps to reduce the army's baggage and free it from a heavy logistical "tail" that could slow down its movement. As a result, the Austrian army, like the French, largely lived off the land, acquiring supplies from the local populations by requisitioning. That had been one of the goals of jumping rapidly into Bavaria, since it allowed the Austrians to feed tens of thousands of their soldiers at someone else's expense. The French were well aware of this fact and saw no difference between their system of logistics and the Austrian system.*

---

*Alfred Krauss, *1805: Der Feldzug von Ulm* (Vienna: L. W. Seidel, 1912), pp. 179, 284–285. As Napoleon wrote to Eugène, "When one has long-prepared magazines, one can sometimes avoid using requisitions; but everywhere else they are indispensable. The Austrians requisition in Germany, they requisition in Venice; one cannot feed great armies otherwise." Napoleon to Eugène, 22 September 1805, *Corr. de Nap.*, doc. 9258.

This method of supply had two results for the Austrian army, one obvious and one less so. As the French marched rapidly from Boulogne to Munich, they found it difficult to arrange supplies and forage efficiently. So too did the Austrians in their race from the Inn to the Iller. Even after Austrian troops had reached the Iller line, constant movement and Mack's last-minute changes to the logistics administration continued to produce chaos in this area, which hindered the efficient supply of some Austrian units.[75]

This Austrian reliance on foraging had a more subtle consequence as well. Southern Germany was a rich area at this time with an ample agricultural surplus, along with a dense road network that facilitated rapid, dispersed, and complex maneuvers. This region of Europe was as perfectly (and uniquely) suited to Napoleon's style of warfare as the Iraqi desert was to the American style of warfare in 1991 and 2003. Even in Bavaria, Baden, and Württemberg, however, there were relatively few major cities from which to draw supplies for thousands of men over a long period of time, and the Austrians had no more success prepositioning supplies than the French did. The French armies were racing rapidly from town to town, however, and moved on before they had exhausted the local supplies. The Austrians, on the other hand, remained largely stationary, shifting units from place to place in a confined space. This fact had a profound operational consequence.

The Austrians could not have supplied their army in this manner if Mack had concentrated it in one or two main bodies. Troops thus concentrated would have eaten all of the available supplies in no time and then been forced to starve, set up a magazine system, for which no preparations had been made, or disperse in order to forage further afield. This is one of the reasons why Mack adopted such a dispersed deployment to begin with. That deployment allowed him to draw from the considerable resources of Ulm, Augsburg, Memmingen, Bregenz, Kempten, Stockach, Biberach, and so forth, and thereby support his stationary army until the Russians arrived and offensive operations could begin. The corollary was that the Austrian army had to remain dispersed for as long as possible. Once Mack concentrated it in any one place, he would be forced to begin moving it and keep it moving—or disperse it again.[76]

Foraging as a system of supply thus had distinct limitations and was by no means the positive good that some students of the French revolutionary armies claim. It required the army to stay constantly in motion through prosperous lands with a dense road network that would facilitate sending different units along distinct lines of march. When those conditions were not met, as we shall see in some of Napoleon's later campaigns, the consequences were serious. For Mack's army, the consequence was the forced dispersal of the Austrian army at a time when concentration became essential.

Just as the Austrians suffered from the reverse of the logistical problems that beset the French, they also suffered from the reverse of the command

NAPOLEON I,
EMPEROR OF THE FRENCH

ALEXANDER I,
TSAR OF RUSSIA

FRANCIS II, HOLY ROMAN EMPEROR,
EMPEROR OF AUSTRIA

FREDERICK WILLIAM III,
KING OF PRUSSIA

ARCHDUKE CHARLES OF AUSTRIA

ARCHDUKE FERDINAND D'ESTE

COUNT LUDWIG COBENZL,
AUSTRIAN FOREIGN MINISTER

BARON KARL VON MACK,
AUSTRIAN QUARTERMASTER-GENERAL

P. P. Dolkgorukii,
Russian Imperial Aide-de-Camp

General M. I. Kutuzov,
Commander of the Podolian Army

General P. I. Bagration,
Commander of the
Russian Vanguard

Grand Prince Constantine
Pavlovich of Russia

N. N. NOVOSIL'TSEV,
RUSSIAN STATESMAN

COUNT A. R. VORONTSOV,
RUSSIAN FOREIGN MINISTER

COUNT S. R. VORONTSOV,
RUSSIAN AMBASSADOR TO
GREAT BRITAIN

PRINCE A. A. CZARTORYSKII,
RUSSIAN DEPUTY FOREIGN MINISTER

MARSHAL LOUIS NICOLAS DAVOUT

MARSHAL ALEXANDRE BERTHIER

MARSHAL JEAN LANNES

MARSHAL ANDRÉ MASSÉNA

MARSHAL JEAN BAPTISTE JULES
BERNADOTTE

MARSHAL MICHEL NEY

MARSHAL JEAN-DE-DIEU SOULT

GENERAL GÉRAUD CHRISTOPHE
MICHEL DUROC, FRENCH ENVOY
AND COMMANDER

BARON K. F. VON TOLL,
RUSSIAN GENERAL

COUNT JOSEPH VON COLLOREDO,
AUSTRIAN MINISTER

COUNT PHILIPP VON STADION,
AUSTRIAN AMBASSADOR TO RUSSIA

KARL AUGUST VON HARDENBERG,
PRUSSIAN FOREIGN MINISTER

GENERAL F. F. WINTZINGERODE,
RUSSIAN ENVOY

PRINCE JOHANNES OF LIECHTENSTEIN,
AUSTRIAN COMMANDER

PRINCE CARL VON SCHWARZENBERG,
AUSTRIAN ENVOY AND COMMANDER

CHARLES, EARL WHITWORTH,
BRITISH AMBASSADOR TO FRANCE

arrangements at the highest level. Napoleon hypercentralized his control of the army and refused to create a command echelon between himself and the corps commanders. Mack constantly competed with Ferdinand for control of the single, much smaller Austrian army.

As we have seen, Mack's efforts to take effective command of the army in Germany did not fully succeed, for he was unable to force Ferdinand away from headquarters or deprive him of operational control. Ferdinand's efforts to destroy Mack's plan and take independent command likewise came to naught during Francis's brief foray into the theater of war. Thereafter, Mack and Ferdinand were bitter enemies and rivals for control of the army. Their respective ex post facto descriptions of the campaign reflect this rivalry and the concomitant efforts to shift the blame to the other.[77] The Austrian reaction to a dawning understanding of Napoleon's plan was powerfully conditioned by this rivalry and mutual dislike. Where Napoleon's movements were characterized by inadequate coordination among his subordinates, the Austrians were frequently paralyzed by a fight for control of the campaign.

For all that, the French troops marched on, day by weary day. By October 5, they were nearing their designated positions along the Danube east of Ulm. Once the French had secured the bridges across the river and established themselves on the southern bank, the Austrians would find escape difficult. Their best hope was to concentrate and move rapidly toward the east or south. It was unfortunate for the allies that decisive action was the one thing least likely to emerge from the headquarters of Mack and Ferdinand.

Paralyzed

The decision to stay and hold the Iller line anchored on Ulm was taken on September 22. The next day, Mack sent a sizable corps under the command of FML Kienmayer to the vicinity of Ingolstadt to observe Bernadotte's corps. In the last three days of September, Napoleon's troops crossed the Rhine and marched toward a line that would place them deeply in the rear of the Austrian position, a line that they reached by October 6–7. By then the Austrian position had become critical. The first and most important question we must consider is, Why did Mack not react more efficiently to the impending French envelopment?

As Mack perceived it, the situation did not change between September 22, when he had won the fight over the deployment of the army, and the beginning of October. Mack knew on September 22 where the French corps were going to concentrate and presumably cross the Rhine. With that information in hand, he concluded that Davout, Marmont, and Bernadotte, and possibly Soult as well, were heading for Bohemia to meet the Russians while Ney, Murat, and

Lannes came to attack him near Ulm. However well- or ill-founded this conclusion might have been on September 22, nothing happened before the end of the month that should have caused Mack to revise it.

As the French army began crossing the Rhine, Mack found yet another argument to bolster his interpretation of events. He had realized that Marmont's corps was to link up with Bernadotte's near Bamberg and Würzburg and believed that "there can be no more doubt . . . that it seems to have the aim of simply protecting the Elector of Bavaria for the moment."[78] This evaluation was correct in a way. Napoleon had sent Bernadotte racing to Würzburg initially precisely for that purpose. It was only as he learned of Mack's own movements and began to see greater possibilities that he developed a new, more ambitious plan for Bernadotte, Marmont, and the Bavarians to execute.

Mack did not see the possibilities inherent in Bernadotte's position at Würzburg because he did not believe that Napoleon would violate Prussian neutrality or that Frederick William would give him permission to cross his territory. He never considered the danger Bernadotte's wing posed to his own forces, and he even doubted that it endangered Bohemia, since the marshal could only get from Würzburg to Bohemia if Frederick William gave his permission.[79]

In his self-justification, admittedly written eight years later, Mack argued this point even more strenuously. He noted that Francis was aware of the location of Bernadotte's army when he decided to allow Mack to occupy the Iller line, and that his only orders regarding Prussian territory were to forbid any Austrian from violating it on pain of death. Right after Francis had left, the Prussian king declared that he was mobilizing his entire army to defend his neutrality, "so that I could concern myself with the [French] violation of neutrality even less."[80]

We should be slow to take Mack's word for what went on in his mind in a document written with the explicit intention of clearing his name eight years after he had been court-martialed.* Yet every part of this explanation can be supported by the correspondence of September 1805. Frederick William announced that he was mobilizing his army to defend his neutrality. Francis was aware of Bernadotte's location when he approved the position on the Iller line. Mack did refer at the time to his belief that the French would not be able to cross the Prussian territory of Ansbach that separated Bernadotte's army from the right flank of his own. He even pointed out with some justice how well founded that belief was. His declaration that "there is no example in ancient or modern history of such a wanton and defiant provocation being made to an

---

*On the other hand, it is no more appropriate simply to take Ferdinand's word for what happened, as the Austrian historians do, or to ignore the detailed, thoughtful exposition of Mack's thought process that he provides in his self-justification. When both documents are compared with the available evidence, Mack's is generally more accurate, at least in these early passages.

already-prepared military power of such an enormously high number and quality [of troops] as Prussia" might be exaggerated, but it contains a grain of truth. By sending Bernadotte through Ansbach, Napoleon risked bringing 200,000 Prussian troops into the field against him to outflank Mack's army of less than 50,000 men. Mack's conviction that Napoleon would not do such a foolish thing turned out to be wrong, but it was not insane.

It did not require clairvoyance to recognize the possibility that Napoleon might be, from Mack's perspective, foolish enough to cross Ansbach. Ferdinand wrote Francis on September 28 warning him that Marmont's corps and the Bavarians were marching to link up with Bernadotte.[81] It was possible, he allowed, that this force was earmarked for Bohemia, but it was more likely going to confront Kienmayer's corps on the Danube. Ferdinand pointed out that only by marching to the Danube could Bernadotte's army remain coordinated with the main body of the French force.

He also pointed out that such an attack would gravely jeopardize the right wing of the Austrian army. The entire Iller line could be compromised and the Austrian lines of communication cut completely. But Ferdinand stopped short of making recommendations. The reason for this restraint was obvious if unstated. Less than a week before Francis had clipped the army commander's wings by siding with Mack on the army deployment question. Ferdinand had no new information about Napoleon's intentions and could only report that the French were behaving about as expected. He did not have enough ammunition to restart a debate he had just lost. Once again he did not address the central point. Mack conceded all of the information in Ferdinand's note. He would only have added (had they been speaking to one another) that he did not believe Napoleon would violate Prussian territory. The debate was not about the location of the French forces or even their theoretical capabilities. It was simply about their intentions, and Ferdinand had no more light to shed on that question than Mack had. The conflict within the Austrian high command continued to take its toll, and yet another timely opportunity to reconsider the army's position came and went unheeded.

Subsequent reports seemed to undermine Ferdinand's conviction. On October 1, he reported to Francis that Bernadotte was still in Würzburg and that the Bavarian troops had retreated even farther north from their original positions. He noted that they scrupulously avoided violating Prussian neutrality in doing so.[82] The movement of French troops from the west, however, was clear. Ferdinand reported activity in the Black Forest, as well as camps at Heilbronn and Stuttgard. He confined himself to passing on these reports and offered no comments of his own.

In the meantime Mack worked hastily to construct a defensive line. He ordered the concentration of laborers and materials at Lindau, Ulm, and Memmingen to fortify those places, working "day and night." The Austrian fortification efforts must have been significant, since numerous reports to French commanders mention them and the corvée labor that worked on them. Mack's efforts at fortification did not endear the Austrians to the Bavarian population.[83]

This frantic effort at fortification was part of the overall plan that Mack had never reconsidered. Given that he had determined to hold the Iller line, it made sense. He knew that Napoleon was coming for him with greatly superior forces, and he needed a way to even the odds. The need to fortify a defensive position for his troops was one of the reasons for jumping into Bavaria in the first place.

Once again, however, the conflict in the Austrian high command compromised the leaders' ability to evaluate the situation and respond to it. It is not clear what intelligence Mack saw about the French movements or when. Ferdinand apparently did not keep him informed (hardly surprising, in view of relations between the two men at this point), and Mack concentrated on his fortification efforts. The most unfortunate aspect of this arrangement was that the man who was receiving and evaluating the intelligence, Ferdinand, had already been excluded from making strategic and operational decisions for the army. The man who was authorized to make those decisions was concerning himself instead with the minutiae of fortifying small cities and towns.

The Austrians' efforts to understand French movements were also complicated by the nature of their own deployment. Mack had flooded southeastern Germany with Austrian pickets, and the French troops reported nearly constant contact with them shortly after they crossed the Rhine. Naturally enough, those pickets made contact reports that were consolidated by Austrian corps commanders seeking to understand what they were facing. On October 3 Kienmayer provided Ferdinand with a detailed report of the movements and current positions of the four infantry corps of the right wing of the French army.[84]

The report showed French troops at or approaching Geislingen, Schwabisch Hall, Stuttgart, and Vellberg, and revealed that their destinations were positions on the Danube below Ulm. The report accurately identified Nördlingen as the target of one of the corps. The conclusion drawn by the author of the report, Wallmoden, was that the "main body of the French is moving against Ulm."[85] Wallmoden noted that he had no real information about Bernadotte's movements, but he was believed to be heading for Bamberg.

The lack of information about Bernadotte's corps, as well as Marmont's and the Bavarians', is not surprising. Wallmoden wrote from Ellwangen, a small town on the road from Heilbronn to Nördlingen and Donauwörth. He was piecing together intelligence based on the contact reports of pickets and word of French foragers' efforts ahead of the main army. But the Austrians had no pickets in Ansbach or north of it. Nor were the Bavarians sufficiently friendly to the Austrians to pass on word of French movements of their own accord. The Austrian respect for Prussian neutrality provided Bernadotte's wing with a screen more effective than any cavalry could have been. The lack of information from the north, combined with abundant information from the northwest and west, helped prevent the Austrians from recognizing the danger in a timely fashion. This was a stroke of luck for Napoleon, who had not planned it and did not seem to recognize it as it occurred, but it was the sort of luck that a skilled commander can expect to have now and then.

In the meantime, Mack abandoned his preoccupation with earthworks and turned his attention back to the situation before him. His perception of that situation emerges most clearly from the new disposition he sent to the army on October 5.[86] Unaware of Bernadotte's mission, Mack believed that he had to deal only with the four infantry and one cavalry corps of the right wing of Napoleon's army. Clearly he had accepted Wallmoden's conviction that those corps were converging on the Danube somewhere in the vicinity of Ulm. Mack prepared his army to respond.

First he ordered the army to concentrate into a tight body near Ulm, ready to cross the Danube en masse at a moment's notice. Kienmayer's corps would remain concentrated near Donauwörth. Jellachich would mass his forces near Biberach. Mack intended by this deployment to gain maximum flexibility. It might be wisest, he wrote, to attack one or more of the French columns as they advanced. In that event, the main body at Ulm would cross the river and either take up prepared positions on the other side or march to take one of the French columns in the flank or rear. Kienmayer's corps would cross at Donauwörth, assuming it did not face insurmountable odds, and march upstream either to assist the main body or attack another column in the flank or rear. Jellachich's corps would make sure that no threat was emerging from the Black Forest, and then it too would cross the Danube and march downstream to operate against the flank of any French column it might find, or to assist the main body. If Jellachich encountered forces too strong to attack, he was to withdraw to Memmingen. If Kienmayer found himself in difficulty, he was to withdraw to Ingolstadt. There was no consideration of what the main body would do if it encountered overwhelming forces, but Mack intended to remain with the main body and command it as circumstances dictated.

These dispositions reveal that Mack did not believe he was facing forces so overwhelming that his troops could not hold the Danube line against them. Clearly he had already shifted the defensive orientation of the Austrian position, at least in his mind. The Iller line had become irrelevant, and Mack finally recognized (although not explicitly) that his efforts to defend Lindau, Biberach, and so on had been wasted motion. The Danube was now the defensive line, running from before Biberach to Donauwörth. It was, as Mack noted in his self-justification, a formidable river with a fortified city in the center of the line. He clearly believed that he could hold it.

He also believed that his lines of communications and withdrawal were still secure. Kienmayer could fall back safely on Ingolstadt, which Mack did not believe was threatened, and Jellachich would be able to make it to Memmingen and then farther east. Although he did not explicitly consider it, Mack probably assumed that he would be able to withdraw the main body from Ulm to the east or southeast if necessary.

This disposition betrays no panic, and the usual exhortations to march by day and night or with the greatest possible speed are missing. Mack appears to have sized up the French advance, rejected the notion that Bernadotte presented a danger to his flank, and simply prepared to fight, as he had always intended, to hold the French off until the Russians arrived.

Remarkably, this is the first operational order to the Austrian army in Germany specifically assigning a role to the Russians; they were to march as rapidly as possible toward Ingolstadt or Neuburg, anchoring the army's right flank. Mack is not clear about when he expected the Russians to arrive, but he hoped to expedite that arrival by mounting the Russian troops on carts, as the Austrians had done during the trip through Moravia. He might find it wiser, he wrote, to await the Russian linkup with Kienmayer before beginning overall offensive operations in conjunction with them.

Assuming the validity of Mack's belief that Bernadotte, Marmont, and the Bavarians were not his concern, this plan was sensible, intelligent, and on a par with what Napoleon himself might have come up with. Mack envisioned his army as three corps operating independently but working toward the same goal. He imagined that they might face one, two, or three different fights depending on the circumstances, and he gave his subordinate commanders responsibility for taking the initiative and acting according to their perception of those circumstances. This was a modern and creative plan that allowed for initiative and flexibility at several levels. The only problem, of course, was that one of its fundamental assumptions proved to be devastatingly incorrect.

Davout, Bernadotte, and Marmont entered Prussian territory on October 3.[87] Kienmayer's pickets learned of this event quickly, but Kienmayer did not report the movement to Ferdinand until October 6.[88] Once again the fact that the Austrians had respected Prussian neutrality placed them at a severe disadvantage from the standpoint of gathering timely intelligence. Nevertheless, by October 6 Kienmayer was able to evaluate Napoleon's goals correctly: "All reports agree that the enemy wishes to cross the Danube at Donauwörth, Neuburg, and Ingolstadt." The mystery was over and the game was up. Mack faced the collapse of all of his plans and preconceptions and the prospect of limitless disaster. Once again we shall see how he and Ferdinand were almost uniquely ill-suited for responding to such a crisis.

16

The Battles of Ulm

When Mack learned that Bernadotte was crashing through Ansbach on his way to the Danube, he saw that the situation was dire. At Ingolstadt Napoleon's troops were in excellent position to cut off the Austrian army from reinforcements and its primary lines of communication. The stage was set for disaster. Yet Mack was not without options. He almost certainly could not have retrieved the situation and stabilized his position, but neither was all inevitably lost. To recover from this situation would have required intrepidity combined with realism, bold and rapid decisionmaking, and instant execution. These were precisely the traits least in evidence in Mack's command.

A Poor Decision

It is not clear that Mack and Ferdinand considered their operational options with any degree of care when they learned of Bernadotte's movement, since on the day Kienmayer wrote Ferdinand with the bad news, Ferdinand sent Francis a plan that involved trying to hold Ulm.[1] Napoleon's coup had destroyed any notion of withdrawing to the east, but the Austrians could have withdrawn to the south along a line that ran Ulm-Memmingen-Kempten and probably toward Innsbruck. Napoleon's troops would have been hard-pressed to beat the Austrians to Innsbruck, and the passes and defiles of the Tyrolean Alps could have offered Mack's army formidable defensive positions.

Such a retreat would have had the additional advantage of drawing Mack's forces closer to reinforcements from Archduke John's army in the southern Tyrol and even to forces drawn from Charles's army in Italy. It would have been risky, since it required a skillful rearguard commander who could keep Ney's and Murat's forces at bay, but this was a plan that offered some hope of saving the bulk of Mack's forces.

Mack explained his decision to stand at Ulm in his self-justification of 1813.[2] It was not true, he said, that he had simply marched around "in many small columns" (for which his accusers had taken him to task) and allowed himself to be completely cut off from the homeland. There were "many days free to withdraw ourselves toward Vorarlberg and Tyrol." To do so, however, would have been to move away from the oncoming Russian army, from the second Russian army that was supposedly following it, from reinforcements being prepared in Austria, and from Vienna. It would have exposed Kienmayer's Corps to probable destruction, and Mack was concerned that Napoleon would fall on the hapless Russians and destroy them as well. Above all, he likely feared leaving Napoleon an open route to the Austrian capital, and his was the only Austrian force capable of defending Vienna. He ignored the advantages of terrain and reinforcements available to him if he had retreated south.

Mack's logic here was faulty. Retreating south would have exposed Kienmayer, and possibly the Russians, to destruction by Napoleon's superior forces. It would have left the road to Vienna open. It would have drawn Mack away from reinforcements being prepared for his army. But attempting to hold Ulm was still the wrong decision to make.

Mack could protect Kienmayer, the Russians, and Vienna only if he could hold off the crushing weight of the Grande Armée. He would have to concentrate his army rapidly, hold the river crossings around Ulm, and launch a series of lightning strikes against oncoming French columns. Mack's belief that he could do these things reflected his usual exaggerated self-confidence and his inability to recognize the limitations of his army. That self-confidence apparently prevented him from considering the possibility that he could endanger Kienmayer, Vienna, and the Russians, and lose his army too.

Self-confidence probably led Mack to imagine that Kienmayer and the Russians, whose forces together numbered about the same as the rest of Mack's army, would be helplessly smashed by an enemy Mack believed he could defeat. If he had evaluated the situation more impartially, he might have recognized another advantage of a withdrawal on Vorarlberg. It would have bought time for the Russians to arrive, and they would have arrived on Napoleon's flank and rear, assuming that the emperor chased Mack's army. If Napoleon turned to face the Russians instead, then Mack would have had the opportunity to fall on his flank or rear. Assuming that the Russians and Kienmayer were competent, the withdrawal on Vorarlberg would have opened more promising possibilities for the allies to retrieve the situation.

Mack clearly hoped that he could hold the French long enough for the Russians to arrive and fall on their flank as they attacked him at Ulm. The problem was that this belief required Mack and his army to succeed in the hardest possible option. Nothing would be harder than to respond instantly to an unforeseen calamity and fight perfectly facing the danger of annihilation at every turn.

The news of the changing situation seemed to unhinge the quartermaster general. His report to Francis on October 6 reveals his state of mind.[3] The enemy, he wrote, had advanced on Ulm, but the Austrians were standing firm. He anticipated an attack on Günzburg, but by the morrow twenty-five battalions would be present to defend the bridge. "The enemy," he continued, "seems to have based all his hopes on" seizing the crossings at Günzburg "and thereby threatening our rear and destroying our communications from Ulm, but we are and will continue standing firm here, since Memmingen is already defensible so that our supply does not come *along the Danube.*"* Mack continued, "Even if [the enemy] crossed much further down the Danube and even moved toward the Inn," the Austrian army would stand firm and abandon neither Ulm nor the left bank of the Danube. Napoleon exposed his lines of communication even as he attacked Mack's, and was placing himself between the Austrians and the advancing Russian army as well.

So far, so bad. Mack intended to hold his position whatever happened and ignored the fact that he would have to drive through two or three French columns to get at one of Napoleon's lines of communication. There was another line that ran back to Hanover and could support Bernadotte, Marmont, and the Bavarians, to the extent that lines of communication are vital to an army that is living off the land. Attacking Napoleon's lines of communication would have placed the Austrian army in a position to be attacked from all sides by superior forces, moreover. This scheme was clearly nonsensical.

It reflected Mack's momentary derangement. "If I ever had hopes for a successful outcome," he continued, "I have them still . . . Oh, if only Your Majesty had not had to leave again the army for which You have prepared the first victory, which God will probably grant before the arrival of the Russians. Before tomorrow evening we will have concentrated more than 80 battalions, and then we will not delay to move actively into the rear of the enemy who wishes to take us in the rear." This note makes Pollyanna look like a skeptic.

It is hard to explain Mack's decision to stand at Ulm without reference to his personality. His self-confidence was clearly an important part of this decision, but so too was his insecurity. Would the emperor countenance a retreat in spite of his orders, even in an extreme situation? Would a retreat not be an admission of failure and incompetence, especially in light of Ferdinand's previous complaints and accusations? Could Mack's control of the army survive such admissions? Could Mack survive another ignominious campaign after the disastrous campaign in Naples? Was it not preferable to stake all to win all by seeking a glorious comeback on the banks of the Danube? Posthumous psychoanalysis is always dangerous, but it is hard to imagine that none of these

---

*Emphasis in the original. Mack was fond of underlining phrases, the importance of which is not always obvious.

issues flitted through Mack's mind as he contemplated his situation and dismissed all options but one. However that may be, the decision was made quickly. The Austrian army would not withdraw to the Tyrol but stand and fight on the Danube.

Ferdinand was not as confident as his colleague, or as vague. He reported to Francis that he had agreed with Mack to assemble a large force near Ulm to strike the right wing of Napoleon's army under Ney and possibly Soult in order to prevent that wing from joining Bernadotte's forces.[4] As for dealing with those corps, Ferdinand could only hope that it would be possible for some force to fall on their flank. That force could only come from the Russian army, since Ferdinand noted that Kienmayer had orders to withdraw to Landshut and try to link up with the Russians if he found the forces before him overwhelming (as they surely would be). Ferdinand intended to remain with the main army at Ulm "in order from there to operate in the rear of the French army." He was ordering the headquarters of the army moved from Mindelheim to Ulm.

The next day, Mack drafted a more thoughtful reflection on the current situation that was similar to the plan Ferdinand had outlined for Francis.[5] The main army would concentrate between Ulm and Günzburg with forces on both sides of the Danube. Jellachich was to race "day and night" with the "greatest possible speed" toward Ulm. If he found no enemy before him, he would march toward Stuttgart to attack the enemy's lines of communication; if that was not possible, he would go to Ulm. According to Mack's calculations, Jellachich had sixteen infantry battalions, six jaeger companies, and six cavalry squadrons, or perhaps 15,000 men, to raid the lines of communication of three or four French corps (Ney, Murat, Lannes, and possibly Soult). Kienmayer was to keep his force concentrated near Ingolstadt but maintain contact with the main body through a cordon along the Danube.

Mack's fancy had not deserted him. He noted that the enemy seems "to have the aim of repeating his game of Marengo whereby he would take the army in the rear and cut it off from" Austria. But Ulm, he argued, was already a strongly fortified position, and it covered the roads to the Tyrol admirably. If the enemy wished to advance, he would have to take Ulm, and Mack believed that he could make the cost of such an undertaking very high. Even at this late date, when the survival of his army was on the line, Mack was still talking about protecting the Tyrolean passes. It is impossible to know if he was clinging to the shreds of the original war plan or if he was using this issue as an excuse to justify his desired course of staying and fighting for Ulm.

The Austrian army now deployed according to the new plan. The main body divided into two groups. One group of twenty-eight battalions and thirty squadrons under Schwarzenberg's command was concentrated in Ulm and the small towns on the left bank of the Danube. The second, under Werneck, comprised thirty battalions and twenty-four squadrons and occupied Günzburg.[6]

Kienmayer's corps of nineteen battalions and thirty-four squadrons continued to be concentrated around Ingolstadt and Donauwörth.[7] It was too late for the smooth deployment that Mack had hoped for, however, or for the calm and calculated ripostes he hoped to direct against the oncoming French. As the leading French forces began to make contact with Austrian detachments along the Danube, the situation moved entirely out of Mack's hands. The decision to stay at Ulm was the last decision Mack made freely. Hereafter, all of his actions would be tightly constrained by the encircling French forces.

Encirclement

By October 6–7 Napoleon had achieved an extremely advantageous position against the Austrians. His forces were ready to cross the Danube at multiple places and cut Mack's army off from the Vienna road, the Russians, and reinforcements. An encirclement is a complicated maneuver, however, especially when there are armies outside of the encircling forces that could attempt to relieve those trapped within. A large army trapped in an encirclement with a reasonable amount of supplies, moreover, can sometimes prolong the operation until other forces come to its assistance. This was the case with the Soviet encirclement of the German 6th Army at Stalingrad in 1942—a successful operation that taught the Soviets what not to do in future encirclements.[8]

Napoleon needed to do something quickly with the Austrian forces he had trapped, before the Russians, of whose movements he was only vaguely aware, arrived in his rear. His task was complicated by the fact that he did not know with any degree of precision where Mack's forces were deployed, where they were moving, or what Mack's intentions were. The Austrian pickets had kept French scouts away from the main bodies of Austrian troops, and Napoleon's spies sent in a series of mutually contradictory reports about where the Austrians were and what they were doing. The Austrians' reaction to their realization of Napoleon's intentions was to put tens of thousands of troops in motion in various directions, further complicating Napoleon's efforts to understand what was going on.

Napoleon was aware that Kienmayer's Corps had been dispatched to Ingolstadt, although he was not aware of the size of that corps and his agents, as usual, exaggerated it considerably.[9] He was also aware that a large body of Austrian troops remained in the vicinity of Ulm and Memmingen, and that the army's supplies were housed in the latter town. His approach to the Danube generated a series of Austrian movements along the river in both directions. He had to try to understand, above all, whether Mack was holding at Ulm or retreating to the east and, if so, where. He had little accurate information on which to rely.

As early as October 3, Napoleon began to receive reports indicating that Mack might be intending to withdraw his entire army behind the Lech.[10] More confident reports indicated that there were definitely Austrian troops moving down the Danube from Ulm toward Donauwörth and Ingolstadt.[11] Napoleon accordingly contemplated the contingencies of an Austrian attack against Soult from Ulm and a strike against Bernadotte near Neuburg or Ingolstadt.[12]

The next day, the reports became more confused. Murat wrote that there was a small force in Ulm but many troops were arriving from Memmingen and farther south. A sizable force, on the other hand, had moved out of Ulm toward Günzburg. But Murat was circumspect: "Your Majesty can see from all these reports that the enemy seems to be making his retreat; but I believe that his principal forces are still on the Iller, being persuaded that they were advanced to the defiles of the Black Forest."[13] Other reports from that day confirmed that there were few troops in Ulm and described confusing troop movements throughout the Austrian deployment.[14] Therefore Napoleon confined himself to considering the minutiae of the approach to the lower Danube in orders that emphasized continued flexibility in his thought.[15] He had clearly not yet accepted the idea, however, that Mack had withdrawn from Ulm or was planning to do so: "It seems that the enemy has already sent something toward Donauwörth and Ingolstadt; nevertheless his movement is weak and I do not think it entire. He still occupies Stockach, Memmingen, and the Tyrol."[16] He demanded news above all.[17]

On October 5, Murat offered the emperor more news but appended a contradictory evaluation. "Everything that I learn," he wrote, "confirms that the Austrians are retiring on Donauwörth, which I can hardly believe." He continued, "It is more reasonable to suppose that the troops that they have passed to the right bank of the Danube have no other destination than to mask their movements toward Augsburg. I am told that the enemy has cut all the bridges. There are many troops at Ulm, according to other reports, and this ought to be true." If the Austrians intended to attack the French lines of communication, Murat reasoned, then they would have to concentrate a substantial force at Ulm in order to protect the rear of their advancing columns. If they wanted to cover the retreat of their forces from advanced positions such as Stockach, they would do the same. Despite the word he was receiving of movements to the east, Murat could not accept the idea that Mack was abandoning Ulm at that juncture.[18] In subsequent notes that day, Murat confirmed that there was still a large concentration of Austrian forces around Ulm and Memmingen, and argued that the purpose of that concentration was surely to protect the withdrawal of the more advanced elements of the army, rather than to attack the French flanks.[19]

At the same time, however, the leading elements of the corps of the center and left wing of the army began to report the presence of large Austrian forces at Donauwörth and Ingolstadt more accurately. Soult claimed that there were 7,000–8,000 Austrians at Nördlingen, while Davout wrote of a sizable Austrian force that was intending to attack Bernadotte.[20] That same day Napoleon ordered Ney to join Lannes, Soult, and Murat in concentrating and crossing the Danube at Donauwörth.[21]

Once again, it is important to consider the complexities of an envelopment. Since he had recognized the opportunity to trap Mack's army in late September, Napoleon had abandoned the idea of racing for a frontal assault and began to plan a full-scale encirclement. Encircling an enemy army requires moving far enough away from its main forces to prevent their escaping from the trap once they see it closing. If Napoleon believed there were sizable Austrian forces at Ulm, it would have made no sense for him to direct his army to Ulm. The march to Donauwörth, well to the east of Mack's army, was a natural maneuver to ensure that he caught all of the enemy force in the trap. Far from reflecting an erroneous belief that the Austrians had left Ulm, as one historian claims, calling it a "blitzkrieg to nowhere," this movement was precisely correct as the first step in enveloping the Austrians on the Iller.*

Napoleon's dispositions suffered from the opposite flaw. The French corps arrived on the Danube roughly in sequence from west to east. Ney and Murat got to the vicinity of Ulm first, then Soult and Davout marched on Donauwörth, and finally Bernadotte and Marmont began to arrive at Ingolstadt. Napoleon knew there was a substantial Austrian force in and around Neuburg and Ingolstadt that he could have endeavored to trap. Instead, the order of arrival of his corps virtually ensured that it would escape. Napoleon had no forces moving to the east of Kienmayer's Corps to prevent or even threaten its withdrawal, and the early arrival of Soult and Davout at Donauwörth gave the Austrian commander ample time to recognize his danger and react. Napoleon's method of encirclement can be criticized on the grounds that it was too shallow, not too deep.

Clearly Napoleon believed that the main Austrian body was at Ulm. He had sent his main body to Donauwörth to ensure that it could not break out from the trap. The same day thus brought orders to Soult and Murat to seize Donauwörth, surprising the Austrians there and taking the bridge if at all possible, and the comment to Soult that "the enemy has only today started to perceive our movement and has concentrated at Ulm."[22] The order to Ney to move to Donauwörth was repeated as well.[23] Napoleon also directed Lannes's

---

*See Owen Connelly, *Blundering to Glory: Napoleon's Military Campaigns* (1987; Wilmington, Del.: Scholarly Resources, 1999), p. 80. Connelly's discussion takes no account of the intelligence Napoleon was receiving, not even acknowledging the existence of Kienmayer's corps around Ingolstadt. Connelly also pays no heed to Napoleon's intention of encircling rather than confronting Mack's army and does not consider what movements would have been appropriate for such a mission. He implies that Napoleon's failure to direct his main body straight at Mack's main body was folly.

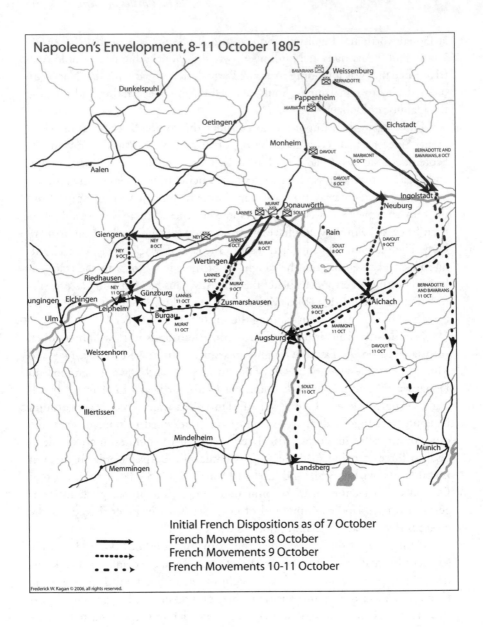

Napoleon's Envelopment, 8–11 October 1805

Dunkelspuhl

Oetingen

Aalen

Monheim

Pappenheim

BAVARIANS
Weissenburg
BERNADOTTE

MARMONT

Eichstadt

DAVOUT

MARMONT
8 OCT

BERNADOTTE AND
BAVARIANS, 8 OCT

DAVOUT
8 OCT

Giengen

NEY
8 OCT

NEY

LANNES MURAT Donauwörth
SOULT

Ingolstadt
Neuburg

NEY
9 OCT

LANNES
8 OCT

Wertingen

MURAT
8 OCT

Rain

DAVOUT
9 OCT

SOULT
8 OCT

Riedhausen

LANNES
9 OCT

MURAT
9 OCT

NEY
11 OCT

Günzburg

LANNES
11 OCT

ungingen Elchingen

Leipheim

Zusmarshausen

BERNADOTTE
AND BAVARIANS
11 OCT

Aichach

Ulm

Burgau

MURAT
11 OCT

SOULT
9 OCT

MARMONT
11 OCT

Weissenhorn

Augsburg

DAVOUT
11 OCT

SOULT
11 OCT

Illertissen

Munich

Mindelheim

SOULT
11 OCT

Memmingen

Landsberg

Initial French Dispositions as of 7 October

French Movements 8 October

French Movements 9 October

French Movements 10–11 October

Corps to the same destination.[24] Consequently on October 6 three infantry and one cavalry corps descended on Donauwörth, Davout's Corps was marching to a position between Donauwörth and Neuburg, and Bernadotte's army was headed for Ingolstadt. The objective of this maneuver was the encirclement of Mack's main body at Ulm.

Napoleon did not know the exact size, location, and intentions of the Austrian forces around Donauwörth, Neuburg, and Ingolstadt. Davout assured him that the forces before him at Neuburg were considerable; Napoleon already had the reports of about 6,000 Austrians at Donauwörth.[25] The river was a formidable barrier to cavalry scouts and the spy reports were less than helpful. So Napoleon focused his attention on seizing the critical bridges and getting across the river as quickly as possible. He also considered the possibility that the Austrians would try to form another defensive line along the Lech. He therefore ordered Soult to throw pontoon bridges across the Danube downriver of the mouth of the Lech "in order to turn that position," although he noted that he would not hesitate to use the bridge at Donauwörth, several miles upriver, if Soult managed to take it relatively intact.[26] Considering Napoleon's ignorance of the Austrians' positions and intentions, this was a reasonable precaution.

These orders led to the first significant combat of the war, as Kienmayer's forces tried to hold the crossing at Donauwörth and then destroy the bridge before withdrawing. The reports Napoleon had been receiving of marches down the Danube to Ulm and east of Ulm reflected the orders Mack had given to concentrate the army near Ulm and around Günzburg. The purpose of that concentration, as Murat rightly surmised, was not to withdraw to the east but to prepare to stand and fight. Mack hoped to attack Napoleon's forces as late as October 6, and he ordered Kienmayer to move up the Danube, if possible, to support that attack.[27] By the next day, however, word of Bernadotte's movements undid Mack's offensive plans, and he told Kienmayer to stand down and wait around Ingolstadt and Neuburg.

In Mack's mind, the question was where and how to attack the exposed lines of communication that he supposed Napoleon was presenting to him. He had clearly not considered how he would defend the Danube line from Napoleon's assault, and he made few meaningful preparations for that defense. If he had considered the problem carefully, he would have recognized the urgency of defending not only Ingolstadt and Neuburg but Donauwörth, the major crossing halfway between Kienmayer's Corps and the main body. Instead it was Kienmayer who took the initiative to defend this critical crossing, and on the night of October 6 he sent an infantry battalion and two cannons to hold the bridge and destroy it if necessary.[28]

When French dragoons approached the Donauwörth bridge the next day, they encountered this meager force, which had already cut the bridge. They quickly drove the Austrians off and rebuilt the bridge, and then gave chase to the Austrians withdrawing east toward Rain.[29] Murat had sent a second force across the river at Donaumünster, hoping to trap the entire Austrian force defending Donauwörth, but these troops arrived after the Austrians were already leaving and could only join in the pursuit.[30] The pursuit was not successful, however, as the Austrians made it across the Lech, where Kienmayer had stationed two infantry battalions and light cavalry as a receiving force.[31] Murat waded across the river with some of his troops and got all the way to Rain but could not force the Austrians to do battle. Soult reported the resulting rumors that there were 25,000 Austrians at Rain, where a large camp had been prepared. He thought that number exaggerated, however, and other information confirmed a very large Austrian force at Ulm.

The damage for the Austrians had already been done, however. The immediate crossing of the Danube at Donauwörth and the pursuit of Kienmayer's forces to Rain placed the lead elements of the French center directly between Kienmayer and the main Austrian force, now moving toward Günzburg from Ulm. Kienmayer recognized that he was outmatched and followed his orders, commanding his forces to withdraw from Ingolstadt and Neuburg to Aichach.[32] Although this route held open the possibility of linking up with Mack's army if Mack had begun withdrawing to the south as well, Mack's determination to keep his force concentrated at Ulm and Günzburg ensured that he would be rapidly cut off from Kienmayer. The initial French crossing of the Danube had already begun to split the Austrian army apart.

On receiving this news, Napoleon began to plan the liquidation of the encircled enemy forces. He sent a warning to Ney on October 7, ordering him to prepare to attack Ulm the next day in coordination with Soult, whose forces would be coming from Donauwörth.[33] He added, "The Emperor will in the mean time march on Augsburg and Landsberg in order to cut off everything the enemy still has on the Iller." This order made sense. Napoleon knew that the Austrian army had been deployed mainly to the southwest of Ulm. He knew that Mack was working to concentrate it at Ulm, but he had received numerous reports indicating that that process was not complete. If he had simply turned his forces from Donauwörth to Ulm, he would have allowed Austrian troops at Memmingen, Stockach, and elsewhere a free passage to the east via the main road through Augsburg. Instead, he directed two corps against Mack's concentration at Ulm and moved with the rest to chase Kienmayer's troops and cut off the retreat of the other Austrian forces.

This movement was normal in an encirclement. It is customary in such operations to construct two rings around the enemy. The inner ring deprives the enemy of freedom to maneuver and ultimately forces him to fight or surrender. The outer ring ensures that debris from the encircled enemy forces cannot escape and that external reinforcements cannot hinder the reduction of the trapped troops. It might be objected that Napoleon did not allocate his forces appropriately, since he sent only two corps against the Austrian main body and kept five others with him in the outer ring of the encirclement. There is no merit in this objection, however, since Ney's and Soult's Corps were two of the largest in the Grande Armée and totaled more than 60,000 men.[34] They were more than a match for anything Mack had in Ulm.

It was not until word arrived of the French seizure of Donauwörth that Mack finally recognized the horrible position he and the Austrian army were in. "Since my courier of yesterday evening," he wrote to Francis, "our position has become alarming. We have confirmed the unfortunate news that Bernadotte has forced Ansbach, whereby he gained many marches whereby he has arrived sooner on the Danube."[35] He tried in this note to put a steely face on the disaster: "We will do everything possible in order to defeat him or to find our junction with the Russians without fighting, but everything has become much more difficult because of this unfortunate event which no one thought possible." The only immediate response he could think of was to beg Ferdinand to "break out" of Ulm with half of the forces there and march "instantly" toward Burgau on the Augsburg road.[36] It is not at all clear what Mack imagined would happen at that point.

By the next morning, Mack had a new plan.[37] All hope of joining with the Russians had been lost, he wrote, since Napoleon now occupied the line of the Lech and Mack had no realistic prospect of breaking through that line by himself. But Ulm was a strong position and there was a lot of ground between Ulm and the Lech from which to draw supplies. The route to the Tyrol also remained open. Mack proposed therefore that Kutuzov hold his columns at the Inn until they had all assembled and their artillery and trains had caught up. Then Kutuzov was to march against Napoleon's line on the Lech. This movement would force Napoleon to divide his forces and give Mack the opportunity to beat those left in front of him. Alternatively, it would allow Mack to strike against Napoleon's lines of communication to the north and northwest. He continued to argue that such raids were safe, since the army could readily fall back on the prepared positions at Ulm in the event of misfortune on the battlefield.

As usual, Mack's notions reflected a lack of understanding of time–space relationships in war. He knew that Kutuzov could not hope to have his army fully assembled on the Inn before October 24. It was five to six days' march from Braunau to the line of the Lech. Therefore Mack had to hold his position at Ulm until the end of October, at least three weeks, in the face of the entire French army. He did not consider the possibility that Napoleon would move to finish him off in that time or constrict his movements to deprive him of the supplies he needed to keep his army alive. On the other hand, Mack had no good options. He might have tried to withdraw south toward the Tyrol, but that movement had become very risky with the French advance to Donauwörth. Like a mouse caught in a trap of its own devising, Mack had options that were better or worse than others, but he was unlikely to find a way out of his predicament.

Naturally Ferdinand disagreed with Mack's recommendation. He wanted to escape from Ulm to the east and link up with Kienmayer and the Russians; he agreed to Mack's plan for offensive operations only if withdrawal proved impossible. Subsequently he claimed never to have believed that Mack seriously accepted the need to link up with the Russians. Mack only mentioned it when he had already "concluded" that it was impossible. This disagreement may have contributed to the vague and confusing orders sent to FML Auffenberg that led to the Battle of Wertingen, discussed below.[38]

Mack nevertheless prepared to take the offensive. On October 8 he ordered the entire main body to concentrate at Günzburg. The purpose of this move was not to break out of the encirclement, for Mack had already dismissed that idea as impracticable, nor is there any evidence that Mack had convinced himself that Napoleon was in retreat after hearing of a British landing at Boulogne.[39] Rather, Mack was preparing to attack Napoleon's communication lines from his base at Ulm. To facilitate that attempt, he ordered Kienmayer to draw Napoleon's forces away from the Lech east toward Augsburg and Munich. Kienmayer was to put forth the rumor that Mack was trying to withdraw with the entire army and that headquarters would soon be moved as well. In this way Mack would be freed up to hit Napoleon's "open" flank. Kienmayer had no difficulty "drawing" Napoleon toward Augsburg and Munich, since that was where Napoleon was sending the bulk of his forces anyway. Mack, however, would find it much harder than expected to take advantage of splitting up the French army.

The key to the success of this maneuver, as Mack himself recognized, was seizing the bridges over the Danube at and around Günzburg. Unfortunately for the Austrians, however, Napoleon and his marshals had also recognized the importance of seizing those bridges, and they acted more rapidly and effectively.

Napoleon's success in this endeavor was fortuitous, since he completely misjudged Mack's motivations and intentions. "It is impossible," Berthier wrote to Ney, "that the enemy, having learned of the crossing of the Danube and the Lech, as well as the terrible fate that must have befallen the body of troops that he had beyond the Lech, is not seriously thinking of retreating."[40] Mack would first try to withdraw to Augsburg, he continued, but he would find that he was too late. Then he would try to retreat to Landsberg. If the French troops arrived in time, Mack might offer battle or try to march to the Tyrol. But Napoleon believed that he would offer battle and ordered Ney to get ready.

Napoleon dismissed the notion that Mack might think of crossing the Danube and attacking his trains. He did not believe that the quartermaster general was sufficiently "insane" to separate himself from his stores at Memmingen and the route to the Tyrol. Accordingly, he ordered Ney to march at once to

Günzburg and seize the bridges there. The implication was that this should not be a risky maneuver, since Mack was certain to be anywhere but there.

All of Napoleon's judgments about Mack's possible movements were wrong, and he sent Ney marching on a collision course with the main body of the Austrian army.* But Napoleon hedged his bets as usual. He instructed Ney to augment his forces by combining with several other units in his vicinity and coordinate with some of Murat's cavalry divisions to protect the vital trains, "if ever the enemy should commit the idiocy of wanting to penetrate" into the rear of the Grande Armée. The rest of Murat's cavalry, as well as Lannes's Corps, were marching up the Danube behind Ney and would be in a position to support him rapidly if he found himself in danger from an unexpected Austrian attack.

Napoleon had no information about what Mack actually was doing that would support the interpretation he had placed on events. He had simply put himself in Mack's place and tried to imagine what he would do if he had somehow committed the series of mistakes that Mack must have made in order to occupy such a terrible position. From that reflection, Napoleon emerged with unwarranted confidence in his conclusion.

It is not that Napoleon thought of intelligent things for Mack to do while the quartermaster general concocted a stupid option. By October 8 it was too late for Mack to withdraw to the east. His army would have been destroyed instantly as five French corps fell on his troops strung out in march columns along a single main road. Mack was bright enough to recognize that fact, and Napoleon only insulted his intelligence by imagining that he would choose such a foolish course of action. Mack's determination to attack Napoleon's flank may have been simply foolishness of another variety, but at least it was not tantamount to immediate suicide.

Napoleon's success in this phase of the campaign did not result from his ability to read the enemy. He had consistently misread Mack throughout the campaign. His success came, rather, from his ability so to constrain Mack's options that it hardly mattered which he chose. It helped that Mack's previous foolish decisions made the quartermaster general complicit in that process of constraint. The fact that Napoleon believed that he could read his enemy and predict his actions would generate problems in future campaigns in which he was less able to eliminate good options the enemy might choose.

Although Mack's and Napoleon's orders appeared to set up a fateful collision in the vicinity of Günzburg, the climax was diverted by an unexpected collision. On the morning of October 8, elements of Murat's and Lannes's Corps encountered FML Auffenburg's forces at Wertingen on the road from

---

*This incident would have been a better ground for Connelly's critique of Napoleon's handling of this part of the campaign, but Connelly ignores it completely. In fact, he misdates several of the critical orders and events. Connelly, *Blundering to Glory*, p. 80.

Donauwörth to Günzburg, and engaged them in the first serious battle of the campaign.

The Battles of Ulm

The Library of Congress subject heading for this part of the campaign of 1805 is "Ulm (Germany)—Capitulation, 1805," as compared with "Austerlitz, Battle of," or "Waterloo, Battle of," for example. This distinction implies that there was no combat meaningful enough to be called a battle and that the important fact is that the Austrian forces capitulated (without a fight). It is true that there was no major engagement of large armies at Ulm, and that the main bodies did not, in the end, fight each other. But it is not true that the Austrians surrendered without fighting or there was no significant combat. Between October 8 and October 14 the French and the Austrians fought a series of running battles that were small individually but involved tens of thousands of troops overall. They played an important part in the ultimate outcome of the campaign.

Wertingen, October 8

Napoleon had secured the critical crossing at Donauwörth and now sought to close the trap completely. Aware that Kienmayer was retreating to the south, Napoleon sent Soult toward Augsburg to cut him off and take that critical city with Davout chasing after him from Neuburg via Aichach.[41] He instructed Bernadotte and Marmont to seize Ingolstadt at once and then head toward Augsburg.[42] While those four corps raced to complete the outer encirclement, Napoleon ordered Ney, Lannes, and Murat to finish the inner ring. He sent Lannes and Murat toward Wertingen and Zusmarshausen respectively with the objective of cutting the Ulm–Augsburg road as well as the Ulm–Landsberg road.[43] The intermediate objective of these advances was Burgau. From that position Lannes and Murat would be able to support Ney, whom Napoleon had ordered to seize Günzburg and its bridges.[44]

The confusion of October 7 in Austrian headquarters led Mack to order FML Auffenberg to take his division of about 5,000 infantry and 400 cavalry from Günzburg to Wertingen.[45] The precise purpose of this order is not clear.[46] The author of the undated covering note for Auffenberg's report asserts that his mission was to observe the French forces streaming over the Danube at Donauwörth. It is also possible that Auffenberg's force was intended to guard the flank of the main body as it concentrated at Günzburg in preparation for the attack on Napoleon's flank. If so, it was too small, too far away, and inadequately supported, although there are indications that Auffenberg expected Werneck's entire corps to follow him toward Wertingen.[47]

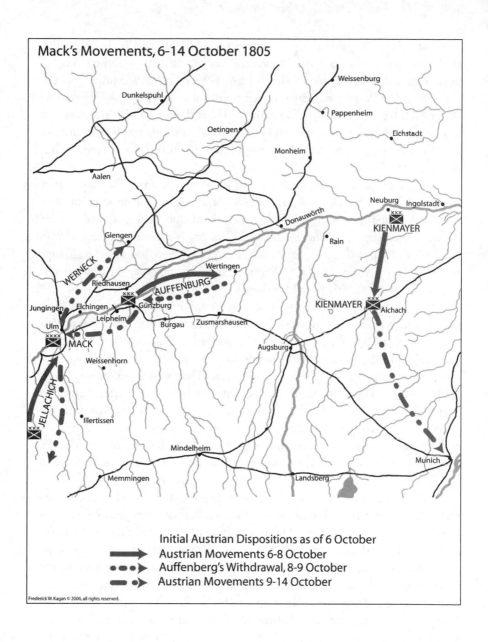

Mack's Movements, 6-14 October 1805

Weissenburg
Dunkelspuhl
Pappenheim
Oetingen
Eichstadt
Monheim
Aalen
Neuburg Ingolstadt
Donauwörth
KIENMAYER
Giengen
Rain
WERNECK
Wertingen
Riedhausen
AUFFENBURG
Jungingen Elchingen Günzburg
KIENMAYER
Ulm Leipheim Burgau Zusmarshausen
MACK
Aichach
Weissenhorn
Augsburg
JELLACHICH
Illertissen
Mindelheim
Munich
Memmingen Landsberg

Initial Austrian Dispositions as of 6 October
Austrian Movements 6-8 October
Auffenberg's Withdrawal, 8-9 October
Austrian Movements 9-14 October

Auffenberg did not clearly understand his purpose and had not considered what he would do if the French approached in large numbers. He reported receiving the order to march from Günzburg to Wertingen on the evening of October 7, marching for ten hours, and arriving in Wertingen by about 8:00 on the morning of October 8. He had time to post his troops in positions around the town and send out reconnaissance parties (which did not pick up any evidence of the enemy, despite the proximity of the French), but not to do much else.

Auffenberg was thus at an enormous disadvantage from the start. Apart from the fact that the forces of Lannes and Murat converging on him outnumbered his troops significantly, he had no clear mission, little awareness of his own and the enemy's situation, no means of asking for reinforcements, and no good idea of what to do if the French attacked. When Murat's Cavalry appeared on the eastern side of Auffenberg's position, however, he and his soldiers attempted valiantly to hold them off.[48]

Murat's cavalry divisions—Klein's 1st Dragoons, Beaumont's 3rd Dragoons, and Nansouty's Cuirassiers—were the first to arrive. In contrast with Auffenberg's troops, these cavalry divisions had a clear objective (Zusmarshausen) and expected a fight.[49] Coming from Rain, they rode up the Lech to Nordendorf and then west toward Wertingen. They struck Auffenberg's outposts and quickly drove them off, seizing the bridge over the Zusam to Wertingen with little difficulty. Fearing that the Austrians would retreat toward Burgau, Klein took his division southwest to cut them off. He could not find a place to cross the Zusam until he reached Roggden, about a mile and a half southwest of Wertingen.[50] Auffenberg concentrated his forces in Wertingen and made no serious effort to hinder Klein's movement.

In the meantime, Lannes's forces had begun to arrive from the north-northwest, along the road from Donauwörth via Pfaffenhofen, led by Oudinot's grenadiers division. Oudinot led his troops along the wooded ridge to the north and west of Wertingen and soon threatened to outflank Auffenberg's position from the west. Seeing his danger, Auffenberg began moving his force to the southwest, initially attempting to reconcentrate them on the heights southwest of Wertingen. It was too late. Klein attacked from Roggden and Murat ordered Beaumont to attack through Wertingen while Oudinot's grenadiers were advancing from the west. The French cut the Austrians to pieces, effectively destroying Auffenberg's Corps and taking between 1,000 and 2,000 prisoners. The remnants escaped toward Günzburg.

Ironically, the Battle of Wertingen convinced Murat that the Austrians were attempting to march from Ulm via Günzburg to Augsburg, although he thought the affairs of the day would probably change their minds.[51] He had learned from the prisoners that Mack was at Günzburg and that the army's trains had been ordered to Zusmarshausen (which was false). A more important

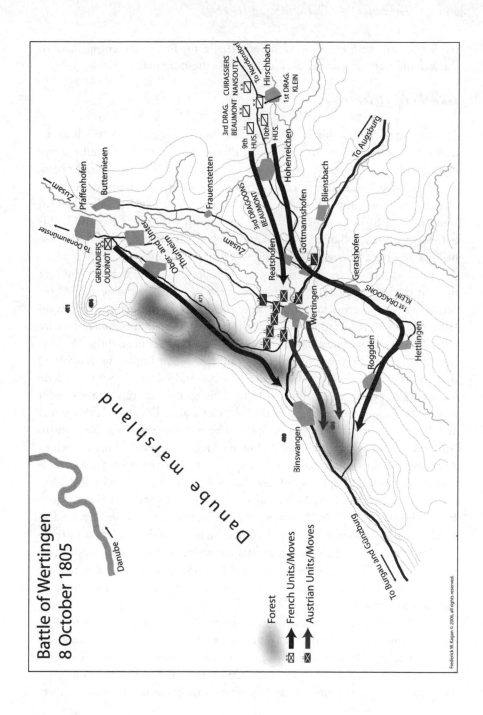

Battle of Wertingen
8 October 1805

Danube

Danube marshland

Zusam
Pfaffenhofen
Butterniesen
To Donaumünster
GRENADIERS
OUDINOT
Ober- and Unter-
Thürheim
Frauenstetten
Zusam
Reatshofen
3rd DRAGOONS
BEAUMONT
9th HUS.
10th HUS.
3rd DRAG.
BEAUMONT
CUIRASSIERS
NANSOUTY
To Nordendorf
Hirschbach
1st DRAG.
KLEIN
Hohenreichen
Gottmannshofen
Bliensbach
To Augsburg
Geratshofen
1st DRAGOONS
KLEIN
Wertingen
Roggden
Hettlingen
Binswangen
To Burgau and Günzburg

Forest
French Units/Moves
Austrian Units/Moves

Frederick W. Kagan © 2006, all rights reserved.

result was that the French had won decisively in the first major engagement of the war and were now firmly astride the Ulm–Augsburg road.

Günzburg, October 9

Another important result of the Battle of Wertingen was that Mack abandoned the notion of moving east along the right bank of the Danube. After toying with the idea of trying to break out toward the Lech on the right bank of the Danube, he decided instead to cross the river at Günzburg, where most of the army was assembled, and operate along the left bank, possibly toward Ingolstadt with the goal of ultimately linking up with the Russians.[52] This half-formed plan collapsed immediately as Ney's troops moved to seize the bridges over the Danube at Günzburg.

On October 8, Ney was still operating under the orders Berthier had sent him the day before, instructing him to prepare to attack Ulm the next day.[53] He accordingly set his army marching toward the Danube and then upriver toward Ulm, and even instructed an officer at the head of a small detachment to seize Ulm if the Austrians had abandoned it or were holding it only lightly.[54]

On that day, however, Berthier sent him new orders implicitly recognizing that the Austrians probably held Ulm in force and instructing Ney to seize Günzburg as rapidly as possible.[55] On October 9, Berthier renewed the order to seize Günzburg, reminding Ney that Napoleon aimed to encircle the enemy at Ulm and prevent him from escaping. Once across the river, Ney was to "observe the corps at Ulm" and follow if it moved toward Donauwörth or Augsburg. Berthier instructed Ney to keep a strong force between the Austrians and Donauwörth but did not indicate that Ney was to attack Mack's army.[56]

Accordingly, Ney halted the army northeast of Ulm and sent General Jean Pierre Firmin Malher's 3rd Division to seize Günzburg and establish a bridgehead over the Danube.[57] He indicated that he believed the Austrians were retreating from the left bank and that Malher would not find much opposition to his crossing. Owing to the failings of the campaign maps available to him, Ney instructed Malher to seize the bridge at Reisensburg rather than the main highway bridge at Günzburg.[58]

Malher, despite this mistake in his orders, divided his division into three columns aimed at the bridge at Leipheim and the two bridges at Günzburg. He did not trouble about the bridge at Reisensburg, which did not carry a highway.* The rightmost column, marching toward Leipheim, found itself slogging through a swamp and gave up. The center column, consisting of three

---

*Malher to Ney, 10 October 1805, in Alombert-Goget and Colin, *La campagne de 1805*, vol. 3, pt. 1, p. 374. This report indicates that Malher thought he was sending a column to the bridge at Reisensburg, but he did not do so; that column crossed at the eastern Günzburg bridge, according to the Austrian reports.

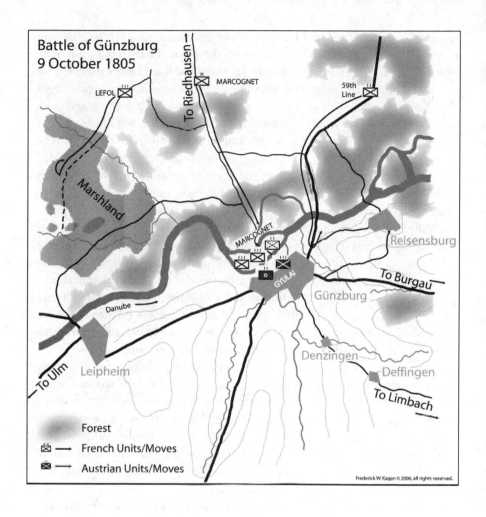

Battle of Günzburg
9 October 1805

To Riedhausen

MARCOGNET

LEFOL

59th Line

Marshland

MARCOGNET

MARCOGNET

GYULAI

Reisensburg

To Burgau

Günzburg

Danube

To Ulm

Leipheim

Denzingen

Deffingen

To Limbach

Forest

French Units/Moves

Austrian Units/Moves

regiments, marched toward Günzburg and encountered a strong Austrian picket of Tyrolean Jaegers. The contact with these forces alerted the main body of defenders at Günzburg, who hastily destroyed the main bridge there.[59]

The Austrian army had been marching and countermarching up and down the Danube for the past two days in a nasty mix of wind, rain, snow, and cold. On October 8, Mack marched the main body out of Ulm to Günzburg. The next day, he decided to move to Burgau and put the army in motion. When he reconnoitered the ground near Burgau, however, he and Ferdinand decided that the movement there was unwise, and he countermanded it. The army then withdrew to a position facing east between Limbach and Reisensburg. A small body of troops under General d'Aspré was sent across to the left bank to guard the bridges and learn of the French movements. The Tyrolean jaegers who first made contact with Ney's advancing regiments belonged to this force.[60]

When the Austrian defenders at Günzburg had thrown down the main bridge, the unfortunate jaegers found themselves cut off on the other bank and 200 of them, along with two cannons and General d'Aspré himself, fell into Malher's hands. In the meantime, the Archduke Charles's infantry regiment was rushed back to defend the main bridge, where it established a formidable defense with two or three infantry battalions and twenty cannons.[61]

The terrain of the area offers a naturally strong position for defending against a river crossing. Both banks are relatively flat and were wooded at the time, but there are rises on the southern side (where the town is) on which cannons may be emplaced with advantage. The main bridge crosses from Günzburg to a small island made by two arms of the Danube and connected to the "mainland" by yet another bridge. This island is perfectly flat and all of it is well within range of guns positioned on the rises north of the town. The Austrians used those guns to murderous effect.

Malher employed more courage than intelligence in his attacks. His forces tried to rush across the first bridge onto the island and from there onto the second bridge, but they were swept by withering fire from the Austrian cannons and, as they approached the river, from the muskets of Austrian infantrymen on the other bank. The French could only bring forward four cannons to meet the Austrian onslaught, and the Austrian gunners cut the crews of those field pieces to shreds.[62] The French infantry labored under this bombardment to rebuild the bridge, but they did not have the necessary materials and the fire of the defenders was too hot. Malher finally called a halt and stationed the men of the center column along the bank, abandoning the attempt to cross there.[63]

The Austrians had thus won the first round of the Battle of Günzburg, but Mack then took a hand. He decided to send the army across the highway bridge east of Günzburg to march on Giengen and then Nördlingen, across the rear of Napoleon's army in an attempt to link up with the Russians.[64] FML

Gyulai was accordingly sent to that bridge, which had been partially destroyed, with seven infantry battalions and fourteen cavalry squadrons in order to repair it and make a bridgehead on the other side of the river. The rest of the army would cross at night.[65]

Gyulai followed orders and before long he had the bridge restored. Just at that moment, in an example of perfect timing that would be suspect if it appeared in a work of fiction, the French 59th Infantry Regiment, which had been sent originally against that bridge, arrived after a delay. In a densely packed column the regiment rushed the bridge, pushing the Austrian defenders into the river, and raced onto the right bank.* Austrian infantry and cavalry rushed to the scene and drove the French back. They were unable to dislodge the French, however, and did not summon reinforcements. The French held the south end of the highway bridge at the end of the day.

Having snatched defeat from the jaws of victory at Günzburg, Mack now abandoned his plan to march across the river and attack Napoleon in the rear. He ordered the Austrian army to march back to Ulm.[66] This decision did not result merely from a funk, however, for there was more bad news than the loss of the bridge at Günzburg. While that battle was being fought, General Louis Henri Loison led the 2nd Division of Ney's Corps to seize the bridge over the Danube at Elchingen, about halfway between Günzburg and Ulm. The fight there, where only a single Austrian regiment had been stationed, was not even close.[67]

The French now controlled most of the Danube bridges except those at Ulm. During the night of October 9–10, Malher's entire division crossed, Loison's division held at Elchingen, and General Pierre Dupont's division advanced toward Ulm. The other French corps had crossed the river and were streaming toward Augsburg, with the exception of Lannes, whom Napoleon had stationed between Augsburg and Zusmarshausen.[68]

Mack's orders and decisionmaking during this battle are difficult to understand. In his self-justification he focused on his plan to march across to the left bank of the Danube. Since Napoleon's army had almost entirely crossed to the right, he argued, it was possible to race across the left bank toward Bohemia, where he could draw supplies and reinforcements. Then Napoleon would have found himself in a most unfortunate situation.[69] But why did

---

*Krauss, *Der Feldzug von Ulm*. The French sources do not explain why the 59th Regiment arrived at the bridge so late; they also seem unaware that the Austrians had rebuilt the bridge after having partially destroyed it (for an exception, see Lannes to Berthier, 9 October 1805, in Alombert-Goget and Colin, *La campagne de 1805*, vol. 3, pt. 1, p. 397). The confusion may stem from the fact that the colonel of the 59th was killed in the action. Malher to Ney, 10 October, p. 374; Journal of Operations of the Artillery . . . Battle of Günzburg (p. 385) mentions that the attack of the 59th did not begin until 7:30 P.M. but offers no explanation; the daily report of 6th Corps for 9 October (p. 387) implies that the 59th had had to fight its way to the bridge in the first place, but there is no account of such combat in the Austrian reports, although it is possible that it fought through more of d'Aspré's pickets.

Mack order the highway bridge rebuilt just in time for the French 59th Regiment to charge across it and win the battle?

Of the fight, Mack said that d'Aspré somehow failed to inform him of the approach of the French throughout the seven or eight hours of contact, and we must presume that the defenders of the two bridges, including the ones who executed his orders to rebuild a bridge, also failed to tell him that they were engaged in combat. Mack claimed that he was so absorbed in developing dispositions for the army's further movement, "which demanded not only all my time, but all my attention," that he did not hear the fierce cannonade going on during those seven or eight hours not more than a few kilometers from his position. This last point is especially remarkable since Murat wrote to Ney from Zusmarshausen, "cannon is heard from your direction," and Napoleon, who was then at Donauwörth, "thinks it is yours."[70] The battle could also be heard in Ulm.[71] It is difficult to avoid seeing a rough similarity between Mack and the fictional Captain Queeg of *The Caine Mutiny*, who blamed his mistakes on those around him.

It is possible, of course, that Mack's account is accurate. He may have remained oblivious to the battle raging nearby as he immersed himself in drafting a disposition for crossing the river and then commanded the bridge rebuilt and ordered his troops to begin the crossing with no idea of what he was sending the troops into.

It is a little surprising, if that was true, that Ferdinand makes no mention of it. His account implies that Mack knew what was going on and decided to order the crossing, presumably unaware that the French 59th Regiment was bearing down on the bridge. The Austrians had stopped the French from crossing at the middle bridge, and the rightmost French column turned back from the bridge at Leipheim without firing a shot. It is easier to believe that Mack did not have good intelligence about French dispositions beyond the contact already established and believed that there was still a clear road from Günzburg to Giengen because it suited his plans. In that case both the ill-fated order and the foolish attempt at self-defense accord with what we know of Mack's personality.

Haslach-Jungingen, October 11

The bedraggled Austrian army streamed back into Ulm during the night and early morning of October 10. The soldiers had been marching and countermarching pointlessly for days in terrible weather. Since the army commander had no clear idea of what he was doing, the soldiers and their officers must have been really confused. Confusion of that sort, coupled with personal discomfort and fear, quickly erodes discipline and courage.

Worse still, the decision to retreat to Ulm was made suddenly in the aftermath of the unexpected defeat at Günzburg. Mack had drawn up no careful dispositions. There was no time to realign the troops after the series of frenzied rushes toward the fights at the bridges. The regiments became intermingled and order broke down. When a horse artillery battery raced through Günzburg, panic spread through the troops, further disarranging them.[72] Worse still, the endless marching coupled with two battlefield defeats had left many regiments with as few as 800 men.[73] Mack's army had sunk to a very low point indeed.

Mack remained confident and determined. The quartermaster general returned at once to his desk and began drafting new plans, dispositions, and operations orders. The many orders, dispositions, and memoranda that survive in Mack's atrocious handwriting allow us to picture him vividly. Full of nervous energy, no doubt keyed up by tension and lack of sleep, Mack must have spent hours at his desk with the rain pounding on the roof of whatever shelter he had found, scribbling away. He lived in a world of his own imagining, and the harsh reality of the army's marching, fighting, and losing made no impact on him. Because he accompanied the army in its disorderly retreat from Günzburg, he must have seen the soldiers in their misery, exhaustion, and confusion. He could not have been unaware that troops continued to straggle into Ulm for nearly twenty-four hours after he ordered the movement. Yet the disposition that emerged from his frantic scribbling was an order to move from Ulm to Heidenheim that very night, after midnight.[74]

Mack apparently realized (or was told) that this order was impossible and he abandoned it, but he was not completely deterred. He spent the night of October 10 drafting a lengthy, detailed disposition for a movement to begin the following afternoon.[75] The army would cross the Danube and march through Heidenheim and Giengen toward the east, with all the benefits that Mack had come to attribute to such a maneuver. Surprisingly, he also proposed to send detachments toward Stuttgart and Strasbourg, presumably to disrupt Napoleon's communications and force him to divide his army. He hoped in this way to take pressure off the Russians and allow them time to concentrate on the Inn, presumably to support his subsequent operations from his new base in Bohemia. Mack soon abandoned this project too, deciding instead to remain in Ulm, where he would be "safe as houses."[76] All of Mack's frenetic planning and writing led the Austrian army to remain stationary in Ulm on October 10–11, unintentionally granting it a much needed rest.

Napoleon came close to committing a significant blunder at this point. He continued to believe that Mack had abandoned Ulm and was trying to escape to the east or southeast. He lost contact with Ney for a brief time, no doubt contributing to this conviction, but Berthier wrote Ney, "As for Ulm, it is impossible that the enemy occupies it in force; if he occupies it with 3,000 or 4,000 men, send a division to chase him away; if he occupies it with forces much greater than that, go there with your entire army, seize the post, and take a good number of prisoners."[77]

In this context he sent most of the army toward Augsburg. Berthier wrote to Lannes, "It seems the enemy is retiring in force" and "the whole army will be entirely concentrated" at Augsburg.[78] This comment is interesting in light of the fact that Napoleon did not order Ney to march to Augsburg. He ordered him to drive the Austrian rear guard, as he supposed, out of Ulm and then "guide yourself according to the enemy's movements, either on Augsburg, or on Landsberg, or on Memmingen."[79] It was not that Napoleon believed the Austrians were retiring. He also meant to chivvy them out of their position and drive them in the desired direction.

Napoleon misread Mack once again and ordered Ney to attack a partially fortified position held by an army nearly twice the size of his corps. He had also moved the other corps that might have supported Ney farther from Ulm, thereby exposing his marshal to considerable short-term danger. Here Napoleon missed an opportunity to constrain Mack's options further. If he had read the situation correctly and sent Lannes and Soult racing toward the southeast and south of Ulm, close to the city, he might have hastened the end of the campaign. In part because of his stubbornness in misreading Mack and in part because of the difficulties in communication, however, Napoleon allowed Mack more breathing room and allowed the Austrians to protract the campaign.

Ney was aware of the miscalculation in his master's thinking after the fight at Günzburg. He wrote at once to Berthier, "The enemy is stronger at Ulm than one had thought; he has received from Günzburg a reinforcement of 15,000 men."[80] He noted incorrectly, however, that "it seems that Ulm will form the left flank of his line of battle." Even in such close proximity, Ney had difficulty understanding the precise position and, even more, the intentions of the Austrians. On October 10 he reported that both Mack and Ferdinand had been present during the Battle of Günzburg, which suggested that the entire Austrian army had been there or nearby, but he still did not understand what Mack was doing at that moment. He wrote that the captured Austrian General d'Aspré, whom he was sending to Napoleon for interrogation, could tell the emperor "that the Austrian army was disposed to make a great effort against my corps, but the attack of Günzburg has frustrated everything. The Austrians are retreating toward Biberach."[81] Did this error result from disinformation by d'Aspré? Did the Austrian general really think that Mack was going to Biberach, or was he guessing based on what he thought Mack should do? Or did Ney simply decide that that is what Mack was going to do, since it seemed to him the only sensible option? At all events, Napoleon must be forgiven somewhat for continuing to believe that Mack was withdrawing from Ulm, since his marshal on the spot thought so as well.

As soon as he learned of the Battle of Günzburg and apparently before he received Ney's report, Berthier sent the marshal new orders: "It remains now to take possession of Ulm, which is important from all points of view." What Napoleon expected Ney to do precisely is unclear. In one sentence he instructed Ney to "surround" Ulm, but two sentences later Berthier wrote, "Immediately after Ulm has been taken." He did not imagine the operation would be difficult, for he ordered Ney to move at once from Ulm to Memmingen or wherever the Austrian army went.[82]

This was a poorly written order. If Ney was to surround Ulm, the supposition must have been that Mack's whole army was not in that city and that Ney would completely destroy whatever forces were there. But in that case where was Mack's army? If it was nearby, as seemed likely from the reports of the Battle of Günzburg, then Ney was running a big risk by encircling even a rear guard at Ulm while Mack could turn on him and relieve his trapped forces. If it was not nearby, of course, then the order to "follow it as closely as possible" makes no sense. It seems likely that Napoleon, still operating on inadequate intelligence, had not fully adjusted his perception of the battle space to reflect the reality that Mack had not been retreating for as long as he had thought and therefore was not where Napoleon had expected him to be. This is an example of the inflexible thought that cropped up from time to time when Napoleon was convinced that he understood what was going on.

The confusion in regard to Ney's orders is surprising considering that Napoleon otherwise responded to the news of the Battle of Günzburg flexibly and intelligently. For the first time, he explicitly gave Murat command over the right wing of the army, comprising his own corps, Ney's, and Lannes's.[83] He wrote to Lannes, "All of the information that the Emperor has received leads him to believe that the enemy will offer battle at Ulm or a little higher [up the Danube]." Lannes was to march through Burgau toward Ulm and support Ney as he attempted to reduce the Austrian position there. He warned that the enemy might be "in great force and resolved to offer battle before Ulm," in which case Lannes should move slowly and should not attack before all his forces were in position.[84] His orders to Murat were vague, requiring the new commander of the right flank only to keep the corps in support of one another and to do the greatest possible harm to the enemy.[85]

As Napoleon reestablished the inner ring of the encirclement that he had erroneously begun to dismantle the day before, he kept the left wing of his army racing toward the southeast. He sent Soult to Landsberg and Bernadotte and the Bavarians to Munich, while Davout held at Aichach.[86] Although Napoleon apparently did not recognize it, he had now ensured that Mack could not escape. From Landsberg, Soult was in an excellent position to cut off any Austrian attempt to move to the south, and Mack could not hope to break through the French forces at Augsburg and Munich. The farther south Napoleon drew his army, the more opportunity he presented to Mack to reconsider his plan to drive along the left bank of the Danube, should he be so inclined.

Napoleon's decision to give Murat command over Ney and Lannes reflected his increasing preoccupation with the Russian threat. On October 9, Bernadotte wrote that he had received word that the first Russian column was about to arrive in Regensburg, squarely on the flank of the French army and in a good position to march into its rear.[87] The next day, Davout wrote that the Russians were expected at Braunau that very day and in Munich on October 16. He also noted that Kienmayer's Corps in Munich was receiving reinforcements and that the overall Austrian army in Swabia numbered between 40,000 and 50,000 men.[88] Napoleon's letter to Ney of October 10 noted for the first time that the army was moving toward Munich "in order to await there the Russians, who have just debouched."[89] The order to Bernadotte to move to Munich from the previous day, by contrast, had not mentioned the Russians at all.[90]

The Russians were not about to descend on Regensburg; they would not arrive even in Braunau until October 20. These dispositions reveal that Napoleon had not really factored the Russians into his plans for this campaign and was forced to scramble as rumors of their impending arrival surfaced more realistically. Had the Austrians possessed the 80,000 men in Bavaria that Napoleon believed to be there, and had the Russians been closer than they were (as many reports to Napoleon had indicated), Napoleon's forces might have found themselves in an unsettling position.

On the other hand, they might not. Napoleon had skillfully encircled the Austrians at Ulm with two rings, and Mack would have had to break through Ney, Lannes, and Murat in order to threaten the rear of Soult, Davout, Bernadotte, and Marmont as they confronted the Russian forces joined with Kienmayer's Corps. Napoleon could reasonably expect both of his separated forces to hold their own. The brief moment when he almost let Mack out of the trap would have put his forces at much greater risk, but he recovered from that error rapidly and with agility.

The overall operational situation was well in hand, therefore, when Ney began pushing his forces forward toward Ulm on October 11. Ney continued to believe he was facing a small rear guard in Ulm: "The enemy has been struck with a terror of which there are few examples; he is retiring on Biberach in order to save himself in the upper Tyrol; all his retreats have been cut off toward Kempten and Füssen; it is therefore likely that Archduke Ferdinand will have left only a weak garrison at Ulm with orders to hold to the last extreme."[91] Accordingly, Ney sent the 2nd and 3rd Divisions marching toward Ulm along the right bank of the Danube.[92] He ordered Dupont's 1st Division to close on Ulm, demand the surrender of the fortress, and then advance to Haslach and Thalfingen, if possible. Baraguey d'Hilliers was to support this movement with his cavalry, although he did not receive the order until the day of the battle.[93]

The stage was thus set for one of the worst blunders of the French maneuver. Dupont, with one infantry division supposedly supported by one dragoons division, was sent to seize a partially fortified city defended by the entire Austrian army. Worse still, Dupont advanced across the open and nearly featureless plain northeast of Ulm. Dupont's order resulted from ignorance of Mack's position and intentions, as well as extreme arrogance and a conviction that the Austrians were already beaten and need not be taken seriously. To everyone's surprise, however, they held their own.

Dupont's 32nd Infantry Regiment marched from its position at Haslach toward Ulm and encountered elements of four Austrian regiments waiting to receive it near Bolfingen.[94] Scorning cleverness, the 32nd charged into the teeth of the Austrian defenses and was driven back after hard fighting. The Austrians, sensing the opportunity to inflict a serious blow on Ney's Corps, sent several infantry and cavalry regiments to Jungingen, from which they hoped to envelop Dupont's force and destroy it. Dupont, however, detected this movement and decided to preempt the Austrian attack. With his remaining forces he raced to Jungingen and took the Austrian regiments forming up there by surprise, capturing at least a thousand prisoners.* The weight of the Austrians' attack drove these forces back to Haslach, where they held as night fell.

Baraguey-d'Hilliers had not received Ney's order to support Dupont until he arrived at Allbeck on the day of the battle. His arrival there was fortuitous, for he managed to drive off some adventurous Austrian cavalry that had been raiding Dupont's headquarters and trains. His late arrival led to an extensive inquisition, since Ney accused him of dereliction of duty, but his failure was clearly unintentional.[95] Some of the French officers thought that if Baraguey-d'Hilliers had arrived promptly the battle might have been won. That is clearly ridiculous, given the great disparity in forces and the fact that the Austrians fought tenaciously. Dupont was forced to fall back to Allbeck and join Baraguey-d'Hilliers there, having utterly failed in his mission.

It is difficult to tell what effect the Battle of Haslach-Jungingen had on Napoleon and his plans. Apparently Napoleon did not learn of it until October 12. In the meantime, however, he had already decided that Mack was probably concentrating his army near Ulm and warned Murat that "the enemy, surrounded as he is, will fight; he is receiving reinforcements from the Tyrol and from Italy; he can thus oppose you within a few days with more than 40,000 men."[96] Murat, however, disposed of 50,000–60,000 men with Lannes's and Ney's Corps, so Napoleon ordered him to march as close to Ulm as possible and be ready to concentrate all his forces to crush the Austrians if

---

*Dupont claimed to have taken 7,000 prisoners, which is absurd; the official bulletin announcing the victory claimed only 1,500 (Krauss, *Der Feldzug von Ulm*, p. 404).

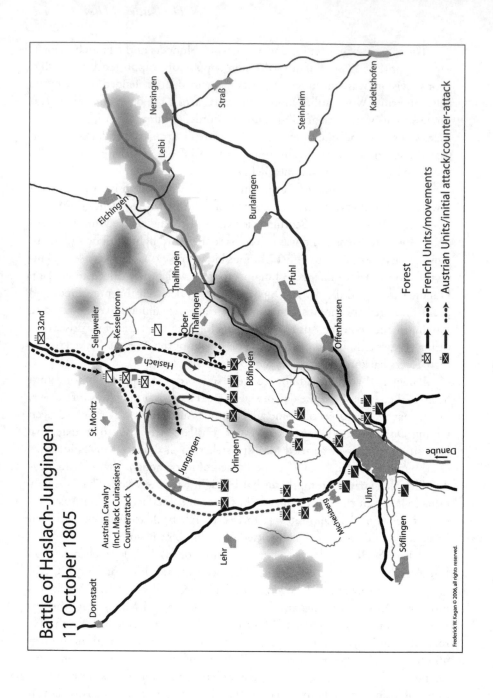

Battle of Haslach-Jungingen
11 October 1805

Forest

French Units/movements

Austrian Units/initial attack/counter-attack

32nd

Kadeltshofen

Steinheim

Straß

Nersingen

Leibi

Burlafingen

Elchingen

Pfuhl

Thalfingen

Offenhausen

Ober-Thalfingen

Seligweiler

Kesselbronn

Haslach

Böfingen

Danube

St. Moritz

Jungingen

Örlingen

Ulm

Austrian Cavalry
(Incl. Mack Cuirassiers)
Counterattack

Michelsberg

Söflingen

Lehr

Dornstadt

Frederick W. Kagan © 2006, all rights reserved.

they attacked. If the Austrians somehow escaped the trap, Napoleon concluded, they would be stopped on the Lech. A sense of urgency entered this note with the statement that the Russians were coming rapidly.

Murat made preparations for a battle on October 13. The army, he wrote Napoleon, would be concentrated by then with Lannes's Corps and two of Ney's divisions on the right bank of the Danube, and Dupont's division on the left. Murat proposed to launch a frontal assault across the river, although he promised to use several "false attacks" to divert the Austrians. He thought that there were about 35,000 Austrians at Ulm, but he was confident that his forces would carry the day.[97]

On October 12, Murat informed Napoleon briefly of the Battle of Haslach-Jungingen and reconfirmed his intention to attack Ulm the next day.[98] But Napoleon had decided against the attack. He believed that Mack was concentrated with his left resting on Ulm and his right on Memmingen. He therefore ordered Soult to race with his corps from Landsberg to Memmingen to be ready to turn Mack's right flank.[99] In the meantime, he ordered Murat to wait until October 14 to launch his attack in order to give Soult time to arrive in force.[100]

Napoleon took the prospect of this battle very seriously. He ordered Murat to have his generals inspect their weapons and battle supplies. In addition to Murat and Soult, he also warned Bessières of the impending battle. He ordered Marmont to race toward the Iller and take up a position near Krumbach. He also warned General Dumonceau, the commander of the Batavian Division; General Rivaud, the commandant at Augsburg; General Godinot; the intendant-general (chief logistics officer); and Davout.[101]

Moreover, he completely altered the balance of his deployment. Before October 12, he had provided only two infantry and one cavalry corps to deal with what he thought were the remnants of Mack's force near Ulm, while the other four infantry corps and the Bavarians held the triangle Munich-Augsburg-Landsberg. Now Napoleon sent Marmont and Soult racing toward the Iller, which would allow him to concentrate four infantry and one cavalry corps against Mack, while only Bernadotte, Davout, and the Bavarians held Munich and its environs.

The only possible conclusion is that on October 12 Napoleon recognized that the main Austrian army was still in the vicinity of Ulm and had not made a serious attempt to break out in any direction. As soon as he had recognized that fact, which the Battle of Haslach-Jungingen probably served to emphasize, he concentrated the bulk of his army toward Ulm in order to destroy Mack immediately. This shift in the balance of his deployment suggests that he had been envisioning Soult and Marmont not only as elements of the outer ring of an encirclement, but also as a sort of roving reserve. If Mack's army or a significant element of it suddenly showed up east of Ulm, then Soult and Marmont would be able to deal with it at least until the rest of the army arrived. At any event, as soon as Napoleon had become convinced of the actual location of Mack's army, he sent Soult and Marmont racing to assist in its destruction.

But there was no battle on October 14 because Napoleon gave no orders for it. Instead, by the dawn of that day he had again changed his mind about how best to proceed and opted for a different course. The reason for this change of heart most probably lies in the dawning recognition that he had once again misconstrued Mack's deployment and intentions.

On October 12, Murat reported that a captured Austrian officer claimed that Mack's army—80,000-strong—was concentrated on the left bank of the Danube and had no troops on the Iller.[102] This report tallied with the events of the previous day, when the Austrians had been strong enough on the left bank to inflict on Dupont what even Napoleon saw as a significant defeat.* It is not likely that Napoleon accepted the inflated strength estimate of the Austrian army, even though he had independent confirmation of that estimate from another source.† He did not act as though he thought he was facing 60,000–80,000 Austrians at Ulm. What mattered now was not the strength of the enemy, but his position.

Early in the morning of October 13, Napoleon received another confirmation of Mack's deployment. Murat forwarded a letter from Lannes reporting on a prisoner who said that there was only a small reserve of 4,000–5,000 men still in Ulm and that the main Austrian forces were all on the left bank of the Danube.[103] Lannes concluded from this disposition that the Austrians were preparing to attack along the left bank in order to drive toward Bohemia and escape. Murat passed his message on but strongly disagreed with it. Would the Austrians really march in such a fashion as to cut their lines of communication to the Tyrol, he asked? Would they not have learned from the experience of October 11 that if a single division could do them so much harm, they had no chance of escaping? Surely they had simply concentrated in the best place they could find to await the outcome of a battle to decide the campaign.

---

*Dupont and Ney claimed a victory, and Murat's report condemned the order to attack but praised the attackers; yet Napoleon harshly criticized Ney for exposing a division to being manhandled. See Dupont to Sanson, 13 October 1805 (in Alombert-Goget and Colin, *La campagne de 1805*, vol. 3, pt. 1, p. 523): "the success of my division was very brilliant." Ney noted that Dupont's battle, "although extremely brilliant," was only partially successful due to Baraguey d'Hilliers's failure to appear in a timely fashion. (Ney to Berthier, 12 October 1805, p. 525). Berthier thundered: "His Majesty was pained that you ordered the attack of Ulm with Dupont's division alone, which led to the crushing of two regiments of dragoons and artillery, whatever the courage of the troops might have been. . . . Events can disrupt the best laid plans, which restores the morale to an army that does not have any" (Berthier to Ney, 13 October 1805, in Alombert-Goget and Colin, *La campagne de 1805*, vol. 3, pt. 2, p. 698).

†Appreciation of the Austrian Army under the Orders of Archduke Ferdinand, dated after 10 October 1805, and presumably before Ferdinand left the army on 14 October, in Alombert-Goget and Colin, *La campagne de 1805*, vol. 3, pt. 1, p. 581. This table gives the total strength of the Austrian army in Bavaria, including Kienmayer's corps, as 86,500 men.

Napoleon did not change his plans out of a fear for his supply lines or belated realization of his dangerous situation, as some have suggested.* Yet he completely abandoned the plan of attacking Ulm on October 14 and changed his dispositions to support a different operation. Why? The answer almost certainly lies in his new understanding of the Austrian deployment. Napoleon had been preparing a battle to fight for the Iller. Ney had one division on the left bank of the Danube and two marching toward Ulm along the right. Lannes held a position on the lower Iller near the confluence with the Danube. Soult was marching through Memmingen toward Illertissen, slightly upriver from Lannes. Clearly the purpose of this deployment was to support an attack across the Iller and then across the base of the triangle formed by the Iller and the Danube. In this way, Napoleon would cut the Austrians off from any retreat to the south and possibly even crush their army between the two rivers.

But the Austrians were not on the Iller. They had retreated to a position on the Danube at and below Ulm. To launch an attack such as Napoleon had originally contemplated made no sense. He did not need two corps to cut the undefended lines of communication from Ulm to the Tyrol. There was no hope of trapping the Austrians between the rivers. The approach to Ulm from the south between the rivers, furthermore, is the worst possible way to attack the city, since it would funnel the French forces into a tight and compact mass right at the crucial moment and permit the Austrians to trap them against one or the other river, if they moved quickly enough. To march across the Iller, then across the Danube, then up the left bank from above Ulm would have exhausted the troops to no purpose. As soon as he had learned that the Austrians were concentrating on the left bank below Ulm, therefore, Napoleon abandoned his battle plan and sought a different solution.

The core of Napoleon's new plan was to shift his forces to the north in order to engage Mack's army in Ulm from a position on the left bank of the Danube, avoiding the need to fight across rivers. On October 13 he ordered Ney to seize the bridge and the heights at Elchingen, regain Albeck and occupy it with Dupont's division, station a second division near the Elchingen

---

*One historian has seized on these messages and Napoleon's rebuke to Ney sent later on October 13 to argue that Napoleon had "finally realized his errors." "The thought of what Mack could do," he continues, "almost overwhelmed him" (Connelly, *Blundering to Glory*, p. 82). He then paints a portrait of Napoleon "scrambling back to Ulm" in a desperate effort to save his trains, which were then at Ellwangen. This interpretation is not supported by the evidence. Nowhere does Napoleon give any indication of concern for his trains, for one thing. For another, Napoleon did not, as Connelly claims, order Murat, Ney, and Lannes to "recross the Danube and engage the Austrians at Ulm," as we shall see. For still another, the rebuke to Ney (Berthier to Ney, 13 October 1805, in Alombert-Goget and Colin, *La campagne de 1805*, vol. 3, pt. 2, p. 698) was not for crossing the Danube, as Connelly asserts, but for failing to retake the bridge and heights near Elchingen, which he had been ordered to do several times, and for attacking Ulm with a single division. Only the latter criticism is unfair, since Napoleon himself ordered Ney to take Ulm quickly and with relatively little force, although it is possible that the sequence of orders and events became confused in Napoleon's mind.

bridge, and maintain a vanguard at Burlafingen, on the right bank of the Danube.[104] He instructed Lannes to seize the bridge over the Iller at Ober-Kirchberg and hold it until Soult or Marmont arrived.[105] He then told Lannes to seize Pfuhl, a small town on the right bank near Ulm, on the next day.[106] He ordered Marmont to race to the Iller near Ober-Kirchberg and "interrupt all of the enemy's communications by sending your left advanced posts as close as possible to Ulm," although Marmont wrote back to say that he could not arrive so rapidly at this destination.[107]

It is clear from these dispositions that Napoleon's priority was fighting a decisive battle with Mack near Ulm, rather than trapping him in the city, let alone winning without a fight. He wrote to Soult, "I am letting you know that the entire enemy army is in Ulm; it is essential that you come to form the left of the Emperor['s army] and to cut the enemy's route to Biberach."[108] Soult was at that moment just arriving at Memmingen, forty-five kilometers from Ulm and a considerable distance from the Ulm–Biberach line. If Napoleon's highest priority had been cutting off Mack's retreat to the south, then he would have sent Lannes across the Iller at once, since he was in a position to cut that line closer to Ulm and more rapidly. Instead, he moved Lannes north to support a battle on the left bank of the Danube. If he had been unwilling to separate Lannes from Ney, since he expected a significant battle near Albeck, then he could have ordered Marmont to cross the Iller because even Marmont was closer than Soult. Instead, Napoleon focused on concentrating the greatest possible force in the immediate vicinity of Ulm, gradually shifting it north to support the expected battle.

Napoleon had postponed that battle by a day, however, since he needed to shift his forces to engage the enemy properly. The main activity for October 14 was to be Ney's advance on Albeck, supported by Lannes if necessary. Napoleon thought this advance would possibly trigger a significant battle north of Ulm, but anything that got the Austrians to fight beyond their entrenchments and fortifications could only be a good thing.[109]

The Collapse of the Austrian Army, Part 1

If the Battle of Haslach-Jungingen had relatively little effect on Napoleon's plans, its impact on the Austrian army was much greater. Perhaps the most important consequence in the long run was that Ferdinand finally decided to oppose Mack openly. He found the quartermaster general's behavior during the fight and afterward so disgraceful that he refused to work with him.

Mack behaved poorly throughout the run-up to the battle, but from his account of the fight, which he forced Ferdinand to send forward as the official "relation" of the combat, it seems that he did pretty well. He makes it sound as though he sent the Austrian left to encircle Dupont's division and carried through that maneuver. The truth was rather different. As part of a scathing general indictment of Mack's performance, Ferdinand reported to Francis that it was not Mack but Schwarzenberg who ordered the maneuver and carried it out with the assistance of FML Klenau.[110] "Mack," he notes laconically, "was present himself." Ferdinand does not mention what Mack was doing during the battle, but apparently he had placed himself at the head of the Mack Cuirassiers Regiment and led the charge to Jungingen.* If this is true, it would go a long way toward explaining Ferdinand's disgust with Mack and refusal to work with him.

Having decided to denounce Mack once and for all, Ferdinand compiled a long list of Mack's misdeeds.† The quartermaster general, Ferdinand wrote, spent his days drafting orders. He would produce at least two contradictory orders every day and give them to Ferdinand to carry out. Consequently the army marched back and forth to no purpose and accomplished nothing. This pointless movement, he continued, had ruined the army more than any action of the enemy. The end was arriving fast, though, according to Ferdinand. The army's position was "critical," and although it was possible that unforeseen events would save it, the "probabilities" were against it.

Ferdinand's screed served to soothe his conscience more than anything else, since he thought that the end would arrive long before Francis would be able to receive and respond to his letter.‡ It really was, however, the beginning of the end of the Austrian army, for Ferdinand was prepared to take dramatic steps to separate himself from the incompetent quartermaster general.

Mack, in the meantime, had been planning feverishly. First he reorganized the Austrian army into four corps, commanded by FML Schwarzenberg, FML Riesch, FML Werneck, and FML Jellachich. Each corps was subdivided into a vanguard, main body, and reserve, each of which might consist of one or more brigades.[111] This organization replicated the French corps-division-brigade system, only with different names. A more important difference was that Mack continually changed the affiliations of units to higher headquarters, so that commanders never developed a comfortable relationship with superiors or subordinates.

From documents captured from Dupont during the Battle of Haslach-Jungingen, Mack learned that Napoleon was shifting his lines of communication to the north.[112] Convinced that Napoleon feared for his communications, Mack developed a plan to attack them. He accordingly ordered Werneck to

---

*Krauss, *Der Feldzug von Ulm*, p. 405 n. 1. Krauss offers no source for this fascinating fact, and it is not corroborated in any of the other accounts that I have been able to find.

†For those following along with the *Caine Mutiny* analogy, Ferdinand here plays a Maryk who actually presents his "book" on Queeg to Halsey.

‡Imagine a Maryk who dispatches his "book" to Halsey just as the *Caine* enters the typhoon.

lead his corps on October 12 through Geislingen to Stuttgart, and even farther toward the Rhine if possible, while Mack led the rest of the army toward Heidenheim. When Werneck objected to this plan, Mack proposed to relieve him and take command of his corps, but Ferdinand and the other generals talked him out of it. Mack regretfully abandoned this plan and developed another.[113]

The new plan, crafted on October 12 for operations the next day, took advantage of Mack's conviction that the enemy's right wing was weak, a conclusion that Napoleon had rightly feared Mack would draw from the Battle of Haslach-Jungingen.[114] This plan concentrated the corps of Schwarzenberg, Riesch, and Werneck against Dupont's division near Albeck, while Jellachich held the Ulm fortifications. The idea was for Werneck's Corps on the right to distract and hold the French while Schwarzenberg and Riesch drove through Jungingen and beyond to the north.[115]

Before he could execute this plan, however, Mack learned that the French were advancing on Weißenhorn, threatening his communications with the Tyrol. In response, Mack ordered Schwarzenberg to send one of his "divisions," commanded by FML Klenau, to Weißenhorn while Jellachich took half of his corps toward Fahlheim, thus forming a line running from Fahlheim to Weißenhorn against Ney and Lannes. This disposition did not last long either, however. When Mack learned that Dupont had largely withdrawn from Albeck and Langenau, he reverted to his previous plan, albeit with a significant modification.[116]

Now Mack sent Jellachich south along the road toward Ochsenhausen with orders to retreat to Lindau if necessary. Schwarzenberg's Corps was to remain in and around Ulm, conducting cautious reconnaissance that did not pull too many troops too far away from the city. Mack ordered Werneck to divide his corps in half and march it in echelons to Heidenheim, while Riesch was to follow Werneck and support him as necessary. But this order suffered yet another change, as Mack decided to send Klenau's division to Weißenhorn while Jellachich marched to Ochsenhausen. Werneck was to drive through Albeck toward Heidenheim, followed by Laudon, commanding one of Riesch's divisions. The rest of Riesch's Corps was to follow toward Heidenheim accompanying the army's baggage.[117]

The commanders had hardly read this order when they received word to meet Mack at once.[118] The main change made at that meeting was that Mack now focused on sending Riesch along the Danube to cut all bridges as far as Donauwörth. He then proposed two alternatives. If the French did not hold Donauwörth or held it only lightly, then the army would march along the Danube toward Bohemia. If Napoleon held Donauwörth firmly, however, then the army would march north, presumably skirting Ansbach, through upper Pfalz toward Bohemia.[119]

These plans were senseless. Among other mistakes, they divided the army at its moment of greatest danger, sending a quarter of it marching south while the other three quarters marched north. Why did Mack send Jellachich toward the Tyrol? There is no good answer. One historian, following a hostile source, speculates that Mack was trying to get rid of the troublesome former quartermaster general of the army, Mayer, whom he sent along on that expedition.[120] It seems more likely that Mack was confused and forgot that if he was marching the main army toward Bohemia, then it was no longer necessary to defend the lines of communication to the Tyrol. Or perhaps he recognized that the army was more or less doomed and decided that it stood a better chance of survival if broken into several detachments. This last interpretation is supported by Mack's constant preoccupation with finding ways to force Napoleon to divide his forces.

However that may be, none of these plans were executed, for Mack soon received shocking news: the British had landed at Boulogne and revolution had broken out in France.* This nonsense persuaded Mack that Napoleon's movements back toward Ulm were part of a general retreat toward the Rhine. Consequently he ordered his corps to move to positions from which they could conduct a pursuit. Riesch was to march down the left bank of the Danube toward Donauwörth; Schwarzenberg back through Ulm to the right bank of the Danube and down toward Günzburg and also toward Weißenhorn; Werneck toward Aalen; and Jellachich toward Memmingen but not as far south as Lindau, since he was supposed to pursue Napoleon's fleeing troops.[121]

This order, amazingly enough, actually had consequences, for Riesch set off down the Danube and reached Thalfingen and Elchingen.† The roads, Riesch wrote, were terrible and in places the horses had to wade through chest-high water. Riesch apparently thought about turning the column around and marching back to Ulm but did not want to become separated from the other half of his corps under Laudon. Turning back would also mean that he had failed to accomplish his mission. As he was mulling the situation over, he heard the sound of cannon and musket fire from the direction of Elchingen. Grabbing the lead units of his corps, he rushed toward that town and there saw Laudon engaged directly on the Elchingen bridge with the French.

Riesch had not expected to find the French in force closer than Günzburg, and he did not believe that Laudon could drive the enemy away from the

---

*Krauss, *Der Feldzug von Ulm*, p. 425. Chandler dates the arrival of this "news" incorrectly to October 7 and uses it to explain all of Mack's subsequent plans and movements. Chandler, *Campaigns of Napoleon* (New York: Macmillan, 1966), pp. 396–397.

†Riesch implies that he started moving according to the previous order and does not indicate that he received a new one. This is possible, since his mission was largely unchanged from the one to the other. Riesch, Relation about the Movement and Battle at Elchingen, 16 October 1805, KA AFA 1805 Deutschland, X/158.

bridge, whose right bank end they still held, before nightfall. He was also concerned for his troops, who were exhausted by their difficult march and facing a more imminent threat than Riesch had anticipated. Accordingly, he ordered Laudon to break off the fight, posting defenders on the Austrian side of the bridge, and he encamped his forces near Elchingen.[122]

The Austrian generals' loss of confidence in Mack can be clearly felt from this example. Riesch probably had the force available to beat back the French and even take, or at least destroy, the bridge. He certainly had the force necessary to screen the position and march on toward his destination. The lack of initiative and aggressiveness Riesch demonstrated reflected his belief that Mack did not know what he was doing, did not know where the French were, and was giving the army dangerous and foolish orders. This belief caused Riesch to act timidly and cautiously at a time when enthusiasm and aggressiveness were essential for success. But it was Mack who had robbed the army of those traits by his exhausting marches and confusing orders.

Riesch was correct to believe that Mack did not know what he was doing, since the quartermaster general's plans were based on a false notion of where the French were and what Napoleon intended. As Laudon fought Malher for control of the Elchingen bridge, Dupont's division was recovering at Brenz, a half-day march northeast of Elchingen, and Loison's 2nd Division was marching toward Nersingen, on the right bank of the Danube opposite Elchingen. Riesch should have been able to batter his way past Ney's Corps, especially thus dispersed, but it was not possible for him to walk to Donauwörth, destroying bridges as he went, as Mack had originally ordered. The stage was set for a showdown at Elchingen.

Mack remained undaunted. On October 14, he issued an order that began, "The enemy army is retreating toward the Rhine, two columns of which will cross the Iller at Memmingen and Illertissen, the third, probably Bernadotte's, latched-onto by Kienmayer's Corps stationed at Munich and Dachau, will at the same time cross the Danube at Donauwörth" and will continue on through Nördlingen toward Mannheim. The middle enemy column, Mack continued, would cross the Danube at Ehingen and Riedlingen and then retreat through Stuttgart to Karlsruhe.[123]

Mack ordered Jellachich to take responsibility for the left (southernmost) column. He instructed Schwarzenberg to attack the middle column in the rear, Werneck to make forced marches toward Stuttgart, and Kienmayer to attack the flank and rear of Bernadotte's Corps. The order did not clarify Riesch's role, and he did not even realize that his advance toward Heidenheim had been canceled.[124] When Mack became aware of this problem, he simply instructed Riesch to operate together with Kienmayer to destroy Bernadotte's Corps.[125] The fight at Elchingen on October 13 seemed to

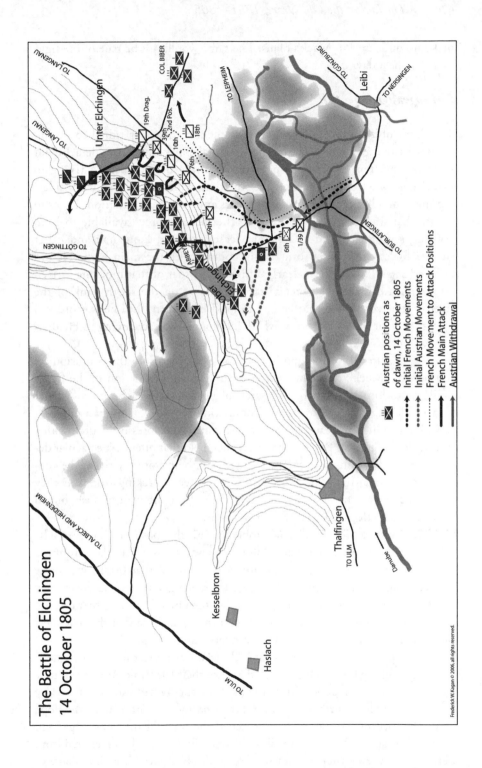

The Battle of Elchingen
14 October 1805

TO LANGENAU
TO LANGENAU
TO GÖTTINGEN

TO ALBECK AND HEIDENHEIM

TO ULM

Unter Elchingen

COL BIBER

19th Drag.

39th
2nd Pos.
10th
18th
76th
69th
ABBÉ
6th
1/39

Ober Elchingen

TO LEIPHEIM

TO BURLAFINGEN

Leibi

TO GÜNZBURG

TO NERSINGEN

Thalfingen

Danube

TO ULM

Kesselbron

Haslach

Austrian positions as
of dawn, 14 October 1805

Initial French Movements

Initial Austrian Movements

French Movement to Attack Positions

French Main Attack

Austrian Withdrawal

make no difference in Mack's plans. The same would not be true of the fight there the next day.

Elchingen, October 14

The Battle of Elchingen is a testimony to the fact that operational confusion can translate into tactical failure and can make a skillful army detachment seem incompetent.[126] Riesch spent the morning of October 14 trying to make sense of Mack's orders and the situation, which was difficult considering the contradiction between those orders and the actual situation. Eager to clarify that situation, Riesch scattered the meager forces available to him, sending a vanguard under General Mecsery toward Langenau and other smaller forces to the west to maintain contact with the main body. He did not understand his mission clearly. But Mack's order of that morning arrived after Riesch had seen the French forces massing on the south bank of the river, and he concluded that he had to hold Elchingen until he was ordered to withdraw or follow the army, which he thought was advancing to Heidenheim, as a rear guard.[127]

Riesch suffered from a number of problems apart from the confusion resulting from Mack's detachment from reality and the reduction in the forces available to him through the dispatch of numerous detachments. At first glance, Elchingen seems to have a dominating position. The town climbs a steep hill to a high plateau. Just to the east stands an impressive church with a walled cloister garden. Beyond that is an open field that offers a spectacular defensive position against any enemy trying to climb up from the river. The gentle slope offers virtually no undulations to protect attacking troops as they advance, allowing the defenders to keep them under fire continuously out to the maximum effective range of their weapons.

There were also a number of problems with this position, however. The hill and the town are more than a kilometer away across a flat plain from the bridge over the Danube. Consequently the defense of that bridge was more difficult than it initially appeared. Once the French got across, moreover, they had room to rally and realign their forces and then march freely, either directly toward the town or to the right or left, and there was little that the defenders on the hill or in the town could do to hinder them.

Although the slope to the east of Elchingen was perfect for the defenders, there was nothing on which they could anchor their left flank. As a result, they were vulnerable to an attack on that flank if the enemy had substantial cavalry forces or enough infantry to get around their position. Contrariwise, the slope of the hill became steeper as it approached the walls of the cloister garden. Troops that had the hardiness to climb it would find themselves sheltered from defenders in the cloister for much of their climb. Apart from the village of

Elchingen, moreover, which was almost directly opposite the bridge, there was nothing on which to anchor the right flank of a defending force either. Riesch thus had to defend his position with both flanks open and a significant terrain-induced vulnerability at the seemingly impenetrable center of his line.

Worst of all, however, Riesch had very little cavalry, an inadequate number of cannons, and not enough ammunition or powder for them or the infantry. Mack had unwisely shorn away much of Riesch's cavalry just as he was setting out toward Elchingen on October 13. The weakness in artillery and ammunition resulted from the loss of many cannons and supply wagons to the terrible roads from Ulm along the Danube to Elchingen.[128] As it turned out, however, the most significant problem Riesch faced was his preoccupation with the operational situation.

The French attack came at 8:00 A.M., allowing the various detachments Riesch had ordered to leave the area (although the French were not aware of that movement). General Loison's 2nd Division of Ney's Corps stormed across the partially dismantled bridge and drove rapidly through the weak defenses Riesch had established to cover it. Riesch had ordered those defenders to use canister from their cannons to keep the French at bay, but apparently the canister had been lost with the supply wagons on the march from Ulm to Elchingen.[129]

The French quickly reformed and broke into two groups. The 6th Light Infantry Regiment marched on the village of Elchingen, while the 1st Battalion of the 39th Line Infantry Regiment marched to the right to climb the deadly slope toward the plateau. The 6th Light found the going relatively easy, for the Austrian defenders broke quickly and took flight. The 39th had a much harder time. Attempting to climb the gentle slope without any reserve or cavalry, the regiment took a fearful beating from the Austrians on the crest. It was soon forced to withdraw to the plain before the bridge.

In the meantime, Ney had gotten a light cavalry brigade, the 2nd Battalion of the 39th, and two more infantry regiments (the 69th and 76th Line) across the river and into formation. Ney sent these three infantry regiments again up the slope east of the cloister garden, while the French pushed out of the village Elchingen and their cavalry struck both of the Austrian flanks.

Nevertheless, it was not easy to dislodge the Austrian defenders. Infantry and the little cavalry that Riesch had available threw back the French attacks on the Austrian left flank three times, while the infantry and artillery stationed along the crest of the slope more than held their own. The weakness of the position of the cloister, however, soon became apparent. Having gained control of the village of Elchingen, the 6th Light now began to attack the cloister. Ney concentrated all available artillery on the walls and the courtyard beyond, which had been filled with Austrian troops. The troops scattered rapidly. The artillery finally breached the cloister's wall—the spot was repaired and is now marked with a plaque and is called Ney's gate—and the infantry began to pour through. Eyewitness accounts indicate that the Austrians continued to resist fiercely, even in this bad situation, and fought with bayonets and knives when their ammunition ran out.[130]

The end, nevertheless, was no longer in doubt. The French were streaming into and around the cloister wall. Cavalry charges on both flanks had forced the defenders to form square, since they did not have enough of their own cavalry to defend themselves from attacks on their flanks and rear.* These formations created further gaps in the Austrian line that the French were not slow to exploit.

The situation was dangerous for Riesch, but his account indicates that he feared less the danger in the tactical situation than that inherent in the operational situation as he understood it. As the battle at Elchingen progressed, Riesch heard from two of his detachments. One under Colonel Biber had been sent out toward Leipheim to reconnoiter. Hearing the battle noise in his rear, Biber attempted to get back to Elchingen to assist. He was intercepted, however, by the 18th Dragoons Regiment of Bourcier's Dragoons Division, attached to Ney to support this attack. The 18th Dragoons drove Biber's confused, unsupported force off without much difficulty, and Riesch probably watched the affair from the Elchingen heights.

That was distressing, but Riesch was much more upset to hear from Mecsery, whose detachment at Langenau had run into Dupont's Division marching to retake Albeck. Dupont and Mecsery exchanged attacks briefly and then Dupont withdrew, believing it was more important for him to secure the army's communications at Günzburg than to reach his assigned objective.[131] Mecsery, in the meantime, reported that there were 10,000 French troops at Langenau (thereby doubling the strength of Dupont's division), trying to march toward Albeck. Rumor of a French advance toward Albeck was further confirmed by another detachment Riesch had sent out toward that town.[132] The field marshal, accordingly, ordered a retreat. "Since I now was entirely outflanked on my left and the enemy was in the place from which I should have expected reinforcements according to the disposition," Riesch explained, he decided to withdraw rather than risk complete encirclement.[133]

This was the correct decision. As the battle continued, Ney had brought Malher's 3rd Division across the bridge and into position to the south-southwest of the town. If Riesch had tried to hold, Ney would hardly have been able to resist sending Malher around to trap the Austrians completely. Why Ney did not try to do so is not clear. One source suggests that he was misguidedly determined

---

*Infantry unsupported by cavalry adopted a square formation in which ranks faced outward on all four sides with senior officers, artillery, and supplies in the center when they were attacked by enemy cavalry. This formation was generally successful against cavalry attacks, but it severely limited the firepower and the mobility of the defending formation, making it more vulnerable to infantry attacks if the enemy had infantry nearby to operate in conjunction with his cavalry.

to ensure that Loison got the full credit for defeating a superior enemy in a strong position without support.[134] Whatever his reason, it allowed Riesch to withdraw his corps toward Ulm.

Elchingen was not a pretty battle for either side. Ney made little effort to maneuver and instead ordered a series of frontal assaults against prepared defenders standing on good terrain. He had the opportunity to trap Riesch's Corps and destroy it completely, but did not do so. Riesch did not maneuver at all. Having stationed his troops in a strong position, he maintained no meaningful reserve with which to plug the holes that inevitably appear in any battle line, or to meet the flank attacks even more inevitable considering the position he occupied. Instead of concentrating his forces for an important fight, he dispersed them in small detachments sent out in every direction. He avoided having those detachments at least, and his entire force at worst, trapped by the French only because Ney chose to impale his corps on the strongest enemy positions he could find.

Endgame

The Battle of Elchingen broke the back of the Austrian army. This was not because the Austrians had been hoping to escape and Loison's victory blocked the door. There was still at least one escape route open even on October 14, although Mack would have no chance to use it. The army collapsed because this battle destroyed any trust that Ferdinand and the Austrian generals might have had in Mack, and any willingness to continue to follow him. The army split at the top, its will to continue resisting died, and its capitulation became inevitable.

The first and most dramatic split came immediately. Almost as soon as Ferdinand had learned of the Battle of Elchingen, he and some of the other generals called on Mack and demanded that the quartermaster general give orders to withdraw the army. When Mack refused, Ferdinand announced that he would not give Napoleon the honor of capturing a member of the imperial house: he was leaving the army. He added that his presence had long been unnecessary, since Mack had taken effective command long since. Mack protested, and notes flew between the two men who could hardly face or speak to each other, but the end was never in doubt. At 11:00 P.M., Ferdinand set out from Ulm with FML Schwarzenberg and Feldzeugmeister Kollowrat and eleven squadrons of cavalry. They rode to Geislingen and the Bohemian frontier, making it beyond the ring of French encirclements without incident.[135]

Mack remained undaunted to the end. He persisted in the conviction that Napoleon was retreating to the Rhine and would pass Ulm without assaulting it. He therefore gave orders to his remaining troops to concentrate around the city, except for Werneck's Corps at Heidenheim, now cut off from Ulm, and prepared to await Napoleon's departure and the arrival of an Austrian relief army (it is impossible to say what he had in mind, since none was on the way) and, of course, the Russians.

Napoleon had finally recognized the true situation and seen what to do. He moved all of Ney's and Lannes's Corps across the Danube and concentrated them in a line from Mähringen, about five kilometers northwest of the city, to Thalfingen, a few kilometers down the Danube. He ordered Marmont to occupy Pfuhl and keep the Austrians from breaking out back across the Danube. Soult was already marching to cut off the line of retreat to Biberach (although Jellachich's Corps had already gotten past him to the south).[136]

On October 15, Napoleon ordered an assault from the north that easily drove the Austrians off the Michelsberg, a dominating hill northwest of the city.[137] From that position, Napoleon could rain death on Ulm, its unfortunate inhabitants, and the Austrian army at will. Soldiers who had been camping in the streets suddenly had to find shelter. Since the city gates were closed, dead horses could not be buried. Supplies, of course, were hard to find.

Still Mack did not lose heart. "In the name of His Majesty," he declared, "I make all Generals and Officers responsible on their honor, their duty, and their own fortune, no more to allow the word 'surrender' to be used, but to think only of the most steadfast and stubborn defense."[138] The enemy army was exhausted, without food or supplies of its own, and retreating to France as rapidly as it could. The Austrian army could hold out until relief arrived. There was no question of starvation, he added, since there were 3,000 horses, and to emphasize that point, he declared, "I will myself be the first to eat horseflesh."

But Napoleon had already sent an emissary to demand the army's surrender; although Mack received the emissary alone, the other generals had to be informed. He told them that he had rejected Napoleon's demand and repeated the reasons for his confidence they had heard so often before. He would only allow himself to be overruled by the unanimous written demand of all of the senior officers of the army, he insisted.

They obliged. In a note signed by seven lieutenant field marshals and two major generals, Mack's officers showed that their willingness to serve under him, listen to his blandishments, place any confidence at all in his self-confidence, had come to an end. They insisted that he save what he could of the army and avoid a pointless and inevitable slaughter. They demanded that he surrender.

This was the moment when Mack should have broken down. Betrayed by officers he had trusted, he should have collapsed emotionally like Captain Queeg of the *Caine* during the mutiny. Amazingly, he did not do so. He accepted his officers' demand grudgingly and then attempted to conduct a protracted negotiation with Napoleon that ended with a face-saving compromise. On October 17 Mack and Napoleon agreed to a capitulation whereby Mack's army would march out of Ulm with full military honors. But he could wait,

Napoleon conceded, until October 25 to do so. And if, before that date, a relief army strong enough to lift the siege arrived, then Mack would be free to march his own army out and join that relief force, fighting Napoleon once again. If not, the officers would be released on their word of honor and the soldiers would be taken as prisoners of war to France.[139] Mack, believing as he did that the Russians would arrive before that time, was delighted. His generals, believing that this meant the end of the war for them, were no doubt relieved.

Is it possible that Mack insisted on the unanimous, written demand of his generals that he surrender in order to avoid the onus of the surrender? It is possible but not likely. Mack was one of those people who never believed himself beaten. He always saw hope and chances for success, even if he had to depart from reality to do so. This self-confidence is an important trait in a general, and Napoleon fully shared it. But Mack had neither the competence to back it up nor the charisma to persuade his subordinates to trust and follow him. In him, this self-confidence was the cause of periodic disaster.

Mack's personality shattered the senior leadership of the Austrian army and fragmented it virtually from the outset of the campaign. It held together for as long as it did because of the professionalism of the senior officers and their need to believe that their commander knew what he was doing. When that belief finally collapsed in the wake of the Battle of Elchingen, all was lost. Possibly the Austrian army in Bavaria suffered from a terminal disease the moment it crossed the Inn, or even from some later date. In the end, however, it was Mack—not Napoleon—who killed it.

17

Advance
and Retreat

Between August 22 and December 2, 1805, the Russian Podolian Army under the command of Mikhail Illarionovich Kutuzov marched more than 1,000 miles from Brody on the Austro–Russian frontier to Braunau on the Austro–Bavarian border, and back to Austerlitz.* The average daily march over that entire period was ten miles, counting rest days, battle days, and inactive days. The real average was much higher. Considering that a significant number of those marches took place with Napoleon's troops snapping at the rear guard's heels and that the army, duly reinforced, marched proudly into battle at the end of all that movement, the accomplishment was impressive indeed.

The approach march from the Russian border to Braunau was impressive—600 miles in fifty-nine days. But when Kutuzov's army arrived on the Inn on October 20, it found Mack's army in ruins. The entire concept of the war had perished and Napoleon had nearly 200,000 troops in hand to confront Kutuzov's force of perhaps 40,000. Thus began the first of several epochal Russian retreats in the face of Napoleon's troops.

The Advance

The Podolian Army crossed the Austrian border on August 25, 1805, five days behind schedule.† The march had been meticulously planned and prepared.

---

*Alexander designated Kutuzov's force the Army of Podolia because it concentrated in that region before crossing the Russian border.

†It was actually nine days behind the original schedule, which had called for the Russians to begin their march on August 16 and arrive at Braunau on October 16. The dates had been changed during the

Most of the lengthy conference on July 16 between Wintzingerode, Mack, Schwarzenberg, and Collenbach concerned the details of march routes, command arrangements, communications, logistics, and so on. Francis sent one of his senior staff officers, General Strauch, to the Russian army at Brody as a liaison. He also sent a captain from the quartermaster general staff and eighteen staff officers to form the campaign staff for Kutuzov's army.[1] The Austrians were entirely responsible for supplying the Russian army as it passed through their territory.

Kutuzov's appointment as commander of the first Russian army to meet the enemy under Alexander was in some ways a surprise. Although the fifty-eight-year-old general had a distinguished record of combat against the Turks over many years, including service with the legendary A. A. Suvorov, his star had been on the wane since Alexander's ascent to the throne.* His career had suffered the ups and downs inevitable under Paul's erratic reign, but at the time of Paul's death he commanded one of the armies Paul mobilized on the Prussian border in 1801 in support of the renewed League of Armed Neutrality against Great Britain.[2]

Alexander had seemed initially well disposed toward Kutuzov, for he made him governor-general of St. Petersburg and Finland soon after taking the throne. Imperial favor, if such it was, soon vanished, however. In August 1802, apparently seizing on an incident in which an officer had concocted a phony assassination scheme (in order to gain credit with the tsar when he "exposed" the scheme), Alexander dismissed Kutuzov. Kutuzov took the hint and submitted a request for a year's leave, which was quickly granted.[3]

There may have been a darker motive for Alexander's dislike of Kutuzov: he had dined with Paul on the night of his assassination, making him the last person not complicit in the plot to kill Paul to have seen the tsar.[4] Since Alexander's official explanation was that Paul died from an apoplectic stroke, Kutuzov's testimony that the tsar had been perfectly healthy and normal just hours before his death could have been quite damning. In this scenario, Alexander may have given Kutuzov the governor-generalship of St. Petersburg

---

conference between Wintzingerode, Mack, and others on July 16, 1805. The protocols of that conference can be found in multiple copies in the Kriegsarchiv (KA AFA 1805 Deutschland, VII/1⅓, VII/30, XIII/96), in L. G. Beskrovnyi, *M. I. Kutuzov: Sbornik dokumentov* (Moscow: Voennoe Izdatel'stvo, 1951), vol. 2, doc. 1 (all subsequent references to this series are to this volume); Léopold Neumann, *Recueil des traités et conventions conclus par l'Autriche avec les puissances étrangères, depuis 1763 jusqu'à nos jours* (Leipzig: F. A. Brockhaus, 1856); etc. The march order for August 25 for the 1st Column (commanded by P. I. Bagration) can be found in Iu. I. Zhiugzhda, ed., *Dokumenty shtaba M. I. Kutuzova, 1805–1806* (Vilnius: Gosudarstvennoe Izdatel'stvo Politicheskoi i Nauchnoi Literatury, 1951), doc. 4.

*The date of Kutuzov's birth is customarily given as September 16, 1745, which would make him sixty years old in September 1805. A recent biography, however, has found archival evidence that he was in fact born in 1747. Iu. N. Guliaev and V. T. Sogliaev, *Fel'dmarshal Kutuzov* (Moscow: Arkheograficheskii Tsentr, 1995), 1:18–19.

in order to keep him close and keep his mouth shut. By August 1802, however, the tsar had grown confident enough to dismiss Kutuzov and perhaps weary of a continual reminder of his guilt. However that may be, by the end of 1802 Kutuzov was back on his estate, and his repeated pleas to the tsar for reinstatement in some capacity fell on deaf ears.

Kutuzov's biographers offer no good explanation for Alexander's sudden turn to him in 1805. Apparently Alexander initially intended to give command of the Podolian Army to General Mikhel'son but changed his mind at a late date.[5] Perhaps Kutuzov's seniority and military record made it impossible for Alexander not to appoint him. This explanation is more likely, considering that the tsar had to find commanders for seven separate armies, one overall "army group" command, and the commands of several independent corps.* It was virtually inconceivable in such a circumstance for Alexander to find no place for so distinguished a general.

It may be that Alexander recognized the diplomatic subtleties that would face the commander of the Podolian Army. He would have to interact with not only Austrians but also numerous small German princes in whose territories the allies expected to be maneuvering. Kutuzov had served as an emissary to the kings of Prussia and Sweden in the previous six years. His diplomatic experience would serve him well amid the complications of the Third Coalition.[6]

Alexander's instructions to Kutuzov show that the tsar placed a premium on this experience and sought to rely on Kutuzov's judgment and subtlety.[7] These instructions heavily emphasized the political purpose of the operation. Kutuzov was to announce loudly wherever he was that Russia had no territorial ambitions and that, considering Russia's expanse and power, such ambitions were unnecessary. He was to bring over to the coalition as many German princes as possible. If he found himself moving into France, he was to bear in mind Alexander's expectation that the majority of the French people would enthusiastically welcome the coalition as long as it was clear that the aim was simply removing Napoleon from power. Alexander read his general into the diplomatic situation in great detail, accompanying his instructions with a mass of diplomatic correspondence, as well as the protocols of the allied conference of July 16, which were to be his guide in dealing with the Austrians.

The tsar understood the importance of unity of command, even if he was not enthusiastic about subordinating his armies to Austria's generals. As long as the emperor himself, Archduke Charles, or some other "prince of the blood" commanded the Austrian army in Germany, Kutuzov was to accept the orders

---

*In addition to Kutuzov's Podolian Army, Alexander mobilized three along the Prussian frontier (all three under the command of General Mikhel'son), one to land in Pomerania, one to watch the Turkish frontier, and one to land in Naples. See below for a fuller discussion of the grand strategic picture.

of that commander. The Austrians could divert the march of this Russian army as necessary, including to Italy if the situation required it. Alexander wanted Kutuzov to ensure that the dangers and burdens of the war were shared equally, but in the event the Austrian commander ordered Kutuzov to a place of greater danger and risk of loss, Kutuzov was to execute those orders, reporting in detail to Alexander afterward. Considering the inherent weaknesses in the coalition, these instructions reflected a solid understanding of what would be required to win, as well as a willingness to subordinate Alexander's immediate interests in pursuit of the larger goals of the coalition.

The intense preparations for the march of the Russian army resulted in a surprisingly smooth movement. Alexander had broken Kutuzov's army into six columns, each of between 8,000 and 10,000 men, composed of infantry, artillery, and cavalry.[8] The purpose of this organization of the army was to ensure that each column would arrive at the Inn able to fight on its own and take part in whatever operations were under way at the moment of its arrival.[9] Consequently the Russian army was broken down into six small corps that would march along the same road at two-day intervals. The overall strength of the army as it crossed the frontier was about 46,000 men.*

The army was weakened, however, when the 6th Column was diverted toward the Turkish frontier as the result of Alexander's growing fear that the sultan intended to take advantage of the tsar's preoccupation with Napoleon to attack.† This decision reduced the army by about 7,500 men to 38,500.‡ Alexander apparently did not intend to leave Kutuzov's army weakened, since he ordered three different infantry and one dragoon regiments to form a new "6th Column" attached to the Podolian Army.[10] Within days he ordered the original regiments of the 6th Column to march to join Kutuzov's army, and the replacements he had designated to stay on the Moldavian

---

*It is difficult to establish the exact size of Kutuzov's army, since the archival documents do not agree. Two, reproduced in Beskrovnyi, *Kutuzov,* doc. 4, give the strength as 56,713 and 48,536. The first figure includes noncombatants—the essential camp followers who fulfilled transportation and other logistical duties for the force. It is not clear whether or not the second figure includes them, which may explain the difference. A. I. Mikhailovskii-Danilevskii, *Opisanie pervoi voiny Imperatora Aleksandra s Napoleonom v 1805-m godu* (St. Petersburg: Independent Corps of the Internal Guard Press, 1844), pp. 33–34, lists the strengths of each column and gives a total of 46,405—a number that likely came from still other official documents.

†Kutuzov to G. V. Rozen, 9 September 1805, in Zhiugzhda, *Dokumenty,* doc. 9. One Cossack Regiment and half a Pioneers Company were first detached from the 6th Column and given to the 5th (Kutuzov to Mal'tits, 9 September 1805, in Zhiugzhda, *Dokumenty,* doc. 8). See also Lieven to Kutuzov, 3 September 1805; Kutuzov to Alexander, 9 September 1805; and Kutuzov to Rosen, 9 September 1805 in Beskrovnyi, *Kutuzov,* docs. 8–10.

‡According to Mikhailovskii-Danilevskii, *Opisanie,* p. 34, the 6th Column consisted of 8,155 men. A Cossack Regiment should have had about 520 men; the half company of pioneers would have been a mere handful.

frontier.* Fears for the security of Russia's southern border largely evaporated with the signing of a new Russo–Turkish treaty on September 23, so the net result of all these tergiversations was simply to delay the march of the 6th Column by more than a month for no purpose.†

In the meantime, the five-day delay in the beginning of the Russian march had already begun to concern Francis. On August 23, he wrote Baillet de Latour, the president of the Hofkriegsrat, that he had not yet heard anything about the Russians entering Austria. Since the whole plan, he wrote, was based on the date of the Russian entry, this delay placed Austria in great danger. He ordered de Latour to haunt Charles, waiting for word of the Russian advance.[11]

Six days later, Francis received word from Alexander that the movement of all of the Russian armies would be delayed—Kutuzov was to march on August 22, two days late, and the second Russian army commanded by General Buxhöwden would not cross the frontier until September 16, three weeks late.‡ Alexander blamed the Austrians' failure to adhere to the coalition treaty in a timely fashion for these delays. Razumovskii reported that the receipt of this message produced "a painful sensation," which he spent three days attempting to soothe.[12] His attempts were only partially successful, for although Cobenzl claimed to understand and sympathize with the need for the delay, he insisted that the Russian troops accelerate their march in order to make good the loss of time.

This was not the first time the Austrians had made such a request. As early as August 2, Razumovskii wrote Wintzingerode, who was temporarily commanding the Podolian Army, asking him to speed up the Russians' movements, and he repeated that request on August 25, before the Austrians had received official word of delays in the march.[13] It is not clear what triggered the first request, but the second probably resulted from Francis's foreboding at the

---

*Lieven to Kutuzov, 21 September 1805, in Beskrovnyi, *Kutuzov*, doc. 25. Mikhailovskii-Danilevskii is right to say that when the Austrians protested the change in plan, Kutuzov responded with bravado ("it is not the number of troops, but their courage" that matters). But his implication that this protest and an Austrian promise to cover the Turkish frontier was what changed Alexander's mind seems unfounded in light of the plans to replace the reassigned troops. Mikhailovskii-Danilevskii, *Opisanie*, p. 35; Kutuzov to Razumovskii, 23 September 1805, in Beskrovnyi, *Kutuzov*, doc. 37.

†According to the original plan, the 6th Column should have crossed the frontier around September 4. Its predecessor, the 5th Column, had done so on September 2 (Zhiugzhda, *Dokumenty*, doc. 6). It is not clear when Kutuzov received word that he had regained control over the original regiments of the 6th Column, but the order to him (Beskrovnyi, *Kutuzov*, doc. 25) was dated September 21, and he clearly had not received it by September 23. Allowing several more days for the order to arrive and for Kutuzov to get the column moving again, it seems unlikely that it could have crossed the frontier much before the beginning of October, or nearly a month late. The text of the Russo–Turkish Treaty can be found in VPR, vol. II, doc. 184.

‡Czartoryskii to Razumovskii, 15 August 1805 (received on 29 August), VPR, vol. II, doc. 158. The delay in the movement of Buxhöwden's army will be considered in more detail in a subsequent chapter.

lack of news from Brody. On September 19 Razumovskii wrote once more, and this letter received a response.

Because of Alexander's delay in naming him commander of the Podolian Army, Kutuzov did not arrive with the troops until September 21. Apparently Wintzingerode had neither replied to nor forwarded Razumovskii's messages, which Kutuzov found waiting for him on his arrival. Somewhat piqued by the fact that the letters had been addressed to Wintzingerode and not to him, Kutuzov nevertheless threw himself into the task of accelerating the army's march. He wrote back to Razumovskii, promising to do everything in his power to accede to the emperor's wishes, and then wrote to Cobenzl with a similar message.[14]

In accord with the proposals of the Austrian court, the Russian troops proceeded by forced marches—four post miles (about 15 miles) per day. In addition, the Austrians provided enough carts to carry half of the infantry another four post miles at a time. In this way, the Russian infantry was able to move between twenty-eight and thirty-eight miles per day. Kutuzov complained to Razumovskii about the strain this speed imposed on the troops, and he refused to try to move the artillery and cavalry just as rapidly, pointing out that simply doubling the horses' forage, as the Austrians proposed, would not make them move twice as fast or far. As a result, the Russian infantry soon began to outstrip its cavalry and artillery, as well as its supplies. Kutuzov was forced to break his army into two separate commands, one for the racing infantry, the other for the lagging cavalry and artillery.[15] He even accepted a subsequent Austrian request to have the troops rest every fifth day instead of every fourth.*

The Russian army moved with great speed and determination. P. I. Bagration's first column conducted march–ride combinations that lasted more than twenty-four hours at a stretch and brought the troops nearly 100 miles in four days.[16] Even the Austrians, desperate for more speed, were impressed by Bagration's efforts.[17] They recognized that the Russian artillery falling behind the infantry would expose the Russians to danger or at least ineffectiveness when they arrived on the Inn, and so they prepared to lend Kutuzov some of their reserve artillery to make up for the deficiency.[18]

By the beginning of October, things appeared to be well under control from Kutuzov's perspective. The army was moving forward in a rapid but stable way, and he felt he could absent himself from his troops for a few days to meet with Francis and the Austrian leadership in Vienna in order to hammer out the last few details. The meeting went well. Francis expressed his con-

---

*He initially rejected this request because of the bad weather and his soldiers' worn shoes (Kutuzov to Razumovskii, 1 October 1805, in Beskrovnyi, *Kutuzov,* doc. 49; Kutuzov to Strauch, 1 October 1805, doc. 52), but relented when the weather improved (Kutuzov to Alexander, 4 October 1805, doc. 56). Leo Tolstoy picked up on the poor condition of the soldiers' boots in *War and Peace,* Norton Critical ed., 2nd ed. (New York: Norton, 1996), pp. 96–99, describing a fictitious review at Braunau during which Kutuzov pointed out the problem to an Austrian observer.

tentment with the Russian troops and promised to work out the remaining details about their supplies and equipment.[19]

The atmosphere in Vienna at the time was surprisingly upbeat. The ongoing Russo–Prussian negotiations were a major preoccupation in Vienna as well as St. Petersburg, as we shall see.* It was in the context of those negotiations that the news of Bernadotte's march through Ansbach arrived in Vienna, and so it was not evaluated properly. The Austrians and Kutuzov reacted to that news with relief and pleasure, since it seemed to ensure that Frederick William would join the coalition, allow Alexander's troops through Prussia, and even add his own formidable army to the fray. It was hoped that since he had already given orders to mobilize that army, it would be swinging rapidly westward.[20] The Russians, of course, did not know how devastating Bernadotte's march was for the security of Mack's army, and their hosts apparently did not think of that fact or did not trouble to explain it to Kutuzov or Razumovskii.†

Consequently as Kutuzov's army began to arrive in Braunau in the second week of October, it was unprepared for serious combat. The forced marches had destroyed the fine organization that would have enabled each column to march into battle on its arrival at the Inn. The infantry now advanced without cavalry or artillery but could hardly go straight into battle in that condition. The soldiers were exhausted and their shoes were in terrible condition, since they had marched tirelessly through inclement weather and along bad roads. Above all, Kutuzov did not recognize the trap he was racing into. Neither Mack nor Ferdinand had kept him apprised of a danger that they, for the most part, had not foreseen, and when realization dawned at the end of the first week of October, they were too busy to worry about putting Kutuzov in the picture. Kutuzov's understanding of the situation was so distorted that on October 17 he sent a message to his army about the "victory" won by the Austrians over Ney at Haslach-Jungingen.[21]

In the meantime, Kutuzov set about organizing his army into battle formations as it arrived. As the first three columns approached Braunau, he broke them into two divisions commanded by Dokhturov and Miloradovich. Each division consisted of two brigades. These brigades comprised only infantry formations at this time, of course, since the artillery and cavalry had not yet arrived.[22] He also took the time to issue an order about the "tactics" of the Russian army that combined brief discussions about the command hierarchy

---

*This topic will be considered in more detail in a subsequent chapter.

†Judging from Razumovskii's correspondence, it seems that the full significance of the march through Ansbach was not felt in Vienna until October 11, when Mack's evaluation of the situation arrived. Kutuzov had already left to rejoin his army, and it is not clear that the significance of the news was passed on to him. Razumovskii to Czartoryskii, 11 October 1805, in Vasil'chikov, *Les Razoumowski*, p. 263.

with the exhortation to use bayonets and battalion columns when possible.* This order indicates that as late as October 17, Kutuzov expected to march forward and attack the French where he found them.[23]

Two days later he learned the truth. Although he had not received any word from Ferdinand or Mack, Kutuzov had decided that the rumors he was hearing were true. Mack's army had been trapped and defeated at Ulm and Memmingen, and had been taken prisoner. Although he initially feared that Napoleon's lead corps were racing to attack him immediately, he quickly realized that this was not the case. He would have time to concentrate his forces and decide what to do. Doing it, of course, would be another matter entirely.[24]

Wreckage

As Napoleon's corps closed the trap on Mack's army at Ulm, the Austrian army exploded. Jellachich took a substantial force south toward the Tyrol. Werneck's Corps, which had been serving as the vanguard for the general advance along the left bank of the Danube, was cut off by the Battle of Elchingen. Another force was trapped at Memmingen. Ferdinand broke out of Ulm at the head of a sizable cavalry force just as the trap was closing. Kienmayer finally led a large corps toward Munich and farther east, successfully retreating in front of Bernadotte's advance. Together these forces amounted to 25,000–30,000 troops.

Napoleon's delay in closing the trap at Ulm had facilitated some of this explosion, and his forces now paid the price for that delay. Dupont's weary infantrymen, who had borne the brunt of the fighting near Ulm, raced after Werneck's and Ferdinand's forces, accompanied by Murat's Cavalry and troops from Lannes's Corps. Soult largely abandoned the effort to close the lines of retreat south of Ulm in order to reduce the sizable enemy force at Memmingen. Marmont tried to pursue Jellachich, but to no avail. Napoleon made no effort to chase Kienmayer or delay his retreat.

By October 18, Murat's Cavalry had picked Werneck's infantry to pieces and forced the Austrian general to surrender his remaining 6,000 troops. Soult's reduction of Memmingen produced a surprising 4,600 prisoners—the marshal had not thought there were half that many in the town. The capitulation of Ulm netted some 25,000 Austrian troops. Combined with the prisoners taken at the battles that had preceded the capitulation, the French took nearly 50,000 prisoners in this brief campaign.[25]

---

*Such exhortations were traditional for those who had served with or under the great A. A. Suvorov, and emphasize once again how nonsensical is the idea that the coalition armies were somehow less "advanced" than the French in their adoption of the column formation for the attack and in their reliance on the bayonet charge.

Kienmayer, Jellachich, and Ferdinand had all escaped, and the Russians were arriving in force at Braunau, while reports erroneously indicated that another large Russian army was on the way and would arrive within a few weeks. The Austrians, Napoleon learned, were raising a *levée en masse* in the Tyrol to defend the Alpine passes and possibly free up their troops to strike at the French flank.[26] The Prussian response to Bernadotte's violation of their neutrality remained unclear, but Napoleon was aware of frantic allied diplomatic activity aimed at Berlin. His own forces were scattered all over Bavaria from the Tyrolean Alps to Ingolstadt and from Ulm to east of Munich. Napoleon had won the first campaign brilliantly but was far from winning the war. The question he now faced was how best to exploit his stunning victory.

The operational level of war—the level between tactics and strategy that focuses on maneuvering armies and corps—consists of two major parts.* The lower part concerns moving armies and their major subunits (corps and divisions) against the enemy so as to set the terms of battle most favorably. Napoleon's maneuver to Donauwörth and Augsburg was a brilliant example of this part of the operational level, since he set the terms of battle so much in his own favor that Mack was forced to surrender rather than accept certain defeat and annihilation.

The higher part of the operational level concerns linking battles and campaigns together to achieve larger objectives. Sometimes it is a matter of combining military activities occurring simultaneously in a theater, as the allies intended to do when Kutuzov's army had arrived in Germany to operate together with Ferdinand's. At other times the issue is properly sequencing the operations of a single army—in this case, Napoleon's transition from defeating Mack to attacking Kutuzov's auxiliary army. Napoleon was not remotely as skillful or successful at this higher operational level as he was at the lower.

He seems to have had no clear plan for what he would do after he defeated the Austrian army in Bavaria. His original idea at the end of September had been to defeat the Austrians quickly, pounce on the Russians, and then march toward Italy in order to cooperate with Masséna in destroying Charles's army.[27] Two weeks later, he had narrowed his focus. Now he expected the Army of Italy to defeat the Austrian forces in front of it, weakened by the dispatch of reinforcements to Germany. He thought it possible that "those famous Russians" would even attack Bernadotte and demanded positive intelligence about them. "I am awaiting that" intelligence, he said on October 11, "before making a

---

*This discussion departs from the definitions and treatments of the operational level that are standard for the U.S. armed forces and for many military historians. The differentiation of the operational level into distinct parts is a concept found primarily in Soviet military theory, and even there the concept is neither well nor consistently developed. Most military officers and military historians agree that maneuvering armies or large subunits (corps and divisions) in order to set the terms of a battle is operational-level conduct, as is the linking together of multiple battles in a campaign. The only new thing is the argument that these two activities comprise distinct parts of the same level of war, and that it is possible to be skillful at one and inept at the other.

decision. I will march on them with 90,000 men and I hope, with God's help, to have them continue their route to France" (as prisoners of war).[28] He still expected to march south after dealing with the Russians in order to "fall on the rear of the Austrian army" as Masséna drove it out of its positions on the Adige.[29] "I would already be there," he concluded, "if I had not found myself occupied here afresh with 50,000 Russians who have just arrived."

A week later, the emperor came to the conclusion that he faced only 25,000 Russians rather than original estimates of double that strength.[30] And he decided to march not south but east, toward Vienna. He wrote the elector of Bavaria, "In a few days, I am going to maneuver on the Inn . . . I hope to do such a job on Austria right in the center of her hereditary lands, that I do not think she will even try to trouble her neighbors."* To Otto he wrote, "I am going in a very few days to the Inn in order to try to seize the Russian army and make all the misfortunes of war felt in the hereditary estates."[31] He told Soult not to worry about the Austrians to his south because "when the Emperor has beaten the Russians and will be marching on Vienna," all the Austrian forces in the Tyrol will beat a hasty retreat.[32]

This note to Soult also contains an important comment: "We must not leave the initiative to the enemy." To that end, he ordered Soult to hasten to Landsberg and ready himself to operate on the Inn. Despite this declaration of the need for speed, Napoleon did not complain when Soult chose to march south instead of east for a day. He even granted him a day's rest before ordering him to proceed to Munich, where he did not arrive until October 25.[33] This behavior hardly supports the notion that Napoleon was in a great hurry.

Napoleon's treatment of Soult was not exceptional in this regard. His actions throughout the period following the Battle of Elchingen show that he placed no real premium on the need for a rapid transition from fighting Austrians to fighting the Russians. The French forces had arrived at approximately their final positions by October 14–15, although Murat's and Lannes's Corps hared off after Ferdinand's escaping forces briefly between October 15 and October 18 or so. Napoleon made no move to pursue Kutuzov's army until October 25. In the intervening ten days, he was occupied with reducing Ulm, chasing Werneck and Ferdinand, attempting vainly to placate the Prussians about Ansbach, and, above all, reorganizing the Grande Armée's logistics.

Supply issues may go a long way toward explaining Napoleon's delay. His explanation to the intendant-general (the officer charged with overseeing the army's logistics) about the need to reorganize his logistics system at this point

---

*Napoleon to the Elector of Bavaria, 23 October 1805, *Corr. de Nap.*, doc. 9418. The hereditary lands are those the Habsburg monarchs held as archdukes of Austria—the present Austrian states of Upper and Lower Austria stretching from the Inn to the Slovakian border. These comments indicate that Napoleon had abandoned the notion of marching south toward modern Slovenia in order to operate in tandem with Masséna's army.

in the campaign should put paid to the notion that Napoleon saw the French army's lack of magazines as an advantage:

> We marched without magazines; we were constrained to do so by the circumstances. We have had an extremely favorable season for that, but, although we have been constantly victorious and have found legumes in the fields, we have nevertheless suffered a great deal. In a season in which there are no potatoes in the fields, or if the army had suffered some reverses, the lack of magazines could have led us to greater misfortunes.[34]

The correspondence of his marshals in this period is riddled with complaints and fears about supplies and the discipline problems resulting from their lack.[35] Napoleon therefore had Augsburg converted into a large fortified base to support subsequent army operations, and he spent a considerable amount of time and effort reorganizing communication lines back to France, as well as ensuring the proper supply of his various corps. This determination to create the logistical basis for subsequent movement may have helped delay Napoleon's movement against the Russians at this point.

Napoleon's poor understanding of the Russians' movements and intentions may also have played a role. The first Russian troops began arriving at Braunau around October 15, and the last infantry column arrived on October 19, along with the first artillery column. The rest of the artillery and cavalry continued to trickle in over the next few days.[36] Napoleon, however, did not know any of this.

At first Napoleon thought that the Russians had arrived earlier than they did. He wrote on October 5 that 22,000 Russians were in Vienna; Bagration's first column only arrived at Krems (the closest the Russian infantry got to Vienna) on October 3.[37] He wrote Joseph that "the Russians are starting to arrive," presumably on the Inn, on October 10, five days early.[38] According to this time line, the Russians would have been concentrated on the Inn by about October 15, and Napoleon's decision not to send Bernadotte racing after them would have made sense, since the French could not have arrived at Braunau before Kutuzov had his army in hand and organized.

Yet by October 19, Napoleon had revised his previous estimates and decided that there were only 12,000 Russians on the Inn to be followed by the remaining 13,000 over the next eight days.[39] This estimate was also wrong, since the Podolian Army had close to 35,000 troops on the Inn by October 19, with the rest expected over the next two or three days. More importantly, Napoleon clearly identified the possibility of striking the Russians before they concentrated but chose to do nothing about it. He continued to organize his logistics and slowly concentrate the army toward Munich for the next six days, giving plenty of time, according to his own calculations, for Kutuzov to finish gathering and organizing his forces.

Had Napoleon sent Bernadotte, the Bavarians, and Davout racing toward the Inn anytime between October 15 and 20, they would have fallen on an exhausted, disorganized Russian force probably incapable of offering serious resistance in combat, let alone significant maneuvering. The forces that Kienmayer rallied to Kutuzov at Muhldorf had been worn out by constant fighting and marching, as well as the emotional exhaustion of defeat. By waiting until October 25 to move east, Napoleon gave Kutuzov critical time to gather his wits and his army and decide what to do—he gave him the initiative he had told Soult he intended to keep himself.

The available evidence does not support an unequivocal explanation for Napoleon's decision. If concerns about logistics were paramount in forcing the emperor to delay his campaign, that fact would speak volumes for the problems the foraging system of supply posed for the French army. If Napoleon somehow hoped that his destruction of Mack's army would lead directly to peace, for which there is some evidence, then he badly underestimated the resolve of the Austrians and the strength of even this fragile coalition.* What is incontestable, however, is that Napoleon had no clear idea of what to do after defeating the Austrians. He had given little thought to what the subsequent campaign would look like or how he would link it to the one just completed. The result of that failure to think through the course of the war beyond the first campaign was an operational pause of eight days. The consequences of that pause shaped the course of the rest of the war.

Retreat

Kutuzov arrived in person at Braunau on October 9 and found himself in a difficult position. He received a letter on October 12 from Ferdinand explaining that the Austrian army of 70,000 men was concentrated at Ulm and Memmingen, that Napoleon's maneuver through Ansbach had temporarily cut the Austrians off from the Russians, but that the army was hale and could hold out for a considerable time.[40] Kutuzov did not receive direct word from Mack or Ferdinand until October 23, when Mack arrived in Braunau bringing confirmation of the great defeat his army had suffered.†

---

*On October 12 Napoleon wrote to Murat, "The day after tomorrow the Austrian army will have [ceased to] exist, and this terrible blow will have put an end to the entire war." *Corr. de Nap.*, doc. 9377.

†Mikhailovskii-Danilevskii, *Opisanie*, pp. 53–56. Once again, Tolstoy captures this scene vividly: "The door of the private room opened and Kutuzov appeared in the doorway. The general with the bandaged head bent forward as though running away from some danger, and, making long, quick strides with his thin legs, went up to Kutuzov. 'You see the unfortunate Mack,' he uttered in a broken voice." Leo Tolstoy, *War and Peace*, ed. and trans. George Gibian (New York: Norton, 1996), p. 107. Given Mack's personality and subsequent performance, as well as Kutuzov's description of the meeting, it is unlikely that Mack behaved in such a fashion, but Tolstoy had the artist's sense of what would have been fitting.

Rumors of French movements and Austrian disasters had filtered quickly into the camp at Braunau and back to Vienna. The Austrians responded by trying to persuade Kutuzov to race forward, take Munich, and relieve Mack and Ferdinand. General Merveldt, whom Francis had sent to take command over the remnants of the Austrian armies collecting at Braunau, made such a proposal on October 20.[41] As late as October 23, the Austrian court was still sending Merveldt orders to get Kutuzov to march toward Ulm and free the army trapped there, unaware that Mack had already surrendered.[42]

But Kutuzov was a cautious man, the opposite of the mercurial, arrogant Mack. When he first heard convincing rumors of Mack's defeat, he wrote only that he intended to act in accord with the enemy's movements.[43] Rejecting Merveldt's requests, Kutuzov resolved to "move closer to the right bank of the Danube" and await the orders of the Austrian court.[44] The precise meaning of this phrase is unclear, since from Braunau the Danube lies to the north, well away from the main lines of communication to anywhere. But from Passau, on the Danube north of Braunau, the river moves southeast toward Linz, which lies along the main Vienna-Braunau-Munich road. "Moving closer to the right bank of the Danube" was probably a euphemism for withdrawing to Linz. This likelihood is strengthened by the fact that the next day Kutuzov wrote Alexander that he might be obliged to withdraw to Vienna, since he was in danger of being cut off by enemy forces three times the size of his own and was the only force capable of defending the Austrian capital.[45] The next day, Mack arrived at Braunau.

The terms of the original capitulation agreement between Mack and Napoleon stipulated that the Austrians could wait until October 25 to surrender, assuming that an allied army large enough to lift the siege did not appear before Ulm first. It appears, however, that Mack became uneasy trapped in his now meaningless fortress and apparently unable to get word of his fate out to the world. In a conversation with Napoleon on October 19, he became convinced that his position was hopeless and that no allied army could relieve Ulm in time. He also became concerned about the danger facing the Austro–Russian army concentrating at Braunau. He therefore agreed to hand Ulm over on October 20, as long as Berthier gave his word of honor that the Russians were too far away and too weak to lift the siege.[46] Berthier did so, Napoleon accepted the agreement, the garrison of Ulm surrendered on October 20, and Mack raced to Braunau.

His arrival dramatically changed the situation in Kutuzov's headquarters, since Mack told Kutuzov that the Austrian army of Germany no longer existed and pressed him to withdraw to a more defensible position. In a conference between Kutuzov, Mack, and Merveldt, there was no more discussion of advancing into Bavaria or holding the Inn line. Now the only question was whether to withdraw toward Vienna or Bohemia, in hopes of linking up with

Buxhöwden's army, the force delayed on the Prussian frontier but now advancing to join Kutuzov. Kutuzov rejected the idea of such a withdrawal at this stage, however, since it would uncover Vienna (and probably also because he did not know where Buxhöwden was). He decided instead to retreat east, toward Lambach or Linz.[47] Orders for the withdrawal were issued on October 24 for a movement to begin the following day to Ried.[48]

Napoleon's delay had cost him an opportunity. Between the time that Bernadotte, Davout, and the Bavarians had arrived at Munich and Napoleon's order to begin the chase on October 25, Kutuzov had managed to reorient himself, evaluate the situation properly, choose a course of action, and begin executing it. If Napoleon's troops had set out from Munich on October 19 or 20, they would have arrived at Braunau by October 25 at the latest, just as the Russians were setting out to the east. As it was, Napoleon began moving east on the same day that Kutuzov did, and the Russians retained a five-march advantage over their pursuers.

Mack's conversation with Kutuzov and Merveldt did more than let the Russian commander know that he needed to withdraw, however. It also sowed another seed of distrust between the Austrians and the Russians. Mack, who never guarded his tongue, apparently let it wag freely during what was probably the first proper meal he had eaten in a long time. Rations had been very short in Ulm the past several days. He not only told Kutuzov about the strength and disposition of the French army and the fate of his own, but he also recounted in detail the conversation he had with Napoleon. He probably aimed to emphasize his own importance by showing Kutuzov how the French emperor had treated him, but even his colleague Merveldt seemed to feel that he was talking too much.

Kutuzov was interested to learn that Napoleon had asked Mack to tell Francis that he wanted peace and was prepared to make sacrifices to achieve it. Kutuzov concluded that Mack knew more than he was telling, a conclusion strengthened by the fact that apparently Merveldt did everything but kick Mack under the table to get him to stop talking. Kutuzov wrote Razumovskii and Czartoryskii at once, warning them that the Austrians might be negotiating secretly with the French, and that Napoleon might persuade them to abandon a war that was not going well for them anyway.[49]

In truth, there was little that Mack left out of his conversation with Napoleon. The emperor had made a spirited attempt to understand how Mack could have allowed himself to get locked up in Ulm, but probably came away disappointed in the result. He then made a series of propositions about treating with Austria. Mack rejoined that Francis would never negotiate without Alexander, and Napoleon responded that he would be happy to discuss peace with Alexander's envoy as well. Although Mack pressed Napoleon about changes in the Austrian borders in Italy and reported that Napoleon made no demur, the

French emperor was clearly far more interested in having Austria join him in the war against Britain than in any detailed territorial arrangements.[50]

Napoleon was probably just amusing himself at Mack's expense. Napoleon may have believed that the defeat he had just inflicted on Austria was so severe that the promise of negotiations on favorable terms might cause Francis to drop out of a coalition he had never been enthusiastic about joining. Mack, of course, had been foolish enough to tell Napoleon that it was only the "threat" of Russian armies on the Austrian eastern frontier that "forced" Francis to fight in the first place. There was little enough here, in fact, for the Russians to be worried about. Francis and Cobenzl were shrewd enough to know that Napoleon had promised no terms advantageous enough to counterbalance the price of infuriating Alexander. For a coalition weakly bound together to begin with, however, Mack's report of this conversation to Kutuzov was an additional source of weakness. With all this in mind, Kutuzov began the long road back toward Vienna, and Napoleon sent his troops chasing after him.

The Chase

By the time Napoleon ordered the Grande Armée forward in pursuit of the Russians, he had lost contact with both Kutuzov's army and Kienmayer's force and did not have a good idea of what the allies were doing. The initial order to Murat, for example, manifested both vagueness about the position of the allied force and a demand for intelligence about the enemy.[51] Napoleon was also unsure of the movements of Austrian troops in the Tyrol, from Italy, and from elsewhere in the monarchy. On October 27 he wrote Joseph that within two weeks he expected to face 100,000 Russians and 60,000 Austrians drawn from Italy and reserves. "I will defeat them," he concluded, but "this will probably cost me some losses."* The next day, Berthier wrote Murat that the emperor was "impatient for news of the enemy" and a similar demand for news of the Austrians around Salzburg and in the Tyrol went to Bernadotte on October 29.[52]

The only operational or strategic intelligence Napoleon seems to have received in this period came from the normally reliable Bacher at Ratisbonne and from French diplomatic agents elsewhere in Germany. They reported that the "second Russian army," commanded, so they erroneously thought, by Mikhel'son [actually by Buxhöwden], was a matter of four or five marches

---

*Napoleon to Joseph, 27 October 1805, *Corr. de Nap.*, 9431. This document undermines Mikhailovskii-Danilevskii's argument that Napoleon intended to defeat Kutuzov's army not only before the Prussians could enter the war in force, but before Kutuzov could link up with the Russian and Austrian reinforcements behind him (Mikhailovskii-Danilevskii, *Opisanie*, pp. 82–83). Because of his faulty intelligence about the position of those Russian and Austrian reinforcements, Napoleon does not initially seem to have had any such intention.

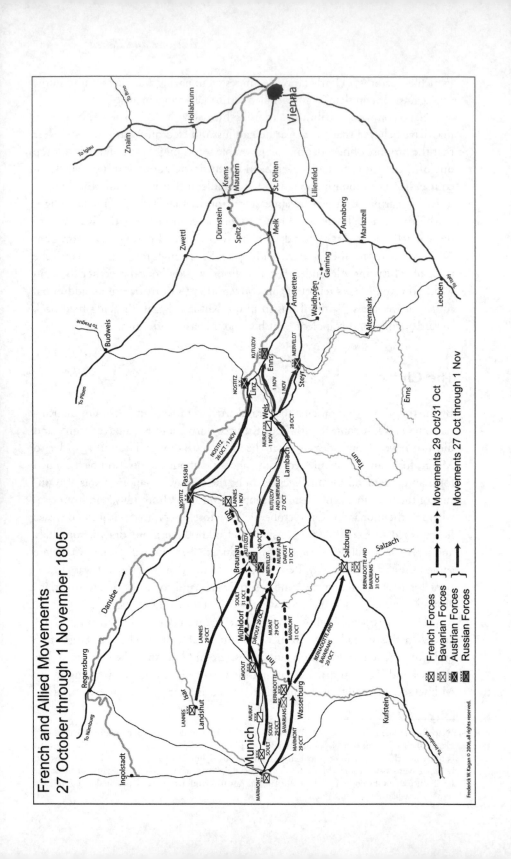

French and Allied Movements
27 October through 1 November 1805

Frederick W. Kagan © 2006, all rights reserved.

away from Braunau. Kutuzov intended to withdraw to Wels in order to link up with this force, which would swell his ranks to around 80,000. At the same time, Charles was said to have received command of the Austrian army in Germany and to be racing up from Italy at the head of 20,000 men.[53] The only truth in these reports was that Kutuzov was retreating.

Faced with such a confused situation, Napoleon proceeded cautiously. The first movement order, issued on October 25, sent the army along three roads toward the Inn. Two corps (Marmont and Ney) were ordered to Landshut; Lannes, who was already concentrated at Landshut, was ordered forward to Vilsbiburg; Davout and Soult were sent out along the road to Mühldorf; Bernadotte and the Bavarians were sent to Wasserburg on the road to Salzburg, which they were to take; Augereau's Corps, which was just arriving in the theater, was ordered to Kempten.[54] In this way, the Grande Armée was formed into a line capable of concentrating and enveloping the enemy wherever it might encounter him. This deployment also facilitated foraging, on which, despite Napoleon's best efforts to establish a magazine system, the army would still have to rely for food.

Napoleon seems to have had some concern for his southern flank. Not only did he order Bernadotte to seize Salzburg, but he directed Augereau to Kempten and then sent Marmont to Wasserburg, presumably as support for Bernadotte.[55] When he changed his mind two days later, sending Marmont instead toward Steyr, for reasons we will explore in a moment, he ordered Ney to Innsbruck instead.[56] He thereby diverted three corps to the task of maintaining security on his southern flank against Austrian forces in the Tyrol and against reinforcements coming north from Italy.*

From virtually the outset of this campaign, therefore, Napoleon broke his army into two major parts. One composed of three corps watched the Tyrol and the approaches from Italy, while the other, composed of four infantry and Murat's Cavalry Corps, chased after Kutuzov's army. The separation between these two forces did not seem crucial, however, since Napoleon expected the Russians to stand and fight at Wels on the Traun or near Steyr on the Enns. He therefore ordered Marmont to race to Steyr in order to "turn all the positions of the enemy," whether Kutuzov stood at Wels or near Steyr.[57] He warned Bernadotte to be ready to march at a moment's notice, since "if [the enemy] effects his project of awaiting us at Wels or at Steyer, you will be in a position to be able to participate in the battle."[58]

The contrast between Napoleon's campaign planning during this phase of the war with that during the Ulm phase is striking. He seems to have made no

---

*On October 28 Berthier warned Bernadotte that a column of 12,000–15,000 Austrians was marching on Salzburg from the Tyrol and ordered the marshal to take the Austrians prisoner. His care to inform Bernadotte of the positions of Augereau and Ney indicates that he saw these three corps as likely to interact on the French southern flank. Berthier to Bernadotte, 28 October 1805, in Alombert-Goget and Colin, *La campagne de 1805*, vol. 4, pt. 1, p. 253.

detailed plans for compelling the Russians to fight. Relying on vague intelligence, he hoped that Kutuzov would stop and fight of his own accord, once he had united with the reinforcements that Napoleon believed (erroneously) were a small distance behind the Russian army. There is no evidence that Napoleon considered his alternatives in the event the Russians refused to fight at Wels or Steyr or foresaw that in the event his army would have been permanently divided, since Bernadotte, Augereau, and Ney would not be able to catch up with the main body. Although Napoleon had the larger force and, in principle, the better position, he was nevertheless leaving the initiative in the allies' hands—a battle would occur when and where Kutuzov chose.

Splitting the Coalition

Kutuzov had decided to avoid battle until he evened the odds. Although he initially wrote Francis that he intended to retreat to Lambach or perhaps Linz, his reports to Alexander show that he had already considered the possibility of marching back to Vienna.[59] Above all, he wrote Czartoryskii, he urgently needed to learn where Buxhöwden was "in order to know whether that army was near me or not so that I can make my dispositions accordingly."[60] For Kutuzov, the next few weeks would be an unremitting effort to link up with reinforcements before confronting the Napoleonic juggernaut.

Which reinforcements should the Austro–Russian army attempt to link up with? This question exacerbated the damage inflicted on the coalition's cohesion by Mack's surrender and the report of Mack's conversation with Napoleon. Kutuzov wanted to link up with the Russian reinforcements marching behind him and, if possible, with Prussian troops as well, if Prussia actually put her army in motion against the French. This was the option that Alexander preferred as well.[61] This option, however, drew the Austro–Russian army to the east and possibly the north, since those were the directions from which such reinforcements would come. Kutuzov even considered marching north from Braunau into Bohemia, as we have seen, in the hope of linking up with Buxhöwden's army sooner. The Austrians' hopes, by contrast, looked south.

Until word of Mack's arrival in Braunau and the details of his army's destruction reached Vienna, the Austrians had rejected rumors of the disaster at Ulm and insisted that Kutuzov race forward into Bavaria to rescue Mack.[62] As soon as the Austrian high command became convinced of Mack's complete capitulation, attention turned to maintaining communications with the armies of Archduke John in the Tyrol and Archduke Charles in Italy. De Latour accordingly ordered Merveldt to withdraw behind the upper Inn and hold Salzburg for as long as possible to await the arrival of

Charles and his reinforcements from Italy, which would bring the strength of the allied armies up to 90,000 men. Since these reinforcements could not arrive in less than a month, however, de Latour recognized that Merveldt (and Kutuzov) might have to withdraw from the Salza. In that case, he ordered Merveldt to retreat by one of two routes to Leoben to link up with Charles far to the east and south.[63]

This order, which should have reached Merveldt within two or three days, remained unexecuted, however, and the Austrian troops continued to march toward Vienna together with the Russians. The first combat of this phase of the war took place between the Austrian rear guard and Murat's advancing cavalry at Ried on October 30. The French came upon an Austrian infantry detachment of 4,000–6,000 men near Ried and attacked at once. Austrian cavalry soon arrived to support the infantry but could not prevent the infantry from being driven into a defile. Murat ordered a number of his dragoons to dismount and, together with the still mounted chasseurs, they cut the Austrian infantry to pieces, taking 500–600 prisoners.[64] This minor combat, which resembled some of the fights around Ulm, had a very different operational result from those earlier battles. Although the Austrians left dead and wounded as well as prisoners in French hands, Murat's Cavalry was not able to divert the Austrian rear guard from its purpose. At the end of the day, the Austrians successfully broke contact and the retreat of the Austro–Russian army continued unimpeded. The combined army marched from Ried to Lambach on October 27, to Wels on October 28, and to Enns on November 1.[65]

The first Russian encounter with Napoleon's troops took place at Lambach on October 31. Kutuzov had sent four jaeger battalions, one squadron of the Pavlograd Hussars Regiment, and part of a horse artillery company to rescue four Austrian battalions attacked by the French.[66] The French 3rd Dragoons Division, supported by infantry from the 1st Division of Davout's Corps, attacked the combined force near Lambach, driving it off but failing to destroy or capture a significant part of it. Kutuzov reported suffering about 100 killed and fewer than 50 wounded.[67] Once again this engagement did not prevent or delay the retreat of the allied armies. It demonstrated, however, that Austrian and Russian troops could cooperate successfully at the tactical level. Kutuzov subordinated the Russian troops directly to Merveldt's command for the duration of the fight.[68]

By November 1 the Russian army had taken up a strong position on the river Enns near the town of that name. It remained in that position for two days, a delay that coincided with several reevaluations of the allied operational and strategic position. Kutuzov had ordered Merveldt's force to the town of Steyr, in order to cover his southern flank from any French efforts at envelopment. A smaller Austrian detachment under General Nostitz, which

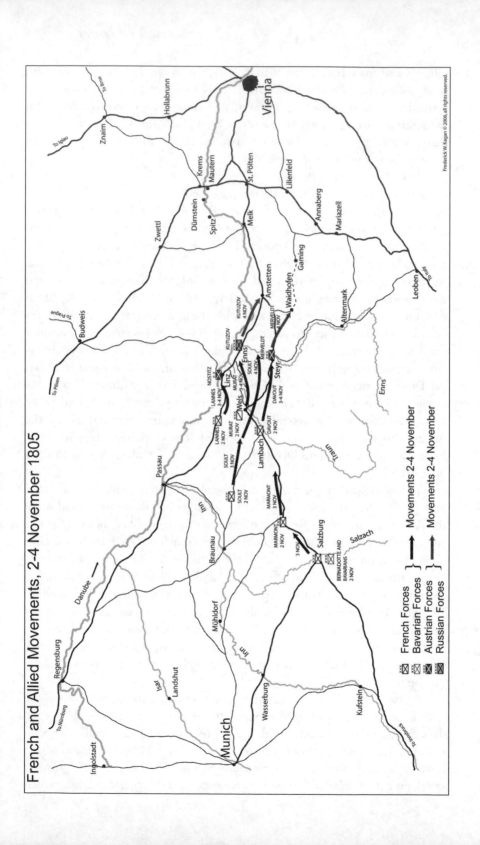

French and Allied Movements, 2–4 November 1805

had withdrawn from Passau along with the rest of the allied army, had been ordered to destroy the bridge over the Danube at Linz, thus securing Kutuzov's right.* Kutuzov and Merveldt began constructing fortifications in order to hold the river line.

The effort to hold the Enns line resulted from a meeting between Francis and Kutuzov at Wels to coordinate strategy for the forthcoming campaign. Francis had requested the meeting on October 26. He rode out from Vienna at once, met with Kutuzov on October 28, and rode back immediately to his capital.[69] This visit gave rise to a rumor among the French that Francis had come out to Wels on his way to Braunau, unaware that Mack's army had surrendered, and that he had withdrawn precipitously and with his hopes dashed on learning the truth.[70]

Francis had come to Wels, rather, to exhort Kutuzov to hold a line as far west as possible until reinforcements, both Russian and Austrian, could arrive to assist him. His orders were "to avoid defeats, to preserve the army whole and unharmed, not to enter into battle with Napoleon, but to hold him off at every step giving time for Archdukes Carl and John and the corps coming from Russia to reach the theater of war."[71] Kutuzov did not entirely accept Francis's plan of fighting for every step of the way, since he feared exposing his army to a major engagement from which he would not be able to extricate it.[72] He clearly hoped, nevertheless, to hold at Enns and Steyr for some time.

The arrival of the Russian army at Enns was dramatic. The last Russian troops crossed the bridge with Murat's vanguard on their heels. Taking advantage of the fact that the bridge had already been loaded with combustible material, a squadron of the Pavlograd Hussars, having already crossed the river, raced back to the bridge and managed to ignite it under musket, cannon, and cartridge fire from the French. The successful destruction of this bridge promised the Russians a much needed respite.† Napoleon, however, had other ideas.

---

*Mikhailovskii-Danilevskii, *Opisanie*, p. 89. Merveldt's force had been marching along a road south of and parallel with Kutuzov's line of retreat since leaving Braunau.

†Mikhailovskii-Danilevskii, *Opisanie*, p. 89; Bagration to Kutuzov, 4 November 1805, in Zhiugzhda, *Dokumenty*, doc. 82; Murat to Napoleon and Belliard to Berthier, 4 November 1805, in Alombert-Goget and Colin, *La campagne de 1805*, vol. 4, pt. 1, pp. 489–492. The French accounts focus on chasing the Russians into Enns and describe the burning of the bridge only briefly. Belliard's account makes it clear that the Russians destroyed the bridge and burned the wood needed to repair it. This scene is described vividly and with reasonable accuracy in its main details in *War and Peace*, pp. 117–128. The "Karl Bogdanych Schubert" commanding the squadron of the Pavlograd Hussars in which Nikolai Rostov was serving was in reality Colonel O'Rourke, the commander of the squadron that actually burned the bridge. Tolstoy presumably transformed him from an Irishman (or perhaps a Russian of Irish descent) into a German in order to suit the Slavophile predilection of the time to blame the Russian army's misfortunes on its "excessive" reliance on German officers, a theme that runs throughout *War and Peace*.

Steyr

Problems of logistics and Austro–Russian movements continued the process of breaking up the main body of the Grande Armée that Napoleon's diversion of three corps to the Tyrol had begun. As Lannes' Corps approached Braunau, Napoleon decided that he could not have so many corps traversing the single road Braunau-Ried-Wels that the Russians had previously advanced and then retreated upon. Berthier accordingly sent Lannes to the north, along the left bank of the Inn, to cross the Inn at Schärding instead, "because the enemy is withdrawing and because we are having the greatest difficulty in living."[73] This order imposed on Lannes a lengthy detour that would either delay his arrival on the presumed battlefield or exhaust his troops—or both. It is further evidence of the difficulties the French method of logistics imposed upon Napoleon as he moved away from the fertile lands and dense road network of southwestern Germany.

In the wake of the fight at Lambach, Kutuzov had sent Merveldt's Corps to Steyr, as we have seen, hoping to cover his left flank and support his position farther down the Enns at the town of the same name. Murat duly reported this movement, and Napoleon reacted immediately by sending Davout from Lambach toward Kremsmünster on the road to Steyr, rather than the road to Wels where Murat's Corps was and where Soult's Corps was headed.[74] Steyr is less than a day's march from Enns, of course, and this movement eased the congestion on the main Braunau-Linz-Vienna road. This diversion also left the reconcentration of the Grande Armée to some extent in the allies' hands, assuming that Davout continued to follow Merveldt's weak corps and that Merveldt did not immediately rejoin Kutuzov.

It is difficult to know what was in Napoleon's mind at this point in the campaign. He wrote little himself at this time, and the orders he sent through Berthier contain little explanation of his intentions or even his understanding of the enemy situation. At no point did he make it clear to Murat, commanding the vanguard of his army and authorized to control the nearest following infantry corps, what his objective was. Most historians have assumed that Napoleon intended to catch and destroy Kutuzov before the Russians could link up with their reinforcements, but there is no direct evidence to support that assumption, while there is direct evidence that contradicts it. The explanation surely lies, in part, in the enormous difficulty Napoleon encountered in obtaining accurate intelligence about the allied war effort.

Once the French army began passing through towns from which the Austro–Russian army had just retreated, Napoleon had a perfect picture of the size and composition of that enemy army (in contrast with the vagueness and mistakes that characterized his understanding of the size of Mack's army right up to its surrender).[75] He generally knew in a timely fashion from Murat's reporting where the allied army was and what road it had taken. Estimates of Kutuzov's intentions, however, varied wildly, and reports of the movements of other allied armies continued to be confusing, contradictory, and frequently fictional.

Most reports indicated (accurately) that Kutuzov intended to continue withdrawing to the east, but differed about where he would make a stand.* But as the Russians marched toward Linz (on the road to the east), Murat had to wonder if Kutuzov did not intend to continue marching north into Bohemia to link up with the (nonexistent) reinforcements thought to be marching through Prague.[76] The next day he reported that Kutuzov would certainly withdraw to Amstetten, where he would join with the 50,000 men of Mikhel'son's army.[77] Reports about that army, which was actually commanded by Buxhöwden and was weeks away, about the Russian armies on the Prussian frontier, about the Prussian armies, and about movements in Italy were uselessly vague or inaccurate.[78]

The lack of concrete intelligence, concerns about logistics, and fears of exhausting his army, which had already marched so far so fast, clearly knocked Napoleon off stride. In a most uncharacteristic note, he ordered Murat not to move too rapidly. "We must march with prudence," he wrote. "The Russians are not yet subdued; they also know how to attack." He warned against exposing Davout's flanks by an unwary advance and assigned a limit of advance—a very unusual action for a commander who normally spurs his subordinates to the fastest possible movements.[79] Oddly enough, Napoleon had written the day before to Talleyrand that the Russians "have no chief; panic fear has taken possession of them," and just two days later he wrote Eugène that the Russians were "subdued" (*entamé*).[80] These contradictions do more than highlight the difficulties of using Napoleon's correspondence.[81] They also show the emperor's discomfort with the situation by revealing his need to paint the situation in brighter colors to his distant subordinates than he himself actually saw.

We can only surmise Napoleon's intentions in sending Davout toward Steyr instead of Enns. Logistics may have played a role, but his greatest motivation was likely a desire to outflank Kutuzov's army and destroy it. This interpretation is supported by the fact that Napoleon ordered Soult to march from Wels to Kronstorf, on the Enns between the town of Enns and Steyr.[82] With Murat advancing on Enns, Soult on Kronstorf, and Davout on Steyr, Napoleon was in a good position to turn Kutuzov's left flank and possibly even pin him against the Danube, which moves southeast from Linz down to Wallsee, well to the rear of Enns. Napoleon's orders to Marmont to race to

---

*Interrogated Russian prisoners claimed that the Russians would withdraw all the way to Vienna, while another report indicated that they would make a stand between St. Pölten and Melk. Report of the Interrogation of Two Russian Prisoners, 1 November 1805, in Alombert-Goget and Colin, *La campagne de 1805*, vol. 4, pt. 1, p. 388.

Lambach and then Kremsmünster and to Bernadotte to rush from Salzburg to Steyr indicate that he thought that a decisive battle, probably on the Enns, was imminent.[83] Napoleon's decisions may have been influenced by Davout's report of November 3 that the Russians intended to hold at Enns and that "Michelson's" army was still on the Russo–Polish frontier.*

It is not clear why Davout had such an easy time crossing the Enns at Steyr in the face of Merveldt's Corps, which had already burned the bridges over the river and in principle only had to defend against a crossing by boat.† This crossing is especially surprising in view of the fact that Merveldt apparently disposed of nearly 22,000 troops.‡ According to the French accounts, the Austrians defended the crossing tenaciously at first, firing muskets and artillery from the houses along the right bank of the river and inflicting heavy casualties on French troops brave enough to try to cross. When the French managed to bring up their own artillery, however, they silenced the Austrian defenders by setting the houses on fire. The left bank is much higher than the right at that point, which favored the French. Since the Austrians had failed to burn the boats on the Enns when they burned the bridge, moreover, the French were able to ferry a small number of troops across the river. The first thirty of these troops apparently sufficed to drive the Austrians off entirely.[84] It is difficult to imagine how Merveldt decided to withdraw 21,000 Austrian troops simply because thirty Frenchmen crossed the Enns on boats!

Merveldt likely withdrew in response to the developing operational situation. As the French fought to establish a foothold on the right bank of the Enns at Steyr, they were also advancing to the north and south of that position. Davout had ordered a regiment to secure the crossings farther up the Steyr and the Enns and Steinbach and Ternberg, respectively. These positions would have allowed him to envelop Merveldt's Corps from the south.[85] At the same time, Soult was working to cross the Enns at Kronstorf, halfway between

---

*Davout to Berthier, 3 November 1805, in Alombert-Goget and Colin, *La campagne de 1805*, vol. 4, pt. 1, p. 455. This report was quite right; but it was never Mikhel'son's army that Napoleon had to worry about imminently, and Buxhöwden's army was much farther along toward Moravia.

†I have not been able to locate Austrian accounts of this fight, and neither Moriggl nor Angeli narrates it. Moriggl, *Der Feldzug von Ulm*, pp. 553ff.; Moriz Edlen von Angeli, *Erzherzog Carl von Osterreich als Feldherr und Heeresorganisator* (Vienna: Wilhelm Braumüller, 1897), p. 287. The French accounts all state that the bridges had been burned before they arrived. 3rd Corps, Topographical and Military Notes for 4 November 1805, in Alombert-Goget and Colin, *La campagne de 1805*, vol. 4, pt. 1, pp. 483; and Journal of the Reserve Artillery of 3rd Corps, p. 484.

‡That was the number used for planning purposes by the Hofkriegsrat during its planning session on 4 November (KA AFA 1805 Deutschland, XI/12½). The only reference to the strength of this force in the French documents is a report from Lambach on November 1 that gives the strength of Merveldt's corps as 12,000. In Alombert-Goget and Colin, *La campagne de 1805*, vol. 4, pt. 1, p. 388.

Enns and Steyr.* Since Merveldt was confronted with the threat of envelopment from both sides and faced a dangerous situation at the main crossing point, his decision to withdraw without seriously contesting the crossing makes sense.

With the French across the Enns at Steyr, Kutuzov's position at Enns became untenable. It is quite possible that Kutuzov had already decided to withdraw on November 3, perhaps as he saw Davout maneuvering toward Steyr and Soult toward Kronstorf. He had already ordered Dokhturov to take part of the army to Amstetten on November 4, and followed rapidly with the rest.† Merveldt's rapid withdrawal may have been little more than the execution of a planned retreat already under way. After Davout's crossing, however, Kutuzov had to be concerned with French troops advancing from not only Enns but Steyr as well.[86]

Merveldt's decision to march southeast instead of toward Amstetten exacerbated this problem, and it is not entirely clear why the Austrian field marshal made that decision.‡ He may have been acting belatedly on the Austrian plan to maintain communications with Charles's armies coming from Italy, although it is hard to explain why he chose this moment to do so. A French account suggests that the position of the troops at the end of the fight had something to do with it: Merveldt could not take the Amstetten road without running the gauntlet of French batteries trained on it.[87] Whatever the reason for this decision, the result was clear. Apart from a small detachment of four infantry battalions and four cavalry squadrons commanded by Nostitz and

---

*4th Corps, Order, 4 November 1805, in Alombert-Goget and Colin, *La campagne de 1805*, vol. 4, pt. 1, p. 486. On the other hand, Soult concluded that he could not cross the river quickly, since his engineers told him it would take three days to bridge the Enns at that point. Still, however difficult the bridging operation, the crossing was undefended. Paul Claude Alombert-Goget, *Campagne de l'an 14 (1805). Le corps d'armée aux ordres du Maréchal Mortier. Combat de Dürrenstein* (Paris: Berger-Levrault, 1897), pp. 20–22.

†Kutuzov to Dokhturov, 3 November 1805, in Beskrovnyi, *Kutuzov*, doc. 147. Mikhailovskii-Danlievskii reproduces a letter from Kutuzov to Miloradovich from mid-1806 in which Kutuzov asserts that the loss of Steyr forced him to withdraw and he accepts this testimony as the basis of his own account (*Opisanie*, p. 90). It is difficult to square this account, however, with the order to Dokhturov of November 3, to move to Amstetten with a considerable part of Kutuzov's force before Davout had even begun his attack.

‡Angeli, "Ulm und Austerlitz," p. 287, ascribes it to frustration with Kutuzov's refusal to carry out Francis's orders to hold as far to the west as possible; Moriggl, *Der Feldzug von Ulm*, p. 557, attributes it to the plan developed at the end of October for Merveldt to withdraw into the Steiermark in order to preserve a line of communication with the armies coming from Italy (although he does not refer directly to that plan). Mikhailovskii-Danilevskii, *Opisanie*, p. 90, attributes it to the "arrival" from Vienna of orders to march through Mariazell and Annaberg to defend the approaches to Vienna, but does not note the fact that those orders had been issued nearly two weeks earlier. The two notes by Francis to Kutuzov of November 4–5 (in Beskrovnyi, *Kutuzov*, docs. 152, 156) also cast doubt on the probability that Merveldt was following orders, since Francis took it for granted as late as November 5 that Merveldt would be with Kutuzov in person, which the orders he was supposedly following did not specify. See the next chapter for more detail on the Austrian plans in early November.

Kienmayer respectively, still left with the Russian force, the allied armies had separated once again into their component parts, fracturing the fragile alliance still further.[88]

Amstetten

Kutuzov's delay at Enns enabled Murat's forces to close up and gain a brief rest, and for Lannes's Corps to arrive after its detour to the north. As the Russian army withdrew from Enns, its rear guard, commanded by Prince Bagration, was harassed continuously. Skirmishes raged between Bagration's troops and Murat's dragoons from Altenhofen, where contact was first made, all the way to the heights of Amstetten.[89] Serious engagements occurred at Strengberg and Oed, and by the time the Russians were approaching Amstetten, Kutuzov realized that Bagration's soldiers were in grave danger if left by themselves. He therefore sent Miloradovich with three infantry regiments to establish a receiving position at Amstetten and thereby allow Bagration and his troops to counterattack long enough to break contact.[90]

The actual events of the battle are confused. Miloradovich claims that he ordered one of his regiments to charge with bayonets at a critical moment, but the French accounts focus on the intense fusillades that characterized the battle from their perspective.[91] Both sides claim to have driven the other into disorderly retreat.[92] Both sides claim to have been outnumbered. The French seem to have exaggerated the numbers of casualties inflicted and prisoners taken. Because that part of Austria was sparsely endowed with villages and towns and because most of the fights were more or less unexpected meeting engagements, it is difficult to pinpoint the precise location of some of the battles. Bagration's account is too laconic to be useful.* Consequently reconstructing a narrative of this battle with any degree of tactical or terrain specificity is impossible.

If the specific events and causal relationships of the battle are largely lost to history, its significance is not. This was the first fight in which a major part of the Russian army opposed a significant number of French troops in the open. Both sides acquitted themselves very well, and both managed to draw off in good order at the end of the fight. Above all, the skillful maneuvering of the Russian force, including the timely arrival of Miloradovich and his intelligent application of the reserve forces at his disposal, prevented the possible collapse of the rear guard. That maneuvering allowed the Russians to break contact when evening fell and continue their retreat unhindered. In the first

---

*Bagration to Kutuzov, 6 November 1805, in Zhiugzhda, *Dokumenty*, doc. 84. The sparseness of this account is characteristic of Bagration, unfortunately for the historian.

major clash between the French van and the Russian rear, Napoleon's troops had been unable to force Kutuzov to stand and fight.

As telling as the fact that the French did not force the Russians to fight, however, is the fact that they do not seem to have tried. Reporting to Berthier on the outcome of the battle, Belliard summarized its positive outcomes: 1,500–1,800 prisoners taken along with 40 munitions wagons and 100 horses. More important, however, was the "incalculable advantage of surprising the Russian army, of *forcing it to a precipitate retreat,* to scattering part of it and demoralizing the rest."[93] This conclusion, written by Murat's chief of staff, indicates total confusion about the objective of the pursuit.

There was no need to "force" the Russian army to a "retreat," hasty or not—Kutuzov was withdrawing of his own accord to meet up with reinforcements. Surely the purpose of the attack launched at Amstetten was to pin the Russian army in place and allow other French forces to maneuver around it, cut it off, and destroy it completely. But Belliard apparently had no idea of the necessity for doing any such thing, and Murat seems to have made little or no effort to maneuver around Bagration's defending forces (whose left flank was unprotected for much of the fight). Apparently Murat was chasing the Russians merely to be chasing them and with no clear idea of what he should have been trying to accomplish.

His confusion was somewhat justified, although he should have seen the desirability of pinning the Russians in place rather than driving them in the direction they already wanted to go. As we have seen, Napoleon never gave Murat clear orders about his mission, never made his own intentions clear, never clearly defined the objectives of this phase of the campaign. In contrast with the Ulm campaign, Napoleon's own view of the situation may never have crystallized sufficiently for him to pass on a vision to his subordinates. The emperor may have found it difficult to formulate such a vision when the enemy steadfastly retained the initiative. Or Napoleon may have suffered from a problem similar to the one that afflicted Lee at Gettysburg: he did not understand Kutuzov and did not know how to read him or guess his intentions.

Whatever the reason, the Battle of Amstetten, like the fights that had preceded it, gained Napoleon nothing. Kutuzov continued his withdrawal relatively unfazed and in good order. Murat's gallant, exhausted troops had to arise the next day and continue their so far fruitless pursuit. The confusion about the objectives of this phase of the campaign, however, was about to take on a dramatic new significance.

18

The End
of the Chase

The early days of November brought the campaign toward a critical point. Napoleon's forces were becoming spread out across southern Germany and Austria, his logistical situation was deteriorating, and the prospect of Prussian intervention and an allied war effort in northern Europe was increasing. Napoleon's inability to catch Kutuzov and force him to stand and fight was reducing his chances of bringing the campaign to a rapid conclusion.

The situation for the allies was more promising but still tense. With Charles marching north from Italy, Russian reinforcements racing through Moravia, and Prussian troops mobilizing to the north, the allies had an opportunity to turn things around. In the meantime, however, the pressure on Kutuzov's army made it necessary to decide whether to abandon Vienna and consider what would happen once Kutuzov swung north, away from the main body of the remaining Austrian forces. Napoleon's decisionmaking was hampered by the difficulty he faced in bringing the war to a speedy conclusion if the allies chose to avoid battle and concentrate their forces. The allies faced the collapse of mutual trust in the wake of Ulm, the emotional damage done by that defeat and the prospect of losing Vienna, and the absence of any agreed-on method for developing allied strategy and grand strategy.

Rethinking the War

The need to establish the allied army at what was thought to be a defensible position along the Enns spurred the allies to reconsider their approach to subsequent operations. Francis accordingly convened a session of the Hofkriegsrat, which issued its recommendations on November 4, ironically, the same day the allied army abandoned the Enns position. Francis apparently accepted the report, since his letters to Kutuzov of November 4 and November 5 reflect its major recommendations.*

The memorandum began with a comprehensive review of the forces available or soon to be available in Austria, the primary theater of operations: Merveldt's Corps, Kutuzov's army, the Duke of Württemberg's force near Vienna, the 6th Column of the Russian Podolian Army now advancing toward Krems, Buxhöwden's army coming up behind it, the Russian Guards Corps under Grand Prince Constantine (Alexander's younger brother), the (from the Austrian perspective) third Russian army, and Austrian troops in Bohemia. These forces totaled nearly 182,000 troops, and this list takes no account of troops coming from Italy or the mobilizing Prussian army.

The Hofkriegsrat drew the obvious conclusion from this review: the allies should postpone major combat until they had assembled all or most of these forces in one place. The Hofkriegsrat did not contemplate an attempt to defend Vienna, should the army be driven away from its position on the Enns. This decision was wise, considering that most of the city at that time was on the right bank of the Danube and virtually indefensible against a major attack from the west. The Russian army, the War Council concluded, should cross the Danube at Krems. Buxhöwden's army should position itself northeast at Hollabrunn, and Württemberg's Corps should hold a position to the north along the road to Brünn. These forces should defend and observe the left bank of the Danube.

The Hofkriegsrat ruled out the possibility of undertaking offensive operations before all of the forces had assembled, around December 15. At that point, the unified armies would recross the Danube at Krems while Ferdinand led his force across at Linz. If the French managed to cross the river before then, the allied armies would fight hard to retain control of the Marchfeld, the area east of Vienna, and communications with Hungary.

The Hofkriegsrat was not aware that Merveldt was intending to march away from Kutuzov when the allies abandoned the Enns line. It suggested instead that Merveldt's Corps continue to withdraw with Kutuzov to St. Pölten, always keeping his southern flank secure. When Kutuzov retreated to Krems, Merveldt would accompany him with a small rear guard; he would also become the quartermaster general of the Russian army. He was to send a small detachment (two infantry battalions and six cavalry squadrons) to Wiener Neustadt to protect the southern approaches to Vienna. Kienmayer would

---

*Answers to Questions Presented to the Assembled War Council by Order of His Majesty on 4 November 1805, KA AFA 1805 Deutschland, XI/12½; Francis to Kutuzov, 4–5 November 1805, in L. G. Beskrovnyi, *M. I. Kutuzov: Sbornik dokumentov* (Moscow: Voennoe Izdatel'stvo, 1951), vol. 2, docs. 152, 156. Issues of grand strategy, including operations in Italy, Prussia, and northern Europe, will be considered in subsequent chapters.

then take the remainder of the force back along the road to Vienna, retreating to Perschling as slowly as possible.*

The essential concept of this plan was to find a defensible position that Kutuzov could hold while the Austro–Russian armies coalesced around his force. The Hofkriegsrat naturally wanted to ensure that this position was as far south as possible in order to facilitate joint operations with Archduke Charles (who received a copy of the full memorandum). In order to support this plan, the Hofkriegsrat recommended constructing a fortified bridgehead at Krems that Kutuzov could easily hold.

As a strategic concept this plan made good sense and was a surprisingly intelligent response to the situation. It was, however, obsolescent by the time it was drafted. Not only had Merveldt already detached his entire army from Kutuzov, but the French were rapidly rebuilding the bridge over the Danube at Linz and Napoleon had already put three divisions across the river to operate along the left bank. The notion that Kienmayer—or anyone—could have withdrawn the small force assigned to him slowly across the mostly flat plain between St. Pölten and Vienna pursued by one or more French corps was nonsensical.

Francis nevertheless accepted the plan and immediately transmitted the relevant parts of it to Kutuzov.[1] The next day, he sent Kutuzov another message and a new assistant, FML Schmitt, to help Merveldt, whom Francis assumed Kutuzov would use at advanced outposts. At the same time, Francis impressed on Kutuzov the importance of "preserving my capital from the disasters that threaten it in the event of your being obliged to abandon the right bank of the Enns." If such a retreat did become necessary, Francis insisted that it be made "step by step."[2]

There had been no time to inform Alexander of the Hofkriegsrat's decisions, so the note the tsar sent his general on November 5 concluded, "I can only be at peace if I know that you have committed yourself to taking upon yourself the high responsibility of defending Vienna."[3] Alexander added that Kutuzov must bear in mind that "you are the leader of the Russian army," and that he must uphold the honor of Russian arms, come what may. In particular, the tsar insisted that if it came to a battle, Kutuzov should attack and not simply hold a position waiting for the French to strike him.

The tsar's immaturity and inexperience is evident in this note. To insist that Kutuzov always attack an enemy that was eager for battle and could bring

---

*This document seems to indicate that Merveldt's withdrawal from Steyr to the south was not in accord with clear orders from Vienna, since it was incompatible with these recommendations. Either Merveldt chose that moment to act on the previous orders (it is not clear whether or not they were ever formally rescinded), or he had just received those orders (unlikely, but possible in a world of hand-carried messages), or he withdrew south in response to battlefield events, as the French accounts suggest. Clearly the accepted understanding of this event—that the Austrians ordered Merveldt to abandon Kutuzov at Steyr—cannot stand.

overwhelming force to bear rapidly was asking him to commit suicide. The admonitions to preserve the "honor" of Russian arms made sense in the grand strategic context. Considering the humiliation the Austrians had just inflicted on themselves, Russia stood to gain a great deal by emerging from this parlous situation with an intact, seasoned army. From an operational perspective, however, this advice ignored the harsh realities of the situation. Alexander understood even less than Francis and the Hofkriegsrat that a false move would lead to the complete destruction of Kutuzov's army; the Russian general had to bend every effort to survival. He could not afford to consider the niceties of honor, keep his force always attacking the enemy, or retreat "step by step."

The only practical consequence of this allied planning process was to grant Kutuzov an Austrian blessing for the retreat to Krems and impress on the Russian general the need to hold his position at Krems indefinitely. Kutuzov undertook to do his best in that regard at least.

To the Left Bank

The differences between Austria and southern Germany continued to make themselves felt in Napoleon's campaign plans and operations as the campaign rolled down the Vienna road. The sparser road network constricted Napoleon's options and forced him to send too many troops down a limited number of roads. In Germany he had been able to assign each corps its own route, but efforts to do the same thing in Austria failed. Soult, for example, found that the bridge over the Enns at Kronstorf, where he was supposed to cross, could not easily be rebuilt and reported that the effort to do so would probably cost him three days.[4] Rather than lose the time, Napoleon decided to send Soult to Enns to cross there and follow in the wake of Murat's and Lannes's Corps. Three corps now raced along the same road, one after the others. Napoleon became concerned that this march column was too long and ordered Murat to condense his formations as much as possible "so that the tail can come to the assistance of the head."[5]

Napoleon was also concerned about feeding so many troops marching along a single road that, according to Murat, the Russians had "ravaged" and from which they had "taken everything."[6] He took several steps to remedy these problems. First, he formed a flotilla to operate along the Danube to transport supplies from French depots upriver to the troops marching along its banks farther down.[7] Second, Napoleon took advantage of this flotilla to ferry some of his troops across to the left bank of the Danube. On November 6 he formed a new corps under the command of Marshal Mortier and composed of Gazan's, Dupont's, and Dumonceau's Divisions taken from Lannes's, Ney's, and Marmont's Corps respectively.[8] He subsequently ordered General Klein's Dragoons Division to cross the river and operate with Mortier.[9]

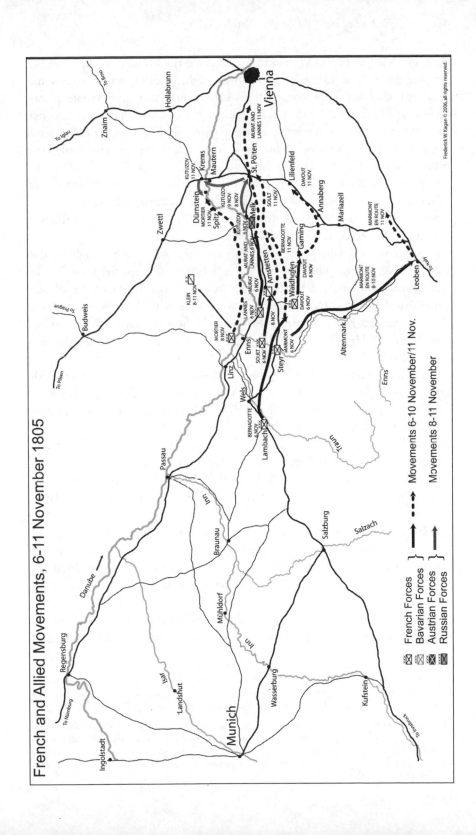

French and Allied Movements, 6–11 November 1805

KUTUZOV
11 NOV

Krems

Mautern

KUTUZOV
9 NOV

Dürnstein

MORTIER
11 NOV

Spitz

KUTUZOV
8 NOV

KUTUZOV
8 NOV

Melk

St. Pölten

MURAT AND
LANNES 11 NOV

Vienna

Lilienfeld

SOULT
11 NOV

DAVOUT
11 NOV

Annaberg

Mariazell

MARMONT
EN ROUTE
11 NOV

Zwettl

BERNADOTTE
11 NOV

Gaming

MURAT AND
LANNES 8 NOV

MURAT
6 NOV

Amstetten

DAVOUT
8 NOV

Waldhofen

DAVOUT
6 NOV

MARMONT
EN ROUTE
8–10 NOV

Altenmark

Leoben

To Italy

KLEIN
8–11 NOV

Budweis

To Prague

To Pilsen

MORTIER
8 NOV

LANNES
6 NOV

Enns

SOULT
6 NOV

MARMONT
6 NOV

Steyr

Linz

Wels

Enns

BERNADOTTE
6 NOV

Lambach

Traun

Passau

Inn

Braunau

Salzburg

Salzach

Danube

Mühldorf

Inn

Wasserburg

Munich

Kufstein

To Innsbruck

Regensburg

To Nürnberg

Isar

Landshut

Ingolstadt

Hollabrunn

Znaim

To Iglau

To Brno

Movements 6–10 November/11 Nov.

Movements 6–10 November

Movements 8–11 November

French Forces
Bavarian Forces
Austrian Forces
Russian Forces

Napoleon instructed Mortier to march along the left bank of the Danube, keeping just behind Lannes's Corps on the right. Mortier was to supply his army entirely from the resources on his bank of the river, and Napoleon forbade him to draw on the magazine at Linz. Further, the emperor instructed the newest corps commander to gather enough supplies that he could send some over the river to support the corps marching along the right bank. Another obvious advantage of establishing the new corps was that it could operate against the Russians if they crossed the Danube at Krems.[10] Napoleon's initial instructions make no reference to such an eventuality, however, and his plans for operations on the right bank at this time make it clear that he did not expect Kutuzov to cross, as we shall see.*

Napoleon thought that the Russians intended to stand and fight in the vicinity of St. Pölten. The fact that Kutuzov had abandoned the Enns line so readily and yet fought so determinedly at Amstetten combined with Napoleon's belief that the "second Russian army" was fast approaching Krems to convince the emperor that Kutuzov intended to hold the heights near St. Pölten to defend Vienna.[11] He lost no time in preparing for what he hoped would be a decisive battle.

Davout's success at Steyr together with Merveldt's mistaken retreat south offered Napoleon a promising opportunity to envelop and destroy Kutuzov's force if it tried to fight at St. Pölten. Napoleon thus ordered Davout to race from Steyr to Waidhofen and then to Lilienfeld. "If the enemy holds at St. Pölten," he noted, "you will find yourself having outflanked his left and you will be able to march on him while Marshals Lannes and Soult march along the Vienna highway to try to outflank his right." Napoleon also sent Marmont to Waidhofen and Bernadotte to Steyr, presumably to support Davout's flanking maneuver, if necessary.†

In an unusual move, Napoleon sent General Mathieu Dumas as a special emissary to Davout, with detailed instructions about Napoleon's intentions and orders to scout the various march routes.[12] These instructions considered the possibility that Kutuzov would link up with the second Russian army before the battle and conversely that he would not be able to do so. In the first case, Napoleon ordered Davout to turn the flank of the Russian armies but not envelop them completely. In the second case the emperor aimed for a more decisive

---

*Napoleon nevertheless made an oblique reference to the idea of Mortier's operating against Kutuzov on the left bank in a letter to Murat of 7 November 1805: "The Russians, who are not expecting this maneuver, may become its victims." Alombert-Goget, *Campagne de l'an 14*, p. 27.

†Berthier to Davout, Marmont, and Bernadotte, 5 November 1805, in Alombert-Goget and Colin, *La campagne de 1805*, vol. 4, pt. 2, pp. 529, 531, 532, respectively. The purposes of Marmont's and Bernadotte's advances may also have been to relieve Davout of the need to worry about Merveldt or secure the right flank of the French army against troops coming from Italy; Napoleon offers no explanation in any of these letters.

blow. He instructed Davout to arrange with Marmont and Bernadotte so that the former attacked the Russians' left and the latter their front while Davout attacked from the rear. He also wanted Davout to cut off any escape route through Lilienfeld. He was to "throw the enemy into the Danube." These plans, of course, did not consider seriously the possibility that Kutuzov would not hold at St. Pölten but would instead continue his withdrawal to Krems and beyond.

As the French vanguard approached St. Pölten, confusion arose between Napoleon and Murat about the objective of the French advance, and it shaped the rest of the campaign. On November 6 Murat reported, "All the Russian generals say loudly that they are not strong enough to risk a battle and that one must not be surprised to see them decide to cross to the left bank of the Danube at Krems." "Thus," he continued, "I see nothing else that can delay for a minute the march of Your Majesty to Vienna."[13]

But what was the objective of the campaign: the capture and destruction of Kutuzov's army or the seizure of the Austrian capital? To this point, the two goals had seemed inseparable, since the Russian army was retreating along the Vienna road. These objectives diverged, however, once it became likely that Kutuzov would march to Krems rather than Vienna. Murat found himself without clear instructions from the emperor about which objective to prefer at that point. He decided, for no very good reason, that the real goal must be Vienna.

Napoleon might have set his subordinate straight if another issue had not arisen to confuse their correspondence further. Murat's report crossed a message from Napoleon in which the emperor berated Murat for not informing him the moment he had joined battle at Amstetten. "If I had known that the enemy was there," he wrote, "I would have made my dispositions at once."[14] What Napoleon thought he would have done is not clear, since the battle was joined and over before he could have taken any effective action. Considering that Napoleon was still at Linz at the time, the battle would have been over long before a courier sent as it began could have reached him. This anger probably reflects Napoleon's frustration with the campaign and with his inability to catch Kutuzov's army more than a legitimate complaint against Murat, although the marshal should have sent off a contact report at once. Napoleon wrote on the same day to Cambacérès, "We are a few days from Vienna. We have only hurt the Russians a little. However fast we've been marching, they have retreated faster still."[15]

Murat took Napoleon's reproach to heart. He wrote back at once, complaining that the emperor had misprized his success at Amstetten. Napoleon's note "seems to bring me your reproaches for yesterday's affair, instead of the evidence of satisfaction that I would have been happy to give the troops who had fought so gloriously." When Napoleon crossed the battlefield, the aggrieved marshal continued, he would see for himself how significant the fight had been.[16] The emperor attempted to clarify the nature of his reproach for his affronted subordinate: "I do not know where you got the idea that I was discontent with the Battle of Amstetten; I was [discontent] with the fact that you had not written me."[17] He did not attempt to clarify the objective of the campaign, however.

One reason for this lapse was probably Murat's November 6 focus on the prospect of trapping the Austrians near Ybbs, whether they wanted to fight or not. Napoleon was very excited about that prospect and hoped for a decisive battle with the Russians at St. Pölten.[18] By the next day it had become clear that Murat's effort had failed, and he once more contemplated the prospect of a fight on the "immense plain" that lies before Vienna stretching to and beyond St. Pölten. Although the marshal doubted that the allies would try to defend St. Pölten, having already abandoned many superior defensive positions, he nevertheless prepared to mass his corps and Lannes's troops against Kutuzov should he make such a mistake. There was no mention of a Russian retreat to Krems in this letter.[19] Four and a half hours later, however, Murat wrote to pass on the word that the Russians were sending their baggage to Krems and the rumor that they intended to retreat to Bohemia. "A report that I have just received at this moment," he concluded, "confirms that the Russians are marching toward Krems. If I can find a practicable route that leads directly to that point, I will send some parties of light troops out there."[20]

At this point Napoleon should have clarified his objectives, and in the ordinary run of events he probably would have. He needed to tell Murat precisely what the aim was and what course the marshal should take if the Russians withdrew to Krems, leaving Vienna uncovered. Nothing in their previous correspondence gave Murat anything like adequate guidance for taking such a decision on his own. Nor had Napoleon made clear, either to Murat or to Mortier, what role the newest corps was supposed to play in the operation. It was time for an informative note laying out the objectives or at least the immediate possible courses of action, for the benefit of the vanguard commander and probably for Lannes and Mortier as well.

Napoleon sent no such clarifying document. His response was vague and confusing.[21] He ordered Murat to send outposts to the outskirts of Vienna if the allies did not offer strong resistance. Murat was to concentrate his own forces and those of Marshal Soult. Bernadotte, Napoleon wrote, would soon be arriving at Amstetten, presumably to reinforce the vanguard. These orders suggest that Napoleon still expected a decisive battle in the plain before Vienna. That suggestion is not necessarily undermined by the reflections that followed those orders: "It is probable that if the Russians have recrossed the Danube it is because they have learned of the passage of Marshal Mortier, which will lead them to cover Vienna on the left bank. Try to gather up as many Russians as you can. I see them arriving with great pleasure; there are already 500 or 600."

Making sense of this note is difficult. First, the Russians had not yet crossed the Danube at Krems. Second, if they had, then why should Murat worry about concentrating Lannes's Corps with him and about Bernadotte's position? Why did Napoleon not refer to securing the bridges over the river near Krems? Why did he give Murat no direction of march, or choose between the two options of marching to Vienna or chasing the Russians? It is interesting that the only directional order he gave was to send outposts toward the Austrian capital. Napoleon made no comment about the small number of forces Murat had dispatched toward the Danube. Above all, the instruction to "gather up" as many Russians as possible is far from an order to attack, envelop, or cut off the Russian army. Murat can be forgiven for not clearly divining Napoleon's intentions from this vague and confused missive.

Murat received no further guidance from Napoleon or Berthier for three days, leaving him to decide whether to follow Kutuzov or march on Vienna.[22] Perhps the emperor was distracted by the manifold military and diplomatic activities he was overseeing. On November 8 he met with the elector of Bavaria to thrash out the details of Bavaria's reward for supporting France. He even wrote Murat on that day, "The Elector of Bavaria is here, which is greatly occupying me."[23] At the same time, Napoleon was conducting a delicate negotiation with Francis in hopes of persuading Austria to leave the Third Coalition.* He was also monitoring the situation in Berlin as it developed after Bernadotte's and Davout's troops marched across Ansbach.† For whatever reason, Napoleon left his vanguard commander in the dark about his specific desires and intentions during a crucial period of the campaign.

Kutuzov decided on November 8 that he would march from St. Pölten to Krems the next day. As he subsequently explained to Francis, he had learned that Mortier was marching along the left bank of the Danube to cut him off, although he seems to have been intending to march to Krems for some time.[24] Murat, as we have seen, had already picked up intimations of Kutuzov's intention and his preparations for the withdrawal to Krems. Now he reported, confusingly, that Kutuzov intended to withdraw "from St. Pölten to Krems *and* Vienna."[25] It is not possible to march from St. Pölten to Krems and Vienna at the same time, since Krems is due north and Vienna due east, along different roads. Murat ordered his corps to take up positions directly fronting St. Pölten and made no serious effort to send cavalry racing toward Mautern, the town opposite Krems, to cut the bridge and keep the Russians on the right bank of the Danube. There is no excuse for this failure except Murat's limited vision combined with the vagueness of

---

*Napoleon to Talleyrand, 9 November 1805, *Corr. de Nap.*, doc. 9468. This negotiation will be considered in greater detail subsequently.

†Talleyrand to Napoleon, 29 October, 31 October, 11 November 1805, in Pierre Bertrand, ed., *Lettres inédites de Talleyrand à Napoléon, 1800–1809* (Paris: Librairie académique Didier, 1889), docs. 117, 118, 120. Unfortunately the correspondence does not include any letters between 1 November and 11 November. Talleyrand was in Munich during this period, so his letters should have taken a day or two to reach Napoleon. The complexities caused in Prussia by the violation of her territory at Ansbach are considered in greater detail in Chapter 20 below.

Napoleon's orders. A competent vanguard commander would have made every effort to prevent the Russians from escaping, whereas Murat simply prepared for a decisive battle near St. Pölten, which even he did not believe likely.

Murat's report of Kutuzov's departure reveals that he had no idea that he was supposed to trap and destroy the Russians. On November 9 he informed Napoleon that "all the Russians have retreated toward Krems."[26] He established a division to "observe" the road the Russians had taken and sent a brigade to "pursue" the Russians, with another brigade in support! Those two brigades would ride "as far as Krems in order to *assure themselves that the enemy has entirely crossed* to the left bank of the Danube."*

Murat explained his immobility in the vicinity of St. Pölten, if not his failure to trap or pursue the Russians aggressively. He had learned that Kienmayer had led the small Austrian force that joined the Russians toward Vienna, and he feared marching either toward Vienna, which would "offer a flank to the Russian army," or toward Krems, because then "I would have feared the Austrians." When Soult's Corps came up from Mölk to "cover the route from Krems," however, Murat wrote that he would be confident to "continue my march toward Vienna." Apparently he decided that the Russians were withdrawing to Russia and abandoning the campaign. Murat was convinced that the right aim was the seizure of the Austrian capital to end the war rapidly. He subsequently wrote to Napoleon that the emperor's "open" declaration to him at Linz that "he wanted to go to Vienna and that he wanted to arrive there in a position to negotiate" had convinced him to advance on the capital.[27]

With calm insouciance and a complete failure to understand the operational and strategic significance of what he was doing, Murat allowed Kutuzov to march over the Danube and burn the bridge spanning that fast and deep current without firing a shot. Murat thereby exposed Mortier's small corps to single combat with the entire Russian army, which outnumbered it significantly, on terms of the Russians' choosing. We shall explore that combat presently.

When Napoleon learned of Murat's blunders, he was furious and sent Murat a blistering verbal assault. "I cannot approve your manner of marching," he wrote. "You go like a scatterbrain without at all weighing the orders that I have given you." The "extraordinary circumstance" that the Russians had marched to Krems instead of Vienna, the emperor ranted, should have shown Murat that he could not continue without new instructions. "Without knowing what projects the enemy might have nor understanding what my wishes might be in this new order of affairs, you go to stuff my army into Vienna," he continued. Napoleon claimed to have sent Murat orders through Berthier to follow the Russians "with your sword in their kidneys," but "it is a singular way of pursuing them to separate yourself from them by forced marches."

---

*Emphasis added.

"I search in vain," he added, "for reasons to explain your conduct." Napoleon also noted dourly that Murat's mistakes had exposed Mortier to heaven knew what sort of debacle and blamed the marshal for seeking glory in capturing Vienna rather than following less glamorous orders. But, Napoleon concluded, "there can be no glory where there is no danger."[28]

Napoleon's criticism was at once justified and unjustified. Murat should have seen that destroying the Russians, which required timely and efficient maneuvers, was more urgent than seizing an undefended capital. His decision to let the Russians go in favor of marching into Vienna with banners flying (and Napoleon's suspicion that Murat hankered for that scene was probably well founded) was the height of military folly.

Napoleon also bears substantial blame for this mistake. Murat had first suggested that Kutuzov might go to Krems rather than Vienna on November 6, and he repeated the warning each day until the Russians actually crossed the river. At no point did Napoleon direct Murat to follow the Russians, even when Murat intimated that he planned to go to Vienna. Napoleon's other military and diplomatic activities distracted him from paying heed to the most important of his undertakings at a crucial time. Likely some of the venom in his long-distance tongue lashing of Murat came from a recognition of his own failure in this regard.

Whatever the causes and wherever the blame might fall, the result of these maneuvers was to allow Kutuzov to escape from the right bank of the Danube and from the immediate danger of being forced to fight the bulk of Napoleon's army. All that now stood between Kutuzov and the substantial reinforcements rushing through Moravia was the newest corps of the French army under the command of its least experienced corps commander. If Mortier could somehow hold Kutuzov in place near Krems for a time, or even if he could have chased the Russians from Krems and pursued them aggressively, the situation might have been salvaged. Much depended on the Battle of Dürnstein, which ensued from this unexpected confrontation.

Dürnstein

Murat's decision to march on Vienna instead of pursuing Kutuzov's army toward Krems not only allowed the Russians to escape across the Danube unopposed but also offered Kutuzov his first real opportunity for a small counteroffensive operation. Kutuzov was fortunate that the target of this operation was the least experienced of Napoleon's corps commanders, whose corps would have to defend itself in the most unfavorable conditions.

Although Mortier was among those created marshal in 1804 when the title was established, he had slightly less combat experience than many of the others. The half-English son of a cloth merchant, he joined the revolutionary

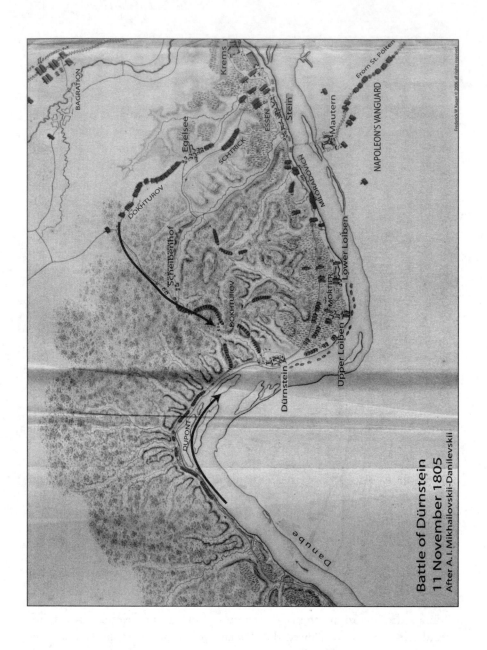

Battle of Dürnstein
11 November 1805
After A. I. Mikhailovskii–Danilevskii

armies in 1791 when he was twenty-three. By 1799 he had been promoted to *général de division,* but he did not command a division during the Italian campaign of 1800, as most of the original marshals did. He oversaw the occupation of Hanover in 1803, although there was little fighting in that incident. He had never really commanded a large unit in combat, therefore, when he took command of a corps for the first time in November 1805.[29]

Mortier's new command was challenging from the start. The divisions that composed it had all been detached from other corps, had never fought together before, and were not physically together when Mortier took up his new post. The lead division of General Honoré Gazan, a veteran of the revolutionary wars who had commanded a division in Switzerland and in Italy, was at Linz, as was the cavalry division commanded by General Klein. The other two divisions, Dupont's and Dumonceau's, were forty-three miles away at Passau. Mortier's new command would have been a formidable force, for it mustered some 16,000 infantry and cavalry when it was formed.[30] It would prove impossible, however, for Mortier to bring the half of his force to bear against Kutuzov.

The dispersion of his corps and the confusion of his orders complicated Mortier's task from the outset. On the day the corps was formed, General Klein, commander of the cavalry division who had been ordered to lead the way along the river road, demurred. The terrain along the river road was ill suited to cavalry, he complained, and much better suited to Gazan's Infantry Division, which was already moving ahead. He proposed to take his entire cavalry division north toward the village of Zwettl, thirty-seven miles from his camp near the Danube, but still twenty-eight miles from Krems.[31] His plan was not entirely without merit. The route Klein proposed was only ten miles longer than the road Mortier had been ordered to take. What is more, it would have the advantage of providing a second line of advance for Mortier's corps that otherwise had to move in column along a single road.

Klein's concern about the suitability of the terrain for cavalry was also well founded. From Linz to Melk, the north bank of the Danube is relatively flat and the road that runs along it relatively good, although the roads along the left bank of the Danube are worse than those along the right, which connect the major cities of Vienna, Linz, and Salzburg. From Melk to Krems, however, the character of the land changes dramatically. Mountains of 1,500 to 2,000 feet drop steep escarpments and cliffs right down to the river, broken only by a narrow road running through a cutting sometimes only a few yards wide. Where the land flattens out or the slope of the hill permits terracing, densely planted vines and apricot trees mark the landscape. The fruits and wines of this region, the Wachau, are extremely good, but their trees and vines, combined with the dramatic rise and fall of the hills cut by many deep ravines, make this an area best avoided by armies.

If Klein's plan made sense, however, it had the fatal flaw of going contrary to both Mortier's desires and Napoleon's intentions. Unwilling to part with all of his cavalry but apparently unable to prevent Klein from going, Mortier demanded that Klein leave him a regiment of his cavalry, despite protests that it would leave the cavalry division too weak if it encountered enemy forces.[32] The parting does not appear to have been amicable. Worse still, Klein rapidly discovered that the terrain north of the Danube along the road he proposed to take was not much better than what he would have found between Melk and Krems. Having set out to the north on November 8, he had managed only fifteen miles of his route by November 10 when Napoleon, angered by his march away from Mortier, reminded him that he was under Mortier's orders and commanded him to rejoin the corps.* The net result of these maneuvers was that Mortier's Corps Cavalry was scrabbling around in the hills north of the Danube immediately before and during the Battle of Dürnstein instead of scouting and screening ahead of the infantry.

Even as Klein headed north on November 8, Murat was receiving word that Kutuzov had directed his baggage and artillery to head north toward Krems. He reported that fact to Napoleon, together with the fact that he had asked Mortier to press toward Krems with all possible speed, presumably to seize Kutuzov's baggage train or possibly to block Kutuzov's retreat.[33] By the end of the day he reflected contentedly, "If it is true that the Russians are retiring through Krems, Marshal Mortier can do them a great deal of harm."[34]

But Mortier was not in as good a position to harm Kutuzov's force or hinder his retreat as Murat hoped. November 9 found Mortier with the leading division (Gazan's) only at Marbach, thirty miles from Krems, while Dupont's Division was thirty-two miles behind him at Grein with Dumonceau's Division following.[35] But Kutuzov had ordered the Army of Podolia to move from St. Pölten to Krems (15 miles or so) on November 8, and he was established in position at Krems by the time Murat was reflecting complacently about the damage Mortier was likely to inflict on him.[36] Mortier, obedient to Murat's request, hastened to move forward more quickly, but his troops could only move so fast. November 10 found Gazan's lead division at Spitz and pushing pickets forward by boat to Dürnstein and the neighboring villages of Ober Loiben and Unter Loiben. But Dupont's Division was still a day's march behind.

Kutuzov was much better informed about Mortier's position than Mortier was about his, and he determined to take advantage of the opportunity presented to him. Mortier had happened upon a collection of boats at the town of Weitenegg, near Melk, on November 9, and had mounted the 4th Light Infantry Regiment and the 100th Infantry Regiment on those boats the sooner to

---

*Napoleon's ability to involve himself in this relatively trivial dispute between a corps commander and one of his subordinates throws into even sharper relief his failure to address the fundamental goals of the campaign with Murat.

get them to the vicinity of Dürnstein. A five-hour boat ride along the rapidly flowing Danube brought them to that town, where the 100th disembarked. The 4th continued farther downstream to the villages of Ober and Unter Loiben. Instead of consolidating a position in those villages, however, the soldiers of the 4th took to looting, and some were taken in their turn by Russian outposts.[37] In this way, Kutuzov learned that Mortier's lead division was at Dürnstein. On November 10, he confirmed the reports of his prisoners through informers who added that Mortier had only Gazan's Division with him, that most of the cavalry had gone toward Zwettl, and that Dupont's and Dumonceau's Divisions were at least as far back as Spitz.[38] Kutuzov decided to take advantage of this situation to inflict a stunning blow on Mortier and his corps.

Between Weissenkirchen and Krems the Danube travels through an S-shaped valley with a strong current. On both sides, hills climb virtually from the river's edge to peaks more than a thousand feet above the water. Deep ravines cut these hills at regular intervals. The town of Dürnstein is nestled between the river and a peak almost 2,000 feet high, the Schlossberg, on top of which stand the ruins of the Schloss Dürnstein. In that medieval castle England's King Richard the Lionheart, seized for ransom on his way home from the Third Crusade, was held prisoner. To this day, Dürnstein retains a medieval appearance; in the early nineteenth century its walls and gates were still largely intact.

To the east along the Danube from Dürnstein a small plain a little over half a mile wide opens between the river and the hills. This plain was filled with vineyards then as now, separated from one another by low stone walls, their trellising presenting a serious obstacle to movement.* The main road in that direction passes through the villages of Ober and Unter Loiben and then clings to the bank of the Danube, through a defile hardly wider than the road itself, to the village of Stein, neighbor to the town of Krems. The hills bordering this plain to the north are steep but climbable. Beyond those hills, the land falls off gently and the going is easier. Today the Austrian hiking club has marked out many hiking trails that follow the ravines from the Danube's side through these hills to the villages of Scheibenhof and Egelsee that lie north of Dürnstein and Stein respectively. To this day, however, no roads cross those hills.

---

*It is not clear how densely the vines covered the plain on which Ober and Unter Loiben sit in 1805. Rainer Egger describes it as "wine country," and his account mentions the importance of the vines in slowing the movement of the various armies in *Das Gefecht bei Dürnstein-Loiben, 1805: Militärische Schriftenreihe* (Vienna: Heeresgeschichtliches Museum Militärwissenschaftliches Institut, 1986), 3:12. Local residents say that the plain was more open and less heavily planted at the time, and a contemporary picture of the battle now hanging in the Hotel Richard Löwenherz in Dürnstein seems to show a relatively open plain. Certainly it is difficult to imagine any important infantry fight taking place in the dense fields of wires supporting countless grapes that now cover the plain and the hillsides behind it as well. Numerous contemporary reports, nevertheless, refer to the vineyards on the plain around the Loibens, which the French found to be a serious obstacle. I am grateful to Franziska Thiery, the proprietress of the Hotel Richard Löwenherz, for the insights and resources about local history that she shared with me, as well as for her wonderful hospitality.

Kutuzov was aware of these circumstances not only because he observed them but because Emperor Franz had sent FMS Heinrich von Schmitt to serve him in the capacity of quartermaster general, a duty he had performed for numerous Austrian commanders in previous wars against Napoleon. Schmitt reported to Kutuzov that there was a trail that led from Stein through Egelsee and Scheibenhof, emerging in one of several defiles to the west of Dürnstein. Kutuzov wasted little time in deciding to attempt to use this trail to place a large force in the rear of Gazan's Division, cutting it off from the rest of Mortier's Corps and affording him time to destroy it.[39]

To accomplish this aim, Kutuzov divided his force into five parts. To Bagration he entrusted the vanguard, composed of three infantry and elements of two cavalry regiments. Bagration's task was to occupy the village of Imbach along the road from Krems to Zwettl and protect Kutuzov's rear from Klein's Cavalry Division, which he knew to be headed toward Zwettl. Miloradovich received command of the left column, composed of four infantry battalions, with orders to defend the village of Stein, make contact with Mortier's forces on the plain between Stein and the Loibens, and pin them there to facilitate their envelopment. Schtrick had charge of the center column composed of two infantry regiments, six infantry battalions, and one cavalry battalion. That column was to move out from Stein through Egelsee and then filter through the hills near Stein to protect the flank of Miloradovich's forces and menace those of Mortier's as they attacked. The most daunting task, however, went to Dokhturov and the right column. That force, consisting of four infantry regiments and a cavalry battalion, was charged with making the long march from Stein through Egelsee and Scheibenhof to emerge from the defiles west of Dürnstein.[40] It was set in motion on November 10, and based on Schmitt's reckoning, expected to arrive at the defiles early in the morning on November 11.[41]

Kutuzov's plan relied on knowledge of the terrain, which he obtained from local inhabitants. An Austrian hunter named Andreas Bayer led Dokhturov's Column through the wooded hills from Egelsee to Dürnstein and beyond, and a local official was apparently present during the allied planning sessions to offer advice about the lay of the land.* It was equally important to the allies' success, however, that Mortier remain unaware of their plan. The new marshal was very obliging in this regard.

Although the detachment of Klein's troops deprived Mortier of much of his cavalry, Mortier had retained the 4th Dragoons Regiment, which marched at the head of his column.[42] Neither these cavalry nor the light troops accompanying Gazan's Division were sent into the hills northeast of Dürnstein, nor does Mortier appear to have undertaken any meaningful scouting beyond the

---

*Egger, *Das Gefecht bei Dürnstein-Loiben*, p. 17; Wilhelm von Kotzebue, *Versuch einer Beschreibung der Schlacht bey Dürnstein am 11ten November 1805* (N.p.: A. von Kotzebue, 1807), p. vii. The "Jäger von Dürnstein" has become a local legend and stories about him abound in the area.

failed effort to send pickets forward by boat, which ended up giving Kutuzov more information than Mortier received. Mortier was convinced that Kutuzov was retreating and he was facing only a rear guard attempting to hold at Stein; he would not need to be concerned about his flanks or counterattacks. He therefore charged heedlessly across the plain between Dürnstein and Stein, ran straight into Miloradovich's force, and pinned himself in a perfect position to facilitate the planned allied envelopment.

From the French perspective, the Battle of Dürnstein was a fierce struggle for control of that plain. On November 10, the French had beaten off the Russian pickets in the Loibens and occupied those villages during a long, cold night.[43] At about 7:00 A.M. the next morning, the Russians advanced from their positions at Stein in two columns, one moving along the bases of the hills to the north, the other straight down the main road from Stein to Dürnstein, which was lined on either side with high stone walls.*

At first the Russians encountered only pickets in the villages of Rothenhof and Unterloiben, which they drove off with relative ease, despite the fact that the French barricaded themselves in houses and on roofs from which they had to be dislodged one by one.[44] Gazan responded to this advance by ordering the 4th Light Infantry Regiment and the 100th Line to counterattack, keeping the 103rd Line in reserve.[45] Miloradovich met the challenge by sending his own reinforcements into the fight, temporarily stabilizing the struggle for the village.[46]

At 10:30 A.M., Mortier committed the 2nd Battalion of the 103rd of the Line to the fight.† The fight for the villages was so finely balanced that this small reinforcement was enough to turn the tide dramatically. The Russians broke and fled, abandoning Unterloiben and a field littered with their dead and wounded, including a significant number of senior officers, about 200 prisoners, and two cannons. Gazan committed the other two battalions of the 103rd to the attack,

---

*Egger, *Das Gefecht bei Dürnstein-Loiben*, p. 15; Report of M. A. Miloradovich to Kutuzov about the Battle of Krems, 21 November 1805, in Iu. I Zhiugzhda, ed., *Dokumenty shtaba M. I. Kutuzova, 1805–1806* (Vilnius: Gosudarstvennoe Izdatel'stvo Politicheskoi i Nauchnoi Literatury, 1951), doc. 99 (the Russians call this fight the Battle of Krems); Relation of the Battle of Dürnstein by Colonel Talandier (who participated in the battle as a newly minted sergeant), in Alombert, *Combat de Dürrenstein*, p. 105. These walls were subsequently removed, and the road across the plain, north of the one used for automotive traffic that largely follows the river, is now open on both sides.

†Colonel Talandier, extract from the Account of the Battle of Diernstein, cited in Alombert-Goget, *Combat de Dürrenstein*, pp. 104–120; Taupin, Colonel of the 103rd Line Infantry Regiment, to the Major General, 18 December 1805, in Alombert-Goget, *Combat de Dürrenstein*, pp. 120–122. Talandier states that it was the 1st Battalion, but as Alombert points out, it is much more likely that he was mistaken than that Taupin, the commander of the 103rd Line, was in error. Kotzebue (*Schlacht bey Dürnstein*, pp. 30–31) states that this counterattack involved all but 200 men of the French reserve, and Egger (*Das Gefecht bei Dürnstein-Loiben*, p. 15) follows him in that assertion. Taupin's and Talandier's accounts, however, indicate that this is an exaggeration and that Gazan and Mortier continued to maintain reserves of at least two line battalions at this point. There is also a disagreement about time; Egger and Kotzebue place the time of the French counterattack at 11:00, but the French give it as 10:30.

and the French drove the Russians all the way back to the defile in front of Stein. They also pushed the Russians off the hills northwest of Stein and threatened to break into the rear of the enveloping columns of Dokhturov's force.

Kutuzov was not a passive spectator during this struggle. He sent his adjutant (and son-in-law), Count Tisenhausen, to Miloradovich with instructions to withdraw slowly, and Miloradovich instantly dispatched Tisenhausen and other officers with reinforcements to set first the left and then the right flank in order and restabilize the situation.[47] At the same time, Kutuzov apparently ordered part of Dokhturov's Column under the command of General Schtrick to counterattack over the hills from Egelsee toward Loiben, halting the advance of the French toward the rear of the enveloping column and retaking the heights with some difficulty.* These forces probably cooperated with reinforcements sent by Miloradovich into the hills on the right flank as well.[48] The French were too strong, however, and they pushed the Russians back to the very gates of Stein, where they were stopped by the narrowness of the defile and murderous canister and musket fire laid down by the reserve forces of General Essen, whom Kutuzov had ordered to defend the town.[49] Nevertheless, they felt they had won a significant battle.[50] Little did they know that the real fight was just beginning.

Dokhturov's Column had a terrible time marching from Krems to the Danube beyond Dürnstein. Although Austrian accounts sneeringly refer to the Russians' "usual" delays in marching, the truth is that the movement was extremely difficult.[51] The road from Krems to Egelsee is steep and winding, and the Russians were exhausted from days of forced marches and limited rations. Further delays ensued when the troops reached Egelsee and then Scheibenhof, as they attempted to gather the scarce supplies in those tiny villages before assembling or proceeding.[52] Moving toward the river from Scheibenhof, moreover, the troops had to march along narrow forest tracks and down steep, rocky defiles. The fact that the local hunter Andreas Bayer was needed to show them the way testifies to the terrible conditions under which they marched. As a result, Dokhturov's Column fell hours behind schedule in its effort to turn the French flank, and the fierce fighting on the plain between Dürnstein and Stein was more prolonged than anyone had anticipated.

---

*Egger, *Das Gefecht bei Dürnstein-Loiben*, p. 16. There is no mention of Kutuzov's order in the sources, but since Dokhturov was at the head of his column it seems clear that the diversion of these troops could only have resulted from the overall commander's orders. Miloradovich notes that Kutuzov sent him several adjutants and officers to replace his losses at this juncture. Mikhailovskii-Danilevskii, *Opisanie*, p. 103, notes that the unit which attacked from Egelsee was the Butyrskii Regiment under the overall command of General Mal'tits (Disposition of Columns for the Attack of the Enemy near Weissenkirchen, 10 November 1805, in Beskrovnyi, *Kutuzov*, vol. 2, doc. 167). Schtrick's report to Kutuzov concentrates on recommending officers and soldiers who performed well in combat and provides little specific detail about the engagement. Schtrick to Kutuzov, 15 November 1805, in Zhiugzhda, *Dokumenty*, doc. 101.

On reaching Scheibenhof, Dokhturov detached a large force under General Urusov to hold the nearby heights.* He continued with the rest of his column along the Pfaffental defile toward the Danube at the hamlet of Wadstein.† When he reached the Danube road, Dokhturov further divided his forces. He stationed two battalions of the Viatka Regiment under the command of Lieutenant Colonel Gvozdev at the base of the defile facing toward Weissenkirchen and sent his vanguard (two battalions of the 6th Jaegers Regiment and one of the Jaroslav Regiment under the command of Major General Ulanius) toward Dürnstein.[53] Ulanius reached Dürnstein and quickly overran the sparse French defenders there while Dokhturov collected the rest of his troops and followed.‡

Dokhturov sent Ulanius into the hills northeast of Dürnstein while he led his four battalions along the main road toward Stein. He even retook the Loibens before Mortier and Gazan were able to respond.[54] Miloradovich heard gunfire from Dürnstein at around 5:00 P.M. and immediately opened an attack, hoping to crush the French in the plain once and for all.[55] But the French withdrew slowly before Miloradovich while attacking Dokhturov's forces near Dürnstein. Russian soldiers attempting to retake the Loibens became frustrated and set fire to the villages instead, hoping to drive out the French defenders, but in reality preparing horrible deaths for their own and French wounded left in the village houses.[56]

The French counterattack against Dokhturov took advantage of the fact that the Russian troops advancing from Dürnstein were confined between the high, narrow stone walls that lined the main road. The French set up cannons and laid down brutal musket fire against the unsuspecting Russians. As the lead troops recoiled, those in the rear broke down the walls and all began to retreat in disorder.§ At the same time, French troops attacked the Schlossberg but were repulsed by Urusov's forces stationed on the height.[57] Had he arrived

---

*Report of D. S. Dokhturov to M. I. Kutuzov about the Battle of Krems, 20 November 1805 in Beskrovnyi, *Kutuzov*, doc. 198; Report of Major General Urusov to D. S. Dokhturov About the Battle of Krems, 16 November 1805, in Zhiugzhda, *Dokumenty*, doc. 97. It is not clear from these accounts which heights Urusov was holding. Most likely it was the Starhemberg and/or the Schlossberg, the peaks behind the Schloss Dürnstein. Urusov was given command of two battalions each of the Briansk and Jaroslav Regiments, one battalion of the 6th Jaegers Regiment, and two battalions of the Mariupol' Hussars Regiment.

†Dokhturov's remaining forces included two battalions of the 6th Jaegers Regiment, the Grenadiers Battalion of the Jaroslav Regiment, and the Moscow and Viatka Regiments.

‡Dokhturov thus had four battalions with him: three of the Moscow Regiment and one of the Viatka Regiment. This depiction differs significantly from that presented by the Austrian narratives, which are the only sources that describe this battle in detail. See Appendix A for a discussion and justification of the differences.

§Colonel Talandier, Extract from the Account of the Battle of Diernstein, cited in Alombert-Goget, *Combat de Dürrenstein*, pp. 104–120. This report is not corroborated by the Russian sources, but it should be generally accepted because of what follows.

earlier in the day, Dokhturov might have been able to rally his troops and per-haps receive reinforcements from Urusov in order to stabilize his hold on Dürnstein and trap the French. By the time his fight began, however, Dupont's forces were near at hand.

Dupont had not intended to race toward Dürnstein on November 11. Mortier had no idea of the Russian position or intentions and had not ordered Dupont to close the gap between his and Gazan's Divisions. When Dupont heard the beginning of the fight at Stein—sound carries well among the steep cliffs that line the Danube in this region—he hastened his march. When the sound diminished, however, either because of a trick of the acoustics or a lull in the battle, Dupont, who had also learned of Mortier's "success" in pushing toward Stein, slowed down once more. He decided, however, to send the 1st Hussars and 9th Light Infantry Regiments to Weissenkirchen and ordered them to send outposts toward Dürnstein. He deployed the 32nd Line Infantry Regiment between Weissenkirchen and Spitz and the 96th Line in Spitz.[58]

At 4:00 P.M., the outposts of the 1st Hussars reported that Russians were descending from the defiles before Dürnstein and the hussars and the 9th Light began to attack them. The odds were heavily in the Russians' favor at first. The road between Dürnstein and Weissenkirchen is very narrow and is bordered for most of its length by steep hills. Although the Russians faced a hussars and a light infantry regiment with only two battalions, it is unlikely that the French were able to develop their full combat power with any degree of efficiency. A terrible melee ensued that the arrival of the 32nd Line only intensified.

Gvozdev, the commander of the two Russian battalions, was very hard-pressed. Dupont's troops kept moving up the hills into his flank and threaten-ing to envelop him, and Gvozdev was forced back toward Dürnstein.[59] He broke free momentarily and began preparations to march in order to rejoin Dokhturov's Column, but he received orders from the commanders standing atop the Schlossberg that he must hold and withdraw as slowly as possible. He set about that grim business with determination.

From the Schloss Dürnstein it is easy to see the location of this battle, and Russian observers there were surely aware of what was going on, whether or not Gvozdev managed to get word out. The allied leaders knew that it was not enough to order Gvozdev to hold, and so FML Schmitt took a battalion of the Briansk Regiment to support Gvozdev, thus evening out the odds.* Dupont describes the ensuing scene: "It was night, everyone was mixed together, the soldiers were fighting body to body. We remained in this position as extraordi-nary as it was horrible for close to an hour." Both sides thought the other would surrender, and some Russian soldiers laid down their arms only to take them up again when the French let down their guard.[60]

---

*See Appendix A.

In the end, the greater weight of the French forces prevailed, and Gvozdev managed to break free for the last time and "follow the traces of the column without the least hindrance," thereby opening the road for Dupont's advance.[61] Dokhturov decided to withdraw, pressured from east and west in a darkness lightened only by the fires of the Loibens, without cavalry or sufficient artillery, having left both behind when the column came to nearly impassible defiles. He pulled his column back up into the mountains around the Schlossberg and allowed Dupont's troops to link up with the bedraggled remnants of Gazan's Division.[62]

This relief came not a moment too soon for Mortier. Although the French fought gallantly and desperately, there was more than one moment of panic in their ranks, and large numbers of French troops, including a general and other senior officers, attempted to flee across the Danube in boats. Not all were successful: the boat carrying General Graindorge became caught in the piers of the burned Danube bridge and its occupants were taken prisoner.[63] Despite the arrival of Dupont's troops at Dürnstein, Mortier had lost his stomach for further adventures. As the Russians withdrew once more toward Krems, Mortier had most of his corps ferried across the Danube to lick its wounds.*

It is not possible to fix the number of casualties in this battle with any precision.[64] Dupont reported a loss of 106 killed and wounded (which seems low for the ferocity and duration of combat he described). The Russians claimed they lost 2,000 men and took 1,500 French prisoners. An officer of the French 4th Hussars Regiment declared that his unit was destroyed.[65] Napoleon called it "a day of massacre," claimed that the French had killed or wounded 4,000 Russians and taken 1,300 prisoners, and admitted that Mortier suffered "considerable" losses.[66] An Austrian account proposes more than 5,000 casualties for the French and 4,000 for the Russians.[67] The loss in lives was certainly great.†

For Kutuzov, however, the price was worth it. Whatever casualties he had inflicted on the French, he had rendered Mortier's Corps *hors de combat* for the remainder of the campaign. More importantly, he had finally managed to break contact completely and believed himself free to continue his withdrawal toward the oncoming Russian reinforcements without worrying about his rear.[68]

Dürnstein was a remarkable battle that undermines the traditional image of Kutuzov and the Russian and Austrian armies. When Kutuzov learned of

---

*Alombert-Goget, *Combat de Dürrenstein*, pp. 153–154. Mortier established his headquarters and those of his divisions on the right bank of the river. Dumonceau's troops relieved Dupont's in position at Weissenkirchen and Spitz.

†Egger (*Das Gefecht bei Dürnstein-Loiben*, p. 21) points out that the economic losses to the region were also staggering, including the destruction of the vineyards on the plain of the Loibens and also at Dürnstein and Krems. The damage has long since been repaired and the vineyards of the Wachau (including Dürnstein and the Loibens) and the Kamptal (including Krems) now produce some of the best Rieslings and Grüner Veltliners in the world.

the mistake Mortier had made in advancing too rapidly, without proper reconnaissance and in too dispersed a manner, he took counsel about how best to inflict a stunning blow on the enemy. FML Schmitt offered a complicated maneuver scheme, as Austrian staff officers were prone to do, and Kutuzov accepted it without demur. Surprisingly, it went off. There were hitches, primarily Dokhturov's inability to achieve his designated position on the Danube in time. But the failure of timing did not upset the overall effect. Russian troops under Russian commanders and Austrian staff officers carried out Schmitt's complicated movement, maneuvered in a flurry of independent detachments, surprised the enemy and were surprised by him, and won. We are familiar with the Russians as fierce fighters and with their skill in retreating. At Dürnstein they demonstrated that they were skillful maneuverers, sometimes more skillful than the French.

Nor can we accept the image of Kutuzov that Tolstoy painted so deftly in *War and Peace*. Fat, lugubrious, passive, Tolstoy's Kutuzov plays no important part in battle, rarely gives an order, and generally does not understand what is going on.* But Kutuzov was no such general. He adopted and implemented a complex plan and then continued to oversee the battle and issue orders to his subordinates that they executed to good effect. He had more control over the situation than Mortier, even though a substantial part of the fight occurred beyond the range of his communications. At Dürnstein we see a skillful, aggressive Kutuzov seizing on an enemy's mistake and making him pay for it. We shall have to seek other explanations for Kutuzov's apparent lassitude at subsequent battles.

Austrian failures undid Kutuzov's success, however. Within two days of leaving Krems, Kutuzov learned that the Austrian troops set to guard the bridges over the Danube at Vienna had failed and that Murat's Cavalry was once again racing to cut him off from reinforcements. The chase, which the Russians had thought finally over, was on again.

Schöngrabern

Napoleon was furious when he understood what Mortier was facing. He transferred his headquarters from Mölk to St. Pölten in order to get word faster. He

---

*Tolstoy does not narrate the Battle of Dürnstein in *War and Peace*, despite the fact that Prince Andrei first saw combat and was lightly wounded there. Tolstoy preferred instead to describe the chaotic melee at Schöngrabern in great detail, probably because it suited his larger thesis about the chaotic, incomprehensible, and uncontrollable nature of combat and the irrelevance of senior leaders in such fights. He would have been hard-pressed to support such a thesis with the Battle of Dürnstein. *War and Peace*; Alombert, *Combat de Dürrenstein*, pp. 128–132; Egger, *Das Gefecht bei Hollabrunn und Schöngrabern, 1805. Militärhistorische Schriftenreihe* (Vienna: Heeresgeschichtliches Museum, Militärwissenschaftliches Institut, 1974), 27:148–173.

berated Soult for following Murat's orders (much to the marshal's confusion and discomfiture) and commanded him to rush in person to Mautern to get the news.[69] "Officers, aides-de-camp, everyone who was at hand he sent for news."[70] He sent a fiery telegram to Murat (His Majesty's "will was not that you rush to Vienna like children") and partially relieved him of his pseudo-command of the vanguard by informing him that he would send orders directly to Davout and Soult.[71] During the day following the battle, in which he received little reliable news, he was wracked by the fear that the Russians had captured a substantial portion of Mortier's Corps, perhaps even Mortier himself.[72]

One of the predominant characteristics of this part of the campaign is that Napoleon did not continually consider and develop alternative plans as he had done in the preceding months.* The collapse of the possibility of naval success in August had been followed by clear and purposeful movements supported by previous preparations. His consideration of alternate possible scenarios during the Ulm campaign had been mirrored in constant troop movements and readjustments of his deployments and marches. But in November 1805 Napoleon had made no remotely adequate preparations for the possibility that Kutuzov would cross the Danube at Krems. When the Russians had done so and had crushed Mortier's Corps as well, Napoleon found no good plan ready to hand. Instead, he screamed at Murat and, unjustly, at Soult, and commanded the disgraced marshals to cross the Danube at Vienna immediately.[73]

This task should have been difficult if not impossible. The Danube in 1805 flowed through Vienna in a different channel from the ones it now has. Three main arms divided the left and right banks, spanned by three bridges, the longest more than 550 paces across. The Austrians guarded the bridges with a detachment of 13,000 men and had prepared them for rapid demolition.[74] If they had executed their plans, Murat would have found himself standing before a broad, fast river and gazing at the smoldering remnants of the only good way across it, just as Napoleon's officers were doing upstream at Mautern. Ordering a subordinate to achieve a nearly impossible goal to retrieve a desperate situation can hardly be called developing an alternative plan.

Napoleon's angry letters to Murat crushed him. "The Prince was extremely affected by the letter Your Majesty wrote him the day before yesterday," General Bertrand wrote the emperor. "He has lost courage, energy, and activity. He constantly returns to the thing that is affecting him so profoundly. . . .

---

*The image popular among modern historians that Napoleon collected himself and calmly proceeded with an alternate plan at this juncture is incorrect. David Chandler writes, "Nevertheless, the French Emperor was the master of the alternative plan and had already devised an improvised *manoeuvre sur Hollabrun* to remedy the damage" (*Campaigns of Napoleon*, p. 406); David Gates writes, "However, Napoleon was already adjusting his army's dispositions to renew the pressure on the Russians" (*The Napoleonic Wars, 1803–1815* [New York: Arnold, 1997], p. 26).

Today he can certainly not serve Your Majesty as he could have before. His head is not with him."[75] Murat himself wrote Napoleon, "[Berthier]'s letter distressed me; Y[our] M[ajesty's] shattered me, and nevertheless I do not deserve such cruel treatment." He went on to defend himself at length and with some justice.* The prospects were not good for a plan to recover rapidly from this setback.

Napoleon at first assumed that the Austrians would cut the Vienna bridges as they and the Russians had done at all previous river crossings. He urged and then ordered Murat to "surprise" them if they were still intact, but he also ordered massive preparations for crossing the Danube using boats or finding a way to bridge it. He told Bernadotte to prepare to cross near Mölk and Murat near Klosterneuburg.[76] He was confident that he could get across the river, but he could not have been certain about when. In addition, he had no good idea of what the Russians intended to do. On November 13 he was still unsure whether they meant to remain at Krems (which he rightly regarded as idiocy) or withdraw, either to Moravia or Bohemia.[77] Only on that day did Soult and Mortier report that the Russians had abandoned Krems during the night and were marching for Moravia.[78]

Murat seemed to recover his spirits somewhat at the prospect of redeeming himself by seizing the Danube bridges against all odds. He negotiated an unopposed passage through Vienna, taking advantage of the rebellious mood of the population resulting from the heavy taxes Francis had levied to pay for the war and from the departure of the emperor and his court to the safety of Brünn. On November 13, the lead elements of Murat's Corps, including Oudinot's and Suchet's Divisions, marched to the right bank head of the Tabor bridge and halted there, facing the Austrian defenders.[79]

The overall Austrian commander at this position was FML Carl Auersperg, who last held a command twelve years ago and had only reluctantly accepted this one six days before. Murat's slow pursuit had allowed FML Kienmayer to join him there. Auersperg had orders to maintain his headquarters and his forces opposite the left bank bridgehead. He had withdrawn both to a position farther north, however, because he found the ground in front of the bridge to be poor as a tactical position and lacking in good drinking water. Consequently he was some distance away from the crisis point at the decisive moment.[80]

---

*Murat to Napoleon, 13 November 1805, in Alombert, *Combat de Dürnstein*, p. 178. Murat's explanations of his actions vary considerably over the course of his correspondence with Napoleon, and it seems clear that he was more intent on finding a tone that would placate his master than on making clear his true feelings. Most of them, however, contain the conviction that Napoleon wanted him to seize Vienna in order to facilitate negotiations to end the war. Murat's knowledge of repeated messages between Napoleon and Francis (see below) no doubt reinforced this belief.

Murat took advantage of the fact that a senior Austrian envoy, FML Gyulai, had crossed the lines the day before with a diplomatic message to Napoleon, part of a negotiation begun in November.[81] Both Napoleon and the Austrian commanders placed high hopes in these exchanges. On November 12, Count Wrbna, the commander of the Vienna garrison, ordered Auersperg not to burn the bridges prematurely so that couriers could use them to move back and forth. That same day, Auersperg wrote to Kienmayer of these events and noted "the burning of the bridges will probably not be necessary any more."[82] Napoleon also seemed to place some hope in the negotiations. He ordered Murat to send Gyulai, or anyone else asking to speak to him, to imperial headquarters at once. He even said that if Gyulai asked Murat to suspend his march on Vienna, he should do so.[83]

In the end nothing came of these negotiations. Francis was not ready to agree to terms that would satisfy the victorious Bonaparte. But the fact that negotiations were under way was known to both Kienmayer and Auersperg and could hardly have been kept secret from the troops guarding the Vienna bridges—and watching the imperial couriers go back and forth.[84] Generals Bertrand, Moissel, and Lanusse approached the troops and demanded to speak to Auersperg who, they said, had asked them to come earlier that morning. Their action caused confusion in the Austrian lines, strengthened by the fact that Wrbna had allowed Murat's troops free passage through the city. Auersperg came to the conclusion that an armistice had been signed and Bertrand and his colleagues did everything in their power to strengthen that belief.

They asked if Auersperg was on his way to the meeting. The commander of the Austrian troops at the bridge, Colonel Geringer, whom Kienmayer had informed of the negotiations, raced off to find out.[85] The French generals insisted that Geringer forbear from firing the bridge or take full responsibility for violating the armistice; for their part, they promised not to take the bridge by force. When Auersperg and Kienmayer learned of these events, they fell to arguing. Kienmayer wanted to destroy the bridge at once but Auersperg demurred. As they were thus debating, the French acted. Relying on the confusion they had sown among the Austrian troops and the fact that they had managed to drive off the soldiers' commanders, Oudinot's grenadiers rushed the bridge and seized the Austrian guns that were supposed to protect it.

Auersperg and Kienmayer arrived at this point and demanded to speak to Murat. The situation was already well in the marshal's hands, however, and there was not much for Auersperg to do. His declaration to Murat that he was "more French than you might think," however, was a worrisome indication of his state of mind. Kienmayer's willingness to promise to "separate himself from the Russians" in return for Murat's pledge not to fire on his withdrawing troops showed that the infection had spread. These declarations clearly reflected more than the demoralization of the moment; the catastrophe at Ulm had hit the Austrians very hard indeed.*

The seizure of the Tabor bridge reversed the overall situation once again. Murat's Cavalry, followed by Soult's and Lannes's infantry, began racing north from Vienna to try to cut the Russians off before they could reach Moravia. The breathing spell that Kutuzov had hoped to enjoy after his victory at Dürnstein evaporated. If he and Francis had still been clinging to the notion of holding the notional fortified bridgehead at Krems while awaiting reinforcements, the situation would have been dire. But Francis had already changed his mind.

The Austrian emperor had decided that the most important priority was to unite Kutuzov's army with the reinforcements coming from Moravia. On November 12, he ordered the Russian commander to abandon the position at Krems and march toward Olmütz as rapidly as possible. He told Kutuzov that he had ordered Buxhöwden to advance by forced march to join him, and Auersperg to send word at once if forced to retreat.[86] Kutuzov prepared his army for the march that very day, acknowledged Francis's note the next day, and promised to have the army moving early in the morning of November 14. He also notified Ferdinand that if the two armies were to link up, it would have to be in Moravia.[87] A bright spot on the horizon was the arrival of the 6th Column of Russian troops at Hollabrunn, which more than made good the losses sustained at Dürnstein.[88]

The need to link up with that column, however, along with Francis's injunction to proceed along the Vienna–Olmütz road, forced Kutuzov to march through the inhospitable country northeast of Krems. Few major roads crossed the area and Kutuzov's line of march was a confused zigzag around woods, fields, and streams.[89] During this march Kutuzov learned of Murat's coup. Francis wrote him two notes on November 14. The first indicated only that the French had managed to get a corps across the Danube at Vienna and that he had found it necessary to replace Auersperg with Prince Liechtenstein. Francis mused briefly on the possibility of Kutuzov's repeating the Dürnstein maneuver—another such victory, he thought, could be "most decisive." On balance, however, he thought it better for Kutuzov to withdraw and link up with the reinforcements.[90]

---

*The account of these events in Chandler gives all credit to Murat and Lannes (*Campaigns of Napoleon*, p. 407). If that had been the case, it is extremely unlikely that Murat, eager to demonstrate his prowess and redeem himself in Napoleon's eyes, would have given the credit in his own report (which Chandler does not appear to have consulted) to Bertrand and his colleagues. Christopher Duffy's contention that Auersperg's debacle "denotes a failure of the will and intellect, if not downright imbecility" (*Austerlitz, 1805* [London: Seeley Service, 1977], p. 64) ignores the confusion resulting from the diplomatic negotiations then under way and the general collapse of Austrian will after Ulm. By subtly emphasizing some aspects and deemphasizing others, historians have removed Austrian decisionmaking from its political and diplomatic context and thereby exaggerated the incompetence of the Habsburg army or at least its senior leadership.

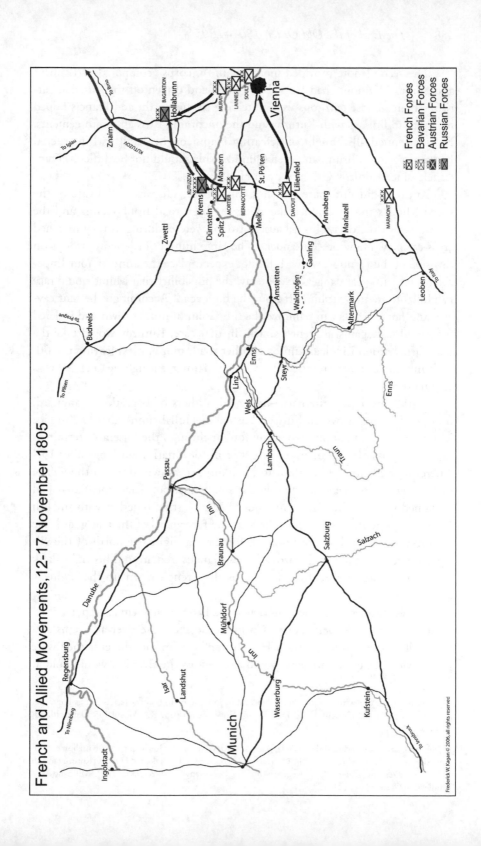

French and Allied Movements, 12–17 November 1805

French Forces · **Bavarian Forces** · **Austrian Forces** · **Russian Forces**

Vienna

BAGRATION
Hollabrunn
MURAT
LANNES
SOULT

To Brno
To Igalu
Znaim

KUTUZOV

Maurern
St. Pö ten

KUTUZOV
Krems
Dürnstein
Spitz
MORTIER
BERNADOTTE
Melk

DAVOUT
Lilienfeld
Annaberg
Mariazell
MARMONT
Leoben

Zwettl

To Prague
Budweis

To Pilsen

Amstetten
Gaming
Waidhofen
Altenmark

Enns
Steyr

Linz
Wels
Enns

Lambach
Traun

Salzburg
Salzach

Passau
Inn

Braunau

Danube

Regensburg

To Nürnburg

Isar
Landshut

Mühldorf
Inn

Wasserburg
Kufstein

Munich

Ingolstadt

To Innsbruck

The second note provided more detail. A "corps" composed of Lannes's and Soult's "divisions" had crossed at Vienna and driven off the Austrian garrisons there. Those garrisons were retreating to the north, and Francis hoped for them to link up with Kutuzov and the oncoming Russian reinforcements. He abandoned all thought of defeating Napoleon in detail and instructed Kutuzov to get to Brünn and even Olmütz. This should not be difficult, Francis felt, since Kutuzov was "already in Hollabrunn."[91]

Kutuzov did not share Francis's confidence. He was well aware of the speed Murat's troops could make along the high road from Vienna and the contrast with the delays his exhausted troops were enduring as they marched cross-country. He wrote Alexander, "The large number of [enemy] troops on this side of the Danube, which I did not expect, place the army of Your Imperial Majesty in great danger." He foresaw the possibility that Murat would race to Hollabrunn and cut him off from the high road. Accordingly, he sent cavalry and horse artillery to reinforce the 6th Column in that town and ordered it to hold fast against a French attack. In that case, Kutuzov would take the main army around Hollabrunn by another road, more or less leaving the 6th Column to its fate, provided it could hold long enough against Murat's vanguard.[92]

In the end it was the battle-hardened soldiers of Bagration's vanguard, now the rear guard (which Kutuzov rushed to Hollabrunn), that had to face Murat, Soult, and Lannes. Bagration fought through the miserable terrain as rapidly as possible and managed to get to his destination on November 15.* There he found the ground not to his liking, so he withdrew to the village of Schöngrabern. Bagration posted the small Austrian detachment that had remained with the Russian army under FML Nostitz, together with the 6th Jaegers Regiment, south of the village as the rear guard of the rear guard. He deployed the main body of his small force on a slight rise north of the village. There he waited as Kutuzov's forces maneuvered around his right flank and rear on the road to Brünn—and as the French raced up the highway from Vienna.†

As Murat opened up the route across the Danube at Vienna, Napoleon developed a new plan. Bernadotte's Corps would cross the river at Krems and then follow the Russians toward Hollabrunn, Znaim, or wherever they were going. Mortier's battered troops would also recross the river but would hold at

---

*The 6th Column was withdrawn from Hollabrunn to join the main body at Jetzelsdorf as Bagration moved into position. Hohenlohe to Francis, 17 November 1805, KA AFA 1805 Deutschland, XI/68½.

†Bagration's rear guard included the Podolia, Azov, and Kiev Grenadiers Regiments, one battalion each of the Novgorod and Narva Regiments, the Chernigov Dragoons, and the Pavlograd Hussars (Kutuzov march order from Krems to Znaim, 12 November 1805, in Beskrovnyi, *Kutuzov*, doc. 169). Mikhailovskii-Danilevskii, *Opisanie*, pp. 121–122.

Krems to serve as Bernadotte's reserve. Napoleon did not imagine that Mortier's men would see combat unless the Russians were stupid enough to try to march on Linz. At the same time, Murat, Lannes, and Soult would cross at Vienna and race up the Vienna-Brünn road. Napoleon hoped that this force, operating together with Bernadotte's Corps, would trap Kutuzov in a vice and destroy his army before he could link up with Buxhöwden.[93]

Bernadotte, however, made a long job of getting across the river, probably because there were not enough boats at Krems to ferry two entire corps (which Napoleon estimated at about 25,000 men total) rapidly.* Napoleon's sharp tongue could not overcome this physical constraint, and Bernadotte did not get across until November 16.[94] In the meantime, Murat was having a hard time determining what the Russians were doing. He knew that they were retreating on Znaim and that their headquarters was at Hollabrunn. He rightly identified Bagration's forces as the rear guard, noting that those forces had been serving as the rear guard since Braunau. He knew that Kutuzov had received some reinforcements but that the larger reinforcement was still a distance away. But he did not know, as he approached the Russian position on November 15, in what strength the Russians held Hollabrunn and he was reluctant to attack before the infantry had come up.[95]

Murat also seemed confused about the purpose of his maneuver. He understood that the immediate purpose of Napoleon's operational plan was to "fall on the enemy and prevent his juncture with the reinforcements that await him at Olmütz." But he was also impressed by the collapse of Austrian morale he had seen in Vienna and during his march north. Two Austrian battalions, he reported, had offered to fight with him against the Russians and their own government. "All the Austrians," he continued, "are separating from the Russians, this is positive, Sire, it is truly an extraordinary thing; Your Majesty will be surprised yourself by it; the Austrian officers no longer conceal it: they all want the Emperor Napoleon to command them."[96]

These words contain a great deal of exaggeration, of course. Many tens of thousands of Austrian troops across the monarchy remained true to their oath and continued to march and fight for Francis and their homeland. It is the impact this belief had on Murat that is important here. Napoleon's vanguard commander clearly saw Austria as a defeated country. In his mind, only the continued presence of the Russians protracted the war, and the Russians seemed eager to withdraw as rapidly as possible. Perhaps because of the tensions and resentments that existed between the marshal and his commander, Murat did not communicate these thoughts clearly to Napoleon. Napoleon, for his part, did not read his subordinate's mind. The French emperor be-

---

*Bernadotte reported that he had only fourteen boats of various sorts and not enough men to operate them or to bridge the river. Bernadotte to Napoleon, 16 November 1805, SHAT C² 8.

lieved that the Austrians were far from defeated—Francis's unwillingness to meet his peace demands convinced him of that—and he strongly doubted that the Russians were withdrawing in order to abandon their allies. Napoleon continued to see the campaign ending with a decisive battle that he needed to prepare for; Murat saw the campaign as effectively over, but for the signing of the peace treaty. Murat, then, approached Hollabrunn uncertain of the size of the enemy before him and confident that the war had already been won. He was an easy mark for the deception the Russians now played on him.

The game began on November 15, when Murat sent word to Nostitz during an exchange of skirmishing fire that an armistice had been signed and he need fight no longer.* Nostitz was deceived and his small force marched off the field. The Russian troops that had been holding the advanced outpost south of Schöngrabern with Nostitz's troops were forced to withdraw and join the main body.

Murat tried the same trick with Kutuzov, but the Russian commander turned that trick back on him. Kutuzov sent Wintzingerode back to Murat offering to withdraw Russia's forces entirely from the Habsburg monarchy if Murat would permit them to march unmolested. Kutuzov never intended to honor this agreement and probably never expected Napoleon to ratify it. Rather, he meant to gain as many days of respite as possible during the armistice that held while the two sovereigns mulled over the agreement.[97]

Murat fell for the ploy. He wrote to Napoleon, somewhat defensively, that he was not ready to attack Bagration, since he did not have enough infantry available. The armistice required both armies to stay in position until it was ratified, which Murat considered an advantage, since the Russians might otherwise slip off in the night. Above all, he believed that this armistice was the "preliminaries of peace that I know to be the object of your desires." In the worst case, he concluded, Napoleon could disavow the armistice and Murat, having given the Russians the stipulated four hours' warning, would attack and demolish them.[98] The next day, he assured Napoleon that the Russians had abided by the terms of the armistice—Bagration's force was right where it had been the day before.[99]

Murat was fortunate that the telephone had not yet been invented, still less the video teleconference. He was thus spared from actually hearing or

---

*Egger, *Schöngrabern*, pp. 13–14; Hohenlohe to Francis, 17 November 1805, KA AFA 1805 Deutschland, XI/68½; Kutuzov to Alexander, 15 November 1805, in Beskrovnyi, *Kutuzov*, doc. 175. Murat, on the other hand, claims that it was Nostitz who approached him (Murat to Napoleon, 15 November 1805, in Le Brethon, *Lettres et documents*, doc. 2247). There is no corroboration for Murat's version of events, whereas the Russian and Austrian accounts tally with each other. Since Kutuzov declares that Murat sent a messenger to him with the same message, moreover (Kutuzov to Alexander, 19 November 1805, in Beskrovnyi, *Kutuzov*, doc. 187) the reconstruction of events that makes the most sense is that the French marshal sent messengers to both Nostitz and Kutuzov at around the same time.

seeing Napoleon when the emperor received word of this latest mistake. "I cannot find the terms in which to express my discontent with you," Napoleon thundered. "You command only my vanguard and you have no right to make an armistice without my orders; you are making me lose the fruits of an entire campaign. Break the armistice at once and march on the enemy. . . . You have let yourself be duped by an aide-de-camp of the [Russian] emperor; I cannot imagine how you could have let yourself be duped at this point."[100] Napoleon was right, of course. As Murat placidly contemplated the service he had done his master by making the armistice, Kutuzov's troops were receding at forced marches from their rear guard. Murat truly seemed to have snatched defeat from the jaws of victory. The Russians gained an even greater advantage from Murat's folly than they had any right to expect, moreover, owing to the circumstances in which the battle was fought.

The Battle of Schöngrabern cannot be accurately reconstructed in detail. Napoleon's arrival on the field the day after the battle obviated the need for Murat to provide him with a written narrative of an event that he probably preferred to forget.[101] The Austrian narrative of the battle is more concerned with Nostitz's behavior than with the fight itself, for obvious reasons, and for the Russian accounts we must rely on the laconic Bagration.*

The odds were as uneven as they had been at Dürnstein, only tipped in the other direction: 25,000–30,000 Frenchmen including substantial cavalry forces faced 6,000–8,000 Russians on nearly open terrain. Kutuzov was certain that he was sending Bagration and his troops to their death, consoling himself with the thought that he was thereby saving the rest of the army. "'Well, good-by, Prince,' said he to Bagration, 'My blessing, and may Christ be with you in your great endeavor!' His face suddenly softened and tears came into his eyes. With his left hand he drew Bagration toward him, and with his right, on which he wore a ring, he made the sign of the cross over him."† Kutuzov rode off expecting to hear nothing more from his rearguard commander.

Murat deployed his forces during the armistice (in violation of its terms), sending detachments to the left and right of Schöngrabern in preparation for the planned envelopment of Bagration's troops. Bagration spread his line thin and managed, despite his numerical inferiority, to maintain a reserve with him at Grund, along with the massed artillery at his disposal. He expected to

---

*Hohenlohe to Francis, 17 November 1805, KA AFA 1805 Deutschland, XI/68½; Bagration to Kutuzov, 17 November 1805, in Beskrovnyi, *Kutuzov*, doc. 180; Kutuzov to Alexander, 19 November 1805, in Beskrovnyi, *Kutuzov*, doc. 187; Mikhailovskii-Danilevskii, *Opisanie*, pp. 128–131. I have found no French accounts of this battle in the printed sources or in the SHAT.

†Tolstoy, *War and Peace*, p. 145. Although the words and the precise actions reflect literary license, Kutuzov's reports show that the emotions Tolstoy represents were real and vivid.

have the four hours' warning promised him in the armistice before any attack began, although Nostitz's defection had deprived him of the ability to ensure advanced warning of any French movements.

When Napoleon's message arrived in the afternoon of November 16, it galvanized Murat into furious and unwise action. Rather than taking the time to deploy his forces carefully, he accepted Napoleon's screed at face value and launched the attack at once. His artillerymen immediately began shelling the Russian lines, and the Russian gunners near Grund responded vigorously. Whether accidentally or not, the Russians managed to set the village of Schöngrabern on fire. Oudinot's grenadiers and the cavalry reserve gathered in the village to attack the Russian center were caught up in the maelstrom. Worse still, they feared that stores of ammunition and powder in the town would go up. They therefore began trying to put out the fire and move their volatile stores away from it, giving Bagration's center a respite, by his own reckoning, of about two hours.

This delay was unfortunate for the French; Murat was not able to start the attack until 5:00 P.M. on this cold, short November day. While his center was dealing with the fire in Schöngrabern, Soult's Corps on the left wing attacked the Russian right under Ulanius with infantry and cavalry. Considering the French numerical superiority, it is difficult to understand how the Russians beat off their attacks. Bagration's troops had one significant advantage—they had no need or intention of holding their ground. As Soult's troops pressed, Ulanius beat them off and withdrew, along with the rest of the Russian line.

Lannes's attacks on the Russian left were more successful, cutting the Russian battalions off from one another and threatening to envelop them. Bagration combined retreat with the timely commitment of his reserves to the threatened sectors to beat off the French attacks, but darkness and confusion played a greater role than the Russians' skill in saving the day. By the time Oudinot and the French center finally got into action, it was too dark and the situation too confused for their attack to be decisive. The failure of the French center to carry the day persuaded Murat to call off the struggle late in the evening. He had obviously failed to break through the rear guard and could not prevent Kutuzov's army from slipping away.

Kutuzov was overjoyed to see Bagration the next day. "I will not ask about your losses," he declared. "You're alive—that's enough for me!"[102] He called for Alexander to promote Bagration and rain awards on him—which the tsar did. Murat's confusion and thoughtless preparation for battle had saved Bagration's detachment from certain annihilation—and Kutuzov's army from the same fate, if its commander is to be believed. It allowed most of Bagration's troops to rejoin the main Russian army, which proceeded unmolested along the road to Brünn and Olmütz, where it finally linked up with the oncoming reinforcements. The chase had ended. The Russians had escaped.

Conclusion

Napoleon did not initially intend to cut the Russians off from their reinforcements, since his faulty intelligence suggested that the task was impossible. When he recognized the opportunity to do so, however, he eagerly embraced it and hurled his army across the length of Austria in an effort to destroy Kutuzov's isolated army. The odds were overwhelming and the Russians should have had no chance to escape even an ordinary general, let alone one as talented as Napoleon.

Napoleon's defenders would like to argue that the fault was Murat's, and the repeated errors the cavalry commander made give credence to this interpretation. But the emperor must share some of the blame. His communications with his vanguard commander were intermittent and unclear. He never specifically told Murat what his mission was, and he was deaf to the indications in Murat's letters that the vanguard commander did not understand what was desired of him. On some occasions, Napoleon's multifarious obligations as head of state clearly distracted him; at other times explanations for this miscommunication are harder to find. The miscommunication was central, however, to Napoleon's failure to chase down and destroy an isolated enemy army.

The Russians, on the other hand, performed brilliantly. Outnumbered nearly 5 to 1 by an army fresh from a stunning victory, Kutuzov and his generals retreated the length of Austria and emerged in Moravia with an intact and battle-worthy force. French mistakes made Kutuzov's escape possible, but his own actions turned the possibility into reality. At Amstetten, Dürnstein, and Schöngrabern, Kutuzov skillfully deployed his meager forces and maneuvered them well. The Battle of Dürnstein was particularly impressive in its use of terrain, surprise, deception, and determined maneuver. Kutuzov positioned himself well to oversee and direct operations, and he and his subordinates retained full control over the course of a confused battle spread over miles of rugged terrain. At Schöngrabern, Bagration showed both skill and determination while winning one of the most impressive defensive victories of the war. Individual Russian soldiers fought as well or better than their vaunted French opponents, who had nothing but grudging praise for them in their reports. Against all odds and despite the repeated failures of his allies, Kutuzov managed not only to save his army but to preserve and even enhance its honor.

Above all, Napoleon's failure to crush Kutuzov forced him to reevaluate his strategic position and choose a new course of action. The situation was much darker for him than it had been a month earlier, for hundreds of thousands of allied troops were swirling all around him and his own army was spread out across Austria. To understand Napoleon's predicament fully, we must turn back now to the other operations, both diplomatic and military, that were carried out during his fruitless chase.

19

Forgotten Theaters

Italy

The War of 1805 was the most complex of the Napoleonic Wars before 1813. As the Russians retreated from Schöngrabern toward Brünn and Olmütz, hundreds of thousands of Austrian, Prussian, Swedish, British, and other Russian forces were in motion elsewhere in Europe. Few of these forces saw battle; none participated in the events that decided the outcome of the war. Yet we cannot simply ignore them. The commanders of the time factored them into all of their decisions and they thus profoundly influenced the decisive campaigns of which they formed no physical part. It is not possible to evaluate Napoleon's decisions or those of his enemies without understanding the full context in which they were made.*

---

*The principal modern historical accounts of this war make no significant mention of theaters other than southern Germany, Austria, and Moravia. See David Chandler, *The Campaigns of Napoleon* (New York: Macmillan, 1966); Scott Bowden, *Napoleon and Austerlitz: An Unprecedentedly Detailed Combat Study of Napoleon's Epic Ulm-Austerlitz Campaigns of 1805* (Chicago: Emperor's, 1997); Christopher Duffy, *Austerlitz, 1805* (London: Seeley Service, 1977); David Gates, *The Napoleonic Wars, 1803–1815* (New York: Arnold, 1997). Even in a biography of Archduke Charles, Gunther Rothenberg offers a scant four pages on the theater in which Charles commanded (Gunther E. Rothenberg, *Napoleon's Great Adversary: Archduke Charles and the Austrian Army, 1792–1814* [New York: Sarpedon, 1982]). More detailed descriptions of the Italian campaign can only be found in some of the Austrian narratives, such as the following: Alois Moriggl, *Der Feldzug von Ulm und seine Folgen für Oesterreich überhaupt und für Tirol insbesonders* (Innsbruck: Verlag der Wagner'schen Buchhandlung, 1861); Oskar Criste, *Erzherzog Carl von Osterreich* (Vienna: Wilhelm Braumüller, 1912); and Moriz Edlen von Angeli, *Erzherzog Carl von Osterreich als Feldherr und Heeresorganisator* (Vienna: Wilhelm Braumüller, 1897). I have located only one short pamphlet that addresses the Battle of Caldiero (nearly comparable in scale, if not significance, to Austerlitz) in any detail: Karl Schikofsky, "Die Schlacht von Caldiero 1805," *Separatabdruck aus dem Organ der Militärwissenschaftlichen Vereine* 71, no. 2 (1905): 158–184. The absence of detailed modern studies of these events outside of the decisive theater is understandable. Most accounts of the Napoleonic Wars focus on events at which Napoleon was present; the overwhelming majority of military accounts focus on battles. Since Napoleon was never in Italy or Prussia during this campaign and there were no battles apart from Caldiero, ignoring them seems quite natural. It is, nevertheless, a serious mistake.

The fact that the largest of the allied armies, Charles's force in Italy, did not take part in the decisive events of the war does not mean that it could not have done so, had Austria's senior commanders made different decisions. Nor was it inevitable that the 200,000 Prussian troops mobilizing in response to Russian threats and then Napoleon's violation of Prussian territory would see no combat in this war. The nonparticipation of these nearly 300,000 troops, which could have crushed Napoleon's overextended forces had they been used skillfully, is as important to understand as the movements of Napoleon's 150,000 men or Kutuzov's 45,000. Before turning to the decisive battle of the war, we must first follow the movements of troops in other theaters, as well as the decisions of their commanders.

Plans

The Austrian and allied war plans placed the largest single army in Italy with the mission of launching an attack as soon as war broke out. Francis entrusted Charles with the command of that army, thereby ensuring it high priority in its plans and operations. Yet Charles never launched an attack, fought one battle, and then withdrew after hearing of Mack's capitulation at Ulm. These nonevents are as puzzling as the dramatic events taking place to the north and require as much explanation.

The obvious personal differences between Mack and Charles played no small role in the different campaigns in their respective theaters. Where Mack was aggressive and determined, Charles was fearful and passive. Mack played an important part in driving Austria to fight a war that Charles heartily opposed. Nothing could be less surprising than that the one waged a campaign in Germany so aggressive that it bordered on foolhardy while the other turned a plan for a massive offensive into a headlong retreat.

These superficial differences do not explain the differences in the two campaigns, however. Charles was an experienced professional commander. Whatever his misgivings about fighting the war, he put his whole heart and mind into performing his duty. Neither Francis nor Mack ever rebuked him for his passivity, questioned his preparations or actions, or wondered at his decisions. There was more here than differing personalities or policy disagreements.

In 1805 the Italian theater differed from the German in two crucial respects: it was farther from the core Habsburg lands, and it was the only Austrian territory bordering French territory. It is more than twice as far from Vienna to Verona as it is from Vienna to Innsbruck as the crow flies. As the soldier marches, the distance is even greater, since the road to Innsbruck is a more or less straight highway along the Danube plain for most of its length, whereas the Verona road crosses several mountain chains.* Consequently Mack's army was concentrated and ready for action along the Bavarian border six or eight weeks before Charles's finished concentrating along the Adige.† Aware of this delay in the mobilization of the army he was to command, Charles did not arrive in Italy until September 20.[1]

The differential mobilization schedules for the two armies highlight a crucial element of the Austrian war plans. They all described the Italian army beginning hostilities by crossing the Adige at the start of the war. Yet it was clear from the moment the mobilization schedules had been drafted (a process in which both Mack and Charles had a hand) that the army in Germany would advance into Bavaria weeks before the Italian army crossed the border. The explanation is simple: the Austrians did not imagine that the advance of the Germany army would lead to a rapid, decisive engagement. For the Austrians, the movement was preparation for the war to follow rather than the opening of hostilities. The real war would begin when Charles crossed the Adige sometime in late October.

The second major difference between the two theaters also affected these calculations. Since Austria shared a border with an occupied French satellite only in Italy, the commanders in that theater were the only ones who had to defend against a surprise attack.‡ As war approached and Mack focused on concentrating and preparing the German army for attack, therefore, Charles and his subordinates were preoccupied with the problem of defending Italy from the French.

In late April 1805 Napoleon ordered the concentration of a large force for him to review as part of his Italian coronation procession.§ Those orders massed around 30,000 soldiers close to the Austrian borders. Austrian

---

*Charles noted to Francis that it would take sixty-six days to mobilize an army on the Italian border and only thirty-eight days to form one on the Inn. In addition to the greater march distances involved, the Austrians were proposing to mobilize a much larger army on the Italian border, which would have required more time in any case. Charles to Francis, 18 May 1805, KA AFA 1805 Italien, V/11a.

†As Mack's army began marching into Bavaria in early September with the final troop contingents closing up in the rear, the army in Italy was projected to have a little over half of its programmed infantry and about 40 percent of its cavalry units. (KA AFA 1805 Italien, VIII/ad2c). The last eight infantry regiments were not scheduled to join Charles's army until October 25.

‡Westernmost Vorarlberg shares a frontier with Switzerland, but the French garrison of Switzerland was known to be small and the terrain in that area so favors the defender that the prospect of a French attack was not terrifying. Charles nevertheless considered the plans and requirements of defending western Tyrol carefully. "Secret Instruction of H[is] Royal Highness the Archduke War Minister about the Defense of the Tyrol," n.d., KA AFA 1805 Italien, I/5.

§See above, Chapter 7, for a discussion of the role this concentration played in shaping Austria's course for war.

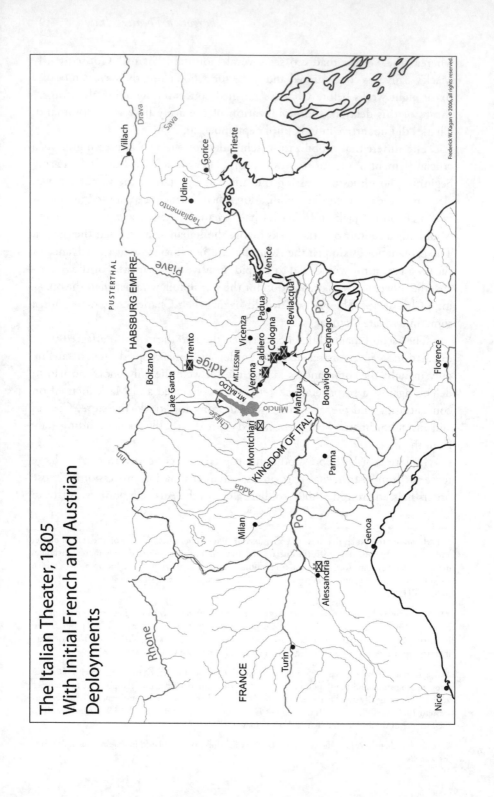

The Italian Theater, 1805
With Initial French and Austrian
Deployments

Villach

Drava

Sava

Gorice

Trieste

Udine

Tagliamento

PUSTERTHAL

HABSBURG EMPIRE

Piave

Venice

Trento

Bolzano

Lake Garda

Adige

MT. LESSINI

Vicenza

Padua

Caldiero

Cologna

Verona

Bevilacqua

Po

Legnago

Florence

Chiese

MT. BALDO

Mincio

Mantua

Bonavigo

Montichiari

KINGDOM OF ITALY

Parma

Inn

Adda

Milan

Po

Genoa

Rhone

Alessandria

FRANCE

Turin

Nice

intelligence inflated that number to around 40,000, however, which Charles at first accepted.[2] In truth, even the 30,000 troops concentrated in large formations that Napoleon actually brought into Italy posed a serious threat to the Austrian defenders there, who numbered fewer than 20,000 men spread out in garrisons at Verona, Vicenza, Venice, Padua, and elsewhere.* The commander of those troops, General of Cavalry Count Heinrich Bellegarde, had no illusions about his ability to hold off a French attack and frankly warned Charles that he could not do so without reinforcements.[3] Charles accepted this evaluation and wrote the emperor that he should order another 20,000 troops to concentrate near the Italian border as reinforcements if he believed Napoleon might launch a surprise attack.[4] Charles, however, was skeptical that Napoleon had any such intention and feared that the proposed reinforcements would be provocative.

He nevertheless recognized that leaving Bellegarde without the means to defend himself against a sudden attack would be irresponsible unless Francis was certain there would be no attack. Francis was determined to avoid provoking or committing to a war at this time, a determination that Charles heartily seconded. The archduke's demand for a declaration that no war was possible at that time therefore occasioned great handwringing.[5] In the end, the emperor accepted a compromise. He authorized Bellegarde to concentrate his forces near the Adige and gave him the authority to take command of neighboring troops in the Tyrol and to his rear if it became necessary, and he made limited reinforcements available to the exposed commander. Charles reckoned that these orders would bring Bellegarde's strength up to about 33,000 men within a month or so. When all of the soldiers on leaves had been recalled (or replaced), Bellegarde's forces would number nearly 49,000, although this process would require two months.[6] Charles was confident that with these reinforcements Bellegarde could hold off Napoleon's troops, now estimated at between 30,000 and 40,000 men.[7]

Charles's confidence did not last long, however. By June, he was considering the defense of Venice and the Tyrol against a French surprise attack, and more reinforcements were on the way to Italy.[8] One likely cause of this renewed unease was the arrival of word that Napoleon intended to

---

*March Plan, 10 March 1805, KA AFA 1805 Italien, III/1; Deployment of Austrian Forces in Italy at the end of March 1805, KA AFA 1805 Italien, II/4. (This document is located in folio III, as it should be. Its *signatur* seems to be mistaken.) Neither of these documents gives complete troop strengths, although they indicate the presence of twenty-two infantry battalions and a handful of cavalry squadrons. In late May, Charles sent Francis a table giving the strength of Austrian forces then in Italy as twenty-one fusiliers battalions, fourteen grenadiers companies, and sixteen cavalry squadrons, for a total strength of 19,508 men (of whom 2,302 were in cavalry formations). KA AFA 1805 Italien, V/12b.

annex Genoa to France.* Concern for the defense of these areas continued into July.[9]

Francis's decision in July to join the Anglo–Russian coalition against France changed the discussions about the defense of Italy, although less than might have been expected.† At the end of the month, Charles sent Francis a lengthy memorandum proposing measures to prepare the armies for the proposed war, which the emperor approved.[10] Charles had not yet given much thought to the tasks the war plan would impose on the army he was to command in Italy. The thrust of the preparations was to allow the Austrian army in Germany to seize as much of Bavaria as possible quickly to forestall the French there, while the army in Italy readied itself to resist the expected Napoleonic onslaught. Charles broke the mobilization of the Austrian army into six "epochs," indicating how many troops would be available to each army during each time period. He did not, however, consider what the Austrian army in Italy would do once it completed its mobilization.[11]

This fixation with defensive operations resulted from the weakness of the Austrian forces in Italy throughout August and September 1805 and their need to hold a number of critical positions throughout the theater. In mid-August, only thirty-five of the fifty infantry battalions in Austrian Italy were concentrated along the Adige at Bevilaqua, Caldiero, and Cologna. Ten battalions were stationed in Venice, and another five had been sent toward Trento in the southern Tyrol. Thus Charles reckoned that he had only 17,500 men available on the main attack corridor.[12] He thought that Napoleon, by contrast, had about 30,000 men concentrated southwest of Lake Garda around Montichiari, some thirty miles from Verona, with another 10,000 stationed at Marengo (which was another 87 miles to the west). Napoleon's main body was closer to the main Austrian forces on the Adige than the Austrian reserves at Venice and Trento and was almost twice as large. According to the deployment plans, moreover, Austrian forces on the Adige could not expect to achieve parity with Napoleon's supposed

---

*Napoleon ordered Talleyrand to inform Francis of the likelihood of this event on June 1; word may have reached the emperor as early as June 7, when Charles wrote to Hiller that the emperor had decided to make his forces in Italy ready for war if it became necessary. Edouard Driault, *Napoléon en Italie (1800–1812)* (Paris: Librarie Félix Alcan, 1906), pp. 335–336; Charles to Hiller, 7 June 1805, Italien, VI/3½. He had certainly learned of it by the time the new reinforcements were dispatched to Pettau.

†Cobenzl presented Francis with a recommendation to join the coalition on July 2. Francis approved it around the middle of the month. His undated approval, reproduced in Adolf Beer, *Zehn Jahre österreichischer Politik, 1801–1810* (Leipzig: F. A. Brockhaus, 1877), pp. 496–498, contains references to the conference between Wintzingerode, Charles, and others of July 16 as being contemporaneous. Austria formally adhered to the coalition on August 9. See above, Chapter 7, for a discussion of these events.

strength at Montichiari until mid-September.* They would not be in a position to undertake offensive operations until well into October. Throughout August and much of September, they would face the threat of a sudden and overwhelming French attack. If such an attack occurred, Charles could think of little more than to have the defenders around Caldiero abandon their position and retreat north toward Trento.[13]

Part of the problem the Austrians faced was inherent in the terrain of northern Italy. Since the Adige split Verona in two and the French held half of it, they could attack from a concentrated position around the city and strike defending forces spread out in a long arc from Venice to the Tyrolean Alps. In particular, a French force crossing the Adige at Verona could march either north along the river's valley toward Trento and the Tyrolean passes, or east through Vicenza toward Padua and the road toward Vienna. It was not enough to hold Verona, however, since the French could also cross the Adige to the south at Legnago, a smaller town that also spans the river. Any Austrian defense had to cover both crossings as well as the eastern shore of Lake Garda, had to garrison Venice, and had to maintain sizable reserves at Trento and Padua. Unless the overall force was very large, moreover, each particular detachment faced the possibility of being overrun by superior French forces before the others could come to its assistance.

Francis's refusal to make the necessary preparations for the possibility of a war with France in the first half of 1805 badly exacerbated this problem. Afraid to provoke Napoleon by increasing his forces near Italy, the Austrian emperor contented himself with establishing a cordon ostensibly to protect against an outbreak of yellow fever. When he became aware of Napoleon's concentrations at Marengo and Montichiari in May, moreover, Francis underreacted by sending only a handful of regiments in the general direction of Italy. These troops had not yet reached their destinations when Napoleon's annexation of Genoa, combined with the exigencies of the Russian court, persuaded the reluctant emperor to join a coalition treaty that meant inevitable war.

In the German theater, as we have seen, Francis's delays created problems for the Austrian mobilization. Mack had overcome those problems through his own frenetic energy and also because of the small distances between the permanent stations of the troops that would compose his army and their final

---

*Charles overestimated that strength by 10,000 men or more, as we have seen. It is difficult to obtain a precise understanding of the deployment plan from the Austrian documents, which disagree with one another substantially about the pace of the deployment. See, e.g., KA AFA 1805 Italien, VIII/2 and VIII/ad2c, and compare with Angeli, *Erzherzog Carl von Oesterreich*, 3:48. According to these various estimates, the Austrians could expect to achieve parity with what Charles thought Napoleon had in Montichiari between September 7 and 12 or thereabouts. In reality, the deployment followed the slower estimates more closely than it did the faster ones.

destination on the Inn. The greater distances that troops destined for Italy had to cover magnified the impact of Francis's prevarications. It was not possible for the Austrian army to mobilize a large force rapidly on the Adige. The delays that political considerations imposed on the mobilization drove its commanders to think in terms of defense and ignore the role their force was intended to play in the forthcoming campaign.

It is important to bear in mind that Charles, Francis, Mack, and the other Austrian leaders all believed that Italy would be the scene of the initial decisive battles. They expected Napoleon to reinforce his army in northern Italy and even attack in that theater. Charles had argued all along that an Austrian defeat in Italy would open the road to Vienna that Napoleon had nearly taken in 1797 and 1801. In this context, it was not surprising that the Austrians thought mainly of defense nor even that they tended to count every Frenchman twice. Intelligence collection, even in the modern period, is frequently shaped by what the collectors expect to find.

The Austrian preparations in Italy were further complicated by the relationship between that theater and the Tyrol. Charles had broken the Italian army in two, one part based at Venice, the other around Caldiero. The smaller Tyrolean army consisted of three major bodies. The largest occupied the southern Tyrol with its base around Trento. A second, designated for the control of central Tyrol, consisted of two smaller groups, one in the upper Inn valley and the other along the upper Adige valley. The third major body covered the northern Tyrol around Innsbruck.[14]

The activities of the Tyrolean armies were crucial to the Italian army commander, since only they could protect the flank and rear of the main body concentrated around Caldiero. Therefore Charles undertook a detailed, professional study of Napoleon's possible routes of attack and the ways in which the Tyrolean army could meet them.[15] The French, he argued, might cross at Verona and fight the main body of the Italian army near Caldiero. They might, on the other hand, march up the right bank of the Adige toward Trento, either to get into the Tyrol or outflank the main Austrian army to the south. Still another possibility was that the French might march up the western shore of Lake Garda and attack Trento from the southwest. They might even make an amphibious landing on the northern shore of the lake in support of such a maneuver. Charles also considered the remoter chances that the French might march up the Chiese river valley and attack Trento from the west or even the northwest, and that they might attack through the Tyrol itself, along the upper Inn and upper Adige valleys, through Bolzano and into the valleys of the Tagliamento or the Piave directly into the Austrian rear. He considered this last possibility the most dangerous, since it offered the French the opportunity to cut off the entire Austrian force.

Charles then considered the possible Austrian responses to these various French moves. In sharp contrast to the despondency that characterized his letters to his elder brother, Charles approached this problem with a professional brisk-ness that did not consider the likelihood of success but only the best ways to achieve it. If Trento were a significant fortress, he wrote, the Austrian defenses would be much easier to plan and conduct. The weakness of that position, how-ever, meant that they could not rely on it to hold out by itself against a siege, and that it must therefore be protected and covered as the pivot of Austrian mancu-vers in northern Italy. He advised breaking the southern Tyrolean army into a number of smaller groups, of which the largest would hold Trento itself. The sec-ond largest would hold Monte Baldo, which lay between the Adige and Lake Garda. This force would cooperate with a detachment from the main Italian army stationed along Monte Lessini, covering the western bank of the Adige. If the Austrians could hold these two positions, Trento, and Caldiero, then the army would be secure unless the French came through the central Tyrol and di-rectly into the valley of the Tagliamento. Charles had no suggestions for how to prevent such an eventuality with the forces at hand, although he hoped that the French would not be wise enough to recognize its potential.

The professionalism of Charles's study extended to the details. For one thing, he exhorted Bellegarde to remember that standing on the defensive was not enough. At some point the Austrian forces would have to go over to the offensive, either to take advantage of the inevitable enemy mistakes or to pursue the further objectives of the campaign. For another, he ordered the dispatch of a series of staff officers to reconnoiter important routes of march and terrain to support further planning. He entrusted Bellegarde and his other subordinates with determining, based on the terrain, the best spots in which to concentrate their forces within the general guidelines he had provided. He continually referred Bellegarde to the "quartermaster general staff" for the development of detailed plans.

This staff was extremely active. The archives contain numerous memoranda from its majors and colonels with proposals for troop deployments, troop move-ments, and reports on terrain reconnaissances.[16] This professionalism contrasts with the amateurishness of most of the planning and staff work in Germany. The careful consideration of possible enemy movements, the identification of points of vulnerability or opportunity based on terrain, the empowering of subordinate officers not only to gather information but to make decisions about operational deployments were all lacking in Mack's army.* Mack himself went to reconnoiter the position of each fortress he hoped to build along the Iller line, and neither he nor his staff made any serious effort to consider possible French courses of action and appropriate responses to them before operations began. They forgot, as Charles did not, that in war the enemy has a vote in what happens.

---

*Charles firmly placed the responsibility for deploying the South Tyrolean army on that army's commander, although he set some general parameters. See Charles to Bellegarde, 1 September 1805, KA AFA 1805 Italien, IX/7; Zach to Lieutenant Colonel Meyer, 3 September 1805, IX/ad26.

Charles, unlike Mack, sought to educate his senior subordinates in his vision of warfare. He encouraged Bellegarde to consider the morale factors in war when making his dispositions and planning his marches. In response to complaints from the southern Tyrolean army about the inadequacy of its forces, he not only clarified the problem but explained that those commanders would have to rely on their "military genius" to solve future problems.[17] They should not seek set rules but should shape their actions according to circumstances guided by that "genius." Above all, they should recognize that they could not simply stand on the defensive. They should always be asking themselves whether there was not a way to maneuver, to turn the enemy's flank, to attack in one valley while retreating in another, and so on. Although cautious at the strategic and grand strategic levels, Charles remained aggressive in principle at the operational level. He sought to convey a sense of intelligent aggressiveness to his subordinates as he was empowering them to make their own independent evaluations and decisions.*

When he received a request from the central Tyrolean army under Auffenberg to increase its forces so that it could cover all the terrain assigned to it, Charles demonstrated his ability to insist on appropriate risk taking.[18] That force was simply an intermediary corps, he wrote, with the mission of securing the communication between the right flank of the Italian army and the left flank of the German. It did not need to have enough force to address all possible contingencies on the terrain it held, but only enough so that it could defeat an enemy that intelligence reported was weaker than it was. Its commander would have to rely on his military skill to maneuver his inadequate forces better than that enemy, since he was engaged in what modern observers would call an "economy of force mission"—one whose secondary importance justified only the smallest possible deployment of troops.

Charles put great effort into coordinating the activities of neighboring armies, especially when their missions and areas of responsibility overlapped— something Mack ignored. Charles knew there was a danger that the Italian and southern Tyrolean armies might not cooperate sufficiently in the defense of the Adige valley in the Monte Baldo–Monte Lessini area. He therefore delineated the areas for which his own force would be responsible and specified those that the Tyrolean army had to cover but avoided prescribing the occupation of specific tactical locations.[19] In this regard Charles's planning was better than Mack's. Mack did not coordinate the activities of his army with the army in

---

*These instructions stand in sharp contrast to the traditional image of Charles as a military theorist (as, for example, in Azar Gat, *The Origins of Military Thought from the Enlightenment to Clausewitz* [Oxford: Clarendon, 1989], pp. 97–107). At a minimum, historians must reckon not only with the theoretical works that Charles published following the War of 1805, but also with his plans and actions in that war and the vision of warfare he presented there. Such a reexamination will reveal, among other things, the complicated relationship between politics, military theory, and military experience.

the northern Tyrol, nor develop intelligent plans for cooperating with the Russian army when it arrived. Charles was clearly the superior operational-level commander.

The differences between the ways in which the two armies functioned stemmed primarily from three factors. First, Charles was a more talented and professional general.* In the revolutionary wars he held commands, whereas Mack held only staff positions. This experience prepared him for the challenges of executing war plans and not merely writing them. His superior understanding of the nature of war and the problems that arise enabled him to write better plans. Charles's theoretical writings are also more intelligent and insightful than Mack's. Charles wrestled with some of the deeper issues of war where Mack was mostly concerned with trivialities.† Although Charles's understanding of war was limited and sometimes naive, it was nevertheless better than Mack's.

Second, Mack was a frenetic, panicky micromanager who insisted on seeing to all details himself. Such leaders undermine staffers' efforts by making them irrelevant and by failing to empower senior staff officers. In addition, Mack was constantly in a state of emergency, "throwing himself at the feet" of senior leaders who opposed his plans and insisting that every order be executed instantly. Such a personality exhausts staff officers who become numbed to the urgency and emergency. Charles embodied calm and rationality, at least toward his subordinates, even during critical moments of the campaign.

Finally, Mack's presence as de facto commander of the army theoretically entrusted to Archduke Ferdinand undermined normal staff function still further. Mack had no appropriate relations with the staff of that army and, beyond that, detested its head, Quartermaster General Mayer. Although Charles, like Ferdinand, did not arrive at the head of his army until late in September, it functioned perfectly well and smoothly prior to his arrival under the capable if uninspired command of Bellegarde.

One critical conclusion emerges from this study: the performance of the Austrian army in Bavaria was below the normal standards of the Austrian army

---

*This fact highlights one of the problems with standard critiques of the "ancien régime" armies: relying on nobles for their officer corps produced worse leaders than the French army, which theoretically permitted promotion based on merit. Mack rose from the commonality purely on the strength of his performance. Charles held command because of his birth. Charles was the better commander. In the aggregate, it is to be expected that the French model would produce better commanders overall than that of the ancient régime, but military skill is not inversely proportional to noble rank.

†Mack was preoccupied, especially in the years leading up to 1805, with drafting detailed plans for reorganizing the tactical and operational units of the Austrian army. His ideas were not necessarily less valid than those of his contemporaries, but they largely ignored many of the deeper issues of the nature of war and the relationship between attack and defense that Charles sometimes addressed. See, e.g., Mack, "My True Wishes for the Improvement of the I[mperial and] R[oyal] War Establishment," 1805(?), KA Nachlaß B/573 (Mack), 10.

of the time. The chaos and confusion that characterized its staff work and planning did not represent customary Austrian practice but resulted instead from the uniquely dysfunctional command relationships at its head, and from the personality of Mack. The higher standard of performance of the Italian general staff and commanders was more representative of what the army could do.*

The quality of Charles's performance and that of the Austrian staff in Italy was nevertheless limited. Charles explicitly refused to consider the relationship between his army and the Austrian force in the northern Tyrol, to say nothing of the Austrian army heading for Bavaria. He did not consider the possibility that forces might need to move between Italy and Germany according to the circumstances, nor did he reflect on the ways in which movements in one theater might affect operations in the other. Considering that the marching distance between Trento and Innsbruck is only about six days, this was a serious failing.

This failing reflected the problems Austria's command structure posed for the development and execution of the coalition war plan. The only person who was responsible for coordinating the activities of all of the theaters in which Austrian troops were operating was Francis. He might have succeeded in that difficult task with the aid of a robust staff, but the head of that staff was Mack, who ignored all theaters except the one he wished to make his own. Charles retained the title of war minister and theoretically could have concerned himself with all the various armies, but his relations with both Francis and Mack precluded his interference in the operations of the German army. Therefore he confined himself to thinking about a single theater in isolation from the others. Of all the contingency plans he developed, none addressed the contingency that he actually faced in October 1805.

Intermittent Contact with Reality

As September progressed, Charles was forced to confront two realities. Mack's growing awareness of the threat he faced led to a series of transfers of troops from the Italian and Tyrolean armies to the German. By the end of the month, moreover, Charles had discovered that the units remaining in his armies were

---

*Mack's performance in 1805 was below the standard he had set himself as a staff officer years earlier. If his plans for allied operations in 1794, 1796, and 1797 failed, they were nevertheless more carefully and thoughtfully developed than his movements in Bavaria in 1805. See Baron Christian Karl August Ludwig von Massenbach, *Nähere Beleuchtung des dem k. k. Obersten und Chef des Generalstaabes Freyherrn von Mack zugeschriebenen Operationsplans für den Feldzug 1794 des Oesterreichisch-Französischen Krieges* (Berlin: Johann Friedrich Unger, 1796), 1:1–8; "Consideration of How and How Many Troops Would Suffice for the Defense of the Rhine or an Offensive on the Other Side of This River," 1796(?), KA, Nachlaß B/573 (Mack), 1; and "Memorandum About the Forthcoming Operations," 1797(?), KA, Nachlaß B/573, 2. These documents are not up to Charles's standard, but all are better than what Mack actually produced prior to the beginning of hostilities in 1805.

significantly below the strength reports he had been seeing in Vienna. These two facts combined with an increasingly mistaken evaluation of the strength and intentions of the French troops in Lombardy to paralyze the archduke and transform his understanding of the campaign.

Mack had begun to realize the danger he faced in Germany by the end of August and immediately requested reinforcements drawn from Italy and the Tyrol.[20] The first transfer occurred in mid-September, as Francis sent three regiments from Auffenberg's army in the northern Tyrol and two from Charles's army in Italy to Ferdinand's German army.* Mack's panic had reached a crescendo by that time, however, and he began to demand complete control over the Tyrolean forces and additional reinforcements from Italy. Following a tense meeting with Mack and Ferdinand, Francis ordered another five infantry and two cavalry regiments from Italy to Germany.[21] Charles had thus lost some 28 infantry battalions out of an army that was supposed to number 144 but had received about half of that strength by mid-September. This detachment of 20 percent of his total programmed strength was bad enough, especially in light of the difficulties Charles foresaw in defending his army against French operations in the southern Tyrol. Worse was to come.

Charles arrived in Padua, the headquarters of the Italian army, on September 20, 1805. He found that the situation on the ground differed dramatically from the one he had thought he would find when he left Vienna. The first problem resulted from the hasty mobilization that Francis had decreed. Charles had initially insisted that the mobilization would take six months, but Mack promised to do it in two, a promise that contributed to his elevation. Mack managed to make the German army sufficiently mobile to accomplish its initial missions by rushing to the theater, which was closer to metropolitan Austria and better able to supply its wants. Charles did no such thing, however, and his subordinates in Italy could not find the means with which to supply the army. As a result, Charles found his troops badly clothed, badly equipped, and lacking in basic means of transportation, especially horses. "The more I get into the details," he wrote to his favorite uncle, Duke Albert of Sachsen-Teschen, "the more I find that we are lacking everything to enter a campaign."[22]

The most important thing Charles lacked was soldiers. The archives contain numerous reports from August and September that list the "current" strength of regiments and battalions down to the individual soldier.[23] According to those records, there were on September 20 exactly 74,348 troops along the Adige line, 10,103 around Trento, 6,999 in Venice, and another 3,278 scattered around in specialized detachments for a grand total of 94,728 men, including 3,868 cavalry. The reality was rather different.

---

*[Francis] to Baillet de la Tour, 16 September 1805, KA AFA 1805 Italien, IX/195. See Chapter 14 for a more complete examination of this order and its effects.

One of the shortcuts the Austrians had to take in order to meet Mack's accelerated mobilization schedule was to skip the thoroughgoing review of regimental rosters that would normally accompany mobilization.[24] This review was essential in the transition from a peacetime footing to a war footing, as it allowed the leadership to find out how many of the soldiers nominally on the rolls were sick, detached, or absent—with or without leave. It was even more important in an army that had sent a large number of its troops on extended leave in the preceding five years in order to save money. Such reviews take time, however, and the Austrians could not afford to waste any moments in setting their troops in motion for distant Italy. As a result, they failed to establish a clear "ground truth" for the number of soldiers in each unit.

Even before he arrived in Padua, Charles ordered such a review to be conducted by the end of September.[25] If the Italian army completed it, however, no record remains in the archives. It is possible that such records were destroyed, since they would have revealed, among other things, that the Austrians had failed to honor their treaty obligations to maintain a certain number of troops in the field. In this regard, the British and the Russians may have been too compliant, since it was once normal to station British officers with troops for whom Britain was paying in order to keep accurate tallies of their numbers. It appears that the trust Alexander insisted on showing Francis during the treaty negotiations was unwarranted in this case.*

The most damaging result was not that the Austrians deluded their allies, however, but that they had deluded themselves. The troop levels maintained in Vienna suggested that infantry battalions in the Italian army averaged 500 men in strength. When Charles had toured his command and reviewed many of his troops, he realized that his battalions actually numbered around 425 soldiers each.† The difference is significant, since it meant that Charles's army probably contained only about 70,000 infantrymen instead of the 87,582 he

---

*The initial British drafts of the Anglo–Russian convention stipulated that British subsidies would be based on the number of Austrian (and Russian) soldiers actually with the colors. Apparently the British meant to have a representative muster each regiment and tally the total before paying the subsidy. This stipulation was dropped from the final treaty because of Austrian and Russian objections. See Mulgrave to Leveson Gower, 21 January 1805, in John Holland Rose, *Select Despatches from the British Foreign Office Archives Relating to the Formation of the Third Coalition against France, 1804–1805* (London: Offices of the Royal Historical Society, 1904), doc. 57; Leveson Gower to Mulgrave, 6 March 1805, doc. 65; and Mulgrave to Leveson Gower, doc. 68. Leveson Gower described the discussions leading to the abandonment of this clause in Leveson Gower to Mulgrave, 12 April 1805, doc. 72. See especially p. 136 and footnote.

†Charles to Albert, 28 September 1805, in Criste, *Erzherzog Carl von Oesterreich*, vol. 2, appendix XL/3. Charles writes that his battalions numbered between 300 and 400 men. Strength figures from this time show that the average was about 425 men per battalion. There is nothing unusual in a divergence between "official" strength figures and "ground truth" in military units. Charles's reactions to this problem, however, together with his official statement that the Austrians had abandoned normal procedures for keeping track of their troops during mobilization, make it clear that the situation in

expected to find on his arrival. Stripped of the detachments in Venice, Trento, and the Tyrol, Charles had only about 55,000 soldiers facing Masséna across the Adige.*

Charles wasted no time complaining to Francis about his problems.[26] The "deployable complement" of his army, he wrote two days after his arrival, was "still very weak." Part of the problem was that soldiers on leave were refusing to return to their units, and the military police were unable to round them up efficiently. Writing to Uncle Albert, he noted that there were as many as 20,602 absentee soldiers (an average of about 100 per battalion)—"a small army."† The Austrian high command had been counting on those soldiers to bring their units to full strength, since even the paper strength of the battalions was considerably below their full authorized wartime allowance.[27] The absentees may help explain the discrepancy between the troop strength on the rolls in Vienna and the reality in Italy. Charles reported being obliged to leave behind "significant detachments" of infantry in the Austrian provinces in order to assist the military police in their task.

According to reports he had seen in Vienna, Charles had taken command of an army numbering, he thought, about 95,000 soldiers including almost 7,500 cavalry and expecting the imminent arrival of another 10,000 troops and 3,500 horses. After he sorted through the confusion in the field, he found that he had only 85,000 soldiers, of which 8,000 were cavalry even including the new arrivals. More than 15 percent of his infantry had evaporated into thin air. The troops transferred from his armies to Mack's numbered about

---

1805 was serious and noteworthy. One example shows the problem in extreme form: Charles wrote Albert on October 1 that he had just reviewed the regiment Wenzel Colloredo and found it to have some 192 soldiers per battalion; the strength listed for that regiment on September 20 showed it to have 475 men per battalion (Charles to Albert, 1 October 1805, Criste, *Erzherzog Carl von Oesterreich*, appendix XL/4; KA AFA 1805 Italien, IX/ad238).

*This fact would also mean that the numbers customarily given for the strength of the Austrian army in this campaign are wrong, since they rely on the fictional data maintained in Vienna. See, e.g., Duffy, *Austerlitz*, p. 38; Rothenberg, *Napoleon's Great Adversary*, p. 110. Rothenberg's figure is drawn from Schönhals, *Der Krieg 1805 in Deutschland, nach Österreichischen Originalquellen* (Vienna: Selbstverlag der Redaction der Österreichischen Militärischen Zeitschrift, 1873), pp. 22–23, which is calculated based on the (erroneous) assumption that each battalion had 500 men. There is no way to prove this point, however, since the archives do not contain the results of Charles's review. On September 27, Charles wrote Francis that he had a deployable strength of 77,000 infantry and 8,000 cavalry, of which 25,000 were detached in the Tyrol, Venice, and elsewhere, leaving 60,000 men on the Adige (KA AFA 1805 Italien, IX/285½). This tally does not include the five infantry and two cavalry regiments he was sending to join Ferdinand, but it does include a number of units newly arrived in the theater.

†Charles to Albert, 3 October 1805, Criste, *Erzherzog Carl von Oesterreich*, vol. 2, appendix XL/5. It is not entirely clear how these soldiers related to the deficit discussed above. The order of battle for September 20 identifies 17,397 soldiers on leave (KA AFA 1805 Italien, IX/ad238) above and beyond the 94,728 nominally present for duty. The Austrians counted on getting these soldiers back to the colors, but the discrepancy between the paper strength and the actual strength of the battalions in Italy was probably unrelated to this issue.

19,000 infantry and perhaps 2,400 cavalry. More than 20,000 soldiers remained absent without leave throughout the inner Habsburg lands. Charles lost nearly 40 percent of an army once supposed to include more than 136,000 troops even before he completed his mobilization.

Charles's 85,000 men formed a substantial force even so, although he had to subtract the 25,000 troops detached in the Tyrol, Venice, and elsewhere. The question was, What French strength did the Austrian army face? The Austrian intelligence effort initially did better in Italy than either Napoleon or Mack did in Germany in finding an answer. In mid-September the Austrians had identified a total of seventy-eight infantry battalions and sixty cavalry squadrons available to Masséna. Estimating the strength of a battalion at 600 men, this meant that there were 46,000 infantry and 6,000 cavalry in French Italy.[28] Charles exaggerated this number in his report to Francis, claiming that Masséna had about 70,000 soldiers in Italy or marching toward it.[29] He remained steadfast in this estimate, increasing it only to 74,500 by the end of the month, despite a report that he received and forwarded suggesting that the French actually had between 125,000–130,000 troops in the peninsula.[30]

The Austrian intelligencers did reasonably well in tracking the units of Masséna's force. Of the twenty infantry regiments composing that army on October 18, the Austrians had correctly identified sixteen by September 19.[31] Nor was Charles's estimate of the overall strength of the French army in Italy that far off: including garrisons and troops in depots and rear areas, Masséna mustered 65,235 soldiers in mid-October, although he had only 41,365 on the Adige. The Austrians overestimated the average strength of the French battalions, reckoning them at about 600 when many had between 300 and 400. Even so, their intelligence in Italy toward the end of September was nearly perfect compared with the 50–100 percent error rate Mack and Napoleon sustained in their estimates of each other's strengths in and around Bavaria.

Thus at the beginning of October about 85,000 Austrians faced around 65,000 Frenchmen in northern Italy and the southern Tyrol. Subtracting garrisons and detachments from both forces left around 60,000 Austrians staring across the Adige at 40,000 French troops. The importance of the nearly 50,000 troops "missing" from the Austrian army becomes immediately apparent. If Charles had those troops or even knew they would arrive presently, he could have reckoned on numerical superiority sufficient to offer the prospect of successful offensive operations. As it was, however, he had to abandon the idea of undertaking an offensive; he was even nervous about his ability to withstand a French attack.

He detailed his argument for Francis. Even if he was fortunate enough to make a successful crossing of the Adige, he would need 40,000 troops to blockade Mantua, Peschiera, and Legnago, leaving only 20,000 to conduct further operations in northern Italy. The large detachments Francis had sent from Italy to Germany, together with the problems resulting from the inadequate mobilization, forced Charles to confine himself to the "strictest defensive" posture in the hopes of preserving his army and protecting the Habsburg lands. In the event of further significant detachments, however, he wrote, "I will not be able to remain responsible even for this goal."[32]

These reflections eroded Charles's will and judgment. The next day, he wrote Uncle Albert that Masséna had thirty infantry and fifteen cavalry regiments, not including reinforcements of 12,000 men that he had just received. "This would make 102,000 men and 6,000 cavalry at full strength, 108,000 in all. But let us count it at only 85,000, [and] it is much stronger than I am, my 'deployable strength' does not comprise as many men as are needed to defend the land between the frontier of the Grisons and Venice."[33] This circumstance "forces me to renounce the offensive and to remain on a poor defensive that I fear I will not be able to sustain for very long." It is not clear how Charles conjured these French reinforcements, but he had begun to degrade the generally good estimates of Masséna's strength that his intelligencers had provided to him and to move closer to fantasy and despondency.

Charles also detailed to Francis the other weaknesses of his force. He did not have remotely enough horses to transport supplies and move artillery. His logisticians had encountered serious problems in obtaining basic foodstuffs. His military treasury was nearly empty, complicating his efforts to remedy other deficiencies. These failings were fully as important in driving Charles to caution as the paucity of his forces. The lack of horses particularly troubled him, since it would prevent him from shifting artillery around the theater, thereby impeding all movement either to the front or to the rear. Thus he feared that he could neither take advantage of any victories he might win nor safely withdraw his army in the event of setbacks. He complained to his brother that little assistance had been forthcoming, although he had repeatedly warned the Hofkriegsrat of these problems.[34]

Francis and the Hofkriegsrat were preoccupied with more serious matters. By the end of September the possibility of a crisis in Germany was apparent, and the Austrian court had responded by trying to get the Russian Podolian Army to Bavaria as rapidly as possible.* As far as Francis was concerned, since Charles was in no real danger, he merited little attention.

This neglect (Charles apparently received only one note from Francis for the month on October 5) had two bad effects. First, Francis missed the opportunity to reevaluate the shape of the campaign and to adjust Charles's mission and operations to accord with the situation developing in Germany. By October 1 it was apparent that an Austrian offensive in Italy was a foolish undertaking,

---

*See above, Chapter 17.

since the assumptions that underlay the overall campaign plan had been shown to be dangerously wrong. The question of the day should not have been accelerating the Russian march, a purely technical problem, but how the Austrian armies should react to the new situation.

A regiment can march from Trento to Innsbruck in six days.[35] A larger force would take somewhat longer. Had Francis ordered a large force to rush from Italy to Bavaria following his meeting with Mack and Ferdinand on September 22, it would have been emerging from the Alpine passes throughout the last two weeks of October. The arrival of such a force, together with the troops that Kienmayer and Jellachich managed to salvage from the wreck at Ulm, would have transformed the situation in Bavaria. They might have forced Napoleon to split his forces in order to contain them while dealing with Kutuzov or, with greater luck, they might have struck Napoleon's flank as he pursued the Russians. In either case they would have altered the shape of the campaign.*

This large-scale transfer did not occur for three reasons. First, Mack did not ask for it. Deluded and self-confident, he was unwilling to recognize or admit in late September the magnitude of the danger he faced. Second, Francis did not see himself as the overall commander. He confined himself to mediating among the army's senior leaders rather than attempting to generate his own vision and giving his own orders. The absence of a real staff to support him was an important element of this failing, but Francis's personality played a large role as well. Charles was the military genius in the family, and Francis never tried to step into his shoes. Third, Charles's increasing fixation with the incapacity of his army and his resentment over being demoted and excluded from the planning and conduct of the campaign in Germany focused his attention narrowly on his own theater and the dangers he faced there. He responded nimbly to the limited requests Francis made of him but might well have balked at larger ones. He feared exposing his army to defeat without saving Mack's, considering that troops sent from Italy might fail to arrive in Germany on time.[36] These personal, structural, and military factors combined to prevent the Austrian senior leadership from seeing, let alone seizing, the only real opportunity to redress the mistakes they had made in their initial deployments and plans. Francis's failure to keep Charles abreast of the situation in Bavaria only exacerbated these problems.

The emperor's silence probably increased Charles's sense of isolation and helplessness and caused him to focus on the futility of the exercise in which he

---

*Arguments advanced in Charles's defense frequently miss the point by asserting that his troops could not have gotten to Ulm in time to prevent Mack's capitulation. That is true, but they could have revolutionized the disastrous situation *following* Mack's surrender had they begun emerging in large numbers from the Tyrolean Alps toward the end of October. See, e.g., Karl Schikovsky, "Die Schlacht von Caldiero 1805," *Separatabdruck aus dem Organ der Militäriwwsenschaftlichen Vereine* 71, no. 2 (1905): 157–184.

was engaged. From the end of September at the latest, Charles knew that all was not going according to plan in Germany, although he lacked details. His imagination was not slow to fill them in, however, convinced as he was of Mack's complete incompetence. He pictured the defeat in Germany vividly even before it happened.[37] Foreknowledge of such a disaster without any detailed information is discouraging. A truly professional and emotionless commander would have begun developing contingency plans similar to those Charles had worked on before arriving in Italy. But the feeling of doom that pervaded Charles's headquarters as the result of the inadequacies of his own army, coupled with his confidence that any day he would receive word of the loss of the Austrian army in Germany, worked on his emotions and sapped his professionalism. Austria's most talented senior commander focused his attention on the situation before him, magnifying the dangers he faced and minimizing his own capabilities. Ignorance of affairs led to despair, which led to paralysis. As the decisive events unfolded in Bavaria, Charles and his army might as well have been in South Africa.

A Muffled Clash

For the Austrians, Italy slipped from being the primary theater of action, at least initially, to complete irrelevance in the face of disaster elsewhere. To Napoleon and the French it was never more than a sideshow. Despite the differences between the French and Austrian command structures and the personalities at their heads, Napoleon did no better at coordinating operations in the two theaters than his enemies. He did not miss any important opportunities, however, since the decisive events of the war occurred in Germany and Austria, as he had expected. His failures as a grand strategist in this campaign, nevertheless, prefigured subsequent similar failures of much greater moment.*

The editor of Masséna's correspondence wrote, "Napoleon calculated thus sometimes: he preferred that one only grew in his shadow."[38] The emperor may have deliberately minimized any possible role for Masséna in the campaign to ensure that his own feats of arms in Germany were not upstaged in Italy—as he had done to numerous senior commanders in previous wars.

It is more likely, however, that Napoleon simply did not believe that anything important could happen in a theater that did not include his presence. He did not worry about Masséna's upstaging him because he knew it would not happen. Neither did he worry that the Austrians could do anything in

---

*The term "grand strategist" here refers to the commander who coordinates operations in distinct theaters. Napoleon was a grand strategist in the way that Roosevelt, allocating resources between Europe and the Pacific, was a grand strategist (although Napoleon was far less effective at this level).

Italy that he could not undo with a victory on the Danube—and he never doubted his victory there.

Napoleon made no real effort to coordinate the operations of the two major armies in this war and assigned Masséna a purely defensive objective throughout the campaign. As Napoleon learned that the Austrians were neither increasing their forces in Verona nor fortifying the heights around that town, he concluded that Masséna could safely try to seize it. The goal of such a seizure was to establish a defensible beachhead that would preclude an Austrian attack in that direction. Napoleon thought that the small French force in Legnago could hold out indefinitely by opening the Adige dikes and flooding the lower river valley—a tactic that would impede French advances as thoroughly as Austrian. In this way, the French would compel the Austrians to attack between a narrow corridor bounded by French-held Verona on one side and Legnago on the other. Napoleon was confident that Masséna could crush such an attack.[39]

In the worst case, however, a successful Austrian drive across the Adige would bring the Austrians only to the strong fortress of Mantua, which Napoleon ordered well stocked.[40] In previous wars Mantua had shown that it could hold out for a considerable period of time even against a determined foe, and Napoleon believed that he would dispatch the Austrian and the Russian forces in Germany long before the fortress fell. Even in the unlikely event that the Austrians took Mantua rapidly, however, they would have to fight through a series of other fortresses and across a number of river lines.[41] In the worst of worst cases, the Austrians might seize all of northern Italy—whereupon a victorious Napoleon would descend on them from the northeast and take it all back. This eventuality would be unfortunate, in light of the fragility of Napoleon's new Italian empire, but Napoleon rightly believed it to be extremely remote.

Interestingly, Napoleon did not consider the possibility of having Masséna try to pin Charles's army and prevent reinforcements from going to Germany. He might have ordered Masséna to launch an attack timed with his movements in Germany or fall on Charles the moment he began to withdraw. On the contrary, when Napoleon wrote Masséna that Austrian troops in the Tyrol and at Trento were being sent to Bavaria, he added, "I would be delighted by this news, since I will be much eased by everything that can reduce the number of troops that are before you. I can rid myself of this army on the Iller promptly."[42]

In principle, this failure was a mistake. If the war had become protracted, Charles's army could have made it back to Vienna and influenced the ultimate outcome, perhaps decisively. Napoleon had a definite interest in seeing that it did not do so. If the Austrians had moved aggressively to transfer large forces over the Alpine passes (as Napoleon and the Russians had done in previous campaigns), they might have interfered with the course of operations even in Bavaria. The only reason to ignore these contingencies was Napoleon's supreme arrogance. He *knew* that he would end the war before Charles's army could get anywhere that mattered, and he *knew* that he could crush Mack in Bavaria no matter what reinforcements he received. And he was right, of course. In future campaigns, however, the conviction that Napoleon could force a rapid ending to a war almost at will would prove unfounded.

Masséna's job seemed very simple at first glance: seize the undefended part of Verona and attack the Austrian positions around Caldiero if it seemed advisable.[43] Considering the disorganization and weakness of the Austrian position, neither task should have been difficult. Things appeared different for the French commander in Italy, however. His situation, in fact, was virtually identical with Charles's in many respects.

Before late July Napoleon had not expected war to break out on the continent, and consequently he made no meaningful preparations to mobilize armies along his frontiers. In Germany he benefited from the fact that the Army of England had been training in full readiness to cross the Channel at a moment's notice. It was fully mobile, with the horses needed to move cannons and transport supplies. Its units were fully manned. It even had some supplies. It could march into Germany at Napoleon's command, although it suffered, even so, from serious logistical failings that resulted from its hasty change of direction, as we have seen.

The Italian army, on the other hand, lacked horses, food, wagons, cannons, ammunition, uniforms, money, and men. The fortresses on which Napoleon relied as a second line of defense were not ready. Many lacked necessary cannons, some required extensive repairs and improvements to be siegeworthy. Like the Austrian army in Italy, Masséna's "was almost entirely lacking in critical things."[44] Unlike Charles, however, Masséna did not simply complain about these failings and the impossibility of making them good. He began to requisition what he needed from the rich surrounding countryside and started to put his army and its fortresses in order. He came up against an unexpected stumbling block, however, in the twenty-year-old viceroy of Italy, Napoleon's stepson Eugène Beauharnais.

Eugène had little experience in his new role, since Napoleon had not left Milan until early June. The young viceroy faced the difficult task of forming a viceregal government over his new subjects in the face of constant micromanagement by his stepfather. Napoleon repeatedly took Eugène to task for not fulfilling his responsibilities properly, and he even had Duroc write the viceroy a letter "on his own," passing on more Napoleonic admonitions.[45]

If the young viceroy was beaten down by an overbearing emperor, however, he was also impressed by the complexity of the scene around him and the latent hostility among many of his new subjects to their novel status. He was eager not to inflame the opposition further in the process of mobilizing the army, and he lent worried ears to Italians' complaints about outrages perpetrated by Masséna.

Napoleon decreed that the Kingdom of Italy and the Empire of France would split the cost of Masséna's force but did not indicate what proportion each state would bear or what the mechanics of this division would be. This decision complicated the situation still further. As a result, Masséna not only lacked the cash necessary to pay for requisitioned materials and animals, but he frequently did not know whether to issue receipts in the name of France or Italy. As a result, he did not issue them at all. Eugène dug in his heels and attempted to rein in Masséna's requisitions; Masséna continued them anyway under pressure to get his army ready to fight. Both complained loudly to Napoleon.[46]

Napoleon solved the problem without solving the problem. He did not clarify the administrative details or explain how much money should come from Italy and how much from France. Instead, he chastised Eugène roundly for failing to understand that in wartime support of the armies is the only thing that matters. He expressed his surprise that Eugène should seem troubled by requisitions. All armies requisition in wartime, Napoleon declared. If the Austrians were in Italy, they would be requisitioning much more. There is no way to support a large army other than by requisitioning, he declared, and Eugène had better accustom himself to the practice.[47]

Much of this criticism was unfair. Eugène had never complained about the requisitions themselves. He had merely pointed out that Italy was a part of the French empire and not hostile terrain and that Masséna was obliged at least to provide receipts for property taken. This point was valid, and Napoleon's reaction reveals much about his attitude to the new portions of his empire. As we have already seen, Napoleon refused to allow the semiautonomous states under his control to behave in ways that countered French interests. He simply extended this principle in wartime—the satellites must bear all necessary burdens to support France's wars. If those burdens caused resentment among the new subjects, that was too bad. Nothing could be allowed to undermine the armies. These views are much more worrisome as general statements than as specific responses to an emergency situation. It was easy to argue in July, August, and September 1805 that Italians' concerns must bow to the need to get an army ready to face Charles. The implication that military concerns should at all times supersede concerns for the long-term stability of new regimes in conquered lands boded ill for the overall stability of the growing French empire.

Despite these trials and tribulations, Masséna got his army ready for war. Napoleon had always intended for Masséna to seize the Austrian part of Verona at the outset of the campaign. He believed that such a move would prevent the Austrians from crossing there in turn and would provide Masséna with a well-defended bridgehead across the Adige. The emperor presumably imagined that this bridgehead would facilitate subsequent movements into Austrian Italy, but he made no mention of such operations in his instructions to his commander.[48]

Masséna, for his part, was pessimistic about the prospects for a successful offensive, even of the limited scope Napoleon proposed. He promised only to hold the Adige line and retreat step-by-step, fighting all the way, if the Austrians attacked in force.[49] Perhaps in response to his marshal's defeatism, Napoleon authorized him to enter into a convention with Archduke Charles whereby neither army would attack the other without giving five or six days' notice. Seemingly, in this way Masséna could pin Charles's army on the Adige without having to fight it, giving Napoleon more time to destroy the Austrians in Germany and come to Masséna's aid.* The emperor then changed his mind again, telling Masséna on September 23 not to sign a convention if he had not already done so but seize the "best opportunity he would have" of attacking and preempting an imminent Austrian strike.† The damage, however, had already been done; Masséna had begun negotiations with Charles for an armistice.

When Masséna's envoy reached Charles, the latter struck a pose. Since there had been no declaration of war, he wrote, there were no hostilities in view that would require an armistice. Only if the pacific intentions of the Austrian emperor were rebuffed would a truce be necessary. He nevertheless deigned to send a representative back to Masséna to see what could be worked out.[50] Of this response Charles wrote, "Despite my poor situation, I paid him back with impudence."[51] The archduke probably intended to persuade Masséna that he felt his position strong enough that he had no need of an armistice. This appears to have been the effect produced: Masséna ordered his divisions to be ready to cross the Adige if nothing came of the talks.[52]

But Charles had never intended to refuse such a suitable offer. Considering his perception of his own weakness, he could hardly do otherwise. The convention, concluded on September 30, bound both sides to give five days' notice before hostilities could commence at noon on the sixth day. It immediately improved Charles's mood: "This puts me a little more at ease because judging

---

*Koch, *Mémoirs de Masséna*, vol. 5, p. 70. This explanation is somewhat suspect. Koch offers no quotations or specific documentary references for this order (no such document appears in Napoleon's published correspondence), and his account posits that Napoleon had intended for Masséna to pin Charles in Italy, whereas there is considerable evidence to the contrary. Masséna did, nevertheless, make such a convention with Charles and he would hardly have done so without Napoleon's prior approval. The timing is also problematic. The Napoleonic missive to which Masséna might have replied with pessimism (and Masséna's letter is not reproduced either) was sent on September 18. The next Napoleonic letter, telling Masséna not to sign the convention if he had not already done so, was sent on September 23 (see below). Five days is not enough time for a letter to get to Masséna, for him to respond, and for his response to make it back to Napoleon.

†Berthier to Masséna, 23 September 1805, *Corr. de Nap.*, doc. 9262; Koch, *Mémoires de Masséna*, pp. 72–73. Note that Koch inserts paraphrases and quotations from Berthier's portion of the letter that do not appear in the *Corr. de Nap.* Possibly Koch is correct to do so—the *Correspondance* was redacted, after all. But since these departures from the generally available evidence have the effect of exonerating Masséna's decision to sign a convention rather than execute Napoleon's original intentions, it is also possible that they are spurious.

by the example of what Masséna did in 1799 I could never be sure of not being surprised in my cantonments without a declaration of war, and consequently defeated, since I have had to extend them [over a wide distance] . . . because of the lack of subsistence. Five days gives me the time to reassemble my troops and does not give Masséna enough time to make detachments."*

Within a few days Charles received even better news: Ferdinand had canceled the march of four of the regiments Charles was ordered to send him from Italy. These units were on their way back to Trento. Charles even thought that "this reinforcement puts me at my ease and will possibly give me the means to make some sort of offensive operation at the beginning of the campaign, if I have enough supplies and artillery horses by then."[53]

Masséna had been speedily provisioning his fortresses and readying his troops. By the end of the first week of October he felt ready, and on October 8 he announced to Charles that he was terminating the truce; hostilities could commence anytime on or after October 14. News that the Neapolitans had come to terms and that Saint Cyr was on his way north with a large force buoyed Masséna still further. He had no need to fear for his right flank, whether or not Napoleon placed Saint Cyr's troops under his control.[54]

Charles received Masséna's message with equanimity. He continued to refuse to initiate hostilities, believing that such was the emperor's will (he had not heard from Francis since September 23), but he was not alarmed at the prospect of a French attack. He was gathering his forces steadily into camps near Verona and Caldiero and "in these positions we will await tranquilly if and when the French begin hostilities."† At some point during these preparations he must have received a note from Francis indicating that hostilities had begun in Germany (somewhat inauspiciously), but providing neither details nor guidance.[55] Even this news did not shake him.

On October 13, however, Charles received an order passed through FML Hiller, one of the Tyrolean commanders, ordering the regiments Charles had originally sent to Ferdinand and that Ferdinand had sent back to Charles to race once again for Innsbruck.[56] Archduke John, commanding in the Tyrol, was panicking because he thought that 20,000 Frenchmen were marching on Innsbruck and he had to find a way to defend it.

---

*Charles to Albert, 3 October 1805, in Criste, *Erzherzog Carl von Oesterreich*, appendix XL/5. See above, Chapter 15, for a discussion of the relation of logistics to army deployments in this era.

†Charles to Albert, 9 and 12 October 1805, in Criste, *Erzherzog Carl von Oesterreich*, appendices XL/7 and 8. The concentration orders for the Italian army are in Disposition, 9 October 1805, KA AFA 1805 Italien, X/57 and X/ad57. Charles notified Francis of the imminent beginning of hostilities on the same day (KA AFA 1805 Italien, X/58½). To understand the relative timing of the two theaters, we should recall the major events of the German theater of this time, especially the Battles of Günzburg (9 October), Haslach-Jungingen (11 October), and Elchingen (14 October). Mack and Napoleon signed the armistice on 17 October, and Mack formally surrendered his army on October 20. The Italian campaign was thus beginning almost precisely as the German campaign was winding to its conclusion.

Charles finally rebelled. He was on the eve, as he thought, of a French attack and faced with an order to send soldiers on their third forced march across the Alps in the space of a few weeks. He refused, pointing out that the likeliest result of such an order would be that the troops would not reach Germany in time to affect the outcome and would, in any event, be so exhausted by these marches and countermarches as to be worthless when they arrived.[57] He wrote to Francis explaining why he had disobeyed orders and to Albert that "I would prefer that the Emperor be angry at the action that I have just taken than that, by a blind obedience I had abandoned a part of the Tyrol to the enemy without even having his troops get to Germany in time and in a state to be helpful."[58]

This decision was fateful and wrong. It was based on a faulty perception of Napoleon's movements in Bavaria. Although it is true that the French advance through Ingolstadt and Donauwörth toward Munich could have looked like a dash for Innsbruck, Napoleon had no such objective in mind in mid-October. As we have seen, the emperor kept his forces concentrated between Munich and Ulm until October 25. Only on that day did he order Bernadotte to seize Salzburg.[59] Napoleon did not order Ney to march on Innsbruck until October 29, and his movement did not begin until two days after that.[60]

Consequently if Charles had acted quickly on the order to send troops to Innsbruck, they would have reached that city well before the French arrived, even if they had to march from the southern portion of Charles's command. If Napoleon had picked up this movement and hastened to send troops to Innsbruck, that would have been even better for the allies. The dispatch of Ney to Innsbruck was an afterthought. His command, fought out and exhausted by the battles around Ulm, was Napoleon's least combat-worthy corps. It was also the one farthest west (apart from Augereau's Corps, just arriving in the theater of operations). Napoleon clearly sent Ney to Innsbruck to protect his right flank from a threat he did not expect to be very great.

If Charles had sent an apparently sizable force toward Innsbruck (and all commanders at this time were inclined to magnify the estimates of enemy forces marching on their flanks), Napoleon might well have made the protection of his flanks a higher priority, probably dispatching a corps farther advanced to the southeast: Bernadotte, Marmont, Davout, or even Lannes or Soult. Such a movement would have weakened the forces pursuing Kutuzov, possibly affecting the course of operations along the Danube. If Napoleon had failed to reinforce his flank in a timely fashion, Charles's transferred forces could have become the nucleus of a small revitalized Austrian army on the southern Bavarian border, able to strike at Napoleon's lines of communication as the French army advanced into the hereditary lands. In either case, Charles was wrong to assume that any force sent on October 13 was doomed to make an exhausting march and arrive too late.

Charles's decision was influenced by his conviction that the evil Mack was at the root of the problem: "I believe that all of this is a trick of the all-powerful Mack who, angry that my cousin had turned back these regiments, has addressed himself surreptitiously to Vienna to get H[is] M[ajesty] to give this order directly."[61] This assumption was also wrong: Mack had canceled his demand for the additional regiments and then changed his mind. Ferdinand, who had largely abdicated responsibility for the affairs of the army under his nominal command following the meeting with Mack and Francis in mid-September, had little to do with this dispute.[62]

Charles's decision should not be instantly dismissed as the result of personal pique or imperial clannishness, however. He knew virtually nothing about what was going on in Germany because no one kept him apprised of events in the theater neighboring his own. He knew that Mack had usurped power in his cousin's army, but not how matters actually stood in that army at any given moment. He knew that things were going badly in Germany, of course, since French troops marching on Innsbruck must mean that Mack's army was in serious trouble. But he had no idea of what danger his own troops consequently faced from the rear. And he knew that he was in danger of exhausting and demoralizing his own army by sending it piecemeal marching back and forth across the Alps.

Charles's decision to withhold reinforcements for the German theater at a critical time resulted in large part from the breakdown of the Austrian command and control system at the strategic and grand strategic levels, and the consequent collapse of communications between the overall leader and the theater commanders, and among the theater commanders themselves. Francis's failure to establish a robust leadership presence supported by a suitable staff condemned Charles and Ferdinand to fight confused and unconnected battles in theaters that were less than a week's march from each other. The only thing that is surprising in this context is that Charles continued to cooperate with the increasingly shrill demands from Germany as long as he did.

To the archduke's surprise, the termination of the truce did not lead to an immediate French attack.[63] The passing days brought more rumors, however, of the collapse of the situation in Germany and the ripple effect of that collapse into the Tyrol. Several regiments were sent marching from the Tyrol toward Innsbruck, and Charles felt that his right flank was being exposed to an attack by the full force of the French army in Bavaria. He felt obliged to reposition troops within his own theater in order to cover the deficiencies created by the collapse of the situation in the Tyrol. As Charles was mulling these rumors, worse news arrived: the Neapolitans had ratified their treaty with Napoleon and Saint Cyr's army was on its way north.[64]

Charles did not panic, at least not officially. His letter to Francis delivering this news focused instead on the need to redirect the Russian troops at Corfu to

Venice rather than Naples. From Venice the Russians would be in a position to either support Charles's attack (probably by helping cover his increasingly exposed left flank) or operate with the Venetian garrison to prevent or delay a French advance into Austria in the event of "misfortune" on the Adige.

The next day, although still without official word from Germany or Francis, Charles concluded that Mack's army had been defeated: "We must have been beaten in Germany since the French are daring to advance so far right up close to the Iser."[65] When small arms fire broke out and spread along the entire French line along the Adige, Charles concluded that Masséna had learned of a French victory in Bavaria of which the archduke had not been informed.[66] He reacted intelligently. Noting that John was mobilizing the Tyrolean militia to defend against a French invasion, Charles decided to move his headquarters closer to the Adige. "I would hope," he wrote, "that the enemy will see in this that I am ready to attack and to conquer all of Italy in the blink of an eye."[67]

This attempt at bravado contrasted sharply with Charles's own sentiments. At the first word of Ferdinand's new plight, the archduke reverted to his previous gloomy pessimism about his army and its prospects. "Our situation is still the same," he wrote Albert on October 13. "We are lacking everything, and I am surprised that our soldiers do not revolt or desert." The troops lacked clothing, supplies, shoes, hats, and even weapons. The magazines were as empty as the army's coffers "despite the immense [amount] of money that we had, according to what Mack had told me." He concluded, "One would need more than the resignation of a Trappist Monk to serve here."[68]

Even his tone in regard to Francis changed somewhat. He obliquely chastised the emperor for allowing Mack to open hostilities "prematurely" and for not informing Charles of the movements in Germany, "as I was justified in hoping" that Francis would do.* But Charles did not confine himself to complaining. He wrote that if the enemy actually was in the Tyrol, he must take aggressive action. He would have to abandon his position on the lower Adige and race for the upper Adige valley, hoping to forestall the French before they could get into the Pustertal, whence they could cut off supplies to the Austrian army. Charles feared that the French might make it to the southern Tyrol ahead of him, that they might defeat his army as it was strung out in small detachments, that he would not be able to sustain a large army in the poor regions of the Tyrol. The urgency was so great, however, that he would have to "leave all that to fate."

Charles did not act on this determination, however, for two reasons. First, Masséna finally struck on October 18. While making feints at various points

---

*Charles to Francis, 16 October 1805, KA AFA 1805 Italien, X/152¼. It was not Mack who opened hostilities thus "prematurely," but Napoleon, who had made up his mind to attack the Austrians much sooner than the plans anticipated.

along the Adige line, the French troops rushed the bridge over the Adige before the Castelvecchio in Verona and beat off the attempts of the local Austrian commander, FML Vukassovich, to push them back. Since Charles had opted to keep most of his forces in central locations rather than spread out along the river line, Masséna's concentrated troops were able to overwhelm the limited reinforcements Vukassovich could bring to bear and consolidated their bridgehead rapidly. They also took a number of Austrian cannons that Vukassovich had placed in an exposed position despite Charles's clear orders not to do so. The archduke felt it necessary to relieve Vukassovich of his command, as an example to the other commanders about the importance of following orders meant to preserve the army's limited mobile artillery park.[69]

Charles did not immediately understand what had occurred, however. His initial report to Francis described French crossings at Verona and Bonavigo that were repulsed as Austrian reinforcements arrived. The French, he thought, had completely abandoned their positions on the left bank of the Adige at Bonavigo, leaving only a small outpost on the Austrian bank at Verona.[70] In truth, the French attack at Bonavigo was a feint designed to draw forces away from Verona, and the commander there withdrew when he succeeded in doing so.[71] Charles rapidly recognized his error, and he realized that the French were across the Adige at Verona in force and were building a large fortified bridgehead. Losses in men and in artillery had proved greater than initially reported.*

By October 22, Charles realized that the initial reports of 20,000 Frenchmen marching rapidly on Innsbruck were vastly exaggerated. Coupled with the fight at Verona, that realization may explain his delay in marching into the Tyrol as he had originally proposed.[72] The collapsing strategic and grand strategic situation, however, weighed more heavily on Charles than the French army immediately before him. He learned that Saint Cyr's army of 20,000–24,000 men was racing to join Masséna. This accretion of strength would destroy the parity Charles believed existed between the two armies in Italy and give Masséna a decisive advantage. He had also learned that Augereau's Corps of 30,000 men was marching rapidly toward the northern Tyrol, that Jellachich had withdrawn from Ulm but lost many of the troops he was trying to save, that Auffenberg had surrendered many troops at Wertingen, that Kienmayer had been driven back to Dachau, and that a smaller French corps than originally reported was on the road to Innsbruck.

Charles once again took immediate action and contemplated more dramatic decisions. He ordered the Austrian forces in the Tyrol to concentrate in

---

*Charles to Francis, 22 October 1805, KA AFA 1805 Italien, X/197¼; Bellegarde to Charles, 20 October 1805, KA AFA 1805 Italien, X/180. Charles was generally disappointed with his subordinates' quality of reporting, as well as their actions in defense of the advanced posts of the Austrian army along the Adige. See Charles to Davidovich, 19 October 1805, KA AFA 1805 Italien, 162.

order to defend themselves better against the multiple threats they faced, and he sent John back toward Innsbruck to take command of this coalescing army.* He also contemplated, once again, the possibility of racing with his army into the Tyrol. In writing to Albert, Charles took a gloomy satisfaction in having predicted the course events would take: "If one could feel satisfaction from what has happened I would feel it from having predicted everything." He added, "To continue my prophecies, I believe that Napoleon, after having taken and destroyed our army in Germany, will fall on the Russians, defeat them as well, and while pursuing them with one part of his forces toward Vienna will send the other by Salzburg toward Spital to seize the Pustertal." He then asked, "What shall I do then?"[73] He evaluated the alternative courses of action open to him:

> Should I rush to the defense of Vienna? But from Verona to Vienna the road is twice as long as from the Inn. Should I throw myself into the Tyrol? But despite my prayers so often repeated to Vienna the Tyrol has magazines neither for the country nor for the troops that are there. They live from day to day from what they get through the Pustertal. Thus this would expose me to being trapped in these mountains to be blocked there from all sides and to have to lay down my arms from the lack of supplies.
>
> Should I retire on Villach? But that would put me between two fires, between the enemy coming through the Pustertal and Masséna who will follow and harass me during my retreat.
>
> What is there then left to do?
>
> To order John to abandon the northern Tyrol in order to retreat by forced marches on Brixen and from there to Villach when he learns that the Russians have suffered a defeat, so that he will not risk being surprised by the enemy in the Pustertal.
>
> To have Hiller make the same maneuver in order to reunite with my brother at Brixen while there is still time.
>
> To leave a sufficient garrison in Venice and to retire with the main part of the army through Gorice on Laibach so as not to be surprised by the enemy at Laibach, to reunite with John between this city and Klagenfurth, to take a position having my rear free, having Hungary behind me. But this maneuver is difficult, a retreat facing an enemy superior in forces because of the arrival of the troops from Naples without exposing myself to a defeat will demand great study and will be the worse because the bad weather and the lack of everything will hold me up in my marches and

---

*Although many secondary accounts describe John as the commander of the Austrian army in the Tyrol, this was not the case. Charles had the overall command of those forces, as well as the forces in Italy, and the young John was assigned to him as an "ad latus," whom Charles could use as a commander if he so chose. (Appointment orders, 31 August 1805, KA AFA 1805 Italien, VIII/135.) During October John shuttled back and forth between the Tyrol and Charles's headquarters in Italy several times.

will hinder my maneuvers. I will consider myself fortunate to arrive in Carniola with half or a third of the army that I have right now.[74]

It is difficult to evaluate Charles's decision fairly at this point because the alternatives he faced were so dangerous and uncertain. John still held Innsbruck and the Alpine passes, so that Charles could have rushed with a large part of his army toward Bavaria. If he had done so, it would surely have altered the face of the campaign fundamentally, since Napoleon would have had to divert substantial forces to deal with the threat suddenly erupting in his rear. Masséna's forces were not well positioned to prevent such a maneuver, since even with the occupation of the Austrian portion of Verona, the French in Italy would have to run the gauntlet Charles had set up in and around Trento, nor did Masséna have orders to prevent Charles from leaving Italy.

Even so, Charles would have been accepting enormous risks in rushing into the Tyrol at this juncture. Masséna would not have been able to prevent him and would have found much difficulty in following him, but he could well have occupied Charles's lines of communication back to Austria. If Napoleon's troops had moved swiftly enough, they might have trapped Charles in the Tyrolean Alps where he would have had to surrender. The advantage in the move lay all in surprise—Napoleon did not expect Charles to undertake such a daring operation. The main risk lay in exposing the last standing Austrian army to defeat by starvation. Charles chose the more prudent course by deciding to withdraw to the east, even though it meant abandoning a risky chance to retrieve the disastrous situation.

The decision to retreat toward Gorice rather than Villach and to aim at Hungary was also problematic. The safest course for Charles to follow was more or less due east. In that way he could reasonably hope to ensure that Napoleon's troops did not get in behind him and cut him off. Therefore this was the best way to secure his army, but it pulled Charles's army farther away from the future theater of war, if Napoleon raced toward Vienna as Charles expected him to. Charles probably would not be able to participate in subsequent operations, including operations resulting from the arrival of Russian reinforcements or even Prussian troops.

Charles's mistrust of Austria's coalition partners no doubt played a significant role in this decision. He had doubted all along that the Russians would arrive in force enough to change the outcome, and to this point in the campaign his fears had been realized. He continued to disbelieve in the possibility of Prussian intervention despite Napoleon's violation of the neutrality zone. He clearly felt that the best he could do was to maintain an Austrian army in order to improve Francis's dismal bargaining position when his allies finally abandoned him, as Charles was sure they would. The poison resulting from the weakness of the coalition helped drive Charles to a course of action virtually ensuring that his army would play no further part in operations.

Having made up his mind, Charles wrote John ordering him to abandon his preparations in the Tyrol and march his reunited army east to link up with the Italian army.[75] John was surprised to receive this order, since he had only arrived in Innsbruck a week or so before and had been preparing to defend the Tyrol against the expected French invasion. He was hastily repairing and provisioning fortresses, mobilizing the local militia, concentrating his limited forces farther east, and preparing to wage a guerrilla war in the Alpine passes.[76] Instead, Charles now ordered him to concentrate all available troops and march to Villach.

Francis apparently played no role in these decisions. Charles informed the emperor of his decisions but began to implement them before Francis could respond, even if he had wanted to. Unfortunately for the Austrians, Charles only began to act decisively as an overall theater commander once he decided that the war was lost and he could only save the pieces. There is every reason to imagine a much more favorable outcome of the campaign for Austria had someone, either Charles or Francis or even Mack, been coordinating the activities of all of her armies throughout the war.

Charles could not implement his decision to begin the retreat immediately, however, because Masséna chose this moment to renew his attack. Masséna had been steadily building up his forces and his bridgehead at Verona since the attack on October 18, and an undeclared truce had held since that time. On October 29 he finally struck. Charles had chosen his position well. Disdaining to spread his forces thin in an effort to prevent the French from crossing the Adige, Charles had instead concentrated his troops around a series of fortifications a short distance east of the river near the village of Caldiero. His outposts and vanguards near the French crossings delayed Masséna's advance and tired and bloodied his troops, with the result that the Austrians were well able to hold their fortifications throughout the day.

When the French withdrew during the night, Charles decided to strike a blow himself in order to gain space for his withdrawal. He accordingly renewed the battle on October 30, driving hard at Masséna's concentrations. The battle was balanced, which was natural considering that the two sides had nearly equal forces, and when the day ended, Charles was able to withdraw once again while Masséna's troops collected themselves. The Austrians had caused sufficient disorder in the French ranks that Masséna was not immediately able to follow when Charles retreated out of the theater.*

---

*The tactical details of the Battle of Caldiero, although fascinating, are not sufficiently important to this narrative to merit a detailed exposition. A French account, with some supporting documents, can be found in Koch, *Mémoires de Masséna*, pp. 91–103. Austrian accounts are in Karl Schikofsky, "Die Schlacht von Caldiero 1805," *Separatabdruck aus dem Organ der Militärwissenschaftlichen Vereine* 71, no. 2 (1905): 158–184; Moriggl, *Der Feldzug von Ulm*, pp. 511–529; Angeli, *Erzherzog Carl von Oesterreich,* 3:103–135.

Conclusion

The failure of Charles's large army to participate in the decisive events of the War of 1805 was by no means predetermined. Numerous decision points came and went at which the archduke could have chosen to march north and thereby alter the flow of the war—including one as late as the end of October. Each time, Charles chose an easier, safer, and more passive course. It is easy to blame him for this passivity and to describe him as an "old school" general more interested in maneuver than in combat and unwilling to risk his army in a hard fight. Such an accusation is unfair, especially considering the hard fighting Charles put in at Caldiero, including a second day's struggle that he himself initiated by preempting Masséna.

The single most important factor that led Charles away from riskier options that might have changed the course of the war was the complete absence of any central leadership presence on the Austrian side, to say nothing of the coalition side. In Charles's place, to be sure, Napoleon would have been over the Alps and into Bavaria by the middle of October, no doubt in contravention of a series of orders from Paris—behavior he found normal in the earlier Italian campaigns. But Charles was not Napoleon and Francis was not the Directory.

Francis was firmly enough in command of the Austrian armies throughout 1805 to ensure that Mack's plans were developed and implemented, even if that meant demoting his own brother. He made the critical decisions of war and peace, and no one, especially Charles, disputed his right to do so. To have made such violent and risky decisions as those entailed in turning the army north without any orders or approval from Francis would have gone against all of Charles's beliefs, understanding, and training. It was asking too much of him to expect him to do so.

The real blame for Charles's inactivity, therefore, lies with the emperor himself. Only Francis could have ordered Charles to take decisive action or empowered him to make the decision himself. He did neither. Instead, Francis focused on defusing the explosive situation he and Mack were creating in Germany and left no one in overall command and control of Austria's armies. The result was as might have been expected. Charles allowed himself to be driven by his mistrust of Austria's allies and his premonitions of military disaster into choosing what seemed to be the safer course. As a result, however, he opened the field for Napoleon to decide the war on his own terms—the most dangerous thing to do.

20

Forgotten Theaters

Germany

Prussia's involvement in the War of 1805 is another of the great might-have-beens of history. Napoleon's violation of Prussian territory at Ansbach drew the Prussians toward the coalition and might have drawn them into the war. Prussia's army, thought to be excellent if small, would have been ideally positioned to strike Napoleon's exposed flanks and rear, potentially cutting off the Grande Armée from France. What would have happened then is hard to say—Napoleon might have won a series of battles against the Russians, the Prussians, and even Charles's returning army, thereby giving him an even greater victory than what he actually achieved at the end of 1805. He might have lost one or more of those fights, however. What is certain is that had the Prussians intervened effectively, the course of the war—and the next ten years of European history, at least—would have been different. Although many contemporaries and most historians believe that Frederick William's failure to participate in the war was inevitable, the truth is that this nonevent was one of the most contingent elements that shaped the War of 1805.*

---

*The common wisdom that the War of 1805 proceeded in some way according to Napoleon's plans, together with the nearly universal admiration for his skills, has lent an aura of inevitability to the events and nonevents of that year. No historians have carefully examined the reasons for Charles's nonparticipation in the decisive events, since they have seemed to most obvious. Although Frederick William's failure to take part in the military events of 1805 has been studied to a greater extent, most still see that failure as inevitable. This results at least partially from the efforts of one of the principal participants to make it so. Hardenberg argued that the king never really meant to go to war. *Eigenhändige Memoiren des Staatskanzlers Fürsten von Hardenberg*, ed. Leopold von Ranke (Leipzig: Duncker & Humblot, 1877), vol. 2, passim. Thomas Stamm-Kuhlmann, in *König in Preußens großer Zeit: Friedrich Wilhelm III. Der Melancholiker auf dem Thron* (Berlin: Siedler Verlag, 1992), relies heavily on Hardenberg's memoirs to make the case for the king's "melancholy" and lassitude. Brendan Simms, *The Impact of Napoleon: Prussian High Politics, Foreign Policy and the Crisis of the Executive, 1797–1806* (New York: Cambridge University Press, 1997), offers a more nuanced view. Largely

The Russo-Prussian War of 1805

The Russian court was divided and confused about how best to deal with Prussia, despite plans to force Frederick William to fight that it had agreed on with Austria. While Adam Czartoryskii continued to dream of a war with Prussia that would lead to the reestablishment of a united Polish kingdom under Alexander's scepter, the tsar vacillated between anger at Frederick William's supposed pusillanimity and his own reluctance to fight the monarch he liked best among all the rulers of Europe. The tsar's staff continued to draw up plans for war with Prussia. Czartoryskii laid the political groundwork for not only the war but the subsequent resurrection of Poland. But the tsar's commitment to fight the war that some of his subordinates were eagerly preparing for him remained unclear.

The extent of Czartoryskii's determination to start a war with Prussia in order to reunite Poland will forever be shrouded in obscurity. Certainly Prince Adam hoped to take advantage of growing Russo–Prussian tensions to favor his homeland, but it is not clear that he was actively working for war between the two states in order to fulfill that aim.* In later years he declared, "I must admit that the improbability of Prussia entering into the concert of the Powers was not what I most regretted. I did not neglect any argument calculated to persuade her, but I foresaw with satisfaction the necessity of disregarding her interests in the event of a refusal, for in that case Poland would have been proclaimed a Kingdom under the sceptre of Alexander."[1] He therefore began to lay the diplomatic and political groundwork in Vienna and Poland to ensure that Poland would benefit if war broke out between Alexander and Frederick William. These preparations coexisted with his strenuous efforts to induce Frederick William to join the coalition.

When the tsar decided, against the wishes of his advisers (including Czartoryskii), to leave St. Petersburg and join his army at the front, Prince Adam brought him to his estate at Puławy, where Alexander and his entourage stayed from September 30 until October 16.[2] The Czartoryskiis had gathered a large part of the Polish nobility, including a number of beautiful young women to grace the dance floors for the evening balls. Prince Adam wore simple black clothes that set off a single decoration: the Polish Order of Virtute Militari that he had received for valor in combat against the Russians in 1792.[3] As the Polish nobility flattered and charmed Alexander, word flew round the district that the Russian tsar was about to liberate Poland from the partition and servitude to which his grandmother had subjected her.

---

ignoring the king, he suggests that Hardenberg's delaying approach was designed to secure better terms for Prussia's entry into the coalition. See below for specific discussions and references.

*W. H. Zawadzki, in *A Man of Honour: Adam Czartoryski as a Statesman of Russia and Poland, 1795–1831* (Oxford: Clarendon, 1993), pp. 127ff., considers the evidence for a concrete plan to despoil Prussia of her Polish possessions and comes to a balanced and cautious conclusion that such a plan certainly existed for the event of a Russo–Prussian war, but not as a plan to incite such a war.

Czartoryskii went even further and began preparing the way in Vienna for a revision of all the eastern European borders, In early October he wrote to the Russian ambassador to Austria, Razumovskii, that war with Prussia was coming to seem inevitable because of Frederick William's continuing timidity. Russia had to consider her aims in such a war, and those could only be the reestablishment of Poland under Russia's control. Austria would naturally insist on compensation for the Russian acquisition of Prussia's Polish territories, and that could be easily arranged: Francis should help himself to both Bavaria and Silesia. Even if he had to give up Austria's Polish territories, he would nevertheless find himself more than compensated. Czartoryskii did not mention that his plan would effectively destroy the Prussian monarchy, which neither escaped nor troubled Russia's Polish foreign minister.[4] Prince Adam justified this ruthless plan in part based on the need to secure the Poles' support for the Russian war effort. He expected a veritable deluge of Polish volunteers to help the Russians fight Prussia to secure an independent Poland.[5]

The tsar countenanced Czartoryskii's declarations and allowed his foreign minister to insert articles into the instructions for the commanders of his armies on Prussia's frontiers to work in various ways to gain the Poles' confidence and support.[6] He refused, however, to commit himself to the support of this adventure. Frederick William's continued recalcitrance forced Alexander nevertheless to prepare for the war, and he did so with grim determination.

The Russian plans for a war against Prussia were as complex as the Austrian program for defeating Napoleon. Three Russian armies were concentrated on the eastern Prussian frontier. The Army of Volhynia, commanded by General Buxhöwden, consisted of 50,000 troops formed at Brest-Litovsk. Its mission was to march either on Warsaw or through Silesia toward Bohemia to support the operations of Kutuzov and the Austrians, depending on whether Frederick William chose to fight with or against Alexander. The Army of the North, commanded by General Bennigsen, was to march with its 47,000 men in two corps through Prussia to Hanover, there to link up with the Russo–Swedish army commanded by General Tolstoy. The Army of Lithuania was forming up more slowly. One of its columns, 12,000 strong and commanded by General Essen, was to cross the frontier at Brest-Litovsk and rush to support General Buxhöwden's force; the other 33,000 soldiers in this army were then to concentrate at Brest-Litovsk, presumably as a reserve.[7]

The war plans relied on surprising the Prussians before they could mobilize and prepare their forces, and on rapidly seizing crucial fortresses and positions. The armies were to avoid sieges and minimize the alienation of local populations (not only Polish) as much as they could. The concept of these operations was to shock Frederick William by bringing more than 160,000 troops to bear against his unready army from the north, east, and south. The armies were not ordered to seek out and engage Prussian troop concentrations but to bypass them whenever possible: why destroy an army that you hope to force into battle against a common enemy later? The Russians were confident that they could coordinate the movements of six or seven major troop concentrations spread out in an arc of several hundred miles and operating against a dispersed foe, but they hoped the Prussians would lose their will to fight quickly and that no serious battles would ensue.

These plans and preparations, both military and diplomatic, show how seriously Alexander contemplated war against Frederick William. The mobilization of these large forces, in addition to Kutuzov's army and Lacy's force designated for the invasion of Naples, was costly. The destruction of Prussia's army was not something lightly to be enterprised. The complications resulting from any effort to resurrect Poland would be far-reaching. Reluctant though he proved to execute these plans, the tsar was ready to do so if necessary.

Not all of Alexander's servants were as enthusiastic about the prospect of a Russo–Prussian war as Czartoryskii, however. The Russian ambassador in Berlin, Alopeus, sympathized with the country in which he was accredited and had the normal desire of diplomats to avoid war. Czartoryskii encountered opposition to his plans for pressing Frederick William from an unlikely source as well: a twenty-eight-year-old noble named Peter Petrovich Dolgorukii.*

Dolgorukii was the scion of a leading noble house of Russia.[8] He was enrolled in the ranks of the Izmailovskii Guards Regiment at the age of one and became a major at fifteen. Four years later he was a lieutenant colonel commanding a garrison regiment, but garrison duty bored him. He wrote to Tsar Paul asking for a transfer to a line regiment, but the tsar (wisely) refused. Undaunted, Dolgorukii wrote again, repeating his request. This time the tsar not only rejected it but berated his obstreperous young lieutenant colonel and instructed him not to bother his monarch again. Dolgorukii remained intrepid. He wrote next to Grand Prince Alexander, repeating his request. The young heir to the throne, almost exactly Dolgorukii's age, was more amenable. Within a year Dolgorukii had received command of Smolensk and its garrison and a promotion to the rank of colonel.

Handsome, witty, and strong, Dolgorukii was also self-confident, precocious, and unwilling to accept either rejection or advice. His intelligence was not tempered by experience or by an understanding of his own limitations. He was a dangerous adviser for an equally inexperienced young monarch, but Alexander was no doubt drawn to his energy, confidence, and youth.

Dolgorukii was a passionate Russian patriot and despised Czartoryskii as a foreigner. He once declared directly to the beleaguered foreign minister, who was always sensitive to precisely this thrust, "You think, my dear sir, like a Polish prince, but I think like a Russian."[9] His opposition to Czartoryskii ranged

---

*His name is sometimes incorrectly rendered Dolgorukov.

Dolgorukii against the other powerful members of Alexander's Unofficial Committee, including Novosil'tsev and Stroganov, but the self-confident young man did not mind. One could almost sense his excitement at the thought of winning such an apparently unequal battle. When Alexander sent Dolgorukii on a special mission to Berlin in September, he sent a powerful ally to help his ambassador fight against the precepts of his foreign minister.

Alopeus reported from Berlin on September 6 that the only hope of bringing Prussia around was a direct meeting between the two sovereigns, but he believed that such a meeting would achieve its purpose. Karl August von Hardenberg managed to convince the Russian envoy that if Alexander's troops crossed the Prussian border without a prior arrangement, Prussia would fight with France against the coalition.[10] When Hardenberg held out the possibility that Prussia might participate in the next year's operations, Alopeus believed this was the best that could be hoped for, even if Alexander had been willing to fight a war he disliked.

Alopeus nevertheless delivered an ultimatum to Hardenberg on September 18, as he had been ordered: If Prussia did not adhere to the coalition at once, Russian armies would cross the border by September 28.[11] This ultimatum arrived right after Hardenberg and Laforest exchanged notes consummating the failure of the most recent effort at a Franco–Prussian treaty.[12] Frederick William was stubbornly determined to remain neutral, whatever blandishments Napoleon offered and threats Alexander made.

The king's behavior at this pass is odd. Here was a large Russian army on his eastern frontier with a smaller Russo–Swedo–British force ready to descend on Hanover. The tsar threatened to use this army to invade Prussia if the king resisted an alliance. Frederick William was ready to fight Alexander to avoid making that alliance. Here was Napoleon offering an offensive–defensive alliance *and* Hanover. The safest course of action would have been to take the proffered alliance, seize Hanover, and fight the Russians with Napoleon's definite aid. Rejecting Napoleon's offer while preparing simultaneously to fight the Russians was a far riskier path that opened the possibility of limitless Prussian defeat without any guarantee of outside assistance. This was hardly the course of action that a timid or cowardly monarch would have chosen.

On learning of the Russian ultimatum, Frederick William did not resurrect the prospect of a French alliance but mobilized his army instead. The prospect of imminent war on the continent had led the king to order a partial mobilization of 80,000 troops on September 7.[13] The Russian ultimatum of September 18 led to the usual committee meeting in Berlin. The conference, which included Hardenberg, Haugwitz, Brunswick, and a number of other senior generals, recommended that the king immediately mobilize his entire army and send a large force marching to the Vistula. It also recommended that he accept Alexander's offer of a direct meeting between the two monarchs in order to gain time. The mobilization order was sent off at once and had been largely executed by October 1. A courier with the king's letter to Alexander left Berlin on September 20.[14]

Alexander had already changed his mind by the time this message reached him. On September 17, Czartoryskii wrote to Alopeus that his warning message of September 6 had persuaded Alexander to meet with Frederick William before ordering his troops to cross the Prussian frontier.* The courier with this message raced from St. Petersburg to Berlin and created a dramatic scene when he arrived on September 27, the day before the Russian troops were to cross the border. Alopeus had met Hardenberg early that morning at the minister's request, and Hardenberg warned the ambassador once again that if the Russians crossed the frontier the result would be "catastrophes for the good cause." Alopeus returned home to find Alexander's courier panting and dusty from his arrival. On reading the dispatch, he hastened back to Hardenberg but encountered a problem: Duroc and Laforest had requested a meeting and were expected to arrive at any moment.†

Hardenberg smuggled Alopeus into a room he did not normally use for audiences in order to prevent an awkward meeting between the French and Russian representatives. He was delighted with the news Alopeus brought him and noted the timeliness of the message. He had been planning to meet with the French representatives and then see the king. Alopeus asked if the French were still offering Hanover to Prussia. "Ah! It is a question of much more," Hardenberg replied. "They are proposing an alliance and much more beyond to us."[15]

In truth, Duroc and Laforest were making yet another effort to force Frederick William to join with Napoleon, even secretly. If Prussia would only make a few demonstrations with her troops, the fear of being attacked from the north would force Austria and Russia to their senses. Frederick William would thereby restore peace to the continent—his dearest wish—at virtually no risk. "The king of Prussia would then have Hanover with everyone's consent."[16]

When Alexander suspended his army's movements, Frederick William rejected this alliance offer and tried once again to get Napoleon to recognize

---

*Czartoryskii to Alopeus, 17 September 1805, VPR, vol. II, doc. 181. Zawadzki, *Man of Honour*, p. 130, may be reading more "thinly concealed" anger into this letter than its content strictly justifies. The note merely makes it clear that Czartoryskii placed the entire responsibility for the course of action Alexander had chosen on Alopeus—for good or ill. The argument that Austrian pressure to avoid a war with Prussia had contributed to Alexander's decision to suspend the march of his troops (Zawadzki, *Man of Honour*) misreads the timing of events—word of the Austrians' request to avoid provoking a war with Prussia only arrived in early October, long after Alexander had suspended the march of his armies. Czartoryskii to Razumovskii, 10 October 1805, VPR, vol. II, doc. 189 n. 316.

†Alopeus's account of this interview is unaccountably missing from VPR, vol. II. This version comes from Metternich, to whom Alopeus subsequently described the scene and to whom he showed his instructions (Metternich to Colloredo, Wilhelm Oncken, *Österreich und Preußen im Befreiungskriege* [New York: Georg Olms Verlag, 1998], pp. 580–581).

Prussia's neutrality—and evacuate Hanover as well, so that Frederick William could incorporate it into the neutrality zone. Hardenberg tried to persuade Napoleon's envoys that such actions would serve France's interests better than an alliance, since they would secure Napoleon's northern flank.[17]

The next day Duroc and Laforest offered Prussia a treaty that recognized the neutrality of northern Germany and gave Prussia temporary possession of Hanover. In return, however, Napoleon demanded a substantial indemnity for the occupation of Hanover, denied Prussia any permanent rights to the Electorate, and insisted that Frederick William guarantee Holland from all invasions by the British or their allies.[18] Hardenberg called a conference to consider how best to respond to this proposal.

It would be most unwise, he pointed out, to make arrangements with France before Frederick William had met with Alexander. If the tsar abandoned his plans of forcing Prussia to join the coalition—something that was by no means clear in Berlin at that time—then a Franco–Prussian arrangement could harm the renewal of Russo–Prussian ties. If, on the other hand, Alexander still meant to invade Prussia if Frederick William did not do his bidding, then it would behoove the king to make Napoleon a friend and even an ally. Therefore Hardenberg proposed that the king reiterate his neutrality and offer an armed mediation between Napoleon and Alexander, keeping open all options in the event that such mediation failed.[19]

Frederick William, who was present at this conference, was unusually out of temper. He had already decided, according to Hardenberg, to avoid meeting Alexander by fabricating a pretext; he was clearly terrified of a face-to-face confrontation with the tsar that he expected to be unpleasant. After wrangling about various courses of action, the king dismissed the meeting without coming to any conclusions at all.[20]

Part of the problem was that Frederick William did not want to make decisions in the presence of his senior advisers. Consequently he ordered Hardenberg to brief his cabinet secretaries, Beyme and Lombard, so that the king could make up his mind in their more congenial company. Beyme reported the results of that meeting to Hardenberg on October 3. The king rejected the French proposals entirely. Prussia would remain strictly neutral. Frederick William would take Hanover but only for the purpose of ensuring its neutrality now that Napoleon had unilaterally withdrawn Bernadotte's forces from the Electorate—and only if the British did not reclaim it first. Hardenberg passed this message on to Laforest the next day, and the French ambassador, who declared himself unable to negotiate such an agreement, promised to send to Napoleon at once. The Prussians' attention was drawn back to the east immediately, however, as Dolgorukii arrived in Berlin that very day.[21]

Although Dolgorukii bore the good news that Alexander was willing to suspend the march of his troops until after his meeting with Frederick William, he also brought the bad news that the tsar remained determined to force the king to agree to the transit of his armies through Prussian territory at least. Alexander's note did not renew his demands for an alliance or for Prussia's active participation in the coalition, although Dolgorukii pressed for them during his interview and a subsequent letter from Alexander hinted at them.[22] Frederick William persisted in his refusal to consider Alexander's demands and proposals, however, and Dolgorukii prepared to take his leave, having failed in his mission. But once again, with timing worthy of a Hollywood script, a courier arrived just as Dolgorukii was leaving. Napoleon's troops had violated Prussian neutrality at Ansbach.[23]

This courier's arrival revolutionized the situation in Berlin, as we shall see, but also at Puławy, where the Russians were in despair before Dolgorukii's letter arrived there. On October 10, Czartoryskii penned a lengthy note to Razumovskii to apprise him of the situation.[24] Alopeus, he wrote, had destroyed Russia's position. The plan had been to force Prussia's hand by threatening her with overwhelming force before her army was prepared to fight, but Alopeus's delays and determination to find a peaceful resolution had ruled out any possibility of catching the Prussians napping. Now Alexander had to contemplate a serious war against a strong and prepared enemy. Worse still, Francis, preoccupied with events in Bavaria, had sent word begging Alexander to avoid a war with Prussia that could only complicate his already delicate situation. Circumstances had conspired to strengthen the tsar's unwillingness to fight Frederick William beyond any hope Czartoryskii might have had of overcoming it.

Czartoryskii may have been shrewd enough to abandon his plans for a Russo–Prussian war, lest they shake apart the coalition that was already fighting Napoleon.* Both he and Alexander recognized that they still faced a significant problem, even apart from the damage the delays were doing to the coalition war plan. Alexander had mobilized large armies and then joined them in the field— the first tsar to do so since Peter the Great.† Czartoryskii was not just trying to fan the dying embers of a Russo–Prussian conflict when he noted, "Not only for the general well-being of affairs but also for the honor of the emperor it is necessary to obtain something real that will be at the same time visible, so that Europe cannot say that the emperor advanced an army, joined it in person and finished by withdrawing before the will of the King of Prussia."[25] Alexander

---

*Patricia Kennedy Grimsted, *The Foreign Ministers of Alexander I: Political Attitudes and the Conduct of Russian Diplomacy, 1801–1825* (Los Angeles: University of California Press, 1969), p. 137, makes a nicely nuanced point: Czartoryskii the diplomat may have recognized the end of his hopes for a revived Poland at this point, but Czartoryskii the Polish patriot still hoped that all was not lost.

†Alexander's imperial biographer, among others, makes much of this point, but it is less impressive than it sounds. Between Peter's death in 1725 and Alexander's accession, men ruled Russia for about seven years (Peter III, 1762–1763 and Paul, 1796–1801). Since Peter III rushed to end a war, not fight one, and Paul sent only a limited expeditionary force to fight in Italy, neither really had the opportunity to take the field. The tsaritsas who ruled for the other sixty-nine years of this period did not join their armies or attempt to command them directly.

told the Austrian envoy Baron von Stutterheim, "I would compromise myself if I retreated now; we must go forward and carve an arrow out of every piece of wood. We will incite Poland to revolt against Prussia."[26] Chagrin at the humiliating position in which he found himself might have driven Alexander to war with Frederick William, even against his real wishes. This was the situation that Napoleon revolutionized when he sent Bernadotte, the Bavarians, and Davout marching through Prussian territory in Franconia.

The Aftermath of Ansbach

It is almost axiomatic for historians of this period that Frederick William never seriously intended to fight Napoleon following the violation of Prussian neutrality at Ansbach.[27] This axiom rests in considerable part on the fact that Prussia did not fight France in 1805 and, to a lesser but still important extent, on Hardenberg's presentation of the situation. When the king exploded on hearing of Napoleon's treachery and sought to order Laforest and Duroc from Berlin, Hardenberg restrained him, arguing that the proposed measures constituted a declaration of war and noting, "I foresaw, what is more, that after the initial ardor had cooled, such steps would not in any case have been followed-up on."[28] The image that emerges is of a monarch so scared and unwilling to fight that even his bellicose utterances do not merit being taken seriously.

Hardenberg, like most modern historians, underestimated the impact of Napoleon's violation of Ansbach. It was natural for him to do so. Before the courier arrived from Franconia, Hardenberg had been pacing the chambers of the palace, disconsolately reflecting that these were the very rooms in which Frederick the Great had lived, walked, and decided the affairs of Europe. In despair at his inability to move the king to a sound policy, Hardenberg contemplated resigning and leaving the field clear for his rival, Haugwitz. Having failed to persuade Frederick William to act boldly, even in the face of clear provocations, Hardenberg could hardly be expected to leap with optimism at the newest provocation. His despondency clearly conditioned his reaction to and reporting of these events.*

The evidence for Frederick William's continued "cowardice" is drawn from the records of the diplomatic negotiations that followed the violation of Prussia's

---

*Hardenberg was later accused of being insufficiently anti-French, and his memoir was in large part an effort to show his longtime opposition to Napoleon. At this decision point he is laying the groundwork to argue that he could not force the king past the point at which the king wanted to stop, and that the real blame lay with Frederick William, not him. His despondency about the king's pusillanimity and the references to Frederick the Great (which closely echo the subtle but devastating scorn A. S. Pushkin later heaped on Alexander I in *The Bronze Horseman*) are all a part of this argument. As Simms points out (*Impact*, p. 194), moreover, it was in Hardenberg's interest at the time to make it seem as though Frederick William was not really willing to fight—the best way to ensure that Prussia would enter the coalition on the most favorable possible terms.

neutrality. At the inevitable conference held on October 7 to consider the crisis, Hardenberg, Brunswick, Schulenburg, and Möllendorf recommended that Frederick William allow Russian troops free passage across Prussia, seize Hanover, prepare his army for war against France, and declare his "armed mediation" in the conflict between the coalition and Napoleon.[29] The fact that the king declared only that he would mediate between the warring sides, together with the fact that he refused to join the coalition immediately, led contemporaries and subsequent historians to conclude that Frederick William was seeking a way out of fighting. A closer examination of the diplomatic record undermines this belief, and an examination of Prussia's military preparations all but destroys it.*

At another conference held on October 9, Frederick William largely accepted his advisers' proposals.[30] This meeting naturally focused on the terms to be demanded of the coalition for Prussia's entry. The king insisted on three main items: a large subsidy from Britain for the mobilization and maintenance of all of Prussia's troops, the establishment of terms to be offered to Napoleon in an attempt to bring peace to the continent, and Hanover, as part of a general improvement of Prussia's western frontiers aimed at making the state more compact and less vulnerable to such insults as she had just suffered.

In the meantime, Laforest and Duroc were well aware of the magnitude of the initial explosion. They knew that the king had sought to throw them both out of his realm, that even military officers they had regarded as reliably pro-French, such as Brunswick and Möllendorf, now cried loudly to avenge the honor of Prussian arms, and that Lombard, who had visited them discreetly on October 7, despaired of his ability to control the growing anti-French rage in the ruling circles.†

The French envoys did their best to minimize the damage Bernadotte's march had caused to Franco–Prussian relations. The whole thing was simply a misunderstanding, they said. Since the Prussians had permitted French (and other) armies to cross their isolated territories in Franconia during the revolutionary wars, they claimed, Napoleon had taken for granted that those territo-

---

*Prussia's military preparations during this period remain unclear, since many of the archival records held at Potsdam were destroyed during Allied bombing raids in World War II. A helpful compilation (prepared long before that conflict) is in "Die Preussische Kriegsvorbereitungen und Operationspläne von 1805," *Kriegsgeschichtliche Einzelschriften* 1 (1883): 1–101. These documents must be handled with care, since the thesis of this work is that Prussia was ready to go to war in 1805. Of the secondary sources cited in this chapter, only Simms appears to have used this source, which may help explain why only his account offers a nuanced discussion of Prussia's behavior in this period.

†Laforest to Talleyrand, 9 October 1805, in Paul Bailleu, ed., *Preussen und Frankreich 1795 bis 1807: Diplomatische Correspondenzen*, Publicationen aus den königlichen preussischen Archiven, 8, 29 (Leipzig, 1881–1887), vol. 2, doc. 291; Duroc to Napoleon, 9 October 1805, doc. 292. This document gives credence and color to the charges against Lombard that Hardenberg levies in his memoirs (Ranke, *Denkwürdigkeiten*, 2:264–268). The French envoys believed that Lombard was working as hard as he could to prevent a breach, even as the Prussian king was deciding to make one.

ries were not included in the neutrality zone about which he was then negotiating with Frederick William. The Austrians had already violated Prussian
neutrality even in this war, they (falsely) declared, so that the Prussians could
have no reasonable complaint against a "similar" French action.[31]

These attempts at pacifying the Prussians had the effect of throwing gaso-
line on a fire. During previous wars the French had used Prussian territory as a
result of explicit agreements between the two states, Hardenberg rejoined. No
such agreements were even being mooted in 1805, let alone concluded. Nor
had the Austrians violated Prussian territory; on the contrary, they had been
careful not to do so, and the one small Austrian unit that had crossed the border had been disarmed immediately. Hardenberg could not see what "misunderstanding" could possibly have led Napoleon to order tens of thousands of
troops to march through the heart of a Prussian province.*

Although it is impossible to know for sure what Napoleon was thinking
when he sent his troops crashing through Ansbach, it is unlikely in the extreme that he expected the Prussians to react as they did.† Part of the problem
was Napoleon's usual inability to see the other side's perspective, as well as the
habitual mistakes aggressive leaders make when dealing with weaker powers:
he did not recognize that Frederick William could retreat no further without
forfeiting all sense of honor and dignity. Napoleon sincerely believed that the
Prussians would side with him when the chips were down. He may have
hoped that his small-scale invasion of Ansbach would have the same effect that
Alexander hoped his large-scale invasion of Prussia would have. Napoleon may
have believed the propaganda line he pursued unsuccessfully after the fact:
since French armies had routinely traipsed across Ansbach and Bayreuth in
previous wars, Frederick William would not complain if they did again. This
explanation seems the more likely in light of the fact that Napoleon made no
diplomatic preparations for the repercussions of his troop movements and
there is no evidence before the event that he even considered the possibility of
such repercussions. For Napoleon, this issue was the result of a misunderstanding (together with a monumental insouciance).

Even if the Prussians wanted to accept such an interpretation, however,
they could not readily do so for two reasons. First, Napoleon put Prussia's
standing as a great power on the line when he treated her like one of the minor
German states. The conferees of October 7 concluded first and foremost that

---

*A series of notes from Hardenberg to Duroc and Laforest are reproduced in Ranke, *Denkwürdigkeiten*,
2:288ff. Mack ordered his troops to respect the Prussian border states scrupulously, as we have seen; he
relied, in fact, on the neutrality of Ansbach to protect the right flank of his army.

†His notes to Duroc and Talleyrand reflect some surprise but much complacency about the Prussian
reaction, of which he had only heard rumors at that point. If he had been expecting an explosion, he
would likely have prepared a stronger diplomatic position for himself and would have done so much
earlier in the game. *Corr. de Nap.*, docs. 9316, 9326.

Napoleon's action "attacked and put in danger the honor and dignity of His Royal Majesty, as well as the independence and security of Your Majesty's Monarchy much more than all of the previous actions of the Russians" and second, "that it is quite impossible for a great state to allow such an offense to its sovereignty to go unpunished."[32]

Nor was it possible, they continued, simply to "throw themselves into the arms of an ally . . . with the loss of their honor" by joining France in a war against the coalition, for which Prussia did not have the necessary resources. Even if the French won such a war, Prussia could expect nothing better than the vassal status of French satellites such as Spain, Holland, and Naples.* Frederick William's advisers came to the conclusion that possible defeat at the hands of Napoleon was preferable to the definite loss of Prussia's great power status, and the king endorsed their conclusions and recommendations.

The second major problem Napoleon's violation of Prussian neutrality caused was that it compromised Frederick William before the coalition. As Hardenberg and others repeatedly declared, Bernadotte's movement through Ansbach was not something mere words could atone for. It gave Napoleon a definite military advantage over the Austrians at the same time that Frederick William was denying the Russians similar advantages, and after he had denied the Austrians the right of transit across the same territory Napoleon invaded. If the Prussians took no action other than to demand and accept an apology, the Russians were certain to believe that a secret pact existed between Berlin and Paris and would attack Prussia as an ally of France. In that event, Prussia would reap all the disadvantages of the French alliance with none of the benefits.[33] For all of these reasons, Frederick William found it impossible to accept the reassurances and continued blandishments that Napoleon and his agents offered in recompense for their "misunderstanding."

Prussian diplomacy nevertheless moved with a slowness that maddened coalition leaders even after this conference. Part of the reason for it was a natural desire to gain time for Prussia's army to reach advantageous positions from which to accept war with France when it came. Having decided to join the coalition, Hardenberg was also determined to obtain the best possible terms for Prussia from her would-be partners.[34] The initial British reaction to Hardenberg's soundings about subsidies revealed the soundness of this strategy. British ambassador Sir Francis Jackson told Hardenberg that Prussia's situation with regard to subsidies was different from that of Russia and Austria because "the two imperial courts were making war from motives long recognised by them as essential to the welfare and independence of Europe, whilst Prussia had an of-

---

*Ranke, *Denkwürdigkeiten*, 2:271. The inclusion of Naples in this list is bewildering, since the Neapolitan court was steadfastly anti-French until circumstances (including a massive earthquake) forced its capitulation.

fence of the gravest nature to avenge."[35] It behooved Prussia both to prepare for war and make it seem as though she did not really need or intend to fight.

The seriousness of Frederick William's war preparations and the optimism with which his generals made their plans strongly suggest, nevertheless, that he and they believed that war was likely and winnable. Throughout September the Prussians had been readying for war against Russia. That effort both helped and harmed the mobilization against France.[36] On the one hand, it had the disadvantage of sending a considerable part of the Prussian army east and north (to defend against the Russo–Swedish army sailing toward Mecklemburg and Hanover), and therefore away from the likely theaters of a Franco–Prussian war. On the other hand, it meant that the army was completing its mobilization when Frederick William decided to court war with Napoleon, and many of the regiments had not yet reached their designated positions for fighting the Russians when new orders were issued on October 9.[37]

Those orders had the Prussian troops in Ansbach pull back into Bayreuth and concentrate there to await reinforcements from Silesia. Other troops were to join with the elector of Hesse and his force of more than 10,000 good troops, already mobilized in a vain attempt to keep Bernadotte from passing through his territory earlier on.[38] Brunswick was to take a sizable force into Hanover to seize the Electorate (before the British could get there).[39] On the recommendation of a staff officer who pointed out that Prussian troops in Bayreuth would be exposed to defeat by French detachments and hard-pressed to find adequate sustenance, that concentration was subsequently shifted north into Thuringia.[40] This change would delay Prussia's effective engagement in the war but would secure the mobilization of Saxon and other German troops more surely, it was argued.

The Prussian war plans developed in this period require careful consideration. In general, they sent the bulk of the Prussian army to the west and northwest of Germany.* When these plans were drafted in mid-October, this deployment made sense. Napoleon's entire Grande Armée was in Bavaria fighting the Austrians around Ulm, a Russian army was marching on the Inn, and Charles had what was thought to be a vast army in Italy and the Tyrol. Although the Prussian forces would require some time to reach their designated concentration areas, it was far from fanciful to imagine that they could best serve the coalition by moving west. As the Franco-Austro-Russian conflict began to shift rapidly east, however, its movement challenged Prussian creativity and flexibility.

In the meantime, Frederick William had put his army of nearly 200,000 men on a war footing and sent much of it racing toward France, while his

---

*"Die Preussische Kriegsvorbereitungen," *Kriegsgeschichtliche Einzelschriften*, p. 16. Eighty-seven and a half infantry battalions were designated to occupy Thuringia, Hesse, and Hanover. Twenty battalions concentrated in Silesia and forty-six battalions remained in reserve, mostly in the general vicinity of Berlin.

senior commanders worked hard to develop the best plans for fighting Napoleon. Brunswick's troops had taken Hanover (without a fight) by October 25, and a regiment had also moved into Bremen.[41] Although Frederick William thus secured his most important goal, he also put himself dangerously at odds with Napoleon, with whom he had steadfastly refused to make an agreement authorizing such a movement. If this was inching cautiously toward war, as most historians would have it, it was inching very quickly for a state that had been completely demobilized only six weeks before.

As preparations for war advanced inexorably and smoothly, however, politics in Berlin reached a crisis. Frederick William had decided to recall Haugwitz to the post of foreign minister without dismissing Hardenberg. The two men would henceforth share responsibility for the office.[42] It is unclear why Frederick William made this decision, but it represented the culmination of his policy of setting his advisers against one another to avoid getting bold advice from them. Hardenberg saw it as the culmination of a campaign of intrigue against him by Lombard and Haugwitz, and there is no reason to doubt that assertion.*

Hardenberg fought in vain to defend his prerogatives, even offering his resignation, which was refused. The king claimed that he needed the best advice from all of his best advisers at this critical pass, and he left Haugwitz and Hardenberg to work out the complexities of sharing an office. Whether this decision secured better advice for the king is questionable. It plunged Prussian high politics into confusion at a critical moment, however, for the battle had hardly been fought out and Hardenberg defeated, when Alexander arrived in Potsdam on October 25.

When the king explained to the tsar his decision to allow Russian troops free passage across his territory on October 9, he made a desperate effort to put off the royal meeting once more, pleading that the exigencies of the new situation did not permit him to leave Berlin at that time.[43] But Alexander was too excited by the sudden improvement of his fortunes to be so easily put off, and he left Puławy right after Dolgorukii arrived there on October 16 with the good news.[44]

One side effect of this news and the tsar's sudden joyful departure was the complete collapse of the hopes that Czartoryskii and his friends had for the resurrection of Poland. The foreign minister's relationship with the tsar suffered directly, as Prince Adam realized that Alexander had never taken his aspirations seriously. The tsar had pursued the reunification of Poland only as long as he could not get what he really wanted—a tight relationship with Frederick William.[45]

Czartoryskii accompanied Alexander to Berlin with a heavy heart, while the tsar enjoyed the parades and balls thrown in his honor. His cheer no doubt diminished as he followed the course of the negotiations, however, for Freder-

---

*Court intrigue is not incompatible with royal decisionmaking and desires. It is far too easy to be captivated by the controversies swirling around Frederick William's servitors and thereby lose sight of the fact that the king nevertheless played the decisive role in events.

ick William refused Russian requests to make a rapid demonstration in order to take the pressure off the suffering Austrians. The king seems to have hoped that he could put off active operations until the following year, although that delusion was short-lived.[46]

Although some might see evidence that Frederick William never intended to fight in his declaration that he would only join the coalition following the failure of his armed mediation, the details of his position belie that interpretation. Declaring that "honor demands a ringing satisfaction, the security of the State, strong measures," the king proposed to offer mediation to Napoleon on the basis of a strict return to the status quo as of the Treaties of Lunéville and Amiens. He specifically insisted that Napoleon evacuate and return independence to Holland, Switzerland, and Naples; immediately separate the crown of Italy from that of France; indemnify the king of Sardinia by giving him Parma, Plaisance, Genoa, Lucca, and possibly the Ionian Islands; and agree to revise borders in Italy to provide more security for Austria.[47]

It is possible to look at these terms and speak of a "negotiation" with Napoleon only by ignoring Napoleon's public and private statements and actions over the year preceding these conferences. There was never the slightest possibility that Napoleon would even treat with a Prussian representative about such terms, let alone agree to them. Nor was Frederick William so deluded. He noted that if this course of action "leads me to war, *as I must foresee only too well,* at least it will have exhausted both my sacrifices and the wrongs of the enemy."[48] However much he disliked the prospect, Frederick William clearly understood that he was well along the road to war.

The final treaty, concluded at Potsdam on November 3, committed Frederick William to go to war that very year.[49] The king undertook to send a representative to Napoleon as soon after the ratification of the agreement as possible, and to begin hostilities no later than four weeks after the departure of that emissary, unless Napoleon returned a favorable reply—which no one expected him to do. It was possible for Frederick William to delay the emissary's departure within limits, of course, but he was absolutely bound once he had done so to follow through on his commitments or incur the bitter wrath of Alexander.

Some have suggested that Frederick William was willing to incur Alexander's wrath and he gave Haugwitz, whom he chose as his emissary to Napoleon, verbal instructions to make a deal with the French emperor.[50] This idea is plausible but difficult to accept without more evidence than seems to be available. In the first place, Frederick William allowed his senior military officers to mobilize the Prussian army fully and get it to jumping-off positions for the war on France. There is no indication that these officers held back in any way from completing their tasks as rapidly as possible.

If the king accepted the cost and danger of such preparations as a cloak for his real intentions, we would have to accept, then, that he was ready for an enraged Alexander to destroy his state when he reneged. The preparations for war took the Prussian army far to the west. At the same time, Russian armies were moving into Prussian territory in large numbers from the east. The result was that Alexander's troops would have been ideally positioned to seize Berlin and destroy its small covering forces, as well as strike at the larger Prussian troop concentrations as they tried to move back toward metropolitan Prussia. The king could not have been unaware of this state of affairs. It is not impossible that he was willing to accept such a risk, but it sorts ill with what the same contemporaries and historians write of him to imagine him coolly undertaking a step worthy of Frederick the Great's wildest and most dangerous gambles. A coward takes up no such risky position. It is much more likely, if we must take the king's unwillingness to fight for granted, that Frederick William ran the risk of war hoping against hope that peace would break out.

By the beginning of November Prussia's diplomatic plans depended almost entirely on the military situation—a good sign of the imminence of war in the minds of the leaders. Brunswick composed two evaluations of the current state of affairs and recommended deployment plans, one on November 1, the other shortly thereafter.[51] The duke assumed the following military position: the Austrians held the Tyrol with 40,000 men and Charles's army in Italy had been reduced to 50,000; Kutuzov's army together with the remnants of Mack's was thought to include 70,000 soldiers on the Inn. Although intelligence reports indicated that Napoleon had 150,000 troops in Bavaria and another 80,000 recruits forming in France, Brunswick put French strength on the Isar at only 90,000.[52]

As long as the Austrians held the Tyrol, Brunswick wrote, Napoleon would not be able to advance toward Vienna; who would leave 40,000 troops holed up in mountain fastnesses in winter on the flank of an army of 90,000? The Prussians, as well as the Russian troops moving through Prussia at that moment, would do best to concentrate in Bohemia and Franconia. This concentration would put Napoleon between two fires. If he chose to attack the Austro–Russian army in front of him, the Prussians would cut him off from France and finish him off in cooperation with their allies. If he chose to attack the Prussians, Brunswick declared that the allies would then have "a beautiful game" in following on Napoleon's heels.

Most of Brunswick's assumptions were wrong, as we have already seen. For one thing, he misestimated the relative sizes of the opposing armies: Napoleon had nearly 180,000 men in Bavaria facing not more than 50,000 or so allies on the Inn with maybe 25,000–30,000 Austrians in the Tyrol. Furthermore, Napoleon did not fear enemy formations on his flanks as a more cautious general might have. Confident that Ney's and Augereau's corps could mask anything the Austrians might have in the Tyrol, Napoleon ignored those enemy formations as he rolled after the Russians toward Vienna with the bulk

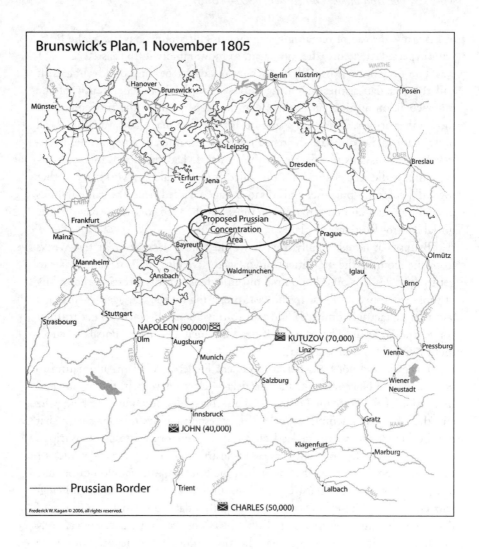

Brunswick's Plan, 1 November 1805

Münster · Hanover · Brunswick · Berlin · Küstrin · WARTHE · Posen

Leipzig

Erfurt · Jena · Dresden · Breslau

Proposed Prussian Concentration Area

Frankfurt · Prague

Mainz · Bayreuth · BERAUN · Olmütz

Mannheim · Waldmunchen · Iglau · Brno

Ansbach

Strasbourg · Stuttgart

NAPOLEON (90,000) · Ulm · Augsburg · KUTUZOV (70,000) · Linz · Vienna · Pressburg

Munich

Salzburg · Wiener Neustadt

Innsbruck · Gratz

JOHN (40,000)

Klagenfurt · Marburg

——— Prussian Border · Trient · Lalbach

CHARLES (50,000)

of his army. Instead of remaining stagnant in and around Bavaria as the Prussians expected, therefore, the war began to move rapidly to the east.*

The Brunswick plan had another set of advantages and disadvantages. It had the Prussian armies operating almost completely independently of the other coalition armies, yet their operations depended on the movements of those other armies. This plan made up for the fact that there was no central body that could coordinate the movements of the different allied armies by allowing the Prussians to operate on their own. It had the disadvantage, however, that it did not ensure that the allied forces would be working together toward a common purpose. This disadvantage resulted from the same failures in coalition staff and command structures that had led to serious flaws in the initial Austro–Russian war plan.

Brunswick noted, finally, that it would take at least four or five weeks from the moment the movement orders were given for the Prussian armies to get to their destination. He pointed out in defense of this assertion that many of those troops were still far to the east (preparing for the war against Russia, a fact that he tactfully omitted) and had to travel long distances to get to their concentration areas. The four-week deadline included in the Potsdam agreement resulted from this calculation.

Haugwitz did not leave Berlin to present Frederick William's ultimatum to Napoleon until November 14, and this delay—eleven days from the signing and ratification of the Potsdam Accord—has also been used to argue that Haugwitz and the king were attempting to shirk their responsibilities to their allies. That may be, but Haugwitz provided a detailed explanation for the timing of his trip in the memorandum he drafted to serve as his instructions during the negotiations.†
Brunswick had determined, he wrote, that the Prussian army would not be fully ready for offensive and defensive operations until December 15. Although Haugwitz empowered himself to accept a truce with a date somewhat in advance of that, he tacitly assumed that Napoleon would not accept a truce. He carefully planned his trip down to Vienna, the time allotted for negotiations with Napoleon (only four days—Haugwitz doubted that Napoleon would take longer than that to negotiate anything), and the time necessary for his trip back to Berlin. The whole purpose of the timing of the trip was to ensure that when Haugwitz returned with Napoleon's refusal to negotiate, the Prussian army would be ready for the war that would inevitably follow.[53]

---

*It is easy to see in Brunswick the "traditional eighteenth-century" general who is overly concerned about his lines of communication and sees victory in war as resulting from superlative maneuver on the enemy's lines. Even modern generals are normally very concerned about their flanks; the Pattons of this world are exceptional.

†Ranke, *Denkwürdigkeiten*, 5:185–189. It was customary for ambassadors and envoys to draft their own instructions prior to negotiations or taking up their offices. The monarch and his foreign minister normally amended and approved these instructions and then gave them official standing.

Historians also argue that Haugwitz's instructions left him so much leeway in negotiations as to allow him to make peace instead of war if he so chose.* In fact, the places where Haugwitz entrusted himself with judgment were specific to particular parts of the negotiation. The document does not give Haugwitz the power to change the purpose of the negotiation completely, whatever its author might have had in the back of his mind. This is an important point because it means that Frederick William did not explicitly give Haugwitz the authority *not* to present Napoleon with the ultimatum if he chose. If Haugwitz took such a step, it would be entirely on his own initiative, whatever "leeway" the instructions gave him on other matters.

It is interesting, nevertheless, that Haugwitz foresaw the possibility of Austria making a separate peace before or during his own negotiations, possibly as the result of a military defeat. In that case (and only in that case, according to the instructions), Haugwitz authorized himself to soothe Napoleon's feathers ruffled by the Prussian declarations and mobilizations. Since the Prussians thought that the allies were not planning to recommence active operations until December 15 anyway, however, this point seemed likely to be moot when Haugwitz left for Vienna.

If Frederick William was really determined to avoid fighting Napoleon in 1805, finally, he threw away a perfect opportunity to escape from the Potsdam treaty almost blamelessly. For when Lord Harrowby arrived in Berlin in late November to discuss the terms of the Anglo–Prussian accord essential to completing the Russo–Prussian agreement, he announced that he could not even discuss the possibility of giving Hanover to Prussia because His Britannic Majesty's British ministers were never empowered to discuss Hanover at all.† Harrowby insisted that the Prussians accept Holland and a variety of other *western* German territories instead of the coveted Electorate—territories that would move the Prussian border farther west and would ensure Prussia's involvement in any future war against France. That, of course, was precisely the intent of the British negotiator, as the Prussians understood perfectly well.[54]

Since the Prussians had declared over and over again that Hanover was an essential condition for their participation in the coalition, Frederick William could have chosen to regard this British refusal to discuss the matter as an obvious deal breaker. To do so might even have been relatively safe, since however

---

*Simms gives this argument too much credence: "He was always meant to judge on the spot" (*Impact*, p. 208).

†Simms, *Impact*, p. 203. When Simon Vorontsov approached Pitt in September about the possibility of offering Hanover to Prussia, Pitt responded that "no minister would be imprudent enough to make such a proposal to the King" and that he would conceal the Prussian demand from George III lest the shock of this outrageous demand kill the old man or drive him finally insane. Vorontsov to Czartoryskii, 29 September 1805, in Gielgud, *Memoirs of Prince Adam Czartoryskii*, 2:79–84. See also Mulgrave to Harrowby, 23 November 1805, in John Holland Rose, *Select Despatches from the British Foreign Office Archives Relating to the Formation of the Third Coalition Against France, 1804–1805* (London: Offices of the Royal Historical Society, 1904), doc. 108.

piqued Alexander would have been about the king's *volte face*, a large part of the blame would have fallen on the intransigent British. Frederick William could claim that he had done nothing but abide by his own agreements with the tsar.

But the king chose no such escape. Although he steadfastly refused to accept the Netherlands and continued to insist on Hanover, he allowed the pressures of the geostrategic situation to overcome even that insistence. By early December (but before news of the Battle of Austerlitz had reached Berlin), the Prussians had agreed to accept only a "temporary occupation" of Hanover, and the British had agreed to defer the negotiations over Prussia's territorial gains until a later time.[55] This agreement implied that Prussia might not receive Hanover, but it put the Prussians at an even greater risk. Their bargaining power with London would never be greater than it was in November 1805. Terms negotiated after they had already done their part might fall short of what they could have hoped to obtain by threatening to pull out of the coalition. By the beginning of December, Frederick William was accepting the risk of fighting a war with Napoleon for no clear benefit at all.*

It seems clear, therefore, that the Prussian king and most of his court had decided to go to war with the coalition against Napoleon except in the unlikely event that the French emperor accepted the harsh and almost anachronistic terms now presented to him. Even Haugwitz—who told Laforest before he went that the king could be brought round, that no Russo–Prussian treaty was signed at Potsdam, that only the ill-intentioned Hardenberg was pressing for war, and that he and Lombard would keep Hardenberg in check—repeatedly advised Frederick William to mobilize as large an army as possible on the Silesian border to prevent a French invasion. He warned that such an invasion might follow if the Austro–Russian army retreated onto Prussian territory, but he did not recommend that Frederick William take steps to prevent the allies from doing so.[56] Lombard had declared as early as October 19 that Prussia was effectively at war with France, and that the diplomatic prevarications he and Haugwitz recommended served mainly to cover the mobilization of the Prussian army.[57]

Nor did that mobilization ever slacken during this period. Prussian troops continued to close up on their jumping-off points in Prussia's western holdings, and Frederick William began provisioning his Silesian fortresses as well.[58] Unfortunately for the coalition, Haugwitz's recommendations to shift the concentration areas of the armies went unheeded.[59] The reason for this failure is unclear, although the difficulty of radically changing the concentration areas during a mobilization, together with the desirability of fighting on Napoleon's lines of com-

---

*These negotiations also put paid to the idea that it was "Pitt's gold" that drew Prussia into this coalition, since the king committed himself to war before negotiating a subsidy treaty with the British. Nor was that agreement, when finally concluded, so lucrative as to make war for money attractive, even had Frederick William not been one of the most pacifistic monarchs in modern history.

munication and the possibility of seizing all territorial objectives at the outset of hostilities, all probably played a role. Nor was the Prussian Silesian frontier as uncovered as Haugwitz made out, since in addition to the large allied army there, several other Russian formations were on the march to join it. Thus by the middle of December the Prussians would have had nearly 200,000 troops, and the Russians some 100,000, converging along Napoleon's northern flank from Moravia to the Rhine. And there is every reason to imagine that they would have launched offensive operations by December 15 with the aim of destroying Napoleon's army.

Conclusion

Napoleon's violation of Prussian neutrality at Ansbach was a strategic gamble fraught with risk. Had Napoleon understood Frederick William and his position better in October 1805, he could have guessed at the reaction. Threatened with total humiliation and the sort of treatment normally reserved for second- and third-class German states, Frederick William could not tolerate such an assault on his dignity. The fact that he was at that very moment mobilizing his army to fight Alexander over the mere threat of a similar affront exaggerated his response. The delay in Prussia's activity following this event resulted not so much from an unwillingness to fight as from the need to prepare Prussia's army for the war. In this fact we see the fateful consequences of Frederick William's earlier failures to mobilize.

The Prussian king should have put his army on a war footing in response to Napoleon's seizure of Hanover in 1803. Had he done so, he would have been in a vastly better bargaining position throughout the subsequent period of rising tension on the continent. And in the fall of 1805 he would have been able to intervene quickly and decisively, either through the mediation he proposed or through military intervention. His failure to mobilize in the face of Napoleon's military preparedness consistently undercut his diplomatic efforts at peace and trapped him into passivity even when war crossed his frontiers. Just as the Austrians found their options sharply constrained as a result of their demobilization, so Frederick William and the Prussians were forced into passivity even after they had, surprisingly, decided to take action. When an aggressive, powerful state has a mobilized army ready to hand, those who must do business with that state—either peacefully or in conflict—suffer badly if they do not have similarly ready military forces.

George Kennan once declared, "You have no idea how much it contributes to the general politeness and pleasantness of diplomacy when you have a little quiet armed force in the background."[60] There can be little doubt that European diplomacy between 1803 and 1805 would have been more polite and more pleasant—at least for the states that ultimately allied against

Napoleon—if France had not been the only power with a "little quiet armed force in the background."

Even so, when the war reached its climax in late November, Napoleon's aggression had added another powerful state to the lists of his enemies.* He gained an advantage over the Austrians in the operational maneuvers in Bavaria, and that advantage helped him eliminate an entire Austrian army without having to fight a pitched battle. But Mack's army numbered only 50,000 men. Frederick William's numbered four times that many. It is difficult not to question the wisdom of Napoleon's calculations and miscalculations in this matter.

Although Napoleon's decision flowed at least as much from a misperception of Frederick William as from any willingness to take on the Prussian army, it is worth noting a basic characteristic of the French emperor's way of waging war. We have already seen how little thought Napoleon gave to the problem of long-range planning. He focused all of his attention on the immediate tasks at hand and made decisions, frequently brilliant, to optimize his chances in dealing with those tasks. He rarely considered the long-term implications of those decisions, however, or how well his initial successes would lay the groundwork for final success in the war, let alone overall success in attaining his ultimate objectives (which were generally unclear in any case). This flexibility gave Napoleon significant advantages in dealing with enemies almost too preoccupied with the long term, but it also entailed significant risks. In 1805 it meant accepting the risk of adding a large, powerful army to the ranks of his enemies at the worst possible moment.

As contingencies and miscalculations led Napoleon to the brink of disaster in late November, however, contingencies and the coalition's miscalculations, as well as Napoleon's skill as a battlefield commander, brought him back from that brink. We now turn our attention to one of the unlikeliest, yet in retrospect most inevitable of all events in the Napoleonic wars: the Battle of Austerlitz.

---

*In considering whether Prussia was or was not "really" a member of the coalition at this point, we should recall that both Russia and Austria had earlier made their own participation in the alliance contingent on attempts at "mediation." Neither they nor Frederick William ever doubted the likely outcome of such attempts.

21

Setting the Terms of Battle

Napoleon faced a dangerous situation after the Battle of Schöngrabern. The Russians were concentrating a growing force northwest of Brno. Charles had broken free of Masséna and was on the road to Graz and from there to Vienna. The entire Prussian army was mobilizing to attack Napoleon's lines of communication in Bavaria and Holland. The Prussians had already seized Hanover. British, Hanoverian, Swedish, and more Russian troops were on the march in northern Germany. Even more Russian forces were on the way to Moravia and Bohemia. Napoleon was obliged to scatter his forces across the length of Austria and soon found himself facing the main allied army in Moravia at a significant numerical disadvantage.

Bonaparte's failure to plan beyond the initial operations of this campaign, together with his failure to catch Kutuzov's army and destroy it before it could link up with Russian reinforcements, had brought him to this terrible pass. If the allies played the hand they had been dealt with moderate intelligence, it seemed, victory would surely be theirs. Napoleon sought salvation in a decisive battle. The allies had no reason to accept such a battle in November or even early December. The emperor's task was to find a way to either force or trick them into fighting before they could bring their overall crushing numerical superiority to bear against him.

If the coalition had considered only military factors, this task would have been nearly impossible. The allied commanders were well aware of the advantages they held and of the danger of throwing away those advantages in an unwise battle. Left to themselves they would have taken no such risk. But the generals were not left to themselves, for both Francis and Alexander accompanied their armies into the field, along with their advisers and hangers-on. The emperors wrested control of the campaign away from their generals, thus bringing the weight of court intrigue and personality to bear on military decisionmaking. Worst of all for the allied cause, it was Alexander, newly arrived in the theater and totally unversed in war, who took the lead. He immediately made a series of decisions that allowed Napoleon to escape from the trap he had set for himself.

The Military Situation in Late November 1805

The French

Napoleon's dash across Austria after Kutuzov forced him to dispatch a significant part of his army to protect his flanks and lines of communication. He thus ordered Ney's corps, exhausted from the fighting around Ulm, into the Tyrol and to Innsbruck, where it remained throughout most of November. Augereau's Corps, arriving from France, assisted Ney in clearing up the remaining Austrian resistance in Bavaria and the Tyrol.* Napoleon ordered Marmont's Corps to Leoben, Bruck, and ultimately Graz in order to keep Charles away from the serious fighting.[1] Davout's Corps held Vienna and its environs, able to support Marmont if necessary. Napoleon sent Bernadotte and the Bavarians to Budweis and toward Bohemia in order to watch his northern flank and prevent Ferdinand from forming a more substantial force from the debris of the Austrian army at Ulm. Mortier's corps, still battered from the drubbing it had taken at Dürnstein, took no part in the rest of the campaign.[2]

The emperor took only Murat's, Lannes's, and Soult's Corps, as well as the Imperial Guard and the Grenadiers Division, with him to meet the allies in Moravia. He could reasonably expect to rally Bernadotte and Davout to him if he had warning of an impending battle. Even so, he could only hope to meet the main allied army with four infantry corps, his cavalry, guards, and grenadiers for the decisive battle. Strategic consumption and the pace of the campaign had cost him four infantry corps (Ney, Augereau, Mortier, and Marmont)—nearly half his army.†

The Russians

Once Kutuzov escaped from Napoleon's efforts to trap and destroy him, the Russians' prospects improved dramatically. Kutuzov led his army through

---

*Although Napoleon periodically sniped at Augereau for failing to keep him informed (he asked Ney to send someone to the marshal "to find out if he is alive or dead"), Augereau was in fact doing his job. Augereau to Napoleon, 18 November 1805, SHAT C² 8.

†"Strategic consumption" is a technical term that refers to the depletion of the combat power of an advancing army as the result of detachments left behind to protect supply depots, critical communications points, and the flanks of the advance. In general terms, the farther an army penetrates into enemy territory, the more combat power it loses to strategic consumption.

Znaim to Brno, Vyškov, and ultimately to Olmütz. When Dolgorukii arrived back at Puławy on October 16 with the news of Napoleon's violation of Prussian territory and the king's immediate reaction, Alexander reorganized the army he had been assembling under General Mikhel'son to invade Prussia.[3] He now ordered Mikhel'son to form two corps commanded by Buxhöwden and Bennigsen, and to reinforce both Tolstoi's and Kutuzov's armies with some of his cavalry. He sent Buxhöwden rushing southwest to link up with Kutuzov. He ordered Bennigsen to march through Warsaw to Breslau and thence move "according to circumstances."[4] The tsar then raced to Berlin and did not leave until early November. Along the way he dallied for a few days in Weimar with his sister and arrived at Olmütz on November 18.[5]

The tsar's optimism eroded rapidly as he neared the theater of war. On November 14 he wrote Frederick William, "Matters are in a much more alarming state than we supposed when I left Berlin, and each moment is precious. The fate of Europe is in your hands, Sire. Myself, I am nervous about my troops. They have already fought with courage, but sustaining alone the efforts of such considerable [enemy] forces they can only cede to the number [sic]."[6] Upon his arrival at Olmütz, the tsar wrote again, "I am abandoning all the forms because you have allowed me, Sire, to address you as my friend. I have never needed one more. Our position is more than critical, we are absolutely alone against the French, and they are following on our heels continually. Today the headquarters are already at Olmütz, which is neither provisioned nor in a state of defense."* Alexander begged the king to hasten the movement of his troops, which Frederick William refused to do because it was impossible for them to move any faster.[7]

The tsar reorganized his armies in Prussia once again in response to his new perception of the urgency of his situation. He subordinated Buxhöwden's army directly to Kutuzov, detached Essen's corps from Bennigsen's army, and ordered it to race to Olmütz as well. He commanded Bennigsen to march as rapidly as possible with the rest of his force into Bohemia to join with Archduke Ferdinand and the remnants of Mack's army there.[8] Mikhel'son was to gather up what was left of the "reserve army" on the Prussian frontier and concentrate it opposite Galicia to be ready to support or receive Kutuzov's army as necessary. Mikhel'son supposedly threw himself into a chair and burst into tears on receiving the news that he was being sent back to Russia and would not be allowed to fight Napoleon.[9]

---

*Alexander to Frederick William, 19 November 1805, in Bailleu, *Briefwechsel*, p. 84. Alexander repeatedly reminded Frederick William that the latter had permitted him to drop all the "forms" of address normally used between sovereigns. The king seemed somewhat bemused by this insistence. It is difficult to know whether Alexander was trying to emphasize the tie of friendship that bound the two into an alliance, or whether this insistence reflected the tsar's known distaste for pomp and ceremony and his determination not to use it with a sovereign he regarded as a real friend.

Bennigsen, on the other hand, sent Essen's troops marching toward Olmütz as rapidly as possible but wrote that he would only be able to follow more slowly. He had encountered great difficulty in getting across the Neman, the Bug, and the Vistula on his way through Poland, and he wanted to receive direct confirmation from the tsar (rather than an order relayed through Mikhel'son), before dramatically shifting his direction and speed of march.[10]

The net result of these orders was that Buxhöwden's army and Constantine's force joined Kutuzov at the beginning of the last week of November. These forces, together with a number of hastily raised Austrian battalions commanded by Prince Liechtenstein, brought the Russian force at Olmütz to around 82,500 men.[11] Perhaps 12,000 troops under General Essen were racing to join them there, and yet another 30,000 under Bennigsen were following them more slowly. The tsar had also established a substantial reserve army of around 50,000 troops on the Russian–Austrian border. The force at Olmütz was only "alone" against the French army if Alexander chose to allow it to be.

The Austrians

The destruction of Mack's army at Ulm left the Austrians with only two meaningful forces in the field: Charles's on the Adige and John's in the Tyrol. When Charles learned of the disaster in Bavaria at the end October, he withdrew both forces to the east, as we have seen.* Afraid of being cut off by French troops crashing across the Alps, Charles also feared that the French might cut him off from John before they could link up. He therefore ordered both armies to withdraw nearly due east in November.[12]

His own army marched through Fontaniva, Albaredo, Fontanafredda, and Palmanova into what is now Slovenia. Word that Marmont's troops were in Graz, Leoben, and Bruck convinced the archduke to continue moving east rather than trying to race north.[13] John, in the meantime, drew his meager forces out of the Tyrol and reached Villach on November 17.[14] Charles accordingly decided to meet up with John in Celje (in Slovenia), safely to the south of French outposts in Graz, which he did on November 26.[15]

The archduke considered driving through Marmont's positions around Graz and Leoben, but reflected that even a successful battle would waste time. He decided instead to march farther east through Pettau (modern Ptuj) to Körmend, which he believed he could reach by about December 6 or 7.†

---

*See above, Chapter 19.

†Charles to Francis, 30 November 1805, KA AFA 1805 Italien, XI/351½. Charles thereby disregarded the advice of one of his subordinate commanders, who suggested that it would be easy to drive through Marmont's force (Chasteler to Charles, 29 November 1805, KA AFA 1805 Italien, XI/326).

There he would be in a position to divert Napoleon's attention and even threaten his rear if the allies were successful in Moravia.

Two considerations governed Charles's actions throughout this retreat. First, he was determined to link up with John's army and not allow it to be trapped and cut to ribbons by Ney's and Marmont's advancing troops.[16] Second, he was well aware of the fact that he commanded the only remaining Austrian army of any importance, and he was determined not to lose it in a foolish engagement.* It is difficult to evaluate the wisdom of these convictions. Charles's army retreated rapidly in a tough situation, through difficult terrain chased by Masséna's army and threatened from the north by Ney and Marmont. If he had raced even faster and tried to brush past, or drive over, Marmont's troops at Graz, he would have posed a serious threat to Napoleon's southern flank. At a minimum, he might have compelled the emperor to retain Davout's corps in and around Vienna, with consequences that will become plain later on.†

Such a movement would have taken some time, as Charles noted, but probably less than the time spent marching the longer distances he proposed. It seems likely that Charles mainly feared losing or severely damaging his army and leaving Austria helpless. We must recall in this regard the archduke's inordinate distrust of the Russians and the Prussians.‡ He feared not merely that Napoleon would impose a harsh peace on Austria, but that an Austria deprived of her armies would be at the mercy of Alexander and Frederick William as well—and he believed neither in that mercy nor in their staunchness as allies. The weaknesses of the coalition and Austria's internal political battles once again led Charles to take the more cautious road and to turn away from chances to swing the course of events away from the disastrous path they were on. Nevertheless, Charles's maneuvers would have had the effect of bringing perhaps 50,000–75,000 troops to within a few days' march of Vienna by the end of the first week in December.

By the middle of December, the coalition could reasonably expect to have nearly 500,000 troops converging on Napoleon's army and its lines of communication. Amazingly, the grandiose plans for assembling a crushing numerical superiority developed early in 1805 appeared to have come off, although farther east than anyone had expected. Considering that the Grande Armée had numbered only about 200,000 when it set out, the odds were powerfully in

---

*This determination is clearest in his decision not to attack Marmont at Graz at the end of November. See Charles to Francis, 30 November 1805, KA AFA 1805 Italien, XI/351½.

†Napoleon promised Marmont that he would reinforce him if he found himself confronted by a superior force—as Charles's army certainly was. Napoleon to Marmont, 15 November 1805, *Corr. de Nap.*, doc. 9495.

‡He reported to Francis the rumor that had emerged from Kutuzov's phony offer to Murat of an armistice before the Battle of Schöngrabern, taking it much more seriously than it deserved. Charles to Francis, 26 November 1805, KA AFA 1805 Italien, XI/290½.

the allies' favor, even counting the 40,000 or so troops Masséna was bringing up after Charles and the force Napoleon was hastily assembling along the French frontier from Holland to Strasbourg.* What is more, the allies' troops were fresh. The 200,000 Prussian and north German troops, as well as Bux-höwden's, Bennigsen's, Constantine's, and Essen's forces, had not yet seen any combat, although they had done a lot of marching. The battle-weary troops of Kutuzov's army formed only a small core of the coalition force. Napoleon had placed himself in the gravest danger by his actions, and only allied mistakes or miracles could save him. The emperor applied himself to generating both.

The Lure of Battle

On the face of it, the allies' best course of action was to remain on the defensive until the overwhelming forces converging against Napoleon were close enough to participate in a decisive battle or campaign. They chose not to do so. The reasons for this decision are obscure. The Russians' standard explanation is that the want of supplies at Olmütz made the position untenable and left them no choice but to fight.† Modern historians tend to credit Napoleon with tricking Alexander into making this decision.[17] Napoleon clearly tried to persuade the tsar that he was weak, fearful, ready to withdraw, and even more ready to make peace, as we shall see, but he undertook this ruse only several days after the allies had already chosen to advance and accept battle. The real reasons for this decision probably have more to do with the strategic and grand strategic context of the war than with these tactical and operational issues.

The logistical explanation does not really explain everything, however. Supplies at Olmütz were a problem, to be sure. Although the Austrians had made considerable efforts to prepare supplies for the campaign before it began, they never imagined that the fighting would stretch all the way back to Moravia, and the camp at Olmütz was not well stocked. Enormous quantities

---

*In November 1805, Napoleon ordered the formation of the "Army of the North," consisting of six divisions: two at Anvers, two at Mainz, and two at Strasbourg. Marshal François Joseph Lefebvre was given command of the new organization with the following charge: "You have seen from the organization of the Army of the North that I have provided for the immediate necessity of guaranteeing us against surprise attacks by our enemies . . . The King of Prussia has assured me that he wishes to maintain the strictest neutrality; I have the right to count on that. Conduct yourself always well and honorably toward the Prussians." Napoleon, Decree, 8 November 1805, *Corr. de Nap.*, doc. 9466; Napoleon to Lefebvre, 15 November 1805, doc. 9488.

†Alexander to Frederick William, 6 December 1805, in Bailleu, *Briefwechsel*, doc. 84; Mikhailovskii-Danilevskii, *Opisanie*, pp. 153–154. Mikhailovskii-Danilevskii also asserts that the Austrians somehow pushed the Russians into fighting in order to end the war sooner, believing that both victory and defeat would lead more rapidly to peace than further campaigning. Theodor von Bernhardi, *Denkwürdigkeiten aus dem Leben des kaiserliches russisches Generals von der Infanterie Carl Friedrich Grafen von Toll* (Leipzig: Otto Wigand, 1865), pp. 163–164, rightly takes issue with this explanation, for which there is no evidence.

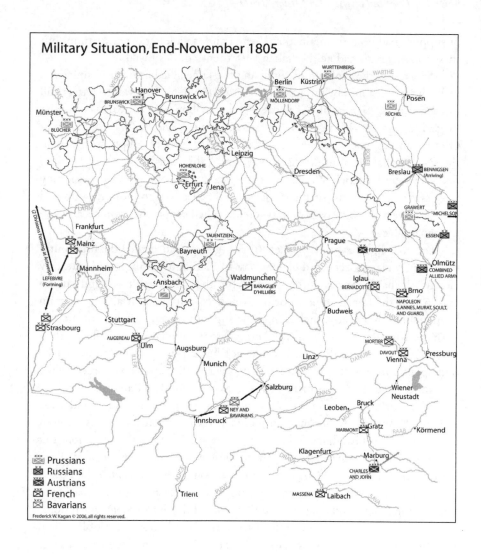

Military Situation, End-November 1805

WÜRTTEMBERG

Berlin Küstrin

Hanover MÖLLENDORF Posen

BRUNSWICK Brunswick RÜCHEL

Münster

BLÜCHER

Leipzig

HOHENLOHE Dresden Breslau BENNIGSEN (Arriving)

Erfurt Jena

GRAWERT MICHELSON

Frankfurt ESSEN

Mainz TAUENTZIEN Prague FERDINAND

Bayreuth

LEFEBVRE (Forming) Mannheim Olmütz COMBINED ALLIED ARMY

Ansbach Waldmunchen Iglau

BARAGUEY BERNADOTTE

D'HILLIERS Brno

Budweis NAPOLEON (LANNES, MURAT, SOULT, AND GUARD)

Strasbourg Stuttgart

AUGEREAU MORTIER

Ulm Augsburg Linz DAVOUT Pressburg

Munich Vienna

Wiener Neustadt

Salzburg Bruck

NEY AND Leoben

BAVARIANS MARMONT Gratz Körmend

Innsbruck

Klagenfurt Marburg

CHARLES AND JOHN

Trient MASSENA Laibach

12 Divisions Forming at Antwerp

Prussians

Russians

Austrians

French

Bavarians

Frederick W. Kagan © 2006, all rights reserved.

of supplies had been maintained at Vienna and, to a lesser extent, Brünn, but these the Austrians had neither taken with them nor destroyed.

As a result, the problem of supplying the large allied army at Olmütz was real. There were four obvious solutions to that problem. One was to retreat still further, into Russian Poland if necessary, thus falling back on Russia's frontier magazines and the rich reserves of western Ukraine. Another was to remain at Olmütz and set about establishing the necessary lines of supply to maintain the force in that excellent defensive position. A third was to retreat to Prussian Silesia, where Frederick William was frantically garrisoning and provisioning fortresses to support just such a maneuver.[18] The last was to move forward and seek decisive battle with Napoleon before the allied supply situation became too unmanageable.

Kutuzov and some of the other Russian generals advocated the first course of action.[19] Having retreated all the way from Braunau to Olmütz, Kutuzov clearly felt that there was nothing magical in that Moravian town and saw no reason why the retreat should not be prolonged until actions already in train brought the allies nearly unchallengeable superiority and certainty of success. Perhaps Kutuzov had a healthier respect for Napoleon's capabilities than Alexander's entourage did. This would not be surprising considering that he had spent two months in dangerous contact with Napoleon's forces, while Alexander's young advisers had never seen a soldier of the Grande Armée.

The allies made some effort to supply themselves in the area but found it too difficult.[20] Apparently no one considered withdrawing toward Prussia, even though substantial Russian reinforcements were coming from that direction. But the decision to advance toward Brno from Olmütz was not taken for want of any better alternative. Alexander, Francis, and their political advisers chose this option because they believed they saw an opportunity not necessarily to end the war at once, but to facilitate other operations that would bring it to a rapid conclusion.

The allies at Olmütz were well aware of the overall movement of Prussian, Russian, and Austrian troops across central Europe. They knew that a large Prussian army was preparing to descend on Napoleon's lines of communication, and that Charles could be in Vienna in a few weeks. They also saw that Napoleon had greatly overextended himself and consequently presented them with a possibly fleeting opportunity.

On November 24, Cobenzl wrote from Olmütz that the combination of Kutuzov's, Buxhöwden's, and Liechtenstein's forces comprised 70,000 men, not including the 11,000 men of the Russian Imperial Guard who were expected to arrive at any moment.* The allied army was therefore "able to retake the offensive

---

*Cobenzl to Metternich, 24 November 1805, HHSt, Rußland Varia II, 240. This note also destroys the argument Mikhailovskii-Danilevskii makes about Austrian duplicity, since it reveals that Cobenzl had informed Alexander and received his approval for the peace overtures to be made to Napoleon.

immediately against the French who have advanced into Moravia." The thought that Bennigsen's force was ready to cross into Bohemia strengthened Cobenzl in this belief. He ordered Metternich to press Frederick William to march as rapidly as possible, and change the direction of his march if possible, to bring it closer to the allies' main army. If the Prussians fell on the flank and rear of the French army "at the same time that the Austro–Russian troops occupy this same army from the front, we can count on an easy and certain success." In another note of the same date, Cobenzl added that the 100,000 troops that the allies would have within a few days were "in no way disposed to give ground to the French, and were preparing on the contrary to retake the offensive immediately."* Alexander thought that "perhaps we may be able to finish this war in a single campaign because of the risky position in which Bonaparte finds himself."†

As the campaign neared its climax, the heads of state and their diplomatic advisers once again began to think in terms of vast combinations of hundreds of thousands of troops acting in a coordinated fashion over hundreds of miles of separation. The allied force at Olmütz was to "occupy" Napoleon while 150,000 Prussians fell on his "flank." The validity of these notions—and there was some—was more than obscured by their vagueness. The same problems that had bedeviled the coalition's war plans at the outset of the campaign returned to complicate allied decisionmaking at the end of it.

This development was natural for three reasons. First, Alexander and Francis arrived on the field of battle, bringing along all their courtiers and diplomats. The diplomats, including Cobenzl, traveling with the army for the first time in the war, now could claim to understand the military situation and therefore to influence it. Second, the accession of Prussia to the coalition in early November raised the importance of diplomacy—and the men who conducted it—to new heights. Cobenzl, Czartoryskii, Alexander, and Francis had to ensure that Frederick William joined the fray. Their considerations of that prospect, which the military commanders did not have to evaluate in any detail, naturally led them to trust their own understanding of the campaign more than that of their professional commanders. Their trust in those commanders was further undermined by the fact that Kutuzov, Buxhöwden, Bennigsen, and the other generals were concerned only with their own armies and operational

---

*Weyrother corroborates the significance of the perceived power of the allied army in convincing the two emperors to seek battle rather than withdraw. See his Diary for 11 November through 2 December, KA AFA 1805 Deutschland, XIII/59.

†Alexander to Frederick William, 28 November 1805, in Bailleu, *Briefwechsel*, doc. 83. This letter mentions the visit of General Savary, part of Napoleon's ruse, it is true. But if Alexander was strongly influenced at this pass by Napoleon's supposed weakness and readiness to negotiate, it is odd that he makes no mention of it in his note. The emphasis on the position of the French army, rather than the fear of its commander, suggests that Alexander was still influenced by the strategic issues that originally convinced Francis and the Austrians to push for early decisive action.

sectors. *Only* the diplomats and heads of state thought about the grand strategic, or even the strategic, situation. This problem arose, again, from the allies' failure to establish an overall military command and staff structure to plan for the entire coalition's operations.

On November 26 Kutuzov ordered the army to break camp at Olmütz and march toward Brno.[21] He did so with a heavy heart. Having opposed the emperors' decision to advance rather than withdrawing or even waiting for a more auspicious moment to attack, Kutuzov did not resign his command or attempt to sabotage the decision.* Nor did Alexander relieve him. The tsar mistrusted Kutuzov, who was an aging holdover from previous reigns, and he surely disliked the advice Kutuzov gave him to begin his military career by withdrawing in the face of a numerically inferior foe. He knew too well, however, that he himself was unfit to take actual command of the army, and he could not readily demote the man who had saved his army and fought so gallantly against overwhelming odds by placing him under the command of a more junior and less experienced officer. The resulting tension within the allied high command, however, boded ill for success in either battle or campaign.

Kutuzov's reluctance to leave Olmütz was based on a sound appreciation of the limitations of the army under his command, not merely on a fear of Napoleon's capabilities. The combat power of that force was significantly smaller than its size would have suggested. It was composed of Austrian reserves hastily conscripted from the streets of Vienna, remnants of the Austrian survivors of Ulm, Kutuzov's weary troops who had just traversed the length of Austria with Murat's cavalry snapping at their heels, Russian reserve formations drawn from all over the empire, and the Russian Imperial Guard that had marched in proud formation all the way from St. Petersburg. These forces did not have common organizations, equipment, doctrine, techniques, or even a common command language. Few of the units had worked together before, few officers knew their superiors or subordinates. Many of these men, both Austrian and Russian, had never conducted maneuvers with forces larger than a regiment. The columns that were put together for the advance from Olmütz to Austerlitz were ad hoc affairs with no internal cohesion. They moved together for the first time when they set out from the Olmütz camp.†

---

*Mikhailovskii-Danilevskii points out that Kutuzov's actions at this pass stand in sharp contrast to those of Suvorov when faced with Hofkriegsrat decisions of which he did not approve. Suvorov's opposition was much easier, considering that he was arguing with a committee hundreds of miles away serving a foreign master. Kutuzov would have had to oppose his own sovereign in person. Mikhailovskii-Danilevskii, *Opisanie*, p. 156.

†The order to move out from Olmütz, which also designated the composition of the various columns for the first time, reflected a real concern with not only the danger of meeting Napoleon but also keeping order even during an unopposed march in a large polyglot composite force. Zhiugzhda, *Dokumenty*, doc. 137.

This force was not representative of the Austrian or the Russian armies. It was considerably less responsive and flexible than the forces both Austrian and Russian generals were accustomed to working with. It was unlikely to find success in complicated or rapid maneuvers, and its subordinate units and their commanders could not be relied on to seize the initiative or respond aggressively and flexibly to changing circumstances. It was an army that required either weeks of training or a great deal of caution in its employment. It was given neither.

Although the strategic and grand strategic situation was important for persuading the emperors to act, the operational situation provided the more aggressive military officers with a strong argument for advancing immediately. Napoleon's occupation of a position to the east of Brno seemed to offer the enticing possibility of cutting him off from that city and, thereby, from his lines of communication and reinforcements to the south in Vienna and to the west in Bohemia. A rapid, decisive turning movement south of Napoleon's position promised to catch him at a point of weakness. It might force him to withdraw from the area. It might trap him away from his supplies and reinforcements. Or it might force on him a decisive battle on terms favorable to the allies. In any case, a turning maneuver promised to change the terms of the campaign dramatically in the allies' favor.[22]

Thus the allies left their excellent position at Olmütz and abandoned any further retreat. On November 24 they decided to advance toward Brno to take Napoleon in his right flank, isolate him, and destroy him.[23] Delays in gathering supplies and writing the necessary dispositions postponed the execution of that decision until November 27.* The execution proved less sound than the concept. The allied army could not undertake rapid and decisive maneuvers and required more than three days to cover the distance from Olmütz to Austerlitz, enabling Napoleon to concentrate reinforcements from near and far to even the odds. The alliance was moving toward battle without a clear understanding of the limitations of its own forces.

Napoleon's Trap

By about November 20 Napoleon's troops had taken up positions they would hold for more than a week: Murat, Soult, Lannes, the Imperial Guard, and the

---

*Kutuzov to Kh. I. Lieven, 25 November 1805, in L. G. Beskrovnyi, *M. I. Kutuzov: Sbornik dokumentov* (Moscow: Voennoe Izdatel'stvo, 1951), vol. 2, doc. 218. Modern historians are too quick to point to these delays as evidence of incompetence among the allied generals. They ignore the uniquely poor organization and situation of this ragtag army. See Duffy, *Austerlitz*; Scott Bowden, *Napoleon and Austerlitz: An Unprecedentedly Detailed Combat Study of Napoleon's Epic Ulm-Austerlitz Campaigns of 1805* (Chicago: Emperor's, 1997); and David Chandler, *The Campaigns of Napoleon* (New York: Macmillan, 1966).

grenadiers in Brno and Austerlitz; Bernadotte at Iglau; Mortier and Davout in Vienna and Pressburg; Marmont at Graz; Ney and Augereau in the Tyrol.[24] Apart from minor cavalry actions and the operations of Ney and Augereau far to the west, the French troops saw no combat and little movement. Napoleon was giving his weary and disillusioned troops a rest while he tried to understand the new shape of the campaign and to find a path to victory.

Napoleon was well aware of the movements of the allied troops across Europe. Marmont watched in frustration as Charles's army paraded in front of his own troops on its way toward Vienna—and sent in frequent reports on that movement.[25] Bernadotte reported on the movements of Ferdinand's small detachment in Bohemia.[26] A French agent sent in a remarkably accurate description of the Prussian deployments and plans.[27] Ségur describes Napoleon in this period: "afflicted by the news of the disaster of Trafalgar, the increasingly hostile dispositions of Prussia, and already tired from his own inaction, he was disquieted by the system of temporization that the Russian army seemed to have adopted." Ségur recognized that "each day increased the danger of our isolated and so distant position. Napoleon, having ventured to the depths of Moravia with 65,000 combatants near him while 150,000 Prussians menaced the entire left flank of his retreat, saw Alexander and 90,000 Russians and Germans holding him in front; the Archduke Ferdinand and 20,000 Austrians advanced in Bohemia on his rear, and at the same time Archduke Charles and 40,000 other Imperials, already in Hungary, raced against his right!" He concluded, "That is why, on November 26, impatient, after an entire night of work, he wrote to Emperor Alexander and sent Savary, his aide-de-camp, to compliment him and sound his militant or pacific dispositions."[28] Ségur was probably right.

At all events, Napoleon began a significant diplomatic campaign that may have been intended to bring the war to a swift conclusion. He had written to Francis on November 17, trying to persuade the emperor that the Russian troops in his territories were more dangerous to him than Napoleon and that he should therefore make a separate peace.[29] When he learned that Haugwitz was on his way to meet him, his first thought was to command Talleyrand to find out exactly what the Prussians wanted and what they planned to do. He repeated several times that Talleyrand was to "find out what he wants."*

On November 25 Francis made a last attempt to reach out to Napoleon on his own hook, sending Count Stadion and Count Gyulai with full powers to negotiate a treaty. The main purpose of this mission was to "second" ("observe" might be a better word) Haugwitz's discussions with Napoleon. Cobenzl's

---

*Napoleon to Talleyrand, 22 November 1805, *Corr. de Nap.*, doc. 9516. This note undermines the notion current in some modern accounts that Napoleon coolly received Haugwitz with no thought from the outset but to put off his mission until he had finished off Alexander's army. There was nothing cool about his initial reaction to Haugwitz's mission.

description of this mission to Metternich makes it clear that he had no expectation of success.[30]

Napoleon regained his composure and form in reacting to this deluge of envoys. He ordered Haugwitz held up at Iglau when he arrived there, not so much to delay the delivery of his embassage as to ensure that his path did not cross that of Stadion and Gyulai.[31] He also instructed Talleyrand to negotiate with the Austrian emissaries on the basis of the cession of the Venetian terra firma to France and Swabia and the Tyrol to Bavaria.

Stadion naturally refused to negotiate on these terms and resisted Napoleon's efforts to separate Austria from her allies. He also attempted to negotiate jointly with Haugwitz, which Napoleon refused to allow, and to convince the Prussian emissary to support the alliance firmly, which Haugwitz refused to do.[32] He did not doubt, however, that Napoleon was seriously negotiating—the length of their meeting alone convinced him of that fact. And there seems no reason to doubt Napoleon's initial sincerity in these negotiations—even Ségur believed in it at this point.[33] There is every reason to imagine that even the dispatch of Savary to Alexander on November 26 was genuine. Concerned about the worsening situation before him, Napoleon decided to divide his enemies diplomatically.

He found the going difficult, however, as the Austrians proved intransigent. Gyulai insisted that Austria be indemnified in Germany for the loss of Venice. "He talked to me of the Teutonic Order, of the [Imperial] Diet at Ratisbonne, and I don't know what else," an exasperated emperor wrote to Talleyrand.[34] Whatever else was going on, Francis was not yet willing to make peace "at any cost," as Napoleon's agents had previously reported.[35]

On November 28 Russian cavalry covering the advance of the allied army attacked French outposts near the town of Vyškov, between Olmütz and Austerlitz.[36] This event, which had an important influence on Alexander, showed Napoleon an opportunity to change the course of the war again.* Napoleon's most important problem throughout the campaign following Mack's capitulation was Kutuzov: he would not offer battle. To the extent that Napoleon had thought about events after Ulm at all, he had clearly imagined a series of rapid maneuvers culminating in one or more decisive battles that, taken together, would end the war. Kutuzov had confounded him by not fighting. If the Russians had continued in that course at Olmütz, as Ségur points out, Napoleon would have been hard-pressed to find a way out of the trap he

---

*Ségur also presents this event as one that changed Napoleon's attitude (*Histoire et mémoires*, p. 446). The historian must use Ségur's memoirs with caution. They were written long after the event, colored by subsequent events, and heavily influenced by his own complex feelings toward Napoleon. In this narrow time frame they seem to condense a general atmosphere reflected in the available documents quite accurately. Considering that Ségur was actually with Napoleon at this time, it seems appropriate to give his account greater credence at this point than it might deserve at others.

had set for himself. He greeted the news that the allied armies had advanced from their secure position with joy and began developing stratagems to encourage their aggressiveness even further, as we shall see.

In characteristic fashion, however, Napoleon continued the incompatible policy of negotiating with the Austrians even as he prepared to lure them and their allies into a climactic battle. Although Alexander's advance changed the character of Napoleon's dealings with the tsar, he continued to support Talleyrand in a sincere effort to make a separate peace with Francis.

Talleyrand met with Stadion and Gyulai for the first time on November 30, although that meeting was brief and vague, since Talleyrand had not yet received clear instructions from Napoleon.[37] The emperor soon supplied that deficiency in a surprising manner—he wrote his foreign minister that he had relaxed his demands. "Monsieur Talleyrand," he wrote, "I wish to make peace promptly." The Austrians could have Salzburg. The elector of Salzburg (a Habsburg prince) could have Venice as long as the Austrians did not station any troops there. Bavaria would become a kingdom and control all of the formerly independent principalities within and just beyond its borders, but there was no more mention of giving it the Tyrol. His own aims in Italy were restricted to gaining all of Verona, Legnago, and the fort of Chiusa. Napoleon even declared that there was no difficulty about "separating the crowns of Italy and France," although he put off the details of that issue. He demanded other compromises too, including large monetary payments, but these terms were softened from his original bargaining position.[38]

This offer was certainly sincere and not part of a ruse designed to persuade the allies to fight. Napoleon informed Talleyrand in the same note that he expected a decisive battle with the Russians on the next day, "although I have done much to avoid it, since it is blood spilled to no purpose." Talleyrand hastened to draw up a treaty encapsulating Napoleon's wishes, although the Battle of Austerlitz intervened before he could negotiate seriously with Stadion and Gyulai on this basis.[39]

There was considerable wisdom in this approach. If Napoleon had actually persuaded Francis to make a separate peace with him, Alexander's departure with his army would have been virtually assured and Napoleon could have consolidated his gains without risking a battle that even he might not win in the depths of Moravia surrounded by enemies. If diplomacy failed and battle ensued, it would still be necessary to negotiate with Francis or his envoys to end the war. Nothing was lost by beginning the process early—or was it?

Napoleon's willingness to accept very modest gains for his notable victories even as late as November 30 suggests two conclusions. First, he was far from certain that he could easily transform the military situation with one quick battle. If he had been sure of fighting and winning a decisive battle, then it was folly to offer Francis any terms at all in advance of that victory and risk having him accept those terms when Napoleon could insist on so much more after the fight.*

Second, he had no clear goal in mind for this war. The terms he offered Stadion and Gyulai on November 30 did little more than give France a slightly more defensible frontier in Italy and strengthen Bavaria as a French buffer and ally. They would not have changed the face of Europe dramatically and would hardly have been worth the cost of the war. The emperor's willingness to offer them so late in the campaign underlines the fact that Austria was never his main target, still less an intended victim.

These diplomatic negotiations reveal Napoleon's state of mind and intentions, but they were made obsolete when Napoleon began to seek battle again after the combat at Vyškov on November 28. In contrast to the sincere overture Napoleon proposed to Francis, his initial note to the tsar, sent with Savary on November 26, was simply a baited hook.[40] Alexander's response was polite and pacific.[41] Napoleon seized on it to send Savary back to request an interview between the two sovereigns.[42] But the minor triumph at Vyškov had turned the heads of the young men in Alexander's entourage and now had a strange effect on Alexander himself.

Vyškov was the first combat the tsar had ever seen.[43] In this regard, Alexander was unique among continental monarchs of his day, for Francis, Frederick William, and of course Napoleon had all seen substantial fighting before taking their respective thrones. Alexander was excited, even galvanized, by the spectacle of fifty-six Russian squadrons routing eight French squadrons on an open field. As he wandered among the dead and dying, however, he was overcome by another emotion. Calling for assistance for all who showed any sign of life, Alexander became melancholy and did not eat for the rest of the day.† His confidence in the possibility of victory over Napoleon had increased; his enthusiasm for battle in general had declined.

---

*Those who might wish to argue that this softening of Napoleon's diplomatic stance was part of some ruse either to trick Francis into withdrawing his forces or lure the allies to the attack must accept the corollary: Napoleon was willing to violate diplomatic norms flagrantly at the most critical junction of his career. If Francis had accepted his terms as the basis of a negotiation and Napoleon had then withdrawn them or changed them dramatically, he would have put himself hopelessly in the wrong before virtually the whole of Europe, considering the number of sovereigns and envoys present in both camps. Napoleon was always careful, on the contrary, to cloak his violations of international norms with self-righteous justifications, something that would have been virtually impossible in this case. It is inconceivable that this offer was other than sincere.

†N. V. Shil'der, *Imperator Aleksandr Pervyi: Ego zhizn' i tsarstvovanie* (St. Petersburg: Izdanie A. S. Suvorina, 1897), p. 135. This description of Alexander's melancholy may have been made up or exaggerated in order to paint the tsar in a more human and attractive light. It is at least equally plausible, however, that it is near the truth. Alexander was a young, inexperienced, emotional, and highly strung man. The remnants of a battle are upsetting, seen up close for the first time. It would have been odd had the tsar not been disturbed by the sight.

Alexander had refused to meet Napoleon personally but sent in his place the irrepressible Dolgorukii (presumably to place the two emperors on the same footing, since Napoleon had sent Savary, his aide-de-camp). Napoleon had come to his front line, either out of curiosity or out of eagerness to hear Alexander's terms, Ségur says.[44] He met Dolgorukii in front of his troops. By all accounts Dolgorukii was as insufferable as only an arrogant, inexperienced young man can be. He refused to use the correct forms of address to Napoleon and demanded that Bonaparte withdraw from all of his new conquests, as well as Belgium! Napoleon kept his calm for some time but finally exploded in the face of Dolgorukii's arrogance and bade him off after an interview of about fifteen minutes.[45]

Dolgorukii returned to the tsar quite pleased with himself and having concluded that the French army was in a pitiable state. "Our success is certain," he declared. "We must only move forward and the enemy will withdraw, as they withdrew from Vyškov."[46] He was particularly unimpressed with Napoleon himself, apparently. Having arrived at the first enemy camp, he told General Langeron, "he saw emerging from the trenches a small figure, very greasy and dressed in an exceedingly funny manner," and was shocked to discover that this was the redoubtable Bonaparte!* Dolgorukii spread his misevaluations of Napoleon and his army broadly through the senior officers of the combined army, and they encouraged the hotheads among them to press harder than ever for battle.

Although Dolgorukii's bravado turned to Napoleon's advantage by encouraging Alexander in his determination to seek battle, we cannot credit Napoleon with cleverness or subtlety here. His emotions on hearing Dolgorukii's tone and words are not compatible with the notion that he had set out to trick the Russians into believing that he was weak and cowed. We have already seen several occasions when Napoleon tempered his wrath and submitted to impertinent nonsense for far longer than fifteen minutes when he believed it would suit his cause. It is not credible that he was unable to contain his anger when the stakes were so high, having done it before when the stakes were much lower.

Most likely, he honestly hoped that Alexander had come to his senses and was willing to parlay.† The evidence of the other negotiations Napoleon had

*Alexandre-Arnauld Langeron, *Zapiski Grafa Lanzherona, ego sed'maia kampaniia v Moravii i v Vengrii v 1805 godu* (St. Petersburg: n.p., 1900), p. 19. Langeron's account is self-serving and inaccurate, as we shall see (Chapter 22). This portion of the account is very much in keeping with Dolgorukii's character, however, and there is no reason to doubt it.

†This is not the consensus view of modern historians. Duffy (*Austerlitz*, p. 76), Gates (*Napoleonic Wars*, p. 29), and Chandler (*Campaigns of Napoleon*, p. 410) all assert that Savary's first mission was part of a ruse to gain intelligence about the allied disposition. Chandler even asserts (*Campaigns of Napoleon*, p. 409) that Napoleon had foreseen the need to prepare such a trap as early as November 14—two days before the Battle of Schöngrabern! All of these accounts either misstate the date of Savary's mission and its relationship to other events, or cover the discrepancies with vagueness. None of them offer evidence to support their interpretation, and none of them consider the sequence of events between November 20

already set in motion suggests that he hoped above all to sow discord among the allies and entrain them in separate and contradictory negotiations, all as a prelude to disrupting the coalition without a battle. If this were true, his fury at hearing Dolgorukii would have been the anger of a man hoping to talk seriously about serious matters who encounters a blithering fool. Bonaparte's wrath probably resulted less from Dolgorukii's tone and insolence than from his own frustration with his failed plans for a diplomatic solution.

Napoleon adroitly abandoned a hopeless course of action for a more promising one, as usual. He had already been preparing for the eventuality of a battle near Austerlitz for some time, and now he put his knowledge of the terrain and his newfound understanding of Alexander to good use. He developed a plan that would simultaneously lure the Russians into a fight and might achieve a decisive victory.

The fight at Vyškov had persuaded Napoleon that a real battle in the immediate future was possible, just as he had begun to fear that he would be hard-pressed to force the allies to fight. He responded immediately by ordering Bernadotte, Davout, and Marmont to race with their corps toward Brno.[47] Modern historians have taken this order to be a part of the trap that Napoleon was setting for the allies. By keeping only Soult, Lannes, Murat, the grenadiers, and the Imperial Guard with him at Brno, it is said, Napoleon deceived the coalition leaders into thinking that he was weaker than he was, always knowing that he could bring Bernadotte and Davout to bear at the decisive moment.[48] This explanation is possible, but others are more likely.

Napoleon did not concentrate the bulk of his army at Brno to begin with not out of any hope of tricking the allies but to deal with the strategic situation, as we have seen. He could not afford to allow Charles's army to retake Vienna and thereby cut him off from its massive stores of supplies and his own lines of communication. Nor could he allow Ferdinand's reviving army to ravage his communications from Bohemia. He was also concerned about keeping order in Vienna. Bernadotte, Davout, and Marmont performed these vital services, which kept them separated from Napoleon's main body.

---

and 30 in any detail. Even the accounts of eyewitnesses trying to make the case for Napoleon's omniscience are contradictory. Thiébault makes great efforts to show that Napoleon had formed his plan for tricking the allies into fighting him exactly as they did at Austerlitz as early as November 21. But he also reports that Napoleon declared that Austerlitz would be the scene of a decisive battle "within two *months.*" *Mémoires du Général Baron Thiébault* (Paris: Librairie Plon, 1895), 3:457; emphasis added. This strange statement seriously calls into question the notion that Napoleon knew on November 21 that he would fight a decisive battle of a certain type at Austerlitz on December 2. Savary gives no indication that he thought Napoleon's peace overtures anything other than genuine. In his own discourse with Alexander during his first mission, his tone was confident, even haughty. There was no suggestion of an approach designed to persuade Alexander of Napoleon's weakness or intention to withdraw. Désiré Lacroix, ed., *Mémoires du Duc de Rovigo pour server à l'histoire de l'Empereur Napoléon* (Paris: Garnier Frères, 1900), 2:53–64.

If Napoleon had concentrated these troops at Brno prematurely without knowing that a decisive battle would ensue quickly, the strategic situation could have collapsed on him entirely. He also would have badly compromised his logistical situation. The stocks at Brno, although ample, would not have maintained the entire Grande Armée indefinitely. His situation demanded that he keep his army dispersed for as long as possible, concentrating only when he was sure that he could have a major battle soon.

The great risk that he took nearly did not pay off. If the Battle of Austerlitz had occurred not on December 2 but a day or two earlier as Napoleon had imagined it would,* only Bernadotte's corps would have arrived. Davout's troops did not reach the battlefield until the night of December 1 through December 2, as we shall see, and Marmont's did not get there at all. Once again, contemporaries and historians have credited Napoleon with divine foresight, omniscience, and omnicompetence, ignoring the large amount of luck that assisted him at this critical pass.

If Napoleon had not deliberately set this trap, however, the allies sprang it on themselves. The difficulty of moving a large, ill-coordinated army even the short distance from Olmütz to Austerlitz led to significant delays, which gave Davout time to race north from Vienna. This trap resulted more from the allies' failure to understand the limitations of their own forces than from any plan of Napoleon's. The net result was to drive the campaign toward a climactic battle just where Napoleon wanted to fight it.

The Ground and the Options

The terrain in the vicinity of what would become the battlefield of Austerlitz presented a number of excellent defensive positions. Perhaps the best one for an army defending against an enemy marching west along the Brno-Olmütz road was the hill the French soldiers dubbed the "Santon," seeing in the church on its summit a similarity to Turkish tombs they had encountered during the Egyptian campaign (a *santon* in French is a religious artifact). Napoleon saw the value of that position as soon as he came into the area, and his first orders were to fortify it even further, rendering it virtually impregnable.[49] The hill called the Zuran, Napoleon's headquarters during much of the battle, is less imposing in height but not in defensibility. What it lacks in feet it makes up for with a gentle forward slope that offers a marvelous killing field for those who hold its crest.

---

*See, e.g., Napoleon to Talleyrand, 30 November 1805, 4:00 P.M. (*Corr. de Nap.*, doc. 9532), in which he writes, "There will probably be a very serious battle with the Russians tomorrow" (i.e., December 1).

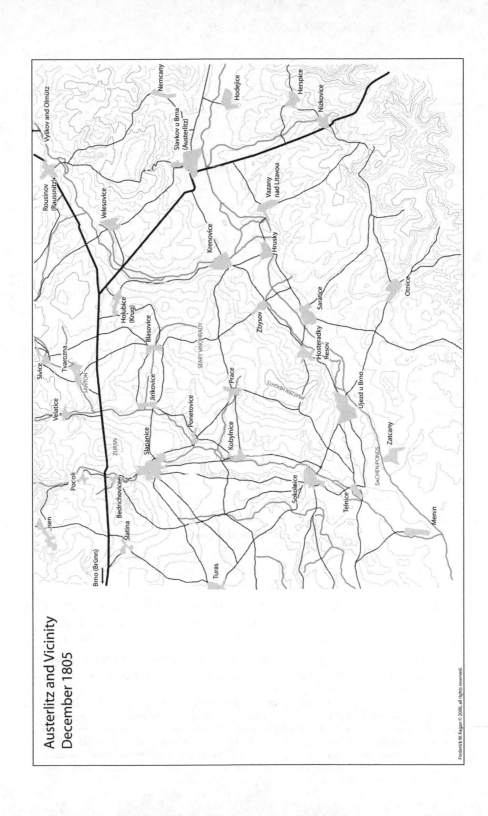

Austerlitz and Vicinity
December 1805

The heights to the south and east of these two positions, the Stare Vinohrady (old vineyards) and the Pratzen heights to the southwest, are relatively less useful as defensive positions against an army attacking from the east than one attacking from the west. Soult, whose troops at first occupied a position east of these heights, asked Napoleon to give him a new position on November 24, because "the environs of Austerlitz do not offer any advantageous [positions]; the land is so open and so revealing that half of the regiments have to serve as guards for the other half."[50] Behind them to the west lies the valley of the Goldbach stream dotted with a series of villages in order from south to north: Menin, Telnice, Sokolnice, Kobylnice, and Slapanice.* The stream was not easily fordable, and the bridges were located mostly in the villages, giving them a tactical importance they would not otherwise have had and rendering the task of defending the line of the Goldbach stream much easier. To the south of Telnice lay two shallow ponds around the village of Sacsan. To the north of the Santon at a short distance lay the foothills of the mountain range known as the "Moravian Switzerland."

If Napoleon had continued to hold the Pratzen heights and the Stary Vinohrady, the allies probably would not have been able to defeat him. Attacks against the heights themselves, including the Santon, would have failed in the face of determined resistance, and any effort to drive through the valley between the Stary Vinohrady and the Santon–Zuran complex would have been exposed to attack from heights on three sides and even the rear.

It might have been possible to march south of the Pratzen heights and the Sacsan ponds in an effort to turn the flank of this position, but such an attempt would have failed. For one thing, it would have required a long march over rough terrain with no meaningful roads. Keeping baggage and artillery up with the combat forces would have been difficult and would have slowed the march in the extreme. Southeast of the Pratzen, the land becomes extremely rugged. An army attempting to envelop the position on the Pratzen would therefore have to remain very close to it. The flank march would have to be conducted over rough terrain under the French guns and would be vulnerable to an attack on an extended and vulnerable flank.

Napoleon, who examined this terrain in minute detail from the moment he arrived at Brno, understood this situation perfectly. Standing on the Pratzen heights, he declared, "Master of this beautiful position . . . I could stop the Russians; but then I would only have an ordinary battle whereas by abandoning it to them and refusing my right, if they dare to descend from these heights to envelop

---

*In this narrative, most village names are given according to their current Czech names to aid visitors to this fascinating battlefield and to avoid the confusion common in the accounts of this battle resulting from the inconsistent translation of Habsburg names into French, Russian, and English. These villages were most commonly known at the time as Menitz (or Melnitz in some French accounts), Telnitz, Sokolnitz, Kobelnitz, and Slapanitz (or Schlapanitz). I shall continue to refer to Austerlitz (now called Slavkov u Brna) and to use the spelling "Pratzen" rather than the Czech "Prace" because these names have become familiar to military historians.

me, they will be lost without recourse!"* These were Napoleon's words on November 30, 1805, as he gazed toward Austerlitz and the advancing Russian army. By following through on this insight, Napoleon set the terms of the imminent battle so strongly in his favor that the outcome of the fight was almost certain.

He also increased the probability that a battle would indeed take place. It is unlikely that the allies would have accepted battle had Napoleon continued to hold the Pratzen heights, and Napoleon knew it. Faced with the choice between launching a frontal attack on an obviously strong defensive position or withdrawing to await further developments, it is nearly certain, considering the divisions inside the allied camp about what to do, that Kutuzov's arguments against fighting would have been unanswerable.† By withdrawing from the Pratzen, Napoleon enticed the allies to attack.

In addition to the likelihood that the allies would refuse to attack such an obviously strong position, moreover, the Santon-Zuran-Pratzen position posed another difficulty for Napoleon: it virtually precluded any chance of a decisive victory. If the allies had attacked those positions head-on, the French forces would have driven them back. The pursuit and destruction of the allied force following such a fight, however, was less certain. An attack on the Santon-Zuran-Pratzen position would not require the allied army to break up into smaller independent units; two or three corps-size elements would have been appropriate to attack that position, and the terrain and likely scheme of maneuver would have kept those elements in contact with each other. Therefore Napoleon would not have been able to defeat the allies in detail, nor was it likely that they would scatter when defeated to facilitate his pursuit and exploitation of the victory. It would have been an ordinary battle that left the allied forces combat worthy even after being defeated.

Given the strategic context, Napoleon could not afford such a battle. Allied reinforcements were approaching in overwhelming strength, whereas Napoleon had none. To extricate himself from his horrible predicament, he had to win a victory so clear and devastating that the allies would make peace without bringing their enormous advantages to bear against him. The battle could not simply be a victory; it had to have a crushing emotional content as well.

---

*Ségur, *Histoire et mémoires*, pp. 451–452. Ségur dates this remark to November 30. Thiébault, however, dates the identical remark to a reconnaissance of 21 November (*Mémoires du Général Baron Thiébault*, p. 457). Both dates are problematic. By November 30, Napoleon had already withdrawn his troops from the Pratzen heights, so the declaration seems irrelevant. On November 21, the Russians were nowhere near those heights and Napoleon had no reason to be sure that he would fight a battle there, the ex post facto efforts of his admirers to the contrary notwithstanding. It is certain, however, that he reviewed the area that would become the battlefield of Austerlitz carefully, and he may have decided even as early as November 21 how he would fight a battle there if the allies obliged him.

†Napoleon did not know of the dissensions in the allied camp, but he had been campaigning against Kutuzov for more than a month and knew how reluctant that general was to accept battle on any but the most advantageous ground.

Napoleon therefore ordered Soult's corps, the one farthest advanced beyond the Pratzen, to withdraw beyond the heights on November 29.[51] By abandoning the Pratzen heights to the allies and concentrating his forces at the Santon-Zuran complex, Napoleon transformed the conditions in which the battle would be fought and made such a victory possible. An allied attack against the fortified Santon position continued to hold out little prospect for success—and therefore was unlikely. Perhaps the most promising course of action the allies could have pursued would have been to attack from the Pratzen-Stary Vinohrady position directly against the Zuran and along the Brünn-Olmütz road against the Santon. With reserves left on the Pratzen, such an attack would have been relatively safe and might have succeded despite the imposing defensive strength of the Santon-Zuran position. It would deprive the allies of any real chance either to destroy Napoleon's army or to cut it off from its reinforcements. Even if the attack were successful, Napoleon would likely have been able to withdraw along the road back to Brno, rally, and prepare to regain the initiative. The allies, no less than Napoleon, sought a decisive battle, not merely a victory, and were likely to avoid such a straightforward plan.

That left an envelopment of Napoleon's right flank as the only promising option for the allies. If they tried that, Napoleon could predict what the battle would look like. The distance from the highway to the south end of the Pratzen is great enough that the allies could not hold the entire line and still concentrate sufficient force to attack. By abandoning the Pratzen, Napoleon forced them to choose between abandoning the highway and with it their lines of communication and withdrawal, or dividing their forces into units that had no direct contact with one another, thus offering Napoleon the opportunity to split up the enemy army and defeat it in detail.

By abandoning the heights, Napoleon not only confirmed the allies in their decision to attack him, but he set the terms of the resulting battle so decisively that he could predict with near certainty what his enemy would do. This allowed him to prepare a counter-thrust that would be devastating and might well be decisive.

The Allied Plan

The coalition army left Olmütz aiming to swing round Napoleon's right flank and cut him off from Vienna.[52] The execution of this plan was complicated by the fact that the allies had lost contact with the French army and did not know exactly where they would encounter it.* This lack of intelligence, combined with

---

*See Stutterheim, La Bataille d'Austerlitz, p. 23. The French had lost contact with the allied army, which was why Napoleon was surprised (and delighted) by the combat at Vyskov on November 28.

inexperience and confusion caused by the different allied contingents, made the coalition's advance cautious and tentative. A bold rush down the Brno-Olmütz road followed by a quick swing to the left might have surprised Napoleon and forced him to fight in a less advantageous position. The allies' slow advance, however, gave him every opportunity to see them coming and make his plans.[53]

Every day's march was the subject of a detailed and careful disposition. The first of these, for the march that occurred on November 27, was the most detailed and cautious of all because the allies believed they might encounter the French that very day and stumble into a meeting engagement. Much of the disposition is concerned with how the various columns should assist one another in that eventuality.[54] By the end of that day, allied reconnaissance had painted a reasonably clear picture of the French deployment.[55] Therefore the dispositions for November 28 included not merely a march order for the whole army but a detailed plan for the attack of Bagration's vanguard against the small French outposts at Vyškov.[56]

The fact that almost every march disposition changed the composition of the columns into which the allied army had been divided increased the confusion in it.[57] It is easy to lay too much emphasis on the fact that Napoleon's corps remained together throughout a campaign and thereby cohered at many levels, improving their combat power and flexibility, considering the dramatic changes in the makeup of Lannes's and Ney's corps over the course of the Ulm campaign, to say nothing of the creation of Mortier's corps from three divisions taken from those and other corps. Consequently it cannot be the case that the stability of the corps system generated its main benefit. The varying composition of the allied columns over the course of a five-day march to contact, however, hindered the development of the coherence necessary for the heterogeneous force Kutuzov had under his nominal command. The deliberate marches nevertheless brought the allies to the battlefield and allowed their leaders to focus on their plan for the combat that was to follow.

The allies' conduct of the battle requires more careful consideration than it has received. At first glance, it appears that they fell into every trap Napoleon laid for them. The plan they developed and executed was so clearly the one for which Napoleon was prepared that it was subsequently asserted that he had somehow possessed himself of it before the battle began.* The plan was so terribly flawed and so lacking in military sense that it seemed drafted by idiots, but

---

*Langeron suggests that Weyrother leaked the plan in advance to Savary during the latter's stay at Olmütz (*Zapiski Grafa Lanzherona*, p. 18). This nonsensical idea is surely a part of the Russian effort to blame the catastrophe on the perfidious, incompetent, and cowardly Austrians. Among other things, there is considerable evidence, as we shall see, that the battle plan was not prepared prior to December 1, long after Savary had left the allied camp. If Weyrother had told the envoy that the allies intended to attack Napoleon (for which there is no evidence), he was adding nothing to the knowledge that Napoleon gained from the combat at Vyškov.

the truth is more complex. Although the plan contained serious flaws that nearly doomed it from the outset, there were reasons for those flaws. The people who drafted and executed the plan for this battle were trained officers with long experience in wars. They were not idiots. They were, however, operating in a political environment and an intellectual atmosphere that made clear thinking difficult and silenced those who might have objected to a bad plan.

The plan was the brainchild of Major General Franz von Weyrother, one of the senior remaining officers of the vaunted Austrian general staff.[58] When FML Schmitt was killed during the Battle of Dürnstein, Weyrother took over his position as chief of staff of Kutuzov's army, and he held that position before and during the Battle of Austerlitz. Weyrother was an experienced staff officer. He served throughout the campaigns against revolutionary France, drafted dispositions for General Alvinczy's army in 1796, and was chief of staff for General Kray, commander of the Austrian army in Italy, during the War of the Second Coalition (1799–1801). His command experience was less extensive; he never commanded a unit larger than a regiment.

The results of Weyrother's staff work during the Italian campaigns had not been successful, and it was ominous that it had been Napoleon who had undone Weyrother's efforts then. Like Mack, Weyrother had a penchant for complex maneuvers.* During the Italian campaigns Austrian armies had split into smaller units and attempted sophisticated independent movements aimed at trapping Napoleon or falling on his flank. The results were mostly disastrous, as these plans allowed Napoleon to exercise his love of defeating his enemies in detail to the full.

The allies nevertheless had every reason to feel confident about the prospect of a battle near Austerlitz, since they knew the terrain better than Napoleon did. Not only was it their home turf, but in late August 1804 they had assembled a large exercise camp at Turas on the very site of the battle of 1805.† The Austrian forces in that exercise broke into two parts and staged two mock battles in which one sought to cross the Goldbach stream in the vicinity of Slapanice while the other tried to prevent it. The lessons of those exercises should have been cautionary for the plan that Weyrother eventually composed, since the lead troops of the attacking force found it difficult to get across the stream and form up properly on the other side, ready to meet

---

*See above for a brief discussion of this Austrian penchant and its role in Mack's planning for the Ulm campaign.

†Archduke Charles's detailed evaluation of these exercises has survived and gives us a general idea of what they were like (KA Memoiren, 6 Abtheilung, 188). For an Austrian army to fight near Austerlitz in 1805 was rather like an American force fighting at one of its training areas in Germany or California. The advantage that intimate knowledge of the terrain gives an army is well-known to U.S. army units who fight the permanent "opposing forces" that train and fight almost every week on the same ground. Mikhailovskii-Danilevskii asserts that Weyrother was present during this exercise (Mikhailovskii-Danilevskii, *Opisanie*, p. 175).

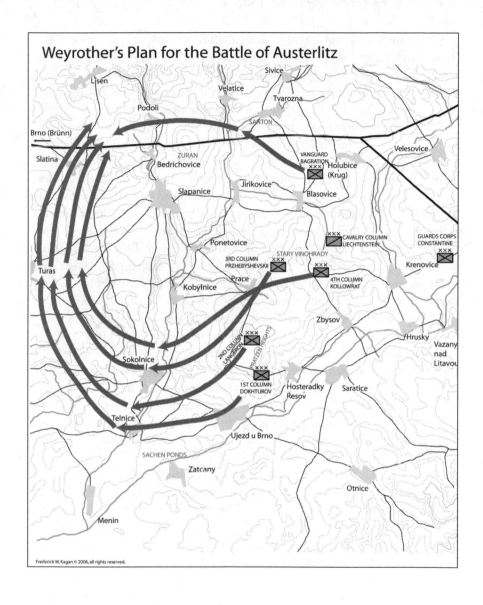

Weyrother's Plan for the Battle of Austerlitz

Sivice

Velatice

Tvarozna

Lisen

Podoli

SANTON

Brno (Brünn)

ZURAN
Bedrichovice

Slatina

VANGUARD
BAGRATION
XXX

Holubice
(Krug)

Velesovice

Jirikovice

Slapanice

Blasovice

Ponetovice

CAVALRY COLUMN
LIECHTENSTEIN
XXX

GUARDS CORPS
CONSTANTINE
XXX

Turas

3RD COLUMN
PRZHEBYSHEVSKII
XXX

STARY VINOHRADY

4TH COLUMN
KOLLOWRAT
XXX

Krenovice

Prace

Kobylnice

Zbysov

Hrusky

Vazany
nad
Litavou

2ND COLUMN
LANGERON
XXX

PRATZEN HEIGHTS

Sokolnice

1ST COLUMN
DOKHTUROV
XXX

Hosteradky
Resov

Saratice

Telnice

Ujezd u Brno

SACHEN PONDS

Zatcany

Otnice

Menin

attacks. Both sides found it hard to navigate the confusing terrain in this vicinity and coordinate the activities of the cavalry with the infantry. These problems came back to haunt the coalition in 1805. Before the battle, however, the intimate knowledge of the terrain gained from those exercises simply increased Weyrother's confidence in the plan he was developing.

Weyrother's scheme divided the allied army into five infantry columns, a cavalry corps, and a reserve.[59] Numbered from south to north on the battlefield, the first four infantry columns were arrayed along the Pratzen heights that Napoleon had abandoned, the fifth along the Olmütz-Brno road, and the cavalry column on the Stary Vinohrady; the reserve was stationed on the reverse slope of that hillock. The first three columns were nominally united under the command of Buxhöwden. The fourth, stationed close to the center of the battlefield near the summit of the Pratzen heights, consisted of two parts. One, composed of Russian troops, was commanded by Miloradovich. The Austrian contingent was under the command of Kollowrat. This divided command was offset by the fact that Kutuzov had stationed himself with this column. The fifth column, also called the vanguard, was commanded by Bagration, the cavalry column by Austrian Prince Liechtenstein, and the reserve by Grand Prince Constantine.*

The plan was for the first four columns to descend from their positions on the Pratzen and sweep forward over the Goldbach brook, move into position in the rear of the French army near Turas, and then assault the Zuran-Santon position from the direction of Brno. Bagration's fifth column was to hold its position until it saw the approach of the other four from the French rear, at which point it was to join in the attack, supported by Liechtenstein's cavalry and, if necessary, the Russian Imperial Guard in reserve.

Although Buxhöwden nominally commanded the first three columns, the burden for the maneuver in fact fell on the column commanders. The 1st Column was subdivided into a vanguard under the command of General Kienmayer, which was to maintain a mobile flank guard ahead and to the left of the main body of the column, commanded by Dokhturov. The initial target of that column was the village of Telnice. The 2nd Column, commanded by a French émigré who had taken service with the Russians, Count Langeron, was to advance into the gap between Telnice and Sokolnice. The 3rd Column, commanded by Przebyshevskii, was to attack Sokolnice. The 4th Column would advance toward Kobylnice, although the precise location at which it would cross the Goldbach was not clear.

The plan was deeply flawed. First and foremost, it took no account of the possibility that Napoleon might take action instead of waiting for the allied wings to crush him like hammer on anvil. Weyrother knew that Napoleon's

---

*The widespread tendency to call Constantine a "grand duke" is odd. Both the Russian *velikii kniaz'* and the German equivalent *Großfürst* translate into English as "grand prince."

forces were concentrated in the vicinity of the Santon and the Zuran; nevertheless, the plan left the Pratzen heights completely barren from the outset of the battle and exposed the allied armies to precisely the sort of devastation Napoleon was able to wreak by seizing them.

Second, the plan did not consider the Goldbach stream as an obstacle or the possible difficulties of rapidly seizing and crossing the bridges in the villages of Telnice and Sokolnice. A related problem was that the plan did not make clear when the allied armies were to deploy from column to line. Clearly they would leave the Pratzen in column; presumably Weyrother intended that they would remain in column across the Goldbach bridges, since he did not seem to consider the likelihood that that crossing would be seriously opposed. He probably imagined that the columns would remain in column formation until they reached the vicinity of Turas, where they would form into line for the final assault from Napoleon's rear. These failures were remarkable in light of the Austrian exercises of the previous year, which had highlighted precisely these issues. Count Bubna, an Austrian colonel present at this meeting, supposedly warned Weyrother, "Just don't make the same mistakes as [we made] at the maneuvers last year."[60]

Still another problem was that the left and right wings of the allied army were not well coordinated. The march of the allied left would take several hours even without opposition, but Bagration's "vanguard" could be in contact with Lannes's forces within minutes. What if Lannes attacked? What if Napoleon began shifting forces from his left flank to his center and right to meet the allied attack? The plan offered no guidance except that Bagration was to hold his ground until the allied left wing was in position behind Napoleon's main body and then attack. With Napoleon's main body between the allied left and right wings, coordination would be impossible.

Weyrother worked on this complicated disposition throughout the day of December 1 and presented it to a meeting of the column commanders at midnight. Accounts of this meeting agree on the essentials.[61] Weyrother presented his plan confidently, even arrogantly, and most of the generals appeared to pay it little attention. Weyrother had also drawn up a map of his scheme, which few of the generals bothered to look at carefully. Langeron claims that Kutuzov fell asleep before Weyrother finished. According to one account, Bagration challenged Weyrother about the inactivity of his corps;* according to Langeron's self-justificatory account written twenty years later Langeron challenged Weyrother on the problem of the Pratzen.† Neither challenge, if they were indeed

---

*Bernhardi, *Denkwürdigkeiten aus dem Leben*, 1:177. It is by no means clear, however, that Bagration was present at the meeting.

†Langeron, *Zapiski Grafa Lanzherona*, p. 23. This account is highly suspect, and the speech Langeron claims to have made at this meeting is improbable. At least one (anonymous) student of this meeting agrees: "Judgment of General Weyrother," KA AFA 1805 Deutschland, XII/ad12¼.

made at that time, generated any discussion or resulted in any change to the plan. Weyrother drafted his disposition in German, and Major von Toll, a Russian staff officer, was told to translate it during the night.[62] Copies were not prepared until early in the morning, and only the most senior commanders were given time to copy them down. Some units set out to execute the disposition even before they received it.[63]

Histories of the battle dramatically describe these details to show the incompetence, chaos, and confusion that reigned in the allied camp and, presumably, help explain the outcome of the battle.* In reality most of them are irrelevant. The column commanders paid little attention to the terrain because they had Austrian column guides to lead them; with such assistance the terrain did not seem all that complicated. This omission was unprofessional and led to unfortunate consequences for General Langeron, especially. But the outcome of the battle would not have been materially altered had the column commanders followed the discussion assiduously. Kutuzov's alleged catnap is even more entertaining and even less important. Without doubt, Kutuzov knew the outlines of the plan before Weyrother briefed it. Experienced soldier that he was, he almost certainly perceived its inadequacies. But, as we have seen and shall explore further, he was unable to protest to any effect. His nap may well have been the most effective and safest possible way to convey feelings he could not otherwise express. In any event, he understood the plan clearly enough the next morning when the battle began.

The real problem with the meeting was not Kutuzov's nap or the officers' inattentiveness but the absence of argument. In a truly professional military force, a staff briefing is not merely an opportunity for a staff officer to show off his intelligence, but a chance for senior and experienced commanders and other staff officers to consider the proposed plan and recommend alterations necessary to ensure success. There should be give-and-take and open discussion with the objective of developing the best possible plan, not stroking the egos of commanders and staff officers. Such a model meeting is not the invariable norm even in the most professional modern militaries, to be sure, but the silence and lack of discussion that greeted the presentation of this obviously flawed plan to a group of senior and experienced officers merits notice.

It is unlikely in the extreme that the plan's flaws were hidden from the commanders. The problem of who could voice objections, however, was considerably more complicated. Although Kutuzov was nominally commander in chief, Alexander had repeatedly made plain to him that he did not really command. Kutuzov's advice to remain on the defensive had been rejected, his plea to take

---

*Duffy, *Austerlitz*, pp. 97–98; Chandler, *Campaigns of Napoleon*, pp. 417–420. Bowden (*Napoleon and Austerlitz*, pp. 303–308) is egregious in this regard, misrepresenting Alexander's personality and state of mind and ignoring the problems the allies faced. He particularly errs in identifying the failings of this makeshift combined army as those common to "armies of the *ancien régime*."

time to train the army dismissed. Once when he inquired about a disposition to be issued to the army under his command, Alexander informed him that it was none of his business.[64] Since Weyrother had Alexander's confidence and Kutuzov did not, the outcome of any protest Kutuzov might have made was foreordained. Kutuzov was not one to waste energy combating the inevitable.

Kutuzov's silence more or less ensured that the other Russian generals kept their peace. After all, he was not only the commander in chief of the army but the senior Russian commander on the scene, second only to Tsar Alexander, who was not present at the meeting. The meeting could not have been a comfortable one, for tensions between Austrians and Russians had been running high ever since the debacle at Ulm. Those tensions were inflamed by news that Francis had made several efforts to negotiate with Napoleon (the Russian generals do not seem to have known that Alexander was a party to most of these efforts). In addition, the Austrians resented the Russians' arrogance toward them. In such a charged atmosphere it was unlikely that Russian soldiers would fail to take the lead from their chief and attack a plan that seemed to have his at least tacit approval.*

The Austrians demonstrated even greater solidarity behind their spokesman, Weyrother. Austria's humiliations had not stopped with Mack's surrender. Auersperg's failure to defend the bridge over the Danube at Vienna and Nostitz's withdrawal from the field at Hollabrunn rankled and seemed to prove that Ulm had not been a fluke. The Austrians were desperate to redeem themselves at all costs and to show themselves worthy of consideration in the peace following allied victory.

For years Austria's leaders had feared that a new war would exhaust the empire without conferring any greater security or benefit on it. With Austria's prestige dropping to new lows, the danger that peace, even following a victorious battle, would not generate advantages for Vienna was very real. In such a situation, the Austrian generals could hardly undercut Weyrother, especially since he had secured Alexander's approval. The truth was that allied generals would have been hard-pressed to make any serious demur to Weyrother's plan because of the complex political background surrounding the battle.

The question remains, however, why Weyrother himself did not see and address the flaws that are so obvious, at least in hindsight. Part of the answer surely lies in the Austrian fixation with complicated maneuver plans described above. In the context of developing such a plan, where the emphasis is on the complexity and interrelationships of the various subunits and their maneuvers, it is easy (if dangerous) to lose sight of what the enemy might do to undermine the plan.

---

*This is one of many reasons for doubting the veracity of Langeron's and Toll's claims about opposition at the meeting.

Another possible reason for Weyrother's failure to address the plan's problems may have been confusion between the initial objectives that guided the army when it set out from Olmütz and the goals that Weyrother sought to achieve concretely on December 2. When the army began to march toward Brno, the goal was to envelope the three corps Napoleon had brought with him east of that city, cut the lines of communication to Vienna and Bohemia, and defeat Napoleon in detail. This objective could be achieved less by a battle plan than by a scheme of operational maneuver. The difference is important. While considering activities at the tactical level—the level of battle—the planner must always keep in mind the presence of the enemy and the imminence of enemy interference with the plan. Units on the flanks of the advance must be prepared at all times to meet with enemy attacks, and contingency plans must be prepared to respond to such attacks. If forces are not marching in line formation—if they are not deployed for battle—they must nevertheless be prepared to deploy in short order, and plans for that deployment must be worked out.

In operational maneuvers, however, the situation is somewhat different. Although where the enemy is and what he might do must always be considered, units conducting operational maneuvers are not generally in direct contact with the enemy.* That means they can reasonably expect to have some warning before an enemy attack to prepare defenses and deploy if necessary. During operational maneuvers the emphasis is generally on speed of movement, and speed is best obtained by traveling in column, not in line. Although certain units are normally designated to guard the flanks, even those flank guards are likely to travel in line in order to keep up with the rest of the formation.

The original allied plan had been one of operational maneuver. It should have emphasized speed and moving to avoid contact with the enemy, which would have slowed down the advance.† The difficulty was twofold. First, the nature of the allied army prevented rapid movement, allowing Napoleon to gather reinforcements. But second, the nature of the terrain virtually precluded an operational envelopment. Along the road from Olmütz to Brno, the mountainous region north of the highway known as the Moravian Switzerland is much closer to the road at Brno than at Olmütz. Rough terrain south of the

---

*This statement is more true for the nineteenth century and before than the twentieth. Armored warfare made it possible for units to conduct prolonged operational movements in nearly constant contact with the enemy, as the Germans and Soviets did in Russia, or the Germans and the Americans did during the Battle of the Bulge. In the nineteenth century such situations were less common, since armies tended to concentrate into a few large groups. When they were not fighting one another on the battlefield, their forces were not normally in contact with one another.

†The advance would have slowed not so much because of the combat, as because of the need to deploy from march columns into fighting formations. This issue persisted well into the twentieth century. The goal of defenders throughout World War II was to force advancing armored columns to deploy and thereby slow down; the goal of the attackers was to pulverize their adversaries so that they could continue to travel in march columns, as Patton did on much of his charge across France.

Pratzen heights similarly converges toward the highway. Finally, the Sacsan ponds pose a nearly insuperable obstacle to significant movement to the south from the Pratzen. The terrain thus conspires to funnel operations into a very tight maneuver corridor as an army approaches the Goldbach stream from the east. Since there are no significant roads running parallel to the main highway, any movement to the south or north must be cross-country, which further reduces the speed of an advance.

When the allies first conceived of enveloping Napoleon's army without knowing exactly where and how it was deployed, it was easy to imagine an operational envelopment safely removed from the danger of an immediate attack. Although the situation on the actual battlefield prevented such operational maneuvers and forced the allies into a tactical situation, Weyrother may not have fully adjusted to the change in focus and situation. Alexander was certainly thinking in terms of an operational envelopment as late as November 28.[65] The plan reads as though it were fundamentally an operational maneuver into the rear followed by a tactical engagement. Weyrother should have noticed that the situation was otherwise, but in the pressure to develop a plan that would work—and thereby restore Austria's honor and prestige—he may well have become confused.

The last reason that must be advanced in Weyrother's defense is that the terrain does not support or permit a good plan of attack from the positions the allies occupied on December 1. Although solutions can be found to the problem of abandoning the Pratzen heights, other critical and probably fatal problems remain much less tractable. The Goldbach stream and the villages that dot it are actually a formidable obstacle, as we shall see, and would have slowed down the allied advance in almost any circumstances. The differential distance that the left wing must cover to get into attack position, as opposed to that which the right wing must cross, renders a coordinated attack highly problematic. In almost any circumstances the battle would likely have broken into two separate engagements with Napoleon shifting forces from one to the other. Obviously better plans could have been developed than the one Weyrother adopted and a more professional staff meeting might have helped develop them. Nevertheless, it is doubtful that the allies could have won the battle on that ground, and nearly certain that they could not have won a decisive victory.

The wiser choice would have been to decline the attack and either hold position on the Pratzen or withdraw to Olmütz and even beyond. But just as the internal coalition tensions rendered intelligent planning impossible, so they also made any notion of abandoning the fight inconceivable. Alexander had not been willing to retreat from Olmütz. He certainly would have resisted withdrawing from before Napoleon's cannons even more fiercely. The Austrians, desperate to maintain and gain face before Alexander, could not possibly have suggested a withdrawal. And Kutuzov, much though he would probably have liked to do so, certainly knew that any such suggestion coming from him would be rejected out of hand. The allies suffered from the positive feedback of fear and honor. Once started down the path of attacking Napoleon, they were driven willy-nilly into accepting battle on the worst possible terms by their own unwillingness to appear weak to one another.

Conclusion

Napoleon's plan rested on the assumption that the allies would abandon the Pratzen heights, as indeed they meant to. He intended to cover his entire right wing from Kobylnice down to Telnice with only one division (Legrand's) of Soult's corps. Two other divisions (St. Hilaire and Vandamme) would race up the Pratzen heights supported by Bernadotte's two divisions, newly arrived on the battlefield, and by Murat's cavalry. Lannes's corps would hold the Santon and the highway. Napoleon hoped and expected that Davout would arrive to support Legrand's division in the south, but he made no contingency plan in case he did not.

Once Soult and Bernadotte had seized the heights, the allied army would have been split in two. Napoleon would then focus on destroying it in detail, first the four columns of the allied left wing and then the remaining allied forces. This plan was simple, obvious from the terrain and the likely actions of the allies, and promised to produce a suitably impressive and decisive battle. And so it did. Once the allies committed themselves to a foolish attack, the terrain and their dispositions made clear to Napoleon how the battle had to go. The combination of his skills in setting the terms of the battle and the allies' unwisdom in abetting him in that task resulted in a fight, the course and outcome of which was nearly inevitable before the first shots were fired.

For all that, however, the battle itself was a nearer-run thing than might have been imagined, for the frictions of war came close to undoing Napoleon's plans. Despite the enormous disadvantages the allies laid on themselves before the battle began, its course and consequences can only be understood through a careful examination of battlefield events on the fateful day of December 2, 1805.

22

The Fight
for the Villages

The Battle of Austerlitz consisted of a number of separate but related combats. In the south, the Russian left wing faced Napoleon's right in a fight for the crossings over the Goldbach brook. In the center two divisions of Soult's Corps came crashing down on the allied 4th Column on the Pratzen heights. To the north, Bagration, Constantine, and Liechtenstein became embroiled with Lannes's and Bernadotte's Corps and the French Imperial Guard. Despite its apparent inevitability, the outcome of the battle depended on the issues of these engagements. And at first glance the French victory in the south against the three left-most Russian columns was unlikely.

Telnice

Weyrother's plan called for all allied columns to step off at seven o'clock in the morning, shortly after dawn.[1] The 1st Column consisted of a vanguard commanded by Kienmayer and a main body under the Russian general Dokhturov. The vanguard had four small infantry and seven cavalry regiments divided into four brigades, while the main body, composed of seven infantry regiments, one jaeger battalion, and one Cossack regiment was divided into two brigades.[2] Kienmayer's task was to seize the village of Telnice and then march on Dokhturov's right flank as the latter wheeled the main body to Turas in preparation for the final attack.

Unique among the allied columns, the 1st Column actually stepped off on time.[3] The position on the southern end of the Pratzen heights from which it began its march loomed ominously over the small village of Telnice. In march column with flags waving and drummers drumming, this column must

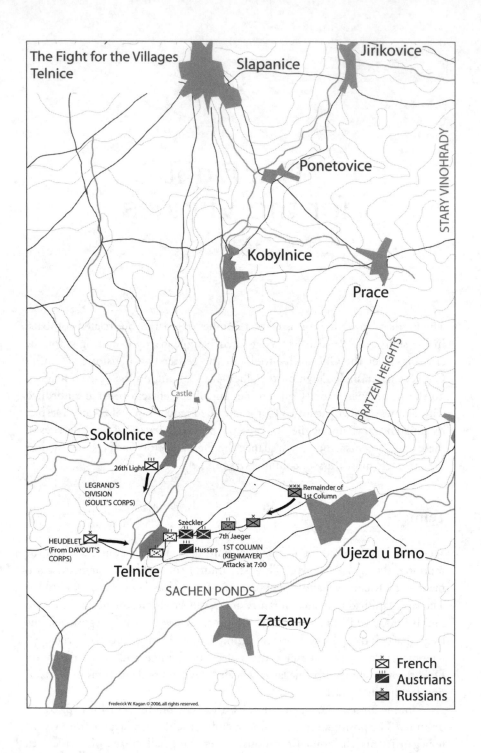

The Fight for the Villages
Telnice

Slapanice

Jirikovice

Ponetovice

STARY VINOHRADY

Kobylnice

Prace

PRATZEN HEIGHTS

Castle

Sokolnice

26th Light

LEGRAND'S
DIVISION
(SOULT'S CORPS)

Remainder of
1st Column

Szeckler

7th Jaeger

HEUDELET
(From DAVOUT'S
CORPS)

Hussars

1ST COLUMN
(KIENMAYER)
Attacks at 7:00

Ujezd u Brno

Telnice

SACHEN PONDS

Zatcany

French
Austrians
Russians

have presented an impressive sight for the French light infantry charged with holding the town. On the other hand, Telnice was a small but crowded village of stone buildings on the eastern side of the Goldbach brook. It is not clear from the accounts how daunting an obstacle the brook was, but the village presented numerous opportunities for a determined defender to hold off a larger attacker. What is more, a series of gentle slopes west of the village both channeled an advance and provided good defensive positions.

Like most of the combat during this battle, the fight for the village of Telnice was a meeting engagement. Forces arrived piecemeal and in small groups, and the outcome turned heavily on which side was the last to bring reinforcements to bear. The initial fight at Telnice pitted the French 3rd Line Infantry Regiment and two battalions of skirmishers from Soult's Corps against two Austrian light infantry battalions and a hussar regiment of Kienmayer's vanguard. At first only one battalion of Austrian Szeckler light infantry fought for the village, and the French defenders made excellent use of vineyards and broken ground outside of the town to hold off the attackers. Even when the 2nd Szeckler Battalion was brought up, the Austrians were unable to drive the French out of their positions. Despite Kienmayer's sending forward three more infantry battalions after that, the Austrians were not able to seize the village they had been attacking for more than an hour.[4]

Finally, at about eight o'clock, the main body of the 1st Column with General Buxhöwden at its head appeared, marching down the slopes from Ujezd toward Telnice. Buxhöwden sent a battalion of the 7th Jaeger Regiment to support Kienmayer's fight for the village and placed a Russian brigade in reserve behind it. With this renewed strength, the vanguard finally convinced the French to withdraw from the village and began consolidating its hold there.[5]

The delay in seizing Telnice, however, gave the French time to bring up reinforcements. Davout's soldiers had been marching almost continuously for three days, and in that time Friant's Infantry Division and Bourcier's Dragoons Division had covered the distance from Pressburg to the battlefield—about ninety miles. They rested briefly and then swung onto the battlefield early in the morning of December 2.[6]

Napoleon had first ordered Davout's forces to Raygern Abbey, a position in the rear of the French right wing from which they could easily be sent to reinforce any weak points on that side of the French line. From there, Davout sent them forward toward Turas. At about eight o'clock, while en route, Davout learned of the plight of the 3rd Line at Telnice and also learned that the allies had not yet attacked the village of Sokolnice.[7] He accordingly ordered both of his divisions to march on Telnice. General Heudelet's Brigade was in the lead, and it reached Telnice at about nine o'clock in the morning.[8]

Davout's troops were not the only French reinforcements headed toward Telnice. The commander of the 3rd Line had also gotten word of his plight back to General Legrand, his division commander, and since the main body of Legrand's troops around Sokolnice was not then engaged, Legrand had ordered the 26th Light Infantry Regiment south to Telnice to assist in the defense.[9] These dispositions, both Davout's and Legrand's, were made hastily in the hope of saving Telnice and stopping the allied advance. Apparently the brigade and regimental commanders involved were not kept informed of the situation.

Heudelet's Brigade arrived at Telnice first and apparently took the allies by surprise. He was assisted in that task by a fog that suddenly blew up and obscured the village and the hills behind it. As a result, Heudelet and the remnants of the 3rd Line drove the Austro–Russian force out of the village again. The Russian Novoingermanland Regiment, sent forward to repair the damage, was caught in the confusion of troops streaming out of the village and began to retreat in disorder that threatened to disrupt the entire column. Buxhöwden had to intervene personally to restore the situation and bring the infantry back to the task at hand.[10]

The French were unable to capitalize on their success and surprise, however, because the French 26th Light, advancing from the north, came upon the 108th Line Infantry Regiment of Heudelet's Brigade unexpectedly and opened fire, mistaking it for the enemy. The fratricide continued in the fog and confusion until one of the officers of the 108th was able to raise the regiment's distinctive eagle and stop the firing. French accounts maintain that amid the fratricide a large number of Russians who were going to surrender took up arms again and continued the fight. The mistake broke the momentum of the French counterattack and allowed the allies to regain the initiative locally.[11]

In the meanwhile, the Austrian hussars had kept their heads and attacked the French streaming into the village and beyond, halting their advance. It appears that at this point Buxhöwden finally brought the full weight of Dokhturov's Column to bear on the task of seizing the village, and the French were hopelessly outnumbered. The Russians attacked Sokolnice at about eight o'clock, and the fighting there was fierce. The defenders of Telnice could no longer hope for reinforcements from the north. Under the pressure of the 1st Column's attacks, therefore, the French drew off from Telnice, mostly north toward Turas and Sokolnice, which had come to occupy the full attention of Soult and Davout.*

---

*Davout does not mention abandoning Telnice, but it is clearly implied. After the discussion of the fratricide, he turns to the developing situation in Sokolnice and describes the movement of his troops away from Telnice to the north. Mazade, *Correspondence du Maréchal Davout*, doc. 127. Soult covers the transition with vagueness, "Rapport sur la bataille d'Austerlitz," in Jacques Garnier, ed., *Relations et rapports officiels de la bataille d'Austerlitz, 1805* (Paris: La Vouivre, 1998), p. 18. Friant makes a similar transition (Mazade, *Correspondence du Maréchal Davout*, doc. 130). Stutterheim, who was present at this spot, states unequivocally that the allies took Telnice (Stutterheim, *La Bataille d'Austerlitz*, p. 66). Buxhöwden is equally unequivocal (Beskrovnyi, *Kutuzov*, doc. 245).

Buxhöwden was thus free to occupy Telnice and consolidate his control of the Goldbach crossing. The Russians and Austrians report that the French had largely disappeared from the plain between Telnice and Turas. It is not clear what happened at that point in this region. After the French were expelled from Telnice, their accounts do not address activities in that area until the conclusion of the battle. Buxhöwden claims that he sent his forces forward and seized Turas.[12] Baron Stutterhcim, who commanded the Szeckler infantry and the Austrian hussars in the initial attack on the village, claims that Buxhöwden settled down in Telnice and refused to move, since he had not made contact with the 2nd Column.[13] The account of the Szecklers implies that they chased the retreating French in the direction of Turas, although it is not clear how far they got or what they did.[14]

The likeliest explanation is that Buxhöwden consolidated the main body of the 1st Column in and around Telnice, and sent advanced parties of light infantry in the direction of Turas. The French, preoccupied by the fights for Sokolnice and the Pratzen, might have failed to pick up this relatively small-scale and confused movement in their rear; and in the end it posed no real threat to their security.

The attack of the allied 1st Column was successful in the sense that it cleared its path of French defenders and set the stage for the advance on Turas as ordered in the disposition. Critical problems that would lead to failure all along the line were already clear even in this successful attack, however. Although the 1st Column had begun the day with enormously greater combat power than the French defenders, more than an hour of unsuccessful fighting had elapsed before that power was brought to bear in any meaningful way. This failure probably resulted in good part from the dispositions themselves and from Weyrother's failure to consider that the advance of his left wing might meet serious opposition in the villages along the Goldbach. Since the columns were literally marching in column formation, two regiments abreast, it took time to bring an entire regiment on line, let alone bring up regiments from farther back in the train. This march order, necessary for a speedy advance to Turas, proved a serious hindrance in the rapid seizure of the village of Telnice, so essential to allied success. It is possible for a well-trained, motivated force to deploy from column to line rapidly and under fire. Unfortunately the heterogeneous allied force was none of these things, and it was confused and disordered in addition.*

As a result, the French won the time necessary to bring up more reinforcements, delaying the allied advance even longer. Since the timing of the battle required a rapid seizure of the villages followed by a quick advance to Turas, these delays would likely have been serious even if things had gone well for the

---

*The Austrians had found this problem daunting when they trained on this spot the previous year. See above, Chapter 21.

allies in the center of the field. As it was, the delays may have served the allies' turn, for the farther the 1st Column advanced before Napoleon's troops crashed down over the Pratzen into its rear, the less likely it was that any of its troops would escape. Since Buxhöwden had not gotten his main body much beyond Telnice, however, he was able to save many of his soldiers from the final rout.

Another problem visible in this attack was the failure to coordinate the actions of the allied columns. The advance of the Russian 1st Column would have been easier had the 2nd and 3rd Columns struck at seven o'clock, as they had been ordered to do. Davout's account makes it clear that he only sent reinforcements to Telnice because Sokolnice was not in danger at the time.[15] But for those reinforcements, Telnice would have been in Russian control as of nine o'clock, and the prospects for further action by the 1st Column would have been that much greater.

What that further action might have been is not clear. Buxhöwden never seriously intended to control the operations of all three columns nominally under his command. Instead he seems to have brushed aside Dokhturov and taken command of the 1st Column, expecting it and the other two columns to follow the orders given in Weyrother's disposition. He could have done a great deal of harm to the French defenders of Sokolnice if he had advanced up the west bank of the Goldbach stream and taken them in the flank. But it is not clear that he seriously attempted to make contact with the columns north of him, let alone concert operations with them. This failure was no doubt due in part to Buxhöwden's limitations as a commander, but it also highlights the weaknesses of the allied army. Never having fought or even trained together, the allied forces did not work well together and were not able to exploit successes they had on one part of the battlefield to help compensate for problems on others.

The result was a hollow victory on the southernmost part of the battlefield. Telnice was taken and the path before the 1st Column lay open, but the delays and Buxhöwden's hesitation to advance left the initiative firmly with Napoleon, and left the decision on the battlefield to other parts of the line.

The Fight for the Pratzen

The advance of the three columns in the center of the allied line was marked by confusion from the outset. All three columns were late in forming up and advancing and were confused about where they were going and how they were to get there. The column commanders did not coordinate their actions and were slow to respond to events that obviously undermined the assumptions of Weyrother's original disposition. Above all, the absence of an

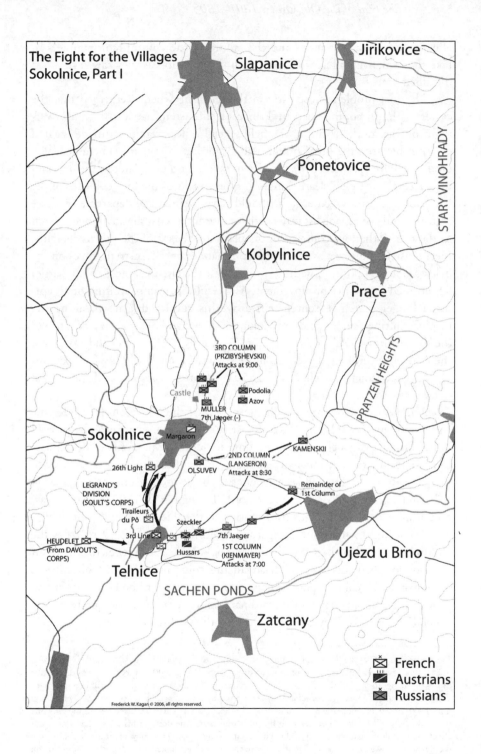

The Fight for the Villages
Sokolnice, Part I

Slapanice

Jirikovice

Ponetovice

Kobylnice

Prace

STARY VINOHRADY

PRATZEN HEIGHTS

3RD COLUMN
(PRZIBYSHEVSKII)
Attacks at 9:00

Castle

Podolia
Azov

MULLER
7th Jaeger (-)

Sokolnice

Margaron

KAMENSKII

26th Light

OLSUVEV

2ND COLUMN
(LANGERON)
Attacks at 8:30

Remainder of
1st Column

LEGRAND'S
DIVISION
(SOULT'S CORPS)

Tiraileurs
du Pô

Szeckler

7th Jaeger

Ujezd u Brno

3rd Line

HEUDELET
(FROM DAVOUT'S
CORPS)

Hussars

1ST COLUMN
(KIENMAYER)
Attacks at 7:00

Telnice

SACHEN PONDS

Zatcany

French
Austrians
Russians

effective overall commander and the failure of the column commanders to take the initiative and act in accord with the situation as they saw it doomed the allied army.

The first problem arose early in the morning when it emerged that the cavalry column commanded by Prince Liechtenstein had made camp overnight on the southern end of the field several miles away from its designated position between the 4th Column and Bagration's vanguard. The allied plan did not call for Liechtenstein's Cavalry to take action until later in the day, and the success of the plan clearly hinged on the attacks of the four columns of the left. Consequently Liechtenstein should have awaited the departure of those columns and then made his way north, or else accepted a slightly longer march to the rear of the four columns in the plain to the east of the Pratzen heights. Liechtenstein, however, as the overall commander of the Austrian forces on the field (a nominal position without meaning in the circumstances of the battle) felt entitled to priority of movement. As a result, instead of waiting or accepting a longer march, Liechtenstein drove his cavalry due north along the heights, cutting the 2nd and 3rd Columns in two and delaying the advance of the 4th Column.* As a result, the three columns of the center did not begin their advance until eight o'clock, more than an hour late. This fact explains Davout's movement to Telnice at eight o'clock after hearing that the allies had not yet attacked Sokolnice.

The next problem arose with the march of the 2nd Column under the command of General Louis Alexandre Arnault Langeron. Langeron had served in the French army before the revolution, including commands in the American revolutionary war, but had left the country thereafter and taken service with the Russians. He had seen combat with Suvorov against the French in Italy and was generally well thought of.[16] December 2, 1805, however, saw him at his very worst, and his contribution to the allies' defeat was not small.

According to the plan, Langeron's Column was supposed to cross the Goldbach somewhere between Telnice and Sokolnice; the precise crossing point was not specified. Like the other advancing columns, the 2nd Column was accompanied by column guides presumably familiar with the local terrain and provided by the Austrians. In the ordinary course of events, the quartermaster general of the army, Weyrother, would have directed the operations of the col-

---

*Stutterheim describes the problem but mitigates Liechtenstein's responsibility (*La Bataille d'Austerlitz*, p. 71). Buxhöwden mentions that Langeron's column stepped off at 8:00 A.M. but does not discuss the causes or the significance of that fact (Beskrovnyi, *Kutuzov*, doc. 245). Alexandre-Arnauld Langeron, in *Zapiski Grafa Lanzherona, ego sed'maia kampaniia v Moravii i v Vengrii v 1805 godu* (St. Petersburg: n.p., 1900), p. 29, describes the problem in detail. In Liechtenstein's defense, his force was the only one that linked the allied left and center with the allied right, and the delay in his arrival had important effects on the allied right wing in the fight. The results of his delaying the movement of the columns of the left wing, however, were more significant. See the following chapter for a discussion of events on the allied right.

umn guides and ensured through his subordinates that the column guides knew what they were doing. Either this direction was missing in the general haste and confusion of the early morning, or the guides of the 2nd Column did not benefit from it, for they led that column directly to the south side of the village of Sokolnice rather than to a point between the two villages. Langeron probably did not notice the error until the 2nd Column had arrived at the wrong place. Certainly he did not prevent or correct the guides' mistake.*

The significance of this error was great. If the 2nd Column had crossed the Goldbach between Telnice and Sokolnice by 8:30 or even a little later, it would have faced no opposition. The elements of Davout's and Soult's Corps fighting at Telnice and then at Sokolnice were fully engaged with those activities and could not have spared troops to deal with 2nd Column. After the crossing, furthermore, Langeron would have been marching across open fields, not fighting through built-up areas as the 1st and 3rd Columns had to do in the villages. There is every reason to believe that Langeron's attack would have made rapid headway. Such a rapid advance would almost certainly have unhinged the French defense at Telnice and probably at Sokolnice as well by presenting the desperately fighting defenders with the imminent threat of an attack from the flank and rear. In other words, it is quite possible that if the 2nd Column had advanced as ordered in the plan, the allied left wing might have made a success of its attack and the course of the battle might have been different.

The 2nd Column slammed into Sokolnice sometime between 8:30 and 9:00. Langeron's Column was divided into two brigades. One, under Major General Olsuvev, consisting of three infantry regiments and the 8th Jaeger Regiment, marched in the lead while the second, commanded by Major General Kamenskii II and including the Riazhsk and Fanagoria Infantry Regiments, marched well in the rear.[17] Sokolnice was held by a limited force drawn from Legrand's division of Soult's Corps, and those forces could not have held out long against two allied columns but for some quirks of the terrain and the appearance of French forces on the Pratzen heights behind Langeron and the 3rd Column.[18]

The 3rd Column under the command of Lieutenant General I. Ia. Przebyshevskii attacked Sokolnice castle north of the town. Przebyshevskii complained not only that he was delayed by Liechtenstein's Cavalry but that his column guides led him across open plowed fields instead of roads or tracks. He was forced to bring up his engineers and bridge ditches three times to get his artillery forward, and consequently he began his attack even later than Langeron did.[19] He then discovered that Sokolnice castle was a formidable obstacle indeed.

---

*Buxhöwden describes this mistake with vicious clarity in a letter to Kutuzov of 21 January 1806 (Beskrovnyi, *Kutuzov*, doc. 25). Langeron does not mention it in *Zapiski Grafa Lanzherona*.

The castle sits on a hillock northeast of town on the west bank of the Goldbach. It is now a hospital, and the green, well-maintained grounds are tranquil and quiet. The wall that surrounds those grounds is intact and presents a serious obstacle to movement, while the building itself is imposing. It is rectangular with a large internal courtyard, and the arched passageways would have been easy to bar and hold, while sharpshooters crouching in upper floors would have had their pick of targets approaching it. The hill it stands on provides an ideal location for stationing artillery against approaching troops. It is not a position to be seized lightly, and Przebyshevskii found it hard going.

The French at first defended Sokolnice only lightly—Margaron's Light Cavalry Division and the 26th Light Infantry Regiment under the command of Colonel François-René Cailloux, Baron Pouget. When the 3rd Line and the Tirailleurs du Pô were driven away from Telnice before Davout's arrival, however, they retreated toward Sokolnice and took up position in and to the rear of the town.[20] Shortly thereafter Legrand ordered the 26th Light to move south toward Telnice to stop the Russian advance, if the town could not be retaken. When this unit became involved in the fratricide incident with Heudelet's 108th line, it withdrew to the north, although it is not entirely clear what became of it. As a result, when the 2nd and 3rd Columns converged on Sokolnice, they found it held initially only by the remnants of the 3rd Line, the Tirailleurs du Pô, and Margaron's Cavalry, which had emplaced its six light guns on a hill near Sokolnice castle overlooking the entire village.*

As Langeron advanced through the town from the south, Przebyshevskii sent Major General Müller III with two battalions of the 7th Jaeger Regiment to seize critical positions necessary for attacking the castle, which he did with some difficulty. As Müller approached the castle, however, Margaron's battery opened fire, wounding Müller and seriously damaging the column that was

---

*The placement of Margaron's guns can be found in General Staff Account, p. 95. The question of the movements of the 26th Light, the 3rd Line, and the Tirailleurs du Pô is difficult to resolve precisely. Most accounts mention the 26th only in connection with the fratricide incident; many accounts exclude it entirely. Some claim that it was sent south from the vicinity of Kobylnice toward Telnice but was diverted to Sokolnice as the fighting broke out there (Duffy, *Austerlitz*, p. 105). This version is highly improbable. First, it is clear that the 26th Light was deployed in or near Sokolnice from the outset (see, e.g., Soult's marginal comment on Stutterheim's account in Garnier, *Relations et rapports officiels*, pp. 107–108). Second, if it never made it past Sokolnice, then how did it come to fire on the 108th Line as that unit fought in and around Telnice? It is, on the other hand, a problem that the departure of the 26th Light prior to the attack of the 3rd Column would seem to leave no troops at all in Sokolnice, with the possible exception of Margaron's Cavalry. It is possible that Przebyshevskii originally encountered that cavalry only, for what chiefly held him up in his initial attack, as we shall see, is the fire from Margaron's battery. It is more likely, however, that the retreating 3rd Line and Tirailleurs du Pô moved from behind Sokolnice into the castle and the village as they saw the 3rd Column approaching, and that it was those tired forces, supported by Margaron's Cavalry and guns, that the Russian 2nd and 3rd Columns initially encountered. The account of the 26th Regiment's commander, Colonel Pouget, is brief, incoherent, and uninformative. See Thierry Rouillard, ed., *Florent Guibert: Souvenirs d'un sous-lieutenant d'infanterie légère (1805–1815) et François-René Cailloux, dit Pouget: Souvenirs de guerre (1790–1831)* (Paris: La Vouivre, 1997), p. 94.

crossing the river and trailing up the slope. Müller reported encountering strong enemy forces and Przebyshevskii hastened to send him reinforcements that enabled him to hold onto his gains. To minimize his losses from the French cannon on the hill, Przebyshevskii commanded three of his five infantry regiments to close up under the castle walls, ordering Lieutenant General Wimpfen to keep the Azov and Podolia Regiments with him in reserve, probably east of the Goldbach.

In the meantime, the jaegers and the regular infantry reserves succeeded in taking the castle and the village of Sokolnice itself.[21] The remnants of the 3rd Line and the Tirailleurs du Pô, as well as Margaron's Cavalry, withdrew to the imposing heights ringing the town to the southwest and west and there hoped to delay the Russian breakout until reinforcements could arrive.[22] Despite delays and confusion, the 2nd and 3rd Columns were making progress; the same cannot be said for the 4th Column, which ran into catastrophe almost immediately.

This column was the latest of all in getting started. This delay resulted in part from the disposition, since the 4th Column began the day east of the village of Prace and had to wait for the 3rd Column to march through that village roughly from north to south before it could advance to the west. The movement of Liechtenstein's Cavalry across the battlefield, which delayed the advance of the 3rd Column, therefore also delayed the advance of the 4th, since the latter had to wait until the former had cleared the village of Prace. It also appears that Kutuzov allowed himself some childish petulance in refusing to issue the order to advance until Alexander himself commanded it.

Alexander appeared on the battlefield at nine o'clock, accompanied by Emperor Francis and the leading members of his suite. He approached Kutuzov and saw that the 4th column was still motionless. He exclaimed, "Mikhailo Larionovich! Why aren't you advancing?" Kutuzov responded, "I am waiting until all of the troops of the column are assembled." Alexander replied, "But we are not on the Empress's Field [a parade ground] where the parade does not begin until all of the regiments are up." Kutuzov answered, "My Lord! It is because we are not on the Empress's Field that I have not begun. Since you order it, however!" And he gave the order to advance.* Kutuzov might have feared abandoning the Pratzen heights to the enemy and sought to delay the movement of the 4th Column for as long as possible.[23]

General Miloradovich, who commanded the Russian element of the column, had created a small vanguard consisting of two battalions of infantry from the Novgorod Regiment and the Grenadiers Battalion of the Apsheron

---

*Mikhailovskii-Danilevskii, *Opisanie*, pp. 181–182. Mikhailovskii-Danilevskii attributed this exchange to P. M. Volkonskii, who, he claimed, was standing near Kutuzov at the time. Toll indicated that Kutuzov refused to give the order to advance until Alexander commanded him to do so, although he did not reproduce this exchange. Theodor von Bernhardi, *Denkwürdigkeiten aus dem Leben des kaiserliches russisches Generals von der Infanterie Carl Friedrich Grafen von Toll* (Leipzig: Otto Wigand, 1865), p. 181.

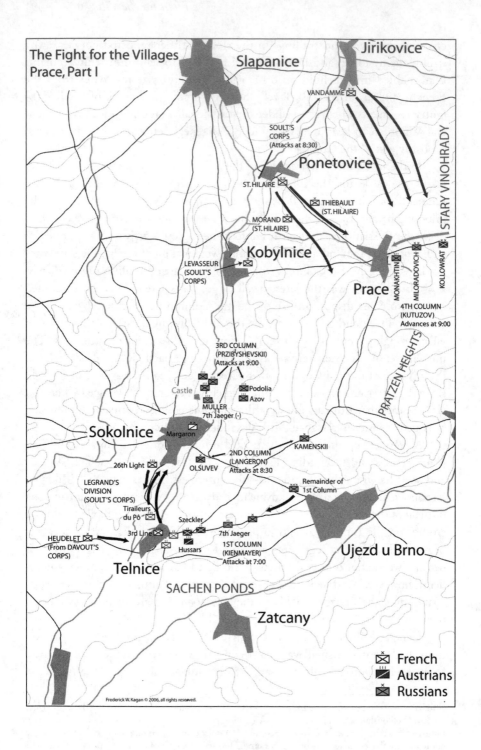

The Fight for the Villages
Prace, Part I

Slapanice

Jirikovice

VANDAMME ⊠

SOULT'S
CORPS
(Attacks at 8:30)

Ponetovice

ST. HILAIRE ⊠

STARY VINOHRADY

THIEBAULT ⊠
(ST. HILAIRE)

MORAND ⊠
(ST. HILAIRE)

Kobylnice

LEVASSEUR
(SOULT'S
CORPS) ⊠

Prace

MONAKHTIN ⊠
MILORADOVICH ⊠
KOLLOWRAT ⊠

4TH COLUMN
(KUTUZOV)
Advances at 9:00

PRATZEN HEIGHTS

3RD COLUMN
(PRZIBYSHEVSKII)
Attacks at 9:00

Castle ⊠
⊠
⊠
⊠ Podolia
MULLER ⊠ Azov
7th Jaeger (-)

Sokolnice
Margaron

26th Light ⊠

OLSUVEV ⊠

2ND COLUMN
(LANGERON)
Attacks at 8:30

KAMENSKII ⊠

LEGRAND'S
DIVISION
(SOULT'S CORPS)

Tiraileurs
du Pô ⊠

3rd Line ⊠

Szeckler ⊠
Hussars ⊠

7th Jaeger ⊠

Remainder of ⊠
1st Column

HEUDELET ⊠
(From DAVOUT'S
CORPS)

Telnice

1ST COLUMN
(KIENMAYER)
Attacks at 7:00

Ujezd u Brno

SACHEN PONDS

Zatcany

⊠ French
◪ Austrians
⊠ Russians

Frederick W. Kagan © 2006, all rights reserved.

Regiment, together with two guns, under the command of Lieutenant Colonel Monakhtin. He assigned this vanguard the task of taking the village of Prace in the first instance, in advance of the arrival of the main body of the column.* At approximately nine o'clock in the morning, Monakhtin and his small force moved into the village of Prace, followed by the rest of Miloradovich's Russians in march columns, and they in turn were followed by the Austrian contingent of the 4th Column.

The entire column, including the emperors and Kutuzov, was unaware of the fact that Napoleon had stationed Soult's Corps to their front and right at a very short distance and that Bernadotte's Corps was waiting in the wings farther north. Napoleon had stationed St. Hilaire's Division in the defile in front of Ponetovice and Vandamme's Division in that before Jirikovice. Levasseur's Brigade of Legrand's Division was stationed in column before Kobylnice to serve as a reserve for the forces attacking the Pratzen.[24] These forces remained unknown to the allies for several reasons. First, the 4th Column was wending its way along the road from the east of Prace toward the village, and that road runs through the defile that separates the Pratzen heights south from the Stary Vinohrady to the north. It does not provide a good position from which to observe the villages of Ponetovice and Jirikovice, which are screened by the shoulder of the Stary Vinohrady in their own defiles. The village of Prace is nestled deeply into the defile and has no value as an observation point.

Nor does it appear that the allies sent out scouts to the heights immediately in front of them. The Cossack pickets that one would normally expect to see in front of any advancing Russian force appear to have been absent.† This serious lapse in professionalism was the more important because the weather was conspiring with Napoleon as well. The early morning of December 2 was overcast and foggy, and heavy fog lingered in the defiles occupied by Soult's troops even after it started to clear off the rest of the battlefield. The fog did not begin to lift from those positions until eight o'clock in the morning, and it dissipated gradually. Only cavalry pickets moving in advance of the allied formations could have identified the French troops waiting to counterattack.

---

*Miloradovich's report to Kutuzov states that this vanguard was to take the village of Slapanice, "according to the disposition . . . located a mile from the camp" (Report of M. I. Miloradovich to M. I. Kutuzov About the Battle of Austerlitz, in Beskrovnyi, *Kutuzov*, no. 238, p. 230). It seems certain that Miloradovich was confused about the name of the village to which he was referring, since Slapanice is over three miles from the original encampment of the 4th Column, and Weyrother's disposition did not foresee the 4th Column having anything to do with Slapanice at this stage of the battle. Kutuzov's account simply mentions that the vanguard moved to take the village in front of the column, which would have been Prace.

†Ermolov says, "The infantry columns, comprised of a large number of regiments, did not have with them a single cavalryman" (Fedorov, *Zapiski A. P. Ermolova*, p. 54). This statement is only slightly exaggerated. According to the order of battle developed by the Austrian general staff after the event, the 3rd Column had five squadrons of cavalry and the 4th had two, but the 1st (apart from Kienmayer's detachment) and the 2nd had none. KA AFA 1805 Deutschland, XIII/ad13k. Langeron, the 2nd Column commander, nevertheless says that he did have Cossacks with him (Langeron, *Zapiski Grafa Lanzherona*, p. 30).

The loss of the fog posed a dilemma for Napoleon and the opportunity for him to demonstrate that wonderful sense of timing for which he is famous. The fog first cleared off the Pratzen heights and the sun began to shine on the Russian troops moving off them to the southwest. Napoleon wanted to wait for the Russians to denude the heights entirely as he expected them to do and as they had planned to do. The gradual disappearance of the fog from the defiles in front of Ponetovice and Jirikovice, however, also began to expose Soult's forces to the view of the allies, and every minute of delay increased the chance that the allies would realize their mistake and take countermeasures.

Soult, who stayed with Napoleon at the village of Ponetovice, was concerned about this problem and niggled at Napoleon to let him advance at once. But Napoleon told him to be calm and asked him how long it would take him to reach the peak of the Pratzen heights. Soult replied that it would take twenty minutes.* Napoleon ordered him to wait fifteen minutes before ordering the attack.

Napoleon's delay allowed the allies time to clear the Pratzen of all troops except the 4th Column. It is not clear, however, that Napoleon was aware of the position of that column. Just as the terrain screened his troops from the allies' view, so too it probably hid the 4th Column from Napoleon. The French troops that first encountered the allies may have been taken almost as much by surprise as the allies were.†

The 4th Column marched to its destruction oblivious of the fate that awaited it. Major Toll rode in advance of Monakhtin's vanguard with only a single Cossack for escort. He passed through Prace and rode up the shoulder of the Pratzen height to the south in order to gain a point of vantage. He was rewarded almost at once with the sight of a mass of troops marching up toward the summit of the hill. He claims that he at first took them to be part of the tail of the 3rd Column, although he should have known from their direction of march, to say nothing of their uniforms, that this was impossible. As he continued to ride toward them, however, he was rapidly disillusioned when he heard bullets start to whistle around his ears. Apprehending his error at last, he wheeled his horse

---

*Ségur, *Histoire et mémoires* (Paris: Librairie de Firmin-Didot et Cie., 1877), p. 466, claims that Soult said it would take ten minutes. Thiébault, however, claims that Soult answered twenty minutes (*Mémoires du Général Baron Thiébault* [Paris: Librairie Plon, 1895], p. 457). Soult noted in his commentary on Kutuzov's account (in Thierry Rouillard, ed., *Alexandre Andrault de Langeron: Journal inédit de la campagne de 1805* [Paris: La Vouivre, 1998], p. 140), that he responded "less than twenty minutes." The distance between Ponetovice and the Pratzen heights is about one mile with a climb of three hundred feet. Soult's men could have been expected to cover that distance in ten minutes on the run with no opposition, but they did not advance at the run and they did encounter opposition. Twenty minutes was a far more reasonable answer.

†The French accounts do not indicate any such surprise. On the other hand, most of them gloss over the fight for the Pratzen heights with little detail. None of the accounts of Napoleon's decision to attack mention the presence of the 4th Column; they all seem to suggest that Napoleon thought that his troops would find the heights empty.

and went racing back toward Monakhtin's troops to give the warning. It was already too late.[25]

Soult's attack consisted of three drives. Morand's Brigade of St. Hilaire's Division attacked toward the Pratzen heights while Thiébault's Brigade of the same division attacked to seize the village of Prace. Vandamme's entire division swept over the southern shoulder of the Stary Vinohrady and onto the eastern shoulder of the Pratzen heights.* The rightmost brigade of Vandamme's Division under the command of General Varé was supposed to wait in reserve, but the enthusiasm of the troops and officers got the better of its orders, and it attacked to the left of the village.[26] In this way, the 4th Column was taken entirely unawares and struck almost simultaneously on the front and along the entire length of its right flank. This situation would test even the best-trained unit to the limit. It is not surprising that the 4th Column failed the test. It is surprising, in these circumstances, that the fight for the Pratzen lasted for three hours.

Monakhtin's small force passed through Prace and confronted Thiébault's Brigade to the front nearly at once. It would almost certainly have seen Morand's Brigade moving south onto the heights to its left and Vandamme's Division of three brigades mounting the heights to its right, with Varé drawing close on its right flank and rear. Three Russian battalions unexpectedly, and briefly, confronted a French corps moving to surround them. Monakhtin did not panic. He deployed his vanguard into a line and had his soldiers lie down. The French were not expecting to find significant Russian forces at Prace and had taken no precautions against such a surprise. As a result, the vanguard rose and fired at point-blank range into the lines of the oncoming French, driving them off in disorder for the moment. The respite was short, however, as Thiébault brought up his other battalions and drove the vanguard from the village with a bayonet charge.[27] Monakhtin's two guns were lost and the vanguard collapsed; the two battalions of the Novgorod Regiment went racing in disorder to the rear.†

Miloradovich did the best he could with his limited resources. Seeing a powerful French force sweeping up at him, he sent Major General Repninskii with the Grenadiers Battalion of the Novgorod Regiment to hold the heights

---

*Thiébault (*Mémoires du Général Baron Thiébault*, p. 461) and Soult (Garnier, *Relations et rapports officiels*, p. 19). Soult claims that he expressly instructed St. Hilaire to avoid the village of Prace; however that may be, Thiébault is explicit that the plan for his brigade was to take the village. As Soult indicates that St. Hilaire accompanied Thiébault's brigade, it is unlikely that Thiébault's account is incorrect on this point. It is more likely that Soult was attempting to blame the initial difficulties in taking the village (which he does not describe) on St. Hilaire.

†From Miloradovich's account. Kutuzov describes the collapse of the Novogorod Regiment with perhaps excessive rancor in his "Relation of M. I. Kutuzov to Alexander I about the Battle of Austerlitz," 13 March 1806, in Beskrovnyi, *Kutuzov*. Toll also mentions the flight of the Novgorod troops and implies, as Kutuzov does, that they did not fight at all (Bernhardi, *Denkwürdigkeiten aus dem Leben*, p. 183). It is more likely that the rapid deployment and charge Miloradovich describes as taking place prior to the flight made less impression on Toll, who saw it, and Kutuzov, who heard of it, than the panicked flight that followed.

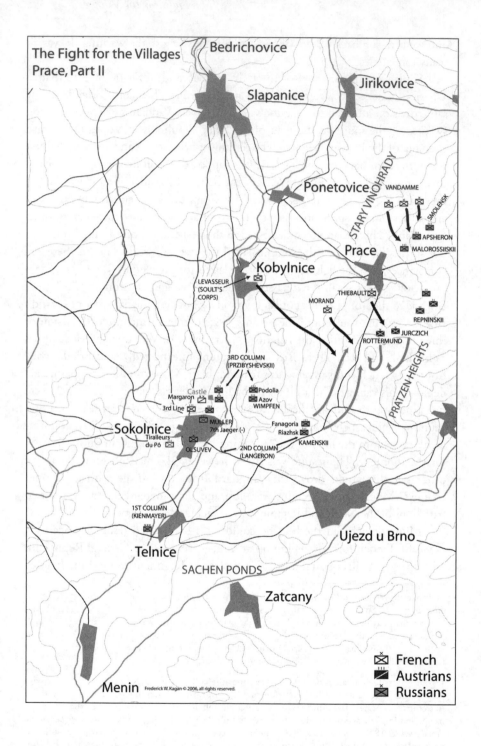

The Fight for the Villages
Prace, Part II

Bedrichovice

Slapanice

Jirikovice

Ponetovice

STARY VINOHRADY

VANDAMME

SMOLENSK

APSHERON

MALOROSSIISKII

Prace

Kobylnice

LEVASSEUR
(SOULT'S
CORPS)

MORAND

THIEBAULT

REPNINSKII

JURCZICH

ROTTERMUND

PRATZEN HEIGHTS

3RD COLUMN
(PRZIBYSHEVSKII)

Castle

Margaron

3rd Line

Podolia

Azov
WIMPFEN

MULLER
7th Jaeger (-)

Fanagoria

Riazhsk

KAMENSKII

Sokolnice

Tiraileurs
du P6

OLSUVEV

2ND COLUMN
(LANGERON)

1ST COLUMN
(KIENMAYER)

Ujezd u Brno

Telnice

SACHEN PONDS

Zatcany

French
Austrians
Russians

Menin Frederick W. Kagan © 2006, all rights reserved.

behind the village of Prace along with two Austrian battalions. He hoped that these forces would be able to receive the fleeing vanguard and allow it to regroup. He also sent his remaining Russian regiments, the Malorossiiskii Grenadiers, the Smolensk, and the Apsheron Regiments, which Kutuzov had ordered to deploy into battle formation, to advance to meet the enemy "either to drive him off or, at least, to stop his efforts in order to give the Austrians time to occupy a position to the rear."[28] The Austrian component of the 4th Column under the command of General Kollowrat was moving to take position along the shoulder of the Pratzen heights to hold that critical position.*

These movements were completed, and an Austrian line stretched along the shoulder of the Pratzen to the left of the Russians with Repninskii's ad hoc collection of troops at its extreme left flank. Monakhtin's vanguard had evaporated entirely. The Novgoroders swept away the Apsheron Grenadiers Battalion in their flight and all ran off the battlefield despite Repninskii's efforts to rally them.

The 2nd and 3rd Columns, meanwhile, were still in and around the village and castle of Sokolnice when they received word that the French were on the Pratzen heights. In that position French troops on the heights were an imminent danger. The situation required an aggressive response if it was to be retrieved. It was unfortunate from the allied perspective, therefore, that their two weakest commanders were the ones challenged to transcend themselves.

Langeron, who had for some reason stationed the few Cossacks attached to 2nd Column on his right flank and rear, first learned at 9:30 that the French were on the heights from one of those scouts. He did not believe the report, however, thinking that the scouts had taken the Austrians for French, although he realized that the reported direction of their march was odd. Fortunately Count Kamenskii had command of the two regiments Langeron had left as a reserve well to his rear near the heights, and he was not so easily confused. He at once reoriented the Fanagoria and Riazhsk Regiments, which he commanded, and marched them up the heights against the French. Langeron believed him when he reported that he was engaged in fighting the French on the heights a few minutes after the Cossack courier arrived.[29]

Kamenskii's two regiments took Morand's 10th Light Infantry Regiment in the flank as it moved onto the Pratzen heights and disrupted it. St. Hilaire was forced to rush to Thiébault and demand one of his battalions to restore the situation there, which remained precarious for some time. In the meantime, Thiébault watched the Austrians moving up to take their positions on the heights. He was puzzled because they took no action against him and even

---

*Kutuzov's account claims that Kutuzov gave the order for this movement. The Austrian accounts credit Kollowrat with the decision to send the Austrians to hold the Pratzen heights. See KA AFA 1805 Deutschland, XII/12½; XIII/13. It is possible that both commanders reached the same conclusion at the same time.

more confused when an officer approached him and Morand, who was with him at that time scouting out this apparent threat, and said, "Don't shoot! We're Bavarians!" and then withdrew.

Thiébault took counsel with St. Hilaire. The latter was concerned about the possibility of a diplomatic incident arising if the troops in front of Thiébault really were Bavarians, but Thiébault did not believe it. He made preparations in case it turned out that they were in fact Austrians. His premonitions were proved right when an officer from Kamenskii's Brigade was observed riding up to an officer among these "Bavarians" and engaging in conversation for some while before riding off. Accordingly, Thiébault drew up the three guns of which he disposed, as well as six more that Napoleon had just sent to his sector, masking them behind his infantry. He loaded them with canister and shot, and prepared more rounds on the ground next to the guns to facilitate rapid loading. When he opened fire, his guns and the muskets of his well-trained infantry cut great swaths in the ranks of the Austrians, who broke and ran within a few minutes, having sustained heavy losses.*

The Austrian regiments, commanded by Jurchich and Rottermund, were far from being crack troops. They were newly raised formations that included many soldiers previously deemed unfit for service. They were not well trained.[30] It was probably these considerations that had led Kollowrat to attempt the Bavarian ruse in order to avoid or at least delay their encounter with crack French infantry; he surely did not foresee that Thiébault would take advantage of his ruse in such a devastating fashion. The French guns having torn the ranks of these recruits to shreds, no one was surprised when they ran. The amazing thing, however, was that they stopped running as they came upon Kamenskii's steady troops and re-formed a ragged but determined firing line, ready to go back into battle.†

The combined Austro–Russian line then began a counterattack at bayonet point in a dense formation with closed ranks. The French returned accurate and murderous fire that tore holes in the ranks of the advancing allied force,

---

*This account is from Thiébault, *Mémoires du Général Baron Thiébault*, pp. 469–472. The story is told rather differently in the Austrian accounts, although they agree that the French opened a withering fire at a certain point. The lack of corroboration of the story of the Bavarian ruse in the Austrian sources is not surprising, since it reveals their failure to fight aggressively and indeed their effort to avoid combat that led to disaster. Thiébault's story, on the other hand, explains why all the allied observers condemned the Austrians for running without fighting while Toll defends them by pointing to the casualties they took. The immediate collapse of the Austrian line is explicable if we consider that they probably took most of the 2,400 casualties Toll mentions within ten minutes of firing. See Bernhardi, *Denkwürdigkeiten aus dem Leben*, p. 184.

†Thiébault mentions that the Austrians re-formed after his cannonade (*Mémoires du Général Baron Thiébault*, p. 474). The Austrian account does not mention the Bavarian ruse but ascribes the initial passivity of the Austrian line to confusion resulting from the apparent similarity of the French uniforms to those of the Russians (KA AFA 1805 Deutschland, XIII/13). This account also states that these troops re-formed once they met up with Kamenskii's brigade (p. 22 reverse).

but the allies did not falter. The rush, accompanied by the "hurrahs" the Russians customarily loosed during a charge, ground to a slow, painful advance. The French, however, were unable to stop it completely and were forced to give ground to maintain their formations and order. A furious melee ensued that lasted for more than twenty minutes as the French and the allies battled for the summit.

Kutuzov had by this point abandoned all pretext of actually controlling the allied army, despite his nominal position as commander in chief, and had become in effect the commander of the 4th Column. During this fight he and his aides, together with Weyrother and the general staff, rode among the troops encouraging, exhorting, and leading them on in this desperate fight. The emperors were within sight of the fight for most of its duration. As allied troops came streaming off the heights during the fight, Aléxander tried to stop them, crying, "I am with you, I am sharing your danger, stop!" It was to no avail.[31] Kutuzov was wounded in the cheek, streaming blood, but refused the attentions of Alexander's medic: "Thank the Tsar and tell him that my wound is not dangerous, but over there is the fatal wound!" pointing at the French.[32] Kutuzov's son-in-law, F. I. Tizenhausen, an adjutant with headquarters, attempted to rally a battalion that had broken by seizing its standard and running forward, but was shot dead. Kutuzov likely witnessed his death.*

If the situation was horrible for Kutuzov, it appeared so desperate to the French that St. Hilaire hastened to Morand and Thiébault to discuss the possibility of withdrawing from the field: "This is becoming untenable, and I propose to you, messieurs, that we take up in the rear a position that we would be able to defend."[33] Even before the brigade commanders could respond to this proposal the commander of the 10th Light Infantry Regiment, Colonel Pouzet, who had overheard the conversation while riding nearby, leaped from his horse and exclaimed, "Withdraw us, General[?] . . . If we make one step backward we will be lost. We have only one way to leave here with honor and that is to rush head down at whatever faces us and, above all, not to give our enemies the time to reckon with us." Thiébault cried in response, "Bravo, Colonel Pouzet! This is one of the best moments of your life." The brigadiers returned to their brigades and the horrible melee continued.

Finally, Levasseur's Brigade of Legrand's Division, which had been held in reserve near Kobylnice, advanced up the Pratzen and took Kamenskii's Brigade in the right flank (it is unclear who gave the order for this advance). This attack, together with a final charge by St. Hilaire's Division, broke the allied line and forced the allies to move away from the 2nd Column and almost off the Pratzen plateau, the Austrians toward the village of Hosteradky-Resov and

---

*Mihailovskii-Danilevskii, *Opisanie*, p. 184. It is also likely that this event was the model for Prince Andrei's seizure of a standard in Tolstoi's narrative of Austerlitz, and his subsequent wounding.

the Russians toward Krenovice.* Near the latter village Kamenskii re-formed his brigades and remained in good order at the foot of the hill until the very end of the battle, helping to enable the withdrawal of the remnants of the three left-most columns.

The performance of the 4th Column was not as bad as might have been expected, despite its ultimate failure. Caught in march column by an attack from the front and the flank, it could have disintegrated instantly and been cut to pieces. Instead its commanders were able to deploy it into battle formation and maneuver it toward a critical defensive position. Once there, it fought with great stubbornness and determination and was only broken when fresh French troops came up and struck its flank as it was attacked once again from the front.

The battle for the Pratzen heights was a meeting engagement for all concerned. The French had not expected to find the 4th Column in position near Prace, and the allies had not expected to fight the French in that area at all. Both sides reacted to the initial encounters with surprising alacrity and agility, and the fight was finely balanced right up to the end. The key to the French success was the availability of one last reserve force to enter the fray at a decisive place and time. If the other column commanders had been quicker to perceive and react to the crisis in their rear, it is not at all certain that the allies would have lost the heights at that point.†

Indeed, when Langeron left Sokolnice to evaluate Kamenskii's situation, he had the opportunity to disengage some of his forces from the fight for the village that was then winding down and bring Kamenskii some reserves. He castigates himself in his memoir for failing to do so (although he offers no explanation for this failure); he also blames Buxhöwden, the overall commander of the three left-most columns, for failing to act decisively in this crisis.[34] Both charges are valid.

The greatest weakness in the allied army was not the tactical proficiency or determination of its soldiers or even the competence of its officers. The skill with which both officers and men responded to the unforeseen crisis on the Pratzen heights is testimony enough to their quality. The real problem was that the column commanders did not really command their columns and neither Buxhöwden nor Kutuzov really influenced the battle other than in

---

*Thiébault mentions that Levasseur's Brigade was supposed to be in reserve, but nothing was heard of it throughout the initial battle for the Pratzen. He remarks that it finally appeared "to our astonishment" at the end of the fight with Kamenskii's brigade (Thiébault, *Mémoires du Général Baron Thiébault*, pp. 473, 479). Toll states that Kamenskii was forced to withdraw following an attack by five battalions of Legrand's division that had been stationed near Kobylnice (Bernhardi, *Denkwürdigkeiten aus dem Leben*, p. 185).

†The fact that Napoleon could have brought Bernadotte's Corps and the full weight of the Imperial Guard into the fight if necessary, however, makes it enormously unlikely that he would have failed to take the heights eventually if he was determined to do so. The shape of the battle resulting from such a movement, however, would have been very different.

their immediate vicinity. Buxhöwden and Kutuzov abdicated their responsibilities, while the column commanders were preoccupied with following Weyrother's plan and were slow and unwilling to make changes to it—or to throw it away entirely as the situation so obviously demanded. This weakness at the highest tactical levels struck the allies fatally and gave Napoleon command of the Pratzen and the battle.

Sokolnice

As the French gained the upper hand on the Pratzen heights, the full import of the delays in the movement of the 2nd and 3rd Columns became clear. Had those columns stepped off promptly at seven o'clock and had they rapidly seized and passed through the villages of Telnice and Sokolnice, as was likely if the 2nd Column had followed the course prescribed for it, then by the time of the fight on the Pratzen they would have been well away and marching toward their further objective at Turas. It is not clear what the result would have been. There is evidence, as we shall see later, that Napoleon was nervous about such an irruption into his rear and that he might have responded in some way that would have made it possible for the allies to recover from their mistaken plan.

What is unclear above all is what the effect would have been of the sight of French troops on the Pratzen heights while allied columns were well on the way to Turas. For in that circumstance, the Pratzen heights themselves would have been far enough away from them to be largely irrelevant—out of any meaningful cannon shot, to say nothing of musketry. Although the allies would no doubt have been disconcerted to find the enemy in their rear, they would have had the Goldbach and the villages between them and the French—excellent strong points and delaying positions, as they found much to their chagrin during the actual fighting. It may be, in other words, that a more or less rigid adherence to the original disposition would not have led to catastrophe, whether or not it produced anything that could be called victory.

The 2nd and 3rd Columns had just finished consolidating their position at Sokolnice when they realized that the French were about to overrun the Pratzen heights, still worrisomely close. When Kamenskii reported to Langeron that he had turned his brigade around and was fighting for the heights, Langeron hastened to join him. Langeron's behavior in this instance is inexplicable. He did not doubt Kamenskii's report, as he had previously doubted the reports of his own observers, that the French were moving onto the Pratzen in force. He had no reason to imagine that his mere presence on the scene would help resolve the crisis. Certainly there was nothing he could observe from the Pratzen itself that Kamenskii's report had not already told him. Yet he abandoned his troops in the village and rode up to Kamenskii merely as a spectator, to a considerable extent abandoning control over his column just at the critical moment. For even as Langeron reached Kamenskii, the situation in Sokolnice suddenly collapsed when fresh French forces attacked and retook much of the town.

Davout learned of the crisis at Sokolnice just as he was driven out of Telnice by the arrival of the main body of the 1st Column, as we have seen. The forces withdrawing from Telnice therefore moved north, arriving at Sokolnice shortly after the Russians had taken it and while they were in the process of expanding their bridgehead. Leaving Heudelet with the battered 108th Line to hold the northern exit from Telnice and thereby guard the right flank of the corps, Davout raced north with four regiments: the 48th and 111th of General Lochet's Brigade and the 15th Light and 33rd Line of General Kister's Brigade.[35]

Learning that the French were fighting for control of the Pratzen heights, Przebyshevskii broke his column into two. He had already ordered Lieutenant General Wimpfen to keep the Azov and Podolia Regiments in reserve near the Pratzen, and he now ordered them to "hinder that enemy movement" from the heights and defend the rear of the 3rd Column.[36] Wimpfen had less initiative than Kamenskii, for he appears to have simply stationed his troops in a defensive position and awaited the French attack from the heights, rather than trying to interfere with the struggle going on in front of him on the Pratzen.

As Lochet drove into Sokolnice at the head of the 48th Line, therefore, he faced two jaeger regiments and six line regiments of the 2nd and 3rd Columns. The Russians were still disorganized, however, and were probably spread throughout the town and the surrounding area on both sides. Langeron states that there was a great deal of confusion, although he claims that he was waiting for further orders from Buxhöwden, which did not arrive.[37] It is not clear what orders Langeron was expecting, but he probably meant that it was time to dress ranks, as the disposition called for, and begin the advance on Turas, since Sokolnice had apparently been taken easily and since the 1st Column had successfully attacked Telnice. To that end, some coordination by Buxhöwden, the overall commander of the four left columns, would have been necessary. The next message from Telnice was sent not by Buxhöwden, however, but by Davout in the form of Lochet's 48th Line.

As the 48th Line drove into the confused Russian outposts, Margaron's Cavalry also attacked and together they drove the Russians back into the village. Lochet then began methodically advancing deep into the town house by house.[38] In his enthusiasm, however, Lochet advanced too far and without waiting for reinforcements, and the Russians did not panic. Instead, the jaegers began moving around the 48th and for a time had it almost completely encircled, while other Russian units moved to cut off the other regiment of Lochet's Brigade, the 111th Line, which was coming up in reserve, from the remaining forces of Friant's Division. The 48th had to hold out

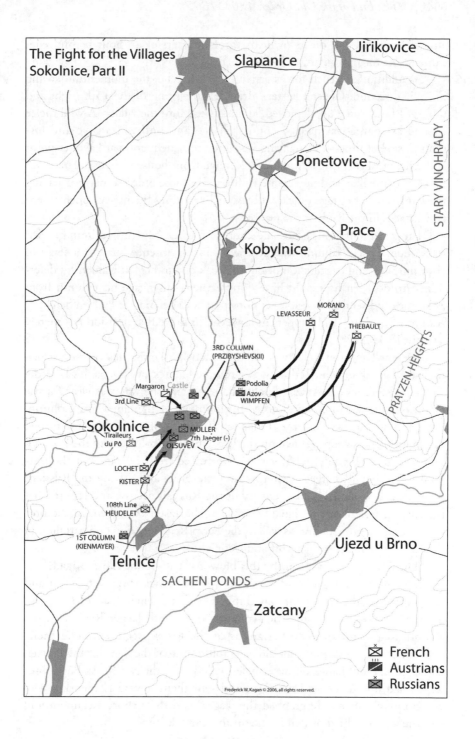

The Fight for the Villages
Sokolnice, Part II

Slapanice

Jirikovice

Ponetovice

Prace

STARY VINOHRADY

Kobylnice

LEVASSEUR

MORAND

THIEBAULT

3RD COLUMN
(PRZIBYSHEVSKII)

PRATZEN HEIGHTS

Margaron   Castle

3rd Line

Podolia

Azov
WIMPFEN

Sokolnice
Tiralleurs
du Pô

MÜLLER

7th Jaeger (-)

OLSUVEV

LOCHET

KISTER

108th Line
HEUDELET

1ST COLUMN
(KIENMAYER)

Ujezd u Brno

Telnice

SACHEN PONDS

Zatcany

French

Austrians

Russians

Frederick W. Kagan © 2006, all rights reserved.

almost encircled and on its own for three-quarters of an hour before relief came in the form of an attack by the 111th to relieve it.[39]

As additional French forces arrived on the scene, the momentum swung in their direction. General Kister's Brigade, consisting of the 15th Light and the 33rd Line, came up, deployed, and attacked into the village. A wild melee ensued as charge was met by countercharge and both sides gave and lost ground several times. The fighting was ferocious, frequently at bayonet point and with muskets firing at point-blank range from house to house. There was no clear battle line, and the regiments fought in loose order, sometimes having to change their frontage quickly, occasionally finding themselves open to enemy attacks in the flank or the rear.[40]

Langeron found this chaos and confusion when he returned from his visit to Kamenskii. His column fought bravely in his absence but lost a sense of clear purpose, and its cohesion began to break down. He left Kamenskii determined to do what he should have done earlier—disengage his column from Sokolnice and send all available reinforcements to defend the Pratzen heights.[*] A number of things had happened, however, to make that decision not merely late but irrelevant.

Even as Langeron rode away from Kamenskii, Levasseur's Brigade struck the latter's flank in conjunction with a renewed attack by Thiébault's Brigade. The allied line on the Pratzen finally shattered and the way was clear for the victorious French to complete the envelopment of the allied 3rd Column. After a brief pause to allow the troops to catch their breath, St. Hilaire turned his division and swooped down on the Russians in Sokolnice with the brigades of Thiébault, Morand, and Levasseur, borrowed from Legrand for the purpose.[41] Thiébault, charged with attacking the castle and driving the Russians out, was overwhelmed by the ferocity of the Russian defense and reports that the carnage was immense. Finally, however, the castle was taken. In the process, the entire 3rd Column as well as the Perm Regiment and one battalion of the Kursk Regiment were cut off and trapped.[42]

The 2nd column was rent by this blow as well—Kamenskii's Brigade was battered and retreating toward Austerlitz with a French corps between it and Langeron. Another regiment was trapped with the encircled 3rd Column, leaving Langeron with only the remnants of the 8th Jaeger Regiment, the Vyborg Regiment, and two battalions of the Kursk Regiment. The encirclement of the 3rd Column should have told him that the fight for the Pratzen had been lost, but Langeron nevertheless haled away the two Kursk Battalions, which had not yet crossed the river, and sent them toward Kamenskii, who was no longer there. He grabbed the jaegers and the Vyborg Regiment and withdrew to join Buxhöwden in the south near Telnice.[43]

---

*Langeron admits that this decision came far too late. See Langeron, *Zapiski Grafa Lanzherona*, p. 32.

It is not clear that Przebyshevskii realized he had been encircled; he only knew that the situation was collapsing around his ears and his soldiers, who had been fighting continuously all day, were running out of ammunition as well as stamina. He decided that further attempts to hold on to the castle and as much of the village as he then controlled would be futile as Wimpfen's reserve-cum-rear guard was crushed in and Wimpfen himself wounded. Accordingly, he took counsel with his column guides about the best way to withdraw from the area and find a secure route back to the rest of the army. Clearly he had no idea where the rest of the army was. In the end, the column guides, no doubt desperate to leave, began to lead him away from the castle, but that move only deprived Przebyshevskii of what cover he had left. Following another fierce cavalry attack to his flank, he surrendered the column and himself.[44] The survivors of the 2nd and 3rd Columns joined with those of the 1st to make their way out of the trap any way they could.

Soult's seizure of the Pratzen heights, given the failure of the Russian left wing to make good its plans, determined the outcome of the battle. The collapse of the 2nd and 3rd Columns ensured that the result would be a *crushing* French victory. Although there was a great deal of other fighting and dying on the field on December 2, almost all of it was peripheral to these central events.

Conclusion

The end of the battle saw the beginning of a series of mutual recriminations among the column commanders that lasted for decades. In a report to Kutuzov, Buxhöwden blamed Langeron for the collapse of his column and obliquely suggested that Langeron's behavior was a fundamental cause for the loss of the battle.[45] He offered as exculpation only the fact that he personally knew Langeron to be brave, but he noted, "There is a difference being in battle as a field grade officer and as a general. Here experience is necessary, in addition to personal courage and theory, developing the necessary character of the commander and presence of mind. [Langeron] had not yet had the chance to stand against an enemy as a general."

This criticism is well founded and valid. Langeron's behavior throughout the battle was inexcusable. He allowed his column to be led to the wrong place. When he was informed of the battle to his rear he at first refused to believe it and then, for no clear reason, abandoned his forward brigade to observe (without participating in) the actions of Kamenskii's Brigade. In the meantime, the forces he had left behind in Sokolnice, badly in need of reorganization and the restoration of a clear purpose and direction, were left headless. When they were attacked, chaos ensued. A significant number were trapped with the 3rd Column and ultimately surrendered. Langeron, returning, sent two battalions away to no purpose and then led the rest south to no avail. The column shattered entirely without achieving any of its objectives. In many respects, its fate was worse than that of the 3rd column. Although that column ultimately surrendered, it remained whole and cohesive and continued to follow orders to the end of the battle. Langeron's burden of guilt was heavy indeed.

But in many respects Buxhöwden was equally culpable, as Langeron pointed out at every opportunity in his own narrative. When he had finally taken Telnice and Davout had drawn off all of his forces except for the 108th Line, Buxhöwden was in a position to advance either north toward Sokolnice or northwest toward Turas and face relatively little opposition. If he had taken either course of action, the French fighting at Sokolnice could have been taken in the flank and rear and, worse still, found themselves between two fires. It is highly likely in that event that most of the 3rd column and much of the 2nd could have been saved.

An even more fundamental criticism that can be levied against Buxhöwden is that he never even tried to fill the role that had been assigned to him as commander of the four left columns. His conduct throughout the battle was as though he saw himself as the commander of the 1st Column and nothing more—a position that was quite unnecessary for him to fill considering that the 1st Column already had an outstanding commander in the person of Dokhturov. As a result, Buxhöwden, who alone could have coordinated the actions of the allied columns, did not do so, and the columns each fought separate and mostly hopeless fights.

This failure of coordination was fatal. The forces of Davout and Legrand tasked with defending Sokolnice and Telnice were vastly outnumbered by the allied columns attacking them. Looking only at the odds, a coalition victory should have been certain from the beginning. The allied failure to coordinate their attacks, however, allowed Davout and Legrand effectively to double their forces by fighting first at Telnice and then at Sokolnice with the same troops. If the attacks on those two villages had proceeded nearly simultaneously, there can be virtually no doubt that the allies would have taken both in short order. Buxhöwden's failure to coordinate those attacks, or to take advantage of his success to assist his sister units, doomed the allies irretrievably on the southern flank.

Buxhöwden never sought to defend himself against these charges, but he did not have to. Kutuzov, bitter and vitriolic in defeat, accepted Buxhöwden's account and blamed Langeron and Przebyshevskii for the collapse of the allied left. The reason was probably a combination of the fact that Buxhöwden, as supernumerary 1st Column commander, had won the only meaningful victory of the day by taking the village assigned to him, whereas Langeron's Column exploded and Przebyshevskii's surrendered with its commander at its head. Kutuzov therefore largely passed on Buxhöwden' recriminations to Alexander, together with his own condemnation of the Novgorod Regiment and Kollowrat's Austrians for fleeing without firing a shot—accusations that were thoroughly and manifestly unfair.[46]

Alexander was not in a good mood after the battle in which his own soldiers went running by him, oblivious of his calls to stand and fight. Accordingly, he added five years to the mandatory service of the soldiers in the two battalions that had run and degraded them and their officers in various other ways, particularly changes in their uniforms.[47] Przebyshevskii was court-martialed first on the charge of surrendering his entire unit to the French at the outset of the battle—and quickly exonerated—and then on the charge of dereliction of duty, of which he was convicted. He was sentenced to serve in the ranks for one month and then to be retired from the service (presumably as a private). Alexander confirmed the sentence in 1810.[48]

Alexander was kinder to Langeron, who did not surrender his column and was not taken prisoner. He merely sent him word through General Lieven: "The Emperor is dissatisfied with your dispositions but, granting you some consideration, asks that you request your retirement."[49] His anger with Langeron soon faded, however, and he was appointed to serve with the army in 1806, although he played no active role in that campaign. We shall meet him again, however, in the campaigns of 1812 and beyond.

With the loss of the Pratzen heights the allies' hopes of victory were dashed. The collapse of the other three columns, which was unnecessary even given Napoleon's dispositions and plans, turned defeat into catastrophe. Even so, the disaster would have been much worse if similar disorder had affected the allied columns to the north. The fight on the northern flank could not have affected the outcome of the battle—that was determined by the collapse of the allied center and south—but it did go a long way toward saving a large part of the allied army.

23

The End
of the Fight

The fight for the villages of Sokolnice and Telnice determined the outcome of the Battle of Austerlitz. Without rapidly seizing those towns and moving on, the allies had no hope of winning. The magnitude of the French victory, however, depended on the outcome of the series of separate but interrelated fights in the center and to the north. Had the allied forces of Constantine, Liechtenstein, and Bagration acted decisively and skillfully, most of the coalition army could have escaped disaster. Had they acted timidly or incompetently, Napoleon might well have destroyed the entire Austro–Russian army. The difference might have been critical, considering the larger operational and strategic situation, although much depended on the allied sovereigns' perceptions of the battle they witnessed.

The combat on the Stary Vinohrady and north along the Brno–Olmütz road presents a real challenge to the historian seeking to narrate it. The French corps of Soult, Murat, Bernadotte, and Lannes and the Imperial Guard and Grenadiers Divisions faced the Russian Imperial Guard commanded by Constantine, Bagration's "vanguard," Liechtenstein's combined cavalry, and elements of the shattered allied 4th Column. None of these units were subordinate to intermediate commanders, as the Russian columns on the left were (theoretically) under Buxhöwden's overall command. Each reported directly to Napoleon or Kutuzov. As a result, these actions were not coordinated with one another. Units were sent piecemeal to take advantage of opportunities or plug holes. The number of interrelated events occurring simultaneously and in a complicated linked series of sequences precludes a simple narrative. Attempting to isolate the individual events and narrate them separately, however, destroys the linkages among them that alone give them meaning. The account that follows therefore aims to explore these events and their relationships at the macrolevel, the more so since other authors have already narrated the battalion-level fights individually.[1]

The Course of the Battle in the Center and North

Napoleon's plans for the northern sector of the battlefield are not entirely clear. His own dispositions offer no insight into the scheme of maneuver he intended to follow.[2] The actual battle plan was delivered orally to the collected marshals on the morning of the battle and there is no detailed written record of it. Berthier's account omits any discussion of Napoleon's battle plan, and Ségur's simply argues that Napoleon planned for precisely what happened. We have already seen the degree to which that argument is groundless.[3] We can only conjecture about Napoleon's intentions based on the initial dispositions and his orders during the battle, although we must always remember the danger of such a proceeding with a mind as agile and responsive as Bonaparte's.*

Napoleon certainly meant for Soult to take the Pratzen heights, and he probably did not expect the marshal to encounter much resistance, as we have seen. He deployed Lannes to face Bagration on the Olmütz road, Murat to link Soult with Lannes, and Bernadotte to serve as a reserve, along with the Imperial Guard. One historian suggests that Napoleon intended for all of these forces to accompany Soult in a sweep southward across the Pratzen, thereby trapping and destroying nearly the entire allied force.[4] This interpretation is unlikely, since Napoleon was aware of Bagration's force and its strength at least, whether or not he knew that Constantine's troops had not moved south along with the other four columns. Lannes was clearly supposed to handle Bagration and any other Russian forces on the northern part of the battlefield, although it is unclear whether Napoleon meant him to advance and crush those troops or simply hold them.† Since Bernadotte's forces were deployed close behind Lannes's in the north, Napoleon probably meant Bernadotte to be ready to support Lannes. It is possible, however, that he also wanted Bernadotte to be able to support Soult, or even to be available to exploit the victory in some way.

---

*Scott Bowden does not offer a detailed reconstruction of Napoleon's plan for the battle (see *Napoleon and Austerlitz*, p. 313). Christopher Duffy does, in *Austerlitz, 1805* (London: Seeley Service, 1977), pp. 88–89, but without benefit of footnotes. He seems to rely entirely on the two dispositions cited above but does not make sufficiently clear that those dispositions offer no guidance about how Napoleon expected the battle to develop.

†Ségur suggests that Napoleon meant for Lannes only to hold off Bagration while Soult split the allied army in two (*Histoire et mémoires*, p. 465). This explanation is plausible and in accord with Napoleon's standard approaches. It may also have been an attempt after the fact to show that Napoleon did precisely what he had always meant to, since Ségur concludes, "Thus was the battle as it was conceived and executed!"

The confusion in the written record about Napoleon's plans contrasts with the specificity of the allies'.* Weyrother's plan had Bagration taking position just west of the Santon hill. Liechtenstein was supposed to support this movement and occupy the Zuran hill with horse artillery. Weyrother imagined that neither operation would face significant opposition. The allied right wing then was to await the successful advance of the four columns of the left; only when they were approaching Slapanice from the south and west was Bagration to advance to link up with them, thus completing the annihilation of the French army.[5] Constantine's Guard Corps was ordered to take position between Blasovice and Holubice and serve as reinforcements for Liechtenstein and Bagration.† The actions of the allied right wing can only be understood in light of the fact that the collapse of Weyrother's plan left those forces without any preliminary guidance and the allied command structure gave them no unifying leader.

When Soult's troops raced up the Pratzen and threw the 4th Column into disorder, Kutuzov and Alexander realized that an emergency had arisen. They first worked with Miloradovich and Kollowrath to establish firing lines on the hills north and south of the village of Prace, as we have seen. They also sent for help. Liechtenstein's combined cavalry corps was still traversing the battlefield from south to north, trying to get to the location designated for it in the initial dispositions. Now Kutuzov ordered Liechtenstein to hasten his movement but also to send troops to help beat off Soult's attack.[6] Alexander informed Constantine of the allied crisis and asked him to send assistance as well.‡

Constantine found himself in a difficult position. Two years Alexander's junior, he was the youngest corps-level commander on the battlefield by a wide margin. Now he commanded the only allied reserve on the battlefield and had only fleeting contact with the allied commanders and senior leaders. He faced a number of difficult decisions that he had to make rapidly and correctly on his own.

---

*The confusion about Napoleon's plans exists on paper only. He knew what he intended to do at the time, and his marshals likely had at least a generally clear picture of what they were supposed to do and how their actions were supposed to fit into the larger scheme.

†The documents of the time refer to the current village of Holubice as Krug, and the current village of Velesovice-Holubice simply as Holubice. Duffy and Bowden follow those documents in this convention. I shall continue to refer to them by their modern names to facilitate the use of modern maps and travel around the modern battlefield.

‡Mikhailovskii-Danilevskii, *Opisanie pervoi voiny Imperatora Aleksandra s Napoleonom v 1805-m godu* (St. Petersburg: Independent Corps of the Internal Guard Press, 1844), p. 192. Both Bowden and Duffy mention this incident without citing the source (*Napoleon and Austerlitz*, p. 365; *Austerlitz*, p. 133). In Bowden's account, it was Miloradovich who sent word, but he offers no evidence to support that assertion, which is unlikely. Miloradovich was fully occupied with the situation at hand, and he had no authority to ask Constantine for assistance, whereas the tsar did, and he was watching the same scene without direct involvement in it. Interestingly, no other Russian account mentions this incident.

History has not been kind to Constantine. He had a reputation for violence, aggressiveness, and thoughtlessness bordering on stupidity. This reputation was somewhat justified. He also had considerable military experience for someone his age, and he was not as unfit to make important decisions in battle as one might imagine.* When Tsar Paul sent Suvorov with an auxiliary army to fight in Italy in 1799, Constantine begged to go with it. The young grand prince had taken a deep interest in military affairs from an early age and was eager to see battle for himself. Paul allowed him to join the army but only incognito, since he did not wish to dignify an auxiliary army with the formal presence of one of his sons. At first, Constantine allowed his arrogance to get the better of him, and persuaded a Russian commander to make a foolish, costly attack. Then Suvorov took him under his wing. Russia's greatest general of that age instructed Constantine in war and gave him opportunities to advise and command at higher levels throughout the campaign. Chastened by his first experience, Constantine learned a great deal from both Suvorov and Bagration, who was also present during that campaign.[7] This experience helps explain Constantine's performance at Austerlitz.

Constantine received Alexander's request for help as he was moving his forces toward their intended concentration area along the Raussnitzer stream north of Krenovice. He at once dispatched a battalion of the Izmailovskii Guards regiment toward the Pratzen, but that unit arrived just in time to be swept away by the collapse of the last allied resistance on the heights.[8] Constantine also took thought for his right flank, sending the Guards Jaegers Battalion to seize the village of Blasovice.[9]

Liechtenstein's Cavalry should have been covering Blasovice and all of the land between the Stary Vinohrady and Bagration's left flank near Holubice, but its delayed march had left a hole in the allied right. Bagration teased out his left somewhat to mind this gap, stationing an artillery battery at Blasovice covered loosely by the Pavlograd Hussars Regiment. He gratefully turned this duty over to Constantine's Guards Jaegers as the grand prince moved tentatively to fill the gap left by Liechtenstein.[10]

Constantine's caution was appropriate for two reasons. First, Liechtenstein's combined cavalry corps arrived shortly after this movement and took up its designated role. Second, the grand prince knew that he commanded the only allied reserve on the battlefield. He did not know the overall situation. Alexander could have told him mainly of the plight of the 4th Column and what he knew of the French dispositions (which was a great deal).[11] The tsar probably did not know how Buxhöwden's troops were doing with any degree

---

*Bowden exaggerates when he asserts that Constantine had "no more qualifications to command other than his birthright" (*Napoleon and Austerlitz*, p. 365). It is true that a young man with as little experience as the grand prince would never have been commander had he not been the tsar's brother, but this characterization improperly dismisses the significant military education he received in a short time, as we shall see.

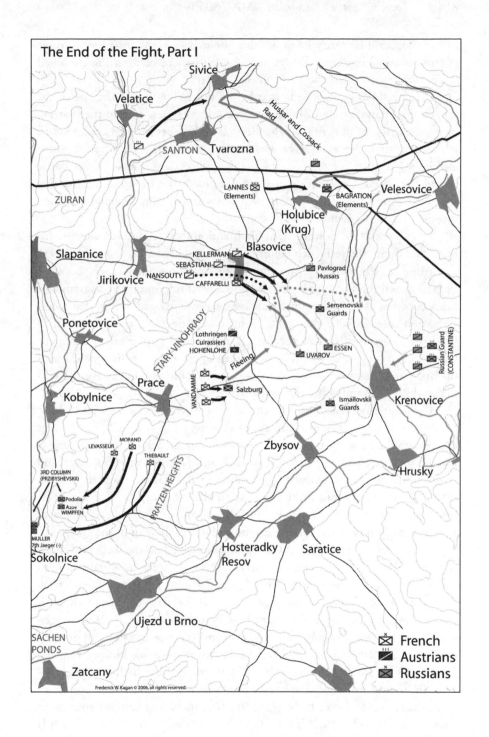

The End of the Fight, Part I

Sivice

Velatice

SANTON

Tvarozna

Hussar and Cossack Raid

ZURAN

LANNES
(Elements)

BAGRATION
(Elements)

Velesovice

Holubice
(Krug)

Slapanice

KELLERMAN

Blasovice

SEBASTIANI

Pavlograd
Hussars

Jirikovice

NANSOUTY

CAFFARELLI

Ponetovice

Semenovskii
Guards

STARY VINOHRADY

Lothringen
Cuirassiers

HOHENLOHE

Fleeing

ESSEN

UVAROV

Russian Guard
(CONSTANTINE)

Prace

VANDAMME

Salzburg

Ismailovskii
Guards

Krenovice

Kobylnice

LEVASSEUR

MORAND

THIEBAULT

Zbysov

3RD COLUMN
(PRZIBYSHEVSKII)

Hrusky

Podolia

PRATZEN HEIGHTS

Azov

WIMPFEN

MULLER
7th Jaeger (-)

Sokolnice

Hosteradky
Resov

Saratice

Ujezd u Brno

SACHEN
PONDS

⊠ French
◢ Austrians
⊠ Russians

Zatcany

of precision, and he surely knew nothing about Bagration's situation. In these circumstances Constantine was right to be cautious in committing the allied reserve without knowing how and where to do it.

It is a little more surprising that he did not follow up on the fate of the Izmailovskii Battalion he had sent on Alexander's request toward the Pratzen, or on the shape of the critical fight there. If he had betaken his command to Alexander's assistance at once, he could certainly have driven off Soult's corps, although it is difficult to predict what the subsequent course of the battle would have been. Constantine may have assumed that he would receive further word from Alexander if more help was needed, thus showing a limited imagination and little initiative.

It is also possible, however, that his attention focused on the danger to his front and right, where French columns that should have been powerful even according to Weyrother's disposition now faced the open spaces between Bagration and the Pratzen heights. When Constantine informed Bagration of his occupation of Blasovice, the latter's response encouraged him in that focus. Bagration congratulated the grand prince on his decision and asked him to hold the village until it had become clear what had happened to Liechtenstein.[12] In any event, Constantine continued to creep cautiously forward with his main body toward a position on the Stary Vinohrady northwest of Krenovice while maintaining his outpost at Blasovice.

Constantine's forward movement came just in time. Lannes and Murat began advancing to the east and south at 8:00 A.M., just as Soult's troops charged up the slopes of the Pratzen heights.[13] The French light troops screening the advance encountered the Russian Guards Jaegers before Blasovice, and an intensifying combat ensued. Constantine fed a battalion of the Semenovskii Guards Regiment into the fight in an effort to keep hold of Blasovice, but it was not enough. Murat brought the weight of Caffarelli's division of Lannes's corps to bear and the French drove the Russians out of the village.[14]

At this point Liechtenstein's Cavalry finally arrived on the scene and threw itself into the battle. At first the Austrian cavalry commander sought to reinforce an attempt by the Pavlograd Hussars to drive the advancing French back into and through Blasovice, but this attack failed.[15] He then detached FML Prince Hohenlohe with an artillery battery supported by the Lothringen Cuirassiers Regiment to take position between Blasovice and Prace in order to cover the left flank of his unit and Constantine's Guard. Noting that the French seemed intent on advancing to Holubice and the highway, Liechtenstein then sent Uvarov to attack their positions around Blasovice once again. The Russian cavalry met intense artillery fire, including canister rounds, as they neared the village, and it took the efforts of Lieutenant General Essen II and Uvarov himself, as well as the timely intervention of the Pavlograd Hussars in the fight, to restore order to the scattered cavalry.[16]

When they had done so, however, Uvarov and Essen led their cavalry in a renewed charge that broke through the French lines. The Grand Prince Constantine Uhlans Regiment, which was in the van of the advance, attempted to exploit this success too far, running headlong into a French artillery battery supported by infantry that decimated it with canister rounds and massed musketry at close range. The regiment lost 400 men in an instant and its commander, Müller-Zakomelsky, was taken prisoner.[17] French cavalry under Generals Kellermann and Sébastiani then struck the rest of the Russian line from front and flank, driving the Russians off in disarray.

This was enough for Bagration. Although his orders were to await the success (!) of the allied left wing before moving, Bagration decided that he could not allow the French to ravage his own left wing and Liechtenstein's cavalry without responding. In one of the rare instances of an allied commander disregarding Weyrother's plan in light of its obvious collapse, Bagration put his entire command in motion and prepared to support Liechtenstein's efforts to drive off Murat's and Lannes's Corps. He may also have hoped to force the French to shift forces from their right and center to meet his attack, thereby facilitating the operations of the hard-pressed allied left, although it is not clear how much he knew about the situation there.*

Bagration accordingly sought to hold Holubice and staged raids north of the road and the Santon hill. He probably intended to prevent the French from turning his right flank, and he may have hoped to draw French troops from farther south to the threatened area.† A force of Cossacks and hussars charged north of the Santon, creating mayhem. They came under murderous fire from the French batteries on that height, however, and from French cavalry that rushed to counterattack. The raid was driven off with heavy losses and in great disorder.[18] The attempt to hold Holubice was less rash but fared no better. The light infantry and cavalry Bagration had ordered to hold the town were overmatched by the advancing French columns and forced to withdraw slowly as well.[19] These retreats occurred in good order, however, and Bagration ended up getting most of his force back to Raussnitz, where he eventually held firm.

As Bagration was struggling with Lannes along the highway, Uvarov continued his desperate efforts to hold off the French advance southeast of Blasovice. This fight, which had helped draw Bagration into the battle, now began to merge with renewed fighting on the Pratzen heights, and the battle developed a

---

*"Report of P. I. Bagration to M. I. Kutuzov About the Battle of Austerlitz," 10 December 1805, in Beskrovnyi, *Kutuzov*, doc. 236. Bagration stresses the reasons for his decision to abandon Weyrother's plan. See also the Austrian General Staff Account, pp. 24, 24 reverse. Duffy (*Austerlitz*, p. 123) is wrong to imply that Bagration began his advance at the beginning of the battle.

†No available source clarifies Bagration's plans or intentions for his attack. He asserts in his report to Kutuzov that he acted "so as not to allow the enemy in any way to take advantage of my flanks" (Bagration to Kutuzov, 10 December 1805, in Beskrovnyi, *Kutuzov*, doc. 236).

new center on the Stary Vinohrady in which the final reserves of both armies became embroiled.

As we have seen, St. Hilaire's Division of Soult's Corps, supported at the critical moment by Levasseur's Brigade, broke the allied fourth column on the Pratzen heights and took possession of that crucial terrain feature. Vandamme's Division of the same corps swept onto the heights to the left of St. Hilaire's and helped defeat Miloradovich's Russians drawn up behind the village of Prace. Vandamme then turned his division toward the east to chase from the heights the last remnants of the fourth column, including the large, powerful Austrian Salzburg Regiment. He succeeded in this endeavor, and the Austrians withdrew, part in good order, part in a streaming mass of broken infantry that ran northeast.[20]

The fleeing Austrian infantry soon found themselves in another desperate fight. After defeating the Grand Prince Constantine Uhlans, Uvarov brought the rest of his unit onto the Stary Vinohrady between Prace and Blasovice, ordered Lieutenant Colonel Ermolov to establish his artillery battery in support, and prepared to await events. He soon found himself under musket fire from the advancing French troops and ordered the Elisavetgrad Hussars Regiment to charge the enemy. A battalion of Caffarelli's division formed square and beat off this attack, and Murat prepared to counterattack in turn.[21]

Just at that moment, however, the Austrian infantry fleeing from the Pratzen heights reached Uvarov's cavalry and threatened to confuse and disorder it. Desperate to maintain his formation, Uvarov and his men sabered the Austrians mercilessly in an effort to drive them off. Murat, who observed this fratricide, thought at first that the Austrians must be Bavarian troops and held off the planned counterattack briefly. He soon realized his error, however, and launched Nansouty's Cavalry division against Uvarov.* This attack, which briefly overwhelmed Ermolov's guns, drove Uvarov's Cavalry back, and Uvarov only reestablished control and order beyond the Rakovec stream.[22]

Constantine was not idle during these events. Although his attention had originally been drawn toward Blasovice and the north, Vandamme's destruction of the last remnants of the 4th Column had drawn it once again to the Stary Vinohrady and the Pratzen heights. He therefore began to march the guard, now consisting of six infantry battalions and ten cavalry squadrons, to his left to Krenovice. From this position he could receive Liechtenstein's defeated cavalry columns and help rally other allied forces on the heights before Austerlitz. He may have imagined that he was also keeping the allied left and right wings connected, although events on the Pratzen had long since put that goal beyond the reach of his meager force.[23]

---

*Report of Prince Murat's Army Corps, in Garnier, *Relations et rapports*; "Report of F. V. Uvarov to M. I. Kutuzov," 7 December 1805, in Zhiugdzha, *Dokumenty*, doc 145. The fratricide is attested in both sources. Murat states it baldly, but even Uvarov admits that the hussars "bravely did everything possible to hold off the enemy, not sparing even the Imperial infantry."

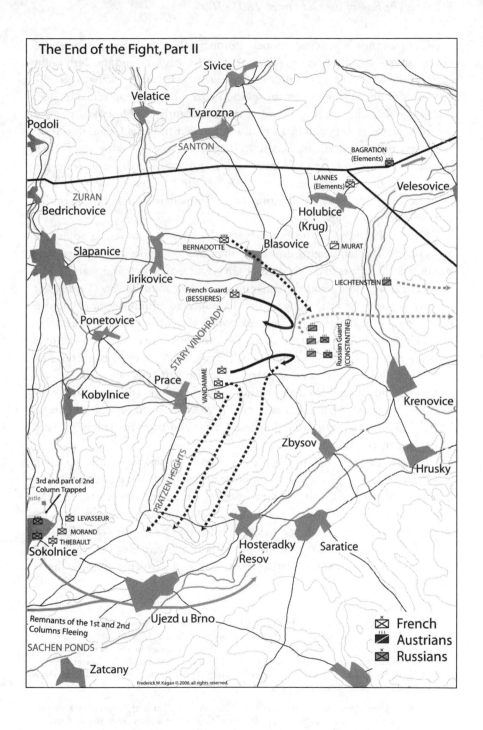

The End of the Fight, Part II

Sivice
Velatice
Tvarozna
Podoli
SANTON
BAGRATION (Elements)
LANNES (Elements)
Velesovice
ZURAN
Bedrichovice
Holubice (Krug)
MURAT
Slapanice
BERNADOTTE
Blasovice
Jirikovice
LIECHTENSTEIN
French Guard (BESSIERES)
STARY VINOHRADY
Ponetovice
Russian Guard (CONSTANTINE)
Prace
VANDAMME
Kobylnice
Krenovice
Zbysov
PRATZEN HEIGHTS
Hrusky
3rd and part of 2nd Column Trapped
astie
LEVASSEUR
MORAND
THIEBAULT
Sokolnice
Hosteradky Resov
Saratice
Remnants of the 1st and 2nd Columns Fleeing
SACHEN PONDS
Ujezd u Brno

French
Austrians
Russians

Zatcany

Constantine's advancing troopers immediately encountered evidence of the collapse of the allied center. A battalion of the 4th Line and the 24th Light Infantry Regiment of Vandamme's Division, which had participated in the final rout of the Salzburg regiment on the Pratzen heights, continued its pursuit too far. Cresting the heights east of Prace jubilantly, they found themselves confronting the cavalry and infantry of the Russian Imperial Guard drawn up in perfect order. The Russian cavalry charged at once, breaking the French battalions as they attempted to form square and wresting the eagle from the 4th Line.[24] Some of these troops streamed off the field, racing by a bemused Napoleon and mechanically chanting "Vive l'empereur!" even as they continued their headlong flight.[25]

Help was at hand for the routed French battalions, however. As Soult's attacks on the Pratzen heights drove the allies away, Napoleon sought to trap Buxhöwden's unfortunate columns fighting at Sokolnice and standing at Telnice. He therefore ordered Vandamme to march south on St. Hilaire's left flank to support the coup de grace that he hoped to administer near Ujezd u Brno. He also ordered Bernadotte to swing his corps south to take Vandamme's place, and he brought up his own Imperial Guard onto the heights themselves.* As Vandamme rallied his bedraggled regiments, Bessières sent two squadrons of light cavalry charging at the Russians. This charge was beaten off, but it facilitated the withdrawal of the 4th and the 24th. Vandamme completed his realignment and marched south to join St. Hilaire as French reinforcements from the Imperial Guard and from Bernadotte's Corps began to arrive on the scene.[26]

In the meantime, one of Napoleon's aides-de-camp, General Rapp, took the Mamelukes—Napoleon's personal horse guard which Rapp commanded—and two squadrons of chasseurs of the Imperial Guard and charged the Russian Guard. Since the Russians were standing amid the vineyards that gave the Stary Vinohrady its name, this attack quickly stalled and fierce hand-to-hand fighting ensued.† Constantine threw the Imperial Horse Guard Regiment into the struggle to free the infantry fighting in the vineyards, which it did. He thereupon decided to withdraw.[27]

---

*"Account of the Battle of Austerlitz by Berthier," in Garnier, *Relations et rapports*, p. 57; Soult, "Rapport sur la bataille d'Austerlitz," in Garnier, *Relations et rapports*, p. 22; Ségur, *Histoire et mémoires*, pp. 467–468. Ségur claims that Napoleon sent him with the message to Bernadotte because he mistrusted Bernadotte's will to advance, and that Ségur found the marshal, indeed, reluctant to move. Considering that Ségur's memoir was written after Bernadotte had defected to the allied side, this claim must be viewed with some skepticism.

†Mikhailovskii-Danilevskii, *Opisanie*, pp. 193–194; "Account of the Battle of Austerlitz by Berthier," in Garnier, *Relations et rapports*, p. 57; Rapp, *Memoirs of General Count Rapp, First Aide-de-Campe to Napoleon* (London: Henry Colburn, 1823), p. 61; Ségur, *Histoire et mémoires*, pp. 470–471. Rapp's account is brief, self-glorifying, and inaccurate in that it conflates several events. Both Mikhailovskii-Danilevskii and Berthier agree that the charge did not succeed and the fighting was fierce.

The French, however, renewed the attack, and Bernadotte's lead regiments arrived to support Rapp's weary troops. The Russian Guard Cavalry renewed its struggle and once more bought the infantry free, though at a hideous cost. One of the Russian Guard Cavalry regiments charged too far and was decimated by a French battery. The others suffered fearful casualties in a struggle that lasted for more than a quarter of an hour: one Russian squadron was reduced to eighteen effectives at the end of the fight, and its commander, Prince Repnin, was captured. The Russians nevertheless were able to break contact and withdraw in some disorder through Krenovice to the heights west of Austerlitz.*

Rapp returned in triumph to Napoleon, bleeding from a wound but glorying in his victory, thus providing Gerard with the model for his famous painting of the battle.† He claimed to have destroyed the entire Russian guard with only his small cavalry force, but in truth it was no such matter.[28] Constantine had withdrawn in the face of superior French forces, especially Bernadotte's arriving corps, and he had salvaged most of his infantry and some of his bedraggled cavalry despite numerous French attempts to destroy his command. It was a creditable performance for a young man in a disastrous battle. Like Bagration's stubborn professionalism to the north, Constantine's sangfroid kept alive the possibility of the allies escaping from Austerlitz with a force that could be regrouped and reformed to await further developments.

When they had beaten off Bagration, Liechtenstein, and Constantine, Lannes, Murat, and Bernadotte all stopped their advances and did not attempt to exploit their victories. Murat explained his decision. His "intention was to continue to push the enemy and to take the heights of Raussnitz and of Austerlitz on which [the enemy] had retired; but to the right they were still fighting with much determination; the prince did not have any news from there." He wanted to protect the lines of communication from Olmütz through Austerlitz to Brno, and "fearing that His Majesty might have need of his troops, he did not want to get too far away and was forced to suspend his

---

*"Brief Description of the Movements of the Combined Austrian and Russian Imperial Armies in the Campaign of 1805 along with a Detailed Description of the Battle that Took Place on 2 December 1805 Between Brünn, Rausnitz, and Austerlitz, Including a Battle Map Drawn by the Imperial and Imperial-Royal Quartermaster General Staff in March 1806," KA AFA 1805 Deutschland, XI/66¼, from now on referred to as Austrian General Staff Account, p. 28; "Account of the Battle of Austerlitz by Berthier," in Garnier, *Relations et rapports*, p. 58; Mikhailovskii-Danilevskii, *Opisanie*, pp. 194–195. The available accounts make sequencing these charges and countercharges difficult. Mikhailovskii-Danilevskii is clear that the French made two separate attacks and the Russians two separate counterattacks (he also conflates these events with the rout of the 4th Line and 24th Light that occurred earlier, however). Berthier's account suggests that it was all part of one movement. Rapp (*Memoirs of General Count Rapp*) implies that he attacked twice, although his account is also condensed. The version presented here is a best guess, but the accounts do not support a definitive description of this combat.

†Ségur notes, however, that Gerard's painting is inaccurate in several particulars (*Histoire et mémoires*, p. 470).

march in order to be close enough still to send His Majesty reinforcements if it was necessary."[29]

It is not clear whether Lannes and Bernadotte held off for the same reasons or if some other factor intervened. We do not have accounts of the battle by either of them, although Napoleon's aide-de-camp, Savary, who was present with the emperor for most of the battle, notes that the emperor was surprised that Bernadotte did not continue his advance toward Austerlitz and the highway to cut off the allied retreat.[30] It is difficult to know what to make of this statement.* Savary claims that the allies were retreating in complete disorder and that Bernadotte could have hindered their attempts to rally the "debris" of the battle. This statement is certainly untrue. Bagration and Constantine both retreated in reasonable order and had rallied their forces before Bernadotte could have intervened. Bernadotte's Corps outnumbered the Russian Guard substantially, of course, and his troops were fresh whereas the Russians were tired after protracted and desperate fighting. But Bernadotte did not have his entire corps ready to face the Russians, and he would have had to pursue retreating forces that could choose their ground to resist him. It is not obvious that Bernadotte alone could have easily crushed the Russian Guard and the remnants of other allied formations that joined it near Austerlitz.

It is also odd that Napoleon, who, Ségur claims, mistrusted Bernadotte from the outset and had his fears confirmed during the course of the battle, then simply assumed that Bernadotte would complete the pursuit without further encouragement. Nor is it at all clear what orders Napoleon had given Bernadotte. The emperor's failure to guide his wayward subordinate is the more remarkable in that Ségur claims that Napoleon could see much of the fighting with the Russian Guard. As was the case with Murat's decision to march on Vienna instead of Krems, the subordinate deserves blame for failing to make the right decision and take the initiative. But Napoleon also deserves blame for losing control of his subordinate at a critical point in the battle.† However that may be, the three allied columns in the north were able to rally their troops and withdraw to safety unhindered.

The struggles in the north were bloody fights in which the French drove the Russians back after hard fighting and the latter recollected themselves rapidly in the rear. The struggle in the south was a catastrophe for the coalition almost from the beginning of the battle. As soon as Bernadotte's lead division

---

*Although Bowden (*Napoleon and Austerlitz*, p. 375) accepts it uncritically.

†It is more difficult to establish precisely what happened during this phase of the battle and especially why, because many of the accounts, both primary and secondary, move into a mode of glorifying the French army and Napoleon and explaining the victory by reference to the superior fighting qualities and determination of the French over their enemies, notwithstanding descriptions of bitter and brutal fighting by both sides throughout the battle.

arrived and the French Guard began driving Constantine's troops away from the Pratzen heights, Napoleon sent Vandamme's Division to the aid of St. Hilaire's Division in the south around Ujezd u Brno and Hosteradky-Resov. His aim was to cut off and destroy the remnants of Buxhöwden's three columns that had been shattered by the fighting around Sokolnice.

Kutuzov had recognized the danger facing the coalition army as soon as he realized that the allies would not be able to hold the Pratzen heights, and had immediately ordered all of the columns to withdraw.[31] Buxhöwden executed this order with the 1st Column and remnants of the 2nd that managed to join him. The allies conducted the withdrawal skillfully, considering their terrible position. Buxhöwden stationed infantry and artillery at critical points to cover the withdrawal all along the route. The delay imposed on Vandamme's arrival by his fight with Constantine facilitated this retreat, since it left the French with few forces around Ujezd as the first allied troops marched by. The fight for the village of Ujezd, as well as an artillery duel between the Russian battery and French artillery moving south to the Ujezd heights, also bought the Russians more time.*

Napoleon's official account of the battle enshrined a myth that the allied columns fleeing across the frozen Sacsan ponds perished to a man when their weight combined with French artillery shattered the ice around them.† In truth, few allied soldiers drowned in the lakes, which were too shallow to swallow up the Russian troops.‡ The casualty figures Kutuzov sent to Alexander make it clear that not many Russians could have perished in icy water. Of the more than 10,000 Russian troops in Dokhturov's command in the 1st Column, only 1,985 were killed or missing in action.[32] Many of those casualties must have come during the hard fighting in the early morning and the grueling retreat. Most of the 1st Column and elements of the other two escaped Napoleon's trap. Allied casualties were nevertheless heavy. Kutuzov reported losing 19,454 dead and missing, and the number of wounded must have been even greater, although the French tended to bayonet wounded Russians, so the total loss may not have been much higher. The French lost at least 8,000 soldiers in the fighting.[33]

---

*These actions are described in great detail in accounts by Stutterheim, Soult, Berthier, Buxhöwden, and others. They are well-known and there is remarkable agreement among the French, Russian, and Austrian versions on most points.

†Thirtieth Bulletin of the Grande Armée, 3 December 1805, *Corr. de Nap.*, doc. 9541. Soult's account, which was written after this bulletin appeared and clearly emulated it in key points, makes a similarly exaggerated reference to this occurrence. See also Ségur, *Histoire et mémoires*, p. 473.

‡Duffy, *Austerlitz*, pp. 148–149, makes this case well. Stutterheim mentions that the ice broke in places on the ponds and "some" troops perished in *La Bataille d'Austerlitz*, p. 97. Bowden, *Napoleon and Austerlitz*, pp. 382–385, leaves the issue open.

Austerlitz: An Evaluation

Why did Napoleon win the Battle of Austerlitz? The verdict of historians is clear: because of the excellence of the Grande Armée, Napoleon's genius, and the utter incompetence of the allies, which typified the failings of the "old regime" armies and their leaders.* This interpretation is invalid. Numerous allied regiments, divisions, and even whole columns fought at Austerlitz skillfully and with determination. Bagration, Constantine, and even Dokhturov brought their columns away from the fight in good order and without taking annihilating casualties. Soult's corps took the Pratzen heights from a confused and disorganized foe, but his troopers knew they had been in a serious fight. Those who would portray Napoleon as the Yankees pitted against a Little League team must ignore the moments when St. Hilaire contemplated withdrawing at the crucial moment on the Pratzen, when the Russian guard routed elements of two French regiments on the Stary Vinohrady, and when Napoleon himself, in a moment of panic, feared that his own reserves marching to battle were allied troops sweeping into his rear.[34] Although it may have been Napoleon's finest victory, Austerlitz was also a near-run thing because of the skill and stubbornness with which the allies attempted to extricate themselves from a terrible situation.

That terrible situation was far more decisive than the supposed superiority of French soldiers over Russians and Austrians. Complicated political and interpersonal considerations led Alexander to order an advance from Olmütz. The ad hoc nature of the allied army and its formations hindered that advance. Political and interpersonal considerations continued to dictate the allies' course as they approached the French positions, and led to the formation and adoption of Weyrother's badly flawed plan. Once the allies set about executing that flawed plan, Napoleon's victory was likely.

The conduct of individual allied formations at critical moments of the battle highlights not their incompetence but their potential squandered by a foolish plan. The 4th Column, suddenly attacked by two enemy divisions of whose existence and intentions it had previously been unaware, could have shattered and fled in all directions. Instead, Kutuzov, Alexander, Miloradovich, and several junior Russian and Austrian officers rallied the troops, formed them into lines, maneuvered them under heavy fire, and very nearly drove off Soult.

---

*Chandler, *Campaigns of Napoleon*, p. 437, writes, "It is interesting to compare Napoleon's mastery with his opponents' ineptness." Bowden's narrative concludes with a veritable paean to Napoleon and his army and a scathing condemnation of every aspect of the allied forces throughout the campaign (*Napoleon and Austerlitz*, pp. 418–437). It is hard to see how Austerlitz was such an impressive victory if Napoleon's opponents epitomized military foolishness and confusion, but the emperor's many glorifiers seek to place Napoleon and the Grande Armée on a different plane from their opponents rather than argue that the French triumphed against worthy foes.

They failed to do so because the allies had no plans to fight on the Pratzen heights and therefore had very few reinforcements available, whereas the French could bring overwhelming numbers to bear if necessary. Kamenskii nevertheless sensed the danger and on his own initiative brought his half of Langeron's Column to Miloradovich's aid. Only the timely arrival of a designated French reserve brigade, Levasseur's, turned the tide back in favor of the French. This is hardly the performance of an incompetent army.

Liechtenstein's Cavalry started the day incorrectly positioned on the battlefield, and his blundering through the advancing allied infantry columns contributed to their disaster. It brought him to the aid of Bagration's and Constantine's troops assailed by Murat and Lannes at a critical time, however. Skillful allied cavalry charges threw the French advance in the north of the battlefield into disorder and allowed the allied infantry to break contact and withdraw with the bulk of their forces intact. If against these successes we must set Langeron's incompetent handling of the 2nd Column and Buxhöwden's total failure to take the initiative with the forces at Telnice, we can also set Bernadotte's failure to pursue the Russian Guard and the failure of Davout and Soult to keep the allies out of Telnice in the first place against the achievements of the Grande Armée. Perhaps the best example of the balance of these enemies at the lower tactical level is the fact that both Alexander and Napoleon watched helplessly as some of their soldiers fled past them off the field. At the level of troops in contact with the enemy, Austerlitz was far from being a battle of giants against pygmies.

The allied failures occurred primarily at the operational level and the grand tactical level—the level at which large formations are deployed and maneuvered on the battlefield. At these levels, failures of planning and virtually nonexistent command and control doomed the allies.

Napoleon played a key role in shaping the battle for the French during the fight. He ordered Soult to advance. He ordered Bernadotte to advance. He ordered Vandamme to change direction. He ordered the guard to advance. Each order played a crucial role in determining the battle's outcome. On the allied side, Buxhöwden gave no orders to any formation other than the 1st Column, despite the fact that both the 2nd and 3rd Columns were nominally under his command. Kutuzov and Alexander sent to Constantine and Liechtenstein for reinforcements, but little resulted from these requests. Kutuzov then ordered the army to withdraw, which it did. At no other time did a column commander, Kutuzov, Alexander, or Buxhöwden, attempt to affect the actions of columns other than those they were with. As a result, the battle for the allies was a series of single engagements pitting individual columns against various better coordinated enemy forces.

This failure did not result from the inability of "traditional eighteenth-century armies" to manage large battles. The Austrians had repeatedly done so during the revolutionary wars with varying degrees of success. Charles managed it over the course of two and a half days during the Battle of Caldiero in this war. Rather, the failure resulted from the ad hoc nature of the army and the confused command structure resulting from the presence of the Russian emperor on the battlefield. It also resulted from the fact that the army's commander, Kutuzov, found himself virtually from the beginning of the battle in the midst of a wild, confusing melee in which he was wounded. It resulted, in other words, from some of the same failings that led the allies to launch this ill-fated attack in the first place.

In evaluating the allied effort at Austerlitz, we must keep in mind how unrepresentative this army was of the normal capabilities of Russian and Austrian forces, still less of "eighteenth-century armies." Political and personal considerations prevented professional allied commanders from thinking and acting as well as they usually did, and hindered the Austrians' normally efficient staff work. These weaknesses presented Napoleon with opportunities and he took advantage of them.

Napoleon's role in the Battle of Austerlitz was not that of omniscient war god but skillful general seizing on and magnifying his enemy's mistakes. Napoleon did not lure the allies into battle until after they decided to fight him. By withdrawing his troops from the Pratzen heights, he offered them the opportunity to commit an error—which they did. He then seized on that error in an obvious way. He accepted a great risk, particularly in the southern part of the battlefield, and he had too many troops in the north. Bernadotte's Corps hardly fought at all, nor did the French grenadiers or most of the Imperial Guard. Considering how hard-pressed Davout and Legrand's division of Soult's Corps were at Telnice and Sokolnice, it is remarkable that Napoleon took no thought to send any of the copious available reinforcements to support them. It is also surprising that he did not directly order Bernadotte, Lannes, and Murat to pursue Bagration and the Russian Guard and complete their destruction, thereby assuring the annihilation of the allied army. Napoleon's victory was tremendous, but not as tremendous as it could have been.

The apparent ease with which Napoleon seized on his enemies' mistakes and punished them should not obscure his skill in doing so. The Grande Armée that he and his marshals had been training for more than two years fought superbly. The corps commanders coordinated their subordinate units skillfully and smoothly. They also worked together as well as might be expected of men who had been working together for many months. Davout and Soult coordinated their activities around Telnice and Sokolnice (apart from the brief fratricide incident); Murat and Lannes fought together in the north as if they had been doing so for decades. St. Hilaire's brigade commanders, confident of their soldiers' skills and resilience, persuaded the shaken general to stand firm on the Pratzen heights at the critical moment. French infantry units broken by Russian cavalry charges rallied and continued the fight. The Grande Armée functioned like the smooth machine it was, and Napoleon deserves credit for choosing its leaders and training them well.

He also deserves credit for balancing control with giving his subordinates the freedom to fight their own fights. He trusted Lannes and Davout to do their jobs and virtually ignored them throughout the battle. He stayed with Soult to control the decisive flow of events and then remained with his advancing guard as Soult's troops moved forward to exploit their initial success. From his position on the Stary Vinohrady he did not attempt to micromanage engagements he could only watch, but he did continue to feel the shape of the battle and intervene at important moments to change that shape to suit his plans. Both in setting the terms of the battle and in managing it, Napoleon showed his mastery of the art of war.

After the Battle

The future course of the war did not depend on Napoleon, however, but on Alexander and Francis. The allies had many options for reconstituting their main army and bringing more soldiers into the fight, but only if they had the will to continue after Austerlitz. The tsar spent the day as badly as a monarch could, and his experiences sapped his will, although he recovered it rapidly. Francis surely enjoyed the spectacle no more, and his determination to continue the fight did not survive.

As the 4th Column collapsed during the desperate fighting on the Pratzen heights, Alexander became separated from not only Kutuzov but also his entourage. Only his surgeon, two Cossacks, and two servants accompanied him away from the Pratzen heights. He spent much of the day alone, helpless, and probably confused about what was going on. Because he played no part in events after about eleven o'clock in the morning, he also had many hours to spend contemplating his mistakes and his failures.

Major von Toll, who led the vanguard of the 4th Column into Prace at the beginning of the fight, caught sight of the tsar after the battle was over. Alexander was riding along with his tiny retinue, visibly in despair. He had never been a good horseman, and when he came to a small ditch in the field, he could not bring his horse to cross it. Only after his surgeon had done so several times, to show how easy it was, did Alexander finally persuade his mount to follow. After a time, the tsar's depression overcame him. He dismounted and sat down on the ground. Then the young man burst into tears.

Toll, who had been debating whether or not to approach his sovereign in his hour of despair, got up the courage to do so. He spoke some words of encouragement to the tsar, exhorting him to remember that a battle lost is not the end of the world, that things are never so bad that they cannot be mended. After a time, Alexander took heart enough to remount and proceed on his way.*

The Austrian emperor's will likewise collapsed following the battle.† The tsar and Francis communicated on December 3, and Francis informed his colleague that he wished to open negotiations with Napoleon.‡ Alexander agreed, and he may even have embraced the idea of simply ending the war at that point—at least at first. But as Prince Liechtenstein, Francis's chosen envoy, rode off to meet Napoleon, Alexander's nerve returned. As Toll noted, the situation that seemed so black early in the morning of December 3 rapidly grew brighter. Many soldiers who had scattered or managed to escape from their French guards found their way back to the army over the next few days, swelling the depleted ranks. Moreover, the allies received immediate reinforcements. Merveldt brought his exhausted force of 4,000 soldiers to join the army almost immediately after the battle, and General Essen I arrived with his 12,000 men from Bennigsen's army on December 6.§ These reinforcements would have restored the army to a respectable strength, able to hold defensively until Charles's army and the rest of Bennigsen's force arrived—to say nothing of the Prussians and their allies. Kutuzov, who fortuitously joined the tsar on the night of December 2, may have pointed out to Alexander that his situation was little worse than it had been before the battle, and there was still every reason to hope for a successful outcome of the campaign.**

---

*This is the version that Toll gives (Bernhardi, *Denkwürdigkeiten aus dem Leben*, pp. 187–188) and Shil'der accepts (N. V. Shil'der, *Imperator Aleksandr Pervyi: Ego zhizn' i tsarstvovanie* [St. Petersburg: Izdanie A. S. Suvorina, 1897], pp. 141–142). Czartoryskii, who accompanied the tsar during the early part of the battle, gives a different story, however (Adam Gielgud, ed., *Memoirs of Prince Adam Czartoryski* [New York: Arno/New York Times, 1971], pp. 108–109). He describes the tsar as extremely depressed (p. 110). He ascribes decisions and actions to Alexander, moreover, that indicate he remained self-possessed and in touch with the battle. Both versions were written after the fact and are suspect because of the prominence they ascribe to their respective authors. Czartoryskii finished his account during his last illness; the manuscript in fact breaks off at this point. Toll's "memoirs," on the other hand, were written by Bernhardi years later from notes and interviews with Toll. I have accepted Toll's version because it accords better with Alexander's personality and because Czartoryskii's depiction of the battle shows that he had no real understanding of what was going on around him. Tolstoy movingly depicts the same scene in detail according to this version, following his superb but inaccurate narrative of the battle. *War and Peace*, ed. and trans. George Gibian (New York: Norton, 1996), pp. 249–250. Tolstoy's description of Austerlitz is one of the finest examples of brilliant narrative technique evoking the feeling of battle while subtly distorting causality. See Kimberly Kagan, *The Eye of Command* (Ann Arbor: University of Michigan Press, 2006), for a discussion of the value and limitations of the "face of battle" technique of battle narration that Tolstoy uses here.

†We have no testimony about Francis's actions during the battle or his state of mind during or after it.

‡It is difficult to find any meaningful evidence about this communication or even to know whether the two sovereigns met (they were close) or simply exchanged notes. Prince Adam Czartoryskii writes that he attempted to unite the two emperors immediately following the battle and failed (Gielgud, *Memoirs of Prince Adam Czartoryskii*, p. 111). When Francis met Napoleon on December 4, however, he apparently declared that he had already spoken with Alexander (Ségur, *Histoire et mémoires*, p. 479). Liechtenstein, the envoy sent to arrange the meeting, arrived at Napoleon's headquarters "rather late" on December 3 (Lacroix,

Francis, however, had had enough. If Alexander ever tried to suggest that the allies might retreat a little more and try to hold on until they could bring their crushing numerical superiority to bear, Francis must have grown disgusted. How many times had he heard that argument? How many times did the Russians think he would fall for it? At the moment, Francis was the emperor of Hungary and some Balkan territories. Napoleon held all of the Austrian hereditary lands including Vienna, Ney commanded in the Tyrol, and Masséna had marched through all of Austrian Italy. Francis may well have decided to heed the advice of sage gamblers: stop doubling your bets before you have lost everything. He was determined to make a deal with Napoleon.*

Alexander respected Francis's right to do what was best for his monarchy and prepared to betake himself and his army back to Russia. He demanded only that Francis not involve him in the negotiations with Napoleon and that those negotiations ensure the peaceful passage of the Russian army out of Austrian territory. He also noted that should Napoleon's demands prove so unacceptable that Francis found himself obliged to break off the negotiations, the tsar was prepared to turn his army around and return it to the fight in support of his ally.†

The behavior of Francis and Alexander at this pass gave rise to bitter recriminations on both sides. Francis declared, "The complete retreat of the Russians which was, if not demanded, at least provoked with solicitude by the Emperor Alexander after the battle, deprived us of a necessary resource at the moment when we had to negotiate the peace."35 Stadion's biographer writes

---

Mémoires, p. 81; note that Bernhardi, *Denkwürdigkeiten aus dem Leben*, p. 189, incorrectly writes that Francis sent Liechtenstein late in the evening of the day of the battle). It seems reasonable to conclude, therefore, that Alexander and Francis met sometime during the morning of December 3.

§Bernhardi, *Denkwürdigkeiten aus dem Leben*, p. 189. Merveldt took command of Kienmayer's force that escaped from Ulm. He separated from the Russians at Lambach and Davout pursued him, finally forcing him to battle at Mariazell. The 4,000 men he commanded were the few who had survived all of these tribulations, including the lost battle.

**This is just a guess. There is no direct evidence about what Kutuzov said to Alexander except the worthy indirect evidence of his character and professionalism.

*There is, again, no direct evidence to support this line of argument—or any line of argument about Francis's decisionmaking in this epoch. We simply do not know anything about the emperor's mind-set, attitudes, or decisions. Conjecture is the only way to offer any sort of explanation. See Rudolfine Freiin von Oer, *Der Friede von Pressburg: Ein Beitrag zur diplomatiegeschichte des Napoleonischen Zeitalters* (Münster: Aschendorfsche Verlagsbuchhandlung, 1965), pp. 109ff., for a detailed consideration of the aftermath of the battle. Von Oer also points out that the absence of reliable sources about the hours and days immediately following the fight makes a detailed reconstruction extremely difficult.

†[Alexander] to [Francis], undated, HHSt, Rußland Varia II, 240, pp. 270–271. Although the letter is not signed, dated, or addressed, it is clearly from Alexander to Francis, and it must have been drafted during the first week of December, judging from its content. Since some of the phrases in it are nearly identical with those of the notes sent on December 6 to Berlin and London, it is likely that this note was drafted at about the same time (VPR, vol. II, docs. 206–207).

that Alexander "ordered the retreat of his troops to Poland, and thereby betrayed Austria. Thus Francis II had to agree to an armistice on December 6."[36] The Russians were even sharper: Mikhailovskii-Danilevskii claims that as Russian blood was flowing like a river in defense of their homeland, the Austrians were meeting in the Kaunitz castle in Austerlitz to press Francis to make peace with Napoleon.* The collapse of the coalition army, which resulted in large part from the weakness of the alliance, fertilized the seeds of mistrust between Russia and Austria that previous events had already sown.

Francis rode to meet Napoleon on December 4 and began the peace negotiations that led to the Treaty of Pressburg between France and Austria. We will consider the details of this negotiation, as well as Prussia's reactions to the Battle of Austerlitz, below. For the moment it is enough to note that Francis's and Alexander's reactions to that battle shattered the fragile coalition irretrievably. As the Russian troops marched away from Austerlitz toward their homeland, Francis's negotiating position deteriorated precipitately and the treaty he later was forced to sign was harsh indeed. Napoleon broke the will to continue fighting in a crucial member of the coalition. He had won the war. It remained to be seen whether he could win the peace.

---

*Mikhailovskii-Danilevskii, *Opisanie*, pp. 218–219. There is no other evidence to support the notion that such a meeting took place. Mikhailovskii-Danilevskii asserts that Francis told Alexander on the day of the battle that he wanted to make peace, and he sent Liechtenstein off at once to do so, a chronology that the French accounts rule out completely.

24

The Peaces
of 1805

To end the account of the War of 1805 with the Battle of Austerlitz or limit the description of the peace negotiations to a brief summary of the terms of the peace is to deprive Napoleon of one of his most impressive achievements. He masterfully manipulated the many parties involved in the negotiations. He concluded five separate peace treaties in a single month. He won earthshaking terms for France. The peace negotiations of 1805 deserve careful examination if only to pay homage to Napoleon's diplomatic skill, which equaled his military skill.

But Napoleon's diplomatic skills lay in getting the peace terms he wanted, not in designing a stable, durable peace. Although the treaties of 1805 gave France more than Louis XIV had ever sought, they were permeated by fault lines that would lead to new wars. In 1801 and 1802 Napoleon negotiated peace treaties based more on the transitory weaknesses and fears of his enemies than on the real correlation of forces in Europe. He did the same in 1805, while dictating even harsher terms. It was not inconceivable that Napoleon's enemies would learn to live with the peace terms he dictated, depending on his own behavior. But it was unlikely.

Napoleon's War Aims

For Napoleon, the War of 1805 was an entirely defensive struggle that he never intended to fight. Having begun it reluctantly, he was initially determined to end it as rapidly as possible in order to return to his main preoccupation— defeating England. Consequently his initial war aims were rudimentary and focused on securing himself a stable peace that would allow him to pursue his war against the "nation of shopkeepers" without fear of distractions beyond the

Rhine. Events on land and sea in October 1805 led to important changes in these aims, but the final peace treaties that Napoleon imposed on Prussia and Austria were largely shaped by the emperor's initial preconceptions about the nature and purpose of the war.

The defensive goal of Napoleon's initial war aims should not obscure their revolutionary nature, however. From the beginning, Napoleon was determined to reduce the power and influence of Austria in western Germany by attacking the constitution and organization of the Holy Roman Empire. He did not decide to abolish the Holy Roman Empire in 1805, although he may have flirted with the idea of taking Charlemagne's crown for himself, as we shall see. Instead, he determined to expand the territory of his minor German allies at Austria's expense in an effort to reward them for their support during the war, encourage them to remain loyal French satellites, and enable them to form a bulwark capable of resisting Austria in future struggles.

Napoleon's war aims developed in four phases. In the first, during August and September 1805, Napoleon recognized that war was inevitable and prepared for it. His war aims in this period reflected the need to secure German allies for the struggle against Austria. Although there are hints in this period of a larger objective, Napoleon's major focus was limited to the formation of a countercoalition. He promised Baden, Württemberg, and Bavaria unspecified but significant territorial gains in return for their support against the coalition.[1] These promises succeeded in their aim, as all three of the targeted electorates allied with Napoleon against Austria.

Napoleon's desperate efforts to bring Frederick William into the war were less successful.[2] Even the offer of Hanover left the Prussian king unmoved despite the tergiversations this offer caused among his advisers. With growing impatience and frustration, the emperor declared on August 22 that he would only give Hanover to the Prussians if Frederick William moved quickly enough to deter the Austrians from fighting; if he did not, then the offer would evaporate.[3] Napoleon did not see Prussia as a threat at this time and was interested in bribing Frederick William to support him only if the king would move rapidly and effectively—something Frederick William was determined not to do.*

Even in this period, however, Napoleon and Talleyrand hinted that greater changes in Germany would follow a decisive French victory. Talleyrand declared in mid-August that Napoleon's treaty with Bavaria, then under negotiation, "would establish . . . the elements of the future organization of the German Empire."[4] Napoleon himself wrote at the beginning of October that

---

*Napoleon's intentions are evident from the fact that by early September he was already moderating his offer to Berlin: the Prussians were to be allowed Hanover only during hostilities and until Napoleon disposed of the Electorate as suited him at the peace. Napoleon to Talleyrand, 12 September 1805, *Corr. de Nap.*, doc. 9203.

"my intention is to include Darmstadt in my German Federation, composed of Bavaria, Darmstadt, Württemberg, and Baden."[5] The phrasing of this note suggests that the idea of a German federation was by no means novel.[6]

As long as Napoleon was bending every effort to organizing his army, putting it in motion, understanding the allies' movements and intentions, and developing his plans, his war aims received little concrete development. Even Talleyrand's activity in this period was confined to forming and shoring up Napoleon's countercoalition, continuing the vain negotiations with Prussia, and providing Napoleon with intelligence about the enemy's troop movements across the continent.[7] The French government at war had no time to think seriously about what the peace would look like.

That situation began to change as Napoleon and Talleyrand gained confidence in a rapid, decisive victory over the Austrians, if not the entire coalition. As Napoleon's corps closed the trap around Mack's forces near Ulm, Napoleon and Talleyrand separately began to think more seriously about France's war aims and goals. The second phase of the development of French war aims thus began in mid-October and lasted into late November.

This phase started with the first serious consideration of French goals on the continent since the peace of Lunéville, as Talleyrand turned his attention fully to the problem. By October 11 the foreign minister had concluded that a crushing French victory over the Austrians was imminent and he began developing terms that he thought Napoleon should offer Francis to end the war.[8] Interestingly, Talleyrand wanted to press moderate terms for the Austrians on Napoleon. In a brief note to Alexandre-Maurice d'Hauterive, the chief of political correspondence of the Foreign Ministry, Talleyrand proposed that Venice become an independent republic and that Austria give all of her possessions in Swabia to the elector of Bavaria "or some other prince." In return, Napoleon would promise to help the Austrians take Wallachia and Moldavia, to "abandon the crown of Italy as [Napoleon] promised to do," and to make an offensive–defensive alliance with Francis, sending all idea of an alliance with Prussia "to the devil." Talleyrand called this sketch "my dream of this evening." Instead of abandoning it, he developed it into a lengthy, well-considered memorandum with details and justifications for the proposed course of action.

Four major powers ruled Europe in 1805, Talleyrand wrote, France, Austria, Britain, and Russia.[9] Prussia was too small in population and territory, too poor in resources, and ruled by too timid a prince to rank as a great power—she was merely "the first of the second-order powers." Of these four great powers, Austria and Britain were natural allies against France. Russia, "separated from [France] by immense distances, is not directly her enemy, but she is [her enemy] indirectly as the natural enemy of [France's] oldest allies," by which Talleyrand presumably meant Poland and the Ottoman Empire. Insofar as the Russians contemplated the conquest of the Ottoman Empire,

"France will be forced to consider them as her enemies." Talleyrand found such a configuration of states to be unstable. Nothing but perpetual war punctuated by meaningless truces could result when Austro–British alliances, frequently supported by Russia, threatened France. Although Talleyrand did not doubt that France could stand up to a large enemy coalition, he sought to attain a more durable peace. Only by separating Austria from Britain and generating antagonisms between St. Petersburg and Vienna, he concluded, could stability be restored to the continent.

Talleyrand therefore proposed that Napoleon impose a moderate peace on Francis. The aim of that peace should be to place buffers between France and Austria to eliminate the sources of friction and hostility between the two states. At the same time, he suggested giving Wallachia and Moldavia to Austria to offset the Austrian losses in Germany and Italy he contemplated demanding and drive a wedge between Austria and Russia. If Austria was rewarded for making peace with two rich provinces—control of virtually the entire length of the Danube and a substantial portion of the Black Sea coast including a good port—she would happily renounce Venice, Triest, Vorarlberg and the Tyrol, and the minor territories scattered throughout Swabia that Talleyrand coveted. The Austrian presence in the Balkans and on the Black Sea, he continued, would make Russia Austria's natural enemy and France, therefore, her natural ally. He even offered a specious argument that depriving the Ottoman Porte of its territories was the best way to strengthen the Turkish empire. The aim of the peace was to make Austria into France's reliable friend and partner, render the pusillanimous Prussians irrelevant, and thereby stabilize Europe as far as the Vistula and the Black Sea.

Napoleon rejected these proposals almost immediately. When he met Talleyrand in Munich on October 27, Napoleon ordered him to prepare a harsh treaty for Francis to sign.[10] He sought to deprive Austria of Vorarlberg, the Tyrol, Venice, and Austria's entire Adriatic coastline. Francis would also abandon the Holy Roman crown, thus bringing Charlemagne's thousand-year empire to an ignominious end. Napoleon offered Francis no meaningful compensation to soften the blow: neither Moldavia-Wallachia nor an alliance. He proposed instead to seek an alliance with Russia. When Talleyrand objected to many of these proposals, Napoleon overruled him. The emperor was determined to eliminate Austria as the dominant power in Germany and shake hands with Alexander over the corpse of the Holy Roman Empire.

Historians hostile to Napoleon see in Talleyrand's Strasbourg memorandum a hopeless effort to rein in Napoleon and persuade him to develop limited goals that the other states of Europe could live with. In this view Napoleon's refusal to accept Talleyrand's recommendations was also a refusal to accept limitations on his power or any need to accommodate the other states of Europe.[11] The reality of Napoleon's thought and action was, as usual, more complex.

Napoleon had not decided in October 1805 to begin a program of unlimited conquest in Europe, and his rejection of Talleyrand's proposal did not reflect such a decision. Rather, Napoleon had always mistrusted Francis and saw Austria as his primary continental enemy. He far preferred doing business with Alexander, believing they had many more interests in common. The rejection of Talleyrand's proposal therefore reflected Napoleon's determination to weaken Austria and reach out to Russia.

Napoleon began to put this program in train immediately. On October 21 he seized all of Francis's possessions in Swabia and levied contributions on those territories to support his armies.[12] Two days after Mack surrendered, moreover, Napoleon ordered that the Austrian prisoners he had taken be dispersed among the various departments of France to provide laborers for those who needed them.[13] On November 2, Napoleon wrote the elector of Württemberg a note that began the dismantling of the Holy Roman Empire. "One must well determine the part of German customs that must be abolished, that only serves to give the Emperor [of Germany] a power for which there is no compensation because it does not offer any guarantee any more; I mean to say, first the Aulic Council, a large part of the attributions of the Diet of Ratisbonne, which in truth is nothing but a miserable monkey-house."[14] His rambling note highlights Napoleon's failure, even at this late date, to think through his aims in Germany. The aim of destroying Austrian power in Germany, however, is quite clear.

Since Napoleon intended to offer Francis no compensation for the brutal peace he meditated, he could only use threats to cow the Austrians into submission following Mack's humiliation. "I would give my brother the Emperor of Germany yet another piece of advice," he declared in a bulletin. "Let him hasten to make peace. This is the moment to remember that all empires have a term; the idea that the end of the dynasty of the House of Lorraine might have arrived should scare him."[15] In a private note to Francis in early November, Napoleon moderated his tone only slightly. He reminded the Austrian emperor that Francis could have ended the war both on land and sea and been "the benefactor of the entire world," but he had chosen not to. He added that Francis would surely recognize the justice of Napoleon's determination to benefit from the advantages his fortunes in war had offered him. The conditions of peace must provide "a guarantee against a fourth coalition with England."[16]

It seemed that Francis might take Napoleon's advice. In early November, he sent Count Ignatius Gyulai, a Hungarian general who had fought at Hohenlinden and had his complete trust, to meet Napoleon.[17] Francis was careful to tell his allies about this mission and explain its purpose to them.[18] He hoped above all to persuade Napoleon to conclude an immediate armistice, hopefully on the Enns, otherwise on the lines currently occupied by the armies. Such an armistice would allow the Austrians to prepare a defense of Vienna, allow the Russians time to arrive to reinforce them, and prevent Napoleon from turning against the Prussians before they were ready to fight. Francis also hoped to learn what Napoleon's war aims really were, imagining quite wrongly that Napoleon had aims as settled and constant as those of the coalition. It does not seem that Francis intended at this time to violate the coalition treaty by making a separate peace with France or even that he had much hope that the negotiations would succeed.* He instructed Gyulai not to negotiate with Napoleon but only refer his terms to Francis.[19]

Gyulai met Napoleon at Linz on November 8. He did not succeed in any of his objectives.[20] Napoleon made it clear that he intended to take Francis's possessions in Swabia, that he intended to "compensate" Bavaria, Baden, and Württemberg, and that he would not compromise on his demands for Venice. He did offer conciliatory language about evacuating Naples and maintaining its independence, as well as vague promises with regard to Holland, Switzerland, and the Kingdom of Italy. Gyulai was unable to secure an armistice, although Napoleon sent him back to Vienna with a moderate note and expected to see him back again very shortly.[21] Gyulai's movements back and forth between Francis and Napoleon with talk of an armistice and a peace sowed confusion in the garrison guarding Vienna's bridges, which Murat took advantage of following the Battle of Dürnstein.[22]

By the time Gyulai returned to Vienna to report to Francis, the Austrian court had already left the city. With some difficulty, Gyulai located the emperor and met him at Poysdorf, sixty kilometers from the capital, on November 11. He reported on his unproductive visit, especially about the unacceptable conditions Napoleon insisted on for an armistice.[23] Francis resolved to send his envoy back again, and Gyulai met Napoleon once more on November 12. In the space of forty-eight hours Napoleon had moved his headquarters from Linz to St. Pölten and adjusted his armistice demands accordingly. Now he insisted on a demarcation line extending from Krems through Graz toward Laibach and down to Trieste.[24] This line was far to the east of Austrian positions in the Tyrol and Slovenia. Napoleon categorically rejected Prussian mediation; he would negotiate with Prussia, he proclaimed, only if Frederick William declared war on him. Nevertheless, the emperor held out hope of continued negotiations, even in the absence of an armistice. If Francis would meet him at the front lines, he declared, they could end the war in an hour. Gyulai had to return to his master with this forlorn hope.

---

*Cobenzl to Metternich, 10 November 1805, in Metternich-Winneburg, *Aus Metternich's nachgelassenen Papieren*, p. 82, indicates the Austrian court's lack of confidence in the outcome of the negotiations. Francis's letters to Napoleon clearly express his determination to make peace only in concert with Alexander (see Francis to Napoleon, 30 October 1805, and 22 November 1805, in Adolf Beer, *Zehn Jahre österreichischer Politik, 1801–1810* [Leipzig: F. A. Brockhaus, 1877], pp. 454–456).

Gyulai reached Brno on November 15 to learn of Murat's coup in Vienna and the danger menacing Kutuzov's army. This situation prompted Francis to write one more letter to Napoleon, although clearly the Gyulai negotiations were leading nowhere.[25] Francis insisted that further discussions depended on Tsar Alexander, ensuring their futility. Since Napoleon had not yet defeated Alexander, he was unwilling to negotiate with him or allow him to mediate in any way.

It is not at all clear whether either side took these negotiations seriously. Francis might have made peace had Napoleon offered him very generous terms, but he certainly had no intention of making peace on any terms the emperor of the French was prepared to accept. Napoleon, for his part, seems to have believed initially that peace was imminent. He wrote to Talleyrand on November 9, "The Emperor of Germany is still in Vienna. He has written me several letters; he wants to come to an arrangement."[26] He ordered Marshal Marmont to "send out negotiators; say that I am master of Vienna, that I am negotiating an arrangement." It was clear, though, that the main purpose of these declarations was to gain time for Marmont's movement.[27] Talleyrand believed that the fashioning of a peace was urgent. On hearing of the Battle of Trafalgar, he wrote Hauterive, "I hope it will place no obstacles in the way of any of the political operations that seem to me appropriate to undertake right now! We have done enough great things, miraculous things, [and] it is time to finish by coming to an arrangement." A week later, Talleyrand reflected the somber mood setting in at imperial headquarters. "We beat [the Russians], we kill them, we take them, and that does not prevent this from being a bad war of which the French soldier will soon become weary because he has to kill too much."[28]

As the negotiations dragged on, however, Napoleon's enthusiasm waned. He turned his attention to ensuring that any real peace negotiations would take place on the basis of a status quo in Germany in which Francis's influence had already vanished. On November 8, Napoleon and Elector Max Joseph of Bavaria agreed to the "mediatization" of all of imperial holdings in Swabia and Franconia; with a stroke of the pen Napoleon gave the lands of all of the imperial nobility in these regions to Bavaria.* They jointly abolished the imperial post and a variety of other imperial perks that the Holy Roman Emperor had retained in German lands.[29] On November 15, Napoleon informed Max Joseph that he had given orders to destroy the fortresses separating Bavaria from the Tyrol; Bavarian troops alone would garrison the conquered Austrian lands there. The hint that Bavaria would gain the Tyrol at the peace was clear.[30]

---

*Imperial knights were those who held their lands directly from the Holy Roman Emperor. The lesser states in which their territories lay had no rights to tax them, recruit from their lands, or judge them in court. "Mediatization" is the term for the process by which these knights were subordinated to the territorial states enclosing their lands, thereby effectively stripping them of their independence and privileges.

Napoleon clarified the link between this advice to his minor German allies and the final peace treaty in a note to the elector of Württemberg. "Things that have to be done at the peace," he wrote, "cause a great deal of embarrassment; when they have already been done, all is easy." He exhorted the elector to do everything he could think of to eliminate the power of the Holy Roman Emperor in his lands so that "in a peace treaty one can simply say: Everything that the electors have done is recognized."[31] As in 1801, Napoleon sought to change the international situation in his favor even as he was negotiating with the Austrians, both to drive them to peace rapidly and to gain a more advantageous treaty.

It seems that Napoleon even imagined that his maneuvers would please Alexander. He asked the elector of Württemberg to persuade his sister to intervene with the tsar, her son, by pointing out "that this will even be advantageous for Russia because it will weaken Austria; that it is not very advantageous for France because she could retain what she is giving to others." It is amazing that Napoleon could so misunderstand Alexander in mid-November 1805 as to imagine that these arguments would have traction with the tsar.

At the same time, Napoleon worked ineptly to sow discord between the Russians and the Austrians. He would have liked, he wrote Francis, to push his outposts to Brno but not as long as Francis was there "because I would not like to do anything that might seem to [Francis] to be meant to be disagreeable to him when my only goal is to pursue the Russian army and lead it to evacuate his states. . . . If Your Majesty wishes to assure me that [the Russians] will evacuate all of your states," he concluded, "I will stop at Brno and cease pursuing them."* He also warned Francis that everyone in Austria hated the Russians, feared them more than the French, and wanted the war to end immediately. This theme of the Austrians' hatred for the Russians also appeared in Napoleon's public statements at this time, probably as the overt complement of his secret diplomatic campaign to drive a wedge between Austria and Russia.†

Evidence that Napoleon had some hope that his negotiations with Francis would lead to peace comes from his disillusionment on deciding that they would not. He wrote to Talleyrand on November 23 that he and Francis "write one another many letters without thereby arriving at anything important.

---

*Napoleon to Francis, 17 November 1805, *Corr. De Nap.*, doc. 9503. Talleyrand confirms that this was the real reason for Napoleon's delay in moving into Brno (Talleyrand to Hauterive, 18 November 1805, in Couchoud and Couchoud, *Talleyrand: Mémoires*, p. 349). Unlikely as it may seem that Napoleon would deny himself a military advantage in order to offer an olive twig to Francis, it is difficult to imagine any other reason for this delay.

†See, e.g., the Twenty-Sixth and Twenty-Seventh Bulletins of the Grande Armée, 18–19 November 1805, *Corr. De Nap.*, docs. 9510–9511. Interestingly, previous public statements had highlighted the supposed hatred of the Germans for the British. See, e.g., the Fifteenth and Twenty-Second Bulletins of the Grande Armée, 31 October and 13 November 1805, *Corr. De Nap.*, docs. 9443 and 9476 respectively.

Cobenzl, who is doing it, thought to deceive me, but he has not succeeded."[32]
There is certainly no indication here or anywhere that Napoleon's offers were
other than sincere, especially considering the close relationship between those
offers and the ultimate peace he dictated. At any time after Ulm, it seems,
Francis could have ended the war by accepting terms not very different from
those he ultimately received. He did not do so primarily because he hoped that
the arriving Russian reinforcements and the imminent participation of the
Prussians would retrieve the situation for him and the coalition.

The "Interior Lines" of Napoleonic Diplomacy

Military theorists have a term that describes the ability of a force surrounded
by numerous enemies to attack them each separately by moving rapidly from
one to the next before the others can react: "operations on interior lines." Such
operations at the grand strategic and strategic levels brought Frederick the
Great his successes against more numerous coalitions. Napoleon made brilliant use of this technique during the Italian campaigns of 1796–1797, and he
would do so again in subsequent wars. The use of interior lines was one of
Napoleon's favorite operational techniques.

It was also, suitably adapted, his favorite technique for handling complex
multilateral negotiations. We have already seen this technique during the negotiations in 1801 and 1802. Napoleon worked to first attain a suitable peace
with Austria. He combined military operations that changed the situation to
Austria's disadvantage with negotiations with minor powers whose results he
could then present as *faits accomplis.* Napoleon forced Austria out of the war
and signed the moderate Peace of Paris with Alexander. Only then did he work
to force Britain to a peace made much more advantageous for France by the
fact that Napoleon had stripped Addington of continental allies. Napoleon's
ability to negotiate with all of the belligerent powers individually and at his
own pace, moving from one to the next before the others could react, allowed
him to dictate peace agreements far more favorable than the objective situation
warranted. He applied this same approach in 1805 in an even more complex
and fluid situation.

Prussia's increasingly hostile and threatening attitude lent urgency to the
negotiations. Napoleon became aware in October that Frederick William had
taken the violation of his state's neutrality at Ansbach badly. By the end of the
month, Duroc was reporting from Berlin that the Prussians had joined the
coalition and would attack France if Napoleon did not accede to their demands. He added that those demands would certainly include compensation
for the king of Sardinia, indicating their harshness and, given the military situation of the time, unreality.[33] Haugwitz's departure from Berlin to meet

Napoleon in late November confused the situation, since he told Laforest a series of lies in an effort to subvert his master's determination to adhere to the Potsdam Accord.* Haugwitz's mission presented Napoleon with a danger and an opportunity. Haugwitz's instructions ordered him to present Napoleon with an ultimatum that would lead to war if rejected. But his arrival at Napoleon's headquarters offered Napoleon a chance to cajole the envoy into taking a different tack. Noticing the danger, Napoleon seized the opportunity.

The third phase of the development of France's war aims and peace terms stretches from the fourth week of November until December 14. In this period, Napoleon was deeply concerned by the possibility that Frederick William would intervene against him, which could prove disastrous for the campaign. In his initial note to Talleyrand about how to deal with Haugwitz he emphasized the need to find out what Frederick William really wanted from France and what he intended to do.[34] Napoleon determined to stall Haugwitz to prevent him from delivering a message that would lead to an open breach, hoping to reach an agreement with Francis in the interim. In this third phase, Napoleon's overriding priority was to force Francis into peace before Frederick William could intervene in the war.

Francis provided Napoleon with an apparent opportunity to achieve this aim by sending Gyulai and Stadion to negotiate with him in the last week of November.[35] As we have seen, the main purpose of this mission was to observe Haugwitz and second him, as well as to prove to the Prussians that the Austrians were serious about trying for peace. No one in the Austrian court thought that anything would come of these negotiations. By contrast, this period found Napoleon at his most diplomatic and flexible. Although he declared on November 25 that he was immovable in his desire to have Venice, the Tyrol, Swabia, and so forth, five days later he proposed a compromise that would leave Austria almost all of Venice and the Tyrol in exchange for more modest gains for Bavaria.[36] Napoleon was well aware that his strategic situation was deteriorating with every passing day, and he briefly came to agree with his foreign minister that it was high time to make peace.

Francis's selection of envoys cast doubt on his sincerity in the negotiations, although it is not clear that Napoleon or Talleyrand understood immediately. Stadion was an odd choice for the duty. He was an imperial count with holdings in southwestern Germany that Napoleon was working to give to Bavaria. Stadion could be counted on to resent that transaction as well as much of what Napoleon was trying to do in that area with a sense of personal grievance. In

---

*See above, Chapter 20. Laforest to Talleyrand, 14 November 1805, in Bailleu, *Preussen und Frankreich*, vol. 2, doc. 305. Haugwitz told Laforest that Prussia had not adhered to the coalition and that there was no accord with Russia—patent lies. It appears, however, that Laforest believed him. Talleyrand passed this information to Napoleon on 26 November (Bertrand, *Lettres inédites de Talleyrand*, doc. 129, p. 193).

1800, Austrian Foreign Minister Baron von Thugut had refused to use Stadion as an envoy in a similar situation, declaring that "it is hardly possible . . . since one must sacrifice the Empire more or less to our interests in Italy, to send a negotiator who depends upon the Empire for his property, his family, and everything that belongs to him."[37] Yet Francis did precisely that in 1805.

Stadion had also served as Austrian ambassador to St. Petersburg where he negotiated, among other things, Austria's accession to the Third Coalition. A Russophile and an imperial noble who had belonged to the small clique of Austrian senior leaders determined to resist Napoleon by arms, Stadion was hardly the figure best suited to mollify Napoleon or pave the way to a rapid peace. He was exactly the right person, on the other hand, to ensure that Austria got the best peace possible under the circumstances. His selection shows Francis's continued determination to retrieve his desperate situation and his unwillingness to throw in his lot with the triumphant French emperor.

Talleyrand found Stadion a stiff, unbending hardliner. After their initial meeting, he described his counterpart as a man "of whom flexibility of character does not seem to me to be the distinctive quality, and who holds the reins of the negotiation in such a manner as to reduce Mr. Gyulai to the role of mute witness." Talleyrand added that Stadion tended to make speeches and seemed affected. He concluded, "These gentlemen showed themselves to be in no hurry," and he did not expect to find the going with Stadion and Gyulai to be at all easy.[38]

The instructions Stadion brought with him, which he probably drafted, were indeed unbending. They insisted that Austria retain the Tyrol, Vorarlberg, and the Adriatic coast of Venice without question. Stadion was to try his best to retain the city and as much of the hinterland of Venice as possible, although here he had some latitude. The instructions foresaw making further small sacrifices in the empire in order to preserve Austria's position in Italy to the greatest possible extent—even, if necessary, transferring the Habsburg elector of Salzburg to Venice and giving part of Salzburg to Bavaria.[39]

Napoleon received Stadion and Gyulai in Brno on November 24 and began trying to break up his negotiating partners in order to defeat them in detail. He first let fall the remark that it would be much better for Austria to conclude a separate peace with him than try to negotiate on behalf of the entire coalition. He drew Gyulai aside before meeting with Stadion, the head of the mission, and asked him to consider whether "Francis would prefer to give Salzburg to Bavaria, to sacrifice Venice, or to see the Tyrol joined to Switzerland."[40] Here Napoleon worked not only to separate Austria from Russia (and Gyulai potentially from Stadion), but also to establish a negotiating position. In the joint meeting with both envoys, Napoleon insisted that he must have Venice; there could be no peace between Austria and France, he said, until Austria had been entirely driven from Italy. He promised that if Stadion and Gyulai made peace at that moment, Austria could retain Salzburg and the Tyrol. If Napoleon had greater success in a continued campaign, however, he would take those territories as well. Napoleon was master of the exploding offer.[41]

The Austrians hastened to move the conversation away from these distasteful ultimata, but rapidly found themselves on even worse ground. When Stadion insisted that Francis wanted to make not just a particular peace with France but a general peace for the entire continent, Napoleon demanded that the Holy Roman Emperor ratify and execute the agreements reorganizing the empire in 1803, as well as abandon age-old rights of his within the empire. Stadion, the imperial count, resisted and the conversation became unpleasant.

No doubt in a final effort to find some leverage with his formidable interlocutor, Stadion mentioned Haugwitz's mission and his desire to meet with the Prussian envoy. Napoleon declared that he did not fear Prussia and believed that Haugwitz was headed to Brno with an "agreeable" message for him. It would be far better for Austria, he repeated, if Francis made a separate peace with him.[42]

For all the unpleasantness of Napoleon's meeting with the Austrian envoys, the positions he took in Brno were less extreme than the one he instructed Talleyrand to pursue the following day. In his own conversation he appeared to hold out hope to Gyulai that Austria could keep two out of three of its main territorial aims, whereas on November 25 he insisted that Talleyrand get both the Tyrol and Venice.[43] It is too easy to see in Napoleon's notes and statements an unreasonable determination to seize all of western Europe and undertake an unlimited expansion of his power. In truth, he was negotiating skillfully.

Clearly Napoleon did not mean everything he said to the Austrians. There is no indication, for instance, that he ever seriously intended to give the Tyrol to Switzerland or make it an "independent state" as he threatened to Stadion and Gyulai. Neither was he remotely as certain of the benevolent intentions of the Prussian court as he made out. The apparent flexibility in his terms, on the other hand, was probably real—as long as the Austrians seized them and made peace at once. If he could end the war rapidly, before the Russians and the Prussians (not to mention Archduke Charles) could bring overwhelming strength to bear against him, Napoleon might have been willing to sacrifice advantages in Germany.

Napoleon sized Stadion up quickly and accurately. To begin the negotiations from anything other than an extreme position would have made it difficult to move the imperial count on the issues that mattered most to Napoleon, such as Venice. The harsh note to Talleyrand was an effort to raise the opening bid as high as possible in hopes of securing a reasonable immediate settlement. The softer note Napoleon sent on November 30, which left the Austrians the Tyrol, most of Salzburg, and almost all of Venice, reflected his real minimum demands for an immediate peace, reduced even further because of Napoleon's trepidation about the overall situation.[44]

The conversation ended with both sides agreeing to begin formal negotiations and settling on Vienna as their location. Napoleon named Talleyrand his negotiator and turned the Austrian delegation over to the experienced hands of his foreign minister.[45] Before the Austrians left Brno, however, Napoleon took Gyulai aside once more and made him an astonishing offer. If Austria would turn over Venice, Napoleon would give Francis Salzburg, Regensburg, the lands of the imperial nobility—and Hanover!* He even spoke vaguely of an alliance with Austria. The goals of this maneuver were clear. Napoleon was determined to retain Venice for the Kingdom of Italy. He also wanted to make peace rapidly. He needed to find a way to compensate Francis in the German empire for the losses in Italy, but not at the expense of his minor German allies. Hanover was a perfect compensation because it was far removed from the interests of Bavaria, Baden, and Württemberg, and because it would permanently estrange Austria from Prussia and Britain as well. It was a skillfully laid snare that the Austrians would find hard to resist.

Napoleon wasted no time in using the negotiations with Austria as a lever against Prussia. He maneuvered to delay Haugwitz until November 28, when he met with the Prussian envoy in Brno.[46] What happened at the meeting is not entirely clear, since Haugwitz's brief report does not seem adequate to describe a four-hour conversation.† Haugwitz wrote that Napoleon received him with a "glacial" air and that "it would have sufficed to let escape one word" that strengthened Napoleon in his belief that Frederick William was on the point of taking up arms against him "to precipitate a separate peace with Austria and to bring the entire weight of [Napoleon's] power against Prussia." Stadion was deeply engaged in serious peace negotiations, he continued, and it was only through the most adroit maneuvering (which, as Hardenberg points out, Haugwitz did not describe at all) that Haugwitz managed to allay the emperor's hostility.

Among other things, Haugwitz took it on himself without any authorization to promise that the Prussians would not permit any attack against Holland from northern Germany, and would allow the beleaguered French troops in Hameln, Napoleon's last foothold in Hanover, to forage for supplies.[47] Haugwitz took this step because in a successful "mediation" between Napoleon and Francis it was essential that Frederick William maintain "his ancient friendly relations" with France. Those relations were even more important because Haugwitz was convinced that Austria was preparing to abandon the coalition altogether. "The moment," he wrote the king, "that the Emperor Napoleon counts you among his enemies, he will make a golden bridge for

*Von Oer, *Der Friede von Pressburg*, p. 86. Von Oer points out that although Napoleon's note to Talleyrand (26 November 1805, *Corr. De Nap.*, doc. 9526) suggests that the Austrians brought up these points, all of the Austrian reports make it clear that it was Napoleon who had done so.

†Hardenberg's ex post facto footnotes show clearly his opinion that Haugwitz had not done justice to his conversations with Napoleon.

Austria. She will not resist it, and you will have thenceforth the entire power of France joined with the Bavarians on your hands."[48]

Haugwitz's accusations were manifestly unjust.* Francis made no effort to violate his agreement not to make a separate peace. On the contrary, he threw away several opportunities to do so in part by insisting that Alexander be a party to any agreement. The selection of Stadion as the chief negotiator practically ensured that peace would not result rapidly from the Franco–Austrian negotiations. Napoleon's skill both in keeping Haugwitz and Stadion from seeing each other and in playing to Haugwitz's desires by exaggerating the importance of the Franco–Austrian negotiations convinced the Prussian envoy that Francis was on the verge of giving up his allies.

By accepting this conviction with no evidence but Napoleon's own word, Haugwitz served his master badly. He made no mention of his primary mission in his initial interview with Napoleon and failed to execute his instructions to lay before the emperor an ultimatum with unacceptable conditions. Virtually from the moment he arrived at French headquarters, Haugwitz abandoned the policy that Frederick William had decided on and began to pursue his own policy of determined reconciliation with France at the expense of Prussia's allies. His repeated accusations that the Austrians were already preparing to abandon the coalition merely added gross insult to serious injury.

The initial meetings between Talleyrand and the allied envoys began to persuade the foreign minister that coming to an arrangement with Prussia might be easier than making the Austrians yield, at least without winning a battle or two. Talleyrand met Stadion and Gyulai for the first serious discussion on November 29. They sparred over the proposed line for an armistice, over whether the peace would be general or separate, and over the terms. Stadion made another effort to insist on joint negotiations with Haugwitz, and Talleyrand turned this proposal aside once more.[49] Talleyrand wrote Napoleon that "Cobenzl is the one who keeps the Emperor of Austria on Russia's side" and "Stadion belongs to Cobenzl and the cabinet of Petersburg."[50] After another meeting a few days later, Talleyrand wrote, "Stadion is not the man whom H[is] M[ajesty] the Emperor of Austria should have chosen if he wanted a prompt peace. He was the Austrian minister in Russia; he concluded the Russian alliance with Austria." Talleyrand did not think Stadion would easily get past the coalition's failure to achieve the aims he had participated in establishing.[51]

Haugwitz, on the other hand, was far more forthcoming. Talleyrand noted that the Prussian minister had "pushed politeness to the point of wearing the grand cordon of the [French!] Legion of Honor for almost the entire

---

*Although the years have not dulled the ardor of those who wish to argue that Austria or Prussia betrayed the coalition and each other, and the charges and counter-charges have obfuscated an issue that the evidence makes simple.

day in Vienna." He added, "I was also pleased enough with him as regards important matters."[52] Talleyrand began by pressing Haugwitz on several key points. Why did the Prussians occupy Hanover? What is the situation of the troops there now? To whom does Hanover belong? Will Prussia allow Sweden and Russia to attack Holland? Was there a convention signed on November 3 between Prussia, Russia, and Austria? Haugwitz once again gave much more ground than his instructions permitted. As he had when speaking with Napoleon, Haugwitz declared that Hanover belonged to France; that since the allies had been allowed to cross Prussian territory, the French would receive similar rights; that there would be no attack on Holland; and that the agreement of November 3 was "a simple declaration" that bound no state to any particular action. Prussia wished only to see peace reestablished on the continent and offered to mediate between the opposing sides on a basis of neutrality.[53] Talleyrand had every right to be pleased.

Even so, both he and Napoleon sensed that Haugwitz was concealing something. After his meeting with the Prussian envoy, Napoleon wrote Talleyrand, "In his conversation with me he used a great deal of finesse, I would even say talent; I still have the idea, however, both from the [king's] letter and from his conversation, that one was uncertain in Berlin about what part to take."[54] Talleyrand declared that although dispatches he received from Laforest in Berlin tended to confirm Haugwitz's statements, "Nevertheless there is in the court of Berlin something bizarre and singular that it is impossible to explain except by the lassitude of conduct and the pusillanimity that explains all."[55] They were right; Haugwitz was violating the instructions he himself had drafted.

Haugwitz's instructions were in some respects vague, but in others quite specific. He was definitely obliged to place before Napoleon the coalition's demands outlined in the Treaty of Potsdam, which included the evacuation of French troops from Switzerland, the independence of Switzerland, Holland, and Naples, and a large indemnity for the king of Sardinia in the territories of the Kingdom of Italy.[56] It is true that Haugwitz had reserved to himself the right to moderate the terms proposed to Napoleon, *if* Napoleon insisted on it and *if* the Austrians agreed. Nowhere in the instructions, however, did Haugwitz suggest that he might fail to offer the coalition's demands altogether and begin negotiations on an entirely different basis, which would have violated the Treaty of Potsdam in its most fundamental meaning.

Haugwitz subsequently defended his actions in Vienna on the ground that they were forced on him by the Battle of Austerlitz.[57] His behavior before that battle gives lie to this claim, however. He did not go to meet Napoleon "with more of an open mind than was strictly compatible with the treaty of Potsdam," as one recent historian puts it.[58] He went willing, perhaps determined, to sabotage the policy his court had agreed on with its allies and pursue his own independent foreign policy, confident that he would be able to make it good when he returned to Berlin. Haugwitz's behavior in Vienna was not that of a cowardly servant of a cowardly master, as it is often portrayed. It was a bold throw with high stakes. Haugwitz sought to end the war, salvage Prussia's relationship with France, and restore his ascendancy in Berlin over his rival, Hardenberg. If Napoleon and Talleyrand were aware that something was fishy in the Prussian camp, they also saw that Haugwitz's behavior offered the promise of splitting up the coalition in another fashion, if the Austrians proved as recalcitrant as they seemed likely to do.

In the meantime, Talleyrand had received Napoleon's order of November 30 to prepare a moderate peace treaty for the Austrians on December 1, and he immediately set to that difficult task.[59] The draft he produced implemented Napoleon's directives as Talleyrand understood them. It gave Austria Salzburg and left Venice in the hands of an Austrian archduke; promised that the Kingdom of Italy would be separated from the French empire at Napoleon's death; offered very limited territorial gains to Württemberg, Baden, and Bavaria; made the last-named electorate into a kingdom; and required the Austrians to pay compensations of five million florins.[60] Talleyrand asked Napoleon if he meant to make Baden and Württemberg kingdoms as well, since the elector of Württemberg was especially keen on this promotion. He also wondered if Napoleon still intended to separate the three electorates (or kingdoms) from the German empire, as had previously been discussed. The draft treaty assumed that Napoleon did not wish to do so.[61]

This last issue was a crucial one. If Napoleon insisted on separating the three electorates from the German empire—making them formally independent—he would be signing the death warrant of the Holy Roman Empire. That organization could not exist in any meaningful form without the participation of southwestern Germany. Such a decision would have been momentous in itself, but it would raise the question of what the new organization of Germany would be. Would these states simply exist as independent buffers? Would they form some sort of "confederation" under Napoleon's tutelage? The future development of central Europe hinged on the decisions Napoleon made in this regard.

Napoleon may have decided not to insist on separating the three electorates from the empire because of Prussia.[62] The only remotely firm position Haugwitz had taken in his initial meeting with Talleyrand was that "he could not . . . conceal the chagrin that the liaisons of the three electoral courts with France gave his court. 'That,' he said to [Talleyrand], 'deranges the system of Germany.'"[63] Laforest passed along evidence that Haugwitz was accurately presenting the views of the court of Berlin on this issue, if no other.[64] Napoleon may have drawn in his horns temporarily to avoid disturbing what promised to be a helpful relationship with the wayward Prussian emissary.

Talleyrand was aware from Napoleon's notes that a battle was imminent, but he did not ask how the outcome of that battle would change his negotiating position.* This omission was intentional. Talleyrand had been arguing since October for the need to sign a moderate treaty with Austria that would make Francis Napoleon's friend and ally against the Russians. He surely recognized the possibility that a Napoleon flush with the success of a new victory in battle would increase his demands dramatically, but he may have hoped to head off that eventuality by plunging directly into negotiations on the basis of the moderate treaty. Interestingly, Napoleon made no effort to prevent or delay beginning negotiations on that basis even as he was preparing for a battle he expected to win—or perhaps he was less sure of a decisive victory than is often made out.

In any event, Talleyrand learned of Napoleon's triumph early on the morning of December 3 and immediately spread the word.[65] Amazingly, he proceeded to begin negotiations with Stadion and Gyulai as scheduled—and on the basis of the moderate peace drafted before the battle. He might have entrammeled himself in the negotiations to an extent sufficient to embarrass Napoleon's inevitable efforts to change the terms, but Stadion's obstinacy prevented such an eventuality. With a determination that the military situation did not warrant even before the Battle of Austerlitz, Stadion fought on almost every point. He even attempted to retain the Holy Roman Emperor's centuries-old precedence in treaties over all other heads of state—even other emperors.[66] The two sides were haggling over minor issues when Napoleon's first post-Austerlitz messages reached Talleyrand and fundamentally changed the nature of the negotiations.

When the battle was over, Napoleon feared that Talleyrand might have compromised him already with the Austrian envoys, and hastened to write a mendacious note:

> . . . an army of 100,000 men commanded by the two emperors has been entirely destroyed. All protocols have become useless. The negotiations are nullified because it is obvious that they were a ruse of war to lull me. General Gyulai wrote to Prince Charles that there would be a battle; he thus acts like a spy. Tell Mr. Stadion that I was not duped by their ruse; that that's why I sent them away from Brno; that, the battle having been lost, the conditions cannot be the same.[67]

There was no ruse in the Austrian negotiations and they were not an effort to lull Napoleon. Apart from their ostensible purpose, Stadion and Gyulai hoped mainly that their presence in Vienna would operate on Haugwitz in a

---

*Compare Talleyrand to Napoleon, 30 November 1805 and 1 December 1805, in Bertrand, *Lettres inédites de Talleyrand*, docs. 134 and 135 respectively. Talleyrand reported in the earlier note his "most lively disquiet" about the dangers of the battle that lie ahead for Napoleon but made no mention in his later note about how the outcome of the battle might change the nature of the treaty he was negotiating.

positive manner, not that it would deceive Napoleon in some way. Napoleon may not have understood the depths of the secret purposes guiding the coalition's envoys, but he had no reason to imagine or complain that he had been duped in any way.

This line of argument was an effective way to break up the negotiations and begin again on different terms, however, and Napoleon hastened to make it public.[68] He also ordered Talleyrand to shift the locus of the negotiations with the Austrians to Nikolsburg while leaving Haugwitz cooling his heels in Vienna. The foreign minister was to rush to Brno to receive new instructions. "I will tell you at Brno what I want to do," the emperor wrote, "do not prejudice anything. Tell the Austrians that the battle has changed the face of affairs; that since they wished to risk and lose everything, they must expect harsher conditions." He also complained that the Austrians "sent negotiators the day they wanted to attack me, to lull me."[69] Considering that Napoleon had known for days that the allies intended to attack him and nevertheless negotiated with them, indeed, that he built his entire battle plan around that knowledge, this last complaint is extravagant nonsense—but useful propaganda.

Talleyrand complied with the summons but tried one last time to persuade Napoleon to pursue moderate peace terms with the Austrians. "Y[our] M[ajesty] can shatter the Austrian monarchy or restore it. Once shattered it will not be in even Y[our] M[ajesty's] power to reassemble the scattered debris and form it again into a single mass. The existence of this mass is necessary, however. It is indispensable to the future well-being of the civilized nations."[70] The foreign minister wrote further that the glory days of Austria were long past and the Habsburgs had been in steady decline for centuries. Although Francis's territories looked expansive on a map, the internal contradictions and centrifugal forces resulting from the empire's polyglot and feudal nature made it infinitely weaker than France. Napoleon had nothing to fear from Austria and nothing to gain from smashing the Habsburg empire to pieces. If he did so, the Hungarians would separate themselves from the wreckage and "too weak to form an independent State, will give themselves to the Russians." Talleyrand reported that he had received reliable word that such a plan was circulating inside Hungary at that moment. If such a union occurred, "the Russians, masters of Hungary, would be all-powerful against Europe."

Talleyrand therefore suggested that Napoleon reread the Strasbourg memorandum and reconsider his rejection of it. At that moment, "beaten and humiliated, [Austria] needs her conqueror to extend a generous hand to her and by allying with her give her back the confidence in herself that so many defeats and so many disasters would deprive her of forever."[71] The foreign minister could readily reconcile the Strasbourg memorandum with the soft treaty he was in the process of negotiating, but he wished to continue the negotiations with someone other than Stadion.

More interestingly from Napoleon's perspective, Talleyrand reported seeing Haugwitz several times. The Prussian envoy, he noted, "received the news of the victory with signs of joy." The foreign minister dismissed Haugwitz and the Prussian court as well, however. "I saw in Mr. Haugwitz's face that the dominant sentiment of his court is fear," he wrote. "I am letting him amuse himself alone and I amuse him with this plan of a general guarantee that is so close to his heart." He finished by noting that while Haugwitz bleated about a general guarantee of the continental peace, "I would be pleased if Y[our] M[ajesty] would authorize me to make an arrangement with these gentlemen [Stadion and Gyulai] that, I am convinced, would assure the peace of the continent for more than a century better than any conceivable guarantees."[72] By December 7 the negotiations had been moved. Talleyrand awaited Napoleon's pleasure at Brno, and Stadion and Gyulai arrived in Nikolsburg.[73]

Did Napoleon ever contemplate offering Francis the sort of lenient terms Talleyrand suggested? The evidence is unclear. The two emperors met on December 4 in the village of Nasiedlowitz. Napoleon says that Francis would have made peace on the spot, but Napoleon resisted doing so. He accorded the Austrians an immediate armistice and promised an armistice for the Russians too, as long as Alexander began to move his army out of Austrian territory as rapidly as possible.[74] The two men began to consider the terms of the ultimate peace treaty, and it seems that Napoleon's initial offer was indeed generous. The Austrians firmly believed that Napoleon had promised not to take any of Francis's German territories, specifically including the Tyrol, although the offer may have been tied to the condition that Alexander close his ports to British shipping. Francis was distressed and surprised when he learned later that Napoleon was demanding the Tyrol, a demand that he called "as unexpected as it is hostile."[75]

Savary offers some insight into the reasons for Napoleon's initial moderation. Although flushed with his astonishing success at Austerlitz, Savary writes that Napoleon was well aware of the dangers inherent in his position after that battle. He knew that the Prussians "had an army united with a Russian corps at Breslau; in addition he had learned from the intercepted dispatches of Stadion that Archduke Charles had arrived on the Danube while the Army of Italy, commanded by Masséna, was still far behind beyond the Julian Alps: it was not therefore impossible that all these united armies could combine into a movement that would force him to run new risks that might compromise the success of Austerlitz." Napoleon therefore eagerly seized on Francis's peace offer in an effort to extricate himself from a strategic situation that was very dangerous even after his magnificent victory.[76] Napoleon's sense of danger at this pass was probably what prompted him to demand that Alexander withdraw his army at once. Only if the tsar did so could Napoleon begin to breathe more easily in the immediate future. Happily for Napoleon, the tsar had already decided to return to Russia as rapidly as possible.[77]

In his note informing Talleyrand of these events, Napoleon nonetheless hinted that he would place harsher demands on the Austrians than the ones Talleyrand had been negotiating.[78] It is possible that the emperor simply meant to take all of Venice, something the terms offered on November 30 had not included but that even the Austrians appeared now to accept as inevitable.[79] Or possibly he intended to double-cross Francis as soon as the Russians left the immediate area and his strategic situation began to clear up. Napoleon certainly intended to drive Francis to peace as rapidly and advantageously as possible in order to free his hands to deal with Frederick William, whose army, massed along the northern flank of the Grande Armée, posed a grave risk to the successes Napoleon had so far achieved.

The victory at Austerlitz was not enough by itself to force Francis to make peace rapidly on terms Napoleon found acceptable. The emperor of the French therefore developed new levers to use on his recalcitrant counterpart. Rumors had been flying around Hungary for some time that the Hungarians would not support a continuation of the war against France. Napoleon had compromised the Archduke Joseph, the Palatine of Hungary, by publishing a correspondence in which the archduke apparently asked Napoleon to treat Hungary as neutral territory.* Davout had sent units marching from Vienna to Pressburg and issued proclamations in Hungarian promising that the French would respect "your independence, your constitution, and your privileges" if the Hungarians remained neutral or supported the French.† Davout kept a watchful eye on Hungary right up until his departure to participate in the Battle of Austerlitz, and the Austrians were well aware of French propaganda efforts in that crucial area.[80] Since a revolution in Hungary would have been disastrous for Austria, these activities increased the pressure on Francis to make peace as quickly as possible.

Napoleon did not stop there, however. On November 28 he ordered his agents to raise a contribution of 100 million French francs on the Austrian territories held by the Grande Armée.[81] This money was to be given to the army as a "gratification" or reward for its performance in the campaign—and probably to offset salary arrears in the army as well.[82] Although Napoleon surely wished to ease the burden of war on France, he no doubt intended this "con-

---

*Von Oer, *Der Friede von Pressburg*, pp. 114–116, shows that the situation was more complicated than this—the French offered Joseph Hungarian neutrality in response to a more anodyne Austrian note. French "misrepresentation" of this correspondence was based at least partly on misinterpretation, however. Certainly Davout suspected the Austrians of dealing in bad faith when he learned that Francis had repudiated the agreement he thought he had made about Hungary. See Davout to Berthier, 22 November 1805, in Charles de Mazade, ed., *Correspondence du Maréchal Davout, Prince d'Eckmühl; ses commandemants, son ministère, 1801–1815* (Paris: Librarie Plon, 1885), vol. 1, doc. 116, p. 184.

†Von Oer, *Der Friede von Pressburg*, p. 114. Pressburg is the German name for the city of Bratislava, now the capital of Slovakia. In 1805 Pressburg was a leading city of the Hungarian part of the Habsburg Empire.

tribution" to increase the pressure on Francis by reminding him of the pain Napoleon could inflict on the large part of his territory controlled by France.

The victor of Austerlitz took additional steps to increase the pressure on Francis. During the meeting at Nasiedlowitz on December 4, Napoleon "granted" Francis's request for an armistice for himself and for the Russians.[83] On December 6 Marshal Berthier and FML Liechtenstein concluded an armistice agreement that was to last for the duration of the negotiations.[84] This armistice, to which Alexander was not a party, committed the tsar of Russia to remove his army from Austrian territory within one month and to allow the progress of that army to be monitored continuously until it had done so. It also forbade the entry of any "foreign army" into Austrian lands, recruitment efforts in Hungary, and the formation of extraordinary militias in Bohemia.

Although Alexander had already told Francis that he intended to leave Habsburg lands as quickly as possible, it is nevertheless strange to find an Austrian emperor guaranteeing the behavior of his former ally, who was not a party to the guarantee. The French also found the tsar's behavior strange. Savary writes, "I could not understand why the Emperor of Russia had not been at the interview with the Austrian Emperor." Napoleon was sufficiently concerned to send Savary chasing after Alexander to receive his agreement to the armistice Francis had accepted on his behalf.[85] Savary's mission reflected the importance of Napoleon's diplomatic accomplishment. By obliging Alexander to withdraw his army and making that withdrawal a central article of the armistice with Austria, Napoleon with one stroke did more to harm Francis's bargaining position than all the shots at Austerlitz had done. Such was Napoleon's perspective on the affair.

Apparently Napoleon was not aware that Alexander had initiated the decision to abandon his ally, thereby breaking the alliance. The tsar did not negotiate either an armistice or a peace with Napoleon because to do so would have explicitly violated the coalition treaty, which forbade separate peace agreements. His loss of will to continue to fight combined with Francis's determination to make peace nevertheless shattered the alliance no less effectively than a separate peace would have done. Napoleon's real diplomatic coup was in convincing Francis to guarantee that the Russians would withdraw and the Prussians would stay out of his lands. Subsequently any Austrian effort to seek external support while taking a firm position in the peace negotiations would result in a legally justified French attack. By accepting these armistice terms, Francis committed himself to making a bad peace.

The Habsburg monarch does not appear to have understood the consequences of his decision, however. Shortly after the conclusion of the armistice, Francis sent Baron Stutterheim to Berlin with a message of desperation. He begged Frederick William to let him know if the Prussian king intended to stand by Austria or not. If so, he would draw out the negotiations and refuse to accept any "too harsh conditions." If Frederick William abandoned him as Alexander had already done, however, then Francis warned that he might have no choice but to accept an alliance with France.[86] Considering that Francis had undertaken to prevent the Prussian army from entering his territory, this was a strange position to take. Indeed, it reflected the unreality that reigned in Austrian counsels at this point—or the catastrophic position in which the collapse of the Third Coalition, triggered by Alexander's withdrawal, had placed the Court of Vienna.

Francis's hope that Frederick William would stand by him induced him to recommence the peace negotiations from a firm and unrealistic position. Whether because Napoleon had requested it or for some other reason, Francis did not send Stadion back as his emissary, but chose Liechtenstein once more instead.[87] The instructions he gave Liechtenstein allowed him to agree to the cession of Venice including much of its hinterland, although not its Adriatic coast, to the Kingdom of Italy. Francis hoped to fob Napoleon off with some minor concessions in Germany, however, while demanding that the French army evacuate Naples and that Napoleon guarantee the independence of Holland and Switzerland. In the event that Napoleon proved difficult, Liechtenstein was to delay in hopes that a good word would arrive from Berlin in a timely fashion: "he still believed that time was working for him!"[88]

Had Francis been aware of the whirlwind of activity taking place in the French court in Moravia he would have been far less sanguine. On December 8 or 9, Talleyrand met with Napoleon for the first time since the Battle of Austerlitz to discuss the details of the peace treaties.[89] Talleyrand apparently attempted once more to mitigate Napoleon's terms for Austria, but he needed clarification of those terms above all. He read Napoleon a twelve-point "questionnaire" about the specifics of the proposed treaty, and his questions reflected his prejudices. Did Napoleon simply mean to take Venice? he asked. And if so, how much of it? Did Napoleon want Vorarlberg, the Tyrol, Lindau, Salzburg, and so forth? Were the three southwestern electorates to be separated from the German empire formally? Was Napoleon willing to give Moldavia and Wallachia to the Austrians? To make a treaty with Francis? In other words, Talleyrand inquired whether Napoleon would accept the moderate peace terms he had already rejected.[90]

Napoleon's partial answers to Talleyrand's questions make his general intentions clear. Francis must renounce the Tyrol, all of Venice, and a collection of other territories in Germany. He must recognize Napoleon as king of Italy as well as the Act of Mediation then governing Switzerland's political organization. Napoleon held back from formally abolishing the German empire, however, and the Bavarian ambassador, Gravenreuth, concluded from his conversations with Talleyrand at about the same time that the French were eager to avoid taking positions in southern Germany that might upset the

Prussians.[91] Gravenreuth later wrote the Bavarian prime minister, "We would have won a lot more without the Prussians."[92] All of the questions relating to Russia were left open. Clearly Napoleon was not yet certain about what position to take with regard to Alexander and wanted to keep all options, presumably including the option of an alliance, alive.

Once Napoleon had explained his goals to Talleyrand, he ordered his foreign minister to conclude treaties with Baden, Bavaria, and Württemberg immediately, probably to present the Austrian negotiators with a series of *faits accomplis*.[93] The diplomatic activity this demand occasioned was impressive. The French foreign office, working out of poor conditions in the middle of Moravia, drafted three treaties in the space of twenty-seven hours, and Talleyrand secured the adhesion of the three electorates in two days. The haste with which the treaties were drafted was reflected in numerous errors, including misnamed geographical features, misdesignated cities, and a requirement that Austria cede a territory already ceded long ago. Talleyrand negotiated and signed the treaty with Baden with the Badenese military commissioner, since there was no diplomatic representative present at that moment and the French were unwilling to await his arrival.[94] The sense of the treaties was clear enough, however: Napoleon wished to "break the German ties without saying the word," as Gravenreuth noted.[95]

The bilateral treaties made Bavaria and Württemberg kingdoms with greatly increased territory and sovereignty exactly like Austria and Prussia had in their German lands. In other words, both states were fully sovereign and de facto independent of the Holy Roman Empire, even if they remained nominal electorates within that empire. The treaties used the phrase "German confederation" for the first time in European diplomatic discourse, although the usage was ambiguous; it seemed to be simply a synonym for "German empire," the traditional designation of the Holy Roman Empire.[96] Napoleon had not yet decided to give the Tyrol to Bavaria, however, and his bilateral treaty with Max Joseph did not mention that conquest. Gravenreuth managed to secure Vorarlberg, however.[97] All three treaties bound the smaller German states to France with offensive–defensive alliances and made them effectively clients.

The electoral negotiators did not simply accept terms already prepared by Talleyrand, however. Each envoy prepared his own "wish list" of territories and conditions and presented them (with the exception of the Badenese minister, who arrived after the treaty had already been signed) as the basis of negotiations. Talleyrand and Napoleon mediated the conflicting desires of these states and occasionally moderated their demands, but the electoral representatives took great initiative in destroying the German empire in southwestern Germany. Napoleon was disappointed that they had not taken more initiative. Talleyrand upbraided Gravenreuth for his master's failure to destroy the last vestiges of Austrian suzerainty in Bavaria on his own, and insisted that he issue peremptory orders to do so at once.[98] The French were eager to ensure that southwestern Germany had acquired its final form before Talleyrand ever sat down to discuss terms with the Austrian envoys.

The deeper significance of the revolution Napoleon was fomenting in the "third Germany" would only become clear after several months had passed, but the treaties of December 10–12 spelled the end of the age-old European balance in that area. Austria had lost all importance beyond her now truncated borders, Prussia was excluded from southern Germany entirely, and now only Napoleon held sway there, supported by three tame vassals. As the Prussians would soon discover, Napoleon's de facto seizure of control in southwestern Germany gave him vastly greater power throughout Germany and Europe. He was well on the way to snatching Charlemagne's crown from Francis's head— and it is possible that he had that very thought in mind.

As early as October 1805, Napoleon had counted up the number of electoral votes he could rely on in an election for the Holy Roman throne and determined that he had only four of ten.[99] This sort of counting continued until April 1806. Napoleon's continuing refusal to abolish the Holy Roman Empire formally or to separate the three southwestern electorates openly from that empire could have been intended to mollify the Prussians, but could also have reflected the emperor's ambivalence about that empire. The archchancellor of the empire, Dalberg, suggested to Napoleon that if he promised to save the empire's constitution, a grateful Germany would present him the crown. In reply, Napoleon criticized Dalberg for trying to incite German nationalism.[100] At a time when the collapse and final end of the empire seemed obvious to many people, Napoleon's determined refusal to destroy it strongly suggests that he considered revising it to suit his own needs. This refusal also eliminated one more bone of contention between Napoleon and Francis, thereby improving the prospect of a rapid peace with Austria that was the emperor's primary goal in the second week of December.

The negotiations for that peace resumed with Liechtenstein's arrival at Brno on December 10. Napoleon met the Austrian envoy while Talleyrand frantically completed arrangements with Baden, Bavaria, and Württemberg. "If you have plenipotentiary powers," Napoleon told Liechtenstein, "I will negotiate with you at once and in 24 hours all will be finished."[101] The two began to discuss terms. Napoleon insisted on taking all of Venice but then allowed Austria to keep Dalmatia and Albania. The emperor demanded, in addition, that Austria cede the Tyrol to Archduke Ferdinand, formerly the Duke of Tuscany, now the elector of Salzburg, and take Salzburg as compensation. Liechtenstein tried vainly to defend the Kingdom of Naples, but Napoleon declared that he would take it as a prize because of its alliance with Britain during the war.[102]

Liechtenstein realized that he was out of his depth as a diplomat (he had always been a soldier) and begged Francis to send Stadion to help him. In response, Francis sent Gyulai to assist Liechtenstein with the diplomatic niceties. He sent with Gyulai a response to Napoleon's initial terms that was remarkable for its stubbornness. The Austrian emperor insisted on retaining Dalmatia and Albania, as well as the Tyrol and Vorarlberg. He ordered Liechtenstein not to agree to excessive financial compensation for France and to insist on an improvement in the border between Austria and the Venetian lands in Italy and between Bohemia and Bavaria. If Napoleon would not retreat from his demand to move Archduke Ferdinand to the Tyrol, then the Tyrol must be held as a Habsburg secondogeniture, as Tuscany was.[103] Evidently Francis still hoped that Frederick William would come to his aid in time to allow him to escape a disastrous treaty.

As soon as the last electoral treaty was signed, Talleyrand took over the negotiations with the Austrian envoys. He complained that the discussions could not have been conducted in a more depressing location. "Brno is a horrible place," he wrote to Hauterive. "There are four thousand wounded here right now; every day there are quantities of deaths. Yesterday the stench was detestable."[104] In this unpleasant environment Talleyrand met with Gyulai and Liechtenstein for the first time on December 12. He began by reading them a proposed treaty incorporating the terms he had just finished negotiating with the three electorates.[105] The Austrians already knew many of the demands Napoleon would make in this treaty, but some of the terms surprised them.[106] They fought hard for Dalmatia, Albania, the Tyrol, and Vorarlberg, and lost on every point. Although Talleyrand promised to forward the suggestion that Ferdinand receive both the Tyrol and Vorarlberg, he held out no hope that the emperor would accept such terms. The Austrians were reduced to begging for financial compensation to Ferdinand for the exchange of wealthy Salzburg for poorer lands.

The French nevertheless offered substantial compensation to Francis for the losses they imposed on him: they would create an electorate for an Austrian prince of the lands formerly belonging to the Teutonic Order and a number of other scattered possessions. Gyulai and Liechstenstein demurred, since those lands were sparse and poor and did not at all compensate Francis for his losses. Talleyrand asked what German lands they would prefer, and Gyulai immediately responded, "Hanover."[107] This suggestion took Liechstenstein by surprise, and the two envoys had to confer for a few moments before Gyulai evidently persuaded his colleague to make the demand. Talleyrand was also surprised and pointed out to Napoleon that to give Hanover to Austria would serve France by alienating Vienna from London and Berlin. It would also drive Prussia "entirely from the French system, strengthen Austrian influence in the empire, furnish the court of Vienna with pretexts and means for agitating in northern Germany, and involving France in wars by the obligation she would have to maintain her work [i.e., the treaty]."[108] Talleyrand passed the idea along to Napoleon for his consideration.

Despite the obvious points of disagreement, Talleyrand emerged from this marathon meeting optimistic. Although Liechtenstein had found it necessary to travel to Hollitsch to meet Francis and receive permission to sign, the foreign minister believed that he would indeed sign no later than December 19.[109] Talleyrand thought that he would even be able to incorporate Napoleon's request to leave vague the questions of when the crowns of Italy and France would be separated and the terms on which Francis might receive back the artillery Napoleon had taken from him during the campaign, as well as other terms relating to Naples.[110] The peace seemed all but made.

Prussian Wild Card

For a brief moment, it seemed that peace with Austria could not come too soon. As Talleyrand was meeting with Liechtenstein, Napoleon was becoming concerned again about Prussia's attitude. "As for Prussia, what does she want?" he asked Talleyrand on December 13. "I do not know at all. It seems that she is sending an army into Silesia. I have not yet seen Mr. Haugwitz."[111] He ordered the continuation of a conscription then under way: "The peace has not been signed. The Russians, it is true, have evacuated the states of the House of Austria by agreement; but as long as the peace is not concluded, we must maintain ourselves in a good position."[112] He warned Fouché that "the opening of negotiations is not a conclusion" and instructed him to renew his activity in keeping the stream of recruits flowing to the Grande Armée.[113] To the elector of Württemberg he declared, "Neither you nor I nor the cabinet of Berlin itself knows what the Prussian armies want." He added that his victory at Austerlitz would probably lead Francis to make peace quickly but noted that he was forming armies in the north to confront the Prussians. He reassured the elector that "you and my allies can only gain from a continuation of the war."[114] He even wrote Masséna in Italy warning him that Charles was in Hungary and very close to Vienna. "At the first hostilities," he added, "he will march on this city; make your dispositions to be in a state to approach it in a few marches at the first order."[115] Napoleon clearly recognized the possibility that the Austrians would delay negotiations until the arrival of a Prussian army in the theater and then attack; he was well aware of the fact that the Grande Armée was not, despite its previous victories, in a very good position to receive such an attack.

By the following day, however, Napoleon's fears were evaporating. He wrote Talleyrand that he was not displeased about the delay in the signing of the treaty with Austria and that Talleyrand would see why from his account of the meeting with Haugwitz. For the Prussian minister had promised to sign a treaty that would oblige the Prussian king not to meddle in the affairs of Italy, recognize the transfer of the Tyrol to Bavaria, give Ansbach to Bavaria, and form an alliance with France. All Haugwitz demanded in return was Hanover.[116]

Haugwitz had gone to Vienna determined to make peace with Napoleon if at all possible, as we have seen. But for the first two weeks in December Napoleon refused to see him or allow him to meet with Talleyrand. The emperor wanted to make peace with Austria first and then deal with the Prussians. It is not clear why Napoleon changed his mind and began to treat with Haugwitz on December 14. He may have felt that the Austrian treaty was sufficiently advanced and promising that he could use it as a lever against Haugwitz, or he may have sensed an opportunity to change the situation by opening negotiations, from his perspective, prematurely.

However that may be, Napoleon and Haugwitz met for an extended session on December 14 and all but came to terms. It is impossible to know exactly what happened at this meeting, since Napoleon left no detailed account and Haugwitz's lengthy report on it is clearly mendacious and distorted.* According to Haugwitz, Napoleon once again greeted him coldly and even angrily, denouncing Prussia's apparent determination to join England and the coalition against France. Haugwitz claimed that he was once again certain that the only choice was between peace with France and immediate war. That Haugwitz should have felt this situation to be worth commenting on is surprising, since he had been sent to Vienna specifically to deliver an ultimatum offering Napoleon a choice between peace and war. Haugwitz's conviction in this regard also seems erroneous. Napoleon had by no means decided on war with Prussia and had made few preparations to wage such a conflict in the near future. The French documents show nearly conclusively that Napoleon was eager to delay matters with Berlin at this time, rather than forcing them to a head.

In order to support the argument that immediate peace was the only sensible alternative, given such a choice, Haugwitz painted the political and military situation as blackly as possible. Austria, he declared, had betrayed Prussia and was even then making a separate peace. Alexander had abandoned Frederick William to his fate, and no aid from Russia could arrive in time to help in a war with Napoleon that would inevitably end in less than four weeks, either in victory or defeat. Prussia was left to her own devices against the redoubtable French army. In such a case, peace was the only wise course to pursue.

Virtually none of these assertions were true. The Austrians had not betrayed Prussia; they were deliberately spinning out the negotiations until Francis had heard back from Frederick William about Prussia's intentions.

---

*Haugwitz's report is in Ranke, *Denkwürdigkeiten*, 5:220–243. Hardenberg sprinkled acidic comments throughout this report, highlighting its mendacity and inaccuracy. Although those comments are distorting in that they are designed to throw Hardenberg in the best possible light and discredit Haugwitz, they are nevertheless closer to the truth than Haugwitz's version in most respects.

Haugwitz had every opportunity to learn that fact, moreover, since he had met with Stadion and the Austrian emissary had wanted to compare notes fully. Haugwitz, for reasons of his own, had been far less eager.[117]

The one clear "betrayal" the Austrians had unwisely committed was to ask openly for Hanover. Napoleon took full advantage of this indiscretion, even showing Haugwitz a leaf of Talleyrand's letter describing his interview with the Austrian emissaries. Haugwitz, in turn, gave this Austrian demand the highest prominence, assuring the king that he could verify Talleyrand's handwriting.[118] It is unlikely that Gyulai's error affected Haugwitz very much, since he had clearly gone to Vienna determined to do precisely what he ultimately did. It was powerful propaganda, however, in favor of the ratification of the agreement that Haugwitz made and helped poison the already tainted relationship between Austria and Prussia.

Nor was the military situation remotely as bleak as Haugwitz portrayed it. Hardenberg calculated that Prussia could count on more than 250,000 troops—her own and her remaining allies'; this number was only mildly exaggerated.* In addition, the Russians had a large army (Mikhel'son's) in and around Prussia's eastern borders. It could well have arrived in time to participate in the rapid campaign Haugwitz described. Finally, Haugwitz's despair took no account of Napoleon's poor situation. Overextended, exhausted, without reliable trained reserves or the promise of any new help from allies, the French emperor was hardly in a position to launch another dramatic lightning war from his makeshift base in Moravia. Prussia had little reason to fear war with Napoleon in December 1805, and Haugwitz had to strain credulity to make the argument that any course but immediate peace was suicide.

Haugwitz may well have feared Napoleon's military prowess excessively, and the reports of the Battle of Austerlitz, which Napoleon steadily embellished in early December, may have played on that fear.† It is more likely, however, that Haugwitz used the general fear of Napoleon's military skill to cloak his own determination to make peace at all costs. Hardenberg suspected that

---

*Ranke, *Denkwürdigkeiten*, 5:226 n. 1. See "Die Preußische Kriegsvorbereitungen and Operationspläne von 1805," in *Kriegsgeschichtliche Einzelschriften, herausgegeben vom Grossen Generalstabe, Kriegsgeschichtliche Abteilung I* (Berlin: E. S. Mittler, 1883–1914), appendix 7, pp. 86–94, for a complete listing of the available Prussian and allied forces, which added up to well over 250,000, although many were designated as reserves in various locations.

‡The Thirty-Third, Thirty-Fourth, Thirty-Fifth, and Thirty-Sixth Bulletins of the Grande Armée (7, 10, 11, 14 December respectively) exaggerated various aspects of the French victory and kept the memory of the battle vivid for many days by parceling out information into multiple dispatches (*Corr. de Nap.*, docs. 9550, 9556, 9559, 9574 respectively). Napoleon did not release another bulletin until December 26, and that one was clearly aimed at intimidating the Austrians (*Corr. de Nap.*, doc. 9616). Perhaps he felt the first four had achieved their effect by helping convince Haugwitz to make peace, and renewed the propaganda offensive only when the Austrians continued to prove obdurate. Historians have been far too credulous in using the information in these reports, since they contained distortions inserted for immediate and important political considerations.

Haugwitz sought to use such a "success" in Vienna to supplant him as sole foreign minister once more.[119] He was probably right.

If Haugwitz served his master badly by deliberately sabotaging his policy and pursuing his own ends, Frederick William had himself partly to blame. Frederick William created the preconditions for Haugwitz's behavior in Vienna by making Haugwitz and Hardenberg compete for his favor and by encouraging them to take opposite positions to balance each other and thereby facilitate a policy of paralysis. It did not follow, however, that the king would welcome this self-serving destruction of his own policy. Haugwitz ran a considerable risk of being disavowed and discredited and of seeing his career destroyed. He was well aware of this risk, and that is surely the reason why he even refused to summarize the terms of the treaty he concluded with Napoleon on December 15 in writing from Vienna.[120] It is why he waited until he had returned to Berlin to prepare the vast memorandum on his mission that served more to argue his case than to report events. It is why he launched into a desperate effort to ensure that Frederick William ratified the treaty he had signed without any authorization.

The Treaty of Schönbrunn, which Haugwitz and Napoleon signed on December 15, gave Napoleon a great deal. It promised an offensive–defensive alliance between France and Prussia guaranteeing the Ottoman Empire, Napoleon's holdings in France and Italy and Bavaria; it also guaranteed the cession of the Tyrol and Ansbach to Bavaria, in advance of any such agreement by the Austrians. It bound Frederick William to give Napoleon the Duchy of Clèves and the principality of Neuchâtel for disposition to whomever he chose. Apparently Napoleon was beginning to look for ways to circumvent his promise not to aggrandize France beyond the Rhine. In return, Prussia received peace and Hanover. Haugwitz thought it was a good trade.[121]

In the process, Haugwitz deliberately and coolly stabbed Austria in the back. In their first conversation, Napoleon played the obvious card of threatening Haugwitz with the prospect of an imminent Austrian treaty: "Talleyrand may already have signed a peace treaty with Austria," he declared, "and in this case I have no idea what our future relations will be."[122] Later that day, however, Napoleon changed his approach. The treaty had not been signed, he said, and the Austrians continued to delay on minor matters. He invited Haugwitz to take advantage of that situation, and the faithless minister did. If Napoleon pronounced these words, he thereby let Haugwitz know that a firm line would support the Austrians and help them either make a better deal or retrieve the situation somehow. Had Haugwitz been loyal to his instructions and to the wishes of the Prussian court, he would have delayed and worked to support the beleaguered ally. Instead, he took ruthless advantage of the situation to further his perception of Prussia's cause, exactly as Napoleon had intended.

Haugwitz's betrayal of Austria transformed the negotiations at Nikolsburg. Napoleon immediately instructed Talleyrand to draft a new treaty for the Austrians giving France everything he wanted. Once he had approved the new treaty, he intended Talleyrand to give it to the Austrians "assuring them that I will not change a single word; that they can choose their part, to make peace or war."[123] What had been a treaty under negotiation was about to become a diktat.

Napoleon's changed attitude placed Talleyrand in a difficult position in several ways. It required that he change the basis of the negotiation substantially, revoking several concessions that he had intimated to the Austrian envoys that Napoleon might accept. It required him to delay the negotiations until he worked out a draft treaty that suited Napoleon. Because the treaty with Prussia was to be secret, he could not explain to the Austrians the reasons for the changed propositions or the delay. He found the location of the negotiations unfortunate for delaying tactics, moreover, because there was nothing for the Austrian envoys to do to amuse themselves. As a result, he complained, "I have them on my hands almost the entire day."[124] Even Talleyrand found it difficult to go through six- and seven-hour conferences day after day with nothing to say.

The foreign minister continued to make minor efforts to mitigate the terms of the treaty Napoleon intended to impose on Francis, but with diminishing zeal as the inevitability of the outcome became clear to him. He slyly suggested to Gyulai that Francis might ask for Moldavia and Wallachia as compensation for his losses in Germany and Italy, and that Napoleon would "use all his influence" to persuade the Ottoman sultan to accept his loss. He probably hoped to use this offer as a way to form an Austro–French rapprochement and to group Austria with France against Russia—his favorite project. Gyulai, who had been foolish enough to ask for Hanover without contemplating the effect of that request on Prussia, was bright enough to realize that an Austrian seizure of the Danubian principalities would lead to hostility and possibly war with Russia. He firmly refused this poisoned pill.[125]

Talleyrand took his case directly to the emperor, although now with great delicacy. The revised draft treaty, he reported on December 16, was likely to encounter significant obstacles at the Austrian court, especially because of the size of the financial indemnities Napoleon demanded. He added, "I must testify that [Liechtenstein] exudes only the [desire for the] reestablishment of a sincere and durable friendship between the two empires."[126] He clearly hoped to stir in Napoleon a desire to rethink the harshness of the terms he was about to impose on his defeated foe, but Napoleon was unwilling to reconsider any of them.

The emperor relented enough to recall Talleyrand to Vienna and away from the unhealthy air of Brno. He also decided to shift the locus of the negotiations to Pressburg, which was closer to Vienna and would facilitate communication between Talleyrand and Napoleon and between Liechtenstein and Francis, who had established his court at Hollitsch.[127] Although he would ultimately reduce his demand for compensations from 100 million francs to 50 million, however, he remained true to his initial intention not to allow the Austrians to change a single word of the draft he ordered Talleyrand to present them.

Nevertheless, the negotiations dragged on as the Austrians tried to salvage some of their ravaged empire, and Napoleon became increasingly impatient.[128] Archduke Charles had been interfering with the supply of Vienna from his base in Hungary for some time, and Napoleon now told Berthier to warn the archduke that any further interference would lead to the renewal of war.[129] Two days later he added orders to begin preparations for concentrating the French army for battle against the Austrians should hostilities be renewed.[130] He told Talleyrand to inform his counterparts of this concentration and to explain it with reference to Charles's violations of the armistice agreement.[131]

Napoleon also began to develop another lever to use on Francis: he raised the specter of revolution in the Habsburg hereditary lands. On December 16, he told Berthier to warn the Austrians that if Charles's embargo on Vienna did not cease, then "the Emperor Napoleon will take measures for the government of this capital."[132] He announced publicly that such a step would mean the destruction of the current social and political order in the Austrian capital and the substitution of a French "constitution" that would be "more appropriate to the times." He left the readers of his announcement to consider to what degree such a "constitution" would accord with the state structure of the remaining Habsburg lands.[133]

This threat to bring the French Revolution into the heart of the hereditary lands struck home. Francis had already seen, fought, and for the moment defeated Jacobin tendencies in the first few years of his reign.[134] He could see the danger of a recurrence in such treacherous times. Archduke Charles feared not merely the rise of French revolutionary "constitutionalism" in the Austrian lands, but also the rise of nationalist rebellion in Poland and elsewhere.[135] This fear was also natural: the ill-considered reforms of Joseph II had fomented a nationalist rebellion in Belgium that nearly led to the loss of that province even before the French Revolution.[136] How much more likely was such a rebellion now, with the Habsburg monarchy suffering devastating defeats and French agents exciting nationalist hotheads wherever they roamed?

Napoleon's threats were powerful, but Francis and his advisers and envoys still dithered, hoping to find a way to avoid accepting unbearable terms. The dithering ended when Archduke Charles arrived at Francis's court on December 20. Francis had asked his brother to meet him "so that you and I can consider our position and what to do henceforth."[137] Charles hastened to meet the emperor and was horrified by the situation at the imperial court. "I have found here a true Tower of Babel," he wrote his uncle. "Everyone advises, orders, disposes, commands—and everyone only says and does stupid things." He resolved to take control of the situation by driving out the foolish courtiers who had led Austria into disaster and continued to risk the survival of the monarchy by failing to understand the situation and by ensuring that a firm peace was signed as soon as possible.[138]

Charles spoke bluntly to his brother. "The monarchy is shaken, all its parts have been torn from their roots, confusion has replaced order, the foundation threatens to collapse if the spirit of Providence does not reign over you and guide your decisions." Peace alone would not cure these problems, he continued. Although the people of the Habsburg lands were still able to distinguish between the emperor and the evil advisers whose counsel had led to such disaster, the time would soon come when they could not do so; then the House of Habsburg would fall. In order to save his throne, therefore, Francis must make peace at once, and Charles volunteered to meet Napoleon to hasten the process. He also insisted that Francis fire Cobenzl and his colleagues. The archduke declared that only one man was fit to take the place of the disgraced Cobenzl—Count Stadion.[139]

To drive his point home and make brutally clear that Francis could hope for no salvation in the renewal of military operations, Charles submitted an evaluation of the military situation and a consideration of the various courses of action open to Austria two days later.[140] Charles had refined the art of presenting a military situation in the blackest possible colors throughout 1804 and early 1805, and his skills did not desert him at this decisive moment. His memorandum once again breathed hopelessness and defeatism. This time those sentiments had considerable justification in reality after the withdrawal of Russian troops and Haugwitz's perfidy (of which Charles may not have been fully aware).

Charles's decisive defeatism combined with Napoleon's determination and Talleyrand's skill and sheer endurance to turn the tide. By December 23 Talleyrand had bullied Gyulai and Liechtenstein into accepting most of the terms Napoleon demanded.[141] The next day, only the article about contributions remained.[142] When Napoleon reduced his demands from 100 million to 50 million francs, only one small problem remained: Gyulai and Liechtenstein were reluctant to sign the treaty before Charles met with Napoleon lest they offend the archduke and anger the emperor by denying his brother the chance to mitigate the terms.[143] Little did they know that Charles's main purpose in seeking the meeting was to capitulate as rapidly as possible. In the end, they signed the Treaty of Pressburg on the same day that Napoleon met with Charles—a meeting that Napoleon ensured had no significance.[144]

The Peaces of 1805

The treaties of Pressburg and Schönbrunn transformed Europe more fundamentally than any international agreements had done since the Peace of

Hubertusberg ended the Seven Years War in 1763 and formally recognized Prussia's rise to great-power status. Austria lost Venice, Vorarlberg, the Tyrol, and all of her holdings, rights, and privileges in southwestern Germany. Prussia acquired Hanover but lost her holdings in Franconia. Bavaria and Württemberg became kingdoms and gained vast expansions of their territory and power. They also became French vassal states, giving Napoleon complete control over southwestern Germany. The Holy Roman Empire lost even the small significance it possessed at the start of the war.

Napoleon had not decided what he intended to do with his new empire, however. He hinted at his true thoughts and motivations to Cambacérès on December 20: "The peace will be made; but, since I have decided to make a peace that will at last put an end to the intrigues of England, it will still take a few days to know the definite outcome of the negotiations."[145] To the last, Napoleon did not understand the nature of the coalition against him. Even in December he believed that Pitt's gold had fomented continental rebellion against him, that the states of Europe served Britain's interests rather than theirs, and that if he weakened the cat's paws of perfidious Albion sufficiently, peace on the continent would ensue.

He did not realize that when he forced the Austrians to agree to crushing peace terms he sowed the seeds of future conflict. Francis never reconciled himself to this peace. He signed it under duress and the threat of further warfare that, deserted by all his allies, he knew he could only lose. If his fear of Napoleon or his mistrust of the other states of Europe changed, there was every reason to imagine that he would hasten to undo a peace he saw as monstrously unjust and as a threat to the existence of his monarchy. The Peace of Pressburg was made at the moment of Austria's greatest weakness and despair. Like the Peace of Lunéville, it would become unstable as those conditions changed, unless Napoleon could find ways to make it acceptable to his vanquished foes.

The Treaty of Schönbrunn was even less stable, since Haugwitz had negotiated and signed it contrary to his instructions, contrary to the wishes of the Prussian court, and without informing the king or his co–foreign minister that he was doing so. It reflected Haugwitz's fear and personal calculations in the context of Napoleon's headquarters; it did not even accurately reflect the prevailing attitudes in Berlin. When Haugwitz returned, a fierce debate broke out about whether or not to ratify the rogue peace he had made on his own accord, and the Prussian court soon found itself in a desperate situation as the full ramifications of Haugwitz's treachery made themselves felt. The story of the War of 1806–1807 is the story of the failure of the Peace of Schönbrunn.*

---

*We will consider the collapse of that peace and the war that ensued in the next volume of this series.

The End of the Third Coalition

The Treaties of Pressburg and Schönbrunn formally dissolved the Third Coalition. Only Russia and Britain remained nominally at war with France, but neither had any plans to fight the victorious Grande Armée, even if both remained unwilling to make peace with Napoleon. The Third Coalition had been weak from the outset. Its members distrusted one another and pursued divergent aims. Its leaders were never able to coordinate their diplomatic or their military activities. Alexander pressed Francis to go to war and then deserted him at the first real check. The nature of the coalition's collapse poisoned relations between its former members still further, sowing the seeds for the failure of subsequent efforts to oppose Napoleon. Europe was plunged into a terrible predicament. The peace ending the war was unstable and liable to collapse at any moment, but the great powers were unlikely to combine to form an effective alliance pursuing clear and positive goals. Napoleon rapidly returned to his preoccupation with the war with Britain and failed to consider how to establish a durable peace on the continent, even one that suited him. The horrors of the War of 1805 merely set the stage for even greater calamities to come.

Conclusion

Napoleon's 1805 campaign and the peace agreements that concluded it ended the old order in Europe and began the transformation of the continent. During the war the major powers conducted diplomacy on the basis of business as usual. The Russians saw the war as a luxury to be pursued or abandoned depending on what best suited their interests. The British continued the policy of supporting continental coalitions against the French Revolution without committing their own main forces to the fight, and only insofar as those coalitions showed real promise of success. The Prussians clung to a neutrality policy nearly a decade old, abandoning it only when the war was already under way. The Austrians continued to find themselves drawn into wars they preferred not to fight. But the War of 1805 changed all that and paved the way for even more dramatic changes to come.

First and foremost, the destruction of the Austrian army and the Peace of Pressburg fundamentally altered the balance of power in Europe. Austria was no longer the dominant power in Germany and the inevitable bulwark of any anti-French coalition. Deprived of the Tyrol, Vorarlberg, Salzburg, all of her Italian possessions, Istria, and Dalmatia, Austria, on January 1, 1806, was weaker than she had been for centuries. And Napoleon dispossessed Francis of a meaningful voice in the affairs of the "third Germany," those minor German states that did not belong to Prussia or Austria. This situation was unprecedented since the time the Habsburgs had gained the Holy Roman crown.

The establishment of France as the dominant power in western Germany was no less dramatic and earth-shaking. Louis XIV at the height of his power did not get within sight of the influence Napoleon wielded in Germany in 1806. Bavaria, Baden, and Württemberg were loyal client states of France, the various appanages of the Holy Roman Empire were destroyed, and Napoleon even acquired German territory to give as a reward to his own French marshals. This development created the preconditions for the Franco–Prussian War of 1870–1871, for henceforth France claimed a dominant role in the affairs of southwestern Germany, and German unification required her consent or defeat.

Prussia's future role in this new Germany remained unclear. Frederick William finally abandoned the neutrality policy, only to have Haugwitz betray him back into it at the last moment for his own purposes. The king's initial inclination toward war at the worst possible moment for Napoleon did not escape the emperor of the French. He accepted Haugwitz's about-face with apparent goodwill, but his trust in Frederick William collapsed. The Prussian king recognized that he had exposed himself completely for no gain at all. The seeds of future tension, if not further conflict, had already begun to sprout.

Alexander learned mostly the wrong lessons from this war. His opposition to Napoleon grew and was complicated by fear. He was no longer eager to cross swords with his upstart brother emperor, but he was also in no mood to abandon his efforts to defend Europe against further French depredations. The events of 1804–1805, however, badly undermined his willingness to trust any ally except Britain. Austerlitz and Pressburg left a bad taste in the tsar's mouth, and he seemed to believe some of his subordinates' exaggerated claims about Austrian perfidy. He was not harsh enough, on the other hand, with Frederick William, who had allowed Haugwitz to defect from the coalition on his behalf at the worst possible moment. The tsar's bad experience with the alliance of 1805 would make it ever harder for him to trust the same coalition partners again in the future.

The British suffered from the same problem in even greater degree. The recent failure to check France by proxy called the whole enterprise into question once more. Napoleon's victory did enormous political harm to the Pitt government, apparently even undermining the aged prime minister's health. Worst of all, the Peace of Schönbrunn began the process of turning Prussia from ally into enemy by requiring Frederick William to seize Hanover on his own behalf, rather than on behalf of its rightful monarch. Napoleon thereby completed the process his military and other diplomatic victories had begun, shattering the coalition and poisoning relations among his potential enemies for years to come.

What did Napoleon learn from the events of 1805? Mainly that he had destroyed the most important potential restraints on his power in western Europe. He had begun to toy with the creation of an empire in 1804, but the events of 1805 rapidly eclipsed that development in his mind. In the aftermath of Austerlitz, Pressburg, and Schönbrunn, the emperor of the French was ready to turn all his energies to the establishment of a true empire worthy of his ambitions. The War of 1805 and the peace agreements that ended it mark the true beginning of the *Grande Empire*.

Appendix

The Battle
of Dürnstein

The account of the Battle of Dürnstein given in the text differs significantly from the only other detailed accounts of that battle, all of which are Austrian.[1] The Austrian accounts assert that Dokhturov's Column was subdivided into multiple groups (Kotzebue mentions three; the others mention four), and that FML Schmitt commanded one of those groups. According to these accounts, Schmitt led approximately six battalions on a long trek up the Danube, past the Pfaffental defile, down which Dokhturov's forces marched to the Heudürrgraben defile further upstream. There, they claim, Schmitt debouched with his forces at the decisive moment, taking Dupont's division in the flank and rear and precipitating its flight.

This account cannot be accepted in light of the Russian sources. None of the Austrian accounts made use of them, either because they were not available (they were not published until 1951) or for linguistic reasons (they are all in Russian).* According to the Russian sources, Dokhturov split his command roughly in half, leaving part under the command of General Urusov in the vicinity of Scheibenhof and taking the other part with him. Dokhturov's report accounts fully for all of the units under his command, making Kirchhammer's contention that there are some battalions unaccounted for untenable.[2] If Schmitt had command of any of these forces, then it is remarkable that none of the Russians who believed that they had command of them mentioned that fact.[3] Nor do the accounts of Urusov and Gvozdev tally with the notion that Schmitt had taken a substantial body of troops and descended with it on Dupont's flank and rear.

---

*Egger notes that "Russian depictions, apart from the works of Mikhailovskii-Danilevskii, were not available." Rainer Egger, *Das Gefecht bei Dürnstein-Loiben, 1805. Militärhistorische Schriftenreihe*, vol. 3, 3rd ed. (Vienna: Heeresgeschichtliches Museum/Militärwissenschaftliches Institut, 1986), p. 33. Kotzebue describes his sources carefully (Von Kotzebue, *Versuch einer Beschreibung der Schlacht*, pp. iii–x), and they are all Austrian civilians present at the time of the battle. The other two articles do not list their sources, but their authors did not make use of Russian materials (and both appeared long before the Russian document sets were published).

Most damaging of all to this version is the fact that it would have made utter nonsense of Dupont's account.[4] If Dupont had suffered an attack on his flank and rear by a force of six battalions and somehow withstood it, it is inconceivable that he would have failed to note such an occurrence proudly. Considering that he had with him only one line regiment, one light infantry regiment, and a regiment of Hussars, however, it is highly unlikely that he could have withstood the force of six Russian battalions attacking his flank at all while two more held the road to the front.* Bottled up in a narrow defile by the two battalions of the Viatka Regiment Dokhturov had stationed there, Dupont's troops would surely have been routed and exterminated if Schmitt had shown up with such a large force in their rear. None of the French, Russian, or Austrian accounts, however, makes mention of such a slaughter, and the French tallies indicate that Dupont lost 106 men killed or wounded.[5]

The final problem is that the account of Schmitt's movement is unnecessary to explain the outcome of the fight between Dupont's troops and the Russians barring the road to Dürnstein. Comparing Dupont's and Gvozdev's accounts provides a coherent and congruent picture of the fight. Dupont's lead light troops made contact with Gvozdev's two line battalions established across the very narrow defile between the river and high ground to the their right. The French were held. Dupont then sent forward the 32nd Line Infantry Regiment and attempted to outflank the Russians along the high ground. Pushed back, Gvozdev retreated slowly and played for time. He reports that he received the reinforcement of a battalion of the Briansk Regiment, which had been left near Scheibenhof with Urusov, at about this time, which enabled him to stabilize the position and hold. The Russian accounts imply that they continued to hold their ground, but the French accounts make it clear that they beat the Russians back from the main Danube road and effected a linkup between Gazan's battered division and Dupont's.† Adding Schmitt's supposed timely arrival to this narrative simply obscures it and forces us to dismiss four contemporaneous commanders' reports of the fight and rely instead on ex post facto logical reconstructions.

If this is the case, then what happened to Schmitt, who was killed fighting gallantly at this battle? The likeliest explanation is that he or Urusov noticed that Gvozdev was in trouble—and it is very easy to observe events near Wad-

---

*Of Dupont's division the following units participated in battle: 1st Hussars Regiment, 9th Light Infantry Regiment, and 32nd Line Infantry Regiment. Alombert-Goget, *Dürrenstein*, p. 130 n. 2.

†Talandier's account, in Alombert-Goget, *Dürrenstein*, pp. 117–118; Taupin's account, p. 123. Even Mikhailovskii-Danilevskii (*Opisanie pervoi voiny Imperatora Aleksandra s Napoleonom v 1805-m godu.* [St. Petersbug: Independent Corps of the Internal Guard Press, 1844], p. 106) concedes that Dokhturov was compelled to abandon the road and let the French escape. Kutuzov's report to Francis implies the same: the victory "would have been even more complete without the arrival of darkness which prevented us not from pursuing the enemy but from taking the entire corps." Kutuzov to Francis, 12 November 1805, KA AFA 1805 Deutschland, XI/46¾.

stein (where Gvozdev and Dupont were facing off) from the Schloss Dürn-stein—or else Gvozdev sent word back to Dokhturov, Urusov, or Schmitt. Dokhturov or Urusov then presumably decided to send the reinforcements about which Gvozdev testifies.

It would have been the most natural thing in the world for Schmitt to accompany those reinforcements. Gvozdev was a junior commander in a very tight spot; Schmitt was a senior, talented, and experienced officer who was not evidently engaged in serious fighting or maneuvering at the time. Throughout the course of the day Kutuzov regularly sent adjutants and senior officers alone or with reinforcements to help junior officers in trouble near Stein. No doubt Dokhturov or Urusov did the same by sending Schmitt to Gvozdev.[6]

Once arrived at Wadstein, Schmitt would have had all the hard fighting he could have wanted. The odds were roughly even—three French line and three light infantry battalions against three Russian line infantry battalions stretched across a narrow defile. We have Dupont's testimony that the fighting was brutal and degenerated into a wild, incomprehensible melee from which he had to order his subordinates to disengage their troops man by man from the enemy. Schmitt no doubt fought gallantly, spurring the men on, and died at some point in that melee.

This revision of the account does not in any way detract from Schmitt's heroism or his contributions to the battle—important points since he was the only hero of this campaign for the Austrians. We must accept, however, that it is extremely unlikely that Schmitt led a large column of troops in this fight.

Notes

Introduction to Napoleon and Europe

1. Carl von Clausewitz, *On War*, trans. and ed. Michael Howard and Peter Paret, paperback ed. (Princeton: Princeton University Press, 1989), p. 608 and esp. n. 1.

Volume Introduction

1. The centrality of Poland in the minds of these rulers, as well as the relative insignificance of France, is amply demonstrated by T. C. W. Blanning, *The French Revolutionary Wars* (New York: Arnold, 1996); and *The Origin of the French Revolutionary Wars* (New York: Longman, 1986).

Chapter 1   The Peace: Lunéville, Paris, Amiens, 1801–1802

1. See David Chandler, *Campaigns of Napoleon* (New York: MacMillan, 1966), pp. 205–249, for a standard treatment.
2. Total exports increased twentyfold between 1780 and 1800, while the value of the grain exported from all of European Russia increased by only four times in the same period. Ragsdale, *Paul I*, p. 32.
3. See I. S. Bliokh, *Finansy Rossii XIX stoletiia, istoriia—statistika* (St. Petersburg: M. M. Stasiulevich, 1882), vol. 1, for a discussion of the state of Russia's finances at the beginning of the nineteenth century. As an example of the parlous condition of those finances, Bliokh points out that the more than 400 million rubles worth of debt and paper money issued by 1801 were equal to more than ten years of the ordinary income of the Russian state (p. 59). In 1801 the Russian state took in about 77 million assignat (paper) rubles, while it spent 107 million, making up the difference by issuing more paper money. In that year (in which Russian forces were engaged in no serious combat), expenditure on the military topped 46 million assignat rubles. There can hardly be a clearer argument for Russia's urgent need for a general pacification of Europe, but only on terms that did not otherwise harm Russia's economy (Bliokh, 1:84–85).
4. See Roderick E. McGrew, "Paul I and the Knights of Malta," in Ragsdale, ed., *Paul I*, 44–75.
5. See T. C. W. Blanning, *The French Revolutionary Wars* (New York: Arnold, 1996) for a narrative of this campaign, its causes, and its consequences.
6. See David Chandler, *The Campaigns of Napoleon* (New York: Macmillan, 1966), for a detailed and now classic account from the French perspective. Blanning, *French Revolutionary Wars,* does an excellent job putting the campaign in context, while Gunther Rothenberg, *Napoleon's Great Adversary: Archduke Charles and the Austrian Army, 1792–1814* (New York: Sarpedon, 1982), provides an Austrian perspective and context.

7. Emperor Francis to Cobenzl, February 21, 1801, cited in August Fournier, *Gentz und Cobenzl: Geschichte der österreichischen Diplomatie in den Jahren 1801–1805, nach neuen Quellen* (Vienna: Wilhelm Braumüller, 1880), p. 14.

8. Currency in circulation had increased from 27.52 million guilders to 91.861 million between 1793 and 1798; the annual deficit increased from 28.59 million to 56.666 million, and the total debt had increased from 390.13 million to 572.044 million. Adolf Beer, *Die Finanzen Oesterreichs im XIX. Jahrhundert, nach archivalischen Quellen* (Prague: F. Tempsky, 1877), pp. 6–7.

9. Military expenditures ranged between 69.5 million guilders in 1793 and a high of 110 million in 1797, not considering the period of the War of the Second Coalition. By contrast, expenditure on all internal programs averaged 10 million guilders annually. Beer, *Finanzen Oesterreichs*, p. 7.

10. Napoleon to Joseph, 21 January 1801, *Correspondance de Napoléon Ier* (Paris: Henrie Plon, 1861), doc. 5315. Hereafter *Corr. de Nap.*

11. Napoleon to Joseph, 13 February 1801, *Corr. de Nap.*, doc. 5367.

12. See, for example, Count Rostopchin's note of 8 October 1800 in SIRIO, vol. 70, doc. 4, pp. 10–11. The conditions are repeated in numerous other notes and dispatches throughout that correspondence.

13. See, for instance, Napoleon's response to Murat's proposal for an armistice of 20 February 1801, in Napoleon to Berthier, 19 February 1801, *Corr. de Nap.*, doc. 5399.

14. Report of Lucchesini, Paris, 17 April 1801, in Paul Bailleu, ed. *Preußen und Frankreich 1795 bis 1807: Diplomatische Correspondenzen*, Publicationen aus den königlichen preussischen Archiven, 29 (Leipzig, 1887), vol. 2, doc. 30.

15. Brendan Simms, *The Impact of Napoleon: Prussian High Politics, Foreign Policy, and the Crisis of the Executive, 1797–1806* (New York: Cambridge University Press, 1997), pp. 102–105.

16. Bailleu, ed., *Preußen und Frankreich*, 1:496, quoted in Simms, *Impact*, p. 82.

17. Simms, *Impact*, p. 85.

18. Napoleon Bonaparte, Note for the Minister of Foreign Relations, Paris, 10 October 1800, in Bailleu, *Preußen und Frankreich*, vol. 2, doc. 4.

19. Report of Lucchesini, 25 January 1801, in Bailleu, *Preußen und Frankreich*, vol. 2, doc. 14.

20. Haugwitz to the Duke of Brunswick, 8 February 1801, in Bailleu, *Preußen und Frankreich*, vol. 2, doc. 16.

21. Simms, *Impact*, p. 84.

22. Haugwitz Memorandum, 21 August 1801, in Bailleu, *Preußen und Frankreich*, vol. 2, doc. 41.

23. Haugwitz Memorandum, 21 August 1801, in Bailleu, *Preußen und Frankreich*, vol. 2, doc. 41.

24. Alexander is the subject of numerous biographies, including Janet M. Hartley, *Alexander I* (New York: Longman, 1994); Allen McConnell, *Tsar Alexander I: Paternalistic Reformer* (Arlington Heights, Ill.: Harlan Davidson, 1970); and N. V. Shil'der, *Imperator Aleksandr Pervyi: ego zhizn' i tsarstvovanie* (St. Petersburg: Izdanie A. S. Suvorina, 1897). This section draws heavily on these sources and on Isabel de Madariaga, *Russia in the Age of Catherine the Great* (New Haven: Yale University Press, 1981).

25. Both documents can be found in Aleksandr Trachevskii, ed., *Diplomaticheskiia snosheniia Rossii s Frantsiei v epokhu Napoleona I, Tom Pervyi, 1800–1802*, vol. 1 (SIRIO, vol. 70); "Rescript to Kolychev," 28 April 1801, doc. 62, pp. 125–137; and "Instruction to Morkov, sent to Paris," 9 July 1801, doc. 93, pp. 201–222.

26. Almost every letter Kolychev wrote back to the Russian court warns of Napoleon's treachery and limitless ambitions. See SIRIO, vol. 70, passim. Alexander warned Morkov that Napoleon might prove impossible and that all Morkov could do in that circumstance would be to await more propitious circumstances for negotiation. See "Instruction to Morkov, sent to Paris," 9 July 1801, SIRIO, vol. 70, doc. 93, pp. 201–222.

27. Instructions to Morkov, 9 July 1801, SIRIO, vol. 70, doc. 93, p. 210.

28. The treaty is document 488 in Martens, *Recueil*, 13:263.

29. The secret protocols are document 489 in Martens, *Recueil*, 13:266.

30. Rescript to Morkov, 16 November 1801, SIRIO, vol. 70, doc. 117, p. 286.
31. Peace of Florence between Naples and France, 28 March 1801, in Michel Kerautret, *Les grands traités du Consulat (1799–1804): Documents diplomatiques du Consulat et de l'Empire* (Paris: Nouveau Monde Editions/Fondation Napoléon, 2002), vol. 1, doc. 23.
32. Report of A. R. Vorontsov, 1 June 1803, SIRIO, vol. 77, doc. 62, pp. 153–157.

Chapter 2   War Renewed, 1801–1803

1. See, for instance, Kurakin to Morkov, 12 February 1802, SIRIO, vol. 70, doc. 135; and Rescript to Morkov, 8/20 February 1802, SIRIO, vol. 70, doc. 141.
2. Conference of the Vice Chancellor with Count Saurau, 12/24 March 1802, SIRIO, vol. 70, doc. 148.
3. See AKV, vol. 18, doc. 117, V. P. Kochubei to S. R. Vorontsov, 2 June 1802, p. 275, for Kochubei's account of the meeting. Czartoryskii's view of the matter can be found in Adam Gielgud, ed., *Memoirs of Prince Adam Czartoryski* (New York: Arno, 1971), 1:281–283. See also N. K. Schil'der, *Imperator Alexander Pervyie: ego zhizn' i tsarstvovanie* (St. Petersburg: A. S. Suvorin, 1897), 2:89–92.
4. Queen Louise left a detailed and glowing description of the meeting, reproduced as "Zusammenkunft in Memel," in Paul Bailleu, ed., *Briefwechsel König Freidrich Wilhelm's III und der Königin Luise mit Kaiser Alexander I,* Publikationen aus den k. Preußischen Staatsarchiven (Leipzig: 1900), 75:531–536.
5. See Albert Sorel, *L'Europe et la révolution française: Sixième partie: La trêve—Lunéville et Amiens, 1800–1805* (Paris: Libraire Plon, n.d.), pp. 232–237, esp. 236.
6. To Talleyrand, Minister of Foreign Affairs, 3 April 1802, *Corr. de Nap.*, doc. 6019.
7. August Fournier, *Gentz und Cobenzl: Geschichte der österreichischen Diplomatie in den Jahren 1801–1805, nach neuen Quellen* (Vienna: Wilhelm Braumüller, 1880), p. 34.
8. Morkov to the Court, 18/30 April 1802, SIRIO, vol. 70, doc. 158, pp. 397–399.
9. Morkov to the Court, 23 May/4 June 1802, SIRIO, vol. 70, doc. 169, p. 422.
10. The agreement can be found as Agreement between Morkov and Talleyrand, 22 May/3 June 1802, SIRIO, vol. 70, doc. 168, pp. 414–415; and Joint Note of Morkov and Talleyrand to the Imperial Diet at Regensburg, Paris, 22 May (3 June) 1802, in A. L. Narochnitskii, ed., *Vneshniaia politika rossii XIX i nachala XX veka: Dokumenty Rossiiskogo Ministerstva Inostrannykh Del,* 1st series, vol. 1 (Moscow: Gosudarstvennoe Izdatel'stvo Politicheskoi Literatury, 1960; hereafter VPR), doc. 81, pp. 221–230.
11. See, for example, Alexander I to Ambassador to the Sardinian Kingdom Ia. G. Lizakevich, 16 (28) May 1802, VPR, vol. I, doc. 77, pp. 205–207.
12. See Patricia Kennedy Grimsted, *The Foreign Ministers of Alexander I: Political Attitudes and the Conduct of Russian Diplomacy, 1801–1825* (Berkeley: University of California Press, 1969), esp. pp. 101–103.
13. Grimsted, *Foreign Ministers*, pp. 91–100.
14. See, for example, Alexander I to Ambassador to the Hague G. O. Shtakel'berg, 16 (28) May 1802, VPR, vol. I, doc. 78, pp. 207–215. The basic outlines of the policy Alexander pursued following Vorontsov's appointment are already apparent in this policy guideline sent to the new ambassador to the Batavian Republic.
15. See François Furet, *Revolutionary France, 1770–1880*, trans. Antonia Nevill (Malden, Mass.: Blackwell, 1999), pp. 226ff.; also Louis Bergeron, *France Under Napoleon*, trans. R. R. Palmer (Princeton: Princeton University Press, 1990), passim.
16. See Napoleon to Rear Admiral Decrès, Minister of the Marine and of the Colonies, 15 January 1803, *Corr. de Nap.*, doc. 6544, for his detailed instructions concerning the expedition sent to India under General Decaen. Napoleon to the King of Spain, 27 November 1802, *Corr. de Nap.*, doc. 6455, contains an offer of territories in Italy for Florida. W. M. Sloane, "Napoleon's Plans for a Colonial System," *American Historical Review,* vol. 4. (April 1899), pp. 439–455, contains a good summary of Napoleon's colonial activity.

17. See Napoleon to Talleyrand, 28 December 1802, *Corr. de Nap.*, doc. 6513, for the violent protest against prominent émigrés in Britain and Napoleon to Talleyrand, 17 November 1802, *Corr. de Nap.*, doc. 6429, for a more moderate demand made of Prussia in this regard.

18. Critical documents relating to the crisis in Switzerland are Declaration to the Five Deputies of Switzerland, 11 December 1802, *Corr. de Nap.*, doc. 6483; Conference That the Ten Deputies, Named by the Two Parties, Had with the First Consul on 29 January 1803, *Corr. de Nap.*, doc. 6560; and Act of Mediation of Switzerland, 19 February 1803, *Corr. de Nap.*, doc. 6590.

19. Napoleon to Alexander I, 20 October 1802, SIRIO, vol. 70, doc. 211, pp. 522–523.

20. Alexander to Napoleon, 21 October 1802, SIRIO, vol. 70, doc. 213, pp. 531–532.

21. A. R. Vorontsov to Morkov, 9 November 1802, SIRIO, vol. 70, doc. 218, pp. 543–546; Alexander to Napoleon, 14 November 1802, SIRIO, vol. 70, doc. 221, pp. 552–553.

22. Napoleon to Talleyrand, 4 November 1802, *Corr. de Nap.*, doc. 6414.

23. Napoleon to Talleyrand, 28 December 1802, *Corr. de Nap.*, doc. 6513.

24. Napoleon to Talleyrand, 6 October 1802, *Corr. de Nap.*, doc. 6364.

25. Sorel, *L'Europe et la Révolution Française*, p. 269.

26. Napoleon to Talleyrand, 29 August 1802, *Corr. de Nap.*, doc. 6276, and Napoleon to Citizen Sébastiani, 5 September 1802, *Corr. de Nap.*, doc. 6308.

27. See his instructions to General Decaen, commander of French forces in India, in Napoleon to Rear Admiral Decrès, 15 January 1803, *Corr. de Nap.*, 8:176–178.

28. Whitworth to Hawkesbury, 21 February 1803, *Papers Relative to the Discussion with France in 1802 and 1803* (London: A. Strahan, 1803), doc. 38, pp. 102–111. This collection was published anonymously sometime after May 1803. It was clearly designed to serve propagandistic purposes, but a number of the letters and documents can be substantiated with other sources, as this one accords, for example, with the description of this conversation given by Lord Whitworth to Russian Ambassador Morkov, reproduced in Morkov to A. R. Vorontsov, 28 February 1803, SIRIO, vol. 77, doc. 22, pp. 46–49.

29. Morkov to A. R. Vorontsov, 28 February 1803, SIRIO, vol. 77, doc. 22, pp. 46–49.

30. Morkov to the Court, 16 March 1803, SIRIO, vol. 77, doc. 29, pp. 63–68.

31. See Stanford J. Shaw, *Between Old and New: The Ottoman Empire Under Sultan Selim III, 1789–1807* (Cambridge: Harvard University Press, 1971), pt. 4, for the Ottoman perspective on this problem; A. M. Stanislavskaia, *Rossiia i Gretsii v kontse XVIII-nachale XIX veka* (Moscow: Nauka, 1976); and Roger V. Paxton, "Russian Foreign Policy and the First Serbian Uprising: Alliances, Apprehensions, and Autonomy, 1804–1807," in Wayne S. Vucinich, ed., *The First Serbian Uprising, 1804–1813* (New York: Columbia University Press, 1982), for the Russian perspective. Many of the relevant documents are in VPR, vols. I and II.

32. Consul General in Jassy A. A. Zherve to Minister of Foreign Affairs A. R. Vorontsov, 4 February 1803, VPR, vol. I, doc. 154.

33. Ambassador to Constantinople A. Ia. Italinskii to Minister of Foreign Affairs A. R. Vorontsov, 16 February 1803, VPR, vol. I, doc. 155.

34. Plenipotentiary Representative to the Republic of Seven United Islands G. D. Mocenigo to Alexander I, 26 January 1803, VPR, vol. I, doc 150.

35. A. R. Vorontsov to Italinskii, 3 January 1803, VPR, vol. I, doc. 147.

36. A. R. Vorontsov to Italinskii, 28 November 1802, VPR, vol. I, doc. 137.

37. Morkov to the Court, 16 March 1803, SIRIO, vol. 77, doc. 29.

38. SVM, vol. 4, bk 1, pt. 2, sec. 2., pp. 271–274.

39. SVM, 4.1.2.2, pp. 113ff.

40. Memorandum of Quartermaster General Sukhtelen to the Military Commission of 15 June 1802, reprinted in SVM, 4.1.2.2, pp. 159–172.

41. Minister of Foreign Affairs A. R. Vorontsov to Ambassador to London S. R. Vorontsov, 19 November 1802, VPR, vol. I, doc. 132.
42. See, e.g., Grimsted, *Foreign Ministers.*
43. A. R. Vorontsov to S. R. Vorontsov, 24 March 1803, VPR, vol. I, doc. 162.
44. See A. R. Vorontsov to S. R. Vorontsov, 24 March 1803, VPR, vol. I, doc. 162, for a discussion of the weakness of the British cabinet at that time.
45. Report of A. R. Vorontsov, 1 June 1803, SIRIO, vol. 77, doc. 62.
46. SVM, 4.1.2.2, pp. 273–275.

Chapter 3   Alexander's Turn Against Napoleon, 1803–1804

1. A. W. Ward, G. W. Prothero, and Stanley Leathes, eds., *Cambridge Modern History* (New York: Macmillan, 1906) 9:209; Edouard Desbrière, *Projets et tentatives de débarquement aux Iles Britanniques, 1793–1805* (Paris: Librairie Militaire R. Chapelot, 1902), 3:36–38.
2. Ward, Prothero, and Leathes, eds., *Cambridge Modern History*, 9:210.
3. Desbrière, *Projets et tentatives*, 3:38–39.
4. Ward, Prothero, and Leathes, eds., *Cambridge Modern History*, 9:211.
5. Christopher D. Hall, *British Strategy in the Napoleonic War, 1803–1815* (New York: Manchester University Press, 1992), p. 104.
6. See, e.g., Napoleon to Berthier, 22 May 1803, *Corr. de Nap.* 6760 and 6761, 23 May 1803; *Corr. de Nap.* 6764, 6 June 1803; *Corr. de Nap.* 6793 and 6794, and others.
7. Napoleon to Rear Admiral Decrès, Minister of the Marine and Colonies, 21 May 1803, *Corr. de Nap.*, 6758 for the letters of marque, and 3 June 1803, *Corr. de Nap.*, 6783, for the naval buildup.
8. Message to the Senate, 20 May 1803, *Corr. de Nap.*, 6755.
9. Words Addressed by the First Consul to the Members of the Senate of the Tribunate, and of a Deputation of the *Corps Législatif,* 25 May 1803, *Corr. de Nap.*, 6766.
10. Extract from the registers of the deliberations of the Government of the French Republic, 22 May 1803, cited in Desbrière, *Projets et tentatives*, 3.63; Napoleon to Citizen Marescalchi, Minister of Foreign Relations of the Republic of Italy, 22 May 1803, *Corr. de Nap.*, 6759.
11. Napoleon to General Berthier, 13 May 1803, *Corr. de Nap.*, 6742, for Hanover; Minister of Foreign Affairs to the French Ambassador at Naples, 13 May 1803, cited in Ch. Auriol, *La France, l'Angleterre et Naples de 1803 à 1806* (Paris: Librairie Plon, 1904), 1:275–281 for Naples.
12. Minister of War to General Gouvion Saint-Cyr, Instructions to General Saint-Cyr, 23 May 1803, reproduced in Auriol, *La France, l'Angleterre et Naples*, 1:295.
13. Decision, 20 June 1803, *Corr. de Nap.*, 6840.
14. Napoleon to Citizen Regnier, Grand Judge, Minister of Justice, 25 May 1803, *Corr. de Nap.*, 6767.
15. Napoleon to Citizen Regnier, 4 June 1803, *Corr. de Nap.*, 6786.
16. Napoleon to General Berthier, 4 June 1803, *Corr. de Nap.*, 6791.
17. Napoleon to Citizen Regnier, 22 June 1803, *Corr. de Nap.*, 6843, and 27 June 1803, *Corr. de Nap.*, 6861.
18. Napoleon to Citizen Regnier, 3 June 1803, *Corr. de Nap.*, 6780, 6781, 6782; 24 June 1803, *Corr. de Nap.*, 6855; and 27 June 1803, *Corr. de Nap.*, 6861.
19. Ward, Prothero, and Leathes, eds., *Cambridge Modern History*, 9:212.
20. David Chandler, *The Campaigns of Napoleon* (New York: Macmillan, 1966), pp. 322–325.
21. See Harold C. Deutsch, "Napoleonic Policy and the Project of a Descent upon England," *Journal of Modern History*, vol. 2, no. 4 (December 1930), pp. 541–568, for a well-researched discussion of this issue, concluding that Napoleon's preparations for an invasion were real.

22. Napoleon to General Berthier, 14 June 1803, *Corr. de Nap.,* 6814. Preliminary projects for the formation of this army dated from April 18. See Desbrière, *Projets et tentatives,* 3:179ff.

23. See letters to Berthier and Cambacérès in this period, *Corr. de Nap.,* 6869–6892.

24. First Consul to the Minister of War, 28 August 1803; reproduced in Desbrière, *Projets et tentatives,* 3:190–202.

25. Auguste Frédéric Louis Viesse de Marmont, *Mémoires du Maréchal Marmont, Duc de Raguse de 1792 à 1841* (Paris: Perrotin, 1857), 2:208. See also Mathieu Dumas, *Souvenirs du Lieutenant Général Comte Mathieu Dumas de 1770 à 1836* (Paris: Librairie de Charles Gosselin, 1839), 3:240–241.

26. Napoleon to Rear Admiral Ganteaume, 7 December 1803, *Corr. de Nap.,* 7359.

27. Some flavor of this training can be found in, for example, the Order of the Day of the Camp of St. Omer, July 3, 1804, which specifies daily target practice with live rounds (most unusual for a peacetime army), and the Order of the Day for July 28, which refers to frequent maneuvers at the division, brigade, and battalion level, also exceptional practice in a peacetime force. AN, AF IV, 1602, plaquette 3, pp. 6, 14.

28. Napoleon to Citizen Talleyrand, 14 August 1803, *Corr. de Nap.,* 7007, contains the ultimatum to which the Spanish succumbed. See also Desbrière, *Projets et tentatives,* vol. 3, for the dual purpose of the camp at Bayonne.

29. Georges Lefebvre and Henry F. Stockhold, trans., *Napoleon: From 18 Brumaire to Tilsit, 1799–1807* (New York: Columbia University Press, 1969), 1:179–180.

30. Alexander was aware of these issues. See Rescript to Morkov, 5 June 1803, SIRIO, vol. 77, doc. 64, pp. 159–164.

31. Envoy in Berlin M. M. Alopeus to Prussian Minister of Foreign Affairs Haugwitz, 31 May 1803, VPR, vol. 1, doc. 181, p. 434.

32. Minister of Foreign Affairs A. R. Vorontsov to Envoy in Berlin M. M. Alopeus, 16 June 1803, VPR, vol. 1, doc. 187, pp. 447–449.

33. See above, Chapter 2.

34. Project of a basis of a Russo–Prussian convention about the Joint Defense of Northern Germany from French Aggression, 4 July 1803, VPR, vol. 1, doc. 195, pp. 463–465.

35. Alexander I to Envoy to Berlin M. M. Alopeus, July 4, 1803, VPR, vol. 1, pp. 459–461.

36. "Duroc: Account of My Mission to Berlin," March 20–27, 1803; Paul Bailleu, ed., *Preußen und Frankreich von 1795 bis 1807: Diplomatische Correspondenzen,* pt. 2, 1800–1807 (Leipzig: S. Hirzel, 1887), doc. 94, pp. 127–132.

37. Simms, *Impact,* pp. 84–86.

38. See Frederick William to Lucchesini, 25 March 1803, Bailleu, *Preußen und Frankreich,* vol. 2, doc. 96, pp. 133–136; 28 May 1803, doc. 102, pp. 145–146.

39. Talleyrand to Laforest, 17 May 1803, in Bailleu, *Preußen und Frankreich,* vol. 2, doc. 101, pp. 142–145.

40. See, for example, Lucchesini's Report, 29 May 1803, in Bailleu, *Preußen und Frankreich,* vol. 2, doc. 104, pp. 148–151.

41. Haugwitz to Frederick William III, 4 June 1803, in Bailleu, *Preußen und Frankreich,* vol. 2, doc. 106, pp. 152–154; Frederick William III to Lucchesini, 6 June 1803; doc. 107, pp. 155–156. The context of Prussia's decisionmaking in this crisis and its subsequent consequences will be considered more fully in Chapter 8.

42. Talleyrand to Morkov, 10 June 1803, SIRIO, vol. 77, pp. 196–198.

43. Oral Note of Morkov to Talleyrand, 6 June 1803, SIRIO, vol. 77, doc. 68, pp. 170–172.

44. Morkov to S. R. Vorontsov, 13 June 1803, SIRIO, vol. 77, doc. 78, pp. 203–205.

45. Morkov to the Court, 14 June 1803, SIRIO, vol. 77, doc. 80, pp. 208–213.

46. Talleyrand to Hédouville, 19 June 1803, SIRIO, vol. 77, doc. 83, pp. 219–221.

47. Report of A. R. Vorontsov, 7 July 1803, SIRIO, vol. 77, no. 99, pp. 246–250.

48. This proposal was sent forward to Paris in slightly modified form on July 19. Project of Preliminary Articles, 19 July 1803, SIRIO, vol. 77, no. 115, pp. 282–285.

49. Hédouville to Talleyrand, 10 July 1803, SIRIO, vol. 77, no. 103, pp. 254–261.

50. Talleyrand to Morkov, 23 July 1803, SIRIO, vol. 77, no. 121, pp. 291–292.

51. Talleyrand to Morkov, 28 July 1803, SIRIO, vol. 77, no. 122.

52. Bonaparte to Emperor Alexander, 29 July 1803, SIRIO, vol. 77, no. 123, pp. 299–300; also in *Corr. de Nap.,* 6957.

53. Talleyrand to Hédouville, 18 July 1803, SIRIO, vol. 77, no. 109, pp. 270–271.

54. A. R. Vorontsov to Chargé d'Affairs in Vienna I. O. Anstett, 18 October 1803, in VPR, vol. 1, doc. 222, pp. 522–525.

55. See Adolf Beer, *Die Finanzen Oesterreichs im XIX. Jahrhundert, nach archivalischen Quellen* (Prague: F. Tempsky, 1877), pp. 3–13.

56. Gunther Rothenberg, *Napoleon's Great Adversary: Archduke Charles and the Austrian Army, 1792–1814* (New York: Sarpedon, 1995), p. 87.

57. Rothenberg, *Napoleon's Great Adversary,* is the only work in English that focuses on Charles. The standard German sources are two multivolume biographies: Oskar Criste, *Erzherzog Carl von Österreich* (Vienna: Wilhelm Braumüller, 1912); and Moriz Edlen von Angeli, *Erzherzog Carl von Österriech als Feldherr und Heeresorganisator* (Vienna: Wilhelm Braumüller, 1897).

58. Rothenberg, *Napoleon's Great Adversary,* p. 91.

59. Rothenberg, *Napoleon's Great Adversary,* p. 87; Criste, *Erzherzog Carl von Österreich,* 2:182–183.

60. See Frederick W. Kagan, *The Military Reforms of Nicholas I: The Origins of the Modern Russian Army* (New York: St. Martin's, 1999), for a brief discussion of the administrative reforms of Alexander's time and for references to the essential works on this subject.

61. Cobenzl to Colloredo, 1 September 1803, Fournier, *Gentz und Cobenzl,* p. 81 n. 3. There is no indication in the documents reproduced in VPR, vol. 1, of this meeting.

62. Cobenzl to Colloredo, 23 September 1803, in Fournier, *Gentz und Cobenzl,* p. 203.

63. Instruction to Metternich, 5 November 1803, in Fournier, *Gentz und Cobenzl,* pp. 203–214.

64. Instruction to Metternich, 5 November 1803, in Fournier, *Gentz und Cobenzl,* pp. 203–214, esp. p. 208.

65. The implementation of this policy of delay is seen clearly in the report of the Russian chargé d'affaires in Vienna, I. O. Anstett, to A. R. Vorontsov of 16 November 1803 (VPR, vol. 1, doc. 230, pp. 545–548), in which Anstett gives a detailed description of a conversation he had with Cobenzl.

66. A. R. Vorontsov to Alexander I, 24 November 1803, VPR, vol. 1, doc. 231, pp. 550–555.

67. Chargé d'affaires in Vienna I. O. Anstett to A. R. Vorontsov, 16 November 1803, VPR, vol. 1, doc. 230, pp. 545–548.

68. A. R. Vorontsov to Austrian Ambassador in St. Petersburg Stadion, 1 January 1804, VPR, vol. 1, doc. 246, pp. 594–599.

69. Adolf Beer, *Österreich und Russland in den Jahren 1804 und 1805* (Archiv für österreichische Geschichte, 1875), 53:138.

70. SVM, 4.1.2.2, p. 283.

71. SVM, 4.1.2.2, pp. 284–285.

72. SVM, 4.1.2.2, p. 284.

73. SVM, 4.1.2.2, pp. 286–289.

74. SVM, 4.1.2.2, p. 289.

75. SVM, 4.1.2.2, p. 270 n.

76. See, e.g., David Chandler, *Campaigns of Napoleon* (New York: MacMillan, 1966), p. 154.

77. SVM, 4.1.2.2, p. 291.

Chapter 4   The Seeds of War

1. See Jacques Godechot, *La contre-révolution, doctrine et action, 1789–1804* (1961; Paris: Presses Universitaires de France, 1984), for a concise and readable account of these insurrections and counterrevolutionary movements. There is a considerable literature on the *vendéen* insurrections and the *chouannerie* of the revolutionary period, but most of those works end prior to Napoleon's ascent to power. The field of revolutionary and counterrevolutionary opposition to Napoleon remains relatively unexplored.

2. Godechot, *La contre-révolution*, pp. 385–386.

3. Godechot, *La contre-révolution*, pp. 398–399.

4. Godechot, *La contre-révolution*, pp. 390–397.

5. See, for example, Napoleon to Talleyrand, 7 June 1803, *Corr. de Nap.*, 6796, regarding émigrés in Spain and Prussia; Napoleon to Régnier, 2 August 1803, *Corr. de Nap.*, 6966, ordering the arrest of one Christin, a member of the Russian delegation; and Napoleon to Talleyrand, 4 August 1803, *Corr. de Nap.*, 6978, demanding that Portugal arrest "de Coigny and all those who foment brigandage in France."

6. See, for example, Napoleon to Régnier, 8 August 1803, *Corr. de Nap.*, 6983; 30 September 1803, *Corr. de Nap.*, 7142; 5 October 1803, *Corr. de Nap.*, 7166; and 3 February 1804, *Corr. de Nap.*, 7519.

7. Napoleon to Régnier, 25 August 1803, *Corr. de Nap.*, 7041.

8. Jean Tulard, *Joseph Fouché* (Paris: Fayard, 1998), p. 166.

9. Napoleon to Régnier, 24 January 1804, *Corr. de Nap.*, 7497.

10. Notes for the Minister of War, 19 January 1804, *Corr. de Nap.*, 7489.

11. Napoleon to Citizen Réal, 11 March 1804, *Corr. de Nap.*, 7610.

12. Napoleon to Marmont, 12 March 1804, *Corr. de Nap.*, 7616.

13. Napoleon to Soult, 7 March 1804, *Corr. de Nap.*, 7594.

14. Napoleon to Dessole, 8 March 1804, *Corr. de Nap.*, 7598.

15. Godechot, *La contre-révolution*, pp. 400–401.

16. Godechot, *La contre-révolution*, p. 401.

17. Tulard, *Joseph Fouché*, pp. 169–170.

18. Napoleon to Berthier, 10 March 1804, *Corr. de Nap.*, 7608.

19. Napoleon to Citizen Harel, Commandant of the Chateau de Vincennes, 20 March 1804, *Corr. de Nap.*, 7638.

20. Godechot, *La contre-révolution*, p. 402.

21. Napoleon to Réal, 19 March 1804, *Corr. de Nap.*, 7631.

22. Arrêté, 20 March 1804, *Corr. de Nap.*, 7636.

23. Napoleon to Citizen Réal, 20 March 1804, *Corr. de Nap.*, 7639.

24. See, for example, David Gates, *The Napoleonic Wars, 1803–1815* (New York: Arnold, 1997), p. 17. It is referred to as "the final provocation" by David Chandler in *Campaigns of Napoleon* (New York: Macmillan, 1966), p. 328. Paul Schroeder sees it as important to Alexander's subsequent actions in *The Transformation of European Politics, 1763–1848* (New York: Oxford University Press, 1994), p. 251. He states that the break in relations between Russia and France resulted from it and led directly to the formation of the Third Coalition and the war, although Schroeder also takes account of the previous irritants and subsequent clashes that actually led to the war. Albert Sorel, the only historian to notice the Russian military buildup of late 1803 and early 1804, best puts this event in its proper context, although even he overstates its significance for Russia. Albert Sorel, *L'Europe et la Révolution Française. Sixième partie: La Trêve—Lunéville et Amiens, 1800–1805* (Paris: Librairie Plon, n.d.), p. 359.

25. See the previous chapter.

26. Napoleon to Régnier, 2 August 1803, *Corr. de Nap.*, 6966.

27. Napoleon to Talleyrand, 8 November 1803, *Corr. de Nap.*, 7252.

28. Napoleon to Talleyrand, 12 December 1803, *Corr. de Nap.*, 7375.

29. Godechot, *La contre-révolution*, p. 391.

30. Napoleon to Talleyrand, 23 March 1804, *Corr. de Nap.*, 7644.

31. A. A. Czartoryskii to Cardinal-Secretary of the Roman Pope E. Consalvi, 13 June 1804, VPR, vol. II, doc. 27.

32. Napoleon to Cardinal Fesch, 13 April 1804, *Corr. de Nap.*, 7474.

33. The record of this meeting is available as Protocol of the Meeting of the State Council, 17 April 1804, VPR, vol. I, doc. 278. Present at this meeting were P. V. Zavadovskii, minister of education, V. Zubov, A. B. Kurakin, soon to be minister of foreign affairs, N. Romantsoff, A. I. Vasil'ev, minister of finance, S. K. Viaz'mitinov, minister of war, P. V. Lopukhin, minister of justice, V. P. Kochubei, minister of internal affairs, Morkov, D. Troshchinskii, A. Ia. Budberg, soon to be minister of foreign affairs, and Czartoryskii.

34. Note of Minister-Resident in Regensburg [Ratisbonne] F. A. Klüpfel to the Diet of the German Empire, 20 April 1804, VPR, vol. II, doc. 1. The immediately following documents convey the news of Alexander's reactions to Prussia, Austria, Oubril in Paris, and others.

35. Note of Oubril to Talleyrand, 12 May 1804, SIRIO 77, doc. 238.

36. Czartoryskii to Oubril, 21 April 1804, VPR, vol. II, doc. 6.

37. D. P. Tatishchev to S. R. Vorontsov, 23 April 1804, AKV 18b, doc. 43. The printed volume has the letter addressed to Alexander Vorontsov, but the content indicates that it must have been sent to Simon.

38. Hédouville to Talleyrand, 20 April 1804, SIRIO 77, doc. 228.

39. Alexander to Razumovskii, 7 May 1804, VPR, vol. II, doc. 14. A similar message was sent to Prussia: Alexander to Frederick William, 21 April 1804, VPR, vol. II, doc. 3. The formal offer of a secret agreement with Prussia was sent on 4 May: Alexander to Alopeus, VPR, vol. II, doc. 12, and Declaration of Russia about Joint Activities with Prussia for the Defense of Northern Germany, VPR, vol. II, doc. 13.

40. Oubril to Czartoryskii, 13 May 1804, SIRIO 77, doc. 239.

41. Napoleon to Talleyrand, 13 May 1804, *Corr. de Nap.*, doc. 7745.

42. Napoleon to Talleyrand, 13 May 1804, *Corr. de Nap.*, doc 7746.

43. Note of Talleyrand to Oubril, 16 May 1804, SIRIO 77, doc. 241.

44. Czartoryskii to Alexander, 17 May 1804, VPR, vol. II, doc. 22.

45. Czartoryskii to Razumovskii, 19 June 1804, VPR, vol. II, doc. 31.

46. Czartoryskii to Razumovskii, 19 June 1804, VPR, vol. II, doc. 31.

47. Cobenzl to the Count d'Antraigues, presumed date of 11 September 1804, reproduced in August Fournier, *Gentz und Cobenzl: Geschichte der österreichischen Diplomatie in den Jahren 1801–1805, nach neuen Quellen* (Vienna: Wilhelm Braumüller, 1880), p. 225–226.

48. Oubril to Czartoryskii, 6 July 1804, SIRIO 77, doc. 264.

49. Napoleon to Talleyrand, 9 July 1804, *Corr. de Nap.*, doc. 7852.

50. Fournier, *Gentz und Cobenzl*, p. 129.

51. Czartoryskii to Razumovskii, 19 June 1804, VPR, vol. II, doc. 31.

52. Napoleon to Soult, 3 June 1804, *Corr. de Nap.*, doc 7801.

53. Napoleon to Brune, 27 July 1804, *Corr. de Nap.*, doc. 7874.

54. Warren to Hawkesbury, 27 April 1804, in John Holland Rose, *Select Despatches from the British Foreign Office Archives Relating to the Formation of the Third Coalition Against France, 1804–1805* (London: Offices of the Royal Historical Society, 1904), pt. 1, doc. 1; Czartoryskii to S. R. Vorontsov, 30 April 1804, in Holland Rose, *Select Despatches*, pt. 1, doc. 3; also AKV 15, pp. 172–178; Warren to Czartoryskii, 27 April 1804, as an appendix to the previous in AKV 15, pp. 176–178.

55. Czartoryskii to S. R. Vorontsov, 30 April 1804, Holland Rose, *Select Despatches*, pt. 1, doc. 3; AKV 15, pp. 172–176.

56. Christopher D. Hall, *British Strategy in the Napoleonic War, 1803–1815* (New York: Manchester University Press, 1992), pp. 104–109. John Charles Fedorak, *Henry Addington, Prime Minister, 1801–1804: Peace, War, and Parliamentary Politics* (Akron, Ohio: University of Akron Press, 2002) undertakes to revise the historical image of Addington and his government fundamentally. He specifically argues that Addington prepared for war and conducted operations once war was renewed intelligently and aggressively. But Fedorak's efforts in this regard fail to consider in any detail the course of the negotiations between Addington's government and Alexander, and the reasons for their failure then and their subsequent success under Pitt.

57. In Hall, *British Strategy*, p. 108.

58. See Fedorak, *Henry Addington*, for a discussion of efforts to disparage and ultimately unseat Addington.

59. Fedorak, *Henry Addington*, pp. 207ff.

60. Count Vorontsov to Prince Czartoryskii, no. 256, 25 June 1804, AKV 15b, doc. 18, p. 212.

61. Lord Harrowby to Count [S. R.] Vorontsov, 26 June 1804, in Holland Rose, *Select Despatches*, pt. 1, doc. 7.

62. S. R. Vorontsov to Czartoryskii, 29 June 1804, AKV 15b, doc. 19.

63. Warren to Harrowby, 24 July 1804, in Holland Rose, *Select Despatches*, pt. 1, doc 13.

64. A good example of this problem can be seen from Czartoryskii to A. R. Vorontsov, 7 May 1804, in Adam Gielgud, ed., *Memoirs of Prince Adam Czartoryski* (New York: Arno/New York Times, 1971), 2:29, in which Czartoryskii apologizes for reacting to the d'Enghien affair before consulting Vorontsov.

65. "Discussion and Notes of State Chancellor A. R. Vorontsov about the Current Conditions of Europe and the Ways in which They Might Affect Russia," 4 August 1804, AKV 11, p. 472. See Counterdeclaration of Russia About Joint Operations with Denmark for the Defense of Northern Germany from French Aggression, 29 March 1804, VPR, vol. I, doc. 270; Declaration of Russia about Joint Operations with Prussia for the Defense of Northern Germany, 4 May 1804 and Declaration of Prussia about Joint Operations with Russia for the Defense of Northern Germany, 24 May 1804, VPR, vol. II, docs. 13, 23; and Russo-Swedish Convention about Joint Operations for the Defense of Northern Germany, 14 January 1805, VPR, vol. II, doc. 89. Note 140 to the last document describes the process of the negotiation for the Russo–Swedish Convention, which began in April 1804 and was well under way when Vorontsov wrote his note of 4 August.

66. W. H. Zawadzki, *A Man of Honour: Adam Czartoryski as a Statesman of Russia and Poland, 1795–1831* (Oxford: Clarendon, 1993), p. 48.

67. Grimsted, *Foreign Ministers*, pp. 106–113.

68. Reprinted in its entirety with textual commentary in Patricia Kennedy Grimsted, "Czartoryski's System for Russian Foreign Policy, 1803: A Memorandum, Edited with Introduction and Analysis," *Canadian Slavic Studies* 5: 19–92.

69. Alexander to S. R. Vorontsov, 22 September 1804, VPR, vol. II, doc. 49.

70. Secret Instructions of Alexander I to N. N. Novosil'tsev, 23 September 1804, VPR, vol. II, doc. 50.

71. See below, Chapter 6.

72. Additional Notes for Instruction Given by His Imperial Majesty to Mr. de Novosil'tsev, 23 September 1804, VPR, vol. II, doc. 51.

73. Schroeder, *Transformation of European Politics*, pp. 259–260.

Chapter 5   Austria's Turn

1. Fournier suggests that the actual budget was hardly reduced at all, although the "official" military budget was reduced significantly, as indicated in Adolf Beer, *Die Finanzen Oesterreichs im XIX. Jahrhundert, nach archivalischen Quellen* (Prague: F. Tempsky, 1877), p. 391. See August Fournier,

Gentz und Cobenzl: Geschichte der österreichischen Diplomatie in den Jahren 1801–1805, nach neuen Quellen (Vienna: Wilhelm Braumüller, 1880), p. 110 n. 3.

2. See above, Chapter 3, for the Russian approach.

3. A significant portion of the memorandum is reprinted in Oskar Criste, *Erzherzog Carl von Oesterreich* (Vienna: Wilhelm Braumüller, 1912), 2:252–257. The entire memorandum is in Albrecht and William, Archdukes of Austria, eds., *Ausgewählte Schriften*, 5:611–641.

4. Criste, *Erzherzog Carl von Oesterreich*, 2:256.

5. Criste, *Erzherzog Carl von Oesterreich*, 2:257.

6. Cobenzl to Colloredo, 9 March 1804, in Fournier, *Gentz und Cobenzl*, pp. 215–219.

7. Cobenzl to Colloredo, 9 March 1804, in Fournier, *Gentz und Cobenzl*, p. 216.

8. Cobenzl to Colloredo, 9 March 1804, in Fournier, *Gentz und Cobenzl*, p. 217.

9. Oskar Regele, "Karl Freiherr von Mack und Johann Ludwig Graf Cobenzl: Ihre Rolle im Kriegsjahr 1805," *Mitteilungen des Österreichischen Staatsarchivs* 21 (1968):142–143; Max Jähns, *Geschichte der Kriegswissenschaften vornehmlich in Deutschland, Dritte Abteilung. Das XVIII Jahrhundert seit dem Auftreten Freidrichs des Großen, 1740–1800* (Munich: R. Oldenbourg, 1891), sec. 130, p. 2117; Moriz Edlen von Angeli, "Beiträge zur vaterländischen Geschichte: IV Ulm und Austerlitz: Studie auf Grund archivalischer Quellen über den Feldzug 1805 in Deutschland," *Streffleur's Oesterrischische Militärische Zeitschrift* 18, no. 4 (1877): 433–435; and Christian Karl August Ludwig Freiherr von Massenbach, *Nähere Beleuchtung des dem k. k. Obersten und Chef des Generalstaabes Freyherrn von Mack zugeschriebenen Operationsplans für den Feldzug 1794 des Oesterreichisch–Französischen Krieges* (Berlin: Johann Friedrich Unger, 1796), 3 vols. See below, Chapter 14, for additional biographical details about Mack.

10. Regele, "Karl Freiherr von Mack," p. 143. Mack's "Instructions for Generals" can be found in full in *Beiträge zur Geschichte des österreichischen Heerwesens. Erstes Heft: Der Zeitraum von 1757— 1814, Mit besonderer Rücksichtnahme auf Organisation, Verpflegung und Taktik* (Vienna: L. W. Seidel, 1872), pp. 127–141. They are not attributed to Mack in that volume, but they are attributed and summarized with a reference to this volume in Jähns, *Geschichte der Kriegswissenschaften*, sec. 130, pp. 2116–2120.

11. Cobenzl to Colloredo, 29 July 1804, in Fournier, *Gentz und Cobenzl*, p. 241.

12. Cobenzl to Colloredo, 27 March 1804, in Fournier, *Gentz und Cobenzl*, p. 220.

13. [Cobenzl] to Stadion, 1 April 1804, in Beer, "Oesterreich und Russland," p. 205.

14. Francis to Alexander, 1 April 1804, in Beer, "Oesterreich und Russland," p. 182.

15. [Cobenzl] to Stadion, 1 April 1804, in Beer, "Oesterreich und Russland," p. 205.

16. [Cobenzl] to Stadion, 11 July 1804, in Beer, "Oesterreich und Russland," p. 229.

17. [Cobenzl] to Stadion, 17 June 1804, in Beer, "Oesterreich und Russland," p. 216.

18. [Cobenzl] to Stadion, 17 June 1804, in Beer, "Oesterreich und Russland," p. 216.

19. The best works on the topic were written at the beginning of the twentieth century. See Edouard Driault, *Napoléon en Italie (1800–1812)* (Paris: Librairie Félix Alcan, 1906); Driault, *Napoléon et l'Europe: Austerlitz: La Fin du Saint-Empire, 1804–1806* (Paris: Librairie Félix Alcan, 1912); Albert Pingaud, *Bonaparte: Président de la République Italienne* (Paris: Librairie académique, Perrin et Cie., 1914). All three are impartial about Napoleon, make excellent use of archival sources, and, most unusually for French scholarship on this topic, are extensively footnoted, especially Driault's works. Alain Pillepich, *Napoléon et les Italiens: République italienne et Royaume d'Italie (1802–1814)* (Paris: Nouveau Monde/Fondation Napoléon, 2003), provides a modern if brief overview.

20. This is the view offered by Pingaud in *Bonaparte*, 1:241–263.

21. This line of argument is presented in Edouard Driault's two works on this subject, *Napoléon en Italie (1800–1812)* (Paris: Librairie Félix Alcan, 1906); and *Napoléon et l'Europe: Austerlitz: La Fin du Saint-Empire, 1804–1806* (Paris: Librairie Félix Alcan, 1912).

22. The biographical sketch that follows is taken from Pingaud, *Bonaparte*, 1:384–395.

23. Pingaud, *Bonaparte*, 1:387.

24. Pingaud, *Bonaparte*, 1:475–476.

25. Marescalchi to Melzi, 9 May 1804; summarized in Pingaud, *Bonaparte*, 2:399–401.

26. Marescalchi to Melzi, 21 March 1804, in Pingaud, *Bonaparte*, 2:398–399.

27. Driault, *Napoléon en Italie*, p. 296. Melzi's letter to Napoleon enclosing the proposal is in Francesco Melzi d'Eril Duca di Lodi, *Memorie-Documenti e Lettere Inedite di Napoleone I. e Beauharnais*, ed. Giovanni Melzi (Milan: Gaetano Brigola, 1865), 2:212–214. The proposal is only reproduced in Driault.

28. Melzi, *Memorie-Documenti*, 2:213.

29. Cited in Driault, *Napoléon en Italie*, pp. 298–299.

30. Napoleon to Melzi, 23 June 1804, in Melzi, *Memorie-Documenti*, 2:215.

31. Letters from Marescalchi to Melzi of June 1804; cited in Pingaud, *Bonaparte*, 2:410–411.

32. Pingaud, *Bonaparte*, 1:391.

33. Melzi to Napoleon, 11 July 1804, in Melzi, *Memorie-Documenti*, 1:216–219.

34. Napoleon to Marescalchi, 28 August 1804, *Corr. de Nap.*, doc. 7968.

35. Report of Moll [to Cobenzl], 9 July 1804, in Pingaud, *Bonaparte*, 2:413 n. 2.

36. "Denkschrift der Staatskanzlei über eine Annäherung an Preußen," 1 September 1804, in Fournier, *Gentz und Cobenzl*, p. 293ff.

37. Fournier, *Gentz und Cobenzl*, p. 141.

38. Fournier, *Gentz und Cobenzl*, p. 142.

39. Fournier, *Gentz und Cobenzl*, p. 146.

40. The treaty is reproduced in F. Martens, *Recueil des Traités et Conventions conclus par la Russie avec les Puissances Etrangères* (St. Petersburg: A. Böhnke, 1902), 2:406–421.

41. Cobenzl to Colloredo, 13 October 1804, in Fournier, *Gentz und Cobenzl*, p. 148.

Chapter 6　The Formation of the Third Coalition

1. "Note of Count S. R. Vorontsov about the Life and Activities of the British Minister, Pitt the Younger," AKV, vol. 15, pp. 453–480.

2. Novosil'tsev's record of that meeting, which Pitt read and commented on, is in Record of a Meeting of N. N. Novosil'tsev with the Prime Minister of Great Britain, Pitt, 25 December 1804, VPR, vol. II, doc. 79.

3. Emphasis in the original.

4. Record of a Meeting of N. N. Novosil'tsev with the Prime Minister of Great Britain, Pitt, 25 December 1804, VPR, vol. II, doc. 79.

5. Record of a Meeting of N. N. Novosil'tsev with the Prime Minister of Great Britain, Pitt, 25 December 1804, VPR, vol. II, doc. 79.

6. This last clause was an addition by Pitt to Novosil'tsev's manuscript for the purpose of underlining the point. See VPR, vol. II, doc. 79, p. 225, n.

7. Deputy Minister of Foreign Affairs A. A. Czartoryskii to Ambassador in Constantinople A. Ia. Italinskii, 28 April 1804, VPR, vol. II, doc. 11.

8. VPR, vol. II, note 61.

9. Czartoryskii to Italinskii, 25 August 1804, VPR, vol. II, doc. 43.

10. The reference to this British statement is mysterious. The editors of *Vneshniaia politika rossii* claim (VPR, vol. II, n. 68) that it is to be found in Lord Harrowby to Count Voronstov, 26 June 1804, in John Holland Rose, *Select Despatches from the British Foreign Office Archives Relating to the Formation of the Third Coalition Against France, 1804–1805* (London: Offices of the Royal Historical Society, 1904), doc. 7, pp. 14–19. There is, however, no such reference in that document (and such

a reference would have been out of place given the contents of the document). On the other hand, when tasked with the statement by Czartoryskii, Harrowby acknowledged making it in "my letter to Count Woronzow of the 26th of June" and British Ambassador to Russia J. B. Warren attempted to clarify it, not to deny that it had been made (Harrowby to Leveson Gower, 10 October 1804; Warren to Harrowby, 24 July 1804, in Holland Rose, *Select Despatches*, docs. 29, 13).

11. Czartoryskii to Italinskii, 25 August 1804, VPR, vol. II, doc. 43.

12. Czartoryskii to S. R. Vorontsov, 30 August 1804, VPR, vol. II, doc. 45.

13. Harrowby to Leveson Gower, 10 October 1804, in Holland Rose, *Select Despatches*, doc. 29.

14. N. N. Novosil'tsev to Alexander I, 5 January 1805, VPR, vol. II, doc. 87. The instruction to Simon Vorontsov was reproduced as doc. 49 and the two sets of instructions for Novosil'tsev as docs. 50–51.

15. Czartoryskii to N. N. Novosil'tsev, 16 February 1805, VPR, vol. II, doc. 103.

16. John Ehrmann, *The Younger Pitt: The Consuming Struggle* (London: Constable, 1996), 3:700, citing Pitt to Harrowby, 20 November 1804.

17. Ehrmann, *The Younger Pitt*, citing Wilberforce, 8 January 1805.

18. Warren to Harrowby, 30 June 1804, in Holland Rose, *Select Despatches*, doc. 8.

19. Warren to Harrowby, 10 July 1804, in Holland Rose, *Select Despatches*, doc. 11.

20. Warren to Harrowby, 30 June 1804, in Holland Rose, *Select Despatches*, doc. 8.

21. Napoleon to the Emperor of Austria, 1 January 1805, *Corr. de Nap.*, doc. 8250; to the King of England, 2 January 1805, *Corr. de Nap.*, doc. 8252; to the King of Spain, 2 January 1805, *Corr. de Nap.*, doc. 8253; to the King of Naples, 2 January 1805, *Corr. de Nap.*, doc. 8254; to the Queen of Naples, 2 January 1805, *Corr. de Nap.*, doc. 8255; and to the Emperor of Russia, 14 January 1805, *Corr. de Nap.*, doc. 8273.

22. Édouard Driault, *Napoléon et l'Europe: Austerlitz, Fin du Saint-Empire (1804–1806)* (Paris: Librairie Félix Alcan, 1912), p. 168.

23. Ehrman, *The Younger Pitt*, pp. 726–728.

24. For the first, see Mulgrave to Leveson Gower, 21 January 1805, in Holland Rose, *Select Despatches*, doc. 57; for the second, see Mulgrave to Leveson Gower, 21 January 1805, in Holland Rose, *Select Despatches*, doc. 58; for the third, see "Official Communication made to the Russian Ambassador at London," 19 January 1805, in C. K. Webster, ed., *British Diplomacy, 1813–1815: Select Documents Dealing with the Reconstruction of Europe* (London: G. Bell, 1921), appendix 1, pp. 388–394.

25. Webster, *British Diplomacy*.

26. Holland Rose, *Select Despatches*, doc. 58.

27. Ehrman, *The Younger Pitt*, pp. 726–727.

28. Czartoryskii to Novosil'tsev, 16 February 1805, VPR, vol. II, doc. 103.

29. Czartoryskii to Novosil'tsev, 16 February 1805, VPR, vol. II, doc. 103.

30. Leveson Gower to Mulgrave, 6 March 1805, Holland Rose, *Select Despatches*, doc. 65.

31. Leveson Gower to Mulgrave, 6 March 1805, Holland Rose, *Select Despatches*, doc. 65.

32. Leveson Gower to Mulgrave, 6 March 1805, Holland Rose, *Select Despatches*, doc. 65.

33. Leveson Gower to Mulgrave, 22 March 1805, Holland Rose, *Select Despatches*, doc. 69.

34. Leveson Gower to Mulgrave, 7 April 1805, Holland Rose, *Select Despatches*, doc. 71.

35. Czartoryskii to [Simon] Vorontsov, 4 (16?) April 1805, AKV, vol. 15, p. 290.

36. Alexander I to S. R. Vorontsov, 15 April 1805, VPR, vol. II, doc. 118.

37. Alexander I to S. R. Vorontsov, 15 April 1805, VPR, vol. II, doc. 118.

38. W. H. Zawadzki, *A Man of Honour: Adam Czartoryski as a Statesman of Russia and Poland, 1795–1831* (Oxford: Clarendon, 1993), p. 115; Patricia Kennedy Grimsted, *The Foreign Ministers of Alexander I: Political Attitudes and the Conduct of Russian Diplomacy, 1801–1825* (Los Angeles: University of California Press, 1969), p. 140. Zawadzki and Grimsted agree on the existence of the conspiracy and some of its figures but differ on the other members, although neither probes the issue in depth.

39. Zawadzki, *Man of Honour*, p. 115.

40. Czartoryskii to Novosil'tsev, 16 February 1805, VPR, vol. II, doc. 103.

41. Czartoryskii to Novosil'tsev, 17 February 1805, VPR, vol. II, doc. 104.

42. Novosil'tsev to Simon Vorontsov, 16 April 1805, AKV, vol. 18, pp. 457–458. Emphasis added.

43. Czartoryskii to Simon Vorontsov, 16 June 1805, AKV, vol. 15, pp. 323ff.

44. Czartoryskii to Simon Vorontsov, 16 June 1805, AKV, vol. 15, pp. 323ff.

45. Czartoryskii to Alexander Vorontsov, 18 June 1805, cited in Zawadzki, *Man of Honour*, p. 122.

46. Ehrman, *The Younger Pitt*, p. 745.

47. Ehrman, *The Younger Pitt*, pp. 752–762.

48. Ehrman, *The Younger Pitt*, p. 766.

49. Ehrman, *The Younger Pitt*, pp. 770–771.

50. Lord Mulgrave to Count Vorontsov, 5 June 1805, in Holland Rose, *Select Despatches*, doc. 82.

51. Ehrman, *The Younger Pitt*, pp. 782–783.

Chapter 7   The Road to War

1. See below, Chapter 8.

2. Archduke Charles, "Ueber den Krieg mit den Neufranken," 1795, Archdukes Albrecht and William, *Ausgewählte Schriften weiland seiner kaiserlichen Hoheit des Erzherzogs Carl von Oesterreich* (Vienna: Wilhelm Braumüller, 1894), 5:7.

3. See Azar Gat, *A History of Military Thought from the Enlightenment to the Cold War* (New York: Oxford University Press, 2001), pp. 97–107, for a brief summary of Charles's thought. Gat's study of this period (as well as other similar studies) is marred by his failure to explore any other Austrian military theorists, some of whom actually developed aggressive doctrines of maneuver *and battle*. This topic is explored more thoroughly in an article now under preparation by the author.

4. "Stand der k. k. Armee mit Ende April 1805," KA AFA 1805 Deutschland, IV/7.

5. Moriz Edlen von Angeli, "Beiträge zur vaterländischen Geschichte. IV. Ulm und Austerlitz. Studie auf Grund archivalischer Quellen über den Feldzug 1805 in Deutschland. A Ulm," *Mittheilungen des K. K. Kriegs-Archivs* 2 (1877): 423.

6. Archduke Charles, "Ueber die politische Lage Europas," 12 April 1804; "Confidentielle Bemerkungen über den politischen Zustand Europas," 23 April 1804, in Albrecht and William, *Ausgewählte Schriften*, 6:3–26.

7. "Confidentielles Promemoria über die Französische Kaiserwahl," 1 June 1804, in Albrecht and William, *Ausgewählte Schriften*, 6:27–30.

8. "Bemerkungen zur Depesche an den Grafen Stadion vom 2. December 1804," 18 January 1805, in Albrecht and William, *Ausgewählte Schriften*, 6:31–32.

9. Francis to Charles, 10 January 1805, in Oskar Criste, *Erzherzog Carl von Oesterreich* (Vienna: Wilhelm Braumüller, 1912), vol. 2, appendix 23, pp. 530–531.

10. Charles to Francis, 18 January 1805, in Criste, *Erzherzog Carl*, vol. 2, app. 24, p. 532.

11. Francis to Charles, 29 January 1805; Charles to Francis, 13 February 1805; Francis, "Entwurf eines Allerhöchsten Handschreibens," February 1805; Francis to Charles, 7 March 1805; Francis to Charles, 18 March 1805, in Criste, *Erzherzog Carl*, 2:533–555.

12. August Fournier, *Gentz und Cobenzl: Geschichte der österreichischen Diplomatie in den Jahren 1801–1805, nach neuen Quellen* (Vienna: Wilhelm Braumüller, 1880), pp. 155–158.

13. Edouard Driault, *Napoléon en Italie (1800–1812)* (Paris: Librairie Félix Alcan, 1906), pp. 309ff.

14. Driault, *Napoléon en Italie*, p. 314.

15. Napoleon to the Emperor of Austria, 1 January 1805, *Corr. de Nap.*, doc. 8250.

16. Francis to Napoleon, 23 January 1805, in Adolf Beer, "Österreich und Russland in den Jahren 1804 und 1805," *Archiv für österreichische Geschichte* 53 (1875): 196–198.

17. Fournier, *Gentz und Cobenzl*, p. 160.
18. Napoleon to the Emperor of Austria, 17 March 1805, *Corr. de Nap.*, doc. 8445; Francis to Napoleon, 16 April 1805 (incorrectly listed as 1804), in Beer, *Oesterreich und Russland*, pp. 198–199; Fournier, *Gentz und Cobenzl*, p. 160.
19. Cobenzl to Colloredo, 7 April 1805, cited in Fournier, *Gentz und Cobenzl*, p. 161 n. 2.
20. Report of Stadion from the end of March 1805, cited in Fournier, *Gentz und Cobenzl*, p. 165 n. 1.
21. Metternich to Colloredo, 18 February 1805, in Prince Richard Metternich-Winneburg, ed., *Aus Metternich's nachgelassenen Papieren* (Vienna: Wilhelm Braumüller, 1880), 1:41.
22. "Record of the Meeting of Minister of Foreign Affairs of Prussia Hardenberg with Ambassador in Berlin M. M. Alopeus and F. F. Wintzingerode," 18 March 1805; and "F. F. Wintzingerode to Deputy Minister of Foreign Affairs A. A. Czartoryskii," 22 March 1805, VPR, vol. II, docs. 112 and 113 respectively.
23. Metternich to Colloredo, 16 May 1805, Metternicht-Winneburg, *Aus Metternich's ausgelassene Papieren*, p. 45.
24. Driault, *Napoleon en Italie*, pp. 328ff.
25. Driault, *Napoleon en Italie*, p. 329.
26. Napoleon to Decrès, 24 May 1805, *Corr. de Nap.*, doc. 8784.
27. Driault, *Napoleon en Italie*, p. 333.
28. Driault, *Napoleon en Italie*, pp. 333–334.
29. Driault, *Napoleon en Italie*, p. 330.
30. Driault, *Napoleon en Italie*, p. 331.
31. Driault, *Napoleon en Italie*, p. 334.
32. Napoleon to Cambacérès, 29 May 1805, *Corr. de Nap.*, doc. 8806.
33. Talleyrand to La Rochefoucauld, 1 June 1805, in Driault, *Napoleon en Italie*, pp. 335–336.
34. *Napoleon en Italie*, p. 336.
35. Napoleon to Berthier, 27 March 1805, *Corr. de Nap.*, doc. 8491; Driault, *Napoleon en Italie*, p. 320.
36. "Most Urgent Reasons," n.d., KA AFA 1805 Italien, IV/2.
37. Charles to Francis, 26 May 1805, KA AFA 1805 Italien, V/7½.
38. Emperor's signed marginal note on the last page of Charles to Francis, 25 May 1805, KA AFA 1805 Italien, V/12.
39. Fournier, *Gentz und Cobenzl*, pp. 166–167.
40. Czartoryskii to Razumovskii, 14 June 1805, VPR, vol. II, doc. 135.
41. Presentation of the Minister to the Emperor, 2 July 1805, in Fournier, *Gentz und Cobenzl*, pp. 304–308.
42. Decision of the Emperor concerning the Presentation of 2 July, in Adolf Beer, *Zehn Jahre österreichischer Politik, 1801–1810* (Leipzig: F. A. Brockhaus, 1877), pp. 496–498.
43. Declaration of Deputy Minister of Foreign Affairs A. A. Czartoryskii to Austrian Ambassador in St. Petersburg Stadion, 9 August 1805; Declaration of Austrian Ambassador in St. Petersburg Stadion about the Accession of Austria to the Anglo-Russian Convention of Alliance of 11 April 1805, VPR, vol. II, docs. 153, 154 respectively.

Chapter 8 Prussia Opts Out

1. Brendan Simms, *The Impact of Napoleon: Prussian High Politics, Foreign Policy, and the Crisis of the Executive, 1797–1806* (New York: Cambridge University Press, 1997), explores these issues in detail, but his account focuses on the "high politics" of the Prussian court while neglecting a real consideration of the thought process and even role of the king in the decision. Phillip G. Dwyer, "Politics of Prussian Neutrality," *German History* 12, no. 3 (1994): 351–373, ignores this decisive

point almost completely focusing instead on the reaction to Napoleon's invasion of Hanover and on Frederick William's decision to go to war following Napoleon's violation of Prussian neutrality during the Ulm Campaign. Thomas Stamm-Kuhlmann explores the decision only from Frederick William's perspective in *König in Preußens großer Zeit: Friedrich Wilhelm III. Der Melancholiker auf dem Thron* (Berlin: Siedler Verlag, 1992).

2. Simms, *Impact*, passim.

3. See Stamm-Kuhlmann, *König in Preußens großer Zeit*, pp. 188–90 for a discussion of the king's perception of his own rationality.

4. Stamm-Kuhlmann, *König in Preußens großer Zeit*, p. 188.

5. Talleyrand to Laforest, 17 May 1803, in Paul Bailleu, ed., *Preußen und Frankreich 1795 bis 1807: Diplomatische Correspondenzen,* Publicationen aus den königlichen preussischen Archiven, 8, 29 (Leipzig, 1881–1887), vol. 2, doc. 101.

6. Stamm-Kuhlmann, *König in Preußens großer Zeit*, pp. 182–183.

7. Stamm-Kuhlmann, *König in Preußens großer Zeit*, p. 183.

8. Ostensible decree to Lucchesini, 28 May 1803, in Bailleu, *Preußen und Frankreich,* vol. 2, doc. 102.

9. Confidential decree to Lucchesini, 28 May 1803, in Bailleu, *Preußen und Frankreich,* vol. 2, doc. 103; Lucchesini's Report, 9 June 1803, in Bailleu, *Preußen und Frankreich,* vol. 2, doc. 112.

10. Lucchesini's Report, 29 May 1803, in Bailleu, *Preußen und Frankreich,* vol. 2, doc. 104.

11. J. W. Lombard to Lucchesini, 6 June 1803, in Bailleu, *Preußen und Frankreich,* vol. 2, doc. 108.

12. Haugwitz to Frederick William III, 4 June 1803, in Bailleu, *Preußen und Frankreich,* vol. 2, doc. 106.

13. Stamm-Kuhlmann, *König in Preußens großer Zeit*, p. 184.

14. Haugwitz to Frederick William III, 4 June 1803, Bailleu, *Preußen und Frankreich,* vol. 2, doc. 106.

15. See above, Chapter 3, for a consideration of this offer from the Russian perspective. Envoy in Berlin M. M. Alopeus to Prussian Minister of Foreign Affairs Haugwitz, 31 May 1803, *VPR,* vol. I., doc. 181, p. 434.

16. Haugwitz to Frederick William III, 8 June 1803, in Bailleu, *Preußen und Frankreich,* vol. 2, doc. 110.

17. Frederick William III to Haugwitz, 9 June 1803, in Bailleu, *Preußen und Frankreich,* vol. 2, doc. 111.

18. Frederick William III to Haugwitz, 9 June 1803, in Bailleu, *Preußen und Frankreich,* vol. 2, doc. 111.

19. Frederick William III to Haugwitz, 9 June 1803, in Bailleu, *Preußen und Frankreich,* vol. 2, doc. 111.

20. Dwyer, "Politics of Prussian Neutrality," pp. 355–358.

21. Stamm-Kuhlmann, *König in Preußens großer Zeit*, p. 181.

22. Frederick William to Alexander, 7 July 1803, in Paul Bailleu, ed., *Briefwechsel König Friedrich Wilhelms III und der Königin Luise mit Kaiser Alexander I,* Publicationen aus den K. Preussischen Archiven 75 (Leipzig, 1900), doc. 35.

23. Frederick William to Lucchesini, 6 June 1803, in Bailleu, *Preußen und Frankreich,* vol. 2, doc. 107.

24. Frederick William to Haugwitz, 15 June 1803, in Bailleu, *Preußen und Frankreich,* vol. 2, doc. 113.

25. Frederick William to Lucchesini, 15 June 1803, in Bailleu, *Preußen und Frankreich,* vol. 2, doc. 114.

26. Frederick William to Haugwitz, 9 June 1803, in Bailleu, *Preußen und Frankreich,* vol. 2, doc. 111.

27. Bericht Lucchesini's, 13 June 1803, in Bailleu, *Preußen und Frankreich,* vol. 2, doc. 116.

28. Bericht Lucchesini's, 25 June 1803, in Bailleu, *Preußen und Frankreich,* vol. 2, doc. 119.

29. The concept of an agreement was in a decree to Lucchesini, 18 June 1803, in Bailleu, *Preußen und Frankreich,* vol. 2, doc. 117. The protests are in Lucchesini to Talleyrand, 30 June 1803, doc. 121, and Frederick William to Napoleon, 7 July 1803, doc. 123.

30. Memorandum of Count Haugwitz, 28 June 1803 (presented to the King on 30 June), in Bailleu, *Preußen und Frankreich,* vol. 2, doc. 120.

31. Memorandum of Count Haugwitz, 28 June 1803 (presented to the King on 30 June), in Bailleu, *Preußen und Frankreich,* vol. 2, doc. 120.

32. Memorandum of Count Haugwitz, 28 June 1803 (presented to the King on 30 June), in Bailleu, *Preußen und Frankreich,* vol. 2, doc. 120.

33. J. W. Lombard to Lucchesini, 16 July 1803, in Bailleu, *Preußen und Frankreich*, vol. 2, doc. 125.

34. J. W. Lombard to Lucchesini, 16 July 1803, in Bailleu, *Preußen und Frankreich*, vol. 2, doc. 125, p. 183 n. 1.

35. Bericht J. W. Lombard's, 24 July 1803, in Bailleu, *Preußen und Frankreich*, vol. 2, doc. 126.

36. Bericht J. W. Lombard's, 24 July 1803, in Bailleu, *Preußen und Frankreich*, vol. 2, doc. 126.

37. Bericht J. W. Lombard's, 24 July 1803, in Bailleu, *Preußen und Frankreich*, vol. 2, doc. 126.

38. Bericht J. W. Lombard's, 24 July 1803, in Bailleu, *Preußen und Frankreich*, vol. 2, doc. 126.

39. Bericht J. W. Lombard's, 24 July 1803, in Bailleu, *Preußen und Frankreich*, vol. 2, doc. 126.

40. Bericht J. W. Lombard's, 30 July 1803, in Bailleu, *Preußen und Frankreich*, vol. 2, doc. 127.

41. See Chapter 3.

42. Napoleon to the King of Prussia, 29 July 1803, *Corr. de Nap.*, doc. 6956.

43. Denkschrift des Grafen Haugwitz, 12 August 1803, in Bailleu, *Preußen und Frankreich*, vol. 2, doc. 130.

44. Napoleon's conviction that the Russian court was Anglophile and the distance between Alexander and his advisers is clearly seen in J. W. Lombard's report, 24 July 1803, in Bailleu, *Preußen und Frankreich*, vol. 2, doc. 126, p. 188; and J. W. Lombard's report, 30 July 1803, doc. 127, p. 192: "What should one think of a court where the ministers think differently from their master and where they change every year?" Talleyrand repeated this charge in a note to Laforest, 10 October 1803, in Bailleu, *Preußen und Frankreich*, vol. 2, doc. 139.

45. A dispatch was sent to Lucchesini and to the Russian court with the proposal on August 15. Bailleu, *Preußen und Frankreich*, vol. 2, p. 196 n. 1; Bailleu, *Briefwechsel*, p. 34 n. 4.

46. Bericht Lucchesini's, 10 September 1803, in Bailleu, *Preußen und Frankreich*, vol. 2, doc. 133.

47. Kaiser Alexander I. an König Friedrich Wilhelm III, 24 September 1803, in Bailleu, *Briefwechsel*, doc. 40 (also in VPR, vol. I, doc. 221 with slightly different content, since it was taken from an earlier draft). This note was communicated to Haugwitz in late October: Haugwitz to Frederick William III, 26 October 1803, in Bailleu, *Preußen und Frankreich*, vol. 2, doc. 142.

48. Frederick William to Lucchesini, 24 September 1803, in Bailleu, *Preußen und Frankreich*, vol. 2, doc. 136.

49. Denkschrift des Grafen Haugwitz, 3 November 1803, in Bailleu, *Preußen und Frankreich*, vol. 2, doc. 143.

50. Aufzeichnung des Grafen Haugwitz, 10 November 1803, in Bailleu, *Preußen und Frankreich*, vol. 2, doc. 144.

51. See Chapter 3.

52. Report of Lucchesini, 4 or 5 February 1804, in Bailleu, *Preußen und Frankreich*, vol. 2, doc. 156.

53. Report of Lucchesini, 30 November 1803, in Bailleu, *Preußen und Frankreich*, vol. 2, doc. 146.

54. Rescript to Lucchesini, 15 December 1803, in Bailleu, *Preußen und Frankreich*, vol. 2, doc. 149.

55. Report of Lucchesini, 30 December 1803, in Bailleu, *Preußen und Frankreich*, vol. 2, doc. 151.

56. Talleyrand to Laforest, 30 December 1803, in Bailleu, *Preußen und Frankreich*, vol. 2, doc. 152.

57. Report of Lucchesini, 4 or 5 February 1804, in Bailleu, *Preußen und Frankreich*, vol. 2, doc. 156.

58. Memorandum of King Frederick William III, mid-January 1804, in Bailleu, *Preußen und Frankreich*, vol. 2, doc. 153.

59. Rescript to Lucchesini, 19 January 1804, in Bailleu, *Preußen und Frankreich*, vol. 2, doc. 154.

60. Report of Lucchesini, 4 or 5 February 1804, in Bailleu, *Preußen und Frankreich*, vol. 2, doc. 156.

61. Memorandum of Count Haugwitz, mid-February 1804, in Bailleu, *Preußen und Frankreich*, vol. 2, doc. 159.

62. Memorandum of Count Haugwitz, mid-February 1804, in Bailleu, *Preußen und Frankreich*, vol. 2, doc. 159.

63. Memorandum of King Frederick William III, mid-February 1804, in Bailleu, *Preußen und Frankreich*, doc. 160.

64. Frederick William to Alexander, 21 February 1804, in Bailleu, *Briefwechsel*, doc. 48.

65. Memorandum of Count Haugwitz, end-February 1804, in Bailleu, *Preußen und Frankreich*, vol. 2, doc. 161.

66. Frederick William to Haugwitz, 13 March 1804, in Bailleu, *Preußen und Frankreich*, vol. 2, doc. 163.

67. Czartoryskii to Alopeus, 17 March 1804, VPR, vol. I, doc. 264.

68. Alexander to Frederick William, 15 March 1804, in Bailleu, *Briefwechsel*, doc. 49.

69. See Chapter 4.

70. Alexander to Frederick William III, 21 April 1804, in Bailleu, *Briefwechsel*, doc. 51. See Lucchesini's report, 14 March 1804, in Bailleu, *Preußen und Frankreich*, vol. 2, doc. 165 for Napoleon's last offer; and Haugwitz to Frederick William, 30 March 1804, doc. 167 for the concept of Frederick William's final rejection. Alexander must have been reacting to an earlier exchange, although it is not entirely clear which one.

71. Haugwitz to Frederick William, 30 March 1804, in Bailleu, *Preußen und Frankreich*, vol. 2, doc. 167.

72. Memorandum of King Frederick William III, mid-February 1804, in Bailleu, *Preußen und Frankreich*, vol. 2, doc. 160.

73. Declaration of Russia about Joint Actions with Prussia for the defense of Northern Germany, 4 May 1804, VPR, vol. II, doc. 13.

74. Alopeus to Czartoryskii, 26 May 1804, VPR, vol. II, doc. 24.

75. Alexander to Alopeus, 16 June 1804, VPR, vol. II, doc. 30.

76. Decree to Lucchesini, 23 April 1804, in Bailleu, *Preußen und Frankreich*, vol. 2, doc. 172.

77. Frederick William III to Napoleon, 28 June 1804, in Bailleu, *Preußen und Frankreich*, vol. 2, doc. 184.

78. Talleyrand to Laforest, 5 May 1804, in Bailleu, *Preußen und Frankreich*, vol. 2, doc. 173.

79. J. W. Lombard to Hardenberg, 8 May 1804, in Bailleu, *Preußen und Frankreich*, vol. 2, doc. 174.

80. Hardenberg to Lombard, 9 May 1804, in Bailleu, *Preußen und Frankreich*, vol. 2, doc. 175.

81. Talleyrand to Laforest, 5 May 1804, in Bailleu, *Preußen und Frankreich*, vol. 2, doc. 173.

82. Alexander to Frederick William, 21 April 1804, in Bailleu, *Briefwechsel*, doc. 51.

83. Lucchesini's report, 26 May 1804, in Bailleu, *Preußen und Frankreich*, vol. 2, doc. 181.

84. Alexander to Frederick William, 3 June 1804, in Bailleu, *Briefwechsel*, doc. 54.

85. Frederick William to Alexander, 11 July 1804, in Bailleu, *Briefwechsel*, doc. 55.

86. Lucchesini's report, 17 May 1804, in Bailleu, *Preußen und Frankreich*, vol. 2, doc. 176.

87. Lucchesini's report, 17 May 1804, in Bailleu, *Preußen und Frankreich*, vol. 2, doc. 176.

88. Decree to Lucchesini, 24 May 1804, in Bailleu, *Preußen und Frankreich*, vol. 2, doc. 178.

89. Hardenberg to Frederick William, 24 May 1804, in Bailleu, *Preußen und Frankreich*, vol. 2, doc. 177.

90. Hardenberg to Lucchesini, 25 May 1804, in Bailleu, *Preußen und Frankreich*, vol. 2, doc. 180.

91. Hardenberg to Frederick William, 6 June 1804, in Bailleu, *Preußen und Frankreich*, vol. 2, doc. 183.

92. Decree to Lucchesini, 4 September 1804, in Bailleu, *Preußen und Frankreich*, vol. 2, doc. 195.

93. Decree to Lucchesini, 12 October 1804, in Bailleu, *Preußen und Frankreich*, vol. 2, doc. 204.

94. Frederick William to Alexander, 11 July 1804, in Bailleu, *Briefwechsel*, doc. 55. See above.

95. Czartoryskii to Alopeus, 9 October 1804, VPR, vol. II, doc. 54.

96. Alexander to Frederick William, 5 October 1804, in Bailleu, *Briefwechsel*, doc. 56.

97. Czartoryskii to Alopeus, 9 October 1804, VPR, vol. II, doc. 54.

98. VPR, vol. II, n. 89.

99. Czartoryskii to Alopeus, 9 October 1804, VPR, vol. II, doc. 54.

100. Czartoryskii to Alopeus, 9 October 1804, VPR, vol. II, doc. 54. Emphasis added.

101. Napoleon to Fouché, 7 October 1804, *Corr. de Nap.*, doc. 8100.

102. J. W. Lombard to Lucchesini, 24 May 1804, in Bailleu, *Preußen und Frankreich*, vol. 2, doc. 179.

103. Decree to Lucchesini, 20 July 1804, in Bailleu, *Preußen und Frankreich*, vol. 2, doc. 188.

104. Lucchesini to Hardenberg, 26 May 1804, in Bailleu, *Preußen und Frankreich*, vol. 2, doc. 182.

105. Czartoryskii to Alopeus, 18 October 1804, VPR, vol. II, doc. 57.

106. Hardenberg to Lucchesini, 22 October 1804, in Bailleu, *Preußen und Frankreich*, vol. 2, doc. 213.

107. Hardenberg to Knobelsdorff, 28 October 1804, in Bailleu, *Preußen und Frankreich*, vol. 2, doc. 214.

108. Simms, *Impact,* p. 162.

109. J. W. Lombard to Hardenberg, 29 October 1804, in Bailleu, *Preußen und Frankreich*, vol. 2, doc. 215; Simms, *Impact,* pp. 161ff., describes both Lombard's role and Hardenberg's subsequent efforts to whitewash his own motives.

110. Frederick William to Napoleon, 30 October 1804, in Bailleu, *Preußen und Frankreich*, vol. 2, doc. 216.

111. Laforest to Talleyrand, 30 October 1804, in Bailleu, *Preußen und Frankreich*, vol. 2, doc. 217.

112. Laforest to Talleyrand, 10 November 1804, in Bailleu, *Preußen und Frankreich*, vol. 2, doc. 222.

113. Frederick William to Lucchesini, 2 November 1804, in Bailleu, *Preußen und Frankreich*, vol. 2, doc. 219.

114. Hardenberg to Lucchesini, 1 November 1804, in Bailleu, *Preußen und Frankreich*, vol. 2, doc. 218.

115. Cited in Stamm-Kuhlmann, *König in Preußens großer Zeit*, p. 191. Emphasis in the original.

116. See Simms, *Impact,* pp. 164–166.

117. Lucchesini's report, 12 November 1804, in Bailleu, *Preußen und Frankreich*, vol. 2, doc. 223.

118. Napoleon to the King of Prussia, 10 November 1804, *Corr. de Nap.*, doc. 8170.

119. Stamm-Kuhlmann, *König in Preußens großer Zeit*, p. 191.

120. Michel Vovelle, ed., *Mémoires de Joseph Fouché, duc d'Otrante* (Paris: Imprimerie Nationale, 1992), p. 222.

121. Simms, *Impact,* p. 164.

122. Note of Alopeus to Hardenberg, 28 October 1804, VPR, vol. II, doc. 60.

123. Stamm-Kuhlmann, *König in Preußens großer Zeit*, p. 192.

124. VPR, vol. II, n. 112.

125. Czartoryskii to Alopeus, 15 November 1804, VPR, vol. II, doc. 71.

126. Czartoryskii to Alopeus, 22 December 1804, VPR, vol. II, doc. 78.

127. August Fournier, *Gentz und Cobenzl: Geschichte der österreichischen Diplomatie in den Jahren 1801–1805, nach neuen Quellen* (Vienna: Wilhelm Braumüller, 1880), pp. 142 144.

128. Metternich to Colloredo, 24 September 1804, in Prince Richard Metternich-Winneburg, ed., *Aus Metternich's nachgelassenen Papieren* (Vienna: Wilhelm Braumüller 1880), doc. 56.

129. Metternich to Colloredo, 24 September 1804, in Metternich-Winneburg, ed., *Aus Metternich's nachgelassenen Papieren*, doc. 56.

130. See Metternich to Colloredo, 17, 20 November 1804, in Wilhelm Oncken, *Österreich und Preußen im Befreiungskriege* (New York: Georg Olms Verlag, 1998; facsimile reprint of the 1879 ed.), docs. 3–4, for Metternich's reaction to the Rumbold affair. Colloredo to Metternich, 15 November 1804, in Oncken, *Österreich und Preußen*, docs. 5–6, gives the Austrian court's official reaction to events at the start of the affair and orders Metternich to start negotiations.

131. Metternich to Colloredo, 4 December 1804, in Oncken, *Österreich und Preußen*, doc. 7.

132. See, e.g., Metternich to Colloredo, 5 December 1804, in Oncken, *Österreich und Preußen*, doc. 8.

133. Hardenberg to Metternich, 26 December 1804, in Metternich-Winneburg, ed., *Aus Metternich's nachgelassenen Papieren*, vol. 1, doc. 60.

134. Colloredo to Metternich, 10 January 1805, in Oncken, *Österreich und Preußen*, docs. 11–12.

135. See, e.g., Instructions to Metternich, 5 November 1803, in Fournier, *Gentz und Cobenzl*, pp. 203–214.

136. Metternich to Hardenberg, 15 January 1805, in Metternich-Winneburg, *Aus Metternich's nachgelassenen Papieren*, doc. 61.

137. Instructions of Alexander to General F. F. Wintzingerode, 28 January 1805, VPR, vol. II, doc. 91.

138. Instructions of Czartoryskii to Alopeus, 28 January 1805, VPR, vol. II, doc. 92.

139. Draft of a Letter for Exchange Between Their Majesties the Emperors of Russia and Austria and the King of Prussia, n.d., VPR, vol. II, n. 152.

140. Notes of a Meeting of the Minister of Foreign Affairs of Prussia Hardenberg with Ambassador in Berlin M. M. Alopeus and F. F. Wintzingerode, 18 March 1805, VPR, vol. II, doc. 112.

141. Wintzingerode to Czartoryskii, 22 March 1805, VPR, vol. II, doc. 113.

142. See Instruction of Alexander I to General F. F. Wintzingerode, 28 January 1805, VPR, vol. II, doc. 91.

143. Memorandum of Haugwitz about the Political Situation in Connection with the Mission of Baron von Wintzingerode 1805, 27 February 1805, cited in Simms, *Impact,* p. 172. This document is paraphrased in Leopold von Ranke, *Denkwürdigkeiten des Staatskanzlers Fürsten von Hardenberg* (Leipzig: Ducker and Humblot, 1877), 2:138–141.

144. Ranke, *Hardenberg,* 2:136–142, implies that Haugwitz's memorandum prevented the king from following his advice, which was to negotiate the alliance. Although his testimony on such matters is generally suspect, given the charged relationship between the two men, both other evidence and logic suggest that it is generally valid in this case.

145. Instruction for General von Zastrow during his Mission to Petersburg, 12 April 1805, in Ranke, *Hardenberg,* 5:137–145.

146. Lucchesini to Hardenberg, 29–30 July 1805, Bailleu, *Preußen und Frankreich,* vol. 2, doc. 259; and Talleyrand to Laforest, 30 July 1805, in Bailleu, *Preußen und Frankreich,* vol. 2, doc. 261. The formal French offer was contained in a long memorandum delivered by Laforest to Hardenberg on 8 August 1805, reprinted in Ranke, *Hardenberg,* 5:145–160.

147. Lucchesini to Hardenberg, 29 July 1805, in Bailleu, *Preußen und Frankreich,* vol. 2, doc. 259.

148. Lucchesini to Hardenberg, 6 August 1805, in Bailleu, *Preußen und Frankreich,* vol. 2, doc. 262.

149. Laforest to Talleyrand, 10 August 1805, in Bailleu, *Preußen und Frankreich,* vol. 2, doc. 264.

150. Laforest to Talleyrand, 10 August 1805, in Bailleu, *Preußen und Frankreich,* vol. 2, doc. 264.

151. Memorandum of Beyme, 16 August 1805, 18 August 1805, in Bailleu, *Preußen und Frankreich,* vol. 2, docs. 267–268.

152. Protocol of the Conference at Halberstadt, 22 August 1805, in Ranke, *Hardenberg,* 5:167–172.

153. Rescript to Lucchesini, 17 August 1805, Ranke, *Hardenberg,* 5:161–164.

154. Laforest to Talleyrand, 14 August 1805, in Bailleu, *Preußen und Frankreich,* vol. 2, doc. 266.

155. Simms, *Impact,* p. 184. The document is paraphrased in Ranke, *Hardenberg,* 2:196–199.

156. Decree to Lucchesini, 9 September 1805, in Bailleu, *Preußen und Frankreich,* vol. 2, doc. 278.

157. Note of the Minister of Foreign Affairs about the Means for Bringing Prussia into the Coalition against Napoleon, 19 August 1805, VPR, vol. II, doc. 160.

158. See, e.g., Lord Mulgrave to Lord G. L. Gower, 11 March 1805, in John Holland Rose, *Select Despatches from the British Foreign Office Archives Relating to the Formation of the Third Coalition against France, 1804–1805* (London: Offices of the Royal Historical Society, 1904), doc. 67, pp. 114–116; and Lord G. L. Gower to Lord Mulgrave, 22 March 1805, in Holland Rose, *Select Despatches,* doc. 69, pp. 121–125; and Czartoryskii to M. M. Alopeus, 19 August 1805, VPR, vol. II, doc. 163.

159. Patricia Kennedy Grimsted, *The Foreign Ministers of Alexander I: Political Attitudes and the Conduct of Russian Diplomacy, 1801–1825* (Los Angeles: University of California Press, 1969), pp. 134–137; W. H. Zawadzki, *A Man of Honour: Adam Czartoryski as a Statesman of Russia and Poland, 1795–1831* (Oxford: Clarendon, 1993), pp. 127–136.

160. Simms, *Impact,* pp. 182–185.

161. Instruction of Alexander I to General F. F. Wintzingerode, 28 January 1805, VPR, vol. II, doc. 91.

162. Simms, *Impact,* p. 190.

Chapter 9   The Opposing Alliances

1. The treaty is reproduced in F. Martens, *Recueil des Traités et Conventions conclus par la Russie avec les Puissances Etrangères* (St. Petersburg: A. Böhnke, 1902), 2:433ff.
2. Article 2 in Martens, *Recueil*, 2:435.
3. Sixth Separate Article, in Martens, *Recueil*, 2:443.
4. First Separate and Secret Article, in Martens, *Receuil*, 2:458.
5. See, for example, the derision aimed at the Austrian army in Gunther Rothenberg, *The Art of Warfare in the Age of Napoleon* (Bloomington: Indiana University Press, 1980), pp. 166–168; Rothenberg, *Napoleon's Great Adversary* (New York: Sarpedon, 1982), p. 38; Scott Bowden, *Napoleon and Austerlitz: An Unprecedentedly Detailed Combat Study of Napoleon's Epic Ulm–Austerlitz Campaigns of 1805* (Chicago: Emperor's, 1997), pp. 121, 135; Martin Boycott-Brown, *The Road to Rivoli: Napoleon's First Campaign* (London: Cassell, 2001), pp. 33, 45; Robert M. Epstein, *Napoleon's Last Victory and the Emergence of Modern War* (Lawrence: University Press of Kansas, 1994), pp. 22–23; Christopher Duffy, *The Army of Maria Theresa: The Armed Forces of Imperial Austria, 1740–1780* (Vancouver: David & Charles, 1977), p. 214 (his description of the Austrian army in *Austerlitz, 1805*, pp. 24–29, is far from flattering, although it focuses more narrowly on Mack, his attempted reforms, and their consequences); and David Chandler, *Austerlitz, 1805: Battle of the Three Emperors* (1990; London: Osprey, 1998), p. 38.
6. Marcel Marion, *Histoire financière de la France depuis 1715. Vol. IV, 1797–1818: La fin de la Révolution, le Consulat et l'Empire, la libération du territoire* (1925; New York: Burt Franklin, n.d.), 4:268–271.
7. Hans Karl von Zwehl, *Der Kampf um Bayern 1805. I. Der Abschluss der Bayerisch-Französischen Allianz. Münchener Historische Abhandlungen. Erste Reihe: Allgemeine und Politische Geschichte* (Munich: C. H. Beck, 1937), 13:45–47; and Josef Gmeinwiser, "Die bayerische Politik im Jahre 1805" (Ph.D. diss, University of Munich, 1928), pp. 9–11.

Chapter 10   The Austrian War Plan

1. See W. H. Zawadzki, *A Man of Honour: Adam Czartoryski as a Statesman of Russia and Poland, 1795–1831* (Oxford: Clarendon, 1993), for Czartoryskii's biography; and "Vorontsov, Aleksandr Romanovich," in V. Fedorchenko, *Imperatorskii dom: Vydaioshchiesia sanovniki* (Moscow: Olma Press, 2001), 1:228–230.
2. See above, Chapter 5.
3. August Fournier, *Gentz und Cobenzl: Geschichte der österreichischen Diplomatie in den Jahren 1801–1805, nach neuen Quellen* (Vienna: Wilhelm Braumüller, 1880); Oskar Regele, "Karl Freiherr von Mack und Johann Ludwig Graf Cobenzl: Ihre Rolle im Kriegsjahr 1805," *Mittheilungen des österreichischen Staatsarchivs* 21 (1968): 142–164; Alois Moriggl, *Der Feldzug von Ulm und seine Folgen für Oesterreich überhaupt und für Tirol insbesonders* (Innsbruck: Verlag der Wagner'schen Buchhandlung, 1861).
4. VPR, vol. I, n. 327.
5. VPR, vol. II, n. 140.
6. Russo–Swedish Convention about combined action for the defense of Northern Germany, 14 January 1805, VPR, vol. II, doc. 89.
7. Norman E. Saul, "The Objectives of Paul's Italian Policy," in Hugh Ragsdale, ed., *Paul I: A Reassessment of His Life and Reign* (Pittsburgh, Pa.: University Center for International Studies, 1979), p. 35. See Alexander to D. P. Tatishchev, 2 March 1805, VPR, vol. II, doc. 108, for evidence that Alexander regarded himself as bound by Paul's treaty.

8. VPR, vol. II, n. 115.

9. Czartoryskii to Razumovskii, 8 November 1804, VPR, vol. II, doc. 69.

10. Czartoryskii to S. R. Vorontsov, 9 December 1804, VPR, vol. II, doc. 72.

11. Czartoryskii to S. R. Vorontsov, 17 February 1805, VPR, vol. II, doc. 105.

12. Czartorsykii to Razumovskii, 8 February 1805, VPR, vol. II, doc. 98.

13. John Ehrmann, *The Younger Pitt: The Consuming Struggle* (London: Constable, 1996), 3:792–793; Richard Hopton, *The Battle of Maida, 1806: Fifteen Minutes of Glory* (Barnsley, U.K.: Pen and Sword Books, 2002), pp. 46–48.

14. Russian Declaration about Combined Actions with Prussia in Defense of Northern Germany, 4 May 1804, VPR, vol. II, doc. 13.

15. Secret Convention of 6 November 1804 between Austria and Russia and Acts Relative to It, 6 November 1804, Léopold Neumann, *Recueil des traités et conventions conclus par l'Autriche avec les puissances étrangères, depuis 1763 jusqu'à nos jours* (Leipzig: F. A. Brockhaus, 1856), vol. 2, doc. 141, pp. 107–112.

16. A. R. Vorontsov to Alexander, 24 November 1803, VPR, vol. I, doc. 231.

17. See above, Chapter 4.

18. See above, Chapter 5 for the Austrian conception of the meaning of the alliance of November 1804.

19. The initial Russian approach is in A. R. Vorontsov to I. O. Anstett, 18 October 1803, VPR, vol. I, doc. 222. The first concrete proposal is in A. R. Vorontsov to Stadion, 1 January 1804, VPR, vol. I, doc. 246.

20. See VPR, vol. II, p. 597, note **.

21. See above, Chapter 5.

22. Observations on the Report from the Russian Court (from the chancellery of the court and of the State), not dated but before 3 March 1804, in Albrecht and William, Archdukes of Austria, eds., *Ausgewählte Schriften weiland seiner kaiserlichen Hoheit des Erzherzogs Carl von Oesterreich* (Vienna: Wilhelm Braumüller, 1894), 5:652–662.

23. Report about the Russian Memorandum, St. Petersburg, 20 December 1803, and the Comments of the Privy Court- and State-Council, 3 March 1804, Albrecht and William, *Ausgewählte Schriften*, 5:611–641.

24. Report about the Russian Memorandum, St. Petersburg, 20 December 1803, and the Comments of the Privy Court- and State-Council, 3 March 1804, Albrecht and William, *Ausgewählte Schriften*, 5:625–629.

25. Report about the Russian Memorandum, St. Petersburg, 20 December 1803, and the Comments of the Privy Court- and State-Council, 3 March 1804, Albrecht and William, *Ausgewählte Schriften*, 5:614–624.

26. Report about the Russian Memorandum, St. Petersburg, 20 December 1803, and the Comments of the Privy Court- and State-Council, 3 March 1804, Albrecht and William, *Ausgewählte Schriften*, 5:619–620.

27. Azar Gat, *The Origins of Military Thought from the Enlightenment to Clausewitz* (Oxford: Clarendon, 1989); Patrick J. Speelman, *Henry Lloyd and the Military Enlightenment of Eighteenth-Century Europe* (Westport, Conn.: Greenwood, 2002); Lee W. Eysturlid, *The Formative Influences, Theories, and Campaigns of the Archduke Carl of Austria* (Westport, Conn.: Greenwood, 2000).

28. Albrecht and William, *Ausgewählte Schriften*, 5:624.

29. Cobenzl to Colloredo, 9 March 1804, in Fournier, *Gentz und Cobenzl*, p. 215.

30. Cobenzl to Colloredo, 9 March 1804, in Fournier, *Gentz und Cobenzl*, p. 215.

31. The Austrian response, dated 1 April 1804, can be found in HHSt, Rußland Varia II, 240, ff. 387–390. It is reprinted in Adolf Beer, "Österreich und Russland in den Jahren 1804 und 1805," *Archiv für österreichische Geschichte* 53 (1875): 182–185.

32. Treaty of Defensive Alliance, 14 June 1792, in F. Martens, *Recueil des Traités et Conventions conclus par la Russie avec les Puissances Etrangères* (St. Petersburg: A. Böhnke, 1902), vol. 2, doc. 43; Act of Accession of the Roman Emperor to the Convention Concluded on 23 January 1793 Between

Prussia and Russia, Declaration Relating to the Partition of Poland, and Secret Declaration Concerning the Alliance between Russia and Austria against Prussia, all dated 1 January 1795, in Martens, *Recueil,* vol. 2, docs. 44–46.

33. Cobenzl to Stadion, 1 April 1804, in Beer, "Österreich und Rußland," pp. 202–205.
34. Cobenzl to Stadion, 1 April 1804, in Beer, "Österreich und Rußland," pp. 205–215.
35. Cobenzl to Colloredo, 9 March 1804, Fournier, *Gentz und Cobenzl,* p. 215.
36. Alexander to Razumovskii, 7 May 1804, VPR, vol. II, doc. 14. The (less specific and informative) formal convention counteroffer of the same date is reprinted as doc. 15.
37. The formal Austrian counterproposal containing that figure is in HHSt, Rußland Varia II, 240, ff. 397–404 (it can be dated by the plenipotentiary powers granted in the following document to 15 June 1804). Cobenzl verbally emphasized this demand to Razumovskii on 3 June 1804 (VPR, vol. II, doc. 25).
38. Razumovskii to Czartoryskii, 15 September 1804, VPR, vol. II, doc. 48.
39. Additional Notes about the Secret Instruction of Alexander to N. N. Novosil'tsev, 23 September 1804, VPR, vol. II, doc. 51.
40. This treaty, dated 6 November 1804, has been published in many places, including VPR, vol. II, doc. 63; Neumann, *Recueil des traités,* vol. 2, doc. 141, and Martens, *Recueil,* vol. 2, docs. 54–55.
41. See Alexander to S. R. Vorontsov, 11 May 1805, VPR, vol. II, doc. 125; Mulgrave to S. R. Vorontsov, 8 June 1805, in John Holland Rose, *Select Despatches from the British Foreign Office Archives Relating to the Formation of the Third Coalition against France, 1804–1805* (London: Offices of the Royal Historical Society, 1904), doc. 86, p. 174. Mulgrave promised to forward a detailed consideration of the Russian plan, but the published documentary record does not contain such a response.
42. Alexander to S. R. Vorontsov, 11 May 1805, VPR, vol. II, doc. 125 and n. 192. See p. 405 for the notation that the document was received on 1 June.
43. Warren to Harrowby, 5 November 1804; Gower to Harrowby, 7 November 1804, 28 November 1804, 8 December 1804, 24 December 1804; Gower to Mulgrave, 22 March 1805, in Holland Rose, *Select Despatches,* docs. 39, 41, 46, 49, 53, and 70, respectively.
44. Gower to Mulgrave, 14 August 1805, in Holland Rose, *Select Despatches,* doc. 99, p. 197.
45. Fournier, *Gentz und Cobenzl,* p. 148.
46. Francis to Charles, December 1804, in Adolf Beer, *Zehn Jahre österreichischer Politik, 1801–1810* (Leipzig: F. A. Brockhaus, 1877), p. 481.
47. Fournier, *Gentz und Cobenzl,* p. 152.
48. Comparison of the Military Power of Austria and Russia (as Possible Allies) with France and Its Allies, as Well as a Proposal for an Operations Plan for the Case of a War with France, 22 January 1805, Albrecht and William, *Ausgewählte Schriften,* 6:33–50.
49. Albrecht and William, *Ausgewählte Schriften,* 6:37.
50. Paul Claude Alombert-Goget and Jean Lambert Alphonse Colin, *La campagne de 1805 en Allemagne* (Paris: Librairie militaire R. Chapelot, 1902–1908), vol. 1, annex, pp. 36–37.
51. Albrecht and William, *Ausgewählte Schriften,* 6:45.
52. Albrecht and William, *Ausgewählte Schriften,* 6:45. On page 43 he still keeps open the possibility of sending the German army all the way to the Iller.
53. "Betrachtungen über die Vorbereitungen und künftigen Operationen der verbündeten k. k. und k. russischen Armeen," in Alfred Krauss, *1805: Der Feldzug von Ulm* (Vienna: L. W. Seidel, 1912), appendix 4. The version forwarded to Charles in February 1805 is reprinted in Albrecht and William, *Ausgewählte Schriften,* 6:60–64. This version differs in a number of minor details and in the major one that the proposal for the actions of the Austrian armies present in the earlier draft has been deleted.
54. Compare Krauss, *Der Feldzug von Ulm,* appendix 4, p. 5, with Albrecht and William, *Ausgewählte Schriften,* 6:62.

692 *Notes:* The Coalition War Plan

55. Krauss, *Der Feldzug von Ulm*, appendix 4, p. 7. This section is omitted from the memorandum reproduced in Albrecht and William, *Ausgewählte Schriften*, vol. 6.

56. Archduke Charles's observations about the use of Russian troops, 25 February 1805, in Albrecht and William, *Ausgewählte Schriften*, 6:55–59.

57. Archduke Charles's report, 25 February 1805, in Albrecht and William, *Ausgewählte Schriften*, 6:65–67.

58. Continued Reports of the FML Mack, February 1805, in Albrecht and William, *Ausgewählte Schriften*, 6:68–75. The document is undated, but Charles's response is dated 25 February 1805.

59. Regele, "Karl Freiherr von Mack," p. 143.

60. Archduke Charles's report, 25 February 1805, in Albrecht and William, *Ausgewählte Schriften*, 6:76–86.

Chapter 11 The Coalition War Plan

1. Operations plan proposed in 1805 by the court of Vienna, Léopold Neumann, *Recueil des traités et conventions conclus par l'Autriche avec les puissances étrangères, depuis 1763 jusqu'à nos jours* (Leipzig: F. A. Brockhaus, 1856), pp. 112–117, reprinted from Comte de Garden, *Histoire générale des traités de paix et autres transactions principales entre toutes les puissances de l'Europe depuis la paix de Westphalie* (Paris: Amyot, 1867), pp. 402–407.

2. Neumann, *Recueil des traités*, p. 113.

3. "Notes of the Minister of Foreign Affairs of Russia about the Austrian Draft Plan for Military Operations," 6 May 1805, VPR, vol. II, doc. 121. Also available as "Remarks about the operation plans proposed by Austria," in Neumann, *Recueil des traités*, pp. 117–121, reprinted from Garden, *Histoire générale*, pp. 407–411. "Response to the German Plan that Was Sent Here from Vienna by Mr. de Wintzingerode," HHSt, Rußland Varia II, 240 (unfoliated, not dated, not signed, interfoliated with a note from Alexander to Razumovskii of 28 April 1805) appears to be a summary of the Russian note made by Stadion, to whom it was probably read before being dispatched to Razumovskii (a standard diplomatic practice designed to ensure that both ambassador and foreign minister were made aware of the same decisions at the same time).

4. The passages referring to internal disaffection in France and hostility among the conquered states are almost uniformly absent from the versions of this note reprinted in Garden, *Histoire générale*, and Neumann, *Recueil des traités*. VPR, vol. II, working from archival materials, supplies the missing text (see the footnotes to doc. 121). The fact that these ideas were communicated to the Austrians is apparent from the summary in HHSt, Rußland Varia II, 240, which refers to this disaffection.

5. Alexander to Razumovskii, 10 May 1805, VPR, vol. II, doc. 122. Two copies of this note can be found in HHSt, Rußland Varia II, 240 (unfoliated), both dated 28 April 1805 (10 May 1805 in new style).

6. This note was presented to Cobenzl at the end of May 1805 (VPR, vol. II, n. 192, where it is summarized briefly). The plan itself is interfoliated with the second copy of Alexander's note to Razumovskii of 28 April 1805 (10 May 1805 new style), in HHSt, Rußland, Varia II, 240 as "A subsequent operations plan proposed by the court of Russia." This copy is almost certainly Stadion's summary of the plan as read to him by Czartoryskii (based on internal evidence). Another copy, possibly sent by the Russian court directly to Vienna, is in KA AFA 1805 Deutschland, VII/29. It is similar to the copy in the HHSt, with one notable exception discussed below.

7. Operations plan, KA AFA 1805 Deutschland, VII/29. This passage is omitted from the version in the HHSt.

8. Comments of the Russian Minister of Foreign Affairs on the Austrian Draft Plan of Military Actions, 6 May 1805, VPR, vol. II, doc. 121.

9. Frederick W. Kagan, "The Austrian Army, 1763–1805," unpublished article in preparation, provides a brief consideration of the nature of allied war planning in the early revolutionary period.

10. Charles's response is "Observations about Russian Negotiations Communicated to Me on the 20th of This Month," 23 June 1805, in Archdukes of Austria Albrecht and William, eds., *Ausgewählte Schriften weiland seiner kaiserlichen Hoheit des Erzherzogs Carl von Oesterreich* (Vienna: Wilhelm Braumüller, 1894), 6:153–162. Mack's is in HHSt, Rußland Varia II, 240 (unfoliated—follows the Russian war plan). This document is undated and unsigned. I ascribe it to Mack for the following reasons. First, it differs enough from Charles's response to rule out the archduke as the author. Second, it was clearly written by a military officer from a military–technical perspective. Third, it repeats several of the arguments that Mack had presented in the exchanges with Charles earlier in the year, especially concerning the importance of keeping the Russian and Austrian contingents separate. Cobenzl's response is in KA AFA 1805 Deutschland, XIII/92, date 17 June 1805. It is not signed. I ascribe it to Cobenzl because it is directly addressed to Francis (which means that Cobenzl probably wrote it and Colloredo presented it), because it considers the Russian proposal primarily from a political standpoint, and because it refers explicitly to the authors' having already presented correspondence from Razumovskii to the emperor—a job that belonged exclusively to Colloredo but that Cobenzl (alone among other officials) unofficially would have participated in.

11. Observations, First Piece, and Second Piece, HHSt, Rußland Varia II, 240 (unfoliated—interfoliated with Alexander's note dated 28 April 1805).

12. Observations about Russian Negotiations Communicated to Me on the 20th of This Month, 23 June 1805, in Albrecht and William, *Ausgewählte Schriften*, 6:158.

13. See above, Chapter 5, for Cobenzl's change of heart and efforts to persuade Francis to fight. The memorandum responding to the Russian plan is in KA AFA 1805 Deutschland, XIII/92. It is dated 17 June 1805, but it is not signed or foliated. See above, note 10, for an explanation of its attribution to Cobenzl (and Colloredo).

14. It seems that Charles's memorandum was responding to some of the points contained in Cobenzl's, including this proposal to delay an Austrian declaration of war until after the Russians had crossed the Austrian frontier; Cobenzl's memorandum predated Charles's by nearly a week. See also "Main Concept" from Charles to Francis, 23 July 1805, KA AFA 1805 Italien, VII/12, for a discussion of the need for the Austrian army to be fully ready for war the moment the Russians crossed the frontier.

15. The Austrian plan is reproduced (translated into Russian) in VPR, vol. II, n. 243.

16. Alexander to Razumovskii, 10 May 1805, VPR, vol. II, doc. 122. A brief biography is in Nikolai Mikhailovich, *General-ad"iutanty imperatora Aleksandra I* (St. Petersburg: Expeditsiia zagotovleniia gosudarstvennykh bumag, 1913), pp. 49–51.

17. Protocols of this conference are in KA AFA 1805 Deutschland, VII/1½, VII/30, and XIII/96. The protocol was translated into French and somewhat condensed in Neumann, *Recueil des traités*, pp. 121–129; and Garden, *Histoire générale*, 412–421.

18. Declaration of Deputy Minister of Foreign Affairs Czartoryskii to Austrian Ambassador in St. Petersburg Stadion, 9 August 1805, VPR, vol. II, doc. 153. The document is also available in HHSt, Rußland Varia II, 240, "Declaration Returned by Prince Czartoryskii to Ambassador Count Stadion 28 July/9 August 1805."

19. Preliminary Declaration Sent by the Ambassador of H[is] I[mperial] and R[oyal] M[ajesty] to His Excellency Prince Czartoryskii, 28 July/9 August 1805," in F. Martens, *Recueil des Traités et Conventions conclus par la Russie avec les Puissances Etrangères* (St. Petersburg: A. Böhnke, 1902), 2:428ff.

20. Czartoryskii to Razumovskii, 15 August 1805, VPR, vol. II, doc. 158.

21. Note of the Ministry of Foreign Affairs about Ways of Drawing Prussia into the Coalition against Napoleon, 19 August 1805, VPR, vol. II, doc. 160; Czartoryskii to Alopeus, 19 August 1805, VPR, vol. II, docs. 161–163.

22. Alfred Krauss, *1805: Der Feldzug von Ulm* (Vienna: L. W. Seidel, 1912), p. 133.

23. *Nähere Beleuchtung des dem k. k. Obersten und Chef des Generalstaabes Freyherrn von Mack zugeschriebenen Operationsplans für den Feldzug 1794 des Oesterreichisch-Französischen Krieges* (Berlin: Johann Friedrich Unger, 1796), 1:1–7.

Chapter 12   Napoleon's War Plans: Decisions

1. Paul Claude Alombert-Goget and Jean Lambert Alphonse Colin, *La campagne de 1805 en Allemagne* (Paris: Librairie militaire R. Chapelot, 1902–1908), 1:20–29.

2. Alombert-Goget and Colin, *La campagne de 1805*, 1:29. The orders are in Napoleon to General Pino, 22 January 1805, *Corr. de Nap.*, doc. 8282; Napoleon to Berthier, 22 January 1805, doc. 8283; and 25 January 1805, docs. 8287–8288.

3. Napoleon to Pino, 22 January 1805, *Corr. de Nap.*, doc. 8282.

4. Talleyrand to Larochefoucauld, 31 January 1805, in Alombert-Goget and Colin, *La campagne de 1805*, 1:29–30.

5. Francis to Napoleon, 23 January 1805, in Alombert-Goget and Colin, *La campagne de 1805*, 1:32–34; also available in Adolf Beer, "Oesterreich und Russland in den Jahren 1804 und 1805," *Archiv für österreichische Geschichte* 53 (1875): 196–198.

6. Napoleon to Berthier, 1 February 1805, *Corr. de Nap.*, doc. 8306; Napoleon to Pino, 1 February 1805, doc. 8307; Napoleon to Melzi, 1 February 1805, in Alombert-Goget and Colin, *La campagne de 1805*, 1:35; Talleyrand to Otto, 9 February 1805, in Alombert-Goget and Colin, *La campagne de 1805*, 1:37–38.

7. Francis to Napoleon, 23 January 1805, in Alombert-Goget and Colin, *La campagne de 1805*, 1:32–34; also available in Beer, "Oesterreich und Rußland," pp. 196–198.

8. Although the Genoese had already complied with all of his demands to attack British shipping interests and supply France with sailors in 1804. Edouard Driault, *Napoléon en Italie (1800–1812)* (Paris: Librairie Félix Alcan, 1906), pp. 330–331.

9. Napoleon to Decrès, 30 May 1805, *Corr. de Nap.*, doc. 8813.

10. Edouard Desbrière, *Projets et tentatives de débarquement aux Iles Britanniques* (Paris: Librairie Militaire R. Chapelot, 1900–1902), vol. 4, pts. 1–2, passim.

11. Desbrière, *Projets et tentatives*, vol. 4, pt. 2, pp. 239–250.

12. Desbrière, *Projets et tentatives*, vol. 4, pt. 2, pp. 341–353.

13. Warren to Harrowby, 23 September 1804, in John Holland Rose, *Select Despatches from the British Foreign Office Archives Relating to the Formation of the Third Coalition Against France, 1804–1805* (London: Offices of the Royal Historical Society, 1904), p. 40. Napoleon to Murat, 26 May 1805, *Corr. de Nap.*, doc. 8791.

14. Napoleon to Berthier, 2 October 1804, *Corr. de Nap.*, doc. 8074.

15. Napoleon to Vice Admiral Villeneuve, 12 December 1804, *Corr. de Nap.*, doc. 8206; and Napoleon to Rear Admiral Missiessy, 23 December 1804, doc. 8231. See also Napoleon to General Lauriston (commander of the ground forces with Villeneuve's fleet), 12 December 1804, doc. 8209; and Instructions for General Lagrange (commander of the ground forces with Missiessy's fleet), 23 December 1804, doc. 8232.

16. Decrès to Lauriston, 11 December 1804, in Desbrière, *Projets et tentatives*, vol. 4, pt. 2, p. 269; Napoleon to Villeneuve, 12 December 1804, *Corr. de Nap.*, doc. 8206 (also in Desbrière, *Projets et tentatives*, vol. 4, pt. 2, p. 273).

17. Napoleon to Missiessy, 23 December 1804, *Corr. de Nap.*, doc. 8231; Instructions to General Lagrange, 23 December 1804, doc. 8232; and Decrès to Vice Admiral Villaret-Joyeuse, Captain-General

of Martinique, or to General of Division Ernouf, Captain-General of Guadeloupe, 26 December 1804, in Desbrière, *Projets et tentatives*, vol. 4, pt. 2, p. 286.

18. Napoleon to the King of England, 2 January 1805, *Corr. de Nap.*, doc. 8252.

19. Desbrière, *Projets et tentatives*, vol. 4, pt. 2, p. 350.

20. Napoleon to the King of England, 2 January 1805, *Corr. de Nap.*, doc. 8252. Emphasis added.

21. Villeneuve to Decrès, 21 January 1805, in Desbrière, *Projets et tentatives*, vol. 4, pt. 2, p. 299.

22. Précis of the Campaign of the Squadron under the Orders of Rear Admiral Missiessy, 8 January 1805, in Desbrière, *Projets et tentatives*, vol. 4, pt. 2, pp. 307–309; Report of the French Expedition of the Division under the Orders of Rear Admiral Missiessy, 26 June 1805, vol. 4, pt. 2, pp. 309–313.

23. Decrès to Rear Admiral Missiessy, 27 January 1805, Desbrière, *Projets et tentatives*, vol. 4, pt. 2, p. 313.

24. Desbrière, *Projets et tentatives*, vol. 4, pt. 2, p. 318.

25. Napoleon to Decrès, 16 January 1805, Desbrière, *Projets et tentatives*, vol. 4, p. 2, pp. 325–326. Also available in *Corr. de Nap.*, doc. 8279.

26. Desbrière, *Projets et tentatives*, vol. 4, pt. 2, pp. 326–327.

27. Desbrière, *Projets et tentatives*, vol. 4, pt. 3, pp. 357–358.

28. Napoleon to Ganteaume, 2 March 1805, in Desbrière, *Projets et tentatives*, vol. 4, pt. 3, pp. 363–366; Napoleon to Villeneuve, 2 March 1805, vol. 4, pt. 3, pp. 366–367; Napoleon to Lauriston, 2 March 1805, vol. 4, pt. 3, pp. 367–369; and Napoleon to Berthier, 3 March 1805, vol. 4, pt. 3, pp. 369–370. These documents are also reproduced in *Corr. de Nap.*, docs. 8379–8384.

29. A fact that Desbrière himself admits. See *Projets et tentatives*, vol. 4, pt. 3, p. 357.

30. Desbrière, *Projets et tentatives*, vol. 4, pt. 3, pp. 370–372.

31. Napoleon to Villeneuve, 2 March 1805, in Desbrière, *Projets et tentatives*, vol. 4, pt. 3, pp. 366–367.

32. Albert Pingaud, *Bonaparte, Président de la République Italienne* (Paris: Librairie académique, Perrin et Cie, 1914), 2:439–445.

33. Napoleon ordered Decrès to prepare a new organization for the port of Genoa on 24 May 1805 (*Corr. de Nap.*, doc. 8784), before the incorporation of the new territory. He ordered the destruction of the customs barriers and the implementation of a regime to smooth the economic transition resulting from the incorporation four days later (Napoleon to M. Collin, 28 May 1805, *Corr. de Nap.*, doc. 8804). He repeated his order to Decrès, with considerable emphasis on the resources available in Genoa, on 4 June 1805 (*Corr. de Nap.*, doc. 8837).

34. See, for example, Napoleon to Decrès, 30 May 1805, in Desbrière, *Projets et tentatives*, vol. 4, pt. 3, pp. 593–594. Also in *Corr. de Nap.*, doc. 8813.

35. See *Corr. de Nap.*, March 1805 through July 1805, passim. Many of these letters along with others from Napoleon to Eugène and many from Eugène to Napoleon are reprinted in A. Du Casse, ed., *Mémoires et correspondence politique et militaire du Prince Eugène*, vol. 1 (Paris: Michel Lévy Frères, 1858).

36. Desbrière, *Projets et tentatives*, vol. 4, pt. 3, pp. 479–488.

37. Telegraphic correspondence between Ganteaume and Napoleon, 24 March 1805, in Desbrière, *Projets et tentatives*, vol. 4, pt. 3, p. 469; vol. 4, pt. 3, pp. 470–471; Ganteaume to Decrès, 3 April 1805, vol. 4, pt. 3, p. 504.

38. Napoleon to Decrès, 11 April 1805, in Desbrière, *Projets et tentatives*, vol. 4, pt. 3, pp. 507–508; also in *Corr. de Nap.*, doc. 8568.

39. Napoleon to Lauriston, 13 April 1805, in Desbrière, *Projets et tentatives*, vol. 4, pt. 3, p. 509; Napoleon to Villeneuve, 14 April 1805, vol. 4, pt. 3, p. 513.

40. Napoleon to Decrès, 27 April 1805, in Desbrière, *Projets et tentatives*, vol. 4, pt. 3, pp. 526–527.

41. Desbrière, *Projets et tentatives*, vol. 4, pt. 3, pp. 525–526.

42. Desbrière, *Projets et tentatives*, vol. 4, pt. 3, pp. 524–528.

43. For a full account of Napoleon's various plans and actions see Desbrière, *Projets et tentatives*, vol. 4, pt. 3, passim.

44. Napoleon to Pino, 13 April 1805, *Corr. de Nap.*, doc. 8581.

45. Napoleon to Talleyrand, 16 April 1805, *Corr. de Nap.*, doc. 8590.

46. Napoleon to Jourdan, 20 April 1805, *Corr. de Nap.*, doc. 8602.

47. Napoleon to Murat, 26 May 1805, *Corr. de Nap.*, doc. 8791.

48. Napoleon to Decrès, 26 May 1805, *Corr. de Nap.*, doc. 8792.

49. Napoleon to Cambacérès, 26 May 1805, *Corr. de Nap.*, doc. 8788.

50. Napoleon to Fouché, 26 May 1805, *Corr. de Nap.*, doc. 8790.

51. Napoleon to Decrès, 29 May 1805, *Corr. de Nap.*, doc. 8808.

52. See Talleyrand to Laforest, 4 June 1805, in Paul Bailleu, ed., *Preußen und Frankreich 1795 bis 1807: Diplomatische Correspondenzen*, Publicationen aus den königlichen preussischen Archiven, 8, 29 (Leipzig, 1881–1887), vol. 2, doc. 255.

53. Napoleon to Cambacérès, 20 June 1805, *Corr. de Nap.*, doc. 8916.

54. Carl Ritter von Schönhals, *Der Krieg 1805 in Deutschland, nach Österreichischen Originalquellen* (Vienna: Selbstverlag der Redaction der Österreichischen Militärischen Zeitschrift, 1873), p. 14; Napoleon to Berthier, 27 March 1805, *Corr. de Nap.*, doc. 8491.

55. Schönhals, *Der Krieg 1805*, pp. 14–15.

56. Alois Moriggl, *Der Feldzug von Ulm und seine Folgen für Oesterreich überhaupt und für Tirol insbesonders* (Innsbruck: Verlag der Wagner'schen Buchhandlung, 1861), p. 47.

57. Eugène to Napoleon, 11 July 1805 in Du Casse, *Mémoires et correspondance*, p. 193.

58. Eugène to Napoleon, 14 July 1805, in Du Casse, *Mémoires et correspondance*, p. 198.

59. Napoleon to Eugène, 23 July 1805, *Corr. de Nap.*, doc. 9005.

60. Eugène to Napoleon, 17 July 1805, in Du Casse, *Mémoires et correspondance*, p. 202.

61. Note of the Minister of Foreign Affairs to Count Philip Cobenzl, 5 Thermidor Year 13 (24 July 1805), *Campagnes de la Grande-Armée et de l'Armée d'Italie en l'an XIV (1805)* (Paris: La Librairie Economique, 1806), pp. 47–50.

62. Napoleon to Eugène, 27 July 1805, *Corr. de Nap.*, doc. 9028.

63. Letter of the Minister of Foreign Affairs to Count Cobenzl, Vice Chancellor of Court and State at Vienna, 17 Thermidor, Year 13 (5 August 1805), in *Campagnes de la Grande-Armée*, p. 51. This letter mentions Wintzingerode's presence in Vienna and guesses at his mission there, but is not more specific.

64. Talleyrand to Durand, 23 July 1805, SIRIO, vol. 82, doc. 29, pp. 90–93.

65. Napoleon to Talleyrand, 31 July 1805, *Corr. de Nap.*, doc. 9032. Napoleon approved the note on 3 August 1805 (Napoleon to Talleyrand, 3 August 1805, *Corr. de Nap.*, doc. 9038), and it was sent out dated 5 August 1805 (Letter of the Minister of Foreign Affairs to Count Cobenzl, Vice Chancellor of Court and State at Vienna, 17 Thermidor, Year 13, in *Campagnes de la Grande-Armée*, pp. 51–59).

66. Talleyrand to Napoleon, 6 August 1805, in Pierre Bertrand, ed., *Lettres inédites de Talleyrand à Napoléon, 1800–1809* (Paris: Perrin et Cie, 1889), doc. 89, pp. 123–125.

67. Napoleon to Talleyrand, 7 August 1805, *Corr. de Nap.*, doc. 9055.

68. Napoleon to Talleyrand, 10 August 1805, *Corr. de Nap.*, doc. 9062.

69. Napoleon to Talleyrand, 12 August 1805, *Corr. de Nap.*, doc. 9068. The note referred to is probably Otto's dispatch of 2 August (in Alombert-Goget and Colin, *La campagne de 1805*, 1:127–129).

70. Declaration of the Court of Vienna given to the Minister of the Emperor of the French, 5 August 1805, Léopold Neumann, *Recueil des traités et conventions conclus par l'Autriche avec les puissances étrangères, depuis 1763 jusqu'à nos jours* (Leipzig: F. A. Brockhaus, 1856), 2:162–167.

71. See KA AFA 1805 Deutschland, VII/24.

72. Napoleon to Talleyrand, 12 August 1805, *Corr. de Nap.*, doc. 9068.

73. Napoleon to Cambacérès, 13 August 1805, *Corr. de Nap.*, doc. 9069.

74. Alombert-Goget and Colin, *La campagne de 1805*, 1:62–63.

75. Napoleon to Talleyrand, 13 August 1805, *Corr. de Nap.*, doc. 9070.

76. Napoleon to Talleyrand, 13 August 1805, *Corr. de Nap.*, doc. 9070; emphasis added.

77. Villeneuve to Decrès, 3 August 1805, in Desbrière, *Projets et tentatives*, vol. 4, pt. 3, pp. 725–727.

78. Desbrière, *Projets et tentatives*, vol. 4, pt. 3, pp. 730–732.

79. Napoleon to Decrès, 13 August 1805, in Desbrière, *Projets et tentatives*, vol. 4, pt. 3, p. 751; also *Corr. de Nap.*, doc. 9072; Napoleon to Decrès, 14 August 1805, in Desbrière, *Projets et tentatives*, vol. 4, pt. 3, pp. 753–755; *Corr. de Nap.*, doc. 9076.

80. Desbrière, *Projets et tentatives*, vol. 4, pt. 3, pp. 733–757.

81. Napoleon to Villeneuve, 13 August 1805, in Desbrière, *Projets et tentatives*, vol. 4, pt. 3, pp. 752–753; Napoleon to Lauriston, 14 August 1805, vol. 4, pt. 3, p. 753; Napoleon to Decrès, 14 August 1805, vol. 4, pt. 3, pp. 753–755; Decrès to Villeneuve, 14 August 1805, vol. 4, pt. 3, pp. 755–756.

82. Napoleon to Villeneuve, 13 August 1805, in Desbrière, *Projets et tentatives*, vol. 4, pt. 3, pp. 752–753.

83. Napoleon to Lauriston, 14 August 1805, in Desbrière, *Projets et tentatives*, vol. 4, pt. 3, p. 753.

84. Napoleon to Talleyrand, 23 August 1805, *Corr. de Nap.*, doc. 9117; see below for a discussion of this note.

85. Napoleon to Talleyrand, 16 August 1805, *Corr. de Nap.*, doc. 9087.

86. Napoleon to Talleyrand, 22 August 1805, *Corr. de Nap.*, doc. 9104; Napoleon to the King of Prussia, 23 August 1805, *Corr. de Nap.*, doc. 9116.

87. Napoleon to Talleyrand, 18 August 1805, in Alombert-Goget and Colin, *La campagne de 1805*, 1:66–67.

88. Napoleon to Talleyrand, 18 August 1805, and other reports and orders described in the text, Alombert-Goget and Colin, *La campagne de 1805*, 1:66–67.

89. Napoleon to Talleyrand, 19 August 1805, *Corr. de Nap.*, doc. 9093; and Napoleon to Eugène, 19 August 1805, doc. 9095.

90. Numerous letters are reproduced in Alombert-Goget and Colin, *La campagne de 1805*, 1:127–135.

91. Villeneuve to Decrès, 6 August 1805, in Desbrière, *Projets et tentatives*, vol. 4, pt. 3, pp. 776–777; vol. 4, pt. 3, pp. 780ff.

92. Napoleon to Villeneuve, 22 August 1805, in Desbrière, *Projets et tentatives*, vol. 4, pt. 3, p. 812; also *Corr. de Nap.*, doc. 9115.

93. Napoleon to Decrès, 22 August 1805, in Desbrière, *Projets et tentatives*, vol. 4, pt. 3, p. 812.

94. Napoleon to Decrès, 22 August 1805, in Desbrière, *Projets et tentatives*, vol. 4, pt. 3, p. 813.

95. Decrès to Napoleon, 22 August 1805, in Desbrière, *Projets et tentatives*, vol. 4, pt. 3, p. 814.

96. Napoleon to Talleyrand, 23 August 1805, *Corr. de Nap.*, doc. 9117. Both Desbrière, *Projets et tentatives*, and Alombert-Goget and Colin, *La campagne de 1805*, cite this letter as evidence of Napoleon's decision to turn east.

Chapter 13   Napoleon's War Plans: Concept and Action

1. See, for example, Napoleon to Berthier, 23 August 1805, *Corr. de Nap.*, doc. 9120.

2. Berthier to Marmont, 28 August 1805, in Paul Claude Alombert-Goget and Jean Lambert Alphonse Colin, *La campagne de 1805 en Allemagne* (Paris: Librairie militaire R. Chapelot, 1902–1908), 1:370.

3. Napoleon to Berthier, 23 August 1805, *Corr. de Nap.*, doc. 9119.

4. Napoleon to Berthier, 23 August 1805, *Corr. de Nap.*, doc. 9120.

5. Napoleon to Dejean, 23 August 1805, *Corr. de Nap.*, doc. 9122.

6. Napoleon to Talleyrand, 25 August 1805, in Alombert-Goget and Colin, *La campagne de 1805*, 1:265; *Corr. de Nap.*, doc. 9130.

7. Alombert-Goget and Colin, *La campagne de 1805*, 1:159, 163.

8. Napoleon to the Elector of Bavaria, 25 August 1805, *Corr. de Nap.*, doc. 9134.

9. Napoleon to Berthier, 25 August 1805, *Corr. de Nap.*, doc. 9132.

10. See Napoleon to Talleyrand, 25 August 1805, *Corr. de Nap.*, doc. 9130, for the sense that the Austrians have stolen a march and that Napoleon must race to prevent them from overrunning Bavaria before he can react.

11. This line of argument follows the excellent reasoning of Alombert-Goget and Colin, *La campagne de 1805*, 1:166–170.

12. Napoleon to Talleyrand, 25 August 1805, in Alombert-Goget and Colin, *La campagne de 1805*, 1:266; *Corr. de Nap.*, doc. 9130.

13. Berthier to Bernadotte, 5 September 1805, in Alombert-Goget and Colin, *La campagne de 1805*, 1:436.

14. Napoleon to Berthier, 23 August 1805, *Corr. de Nap.*, doc. 9121.

15. Napoleon to Saint Cyr, 2 September 1805, *Corr. de Nap.*, doc. 9176.

16. Napoleon to Eugène, 27 August 1805, *Corr. de Nap.*, doc. 9143.

17. Napoleon to Berthier, 30 August 1805, *Corr. de Nap.*, doc. 9163.

18. Napoleon to Saint Cyr, 2 September 1805, *Corr. de Nap.*, doc. 9176.

19. Napoleon to Eugène, 31 August 1805, *Corr. de Nap.*, doc. 9171.

20. Napoleon to Eugène, 27 August 1805, *Corr. de Nap.*, doc. 9143.

21. Napoleon to Masséna, 18 September 1805, *Corr. de Nap.*, doc. 9233; Berthier to Masséna, 17 September 1805, in General Jean Baptiste Frédéric Koch, ed., *Mémoires de Masséna* (Paris: Paulin et Lechevalier, 1850), 5:362–365.

22. Napoleon to Masséna, 18 September 1805, *Corr. de Nap.*, doc. 9233; Berthier to Masséna, 17 September 1805, in Koch, *Mémoires de Masséna*, 5:362–365. The quotation is from the first note.

23. Berthier to Saint Cyr, 2 September 1805, *Corr. de Nap.*, doc. 9176.

24. Napoleon to Villeneuve, 14 September 1805, *Corr. de Nap.*, doc. 9210. This order will be considered below in more detail as it relates to Napoleon's revised plans for the war at sea.

25. Saint Cyr to Berthier, 8 September 1805, in Ch. Auriol, *La France, l'Angleterre et Naples de 1803 à 1806* (Paris: Librairie Plon, 1904), 2:511–514.

26. Alquier to the Minister of Foreign Relations, 7 September 1805, in Auriol, *La France*, 2:516–520.

27. Convention Between Russia and the Kingdom of the Two Sicilies about the Defense of the Kingdom from French Attack, 10 September 1805, VPR, vol. II, doc. 179; also in Auriol, *La France*, 2:525–530.

28. Alquier to the Minister of Foreign Affairs, 16 September 1805 and 20 September 1805, in Auriol, *La France*, 2:543–544, 551–552.

29. Treaty of Neutrality, in Auriol, *La France*, 2:578–579.

30. Minister of Foreign Affairs to the Ambassador of France at Naples, 22 September 1805; Berthier to Saint Cyr, 23 September 1805, in Auriol, *La France*, 2:582–584, 585. The note to Saint Cyr is also reproduced in *Corr. de Nap.*, doc. 9263.

31. Auriol, *La France*, 2:587–588; Marquis de Circello to Marquis de Gallo, 7 October 1805, in Auriol, *La France*, 2:589–593.

32. Alquier to the Minister of Foreign Affairs, 9 October 1805, in Auriol, *La France*, 2:596–598.

33. Ratification of the Treaty of Neutrality, in Auriol, *La France*, 2:594–595.

34. Annulment of the Treaty of Neutrality, in Auriol, *La France*, 2:603–604.

35. Saint Cyr to the Minister of War, 25 October 1805, in Auriol, *La France*, 2:614–616.

36. See above, Chapter 8.

37. Laforest to Talleyrand, 14 August 1805, in Paul Bailleu, *Preußen und Frankreich 1795 bis 1807: Diplomatische Correspondenzen*, Publicationen aus den königlichen preussischen Archiven, 8, 29 (Leipzig, 1881–1887), vol. 2, doc. 266, pp. 360–362. Talleyrand to Laforest, 25 August 1805, doc. 270, contains the foreign minister's response.

38. See above, Chapter 9.

39. Reports of Otto to Talleyrand from 25–26 August 1805, Hans Karl von Zwehl, *Der Kampf um Bayern 1805. I. Der Abschluss der Bayerisch-Französischen Allianz. Münchener Historische Abhandlungen. Erste Reihe: Allgemeine und Politische Geschichte,* vol. 13 (Munich: C. H. Beck, 1937), appendix 5, pp. 186–190.

40. See "Observations on the Draft Treaty that Mr. Otto Presented in July 1805 and Which Was Returned to Him on 8 August 1805" and "Alliance Treaty between the Elector of Bavaria and H[is] M[ajesty] the Emperor of the French dated Würzburg, 23 September 1805," in Gmeinwiser, "Die bayerische Politik," appendices 8–9. Montgelas requested a subsidy both for the army and for the elector himself, but the final treaty promised only a subsidy for the army.

41. Napoleon to Bernadotte, 5 September 1805, *Corr. de Nap.,* doc. 9184.

42. Napoleon to Talleyrand, 12 September 1805, *Corr. de Nap.,* doc. 9203.

43. Napoleon to Duroc, 28 August 1805, *Corr. de Nap.,* doc. 9155.

44. Napoleon to Talleyrand, 19 September 1805, *Corr. de Nap.,* doc. 9240.

45. Duroc to Talleyrand, 3 September 1805; Duroc to Napoleon, 8 September 1805; Duroc to Talleyrand, 18–19 September 1805; in Bailleu, *Preußen und Frankreich,* vol. 2, docs. 274, 277, 285.

46. Napoleon to Duroc, 28 August 1805, *Corr. de Nap.,* doc. 9155.

47. Duroc to Napoleon, 8 September 1805, Bailleu, *Preußen und Frankreich,* vol. 2, doc. 277; but Alombert-Goget and Colin, *La campagne de 1805,* vol. 2, pt. 1, p. 27 n. 1, correct the text of this letter. Where Bailleu has Duroc recommending that Bernadotte pass "through" (*par*) Ansbach and Beireuth, Alombert-Goget and Colin note that the text actually reads "between" (*entre*) Ansbach and Beireuth. This is the only reading of the text that makes geographical sense, since a forced march from either Bamberg or Würzburg would not travel through Ansbach to get to Amberg.

48. Alombert-Goget and Colin, *La campagne de 1805,* vol. 2, pt. 1, p. 27.

49. Alombert-Goget and Colin, *La campagne de 1805,* vol. 2, pt. 1, p. 26.

50. Alombert-Goget and Colin, *La campagne de 1805,* vol. 2, pt. 1, p. 28.

51. Instructions for Vice Admiral Villeneuve, 14 September 1805, *Corr. de Nap.,* doc. 9210.

52. Napoleon to Decrès, 15 September 1805, *Corr. de Nap.,* doc. 9220.

53. See above.

54. Napoleon to Decrès, 13 September 1805, *Corr. de Nap.,* doc. 9209.

55. Napoleon to Decrès, 13 September 1805, *Corr. de Nap.,* doc. 9209.

56. Napoleon to Decrès, 17 September 1805, *Corr. de Nap.,* doc. 9229.

Chapter 14   The Race to the Iller

1. Moriz Edlen von Angeli, "Beiträge zur vaterländischen Geschichte. IV. Ulm und Austerlitz. Studie auf Grund archivalischer Quellen über den Feldzug 1805 in Deutschland. A and B. Ulm," *Mittheilungen des K. K. Kriegs-Archivs* 2 (1877): 395–510; 3 (1878): 283–394; Alfred Krauss, *1805: Der Feldzug von Ulm* (Vienna: L. W. Seidel, 1912).

2. The following biographical sketch is taken from Angeli, "Ulm und Austerlitz," pt. A, vol. 2, pp. 433–435; and Oskar Regele, "Karl Freiherr von Mack und Johann Ludwig Graf Cobenzl: Ihre Rolle im Kriegsjahr 1805," *Mitteilungen des österreichischen Staatsarchivs* 21 (1968): 142–143.

3. The story is told rather differently from Francis's perspective in Cölestin Wolfsgruber, *Franz I. Kaiser von Oesterreich* (Vienna: Wilhelm Braumüller, 1899), 2:137–138.

4. Angeli, "Ulm und Austerlitz," pt. A, vol. 2, p. 439.

5. Angeli, "Ulm und Austerlitz," pt. A, vol. 2, p. 438.

6. See above, Chapter 7.

7. Angeli, "Ulm und Austerlitz," pt. A, vol. 2, p. 444.

8. Krauss, *Der Feldzug von Ulm*, pp. 132–133; KA AFA 1805 Deutschland, VIII/31.

9. Angeli, "Ulm und Austerlitz," pt. A, vol. 2, p. 446.

10. The documents relating to this negotiation can be found in KA AFA 1805 Deutschland, 74, and 74a through 74v, all dating from the first ten days or so of September 1805.

11. Hans Karl von Zwehl, *Der Kampf um Bayern 1805. I. Der Abschluss der Bayerisch-Französischen Allianz. Münchener Historische Abhandlungen. Erste Reihe: Allgemeine und Politische Geschichte.* vol. 13 (Munich: C. H. Beck, 1937), p. 66.

12. Von Zwehl, *Der Kampf um Bayern*, p. 61.

13. Krauss, *Der Feldzug von Ulm*, p. 185; Anon. [a courier] to Schwarzenberg, 11 September 1805, KA AFA 1805 Deutschland, IX/74u.

14. The negotiations and their results are described in von Zwehl, *Der Kampf um Bayern*, pp. 66ff.

15. Krauss, *Der Feldzug von Ulm*, p. 185.

16. Krauss, *Der Feldzug von Ulm*, pp. 180–181.

17. Krauss, *Der Feldzug von Ulm*, p. 181.

18. Mack to Francis, 3 September 1805, KA AFA 1805 Deutschland, IX/1.

19. Mack to Francis, 6 September 1805, KA AFA 1805 Deutschland, IX/5, cited in Krauss, *Der Feldzug von Ulm*, pp. 181–182.

20. Krauss, *Der Feldzug von Ulm*, pp. 184–185.

21. Krauss, *Der Feldzug von Ulm*, p. 179.

22. Krauss, *Der Feldzug von Ulm*, p. 186.

23. Mack to Francis, 21 August 1805, KA AFA 1805 Deutschland, VIII/20½, cited in Krauss, *Der Feldzug von Ulm*, pp. 152–153.

24. Mack to Francis, 6 September 1805, cited in Krauss, *Der Feldzug von Ulm*, pp. 181–182.

25. Mack to Francis, 16 September 1805, cited in Krauss, *Felzug von Ulm*, pp. 186–188.

26. Langenau to Charles, 24 September 1805, KA AFA 1805 HKR Deutschland, IX/1.

27. Allgemeiner Armeebefehl, 27 August 1805, KA AFA 1805 Italien, VIII/100.

28. Mack to Riesch, and General Order to Riesch's Army Corps, 14 September 1805, KA AFA 1805 Deutschland, IX/15, IX/ad15.

29. Anon. to anon., 11 September 1805, KA AFA 1805 Deutschland, IX/10. Another version of the same document, possibly sent to Weyrother, is in KA AFA 1805 Deutschland, XIII/124.

30. Mack to Francis, 16 September 1805, KA AFA 1805 Deutschland, IX/66½; this document is reproduced almost entirely in Krauss, *Der Feldzug von Ulm*, pp. 186–190.

31. Krauss, *Der Feldzug von Ulm*, p. 189.

32. See, for example, the reports in KA AFA 1805 Deutschland, XIII/124.

33. Memorandum about the Report of FML Mack, 9 September 1805, Archdukes of Austria Albrecht and William, eds., *Ausgewählte Schriften weiland seiner kaiserlichen Hoheit des Erzherzogs Carl von Oesterreich* (Vienna: Wilhelm Braumüller, 1894), 6:175–177; this document is also reproduced in Krauss, *Der Feldzug von Ulm*, pp. 182–184.

34. Francis to Mack, 17 September 1805, KA AFA 1805 Deutschland, IX/90.

35. Mack to Francis, 17 September 1805 [sent early in the morning of 18 September], KA AFA 1805 Deutschland, IX/66⅓. This document is reproduced extensively in Krauss, *Der Feldzug von Ulm*, pp. 191–193.

36. Mack to Francis, 16 September 1805, KA AFA 1805 Deutschland, IX/66½.

37. Mack to Francis, 19 September 1805, KA AFA 1805 Deutschland, IX/66¼.

38. KA AFA 1805 Deutschland, XIII/124.

39. Mack to Francis, 19 September 1805, KA AFA 1805 Deutschland, IX/66¼ and Draft Holograph Note to the War President, KA AFA 1805, Deutschland, IX/66¼a.

40. Krauss, *Der Feldzug von Ulm*, p. 202. Krauss does not identify the source for these recommendations, but they seem reasonable given Ferdinand's memoranda of a week later.

41. Krauss, *Der Feldzug von Ulm*, p. 203. The source of Francis's message to Ferdinand is not indicated.

42. Ferdinand to Francis, 20 September 1805, KA AFA 1805 Deutschland, IX/24.

43. Mack to Ferdinand, 20 September 1805, KA AFA 1805 Deutschland, IX/29.

44. Ferdinand to Mack, 21 September 1805, KA AFA 1805 Deutschland, IX/30.

45. Krauss, *Der Feldzug von Ulm*, pp. 207–209, and Disposition for the Concentration of a Corps at Neuburg and Ingolstadt, 23 September 1805, KA Nachlaß B/573 (Mack), 27.

46. Self-Justification of Mack to Emperor Francis, St. Pölten, March 20, 1813, KA Nachlaß B/573 (Mack), 26.

Chapter 15   Napoleon Seizes an Opportunity

1. "Austrian Troops by Army Corps," 29 August 1805, in Claude Alombert-Goget and Jean Lambert Alphonse Colin, *La campagne de 1805 en Allemagne* (Paris: Librairie militaire R. Chapelot, 1902–1908), vol. 2, pt. 1, p. 213.

2. Note on the movements of the Austrians, 2 September 1805, and intelligence reproduced from a German table listing the strengths of various European powers, 4 September 1805; Alombert-Goget and Colin, *La campagne de 1805*, vol. 2, pt. 1, pp. 202 and 211 respectively. The first report lists the Austrian strength as 420,000, but notes that this number seems exaggerated.

3. Note from Lezay-Marnezia, 22 September 1805, in Alombert-Goget and Colin, *La campagne de 1805*, vol. 2, pt. 1, p. 312.

4. Langenau to Charles, 24 September 1805, KA AFA 1805 HKR Deutschland, XI/1.

5. SVM, vol. 4, bk. 1, pt. 2, sec. 2, Information about the Statutory and Mustered Strength of the Army by Branch of Troops and in Sum on 1 January 1805 and 1806, following p. 388. These are the numbers of troops with the colors. The full-strength figures would have been about 18,000 higher.

6. Extract from a Letter from Leipzig, 30 August 1805, in Alombert-Goget and Colin, *La campagne de 1805*, vol. 2, pt. 1, p. 197; Report from Vienna, 4 September 1805, p. 210.

7. Murat to Napoleon, 10 September 1805, in Alombert-Goget and Colin, *La campagne de 1805*, vol. 2, pt. 1, p. 235.

8. Report from Geislingen, 24 September 1805, in Alombert-Goget and Colin, *La campagne de 1805*, vol. 2, pt. 1, p. 327.

9. Napoleon to Duroc, 11 September 1805, *Corr. de Nap.*, doc. 9199.

10. Note: draft of a speech to the French announcing the war with Austria, 15 September 1805, *Corr. de Nap.*, doc. 9216.

11. Otto to Talleyrand, 28 August 1805, in Alombert-Goget and Colin, *La campagne de 1805*, vol. 2, pt. 1, p. 191; unaddressed and unsigned note from 4 September 1805, p. 213; Bertrand to Napoleon, 30 August 1805, p. 196; Note about the movement of the Austrians, 2 September 1805, p. 202.

12. Note about the movement of the Austrians, 2 September 1805, in Alombert-Goget and Colin, *La campagne de 1805*, vol. 2, pt. 1, p. 202; Bertrand to Napoleon, 2 September 1805, p. 200.

13. Compare Alfred Krauss, *1805: Der Feldzug von Ulm* (Vienna: L. W. Seidel, 1912), pp. 128–129, with Alombert-Goget and Colin, *La campagne de 1805*, vol. 2, pt. 1, p. 191ff., especially the reports cited above, "The Most Recent Situation of the Austrian Army," 5 September 1805, in Alombert-Goget and Colin, *La campagne de 1805*, vol. 2, pt. 1, p. 203; and Murat to Napoleon, 10 September 1805, p. 235, in which he estimates that there are 60,000 Austrian troops at Wels in addition to 10,000–12,000 at Braunau—totals that are off by nearly a factor of two.

14. Compare Murat to Napoleon, 17 September 1805, in Alombert-Goget and Colin, *La campagne de 1805*, vol. 2, pt. 1, p. 265, with Langenau to Charles, 24 September 1805, KA AFA 1805 HKR Deutschland, IX/1. Murat to Napoleon, 21 September 1805, Alombert-Goget and Colin, *La campagne de 1805*, vol. 2, pt. 1, p. 305, contains a similar overestimation.

15. Bertrand to Napoleon, 20 September 1805, Alombert-Goget and Colin, *La campagne de 1805*, vol. 2, pt. 1, p. 281. See Langenau to Charles, 24 September 1805 (KA AFA 1805 HKR Deutschland, IX/1) for the number of battalions present by commander on 24 September.

16. Didelot to Murat, 21 September 1805, in Alombert-Goget and Colin, *La campagne de 1805*, vol. 2, pt. 1, p. 299; and Murat to Napoleon, p. 311.

17. Unaddressed, unsigned reports of 24 September 1805, in Alombert-Goget and Colin, *La campagne de 1805*, vol. 2, pt. 1, pp. 325, 327.

18. Berthier to the elector of Bavaria, 28 September 1805, in Alombert-Goget and Colin, *La campagne de 1805*, vol. 2, pt. 1, p. 351. It is not clear whether this message was sent.

19. Otto to Talleyrand, 28 August 1805, in Alombert-Goget and Colin, *La campagne de 1805*, vol. 2, pt. 1, p. 191.

20. Bulletin from Ratisbonne, 11 September 1805, in Alombert-Goget and Colin, *La campagne de 1805*, vol. 2, pt. 1, p. 242. Napoleon fully recognized Bacher's value. See Napoleon to Berthier, 7 September 1805, *Corr. de Nap.*, 9188.

21. Napoleon to Murat, 13 September 1805, Dépêche télégraphique, *Corr. de Nap.*, 9206, and a normal letter sent after it, 9205.

22. Berthier to Murat, 15 September 1805, in Alombert-Goget and Colin, *La campagne de 1805*, vol. 2, pt. 1, p. 256.

23. Murat to Napoleon, 15 September 1805, in Alombert-Goget and Colin, *La campagne de 1805*, vol. 2, pt. 1, p. 258.

24. Murat to Napoleon, 16 September 1805, in Alombert-Goget and Colin, *La campagne de 1805*, vol. 2, pt. 1, p. 263.

25. Murat to Napoleon, 17 September 1805, in Alombert-Goget and Colin, *La campagne de 1805*, vol. 2, pt. 1, p. 269.

26. Bacher to Murat and Didelot to Murat, 17 September 1805, in Alombert-Goget and Colin, *La campagne de 1805*, vol. 2, pt. 1, pp. 272, 277 respectively.

27. Napoleon to Murat, 18 September 1805, *Corr. de Nap.*, 9231.

28. Murat to Napoleon, 18 September 1805, in Alombert-Goget and Colin, *La campagne de 1805*, vol. 2, pt. 1, pp. 274 (telegraph), 276.

29. Murat to Napoleon, 19 September 1805, in Alombert-Goget and Colin, *La campagne de 1805*, vol. 2, pt. 1, p. 279.

30. This note was entered into the *Corr. de Nap.* as "Note determining the movements of the army that would result in the capitulation of Ulm" and dated 22 September 1805 (9254). Alombert-Goget and Colin, *La campagne de 1805*, vol. 2, pt. 1, pp. 29ff., argue convincingly that neither the date nor the title is warranted.

31. "Order determining the deployment of the divisions and corps of the Grande Armée," 17 September 1805, *Corr. de Nap.*, 9227. Alombert-Goget and Colin, *La campagne de 1805*, vol. 2, pt. 1, p. 266, show that this order was also not implemented.

32. Army Order, 20 September 1805, *Corr. de Nap.*, 9245.

33. Berthier to Murat, to Lannes, and to Ney, 20 September 1805, in Alombert-Goget and Colin, *La campagne de 1805*, vol. 2, pt. 1, pp. 284, 286, 287 respectively.

34. Napoleon to Murat, 21 September 1805, in Alombert-Goget and Colin, *La campagne de 1805*, vol. 2, pt. 1, p. 296.

35. Report without author, addressee, or location of 24 September 1805, in Alombert-Goget and Colin, *La campagne de 1805*, vol. 2, pt. 1, p. 325; Report from Geislingen, 24 September 1805, p. 327; and Didelot to Murat, 21 September 1805, p. 299.

36. Murat to Ney, 23 September 1805, in Alombert-Goget and Colin, *La campagne de 1805*, vol. 2, pt. 1, p. 322.

37. Napoleon to Joseph, 26 September 1805, *Corr. de Nap.*, 9266.

38. Napoleon to Talleyrand, 27 September 1805, *Corr. de Nap.*, 9270.

39. Napoleon to Bernadotte, 27 September 1805, *Corr. de Nap.*, 9274.

40. Napoleon to Otto, 28 September 1805, *Corr. de. Nap.*, 9277.

41. Note of the Major General's Bureau, 28 September 1805, in Alombert-Goget and Colin, *La campagne de 1805*, vol. 2, pt. 1, p. 344.

42. Otto to Talleyrand, 28 August 1805, in Alombert-Goget and Colin, *La campagne de 1805*, vol. 2, pt. 1, p. 191; Extract of a Letter from Leipzig, 30 August 1805, p. 197; A report from Vienna dated 4 September 1805 (p. 210), indicated that the Russians would be in Brünn by 12 September, which would indicate that they had begun their march weeks before.

43. Unsigned, unaddressed report of 7 September 1805, in Alombert-Goget and Colin, *La campagne de 1805*, vol. 2, pt. 1, p. 198.

44. Murat to Napoleon, 10 September 1805, in Alombert-Goget and Colin, *La campagne de 1805*, vol. 2, pt. 1, p. 235.

45. Napoleon to Duroc, 11 September 1805, *Corr. de Nap.*, 9199.

46. Circular of Talleyrand, 7 September 1805, SIRIO, vol. 82, doc. 39, pp. 131–132.

47. Durand to Talleyrand, 15 September 1805, in Alombert-Goget and Colin, *La campagne de 1805*, vol. 2, pt. 1, p. 254.

48. KA AFA 1805 Deutschland, IX/70.

49. Bacher to Murat, 17 September 1805, in Alombert-Goget and Colin, *La campagne de 1805*, vol. 2, pt. 1, p. 272.

50. Didelot to Murat, 17 September 1805, in Alombert-Goget and Colin, *La campagne de 1805*, vol. 2, pt. 1, p. 277.

51. Bertrand to Napoleon, 20 September 1805, in Alombert-Goget and Colin, *La campagne de 1805*, vol. 2, pt. 1, p. 281.

52. Murat to Napoleon, 21 September 1805, in Alombert-Goget and Colin, *La campagne de 1805*, vol. 2, pt. 1, p. 305.

53. Murat to Napoleon, 23 September 1805, in Alombert-Goget and Colin, *La campagne de 1805*, vol. 2, pt. 1, p. 319.

54. Report from Geislingen, 24 September 1805, in Alombert-Goget and Colin, *La campagne de 1805*, vol. 2, pt. 1, p. 327.

55. Napoleon to Bernadotte, 27 September 1805, *Corr. de Nap.*, 9274.

56. Napoleon to Otto, 28 September 1805, *Corr. de Nap.*, 9277. Napoleon was probably referring to the town of Kalchreuth, due north of Nürnberg.

57. David Chandler, *The Campaigns of Napoleon* (New York: Macmillan, 1966), p. 391; David Gates, *The Napoleonic Wars, 1803–1815* (New York: Arnold, 1997), p. 22; Scott Bowden, *Napoleon and Austerlitz: An Unprecedentedly Detailed Combat Study of Napoleon's Epic Ulm-Austerlitz Campaigns of 1805* (Chicago: Emperor's, 1997), p. 167. A notable exception is Martin van Creveld, *Supplying War: Logistics from Wallenstein to Patton* (1977, New York: Cambridge University Press, 1986), pp. 40–61, which accurately portrays the difficulties the French encountered in attempting to supply their army as it fanned out across southern Germany.

58. See, for example, Murat to Napoleon, 28 September 1805, in Alombert-Goget and Colin, *La campagne de 1805*, vol. 2, pt. 2, p. 424; Murat to Napoleon, 30 September 1805, p. 441; Murat to Berthier, 30 September 1805, p. 443; Berthier to Ney, 29 September 1805, p. 480; Soult to Berthier, 24 September 1805, p. 501; Soult to the Supply Officer, 25 September 1805, p. 506; Soult to Napoleon, 28 September 1805, p. 519; and many others throughout this document collection. Note that some of these supply shortages occurred in France in spite of orders to prepare supplies in advance of the arrival of the soldiers.

59. Bernadotte to Napoleon, 23 September 1805, in Alombert-Goget and Colin, *La campagne de 1805*, vol. 2, pt. 1, p. 132; William, the elector of Hesse, to Bernadotte, 25 September 1805, in Alombert-Goget and Colin, *La campagne de 1805*, vol. 2, pt. 1, p. 138.

60. Bernadotte to Napoleon, 28 September 1805, in Alombert-Goget and Colin, *La campagne de 1805*, vol. 2, pt. 1, p. 151.

61. Didelot to Ney, 29 September 1805, in Alombert-Goget and Colin, *La campagne de 1805*, vol. 2, pt. 2, p. 481.

62. Bernadotte to Berthier, 3 October 1805, in Alombert-Goget and Colin, *La campagne de 1805*, vol. 2, pt. 2, p. 703; Davout to Berthier, 2 October 1805; p. 648.

63. See above, note 58, for references on this point.

64. Sir Michael Howard, *The Franco–Prussian War: The German Invasion of France, 1870–1871* (1961; New York: Methuen, 1979), p. 63.

65. Napoleon to Berthier, 26 August 1805, in Alombert-Goget and Colin, *La campagne de 1805*, vol. 2, pt. 1, p. 334.

66. The order subordinating Marmont to Bernadotte is rather vague, but the intent is clear. Napoleon to Marmont, 13 September 1805, *Corr. de Nap.*, doc. 9207. A clarification followed: Berthier to Bernadotte, 28 September 1805, in Alombert-Goget and Colin, *La campagne de 1805*, vol. 2, pt. 1, p. 348.

67. See Chandler, ed., *Napoleon's Marshals*.

68. Napoleon to Berthier, 26 August 1805, *Corr. de Nap.*, 9137.

69. Berthier to Murat, 20 September 1805, in Alombert-Goget and Colin, *La campagne de 1805*, vol. 2, pt. 1, p. 284.

70. Berthier to Lannes, Ney, and Soult, 20 September 1805, in Alombert-Goget and Colin, *La campagne de 1805*, vol. 2, pt. 1, pp. 286, 287, 289 respectively.

71. Berthier to Davout, 20 September 1805, in Alombert-Goget and Colin, *La campagne de 1805*, vol. 2, pt. 1, p. 290.

72. Napoleon to Murat, 21 September 1805, in Alombert-Goget and Colin, *La campagne de 1805*, vol. 2, pt. 1, p. 296.

73. Murat to Ney, 23 September 1805, in Alombert-Goget and Colin, *La campagne de 1805*, vol. 2, pt. 1, p. 322; and 24 September 1805, p. 456; Soult to Murat, 23 September 1805, p. 499; Davout to Murat, 24 September 1805, p. 559.

74. Murat to Napoleon, n.d., in Alombert-Goget and Colin, *La campagne de 1805*, vol. 2, pt. 2, p. 397. Internal references date this document to around 25 September 1805.

75. The movements of the Austrian army and their consequences are described in great detail in Krauss, *Der Feldzug von Ulm*, passim.

76. This argument is laid out clearly in Krauss, *Der Feldzug von Ulm*, p. 284.

77. Rechtfertigungsschrift Macks an Kaiser Franz, St. Pölten, March 20, 1813, KA Nachlaß B/573 (Mack); Ferdinand, XIII/106, cited in Krauss, *Der Feldzug von Ulm*, p. 207.

78. Mack to Francis, 27 September 1805, KA AFA 1805 Deutschland, IX/73.

79. Mack to Francis, 27 September 1805, KA AFA 1805 Deutschland, IX/73.

80. Mack, Rechtfertigung, KA Nachlaß B/573 (Mack), 26.

81. Ferdinand to Francis, 28 September 1805, KA AFA 1805 Deutschland, IX/52.

82. Ferdinand to Francis, 1 October 1805, KA AFA 1805 Deutschland, X/8.

83. Mack to Baron Rothkirch and General Crenneville, 1 October 1805, KA AFA 1805 Deutschland, X/9. See also M. Lezay-Marnesia to Marshal Berthier, 2 October 1805, in Alombert-Goget and Colin, *La campagne de 1805*, vol. 2, pt. 2, p. 628; and Division General Tilly to Ney, 3 October 1805, p. 665.

84. Kienmayer to Ferdinand, 3 October 1805, KA AFA 1805 Deutschland, X/18.

85. Wallmoden to Kienmayer, 3 October 1805, KA AFA 1805 Deutschland, X/ad18c.

86. General Disposition, 5 October 1805, KA AFA 1805 Deutschland, X/31a.

87. Marmont to Berthier and Bernadotte to Berthier, 3 October 1805, in Alombert-Goget and Colin, *La campagne de 1805*, vol. 2, pt. 2, pp. 701, 703 respectively; Davout to Berthier, 2 October 1805, p. 648.
88. Kienmayer to Ferdinand, 6 October 1805, KA AFA 1805 Deutschland, X/39.

Chapter 16   The Battles of Ulm

1. Ferdinand to Francis, 6 October 1805, KA AFA 1805 Deutschland, X/40. This plan will be considered in more detail below.
2. Letter of Self-Justification from Mack to Emperor Francis, 20 March 1813, KA Nachlaß B/573 (Mack), 26.
3. Mack to Francis, 6 October 1805, KA AFA 1805 Deutschland, X/43½.
4. Ferdinand to Francis, 6 October 1805, KA AFA 1805 Deutschland, X/40.
5. "Observation about the Status of the Current Situation," 7 October 1805, KA AFA 1805 Deutschland, X/48.
6. Order of Battle and Dislocation for the Army in Germany, 7 October 1805, KA AFA 1805 Deutschland, X/55½.
7. Order of Battle and Dislocation, n.d., KA AFA 1805 Deutschland, X/2 gives a listing of the units belonging to Kienmayer's corps, although that changed somewhat by 7 October.
8. In addition to the many classic accounts of the Battle of Stalingrad, see especially Louis Rotundo, ed., *The Battle of Stalingrad: The 1943 Soviet General Staff Study* (Washington: Brassey's, 1989).
9. See, e.g., Soult to Napoleon, 7 October 1805, in Paul Claude Alombert-Goget and Jean Lambert Alphonse Colin, *La campagne de 1805 en Allemagne* (Paris: Librairie militaire R. Chapelot, 1902–1908), vol. 3, pt. 1, p. 251.
10. Murat to Napoleon, 3 October 1805, in Alombert-Goget and Colin, *La campagne de 1805*, vol. 2, pt. 2, p. 672; Soult to Napoleon, 3 October 1805, p. 684.
11. Murat to Napoleon, 3 October 1805, in Alombert-Goget and Colin, *La campagne de 1805*, vol. 2, pt. 2, p. 675.
12. Napoleon to Davout, 3 October 1805, in Alombert-Goget and Colin, *La campagne de 1805*, vol. 2, pt. 2, p. 714 (*Corr. de Nap.*, 9322); Napoleon to Soult, 3 October 1805, *Corr. de Nap.*, 9323.
13. Murat to Napoleon, 4 October 1805, in Alombert-Goget and Colin, *La campagne de 1805*, vol. 2, pt. 2, p. 729.
14. Lemarois to Napoleon, 4 October 1805, in Alombert-Goget and Colin, *La campagne de 1805*, vol. 2, pt. 2, p. 739; "Information," p. 743; Lannes to Napoleon, p. 746.
15. Napoleon to Murat and Soult, 4 October 1805, in Alombert-Goget and Colin, *La campagne de 1805*, vol. 2, pt. 2, pp. 769–770 (*Corr. de Nap.*, 9339 and 9340).
16. Napoleon to Bernadotte, 4 October 1805, in Alombert-Goget and Colin, *La campagne de 1805*, vol. 2, pt. 2, p. 772 (*Corr. de Nap.*, 9337).
17. Napoleon to Murat, 4 October 1805, *Corr. de Nap.*, 9339.
18. Murat to Napoleon, 5 October 1805, in Alombert-Goget and Colin, *La campagne de 1805*, vol. 2, pt. 2, p. 782.
19. Murat to Napoleon, 5 October 1805, in Alombert-Goget and Colin, *La campagne de 1805*, vol. 2, pt. 2, pp. 788–789.
20. Soult to Napoleon, 5 October 1805, in Alombert-Goget and Colin, *La campagne de 1805*, vol. 2, pt. 2, p. 813; Soult to Berthier, 5 October 1805, in Alombert-Goget and Colin, *La campagne de 1805*, vol. 2, pt. 2, p. 816; Davout to Napoleon, 5 October 1805, in Alombert-Goget and Colin, *La campagne de 1805*, vol. 2, pt. 2, p. 818; Davout to Soult, 5 October 1805, in Alombert-Goget and Colin, *La campagne de 1805*, vol. 2, pt. 2, p. 821.

21. Berthier to Ney and Berthier to Murat, 5 October 1805, in Alombert-Goget and Colin, *La campagne de 1805*, vol. 2, pt. 2, p. 827.

22. Berthier to Soult (two notes) and Murat, 5 October 1805, in Alombert-Goget and Colin, *La campagne de 1805*, vol. 2, pt. 2, pp. 835, 837, 831. The quotation is from p. 837.

23. Berthier to Ney, 6 October 1805, in Alombert-Goget and Colin, *La campagne de 1805*, vol. 2, pt. 2, p. 844.

24. Berthier to Lannes, 6 October 1805, in Alombert-Goget and Colin, *La campagne de 1805*, vol. 2, pt. 2, p. 857.

25. Davout to Napoleon, 6 October 1805, in Alombert-Goget and Colin, *La campagne de 1805*, vol. 2, pt. 2, p. 875.

26. Napoleon to Soult, 6 October 1805, in Alombert-Goget and Colin, *La campagne de 1805*, vol. 2, pt. 2, p. 866 (*Corr. de Nap.*, 9346).

27. Alfred Krauss, *1805: Der Feldzug von Ulm* (Vienna: L. W. Seidel, 1912), p. 302.

28. Krauss, *Der Feldzug von Ulm*, pp. 303, 317.

29. Marches and Historical Reports of the 1st Mounted Dragoons Division, 7 October 1805, in Alombert-Goget and Colin, *La campagne de 1805*, vol. 3, pt. 1, p. 248; Soult to Napoleon, 7 October 1805, p. 251.

30. Reports of the movements, etc., of the corps d'armée of the reserve, 7 October 1805, in Alombert-Goget and Colin, *La campagne de 1805*, vol. 3, pt. 1, p. 247.

31. Krauss, *Der Feldzug von Ulm*, p. 319.

32. Krauss, *Der Feldzug von Ulm*, pp. 318–319.

33. Berthier to Ney, in Alombert-Goget and Colin, *La campagne de 1805*, vol. 3, pt. 1, p. 253.

34. Recapitulation of the Troops of the Grande Armée, n.d., in Alombert-Goget and Colin, *La campagne de 1805*, vol. 3, pt. 1, p. 243.

35. KA AFA 1805 Deutschland, X/58½.

36. Mack to Ferdinand, 7 October 1805, KA AFA 1805 Deutschland, X/58.

37. Mack to Francis and Kutuzov, 8 October 1805, KA AFA 1805 Deutschland, X/63.

38. Krauss, *Der Feldzug von Ulm*, pp. 328–329; Ferdinand to Francis, 8 October 1805, KA AFA 1805 Deutschland, X/70 and Ferdinand to Kienmayer, X/69.

39. This idea is mooted in David Chandler, *The Campaigns of Napoleon* (New York: Macmillan, 1966), p. 396; Christopher Duffy, *Austerlitz, 1805* (London: Seeley Service, 1977), pp. 46–47; and David Gates, *The Napoleonic Wars, 1803–1815* (New York: Arnold, 1997), p. 24.

40. Berthier to Ney, 8 October 1805, in Alombert-Goget and Colin, *La campagne de 1805*, vol. 3, pt. 1, p. 300.

41. Berthier to Soult and Napoleon to Soult, 8 October 1805, in Alombert-Goget and Colin, *La campagne de 1805*, vol. 3, pt. 1, pp. 334–335. Napoleon to Davout, 8 October 1805, p. 341.

42. Berthier to Marmont and to Bernadotte, 8 October 1805, in Alombert-Goget and Colin, *La campagne de 1805*, vol. 3, pt. 1, pp. 349, 351.

43. Napoleon to Lannes and Berthier to Murat, 8 October 1805, in Alombert-Goget and Colin, *La campagne de 1805*, vol. 3, pt. 1, pp. 312–313.

44. Berthier to Ney, 8 October 1805, in Alombert-Goget and Colin, *La campagne de 1805*, vol. 3, pt. 1, p. 300.

45. The size of Auffenberg's division is from Krauss, *Der Feldzug von Ulm*, p. 341. Mack's order has not been preserved, but Auffenberg refers to it in his official dispatch regarding the battle, KA AFA 1805 Deutschland, X/71.

46. Krauss, *Der Feldzug von Ulm*, makes much of this fact, pp. 342–343.

47. Krauss, *Der Feldzug von Ulm*, p. 342.

48. The account that follows is taken primarily from Krauss, *Der Feldzug von Ulm*, pp. 337–342. The brief narrative in Franz Willbold, *Napoleons Feldzug um Ulm: Die Schlacht von Elchingen 14. Oktober 1805 mit der Belagerung und Kapitulation von Ulm* (Ulm: Süddeutsche Verlagsgesellschaft, 1987),

p. 24, is neither informative nor accurate (Willbold claims, for example, that Lannes's objective was Augsburg, which is untrue).

49. Belliard to Klein and to Beaumont, d'Hautpoul, and Nansouty, 8 October 1805, in Alombert-Goget and Colin, *La campagne de 1805*, vol. 3, pt. 1, pp. 314–315.

50. Marches et rapports historique de la 1re division de dragons montés, 8 October 1805, in Alombert-Goget and Colin, *La campagne de 1805*, vol. 3, pt. 1, p. 318.

51. Murat to Napoleon, 8 October 1805, in Alombert-Goget and Colin, *La campagne de 1805*, vol. 3, pt. 1, p. 316.

52. Krauss, *Der Feldzug von Ulm*, p. 359; Disposition, 9 October 1805, KA AFA 1805 Deutschland, X/73.

53. Berthier to Ney, 7 October 1805, in Alombert-Goget and Colin, *La campagne de 1805*, vol. 3, pt. 1, p. 253.

54. See the various dispositions and orders of 8 October 1805, in Alombert-Goget and Colin, *La campagne de 1805*, vol. 3, pt. 1, pp. 302–307. Ney to Crabbé, 8 October 1805, p. 308.

55. Berthier to Ney, 8 October 1805, in Alombert-Goget and Colin, *La campagne de 1805*, vol. 3, pt. 1, p. 300.

56. Berthier to Ney, 9 October 1805, in Alombert-Goget and Colin, *La campagne de 1805*, vol. 3, pt. 1, p. 365.

57. Dispositions of 9 October 1805, in Alombert-Goget and Colin, *La campagne de 1805*, vol. 3, pt. 1, p. 366.

58. Ney to Malher, 9 October 1805, in Alombert-Goget and Colin, *La campagne de 1805*, vol. 3, pt. 1, p. 367.

59. See Krauss, *Der Feldzug von Ulm*, pp. 364–369 for a basic narrative of this battle; Willbold, *Napoleons Feldzug um Ulm*, pp. 25–30, largely reproduces this account.

60. Ferdinand, Account of the Battle of Günzburg, 12 October 1805, KA AFA 1805 Deutschland, X/75.

61. Krauss, *Der Feldzug von Ulm*, pp. 365–366.

62. Journal of Operations of the Artillery . . . Battle of Günzburg, in Alombert-Goget and Colin, *La campagne de 1805*, vol. 3, pt. 1, p. 385.

63. Malher to Ney, 10 October 1805, in Alombert-Goget and Colin, *La campagne de 1805*, vol. 3, pt. 1, p. 374.

64. Ferdinand, Account of the Battle of Günzburg, KA AFA 1805 Deutschland, X/75.

65. Krauss, *Der Feldzug von Ulm*, p. 366.

66. Ferdinand, Account of the Battle of Günzburg, KA AFA 1805 Deutschland, X/75.

67. French accounts are in Alombert-Goget and Colin, *La campagne de 1805*, vol. 3, pt. 1, pp. 368–372. Krauss, *Der Feldzug von Ulm*, pp. 367–368.

68. Berthier to Lannes, 9 October 1805, in Alombert-Goget and Colin, *La campagne de 1805*, vol. 3, pt. 1, p. 396.

69. Rechtfertigung, KA Nachlaß B/573 (Mack), 26, 3rd point.

70. Murat to Ney, 9 October 1805, in Alombert-Goget and Colin, *La campagne de 1805*, vol. 3, pt. 1, p. 390.

71. Krauss, *Der Feldzug von Ulm*, p. 368.

72. Krauss, *Der Feldzug von Ulm*, pp. 367–369.

73. Krauss, *Der Feldzug von Ulm*, p. 377.

74. Krauss, *Der Feldzug von Ulm*, p. 378.

75. Disposition, 10 October 1805, KA AFA 1805 Deutschland, X/92.

76. Krauss, *Der Feldzug von Ulm*, p. 382.

77. Berthier to Ney, 9 October 1805, in Alombert-Goget and Colin, *La campagne de 1805*, vol. 3, pt. 1, p. 390.

78. Berthier to Lannes, 9 October 1805, in Alombert-Goget and Colin, *La campagne de 1805*, vol. 3, pt. 1, p. 396.

79. Berthier to Ney, 9 October 1805, in Alombert-Goget and Colin, *La campagne de 1805*, vol. 3, pt. 1, p. 390.

80. Ney to Berthier, 9 October 1805, in Alombert-Goget and Colin, *La campagne de 1805*, vol. 3, pt. 1, p. 391.

81. Ney to Napoleon, 10 October 1805, in Alombert-Goget and Colin, *La campagne de 1805*, vol. 3, pt. 1, p. 459.

82. Berthier to Ney, 10 October 1805, in Alombert-Goget and Colin, *La campagne de 1805*, vol. 3, pt. 1, p. 460.

83. Note from Berthier, 10 October 1805, in Alombert-Goget and Colin, *La campagne de 1805*, vol. 3, pt. 1, p. 461.

84. Berthier to Lannes, 10 October 1805, in Alombert-Goget and Colin, *La campagne de 1805*, vol. 3, pt. 1, p. 468.

85. Berthier to Murat, 10 October 1805, in Alombert-Goget and Colin, *La campagne de 1805*, vol. 3, pt. 1, p. 461.

86. Berthier to Soult, 10 October 1805, in Alombert-Goget and Colin, *La campagne de 1805*, vol. 3, pt. 1, p. 474; Bernadotte to Berthier, p. 492; Davout to Berthier, p. 483.

87. Bernadotte to Berthier, 9 October 1805, in Alombert-Goget and Colin, *La campagne de 1805*, vol. 3, pt. 1, p. 425.

88. Davout to Napoleon, 10 October 1805, in Alombert-Goget and Colin, *La campagne de 1805*, vol. 3, pt. 1, p. 483.

89. Berthier to Ney, 10 October 1805, in Alombert-Goget and Colin, *La campagne de 1805*, vol. 3, pt. 1, p. 460.

90. Berthier to Bernadotte, 9 October 1805, in Alombert-Goget and Colin, *La campagne de 1805*, vol. 3, pt. 1, p. 423.

91. Ney to Dupont, 11 October 1805, in Alombert-Goget and Colin, *La campagne de 1805*, vol. 3, pt. 1, p. 503.

92. Dispositions for the 6th Corps, 10 October 1805, in Alombert-Goget and Colin, *La campagne de 1805*, vol. 3, pt. 1, p. 500.

93. Ney to Dupont [10 October 1805], in Alombert-Goget and Colin, *La campagne de 1805*, vol. 3, pt. 1, p. 502; Ney to Baraguey-d'Hilliers, 10 October 1805, p. 502 and n. 1.

94. The account below largely follows that of Krauss, *Der Feldzug von Ulm*, pp. 402–406.

95. Documents relating to Ney's accusation and the investigation can be found in Alombert-Goget and Colin, *La campagne de 1805*, vol. 3, pt. 1, pp. 525ff.

96. Napoleon to Murat, 11 October 1805, in Alombert-Goget and Colin, *La campagne de 1805*, vol. 3, pt. 1, p. 559.

97. Murat to Napoleon, 11 October 1805, in Alombert-Goget and Colin, *La campagne de 1805*, vol. 3, pt. 1, p. 559.

98. Murat to Napoleon, 12 October 1805, in Alombert-Goget and Colin, *La campagne de 1805*, vol. 3, pt. 2, p. 610.

99. Berthier to Soult, 11 October 1805, in Alombert-Goget and Colin, *La campagne de 1805*, vol. 3, pt. 2, p. 638.

100. Napoleon to Murat, 12 October 1805, in Alombert-Goget and Colin, *La campagne de 1805*, vol. 3, pt. 2, p. 612.

101. Berthier to Bessières, 12 October 1805, in Alombert-Goget and Colin, *La campagne de 1805*, vol. 3, pt. 2, p. 633; Berthier to Marmont, p. 637; Napoleon to Berthier, p. 645; Berthier to Rivaud, p. 649; Berthier to Godinot, p. 650; Berthier to the Intendant-General, p. 653; and Berthier to Davout, p. 669.

102. Murat to Napoleon, 12 October 1805, in Alombert-Goget and Colin, *La campagne de 1805*, vol. 3, pt. 2, p. 613.

103. Lannes to Murat, 11:30 p.m., 12 October 1805, in Alombert-Goget and Colin, *La campagne de 1805*, vol. 3, pt. 2, p. 681; Murat to Napoleon, 4:00 A.M., 13 October 1805, in Alombert-Goget and Colin, *La campagne de 1805*, vol. 3, pt. 2, p. 682.

104. Berthier to Ney, 13 October 1805, in Alombert-Goget and Colin, *La campagne de 1805*, vol. 3, pt. 2, p. 685.

105. Berthier to Lannes, 13 October 1805, in Alombert-Goget and Colin, *La campagne de 1805*, vol. 3, pt. 2, p. 689.

106. Berthier to Lannes, 13 October 1805, in Alombert-Goget and Colin, *La campagne de 1805*, vol. 3, pt. 2, p. 699.

107. Berthier to Marmont, 13 October 1805, in Alombert-Goget and Colin, *La campagne de 1805*, vol. 3, pt. 2, p. 702; Marmont to Berthier, p. 703.

108. Berthier to Soult, 13 October 1805, in Alombert-Goget and Colin, *La campagne de 1805*, vol. 3, pt. 2, p. 706.

109. Berthier to Lannes and Ney, 13–14 October 1805, in Alombert-Goget and Colin, *La campagne de 1805*, vol. 3, pt. 2, pp. 723–724.

110. Ferdinand to Francis, 12 October 1805, KA AFA 1805 Deutschland, X/109½.

111. Krauss, *Der Feldzug von Ulm*, pp. 414–416.

112. Krauss, *Der Feldzug von Ulm*, p. 417.

113. Krauss, *Der Feldzug von Ulm*, p. 417.

114. Berthier to Ney, 13 October 1805, in Alombert-Goget and Colin, *La campagne de 1805*, vol. 3, pt. 2, p. 698.

115. Secret General Order of 12 October 1805, KA AFA 1805 Deutschland, X/120.

116. Krauss, *Der Feldzug von Ulm*, pp. 418–420.

117. Riesch, Relation about the Movement and Battle at Elchingen, 16 October 1805, KA AFA 1805 Deutschland, X/158 and Mack to Riesch, 13 October 1805, KA AFA 1805 Deutschland, X/ad158a; Mack to Riesch, 13 October 1805, X/ad158c.

118. Riesch, Relation about the Movement and Battle at Elchingen, 16 October 1805, KA AFA 1805 Deutschland, X/158.

119. Riesch, Relation about the Movement and Battle at Elchingen, 16 October 1805, KA AFA 1805 Deutschland, X/158; Mack to Riesch, 13 October 1805, KA AFA 1805 Deutschland, X/ad158d; General Order, 13 October 1805, KA AFA 1805 Deutschland, X/133, and orders to Werneck and Jellachich, X/133b, c, and d.

120. Krauss, *Der Feldzug von Ulm*, p. 423 n. 3.

121. Krauss, *Der Feldzug von Ulm*, pp. 425–428.

122. Riesch, Relation about the Movement and Battle at Elchingen, 16 October 1805, KA AFA 1805 Deutschland, X/158. See Malher to Ney, 13 October 1805, in Alombert-Goget and Colin, *La campagne de 1805*, vol. 3, pt. 2, pp. 684, 688, and the daily report of the 6th Corps, p. 688, for the French side of this little fight.

123. General Order, 14 October 1805, in Krauss, *Der Feldzug von Ulm*, p. 431.

124. Krauss, *Der Feldzug von Ulm*, p. 432.

125. Krauss, *Der Feldzug von Ulm*, p. 433.

126. The most detailed account of this battle is in Willbold, *Napoleons Feldzug um Ulm*, pp. 58–79. See also Krauss, *Der Feldzug von Ulm*, pp. 456–461. The narrative that follows is drawn primarily from those two accounts and that of Riesch himself, Riesch, Relation about the Movement and Battle at Elchingen, 16 October 1805, KA AFA 1805 Deutschland, X/158. The various French accounts are in Alombert-Goget and Colin, *La campagne de 1805*, vol. 3, pt. 2, pp. 726–747.

127. Riesch, Relation about the Movement and Battle at Elchingen, 16 October 1805, KA AFA 1805 Deutschland, X/158.

128. Riesch, Relation about the Movement and Battle at Elchingen, 16 October 1805, KA AFA 1805 Deutschland, X/158.

129. Riesch, Relation about the Movement and Battle at Elchingen, 16 October 1805, KA AFA 1805 Deutschland, X/158; Willbold, *Napoleons Feldzug um Ulm,* p. 66.

130. Willbold, *Napoleons Feldzug um Ulm* pp. 70–72.

131. Journal of Military Operations of Dupont's Division, 14 October 1805, in Alombert-Goget and Colin, *La campagne de 1805,* vol. 3, pt. 2, p. 726.

132. Krauss, *Der Feldzug von Ulm,* p. 460.

133. Riesch, Relation about the Movement and Battle at Elchingen, 16 October 1805, KA AFA 1805 Deutschland, X/158.

134. Willbold, *Napoleons Feldzug um Ulm.*

135. Krauss, *Der Feldzug von Ulm,* pp. 433–434.

136. General Order, 14 October 1805, *Corr. de Nap.*, 9382; Napoleon to Berthier, 15 October 1805, *Corr. de Nap.*, 9383.

137. Krauss, *Der Feldzug von Ulm,* p. 470.

138. Krauss, *Der Feldzug von Ulm,* p. 471.

139. Capitulation of Ulm, 19 October 1805, KA AFA 1805 Deutschland, X/206 $^1/_7$. The capitulation was actually agreed to and signed on 17 October. Krauss, *Der Feldzug von Ulm,* pp. 478–479.

Chapter 17   Advance and Retreat

1. Secret Instruction for Strauch, 2 August 1805, KA AFA 1805 Deutschland, XIII/98.

2. Guliaev and Sogliaev, *Fel'dmarshal Kutuzov,* pp. 184–185.

3. Guliaev and Soglaev, *Fel'dmarshal Kutuzov,* pp. 187–189.

4. Guliaev and Soglaev, *Fel'dmarshal Kutuzov,* p. 188 and note.

5. See Razumovskii to Czartoryskii, 1 September 1805, VPR, vol. II, doc. 172.

6. Guliaev and Soglaev, *Fel'dmarshal Kutuzov,* pp. 172–182.

7. Rescript from Alexander to Kutuzov with Instructions about the Conduct of the War with France, August 1805, in L. G. Beskrovnyi, *M. I. Kutuzov: Sbornik dokumentov* (Moscow: Voennoe Izdatel'stvo, 1951), vol. 2, doc. 3. A note indicates that the dating of this document is difficult, but it surely belongs in the middle of August.

8. Beskrovnyi, *Kutuzov,* doc. 7.

9. "Protocol of the meeting of July 16 between Wintzingerode and the Austrian generals" is available in KA AFA 1805 Deutschland, VII/1½, VII/30, and XIII/96; and (somewhat condensed) in Neumann, *Recueil des traités,* pp. 121–129; and Comte de Garden, *Histoire générale des traités de paix et autres transactions principales entre toutes les puissances de l'Europe depuis la paix de Westphalie,* vol. 8 (Paris: Amyot, 1867), pp. 412–421, point 6.

10. Kutuzov to Grabovskii, 15 September 1805, in Zhiugzhda, *Dokumenty,* doc. 16.

11. Francis to Baillet de Latour, 23 August 1805, KA AFA 1805 Deutschland, VIII/23.

12. Razumovskii to Czartorsykii, 1 September 1805, VPR, vol. II, doc. 172.

13. Beskrovnyi, *Kutuzov,* doc. 34, n. 1.

14. Kutuzov to Razumovskii, 23 September 1805, in Beskrovnyi, *Kutuzov,* doc. 35; Kutuzov to Cobenzl, 27 September 1805, HHSt, Rußland Varia II, 240.

15. Kutuzov, Order to Podolian Army, 23 September 1805, in Beskrovnyi, *Kutuzov,* doc. 36; Kutuzov to Alexander, 24 September 1805, doc. 43; Kutuzov, Order to Podolian Army, 25 September 1805, doc. 44.

16. Bagration to Kutuzov, 3 October 1805, in Zhiugzhda, *Dokumenty*, doc. 30.

17. Strauch to Ferdinand, 4 October 1805, KA AFA 1805 Deutschland, X/23.

18. Langenau to Charles, 24 September 1805, KA AFA HKR 1805 Deutschland, IX/1. See also Kutuzov to Razumovskii, 4 October 1805, in Beskrovnyi, *Kutuzov*, doc. 58.

19. Kutuzov to Czartoryskii, 8 October 1805, in Beskrovnyi, *Kutuzov*, doc. 67; Razumovskii to Czartoryskii, 8 October 1805, Alexander Vasil'chikov, *Les Razoumowski* (Halle: Tausch & Grosse, 1893), vol. 2, pt. 2, pp. 259–260. Razumovskii was present at the meeting.

20. Kutuzov to Czartoryskii, 8 October 1805, in Beskrovnyi, *Kutuzov*, doc. 67; Razumovskii to Czartoryskii, 8 October 1805, in Vasil'chikov, *Les Razoumowsky*, pp. 259–260; Cobenzl to Kutuzov, 12 October 1805, HHSt, Rußland Varia II, 240.

21. Kutuzov to the Podolian Army, 17 October 1805, in Beskrovnyi, *Kutuzov*, doc. 81.

22. Kutuzov to the Podolian Army, 15 October 1805, in Beskrovnyi, *Kutuzov*, doc. 78.

23. Kutuzov to the Podolian Army, 18 October 1805, in Beskrovnyi, *Kutuzov*, doc. 86. A note indicates that the original bore the date 17 October 1805 (new style); the dating of it to October 18 is not explained.

24. Kutuzov to Czartoryskii and Alexander, 19 October 1805, in Beskrovnyi, *Kutuzov*, docs. 87–88.

25. Figures are from the French tallies; Paul Claude Alombert-Goget and Jean Lambert Alphonse Colin, *La campagne de 1805 en Allemagne* (Paris: Librairie militaire R. Chapelot, 1902–1908), vol. 3, pt. 2, pp. 856–866. See also Soult to Napoleon, n.d., vol. 3, pt. 2, p. 770; and Soult to Berthier, 14 October 1805, p. 773. Alfred Krauss accepts this total in *1805: Der Feldzug von Ulm* (Vienna: L. W. Seidel, 1912), p. 505.

26. The mobilization and operations of Austrian forces in the Tyrol are described in great detail in Alois Moriggl, *Der Feldzug von Ulm und seine Folgen für Oesterreich überhaupt und für Tirol insbesonders* (Innsbruck: Verlag der Wagner'schen Buchhandlung, 1861), pp. 185ff.

27. Napoleon to Masséna, 29 September 1805, *Corr. de Nap.*, doc. 9286.

28. Napoleon to Otto and to Bernadotte, 11 October 1805, *Corr. de Nap.*, docs. 9365–9366.

29. Napoleon to Masséna, 11 October 1805, *Corr. de Nap.*, doc. 9369.

30. Napoleon to Soult, 19 October 1805, *Corr. de Nap.*, doc. 9397; Berthier to Soult, 20 October 1805, in Alombert-Goget and Colin, *La campagne de 1805*, vol. 3, pt. 2, p. 989; and Napoleon to Bernadotte, 19 October 1805, *Corr. de Nap.*, doc. 9394, which gives the strength of the Russian army as 30,000.

31. Napoleon to Otto, 24 October 1805, *Corr. de Nap.*, doc. 9419.

32. Berthier to Soult, 18 October 1805, in Alombert-Goget and Colin, *La campagne de 1805*, vol. 3, pt. 2, p. 931.

33. Berthier to Soult, 23 October 1805, in Alombert-Goget and Colin, *La campagne de 1805*, vol. 3, pt. 2, p. 1085; Soult to Napoleon, 19 October 1805, p. 964; Berthier to Soult, 20 October 1805, p. 989.

34. Napoleon to Petiet, 24 October 1805, *Corr. de Nap.*, doc. 9425.

35. Alombert-Goget and Colin, *La campagne de 1805*, vol. 3, pt. 2, passim.

36. Order to the Podolian Army, 15 October 1805, in Beskrovnyi, *Kutuzov*, doc. 79; Kutuzov to Alexander, 19 October 1805, doc. 88.

37. Napoleon to Talleyrand, 5 October 1805, *Corr. de Nap.*, doc. 9344; Bagration to Kutuzov, 3 October 1805, in Zhiugzhda, *Dokumenty*, doc. 30.

38. Napoleon to Joseph, 10 October 1805, *Corr. de Nap.*, doc. 9359.

39. Napoleon to Soult, 19 October 1805, *Corr. de Nap.*, doc. 9397.

40. Ferdinand to Kutuzov, 8 October 1805, reproduced in German and translated into Russian in Mikhailovskii-Danilevskii, *Opisanie*, pp. 40–43. Judging by its tone, this letter was almost certainly written by Mack.

41. Mikhailovskii-Danilevskii, *Opisanie*, pp. 55–56.

42. Anon. to Merveldt, 23 October 1805, HHSt, Rußland Varia II, 240. The author may have been Cobenzl.

43. Kutuzov to Czartoryskii, 19 October 1805, in Beskrovnyi, *Kutuzov*, doc. 87.

44. Kutuzov to Razumovskii, 21 October 1805, in Beskrovnyi, *Kutuzov*, doc. 103; a copy (in French) can also be found in HHSt, Rußland Varia II, 240.

45. Kutuzov to Alexander, 22 October 1805, Mikhailovskii-Danilevskii, *Opisanie*, p. 56; reproduced in Beskrovnyi, *Kutuzov*, doc. 107.

46. Krauss, *Der Feldzug von Ulm*, pp. 496–498.

47. Kutuzov to Francis and to Razumovskii, 23 October 1805, in Beskrovnyi, *Kutuzov*, docs. 108–109. In the note to Francis, Kutuzov declares his intention of retreating to Lambach and awaiting orders; in the message to Razumovskii he writes that he will withdraw to Linz.

48. Order to the Podolian Army, 24 October 1805, in Beskrovnyi, *Kutuzov*, doc. 115.

49. Kutuzov to Razumovskii and Czartoryskii, 24 October 1805, in Beskrovnyi, *Kutuzov*, docs. 113–114.

50. [Mack], "Précis of My Interview with the Emperor of the French," 27 October 1805, KA AFA 1805 Deutschland, X/ad246.

51. Berthier to Murat, 25 October 1805, in Alombert-Goget and Colin, *La campagne de 1805*, vol. 4, pt. 1, p. 179. An order to Davout on the same day exhibited similar confusion about the enemy's position and intentions (p. 180).

52. Berthier to Murat, 28 October 1805, in Alombert-Goget and Colin, *La campagne de 1805*, vol. 4, pt. 1, p. 258; Berthier to Bernadotte, 29 October 1805, p. 279.

53. Bulletin (Bacher), 26 October 1805, in Alombert-Goget and Colin, *La campagne de 1805*, vol. 4, pt. 1, p. 219; Schulmeister to Savary, 26 October 1805, p. 220; Bulletin from Ratisbonne (Bacher), 27 October 1805, p. 250.

54. General Order, 25 October 1805, *Corr. de Nap.*, doc. 9427.

55. Berthier to Marmont, 27 October 1805, in Alombert-Goget and Colin, *La campagne de 1805*, vol. 4, pt. 1, p. 225.

56. Alombert-Goget and Colin do not reproduce many orders to Ney in this period, but the deployment list for October 29 remarks that Ney was ordered to leave Landsberg for Innsbruck by October 31 (in Alombert-Goget and Colin, *La campagne de 1805*, vol. 4, pt. 1, p. 297). This order is also mentioned in Berthier to Bernadotte, 29 October 1805, p. 279.

57. Berthier to Marmont, 28 October 1805, in Alombert-Goget and Colin, *La campagne de 1805*, vol. 4, pt. 1, p. 280.

58. Berthier to Bernadotte, 29 October 1805, in Alombert-Goget and Colin, *La campagne de 1805*, vol. 4, pt. 1, p. 279.

59. Kutuzov to Francis, 23 October 1805, in Beskrovnyi, *Kutuzov*, doc. 108; Kutuzov to Alexander, 22 October 1805, doc. 107.

60. Kutuzov to Czartoryskii, 24 October 1805, Beskrovnyi, *Kutuzov*, doc. 117.

61. Alexander to Kutuzov, 5 November 1805, in A. M. Val'kovich and A. P. Kapitanov, eds., *Fel'dmarshal Kutuzov: Dokumenty, dnevniki, vospominaniia* (Moscow: Arkheograficheskii tsentr, 1995), doc. 121.

62. [Cobenzl?] to Merveldt, 23 October 1805, HHSt, Rußland Varia II, 240; Razumovskii to Kutuzov, 24 October 1805, in Beskrovnyi, *Kutuzov*, doc. 118.

63. [De Latour] to Merveldt, 25 October 1805, KA AFA 1805 Deutschland, X/212½d.

64. Murat to Napoleon, 30 October 1805; Belliard to Berthier, 30 October 1805; 3rd Dragoons Division, Report on the Combats of 8 and 9 Brumaire; and Journal of the 3rd Dragoons Division, in Alombert-Goget and Colin, *La campagne de 1805*, vol. 4, pt. 1, pp. 310–317.

65. Orders to the Podolian Army of 26–27 October and 1 November, in Beskrovnyi, *Kutuzov*, docs. 121, 124, 125, 136.

66. Kutuzov to Alexander, 4 November 1805, in Beskrovnyi, *Kutuzov*, doc. 148.

67. Kutuzov to Alexander, 4 November 1805, in Beskrovnyi, *Kutuzov*, doc. 150; Murat to Napoleon, 31 October 1805; 3rd Dragoons Division—Report on the Combats of 8–9 Brumaire; Journal of the 3rd Dragoons Division; 3rd Army Corps, Daily Report, 31 October 1805, in Alombert-Goget and Colin, *La campagne de 1805*, vol. 4, pt. 1, docs. 341–349. I have not been able to locate an Austrian account of the engagements at Ried or Lambach.

68. Kutuzov to Alexander, 4 November 1805, in Beskrovnyi, *Kutuzov*, doc. 150.

69. Francis to Kutuzov, 26 October 1805 and 29 October 1805, in Beskrovnyi, *Kutuzov*, docs. 122, 132.

70. Murat to Napoleon (three reports), 31 October 1805, in Alombert-Goget and Colin, *La campagne de 1805*, vol. 4, pt. 1, pp. 340–342.

71. The minutes of this meeting and the plan that Francis subsequently sent to Kutuzov are no longer extant. This summary of Francis's "orders" comes from Mikhailovskii-Danilevskii, *Opisanie*, p. 84. See Francis to Kutuzov, 29 October 1805, in Beskrovnyi, *Kutuzov*, doc. 132 and note; Kutuzov to Francis, October 1805, doc. 133 and note. Merveldt seems to refer to this plan in a note to Francis of 30 October 1805 (KA AFA 1805 Deutschland, X/220½), but offers no more specifics.

72. Kutuzov to Francis, October 1805, in Beskrovnyi, *Kutuzov*, doc. 133, citing Mikhailovskii-Danilevskii, *Opisanie*, p. 84. Mikhailovskii-Danilevskii misdates both the meeting and this exchange of notes to before October 27.

73. Berthier to Lannes, 30 October 1805, in Alombert-Goget and Colin, *La campagne de 1805*, vol. 4, pt. 1, p. 327.

74. Murat to Napoleon, 1 November 1805, in Alombert-Goget and Colin, *La campagne de 1805*, vol. 4, pt. 1, p. 382; Berthier to Davout, 2 November 1805, p. 416.

75. See, for example, Murat to Napoleon, 2 November 1805, in Alombert-Goget and Colin, *La campagne de 1805*, vol. 4, pt. 1, p. 429; Report of the Interrogation of Two Russian Prisoners, 1 November 1805, p. 388.

76. Murat to Napoleon, 1 November 1805, in Alombert-Goget and Colin, *La campagne de 1805*, vol. 4, pt. 1, p. 384.

77. Murat to Napoleon, 2 November 1805, in Alombert-Goget and Colin, *La campagne de 1805*, vol. 4, pt. 1, p. 429.

78. In addition to those already cited, see Bulletin [from Dresden], 1 November 1805, in Alombert-Goget and Colin, *La campagne de 1805*, vol. 4, pt. 1, p. 401.

79. Napoleon to Murat, 31 October 1805, in Alombert-Goget and Colin, *La campagne de 1805*, vol. 4, pt. 1, p. 351.

80. Napoleon to Talleyrand, 30 October 1805, *Corr. de Nap.*, doc. 9440; Napoleon to Eugène, 2 November 1805, doc. 9449.

81. Although they emphasize those difficulties. Napoleon's correspondence is a vast trove of information to be approached with skepticism and great care, since the emperor slanted his reporting of events, even to trusted subordinates, in order to produce the desired effects on everyone. The reader can be reasonably certain that Napoleon's letters to immediate subordinates about matters directly concerning them are mostly accurate. All others must be suspected and carefully examined before they receive any reliance or credence. Napoleon's ex post facto explanations of his own intentions are almost always useless to the historian. These difficulties are in addition to the problem that the published *Correspondance* is not always accurate, nor is it complete. See, for example, August Fournier, "Zur Textkritik der Korrespondenz Napoleon I," *Archiv für österreichische Geschichte* 39 (1905): 41–180.

82. This order has not been preserved in the published document collections, but it is referred to in the Emplacements of 3 November 1805, in Alombert-Goget and Colin, *La campagne de 1805*, vol. 4, pt. 1, p. 473, in Soult's order for 4 November 1805, p. 486, and his order to Margaron of the same date, p. 487.

83. Berthier to Bernadotte, 2 November 1805, in Alombert-Goget and Colin, *La campagne de 1805*, vol. 4, pt. 1, p. 414; to Marmont, same date, p. 416; and 4 November 1805, p. 479.

84. Journal of the 3rd Dragoons Division, 4 November 1805, in Alombert-Goget and Colin, *La campagne de 1805*, vol. 4, pt. 1, p. 481; 3rd Corps daily report, p. 482; 3rd Corps Topographical and Military Notes, p. 483; Journal of the Reserve Artillery of 3rd Corps, p. 484.

85. Order (Davout to Gudin), 4 November 1805, in Alombert-Goget and Colin, *La campagne de 1805*, vol. 4, pt. 1, p. 480; the Colonel of the 21st Regiment to Gudin, same date, p. 480.

86. Kutuzov to Dokhturov, 4 November 1805, in Beskrovnyi, *Kutuzov*, doc. 149.

87. 3rd Corps, Topographical and Military Notes, 4 November 1805, in Alombert-Goget and Colin, *La campagne de 1805*, vol. 4, pt. 1, p. 483.

88. Angeli, "Ulm und Austerlitz," p. 287.

89. Journal of the 2nd Dragoons Division, 5 November 1805, in Alombert-Goget and Colin, *La campagne de 1805*, vol. 4, pt. 2, p. 508.

90. Belliard to Berthier, 5 November 1805, in Alombert-Goget and Colin, *La campagne de 1805*, vol. 4, pt. 2, p. 509; Kutuzov to Alexander, 6 November 1805, Beskrovnyi, *Kutuzov*, doc. 157; Mikhailovskii-Danilevskii, *Opisanie*, p. 92.

91. Miloradovich to Kutuzov, 5 November 1805 [misdated in the published collection], in Zhiugzhda, *Dokumenty*, doc. 85; Mikhailovskii-Danilevskii (who dresses up this part of the story), *Opisanie*, p. 92; Belliard to Berthier, 5 November 1805, in Alombert-Goget and Colin, *La campagne de 1805*, vol. 4, pt. 2, p. 509, which is similar to the account in Journal of the Reserve Cavalry Corps, p. 513.

92. Except for one French account claiming that both armies bivouacked in each other's presence (Historical Account of 5th Corps, Précis of the Battle of Amstetten, in Alombert-Goget and Colin, *La campagne de 1805*, vol. 4, pt. 2, p. 517).

93. Belliard to Berthier, 5 November 1805, in Alombert-Goget and Colin, *La campagne de 1805*, vol. 4, pt. 2, p. 509. Emphasis added.

Chapter 18   The End of the Chase

1. Francis to Kutuzov, 4 November 1805, in Beskrovnyi, *Kutuzov*, doc. 152.

2. Francis to Kutuzov, 5 November 1805, in Beskrovnyi, *Kutuzov*, doc. 156.

3. Alexander to Kutuzov, undated, in Mikhailovskii-Danilevskii, *Opisanie pervoi voiny Imperatora Aleksandra s Napoleonom v 1805-m godu* (St. Petersburg: Independent Corps of the Internal Guard Press, 1844), pp. 76–77, reproduced in Beskrovnyi, *Kutuzov*, which gives the date as November 5, 1805, without explaining.

4. Paul Claude Alombert-Goget, *Campagne de l'an 14 (1805). Le corps d'armée aux ordres du Maréchal Mortier: Combat de Dürrenstein* (Paris: Berger-Levrault, 1897), pp. 20–22.

5. Napoleon to Murat, 6 November 1805, in Paul Claude Alombert-Goget and Jean Lambert Alphonse Colin, *La campagne de 1805 en Allemagne* (Paris: Librairie militaire R. Chapelot, 1902–1908), vol. 4, pt. 2, p. 548.

6. Murat to Napoleon, 7 November 1805, in Alombert-Goget and Colin, *La campagne de 1805*, vol. 4, pt. 2, p. 581.

7. See Alombert-Goget, *Combat de Dürrenstein*, pp. 1–20, for the formation of this flotilla and its immediate purposes.

8. Berthier to Mortier, 6 November 1805, in Alombert-Goget, *Combat de Dürrenstein*, p. 23. Alombert-Goget points out several times that this corps, commonly referred to in French accounts as the 8th Corps, did not in fact receive a number. Alombert-Goget, *Combat de Dürrenstein*, p. 28.

9. Berthier to Klein, 7 November 1805, in Alombert-Goget, *Combat de Dürrenstein*, p. 26.

10. Alombert-Goget, *Combat de Dürrenstein*, p. 23.

11. Alombert-Goget, *Combat de Dürrenstein,* pp. 20–21.

12. Instructions Given By Napoleon to General Mathieu Dumas Before His Mission to Marshal Davout, 5 November 1805, in Alombert-Goget and Colin, *La campagne de 1805*, vol. 4, pt. 2, p. 530.

13. Murat to Napoleon, 6 November 1805, in Alombert-Goget and Colin, *La campagne de 1805*, vol. 4, pt. 2, p. 546.

14. Napoleon to Murat, 6 November 1805, in Alombert-Goget and Colin, *La campagne de 1805*, vol. 4, pt. 2, p. 548.

15. Napoleon to Cambacérès, 6 November 1805, *Corr. de Nap.*, doc. 9455.

16. Murat to Napoleon, 6 November 1805, in Alombert-Goget and Colin, *La campagne de 1805*, vol. 4, pt. 2, p. 550.

17. Napoleon to Murat, 7 November 1805, *Corr. de Nap.*, doc. 9461.

18. Murat to Napoleon, 6 November 1805, in Alombert-Goget and Colin, *La campagne de 1805*, vol. 4, pt. 2, p. 549; Napoleon to Murat, 7 November 1805, *Corr. de Nap.*, doc. 9461.

19. Murat to Napoleon, 7 November 1805, in Alombert-Goget and Colin, *La campagne de 1805*, vol. 4, pt. 2, p. 581.

20. Murat to Napoleon, 7 November 1805, in Alombert-Goget and Colin, *La campagne de 1805*, vol. 4, pt. 2, p. 582.

21. Napoleon to Murat, 8 November 1805, *Corr. de Nap.*, doc. 9465.

22. See Alombert-Goget, *Combat de Dürrenstein*, p. 83.

23. Napleon to Murat, 8 November 1805, *Corr. de Nap.*, doc. 9465; Josef Gmeinwiser, "Die bayerische Politik im Jahre 1805" (Ph.D. diss., University of Munich, 1928), pp. 167ff.

24. Order of the Main Duty Department of the Podolian Army and Kutuzov to the Podolian Army, 8 November 1805, in Beskrovnyi, *Kutuzov*, docs. 160–161; Kutuzov to Francis, 11 November 1805, in Mikhailovskii-Danilevskii, *Opisanie*, pp. 96–97.

25. Murat to Napoleon, 8 November 1805, in Alombert-Goget and Colin, *La campagne de 1805*, vol. 4, pt. 2, p. 614. Emphasis added.

26. Murat to Napoleon, 9 November 1805, in Alombert-Goget, *Combat de Dürrenstein*, p. 80.

27. Murat to Napoleon, 11 November 1805, in Alombert-Goget, *Combat de Dürrenstein*, p. 144.

28. Napoleon to Murat, 11 November 1805, *Corr. de Nap.*, doc. 9470.

29. Philip J. Haythornthwaite, *Who Was Who in the Napoleonic Wars* (London: Arms & Armour, 1998), pp. 225–226; Alombert-Goget, *Combat de Dürrenstein*, pp. 326–327; David Chandler, ed., *Napoleon's Marshals* (New York : Macmillan, 1987), pp. 310–330.

30. Alombert-Goget, *Combat de Dürrenstein*, pp. 34–45.

31. Alombert-Goget, *Combat de Dürrenstein*, pp. 65, 75–76.

32. Alombert-Goget, *Combat de Dürrenstein*, p. 76.

33. Alombert-Goget, *Combat de Dürrenstein*, p. 69.

34. Alombert-Goget, *Combat de Dürrenstein*, p. 71.

35. Alombert-Goget, *Combat de Dürrenstein*, pp. 76, 78.

36. Beskrovnyi, *Kutuzov*, docs. 160–161.

37. Alombert-Goget, *Combat de Dürrenstein*, pp. 87–90; Kutuzov to Francis, 11 November 1805, KA AFA 1805 Deutschland, XI/45½.

38. Mikhailovskii-Danilevskii, *Opisanie*, pp. 99–100.

39. Mikhailovskii-Danilevskii, *Opisanie*, p. 100.

40. Beskrovnyi, *Kutuzov*, doc. 167.

41. Beskrovnyi, *Kutuzov*, doc. 166, Mikhailovskii-Danilevskii, *Opisanie*, p. 103.

42. Relation of Colonel Rozat, a commander of one of the squadrons in this regiment, in Alombert-Goget, *Combat de Dürrenstein*, p. 124.

43. Kotzebue, *Beschreibung*, pp. 14ff.

44. Egger, *Das Gefecht bei Dürnstein-Loiben*, p. 14; From the Report of M. A. Miloradovich to M. I. Kutuzov About the Battle of Krems, 21 November 1805, in Beskrovnyi, *Kutuzov*, doc. 199; Kotzebue, *Beschreibung*, pp. 27–28.

45. Colonel Talandier, extract from the Account of the Battle of Diernstein, in Alombert-Goget, *Combat de Dürrenstein*, pp. 106–107.

46. From the Report of M. A. Miloradovich to M. I. Kutuzov About the Battle of Krems, 21 November 1805, in Beskrovnyi, ed., *Kutuzov*, doc. 199.

47. From the Report of M. A. Miloradovich to M. I. Kutuzov About the Battle of Krems, 21 November 1805, in Beskrovnyi, ed., *Kutuzov*, doc. 199. Mikhailovskii-Danilevskii gives the general content of Kutuzov's order in *Opisanie*, p. 103.

48. From the Report of M. A. Miloradovich to M. I. Kutuzov About the Battle of Krems, 21 November 1805, in Beskrovnyi, *Kutuzov*, doc. 199.

49. Essen to Kutuzov, 18 November 1805, in Beskrovnyi, *Kutuzov*, doc. 186.

50. Colonel Talandier, extract from the Account of the Battle of Diernstein [Dürnstein], cited in Alombert-Goget, *Combat de Dürrenstein*, pp. 104–120.

51. Report about the battle at Dürnstein on 11 November 1805, KA AFA 1805 Deutschland, XI/46. This document is anonymous and undated, although it provides accurate detail about the battle.

52. Egger, *Das Gefecht bei Dürnstein-Loiben*, p. 17.

53. Report of D. S. Dokhturov to M. I. Kutuzov about the Battle of Krems, 20 November 1805, in Beskrovnyi, *Kutuzov*, doc. 198; Report of the Commander of the 6th Jaegers Regiment Ulanius to D. S. Dokhturov about the Battle of Krems, 14 November 1805, in Zhiugzhda, *Dokumenty*; Report by Lieutenant Colonel Gvozdev to Major General Urusov About the Battle of Krems, 20 November 1805, in Zhiugzhda, *Dokumenty*, doc. 98; Mikhailovskii-Danilevskii, *Opisanie*, p. 104.

54. Report of D. S. Dokhturov to M. I. Kutuzov about the Battle of Krems, 20 November 1805, in Beskrovnyi, *Kutuzov*, doc. 198; Colonel Talandier, Extract from the Account of the Battle of Diernstein, cited in Alombert-Goget, *Combat de Dürrenstein*, pp. 104–120; Taupin, Colonel of the 103rd Line Infantry Regiment, to the Major General, 18 December 1805, in Alombert-Goget, *Combat de Dürrenstein*, pp. 120–124.

55. From the Report of M. A. Miloradovich to M. I. Kutuzov About the Battle of Krems, 21 November 1805, in Beskrovnyi, *Kutuzov*, doc. 199; Colonel Talandier, Extract from the Account of the Battle of Diernstein, cited in in Alombert-Goget, *Combat de Dürrenstein*, pp. 104–120.

56. Extract from the Journal of Operations of Dupont's Division, in Alombert-Goget, *Combat de Dürrenstein*, 127–130. See also Dupont's letter of 1826 in Alombert-Goget, *Combat de Dürrenstein*, pp. 131–133; Colonel Talandier, Extract from the Account of the Battle of Diernstein, cited in Alombert-Goget, *Combat de Dürrenstein*, pp. 104–120.

57. Report of Major General Urusov to D. S. Dokhturov About the Battle of Krems, 16 November 1805, in Zhiugzhda, *Dokumenty*, doc. 97. There is no reliable French corroboration of this account, although it is not incompatible with the narratives of Talandier and Taupin.

58. Extract from the Journal of Operations of Dupont's Division, in Alombert-Goget, *Combat de Dürrenstein*, 127–130.

59. From the Report of Lieutenant Colonel Gvozdev to Major General Urusov About the Battle of Krems, 20 November 1805, in Zhiugzhda, *Dokumenty*, doc. 98.

60. Extract from the Journal of Operations of Dupont's Division, in Alombert-Goget, *Combat de Dürrenstein*, 127–130.

61. From the Report by Lieutenant Colonel Gvozdev to Major General Urusov about the Battle of Krems, 20 November 1805, in Zhiugzhda, *Dokumenty*, doc. 98.

62. Mikhailovskii-Danilevskii, *Opisanie*, p. 106; Extract from the Journal of Operations of Dupont's Division, in Alombert-Goget, *Combat de Dürrenstein*, pp. 127–130; Colonel Talandier, Extract

from the Account of the Battle of Diernstein, pp. 104–120; Taupin, Colonel of the 103rd Line Infantry Regiment to the Major General, 18 December 1805, pp. 120–124.

63. From the Report of M. A. Miloradovich to M. I. Kutuzov about the Battle of Krems, 21 November 1805, in Beskrovnyi, *Kutuzov,* doc. 199. See Alombert-Goget, *Combat de Dürrenstein,* p. 116 n. 1.

64. See Alombert-Goget, *Combat de Dürrenstein,* p. 137 n. 1.

65. Extract from the Journal of Operations of Dupont's Division, in Alombert-Goget, *Combat de Dürrenstein,* 127–130; Mikhailovskii-Danilevskii, *Opisanie,* p. 108; Colonel Rozat, Memoires, cited in Alombert-Goget, *Combat de Dürrenstein,* pp. 124–127.

66. Twenty-Second Bulletin of the Grande Armée, 13 November 1805, *Corr. de Nap.,* doc. 9476.

67. Egger, *Das Gefecht bei Dürnstein-Loiben,* pp. 20–21.

68. Kutuzov to Alexander, 14 November 1805, in Beskrovnyi, *Kutuzov,* doc. 171.

69. Berthier to Soult and Soult to Berthier, 11 November 1805, Alombert-Goget, *Combat de Dürrenstein,* pp. 139, 143.

70. *Mémoires de Ségur,* cited in Alombert-Goget, *Combat de Dürrenstein,* p. 140 n. 2.

71. Berthier to Murat, 11 November 1805, in Alombert-Goget, *Combat de Dürrenstein,* p. 138.

72. Berthier to Bernadotte, 12 November 1805, in Alombert-Goget, *Combat de Dürrenstein,* pp. 166–167.

73. Napoleon to Murat, 11 November 1805, *Corr. de Nap.,* doc. 9470; 12 November, doc. 9472; to Soult, 12 November, doc. 9473.

74. Egger, *Das Gefecht bei Hollabrunn und Schöngrabern,* 27:2, 6.

75. Bertrand to Napoleon, 13 November 1805, SHAT C² 7. Also cited in Alombert-Goget, *Combat de Dürrenstein,* p. 178 n. 1.

76. Berthier to Murat, 12 November 1805, in Alombert-Goget, *Combat de Dürrenstein,* pp. 160, 174; Berthier to Bernadotte, p. 166; Napoleon to Murat, 12 November 1805, p. 172.

77. Berthier to Bernadotte, 13 November 1805, in Alombert-Goget, *Combat de Dürrenstein,* p. 193.

78. Mortier to Berthier and Soult to Berthier, 13 November 1805, in Alombert-Goget, *Combat de Dürrenstein,* pp. 185, 188.

79. Egger, *Das Gefecht bei Hollabrunn und Schöngrabern,* 27:5–8.

80. Egger, *Das Gefecht bei Hollabrunn und Schöngrabern,* 27:5–6.

81. Moriz Edlen von Angeli, "Beiträge zur vaterländischen Geschichte. IV. Ulm und Austerlitz. Studie auf Grund archivalischer Quellen über den Feldzug 1805 in Deutschland. A and B Ulm," *Mitteilungen des K. K. Kriegs-Archivs* 2 (1877): 395–510; 3 (1878): 308.

82. Moriz Edlen von Angeli, "Ulm und Austerlitz," pp. 322.

83. Napoleon to Murat, 12 November 1805, in Alombert-Goget, *Combat de Dürrenstein,* p. 160.

84. The account of taking the Tabor bridge that follows relies on Murat's narrative of the event in Murat to Napoleon, 13 November 1805, in Paul Le Brethon, ed., *Lettres et documents pour servir à l'histoire de Joachim Murat, 1767–1815* (Paris: Librairie Plon, 1909), p. 146; and Egger, *Gefecht by Hollabrunn und Schöngrabern,* 27:8–11. Allowing for bias, these accounts tally remarkably well. Egger largely accepted Murat's presentation in light of the Austrian sources he had available.

85. Angeli, "Ulm und Austerlitz," p. 322.

86. Franz to Kutuzov, 12 November 1805, KA AFA 1805 Deutschland, XI/48½; also in Anon. "Pis'ma, raskazy i zametki otnosiashchiesia do gosudarstvennei deiatelei: Kn. M. M. Shcherbatova, gr. Arakcheeva, kn. M. I. Golenishcheva-Kutuzova-Smolenskago; gr. P. P. Konovnitsyna, gener. Fulia, A. S. Shishkova, arkhimandrita Fotii i I. N. Skobeleva, 1789–1826," *Russkaia starina* 1 (January-June 1870), p. 496; and Beskrovnyi, *Kutuzov,* doc. 170.

87. Kutuzov to Francis, 13 November 1805, KA AFA 1805 Deutschland, XI/54½; Kutuzov to [Ferdinand], 13 November 1805, KA AFA 1805 Deutschland, XI/55½. A preparatory order was issued on November 12 (Beskrovnyi, *Kutuzov,* doc. 169), and the movement order on November 14 (Beskrovnyi, *Kutuzov,* doc. 172). These documents contradict Kutuzov's subsequent assertion

(followed by Mikhailovskii-Danilevskii) that it was the loss of the Tabor bridge that drove him away from Krems. See Kutuzov to Miloradovich, 8 July 1806, in Mikhailovskii-Danilevskii, *Opisanie*, p. 117 n.

88. Mikhailovskii-Danilevskii, *Opisanie*, p. 114.
89. Movement Order to Etzelsdorf, 14 November 1805, in Beskrovnyi, *Kutuzov*, doc. 172.
90. Francis to Kutuzov, 14 November 1805, Anon. "Pis'ma, raskazy i zametki," *Russkaia starina*, 1:497.
91. "Pis'ma, raskazy i zametki," *Russkaia starina*, 1:499.
92. Kutuzov to Alexander, 14 November 1805, in Beskrovnyi, *Kutuzov*, doc. 171.
93. Berthier to Bernadotte and to Mortier, 13 November 1805, in Alombert-Goget, *Combat de Dürrenstein*, pp. 193, 195; Berthier to Murat, 14 November 1805, p. 207.
94. Bernadotte to Napoleon and Berthier to Bernadotte, 15 November 1805, in Alombert-Goget, *Combat de Dürrenstein*, pp. 210–211. Napoleon's estimate of the corps' strength is in Napoleon to Murat, 15 November 1805, p. 213.
95. Murat to Napoleon, 14 November 1805, in Paul Le Brethon, ed., *Lettres et documents pour servir à l'histoire de Joachim Murat, 1767–1815* (Paris: Librairie Plon, 1909), doc. 2243; 15 November, docs. 2245–2246.
96. Murat to Napoleon, 14 November 1805, in Le Brethon, *Lettres et documents*, doc. 2243.
97. Murat to Napoleon, 15 November 1805, in Le Brethon, *Lettres et documents*, doc. 2247; Kutuzov to Alexander, 15 November 1805, in Beskrovnyi, *Kutuzov*, doc. 175 and 19 November 1805, doc. 187; Hohenlohe to Francis, 17 November 1805, KA AFA 1805 Deutschland, XI/68½. The armistice can be found at KA AFA 1805 Deutschland, XI/71⅓b.
98. Murat to Napoleon, 15 November 1805, in Le Brethon, *Lettres et documents*, doc. 2247.
99. Murat to Napoleon, 16 November 1805, Le Brethon, *Lettres et documents*, doc. 2249.
100. Napoleon to Murat, 16 November 1805, *Corr. de Nap.*, doc. 9497.
101. Egger, *Gefecht by Hollabrunn und Schöngrabern*, p. 17.
102. Mikhailovskii-Danilevskii, *Opisanie*, p. 131.

Chapter 19　Forgotten Theaters: Italy

1. Oskar Criste, *Erzherzog Carl von Oesterreich* (Vienna: Wilhelm Braumüller, 1912), 2:335.
2. Report from Baron von Moll, 27 March 1805, KA AFA 1805 Italien, II/3. (This document is located in folio III, as it should be. Its *signatur* seems to be mistaken.) Charles to Francis, 26 May 1805, KA AFA 1805 Italien, V/7½.
3. Bellegarde to Charles, 9 May 1805 (presented on 17 May), KA AFA 1805 Italien, V/11b.
4. Charles to Francis, 26 May 1805, KA AFA 1805 Italien, V/7½.
5. Charles to Francis, 25 May 1805 (presented on 28 May), KA AFA 1805 Italien, V/12, with the emperor's marginal response accepting Charles's recommendations but refusing to commit on the likelihood of war.
6. KA AFA 1805 Italien, V/12b.
7. Charles to Bellegarde, 25 May 1805 (dispatched on 29 May), KA AFA 1805 Italien, V/12a.
8. Archduke John to Charles, 8 June 1805, KA AFA 1805 Italien, VI/1 concerns the defense of Venice; Charles to Francis (approving and forwarding John's recommendations), 8 June 1805, KA AFA 1805 Italien, VI/ad1. Francis's marginal comment on this last document indicates the emperor's approval as well. Charles to Bellegarde, 21 June 1805, Italien, VI/3, concerns the defense of the Tyrol. Charles to Hiller, 7 June 1805, Italien, VI/3½, contains the order to acquire necessary munitions and artillery to place Austrian Italy in a state of defense. Italien VI/4 contains a march plan for the movement of nine infantry and two cavalry regiments, all but two of which were destined for Pettau (modern Ptuj in Slovenia on the Drava River).

9. Crenneville to Bellegarde, 23 July 1805, KA AFA 1805 Italien, VII/13½; Charles to Bellegarde, 20 July 1805, Italien, VII/28.

10. Consideration of All Preliminary Arrangements Which Would Have To Be Made to Concentrate, Arm, and Supply the Armies, 23 July 1805, KA AFA 1805 Italien, VII/12. Francis's marginal comment approves the recommendations and orders their execution.

11. The appendixes indicating what the strengths of the various armies were to be in each epoch are missing from this document, although they are listed in KA AFA 1805 Italien, VIII/2 and ad2c (there are some variations between these two versions).

12. Charles to Bellegarde, 13 August 1805, KA AFA 1805 Italien, VIII/19.

13. Charles to Bellegarde, 13 August 1805, KA AFA 1805 Italien, VIII/19.

14. Charles to Bellegarde, 14 August 1805, KA AFA 1805 Italien, VIII/24.

15. Charles to Bellegarde, 14 August 1805, KA AFA 1805 Italien, VIII/24.

16. See, e.g., Note of Colonel Richter, 29 August 1805, KA AFA 1805 Italien, VIII/115, Colonel [name unreadable] to Zach, 30 August 1805, VIII/125, and many other items in folios VII and VIII of this carton.

17. Zach to Lieutenant Colonel Mayer, 3 September 1805, KA AFA 1805 Italien, IX/ad26. Zach is clearly reporting Charles's responses to Mayer's initial note.

18. Zach to Czervinska, 6 September 1805, KA AFA 1805 Italien, IX/59.

19. [Charles] to Bellegarde, 14 August 1805, KA AFA 1805 Italien, VIII/24.

20. See above, Chapter 14.

21. Francis to Charles, 23 September 1805, KA AFA 1805 Italien, IX/264½. This document seems to be in Mack's handwriting, and it is unsigned. It was clearly written as though to be sent over Francis's signature, however, since Mack never addressed Charles as "Euer Liebden," a term of formal endearment that only Francis used to the second-ranking member of the ruling house.

22. Charles to Duke Albert of Sachsen-Teschen, 25 September 1805, in Criste, *Erzherzog Carl von Oesterreich*, vol. 2, appendix XL/2. See also the letters of September 21 and 28, appendices XL/1 and XL/3 and many others in this volume for a catalogue of Charles's complaints. We shall examine some of them in greater detail below.

23. A fine example is "Order of Battle and Deployment of the Imp[erial] and Imp[erial] Roy[al] Main Army in Italy," 20 September 1805, KA AFA 1805 Italien, IX/ad238.

24. Orders to conduct a review of troop strength and equipment, 18 September 1805, KA AFA 1805 Italien, IX/214.

25. Orders to conduct a review of troop strength and equipment, 18 September 1805, KA AFA 1805 Italien, IX/214.

26. Charles to Francis, 22 September 1805, KA AFA 1805 Italien, IX/245½.

27. Compare "Complement of the I[mperial and] R[oyal] Army at the End of April 1805" (KA AFA 1805 Deutschland, IV/7), which suggests an average of about 1,000 soldiers per battalion with "Order of Battle and Deployment of the Imp[erial] and Imp[erial] Roy[al] Main Army in Italy," (20 September 1805, KA AFA 1805 Italien, IX/ad238), which suggests an average of 500 soldiers per battalion (including a total for the army of 17,397 furloughed soldiers).

28. KA AFA 1805 Italien, IX/229. See also the report of a debriefing of a deserter from the 8th Light Infantry Regiment, 16 September 1805, IX/196.

29. Charles to Francis, 22 September 1805, KA AFA 1805 Italien, IX/245½.

30. Charles to Francis, 24 September 1805, KA AFA 1805 Italien, IX/275½; and 27 September 1805, IX/285½.

31. Compare KA AFA 1805 Italien, IX/229 with Order of Battle of the Army of Italy on 18 October 1805, in Jean Baptiste Frédéric Koch, ed., *Mémoires de Masséna* (Paris: Paulin et Lechevalier, 1850), 5:appendix 6, p.368.

32. Charles to Francis, 27 September 1805, KA AFA 1805 Italien, IX/285½.

33. Charles to Albert, 28 September 1805, in Criste, *Erzherzog Carl von Oesterreich*, vol. 2, appendix XL/3.

34. Charles to Albert, 25 September 1805, in Criste, *Erzherzog Carl von Oesterreich*, vol. 2, appendix XL/2. See also Charles to Francis, 30 September 1805, KA AFA 1805 Italien, IX/301½.

35. See, e.g., Charles to Francis, 27 September 1805 (KA AFA 1805 Italien, IX/285½).

36. Charles to Albert, 13 October 1805, in Criste, *Erzherzog Carl von Oesterreich*, vol. 2, appendix XL/9.

37. Charles to Albert, 20 October 1805, in Criste, *Erzherzog Carl von Oesterreich*, vol. 2, appendix XL/12.

38. Koch, *Mémoires de Masséna*, p. 74.

39. Berthier to Masséna, 17 September 1805, in Koch, *Mémoires de Masséna*, appendix 3.

40. Napoleon to Eugène, 23 July 1805, 13 August 1805, and 31 August 1805, in A. du Casse, ed., *Mémoires et correspondance politique et militaire du Prince Eugène* (Paris: Michel Lévy Frères, 1858), pp. 206–207, 244–245, and 263–264; Eugène to Napoleon, 28 July 1805 and 7 September 1805, pp. 221–223, 348–352.

41. Napoleon to Eugène, 16 September 1805, in du Casse, *Mémoires et correspondance,* pp. 364–370; Napoleon to Berthier, 22 September 1805, *Corr. de Nap.*, no. 9256.

42. Napoleon to Masséna, 29 September 1805, in Koch, *Mémoires de Masséna*, appendix 5, p. 367.

43. Berthier to Masséna, 17 September 1805, in Koch, *Mémoires de Masséna*, appendix 3, pp. 362–365.

44. Koch, *Mémoires de Masséna*, pp. 52–56; the quotation is from p. 56.

45. Eugène, correspondence from June to September 1805, in du Casse, *Mémoires et correspondance,* passim; Duroc to Eugène, 31 July 1805, pp. 227–231.

46. Koch, *Mémoirs de Masséna*, pp. 56–60; Eugène, correspondence during September 1805, du Casse, *Mémoires et correspondance,* pp. 341ff.

47. Napoleon to Eugène, 22 September 1805, *Corr. de Nap.*, doc. 9258.

48. Napoleon to Masséna, 18 September 1805, *Corr. de Nap.*, doc. 9233; 23 September 1805, doc. 9262.

49. Koch, *Mémoirs de Masséna*, pp. 68–69.

50. Koch, *Mémoires de Masséna*, p. 71.

51. Charles to Albert, 3 October 1805, in Criste, *Erzherzog Carl von Oesterreich*, appendix XL/5.

52. Koch, *Mémoires de Masséna*, p. 71.

53. Charles to Albert, 7 October 1805, in Criste, *Erzherzog Carl von Oesterreich*, appendix XL/6.

54. Koch, *Mémoires de Masséna*, pp. 77–78.

55. Francis to Charles, 5 October 1805, KA AFA 1805 Italien, X/34½.

56. Charles to Albert, 13 October 1805, in Criste, *Erzherzog Carl von Oesterreich*, appendix XL/9; KA, AFA, Italien, 1805, X/124, ad124.

57. Charles to Ferdinand, 13 October 1805, KA AFA 1805 Italien, X/120.

58. Charles to Albert, 13 October 1805, in Criste, *Erzherzog Carl von Oesterreich*, appendix XL/9.

59. Berthier to Bernadotte, 25 October 1805, in Alombert-Goget and Colin, *La campagne de 1805*, vol. 4, pt. 1, p. 175.

60. Berthier to Bernadotte, 29 October 1805, in Alombert-Goget and Colin, *La campagne de 1805*, vol. 4, pt. 1, p. 279. The order to Ney is not preserved in this collection.

61. Charles to Albert, 13 October 1805, in Criste, *Erzherzog Carl von Oesterreich*, appendix XL/9.

62. See above, Chapter 14.

63. Charles to Albert, 15 October 1805, in Criste, *Erzherzog Carl von Oesterreich*, appendix XL/10.

64. Charles to Francis, 15 October 1805, KA AFA 1805 Italien, X/139½.

65. Charles to Albert, 16 October 1805, in Criste, *Erzherzog Carl von Oesterreich*, appendix XL/11.

66. Charles to Francis, 16 October 1805, KA AFA 1805 Italien, X/152½.

67. Charles to Albert, 16 October 1805, in Criste, *Erzherzog Carl von Oesterreich*, appendix XL/11.

68. Charles to Albert, 13 October 1805, in Criste, *Erzherzog Carl von Oesterreich*, appendix XL/9.

69. Charles to Francis, 19 October 1805, KA AFA 1805 Italien, X/161¼. Relations of the fight at Verona are in KA AFA 1805 Italien, X/155 and attachments and X/156. The French account is in Koch, *Mémoires de Masséna,* pp. 85–89; and Report of General Duhesme, 19 October 1805, in Koch, *Mémoires de Masséna,* appendix 7, p. 375.

70. Charles to Francis, 19 October 1805, KA AFA 1805 Italien, X/161¼.

71. Koch, *Mémoires de Masséna,* pp. 88–89.

72. Charles to Francis, 22 October 1805, KA AFA 1805 Italien, X/197¼.

73. Charles to Albert, 25 October 1805, Criste, *Erzherzog Carl von Oesterreich,* appendix XL/14.

74. Charles to Albert, 25 October 1805, Criste, *Erzherzog Carl von Oesterreich,* appendix XL/14.

75. Charles to John, 25 October 1805, cited in Alois Moriggl, *Der Feldzug von Ulm und seine Folgen für Oesterreich überhaupt und für Tirol insbesonders* (Innsbruck: Verlag der Wagner'schen Buchhandlung, 1861), pp. 266–269.

76. Moriggl, *Der Feldzug von Ulm,* pp. 251–265.

Chapter 20   Forgotten Theaters: Germany

1. Adam Gielgud, ed., *Memoirs of Prince Adam Czartoryski* (New York: Arno/New York Times, 1971), 2:96.

2. Zawadzki, *Man of Honour,* pp. 130–131.

3. Alexander Vasil'chikov, *Les Razoumowski* (Halle: Tausch & Grosse, 1893), 2:243; Zawadzki, *Man of Honour,* p. 132.

4. Czartoryskii to Razumovskii, 28 September 1805 and undated, in Vasil'chikov, *Les Razoumowski,* 2:243–250. The first letter (but not the more aggressive second) is reprinted in VPR, vol. II, as doc. 189.

5. Zawadzki, *Man of Honour,* p. 132. These events are described with a somewhat different emphasis in Gielgud, *Memoirs of Prince Adam Czartoryski,* 2:98–99.

6. Alexander countersigned at least one of Czartoryskii's letters to Razumovskii (VPR, vol. II, doc. 189). See also Extract from H[is] I[mperial] M[ajesty's] Instruction to General Michelson, Grand Prince Nikolai Mikhailovich, *Kniazia Dolgorukie, spodvizhniki Imperatora Aleksandra I v pervye gody ego tsarstvovaniia: Biograficheskie ocherki* (St. Petersburg: Ekspeditsiia zagatovleniia gosudarstvennykh bumag, 1902), appendix 5, p. 147, art. 5.

7. Exposée of Political Affairs by Prince Pierre Dolgorouky, mid-August 1805 (the postscript is dated August 14), Nikolai Mikhailovich, *Dolgorukie,* appendix 4, pp. 140–145; Extract of H[is] I[mperial] M[ajesty's] Instructions for General Michelson, September 1805, Nikolai Mikhailovich, *Dolgorukie,* appendix 5, pp. 146–152; Plan of Operations of the Armies of Volhynia, Lithuania, and the North in Case of Aggression against Prussia, 14 August 1805, Nikolai Mikhailovich, *Dolgorukie,* appendix 6, pp. 153–155.

8. See biographies in Nikolai Mikhailovich, *Dolgorukie,* and Nikolai Mikhailovich, *General-Ad"iutanty Imperatora Aleksandra I* (St. Petersburg: Expeditsiia zagotovleniia gosudarstvennykh bumag, 1913), pp. 27–28.

9. Nikolai Mikhailovich, *Dolgorukie,* p. 11.

10. Alopeus to Czartoryskii, 6 September 1805, VPR, vol. II, doc. 177–178.

11. Note of the Minister of Foreign Affairs about the Means to Bring Prussia into the Coalition Against Napoleon, 19 August 1805, VPR, vol. II, doc. 160; Leopold von Ranke, *Denkwürdigkeiten des Staatskanzlers Fürsten von Hardenberg* (Leipzig: Ducker & Humblot, 1877), 2:220.

12. Hardenberg to Laforest, 16 September 1805; Laforest to Hardenberg, 17 September 1805 in Ranke, *Denkwürdigkeiten,* 2:215–220.

13. "Die preußischen Kriegsvorbereitungen und Operationspläne von 1805," *Kriegsgeschichtliche einzelschriften, herausgegeben vom Grossen Generalstabe, kriegsgeschichtliche Abteilung I* (Berlin: E. S. Mittler, 1883–1914), 1:4.

14. Ranke, *Denkwürdigkeiten,* 2:221; *Kriegsgeschichtliche Einzelschriften,* 1:5. Frederick William's letter is reproduced in Ranke, *Denkwürdigkeiten,* 2:222–224; Bailleu, *Briefwechsel,* doc. 71 (although there it is dated September 21).

15. Metternich to Colloredo, Wilhelm Oncken, *Österreich und Preußen im Befreiungskriege* (New York: Georg Olms Verlag, 1998), pp. 580–581.

16. Verbal note, 27 September 1805, Ranke, *Denkwürdigkeiten,* 2:228–237.

17. Ranke, *Denkwürdigkeiten,* 2:240–242.

18. Ranke, *Denkwürdigkeiten,* 2:242–246; see also Hardenberg to Frederick William, 28 September 1805, in Bailleu, *Preußen und Frankreich,* vol. 2, doc. 288.

19. Ranke, *Denkwürdigkeiten,* 2:251–252.

20. Ranke, *Denkwürdigkeiten,* 2:253.

21. Ranke, *Denkwürdigkeiten,* 2:253–258.

22. Alexander to Frederick William, 27 September 1805, in Bailleu, *Briefwechsel,* doc. 72; Ranke, *Denkwürdigkeiten,* 2:259–260; Alexander to Frederick William, 30 September 1805, in Bailleu, *Briefwechsel,* doc. 73.

23. Dolgorukii to Alexander, 6 October 1805, in Nikolai Mikhailovich, *Dolgorukie,* pp. 12–14.

24. Czartoryskii to Razumovskii, 10 October 1805, VPR, vol. II, doc. 189.

25. Czartoryskii to Razumovskii, 10 October 1805, VPR, vol. II, doc. 189.

26. Cited in Zawadzki, *Man of Honour,* p. 132.

27. Paul W. Schroeder writes in *The Transformation of European Politics, 1763–1848* (New York: Oxford University Press, 1994), p. 280, "In reality the Potsdam Convention was not even potentially a turning-point in the war," since Frederick William never contemplated really fighting. Grimsted offers a similar evaluation (*Foreign Ministers,* p. 138) as does Zawadzki (*Man of Honour,* p. 133). Stamm-Kuhlmann, as already noted, identified this period as the best evidence of the "melancholy" that afflicted the king (*König in Preußens großer Zeit,* p. 200). Simms (*Impact,* pp. 191ff.) offers a more nuanced evaluation of Prussian policy that places Frederick William's hesitations intelligently in the diplomatic context.

28. Ranke, *Denkwürdigkeiten,* 2:263.

29. The protocol is in Ranke, *Denkwürdigkeiten,* 2:268–275.

30. The protocol is in Ranke, *Denkwürdigkeiten,* 2:275–278.

31. A series of French communications are reproduced in Ranke, *Denkwürdigkeiten,* 2:279ff. See also Laforest to Talleyrand, 9 October 1805, in Bailleu, *Preußen und Frankreich,* vol. 2, doc. 291; Napoleon to Duroc, 2 October 1805, *Corr. de Nap.,* doc. 9316; Napoleon to Talleyrand, 3 October 1805, *Corr. de Nap.,* doc. 9326; Napoleon to Frederick William, 5 October 1805, *Corr. de Nap.,* doc. 9342.

32. From the protocol of the conference of October 7 in Ranke, *Denkwürdigkeiten,* 2:270.

33. Ranke, *Denkwürdigkeiten,* 2:270–271.

34. Simms, *Impact,* pp. 194–195, is very convincing on this point.

35. Cited in Simms, *Impact,* p. 197.

36. As, Hardenberg noted, some defenders of the king's efforts to preserve his neutrality claimed (Ranke, *Denkwürdigkeiten,* 2:313–314).

37. *Kriegsgeschichtliche Einzelschriften,* 1:6–9.

38. Ranke, *Denkwürdigkeiten,* 2:275–279.

39. *Kriegsgeschichtliche Einzelschriften,* 1:14.

40. Memorandum of Lieutenant Colonel von Kleist, 16 October 1805, in *Kriegsgeschichtliche Einzelschriften,* 1:appendix 4.

41. *Kriegsgeschichtliche Einzelschriften,* 1:18.

42. Ranke, *Denkwürdigkeiten,* 2:301ff.

43. Frederick William to Alexander, 9 October 1805, in Bailleu, *Briefwechsel,* doc. 75.

44. Zawadzki, *Man of Honour,* p. 133.

45. Zawadzki, *Man of Honour*, pp. 134–136; Grimsted, *Foreign Ministers*, p. 139. The bitterness of Czartoryskii's disappointment is displayed in a letter he wrote to Alexander in April 1806 (Gielgud, *Memoirs of Prince Adam Czartoryski*, 2:122–131).

46. The most detailed account of these meetings is in Ranke, *Denkwürdigkeiten*, 2:305–317. Hardenberg was present throughout the conferences.

47. Ranke, *Denkwürdigkeiten*, 2:308.

48. Ranke, *Denkwürdigkeiten*, 2:307, emphasis added.

49. Russo-Prussian Convention About Combined Actions against France, 3 November 1805, VPR, vol. II, doc. 194; also reprinted in Ranke, *Denkwürdigkeiten*, 2:324–332.

50. See Thomas Stamm-Kuhlmann, *König in Preußens großer Zeit: Friedrich Wilhelm III. Der Melancholiker auf dem Thron* (Berlin: Siedler Verlag, 1992), p. 200; Simms, *Impact*, p. 208.

51. Both are in *Kriegsgeschichtliche Einzelschriften*, 1:21–26 (in German) and in Ranke, *Denkwürdigkeiten*, 2:317–324 (in French; Brunswick's translation).

52. *Kriegsgeschichtliche Einzelschriften*, 1:21. Why Brunswick made this error is not clear.

53. Simms, *Impact*, pp. 207–208, makes this point well.

54. Mulgrave to Harrowby, 27 October 1805, in Holland Rose, *Select Despatches*, doc. 100.

55. Simms, *Impact*, p. 206.

56. Report of Count Haugwitz, 20 November 1805 and 2 December 1805, in Bailleu, *Preußen und Frankreich*, vol. 2, docs. 307, 311 respectively; Laforest to Talleyrand, 14 November 1805, doc. 305.

57. Lombard to Hardenberg, 19 October 1805, in Bailleu, *Preußen und Frankreich*, vol. 2, doc. 300.

58. *Kriegsgeschichtliche Einzelschriften* 1, passim.

59. The editors of the *Kriegsgeschichtliche Einzelschriften 1* take the Prussians to task for this failure (pp. 53–55).

60. Cited in John Lewis Gaddis, *Strategies of Containment: A Critical Appraisal of American National Security Policy During the Cold War* (New York: Oxford University Press, 1982), p. 39.

Chapter 21   Setting the Terms of Battle

1. Napoleon to Marmont, 15 November 1805, *Corr. de Nap.*, doc. 9495.

2. See Paul Claude Alombert-Goget and Jean Lambert Alphonse Colin, *La campagne de 1805 en Allemagne* (Paris: Librairie militaire R. Chapelot, 1902–1908), vol. 4; Paul Claude Alombert-Goget, *Campagne de l'an 14 (1805). Le corps d'armée aux ordres du Maréchal Mortier. Combat de Dürrenstein* (Paris: Berger-Levrault, 1897); and SHAT C² 8, passim.

3. SVM, vol. 4, bk. 1, pt. 2, sec. 2, pp. 333–334.

4. Theodor von Bernhardi, *Denkwürdigkeiten aus dem Leben des kaiserliches russisches Generals von der Infanterie Carl Friedrich Grafen von Toll* (Leipzig: Otto Wigand, 1865), p. 155.

5. N. V. Shil'der, *Imperator Aleksandr Pervyi: Ego zhizn' i tsarstvovanie* (St. Petersburg: Izdanie A. S. Suvorina, 1897), 2:132.

6. Alexander to Frederick William, 14 November 1805, in Paul Bailleu, ed., *Briefwechsel König Friedrich Wilhelms III und der Königin Luise mit Kaiser Alexander I,* Publicationen aus den K. Preussischen Archiven 75 (Leipzig: S. Hirzel, 1900), pp. 83–84.

7. Frederick William to Alexander, 23 November 1805, in Leopold von Ranke, *Denkwürdigkeiten des Staatskanzlers Fürsten von Hardenberg* (Leipzig: Ducker & Humblot, 1877), 2:348–349.

8. A. I. Mikhailovskii-Danilevskii, *Opisanie pervoi voiny Imperatora Aleksandra s Napoleonom v 1805-m godu* (St. Petersburg: Independent Corps of the Internal Guard Press, 1844), p. 151; Alexander to Michelson, 20 November 1805, SVM, 4, 1, 2, 2, pp. 350–351.

9. Mikhailovskii-Danilevskii, *Opisanie*, p. 151.

10. Bennigsen to Alexander, 27 November 1805, RGVIA, fond 471, opis' 1, delo 16.

11. Mikhailovskii-Danilevskii, *Opisanie*, p. 146.

12. See KA AFA 1805 Italien, XI, passim.

13. [Name unreadable] to Charles, 15 November 1805, KA AFA 1805 Italien, XI/135; Charles to Francis, 17 November 1805, KA AFA 1805 Italien, XI/153½.

14. Siegenthal to Charles, 17 November 1805, KA AFA 1805 Italien, XI/156.

15. Charles to Francis, 26 November 1805, KA AFA 1805 Italien, XI/290½.

16. See, e.g., Charles to Francis, 11 November 1805, KA AFA 1805 Italien, XI/105½; 17 November 1805, XI/153½; 20 November 1805, XI/209½; finally linking up with John: 26 November 1805, XI/290½.

17. The classic exposition of this view is in David Chandler, *Campaigns of Napoleon* (New York: Macmillan, 1966), pp. 409–412. See also Christopher Duffy, *Austerlitz, 1805* (London: Seeley Service, 1977), pp. 76–77; and Scott Bowden, *Napoleon and Austerlitz: An Unprecedentedly Detailed Combat Study of Napoleon's Epic Ulm-Austerlitz Campaigns of 1805* (Chicago: Emperor's, 1997), pp. 308–312.

18. Frederick William to Alexander, 27 November 1805, in Ranke, *Denkwürdigkeiten*, 2:350.

19. Mikhailovskii-Danilevskii, *Opisanie*, p. 154.

20. [Major General Stutterheim], *La Bataille d'Austerlitz, par un militaire témoin de la journée du 2 décembre, 1805* (Hamburg: n.p., 1806), p. 21.

21. Disposition for the "Offensive Actions of the Allied Forces," from Olshany to Austerlitz, 26 November 1805, in Iu. I. Zhiugzhda, ed., *Dokumenty shtaba M. I. Kutuzova, 1805–1806* (Vilnius: Gosudarstvennoe Izdatel'stvo Politicheskoi i Nauchnoi Literatury, 1951), doc. 137.

22. Weyrother, Diary for 11 November through 2 December 1805, KA AFA 1805 Deutschland, XIII/59.

23. This was the date of the war council at which the advance was decided on, Iu. N. Guliaev and V. T. Sogliaev, *Fel'dmarshal Kutuzov* (Moscow: Arkheograficheskii Tsentr, 1995), 1:217. The records of this council apparently have not survived.

24. Ségur, *Histoire et mémoires* (Paris: Librairie de Firmin-Didot et Cie., 1877), 2:445 is accurate: see SHAT C² 8, correspondence from November 19–22.

25. Marmont to Berthier, 21 and 25 (two letters) November 1805, SHAT C² 8.

26. Bernadotte to Napoleon, 21 November 1805, SHAT C² 8.

27. 17 November 1805, SHAT C² 8.

28. Ségur, *Histoire et mémoires*, p. 446.

29. Napoleon to Francis, 17 November 1805, *Corr. de Nap.*, doc. 9503.

30. Cobenzl to Metternich, 24 November 1805 (first letter of that date), HHSt Rußland II Varia, 240.

31. Napoleon to Talleyrand, 25 November 1805, *Corr. de Nap.*, doc. 9523.

32. Hellmuth Rössler, *Graf Johann Philipp Stadion* (Munich: Herold,1966), 1:212–216.

33. Ségur, *Histoire et mémoires*, p. 446.

34. Napoleon to Talleyrand, 26 November 1805, *Corr. de Nap.*, doc. 9526.

35. Unsigned note, 19 November 1805, SHAT C² 8.

36. Report of P. I. Bagration to M. I. Kutuzov about Combat with the Enemy near Vyškov, Habrovany, and Rousinov, 28 November 1805, in L. G. Beskrovnyi, *M. I. Kutuzov: Sbornik dokumentov* (Moscow: Voennoe Izdatel'stvo, 1951), vol. 2, doc. 227. A French account of this fight by General Guyot, commander of the 9th Regiment of Hussars (written on December 5) is in SHAT C² 8.

37. Talleyrand to Napoleon, 30 November 1805, *Corr. de Talleyrand à Napoléon*, doc. 134.

38. Napoleon to Talleyrand, 30 November 1805, *Corr. de Nap.*, doc. 9532.

39. Talleyrand to Napoleon, 1 December 1805, *Corr. de Talleyrand à Napoléon*, doc. 135.

40. Napoleon to Alexander, 25 November 1805, SIRIO 82, doc. 54.

41. Alexander to Napoleon, 27 November 1805, SIRIO 82, doc. 55.

42. Ségur, *Histoire et mémoires*, p. 447.

43. Shil'der, *Imperator Aleksandr Pervyi*, 2:135.

44. Ségur, *Histoire et mémoires*, p. 447.

45. See the accounts in Ségur, *Histoire et mémoires*, pp. 447–448; Grand Prince Nikolai Mikhailovich, *Kniazia Dolgorukie, spodvizhniki Imperatora Aleksandra I v pervye gody ego tsarstvovaniia: Biograficheskie ocherki* (St. Petersburg: Ekspeditsiia zagatovleniia gosudarstvennykh bumag, 1902), pp. 16–17.

46. Nikolai Mikhailovich, *Dolgorukie*, p. 17.

47. Napoleon to Bernadotte, 28 November at 8:00 P.M., *Corr. de Nap.*, doc. 9531, and n. 1: analogous letters were sent also to Davout and Marmont.

48. Duffy, *Austerlitz*, pp. 76–77; Chandler, *Campaigns of Napoleon*, p. 410.

49. Duffy, *Austerlitz*, p. 72.

50. Soult to Napoleon, 24 November 1805, SHAT C² 8.

51. Soult's order on 29 November 1805 to Vandamme, one of his division commanders, executing this imperial command, is in SHAT C² 8. See also Thiébault, *Mémoires du Général Baron Thiébault*, 3:448.

52. Weyrother, Diary, KA AFA 1805 Deutschland, XIII/59.

53. See Stutterheim, *La Bataille d'Austerlitz*, pp. 38–39.

54. Disposition for the Advance of the Combined Army to Predlitz, 27 November 1805, in Beskrovnyi, *Kutuzov*, doc. 223.

55. Stutterheim, *La Bataille d'Austerlitz*, p. 33.

56. Disposition for the Advance of the Combined Army to the Town of Vyškov, 28 November 1805, in Beskrovnyi, *Kutuzov*, doc. 226.

57. In addition to the two dispositions already cited, see Disposition for the Advance of the Combined Army to Kucherau and Pogdalitze, 29 November 1805, in Beskrovnyi, *Kutuzov*, doc. 228; and Disposition for the Advance of the Combined Army to Austerlitz, 30 November 1805, doc. 229.

58. Biography in the *Allgemeine deutsche Biographie: Auf Veranlassung seiner Majestaet des Königs von Bayern hrsg. durch die Historische Commission bei der Königl. Akademie der Wissenschaften* (Leipzig: Duncker & Humblot, 1875–1912).

59. Disposition for the Attack on the Enemy's Position Around Slapanice and Sokolnice on December 2, 1805, in Beskrovnyi, *Kutuzov*, doc. 233.

60. Mikhailovskii-Danilevskii, *Opisanie*, p. 175.

61. The most colored and least reliable report is in Langeron, *Zapiski Grafa Lanzherona*, p. 23. A brief account is in Bernhardi, *Denkwürdigkeiten aus dem Leben*, 1:175–177. See also Mikhailovskii-Danilevskii, *Opisanie*, p. 175.

62. The German version is in KA AFA 1805 Deutschland, XII/12.

63. Bernhardi, *Denkwürdigkeiten aus dem Leben*, 1:177; V. A. Fedorov, ed., *Zapiski A. P. Ermolova, 1798–1826* (Moscow: "Vysshaia shkola," 1991), p. 54.

64. Shil'der, *Imperator Aleksandr Pervyi*, 2:134.

65. Alexander to Frederick William, 28 November 1805, in Ranke, *Denkwürdigkeiten*, 2:351–352.

Chapter 22   The Fight for the Villages

1. Disposition for the Attack on the Enemy Position Around Slapanice and Sokolnice, 2 December 1805, in L. G. Beskrovnyi, *M. I. Kutuzov: Sbornik dokumentov*, vol. 2 (Moscow: Voennoe Izdatel'stvo, 1951), doc. 233; KA AFA 1805 Deutschland, XII/12. Hereafter "Disposition for the Attack."

2. Organization and Complement, KA AFA 1805 Deutschland, XIII/ad13k.

3. [Major General Stutterheim], *La Bataille d'Austerlitz, par un militaire témoin de la journée du 2 décembre, 1805* (Hamburg: n.p., 1806), pp. 60–61.

4. Soult, "Rapport sur la bataille d'Austerlitz," in Jacques Garnier, ed., *Relations et rapports officiels de la bataille d'Austerlitz, 1805* (Paris: La Vouivre, 1998), pp. 17–18; Stutterheim, *La Bataille d'Austerlitz*, pp. 61–65; "Brief Description of the Movements of the Combined Austrian and Russian Imperial Armies in the Campaign of 1805 along with a Detailed Description of the Battle that Took Place on 2 December 1805 Between Brünn, Rausnitz, and Austerlitz, Including a Battle Map Drawn by the Imperial and Imperial-Royal Quartermaster General Staff in March 1806," KA AFA 1805 Deutschland, XI/66¼, pp. 29ff.

5. A. I. Mikhailovskii-Danilevskii, *Opisanie pervoi voiny Imperatora Aleksandra s Napoleonom v 1805-m godu* (St. Petersburg: Independent Corps of the Internal Guard Press, 1844), p. 178.

6. Davout to Berthier, 6 December 1805, from Charles de Mazade, ed., *Correspondence du Maréchal Davout, Prince d'Eckmül; ses commandemants, son ministère, 1801–1815*, vol. 1 (Paris: Librairie Plon, 1885), doc. 126.

7. Davout to Napoleon, Pressburg, 26 December 1805, in Mazade, *Correspondence du Maréchal Davout*, doc. 127.

8. Davout to Napoleon, 26 December 1805, in Mazade, *Correspondence du Maréchal Davout*, doc. 127.

9. Soult in Garnier, *Relations et rapports officiels*, p. 17.

10. Mikhailovskii-Danilevskii, *Opisanie*, p. 179; "Report of F. F. Buxhöwden to M. I. Kutuzov about the Battle of Austerlitz," December 1805, in Beskrovnyi, *Kutuzov*, doc. 245; Stutterheim, *La Bataille d'Austerlitz*, pp. 65–66.

11. Davout to Napoleon, 26 December 1805, in Mazade, *Correspondence du Maréchal Davout*, doc. 127; Friant to Davout, 3 December 1805, doc. 130.

12. Report of F. F. Buxhöwden to M. I. Kutuzov about the Battle of Austerlitz, December 1805, in Beskrovnyi, *Kutuzov*, doc. 245.

13. Stutterheim, *La Bataille d'Austerlitz*, p. 66.

14. KA AFA 1805 Deutschland, XIII/68.

15. Davout to Napoleon, 26 December 1805, in Mazade, *Correspondence du Maréchal Davout*, doc. 127.

16. "Lanzheron, Liudovik-Aleksandr-Andro," in the *Russkii Biograficheskii Slovar'* (S.-Peterburg: Izdan"ie Imperatorskago Russkago istoricheskago obshchestva, 1896–1918).

17. Langeron, *Zapiski Grafa Lanzherona*, p. 29.

18. Mazade, *Correspondence du Maréchal Davout*, doc. 127.

19. Report of Lieutenant General I. Ia. Przebyshevskii to Alexander I about the Actions of the 3rd Column in the Battle of Austerlitz, 23 July 1806, in Beskrovnyi, *Kutuzov*, doc. 255. See also Langeron's account for the sequencing.

20. "Account of the Battle of Austerlitz, Won on 2 December 1805 by Napoleon against the Russians and the Austrians, under the Command of Their Sovereigns," in Garnier, *Relations et rapports officiels*, p. 94.

21. Przebyshevskii report, in Beskrovnyi, *Kutuzov*, doc. 255, appendix.

22. Soult, "Rapport sur la bataille d'Austerlitz," in Garnier, *Relations et rapports officials*, p. 95.

23. N. V. Schil'der makes this point in *Imperator Aleksandr Pervyi: Ego zhizn' i tsarstvovanie* (St. Petersburg: Izdanie A. S. Suvorina, 1897), 2:140, although his work glorifies Kutuzov and he offers no evidence for it.

24. Soult's account claims that these forces were positioned in front of Kobylnice specifically to deal with the eventuality that occurred, which is unlikely considering the improbability of that particular eventuality (Soult in Garnier, *Relations et rapports officiels*, p. 19).

25. Bernhardi, *Denkwürdigkeiten aus dem Leben*, p. 183.

26. Soult, "Rapport sur la bataille d'Austerlitz," in Garnier, *Relations et rapports officiels*, p. 19.

27. Fernand Calmettes, ed., *Mémoires du Général Bon. Thiébault*, vol. 3 (Paris: Librairie Plon, 1895), p. 468.

28. "Report of M. A. Miloradovich to M. I. Kutuzov About the Battle of Austerlitz," 3 December 1805, in Beskrovnyi, *Kutuzov*, doc. 238.

29. Langeron, *Zapiski Grafa Lanzherona*, p. 30.

30. KA AFA 1805 Deutschland, XIII/13, p. 21 obverse.

31. Langeron, *Zapiski Grafa Lanzherona*, pp. 35–36.

32. Mikhailovskii-Danilevskii, *Opisanie*, p. 184.

33. Calmettes, *Mémoires du Général Bon. Thiébault*, p. 475.

34. Langeron, *Zapiski Grafa Lanzherona*, p. 31.

35. Mazade, *Correspondence du Maréchal Davout*, doc. 127.

36. Przebyshevskii to Alexander I about the Actions of the 3rd Column in the Battle of Austerlitz, 23 July 1806, in Beskrovnyi, *Kutuzov*, doc. 255.

37. Langeron, marginal comments on Stutterheim's account, in Thierry Rouillard, ed., *Alexandre Andrault de Langeron, Journal inédit de la campagne de 1805, Austerlitz, et Karl Freiherr von Stutterheim, Mikhaïl Hilarionivitch Golénistchev-Kutuzov, Relations de La Bataille d'Austerlitz* (Paris: La Vouivre, 1998), p. 110; Soult, "Rapport sur la bataille d'Austerlitz," in Garnier, *Relations et rapports officiels*, p. 110.

38. Soult, "Rapport sur la bataille d'Austerlitz," in Garnier, *Relations et rapports officiels*, p. 95; Friant to Davout, 3 December 1805, in Mazade, *Correspondence du Maréchal Davout*, doc. 130; Davout to Napoleon, 26 December 1805, doc. 127.

39. Friant to Davout, in Mazade, *Correspondence du Maréchal Davout*, doc. 130; Davout to Napoleon, doc. 127.

40. Davout to Napoleon, in Mazade, *Correspondence du Maréchal Davout*, doc. 127; Friant to Davout, doc. 130.

41. Calmettes, *Mémoires du Général Bon. Thiébault*, pp. 479–481.

42. Langeron, *Zapiski Grafa Lanzherona*, p. 33.

43. Langeron, *Zapiski Grafa Lanzherona*, p. 33.

44. Przebyshevskii to Alexander I about the Actions of the 3rd Column in the Battle of Austerlitz, 23 July 1806, in Beskrovnyi, *Kutuzov*, doc. 255.

45. Buxhöwden to Kutuzov, 2 February 1806, in Beskrovnyi, *Kutuzov*, doc. 250.

46. See, e.g., Kutuzov to Alexander, 1 March 1806, in Beskrovnyi, *Kutuzov*, doc. 252.

47. Mikhailovskii-Danilevskii, *Opisanie*, pp. 215–216.

48. "Przhibyshevskii, Ignatii Iakovlevich," in *Russkii Biograficheskii Slovar'*; Mikhailovskii-Danilevskii, *Opisanie*, p. 215.

49. Mikhailovskii-Danilevskii, *Opisanie*, p. 214.

Chapter 23   The End of the Fight

1. Scott Bowden, *Napoleon and Austerlitz: An Unprecedentedly Detailed Combat Study of Napoleon's Epic Ulm-Austerlitz Campaigns of 1805* (Chicago: Emperor's, 1997); Christopher Duffy, *Austerlitz, 1805* (London: Seeley Service, 1977).

2. Orders, 1 December 1805, *Corr. de Nap.*, doc. 9534; General Dispositions, 1 December 1805, doc. 9535.

3. "Account of the Battle of Austerlitz by Berthier," in Jacques Garnier, ed., *Relations et rapports officiels de la bataille d'Austerlitz, 1805* (Paris: La Vouivre, 1998), p. 57; Philippe-Paul de Ségur, *Histoire et mémoires* (Paris: Librairie de Firmin-Didot et Cie., 1877), p. 465. The other marshals, writing their reports to Napoleon or Berthier, did not describe the initial battle plan in any detail to the man who developed it.

4. Duffy, *Austerlitz*, pp. 88–92, esp. p. 92.

5. Disposition for the Attack on the Enemy's Position Around Slapanice and Sokolnice, 2 November 1805, in L. G. Beskrovnyi, *M. I. Kutuzov: Sbornik dokumentov*, vol. 2 (Moscow: Voennoe Izdatel'stvo, 1951), doc. 233.

6. "Brief Description of the Movements of the Combined Austrian and Russian Imperial Armies in the Campaign of 1805 along with a Detailed Description of the Battle that Took Place on 2 December 1805 Between Brünn, Rausnitz, and Austerlitz, Including a Battle Map Drawn by the Imperial and Imperial-Royal Quartermaster General Staff in March 1806," KA AFA 1805 Deutschland, XI/66¼, from now on referred to as Austrian General Staff Account, p. 17; Karl Stutterheim, *La Bataille d'Austerlitz, par un militaire témoin de la journée du 2 décembre, 1805* (Hamburg: n.p., 1806), p. 78.

7. "Konstantin Pavlovich, velikii kniaz', tsesarevich," in *Russkii Biograficheskii Slovar'* (St. Petersburg: Izdanie Imperatorskago Russkago istoricheskago obshchestva, 1896–1918). This entry, nearly eighty-five pages long, amounts to a brief biography.

8. Mikhailovskii-Danilevskii, *Opisanie*, p. 192.

9. Mikhailovskii-Danilevskii, *Opisanie*, p. 191.

10. Austrian General Staff Account, p. 18.

11. Austrian General Staff Account, pp. 16 reverse, 17 reverse.

12. Mikhailovskii-Danilevskii, *Opisanie*, pp. 191–192.

13. Report of Prince Murat's Army Corps, in Garnier, *Relations et rapports*, p. 13.

14. Report of Prince Murat's Army Corps in Garnier, *Relations et rapports*, p. 13; Mikhailovskii-Danilevskii, *Opisanie*, p. 192.

15. Mikhailovskii-Danilevskii, *Opisanie*, p. 192; Austrian General Staff Account, pp. 23, 23 reverse.

16. Austrian General Staff Account, pp. 23 reverse, 24.

17. Austrian General Staff Account, p. 24; Mikhailovskii-Danilevskii, *Opisanie*, p. 192; Report of Prince Murat's Army Corps, in Garnier, *Relations et rapports*, p. 13.

18. Austrian General Staff Account, pp. 30 reverse, 31; Report of Prince Murat's Army Corps, in Garnier, *Relations et rapports*, p. 13.

19. Austrian General Staff Account, p. 30 reverse; Mikhailovskii-Danilevskii, *Opisanie*, p. 197.

20. A. du Casse, ed., *Le Général Vandamme et sa correspondance*, vol. 2 (Paris: Didier et cie., 1870), p. 155; Soult, in Garnier, *Relations et rapports*, p. 20; Austrian General Staff Account, pp. 25 reverse, 26.

21. Report of Prince Murat's Army Corps, in Garnier, *Relations et rapports*, p. 14; "Report of F. P. Uvarov to M. I. Kutuzov about the Battle of Austerlitz," 7 December 1805, Iu. I. Zhiugzhda, ed., *Dokumenty shtaba M. I. Kutuzova, 1805–1806* (Vilnius: Gosudarstvennoe Izdatel'stvo Politicheskoi i Nauchnoi Literatury, 1951), doc. 145.

22. V. A. Fedorov, ed., *Zapiski A. P. Ermolova, 1798–1826* (Moscow: "Vysshaia shkola," 1991), pp. 56–57; "Report of F. V. Uvarov to M. I. Kutuzov," 7 December 1805, Zhiugdzha, *Dokumenty*, doc 145; Austrian General Staff Account, p. 29.

23. Austrian General Staff Account, p. 26 reverse; Mikhailovskii-Danilevskii, *Opisanie*, pp. 193–194.

24. Austrian General Staff Account, p. 27; "Account of the Battle of Austerlitz by Berthier," in Garnier, *Relations et rapports*, p. 57; Soult in Garnier, *Relations et rapports*, p. 22; Mikhailovskii-Danilevskii, *Opisanie*, p. 193. Bigarré, *Mémoires du Gal. Bigarré, Aide de camp du Roi Joseph* (Paris: Ernest Kolb, 1893), pp. 176–177, describes this action with a number of minor errors.

25. Ségur, *Histoire et mémoires*, pp. 469–470.

26. "Account of the Battle of Austerlitz by Berthier," in Garnier, *Relations et rapports*, p. 57; Soult, in Garnier, *Relations et rapports*, p. 22.

27. Mikhailovskii-Danilevskii, *Opisanie*, p. 194.

28. Ségur, *Histoire et mémoires*, p. 470; Rapp, *Memoirs of General Count Rapp*, p. 63.

29. Report of Prince Murat's Army Corps in Garnier, *Relations et rapports*, p. 14.

30. Désiré Lacroix, ed., *Mémoires du Duc de Rovigo pour servir à l'histoire de l'Empereur Napoléon* (Paris: Garnier Frères, 1900), pp. 76–77.

31. "Relation of M. I. Kutuzov to Alexander I about the Battle of Austerlitz," 26 January 1806, in Beskrovnyi, *Kutuzov*, doc. 247.

32. Duffy, *Austerlitz*, pp. 182–183, relying on figures in "Report of Soldiers and Line Horses Killed and Missing in Action on 2 December," 6 January 1806, in Beskrovnyi, *Kutuzov*, doc. 243.

33. Duffy, *Austerlitz*, pp. 156–157.

34. Ségur, *Histoire et mémoires*, p. 469.

35. Francis to Metternich, n.d., cited on p. 360 of Moriz Edlen Angeli, "Beiträge zur vaterländischen Geschichte. IV. Ulm und Austerlitz. Studie auf Grund archivalischer Quellen über den Feldzug 1805 in Deutschland. B. Austerlitz," *Mittheilungen des K. K. Kriegs-Archivs* 3 (1878): 283–394.

36. Hellmuth Rössler, *Graf Johann Philipp Stadion* (Munich: Herold, 1966), 1:217–218.

Chapter 24   The Peaces of 1805

1. Napoleon to Talleyrand, 25 August 1805, *Corr. de Nap.*, docs. 9130–9131; Napoleon to the Elector of Bavaria, 2 October 1805, doc. 9314. Rudolfine Freiin von Oer, *Der Friede von Pressburg: Ein Beitrag zur diplomatiegeschichte des Napoleonischen Zeitalters* (Münster: Aschendorfsche Verlagsbuchhandlung, 1965), pp. 32–37. The Franco-Bavarian Treaty of 23 September 1805 is reproduced in Josef Gmeinwiser, "Die bayerische Politik im Jahre 1805" (Ph.D. diss., University of Munich, 1928), appendix 9, pp. 224–226.

2. See above, Chapter 8 and von Oer, *Der Friede von Pressburg*, pp. 30–31.

3. Napoleon to Talleyrand, 22 August 1805, *Corr. de Nap.*, doc. 9104.

4. Talleyrand to Napoleon, 18 August 1805, in Pierre Bertrand, ed., *Lettres inédites de Talleyrand à Napoléon, 1800–1809* (Paris: Librairie académique Didier, 1889), doc. 92, p. 129.

5. Napoleon to Talleyrand, 2 October 1805, *Corr. de Nap.*, doc. 9307.

6. Von Oer, *Der Friede von Pressburg*, p. 18.

7. Bertrand, *Lettres inédites de Talleyrand*, pp. 128–156.

8. Talleyrand to Hauterive, 11 October 1805, in Paul-Louis Couchoud and Jean-Paul Couchoud, eds., *Talleyrand: Mémoires, 1754–1815*, rev. ed. (Paris: Plon, 1982), p. 344.

9. Talleyrand to Napoleon, 17 October 1805, in Bertrand, *Lettres inédites de Talleyrand*, doc. 111, and Couchoud and Couchoud, *Talleyrand: Mémoires*, pp. 345–347.

10. Von Oer, *Der Friede von Pressburg*, pp. 46–48; Talleyrand to Hauterive, 27 October 1805, Couchoud and Couchoud, *Talleyrand: Mémoires*, p. 348.

11. Paul Schroeder, *The Transformation of European Politics, 1763–1848* (New York: Oxford University Press, 1994), p. 278.

12. Decree, 21 October 1805, *Corr. de Nap.*, doc. 9407.

13. Napoleon to Champagny, 21 October 1805, *Corr. de Nap.*, doc. 9411.

14. Napoleon to the Elector of Württemberg, 2 November 1805, *Corr. de Nap.*, doc. 9444.

15. Ninth Bulletin of the Grande Armée, *Corr. de Nap.*, doc. 9408.

16. Napoleon to Francis, 3 November 1805, *Corr. de Nap.*, doc. 9451.

17. Von Oer, *Der Friede von Pressburg*, pp. 67–69; Francis to Napoleon, 5 November 1805, in Adolf Beer, *Zehn Jahre österreichischer Politik, 1801–1810* (Leipzig: F. A. Brockhaus, 1877), p. 454.

18. Cobenzl to Metternich, 10 November 1805, in Prince Richard Metternich-Winneburg, ed., *Aus Metternich's nachgelassenen Papieren* (Vienna: 1880: Wilhelm Braumüller). pt. 1, vol. 2, p. 82.

19. Von Oer, *Der Friede von Pressburg*, p. 68.

20. Von Oer, *Der Friede von Pressburg*, pp. 69–71.

21. Napoleon to Francis, 8 November 1805, *Corr. de Nap.*, doc. 9464; Napoleon to Talleyrand, 9 November 1805, doc. 9468.

22. See above, Chapter 18.

23. Von Oer, *Der Friede von Pressburg*, pp. 71–72.

24. Von Oer, *Der Friede von Pressburg*, p. 72.

25. Von Oer, *Der Friede von Pressburg*, p. 73; Francis to Napoleon, 15 November 1805, in Beer, *Zehn Jahre österreichischer Politik*, p. 455.

26. Napoleon to Talleyrand, 9 November 1805, *Corr. de Nap.*, doc. 9468.

27. Napoleon to Marmont, 14 November 1805, *Corr. de Nap.*, doc. 9480.

28. Talleyrand to Hauterive, 12 and 18 November 1805, in Couchoud and Couchoud, *Talleyrand: Mémoires*, pp. 348–349.

29. Von Oer, *Der Friede von Pressburg*, p. 57; the document is reproduced on p. 245.

30. Napoleon to the Elector of Bavaria, 15 November 1805, *Corr. de Nap.*, doc. 9484. The orders to blow up the fortresses and transfer control of the Tyrol to Bavarian troops went to Ney the following day (doc. 9500).

31. Napoleon to the Elector of Württemberg, 16 November 1805, *Corr. de Nap.*, doc. 9501.

32. Napoleon to Talleyrand, 23 November 1805, *Corr. De Nap.*, doc. 9519.

33. Duroc to Napoleon, 27 and 30 October 1805, in Paul Bailleu, ed., *Preußen und Frankreich 1795 bis 1807. Diplomatische Correspondenzen*. Publicationen aus den königlichen preussischen Archiven, 8 and 29 (Leipzig, 1881–1887), vol. 2, docs. 301–302.

34. See above, Chapter 20, and Napoleon to Talleyrand, 22 November 1805, *Corr. de Nap.*, doc. 9516.

35. See above, Chapter 20.

36. Napoleon to Talleyrand, 30 November 1805, *Corr. de Nap.*, doc. 9532.

37. Von Oer, *Der Friede von Pressburg*, p. 80.

38. Talleyrand to Napoleon, [29] November 1805, in Bertrand, *Lettres inédites de Talleyrand*, doc. 124. In the text this document is dated November 20, which is impossible; Stadion and Gyulai did not arrive in Vienna until November 28 (Von Oer, *Der Friede von Pressburg*, p. 89). Talleyrand furthermore reports in this note that they had not brought their plenipotentiary powers with them but would do so the following day. He wrote Napoleon on November 30 that they had done so on that day (Bertrand, *Lettres inédites de Talleyrand*, doc. 134).

39. Von Oer, *Der Friede von Pressburg*, pp. 79–80; and "Two Secret Instructions for Stadion, Including the Instruction of 23 November 1805," pp. 247–250.

40. Von Oer, *Der Friede von Pressburg*, p. 81.

41. Von Oer, *Der Friede von Pressburg*, p. 82.

42. Von Oer, *Der Friede von Pressburg*, pp. 82–83.

43. Napoleon to Talleyrand, 25 November 1805, *Corr. de Nap.*, doc. 9523.

44. Napoleon to Talleyrand, 30 November 1805, *Corr. de Nap.*, doc. 9532.

45. Von Oer, *Der Friede von Pressburg*, p. 84.

46. Haugwitz to Frederick William, 2 December 1805, in Leopold von Ranke, *Denkwürdigkeiten des Staatskanzlers Fürsten von Hardenberg* (Leipzig: Ducker and Humblot, 1877), 5:190–195.

47. Haugwitz to Frederick William, 2 December 1805, in Leopold von Ranke, *Denkwürdigkeiten des Staatskanzlers Fürsten von Hardenberg* (Leipzig: Ducker and Humblot, 1877), 5:190–195.

48. Ciphered portion of Haugwitz to Frederick William, 2 December 1805, in Bailleu, *Preußen und Frankreich*, vol. 2, doc. 311.

49. Von Oer, *Der Friede von Pressburg*, p. 91.

50. Talleyrand to Napoleon, 30 November 1805, in Bertrand, *Lettres inédites de Talleyrand*, doc. 134, p. 202.

51. Talleyrand to Napoleon, 2 December 1805, in Bertrand, *Lettres inédites de Talleyrand*, doc. 136, pp. 204–205.

52. Bertrand, *Lettres inédites de Talleyrand*, doc. 137, p. 205.

53. Bertrand, *Lettres inédites de Talleyrand*, doc. 137, pp. 205–207.

54. Napoleon to Talleyrand, 30 November 1805, *Corr. de Nap.*, doc. 9532.

55. Talleyrand to Napoleon, 2 December 1805, in Bertrand, *Lettres inédites de Talleyrand*, doc. 136, p. 205.

56. Memorandum of Count Haugwitz To Serve Him as Instruction During His Voyage to Vienna in November 1805, in Ranke, *Denkwürdigkeiten*, 5:185–189. The Treaty of Potsdam is in F. Martens, *Recueil des Traités et Conventions conclus par la Russie avec les Puissances Etrangères* (St. Petersburg: A. Böhnke, 1902), 2:480ff.

57. See below.

58. Brendan Simms, *The Impact of Napoleon: Prussian High Politics, Foreign Policy, and the Crisis of the Executive, 1797–1806* (New York: Cambridge University Press, 1997), p. 208.

59. Talleyrand to Napoleon, 1 December 1805, in Bertrand, *Lettres inédites de Talleyrand*, doc. 135, p. 202.

60. Draft Treaty, 1 December 1805, in von Oer, *Der Friede von Pressburg*, pp. 250–254.

61. Talleyrand to Napoleon, 1 December 1805, in Bertrand, *Lettres inédites de Talleyrand*, doc. 135.

62. Von Oer, *Der Friede von Pressburg*, p. 98, makes this suggestion.

63. Talleyrand to Napoleon, 2 December 1805, in Bertrand, *Lettres inédites de Talleyrand*, doc. 137, p. 208.

64. Laforest to Talleyrand, 19 November 1805, in Bailleu, *Preußen und Frankreich*, vol. 2, p. 410 n. 1.

65. Von Oer, *Der Friede von Pressburg*, p. 100.

66. Von Oer, *Der Friede von Pressburg*, pp. 99–102.

67. Napoleon to Talleyrand, 3 December 1805, *Corr. de Nap.*, doc. 9540.

68. Thirtieth Bulletin of the Grande Armée, 3 December 1805, *Corr. de Nap.*, doc. 9541.

79. Napoleon to Talleyrand, 4 December 1805, *Corr. de Nap.*, doc. 9542.

70. Talleyrand to Napoleon, 5 December 1805, in Bertrand, *Lettres inédites de Talleyrand*, doc. 138, p. 209. Whether or not Napoleon actually received this note is open to question. See von Oer, *Der Friede von Pressburg*, p. 104.

71. Talleyrand to Napoleon, 5 December 1805, in Bertrand, *Lettres inédites de Talleyrand*, doc. 138, p. 211.

72. Talleyrand to Napoleon, 5 December 1805, in Bertrand, *Lettres inédites de Talleyrand*, doc. 138, p. 212.

73. Talleyrand to Napoleon, 7 December 1805, in Bertrand, *Lettres inédites de Talleyrand*, doc. 139, pp. 212–213.

74. Napoleon to Talleyrand, 4 December 1805, *Corr. de Nap.*, doc. 9542.

75. Von Oer, *Der Friede von Pressburg*, pp. 109–110.

76. Désiré Lacroix, ed., *Mémoires du Duc de Rovigo pour servir à l'histoire de l'Empereur Napoléon* (Paris: Garnier Frères, 1900), 2:82.

77. Lacroix, ed., *Mémoires*, 2:86–87.

78. Napoleon to Talleyrand, 4 December 1805, *Corr. de Nap.*, doc. 9542.

79. Von Oer, *Der Friede von Pressburg*, p. 110.

80. See Davout's correspondence from 17 November through 27 November 1805, in Mazade, *Correspondence du Maréchal Davout*, vol. 1, docs. 115–121, passim.

81. Decree, 28 November 1805, *Corr. de Nap.*, doc. 9529.

82. Napoleon to Daru, 6 December 1805, *Corr. de Nap.*, doc. 9547; "Order," 9 December 1805, doc. 9553.

83. Napoleon to Talleyrand, 4 December 1805, *Corr. de Nap.*, doc. 9542.

84. Armistice Concluded Between T[heir] I[mperial] M[ajesties] of France and Austria at Austerlitz, 6 December 1805, in Léopold Neumann, *Recueil des traits et conventions conclus par l'Autriche avec les puissances étrangères, depuis 1763 jusqu'à nos jours* (Leipzig: F. A. Brockhaus, 1856), 2:181–182.

85. Lacroix, *Mémoires du Duc de Rovigo*, pp. 84–87.

86. Frederick William to Haugwitz, 19 December 1805, in Ranke, *Denkwürdigkeiten*, 2:367–368; von Oer, *Der Friede von Pressburg*, pp. 117–118.

87. Von Oer, *Der Friede von Pressburg*, p. 119.

88. Von Oer, *Der Friede von Pressburg*, pp. 119–120. The quotation is from p. 120.

89. Von Oer, *Der Friede von Pressburg*, pp. 121–130.

90. The "Brünner Questionnaire," in von Oer, *Der Friede von Pressburg*, pp. 256–258.

91. Granvenreuth to Max Joseph, 8 December 1805, in von Oer, *Der Friede von Pressburg*, pp. 259–260.

92. Von Oer, *Der Friede von Pressburg*, p. 128.

93. The following section draws heavily on von Oer, *Der Friede von Pressburg*, pp. 131–140.

94. Von Oer, *Der Friede von Pressburg*, p. 139.

95. Gravenreuth to Max Joseph, 8 December 1805, in von Oer, *Der Friede von Pressburg*, p. 262.

96. Von Oer, *Der Friede von Pressburg*, p. 133.

97. Von Oer, *Der Friede von Pressburg*, p. 134.

98. Gravenreuth to Max Joseph, 8 December 1805, in von Oer, *Der Friede von Pressburg*, p. 260.

99. Von Oer, *Der Friede von Pressburg*, p. 133.

100. Edouard Driault, *Napoléon et l'Europe: Austerlitz: La Fin du Saint-Empire (1804–1806)* (Paris: Librairie Félix Alcan, 1912), pp. 356–360; Napoleon to the Elector Archchancellor of the German Empire, 24 December 1805, *Corr. de Nap.*, doc. 9608.

101. Von Oer, *Der Friede von Pressburg*, p. 141.

102. Von Oer, *Der Friede von Pressburg*, pp. 141–142.

103. Von Oer, *Der Friede von Pressburg*, pp. 142–144.

104. Talleyrand to Hauterive, 11 December 1805, in Couchoud and Couchoud, *Talleyrand: Mémoires*, p. 353.

105. The Treaty Articles Read by Talleyrand to Liechtenstein and Gyulai with Comments by the Austrians, 12 December 1805, in von Oer, *Der Friede von Pressburg*, pp. 262–268.

106. Talleyrand to Napoleon, [12] December 1805, in Bertrand, *Lettres inédites de Talleyrand*, doc. 140, p. 213.

107. The Treaty Articles Read by Talleyrand to Liechtenstein and Gyulai with Comments by the Austrians, 12 December 1805, in von Oer, *Der Friede von Pressburg*, p. 266; Talleyrand to Napoleon, [12] December 1805, in Bertrand, *Lettres inédites de Talleyrand*, doc. 140, p. 216.

108. Talleyrand to Napoleon, [12] December 1805, in Bertrand, *Lettres inédites de Talleyrand*, doc. 140, pp. 216–217.

109. Talleyrand to Napoleon, 14 December 1805, in Bertrand, *Lettres inédites de Talleyrand*, doc. 141, p. 217; von Oer, *Der Friede von Pressburg*, pp. 148–149.

110. Napoleon to Talleyrand, 13 December 1805, *Corr. de Nap.*, doc. 9560.

111. Napoleon to Talleyrand, 13 December 1805, *Corr. de Nap.*, doc. 9560.

112. Napoleon to Champagny, 13 December 1805, *Corr. de Nap.*, doc. 9563.

113. Napoleon to Fouché, 13 December 1805, *Corr. de Nap.*, doc. 9565.

114. Napoleon to the Elector of Württemberg, 13 December 1805, *Corr. de Nap.*, doc. 9567.

115. Napoleon to Masséna, 13 December 1805, *Corr. de Nap.*, doc. 9571.

116. Napoleon to Talleyrand, 14 December 1805, *Corr. de Nap.*, doc. 9573.

117. Report of Count Haugwitz About his Mission to Napoleon, 26 December 1805, Ranke, *Denkwürdigkeiten*, 5:224.

118. Report of Count Haugwitz About his Mission to Napoleon, 26 December 1805, Ranke, *Denkwürdigkeiten*, 5:232.

119. Ranke, *Denkwürdigkeiten*, 5:223 n. 2.

120. Haugwitz, Report, 16 December 1805, in Ranke, *Denkwürdigkeiten*, 2:385.

121. The treaty is reprinted in Ranke, *Denkwürdigkeiten*, 2:389–392.

122. Haugwitz, Report, 26 December 1805, in Ranke, *Denkwürdigkeiten*, 5:231.

123. Napoleon to Talleyrand, 15 December 1805, *Corr. de Nap.*, doc. 9578.

124. Talleyrand to Napoleon, 17 December 1805, Bertrand, *Lettres inédites de Talleyrand*, doc. 145, p. 225.

125. Von Oer, *Der Friede von Pressburg*, pp. 164–165.

126. Talleyrand to Napoleon, 16 December 1805, in Bertrand, *Lettres inédites de Talleyrand*, doc. 144, p. 223.

127. Napoleon to Talleyrand, 16 December 1805, *Corr. de Nap.*, doc. 9582.

128. See Talleyrand's correspondence with Napoleon, 16–24 December 1805, in Bertrand, *Lettres in- édites de Talleyrand*, pp. 222–227; von Oer, *Der Friede von Pressburg*, pp. 175–178.

129. Napoleon to Berthier, 16 December 1805, *Corr. de Nap.*, doc. 9583.

130. Napoleon to Berthier, 18 December 1805, *Corr. de Nap.*, doc. 9587.

131. Von Oer, *Der Friede von Pressburg*, p. 170.

132. Napoleon to Berthier, 16 December 1805, *Corr. de Nap.*, doc. 9583.

133. Von Oer, *Der Friede von Pressburg*, p. 170.

134. See Ernst Wangermann, *From Joseph II to the Jacobin Trials: Government Policy and Public Opinion in the Habsburg Dominions in the Period of the French Revolution*, 2nd ed. (New York: Oxford Uni- versity Press, 1969).

135. Charles to Albert of Sachsen-Teschen, 25 December 1805, in Oskar Criste, *Erzherzog Carl von Oesterreich* (Vienna: Wilhelm Braumüller, 1912), vol. 2, appendix XL/29, pp. 601–602.

136. T. C. W. Blanning, *Joseph II* (New York: Longman, 1994), pp. 171–175.

137. Criste, *Erzherzog Carl von Oesterreich*, 2:371.

138. Charles to Albert, 21 December 1805, in Criste, *Erzherzog Carl von Oesterreich*, vol. 2, appendix XL/27, p. 600.

139. Criste, *Erzherzog Carl von Oesterreich*, 2:372–373.

140. Archduke Charles, "Memorandum on the Resumption of Hostilities at the Breaking-Off of Negotiations," in Moriz Edlen von Angeli, *Erzherzog Carl von Osterreich als Feldherr und Heeresor- ganisator* (Vienna: Wilhelm Braumüller, 1897), vol. 3, appendix 8, pp. 238–240.

141. Talleyrand to Napoleon, 23 December 1805, in Bertrand, *Lettres inédites de Talleyrand*, doc. 146, pp. 226–227.

142. Talleyrand to Napoleon, 24 December 1805, in Bertrand, *Lettres inédites de Talleyrand*, doc. 147, p. 227.

143. Napoleon to Talleyrand, 23 December 1805, *Corr. de Nap.*, doc. 9605; Talleyrand to Napoleon, 25 December 1805, Bertrand, *Lettres inédites de Talleyrand*, doc. 148, pp. 227–228, 26 December 1805, doc. 149, pp. 228–229.

144. Napoleon to Talleyrand, 25 December 1805, *Corr. de Nap.*, doc. 9613.

145. Napoleon to Cambacérès, 20 December 1805, *Corr. de Nap.*, doc. 9593.

Appendix: The Battle of Dürnstein

1. Rainer Egger, *Das Gefecht bei Dürnstein-Loiben, 1805, Militärhistorische Schriftenreihe*, vol. 3 (Vienna: Heeresgeschichtliches Museum, Militärwissenschaftliches Institut, 1986); [H. Heller], "Das Gefecht bei Dürrenstein am 11. November 1805. Nach österreichischen Originalquellen," *Österreichische militärische Zeitschrift*, vol. 1 (1860), 3rd series, no. 9; [Alexander von Kirchham- mer], "Militärische Aufgaben auf geschichtlicher Grundlage, Aufgabe I: Dürnstein 1805," *Österre- ichische militärische Zeitschrift*, vol. 22 (1881), no. 1, pp. 23–38; no. 2, pp. 45–54; no. 4, pp. 95–126; Wilhelm von Kotzebue, *Versuch einer Beschreibung der Schlacht bey Dürnstein am 11. November 1805 nebst einem Plane dieser Schlacht* (n.p.: A. von Kotzebue, 1807).

2. Kirchhammer, "Militärische Aufgaben," pp. 108–109.

3. Dokhturov to Kutuzov, 20 November 1805, in Iu. I. Zhiugzhda, ed., *Dokumenty shtaba M. I. Kutu- zova, 1805–1806* (Vilnius: Gosudarstvennoe Izdatel'stvo Politicheskoi i Nauchnoi Literatury,

1951), doc. 95; Ulanius to Dokhturov, 14 November 1805, doc. 96; Urusov to Dokhturov, 16 November 1805, doc. 97; Gvozdev to Urusov, 20 November 1805, doc. 98.

4. *Journal des opérations de la division Dupont*, cited in Paul Claude Alombert-Goget, *Campagne de l'an 14 (1805). Le corps d'armée aux ordres du Maréchal Mortier. Combat de Dürrenstein* (Paris: Berger-Levrault, 1897), pp. 126–130.

5. Alombert-Goget, *Combat de Dürrenstein*, p. 130 n. 2.

6. See above, Chapter 18.

Bibliography

Abbreviations

VPR *Vneshniaia Politika Rossii (VPR I, II, or III depending on the volume; all are from Series 1).*

SIRIO *Sbornik Imperatorskago Russkago Istoricheskago Obshchestva (identified by volume, SIRIO 70, SIRIO 73, etc.).*

AKV *Arkhiv Kniazia Vorontsova (identified by volume).*

Corr. de Nap. *Correspondance de Napoléon Ier (identified by document number).*

SVM *Stolietie voennago ministerstva, 1802–1902.*

RGVIA *Rossiisskii Gosudarstvennyi Voenno-Istoricheskii Arkhiv (Moscow).*

GARF *Glavnyi Arkhiv Russkoi Federatsii (Moscow).*

SHAT *Service Historique de l'Armée de Terre (Vincennes).*

AN *Archive Nationale (Paris).*

KA *Kriegsarchiv (Vienna).*

HHSt *Haus-, Hof-, und Staatsarchiv (Vienna).*

GStA *Geheime Staatsarchiv (Berlin).*

HKR *Hofkriegsrat (Austrian Kriegsarchiv).*

AFA *Alte Feldakten (in Austrian Kriegsarchiv).*

FML *Feldmarshal-Leutnant (Austrian military rank equivalent to full general, just below field marshal).*

Archives

Austria
Haus-, Hof-, und Staatsarchiv.
Rußland Varia II, 240.
Kriegsarchiv.
Alte Feldakten, 1805, Deutschland, I–XIII.
Alte Feldakten, 1805, Italien, 1804 (XII)–1805 (XII).
Alte Feldakten, 1805, HKR, VII–X.
Nachlaß Mack.
Nachlaß Franz.
Memoiren, 6. Abteilung.
Dürnstein Parish Archive.
Graf, Leopold. *Kriegs-Begebenheiten zu Unterloiben am 11. November 1805.* Typescript of manuscript prepared by Dr. E. Alzinger in August 1982. I am very grateful to Dr. Gottfried Thiery of the Gesellschaft der Freunde Dürnsteins for sending me a copy of this typescript.

France

Archives Nationales.

AF IV 1601. Armée contre l'Angleterre.

Service Historique de l'Armée de Terre.

C² 7, Correspondence de la Grande Armée, 1–15 November 1805.

C² 8, Correspondence de la Grande Armée, 16–30 November 1805.

C² 9, Correspondence de la Grande Armée, 1–15 December 1805.

C² 13, Mémoires militaires; papiers prussiens et russes, renseignements étrangers sur la campagne de 1805 et sur différentes campagnes antérieures des prussiens et des russes.

C² 17, Renseignements divers sur la bataille d'Austerlitz; matériaux de rédaction pour le général Blein; son ouvrage.

C² 200, Expédition d'Angleterre. Corréspondance du chef de l'état-major général avec le premier consul, le directeur de l'administration de la guerre, les ministres et les officiers composant l'état-major général des divers camps, 28 August 1803–17 January 1805.

C² 233, Lettres du general Dumas á Joseph Napoleon sur la campagne de 1805 et la bataille d'Austerlitz.

C² 253, Correspondance du général Andréossy, aide-major général et chef de l'état-major général de la grande armée.

C² 377, Grande armée (4e corps). Correspondance du chef de l'état-major général (généraux Salligny, Morand, Merle), 19 September 1805–17 May 1806.

C² 384, Camps de Bruges. Rapports au général en chef. 11 April–2 August 1804.

C² 390, Grande Armée (3e corps). Correspondance du maréchal Davout, 20 September 1805–25 March 1806.

Published Sources

Alombert-Goget, Paul Claude. *Campagne de l'an 14 (1805). Le corps d'armée aux ordres du Maréchal Mortier. Combat de Dürrenstein.* Paris: Berger-Levrault, 1897.

Alombert-Goget, Paul Claude, and Jean Lambert Alphonse Colin. *La campagne de 1805 en Allemagne.* Paris: Librairie militaire R. Chapelot, 1902–1908.

Albrecht and William, Archdukes of Austria, eds. *Ausgewählte Schriften weiland seiner kaiserlichen Hoheit des Erzherzogs Carl von Oesterreich.* Vienna: Wilhelm Braumüller, 1894.

Allgemeine deutsche Biographie: Auf Veranlassung Seiner Majestaet des Königs von Bayern hrsg. durch die Historische Commission bei der Königl. Akademie der Wissenschaften. Leipzig: Duncker & Humblot, 1875–1912.

Angeli, Moriz Edlen von. "Beiträge zur vaterländischen Geschichte. IV. Ulm und Austerlitz. Studie auf Grund archivalischer Quellen über den Feldzug 1805 in Deutschland. A.and B Ulm." *Mittheilungen des K. K. Kriegs-Archivs* 2 (1877): 395–510; 3 (1878): 283–394.

———. *Erzherzog Carl von Osterreich als Feldherr und Heeresorganisator.* Vienna: Wilhelm Braumüller, 1897.

Auriol, Ch. *La France, l'Angleterre et Naples de 1803 à 1806.* Paris: Librairie Plon, 1904.

Bailleu, Paul, ed., *Briefwechsel König Freidrich Wilhelms III und der Königin Luise mit Kaiser Alexander I.* Publicationen aus den K. Preussischen Archiven 75. Leipzig: S. Hirzel, 1900.

Bailleu, Paul, ed. *Preussen und Frankreich 1795 bis 1807. Diplomatische Correspondenzen.* Publicationen aus den königlichen preussischen Archiven, 8 and 29. Leipzig: S. Hirzel, 1881–1887.

Bartenev, P. I., ed. *Arkhiv kniazia Vorontsova*. Moscow: Tipografiia Lebedeva, 1870–1895.

Beer, Adolf. *Die Finanzen Oesterreichs im XIX. Jahrhundert, nach archivalischen Quellen*. Prague: F. Tempsky, 1877.

———. "Österreich und Russland in den Jahren 1804 und 1805." *Archiv für österreichische Geschichte* 53 (1875): 126–243.

———. *Zehn Jahre österreichischer Politik, 1801–1810*. Leipzig: F. A. Brockhaus, 1877.

Beiträge zur Geschichte des österreichischen Heerwesens. Vol. 1, *Der Zeitraum von 1757–1814. Mit besonderer Rücksichtnahme auf Organisation, Verpflegung, und Taktik*. Vienna: L. W. Seidel, 1872.

Bergeron, Louis. *France Under Napoleon*. Translated by R. R. Palmer. Princeton: Princeton University Press, 1990.

Bernhardi, Theodor von. *Denkwürdigkeiten aus dem Leben des kaiserlisches russisches Generals von der Infanterie Carl Friedrich Grafen von Toll*. Leipzig: Otto Wigand, 1865.

Bertrand, Pierre, ed. *Lettres inédites de Talleyrand à Napoléon, 1800–1809*. Paris: Librairie académique Didier, 1889.

Beskrovnyi, L. G. *M. I. Kutuzov: Sbornik dokumentov*. Vol. 2. Moscow: Voennoe Izdatel'stvo, 1951.

Bigarré, Auguste Julien. *Mémoires du Gal. Bigarré, Aide de camp du Roi Joseph*. Paris: Ernest Kolb, 1893.

Blanning, T. C. W. *The French Revolutionary Wars*. New York: Arnold, 1996.

———. *Joseph II*. New York: Longman, 1996.

———. *The Origins of the French Revolutionary Wars*. New York: Longman, 1986.

Bliokh, I. S. *Finansy Rossii XIX stolietiia, istoriia, statistika*. St. Petersburg: M. M. Stasiulevich, 1882.

Bonaparte, Napoleon. *Correspondance de Napoléon Ier*. Paris: Henrie Plon, 1861.

Bordo, Michael, and Eugene N. White. "A Tale of Two Currencies: British and French Finance During the Napoleonic Wars." *Journal of Economic History*, June 1991, pp. 303–316.

Boulay de la Meurthe, Comte de. *Correspondance du duc d'Enghien et documents sur son enlèvement et sa mort*. Paris: Alphonse Picard et Fils, 1908.

Bowden, Scott. *Napoleon and Austerlitz: An Unprecedentedly Detailed Combat Study of Napoleon's Epic Ulm-Austerlitz Campaigns of 1805*. Chicago: Emperor's, 1997.

Boycott-Brown, Martin. *The Road to Rivoli: Napoleon's First Campaign*. London: Cassell, 2001.

Brethon, Paul le, ed. *Lettres et documents pour servir à l'histoire de Joachim Murat, 1767–1815*. Paris: Librairie Plon, 1909.

Calmettes, Fernand, ed. *Mémoires du Général Bon. Thiébault*. Vol. 3. Paris: Librairie Plon, 1895.

Campagnes de la Grande-Armée et de l'Armée d'Italie en l'an XIV (1805). Paris: La Librairie Economique, 1806.

Casse, A. du, ed. *Le Général Vandamme et sa correspondance*. Vol. 2. Paris: Librairie Académique, 1870.

———. *Mémoires et correspondance politique et militaire du Prince Eugène*. Paris: Michel Lévy Frères, 1858.

Caulaincourt, Armand-Augustin-Louis de. *Mémoires du Général de Caulaincourt, Duc de Vicence, Grand Écuyer de l'Empereur*. Paris: Librairie Plon, 1933.

Chalamet, A. *Guerres de Napoléon (1800–1807), racontées par des témoins oculaires*. Paris: Firmin-Didot et Cie., 1895.

Chandler, David. *Austerlitz, 1805: Battle of the Three Emperors*. London: Osprey, 1990.

_____. *The Campaigns of Napoleon.* New York: Macmillan, 1966.

_____. *Dictionary of the Napoleonic Wars.* New York: Macmillan, 1979.

Charles, Archduke of Austria. *Grundsätze der höhern Kriegs-Kunst für die Generäle der österreichischen Armee.* Vienna: Kaiserlich und Kaiserlich-Königlich Hof- und Staats-Druckerei, 1806.

Coffin, Victor. "A Preliminary Study of the Administrative Polity of Napoleon I." *American Historical Review,* July 1908, pp. 753–778.

Connelly, Owen. *Blundering to Glory: Napoleon's Military Campaigns.* Wilmington, Del.: SR Books, 1999.

Criste, Oskar. *Erzherzog Carl von Oesterreich.* Vienna: Wilhelm Braumüller, 1912.

Desbrière, Edouard. *Projets et tentatives de débarquement aux Iles Britanniques.* Paris: Librairie Militarie R. Chapelot, 1902.

Deutsch, Harold C. "Napoleonic Policy and the Project of a Descent upon England." *Journal of Modern History,* December 1930, pp. 541–568.

Doyle, William, *The Oxford History of the French Revolution.* New York: Oxford University Press, 1990.

Driault, Édouard. *Napoléon et l'Europe: Austerlitz: La Fin du Saint-Empire, 1804–1806.* Paris: Librairie Félix Alcan, 1912.

_____. *Napoléon en Italie (1800–1812).* Paris: Librairie Félix Alcan, 1906.

Duffy, Christopher. *The Army of Maria Theresa: The Armed Forces of Imperial Austria, 1740–1780.* Vancouver: David & Charles, 1977.

_____. *Austerlitz, 1805.* London: Seeley Service, 1977.

Dumas, Mathieu. *Souvenirs du Lieutenant Général Comte Mathieu Dumas de 1770 à 1836.* Paris: Librairie de Charles Gosselin, 1839.

Dwyer, Philip G. "The Politics of Prussian Neutrality." *German History* 12, no. 3 (1994): 351–373.

_____. "Prussia and the Armed Neutrality: The Invasion of Hanover in 1801." *International History Review,* November 1993, 661–687.

Dwyer, Philip G., ed. *The Rise of Prussia, 1700–1830.* New York: Longman, 2000.

Egger, Rainer. *Das Gefecht bei Dürnstein-Loiben, 1805. Militärhistorische Schriftenreihe.* Vol 3. 3rd ed. Vienna: Heeresgeschichtliches Museum/Militärwissenschaftliches Institut, 1986.

_____. *Das Gefecht bei Hollabrunn und Schöngrabern, 1805. Militärhistorische Schriftenreihe,* vol. 27. Vienna: Heeresgeschichtliches Museum/Militärwissenschaftliches Institut, 1974.

Ehrman, John. *The Younger Pitt: The Consuming Struggle.* London: Constable, 1996.

Epstein, Robert M. *Napoleon's Last Victory and the Emergence of Modern War.* Lawrence: University Press of Kansas, 1994.

_____. "Patterns of Change and Continuity in Nineteenth-Century Warfare." *Journal of Military History,* July 1992, pp. 375–388.

Eysturlid, Lee W. *The Formative Influences, Theories, and Campaigns of the Archduke Carl of Austria.* Westport, Conn.: Greenwood, 2000.

Fedorak, Charles John. *Henry Addington, Prime Minister, 1801–1804: Peace, War, and Parliamentary Politics.* Akron, Ohio: University of Akron Press, 2002.

_____. "In Search of a Necessary Ally: Addington, Hawkesbury, and Russia, 1801–1804." *International History Review,* May 1991, pp. 221–245.

Fedorchenko, V. *Imperatorskii dom: Vydaioshchiesia sanovniki.* Moscow: Olma-Press, 2001.

Fedorov, V. A., ed. *Zapiski A. P. Ermolova, 1798–1826.* Moscow: Vysshaia shkola, 1991.

Flayhart, William Henry III. *Counterpoint to Trafalgar: The Anglo-Russian Invasion of Naples, 1805–1806.* Columbia: University of South Carolina Press, 1992.

Fournier, August. *Gentz und Cobenzl: Geschichte der österreichischen Diplomatie in den Jahren 1801–1805, nach neuen Quellen.* Vienna: Wilhelm Braumüller, 1880.

Furet, François. *Revolutionary France, 1770–1880.* Translated by Antonia Nevill. Malden, Mass.: Blackwell, 1999.

Gabillard, Jean, "Le financement des guerres napoléoniennes." *Revue Economique,* July 1953, pp. 548–572.

Gaddis, John Lewis. *Strategies of Containment: A Critical Appraisal of American National Security Policy During the Cold War.* New York: Oxford University Press, 1982.

Gagliardo, John G. *Reich and Nation: The Holy Roman Empire as Idea and Reality, 1763–1806.* Bloomington: Indiana University Press, 1980.

Galasso, Giuseppe. "Das italienische Staatensystem in der Politik Napoleons." *Deutschland und Italien im Zeitalter Napoleons: Deutsch-Italienisches Historikertreffen in Mainz 29. Mai–1. Juni 1975.* Edited by Armgard von Reden-Dohna. Wiesbaden: Franz Steiner Verlag, 1979.

Gallaher, John G. *The Iron Marshal: A Biography of Louis N. Davout.* Mechanicsburg, Pa.: Stackpole, 2000.

Garden, Comte de. *Histoire générale des traités de paix et autres transactions principales entre toutes les puissances de l'Europe depuis la paix de Westphalie.* Vol. 3. Paris: Amyot, 1867.

Garnier, Jacques, ed. *Relations et rapports officiels de la bataille d'Austerlitz, 1805.* Paris: La Vouivre, 1998.

Gat, Azar. *A History of Military Thought from the Enlightenment to the Cold War.* New York: Oxford University Press, 2001.

———. *The Origins of Military Thought from the Enlightenment to Clausewitz.* Oxford: Clarendon, 1989.

Gates, David. *The Napoleonic Wars, 1803–1815.* New York: Arnold, 1997.

Gielgud, Adam, ed. *Memoirs of Prince Adam Czartoryski.* New York: Arno/New York Times, 1971.

Gmeinwiser, Josef. "Die bayerische Politik im Jahre 1805." Ph.D. diss., University of Munich, 1928.

Godechot, Jacques. *La contre-révolution: Doctrine et action, 1789–1804.* Paris: Presses Universitaires de France, 1961.

Grimsted, Patricia Kennedy. "Czartoryski's System for Russian Foreign Policy, 1803: A Memorandum, Edited with Introduction and Analysis." *Canadian Slavic Studies* 5: 19–92.

———. *The Foreign Ministers of Alexander I: Political Attitudes and the Conduct of Russian Diplomacy, 1801–1825.* Los Angeles: University of California Press, 1969.

Guliaev, Iu. N., and V. T. Sogliaev. *Fel'dmarshal Kutuzov.* Moscow: Arkheograficheskii Tsentr, 1995.

Hall, Christopher D. *British Strategy in the Napoleonic War, 1803–1815.* Manchester: Manchester University Press, 1992.

Hartley, Janet M. *Alexander I.* New York: Longman, 1994.

Haythornthwaite, Philip J. *Who Was Who in the Napoleonic Wars.* London: Arms & Armour, 1998.

Heller, H. "Das Gefecht bei Dürrenstein am 11. November 1805. Nach österreichischen Originalquellen." *Österreichische militärische Zeitschrift* 1, no. 9 (1860). 3rd series.

Holland Rose, John. *Select Despatches from the British Foreign Office Archives Relating to the Formation of the Third Coalition against France, 1804–1805.* London: Offices of the Royal Historical Society, 1904.

Holtman, Robert B. *The Napoleonic Revolution.* Baton Rouge: Louisiana State University Press, 1967.

Hopton, Richard. *The Battle of Maida, 1806: Fifteen Minutes of Glory.* Barnsley, U.K.: Pen and Sword Books, 2002.

Howard, Michael. *The Franco-Prussian War: The German Invasion of France, 1870–1871.* New York: Methuen, 1961.

Imperial Russian Historical Society. *Russkii biograficheskii slovar'.* St. Petersburg: Tipografiia Glavnago Upravleniia Udelov, 1914.

Jähns, Max. *Geschichte der Krigswissenschaften vornehmlich in Deutschland. Dritte Abteilung. Das XVIII. Jahrhundert seit dem Auftreten Freidrichs des Großen. 1740–1800.* Munich: R. Oldenbourg, 1891.

James, W. M. *The Naval History of Great Britain During the French Revolutionary and Napoleonic Wars.* Vol. 4, *1805–1807.* Mechanicsburg, Pa.: Stackpole, 2002.

Kagan, Frederick W. "The Austrian Army, 1763–1805." Unpublished article under preparation.

———. *The Military Reforms of Nicholas I: The Origins of the Modern Russian Army.* New York: St. Martin's, 1999.

Kagan, Kimberly. *The Eye of Command.* Ann Arbor: University of Michigan Press, 2006.

Kerautret, Michel. *Les grands traités du Consulat (1799–1804): Documents diplomatiques du Consulat et de l'Empire.* Paris: Nouveau Monde Editions/Fondation Napoléon, 2002.

Koch, General Jean Baptiste Frédéric, ed. *Mémoirs de Masséna.* Vol. 5. Paris: Paulin et Lechevalier, 1850.

Kirchhammer, Alexander von. "Militärische Aufgaben auf geschichtlicher Grundlage, Aufgabe I: Dürnstein 1805." *Österreichische militärische Zeitschrift* 22, no. 1 (1881): 23–38; no. 2 (1881): 45–54; no. 4 (1881): 95–126.

Kotzebue, Wilhelm von. *Versuch einer Beschreibung der Schlacht bey Dürnstein am 11ten November 1805.* N.p.: A. von Kotzebue, 1807.

Krauss, Alfred. *1805: Der Feldzug von Ulm.* Vienna: L. W. Seidel & Sohn, 1912.

Lacroix, Désiré, ed. *Mémoires du Duc de Rovigo pour server à l'histoire de l'Empereur Napoléon.* Paris: Garnier Frères, 1900.

Langeron, Alexandre-Arnauld. *Zapiski Grafa Lanzherona, ego sed'maia kampaniia v Moravii i v Vengrii v 1805 godu.* St. Petersburg: n.p., 1900.

Langsam, Walter Consuelo. "Emperor Francis II and the Austrian 'Jacobins,' 1792–1796." *American Historical Review,* April 1945, pp. 471–490.

———. *Francis the Good: The Education of an Emperor, 1768–1792.* New York: Macmillan, 1949.

Lefebvre, Georges, *Napoleon: From 18 Brumaire to Tilsit, 1799–1807.* Translated by Henry F. Stockhold. New York: Columbia University Press, 1969.

Lombard, Johann Wilhelm. *Matériaux pour servir à l'histoire des années 1805, 1806 et 1807; dédies aux Prussiens, par un ancien compatriote.* Paris: Colnet, 1808.

Madariaga, Isabel de. *Russia in the Age of Catherine the Great.* New Haven, Conn.: Yale University Press, 1981.

Mahan, Alfred Thayer. *The Influence of Sea Power upon the French Revolution and Empire, 1793–1812.* New York: Greenwood, 1898.

Marbot, Baptiste-Antoine-Marcelin. *Mémoires du Général Baron de Marbot.* Vol. 1. Paris: Librairie Plon, 1891.

Marion, Marcel. *Histoire financière de la France depuis 1715.* Vol. 4, *1797–1818: La fin de la Révolution, le Consulat et l'Empire, la libération du territoire.* New York: Burt Franklin, n.d. Reprint of 1925 Paris edition.

Marmont, Auguste Frédéric Louis Viesse de. *Mémoires du Maréchal Marmont, Duc de Raguse de 1792 à 1841.* Paris: Perrotin, 1857.

Martens, F. *Recueil des Traités et Conventions conclus par la Russie avec les Puissances Etrangères.* St. Petersburg: A. Böhnke, 1902.

Massenbach, Christian Karl August Ludwig, Freiherr von. *Nähere Beleuchtung des dem k. k. Obersten und Chef des Generalstaabes Freyherrn von Mack zugeschriebenen Operationsplans für den Feldzug 1794 des Oesterreichisch-Französischen Krieges.* Berlin: Johann Friedrich Unger, 1796.

Mazade, Charles, de, ed. *Correspondence du Maréchal Davout, Prince d'Eckmühl; ses commandemants, son ministère, 1801–1815.* Vol. 1. Paris: Librarie Plon, 1885.

McConnell, Allen. *Tsar Alexander I: Paternalistic Reformer.* Arlington Heights, Ill.: Harlan Davidson, 1970.

McGrew, Roderick E. "Paul I and the Knights of Malta." In *Paul I: A Reassessment of His Life and Reign,* edited by Hugh Ragsdale, pp. 44–75. Pittsburgh, Pa.: University Center for International Studies, 1979.

McKay, Derek, and H. M. Scott. *The Rise of the Great Powers, 1648–1815.* New York: Longman, 1983.

McLynn, Frank. *Napoleon: A Biography.* New York: Arcade, 2002.

Melzi d'Eril, Francesco, Duca di Lodi. *Memorie-Documenti e Lettere Inedite di Napoleone I. e Beauharnais.* Vol. 2. Edited by Giovanni Melzi. Milan: Gaetano Brigola, 1865.

Metternich, Clemens Wenzel Lothar, Fürst von. *Aus Metternich's nachgelassenen Papieren.* Vol. 1. Edited by Prince Richard Metternich-Winneburg. Vienna: Wilhelm Braumüller, 1880.

Meynert, Hermann. *Kaiser Franz I. Geschichte seiner Regierung und seiner Zeit.* Vienna: Verlag von Alfred Hölder, 1872.

Nikolai Mikhailovich, Grand Prince. *General-Ad"iutanty Imperatora Aleksandra I.* St. Petersburg: Expeditsiia zagotovleniia gosudarstvennykh bumag, 1913.

_____. *Graf Pavel Aleksandrovich Stroganov (1774–1817): Istoricheskoe izsledovanie epokhi Imperatora Aleksandra I.* St. Petersburg: Department of Preparation of Government Papers, 1903.

_____. *Kniazia Dolgorukie, spodvizhniki Imperatora Aleksandra I v pervye gody ego tsarstvovaniia: Biograficheskie ocherki.* St. Petersburg: Ekspeditsiia zagotovleniia gosudarstvennykh bumag, 1902.

_____. *Le Comte Paul Stroganov.* Translated by F. Billecocq. Paris: Imprimerie Nationale, 1905.

Mikhailovskii-Danilevskii, Aleksandr Ivanovich. *Opisanie pervoi voiny Imperatora Aleksandra s Napoleonom v 1805-m godu.* St. Petersburg: Independent Corps of the Internal Guard Press, 1844.

Moriggl, Alois. *Der Feldzug von Ulm und seine Folgen für Oesterreich überhaupt und für Tirol insbesonders.* Innsbruck: Verlag der Wagner'schen Buchhandlung, 1861.

Narochnitskii, A. L., ed. *Vneshniaia politika rossii XIX i nachala XX veka: Dokumenty Rossiiskogo Ministerstva Inostrannykh Del.* Vol. 1. First series. Moscow: Gosudarstvennoe Izdatel'stvo Politicheskoi Literatury, 1960.

Neumann, Léopold. *Recueil des traités et conventions conclus par l'Autriche avec les puissances étrangères, depuis 1763 jusqu'à nos jours.* Vol. 2. Leipzig: F. A. Brockhaus, 1856.

Oer, Rudolfine Freiin von. *Der Friede von Pressburg: Ein Beitrag zur diplomatiegeschichte des Napoleonischen Zeitalters.* Münster: Aschendorfsche Verlagsbuchhandlung, 1965.

Oncken, Wilhelm. *Österreich und Preußen im Befreiungskriege.* New York: Georg Olms Verlag, 1998. Facsimile reprint of the 1879 edition.

Paget, Augustus B., ed. *The Paget Papers: Diplomatic and Other Correspondence of the Right Hon. Sir Arthur Paget, G.C.B., 1794–1807.* New York: Longmans, Green, 1896.

Panin, N. P. *Materialy dlia zhizneopisaniia grafa Nikity Petrovicha Panina (1770–1837).* St. Petersburg: Imperial Academy of Sciences Press, 1892.

Papers Relative to the Discussion with France in 1802 and 1803. London: A. Strahan, 1803.

Paxton, Roger V. "Russian Foreign Policy and the First Serbian Uprising: Alliances, Apprehensions, and Autonomy, 1804–1807." In *The First Serbian Uprising, 1804–1813.* Edited by Wayne S. Vucinich. New York: Columbia University Press, 1982.

Petiet, Auguste. *Souvenirs historiques, militaires et particuliers, 1784–1815: Mémoires d'un hussard de l'Empire aide de camp du maréchal Soult.* Edited by Nicole Gotteri. Paris: S. P. M., 1996.

Pillepich, Alain. *Napoléon et les Italiens: République italienne et Royaume d'Italie (1802–1814).* Paris: Nouveau Monde/Fondation Napoléon, 2003.

Pingaud, Albert. *Bonaparte, Président de la République Italienne.* Paris: Librairie académique, Perrin et Cie., 1914.

"Pis'ma, raskazy i zametki otnosiashchiesia do gosudarstvennei deiatelei: Kn. M. M. Shcherbatova, gr. Arakcheeva, kn. M. I. Golenishcheva-Kutuzova-Smolenskago; gr. P. P. Konovnitsyna, gener. Fulia, A. S. Shishkova, arkhimandrita Fotii I I. N. Skobeleva, 1789–1826." *Russkaia starina,* January-June 1870, pp. 478–541.

"Die Preussische Kriegsvorbereitungen und Operationspläne von 1805." *Kriegsgeschichtliche Einzelschriften, herausgegeben vom Grossen Generalstabe, kriegsgeschichtliche Abteilung I.* Vol. 1. Berlin: E. S. Mittler, 1883.

Raeff, Marc. *Political Ideas and Institutions in Imperial Russia.* Boulder, Colo.: Westview, 1994.

Ragsdale, Hugh. *Détente in the Napoleonic Era: Bonaparte and the Russians.* Lawrence: Regents Press of Kansas, 1980.

_____. "Was Paul Bonaparte's Fool? The Evidence of Neglected Archives." In *Paul I: A Reassessment of His Life and Reign,* edited by Hugh Ragsdale, pp. 76–90. Pittsburgh, Pa.: University Center for International Studies, 1979.

Ragsdale, Hugh, ed. *Paul I: A Reassessment of His Life and Reign.* Pittsburgh, Pa.: University Center for International Studies, 1979.

Ranke, Leopold von. *Denkwürdigkeiten des Staatskanzlers Fürsten von Hardenberg.* Leipzig: Ducker & Humblot, 1877.

Rapp, Jean. *Memoirs of General Count Rapp, First Aide-de-Campe to Napoleon.* London: Henry Colburn, 1823.

Rauchensteiner, Manfried. *Kaiser Franz und Erzherzog Carl: Dynastie und Heerwesen in Osterreich, 1796–1809.* Vienna: Verlag für Geschichte und Politik, 1972.

Regele, Oskar. "Karl Freiherr von Mack und Johann Ludwig Graf Cobenzl: Ihre Rolle im Kriegsjahr 1805." *Mitteilungen des österreichischen Staatsarchivs* 21 (1968): 142–164.

Resis, Albert. "Russophobia and the 'Testament' of Peter the Great, 1812–1980." *Slavic Review,* Winter 1985, 681–693.

Ross, Steven T. "The Development of the Combat Division in Eighteenth-Century French Armies." *French Historical Studies,* Spring 1965, 84–94.

Rössler, Hellmuth. *Graf Johann Philipp Stadion.* Munich: Herold, 1966.

Rothenberg, Gunther. *The Art of Warfare in the Age of Napoleon.* Bloomington: Indiana University Press, 1980.

_____. *Napoleon's Great Adversary: Archduke Charles and the Austrian Army, 1792–1814.* New York: Sarpedon, 1982.

Rotundo, Louis, ed. *The Battle of Stalingrad: The 1943 Soviet General Staff Study.* Washington: Brassey's, 1989.

Rouillard, Thierry, ed. *Alexandre Andrault de Langeron: Journal inédit de la campagne de 1805.* Paris: La Vouivre, 1998.

_____. *Florent Guibert: Souvenirs d'un sous-lieutenant d'infanterie légère (1805–1815) et François-René Cailloux, dit Pouget: Souvenirs de guerre (1790–1831).* Paris: La Vouivre, 1997.

Saint-Chamans, Auguste Louis Philippe de. *Mémoires du Général Comte de Saint-Chamans, ancien aide-de-camp du Maréchal Soult, 1802–1832.* Paris: Librairie Plon, 1896.

Saul, Norman E. "The Objectives of Paul's Italian Policy." In *Paul I: A Reassessment of His Life and Reign,* edited by Hugh Ragsdale, pp. 31–43. Pittsburgh, Pa.: University Center for International Studies, 1979.

———. *Russia and the Mediterranean, 1797–1807.* Chicago: University of Chicago Press, 1970.

Schieder, Theodor. *Frederick the Great.* New York: Longman, 2000.

Schom, Alan. *Napoleon Bonaparte.* New York: HarperCollins, 1997.

Schönhals, Carl Ritter von. *Der Krieg 1805 in Deutschland, nach Österreichischen Originalquellen.* Vienna: Selbstverlag der Redaction der Österreichischen Militärischen Zeitschrift, 1873.

Schroeder, Paul W. "Napoleon's Foreign Policy: A Criminal Enterprise." *Journal of Military History,* April 1990, pp. 147–162.

———. *The Transformation of European Politics, 1763–1848.* New York: Oxford University Press, 1994.

Scott, Hamish M. "Aping the Great Powers: Frederick the Great and the Defence of Prussia's International Position, 1763–86." *German History* 12, no. 3 (1994): 286–307.

———. "Introduction: Prussia from Rossbach to Jena." *German History* 12, no. 3 (1994): 279–285.

Ségur, Philippe-Paul de. *Histoire et mémoires.* Vol. 2. Paris: Librairie de Firmin-Didot et Cie., 1877.

Shaw, Stanford J. *Between Old and New: The Ottoman Empire Under Sultan Selim III, 1789–1807.* Cambridge: Harvard University Press, 1971.

Shil'der, N. V. *Imperator Aleksandr Pervyi: Ego zhizn' i tsarstvovanie.* St. Petersburg: Izdanie A. S. Suvorina, 1897.

Showalter, Dennis E. "Hubertusberg to Auerstädt: The Prussian Army in Decline?" *German History* 12, no. 3 (1994): 308–333.

———. *The Wars of Frederick the Great.* New York: Longman, 1996.

Simms, Brendan. *The Impact of Napoleon: Prussian High Politics, Foreign Policy, and the Crisis of the Executive, 1797–1806.* New York: Cambridge University Press, 1997.

———. *The Struggle for Mastery in Germany.* New York: St. Martin's, 1998.

Skalon, D. A., ed. *Stoletie voennago ministerstva, 1802–1902: Glavnyi shtab: istoricheskii ocherk: Organizatsiia, raskvartirovanie i peredvizhenie voisk, vypusk I (period 1801–1805 gg.).* St. Petersburg: Tipografiia M. O. Vol'f, 1902.

Sloane, W. M. "Napoleon's Plans for a Colonial System." *American Historical Review,* April 1899, pp. 439–455.

Sorel, Albert. *L'Europe et la Révolution Francaise. Sixième partie: La Trêve—Lunéville et Amiens, 1800–1805.* Paris: Librairie Plon, n.d.

Speelman, Patrick J. *Henry Lloyd and the Military Enlightenment of Eighteenth-Century Europe.* Westport, Conn.: Greenwood, 2002.

Stamm-Kuhlmann, Thomas. *König in Preußens großer Zeit: Friedrich Wilhelm III. Der Melancholiker auf dem Thron.* Berlin: Siedler Verlag, 1992.

Stanlislavskaia, A. M. *Rossiia i Gretsii v kontse XVIII-nachale XIX veka.* Moscow: Nauka, 1976.

[Stutterheim, Karl von]. *La Bataille d'Austerlitz, par un militaire témoin de la journée du 2 décembre, 1805.* Hamburg: n.p., 1806.

Temperley, Harold, and Lillian M. Penson. *Foundations of British Foreign Policy from Pitt (1792) to Salisbury (1902) or Documents, Old and New.* Cambridge: Cambridge University Press, 1938.

Thiébault, Paul-Charles-François. *Mémoires du Général Baron Thiébault*. Paris: Librairie Plon, 1895.

Tolstoy, Leo. *War and Peace*. Edited and translated by George Gibian. New York: Norton, 1996.

Trachevskii, Aleksandr, ed. *Diplomaticheskiia snosheniia Rossii s Frantsiei v epokhu Napoleona I, Tom Pervyi, 1800–1802*. In *Sbornik Imperatorskago Russkago Istoricheskago Obshchestva*, vol. 70. St. Petersburg: M. M. Stasiulevich, 1890.

Tulard, Jean. *Cambacérès: Lettres inédites à Napoléon, 1802–1814*. Vol. 1. Paris: Editions Kincksieck, 1973.

————. *Joseph Fouché*. Paris: Fayard, 1998.

Val'kovich, A. M., and A. P. Kapitanov, eds. *Fel'dmarshal Kutuzov: Dokumenty, dnevniki, vospominaniia*. Moscow: Arkheograficheskii tsentr, 1995.

Vasil'chikov, Alexander. *Les Razoumowski*. Halle: Tausch & Grosse, 1893. Author's name transliterated as Alexandre Wassiltchikow. French edition by Alexandre Brückner.

Vovelle, Michel, ed. *Mémoires de Joseph Fouché, duc d'Otrante*. Paris: Imprimerie Nationale, 1992.

Wangermann, Ernst. *From Joseph II to the Jacobin Trials: Government Policy and Public Opinion in the Habsburg Dominions in the Period of the French Revolution*. New York: Oxford University Press, 1969.

Ward, A. W., G. W. Prothero, and Stanley Leathes, eds., *The Cambridge Modern History*. Vol. 9, *Napoleon*. New York: Macmillan, 1906.

Webster, C. K., ed. *British Diplomacy, 1813–1815: Select Documents Dealing with the Reconstruction of Europe*. London: G. Bell, 1921.

White, Eugene Nelson, "The French Revolution and the Politics of Government Finance, 1770–1815." *Journal of Economic History*, June 1995, pp. 227–255.

Willbold, Franz. *Napoleons Feldzug um Ulm: Die Schlacht von Elchingen 14. Oktober 1805 mit der Belagerung und Kapitulation von Ulm*. Ulm: Süddeutsche Verlagsgesellschaft, 1987.

Wolff, Jacques. "Les insuffisantes finances napoléoniennes: Une des causes de l'échec de la tentative d'hégémonie européenne (1799–1814)." *Revue du Souvenir Napoléonien*, September-October 1994, pp. 5–20.

Wolfsgruber, Cölestin. *Franz I. Kaiser von Oesterreich*. Vienna: Wilhelm Braumüller, 1899.

Woloch, Isser. *Napoleon and His Collaborators: The Making of a Dictatorship*. New York: Norton, 2001.

Zawadzki, W. H. *A Man of Honour: Adam Czartoryski as a Statesman of Russia and Poland, 1795–1831*. Oxford: Clarendon, 1993.

————. "Prince Adam Czartoryski and Napoleonic France, 1801–1805: A Study in Political Attitudes." *Historical Journal*, June 1975, pp. 245–277.

Zhilin, P. A. *Fel'dmarshal Mikhail Illarionovich Kutuzov: Zhizn' i polkovodcheskaia deiatel'nost'*. Moscow: Voennoe Izdatel'stvo, 1987.

Zhiugzhda, Iu. I., ed. *Dokumenty shtaba M. I. Kutuzova, 1805–1806*. Vilnius: Gosudarstvennoe Izdatel'stvo Politicheskoi i Nauchnoi Literatury, 1951.

Zwehl, Hans Karl von. *Der Kampf um Bayern 1805. I. Der Abschluss der Bayerisch-Französischen Allianz. Münchener Historische Abhandlungen*. 1st series. *Allgemeine und Politische Geschichte*, vol. 13. Munich: C. H. Beck, 1937.

Index

TRUE
BLUE

DAVID BALDACCI

TRUE BLUE

GC
GRAND CENTRAL
PUBLISHING

NEW YORK   BOSTON

Copyright © 2009 by Columbus Rose, Ltd. All rights reserved. Except as permitted under the U.S. Copyright Act of 1976, no part of this publication may be reproduced, distributed, or transmitted in any form or by any means, or stored in a database or retrieval system, without the prior written permission of the publisher.

Grand Central Publishing
Hachette Book Group
237 Park Avenue
New York, NY 10017

www.HachetteBookGroup.com

Printed in the United States of America

First Edition: October 2009

10 9 8 7 6 5 4 3 2 1

Grand Central Publishing is a division of Hachette Book Group, Inc. The Grand Central Publishing name and logo is a trademark of Hachette Book Group, Inc.

Library of Congress cataloging publication is available.

Baldacci, David.
True Blue / David Baldacci.—1st ed.
    p.   cm.
ISBN 978-0-446-19551-5 (regular edition)—
ISBN 978-0-446-54697-3 (large print edition)

To Scott & Natasha
and
Veronica & Mike,
part of my family and four of the coolest people I know

TRUE
BLUE

CHAPTER

1

JAMIE MELDON rubbed his eyes vigorously, but when he stared back at the computer screen it was still no good. He glanced at his watch; nearly two in the morning. He was toast. At age fifty he couldn't pull these all-nighters consistently anymore. He slipped on his jacket and pushed back his thinning hair where it had drifted down to his forehead.

As he packed his briefcase he thought about the voice from out of the past. He shouldn't have, but he'd called; they'd talked. Then they'd met. He didn't want that part of his life dredged up again. Yet he would have to do something. He'd been in private practice for nearly fifteen years, but now represented Uncle Sam. He would sleep on it. That always helped.

A decade ago he'd been a hotshot and highly paid criminal defense attorney in New York, legally hand-holding some of the sleaziest of Manhattan's underworld. It had been an exhilarating time in his career, and also represented his lowest point. He'd lost control of his life, been unfaithful to his wife, and become someone he'd grown to loathe.

When his wife had been told that she had perhaps six months to live, something had finally clicked in Meldon's brain. He'd resurrected his marriage and helped his spouse beat a death sentence. He'd moved the family south, and for the last ten years, instead of defending criminals, he was sending them to prison. Everything about that felt right, even if his financial circumstances weren't nearly as rosy.

He left the building and headed home. Even at two a.m. there was life in the nation's capital, but once he got off the highway and rode through the surface streets toward his neighborhood it grew quiet and he grew more drowsy. The blue grille lights flashing off his rearview mirror jolted him to alertness. They were in a straightaway not a half mile from his house, but one bordered on both sides by trees. He pulled off the road and waited. His hand slid to his wallet where his official credentials were contained. He was worried that he'd dozed off or been driving erratically because he was so tired.

He saw the men coming toward the car. Not uniforms, but suits, dark ones that made their starched white shirts stand out under the three-quarter moon. Each man was about six feet tall with an athletic build, clean-shaven face, and short hair, at least that he could make out under the moonlight. His right hand gripped his cell phone and he punched in 911 and kept his thumb poised over the call key. He rolled the window down and was about to hold up his official creds when one of the other men beat him to it.

"FBI, Mr. Meldon. I'm Special Agent Hope, my partner Special Agent Reiger."

Meldon stared at the ID card and then watched as the man flicked his hand and the familiar FBI shield appeared on the next slot in the leather holder. "I don't understand, what's this about, Agent Hope?"

"E-mails and phone calls, sir."

"With whom?"

"We need you to come with us."

"What? Where?"

"WFO."

"The Washington Field Office? Why?"

"Questioning," Hope replied.

"Questioning? About what?"

"We were just told to make the pickup, Mr. Meldon. The assistant director is waiting to talk to you."

"Can't it wait until tomorrow? I'm a United States attorney."

Hope looked put off. "We are fully aware of your background. We *are* the FBI."

"Of course, but I still—"

"You can call the AD if you want, sir, but our orders were to bring you in ASAP."

Meldon sighed. "That's all right. Can I follow you in my car?"

"Yep, but my partner here has to ride with you."

"Why?"

"Having a highly trained agent riding shotgun for you is never a bad thing, Mr. Meldon."

"Fine." Meldon slipped his phone back in his pocket and unlocked the passenger door. Agent Reiger climbed in next to him while Hope walked back to his car. Meldon pulled in behind the other car and they started on their route back to D.C.

"I wish you guys could have come to my office. I just came from town."

Reiger kept his gaze on the other car. "Can I ask why you're out this late, sir?"

"As I mentioned, I was at my office, working."

"Sunday night, this late?"

"It's not a nine-to-five job. Your partner mentioned phone calls and e-mails. Was he inferring ones that I made or received?"

"Maybe neither."

"What?" Meldon snapped.

"The Bureau's intel division gets chatter and scuttlebutt all the time from the dirtbag world. It might be that someone you prosecuted wants payback. And we understand that when you were in private practice in New York you did not leave on the best of terms with some of your, uh, *clientele*. It could be coming from that sector."

"But that was a decade ago."

"The mob has a long memory."

Meldon suddenly looked fearful. "I want protection for my family if there's some nut out there gunning for me."

"We already have a Bucar with two agents stationed outside your house."

They crossed over the Potomac and into D.C. proper, and a few minutes later neared the WFO. The lead car hung a left down an alley. Meldon pulled in behind it.

"Why this way?"

"They just opened a new underground garage for us to use with a hardened tunnel right into WFO. Quicker this way and under Bureau eyes 24/7. These days who the hell knows who's watching? Al-Qaeda to the next Timothy McVeigh."

Meldon looked at him nervously. "Got it."

Those were the last words Jamie Meldon would ever speak.

The massive electric shock paralyzed him even as a large foot stomped down on the car's brake. If Meldon had been able to look over he would've seen that Reiger was wearing gloves. And those gloves were curled around a small black box with twin prongs sticking out. Reiger climbed out of the car as a twitching Meldon slumped over.

The other car had stopped up ahead and Hope ran back to the second car. Together they lifted Meldon out and leaned him face first against a large Dumpster. Reiger pulled out his pistol with a suppressor on the muzzle. He stepped forward, placed the barrel against the back of Meldon's head, and fired one round, ending the man's life.

Together they heaved the body into the Dumpster. Reiger climbed into the dead attorney's car. He followed his partner's ride out of the alley, turned left, and then headed north while Meldon's corpse finished sinking into the garbage.

Reiger pushed a speed dial button on his phone. It was answered after one ring. Reiger said, "Done." Then he clicked off and slipped the phone back in his pocket.

The man on the other end of the phone did likewise.

Jarvis Burns, his heavy briefcase pressing against his bad leg, struggled to catch up to the rest of the party as they headed across the tarmac, up the metal steps, and into the waiting aircraft.

Another man with white hair and a heavily lined face turned back to look at him. He was Sam Donnelly, the Director of National Intelligence, which essentially made him America's top spy.

"Everything okay, Jarv?"

"Perfect, Director," said Burns.

Ten minutes later Air Force One rose into the clear night air on its way back to Andrews Air Force Base in Maryland.

2

"Sɪxᴛʏ-ᴇɪɢʜᴛ . . . sixty-nine . . . seventy."

Mace Perry's chest touched the floor and then she rose up for the last rep of push-ups. Both of her taut triceps trembled with this max effort. She stretched out, greedily sucking in air as sweat looped down her forehead, then flipped over and started her stomach crunches. One hundred. Two hundred. She lost count. And next came leg lifts; her six-pack ridges were screaming at her after five minutes and still she kept going, driving through the pain.

Pull-ups were next. She could do seven when she got here. Now she lifted her chin over the bar twenty-three times, the muscles in her shoulders and arms bunching into narrow cords. With one final shout of endorphin-fueled fury, Mace stood and started running around the large room, once, twice, ten times, twenty times. With each lap, the lady increased her speed until her tank shirt and shorts were soaked through to her skin. It felt good and it also sucked because the bars were still on the windows. She couldn't outrun them, not for three more days anyway.

She picked up an old basketball, bounced it between her legs a few times, and then drove to the hoop, which was a netless basket hung on a makeshift backboard bolted to one wall. She sank the first shot, a layup, and then paced off fifteen feet to the left, turned, and sank a jumper. She moved around the floor, set up, and nailed a third shot, and then a fourth. For twenty minutes she hit jump shot after jump shot, focusing on her mechanics, trying to forget where she was right now. She even imagined the roar of the crowd as Mace Perry scored the winning basket, just as she had done in the high school state championship game her senior year.

Later, a deep voice growled, "Trying out for the Olympics, Perry?"

"Trying for something," said Mace as she dropped the ball, turned, and stared at the large uniformed woman facing her, billy club in hand. "Maybe sanity."

"Well, *try* and get your ass back to your cell. Your buff time's up."

"Okay," said Mace automatically. "I'm going right now."

"Medium security don't mean *no* security. You hear me!"

"I hear you," said Mace.

"You ain't here much longer, but your ass is still *my* turf. Got that?"

"Got it!" Mace jogged down the hall that was enclosed by stacked cement blocks painted gunmetal gray, just in case the residents here weren't depressed enough. The corridor ended at a solid metal door with a square cutout at the top as a viewpoint. The guard on the other side pushed a button on a control panel and the steel portal clicked open. Mace passed through. Cement blocks, tubular steel, hard doors with tiny windows out of which angry faces peered. Clicks to go. Clicks to get back in. Welcome to incarceration for her and her fellow three million Americans who enjoyed the luxury of government housing and three squares for free. All you needed to do was break the law.

When she saw who the guard was she muttered one word. "Shit."

He was an older guy, fifties, with pale, sickly skin, a beer belly, no hair, creaky knees, and a smoker's caustically cracked lungs. He'd obviously switched posts with the other guard who'd been stationed here when Mace had come through for her workout, and Mace knew why. He'd developed an eye for her, and she spent much of her time ducking him. He'd caught her a few times and not one of the encounters had been pleasant.

"You got four minutes to shower before chow, Perry!" he snapped. He moved his bulk into the narrow passageway she had to navigate through.

"Done it faster," she said as she tried and failed to dart past him.

He spun her around and leaned his heft against her while she braced herself with her palms against the wall. He shoved his fat size twelve boots under the flimsy soles of her size sixes; now Mace was on her tiptoes with her back arched. She felt the brush and then grip of his meaty hand on her butt as he pulled her to him, doggie-style. He'd managed to position them both in the one blind spot of the overhead security camera.

"Little patdown time," he said. "You ladies hide shit everywhere, don't you?"

"Do we?"

"I know your tricks."

"Like you said, I only got four minutes."

"I hate your kind," he breathed into her ear.

Camels and Juicy Fruit are quite a combo. He slid a hand across her chest, squeezing hard enough to make her eyes water.

"I hate your kind," he said again.

"Yeah, I can really tell," she said.

"Shut up!"

One of his fingers probed up and down the cleft of her butt through her shorts.

"There's no weapon in there, I swear."

"I said shut up!"

"I just want to go take a shower." *Now, more than ever.*

"I bet you do," he said in his gravelly rumble. "I just bet you do." One hand riding on her right hip, the other on her butt, he shoved his boots farther under her heels. It was like she was tottering on four-inch stilettos now. What she wouldn't have given for a stiletto, just not the shoe kind.

She closed her eyes and tried to think of anything other than what he was doing to her. His pleasures were relatively simple: cop a feel or rub his hard-on against a chick when he got the chance. In the outside world this sort of conduct would've earned him a minimum of twenty years on the other side of these bars. Yet inside here it was classic he-said, she-said, and no one would believe her without some DNA trace. That's why Beer Belly only pantomimed it through the clothes. And throwing a punch at the bastard would earn her another year.

When he was done he said, "You think you're something, don't you? You're Inmate 245, that's who you are. Cell Block B. That's who you are. Nothing more."

"That's who I am," said Mace as she straightened her clothes and prayed for an early diagnosis of lung cancer for Beer Belly. What she really wanted was to pull a gun and lay his brains—on the off chance he had any—against the gray walls.

In the showers she scrubbed hard and rinsed fast, something you just innately did in here. She'd already experienced her initiation in here after only two days. She'd busted the woman's face. The fact that she'd avoided solitary or time tacked on had not endeared Mace to her fellow inmates. They simply tagged her as a privileged bitch, and that was about as bad as it could get in a place where your cell rep defined every right you had or didn't have. Nearly two years later she was still standing, but she wasn't exactly sure how.

She hustled on, every minute now precious, as she counted down her time to freedom, with both anticipation and dread, because on this side of the wall nothing was guaranteed except misery.

CHAPTER

3

A FEW MINUTES LATER a wet-haired Mace walked through the chow line and received her basic food groups so crapped and fatted up that in any other place—except possibly high school cafeterias and airline coach class—they would be deemed inedible. She swallowed enough of the garbage to keep from passing out from hunger and rose from her seat to throw the rest away. As she passed by one table a drumstick of a calf shot out and she fell over it, her tray clattering away, the goop on it painting the floor a nice greenish brown. Up and down the perimeter line, guards tensed. The inmate who'd done the tripping, a prisoner named Juanita, glanced down as Mace slowly got to her feet.

"You a clumsy bitch," said Juanita. She looked at her crew who sat all around the queen bee Juanita had become in here. "Ain't she a clumsy bitch?"

Every member of Juanita's crew agreed Mace was the clumsiest bitch ever born.

Juanita carried two-hundred-and-fifty-plus pounds on a wide six-foot frame, with each hip the size and shape of a long-haul truck's mud flap. Mace was five-six, about one-fifteen. On the surface Juanita was soft, mushy; Mace was as hard as the steel doors that kept all the bad girls inside this place. Yet Juanita could still crush her. She'd landed here after a sweetheart plea deal for murder in the second in which her tools had included a tire iron, a Bic lighter, and lots of accelerant.

It was said that she liked this place much better than she ever had her world on the outside. In here Juanita was queen bee. Out *there* she was just another GED-less fat chick to punch the hell out of, courier drugs and guns through, or make babies with before the man abandoned her. Outside prison Mace had known a thousand Juanitas. She was doomed from the moment she'd tumbled from the womb.

That might have explained why Juanita had done enough crazy stuff inside here, including two aggravated assaults and a weapons and drugs bust, to tack twelve more years onto her original sentence. At that rate the woman would be here until they hauled her carcass out and slipped it into a potter's field somewhere. Her fat and bones would soon fertilize the earth and no one would either care or remember her.

However, that left the living woman with nothing to lose, and that's precisely what made her so dangerous, because it carved normal societal inhibitors right out of her brain pattern. That one factor turned mush to titanium. No matter how many reps or laps Mace did, she could never match what Juanita had. Mace still had compassion, still had remorse. Juanita no longer had either, if she ever did.

Mace held the fork ready. Her gaze drifted for a moment to Juanita's wide hand planted flat on the table, orange nail polish muted against her skin that was obscured only by a tattoo of what looked to be a spider. An obvious target, the hand.

Not tonight. I already two-stepped with Beer Belly. I'm not dancing with you too.

Mace kept walking and slid her tray and utensils into the dirty bin.

Only as she was leaving did she glance over at Juanita, to find the woman still watching her. Keeping her gaze dead on Mace, Juanita whispered something to one of her crew, a gangly lily white named Rose. Rose was in here for nearly decapitating her husband's sexy plaything in a bar restroom using the gutting knife hubby kept for his fish catches. Mace had heard that the husband hadn't come to Rose's trial, but only because he was so upset she'd ruined his best blade. It was definitely more the stuff of Jerry Springer retro than Oprah couch chatter.

Mace watched as Rose nodded and grinned, showing the nineteen teeth she had remaining in her gaping mouth. It was hard to believe she was perhaps once a little girl playing dress-up, sitting on her father's knee, forming her cursive letters, cheering at a high school football game, dreaming about something other than one hundred and eighty months in a cage playing second fiddle to a bloated queen bee with the mental makeup of Jeffrey Dahmer.

Rose had visited Mace on the second day she'd been here and told her that Juanita was the messiah and what the messiah wanted, she got. When the cell door opened and the messiah appeared, she would like it. Those were the rules. That was just the way it was in Juanita Land. Mace had declined Juanita's offer several times. And before things had truly gotten out of hand, Juanita had suddenly backed off. Mace thought she knew why but wasn't sure. Yet it had led to two years of fighting for her life every day, using her wits, her street smarts, and her newly found muscle.

Mace trudged to Cell Block B and the doors slammed into place behind all of them at precisely seven p.m. So much for another exciting Sunday night. She sat on the steel bed with a mattress so thin laid over it that Mace could almost see right through the damn thing. Over the two years she'd slept on it her body had absorbed every buckle and bend in the old metal. She had three more days to go. Well, now really only two, if she made it through the night.

Juanita knew when Mace was getting out. That's why she'd tripped her, tried to bait her. She didn't want Mace to leave. So Mace sat in her cell, crouched into a hard, tight wedge in the corner. Her fists were clenched and there was something shiny and sharp in each one of them that she kept hidden in a place not even the guards could find. The darkness came and then strengthened into the time of night when you figured nothing much good was going to happen because the evil that was coming scared all the good away. And then she waited some more. Because she knew, at some point, her cell door would open as the guards on the night shift looked the other way in consideration for drugs or sex, or both.

And the messiah would appear with one goal in mind: to never again let Mace experience the light of a free day. For two years she'd been building herself up for this moment. Her buffed body waited with anticipation as adrenaline pumped with each exhalation of breath.

Three minutes later the cell door slid open, and there she was.

Only it wasn't Juanita.

This visitor was tall too, over six feet with the one-inch polished boots she wore. And the uniform was not like that of the guards. She wore it well, not a baggy part or dirt stain to be seen. The hair was blond and smelled good in a way that no hair in here ever could.

The visitor took a step forward, and though it was dark, there was enough light coming from somewhere out there that Mace could see the four stars on each shoulder. There were eleven ranks in the District of Columbia Metropolitan Police Department, and those four stars represented the highest one of them all.

Mace looked up, her hands still clenched, as the woman looked down.

"Hey, sis," said the D.C. chief of police. "What say we get you the hell out of here?"

CHAPTER

4

Roy Kingman pump-faked once and then darted a bounce pass between his defender's legs and into the paint, where a giant with rockets in his legs named Joachim stuffed it home, the top of his head almost above the rim.

"That's twenty-one and I'm done," said Roy, the sweat trickling down his face.

The ten young men collected their things and shuffled off to the showers. It was six-thirty in the morning and Roy had already gotten in three games of five-on-five full-court at his sports club in northwest D.C. It had been eight years since he'd suited up for the University of Virginia Cavaliers as their starting point guard. At "only" six-two without rockets in his legs, Roy had still led his team to an ACC championship his senior year through hard work, smart court sense, good fundamentals, and a bit of luck. That luck had run out in the quarters of the NCAA when they'd slammed headfirst into perennial power Kansas.

The Jayhawks' point guard had been a blur of cat quickness and numbing agility, and, at only six feet tall, could easily dunk. He'd poured in twelve threes, mostly with Roy's hand in his face, dished off ten assists, and harassed the Cavs' normally solid point man into more turnovers than baskets. It was not exactly how Roy wanted to remember his four-year collegiate career. Yet now, of course, that was the only way he could recall it.

He showered, dressed in a white polo shirt, gray slacks, and a blue sports jacket, his standard work wear, threw his bag in the trunk of his silver Audi, and headed to work. It was still only a little past seven, but his job demanded a long, full day.

At seven-thirty he pulled into the parking garage of his office building in Georgetown located on the waterfront, snagged his briefcase off the front seat, chirped his Audi locks shut, and rode the elevator car to the lobby. He said hello to Ned the thirty-something heavyset guard, who was cramming a sausage biscuit into his mouth while leisurely turning the pages of the latest *Muscle Mag*. Roy knew that if Ned had to get up from his chair and simply shuffle fast after a bad guy, he not only would never catch him but someone also would have to perform mouth-to-mouth on old Ned.

As long as it's not me.

He stepped on the office elevator and punched the button for the sixth floor after swiping his key card through the slot. Less than a minute later he reached his office suite. Since Shilling & Murdoch didn't open until eight-thirty, he also had to use his key card to release the lock on the law firm's glass doors.

Shilling & Murdoch had forty-eight lawyers in D.C., twenty in London, and two in the Dubai office. Roy had been to all three places. He'd flown to the Middle East in the private plane of some sheik who had business dealings with one of Shilling's clients. It had been an Airbus A380, the world's largest commercial airliner, capable of carrying about six hundred ordinary people or twenty extraordinarily fortunate ones in ultimate luxury. Roy's suite had a bed, a couch, a desk, a computer, two hundred TV channels, unlimited movies on demand, and a minibar. It also came with a personal attendant, in his case a young Jordanian woman so physically perfect that Roy spent much of the flight time pressing his call button just so he could look at her.

He walked down the hall to his office. The law firm's space was nice, but far from ostentatious, and downright slum-dogging it compared to the ride on the A380. All Roy needed was a desk, a chair, a computer, and a phone. The only upgrade in his office was a basketball hoop on the back of the door that he would shoot a little rubber ball into while yakking on the phone or thinking.

In return for ten- or eleven-hour days and the occasional weekend work he was paid $220,000 per annum as a base with an expected bonus/profit share on top of that of another $60,000, plus gold-plated health care and a month of paid vacation with which to frolic to his heart's content. Raises averaged about ten percent a year, so next cycle he would ratchet to over three hundred grand. Not bad for an ex-jock only five years out of law school and with only twenty-four months at this firm.

He was a deal guy now, so he never set foot in a courtroom. Best of all, he didn't have to write down a single billable hour because all clients of the firm were on comprehensive retainers unless something extraordinary happened, which never had since Roy had worked here. He'd spent three years as a solo practitioner in private practice. He'd wanted to get on with the public defender's office in D.C., but that was one of the premier indigent representation outfits in the country and the competition for a slot was intense. So Roy had become a Criminal Justice Act, or CJA, attorney. That sounded important, but it only meant he was on a court-approved list of certified lawyers who were willing basically to take the crumbs the public defender's office didn't want.

Roy had had his one-room legal shop a few blocks over from D.C. Superior Court in office space that he'd shared with six other attorneys. In fact, they'd also shared one secretary, a part-time paralegal, one copier/fax, and thousands of gallons of bad coffee. Since most of Roy's clients had been guilty he'd spent much of his time negotiating plea deals with U.S. attorneys, or DAs, as they were called, since in the nation's capital they prosecuted all crimes. The only time the DAs wanted to go to trial was to get their in-court hours up or to arbitrarily kick some ass, because the evidence was usually so clear that a guilty verdict was almost inevitable.

He'd dreamed of playing in the NBA until he'd finally accepted that there were a zillion guys better than he would ever be, and almost none of them would make the leap to professional hoops. That was the principal reason Roy had gone to law school; his ball skills weren't good enough for the pros and he couldn't consistently knock down the threes. He wondered occasionally how many other tall lawyers were walking around with the very same history.

After getting some work lined up for his secretary when she came in, he needed some coffee. It was right at eight o'clock as he walked down the hall to the kitchen and opened the refrigerator. The kitchen staff kept the coffee in there so it would stay fresher longer.

Roy didn't get the coffee.

Instead he caught the woman's body as it tumbled out of the fridge.

CHAPTER

5

THEY RODE in a black Town Car, an SUV loaded with security behind them. Mace glanced over at her older sister, Elizabeth, known as Beth to her friends and some of her professional colleagues. However, most people just called her Chief.

Mace turned and looked at the tail car. "Why the caravan?"

"No special reason."

"Why come tonight?"

Beth Perry looked at the uniformed driver in front of her. "Keith, turn some tunes on up there. I don't want you falling asleep. On these roads we'll end up driving off the side of a mountain."

"Right, Chief." Keith dutifully turned on the radio and Kim Carnes's jagged voice reached them in the backseat as she crooned "Bette Davis Eyes."

Beth turned to her sister. When she spoke her voice was low. "This way we avoid the press. And just so you know, I've had eyes and ears in that place from day one. I tried to run interference the best I could for you."

"So that's why the cow backed off."

"You mean Juanita?"

"I mean the cow."

She lowered her voice further. "I figured they'd planned on giving you a parting gift. That was the reason I showed up early."

It irritated Mace that the chief of police had to have the radio playing and whisper in her own car, but she understood why. Ears were everywhere. At her sister's level, it wasn't just about law enforcement; it was about politics.

"How'd you manage the release two days ahead of schedule?"

"Time reduced for good behavior. You'd earned yourself forty-eight whole hours of freedom."

"Over two years, it doesn't seem like that big an accomplishment."

"It's not, actually." She patted Mace on the arm and smiled. "Not that I would have expected it from you."

"Where do I go from here?"

"I thought you could crash at my place. I've got plenty of room. The divorce was final six months ago. Ted's long gone."

Her sister's eight-year marriage to Ted Blankenship had started to unravel before Mace had gone to prison. It had ended with no kids and a husband who hated his ex principally because she was smarter and more successful than he ever would be.

"I hope my being in prison didn't contribute to the downfall."

"What contributed is that my taste in men sucks. So I'm Beth Perry again."

"How's Mom?"

"Still married to Moneybags and the same pain in the ass as always."

"She never came to see me. Never wrote me a single letter."

"Just let it go, Mace. That's who she is and neither one of us is going to change the woman."

"What about my condo?"

Beth glanced out the window and Mace saw her frown in the reflection off the glass. "I kept it going as long as I could, but the divorce took a big slice out of my pocketbook. I ended up paying alimony to Ted. The papers had a field day with that even though the file was supposed to be sealed."

"I hate the press. And for the record I always hated Ted."

"Anyway, the bank foreclosed on your condo four months ago."

"Without telling me? They can do that?"

"You appointed me as your power of attorney before you went in. So they notified me."

"So *you* couldn't tell me?"

Beth glared at her. "And what exactly would you have done if I had?"

"It still would've been nice to know," Mace said grumpily.

"I'm sorry. It was a judgment call on my part. At least you didn't end up owing anything on it."

"Do I have anything left?"

"After we paid off the legal bills for your defense—"

"*We?*"

"That was the other reason I couldn't keep paying on the condo. The lawyers always get their money. And you would've done the same for me."

"Like you ever would've ended up in a pile of crap like this."

"Do you want the rest of the bad news?"

"Why not? We're on a roll."

"Your personal investment account got wiped out like everybody else's in the economic freefall. Your police pension was history the moment you were convicted. You have a grand total of one thousand two hundred and fifteen dollars in your checking account. I talked your creditors into knocking your debt down to about six grand and got them to defer payments until you got back on your feet."

Mace was silent for a long minute as the car rolled along winding roads on the way to the interstate that would eventually carry them into Virginia and then on to D.C. "In all your free time while you were running the tenth largest police force in the country and presiding over the security details for a presidential inauguration. Nobody could've done better. I know that. And if it had been me overseeing your finances, you'd probably be in a debtor's prison in China." Mace touched her sister's arm. "Thanks, Beth."

"I did manage to keep one thing for you."

"What's that?"

"You'll see when we get there."

6

THE SUN was starting to come up when the Town Car turned down a quiet residential street that dead-ended in a cul-de-sac. A few seconds later they rolled to a stop in the driveway of a comfortable-looking two-story frame house with a wide front porch that sat at the very end of the road. The only giveaway that this was where the highest-ranking cop in D.C. lived was the security stationed outside and the portable barricades that had been moved out of the way when they'd turned onto the street.

"What the hell is this for, Beth?" Mace asked. "You never had a security detail at your house before. You usually don't even have a driver."

"Different world and the mayor insisted."

"Has there been a threat?"

"I get threats every day. Stalkers at HQ, here at home."

"I know, so what's changed?"

"Not for you to worry about."

The car slowed and Beth Perry rolled down her window and exchanged a few words with the officers on duty, and then she and Mace headed into the house. Mace dropped the duffel bag containing everything she'd brought to prison with her and looked around. "You're not going to tell me the truth about all the new security?"

"There's nothing to tell. I don't particularly like it, but like I said, the mayor insisted."

"But why did he—"

"Drop it, Mace!"

The sisters did a staredown and Mace finally backed off.

"So where's Blind Man?"

As if on cue, an old fifty-pound mutt with gray, black, and tan markings came into the room. As it sniffed the air, it gave a yelp and bounded toward Mace. She knelt and scratched Blind Man behind the ears and then gave the dog a lingering hug, pushing her nose into its smooth fur as Blind Man happily licked her ear.

"I think I missed this guy almost as much as I missed you."

"He's been pining for you."

"Hey, Blind Man, you missed me, man, you missed me?"

"I still can't believe they were going to put him down just because he can't see. That dog's nose is so keen it's better than having two pairs of twenty-twenties."

Mace rose but continued to stroke Blind Man's head. "You always have been one to bring in strays with special cases. The deaf cat, and three-legged Bill the boxer."

"Everybody and everything deserves a chance."

"Including little sisters?"

"You've lost weight, but otherwise you look to be in great shape."

"Worked out every day. Only thing that kept me going."

Beth looked at her strangely. It took Mace a few moments to interpret. "I'm clean, Beth. I was clean when I went in and I didn't touch anything while I was in there, although let me tell you there were more drugs in that place than at Pfizer's world headquarters. I exchanged meth for endorphins. I'll take a pee test if you want."

"I don't, but your probation officer will as a post-release condition."

Mace took a deep breath. She'd forgotten that she was now officially on probation for a full year because of some complicating factors in her sentencing. If she screwed up they could send her right back for a lot longer than twenty-four months.

"I know the guy. He's okay. Plays fair. Your first meeting is next week."

"I thought it would be sooner than that."

"It usually is, but I told him you'd be staying with me."

Mace stared fixedly at her sister. "Any news on who set me up?"

"Let's talk about it later. But I've got some ideas."

There was something in her voice that made Mace decide not to argue. "I'm starving, but can I grab a shower first? Two minutes a day of cold drizzle over two years gets to you."

"Towels, soap, and shampoo are all set upstairs. I've got the rest of your clothes in the guest bedroom."

Thirty minutes later the two sisters sat down in the large, airy kitchen to scrambled eggs, coffee, bacon, and toast that Beth had prepared. The chief had changed into jeans and a sweatshirt with "FBI Academy" stenciled on the front. Her hair was pulled back in a ponytail and she was barefoot. Mace had on a white long-sleeved shirt and a pair of corduroy pants she'd last worn over two years ago. Snug before, they now rode low on her narrow hips.

"You're going to need new things," said her sister. "What are you now, about one-fifteen?

"A little less." She ran a thumb inside the waist of the saggy pants. "I didn't know I was such a porker before."

"Yeah, a real porker. You could sprint circles around most of the force even back then. No donut runs for Mace Perry."

As sunlight spilled through the windows, Beth watched as Mace took her time with each bite and drank the coffee in careful sips. Mace caught her sister eyeing her and put her fork and cup down.

"Pathetic, I know," Mace said.

Beth leaned across and wrapped long fingers around her sister's forearm. "I can't tell you how good it is to have you back safe. What a relief it is—"

Beth's voice faltered and Mace saw the tall woman's eyes suddenly tear up; the same eyes that had stared down the worst the city had to offer. Like Mace, she'd started as a beat cop in the toughest neighborhoods of D.C. that no tourist would ever have ventured into unless he was tired of living.

The chief hurried over to the counter and poured another cup of coffee, gazing out the window into the small backyard while she regained her composure. Mace returned to her meal. In between bites she asked, "So what was it you kept for me?"

Relieved by this change in subject, Beth said, "Follow me and I'll show you."

She opened the door to the garage and nudged the light on with her elbow. It was a two-bay arrangement. In one parking slot sat Beth's black Jeep Cherokee. The vehicle sitting in the other space caused a grin to spill over Mace's face.

A Ducati Sport 1000 S motorcycle painted cherry red. It was the only thing Mace had ever splurged on. And still she'd gotten it dirt cheap and secondhand from a portly cop who'd bought it after going through a midlife crisis only to realize he was terrified to ride the damn thing.

She stepped down to the garage floor, ran her hand along the upside-down high-performance Marzocchi front forks forged from glorious brushed aluminum. Then her fingers slipped over the Sachs shocks that had softened journeys over some rough terrain when she'd used her private ride to chase down some bad guys off-road. The bike had a removable tailpiece cover to give it a sporty, aerodynamic look, but if you popped it off, it revealed a seat and became a two-person ride. However, Mace liked to ride solo. It had a six-speed gearbox, Marelli electronic fuel injection, L-twin cylinders, and its engine generated nearly a hundred horses at eight thousand rpms. She'd kept the bike far longer than any man she ever had, because she loved this machine far more than any guy she'd ever dated.

"How'd my creditors miss this?"

"I assigned it over to myself, so there was nothing to miss. I did it in lieu of payment for administering your affairs." She held out the key. "Your license still valid?"

"Even if it wasn't, you couldn't keep me off it."

"Nice thing to tell the chief of police sworn to uphold and protect."

"Just *uphold* that thought, I'll be back."

Mace slipped the helmet on.

"Wait a sec."

She looked over in time to see Beth toss her a black leather jacket she'd bought for her when she'd gotten the bike. Mace slipped it on.

Her shoulders had widened enough to where it was a tight fit, but it still felt wonderful, because those shoulders and the rest of the body attached to it were now free.

Mace engaged the engine.

From behind the door to the kitchen there came the sounds of claws scratching and then Blind Man started to howl.

"He's always hated you on that thing," Beth yelled over the roar of the bike's engine.

"But God, it sounds so good," Mace shouted back.

Beth had already hit the control for the garage door. Good thing, because a few seconds later the Ducati roared out of the bay and into the crisp morning air, leaving its signature mark in burned-off tread on the cement.

Before the security detail could even react and move the barriers, Mace had already whipped around the staggered portable walls, angling the Ducati almost parallel to the ground. The machine responded flawlessly, like she and it had already fused into one organism. Then she was gone in a long exhale of Italian-engineered exhaust.

The security detail scratched its collective heads and turned to look back at the chief. She raised her cup of coffee in mock salute to their dedicated vigilance and returned to the house. She kept the garage door open, however. Four years ago she'd lost one garage door to her little sister's overeager entry. She did not plan on repeating that mistake.

CHAPTER

7

Mace knew that D.C. was the sort of town where on one block you were as safe as you would be in the middle of a small town in southern Kansas on Sunday afternoon in front of the local Methodist church. Yet one block over, you better have Kevlar covering every square inch of your body because chances were very good that someone was going to get shot. That was where Mace wanted to be. Her brain was wired to run toward the gunfire instead of away from it. Just like her sister.

She'd been working another assignment when a slot had opened with the Narcotics and Special Investigations Division. She'd applied. Her arrest record was stellar, her late-to-work and tardies nonexistent. She'd impressed the brass board and gotten the position. She'd worked 4D Mobile Force Vice, though it was now called Focused Mission Unit, which to her didn't sound nearly as cool.

She'd started doing jump-outs as a plainclothes, which basically meant you cruised looking for dealers and when you saw them you jumped out and arrested as many as you could. In certain areas of D.C. you couldn't miss them. She could hang as many as she wanted. The only thing holding her back was how much paperwork she wanted to do and how much court OT she could stomach.

She'd cut her teeth on street-level dealers hand-selling rocks and making two grand a day. They were small fish to be sure, but they also shot people. Then there were the scratch-offs. They were either checking a rock of crack in their palm or doing a lottery card, it was virtually the same hand motion. And lots of lottery tickets were sold where Mace worked. Yet she'd gotten so good that she could tell by the motion of the index finger at twenty feet whether it was a rock or merely Lotto. Later, she'd gone undercover in the drug and homicidal hell of the Sixth and Seventh districts. That's when all the trouble really began. That's why two years of her life had vanished.

Mace flew through block after block enjoying her first free day in nearly twenty-four months. Her dark hair whipped out from under the racing helmet as she quickly moved from the fortress of solitude around her sister's house, to fairly decent and safe D.C., then to a neighborhood whose turf battle had not yet been fully decided between cops and bandits, and finally onto ground where the thin blue line had failed to establish even a beachhead.

This was the Sixth District, or Six D in the MPD's carved-up fiefdom. If Mace had a hundred bucks for every time she'd seen a PCP zombie running naked screaming through the streets here at midnight, she wouldn't have been so ticked about losing her police pension. In certain sections of Six D there were shuttered houses, trashed buildings, and cannibalized cars on blocks. At night on virtually every corner here something bad was going down and gunfire was as ubiquitous as mosquitoes. All of the honest hardworking citizens— and that constituted most of the folks who lived here—just stayed inside and kept their heads down.

Even in daylight people moved around on the streets with furtive looks. It was as though they just knew stingers launched from nickel-plated Glocks with drilled-off serial numbers or else hollow-points exploding out of virgin pistols looking for first kills could be heading their way. Even the air here seemed to stink, and the sunlight felt degraded by a cover of hopelessness as thick as the carbon emissions eroding what was left of the ozone.

She slowed the Ducati and watched several of the people walking by on the street. The homicide rate in D.C. was nowhere near what it used to be in the late 1980s and early 1990s when young drug kingpins wearing brutish crowns formed from the tendrils of the crack cocaine era enjoyed their reign of terror. Back then a body violently dropped on average *over* once a day, every single day of the year, including the Sabbath. Yet currently nearly two hundred mostly young African American males every year required a medical examiner's certification as to their cause of death, so it wasn't exactly violence-free either. The men around here craved respect, and they seemed to believe they only would get it in increments of nine-millimeter ordnance. And maybe they were right.

She stopped the bike, lifted off her helmet, and shook free the static from her hair. Normally coming here on a fat-cat motorcycle at any time of the day or night was not smart, particularly if you were white and weaponless, as Mace was. Yet no one bothered her, no one even approached her. Maybe they figured a woman not of color coming here alone on a Ducati was obviously psychotic and thus apt to blow up herself like some suicide bomber.

"Hey, Mace! That you?"

She twisted around on her seat to look behind her.

The gent coming toward her was short and stick-thin with a shaved head. He had a pair of two-hundred-dollar LeBron James sneakers on his feet minus the shoelaces.

"Eddie?"

He approached and looked over the bike.

"Nice, nice shit. Heard you were in."

"I got out."

"When?"

"About five seconds ago."

"Just a deuce, right, so you just be an inmate." He grinned at this insult.

"Just two years, that's right. Not a con. Just a lowly inmate."

"My little brother's already done ten, and he's only twenty-five. No family court crap for little bro. Hard time," he added proudly.

"How many people did he kill?"

"Two. But them assholes both had it coming."

"I bet. Well, two years was plenty long enough for me."

He patted the Ducati's gas tank and grinned, showing teeth so white and perfect that she assumed he'd gotten a nice deal on some veneers, probably bartering some prescription pills for them. Being seen talking to even a former police officer was not smart around here. However, Eddie was just a bottom-level huckabuck, a street thug. Not too bright and not connected at all, and the most illegal thing he'd ever done was to retail bags of processed weed, a few C-rocks, and handfuls of stolen OxyContin pills on the street. The real players here knew that, and they also knew that Eddie had no information about their operations that he could possibly sell to the cops. Still, Mace was surprised he was alive. The dumb and the weak around here were usually eradicated extremely efficiently. So maybe he was wound tighter than she thought. Which could make him useful to her.

"Neighborhood all the same?"

"Some things don't change, Mace. People pop and drop. You know that."

"I know someone screwed me."

His grin faded. "Don't know nothing 'bout that."

"Yeah, but maybe you know somebody who does know."

"You out now, girl. Ain't no good looking in the rearview mirror. There might be something you ain't want to see. Besides, your sister already had her boys come down through here with a fine-tooth comb. Hell, they were just down here last week."

"They were? Doing what?"

"Asking questions, doing their CSI thing. See that's the cool thing having a police chief in the family. Cold case don't never go cold. But I bet she gets some shit for it anyway. Not everybody loves the top blue, Mace."

"Like what shit?"

"How the hell I know? I just on the street getting by."

"Her guys talk to you?"

He nodded. "And I told 'em the truth. I ain't know nothing 'bout nothing." He patted the Ducati's gas tank again. "Hey, can I take it for a ride?"

She removed his hand from the Ducati. "There's an old saying, Eddie, to go forward, you have to go back."

"Whoever said that ain't from 'round here."

She eyed his windbreaker, the way his left elbow was clenched tight to his side, and how he leaned ever so slightly that way because of the weight of what was in his pocket. "You know, bro, if you want to carry a gun and not have the cops know, you're gonna have to learn to walk a straighter line and loosen up your arm."

Eddie glanced down at his left pocket and then looked up, grinning. "Got to protect yourself 'round here, Mace."

"You find out anything, you let me know."

"Uh-huh," Eddie said, his veneers no longer visible.

Mace drove through the neighborhood, drawing more stares from folks sitting on their tiny porches or clustered on the street corners or peering out windows. A lot of peering went on around here, usually to see what the sirens were coming for.

She was not making this circuit just to celebrate her release. She wanted to let certain powers-that-be know that Mace Perry had not only survived prison but also was back on her old turf even if she no longer had a badge, gun, and the might of the MPD gang backing her.

But what Eddie had told her was troubling. Beth had apparently continued to investigate the case long after Mace had gone to prison, devoting scarce police resources to the matter. Mace knew several people who would use that if they could to attack Beth. Her sister had already done enough for her.

She finally turned around and rode back to the house. One of the cops on protection duty waved her down as she approached the barricade. She braked to a stop and lifted her visor.

"Yeah?" she said to the man, a young cop with a buzz cut. She could easily tell that he was an egg, meaning a rookie.

Sit on them until they hatch.

She remembered her T.O., or training officer. He was a vet, a "slow walker" who wanted to pull his shift as easy as possible and go home in one piece. Like many cops back then, he didn't like women in his patrol car, and his rules were simple: Don't touch the radio, don't ask to drive, and don't complain when they went to what cops referred to as the hoodle. It was a gathering place, usually a parking lot, where the police cruisers would cluster and the cops would chill out, sleep, listen to music, or do paperwork. The most important rule of her T.O., however, had been to just shut the hell up.

She'd endured that ride for one month before getting "checked out" by a sergeant and certified to roll on her own. And from that day forward Mace's call signal had been 10–99, meaning police officer in service *alone*.

"I understand you're the chief's sister."

"Right," she said, not desiring to volunteer anything more than that.

"You were in prison?"

"Right again. You got another personal question or will two do it for you?"

He stepped back. "Look, I was just wondering."

"Right, just wondering. So why's a young stud like you pulling barricade action? You oughta be running and gunning and locking up and getting some court OT so you can buy a new TV or a nice piece of jewelry for your lady."

"I hear you. Hey, put in a good word for me with the chief."

"She doesn't need any help from me on that. You like being a cop?"

"Until something better comes along."

Mace felt her gut tighten. She would have given anything to be a blue again.

He twirled his hat and grinned at her, probably thinking up some stupid pickup line.

Her teeth clenched, Mace said, "Piece of advice, don't ever take your hat off while on protective duty."

The hat stopped spinning as he stared at her. "Why's that?"

"Same reason you don't take it off when you're on a suspect's turf. Just one more thing to get in the way of you drawing your gun if something hairy goes down. *Egg.*"

She double-clutched, popped a wheelie, barely avoiding his foot as he jumped back, and roared on into the garage.

CHAPTER

8

HER SISTER was waiting for her in the kitchen, fully dressed in a fresh uniform. A stack of documents was on the table in front of her.

"Homework?" said Mace.

"Daily Folder, Homicide Report, news clips, briefing for internal ops meeting. The usual."

"You wear the four stars so well," said Mace as Blind Man sniffed around her ankles and she scratched his ears.

"How was the ride?"

"Not as enlightening as I'd hoped."

"I *hoped* you'd disappoint me and not go back to Six D."

"Sorry not to disappoint you." Mace poured another cup of coffee and sat down at the table. "Saw Eddie Minor."

"Who?"

"Small-fry huckabuck," replied Mace. "He said your guys were down there asking questions about my case just last week."

Beth put down the folder she was holding. "Okay, so?"

"So you still working it?"

"I work all cases where justice hasn't prevailed."

"Eddie said you might be pissing off some high-ups over this."

"Come on. You're listening to a huckabuck's take on D.C. politics?"

"So it is political?"

"I've obviously forgotten that you tend to take every word literally."

"Is that what the heightened security's for?"

"What do you mean?"

"People gunning for you because you won't let the case go?"

"If there are some higher-ups in town who think I'm being a little overzealous in pursuing what happened to you, they sure as hell aren't going to order a hit on me. They have other avenues they can employ."

"So why the extra security?"

"The number of threats against me has gone up a little. Some of them are credible, so a few extra precautions were in order. I don't like it but I have to live with it."

"Where are the credible threats coming from?"

"Don't lose sleep over it. If I had a dollar for every death threat I've gotten over the years."

"It only takes one, Beth."

"I've got lots of folks watching my six."

"Well, you just got one more added to the group."

"No! You focus on you."

"Beth—"

"Focus on *you*."

"Okay, so what exactly are my options?" she asked bluntly.

"You don't have many."

"That wasn't my question."

Beth sat back, double thumbing her BlackBerry with skill. "You have a felony conviction involving a firearm and you're now out on probation. You obviously can't be a cop anymore with that hanging over you."

"Someone kidnapped me, strung me out on multiple meth cocktails laced with who knows what, and forced me to participate in armed robberies while I was whacked out of my mind."

"I know that, you know that, but that's not what the court found."

"The jury and the judge got steamrolled by an overzealous U.S. attorney who had it in for me and you."

"That overzealous U.S. attorney now heads up the entire office."

The color slipped from Mace's face. "What!"

"A month ago Mona Danforth was named interim U.S. attorney for the District of Columbia by the AG."

"U.S. attorney! Dad's old office?"

"That's right," Beth said with disgust.

"The attorney general named her? I thought they had to be Senate confirmed after the president appointed them."

"The AG gets to appoint Mona for a hundred and twenty days. If the president doesn't name a permanent candidate and have that appointee confirmed by the Senate by then, the authority to appoint goes to the district court. The problem is, the AG, the president, and the district court folks all love Mona. So she's a lock for the job any way you cut it. I expect the president to formally name Mona any day now. And from what I understand the Senate confirmation is a gimme."

"I can't believe that woman is running the largest U.S. Attorney's Office in the country. She has the least morals of any prosecutor I've ever been around."

"She's still out there screaming that you got a sweetheart deal because of your connections. Meaning me, of course. And if we hadn't gotten the sentence knocked down on appeal she might have been crowing instead of screaming."

"*She* ought to be in prison. How many times has she looked the other way when evidence got doctored or else went missing when it didn't cut to her side? How many times has she sat and listened to people on the stand commit perjury by feeding back the lines *she* wrote for them?"

Beth slid her BlackBerry in her pocket. "Proof, little sister. Hearsay won't cut it. She's got everyone who matters to her climb up the ladder snookered."

Mace put her head in her hands and groaned. "This has got to be the parallel world where Superman is evil. How do I get off the ride?"

"You never get off the ride. You just learn to hold on a different way."

Mace looked at her sister through a gap in her fingers. "So, is the political pressure on you coming from Mona and her demented heavyweight supporters?"

"Mona has never been my biggest fan."

"I'll take that as a hell yes."

"And I can handle it."

"But it would be better if you backed off trying to find out who set me up."

"Better for whom? The bandits or Mona? Neither of whom I give a crap about. There is no law against the police investigating crimes. And if we get lucky and nail the bastards, you get your record expunged and also receive an official apology and reinstatement to the force."

"An apology from who, Mona?"

"Don't hold your breath."

"Okay, we were talking options?"

"You can't do anything that would require a security clearance, which in this town cuts out a lot of possibilities, and the overall job market sucks right now."

"If you're trying to pep up my spirits, please stop before I stab myself in the heart with a fork since I can no longer own a gun to use to kill myself."

"You wanted options. I'm giving them to you."

"I haven't heard an option. All I've heard is what I *can't* do."

Beth slid a paper across to her. "Well, here's maybe something you *can* do."

Mace looked down at what was written on the sheet.

"Dr. Abraham Altman? I remember him."

"And he remembers you. Not many college professors run afoul of one of the worst drug crews in Ward Nine."

"That's right. Nice guy, just doing some research into urban issues. The HF-12 crew didn't see it that way and came over to G-town to give him grief."

"And you stepped in and saved his ass."

"You've kept up with him?"

"I was a guest lecturer in criminal justice over at Georgetown when you were in West Virginia. He and I reconnected."

"So what does that mean for me?"

"He's looking for a research assistant."

Mace gaped at her sister. "Beth, I didn't even finish college. My 'graduate work' was sixteen weeks at the police academy, so I'm not exactly the poster girl for research assistants."

"He's doing urban research, specifically into impoverished and crime-ridden areas of D.C. I don't think there's anyone out there more qualified to help on that issue than you. And Altman's got a big federal research grant and can pay you well. He'll be home tonight. Around seven, if you can make it."

"So you arranged all this?"

"All I really did was make a suggestion to Altman. He was already your second biggest fan."

It took a moment for Mace to interpret this remark. "Meaning you're my biggest?"

Beth rose. "I've got to run. I've got testimony on the—"

Her cell phone buzzed. She answered, listened, and clicked off. "Change of plan."

"What is it?"

"Just got word that some big-shot lady lawyer dropped out of a fridge at her law firm. Board's been called," she added, referring to the ambulance. "Bandit apparently long gone."

Mace looked at her sister expectantly.

"What?" Beth asked.

"I don't have anything to do."

"So relax, go sleep on a real bed. There's some Rocky Road in the freezer. Go put some weight on those bones."

"I'm not tired. And I'm not hungry. For food, anyway."

"What, you want to go to the crime scene?"

"Thanks, Beth. I'll follow you on the bike."

"Hold on, I didn't say you could go."

"I just assumed."

"Never assume, Mace. If Dad taught us one thing, it's that."

"I won't get in the way. I swear. I . . . I just . . . miss it, Beth."

"Mace, I'm sorry. I don't think it would be a good idea—"

Mace cut her off. "Fine, forget it. You're right. I'll just go eat some Rocky Road and take a nap. And try not to die from excitement."

She started to walk off, her head down, her shoulders slumped.

"All right, you can come," Beth said grudgingly. "But keep your mouth shut. You're invisible. Okay?"

Mace didn't answer; she was sprinting to her bike.

"And stop whining," Beth called after her.

CHAPTER

9

Roy Kingman had hit thirty-one shots in a row on his behind-the-door basketball hoop. The police had swarmed the place minutes after he'd phoned 911. It still didn't seem possible that he'd gone to make coffee, opened the fridge, and caught Diane Tolliver's dead body before it hit the floor. He'd been asked lots of questions by lots of people, some in uniform and some not. As the other lawyers had arrived at work, word had quickly spread as to what had happened. Several partners and a few associates had stopped by to see him, offering supportive words and also expressions of sympathy, puzzlement, and fear. One fellow lawyer had even seemed a bit suspicious of him.

The cops wouldn't tell him anything. He didn't know how long Diane had been dead. He didn't even know what had killed the woman. There was no blood or wounds that he could see. Although he'd defended accused murderers when he'd been a CJA and had seen his share of autopsy photos, he wasn't exactly an expert on violent death.

He looked at his desk full of work to do and then glanced away. Not today. The clients could wait. He hadn't been Diane Tolliver's closest confidant, but he had worked with her and liked her. She'd taught him a lot. And somebody had killed her and stuffed her in a fridge next to a container of days-old potato salad.

He palmed the little rubber ball, cocked his arm back, and with a smooth motion released his thirty-second shot. It sailed straight and true right to the hoop. Only the door opened and the rubber ball hit Beth Perry in the head instead. She bent down to pick it up and tossed it back to him as he rose from his chair, his mouth agape as his gaze took in the four stars. Not that he needed that to know who she was. The D.C. police chief was in the media spotlight quite a bit.

People marched in behind her. The last one closed the door. The last one was Mace, doing her best to get lost in the crowd. Beth introduced herself and some of the folks with her. She'd already interviewed the first responders and looked at the body. Other than Roy there were no witnesses, at least that they had found so far. The paramedics had preliminarily pronounced Tolliver dead, and the ME was on the way to make that pronouncement official.

As two detectives took notes, the chief guided Roy through the events of the morning and what he knew about the dead woman. Her questions were crisp, her methodology spot-on. This was not by accident; she'd worked homicide for two years.

Roy finally said, "You always do the questioning, ma'am? I thought you'd have, you know, some bigger butts to kick around." He added hastily, "I meant that with all due respect."

In the back of the room Mace smiled at his comment. Beth did too.

Beth said, "I like to keep my hand in things. So you were a CJA?"

"That's right."

"You didn't like it there?"

"I like it here better."

"So no reason you know of that someone would want to harm Diane Tolliver?"

"None that I can think of. She wasn't married. She went out some, no serious dating, at least that she talked to me about."

"Would she talk about things like that with you?"

"Well, probably not," he admitted.

"Were you one of her nonserious dates?"

"No. It wasn't like that with us. She was, well, she was a lot older than me."

"Forty-seven."

"Right. I'm about to turn thirty."

"Okay. Go on."

"Her clients were mostly big companies, most of them overseas. She traveled. We both did. She never mentioned any problems."

"When you say you traveled, you mean together?"

"Sometimes, yeah."

"Where, for example?"

"We have an office in London and one in Dubai too."

"An office in Dubai?"

"Lot of money and development going on there. And they need lawyers."

"Did she usually work late?"

"Only occasionally. I do too sometimes."

"Did you ever work late together?"

"A few times."

"You were the first to arrive this morning? Around seven-thirty?"

"Yes, at least I didn't see anyone else."

"The office space has a security system?"

"Yep. We're each assigned cards, so that'll tell you exactly when she came in."

"And exactly when *you* came in too," the voice said.

Everyone turned to stare at Mace, who'd looked chagrined the second she'd finished speaking. Her sister frowned and turned back to Roy, who had his gaze dead on Mace. He squeezed the rubber ball tight in his hand.

"But you don't need the key card to *leave* the space after hours?" asked Beth.

"No, there's a door release button you push."

"And of course during business hours the security system is turned off?"

He said, "That's right."

"The garage elevator doesn't have a key card access?"

"That's right, but you need a key card to access the garage."

"If you're in a car."

"Yeah, it is a gap in security, I know."

"A real gap," she said, eyeing Roy closely.

He shifted uncomfortably. "Look, am I a suspect?"

"We're just collecting information."

His face flushed. "I called 911. I caught her damn body in my arms. I was just going to make coffee. And I had no reason to kill her."

"We're getting way ahead of ourselves, Mr. Kingman. So just calm down."

Roy took a breath. "Okay. Do you need anything else from me?"

"No, but I'm sure my detectives will have some follow-up. No travel plans to Dubai coming up, I hope?" She was not smiling when she asked this.

"I don't think so, no."

Beth rose from her chair. "Terrific. Let's keep it that way. We'll be in touch."

They all filed out. Mace held back while the others disappeared down the hall.

He eyed her. "Can I help you?"

"I don't know. Did you kill her?"

Roy stood, towering over her. "Are you a cop?"

"No, just tagging along for fun."

"You think murder is fun? Are you some kind of sick freak?"

"Well, if you put it that way I guess I am."

"I've got some work to do." He glanced at the door.

Instead of leaving Mace plucked the ball from his hand. In one motion, she turned and drained the shot, hitting nothing but net.

He said, "Nice mechanics."

"High school girls' basketball. We won the state title my senior year."

He appraised her. "Let me guess, you were the leave-it-all-on-the-court point guard who could score and also play some wicked D, including the occasional knocked-on-their-ass flagrant foul to cold-face the other teams?"

"I'm impressed."

"I'm not."

"What?"

"You just basically accused me of murder. So why don't you get the hell out of my office."

"All right, I'm going."

"Best news I've heard all day."

10

THE D.C. Metropolitan Police Department headquarters was located on Indiana Avenue, near the D.C. Superior Court building. It was named after Henry J. Daly, who'd been a homicide sergeant with twenty-eight distinguished years on the police force before an intruder had gunned him down in the building. It was a multistory structure with lots of people in uniform coming and going. And lots of people not in uniform hanging around either waiting for court time next door or else cooling their heels while friends or relatives had some quality face time with the cops inside HQ. The probation and parole offices, along with the Department of Motor Vehicles, were also located in the Daly Building. That pretty much guaranteed that no one going in or out of the place was particularly thrilled to be there.

The chief's office was in a secure area and one had to pass locked doors and lots of cubicles containing people who brought guns with them to work. The office was a corner suite; the door was a keyed entry. The room was large with nice moldings and two windows. A wall of shelves contained ceremonial mugs and hats, stuffed animals, and stacks of newspapers and official reports. The American flag was in front of one window. There was a small sitting area with an ornate chess set on a coffee table. A plasma screen on a hinged arm hung on one wall. There was also a large wooden desk that had seen a lot of wear and tear over the years. This included numerous coffee cup rings marring the surface and probably a few hundred angry fists slamming down on the wood.

Beth sat on the "chief" side and Mace on the other.

"I took a leap of faith letting you tag along," Beth said as she stared at the stacks of files and phone messages on her desk. "It apparently was a mistake on my part to believe that you might just remain quiet and unobtrusive. I'm not sure how I miscalculated considering it's only happened a few thousand times before."

"It just popped out. I'm sorry."

Beth pointed to the pile of phone messages. "Your little 'pop' has already gotten a lot of attention. The mayor, in fact, wants to know why a recently released convicted felon was even allowed near the crime scene, sister or not."

"I'm really sorry, Beth. I don't know why I did it."

"Just go see Altman tonight and become gainfully employed."

"Is he still at G-town? Because the address you gave me is in McLean."

"He's on sabbatical but the address is for his home."

"McLean? Fancy area. They must be paying professors better these days."

"Wait a minute, didn't you know?"

"Know what?"

"Altman is one of the wealthiest people in the Washington area."

"How'd he make his money?"

"He didn't."

Mace gave her sister a funny look. "What?"

"You used to be a pretty good detective. You'll figure it out." Beth pointed to the door. "Now go, I have to play police chief for a while."

Mace headed to the door but then turned back. "I am sorry about today, sis."

Beth smiled. "If that's all I had to worry about, it would be a very good day."

"What about Mona and the mayor?"

"The mayor's a good guy. I can deal rationally with him."

"And Mona?"

"Mona can go screw herself."

The secure door clicked open and Beth's assistant, Lieutenant Donna Pierce, looked in. "They're here for the meeting, Chief."

"Send them in."

The door opened wider and a man with white hair and dressed in a custom-tailored pinstripe suit walked in, followed by a fellow in a baggy gray suit who limped awkwardly, his fat briefcase in his right hand.

The white-haired gent put out his hand. "It's been too long, Beth."

"Crazy schedules all around, Sam."

"Hello, Chief," said Jarvis Burns, the man in the baggy suit.

"I don't think either of you ever met my sister, Mace."

"Mace, this is Sam Donnelly and Jarvis Burns."

Donnelly gave Mace a searching look. "I'm really surprised we've never run into each other before."

"I've been away for a while."

"I know. What happened to you was a case of prosecutorial overreach. That is my *personal* opinion," he hastily added. "Off the record."

"We know the president loves Mona," Beth said grudgingly.

"And I serve at his pleasure," added Donnelly.

When Mace looked at him inquiringly Beth explained, "Sam is the DNI, Director of National Intelligence."

"Yes, but Jarvis here does all the heavy lifting," amended Donnelly. "I just try to keep everyone playing nicely together."

"Then I'll let you and Beth get to it."

"Nice meeting you, Mace," said Donnelly while Burns opened his briefcase. But his gaze trailed her until the door shut.

"She just got out, didn't she?" said Donnelly as he seated himself at Beth's small conference table.

"That's right."

"Any plans?"

"Some things in the works."

"I hope things come together for her."

"They will."

CHAPTER

11

TWO PATROL COPS, one senior and one junior, were admiring Mace's Ducati when she came out of HQ.

"Nice ride," said the older blue as Mace slid onto the seat.

"Yes, it is," she said.

"Ducati?" he said, looking at the name label.

"An Italian-engineered street machine that once you ride it, you dream about it."

The younger cop checked out her lean, buffed figure and pretty face and his mouth edged into a grin. "Wanta take me for a ride one night? Maybe we can share a dream."

"Get back to your shift and stop wasting time talking to ex-cons!" The voice came with such a bark that both cops and Mace jumped. When Mace saw who it was, her hand went reflexively to the spot where she would normally wear her sidearm.

The two cops faded away as the woman marched forward.

Mona Danforth had on her usual expensive two-piece Armani suit, and a bulky litigation briefcase large enough to carry the fates of several targets of the lady's professional ambition tapped against one shapely leg. To add insult to injury, Mona was tall and exceptionally lovely and not yet forty. The way her blond hair curved around her swan neck Mace had to grudgingly concede would turn most guys to mush. She had legs about as long as Mace's entire body. She'd graduated from Stanford Law School, where, of course, she'd been editor in chief of the law review. She was married to a sixty-five-year-old multimillionaire based in New York who provided all the financial resources she would ever need and wasn't around very much. She lived in a fabulous penthouse with wrap-around terraces near Penn Quarter that he'd bought for her. And her looks, money, and power position weren't even the primary reasons that Mace hated her guts, although they certainly didn't hurt.

Mace knew that being U.S. attorney for D.C. was just another stepping stone on the climb up for the woman. Mace had heard that Mona had her life all mapped out: a short stint as the U.S. attorney for D.C., then attorney general of the United States, next a court of appeals position, and then the prized plum, a lifetime appointment to the United States Supreme Court. When she was wasn't trying and winning cases by any means necessary, including bending the rules until they shattered from the torque, she was lining her pockets with all the political favors she would need to fulfill that ambition.

She had already been to the White House for dinner, not once but twice. Her hubby had been a big donor to the current president's election campaign. Beth Perry, who'd reached the top of her profession on hard work and guts and by playing by the rules, hadn't even been invited once. That still rankled her little sister.

Mona stopped and looked down at Mace, who sat astride her Ducati, her helmet dangling in one hand.

"My God," said Mona. "You look like shit. I figured you weren't nearly as tough as people made you out to be, and I guess I was right. And, hell, you were only in a kindergarten lockup for *two years*. Just think what a hag you'd be if you'd done the proper time in a max. A deuce for that was a joke. Thank goodness for you that big sister was around to hold your sweaty little hand."

Mace slipped on her helmet and fired up her bike. Then she lifted up the visor so she could eyeball the woman. "Hey, Mona, I've been gone for twenty-four months and the best you can do is *interim* U.S. attorney? You need to ratchet up the political humping, babycakes, before your looks *really* slide into your ass."

Mace popped the clutch and sped off. In the side mirror she saw Ms. Interim staring at her. That had been pretty stupid, Mace had to admit, but she had actually shown restraint. What she'd really wanted to do was find a wood-chipper, stuff Mona in it, and get right to work.

She had a chunk of time before she was to meet the rich Altman and she knew exactly how she wanted to spend her first day of freedom. She clicked the Ducati into high gear.

As she roared along down by the river, the seagulls dipped down to grab shiny trash off the muddy Potomac before tilting their wings and angling skyward. The monuments basked in the glow of a warming sun. Tourists wandered around, maps in hand; Secret Service agents hovered at 1600 Pennsylvania Avenue keeping the man safe. Over on Capitol Hill, senators, House reps, and armies of aides and golden-tongued lobbyists shuffled through their elaborate dance of running the country right into the dirt.

In many ways the town was sick, corrupt, maddening, frustrating, and patronizing. Still, Mace couldn't help but smile as the Ducati blew past an Old Town Trolley carrying a load of out-of-towners eyeballing with awe the shrines to Tom, Abe, and the mighty white obelisk to George.

That was because this was *her* town.

Mace Perry was back.

12

Roy Kingman was sitting in the managing partner's office that was only a bit larger than his space, though it did have a water view. Chester Ackerman was a few inches shorter than Roy, and he carried the heft of a man who liked his food rich and often. He had a horseshoe of graying hair around his broad head and a large nose with a bump at the end. Roy guessed he was about fifty-five, though he suddenly wondered why he didn't know for sure.

Ackerman brought in far more business to the firm than anyone else. Roy had always found him sharp, tough, and big-voiced. Today, the man was none of those things. He sat across from Roy, his face sweaty, his hands trembling, and his voice low and croaky.

He wagged his head from side to side. "I can't believe this shit. I can't believe it happened. Here!"

"Just calm down, Chester."

"How the hell am I supposed to calm down? There was a murder three doors down from my office."

"And the police are investigating it, and they're probably already running down some solid leads."

Ackerman lifted his head and stared at him. "That's right, you used to work down there, right?"

"Down where?"

"With the cops."

"I was a defense attorney, so I was actually on the other side. But I know how the police work a crime scene. And this is high-dollar Georgetown, so they'll pull out all the stops. Hell, even the chief herself was down here asking me questions."

Ackerman blurted out, "Who do you think might've done it, Roy?" He looked ten seconds from stroking.

Roy said, "I have no idea who could've done it. I worked with Diane but I didn't really know her personally. You were fairly close to her, weren't you?"

"No, not really. I mean, she never really talked about her personal life with me."

"You talked to the police?" he asked.

Ackerman rose and looked out the window, his hands fingering the striped braces he favored. They had gone out of style sometime in the nineties, only the man apparently hadn't noticed or didn't care. "Yeah. They asked me some questions." He turned around to face Roy. "And I told 'em just what I'm telling you. I'm scared and I don't know a damn thing."

"It could just be random, you know."

"Random, what the hell are you talking about?"

"Guy follows Diane in, kills her, and exits. Maybe it was a simple robbery."

"But there's a guard in the front lobby."

"Ned's more of a joke. I can't tell you the number of times I've come in the building in the morning and he's nowhere to be found."

"What the hell do we pay building fees for?"

"If you want serious perimeter protection, hire a real security firm who'll send a trained person who carries a gun. The only thing Ned can do is whack an intruder with a frozen sausage biscuit."

Roy popped up from the chair. "Is there anyone we need to call?"

The other man looked at him with a confused expression. "Call?"

"Yeah, like her relatives?"

"Oh, I've got folks doing that. Her father's dead, but her mom lives in Florida, retired. Diane didn't have any kids. She has an ex-husband, but he lives in Hawaii."

"Did you just find that out?"

"What?"

"You said you didn't know much about Diane personally, but you know all that."

"I just found out!" Ackerman snapped.

Roy put up his hands in mock surrender. "Okay. That's cool." He headed to the door. "Do you mind if I take the rest of the day off? I don't have anything critical pending and what with everything that's happened."

"No, sure, go on. Get some fresh air."

"Thanks."

"Roy, what was it like? Finding the body?"

Roy slowly turned around. "I hope you never have to find out."

13

Roy grabbed his jacket, waved goodbye to his secretary, and took the stairs instead of the elevator. The police had already questioned Ned, who now sat in his swivel chair with a look of terror interrupted by momentary pangs of what Roy assumed was hunger.

"Hey, Ned. How're you doing?"

"Not too good, Mr. Kingman."

Roy leaned against the marble reception console. "Police give you the once-over?" He nodded. "And *were* you away from the front at any time this morning?"

Ned eyed him a little hostilely. "Am I supposed to talk to you about this stuff?"

"Not if you don't want to, no."

"Guess it doesn't matter. I don't know that much, really."

"So you saw Diane come in?"

"Not exactly."

"Well, either you saw her or you didn't."

"I heard her."

"*Heard* her? Where were you?"

"In the back microwaving my biscuit. It always gets cold before I get here."

"What time was that?"

"Around six. I'd just come on duty."

"But you were eating a biscuit when I came in an hour and a half later."

"I eat like five sausage biscuits every morning, but I try to space them out. I'm a big guy: I need constant fuel."

"Did she come up through the garage elevator or by the front doors?"

"I don't know. Like I said, I didn't see her."

"Okay, so what did she *say* when she came into the lobby?"

"She said, 'Hey, how you doing.' And I called back that I was doing fine. When I got back to the front, she'd already gone up in the elevator."

"You're sure it was her voice?"

"Yeah, I've heard her lots of times. She's usually with someone when she leaves the building, you know, for lunch or stuff, and she has a pretty husky voice for a lady."

"But Ned, not to raise the obvious point, if you were in the back and she couldn't see you, how do you know she was even talking to *you*? More likely she was saying hello to someone else coming in the building the same time as her."

Ned looked puzzled. "I hadn't thought of that."

Roy continued, "The person had to be coming through the front doors. If she'd ridden up with him in the elevator from the garage she would have already said hello. And there's only the one garage elevator, so it wouldn't have had time to go back down and come back up with another person before Diane would've headed up in one of the office elevators."

"You're getting way over my head now, Mr. Kingman."

"Did she routinely say hello to you when she came in?"

"Not exactly, no."

"Does that mean she did it once, twice, every other time? Never?"

"Uh, never."

"Did you hear another person's voice?"

"No, but like I said, I was using the microwave. It makes some noise. And then it makes a big 'ding' when it's done."

"Yeah, I know." Roy glanced up at the security cameras mounted in each corner of the lobby. "Did the police take the security tapes?"

"It's on a DVD. But no, they didn't."

"Why not?"

"Because the DVD loaded in the central board was full from a long time ago."

"But once it got full won't it just record over what's already been filmed?"

"The system here doesn't work that way. The disk gets full, it automatically shuts down until you put a new disk in."

"Well, don't people check it?"

Ned looked red-faced. "I did, I mean sometimes. But nobody ever told me how to really do it the right way, and I got to the point where I thought I might screw up, so I stopped checking it."

"Well, you got that right. You *did* screw up."

Ned said in a whining tone, "But I thought the cameras were just there for looks anyway, you know, to make people *think* they were under surveillance. I mean, *I'm* on duty for security purposes."

"In light of what happened this morning that's very reassuring," Roy said sarcastically. "Did you see anyone leaving between the time you heard Diane and when I came in?"

"There were only a few people who came in during that time. All regulars."

"Anybody from Shilling?"

"Not that I recognized, no."

Roy scrutinized Ned. "Did you maybe take another break?"

"No, I swear, I was here the whole time. Okay, I was reading, but I couldn't have missed someone passing by. The lobby's not that big."

That was true, thought Roy. And anyone coming up from the garage elevator would have to pass right in front of the security desk.

"So are you saying you saw nobody leave during that time?"

"That's right. Just people coming in. I mean, it was early, who'd be leaving?"

At least one person might have, thought Roy. *The killer.* "And you told the cops this?"

"Yeah, everything."

"Does your firm carry lots of insurance?"

"How the hell should I know?"

"Well, if I were you I'd find out, because your screwup affected a law firm big-time. And don't forget, they can sue you without even having to hire an attorney."

"Jesus, do you think they might come after me? I mean, they can't, right? I'm just the security guard. I don't have any money."

"The courthouse is open to anyone, Ned. And, hell, they might go after you just for the sheer fun of it."

Roy walked out into the sunshine. Whoever had killed Diane had probably gone up in the elevator with her. And maybe instead of leaving, that person had then stayed in the building somewhere. He or she might even be there now, working in another office.

Or in my office.

Diane had come in about ninety minutes before he had. Had she been killed immediately and the murderer long gone before Roy got to the office? Or had it happened minutes before he got there? Or had it happened while he was in his office and he hadn't heard a damn thing? He tried to remember how cold Diane's body had been. The fact was, if she'd been in the fridge two days or half an hour, she would still have felt pretty cold to him. Maybe the ME would have a better shot at answering that.

"You look like you're thinking way too hard."

Roy looked to his left where Mace Perry was perched on her Ducati staring at him.

CHAPTER

14

"Wʜᴀᴛ ᴀʀᴇ ʏᴏᴜ doing back here?" Roy asked as he walked over.

"How do you know I ever left?"

"I can see the front entrance from my office. I've been staring out at it the last few hours." He eyed the Ducati. "I wouldn't have missed these wheels."

"Look, I know we got off on the wrong foot. And I came back to try it again."

Roy didn't look inclined to accept her offer, but he said, "I never got your name."

"It's Mace."

"Mace? That's a weapon, isn't it?"

"Yes, I am," she quipped.

"Come on, what's your name?"

"Really, my name is Mace."

He shrugged. "Okay."

Mace looked toward the building. "I saw you talking to the security guard. What did he say?"

Roy looked at Ned through the glass. "Not much. Ned's not exactly all that with it."

"Tolliver might've ridden up in the elevator with whoever killed her. Ned was probably somewhere taking a sugar-slurp break. Killer did the deed and then either walked out or to his office in the building. Maybe at your law firm."

"That's one theory."

"I'll give you another one. You were the one who went up in the elevator with Tolliver, and she used her key card, so that leaves no record of you. You killed her and stuffed her in the fridge. You snuck down the stairs and waited until the guard came back. Then you waltzed in the building from the garage elevator side like it was the first time, so he could time-stamp you in his head. You go up to the office, fuss around at your desk for a while, go to the kitchen, open the fridge, catch the poor lady—which would explain any trace of her being on your person and vice versa—and then you call the cops in a fake-freak voice."

Roy stared at her, his features darkening. "Is this how you try to make a fresh start? By accusing me again?"

"I'm not accusing you. But you're a lawyer. You know what's coming. You were on the scene alone with a dead woman. The cops will go down this very same trail with you at some point. So you better be prepared to answer. You can practice on me."

"Why, so you can go back to the cops, tell them, and they can run holes right through my explanations?"

"I told you, I'm not a cop. And if what you're saying is the truth it would be pretty tough to pin a murder rap on you."

"Okay, I'll play along. I accessed the parking garage with my card. That shows I got in around seven-thirty. Took the elevator up to my office, did some work. Went to make coffee and found Diane. I made the call to 911 at two minutes past eight. Records show she was at the office ninety minutes before I got there. I didn't even know she was there."

"That won't cut it. You could've parked your car down the street, walked into the garage, waited for her to arrive, ridden up in the elevator with her, killed her, left, driven your car to the garage, and the same scenario follows."

"Ned said he heard Diane saying hello to someone. That doesn't fit with your scenario."

"The testimony of morons is always heavily discounted by the blues and the courts. And the fact is, you could've come in when you said, at seven-thirty, gone up in the elevator, killed Tolliver, stuffed her in the fridge, and called the cops. Plenty of time."

"Okay, what's my motive?"

"I'm a purist chick when it comes to a criminal investigation, meaning I eyeball opportunity first. Motive usually comes later. But if it's there, the cops will find it."

"So what should I do? Grab the next flight to a country that has no extradition with the U.S.?"

"Nah, it'll probably be okay."

Roy looked startled. "Probably?"

"I've got a good nose for killers, and it's not twitching around you. So where'd you play basketball?"

"How do you know I did? Just because of the office door hoop?"

"It's partly your height, and the way you walk, and how you dissected my playing career earlier."

"And what's the other part?"

"I saw a set of Audi keys on your desk earlier. I checked the garage here. There was an Audi parked near the entrance, which would peg it as yours since you got here so early. In the backseat were a duffel bag, three basketballs, and four pairs of expensive B-ball shoes that pretty much only collegiate or professional players will put out for."

"University of Virginia Cavaliers."

"I actually already knew that since you also have the big cool orange sticker on your rear bumper."

"You know, you look like the police chief."

"She's a lot taller than me."

"I meant in the face, and the eyes. You both have green eyes, with some flecks of bronze." He looked at her more closely. "And a tiny bubble of magenta in the right one."

Mace studied her eyes in the Ducati's side mirror. Incredibly enough, for the first time, she did see bronze and the pop of magenta.

"I don't know any guys who even realize magenta is a color."

He pointed at her. "I knew I recognized you. You're her sister, Mace Perry. Should've remembered as soon as you said your name." He broke off. "But the newspapers said your name was originally Mason Perry." He looked at her funny. "Mason Perry, Perry Mason the TV lawyer? Is that a coincidence?"

"My father was a prosecutor, but he really wanted to be on the other side. So Mason Perry it was. But I go by Mace, not Mason. In fact, I had it legally changed."

"What does your father think of that?"

"I don't know. He was murdered when I was a kid."

"I'm sorry, Mace. Didn't know."

"No reason for you to."

"But weren't you in—"

"I just got out."

"Okay." He put his hands in his pockets and looked awkwardly around while Mace fiddled with the straps on her helmet.

"For what it's worth, I think you got a raw deal," he finally said.

"Thanks. For what it's worth, I think you're telling the truth."

"You know, the only reason I believe in reincarnation is because of Mona Danforth."

"What do you mean?" she said curiously.

"How else can you explain Joseph Stalin coming back as a girl?"

Mace grinned. "You had run-ins with her as a CJA?"

"I wasn't important enough to actually warrant the lady confronting me head-on. But her lieutenants ground my face into the legal dirt on more than one occasion. And the stories about her around PD are legendary."

"You up for lunch? We can take turns devising torture methods to use on Mona."

"Where do you want to go?"

"Ben's Chili Bowl. I've been dreaming about Benny's half-smokes for two years." She slid off the passenger seat cover. "Hop on."

"I don't have a helmet."

"Then don't hit your head if you fall off. Pretty sure my insurance lapsed."

The Ducati sped off a few seconds later.

CHAPTER

15

"So you just got out and you're messing around with a homicide?" They were sitting at the crowded counter in the legendary Ben's Chili Bowl next to the Lincoln Theater on U Street. Roy bit into his chili dog and licked the mustard off one finger.

"I'm not messing with anything. Just getting acclimated to the outside world."

Mace slowly inserted her half-smoke in her mouth before chewing it up and tonguing her lips. She slid a handful of chili-cheese fries into a pool of ketchup and stuffed them all in her mouth.

The deeply contented look on her face made Roy grin. "You want a cigarette?"

"Maybe."

"Prison food really does suck, doesn't it?"

"Yes, it does."

"I still can't figure who'd want to hurt Diane."

"Did you really know her all that well?"

"Worked with her for about two years."

"That doesn't mean you know her. Ever been to her home?"

"Twice. Once for an office party about three months ago and another time before I joined the firm. She was in charge of associate recruitment."

"Was it a tough pitch?"

"Not really. Lot more money than I'm worth."

"But you're on the billable hours treadmill."

"It's not like that."

"What do you mean?"

"Don't get me wrong, I work full days. But at Shilling we don't have to keep track of billable hours."

"I thought that's how lawyers made their money. Like in the Grisham novels."

Roy shook his head. "We work off retainers. Deep-pocketed, sophisticated clients prefer it that way. We know what the workload looks like and they know what their nut is and they pay it. The firm divvies up the spoils and rewards people for the work they do and the business they bring in. No surprises. And a lot more efficient than sucking clients dry."

"But what if something unusual came up off the retainer radar?"

"We write the agreements to take that into account. Then we get paid more."

"Litigation or deals?"

"Deals. Litigation we hand off to other firms, but retain oversight responsibility."

"So how much do you make?"

"That's private."

"Well, if it were public I wouldn't have to ask you."

"Like I said, more than I'm worth."

"My father said that the law was a noble profession."

"It can be, just not for everyone."

"Yeah, I didn't believe him either."

She finished the rest of her half-smoke in one bite.

Later, as they walked out, he said, "So what are you going to do now?"

"Tonight, I've actually got an appointment about a job."

"Doing what?"

"Research assistant."

"I don't see you in a lab wearing a white coat with eyeglasses on a chain."

"Not that kind. The professor is doing research on urban issues. Apparently in parts of the city I know, or at least knew pretty thoroughly."

"The crime-ridden ones?"

"Bingo."

"Who's the professor?"

"Abraham Altman."

"Bill Altman's dad?"

"Who's Bill Altman?"

"He worked at PD when I was a CJA. He's older than me, about forty-five. Good lawyer. He's one of the noble profession guys."

"I don't know if they're related."

"Abe's a professor at Georgetown and is out-the-butt wealthy."

"Then it is the same guy. My sister told me he was like billionaire rich, but hadn't worked for it."

"That's right. So you know him?"

"I helped him out once."

"But you didn't know he was rich?"

"That didn't factor into what I was helping him with. So how did he get his money?"

"Abe's parents lived in Omaha across the street from a young guy who was starting up his own investment firm. They put all their money with the man."

"Omaha? You don't mean?"

"Yep. The Oracle of Omaha, Warren Buffett. Apparently Abe's parents kept investing with him and the earnings compounded until they were one of the largest shareholders of Berkshire Hathaway. When they died decades later I think it totaled well over a billion dollars even after the tax bite. And it all went to Abe; he was an only child."

"And here I was wondering how a college professor could afford me."

"Just tell him you want six figures, full health, paid vacation, and a 401(k) with an employer match. He probably won't blink an eye."

"How about you tell him for me?"

"What?"

"You can be my negotiator."

"You want me to come with you to see Altman?"

"Yeah, I'll pick you up at six-thirty from your office."

"I wasn't going back to my office."

"Then I'll pick you up at your house."

"Condo. And do you always work this fast?"

"I have ever since I lost two years of my life."

CHAPTER

16

THE D.C. Police Department finally had a first-rate facility to conduct forensic testing, the most important of which was the postmortem. Beth Perry, accompanied by two homicide detectives working the case, walked into the six-floor building located at the intersection of 4th and School streets in Ward Six. In addition to the OCME, or Office of Chief Medical Examiner, the building also housed offices for the Metropolitan Police Department and the Department of Health.

A few minutes later Beth stood next to the chief medical examiner. Lowell Cassell was a small, thin man with a short graying beard and wire-rimmed glasses. Except for the tattoo of a fish on the back of his hand, from his days in the Navy as a submariner, and a small scar from a knife wound on his right cheek suffered when on liberty in Japan while drunk in the Navy, he would've looked like a typical member of a college faculty.

The body of Diane Tolliver lay on a metal table in front of them. Beth and the detectives were here to get at least two answers: cause and time of death. The ME took off his glasses, wiped his eyes, and put the spectacles back on. "Fast-tracked the postmortem as you requested."

"Thanks, Doc. What do you have for me?"

"When I saw the bruising on the neck base I felt sure I'd find ligature marks on the neck or evidence of smothering, with homicidal asphyxia being the cause of death."

"But it wasn't?"

"No, the lady basically had her neck broken."

"Basically? Without full ligature marks?"

"Well, there's more. A lot more, actually. Pretty severe injury."

"Atlanto-occipital disarticulation and not simply a dislocation?"

Cassell smiled. "I forgot how well versed you are in forensic matters. Yes, a *disarticulation* clearly."

With one of the detectives' assistance he turned Tolliver's body on its side and pointed to the base of her neck. "Cranio-cervical junction injury." Cassell pressed his fingers against points along the base of the skull and the upper spine. "Brain stem and upper to mid-cervical spinal cord, above C4."

"Full disruption of the cardio-respiratory regulation centers. Immediately fatal."

"Are you angling for my job, Beth?" he said jokingly.

"No, Doc, do you want mine?"

"Good God no!"

"So someone crushed her neck. What else?"

"Hemorrhages in the soft tissues of the back of the neck and injuries to basilar blood vessels. She also had considerable facial bruising and a cut on her right chin, all pre-death. All fairly straightforward until we get to this."

He opened a laptop and pulled up some images of the inside of Diane Tolliver's head. "The X-rays showed separation of the atlas from the base of the skull. You can see the atlas in the foramen magnum—"

"But the spinal canal isn't visible. Okay, that's classic disarticulation."

"Yes, but the brain stem was also *transected*."

She glanced up sharply from the laptop screen. "Brain stem transection?"

"It's most often seen in car crashes where you have massive deceleration. A basilar skull fracture is what killed Dale Earnhardt at Daytona. Or when there's some sort of lengthy fall involved. The brain stem pops and death is instantaneous."

Beth pointed to Diane's body. "This lady was found wedged inside a refrigerator at her law firm about two hours after she walked in the door of her office. She wasn't driving in the Daytona 500 and she didn't fall off a building."

The ME again pointed to the base of the neck where there was considerable discoloration. "A blow right here did the trick. Her being placed in a refrigerator certainly did me no favors, but there are definite signs of bruising before death at this location."

"A blow? With what, Doc?"

"Now that's the strange part. I found no trace evidence, no hairs, fibers, plastics, metals, or anything else relating to the injured area."

"So what was used to kill her, then?"

"My guess is a blow from a foot."

"A foot?"

Cassell pointed to the abrasions on Tolliver's face. "It could have happened this way. She's held down on the floor, facedown with her chin pressed against the linoleum, which accounts for the cut and bruising there when the killing blow was struck. Then someone, a large, powerful man probably, stomps on the back of her neck with all his weight. Now, if a board or pipe or hammer or bat had been used, they might well have left a patterned injury mark on the skin. But as you can see, there was nothing like that here. However, a human foot is flexible and could well have left no discernible marks. Even a fist would have left some sort of pattern, knuckles or even the shape of a palm, for instance. Plus, of course, you can generate much more force with a leg stomp than an arm strike because you can deploy most of your weight in a downward motion."

"So a foot. But wouldn't a shoe have left a mark?"

"Possibly, although human skin is not as revealing as a nice wet patch of grass or dirt. I may be able to discern an image at the wound area provided you find me a shoe, a patterned sock, or a foot to compare it with."

"Okay, but when have you ever seen a brain stem transection from a weaponless assault?"

"Only once, but it was a nonhuman assault."

She looked at him curiously. "Nonhuman?"

"Years ago I was on vacation at Yellowstone National Park. There unfortunately was a fatality with a camper and I was recruited to perform the autopsy."

"What killed the person?"

"A grizzly bear. Probably the most dangerous predator on land." He smiled at Beth. "Other than man, of course, as we both know so well. Anyway, this unfortunate camper had surprised a full-grown male bear while it was scavenging a carcass."

"But there are no grizzlies in Georgetown, Doc."

"No, but there is at least one person with abnormal strength and skill. That bruise is in the exact spot necessary to transect the brain stem. I doubt the location of the blow was a coincidence."

"So was she already unconscious? Or was someone holding her down? If it was just one bandit you'd think she would have fought back and we'd have defensive trace under her fingers."

"Her cuticles were clean."

"Drugged?"

"Tox reports aren't back yet."

Beth studied the body. "Bandit could've had a gun, ordered Tolliver to lie facedown. Then he kills her. That would only take one assailant."

"Quite right."

"Okay, what else?"

"We took an inventory of her clothes. We found a couple of fibers that were not from her garments."

"Her attacker?"

"Possibly. There was also some soiling on her jacket that seemed odd."

"What kind of soiling?"

"Like grease or dirt, we're analyzing it now."

"Not residue from anything in the fridge that might have spilled on her."

"We inventoried that too. No, it didn't come from that source."

"It's the start of the day, she goes from parking garage to office, and she's got dirt on her clothes. Bandit leave-behind?"

"Probably." Cassell shook his head. "It's still confusing. I spent ten years at the Bronx ME's office."

Beth nodded in understanding. "I know, NYPD says perp, MPD says bandit. Can you give me a window on *when* she died?"

"Extremely problematic, Beth. She was found in a refrigerator set at thirty-eight degrees Fahrenheit and then her body was at room temp for several hours. When I arrived at the crime scene she was very cold to the touch. And then she was parked in one of our morgue freezer beds on arrival here. Now fully freed of those icy conditions, the body is decomposing quite on schedule. She's still in rigor, as you can see." He lifted one of the stiff arms. "But the initial refrigeration forestalled the normal post-death chemical process."

"Stomach contents?"

Cassell clicked some computer keys and then scanned the screen. "At most ME shops unless there's suspicion of a drug overdose or poisoning we don't typically do a detailed gastric content analysis. But I knew if I didn't run it, you'd just tell me to do it."

"Working relationships just get better with age, don't they?"

"She had no breakfast, but apparently she had some dinner last night. About six hundred cc's worth of gastric contents including partially digested red proteins."

"In other words, bits of steak?"

"Most probably, yes. Peas and corn and what looks to be red-skinned potatoes. Spinach too. The stomach and duodenal mucosal lining were a bright green."

"Broccoli will do that as well."

"But broccoli along with corn does not digest readily in the stomach. I would have found parts of it in the gastric content. The corn was there as noted, but no broccoli."

"Anything else?"

Cassell made a face. "This lady liked her garlic. The smell was overpowering."

"Remind me to buy you a pair of clothespins. So time of death? Any thoughts?"

He took off his glasses. "If you've got reliable witnesses on both ends substantiating a two-hour window of when she was killed, I can't do any better than that even with all my fancy equipment and tests."

"I'm not sure yet how *reliable* my witnesses are. What else?"

"When I said we did an inventory of her clothing I forgot to mention that one item was missing."

"Her panties."

"Of course I am assuming that the lady typically wore underwear."

"She was forty-seven years old, a partner in a law firm, lived in a million-dollar town house on the water in Alexandria, and was wearing a Chanel suit when she was *stomped*. I think we can safely assume she was the sort of woman who wears underwear. What did the sex assault workup find? Was she raped?"

"Bruising around her genitalia clearly evidenced a sexual assault."

"Please tell me what I want to hear, Doc."

"The fellow left a few pieces of himself behind."

Cassell led her over to a microscope. She examined the slide under magnification and her smile was immediate. "The holy grail of forensic detection."

"Sperm," Cassell added, with a note of triumph. "High up in the vaginal vault and some deposited on the cervix."

"You said the fellow left *pieces*?"

"Two pubic hairs with root balls that do not belong to the deceased."

"Let's hope we get a database hit. Anything else I should know?"

Cassell hesitated. "Not on the case, no, but I hear that Mace is out. Please tell her I said hello."

"I will."

"How is she?"

"You know Mace. Everything slides right off her back."

"Tell her that there is indeed a heaven and that Mona will never make it there."

Beth smiled. "Will do."

17

Gates. Big gates. And a wall. A long, high wall.

The gates opened when Roy pushed a button on a squawk box out front and announced their arrival. They'd ridden over in Roy's Audi since he didn't want to chance serious head trauma on Mace's bike without a helmet.

"You'll have to get one if you want to ride with me, then," she'd told him.

"I'll think about that," he'd said back.

"The helmet?"

"No, whether I want to ride with you again."

They drove up the winding paved road. The property was set high up on what folks in the D.C. area would call a ridge, although people from places with real mountains would simply call it a slightly elevated mound of dirt.

Mace looked out the window. "I didn't know anyone in northern Virginia had this much land."

"Looks like a compound of sorts," said Roy. He pointed to a large structure whose roof must've been thirty feet high. "I wonder what's in there?"

As they rounded a bend the mansion came into view.

"Damn!" they both said together.

"It looks like one of the buildings on the Georgetown campus," said Roy.

"Only bigger," added Mace.

They pulled to a stop next to a full-size Bentley. Beside that was a two-door dusty and dented Honda, which created the impression of a dinghy next to a yacht. They got out and walked up to two massive wooden doors that would not have looked out of place at Buckingham Palace. Before Roy could ring the bell, one of the doors opened.

"Come in, come in," said the man.

Abraham Altman was of medium height, a few inches taller than Mace, with white hair to his shoulders and a clean-shaven face. He had on faded jeans and an untucked long-sleeved shirt open at the neck that revealed a few curls of gray chest hair. Open-toed sandals covered his long feet. His eyes were blue and active. He was in his seventies but seemed to have the energy of a far younger man.

Altman shook Mace's hand vigorously and then abandoned formality and gave her a hug, actually lifting her up on her tiptoes in his exuberance.

In a rush of words he said, "It's so wonderful to see you again, Mace. Your sister told me what happened. Of course I'd read about it in the papers. I was unfortunately in Asia during the whole debacle or rest assured I would have been a character witness for you. What an injustice. Thank God you came out unharmed."

He abruptly turned and held out his hand to Roy. "I'm Abraham Altman. Please call me Abe."

"Roy Kingman. I know your son Bill."

"Wonderful. That's his Bentley out there."

"He's here?" said Roy.

"No, he's out of the country with his family. He's leaving it here until he gets back."

"Who does the Honda belong to?" asked Mace.

"That's mine."

"So old Bill has a Bentley?" Roy said inquiringly. "Does he still work at the public defender's office?"

"No, he left there last year. He's doing other things now." Altman didn't seem inclined to elaborate. "Come into the library. Would you care for something to drink?"

Roy and Mace exchanged glances. Roy said, "Beer?"

"I was actually thinking of tea. It's late for afternoon tea, of course, but we'll call it evening tea. I admire many things of our English friends, and afternoon tea is one of them."

"Tea's good," said Roy, exchanging an amused glance with Mace as they headed into Abe Altman's humble thirty-thousand-square-foot abode.

18

A SMALL MAN in a spotless gold tunic and brown slacks brought in a large tray with a pot of hot tea, cups and saucers, and some scones and muffins and set it down on a massive ottoman covered in a tasteful striped pattern that seemed inconsequential considering the massive scale of the room they were in. The ceilings were high, the walls paneled in leather, and the bookcases solid mahogany and filled with tomes that actually looked as though they'd been read. There was a metal globe at least six feet tall in one corner and a large and old-fashioned slanted writing desk near one of the windows. Another long, low table had dozens of books on it, most of them open and lying page down.

After the man departed Altman said, "That's Herbert. He's been with me for ages. He handles all domestic duties. I could not get along without Herbert."

Mace said, "We should all have a Herbert in our lives."

Altman poured the tea and handed out the food.

"Quite a place you have here," said Roy as he balanced a teacup and saucer on one thigh while biting into a blueberry scone.

"It's far too large of course for me now, but I have lots of grand-children and I like for them to have a place to come. And I do like my privacy."

"Beth said you had a job offer for me?"

Altman solemnly gazed at her. "Yes. And I have to say that I can never repay you for what you did for me. Never."

Mace looked down, embarrassed by his obvious adoration. "Okay."

Altman glanced at Roy. "This woman saved my life. Did you know that?"

"No, but I can certainly believe it."

"The HF-12 gang," Altman added. "Nasty buggers."

"HF-12?" said Roy.

"Heroin Forever, and there were a dozen in the crew," said Mace. "They were bad guys but not that creative with names. Half of them are locked up."

"The other six?" asked Roy.

"Dead."

"I came to see you several times," said Altman. "But they wouldn't let me in the prison."

"Why?"

"My reputation precedes me. That correctional facility in West Virginia has been the object of my wrath on several occasions."

"You should've talked to Beth. She could've gotten you in."

"I did not want to further add to the distress of your sister's situation." He glanced at Roy. "There's a U.S. attorney who has it in for Mace and her celebrated sister."

"Mona Danforth," said Roy.

"Precisely." Altman turned back to Mace. "There was even talk a year ago of Beth being replaced."

Mace put down her cup. "I didn't know that. She never said."

"Your sister internalizes things, sometimes too much." He gazed keenly at Mace. "And I believe you share that attribute. Fortunately the mayor wisely put a stop to all talk of firing Beth."

"So what is it exactly that you do, Professor?" asked Roy.

"Making the world, or at least the nation's capital, a safer place by attacking problems before the fact and not after."

Roy nodded. "Education, preventative, that sort of thing?"

"I mean giving people a *real* choice between good and evil, right and criminal. It's been my experience that when a real choice is offered, invariably almost everyone chooses the law-abiding path."

Mace said, "Which brings us to why I'm here."

"Yes. The project I'm conducting is based on a research grant I was awarded."

"Beth said it involved going into some of the worse-off areas in D.C."

"Yes. Areas you used to work in when you were with the police force."

"What are you looking for?"

"Hope."

"That's tough to find in those places."

"Which is precisely why I picked them."

"So what would my duties involve?"

"I want you to go and meet with certain people in those areas. I've worked with Social Services to identify ten of them. I want you to talk to them and explain my proposal. If they accept then we'll go from there."

"So Mace would make the initial contacts?" asked Roy.

"That's right." He glanced at Mace. "Is he your representative?"

"Something like that. So what's your proposal?" asked Mace.

"An internship, I like to call it. We will take the people out of their current environment, place them in a totally different environment, and immerse them in a rigorous education and social refocusing program. We will gauge their interests and ambitions and help them to fulfill those goals. We will expose them to opportunities they would otherwise never have."

"Sounds sort of like *My Fair Lady*," said Roy.

"With a critical difference," answered Abe. "The connection to their present world will not be severed. They will have full contact and indeed we will encourage that contact with their present life. The goal of the program is to foster and then spread hope. These folks will serve as ambassadors of hope, if you will."

"But no one can afford to do internships like that for everybody living in poverty," said Mace. "Not even you. So aren't you spreading *false* hope?"

Altman smiled. "What you say is true. No one person can afford to lift all the folks that need help and place them in a different world. But if for every person we help it inspires just one other person to break out of the cycle of disempowerment they're currently in, the benefits can be immeasurably positive. Then we have ten people outside the program who in turn can inspire others. What that also does is gain the attention of government. And a government such as ours does have the financial wherewithal to help large numbers of people."

"Our government is pretty tapped out right now," noted Roy.

"But any government's greatest resource is its citizens. Most studies conclude that less than half the adult population in this country is achieving its potential. If you want to equate that to financial terms, we're speaking of trillions of lost dollars per year. Now, even the cynical folks in D.C. would sit up and take notice of numbers like that. And beyond the government you have the private sector that is constantly complaining that they can't get decent help to fill their job requirements. I have to tell you that some of the most creative and quick-thinking people of my acquaintance are sitting in jail right now. For some folks they see justice in that. For me, I see wasted opportunity. I can't make every criminal into a law-abiding citizen. But if I can make even twenty percent of them choose another path that would enable them to contribute to society instead of detracting from it, it would have an enormously beneficial impact."

"You're definitely an optimist, Abe," said Mace. "I agree that a lot of bandits are smart and savvy and could probably run circles around a lot of business types, but what you're talking about doing is a tall order."

"I've lived my entire life through rose-colored glasses of sorts. Sometimes I'm right and sometimes I'm wrong, but I keep trying because I believe it's worth it."

"But I've been out of the loop for a couple of years. I'm not sure how much help I'd be to you."

"I have no credibility with the people who live in those areas. I realize that. But you do. With you I really believe I can make a difference." Altman took off his glasses and cleaned them with a handkerchief. "So are you amenable to such an arrangement?"

"Well, I don't have—"

Roy cut in. "So what sort of pay are we talking here? And benefits?"

Altman's eyes twinkled. "Now I understand why your friend is here."

"I'm not really good with business stuff," explained Mace quickly.

"I completely understand. Well, your salary will be three thousand a week, plus full health care, transportation, a reasonable expense account, and room and board. The project will last about a year, I would assume. So that would be about a hundred sixty-five thousand dollars as a base salary. And if the project is successful there will be more work to do at similar compensatory levels."

Roy looked at Mace and she looked back at him.

"I think the salary is *adequate*," Roy finally said, while Mace nodded vigorously in agreement.

She said, "I already have transportation, but you said room and board?"

"Hours for this sort of venture will be irregular. Much better if you stayed here at the guesthouse. It's behind the gymnasium complex."

"Gymnasium complex?" asked Roy. "The big building on the left coming in?"

"Yes, it has a full-size basketball court, weightlifting and cardio room, sauna, whirlpool, thirty-meter indoor pool, and a full kitchen and relaxation room."

"A full-size indoor basketball court?" said Roy.

"Yes. I never played the game in school but it has always fascinated me and I love to watch it. Ever since moving to this area decades ago I've been a huge Maryland Terrapins fan. I almost never miss a home game, and have attended the last thirty-seven ACC tournaments." Altman studied Roy. "You look familiar to me now."

"I played point for UVA about eight years ago."

Altman clapped his hands together. "Roy Kingman, of course! You were the one who beat us in the ACC finals."

"Well, I had a lot of help from my teammates."

"Let me see, thirty-two points, fourteen assists, seven rebounds, and three steals. And with six-tenths of a second left you drove to the basket, made a reverse layup, drew the foul, calmly made the free throw, and we lost by one."

"Pretty awesome memory, Abe."

Altman turned to Mace. "So will you do it?"

"Yes."

"Excellent." He pulled a key from his pocket and tossed it to Mace. "The key to the guesthouse. Taped to it is the gate code. Do you have a cell phone?"

"Uh, no."

He opened a drawer, pulled out a cell phone, and handed it to her. "Now you do. Would you like to see where you'll be staying?"

They drove over in a golf cart. The guesthouse was set next to a small spring-fed pond. It was like a miniature of the main house and its level of comfort and the quality of the furnishings and amenities was beyond anything Mace had ever experienced.

Roy looked around at the large, open spaces. "How big is this place?"

"Oh, about six thousand square feet, I suppose. Bill and his family stayed here while their new home was being built."

Roy said, "My condo is twelve hundred square feet."

"My cell was eight by eight," said Mace.

As they rode back to the main house, Altman said, "It's funny, you know."

"What's that?" said Roy, who was sitting in the backseat of the four-person cart.

"Growing up in Omaha with him, I never thought Warren Buffett would ever amount to much."

"People said the same thing about me," Mace quipped.

19

"WHAT YOU'RE DOING is a mistake."

Beth had changed from her uniform into sweats. She'd pumped some dumbbells and done a half hour on the elliptical set up in the lower level of her house. It was nearly midnight yet neither sister seemed sleepy as they sat across from each other in the living room. Blind Man was curled up by Mace's feet.

"I thought you *wanted* me to take the job."

"I'm talking about Roy Kingman. You shouldn't be hanging out with *him*."

"Why not?"

"We haven't cleared him as a suspect in the Tolliver murder, that's why. You're on probation. That means avoiding all contact with people of questionable character."

"But that's the reason I am hanging out with him. To keep tabs on him."

"You could be passing time with a killer."

"Wouldn't be the first time."

"You were undercover then."

"I'm sort of undercover now."

"You're not a cop anymore."

"Once a cop always a cop."

"That's not how it works. And I thought we had this discussion?"

"Maybe we did."

"I'm working the case, Mace. You start poking around then it might get all blown up. And that hurts you and me. You need to focus on moving forward with your life."

Mace sat back and said resignedly, "Okay, okay, I hear you."

"Good, I'll hold you to that. So when do you start with Altman?"

"Two days. And he wants me to move into the guesthouse on his property."

Beth looked surprised. "I thought you'd stay with me for a while."

"I can actually do both. Hang here and hang there when work requires it."

"Okay," Beth said, her disappointment clear.

"I'm not abandoning you."

"I know. It's just been two years without you. I need a big Mace Perry fix."

Mace gripped her sister's arm. "You'll get it. We have a lot of catching up to do."

"Before we get all blubbery, Mom called. She'd like to see you."

Mace punched a pillow she was holding. "That's actually the only thing that *could* make me cry. When?"

"How about tomorrow?"

"Will you come with me?"

"I've got a full schedule, sorry."

"Does she still live on the plantation with all the slaves?"

"The last time I checked she was paying her staff a living wage."

"And hubby?"

"Firmly under her thumb and usually not underfoot."

"How about instead of doing the visit I run naked through Trinidad in northeast with 'DEA' stenciled on my back?"

"Might be safer, actually. Oh, Lowell Cassell said hello. And he also said, 'You tell Mace that there is indeed a heaven and Mona Danforth will never make it there.'"

"I knew I loved him. So what did he find?" She added quickly, "I'm not poking around, just curious."

"Tolliver was raped."

"Sperm leave-behind?"

"Yes. He also found a couple of foreign pubic hairs and a bit of fiber. There were also soil stains on Tolliver's clothing."

Mace rose. "Well, I guess I should get some sleep if I'm going to survive Mom. You turning in?"

Beth had pulled out her BlackBerry and was answering e-mails. "Just two hundred and sixty-three to go."

"You still answer every e-mail in twenty-four hours?"

"It's part of the job."

"You still never turn it off, do you?"

Beth looked up. "Like you ever did?"

"I had some fun."

"I've had fun too."

"Yeah, your ex was a real barrel of laughs. I lost two years, sis, you lost eight."

"I'm not saying it was all Ted's fault. My career—"

"It wasn't like he didn't know that going in."

Beth stopped thumbing the BlackBerry. "Get some shuteye, you're going to need all your energy for Mom."

CHAPTER

20

MACE WAS FLYING along the winding roads leading out to horse country where old money melded, often uneasily, with new. She was going to see her mother but was now lost. Backtracking, she became even more turned around. Finally she stopped her bike at the end of a dirt path surrounded by trees. As she was trying to get her bearings she heard something move to her right. When she looked that way her heartbeat spiked. She reached for her gun, but of course she didn't have one.

"How the hell did you get out?" she screamed.

Juanita the Cow was waddling toward her, Lily White Rose with the nineteen teeth right behind. Juanita carried a wide smile along with a Smith & Wesson .40, while Lily White had her gutting knife. Mace tried to start her bike, but the ignition wouldn't catch. The two women started to run toward her.

"Shit!" Mace jumped off the bike and sprinted to the woods, but her boot caught in a bump in the dirt and she fell sprawling. By the time she turned over the women were standing over her.

"No big-sis bitch to help you now, baby," cooed Juanita.

Rose said nothing. She just cocked her blade arm back, waiting for the word from the queen bee to plunge the serrated edge into Mace's jugular.

"Do it, Lily White. Then we got to get the hell outta here."

The blade flew down with a speed that Mace was not prepared for. It hit her square in the neck.

"No!"

Mace fell out of the bed. She felt warm blood spurt out of her nose as it smacked against the nightstand. She landed awkwardly on the carpeted floor and just lay there.

Blind Man, who'd been asleep on the floor next to where she'd fallen, licked her face and gave off little mournful noises in her ear.

"It's okay, Blind Man, I'm okay."

She finally rolled over, sat up, and backed her way into a corner. She squatted there in a defensive ball, her hands made into fists, her eyes looking out at the dark, her breath coming in waves of uneven heaves. Blind Man lay in front of her in the darkness, his thick reddish nose probably taking in each and every dimension of her scented fear.

An hour later she was still there, her spine digging into the drywall that her sister had painted a soothing blue especially for her return. Only she wasn't thinking of Juanita or the gut-chick Rose. Her images were of herself, strung out on meth, huddled in a corner, her body going through shit it had never suffered before.

She'd never seen any of them, none of the bandits who'd snatched her out of an alley where she had set up an observation post on a drug distribution center in Six D. After they'd injected her multiple times with stuff for three days running she didn't even know her own name. The next thing she vaguely remembered was climbing in and out of cars, holding a gun, going into stores and taking what didn't belong to any of them.

Once, shots had been fired. She recalled pulling the trigger on her weapon by instinct, only no round had come out of the barrel; turned out her weapon wasn't loaded and never had been. She was finally arrested holding an unloaded Sig and enough evidence to put her away for a long time while the rest of her "gang" conveniently had disappeared.

So the little sister of the D.C. police chief was busted for armed robbery while caked on meth. Some dubbed her the Patty Hearst of the twenty-first century. The arrest, the trial, the sentencing, the appeals galloped by in a blur. Mona had gone for the carotid, and the female legal threshing machine had come within one appeal of putting Mace away for twenty years at a max a thousand miles away from D.C. She'd argued forcefully that Mace had gone so deeply undercover that she had eventually succumbed to the dark side. Mace remembered sitting in the courtroom watching the vitriol-spewing DA pointing her finger at her and pounding the counsel table demanding that this "animal" be sent away for good. In her mind, Mace had killed the bitch over a hundred times. Yet when she finally had gotten the twenty-four-month sentence, just about everybody had turned on her and her sister.

When the van that had taken Mace in shackles arrived at the prison the news trucks were all lined up. It seemed the warden was reveling in the national spotlight, because he'd personally escorted Mace through the gauntlet of media and the hostile crowd. Trash was thrown at her along with insults of every conceivable degree of vulgarity. And still she'd shuffled along, her head as high as she could hold it, her eyes dead ahead, staring at the steel outer doors of her home for the next two years of her life. But even for tough Mace, the tears had started to gather in her eyes, and her lips had started trembling with the Orwellian strain of it all.

Then the crowd of onlookers had suddenly parted and a tall figure in full dress blues and four stars had marched out and started walking right next to Mace. The stunned look on the warden's face showed that this development was totally unexpected. The crowds stopped screaming. Nothing else was thrown at Mace. Not with Chief of Police Elizabeth Perry with her gun and her badge striding right next to her sister, her face a block of granite as she stared down the crowd, willing them from hostility to numbness. That image, that final image of her sister next to her before Mace entered the house of hell, was really the only thing that had kept her going over those two years.

It was with this last thought that Mace finally fell asleep right on the floor. Two hours before dawn, she woke with a start, staggered to the bathroom, washed the crusted blood off her face in the bathroom, and got back into bed. Exhausted, she slept for nearly three hours, until her sister gently shook her awake.

Mace sat up in bed, looked around the room with an unsteady gaze.

Beth handed her a cup of black coffee and sat next to her. "You okay?"

Mace drank some of the coffee and lay back against the head-board. "Yeah, I'm good."

"You look a little out of it. Bad dream?"

Mace tensed. "Why? Did you hear anything?"

"No, just thought it was probably normal. Your subconscious probably thinks there are still bars on the doors and windows."

"I'm fine. Thanks for the java."

"Anytime." Beth rose.

"Uh . . ."

Beth looked down at her. "Something on your mind?"

"I remember what a media circus it was when I went to prison. I was just wondering."

"Why there wasn't a media army camped outside on your return?"

"Yeah."

"The easy answer is you're old news. It's been two years. And every day there's some national or international crisis, big company collapsing, people getting blown up, or some psycho with automatic weapons and body armor gunning people down at the local mall. And since you've been away hundreds of newspapers have folded, existing ones have cut their staff in half, and the TV and radio folks usually chase stuff far more bizarre than you to get the big ratings. But just in case, I sort of pulled a reverse strategy on the media grunts."

Mace sat up. "What do you mean?"

"I offered to make you available to them for a full interview. I guess they figured if it was that easy, why bother?"

"That's pretty slick, Beth. Busy day today?"

"Nope, didn't you hear? Last night all crime miraculously went away."

Mace showered and changed and checked her hair, face, and clothes in the mirror. Then she got mad at herself for even doing this. No matter what she looked like, her mother would find something wrong with her appearance. And frankly, it would be easy pickings for the woman.

Minutes later she fired up the Ducati. Immediately, Blind Man started howling from behind the door. She smiled and revved the gas. Soon she was heading due west, left D.C. proper, and entered Virginia over Memorial Bridge. As she cut in and out of traffic, Mace started to think about the upcoming encounter with the woman who had given birth to her over three decades ago.

Part of her would take prison again over that.

CHAPTER

21

MACE RACED DOWN the straightaway of Route 50, weaving in and out of the dregs of the morning rush hour. The one traffic light in Middleburg caught her and she geared down the Ducati, finally braking to a stop. The street parking here leaned to Range Rovers and Jag sedans with an occasional Smart car thrown in for green measure. The small downtown area was hip in an upscale rural way. And here one could, for millions of dollars, purchase a really swell place to live. Years ago Mace and Beth had visited their mother, seen the fancy estate, dined at a nice restaurant, done some window shopping, and then gone back to busting bandits in D.C. One visit for Mace was truly enough.

Though Beth Perry was only six years older than her sister, she had played far more of a nurturing role for Mace than their mother ever had. In fact, the first person Mace could ever remember holding her was Beth, who was already tall and rangy at age nine.

Though he'd died when Mace was only twelve, Benjamin Perry had left quite an impression on his younger daughter. Mace could vividly recall sitting in her father's small den doing her homework while her dad put together his legal arguments, oftentimes reading them to her and getting her input. She had wept harder than anyone at his funeral, the casket closed to hide the gunshot wounds to his face.

As she flew past lavish estates residing majestically on hundreds of acres, Mace knew that her mother had ascended to this level of wealth principally by design. She had methodically hunted and then snared a fellow who'd never worked a day in his life but was the only child of a man who had earned a fortune large enough to allow his offspring to live decadently for several generations. By then both daughters were grown and gone, for which Mace was enormously grateful. She was more coach fare and Target than private wings and Gucci.

Beth had gotten her height from her mother, who was several inches taller than her husband. Mace had always assumed that she inherited both her father's average stature and his pugnacity. Benjamin Perry's career as the U.S. attorney in D.C. had been tragically cut short, but during his tenure he'd prosecuted criminals through some of the most violent years in D.C. history, quickly becoming legendary for his scorched-earth pursuit of bandits. Yet he also had a reputation for always playing fair, and if exculpatory evidence came along, defense counsel always saw it. He had told Mace more than once that his greatest fear was not letting a guilty person go free, but sending an innocent one to prison. She had never forgotten those words, and that made the appointment of Mona Danforth to her father's old position even more difficult for her to accept.

Benjamin Perry's murder had never been solved. His daughters had taken various cracks at it over the years, with no success. Evidence was lost or tainted, witnesses' memories faded away, or they died. Cold cases were the toughest to solve. But now that she was out of prison Mace knew, at some point, she had to try again.

A few miles past Middleburg proper she slowed the bike and turned off onto a gravel path, which would become a paved cobblestone road about a half mile up. She drew a deep breath and pulled to a stop in front of the house. They called it by some Scottish name because hubby was Scottish and took great pride in his clan back home. While Mace and Beth were there previously he had even entered the room dressed in a kilt with a dagger in his sock and a bonnet on his head. That had been bad enough, but the poor fellow had caught his skirt on the sword handle of a large armored warrior standing against one wall, causing the skirt to lift up and reveal that the lord of the manor wore his kilt commando style. It was all Mace could do not to blow snot out of her nose from laughing. She thought she had carried it off fairly well. However, her mother had sternly informed her that her husband had not taken kindly to Mace rolling on the floor gasping for air while he was desperately trying to pull his skirt back down to cover his privates.

"Then tell Mr. Creepy to start wearing underwear," Mace had shot back in earshot of her stepfather. "I mean, it's not like he's got anything down there to brag about."

That had not gone over very well either.

As she rounded a bend the manor came into full view. It was smaller than Abe Altman's, but not by much. Mace walked up to the front door fully expecting a uniformed butler to answer her knock. But he didn't.

The thick portal flew open and there stood her mother, dressed in a long black designer skirt, calf-high boots, and a starched white embroidered tunic shirt over which a gold chain was hanging. Dana Perry still wore her whitish-blond hair long, though it was held back today in a French braid. She looked at least ten years younger than she was. Beth had her mother's facial structure, long and lovely, with a nose as straight and lean as the edge of an ax blade. The cheekbones still rode high and confident. Her mother cradled a comb-teased Yorkie in one slender arm.

Mace didn't expect a hug and didn't get one.

Her mother looked her up and down. "Prison seems to have agreed with you. You look to be lean as a piano wire."

"I would've preferred a gym membership, actually."

Her mother pointed a long finger at her. "Your father must be turning over in his grave. Always thinking of yourself and never anybody else. Look at what your sister's accomplished. You've got to finally get it straight, little girl, or you're going right down the crapper. Do you understand what I'm saying?"

"Do you actually want me to come in, or will your ripping me a new one on the front porch satisfy as a visit so I can get back to the real world?"

"You actually call that garbage pit of a city the real world?"

"I'm sure you've been tied up the last two years, so I can understand you not bothering to come see me."

"As though seeing you in prison would've been good for my mental health."

"Right, sorry, I forgot the first rule of Dana, it's all about *you*."

"Get in here, Mason."

She had lied to Roy Kingman. Her father hadn't named her Mason. Her *mother* had. And she'd done it for a particularly odious reason. Chafing under the relatively small salary her husband drew as a prosecutor, she'd wanted him to turn to the defense side, where with his skill and reputation he could have commanded an income ten times what he earned on the public side. Thus, Mason Perry—Perry Mason—was her mother's not-so-subtle constant reminder of what he would not give her.

"It's Mace. You'd think after all these years you might get that little point."

"I refuse to refer to you as a name of a weapon."

It was probably a good thing, Mace thought as she trudged past her mother, that she could no longer carry a gun.

CHAPTER

22

Roy Kingman had skipped basketball that morning. He passed by Ned, who looked far more attentive than usual and even had the tie on his uniform tightened all the way to his fleshy neck. Ned gave him a jaunty two-finger salute and a confident dip of the chin as though to let Roy know that not a single murderer had slipped past him today.

You go, bro.

Roy took the elevator up to Shilling & Murdoch. The police were still there and Diane's office and the kitchen were taped off while the cops and techs continued to do their thing. He had snatched conversations with several other lawyers. He had tried to play it cool with Mace, who'd obviously seen far more dead bodies than he had, but finding Diane like that had done a number on his head. He kept replaying that moment over and over until it felt like he couldn't breathe.

He walked by Chester Ackerman's office but the door was closed and the man's secretary, who sat across from her boss's office, told him the police were in there questioning the managing partner. Roy finally went to his office and closed the door. Settling behind his desk, he turned on his computer and started going through e-mails. The fifth one caught his eye. It was from Diane Tolliver. He glanced at the date sent. The previous Friday. The time stamp was a few minutes past ten. He hadn't checked his work e-mails over the weekend because there had been nothing pressing going on. He had intended to do so on Monday morning, but then Diane's body had tumbled out of the fridge. At the bottom of the e-mail were Diane's initials, "DLT."

The woman's message was terse and cryptic, even for the Twitter generation.

We need to focus in on A-

Why hadn't she finished the message? And why send it if it wasn't finished?

It could be nothing, he knew. How many flubs had he committed with his keystrokes? If it had been important Diane would have e-mailed again with the full message, or else called him. He checked his cell phone. No messages from her. He brought up his recent phone call list just in case she had called but left no message. Nothing.

A-?

It didn't ring any immediate bells for him. If it was referring to a client, it could be any number of them. He brought up the list on his screen and counted. Twenty-eight clients beginning with the letter *A*. And eleven of them were ones that he and Diane routinely worked on together. They repped several firms in the Middle East, so it was Al-this and Al-that. Another lawyer at the firm? There were nearly fifty here, with twenty-two more overseas. He knew all of the D.C. folks personally. Doing a quick count in his head, there were ten whose first or last names started with *A*. Alice, Adam, Abernathy, Aikens, Chester Ackerman.

The police, he knew, had already copied the computer files from Diane's office, so they already had what he had just found. Still, should he call them and tell them what he'd just discovered?

Maybe they wouldn't believe me.

For the first time Roy knew what his clients had felt like when he'd worked criminal defense. He left his office and took the elevator down, with the idea of simply going for a walk by the river to clear his head. On the fourth floor the doors opened and the sounds of power saws and hammers assailed him. He watched as an older man in slacks, short-sleeved white shirt, and a hard hat stepped on the elevator car.

The fourth floor had been gutted and was being built out for a new tenant. All the rest of the building's occupants were counting down the days until completion, because the rehabbing was a very messy and noisy affair.

"How's it coming?" he asked the man, who was holding a roll of construction drawings under one arm.

"Slower than we'd like. Too many problems."

"Guys not showing up to work? Inspectors slow on the approval?"

"That and things going missing."

"Missing? Like what?"

"Tools. Food. I thought this building was supposed to be secure."

"Well, the uniform at the front desk is basically useless."

"Heard about some lady lawyer getting killed here. Is it true?"

"Afraid so."

CHAPTER

23

ROY HEADED ALONG the riverfront, stopping near one of the piers where a forty-foot cabin cruiser was docked. What would it be like, he wondered, to live on a boat and just keep going? Watch the sunset and grab a swim when he wanted? See the world? He'd seen his hometown, lived in D.C., Charlottesville. He'd visited lots of cities, but only to bounce basketballs on hardwood before heading on. He'd viewed the Atlantic and Pacific oceans at forty thousand feet. He'd seen Big Ben, and sand in the Middle East. That was about it.

He smelled him before he saw him.

He turned, his hand already reaching into his pocket.

"Hey, Captain."

"Roy." The man gave him a quick salute.

The Captain was in his late fifties and the same height as Roy. However, whereas Roy was lean, the Captain was built like a football lineman. He must've outweighed Roy by eighty pounds. It had once all been muscle, Roy was sure, but the streets had made a fatty transformation of the man's once impressive physique. His belly was so swollen now that the bottom three buttons on the jacket could no longer be used. And his body listed heavily to the left, probably as did his spine. Eating crap out of Dumpsters and sleeping on cement did that to you.

Roy called him the Captain because of the marks on his jacket. From what he'd learned of the man's history, the Captain had once been an Army Ranger and had distinguished himself in Vietnam. But after returning home things had not gone well. Alcohol and then drugs had ruined what should have been an honorable military career. Apparently the VA had tried to help him, but the Captain had eventually fallen through the cracks and into a life on the streets of the capital of the country he had once defended with his blood.

He'd been homeless for over a decade now. And each year his uniform grew more tattered and his skin more permanently stained by the elements, much in the same way that buildings became filthy. However, there was no one to come and give him a good power wash. Roy had first met him when he'd worked as a CJA. Before he'd settled on G-town, the Captain's foraging range was wider and his manner more aggressive. He'd had a couple of assault charges, mostly for harassing tourists or office dwellers for money or food. Roy had defended him once, gotten him probation, and then tried to get him help, but the VA was swamped with needy soldiers from current wars, and the Captain had never been good about follow-up.

It was sad, and yet all Roy could do was open his wallet, look into the darkened, grizzled face that housed a pair of dimming, vacuous eyes that indicated the owner was not all there, and say, "How about I get you some food?"

The Captain nodded, pushing a huge hand through his tangle of filthy gray and white hair. He wore tattered gloves that had once been white but were now even blacker than his face. As they trudged along together Roy looked down and noted that the Captain's shoes were really pieces of cardboard held together with twine. He had survived the previous winter and the heavy spring rains, and the night chills were gone now. Yet Roy wondered, as the Captain coughed up some phlegm and spit it out into the Potomac, if the older man could survive another year out here. As he gazed at the Captain's jacket and saw the Combat Bronze and other medals on his chest, including the designation for two Purple Hearts, he thought that a country's warriors deserved better than this.

The Captain dutifully waited outside the café, like an obedient dog, as Roy bought the food. He came back out, handed the bag over, and watched as the Captain settled down on the curb and ate it all right there, drinking down the coffee last. He wiped his mouth with the paper bag and rose.

"What size shoe do you take?" Roy asked.

The Captain looked down at his feet. "Big. I think."

"Me too. Come on."

They walked back to the office building and into the underground garage. From the backseat of his Audi, Roy pulled out a pair of nearly new basketball shoes. "Try these on." He tossed them to the Captain, who was quick-handed enough to snare them both.

He sat down on the cold floor of the garage and stripped off his cardboard and twine. When Roy saw the blackened, raw skin festered with lumps and green-colored cuts, he looked away.

"Good to go," the Captain said a minute later. Roy was sure they would have fit if the man had had to cut off his toes. "You sure, Roy? Bet these cost probably a million dollars, right?"

"Not quite and I've got plenty." He studied the Captain. If he gave him cash it would go for booze or some street drugs that the Captain didn't need in his system. He had driven him to shelters on three occasions, but the man had walked out of each one within a day or so. Roy was not going to take him to live at his condo. His neighbors would probably not approve, and there was no guarantee that the former military man would not suddenly go nuts and use Roy for a cutting board.

"Come around in a couple days and I'll have some more stuff for you, okay?"

"Yes, sir," the Captain said amiably, giving him another snappy salute.

Roy suddenly noticed something missing and wondered why he hadn't before. "Where's your cart?" Like some homeless people, the Captain kept everything he had in an old rusted shopping cart with two busted front wheels. You could hear him coming a mile away just from the screech of metal.

"Some pricks stole it!"

"Do you know who?"

"Damn Vietcong. I'll catch 'em. And then. Look." The Captain reached in his pocket and pulled out a large clasp knife. It looked military-issued.

"Don't do that, Captain. Let the police handle it."

The Captain just stared at him. Finally he waved a big hand at Roy. "Thanks for the shoes."

24

Unfortunately, her mother's husband, Timothy, *was* there. Fortunately, he wasn't wearing a kilt. To Mace, he looked like a person of leisure who desperately wanted to be perceived as a man of the land with a British twist. This translated into an outfit consisting of tweeds, an old-fashioned shotgun vest with holders for the shells, a cute pocket kerchief that exactly matched his checked shirt, and nearly knee-high brown leather riding boots, though there wasn't an equine in sight. When Mace saw him she felt her cheeks begin to quiver and had to look away quickly before the next sound that was heard from her was a snort.

An older woman in a maid's uniform brought coffee and little sandwiches out to the faux English conservatory they were sitting in. She looked as though she would rather be driving tenpenny nails through her skull with a hammer than playing maid for Timothy and Dana. The sandwiches weren't nearly as wonderful as the spread Abe Altman had offered. Still, Mace filled her belly and had her caffeine fix.

The little Yorkie, whose name Mace had been told was Angelina Fernandina, sat on a plump pillow in front of her own little gold tray of high-end vittles, happily nipping away with teeth the size and shape of splinters. Mace inclined her head at precious Angelina. "Do you dress her in clothes too?"

Dana answered, "Only when we travel. Our jet makes her cold."

"Poor thing," said Mace.

"So does Beth still have a menagerie of misfits?"

"Just me and Blind Man, but he's going strong. Probably be alive and well when you're planting old Angie there in the dirt."

Timothy sucked in a breath at this remark and gave Angelina a little pat with the *back* of his hand, which told Mace that he didn't actually like dogs, hair-teased or not.

"So, how's the rural aristocratic life treating you both?"

Timothy daintily patted his lips with a monogrammed napkin and glanced at Dana, apparently waiting for her to respond.

"Timothy has been elected to head up the local planning commission. It's an important position because you wouldn't believe what people want to do out here development-wise. It's a travesty."

You mean like putting up a twenty-thousand-square-foot Scottish castle smack in the middle of farmland and raising your working-class neighbors' property taxes tenfold? Mace thought. But she said, "Congratulations, Timothy. That's great."

His chest puffed out a bit as he swallowed the last bit of sandwich. When he spoke it was as though he were addressing an adoring audience of thousands. "I will endeavor to carry out my duties to the best of my abilities. I take the stewardship that has been granted to me very seriously."

God, you are the biggest prick. "I'm sure you do," Mace said pleasantly.

Dana said, "So what are your plans, *Mason?*"

Mace slowly put down her coffee cup. "I'd actually considered stripping on Internet webcams for food, but then a job offer came along."

"What sort of job offer?"

"An assistant to a college professor."

"Why would a college professor want *you* as an assistant?" scoffed her mother.

"He's blind, on a tight budget, and I'm apparently cheaper than a seeing-eye dog."

"Will you please be serious for once in your life, Mason!"

Okay, I tried playing patty-cakes and I don't like it. "What does it matter to you what I do? I'm sure we can agree that you're a few decades late on playing mommy."

"How dare you—"

Mace could feel her ears burning. She didn't want to go there. She really didn't. "Oh, I always dare. So just back off, lady."

"Then let me explain to you quite clearly why it *is* my business. If you can't support yourself, guess who you'll be running to with your hand out?"

Mace formed fists so tight all of her finger joints popped. She leaned into Dana until their noses were only separated by a bare inch. "I would gnaw off my hand before I came to you or Scotch Bonnet Boy over there for one freaking dime."

A scarlet-faced Timothy scrambled to his leather-booted feet. "I think I'll go do some yoga. I feel my balance is off."

Dana immediately put out her hand for him to take. "All right, dear. But remember, we have dinner tonight with the mayor and his wife at the French Hound."

The moment he'd fled the room, Dana whirled on her youngest daughter. "It's nearly impossible to believe, but I think prison has actually made you worse."

This barb was so weak that Mace simply ignored it and studied her mother in silence for a few moments. "So why are you still all so kissy-kissy to him? You've got the ring. You're legally locked to Lord Bonny Butt."

She said stiffly, "He's a Scottish earl, not a lord."

The truth suddenly hit Mace. "Bonny Butt's got a kick-ass pre-nup, doesn't he?"

"Shut up, Mason! This minute."

"So how does it work? You vest a few diamond bracelets, some cash, and a bushel of Triple A bonds for each year of matrimonial bliss?"

Her mother snapped, "I don't even know why I invited you here."

Mace rose. "Oh, that one is easy, actually. You just wanted me to see how fabulous your life is. Well, I'm duly impressed. I'm happy that you're so obviously happy."

"You're a terrible liar. You always were."

"I guess that's why I became a cop. I can just pull my badge and figure out who's trying to screw with me."

"But you can't be a *cop* anymore, can you?" This came out as a clear taunt.

"Not until I figure out who set me up."

Dana rolled her heavily made-up eyes. "Do you really think that's going to happen?"

"I don't think. I *know* it will."

"Well, if I were you, I'd work very hard for your little college professor. Because I see 'assistant' as being as good as it gets for you from here on."

"Thanks for the encouragement. I'll see myself out."

But her mother followed her as far as the front door. As Mace strapped on her helmet, Dana said, "Do you know how much trouble you've caused for your sister?"

"Yeah, actually I do."

"And of course you don't care at all, do you?"

"If I told you otherwise would you believe me?"

"You make me sick with your selfish ways."

"Well, I learned from the master, didn't I?"

"I spent the best years of my life with your father. We never had any money. Never went anywhere. Never did a damn thing. And we never would."

"Yeah, punishing the wicked and making the world a better place for all was just the pits, wasn't it?"

"You were only a child. You had no idea."

"Oh, I had more than an idea. Talk about me? *You'll* never have it nearly as good ever again. I don't care how many rich *Timothys* you marry."

"Oh, you think so?"

Mace lifted her visor. "Yeah, because Dad was the only man you ever really loved."

"Just please go away!"

Mace noticed the slight tremble in her mother's right hand. "Do you know how lucky you were to have a man that good so in love with you? Beth never had that privilege. And I sure as hell haven't."

She thought she saw her mother's eyes turn glassy before the door slammed shut.

Mace mangled the Ducati's gears in her sudden panic to get out of this place. Maybe her mother was right. Maybe she would never be a cop again. Maybe this was as good as it would ever get for her.

25

Beth read through the report on her computer screen three times. This was something her father had taught her. Read through once for general conceptualization and then a second time for the nitty-gritty details. And then read it a final time, at least an hour after the first reading, but do so out of order, which forced your mind and your eyes from their comfort zones.

Beth refocused. They had scrubbed Diane Tolliver's computer at work and at her home without revealing any surprises. The work computer had yielded a mass of legal documents and research items and correspondence on dozens of complicated deals. The woman's town house in Old Town Alexandria had yielded no clues or leads. They would work outward now, from her job and personal life. Murders were almost never random occurrences. Family, friends, acquaintances, rivals, spurned lovers—those were the categories from which the takers of human life were most often spawned.

She looked down at the one interesting item on Diane Tolliver's work computer. The e-mail she'd sent to Roy Kingman Friday night. The missive was cryptic and she was hoping that Kingman could explain it, but when interviewed by her detectives over the phone he claimed to have no idea what it meant or why it had been sent to him.

They also knew from the electronic records from the garage that Tolliver had left the office Friday night at two minutes before seven and returned at a little before ten, leaving again around ten-forty. The cleaning crew had come in at seven-thirty and left around nine-thirty. They had seen nothing unusual.

What did people do for a few hours on a Friday evening? They had dinner. The fact that she had driven showed it was too far to walk. They were accessing the woman's credit card records to see what restaurant she'd gone to. That would only work if she had paid the bill, of course, but it was a viable lead.

Need to focus in on A-

That was the message she'd sent to Kingman that he claimed not to understand. Was that the whole message or had it been cut off? She might have been interrupted. If so, by whom at that late hour? But she'd been alive on Monday morning. Beth frowned as she thought about her sister hanging around Kingman. Could he crack a brain stem? Yeah, he probably could.

There were other messages Diane had sent over the course of the weekend, all from home. Just routine ones to various friends, and she'd ordered some items for her home from two vendors. Her BMW 735 was in the parking garage in her normal space, and the gate record showed she'd accessed the garage at six a.m. on the dot. Her car had been searched without revealing anything of use.

Tolliver's purse had not been found, so robbery couldn't be ruled out. Yet she'd been raped; that might have been the primary motivation. And then killed to prevent her from fingering who'd done it. No one at Shilling & Murdoch had come into the office over the weekend, including Diane Tolliver.

From what Beth had learned, Tolliver usually got in around nine. So why had she come to the office so early on Monday? They were interviewing everyone who worked at the law firm to verify where they were on Monday morning. However, Beth was really counting on getting a database hit on the sperm.

They could find no one who'd talked to Diane over the weekend. One neighbor reported that he saw her drive off in a hurry on Sunday around nine in the morning but did not speak to her. She lived in an end-unit town house with a garage. She could come and go without interacting with anyone, as she apparently had the weekend before she'd been killed.

There were dirty dishes in the dishwasher and trash that indicated she had eaten in over the weekend. She had a cleaning service that came three times a week, but not over the weekend. Her home phone records showed no calls going out, and the only messages on her voice mail had been from solicitors. She, like many people, apparently used her cell phone to communicate most of the time.

They couldn't find her iPhone because it had presumably been in her purse. But they had requested the phone records from her carrier. She'd made many calls on her cell phone over the weekend. None of them had been to friends or coworkers, though. These were all normal things that one did during a weekend. Tolliver had not known, of course, that it would be the last weekend of her life.

The previous Friday, her last full day at the office, had been spent in meetings with various clients. Three of them were local and had been interviewed, but had told them nothing of interest. Tolliver had seemed perfectly normal to them. Two of her client meetings had been with men from overseas. Both men had flown out Friday night and were now in the Middle East. Neither was obviously her killer.

Her cell phone chirped.

"Hello?"

"You working late?" said Mace's voice.

"Had a community outreach event but it got canceled. What are you offering?"

"Dinner, on me. Pick a nice place. I mean really nice, where you actually have to wear shoes and everything."

"Did Altman give you an advance on your salary?"

"No, I just cleaned out my bank account."

"Mace, what about your creditors?"

"I'll start paying them off with my first paycheck. Let's just have a nice meal."

"Mom was that bad?"

"She's still alive and so am I, so how bad could it be?"

"Okay. How about eight-thirty? I'll call you with the place."

Mace clicked off and Beth went back to her notes.

Her office phone rang.

She picked it up and listened for two minutes.

There'd been another murder.

And this one had cut close to home. A U.S. attorney was dead. Mona Danforth wasn't the one killed. Beth managed to avoid tacking "unfortunately" onto the end of this thought. But they had just discovered Jamie Meldon's body in a Dumpster in northwest Washington.

Oɴ ᴛʜᴇ ᴅʀɪᴠᴇ over Beth spent the time thinking about the dead man. Jamie Meldon was one of Mona Danforth's top assistants and was as unlike his boss as it was possible to be. He was a fine, diligent lawyer who'd made enemies in the criminal world as all good prosecutors did. And one of those enemies might have murdered him. She obviously was not going to make dinner with Mace. But if there was one thing her sister would understand it was that in their line of work the job trumped everything else.

When she got to the crime scene she was not surprised to see the FBI there along with her people. Meldon was a U.S. attorney and thus his murder was a federal crime. What did shock her was seeing her police and forensics personnel packing their stuff up to leave.

"What's going on?" she asked the officer in charge.

"We've been told in no uncertain terms that this is a federal investigation and we are persona non grata."

"Like we've never worked a homicide with the Bureau. Where's the SAIC?" she asked, referring to the special agent in charge.

He pointed to a man in a suit near the Dumpster.

Beth marched over with two of her district homicide detectives in tow. "Can I ask what's going on?"

The man turned around to look at her. "Hello, Beth."

Beth recognized him as soon as she saw his face. "Steve? I didn't think the AD came out to homicides."

Steve Lanier, the assistant director of the FBI's Washington Field Office and a man Beth worked with closely, said, "Well, I can't say the same about you because I know you come to every one."

"Did you know Jamie Meldon?"

"No."

"So why are you here, then?"

He glanced over at a group of men in suits. "Do you know who they are?"

"No, should I?"

"They will be coming over here shortly and informing you that national security interests are at stake and the police will not be involved in this investigation."

"What does national security have to do with a prosecutor's murder?"

"Well, I don't suppose we'll ever find out."

"*We*? They might be able to pull the rug out from under us, but you're the FBI."

"In ordinary circumstances that would be true."

"So what's extraordinary about this?"

"All I can tell you is that it came straight from Pennsylvania."

"The White House?"

"And don't bother asking who they are. They won't tell you."

Beth looked puzzled. "CIA? Langley has no law enforcement jurisdiction. Hell, they can't even operate domestically."

"It may not be the CIA."

"Steve, are you saying you don't even know which agency they're from?"

"That's right."

"Then how the hell did they get access to a restricted crime scene?"

Lanier smiled glumly. "They showed their driver's licenses."

"Are you shitting me! Their driver's licenses?"

"The FBI director himself told me that they would be here, what their names were, and that they should have unfettered access to the crime scene, because they were taking over the investigation. So they didn't have to show me their creds."

"This is unbelievable."

"Yes it is."

"Chief Perry?" said one man in his forties and who was the apparent leader of this little group of unknowns.

"Yeah?" Beth said in a stern tone.

"Perhaps the assistant director here has filled you in on . . . things?"

"That you're trumping my jurisdiction based solely on your legal right to drive a motor vehicle? Yep, he mentioned it, but maybe you can run me through it with particulars, including your names and the agency you work for."

"That won't be happening," said the man pleasantly. "The mayor should be e-mailing you — "

Beth's BlackBerry started buzzing.

"Right about now," said the man, smiling.

Beth checked her device. The mayor was polite and diplomatic but the message was clear. Back off now.

"Can I expect copies of reports?" she asked.

"No."

"Can I see the body?"

"Same answer," said the fellow.

"Will you tell me when and if you find the killer?"

"We'll expect you and your people to be gone in the next two minutes."

The men turned and left.

Beth looked at Lanier. "Do you hate them as much as I do, Steve?"

Lanier said, "Oh, even more than you do. Trust me."

"Care to give me their names? I'm assuming you remember them from the driver's licenses."

"Sorry, Beth, I got my marching orders too."

She stalked back to her car. At least she'd be having dinner with her sister tonight after all.

CHAPTER

27

At the sound of the knock Roy looked up from a contract he was reviewing.

"Yeah?"

The door opened and a young man dressed in corduroy pants, striped shirt, and a cheap paisley tie stood there holding on to the front bar of a mail cart. It was old-fashioned, but even in the digital age sometimes lawyers still needed materials that were actually contained in books or written on real paper.

"Special delivery," the young man said.

"Just put it on the desk, Dave."

Dave came forward clutching the book. "Creepy."

"What's creepy?'

"Ms. Tolliver."

Roy shrugged. "I doubt whoever killed her is going to come back."

"Not what I meant."

Dave put the book down on the desk.

Roy leaned back in his chair. "Okay, don't keep me in suspense."

Dave tapped the book. "This is from Ms. Tolliver."

Roy snatched up the book. "When did she put it in the mail room?"

"Don't know."

"Why don't you know? I thought there were procedures."

"Most of the time folks call and we come and pick up the package. They have a delivery sheet filled out and we put it in the pipeline."

"So why don't you know when this book came in?"

"It was just in the mail room with the sheet filled out. She must've done it herself. I checked with Ms. Tolliver's secretary and she didn't know anything about it."

"But she was killed Monday morning. It's now Tuesday afternoon and I'm just getting this?"

"We didn't deliver the mail yesterday because the police were all over the place. Just getting to it now. I'm sorry."

Roy examined the cover of the book. It was on contract law, an out-of-date edition. Lawyers never sent old textbooks to each other. What would be the point?

"Did you see it in the mail room on Friday?"

"Don't think so."

"But you're not sure?"

"No. I'm not."

"Okay, but did you see it in the mail room on Monday morning?"

"Can't really say. It was so crazy around here. But it had to be there on Monday morning. I mean, she couldn't have done it after she was dead."

"If she was the one who put the book in the mail room, Dave. We have no way of telling if she physically did it or not."

"Oh, right." Dave looked at him nervously. "Am I in trouble?"

Roy sat back, his sudden flame of anger gone. "Probably not. Thanks, Dave. Sorry I got testy. I guess we're all a little stressed out."

After Dave closed the door, Roy looked at the mail slip clipped to the book. It was in Diane's neat handwriting that he'd seen on many documents. The mail form had a date and time-of-day box to show when it had gone into the system; however, Diane had not filled in this information. The form did have his name on it as the recipient, so the book *was* meant for him. There was no reason for her to send it to him. But she had. He flipped through some pages, but it was just an old book.

His phone rang. "Yeah?" His mouth formed a smile when he heard the voice.

Mace said, "You must've billed nearly a hundred hours so far today."

"I told you this is a humane law firm. We don't have to lie by the hour."

"You got time to talk?"

"Sure, when?"

"How about now?"

His door opened and Mace waved to him. Roy shook his head and put down his phone. "Are you always this weird?"

"You haven't begun to see my weird side."

"That is truly terrifying."

"I know. I get that a lot."

28

MACE CLOSED the door behind her and sat across from him. "Thanks for repping me last night with old Abe."

"Just wait until you get my bill." He held up the book. "Diane Tolliver sent this to me in the office mail."

"Okay?"

"Like very recently. But she had no reason to. It's an old text-book."

"Put it down. Now!"

He quickly set the book on his desk.

"Who else has pawed it, other than you?" she said severely.

"At least one other, the mail room guy."

"Great."

"He didn't know any better."

"But *you* should have known better."

"Okay, maybe I should have. But I didn't. So now what?"

"You got a hanky?"

"No, but I do have some tissues."

He handed some over. Mace used one to open the book slowly.

"I glanced through a couple of pages, didn't see any cryptic writing. But we could pour lemon juice on it and see if the invisible ink is revealed."

"Or we could just do this." She held the book by the spine and swung it back and forth, the pages flapping open.

A small key fell out and landed on the desk.

"Don't!" Mace cautioned as Roy reached for it.

Using the tissue, she picked up the key by its ridged end.

Mace said, "Not a safety deposit box key, maybe a post office box."

"That narrows it down to a few hundred million. And we don't even know if this key came from her."

"She ever mention a post office box?"

Roy shook his head. "No."

Mace stared down at the key with such intensity that it seemed that she expected the bit of metal to suddenly confess all its secrets. "And you had no other communication from her?"

Roy started to say no, but then he stopped. He clicked some keys and turned the screen around for her to see. "She sent me an e-mail late on Friday night."

"Do the police know about this?"

"Yep, because they already questioned me about it today. I told them I didn't know what it meant."

Mace read the line. "You sure nothing rings a bell?"

"No, but it's awkwardly phrased. 'Focus in on'? Why not just say 'focus on'?"

"I don't know. You're the guy that gets paid by the word. Any viable candidates for 'A'?"

"Too many. But I didn't think you were on the police force any-more."

"There's no law that says a private citizen can't investigate a crime."

"But—"

"Getting back to the key and e-mail, any thoughts?"

"Well, you can't hold me to anything."

"Just tell me, Roy."

"Chester Ackerman. He's the managing partner of the firm. I spoke with him yesterday. He was really nervous, upset."

"One of his lawyers got stuck in the fridge, there's a lot to be upset about."

"I know, but, and this is just my gut, he seemed scared beyond what the situation would compel, if you know what I mean."

"Like he was scared for his own skin?"

"And I think he was lying about something too."

"What?"

"I don't know. Just something."

"What do you know about him?"

"He's from Chicago. Has a family. Brings in tons of business."

"Okay, so basically you're telling me you know nothing?"

"I've never had a reason to dig much deeper on the guy."

"So maybe now you do have a reason."

"You want me to spy on the managing partner?" he said incredulously.

"And anybody else who seems productive."

"For what is most likely a random killing?"

"Your partner got stuffed in a fridge. Who's to say it doesn't have something to do with this place?"

Roy picked up his rubber ball, and shot at the basket. And missed.

"Mechanics are off. Murder closeup sometimes does that." She perched on the edge of his desk and used the tissue to go through the book page by page. "No mob players on the old client list by chance?"

He shook his head. "We don't do criminal work here. Just deals."

"Business clients get into legal trouble all the time."

"Like I told you before, if it's litigation, we farm it out."

"To what firm?"

"Several, on an approved list."

"We're not making much progress here."

"No, we're not," Roy agreed.

"How much do you make?"

His eyes widened slightly. "Why do you keep asking me that?"

"Because you haven't given me an answer. Don't look all pissed. It's a legit question."

"Okay, more than Altman is paying you."

"How much more?"

"With bonus and profit-share and bennies, nearly double."

"An entry-level cop on MPD pulls less than fifty thou a year."

"I never said life was fair. But just so you know, as a CJA I never made close to fifty a year." He studied her. "So why did you want to know how much I make?"

"Your firm clearly has money, so that's a motive to kill."

"Okay. Maybe I can look into some stuff and get back to you. What are you doing tonight?"

"Dinner with big sis. But I'm free after that."

"What, you never sleep?"

"Not for the last two years."

She pocketed the key still wrapped in tissue.

Roy looked nervously at her. "I don't want a withholding evidence charge leveled against me."

"And I want to find out what the hell is going on around here. I'm like addicted to things that seem to make no sense."

"But you're not a cop anymore, Mace."

"So everybody keeps reminding me," she said, as she left his office.

CHAPTER

29

Mace sat on her bike with material evidence from a homicide investigation ripping a black hole in her jacket pocket. She had just committed a felony in a city where her sister was the top enforcer of the law.

"You are an idiot," she muttered as the Ducati idled at a stoplight. "A moron. A reckless piece of crap that never knows when to say, 'No, don't do that!'" She'd promised her sister she would not do exactly what she was doing. Meddling in the case.

But something had happened to her in prison that not even Beth knew about. She'd read an old news article about an FBI agent who'd been convicted of witness tampering, aiding a mob boss, and helping to transport weapons across state lines. He had protested his innocence the entire time, claiming he'd been framed but to no avail. He was tried, convicted, and served his full sentence. On getting out he'd moved to another state, secretly gone undercover, and infiltrated a violent drug ring. He'd collected a mountain of evidence at great personal risk and turned it all over to the Bureau, who'd made the bust. He'd even gone on the stand to testify against the ringleaders. The media had picked up the story and run with it and the public outcry had been immense.

The thinking was, why would a guilty man have done something like that? He must've been innocent. There had been a clear miscarriage of justice. The public pressure filtered to the politicians on Capitol Hill, resulting in the Bureau going against its own rules and reinstating the agent despite his being a convicted felon. The man had gone on to head up an FBI office in the Midwest and his career had been full of accolades and achievements.

The agent's name was Frank Kelly and a desperate Mace had written to him from prison and explained her situation. Kelly had actually come to West Virginia to see her. He was a big, solid fellow with a no-nonsense attitude. He'd read up on her case and told her he believed her to be innocent. But while commiserating with her situation he'd been blunt. "You're never going to get your record clean. Too many obstacles and crap in the way. Even if you do find out some stuff, proving it to the level necessary will be pretty much impossible. There will always be people aligned against you, people who don't want to believe you. But what you can do is get back in the saddle when you get out. You go out on your dime and nerve, no cop shop backing you up, and lay your ass on the line like I did. Then you have a shot at being able to clean your record de facto, in the court of public opinion. There are no guarantees," Kelly had added. "And I have to tell you I got real lucky. But at least this way you can control your own destiny a little. You at least have a shot. Otherwise, you'll never be a cop again."

"That's all I ever asked for," Mace had told him. "A shot."

He'd shaken her hand and wished her luck.

That's all I want, a shot to be a true blue again.

There were those on the police force who believed that because she was Beth Perry's sister Mace received preferential treatment, when actually the reverse was true. Beth had gone out of her way not to show favoritism and had actually driven Mace harder than anyone else under her. Mace had earned every promotion, every commendation, and every scar, including those hidden and those in plain sight. She'd graduated from the Metropolitan Police Academy with some demerits but a far greater number of superlatives. Instructors who'd handed out these black marks also thought she was, hands down, the best police recruit to join the capital city's thin blue line since, well, since her sister had graduated at the top of her class years earlier.

In record time she'd gone from rookie beat cop to sergeant, and then made the leap to CID, or the Criminal Investigations Division where she'd been assigned to the Homicide and Sex Offenses Branch. She'd cut her teeth on stacks of gruesome murders, sex assaults, and cases so cold the files had turned blue along with the bodies. She'd made up procedures on her own, and while she'd sometimes been dressed down for doing so, many of these same methods were now part of the investigative techniques curriculum taught at the police academy.

During her career she'd made friends because she was loyal and had never rolled on any of them even if they deserved it. And she'd made enemies that she would keep until the day she or they croaked. But Mace had also made enemies who could be convinced that they owed her. That was why she was here.

Mace parked her Ducati in front of the shop with the fancy red awning over the top of which was the name of the establishment: Citizen Soldier, Ltd.

Cute.

She tugged open the door and walked in.

Shelves lined the walls and were filled with pretty much every conceivable personal defense item on the market. Behind barred wall cabinets were shotguns, rifles, and assault weapons just waiting for itchy trigger fingers to set them free. Inside belly-button-high locked display consoles were a wide variety of auto and semi-auto pistols and old-fashioned wheel guns.

"Hey, Binder," she called out to the man in the back near the cash register. "Still selling whack jobs SBRs built from reconfigured AR-15 pistols without getting ATF approval and paying the appropriate taxes?"

Binder wore cammie pants and a tight-fitting black muscle shirt that showed off his buffed pecs, delts, and biceps. Military boots were on his feet. They were worn down and looked like the real deal. That's because they were, she knew. He'd pulled years in the uniform of Uncle Sam but also had some stockade time and a dishonorable discharge because of a little drug dealing on the side that had nearly cost two fresh-from-boot-camp grunts their lives from injecting ill-cooked crystal meth. He wore his hair in a big throwback afro that reminded her of a young Michael Jackson. This was quite remarkable-looking since the man was white, had nearly pupil-size freckles all over his face, and his hair was flame red except where it was edged with gray at the roots.

"*Send in the clowns,*" she sang under her breath.

Binder wheeled around. A Garrett handheld scanner was in one hammy fist and a tactical folding knife in the other.

"Wow, you look really happy to see me," she said.

"When the hell did you get out?" This came out more like a hurled piece of spit than a question formed with words.

"I didn't. I escaped. You want to turn me in for the reward?"

He put the tact knife on a shelf containing a pile of other blades, all with price tags attached. "I'm busy," he grunted. "I know you ain't a cop anymore more, so harassment time is over."

Instead of leaving, she dug into the pile of blades on the shelf and picked up a knife that had twin wooden handles. With a flick of her wrist she flipped free the six-inch razor-edged shaft. "Whoa, a channel-constructed handmade Filipino Balisong with an IK Bearing System. Very cool. But unfortunately their importation into the U.S. was banned in the eighties."

Binder didn't look impressed by this information. "Is that right?"

"And the Balisong can technically be considered a gravity or butterfly knife or a switchblade. They're illegal in D.C. and Maryland and you can't sell 'em in Virginia."

"Somebody forgot to send me the memo. I'll talk to my lawyer."

"Good, while you're doing that I'll call the Five D commander and let him run a second set of eyeballs over your inventory list. If you want to dress in drag I can recommend a very nice facility in West Virginia for the next few years." She eyed his bushy redtop. "And the really good news is you won't even have to get a haircut."

Binder leaned down into her face. "What the hell do you want, woman!"

"Some equipment. And I'll pay, just not full price because I'm poor and cheap."

She held up the Balisong and with a flick closed the blade. "And next time, Bin, hide the plainly illegal shit in the back. I mean, at least make the CID guys work for it. Otherwise they'll get rusty."

"What kind of equipment?"

"My wish list starts with a UV blue-light lamp, fluorescent dye, and contrasting spectacles. FYI, pulling out the cheap made-in-China crap will not make me happy. I got enough lead in my system from eating prison food."

"I've got a nice kit for three hundred plus tax," he mumbled.

"Great, I'll give you fifty for it."

His broad face swelled with anger, making his freckles look like giant amoebas. "That's a ripoff. You know what my damn rent is here?"

"You won't have any rent in prison. But I do know the Aryan Nation scuzzballs *are* partial to redheads."

Binder deflated as quickly as he'd inflated. "What else?" he said sullenly.

"Well, let's have a look-see at all the goodies," she said sweetly.

After she'd finished, she loaded her purchases in a large backpack she'd made Binder throw in for free. A belt with an extra feature loaded in the clasp that she'd purchased from him had already been slipped around her waist and tightened down. She'd paid and was heading to the door when he called out, "Twenty bucks says you're back in prison in six months."

She whipped around. "And I've got fifty that says any illegal shit left in this place gets confiscated in forty-eight hours by MPD's finest."

Binder slammed his fist against the counter. "I thought we had a deal!"

"I don't remember anything about a deal. I just mentioned *switchblades* and you gave me a really nice discount. I thought it was like a code word for preferred customers."

"You . . . are . . . a . . . *bitch*!"

"Took you all these years to figure that out, scumball?"

He eyed the backpack. "What the hell are you going to do with all that stuff?"

"I'm not sitting on the sidelines, Bin."

"What's that supposed to mean?"

"Two years in hell, and the blue ripped right out of my heart, that's what that means."

30

Roy closed the door softly behind him. Playing snoop while homicide detectives were still on the premises was not the smartest career move he'd ever made. Yet there was something about Mace Perry that just made him not want to disappoint the woman. Maybe it was the fact that she could probably kick his ass anytime she wanted.

Chester Ackerman's office looked as though the man never did a lick of work, and without billable hours to be counted up, there was no way to tell if he did or not. Still, he brought in more business than any partner in the firm and in the legal world that was the big stick. It was also principally why he was managing partner. As quickly and as efficiently as he could, Roy opened file and desk drawers, checked the pockets of the man's suit coat that hung on the back of the door, and tried but failed to access his computer records.

He heard footsteps coming and started to panic before those sounds eased away down the hall. He listened at the door and slipped out. He bypassed his office and headed to the mail room. He talked to Dave again, gained no useful information, and next questioned the other mail room guy, who was similarly clueless. He waited until both men headed out with items for delivery before searching through the mail room but finding nothing.

The space had one odd feature, a large dumbwaiter that had been built especially for the mailroom. Shilling & Murdoch also had office space on the fifth floor, and this motorized dumbwaiter ran directly into a storage room set up there for the firm's archives. It was more convenient to keep the materials on-site for ready access. And it was far more efficient to send heavy boxes down a straight shaft than cart them through the office and then down the elevators.

As he stood there a weird thought occurred to him.

He rode the elevator to the fourth floor. When the doors opened the sounds of nail drivers and power saws hit him right in the eardrums. He stepped off and was immediately met by a wiry guy with Popeye forearms covered in colorful tattoos and wearing a yellow hard hat.

"Can I help you, buddy?"

"I work at the law firm on the sixth floor."

"Congratulations, but you can't be here."

"I'm also on the building's oversight committee. We've been notified that there have been some thefts of property from your work site and I was asked by the committee chairman to come down to get further details. It has to do with our property and casualty insurance reporting requirements and also our D&O rider, you understand?"

It was as though the minute he'd passed the bar Roy's ability to bullshit on demand had clicked to a whole new level. Or maybe that was *why* he'd gone to law school in the first place.

It was painfully clear from the expression on Hard Hat's face that he hadn't comprehended one syllable Roy had uttered.

"So what does that mean?"

Roy said patiently, "It means I have to look around and report back and maybe your company will get some money from our overlap insurance coverage to help cover some of the losses."

The man tossed a hard hat to Roy. "Works for me, I'm just the carpenter. Only watch your step, dude. Lawyers fall down and get a boo-boo, I don't even want to think about what that would cost."

Roy slipped on the hat and started walking around the space. One of the passenger elevators had been fitted with pads so the construction crew could bring its materials in because the building didn't have a dedicated freight elevator.

Roy didn't know how many of the construction crew had been given key cards. He found the carpenter and asked this question. The guy was driving screws into a metal wall stud.

"Crew chief has one. He lets me in if I get here before the building opens. Most guys report at eight-thirty, so they can just walk right in."

"When does everyone leave?"

"Right at five-thirty. Work rules."

"No overtime? Weekends?"

"Not for me. I don't want it. I like my downtime. Have to ask the crew chief if anybody else works off the clock."

"Where is he?"

"Long lunch." The man put down his power screwdriver and tipped his hard hat back. "See, that's what I want to be when I grow up. A crew chief."

Roy continued to walk around the space. He heard a machine whirring and was surprised to see the building's day porter. He was standing in front of a microwave set up in a little cubby off the main work area where there was also a fridge.

"Hey, Dan, what are you doing here?"

Dan, a slender man with silver hair and a matching mustache, was dressed in a neat blue work uniform. "Missed lunch. Just warming up some soup, Roy."

"You come up here often?"

The microwave dinged and Dan took the bowl out and started spooning tomato soup into his mouth. "They're paying me a little on the side to keep the place tidy."

"Who? The crew chief?"

"Yep. Worked for him before on a job a couple years ago before I got this gig. He remembered me. Few extra dollars don't hurt. I mean, I get all my work done for the building first, Roy," he added quickly.

"I've got no problems with that. But I hear they've been having some problems?"

Dan nodded. "Stuff missing. Some wrenches and some food. I told the crew chief not to keep food up here, but the guys don't listen. They cram their munchies all over the place. And stuff in the fridge there."

"They ever think of hiring a security guard?"

"Too much money for this small a job. I come up here in the

evenings to clean up, but I'm always gone by seven. Never seen or heard anything."

"They work weekends?"

"No, client won't pay the overtime. Monday to Friday, according to my buddy."

"Any theories on who might be stealing?"

"Not a clue. But I doubt it's anybody from your place, unless you got some folks who'll risk their six-figure careers over a package of Oreos and cans of Pepsi."

Roy left the fourth floor and went back to his office. He had spent nearly an hour learning absolutely nothing. He hoped Mace was having better luck with the key.

CHAPTER

31

Performing this particular test at Beth's house was out of the question even for a risk-taker like Mace. So here she was in the ladies' room at a Subway restaurant.

She'd brought in her backpack, locked the door, put on latex gloves, sprinkled the dye on the key, put on her contrasting spectacles, and turned off the light. She powered up her handheld blue-light wand, and her fifty bucks paid to old Binder scored an immediate dividend.

"Friction ridges, come to Momma," she said softly. There *were* fingerprints on the key. She hit the surface with a magnification lens she had also pried from Binder's cold fingers. During her career Mace had looked at enough inked islands, dots, ending ridges, and other fingerprint ID points to be considered an expert. This print was good and clean with minutiae including a hook, a ridge crossing, and even a trifurcation. The other side of the key wasn't quite as good, but there was still plenty enough for a match.

Thumb and index she assumed, since those were the fingers one normally used to hold a key. She was thinking that the prints probably belonged to Diane Tolliver. How that advanced the investigation she wasn't sure, but at least it would show whether the dead woman had held it. She was surprised that the prints hadn't been wiped away by the key being pressed between the pages of the book, but sometimes the good guys got lucky.

Now she had one more favor to call in before she was done with this piece of evidence. Thirty minutes after visiting this last stop and getting some free service from yet another old "friend," she headed back to Roy's office after placing the key in a plastic baggie to protect the prints. She left the key with Roy and instructed him to turn it over to the police with the explanation of how he'd gotten it. As she was walking across the lobby to leave the building she noticed Ned staring at her. Mace changed direction and headed toward him.

"You're Ned, right?"

"That's right. I saw you and Roy Kingman ride off on your motorcycle yesterday."

"What an eagle eye you have. I bet you see everything that goes on around here."

His chest puffed up. "Not much that I miss. That's why I do what I do."

"Security, you mean?"

"That's right. Thinking about joining the police force, though. Kicking bad guys' asses. You know."

Mace ran her gaze over Ned's fat frame, perhaps a little too obviously because he hastily added, "Gotta drop a few pounds before I do, but it doesn't take me too long to get back in shape. I played ball in school."

"Really, what college?"

"I meant high school," Ned mumbled.

"Good for you."

"Hey, weren't you in here with the cops yesterday?"

"Yes, I was." Before he could ask whether she actually was a cop she said, "So do you have a theory on what happened?"

He nodded, leaned toward her, and said in a hushed tone, "Serial killer."

"Really? But wouldn't that involve more than one murder?"

"Hey, even Hannibal Lecter had to start somewhere."

"He was a fictional character. You know that, right?"

Ned nodded a little uncertainly. "Cool movie."

"So why a serial killer?"

"His M.O.," Ned said confidently.

"M.O.?"

"Modus operandi."

"Yeah, I know what the term means. I was referring to how you were using it in this situation."

"Stuffed his victims in a fridge, right? That's pretty original shit. I bet any day now we're gonna be reading about folks crammed in freezers, or meat lockers, or you know, like . . . um . . ."

"Other cold places?"

"Yeah."

"Maybe small people in under-the-counter fridges."

Ned laughed. "Like Popsicle Mini-Me's. Hey, maybe he'll call himself the Stone Cold Killer. Get it?"

"Yeah, that's real clever."

He leaned over the counter and assumed what he no doubt considered was an ultra-cool expression. "Hey, you ever go out for a drink?"

"Oh, lots of times. I'm one party girl."

"Well, maybe sometime we should do it together, party girl."

"Maybe we should."

He pointed a finger at her and pulled an imaginary trigger with his thumb and made a clicking sound with his mouth. At the same time he winked.

These were the moments when Mace so desperately missed her Glock 37 that chambered .45 G.A.P. "one-shot-and-you-drop" cartridges. The standard issue for MPD was the Glock 17 nine-millimeter, and undercover officers usually got the Glock 26 nine-millimeter, which regular officers routinely carried as their off-duty weapon of choice. Mace had dutifully carried the 17 as a cop, but her off-duty and undercover sidearm had been the 37, a gun she wasn't supposed to have. But she had never been that great at following rules, and the 37's superior .45 stopping power had saved her life on two occasions. Now, of course, she could carry no gun at all.

"Hey, Ned, piece of advice, when pointing even a pretend gun at someone, be prepared to duck or you might end up taking a double tap right here." She twice poked a spot dead center of his forehead.

He looked confused. "Huh?"

She merely winked and started to walk away.

"Hey, babe, I don't even know your name."

She turned back. "Mace."

"Mace?"

"Yeah, like the fire-hot spray in the eyes."

"You got my interest, babe."

"I knew I would."

CHAPTER

32

THE PLACE Beth had chosen for dinner was Café Milano, one of D.C.'s most chic restaurants, where folks loved to go see and be seen, in a Hollywood-esque sort of way. It had a wall of windows looking out onto a quiet street, although tonight there was a string of Carey cars and black government SUVs parked up and down its narrow confines.

The bar emptied out into the dining area so it was a little noisy, but Beth's high-ranking position garnered her a table in what was probably the quietest corner in the place. She had changed out of her uniform and was dressed in a knee-length skirt and a white blouse open at the neck, her blond hair splayed over her shoulders. Her work shoes had been replaced with black heels. The bulk of her security detail waited outside, although two armed plainclothes were at the bar enjoying multiple glasses of ginger ale.

Mace roared up in her Ducati, shook off her helmet, and slipped inside, dodging past a party of suited men and their rental dates, all of whom would have failed a breathalyzer test in any state in the country. Her cop's eyes watched them until they climbed into a white stretch Hummer driven by a sober driver in a black suit.

Mace scanned the room and saw her sister waving. She sat down and slid her bike helmet under the table. The tablecloth was white and starched, the aromas wafting from the kitchen pleasing, the crowd an interesting mix of young, middle-aged, and old, variously dressed in suits, jeans, sneakers, and spike heels.

"You clean up nice, sis," she said.

Beth smiled and gazed at Mace's clothes. Black slacks, low-cut gray clingy sweater, and high strap heels. "Did you do some shopping today?"

"Yep. Like you said, I've lost some weight."

"How were the stilettos on the Ducati's gear shifter?"

"No problem. I just skipped over the even ones."

The waiter came over and Beth ordered them two glasses of wine. After he left she said, "Since you're paying, and driving, let's go easy on the vino. And the list here can get pretty expensive."

"Sounds good. I guess you're not packing tonight."

"Not while drinking alcohol; that's still department policy."

"Is your off-duty carry still the .40 caliber or the Glock 26?"

"Twenty-six, same one I carry on duty."

"Must be nice."

"Nothing nice about having to carry a gun, Mace. It's a necessity in our line of work."

"In *your* line of work."

"Well, tonight, we're both out of bullets."

When the wine came they clinked glasses and Beth said, "Here's to many more decades of the Perry sisters hanging together."

Mace had regained her good humor. "Now that's something I can drink to."

Beth stared over her wineglass. "So your buddy Kingman found a key in a book that Tolliver sent him."

Mace munched on a hard olive roll and tried to look surprised. "Really? Key to what?"

"We don't know."

"Prints?"

"Yes."

"Tolliver's?"

"Yes again, how'd you know?"

"Assumed if she sent it, she had to touch it."

"Why did you go and see that sleazeball Binder today?"

Mace took a long slurp of wine before setting her glass down. "Are you having me followed, Beth?"

"I would not call it followed, no."

"Then what the hell would you call it?"

"I'm having you hovered."

"*Hovered*? Has the world changed so much in two years that I'm supposed to know what that means?"

"Beth!"

They both turned to see the mayor standing there, his entourage columned behind him. He was young and good-looking and had by most accounts done a good job for the city. Yet he was a cagey politician, meaning that the person he looked out for the most stared back at him in the mirror every morning.

"Hello, Mayor, you remember my sister?"

They shook hands. He leaned down and said in a low voice, "Good to see you. Let me know if I can be of any assistance. Right. Take care. Stay out of trouble."

This came out in such a blur of polished speech that Mace doubted the man had stopped for a breath or even heard what he'd actually said.

He stood straight. "Having a girls' night out, are we?"

"I guess we are," said Beth.

"Excellent. How we doing on the Tolliver case?"

"You getting calls?"

"I always get calls, I've just learned the ones to pay attention to."

"And these are such calls?"

"Just keep me in the loop."

"We're making progress. The minute I know more, so will you."

"Good, good."

"About that other case?"

"Right. Sorry about that. Above my pay grade." He turned and was gone as quickly as he'd appeared. His staff shuffled off behind their leader, each with a cell phone out, talking, no doubt, to suitably important people.

"That guy will be in office for life," said Mace.

"Long after I'm gone," replied Beth.

"So, getting back to *hover*."

Beth playfully crossed her eyes. "I thought this was a celebration."

"Fine, but I'm going to need another glass of wine. To celebrate being hovered."

"No, one is enough. And you're going to have plenty to eat and get some fresh air before you ride off on that bike."

"And here I was thinking Mom lived all the way out past Middleburg."

"Mace, please."

"I'm not going to embarrass you further."

"That's not what I meant. A DUI gets you sent back."

"Then let's order before I get totally wasted and you have to perform a field sobriety test right here on the table."

The food was excellent, the service attentive, the people coming up to greet the chief only a dozen or so in number and polite for the most part, except when they were either complaining or groveling.

"You're popular," remarked Mace. "Just think if you were in uniform."

"Maybe I'm too popular."

"What?"

"Don't look now, but here comes our favorite DA."

"Ah, hell, and I've only had one glass of wine and not a single controlled substance all day."

They both turned to watch Mona Danforth marching toward them.

CHAPTER

33

THE LADY was wearing a dress that looked like it cost more than Mace's Ducati. The makeup and hair were perfect, the jewelry tasteful but heavyweight enough to still retain the "wow" factor. The only thing marring the package was the woman's expression. For a beautiful woman Mona Danforth could look very ugly.

"Hello, Mona," said Beth pleasantly.

Mona snagged another chair from an adjacent table, unmindful of whether anyone was actually using it or not, and sat down. "We need to talk."

The statement was directed at Beth, but Mace answered first. "Really, Moan, you've learned to actually do that? Congratulations."

Mona didn't even bother to look at her. "This doesn't concern you."

Mace started to shoot something back, but Beth nudged her leg under the table. "I'm assuming this has something to do with Jamie Meldon's death?"

"Why else would I be sitting here?"

"You know, Mona, we are on the same team here. Police, prosecutor? Do you sense a pattern?"

"I heard you got bumped from the case."

"Didn't even have time to step on any shell casings. Go talk to the mayor. You just missed him. Or the CIA, I'm sure Langley would love to fill you in."

Mace, not knowing what they were talking about, merely hunkered down and listened attentively as she would at any contest where one of the players has the potential to go home all bloody.

"One of my people was murdered in *your* jurisdiction. And you're not going to do anything about it?"

"I didn't say I wasn't going to do anything. But while we're on the subject, what exactly do you want me to do?"

Mona looked incredulous. "You're asking me how to do your job?"

"I know you've just been dying to tell me all these years. So here's your chance. Fire away." Beth sat back and looked expectant.

"This is unbelievable. I'm not a cop."

"But you are the interim chief of the largest federal prosecutor's office in the country outside of DOJ. So if you don't have a suggestion on how to do my job, let me give you some help on how to do *yours*."

"Excuse me?" snapped Mona.

"You're pissed that the case was snagged from MPD? In any event, since Jamie was technically a federal employee his murder falls under the jurisdiction of the FBI. Normally we would support that effort, but for some reason we got a muzzle thrown on us. So here's what you can do. Go talk to your high-up contacts at Justice and find out why we were pulled from the case. Do the same at the legal counsel's office at the Bureau. From there it's a short hop to the intelligence community. It was intimated to me that it was the CIA who yanked the cord, but I don't believe everything I'm told. Maybe it was DHS. You know folks over there. In fact a photo of you and the DHS director was in the Style section of the *Post* just last week. Your dress and cleavage were stunning and his drool was unmistakable. I'm sure his wife really enjoyed seeing that. And when you have everything in a nice box with a big red bow, you bring it all to me and I'll run with it. How's that sound?"

"It sounds like I'm wasting my time."

"Do you want to find out who killed Meldon?"

"Don't be condescending!"

"Then work your contacts. And I'll work mine and maybe we'll meet in the middle. But keep in mind that you may run into a wall at some point. Or you may tick somebody off. And your career might take a hit."

Mona stood. "I'm not listening to any more of this garbage."

Beth continued unperturbed. "Your career might take a hit," she repeated firmly. "But I know that in the interest of bringing Jamie's killer to justice you wouldn't have any compunction about professional sacrifice, right?"

"Don't make an enemy of me over this, Beth."

"By the way, how's Jamie's family doing?"

"What?"

"His wife and kids? I visited them earlier today, to express my condolences and to see if they needed anything. I'm assuming you did that too, wonderful, compassionate leader that you are."

With what could only be termed a snarl, Mona stalked off.

Mace leaned across the table and gave her sister a kiss on the forehead. "I bow before your powers of transforming mere words into machine-gun rounds."

"It didn't really get me anywhere."

"But it was so fun to watch. So what's this about a dead DA?"

Beth filled her in on Meldon's homicide.

"So you don't know anything other than his body was in a Dumpster?"

"A bit more than that. Like I said, I talked to his wife. He'd been working late Sunday night. She was surprised when he wasn't home on Monday morning, but not overly concerned since he slept at the office sometimes. When she didn't hear from him by late morning she called the police. His body was finally found this afternoon."

"And the CIA is involved?"

"Actually, that's not substantiated yet. I was actually told that the pushback directive came from the White House."

"The White House! But you didn't tell Cruella de Vil that."

She smiled. "No, I didn't."

Beth finished her second glass of wine. "Would you like another round?"

"And risk a DUI and being sent to the big house?" Mace said with mock terror.

"You can ride with me. I'll have them load your bike in a pickup truck and bring it to the house."

"You mind if I take a rain check on that offer?"

"Plans later?"

"Maybe."

"Would those plans be Roy Kingman?"

"And is that a problem?"

"I already stated my opinion on that subject."

"I know." Mace rose from the table. "I paid the bill. I did it when I went to the ladies' room."

"You really didn't have to do that, Mace." Beth paused and added, "But it was very sweet."

"Hey, we need to do this more often. But maybe we can aim for fast food next time. Easier on the wallet. Prices have really gone up over the last two years."

Mace turned to leave, but Beth reached over and placed an iron grip on her sister's arm, pulling Mace abruptly back into her seat. In a low voice that still managed to conjure images of razor wire, Beth said, "The next time you remove evidence from a crime scene, I will personally pistol-whip you before I arrest you for obstruction, are we clear on that?" There was not a trace of mirth in the woman's eyes. This was Chief Elizabeth Perry talking now, not sweet sister Beth.

Mace just gaped at her, unable to form a response.

"My techs found minute traces of fluorescent dye on the key. I heard old Binder was running a special on his blue-light print kit this week. I think I might pay him a personal visit tomorrow and shut him down."

"Beth—"

"You went over the line. After I told you not to. I told you to let me handle it. Maybe you don't think I'm good enough to get this done."

"It wasn't that."

Beth squeezed her sister's arm. "You get arrested for interfering in a police investigation, you're going back to prison for a lot longer than two years. And then there will be no way you'll ever be a cop again. I don't care if the president of the United States has your back. Is that what you want?"

"No, of course not. But—"

"Then quit screwing up!" Beth leaned away from her and let go of the arm. "Now get out of here." As soon as Mace stood, Beth added, "Oh, and tell Kingman I said hello."

Mace nearly ran out the door.

CHAPTER

34

DRINKS ON the rooftop lounge of the Hotel Washington," said Mace as she and Roy sat at a table overlooking what was one of the nicest views of D.C.

"It's actually called the W Washington now," he said, as he freed three olives from a toothpick and dropped them one by one into his mouth and chewed slowly.

She pointed straight ahead. "Look, you can just make out the countersnipers on top of the White House." She looked at the street. "And there goes a cruiser on a call. Probably a lousy D&D at a bar."

"Could be a shooting."

"Gunshots get a minimum of two patrol units responding. We'd be hearing a lot more sirens. Probably burglar alarm D.C."

"Burglar alarm D.C.?"

"Burglar alarms go off, you respond, and you find out it's a malfunction. That's the principal action around here in 'safe' D.C. You want bullet banging or PCP zombie sprints, head to Sixth or Seventh district. They put on a great show there."

"You're a walking encyclopedia of local crime minutiae."

"That's *all* I am anymore," Mace said resignedly.

"Problems?"

"No, Roy, my life is five-star all the way."

"That didn't come out right."

"It never does with guys." She stood, leaned over the half-wall, and pointed to her left. "Right over there was the first bust I ever made on my own around here. I'd just been certified to ride alone.

Spotted a guy in a suit buying a bag of rock from a punk hucka-buck. Turns out he was a congressman high up on some anti-drug committee. What a shocker, right?"

As she turned back around, Roy quickly shifted his gaze away from her derriere. There was a tattoo of a cross partly visible where her sweater had ridden up, with the lower half of the cross well down on one butt cheek.

The tattoo artist must've had fun doing that one, thought Roy.

She sipped on her beer and munched some nuts. "So do you want to comment on my butt since you were staring at it for so long?"

Bumps of red appeared on each of Roy's cheeks. "Actually it left me pretty speechless."

"There was a prison guard who was really partial to it too."

He flicked a gaze at her. "Did he ever do anything to you?"

"Let's just say he kept his pants on and leave it at that."

"So you got a tattoo of a cross?"

"Don't all good Catholic girls have a cross on their backsides?"

"I don't know. I've never dated a Catholic girl. My loss, I guess."

"Yes, it is."

"You know, I thought about joining the police academy after college."

"Drive fast and shoot guns?"

He grinned. "How'd you know?"

"Way it is with most guys. There were forty-one recruits in my class. Sixteen-week course. Half washed out before the end. Ex-athletes with beer bellies couldn't even do a push-up. Academy was okay. Learned the phone book, spit and polish, a few training scenarios, but not much about actually being a cop."

"Phone book?"

"Policies and procedures, general orders. Paperwork basically. Plus physical training. Near the end they put me on a Christmas detail in Georgetown by myself with no gun and no orders."

"What'd you do?"

"Wandered around, wrote some parking tickets, and smoked some cigarettes."

"Law school was boring too."

"I started out on the north end of Georgia Avenue. They called it the Gold Coast, because it was relatively safe."

"And?"

"And I hated it. Didn't put on the shield and gun to be safe. I wanted to get into Crime Patrol. They hit the whole city, not some lousy five-block radius. They went after the good stuff."

"Not drug dealers then?"

"Lock up druggies you're just padding crime stats. CP went after the burglars, the armed robbers, the murderers, and the drug dealers turned exterminators. That was where the action was." She paused. "Now I'm on probation and working for a college professor. And I can't even dream about holding my Glock 37 again without heading back to lockup. Whoop-de-do."

"I know we don't know each other that well, but if you ever want to talk about things, Mace, I'm here."

"I'm more of a forward thinker." She stood. "Ladies' room," she said. "Be back in a minute."

After doing her business Mace came out of the stall, went to the sink, and splashed water on her face. As she stared in the mirror Beth's words came at her like hollow-points.

Quit screwing up. Trust me.

Mace didn't want to screw up. She *did* trust her sister. She sure as hell didn't want to go back to prison. Agent Kelly's words also came back to her, though.

She groaned. This was a total mental conflict. Her head felt ready to explode from the pressure.

At least you'll have a shot.

She splashed more water on her face and looked at herself in the mirror again.

"Scrub as hard as you want, the scum won't come off."

Mace whirled around to see Mona Danforth standing by the door.

ARE YOU following me?" Mace snapped at D.C.'s chief prosecutor.

In response, Mona locked the door to the ladies' room.

"If you don't open that door I will use your head to crack it open."

"Threatening an officer of the court?"

"Engaging in unlawful detainment?" Mace shot back.

"Just thought I'd do you a little favor."

"Great. You can slit your wrists in the stall over there. I'll call the EMTs once you've fully bled out."

"I know all about Beth's little plan."

"Really? What little plan might that be?"

Mona snapped open her tiny purse, sauntered over to the mirror, and reapplied her makeup and lipstick while she spoke. Mace so wanted to stuff her in a toilet, blond hair first.

"Why, getting you reinstated, of course. You were set up, drugged up, forced to commit all those crimes, blah blah blah. Poor little Mace. The same crap the jury refused to believe." Mona closed her purse, turned and leaned her butt against the sink counter. "So Beth is sending her best detectives to work on the case in the hopes that some miracle will occur that will prove your innocence."

"I *am* innocent."

"Oh, please. Save it for someone who cares. But it won't work because I'm way ahead of her. In fact, I'm so far ahead of her that I don't mind telling you all about it. Then you can go running to Beth and tell her like you always do when you're in trouble."

Mace tried her best to keep her voice calm. "Tell her what exactly?"

Mona eyed her with clear contempt. "There are six people who would need to sign off on your reinstatement even if Beth finds some evidence of your innocence."

"And if she does I would assume these people would sign."

"It's not that simple. Slam-dunk evidence is never going to happen. If she finds an eyewitness I'll convince them the testimony was coerced by an overzealous police chief who will stop at nothing to see her beloved little sister exonerated. And anything else she brings to the table I'll show it was tainted or even fabricated for the exact same reason. And since I'm not a believer in letting the other side hit first, I've already spoken with all of the necessary signatories, including the dear mayor, who had me over for dinner last week, and laid the groundwork for the overwhelming validity of my argument."

"They'll never believe Beth would invent evidence. That's *your* M.O., not hers."

Mona flushed for an instant at this jab but then regained her composure. "They've come to understand, after much coaching by me, that the usually rock-solid Beth Perry is incapable of thinking clearly when it comes to *you*. She will do anything, even break the law, to help you, though you don't deserve it. I have to admit, Beth has some talent. You, on the other hand, are worthless."

"I'm done listening to this crap." Mace started to move past Mona. The attorney made the mistake of putting a hand on Mace's shoulder to stop her. The next second, Mona's arm was twisted behind her back and Mace had pulled the woman right out of her three-inch heels and pushed her face first against the tiled wall of the restroom, the DA's lipstick smearing it.

"Don't ever lay a hand on me again, Mona."

"Let go of me, you bitch," shrieked Mona as she struggled to free herself, but Mace was far stronger. With one more twist of the arm Mace let her go and headed to the door. A furious Mona straightened her dress and bent down to put her heels back on. "I can have you arrested for assault. You'd go back to prison, where you belong."

"Go ahead and try. Your word against mine. And then the public can get into the debate of why you followed me into the ladies' room and locked the door. Hell, *I* was the one in prison, Mona, don't tell me you're liking the girls now."

"Actually, I prefer to let things just play out. It'll be more fun."

Mace stopped with her hand on the doorknob. "What's that supposed to mean?"

"I can bag two Perrys for the price of one. Beth tries to get you reinstated. I show she crossed the line. She gets dumped from her job and you never wear the uniform again. It's the Christmas that keeps on giving."

Mace slammed the door behind her.

36

WHEN MACE returned to the table Roy obviously sensed something was wrong. "You okay?"

"Yeah, there was just something really disgusting in the ladies' room."

As she finished her Coke in one gulp Roy said, "The cops came and got the key."

"Yeah, I know. Messed up there."

"I did?"

"No, *I* did. I forgot how smart my sister is."

"She knew you'd taken the key?"

Mace nodded. "And if it happens again my butt will be right back in prison."

"Your sister is not going to arrest you."

"You don't know Beth then."

"Mace—"

"Drop it, Roy!"

"Okay." He fiddled with his drink. "I've been thinking about Abe Altman."

Mace said absently, "What about him? Want to renegotiate my deal?"

"I was thinking that there is no way he got a research grant that would pay an assistant six figures."

Now Mace looked curious. "I was wondering that too. What do you think?"

"That he's not taking a salary and he's giving those dollars to you. I mean, it's not like he needs the cash."

"Still nice of him, though," she pointed out.

"Well, it sounds like he wouldn't be here except for you."

"He was exaggerating."

"Why do I think that's bullshit?"

Mace shrugged. "Think what you want."

"I heard a snippet on the news that a DA was found murdered."

"Jamie Meldon. Did you know him?"

"No, you?"

She shook her head.

"I guess your sister has her hands full. That's a high-profile case."

"Actually, she's not working it."

"Why not? He was found in D.C."

"Above everybody's pay grades, apparently."

Mace sat there staring off, mulling Mona's words. She finally looked over at Roy. "Did you have time to do any snooping around your firm?"

"I did."

"And?"

"Ackerman's office was clean. In fact, I'm not sure the guy does anything."

"What do you reckon he makes for doing nothing?"

"Seven figures, easy."

"I hate lawyers."

"But he's a rainmaker. The biggest in the firm. He brings major deals in like clockwork. The worker bees like me get paid well. But the rainmakers get the gold."

"Good for him. What else?"

Roy brought her up to speed on the rest of what he learned, including his inspection of the fourth-floor construction site and his conversation with the construction supervisor and later discussion with the building's day porter.

Mace jumped to her feet. "Why the hell didn't you tell me that before?"

"Tell you what before? I just talked to the guy this afternoon."

"That was the day porter. You said you talked to the supervisor a lot earlier."

"Okay, so?"

Mace dropped some cash on the table for the drinks.

"Where are you going?"

"*We're* going to your office building. Right now."

He stood and grabbed his windbreaker. "My office? Why?"

"Not your office, your office *building*, and hopefully you'll get to see why."

"You want to follow me on your bike?"

"No, I need to hide in the floorboard of your car."

"What? Why?"

"Because I'm apparently being hovered!"

37

THEY RODE up in the elevator to the front lobby from the garage.

"What exactly are we looking for here?" he asked as he followed Mace across the lobby to the office elevators.

"A case I worked about five years ago."

God, if it could only be. Nail the bastard. Get back on the force. To hell with Mona. And they couldn't touch Beth. It would be all me.

"What?"

"Just hang tight. I don't like questions while I'm on the hunt." She slipped her hand into her jacket pocket.

"Are you carrying a gun?"

"No, but a girl can protect herself, right?"

They got in the elevator. When Roy moved to hit the floor button for Shilling & Murdoch, Mace grabbed his arm.

"I said office *building*. We might do your office later."

"Do what in it?"

"You're a real funny guy, Roy."

She pushed the button for the third floor. Moments later they both peered out into the semi-darkened space.

"Now what?" Roy said in a confused voice. "Do we push all the floor buttons and then go running from the building laughing hysterically and look for a car to teepee?"

"Which way are the fire exit stairs?"

He led her down the hall past darkened offices and pointed to a door near the end of the corridor. Mace yanked it open with Roy right behind. She pointed to a door set into the wall by the fire exit door. She opened it. It was a broom closet.

"Are there more of these?"

"There's one on the first floor too."

"Boy, this place has great security," Mace said. "You arm the front doors, hire a security guard, albeit a loser one, and then secure the office elevators and the office suites and you don't secure the garage elevators? And then you have a perfect hiding place for some scumball right in the building?"

"The original building developer declared bankruptcy and the people who took it over finished construction on the cheap, and that didn't include secure garage elevators. No one wanted to pay for a retrofit."

"Well, I bet they will now. Okay, even if you come in through the garage you have to pass by the security desk to get to the fire exit stairs. You said the construction crew checks out at five-thirty and they don't work weekends. Ned comes on at six and exits at six. Exterior doors, office elevator, and your office suite all go secure at eight p.m. and go off at eight a.m. That leaves a huge window."

"Window for what?"

"Oh come on. Did you hit your head on the basketball rim one too many times?"

They continued up the stairs and the next door she opened was to the fourth floor. It revealed almost total darkness. Mace scooted forward and crouched down behind some building materials. Roy knelt next to her. "What are we looking for?" he whispered.

"Know it when I see it."

They crept forward with Mace in the lead. Roy noted that she moved like a cat, no noise, no unnecessary movement. He tried as best he could to mimic her. He did find that his hands were growing sweaty, and his pulse banged in his eardrums.

A minute later she stopped and pointed. Roy saw the dim wash of light coming from a far corner of the space where it wouldn't be directly seen from the windows.

Mace reached in her pocket and pulled something out. Roy couldn't see exactly what it was.

"Now what?" he murmured.

"You stay here. If somebody other than me comes flying past, trip them and then bash them on the head with like a two-by-four or something."

"Bash them on the head? That's a felony assault. And what if he has a gun?"

"Okay, sissy boy, let him kill you and then your survivors can file a civil suit against the bastard for wrongful death. I'll leave it up to you."

She headed on while he took cover behind a large toolbox on wheels. He looked around the floor and picked up a block of wood. His fingers gripped the chunk tightly and he mumbled a prayer that no one would come running by.

And I am not *a sissy boy.*

Two minutes went by. And then the silence ended.

He heard a yell, and then a sound like a long hiss. A scream and a heavy thud caused him to leap up and sprint forward. He tripped over a pile of ceiling panels, tumbled forward, landed on his back, slid a couple feet on the smooth concrete, and came to a stop next to a pair of strappy high heels.

Groaning and rubbing his head, he stared up. The light hit him in the eyes. He put up a hand to deflect the glare.

"What the hell are you doing down there, Roy?" asked Mace, who was holding a work light in a cage that she'd snagged off the floor.

"Coming to save you," he admitted sheepishly.

"Gee, that was sweet. I'll just take it as dumb luck that I didn't actually need you to save me, since we'd both be like dead if I had."

She helped him up.

"I heard a scream and a thud. What's going on?"

She pointed her light downward again. Roy's gaze followed the shaft of illumination. The Captain was lying on the concrete, his big body still shaking.

"What the hell did you do to him?"

"Zap knuckles."

"What?"

She held up a pair of black-coated brass knuckles. "Nearly a million-volt pop. He'll be okay. But right now his nickname is Twitchy."

He pointed to the knuckles. "Aren't those illegal?"

Mace copped an innocent look. "Why, Roy, I don't think so. But just in case they are, don't mention them to anyone."

"You know I am a lawyer and thus an officer of the court."

"But there is such a thing as attorney-client confidentiality."

"I'm not your lawyer."

She slipped a buck from her pocket, slapped it in his hand, and then jabbed him in the side with her elbow. "You are now."

"Why'd you zap the Captain?"

"Twitchy is the Captain? You know him?"

"Yeah, ex-vet who's now homeless."

She ran the light over the Captain's rags and filthy face. "I zapped him because he's a big guy, and I'm just a helpless girl."

"You're not helpless and I'm not even convinced you're a girl." He looked around. "So the Captain must've been the one stealing food and tools."

"Maybe more than that, Roy. Maybe a lot more than that."

"What do you mean?"

"How about killing female law partners?"

"The Captain? No, that's nuts. He wouldn't."

"How do you know him?"

"This is sort of his turf around here. I give him stuff. Money. Food."

"And shoes." Mace pointed her light at the Captain's feet. "I remember seeing those in your car."

"The poor guy was wearing cardboard for his shoes."

"So you only know him from the streets?"

Roy hesitated. "Well, not just from the streets."

"How else?"

"Does it matter?"

"It all matters, Roy."

"I defended him once."

"From what?"

"Assault charge. But that was three years ago."

"Yeah, and I can see that things have really looked up for him since then."

"I'm sure he came here just for food and to get off the streets. It's dangerous out there at night."

"Apparently it's dangerous in here too."

"He couldn't have killed Diane."

"Sure he could."

"How?"

"On Friday he snuck in through the garage after the hammer and nail crew left. A guy like him coming in the front door would have aroused too much attention. Old Ned was probably in the back hooked to a milkshake IV or else he waited until he was gone too. He times his movement across the lobby and hits the stairs. He hides out in that oh-so-convenient broom closet until your friend the day porter does his thing and leaves. Then, when things quiet down, he goes to the fourth floor, which he has direct access to from the fire stairs, and beds down for the night. On Monday he either pops awake when he hears the elevator coming up early in the morning or else he's already up because he knows he has to get back out before people start coming in. He hits the button over there to make the car stop on this floor. The doors open. Tolliver can't see him, but he can see her, a lone female trapped in a metal box, easy pickings. He grabs her and that's it."

"But if he knew Ned comes in at six why wouldn't he have already been gone?"

"You think it's all that difficult to slip past Ned?"

"Or maybe he doesn't have a watch."

She knelt down and lifted up the Captain's left sleeve, revealing a watch. She hit it with the light. "And it's got the right time."

"You said something about a case you worked?"

"Same M.O. Bandit hid in buildings where construction was going on. He'd hit the elevator button when he heard the car coming up or down late at night. If the doors opened and it was a chick all by herself, he'd pounce."

"Ever catch the guy?"

"Did better than that. I went in as bait. He tried to grab me and I shot him right in his most private of areas. The guy had butchered three women. So it was a real pleasure to put him out of commission permanently."

"Okay, but the Captain—"

"Look, the *Captain* maybe only plans to rob her, but things get carried away. I see two Purples and a Combat Bronze on his jacket. What branch was he in?"

"How'd you know it was a Bronze Star for combat?"

"Because of the Valor Device worn with the medal." She pointed to a small V on the Captain's chest above the Bronze Star. "That's only for combat heroism."

"I knew that because my brother is a Marine, but how do you know?"

"I've done my patriotic duty and dated guys from every uniformed branch. They liked to show me their medals. Plus my dad had one from Vietnam. So which branch?"

"Army Ranger."

"So he's both huge and strong and really skilled at killing people." She glanced down at the big man and then over at Roy. "The Captain have a real name?"

"Lou Dockery. I still don't believe he killed Diane."

"Spoken like a true defense attorney. But it's not up to you. In fact, you have to call the cops right now."

"Me?"

"Officially, I'm not here. My sister gave you a number to call. Dockery will be in la-la land for another twenty minutes or so. I suggest you make that call, right now."

Roy looked panicked. "What the hell do I tell her?"

"The truth, but leave the part about me out. Hang on a sec." She picked up a piece of wood and used a small knife to cut her hand, drawing a bit of blood that she smeared on the wood.

Roy looked stunned. "What the hell did you do that for?"

"Because I know my sister. And hang on to the chunk of wood."

"Why?"

"Again, because I know my sister. Now give me your key card."

"Why?"

"I want to have a look-see through old Shilling and Murdoch."

"You're not serious?"

She brandished her zap knuckles. "A million volts' worth of serious."

38

Aᴛᴇʀ ʟᴇᴀᴠɪɴɢ Café Milano, Beth had returned to her office to go over some files and respond to some e-mails. She was on her way home when she got the call from Roy. She ordered in the Mobiles and her caravan turned around in mid-street and galloped to G-town. Roy met them at the front doors and let them in.

"Nice uniform," said Roy as Beth walked in dressed in her Café Milano duds. "Hope I didn't interrupt anything fun."

Beth didn't bite. "Where the hell is Mace?"

Roy's smile disappeared. "I don't know."

Since Beth was wearing two-inch heels she was nearly eyeball to eyeball with the tall Roy. "You want to try that answer again?"

"We hooked up and then we parted company. And I came back here."

"Why?"

"I haven't gotten a lot of work done lately, for obvious reasons. Just trying to catch up. And I was going to make some phone calls."

"At this hour?"

"To Dubai. It's the next day there."

"Thanks for the geography lesson. Where is he?"

"Fourth floor."

He led them to the stairs.

"Why not the elevator?" asked Beth.

Because your little sister has my key card, thought Roy. But he said, "The elevators were acting a little funny when I came down. I don't want to get stuck in one."

They trooped up the steps, two armed plainclothes and a uniform in the lead. Other cruisers and unmarked cars were pulling up out front and a perimeter was being set.

"How did you go from working late to ending up on the construction floor in a confrontation?" Beth asked.

"Heard something."

"From the sixth floor!"

"I meant I heard something on the elevator ride up. Didn't think too much of it, but then I remembered the day porter telling me about stuff going missing from the construction site so I decided to check it out."

"You should've called the police right way. You're lucky you're not dead."

"I guess you're right."

They reached the fourth floor and the lawmen pulled their guns and lights and followed Roy's directions. They found the Captain still on the floor, only he wasn't twitching. He seemed to be asleep.

They gave the okay and Beth and Roy came forward.

She looked at the man on the floor.

"He's a big, tough-looking guy. Ex-military if the jacket and medals are real. How'd you subdue him?" She turned and looked at Roy intently.

Roy bent down and picked up the piece of wood that Mace had given to him. "I used this. You can see the blood on it."

"You whacked him with this? Did he attack you?"

"No, but I was afraid he might. It all happened so fast," he added.

Beth turned to her men. "Get Sleeping Beauty out of here." She glanced at Roy. "I think we can chance the elevator. I need your key card to access it."

Roy patted his pockets and checked his windbreaker. "Damn, I must've left it in my office. Now I can't get back in. I'm sorry, you'll have to use the stairs."

Several more uniforms had joined them and it took all of their combined strength to get the bulky Captain down to the lobby.

Beth said, "I want you to run through everything from the top."

"Okay, hey, you want to go get a drink while we do it?"

"No, Mr. Kingman, I don't want to go get a drink. I want the truth."

"I'm telling you the truth, Chief."

"From the top, then, and don't leave anything out, slick. I'm this close to busting your ass on obstruction, tampering, lying to the police, and for just being *stupid*."

Roy said wearily, "Are you sure you and your sister aren't twins?"

"Excuse me?"

"Never mind." He drew a resigned breath and started talking.

CHAPTER

39

MACE DUCKED through the yellow police tape blocking the kitchen and Tolliver's office and searched each place quickly and efficiently.

After finding nothing she had stared at the inside of the refrigerator for some time. Roy had told her that Diane Tolliver was nearly five-eight, about one-forty. Dead bodies were unwieldy things, she knew, having been around more than her fair share. Whoever killed her had to have really wedged the woman in, or else the body could have easily slumped against the door and pushed it open.

She went over the timeline again that her sister had told her and Roy had supplemented. Because Tolliver had had to use her key card that morning they had a pretty detailed understanding of her movements. The garage entry showed Tolliver had checked in at six. Ned had heard her voice in the lobby a minute or so later. She'd swiped her card in the elevator and entered the premises of Shilling & Murdoch ninety seconds after that. Roy had arrived at the office at seven-thirty and found her at a bit past eight. Mace didn't believe that Tolliver had been alive when Roy got to the office, so she was looking at about ninety minutes for the murder to have occurred and the lady to get stuffed in the icebox.

Tolliver had e-mailed Roy late Friday night. She also had sent him a book with a key in it, probably on the same day. An ex–Army Ranger had been hiding out on the fourth floor and right now was probably the prime suspect. Mace looked at her watch. Gazing out Roy's office window she'd seen the patrol cars pull up to the building. She figured Dockery was already under arrest, and they'd take a DNA sample from him. If it matched, he was done. Neat, tied together. And then Mace could tell Beth the truth of her figuring it out, nailing the guy, and possibly get her old job back.

So what was bothering her?

She trudged back to Roy's office so she could see when they brought Dockery out. Like Roy had said, he had a dead-on view of the front of the building.

She pulled something from her pocket. It was a copy of the key that Tolliver had left in the book for Roy. Mace had had a "friend" make the copy for her after she'd left Binder's goodie shop, with the warning that if he messed up the prints on the original key, she would Taser him until his brain started smoking. That actually would pale in comparison to what Beth would do to her if she found out about the key copy.

She thought of the e-mail Tolliver had sent Roy. *We need to focus in on A.* And the *A* was followed by a hyphen. A seemingly trivial detail, but she knew the seemingly unimportant usually became critical in a criminal investigation. She came by her investigative instincts honestly. Her father had been so good at observing and deducing things that the FBI had asked him to teach a course on fieldwork for them at the academy, a tradition that Beth had carried on.

Roy was right, though. It was awkwardly phrased.

We need to focus in on.

She looked down at the key in her hand. Why not just say, *We need to key on A-?*

"We need to key on A-," she said out loud, hoping something would click in her head. Just a coincidence? Key and key? Key on a key?

She sighed and looked out Roy's office window. Marked and unmarked cars were slung around the front with uniforms and plainclothes standing around, probably wondering when they could either go back on patrol or return to their hoodles and wait for their radios to bark.

No one was coming out of the building yet, so Mace sighed and lifted her gaze from the front entrance to the building across from where she was.

When she saw the neon, at first she couldn't believe it.

"Damn!"

She looked down at her key and back at the flashing sign. How in the hell had she missed it? It was purple! But then again she'd never looked out this window at night. But still. Some detective she was.

She snatched the phone from her pocket and fired off a text to Roy.

Come on, Roy, we need to talk like right now.

CHAPTER

40

Roy snatched a peek at his phone after it started to vibrate in his pants pocket. This did not escape the attention of Beth, who was standing near him.

He looked up from the screen and found her gaze on him.

"Dubai calling?" she said coolly.

"No, just a bud in town."

"Bud's up late."

"We're both night owls."

"Good for you," she said, her tone of skepticism delivered like a cannon shot.

"Are we done here, Chief?"

"For now. But next time you hear strange sounds, call the police."

"You have my word."

"It's a good thing you don't do trial work anymore."

"Why's that?"

"Because your bullshitting skills aren't that good."

She turned and marched out of the building while Roy sprinted for the stairs.

Mace was waiting at the front doors to the law firm.

"What the hell is it?" he said as she grabbed his arm and pulled him into the suite. "Your sister was still with me when you sent the text."

"Come on."

They hustled to Roy's office.

Mace went to the window, Roy beside her. She pointed out. "Tell me what you see."

He scanned the darkness. "Buildings. The street. A pissed-off police chief."

"Think Viagra."

"What?"

"Purple!"

He saw the large purple neon sign over the door of a ground-floor shop in the building directly across from his. "A-1 Mailboxes! That's what the key's for?"

"That's right, genius. Focus in on? Try *key* on A-1. Right across the stupid courtyard."

"She must've figured it was outside my window and the e-mail she sent would be enough for me to figure it out." He looked chagrined. "I've been looking out this stupid window all day. But *you* figured it out."

"Don't feel too bad. If I hadn't looked out the window to see if my big sister was scaling the building like King Kong to grab my butt I never would've seen it."

"But now we can't do anything. The police have the key."

"Roy, Roy, I'm disappointed." She held up her key.

"You made a copy?"

"Of course I made a copy."

"Mace, that's evidence tampering. That's illegal."

"Now do you understand why I put you on retainer? So you can't squeal on me."

"I could lose my license over this!"

"Yeah, but you probably won't."

"Probably again? I don't like those odds."

"Fine, you can sit this one out. I'll check out the mailbox tomorrow."

"But you don't know which mailbox was hers."

"Roy, again, I'm very disappointed in you."

"You have a way to find that out?"

"There's always a way."

"Just so you know, your sister clearly didn't buy my cover story."

"Of course she didn't. Contrary to popular belief, one does not get to be police chief of a major city by being either stupid or gullible."

"Mace, what if she finds out you're investigating this thing on your own?"

"Well, there's always suicide."

"I'm being serious."

"Look, I know it's risky and stupid, but I've got my reasons."

"What are they?"

"Let's just say I had a revelation while taking a pee in the ladies' room. Now give me a ride back to the hotel. I need to pick up my bike."

"Okay, I need some shuteye too."

"I didn't say I was going to bed."

"What are you going to do?"

"Until we can check out the mailbox I need something else to occupy my mind. So I'm going to see some old friends."

"At this hour?"

"They do their best work in the dark."

He stared at her for a long moment. "You're not a cop anymore, Mace. You don't have the shield to back you up. These gangs are dangerous."

"As you should have realized by now, I can take care of myself."

"I'll go with you then."

"No. Me they'll tolerate. You, they'll kill, okay?"

"Don't do this. It's nuts."

"No, this is my world."

41

Mace slowed her ride and then stopped. She'd changed in the hotel bathroom, trading in her Café Milano outfit and strappy heels for worn jeans, leather jacket, and her favorite pair of ass-stomping boots that an FBI Hostage Rescue Team assaulter with a crush on her had had made especially for her. She'd bolted through a series of main roads, back streets, and several alleys that she knew all too well. If anyone still had been tailing her, she was pretty sure that they no longer were. She waited three minutes and then reversed her route just to make certain. Nothing. She smiled.

Hoverees, one, Hoverers, zip.

Mace lifted her visor and did a quick recon. The part of D.C. she was in right now, within smelling distance of the Anacostia River, was not listed on any official map of the area for the simple reason that robbed, assaulted, or murdered out-of-towners were never good publicity for the tourism industry. Even with the new ballpark and attempts at gentrification in nearby areas, there were sections of turf here that even some of the blue tended to avoid if they could. After all, they wanted to go home to their families at the end of the day too.

Mace hit the throttle and moved on. She knew there were eyes everywhere, and she was also listening for the sounds of "whoop-whoop" or collective cries of "Five-O." This was the way the folks around here let it be known that blues were in town. The bandits' network even knew which fleet the MPD used for unmarked cars. Since the fleet purchases were large, the police force had to keep them for about three years. Before Mace had gone to prison, the array of unmarked cars had all been blue Chevy Luminas. Every night she'd heard the whoop-whoops as soon as she pulled down the street in her glow-blue ride. She'd gotten so ticked off she'd started renting cars with her own cash.

In one ear she had a bud connected to a police radio she wore on her belt. She was scanning calls to see where the action was. So far it was a quiet night, at least by D.C. standards. She figured she might find some useful intel at a hoodle.

Along the way she passed a bunch of hoopties, old junked cars lining the street. Many of them, she knew from experience, were probably stolen, used for a crime, and then dumped here. Yet enclosed spaces were popular around here for multiple reasons, so from habit, Mace peered in a few as she passed by. One was empty, one had a syringe shooter getting happy juice up his arm, and the last one was a fornication feature starring two girls and one very drunk guy who she knew would wake up in about an hour with his wallet gone.

Mace pulled slowly into a church parking lot and spotted a trio of cruisers parked side by side hood to trunk. This was a hoodle, the place where cops who'd made their rounds went until the dispatcher's squawk over the radio brought them back to fighting crime. She knew better than to zoom into this little circled wagon train. You didn't want to get drawn down on because you interrupted the rest of a stressed-out patrol officer. She stopped her bike well in front of one of the cruisers facing her, took off her helmet, and waved. Chances were good that she knew at least one of the blues in these rides, and her hunch was proven correct when one of the cop cars blinked its lights at her.

She slipped off her Ducati and walked over. The driver of the first cruiser slid down his window and the man leaned out his head.

He said, "Damn, Mace, heard you got your ass lifted out of West Virginia. Good to see you, girl."

Mace leaned down and rested her elbows on the ledge of the open window. "Hey, Tony, how's hoodle time?"

Tony was in his mid-forties with a thick neck, burly shoulders, and forearms the size of Mace's thighs, all the result of serious gym time. He'd been a good friend to Mace and had provided her with flawless backup on more than one occasion when she'd been with Major Narcotics. Next to him was a Panasonic Toughbook laptop that was about as important to a cop as a gun—although the most important piece of equipment any cop carried was his radio. That was his lifeline to call in help when needed.

Tony flashed a smile. "Quiet tonight. Not so quiet last night. Did the circuit, been here twenty minutes, listening to some tunes." He looked over at the young female cop next to him. "Francie, this is Mace Perry."

Francie, who had short strawberry red hair and braces and looked like she was about fifteen, smiled at Mace. Yet she had a blocky build with buffed shoulders that told you not to mess with her. Both officers wore gloves thick enough that a syringe couldn't penetrate easily. The last thing you wanted was to stick your hand under the front seat of a car you were doing a stop-and-search on and pull it back out with a needle sticking in it. Mace had known one beat cop who'd become HIV-infected that way.

"Hey, Francie, how long you been riding with this big old bear?"

"Six weeks."

"So he's your training officer?"

"Yep."

"You could do a lot worse."

Tony said, "Throwing arrests her way left and right. Getting in her courtroom OT. Being a real gentleman and teacher."

Mace smacked him playfully on the arm. "Hell, you just don't want to do the paperwork."

"Now don't go disillusioning the girl."

"Sometimes I still miss roll call."

Tony cracked a grin. "You're crazy, Mace. Same old, same old. Just doling out bodies and wheels and running around trying to find some damn car keys."

"Beats staring at a wall for two years."

Tony stopped smiling. "I bet it does, Mace, I bet it does."

"Same old same old bandits around here too?"

"Except the ones who're dead."

Mace glanced at the other cruisers. "Anybody I know?"

"Don't think so. They send folks all over the place now."

"So remind me how big your kids are?"

"One in college, two in high school and eating me out of house and home. Even when I pull my full twenty-five and get pensioned out, gonna have to get another job."

"Go into consulting. Doesn't matter what, it pays a lot better."

"So why don't you tell me what the hell you're doing out here at two a.m. on your fancy bike with no gun."

"How do you know I'm not packing?"

"Can you say probation violation?"

Mace grinned at Francie. "You see why he's such a good T.O. Nothing gets by this guy. He looks like a musclehead but the dude's got brains."

"Seriously, Mace, why here?"

"Nostalgia."

Tony laughed. "Go look in a photo album if you want that. Streets ain't never fair, especially around here." He turned serious. "You know that better than anybody."

"You're right, I do. Only they never found out who ripped me. That's not right."

"I know."

"So how many blues think I'm dirty?"

"Honestly?"

"Only way that matters to me."

Seventy-thirty on your side."

"I guess it could be worse."

"Hell yes it could be, considering who you share DNA with."

"Beth is a cop's cop. She came up right from the pavement, just like I did."

"But she's also a gal and you know some still don't like that."

"Well, hang in there, Tony, four more years."

"I'm counting, baby, every damn day."

She looked over at Francie. "And if Tony does pull his gun, just remember to duck. The son of a bitch never could shoot straight."

CHAPTER

42

MACE RODE ON, venturing ever more deeply into an area that she, even with all her risk-perverse ways, shouldn't have gone near without a weapon and a two-cruiser backup. Yet she knew exactly where she was headed. She had to see it; she wasn't exactly sure why, only that she had to. It might have been what Mona had revealed in the bathroom. Mace could accept going down and maybe going back to prison, but what she could not accept was taking Beth with her.

She slowed her bike, very aware of silhouettes on the streets, pairs of eyes at curtained windows, heads eased against tinted car windows, all wondering what she was doing in this area at this hour. The human ecosystem here was both fragile and extraordinarily resilient, and also one that most citizens would never experience. Yet it had fascinated Mace for most of her life. The line between cop and bandit here, she knew, was both as thin and as thick as it could get. No layperson would understand what she meant by that, but any cop instantly would.

She looked up. It was straight ahead. Lodged in the middle of Six D like a glioblastoma among more ordinary tumors. It was an abandoned apartment building that had seen more drugs, death, and perversity than possibly any single building in the city. The cops had hit it time and again, but the bandits always returned, like an anthill after a blast of Diazinon granules. On the roof of this place she'd had her O.P., or observation post, set up, principally because no bandit would ever believe that a cop could infiltrate it. It had taken Mace a month of undercover work to wedge her way into this world, her camera and scopes hidden in her bulky clothing while she bought and sold drugs and fended off the sexual thrusts of an array of predators with her Glock 37 and a fast mouth. That was one of the good things about undercover work in that place. Not having a gun would have seemed suspicious, since everyone else was packing.

The roof had a dead-on view of a drug dropoff used by a trio of Latino brothers who had run one of the most violent gangs in D.C. Mace had been in Major Narcotics at the time, but she was looking for far more than just another drug bust. These guys were suspected in more than a dozen murders. Mace was taking pictures and members of her joint task force were tapping their cell phone conversations in hopes of taking the Lats down for life.

Nothing much had changed about the place. It was still a dump, still mostly abandoned, but no longer a beehive of criminal activity since Beth had placed a police satellite station on the first floor of the building. Two of the Lats had moved to the Houston area, or so she'd heard through the prison grapevine. The third brother had been found in Rock Creek Park, more skeleton than corpse. Word was his older brothers had found him skimming profits off their rock bag trade. Apparently, tough love started at home for those boys. Mace was convinced that the brothers had discovered her undercover surveillance either through the streets, dumb luck, or a mole at MPD and then exacted their revenge.

Why couldn't you have just put a round in my head? Quicker, less painful.

It occurred to Mace now, more vividly than it ever had during her two years in prison, that the bastards who set her up were probably going to get away with it. While lying on that metal bed she'd constructed all these elaborate plans about how she would follow up the most insignificant clue, spend every waking moment on the case, until she got them. And then she would march triumphant to the police station with her captured bandits and all would be right with the world.

Perched on her Ducati, she shook her head in bewilderment. *Did I really believe that?*

Thirty percent of the D.C. blues thought she was guilty. That represented twelve hundred cops. Thirty sounded a lot better than twelve hundred. Mace knew she shouldn't care, that it really didn't matter, but it did matter to her. She eyed the alley where she'd stepped out late at night after staring through a telephoto lens for hours and her life had changed forever. The soaked rag over her mouth that turned her brain to jelly. The strong arms pinning hers to her sides. The squeal of wheels, the fast ride to hell. The needle sticks, the nose snorts, the liquid poured down her throat. The retching, the sobbing, the moaning, the cursing. But mostly the sobbing. They'd broken her. It had taken a lot, but they'd won.

If I catch you, I will kill you. But it doesn't look like I will. And where exactly does that leave me? Hoping a homeless vet goes down for murder so I can say I caught him and get my stripes back?

And what about the key and the e-mail? How could Dockery have anything to do with that? There was obviously more there than what Mace had first thought.

Her mental pirouettes were interrupted when she heard the sound near her moments before she saw him. Her hand went to her pocket. The guy was black with a shaved head, only a few inches taller than she, but about ninety pounds heavier with none of it fat. Bandits, she knew, tended to work out religiously, just so they could outrun and outfight the cops if it came down to it. And it usually did at some point.

"Nice bike," he said. He wore a hoodie, jeans, and tongue-out burgundy-and-white basketball shoes.

Mace lifted her visor. "Yeah, I hear that a lot."

She knew he had a pistol in his right hoodie pocket, and the slight bulge in his pants bottom evidenced the throwaway strapped to the inside of his left ankle. Her hand tightened on the object in her own pocket.

"I bet you do. Probably don't hear this tho'." He pulled out a bulky semi-auto that Mace knew with a glance was an inaccurate knockoff piece of crap, but then you didn't have to be a Marine sniper to drop someone at a distance of two feet. "I want it."

"Can you afford the payments?"

He pointed the muzzle at her forehead. " 'Less they making helmets with Kevlar, I think I can. And pull your hand outcha coat real damn slow or I'll kill you, bitch."

"It's just a phone."

"Show me."

She edged out her phone and held it up. "See, just a Nokia 357."

"You a funny bitch."

"You haven't heard the punch line."

"Yeah? What's that?"

The burst of pepper spray hit him in both pupils. He screamed, dropped his gun, and fell back on the sidewalk clawing at his eyes. She pocketed the pepper spray cannon that looked like a phone that she'd bought from Binder's personal defense shop. "I got the all-inclusive caller plan with self-defense add-on."

She snagged his pistol, dropped the mag, cleared the chamber of the lead round, and tossed the gun into a garbage can. His throw-away, an old .22 wheel gun, got the same treatment after she managed to tug up his pants leg and snag it from the ankle strap while he was gyrating uncontrollably. She got back on her bike and stared down at him still rolling and yelping on the pavement. "What's your name?"

"My eyes are burning out my head, bitch!"

"Then stop trying to rob people. Now what's your name?"

"I'll kill you, bitch. I'll kill you."

"Interesting, but not getting us anywhere. Name?"

"I ain't telling you my damn name."

"Tell me your name and I'll give you something to make the sting go away."

He stopped rolling, but his hands were still crammed against his eye sockets. "What!" he screamed.

"It's in my other pocket. Name?"

"Razor."

"Real name."

"Darren."

"Darren what?"

"I'm dying here!"

"Last name?"

"Shit, dammit. Kill you, muther!"

"Name?" she repeated calmly.

"Rogers! Okay! Rogers!"

"Okay, Darren Rogers." She pulled a small spray bottle from her other pocket. "Look at me."

"What?"

"Look at me, Darren, if you want the burn to go away."

He stopped writhing and sat up on his haunches, his fists still buried in his face.

"It doesn't work that way. Open your eyes and look at me."

He slowly pulled his hands away and managed to keep open his teary, inflamed eyes while his entire body shook with the effort. She sprayed both pupils with the liquid from the bottle. Within a few seconds, Darren sat back and took a deep breath. "What the hell is that shit?"

"Magic."

"Why'd you do me like that?"

"Call me overly sensitive, but it might have been the whole gun-robbery-kill-you-bitch thing."

"You even know where the hell you are? You from Iowa or something? Ain't no monuments 'round here, lady."

"Actually, I was born in D.C. and my office was right here for years."

Darren stood and started to rub his eyes, but she snapped, "You've got the pepper crap on your hands, Darren. Rub your eyes you go right back to screaming, and magic may not strike twice."

He let his hands swing at his side. "What'd you do with my guns?"

"In the can over there. Took the ammo out. By the way, the slider on your semi is for shit; jams every second shot. And your .22 throw-away is only good for a laugh."

"I paid two hundred bucks for that semi."

"Then you got ripped off. It's also about as accurate as a TEC-9 at a thousand yards, which translates to anything you hit with it is sheer luck."

"You know a lot 'bout guns?"

"In many ways, they were once my best friends."

"You a crazy bitch."

"There's that word again."

"What the hell you want to know my name for?"

"You live 'round here?"

"Why, you a cop?"

"No, just curious."

"Grew up couple blocks away," he said sullenly.

"What crew you with? Lots to choose from down here."

"Ain't got no crew."

"What, you failed the initiation?"

"Ain't got no crew," he repeated stubbornly.

"Okay, maybe there are a few freelance gun toters around here and maybe you're one of them."

"So what if I am?"

"So with crappy weapons and no crew how come you're still alive?"

"Why you think they call me Razor?"

"Let me take a wild guess and say because you're really sharp?"

"I get by."

He took a menacing step toward her, one hand shielding his face.

She held up the phone. "Don't even think about it, Darren. This button turns my little phone into a one-million-volt Taser and you into a Fry Daddy."

He dropped his hand and took a step back.

"You got family?" she asked.

"Can I get my crappy guns out the trash now?"

"After I'm gone. They don't call me Razor but I'm pretty sharp too."

"What you doing down here?" He looked around. "Like you say, lotta crews."

"They're too busy popping each other to worry about me. But thanks for the concern."

"I don't give a shit if you get your head blown off. Why should I?"

"Not a reason in the world. Go get your crappy guns, Razor, and enjoy what little time you've got left." She hit the gas and the Ducati roared off.

CHAPTER

43

MACE HEARD the car long before she saw it.

She checked her side mirror. Black sedan, tinted glass, big motor, and the rear passenger-side window easing down. Never a good scenario, especially in this part of D.C.

She hit the throttle and the Ducati leapt forward, but the sedan still muscled up closer. She saw the gun muzzle with a suppressor can through the slit of the open window. The shooter took aim through the scope on his sniper rifle while his partner handled the wheel with an expert touch. The crosshairs settled on Mace's helmet and the man's finger closed on the trigger. Sensing that the shooter had drawn his bead, Mace was about to jump the curb when there was a squeal of rubber. Another car flew between the sedan and Mace, and banged against the big car.

The man fired right at the instant the collision occurred and his shot got screwed. Instead of the round drilling a black hole in Mace's head, the driver's-side window of the car between Mace and the shooter exploded, with glass fragments propelled outward like tiny meteors.

Mace recognized the car that had saved her. "Roy!" she screamed.

The shooter cursed and fired again while his partner slammed the sedan into the smaller Audi. Roy ducked down as the second round zipped over his head and shattered the passenger window. He cut the wheel hard to the left and the Audi punched the sedan's front fender at just the right angle to send the bigger car into a counterclockwise spin. The shooter pulled his rifle back and closed the window while the driver tried to steer the car out of the spin.

Roy hit the gas and the Audi pulled next to Mace. Roy looked at her through the open window.

"I've got your back," he said gamely, glassy debris in his hair, his eyes wide with adrenaline and fear.

Mace lifted her visor and yelled, "Are you nuts!"

"Apparently, yeah," he said a little breathlessly.

"What the hell are you doing here?"

"Like I just said, watching your back."

"They could've killed you."

"But they didn't. Right?"

Mace checked their six.

The sedan had pulled out of the spin and was bearing down on both of them, its eight cylinders popping.

"Well, here they come again."

Roy looked behind him. "Oh, shit. Now what?"

Mace shouted, "Follow me, Roy."

44

THE DUCATI hit ninety on a straight strip of road and then Mace decelerated and leaned into the turn at sixty. The battered Audi barely made the cut, its left rear taking out a line of trash cans on the curb, catapulting days-old garbage in all directions as Roy fought the wheel and finally righted the slide and fell in behind her ride.

Mace flicked her gaze in the mirror and saw the sedan take the turn while barely slowing. Her mind galloped as her observations roared into deductions. Pro driver. So probably pro shooter in the rear seat. She didn't want to find out how good he was. The third shot would not be all that charming for her or Roy.

Mace's knowledge of the area served her well. Whenever she saw the sedan edging up on Roy, she would rip down a side street, forcing the bigger car to fall back a bit. They did this dodge and dart for three more blocks while passing bandits doing business, but not a single blue working the streets that Mace could see.

Lazy asses!

She had no choice but to go for it. Up ahead was the church parking lot. She spied two cruisers still at the hoodle. She leaned into the turn, hit the lot, went fully airborne over a speed bump, and soared right at the twin rides of D.C.'s finest. She braked hard, almost laying the Ducati down, but the rear wheel tread fought the torque and held to the asphalt. The Audi torched the pavement with burned rubber as Roy smashed down on the brakes. Before Mace even got her helmet off or Roy leapt from his car, the cops were out, frozen in classic firing stances, gun muzzles aimed at Roy's and Mace's foreheads.

"Hands on your heads, fingers interlocked, and down on your knees. Now!" screamed one of them.

With slight panic Mace noticed that Tony and his rookie were not among this group. He must've gotten a call and left. She studied the four cops aligned against her. All men, all big, all looking pissed off. And she didn't know a single one. She glanced at Roy, who was taking a step forward, gallantly trying to put his body between her and them. She stopped his gallantry by driving her elbow in his side and pushing him behind her. She knew the look in the cops' eyes. She'd had it herself plenty of times. They were one second and one wrong move from unloading with double taps to the head and heart. Even shitty shooters couldn't miss at this distance, and she doubted any of them were bad shots.

"Hands on your head and fingers interlocked, Roy," she hissed. "And get on your knees. Now!"

They both dropped to the asphalt as the blues approached cautiously, firing lines and trigger fingers still set.

"Some guys in a car tried to kill us," barked Roy.

It was at this moment that Mace noticed the silence. No big sedan, no thumping V-8, no gun muzzle with a can pointed her way. Silence.

"What *guys*?" said one of the cops skeptically.

"In a big black sedan. It was chasing us."

The cop looked around. "I don't see a damned thing other than you two."

Another one pointed out, "All I ever saw were you and the chick on the bike coming at us hard."

"I was here about thirty minutes ago," said Mace. "I was talking to Tony Drake. He was parked here at the hoodle with an egg named Francie."

"You a cop?" asked one of them.

"Used to be. Tony can vouch for me."

The first cop shook his head. "We got here about ten minutes ago. And I don't know any Tony Drake. Or a Francie."

Roy started to get up. "Look, this is crazy."

"Stay down!" roared the second cop. His pistol was aimed right at Roy's skull.

"He's staying down," snapped Mace. "He's not going anywhere. No sudden moves. We're both cool. We've got no weapons."

"We'll see about that," said the first cop, as he holstered his gun and pulled cuffs from his belt. "You two look like you got stuff that would concern me. So you don't mind me searching you and your vehicles?"

Roy eyed the cuffs and said indignantly, "Where the hell are you coming from? We didn't do anything wrong."

"This is a stop, Roy, not a contact," said Mace. "We are definitely not free to go."

The other cop eyed Mace. "What, are you his lawyer?"

"Other way around, actually."

"You said you were a cop. Do I know you?"

Mace started to say something but then stopped. These guys might be part of the thirty percent who believed she was dirty.

"Don't think so."

The first cop was looking at the damage to the Audi. "You hit something, mister."

"How about that sedan and two big-ass rifle rounds?" snapped Roy.

"Right, the sedan," the cop said sarcastically. He nodded to his partner, who snapped the cuffs on Roy first, then Mace.

"Have either of you been drinking?" asked the first cop.

"For God's sakes!" yelled Roy. "They were trying to kill us. We came to you for help and all we're getting is hassled and cuffed."

"Shut up!" snapped Mace.

"In case you didn't figure it out, you're both under arrest," said the second cop.

"What's the damn charge?" exclaimed Roy.

"How about disturbing the peace, reckless endangerment, and assault on a police officer for starters? I thought you two were going to run right into us."

"That is bullshit! Look at my damn car. They shot out the windows. They were trying to kill us! Or at least her. What the hell did you want us to do? Now, can you take the damn cuffs off?" Roy pulled his arms free of the cop's hold.

"Okay, I just added resisting arrest. Anything else you'd care to tack on?"

Roy started to say something but Mace managed to jab him in the side. "It's bad enough. Don't make it worse."

The first cop said, "Lady's right. Now you both have the right to remain silent. You . . ."

As he performed the Miranda, Mace tuned out his words. Busted and not even out a week. Hadn't even had time to see her probation officer. She was completely and totally screwed.

I'm going back to prison.

CHAPTER

45

IT WAS like déjà vu all over again. The barred door slid back and there she was, the stars all in alignment on her broad shoulders.

"It's really not what you think, Beth," Mace said quietly as she sat hunched over on a metal bench at the back of the cell.

Her sister sat down next to her. "So tell me what it is about. Please tell me what the hell you and Kingman were doing down there last night."

"We weren't together. I didn't even know he was there until his car flew in between me and the guys trying to shoot me."

"What guys?"

"Town Car. Tinted windows. Didn't the arresting officers fill you in?"

"I want to hear it from you. License plate?"

"No plates. At least on the front. I never saw the rear."

"Go on."

"They came flying at me. Rear passenger window came down a few inches. Saw the gun muzzle. A rifle barrel with a can attached."

"And they fired at you?"

"Twice. And they would've gotten me if it hadn't been for Roy."

"And then what?"

Mace explained how she had gone back to the hoodle for help. "But my buddy wasn't there, just two cruisers with blues I didn't know. They jumped to the wrong conclusion."

"Their report says they never saw another car."

"It obviously had already peeled off. But Roy's car hit it. You can take paint samples from his ride and see if you can get a match somewhere. And you'll find the rounds either in Roy's car or on the street somewhere."

"We found no slugs, either in his car or on the street, and I've had a dozen cadets from the academy walking the line for the last five hours."

"So you *do* believe me?"

"There's also a line of smashed trash cans that Kingman apparently ran into. You sure the damage didn't come from that?"

"Beth, I'm telling you the truth! There was a black sedan chasing us. Somebody fired a rifle from inside it. The rounds shattered the windows in Roy's car and almost hit him. You sure you didn't find anything?"

"No slugs, no casings."

"Any casings would've ejected in the sedan. They must've gone back and policed the slugs."

"That takes time, which makes it a big risk. Why would they do that?"

"I don't know."

"But who would want to kill you?"

"Do you have a few hours so I can give you a list?"

"Did you tell anyone you were going down there last night?"

"Just Roy. It was a spur-of-the-moment thing."

"Kingman said he met you for a drink after you left me and then he went back to work. And he just happened to find you in Six D later, right before someone tried to kill you?" Beth's frown hardened into a scowl. "Don't treat me like a chump, Mace. I don't deserve that."

Mace hesitated just a moment, but it was obviously enough for Beth. "Okay, when you're ready to actually tell me the truth, *maybe* I'll be waiting on the other side of the bars, okay?" She headed to the door.

"Wait!"

Beth turned back. "I'm waiting."

"I was with Roy at his office building last night while you were there."

"Wow! Never saw that one coming."

"Hey, you asked for the truth so don't rip me for giving it."

"Why were you there?"

"He told me about the construction site and things going missing and it made me think of the Liam Kazlowski case, you remember the elevator guy from five years ago?"

Beth nodded slowly. "I think of him sometimes sitting in his max security cell wondering where his balls went. You always did have excellent aim."

"So Roy and I went there to see if we could catch the guy."

"And calling your sister, the chief of police no less, never entered your mind?"

"For all I knew it was a wild-goose chase. I didn't want to call you out on a hunch. Not when you were dressed so pretty," she added lamely.

Beth's face was so tight, the balls of her cheeks so hard against the overlap of skin, that it looked like she had been shrink-wrapped. "I don't know whether to shoot you or drive you back to prison myself," she said in a low, barely-in-control voice.

"Beth—"

Beth lunged forward, forcing Mace to jerk back flush with the cement-block wall. Her voice came at Mace like the thrusts of a knife.

"Within hours of me letting you walk away from a tampering and obstruction charge and me telling you to stay the hell out of the case, you turn right around and stick your nose right in it. What the hell is the matter with you?" Beth was shouting now. "Will you please tell me how in the hell I'm supposed to get through to you?"

Beth's face was spotted with red anxiety flecks. Mace was pressing the back of her head so hard against the wall it felt like her scalp was being split open.

"It's the only shot I've got to get back on the force," Mace said in a calm voice that belied the emotion churning through her.

"What are you talking about? I told you I was working on it."

Mace hesitated but then decided to just get it out. "Mona's ahead of you."

Beth straightened up. "What?"

"Mona ambushed me in the ladies' room at a hotel where Roy

and I were having a drink. She knew your plan and she's already talked to all relevant parties with the result that even if you dig up people with signed confessions it won't matter. I'm never getting back on the force that way. I've never seen her happier."

Beth slowly sat on the bench next to Mace. "And that's why you—"

"Look, bottom line, it's not your battle, Beth. It never has been. It's mine. If anybody is going to do something, it has to be me. Mona was also hoping that you'd keep pushing on the case so she could nail you with some bullshit misuse-of-resource crap or building a bogus case to help me and then get you fired. I may go down, but I am not taking you with me. I'll go back to prison before I'd let that happen."

The two sisters sat there for a few moments in silence.

Beth finally said, "But if the guy you nailed last night is the killer?"

"Yeah, maybe I have a shot at reinstatement."

"You don't sound convinced."

"I'm not convinced about a lot of things. So has he spilled his guts yet?"

"He hasn't said a word except that he wants a lawyer."

"Really? He's not so stupid, then."

"I don't know if he is or not. He wants your drinking-buddy white knight as his shyster."

"Roy as his lawyer? Why?"

"Says he's the only one he'll talk to. Seems like they were good friends. Funny, Kingman never even mentioned to me that he knew him."

"Roy told me he helped the guy out some. Repped him once on an assault."

"So *you* whacked the guy in the head with a piece of wood, right?"

"He outweighed me by about two hundred pounds."

"It sure was a little piece of wood to knock out a guy that big."

"I built up quite an arm in prison," Mace said defiantly.

"Why'd you go down to Six D?"

"To see where it all went down."

"Where they grabbed you?"

"There was a huckabuck on the street named Razor. Heard of him?" Beth shook her head. "Well, he and I had a chat, then I rode on. About five minutes later, here comes the car with the rifleman. Then Roy showed up and the chase was on. That's all I know. I need you to believe me."

Beth sighed. "I do. A couple of my guys on CP rounds scrounged up two witnesses who saw the car bearing down on you and King-man's Audi coming from out of nowhere."

"And the shots?"

"And the shots."

"If you knew that, why were you giving me the third degree, then?"

"Because I'm pissed at you and I wanted to make you sweat."

"Did your witnesses get a plate number?"

"There were apparently no plates on the rear of the car either."

"Okay. That's interesting."

"You see what happens when you lose my hover guys?"

Mace had a sudden thought. "So how did Roy follow me, then?"

"Why don't you ask him? It seems pretty convenient him show-ing up like that. If I were you I'd go a little slow with the man, not that you've ever listened to me when it comes to the male species."

"First time for everything," Mace said slowly.

"So they fired two rounds and left nothing behind. Not your typical street shooters, because those guys don't police their brass since nobody will squeal on them anyway."

"Does Roy know that this Captain dude wants him as his lawyer?"

"I told him."

"You've already talked to Roy?"

"I wanted to see how your stories matched up."

"Thanks a lot."

"Oh, and if someone is trying to kill you, I'd appreciate if you would confine your rides into the Valley of Death to daylight hours."

She turned back to the door.

"Is this going to screw up my probation?"

"You were never officially charged. Kingman's waiting down the hall." She thumbed the bars. "You're going to work this case, aren't you?"

"What would you do, Beth, if it were you?"

The chief left without answering.

So where're our rides?" asked Mace. She and Roy were standing out in front of the district police station while the sun rose above them.

"Impoundment lot," he said, stretching his arms over his head.

"Are you kidding me?"

"That's what they told me inside."

Mace groaned. "Great. My Ducati's probably been chopped and shopped all over the Northeast by now."

"I doubt your sister would let that happen. My Audi, on the other hand, was pretty beat up. Should we cab it over there?"

It took a few minutes to run down a dilapidated taxi. The cabbie seemed surprised to see them flagging him down.

"What's his problem?" asked Roy.

"Well, we don't look like we belong around here, do we, Roy?"

"Why, because we're white?"

"No, because we're not shoving a gun in his face and asking for all his money."

When the cab pulled from the curb she turned to him. "Okay, how did you show up last night? You followed me, right?"

"Not exactly, no."

"How not exactly?"

"I was waiting for you at the spot where the car came after you."

"I'm not liking where this is going."

"Hey, I'm not in cahoots with the guys in the black sedan."

"Oh, good, glad that's all cleared up. I think this is where you and I part company." She tapped on the cabbie's shoulder. "Hey, buddy you can let me—"

"Mace, will you hear me out! I almost got my head blown off last night."

She turned back to him. "Okay, I'm listening."

"You said you were going downtown. I knew what that meant, or at least I thought I did. To the place where you were kidnapped."

"How did you even know where that was?"

"I Googled you on my iPhone."

"What?"

"I Googled the stories. Two of them had the street location where it happened. I went there and waited, figured you'd show up at some point. You did. Then the car came at you and I, well, I . . ."

"Came to my rescue?"

"A little better than I did with the Captain, I guess."

"So you didn't see Razor, then?"

"Who?"

"Never mind. So why did you do it? I mean, you going there at that time of night in your fancy-pants Audi was pretty stupid."

"As stupid as a chick on a Ducati?"

"That's different."

"Anyway, they'd probably just assume I was looking to buy drugs or a hooker."

She folded her arms across her chest and her suspicious look faded. "I'd be in the morgue right now but for you. Thanks. I owe you."

"I also got us arrested with my big mouth."

"I ran to the hoodle, you were just following."

"You think it was somebody from your past shooting at you?"

"Don't see many street crews using suppressor cans and piloting Town Cars. Their usual method is a double tap to the head and then the sounds of running feet."

"Okay, what now?"

"I get my bike back, hopefully in one piece. And you get your Audi back in several hopefully repairable chunks."

"What about the key to the mailbox at A-1? You want me to check it out?"

"No, I'll check it out."

"What if we check it out together?"

"People are watching, you know. They see you with me, probably not good."

"Hell, I've spent more time with you over the last couple days than I've done with every girlfriend I've ever had."

"Really? Then no wonder things never worked out for you."

The cab dropped them at the impoundment lot. Beth had made arrangements so they weren't charged any fees. Mace's Ducati was parked right next to the small office building. A thick chain wrapped in plastic was wound around the front forks and the other end padlocked to a ten-foot-tall steel post. The bike was in pristine condition. It even looked like someone had washed it.

"Like I thought, your sister was looking out for you," said Roy.

Mace was staring at something. "But I don't think she has the same level of commitment to you." She pointed up ahead.

Across the lot Roy's Audi was parked next to a rear section of fence. The entire left side was crunched from the collision with the Town Car and the heavy trash cans. But someone had obviously come in the night to do some more damage. All its wheels were gone along with the passenger door. Someone had also keyed the entire body of the vehicle multiple times and slashed the convertible top. As they walked over and looked inside they could see that the steering wheel, gearshift, CD player, and built-in navigation system were also missing. The seats were ripped open and the foam torn out. Someone had dumped what looked to be antifreeze on the floorboards, where it had mixed with the glass fragments and two used condoms. The trunk had also been jimmied and the spare taken. All Roy's expensive basketball gear was also gone.

"I'm really sorry about your car," she said.

He sighed. "Hey, this is why people buy insurance policies. You hungry?"

"Starving."

He checked his watch. "I know this place. Eggs are good, the coffee hot."

"I guess you need a ride?"

"Guess so. But I don't have a helmet. And I'm not looking to getting busted again. Once a week is about my limit."

"Not a problem."

Mace walked back to the impoundment lot office and returned a few minutes later carrying a motorcycle helmet. A *police* motorcycle helmet.

"How'd you swing that?" he asked.

"You don't want to know."

She slipped her hand into a small black zippered pocket she'd had built years ago under the Ducati's seat and pulled out her pepperspray cell phone and zap knuckles.

"Didn't really want the cops to find these on me." She put them in the pocket of her jacket. "Popped them in there while we were running from the bad guys."

"Good thinking," said Roy. "Because something tells me you might need them."

CHAPTER

47

THE EGGS were good, the toast slathered in butter, the bacon crispy, and the coffee steamy. They ate their fill and then Mace and Roy sat back. He patted his stomach. "Gotta start playing ball again before I get a gut."

"So the Captain wants you to rep him?"

He took a sip of coffee and nodded. "I don't have any details yet."

Mace fingered her cup. "But you don't think he did it?"

"No, but I'll admit that my judgment is probably a little biased. I like the guy."

"Big teddy bear?"

"With a combat bronze and two Purple Hearts," he said sharply.

"I'm not making fun of him. It's shitty that a war hero is on the streets."

"But if he did kill Diane?"

"Then it's over, Roy, friend or not."

"At least he won't be living on the streets anymore."

"So you going to rep him?"

"I'm not sure. I work for Shilling & Murdoch. They don't do criminal defense work. *I* don't do criminal defense work anymore."

"There's always pro bono. Your firm can't have a problem with that."

"I thought you believed he was guilty?"

"Everybody deserves a good defense. Least I heard that somewhere."

"I'll meet with him, go from there."

She pulled the key out. "Do you want me to let you know what I find?"

"Like I said, I'm going with you."

"You don't have to do this."

"I'll probably lose my license to practice before this is all over."

Mace looked confused. "But you still want to come with me? Why?"

"I have no rational basis for answering that question."

"Meaning you have an *irrational* basis?"

Roy put some cash down for the meal.

"So how are you going to find out which box was Diane's?"

"When I think of it you'll be the first to know. By the way, how much do I have left on my buck retainer?"

"After last night, ten cents. Use it wisely."

When Mace and Roy came out of the diner, Karl Reiger picked them up from his observation post tucked inside the mouth of an alley. Farther down the block Don Hope sat in a pale blue Chevy van, his glass on the same target. When Roy and Mace climbed on her bike and drove down the street, Hope eased the van forward and followed. Reiger backed down the alley, came out on the next street over, and ran a parallel course on their tail. They radioed back and forth on a secure communication line and switched out the surveillance every three blocks to knock down the odds of Mace picking up the tail.

Reiger settled back in his seat. It should have been over last night. And it would have been if the punk lawyer hadn't screwed his shot. That would not happen again. Reiger didn't like killing people, especially fellow Americans, but above all, he was going to survive this, even if no one else did.

48

THERE WAS ONLY one person working behind the counter at A-1 when Roy and Mace walked in. He was young with ear buds and lines dangling to an iPod hung on his belt. His head was swaying to the music as he sorted the mail on the counter. Mace led Roy over to the wall of mailboxes. A quick check showed that while they were numbered, none of the digits on the boxes matched the one Mace had written down from the original key.

"Plan B," she whispered to Roy.

Mace walked over to the guy at the counter. "Hey, dude, got a question."

The kid took one ear bud out but his head kept swinging. "Yeah?"

Mace held up the key. "My aunt fell down the stairs and broke her tailbone. That's the good news."

"That she broke her tailbone?" said the kid, perplexed.

"Yeah, because but for that she wouldn't have gone to the hospital and they wouldn't have checked her out and discovered she had like this weird form of leprosy she contracted in Africa or some crazy place. That stuff'll eat your skin right off. And it's like so contagious that if she like breathes on you, your eyeballs fall out. I've never seen anything like this crap. It's got some long-ass medical name."

"Damn, that sucks," said the kid, his head still swinging to the rhythm.

"Anyway, this is her key and she asked me to get her mail. Only she can't remember which box was hers."

"Oh."

"Yeah. So I can't get the mail. And she has some checks and medical bills she needs. It's a hassle but I'm the only relative she has."

"What's her name?"

"Diane Tolliver." Mace crossed her fingers, hoping that the kid had not read of the woman's murder.

He clicked some keys on the computer. "Yeah, she's got a box here."

"So what's the number?"

The kid took out the other bud from his ear and his expression hardened. "I'm not really supposed to give out that info. Mail regs or something. You know, like terrorist stuff."

"Damn, never thought of that." She looked at Roy. "Well, hell, you better go get Auntie and bring her in here then so she can show some ID." She turned back to the kid. "They couldn't keep her in that hospital anymore because they're not set up for contagious crap like that. So we're driving her to Johns Hopkins. We just got going and then she started screaming about her mail. Between you and me I think this stuff messes with your mind too. You know, like forgetting your mailbox number? I know it screws up your sex drive. Docs say it kills the libido like dead, especially in younger people. Anyway, she's out in the car with boils popping all over the place. And her face? It's like tar sliding off. Now, we got inoculated against this shit so we're good, but if I were you, I'd go hide out in the back or something. And anything she touches in here make sure you clean it up with like Clorox or something. The bacteria can live for like weeks on pretty much anything. An orderly at the hospital found that out the hard way." She looked at Roy again. "Go on and get her. Make it fast. I don't want to get caught in traffic going to Baltimore."

Roy turned to head out the door but the kid blurted out, "It's Box 716. Second to the left on the top row over there."

"You sure?" asked Mace. "I don't want you getting in trouble. And Auntie's right outside. She can walk but she falls a lot because of the boils bursting and her feet slipping in the juice. You ought to see the backseat of my car. It's beyond gross."

The wide-eyed kid took a step back. "No, it's cool. Go on ahead and open it up. Your auntie ain't got to come in here."

"Hey, thanks, man." Roy put out a hand for him to shake. The kid took another step back and picked up a large tub of mail. "Yeah, dude, you're welcome."

Roy and Mace headed to Box 716.

49

Beth was in the front seat of a patrol car heading to a meeting when she finished reading over the e-mail from Lowell Cassell. The medical examiner was comparing the DNA on the sperm left inside Diane Tolliver with the sample they'd taken from the residue of a cup of coffee they'd given to Lou Dockery. It was an old police trick. They had enough to hold Dockery until the test results were back. And even if this DNA sample was suppressed by defense counsel motion they could easily get a search warrant. It wasn't like Dockery could change his DNA in the interim. Beth had ordered the coffee cup tactic because she didn't want to waste time with him unless he was the guy who'd raped and murdered Diane Tolliver.

Her multitasking mind shifted gears for a moment. She was monitoring the radio calls in the Fifth District and did not like the paucity of responses from the scout cars to the dispatcher's calls. She picked up the radio.

"Cruiser One rolling in Five D. Cruiser One rolling Five D. Chief out."

Within seconds the chatter picked up and at least five scout cars were responding to each dispatch. Her driver glanced at her.

"Pays off working your way up from the pavement, Chief."

"You think?" she answered absently. Beth punched in the number. The ME answered on the second ring.

"How long?" she said.

Cassell said, "Beth, you asked me that not ten minutes ago. If it had been before the new lab opened, I'd say two to four weeks. We had to send it out back then."

"But not now. Now you have that fancy lab with all those fancy machines."

"We went back over the chain of custody on the sample found in the deceased and confirmed there was no tampering or alteration. We received the sample from Dockery." He paused and Beth could almost see his grin across the phone line. "You haven't used the coffee ploy in a while."

"I'm getting more impatient in my old age."

"It's not that easy pulling DNA off a sperm sample. The sperm heads are hard."

"As hard as the heads of the guys shooting them into women who don't want them to."

Cassell continued, "Then there is the amplification of the DNA and instrumentation. Next comes interpretation of the results. That's where mistakes are made. I don't want to blow up your case because of an error."

"You won't make a mistake, Doc, you're too good."

"Everyone's human. Normally, the protocols I just described take a full week."

"On TV the forensics team does it every episode in like ten minutes."

"Don't get me started on *that*."

"So give me the bottom line time-wise."

"I've put all other work aside and you'll have it by tomorrow. The next day tops."

"I'll take it tomorrow, thanks, Doc."

She clicked off and leaned back in her seat. A moment later they passed a corner that she instantly recognized. She'd been a rookie beat cop riding solo for only two weeks when a bandit had come tearing out of an alley with a TEC-9 and opened fire at a group of people in front of a shoe shop. To this day no one knew why.

Instantly, Beth had gotten her cruiser between the bandit and the crowd. Using her engine block as cover she'd pulled her sidearm and given him two taps in the head. She hadn't bothered with a torso shot because she'd spotted the edges of body armor poking out of his shirt. It wasn't until thirty seconds later, after she'd run over and confirmed the kill, that she discovered that the last TEC-9 round had killed a ten-year-old boy who'd been holding tight to a box containing his new pair of basketball shoes.

The other eight people in the crowd, including the boy's mother, had been saved by Beth's swift actions. The city hailed her as a hero. Yet she went home that night and cried until the sun rose. She was the only one who knew the truth. She had hesitated before firing. To this day she didn't really know why. Civilians could never understand what went through a cop's mind before they pulled the trigger.

Am I going to die today? Will I be sued? Will I lose my job? Can I get a clean shot off? Am I going to die today?

No more than two seconds went by before she'd ended the nightmare scenario. Yet it was enough time for the bandit to get off one last round. The killing round, as it turned out.

Her most vivid image was the box with the new shoes lying in a pool of ten-year-old blood. After calling in the ambulance she did everything she could to bring the little boy back. Tried to stanch the bleeding using her jacket. Breathed hard into his mouth. Pumped his small chest until her arms felt like they would fall off. But she knew he was dead. The eyes were flat, hard. The mother was screaming. Everything was happening in slow motion. Waiting for help to come; the paramedics pronouncing the boy dead; then the gauntlet of stars and bars, the captain, the district commander, and then, finally, the chief himself. It was the longest wait of her life, and all of it, from beginning to end, barely took ten minutes.

She still could feel the heavy, comforting hand of the chief on her trembling shoulder. He said all the right things and yet all Beth could see were those hard, flat eyes. Ten years old. Dead. Two seconds' hesitation. That's all it took. A deuce of seconds. A pair of eye blinks. That was apparently the difference between going home and playing hoops in your new shoes or heading to the morgue to get your chest cavity emptied.

One more crime stat for the books. And yet it wasn't just a stat. His name was Rodney Hawks. Beth had a photo of him from his fourth-grade class in her office on her shelf. She looked at it every day. It pushed her to work harder, try harder, to never leave anything to chance. To never again hesitate when her gun was cocked and locked on a target that required killing.

The shoe shop was no longer there. It was now a liquor store. But for her it would always be the place where she'd allowed Rodney Hawks to die. Where Beth Perry, who had never failed at anything, *had* failed. And a little boy had lost his life because of it.

Beth took a deep breath and pushed these images from her mind. She looked down at her notes and focused on the present situation. Had the homeless vet raped the power lawyer and then stomped on her neck hard enough to crack her brain stem? And then stuffed her in the fridge and gone about his business? The soiling on her clothes and the bits of fabric found at the crime scene also matched what was found on Dockery's clothing. But that didn't really matter. DNA was better than a print. And DNA from sperm was the gold card, particularly when it was found inside the woman. Taken together with the bruising in her genitals, there was no defense lawyer on earth who could spin that one into a positive.

She put the file down and picked up the phone and called her sister. There was no answer so she left a message letting Mace know that they would have the DNA results back soon. If it matched, Lou Dockery would spend the rest of his life in prison. Beth's mind turned to how Dockery's conviction might get Mace her old job back. Despite Mona putting obstacles in their way, if they could convince . . . Beth suddenly dropped this train of thought.

There was one loose end.

She flipped open the Tolliver file once more and looked at two evidentiary items.

A key. And an e-mail.

We need to focus in on A-

There was more here obviously than a homeless vet on a rampage. Yet the real question was, were they connected?

And then there was a shooter in a Town Car with tinted windows, no plates, and a can on the rifle muzzle aiming right at Mace. Was that from Mace's past or tied to this case?

A deuce of seconds. That's all it took.

She was not going to lose her sister again.

50

THERE WAS NOTHING in the mailbox. Nothing, that is, until Mace felt around the top of the inside of the box and her gloved hand closed around a piece of paper taped there. She unfolded it and read the brief contents.

"A name, Andre Watkins. And there's an address in Rosslyn. I guess for him." She looked up at Roy. "Ever heard of this guy?"

"No, and Diane never mentioned him."

"Did she go out a lot?"

"She liked to go to the Kennedy Center; she liked to eat out."

"Well, she probably didn't go alone."

Mace put the paper back inside the box and closed the door.

"Leaving it here?"

"So the police can follow it up if they figure it out."

"Or we could go and tell them about the letter right now."

"We could," Mace said slowly.

"But you want to solve this yourself?"

"It's a long story, Roy. Don't rag me about it. I'm not sure my answers will make any sense anyway."

Twenty minutes later, Mace had parked her bike in an underground garage and she and Roy were zipping to the tenth floor of the apartment building. A man answered the door on the second knock after looking at them through the peephole. This wasn't a guess, because Mace knew that he had. He was as tall as Roy, though about thirty years older, with a trim white beard to match his thinning hair. He was handsome and his skin was tanned a deep brown. He wore jeans that looked like they'd been ironed and a tuxedo shirt with the tail out. His bare feet were in a pair of black leather Bruno Magli shoes. He looked to Mace like the perfect image of the carefree and elegant aristocrat.

"Andre Watkins?" Mace said.

"Can I help you?"

"I sure hope so. Diane Tolliver?"

"What about her?"

"She's dead."

"I know that. Who are you? The police?"

"Not exactly."

"Then I have no reason to talk to you."

He started to close the door, but Mace jabbed her foot in the way. "She had a P.O. box that had a piece of paper with your name and address on it."

"I know nothing about that."

"Okay, we'll just turn it over to homicide and they can run with it. They'll be by to either talk to you today or arrest you. Or probably both."

"Wait a damn minute. I didn't do anything wrong."

"Well, you're sure acting like you did."

"You knocked on my door, two people I don't even know, and you start asking questions about a dead woman? What the hell did you expect me to do?"

"Okay, let's start over. This is Roy Kingman. He worked with Diane at Shilling & Murdoch. She sent him a clue. That clue turned out to be you. You could be in danger."

"And how do I know you're not the ones who killed Diane?"

"I have to tell you, if we'd wanted to kill you, you'd already be dead. One shot through the peephole." Watkins looked at her inquiringly. "I saw the door shift just a millimeter when you leaned against it to see who was there."

"I think I'm going to end this conversation right now."

"We can go to the Starbucks in the lobby and talk if you'll feel safer. All we want is some information."

Watkins looked over his shoulder into his apartment for a moment and then turned back. "No, that's all right, we can do it in here."

The interior of the residence didn't match the elegance of the man; it was sparsely furnished with what looked like rental pieces, and there was even a purple futon. They sat in the small living room that fronted a sliver of kitchen.

"So how did you know Diane?" Roy asked.

"When she wanted to go out, she'd call me."

"So you two were dating?"

"No, I'm an escort."

Mace and Roy exchanged a glance. "An escort?" said Roy.

"Yes. Diane liked to go out. But she didn't like to go alone. It's fun. And it pays well."

Mace ran her gaze over the cheap furniture. "Work dried up for you?"

"My two ex-wives seem in no hurry to get married again. That's actually why I got into the business. Escorting gives me all the fun of marriage without all the hassle."

"But you two got along?"

"I liked Diane very much. I was devastated when I heard she'd been killed."

"Who told you?"

"The anchorwoman on Channel Seven."

"So no one else knew you two were seeing each other?"

"I don't suppose Diane broadcast it around. She was attractive and smart. I knew she was divorced too. Maybe she'd had it with relationships. I know I have."

"So we're here because Diane left a clue that pointed to you."

"But she never told me anything important."

"Never about work or anything?" asked Roy.

"Well, I knew she was a lawyer at Shilling & Murdoch."

"She didn't talk about anyone she was afraid of? Phone calls or threatening messages she'd gotten? A man who was stalking her, nothing like that?" asked Mace.

"No. Our conversations usually were limited to the events we were attending."

"The police have a man in custody," Roy blurted out.

"What man?"

Mace scowled at Roy and spoke up. "I'm sorry, we can't fill in those details."

"So you have no theories for what happened to Diane?"

"No," Roy admitted. He handed Watkins a card. "If you think of anything, please give me a call."

Watkins fingered the card. "This man in custody? He killed Diane?"

"We'll know soon enough. But whatever Diane was trying to get at, it's a dead end," said Mace. "She must've been mistaken, and anyway the case is closed, at least it is for me. Thanks for your time."

Roy started to speak when they were outside, but Mace whispered, "Wait."

When they were back in the garage Roy turned on her and snapped, "You're just going to drop it? What the hell are you thinking?"

She looked up at him. "I'm thinking that the real Andre Watkins is probably already dead."

CHAPTER

51

"Hey, Captain."

The big fellow looked up. "Hey, Roy. I messed up."

"Why don't we talk about it?"

"Okay, I ain't going nowhere."

Roy looked at the guard next to him. "I need to talk to my client. Alone, please."

The door clanged shut behind Roy as the officer left.

He sat next to the Captain, opened his briefcase, and pulled out a legal pad and a pen. "Why don't you tell me what happened."

"Like I said, I messed up. Took some food. I like the Twinkies. And some tools. Sold 'em. Dumb, huh, but they had lots of tools. Didn't think they'd mind."

Roy looked at him blankly. "Do you know why you were arrested?"

The Captain was staring off now. "Still cold at night. Warm in that building. Guess I shouldn't ate the Twinkies. They were pissed about that, right? And the tools. But it was just a couple of wrenches. Only got three bucks for 'em."

Roy leaned back in his chair. "Did they take anything from you?"

"Who?'

"The police."

"Like what?"

"Prints, bodily fluids?"

"They took my fingerprints." He chuckled. "Had to clean off my fingers so they could make 'em black again. And they gave me some coffee but then they came and took it before I was done. Ticked me off."

"Cheap trick to get your DNA."

"What?"

"But you told them you wanted a lawyer, right?"

"That's right. Ain't no dummy. Twinkie shit. Need a lawyer."

"Okay, maybe we have something to work with in case the DNA comes back bad. But then they'll either just get a search warrant or grand jury subpoena."

"Okay," the Captain said, though it was clear he had no idea what Roy was talking about.

"I checked with the police, they haven't formally charged you with trespass or anything else. But you *were* in the building unlawfully."

"I'm hungry. Got any food?"

"I'll ask the guard in a little bit."

"It's nice and warm in here."

"How long have you been staying in my building?"

"Ain't good with dates." He laughed. "I ain't got no social calendar, Roy."

"Okay, how did you get into the building? Not through the front doors?"

"Garage elevator. Snuck across the lobby. Picked the right time. Recon. I was a scout in 'Nam. I was damn good at recon."

"And the guard?"

"He ain't a good guard. He's almost as fat as me."

"Yeah, I know. Then up the fire exit stairs and onto the fourth floor?"

"Warm in there. And food. Got a fridge. And a toilet. Been a long time since I used a toilet, almost forgot how. I just took the Twinkies, Roy, and the tools. Swear to God."

"How did you know they were doing construction there?"

"Heard some guys talking about it on their lunch break."

"And the tools?"

"Just got three bucks for 'em. Some A-rab on the street. Bet the sonofabitch cheated me. I can give 'em the three bucks and call it square," he added hopefully.

"I don't think they'll go for that."

"'Cause of the damn Twinkies, right?"

"Tell me what happened on Monday, Captain, around six in the morning."

"Monday?" The Captain shook his head. "Monday?" he said again, his brow furrowed, his eyes vacant.

"The day before I gave you the shoes and bought you the food."

"Okay, yeah."

"You were in the building?"

"Oh yeah, always in the building."

"When did you leave?"

"I got me a watch." He held up his arm and slid back his coat sleeve to show it.

"The guard comes in at six."

"He ain't a good guard. He ain't hear nothing. He'd never made it in 'Nam." He added in a knowing tone, "He'd be dead."

"There's a security camera in the lobby." The Captain stared blankly at him. "You didn't know about that?"

The Captain shook his head. "Did it see me?"

"Apparently not. Getting back to Monday, did you see anyone at the building?" The Captain shook his head again. "What time did you leave?"

"Early."

"Show me on your watch."

The Captain hesitated and then pointed to the six.

"Okay, six o'clock. Can anyone vouch for that?" The man looked confused. "Did you see anyone who I can talk to that saw you leave at six, or who you might've talked to right after you left the building?"

"No, sir, ain't nobody like that," he said in a carefree tone.

"Where'd you go?"

"Down to the river. Sat on the wall and watched the sun come up. I like watching the sun come up. Ain't as cold that way."

Roy took a photo out of his pocket. "And you never saw this woman?" He showed him a picture of Diane Tolliver.

"Good-looking woman."

"Do you know her?" The Captain shook his head. "Did you see her on Monday?"

"Nope, but I seen her go in the building sometimes."

"But not on Monday morning?"

"No, sir."

"Did you hear the elevator? You must've been getting ready to leave by then."

"I didn't hear nothing." The Captain wiped his nose with his hand. "You think they got something to eat in this place? I'm real hungry."

"Okay, I'll see about it. So you're sure you didn't see anyone when you left?"

"Went out the garage."

"No cars coming in or out or parked there?"

"No, sir."

Roy took a long breath and nearly choked. In the close confines of the room, the Captain's "aroma" was overpowering.

"I just scoot out. I'm real good at scooting."

Roy put his pad and pen away and stood. "I'm sure you are. I'll go check on that food for you."

"Twinkies if they got 'em. And coffee."

After arranging for some food, Roy left and called Mace.

"How's it look?" she asked.

"An insanity defense is pretty appealing right now." His tone sharpened. "All right, I want to know about Watkins. You just dropped a bombshell and then—"

"Not over the phone, Roy. Let's meet later."

"Where are you?"

"Heading out to start my new job."

52

T̲ʜ̲ᴀɴᴋs ꜰᴏʀ ᴍᴇᴇᴛɪɴɢ with me on such short notice," Beth said.

She sat down across from the two men in a small conference room. Sam Donnelly, the nation's director of intelligence, was as elegantly dressed as ever. Jarvis Burns, his right-hand man, looked just the opposite. His suit looked like it had been pulled from the bottom of a trunk after a months-long journey. The DNI had offices in various places. Today, Beth was in downtown D.C. not far from police department headquarters, in a nondescript building that on the outside looked like nothing special. That was sort of the idea, she knew.

She'd been issued a radio frequency badge on arriving here. It had been encoded with her security clearance levels, which were very high. Still, they weren't high enough. Every room she'd entered, silent alarms had gone off, red lights installed on the ceiling had twirled, and computer screens automatically darkened because she was not cleared to see any of what was going on here.

"Always a pleasure, Beth." Donnelly fiddled with a ring on his finger while Jarvis rubbed his leg.

"Getting worse on you, Jarv?" she asked, eyeing the limb.

"I would not advise anyone getting shot and then stabbed with a bayonet wielded by an enormously skilled and suitably mad Vietcong infantryman. I was lucky enough to have killed him before he killed me. But at least he didn't have to endure this level of pain for the last three decades."

"Nothing they can do?"

"What they did on the battlefield back then sort of sealed my fate. Nerve and bone damage that were basically wrapped in Band-

Aids, ruptured blood vessels that were rerouted in crude ways." He slapped his thigh. "It is what it is and you didn't come here to hear me complain about it. What can we do for you?"

"There was a U.S. attorney found dead in D.C. His name was Jamie Meldon."

Donnelly nodded. "A real tragedy. We were briefed on it."

"Who by?" she said quickly.

Donnelly shook his head. "Sorry, Beth. I can't say specifically, but any such criminal act would come to the attention of the DNI through various channels."

"The crime scene was closed off to us and the FBI. We have no idea who took over the investigation. I've heard that the directive came from the White House?" She paused and looked at Donnelly expectantly.

"That's a neither confirm nor deny answer, Beth."

"Sam—"

He held up a hand. "All right, I can say that I have heard nothing that would connect this to the White House. And I think I would have."

"So who can it be? These guys basically walked off with Meldon's body based on waving around their driver's licenses. And the mayor told me in no uncertain terms to back off. Okay, sometimes that happens. But the FBI got called off too."

Donnelly glanced at Burns. "That *is* very unusual. Would you like me to look into this for you?"

"You're the first person I thought of to do it."

"We've always had a good working relationship," he said. "Your spirit of partnership with the federal side is much appreciated, I can tell you that."

"We have to keep the capital safe."

Burns's features darkened. "If terrorists can successfully attack this city, no American anywhere will feel safe. And the other side would have won."

"Preaching to the choir." She shook their hands. "I'll wait to hear from you."

Burns said, "By the way, how is your sister adjusting to life?"

"She's adjusting. But Mace always goes her own way."

After Beth left, Donnelly returned to his office. Jarvis Burns continued to sit at the table and rub his bad leg. He stopped long enough to type in a text on his BlackBerry and a minute later the door opened. The man with long white hair had changed from jeans and the tuxedo shirt that he'd worn while searching Andre Watkins's apartment into a suit and tie.

"Mace Perry?" said Burns. The man nodded. "And the lawyer?"

"Both there."

"She's probably confirmed that you're not Watkins."

"Should I have just killed them?" the man asked matter-of-factly.

Burns sat back and frowned. "Give me the briefing."

53

MACE PUNCHED the code in the gate box and drove her Ducati through. Altman was waiting for her in the front courtyard. He was dressed as casually as before, but now his hair was tied back in a ponytail. In a backpack Mace carried some clothes and a few other essentials. He escorted her over to the guesthouse and waited while she put her things away before showing her how to operate the TV and stereo system and pointing out the computerized HVAC and alarm system controls. There was even a TV that rose up out of a beautifully carved cabinet at the foot of the California king-size bed in the master suite.

"Pretty snazzy place, Abe."

"My late wife, Marty, designed all this. She had such vision, such style. I can barely match my socks."

"I'm right there with you. So what now?"

"Let's go back to the main house and talk strategy."

Over cups of tea Altman outlined his plan in greater detail.

"I've been working with some wonderful folks at Social Services. They'll be expecting you and will lend you their full cooperation. They have background files on all the people of interest that I've already reviewed. As I told you before, I've selected ten people for the initial phase out of all the possibilities submitted thus far. It will be up to you to make the initial contact with them."

"Okay, what sorts of questions do you want me to ask?"

"Nothing too probing. I want you to set them at ease but at the same time let them know that you understand their situation and that we're not in any way prejudging choices they have made or not made. I'm not trying to take them out of their current world."

"But you are, aren't you?"

"I'm attempting to give them an opportunity to change their circumstances in *their* world for the better."

"That's sort of splitting words, isn't it?"

"Yes, it is. And if you question it, *they* certainly will. They will be very suspicious of my motives. The last thing I want is for them to think this is some sort of freak show. You have to convince them that this is a legitimate endeavor with the goal of making their lives better with the hope that they in turn will make the lives of others in similar circumstances better. There are many success stories out there, but the media almost never want to highlight them."

"Bad news gets better ratings."

"Yes, well, we need positive examples to be heard too."

"Most people I know down there are just looking to survive, Abe. I'm not sure how altruistic they'll be about helping others."

"You may be surprised. But you're right in certain respects, and that's fine, that's to be expected. It's only the initial contact. But it is still critical."

Mace's features clouded. "I'm just a little concerned, you know?"

Altman smiled. "That you have no real experience in this field and the hopes of a nation are riding on your ill-prepared shoulders?"

"Couldn't have said it better myself."

"The answer to that of course is that I know no one who's better prepared to do this than you, Mace. No one. If I did, I would've asked that person. I owe you much to be sure, but this project represents in many ways my life's work. I would not risk it all by choosing someone ill fitted for it. It's simply too important."

"Then I'll do my best for you. That's all I can promise."

"Now, I can have Herbert whip up some lunch. He does an amazing tuna salad."

"Thanks, but I'll take a pass. I'm going to grab a shower at the guesthouse. Then I'll hit some of these contacts."

"Excellent. I really appreciate this."

"Not any more than I do. My options were a little thin."

He put a hand on her shoulder. "Darkest before the dawn. A terrible cliché, I know. Yet so often true. And you may find you like the social sciences even more than police work."

"Actually, police work is basically social science only with a Glock and body armor."

"I think I see your point."

"It's all about respect, Abe. At MPD I was a member of the biggest gang out there. But because we were the biggest, we could never, ever afford to lose a battle."

Altman looked very interested. "How did you manage that?"

"By never going into a situation that I knew I couldn't win."

"I can see that."

"With a toot on my radio I could get help when I needed it faster than any other gang out there. I had to hold my own in a fight for three minutes, that was all. And if I had to thump somebody because they spit on me, I did, because once one blue lets disrespect slide by it endangers all the other blues on the street. Spit now, bullets in the back later. You either love me or hate me, but you will respect the uniform. But the same notion works for the bandits. Most of them are just trying to make a living and the blues are trying to catch them. Rolling Cheerios for a couple thousand a day versus tossing meat at Mickey D's for minimum."

"Cheerios?"

"OxyContin. They're just like you and me but they made different choices."

"And had limited opportunities."

"Right. Each side knows the rules. The bandits don't give a crap about getting their ass kicked or being arrested, or getting shot or being put in prison. Happens to them every day. But don't disrespect them. That is the one unforgivable."

"I think I just learned more in two minutes than I have in the last ten years."

"I'll see you, Professor. Keep the lights on for me." She turned back. "Oh, one more thing. My Ducati sticks out a little bit. Do you have a ride I can borrow?"

"Certainly. Do you want the Bentley or the Honda?"

"It's a close call, but I'll go with the Japanese."

CHAPTER

54

MACE SHOWERED at the guesthouse and thoroughly washed her grimy hair. That was one bad thing about motorcycle helmets: your head sweats like hell in one. As she wrapped herself in a thick robe and strolled around the palatial house that was not even a third the size of the really palatial house next door, it occurred to her that it would be quite easy to get used to this sort of life if you were a normal person, which of course she wasn't. Yet she couldn't help but admire the quality of the furnishings and the high-level skill and attention to detail that had gone into the design and construction. Marty Altman must have been quite talented. It was easy to see from his comments about the lady that Abe had worshipped her.

What would it be like to have a guy worship me?

She dug through her backpack and pulled out a dog-eared notebook. In it she kept a list of contacts she'd used when she was on the police force. She found the name and made the call. It took several handoffs by other people, but she finally reached the lady.

"Charlotte, it's Mace."

"Mace Perry!"

"Come on, do you know any other Mace?"

"Are you still in that awful prison?"

"No, I'm done and out."

"Thank God for that."

"You still enjoying DMV?"

"Oh yeah," Charlotte said sarcastically. "I turned down all those movie offers from Hollywood so I could stay right here and deal with angry people all day long."

"So how would you like to deal with a happy one?"

"That's usually a precursor to you wanting a favor."

"I've got a name and address. And I'd love to get a photo of the guy."

"You're not back on the police force. I would've heard."

"No, but I'm trying."

"It's harder to help out these days, Mace. Electronic eyes every-where."

"How about an old-fashioned fax?"

"Now there's a novel idea."

"So you'll help me? Once more? For old times' sake?"

Mace heard a short sigh. "Give me the name. And your fax number."

Ten minutes later Mace was standing next to the fax machine in the small office on the second floor that Altman had shown her. Two minutes later the fax did its thing and the inked paper slid into the catch bin. Mace snatched it up. It was a copy of Andre Watkins's driver's license.

The real Andre Watkins had short, thick dark hair, wore glasses, and had no beard. His height was listed on the license and she saw that he was also several inches shorter than the guy they'd seen. So she'd been right. She wondered if the real Watkins was indeed an escort. It was such an out-of-the-mainstream occupation that Mace tended to think he probably was. That meant the imposter had dug into the man's background.

Heading back downstairs, she happened on a four-person Jacuzzi tub tucked in a private glass-enclosed space set off from a small den. Hesitating only for a moment, Mace raced to the kitchen, opened the wine chiller set into the wall there, uncorked a bottle of Cab, and poured out a glass. Then she hurried back to the Jacuzzi, figured out the buttons, heated it up, dropped her robe, and slid naked into the hot foamy water. A minute later she snagged her cell off the edge of the tub and phoned Roy.

"Where are you?" she asked.

"I'm at work. I do have a job, remember?"

"Okay, Mr. Grumpy. Guess what I'm doing."

"What?"

"Pampering myself."

"How. Taking target practice? Or zapping homeless people with those knuckle things for laughs?"

"I'm sitting in the buff in a Jacuzzi at Altman's guesthouse drinking a glass of red wine."

"I thought you were going to start your new job?"

"I met with Altman and went over stuff. I'm rewarding myself because I also managed to confirm through DMV that that was not the real Andre Watkins at the apartment today."

"So you were right."

"Yeah, but that leaves a lot of unanswered questions. When will you be done at work?"

"Four-thirty," he said. "I'm checking out early."

"I'll pick you up from work. I'll be in Altman's Honda."

"What happened to the Ducati?"

"Decided to give it a rest. Did you get a rental?"

"All they had available was a Mercury Marquis. It's as big as my condo."

"And your Audi?"

"Can you say totaled?"

"I'm sorry, Roy."

"So where are we going at four-thirty? And what do you need my help on?"

"I'll fill you in when I see you."

"Does it involve getting shot at?"

"Possibly."

"Okay, one request then."

"Tell me."

"The next time you call me while sitting naked in a Jacuzzi sipping wine, you can expect some company."

"Wow, Roy, you're so sexy when you go alpha on me."

55

Roy slid into the front seat of the Honda. "You look nice and refreshed."

"Beats the crap out of the prison showers."

"Got the photo of Watkins?"

She pulled it from her jacket and handed it over.

"He doesn't look like an escort."

"What is an escort supposed to look like?"

"I don't know. Sort of like a model."

"Maybe she went for brains and sensitivity over hunky looks."

"I'm assuming you do the same?"

She hit the gas but the old Honda merely puttered away.

"Just doesn't project the same image as the Ducati, does it?" noted Roy.

"It was either this or the Bentley."

"What tipped you that he wasn't the real Watkins?"

"He didn't want to go down to the Starbucks to talk even though that would have been the safest thing to do from his perspective. I think he was afraid someone from the building who knew the real Watkins might have overheard us and fingered him as an imposter."

"Or he just doesn't like coffee."

"And the guy didn't match the apartment. Three-hundred-dollar shoes, a Hickey Freeman shirt, and professional manicure do not compute with particleboard furniture. And the place had been tossed. Didn't you see the indentations in the carpet from where the hutch, the credenza, the TV cabinet, and the shelving system had been moved?"

"Uh, no, I guess I missed that."

"You notice he grilled us on what we knew and what we were guessing about? We weren't interrogating him so much as he was us."

"So who are they?"

"The only thing I know is they're good."

"What would they have been looking for?"

"Whatever Diane Tolliver left with Watkins."

"So *that's* why you told him you were hanging up the investigation."

She nodded. "It buys us some time. And for all I know that dude is mixed up with the guys who were trying to kill me last night. If they think we're harmless and raising the white flag, well, that's not a bad thing."

"So it looks like this might go a lot further than the Captain. They took his DNA, by the way."

"Let me guess. They used the fresh cup of coffee ploy?"

"How'd you know?"

"They'll check it against the sperm they found on Diane and that'll clear him."

"So it was a rape?"

"Apparently so."

"But, Mace, then it was probably just a random thing. Otherwise why would the bandit rape her?"

Mace gave him an exasperated look. "To make it *seem* like a random crime, Roy."

"But they left sperm behind?"

"And you can bet it won't match up to any database. Just like a weapon can be sterilized, so can sperm, no pun intended."

"Okay."

"If it is connected I'm wondering why the shooters came after me."

"You were at the crime scene."

"Along with a hundred other cops."

"Okay, you've been hanging out with me."

"So why not target *you*? You worked with her. You were down there in Six D all alone waiting for me. They could have easily popped you."

"That's nice to know."

"We need to get into her house."

"Diane's?"

"I struck out in her office. There has to be something at the house."

"I'm sure the police searched it."

"Then we need to search it again."

"Mace, if we get caught, you'll have violated your probation. Can't your sister help us?"

"No."

"Why not?"

"I've got my reasons."

"I'd like to hear them."

Mace sighed. "She's not exactly thrilled with me right now. So how do we get into Tolliver's house? Do you have a key?"

"No, why would I have a key to her house?"

"Well, we have some time to muddle that. Right now we're heading over to check out some stuff for Abe."

"Is that why you wanted me along?"

She glanced at him. "What, you mean for protection?"

"I'm not that stupid. I clearly failed the bodyguard test."

"Not when you put your car between me and the shooter. Those rounds could easily have hit you. That took real courage. But I thought you might enjoy hanging out with me. And bring you back to your old, wild CJA days."

"Long way from Georgetown."

"A lifetime, Roy. A lifetime."

CHAPTER

56

THE PEOPLE at Social Services working with Abe Altman were both extremely helpful and laudatory of the wealthy professor.

"He's a man with vision," said the supervisor, Carmela, a young Hispanic woman with straight dark hair and dressed in a pleated skirt and blouse and flats. "He gets it."

"Well, I hope I *get* it too," said Mace.

They were sitting in the woman's office, a ten-by-ten square with a rusty window AC unit that didn't work. There were water stains on the ceiling and walls. The furniture looked like it had been rescued from the dump and the clunky computer on her desk was at least a decade old. The government purse had clearly not been opened very wide to outfit this place.

She said, "Mr. Altman mentioned that you used to be a cop."

"Don't hold that against me."

"I won't. My older brother drives a scout car right here in Seven D."

"Then he's got his hands full."

"You know this area?"

"Used to be my old stomping ground." Mace glanced down at the sheaf of papers in her hand. "So these are all the names?'

"Yes. We've made contact and they will be expecting you at whatever meeting times you give us. After you called to say you were on your way, I made contact with Alisha, the first on the list. She's expecting you in the next thirty minutes." She glanced at Roy. "You look like a lawyer."

"Mr. Kingman is assisting me in this project."

The woman gave him an appraising look. "You ever been down this way?"

"Was down in Six D just last night if that counts."

She looked surprised. "What for?"

"Looking for some excitement. And I found it."

"I bet. Well, the places you'll be going are a little rough."

"I assume that's why we're going to them," answered Mace. "We'll be okay."

"How rough?" Roy wanted to know.

"Even my brother doesn't like taking calls at some of the places on your list, unless he has a couple units as backup."

Roy glanced at Mace with a worried look. "Really?"

"Thanks, Carmela," said Mace, tugging on Roy's arm. "We'll be in touch."

They climbed back in the Honda. Mace read through the file and said, "Okay, Alisha Rogers here we come."

Roy had been reading over her shoulder. He said, "She's only sixteen and already the mother of a three-year-old?"

"Don't sound so stunned. We left the world of *Leave It to Beaver* a long time ago."

He read off Alisha's address. "Do you know where that is?"

"Yep. Middle of Cheerio Alley. How do you like your Cheerios, Roy?"

"Usually without OxyContin. How exactly are we supposed to go into places where the police don't want to go and come out reasonably healthy?"

"It's a little late to be asking that, isn't it?"

"Humor me."

"We're going to help people, not bust their ass. That'll count for something."

"That's it? We just tell them we're here to help people and the dangerous seas will part? This isn't a Disney flick."

"I never took you for a cynic."

"I'm not a cynic. I just want to go home alive tonight."

Mace's smile faded. "Never a bad goal to have."

57

Aʟɪsʜᴀ ʟɪᴠᴇᴅ in an apartment house that more resembled a bombed-out building in the middle of Baghdad than a residence within an easy commute of the Capitol building. As they pulled into the trash-strewn parking lot where the skeletons of a dozen cars lurked, Roy looked around nervously. "Okay, I've definitely been in Georgetown too long, because we're still in the car and I'm already freaking out."

"There are more sides to life than the rich one, Roy. Sure, there's a lot of crime here, but most people who live in this area obey the law, work really hard, pay their taxes, and try to raise their families in peace."

"I know, you're right," he said sheepishly.

"But keep a sharp lookout because it only takes one bullet to ruin a perfectly good day."

"You could've stopped with raising families in peace."

As they headed to the building on foot they passed men and women huddled in tight pockets on low brick walls, sitting on dilapidated playground furniture, or else standing inside darkened crannies of the building's overhang. All these folks stared at the pair as they made their way to the entrance. Mace kept a brisk pace, though her gaze scanned out by grids, probing gingerly into the shadowy edges before pulling back. As Roy watched her it was like she was using antennae to sense potential threats.

"Okay, are we in imminent danger of dying?" he asked.

"You get that just by waking up every day."

"Thanks for being optimistic."

"Reefer, crack, H, Cheerios, meth, Oxy," recited Mace as they marched along.

"I can smell the pot, but the other stuff?"

Mace pointed to the ground where there were remnants of plastic baggies, elastic straps, snort straws, bits of paper, crushed prescription pill bottles, and even broken syringes. "It's all right there if you know what you're looking for. Which apartment does Alisha live in?"

"File said 320."

They walked inside and the smell of pot, urine, raw garbage, and feces hit them like a wrecking ball. In a low voice Mace said, "Don't even wrinkle your nose, Roy, we got eyes all around the clock face. No disrespect. Can't afford it."

They marched on while Roy's gut churned and his nose twitched.

"Elevator or stairs?" he said.

"I doubt the elevator works. And I don't like being locked in little places where I don't know who'll be waiting for me when the doors open."

"Taking the stairs will probably be dicey too."

"No probably about it. It *will* be dicey."

She opened the door to the stairs, pushing it all the way against the wall in case someone was lurking there. Her gaze moved up, to the next landing.

"Clear, let's hit it."

"What if somebody stops us?"

"Getting jumpy on me?"

"Actually it's been a real struggle keeping my underwear clean since we left the car."

"I know you're the lawyer, but if someone stops us let me do the talking."

"I have no problem with that."

"One thing, though, can you fight?"

"With words or fists?"

"Look around, this is not the Supreme Court."

"Yeah, I can. My Marine brother used to kick my ass on a regular basis until I grew six inches in one summer and started holding my own. Then he taught me the tricks of the trade."

"Marines are good at that. Might come in handy. Last time I was here I was wearing my badge and I barely got out alive."

"Thanks for telling me," muttered Roy.

They reached the third floor and found their way blocked by two enormous men in prison shuffle jeans with the waistbands down to the bottom of their butt cheeks and sporting short-sleeved shirts showing muscular arms so tattooed there was no bare skin left. When they tried to walk around them, the men moved with them, forming a wall that stretched right across the narrow hall. Mace took a step back, her hand sliding to her pocket even as she smiled.

"We're looking for Alisha Rogers. Do you know her?"

The men simply stared back without answering. One bumped shoulders with Roy, knocking him back against the wall.

Mace said, "Alisha knows we're coming. We're here to help her."

"She ain't need no help," said one of the men. He was bald with a neck so thick it seemed like a continuation of his bull-like trap muscles. From down the hall there came the sounds of screaming, the slamming of a door, and then what sounded like shots. An instant later, music started blaring from multiple sources and the screams and shots could no longer be heard.

"So you *do* know her?" Mace continued in a pleasant tone.

"What if I do?"

"There could be some money in it for her too."

"How much money?"

"Depends on how well our meeting goes. And no, we didn't bring the cash with us," added Mace as she spotted one of the guys' hands flit behind his back.

"Who you from?" asked Baldy.

"Social!" said a loud voice. They all turned to see a woman nearly as wide as she was tall marching up to them. She was dressed in a long jean dress stretched to its absolute maximum. A colorful scarf was wound around her head and her long toes poked out from the sandals she wore.

"You know them?" said Baldy.

The scarf lady clutched Mace's hand. "Damn right I do. Now get your sorry asses out the way right now! I am not messing with you today, Jerome, and I mean what I say."

The men moved quietly if grudgingly aside and scarf lady led Mace down the hall while Roy scurried after them, his gaze back on Jerome.

"Thanks," said Mace.

"Thanks doesn't come close to cutting it," Roy chimed in.

"Alisha told me Carmela called a little bit ago and she asked me to be on the lookout for you. But I was taking some laundry down and you got past me. Sorry about those jerks. Barks worse than their bite, but they still bite."

"Were those shots we heard a minute ago?" Roy wanted to know.

"Just a little disagreement probably. No blood no foul."

"What's your name?" Mace asked.

"Just call me Non."

CHAPTER

58

Neither Mace nor Roy probably knew what to expect next. But what they certainly didn't expect was what they found in Alisha Rogers's apartment. The place was clean, smelled of Pine-Sol, and was amazingly tidy, particularly because in the hallway leading to her apartment they had passed twelve large bags of garbage stacked nearly to the ceiling. Maybe, Mace thought, that was the reason why Alisha used so much Pine-Sol.

The furniture was cheap, all probably secondhand, but arranged with some thought and even design. The small windows had what looked to be hand-sewn curtains. A few toys were stacked in one corner in an old cardboard crate that had "Deer Park" stamped on it. From what they could see, the place consisted of only two rooms, the one they were in and another, probably the bedroom, where the door was closed. The "kitchen" had a hot plate and an under-the-counter mini-fridge.

Non had a key to the apartment and had let them in.

"Alisha!" she called out. "Social's here."

There were footsteps in the other room, a door opened, and Alisha Rogers stepped out. A three-year-old boy was riding on her slim right hip. Her hair was long and pulled back and tied with a clip except for a tightly braided ponytail that poked out on the right side of her head. Her eyes were big, her face small, and her lips thin and cracked. At five-three she probably didn't weigh more than ninety pounds, while the little boy had to be almost half that.

Roy looked down at the file he was holding documenting Alisha's background. Roy had seen enough while at CJA that teenage mothers did not really surprise him, though he also knew that a child raising a child was never a good thing. Yet it was far better than leaving the little boy in a Dumpster. He had to admire Alisha Rogers for taking that responsibility when some others didn't.

Non said, "I'm gonna leave you folks to it. Alisha, you need anything I'll be down in the laundry room."

"Thanks, Non," Alisha said, her gaze on the floor as the boy stared at Mace and Roy openmouthed.

Mace stepped forward. "Alisha, I'm Mace and this is Roy. We met with Carmela this morning."

Gaze still on the floor, Alisha said, "Carmela's nice."

"And she was very excited about us meeting with you."

"That's a good-looking boy you have there," said Roy. "What's his name?"

"Tyler," she answered. She lifted one of her son's pudgy fists and did a small wave. When she let go, however, Tyler let his arm drop limply to his side and continued to stare at them, his mouth forming a big O.

"You want to sit down while we talk?" said Mace. "Tyler looks like a load."

While Roy and Mace sat on a small battered sofa with trash-bag-covered foam, Alisha put Tyler down on the floor and sat cross-legged next to him. She snagged a toy out of the Deer Park box and handed it to him.

"You play, Ty, Momma's got to talk to these people."

Tyler plopped down on the floor and obediently started playing with the spaceman action figure from *Toy Story* that was missing an arm and a leg.

Alisha looked up. "Carmela say you folks got something for me."

"To be part of a study," said Mace.

Alisha didn't look happy about this. "I thought it gonna be a job. A real job, you know, with child care and some health benefits."

"No, that's right. The study does have a money and training component."

"How 'bout school?"

"And an education component too. That's considered critical, in fact."

"Ain't got my GED. Dropped out to have Tyler. Went back but couldn't make it work."

"We can help with that. You still want to get your GED?" asked Mace.

"Got to if I want to get out of here. Here's just drugs or Mickey D's if I ain't got no school. Can't take care of Ty good." She reached out and stroked Tyler's wiry hair.

As Mace looked at the little boy's face it struck her that she recognized his features, but couldn't remember from where. "Let's go over the details and we'll see if it's something you're interested in."

"I'm interested in anything that'll get us outta here."

"You and Tyler, you mean."

"And my brother."

"Your brother?" Mace said questioningly. That had not been in the report.

"He just got back."

"From where?"

"Prison."

"Okay. How about Tyler's dad?"

She hesitated, her gaze darting to the floor.

Mace had seen that same maneuver a million times. The lady was about to lie.

"Dead probably. I don't know. He ain't here, that's all."

"How about your parents?" asked Roy.

"My daddy's dead. He sold heroin on the corner a block over from here. My momma left me with my grandma."

"Why did your mother leave you?" Roy asked.

"Had to. She in prison for killing my daddy."

"Oh," said Roy.

"Ain't like he didn't deserve it," she said defensively. "He beat her bad all the time."

"And your grandmother?" asked Mace.

Alisha's big eyes became watery. "Drive-by. She just walking down the street with her groceries and got caught between two damn crews. But she got to see Ty born. He got to see his great-grandma."

"That's pretty rare," said Roy. "Four generations."

"She was only forty-nine when she got killed. My momma was thirteen too when she had me."

Mace was about to ask another question when the door to the apartment opened. When Mace saw who it was she realized where she'd seen Tyler's facial features before.

"What the hell you doing here, bitch?" the man at the door screamed.

Darren Rogers, a.k.a. Razor, the guy Mace had pepper-sprayed, stood in the doorway. A moment later the "crappy" semi-auto pistol was pointed right at her face.

59

WHAT THE HELL *you* doing, Darren?" said Alisha as she jumped to her feet.

He pointed at Mace. "This the bitch what sprayed that shit in my eyes last night. I told you 'bout her."

"Well, in all fairness, I wouldn't have if you weren't pointing a gun at me."

Alisha stared at him. "Did you do that?"

"Hell no. The bitch just shot me with the shit while I was walking by. I never pulled no gun on her ass till right now."

Mace turned to Alisha. "He's also got a .22 caliber revolver in a left ankle holster. And his street name is Razor 'cause, as he told me, he's so sharp."

Alisha put her hands on her hips and scowled at Darren. "How she know all that if you just walking by and ain't pulled your damn gun?"

Darren's face screwed up in frustration. "How I supposed to know that?"

Mace turned to Alisha. "Is he your brother?"

"Hey, you talk to *me*," snapped Darren.

"Okay, are you her brother?"

"Yeah, so what?"

"What were you in prison for?"

"Who told you I was in prison?" Darren glanced darkly at his sister.

She said, "Darren, put that gun away before somebody gets hurt. Look at Ty, he's scared to death."

Unnoticed for the last couple of minutes, Tyler had crawled into a corner and tears were dribbling down his chubby cheeks. He was holding up his spaceman, apparently as a shield. Darren's hostile look instantly melted away. "Ah hell, Ty, I'm sorry, little man." He put the gun in his jacket pocket and hustled over to pick up the child. He held his cheek against Tyler's and talked softly to the little boy.

"He's not crying," said Roy curiously.

Alisha started to answer but Darren beat her to it. "He ain't crying, 'cause he can't talk. Can't make no sounds or nothing."

Mace looked at Alisha. "Have you had him checked out?"

Tears again filled Alisha's eyes. "It was 'cause I doing drugs. Ain't even know I was pregnant. Doctors say that messed up something in Ty's head."

"I'm sorry," said Mace.

Alisha rubbed her eyes. "My damn fault for getting pregnant."

"You got *raped*, Alisha," snapped Darren. "This ain't nothing you did."

"Raped? Did they catch who did it?" asked Roy.

Darren eyed his sister and then looked away in disgust.

"Alisha?" said Mace. "Did you report the rape?"

She shook her head.

"Why not?"

Darren spoke up. "'Cause the dude what raped her is named Psycho. He got the biggest crew around here. You go to the cops on him, you be dead. That's why!"

Mace sat back. "I know about Psycho. The guy's been running his drug and gun op for nearly ten years. That's a lifetime in that line of work. You've got to be real smart and even more dangerous to last that long."

"But the police can protect you," said Roy. He glanced at Mace. "Can't they?"

Darren laughed. "Oh yeah. Sure they can. See, last time the police protected somebody 'round here against Psycho they found his head in a trash bag floating in the Anacostia with a sock stuffed in the mouth. They ain't never found the rest of him. That's some damn fine protection, now ain't it?"

Darren put Tyler down on the floor. "So you tell me what the hell you doing here?"

"How about a chance to get out of here," said Mace.

"Outta here how?"

"I'm working on a project with a professor from Georgetown."

"Georgetown! What the hell that got to do with us?"

"I can explain it to you."

Darren looked like he was about to start shouting again, but then he sat down and motioned at her. "Go on then. Tell me."

Mace spent the next thirty minutes doing just that, filling in the basics first and then building on that. "The professor's theory is that to survive on the streets of virtually any large city requires exemplary intelligence, nerve, daring, risk-taking, and the ability to adapt on the fly. Most people require familial support, a bed, a roof, some food, and relief from danger to function properly."

Darren looked sullen. "Ain't that bad 'round here. Do what you got to do. We *got* a roof over our heads now. Food to eat. And she *got* family now. And ain't nobody coming in that door unless they go through me first."

"But it's not a normal life, Darren," pointed out Mace. "You can't reach your potential if you're always worried about becoming homeless or not having enough food to eat, or waiting for somebody to put a bullet in your head."

"I can take care of myself."

Mace turned to Alisha. "You were selected from the files at Social."

"Why me?"

"You've managed to support a special needs child while getting off drugs and after losing both parents. You currently hold down four part-time jobs while getting Tyler's basic health care needs taken care of out of sheer persistence and more than a dash of ingenuity. And you did all this while just having celebrated your sixteenth birthday. I'd say that was pretty special." Mace looked around the tiny apartment. "And you got this place using forged documents that showed you were eighteen and could legally sign a contract."

Alisha looked frightened. "I had to. After my grandma got killed folks came and took her apartment, kicked us out. After that we was living in a box in an alley off Bladensburg Road. Ain't no place for a child. And Darren was gone."

Darren took her hand. "But I'm back now, baby sister. I take care of you and Ty."

Mace looked over at Darren. She really didn't know what to do with him. "You can't take care of them by robbing people. You'll be right back in prison. Last night if I'd been a cop, you already would be."

Darren whirled on her. "You just get the hell out of here."

"When you go back to prison what happens to Alisha and Tyler? Psycho can come right through that door. Then what?"

Darren started to say something but then just stared at the floor.

Mace said, "So there it is, Alisha. That's the offer."

"You trust this professor dude?" said Darren suddenly.

"Yes I do. And he really cares."

"Why the hell he want to help folks like us?"

Choosing her words carefully, she said, "It's like he's building his own crew."

The angry look faded from Darren's face. "So he be the boss then?"

"Just until you can be your own boss," Mace replied.

Darren looked at his sister. "This shit sounds too good to be true. What next, some fat guy running in here waving a big-ass check with a bunch of balloons?"

Mace said, "Darren, just to be clear, we didn't know you were in the picture. I don't know if the offer extends to you or not."

Alisha stood. "I ain't gonna do nothing without Darren coming too."

"Hold on, hold on, girl," said Darren quickly. "We got to think this through."

Mace stood. Roy did too. She said, "You don't have to make up your mind now. It's your choice. We have other appointments to get to."

Darren eyed her warily. "So if Alisha says no, then he just gets somebody else?"

"That's the plan, yeah. There are ten to start with."

Alisha said quickly, "When do he got to know?"

"A week."

Alisha started to say something but Darren turned to Mace. "You tell your boss that Alisha's gonna do it."

"With you along, you mean? I'll have to check on that."

"No. He ain't got to worry about me. Just Alish and Ty."

"Darren!" cried Alisha. "You ain't know what you saying."

Darren turned to her. "I take care of myself. Always have."

"But you ain't got nobody. The jerks in this building be jumping you already."

"I said I can take care of myself."

"But Darren—"

He turned back to Mace. "You tell the man that Alisha be part of his crew. And Ty too. That's it, no more talking."

"Okay." Mace looked over at Tyler, who was watching all of this from the corner. For the first time in a long time, Mace actually felt a lump in her throat. "They have some great doctors at G-town. They can take a look at your son."

Alisha nodded. "Okay," she said in a low voice.

Mace turned back to Darren. "I thought I had you figured out. But I was wrong. And I'm almost never wrong about stuff like that."

"You listen up, anything bad happens to Alisha or Ty, you got me to deal with." He went into the bedroom and closed the door.

Roy and Mace left the apartment. They hadn't gone ten feet when Non ran up to them, looking scared.

"You two got to get outta here right now!"

"What's up, Non?" asked Mace. "Is Jerome on the warpath?"

"I wish it just be him. Psycho found out you were talking to Alisha. He's coming over here. I think he believes you're the Five-oh and Alisha told you stuff."

"Will he try to hurt her?" Mace said quickly.

"I don't know. But that man is bad news all around."

Mace grabbed Roy's arm. "Come on, this way."

She led him down the hall to a different set of stairs. They fled down them, passing pill poppers, syringe stickers, and one guy fornicating with his lady while smoking a joint.

"What about Alisha and Ty?" asked Roy worriedly.

"I'm trying to call Beth, only I can't get a damn signal in here."

They reached the ground floor, ripped open the door, raced down a short stretch of hall, and then ran outside. And stopped.

A dozen men stood there. One of them, the tallest, stepped forward. He had a big smile and his eyes had the look of a man who was used to telling people what to do.

Roy looked at Mace. "Please tell me that's not Psycho."

Mace didn't answer. She just kept her eyes right on the guy coming at them.

60

Psycho circled them once and then twice, nodding, smiling, and glancing at his men and then back at Mace and Roy. A little taller than Roy, he had on black jeans, a sparkling white T-shirt, and tennis shoes. Several gold chains were visible at the neckline of his tee. His hair was cut so short it was more like a membrane over his scalp. His forearms were veined, muscled, and heavily tattooed. Mace noted that his pupils were normal-sized and his forearms clear of needle marks. You didn't last in that business if you were a user, she well knew. Life and death were often separated by only a rational, nimble decision.

On the third pass he stopped and stood in front of them.

"How's Alisha?" Psycho asked in a surprisingly high-pitched voice.

"Doing okay."

"They say you with Social? Why don't I believe that?"

"We're not cops," said Mace.

"Hey, lady jumped right to it. Must be smart, so I know she's not the blue." His crew laughed. Psycho said, "Then let *me* play the 'blues' part, okay?" Not waiting for an answer, he stood straight and assumed a mock stern expression. "Now you two got anything on your person that might *concern* me?"

Several of his crew guffawed at this.

"Not unless you object to a set of keys and a couple cell phones," said Mace.

"Couple?"

"Yeah, one for business and one for pleasure."

Psycho flicked his hand and two of his men came forward and performed the frisk. One squeezed Mace's butt and he got an elbow driven into his gut for the trouble.

"Whoa, lady got some fire," said Psycho. "You step back in line there, Black," he said to the doubled-over man. "Before you get your ass thumped."

He eyeballed Mace. "So no guns, no badge, that still don't mean no cops. Could be undercover."

"Don't even undercover agents carry guns?" asked Roy. "Especially coming around here?"

Mace let a small groan escape as Psycho turned to Roy. "You got a problem with *around here*? What, you don't like *around here*, Mayonnaise Boy?"

Roy managed to swallow a sudden lump in his throat. "I never said that."

"Yeah, you ain't got to say it. I smell it." He glanced at Mace. "This your old lady?" He ran a tongue over his lips as he checked out Mace. "Fine-looking woman."

"It's a business relationship," said Roy, who instantly regretted having said it.

"A business relationship!" whooped Psycho. "A business relationship?" He turned to his men. "He got himself a business relationship with the chick."

They all laughed, and then Psycho spun around so fast it was a blur. "Then you ain't mind if I do this, then, business relationship dude?" He moved to squeeze one of Mace's breasts, but Roy grabbed his hand and pushed it away.

"Yeah I do mind."

The crew fell silent.

Psycho looked down at the hand Roy had grabbed and then back up, his grin intact. "You really want to go there, mayo?"

"Not really, no. And I won't so long as you keep your hands off her."

"So not you then?" Psycho's arm moved so fast Mace heard the impact before she even saw the swing of the fist. Roy staggered back, grabbing his face, and then fell down. The blood streamed down from his nose, and his eye was already swelling.

Mace quickly moved in front of him. "Look, we talked to Alisha about helping her and her son. That's all."

Psycho shoved her aside. "'Scuse me, bitch, but I ain't done thumping me this asshole."

As Psycho advanced on Roy, Mace reached in her pocket for her Taser phone. But before she could snag it two of Psycho's men grabbed her and held her arms behind her back.

Psycho's foot snapped into Roy's gut, doubling him over.

Mace yelled, "We're leaving, okay? We're outta here right now."

Psycho turned back around. "*I* say when you outta here. And *how* you outta here. Walking or not. Breathing or not. Up to me. Me!"

He faced Roy and aimed a leisurely kick at his ribcage. The next moment Psycho had been spun around and was dumped on his knees. Roy's arms were angled through Psycho's arms and boxed around the other man's head, his blood dripping onto Psycho's scalp.

Roy said, "Seventy pounds of torque to the right and your spine snaps right in half. And there's not a damn thing you can do about it, you prick. And one of your guys pulls a gun, you turn into a corpse."

Psycho could only kneel there, his thick arms stuck uselessly out from his sides.

"They will kill your woman. All I got to do is say it."

"You're going to kill us both anyway. At least I'll have the pleasure of taking you along for the ride."

"What's this pounds of torque bullshit!"

One of Psycho's men stepped forward. "It's Marines. It's how they're trained to kill perimeter sentries. Shit's for real, boss," he added quietly.

Psycho looked up at his guy. "You in the Marines, Jaz?"

"Older brother was. He told me."

"You a Marine?" Psycho said to Roy.

"Would it matter?"

"You kill me, they kill you and the woman. Now if you don't kill me, *I'm* gonna kill you both. How 'bout that?"

Roy looked past where Psycho's men were standing. "How about another option?"

"What?"

"The really manly way to settle disputes."

"Knives? You ain't that dumb. I'll cut your mayo ass up."

"I said *really* manly."

"Meaning what?"

"Meaning basketball. One-on-one. There's a court and a ball right over there."

Mace turned her head to stare at the single netless hoop and the old ball resting next to the support pole.

"Basketball!" roared Psycho. "Just 'cause I'm black you think I play ball?"

Roy glanced down. "No. But you're wearing the same shoes that the UNC team wears on the court. And they're not just for show. They've got black scuffs all over the bottoms and the sides. That only comes from playing ball on the asphalt. In fact, I can tell from the scuff patterns that you're a drive-to-the-hoop and not a pull-up jumper kind of guy."

"So you know your basketball?"

"I'm a fan. Is it a deal?"

"Sure, man, no problem."

Roy tightened his grip on the man's neck. "Don't bullshit me."

"I ain't bullshitting you."

Mace said, "That's a good thing. Because if you say you'll do it and you don't, then you just lost the respect of your entire crew. They may not show it today, or tomorrow, but one day they will. Their boss, who wouldn't take a white boy on in hoops? Rather shoot his ass? Yeah, that's real easy. See, you already let him get the jump on you. And you may try to sound all cool and everything, but you're the one on your knees with another man making the decision whether you live or die. He could kill you right now. But he didn't. What he's offered you is respect. A way to settle this, man to man."

Psycho's superior manner slowly faded as he eyed his troops one by one. None of them would fully meet his gaze.

"So what's it gonna be?" said Mace.

"Play to eleven, a point a hoop and win by two," snarled Psycho. "Meaning *I* win by two. Now you let go of my neck so I can kick your ass."

Roy slowly released the man and Psycho stood, carefully wiping off the knees of his jeans. He looked Roy up and down. "Do you even know *how* to play ball?"

"A little."

"A little don't cut it, *around here.*"

"We can flip a coin to see who gets the ball first."

"Oh, you can have it first. Be the only time you get the damn ball. Oh, and here's one more thing to keep in mind. You win, you both walk. I win, you're both dead."

CHAPTER

61

Psycho stole the ball from Roy by burying a shoulder in his gut and knocking him down before dunking and scoring the first point. He walked back over to Roy, who was slowly getting to his feet. Psycho kicked him hard in the shin.

"That's one."

"That was also a foul," said Roy.

"Ain't no fouls on this court. Just man to man."

"Your ball."

Roy had played against every competition imaginable both on the college basketball court and on the streets. Most guys had one signature move, the best two, the very best three. He let Psycho drive past him and score, taking an elbow shot to the thigh.

That was one move, Roy thought to himself.

Psycho scored again, using a different move.

That was two moves.

He glanced over at Mace, who was staring at him anxiously. He gave her a quick wink and then went back on defense, setting his butt low, his feet and hands spread wide.

Psycho drove again and scored using his first move. Or he would have if Roy hadn't stuffed the ball so hard it knocked Psycho flat on his back on the asphalt.

"My ball," said Roy as he snagged it and dribbled it back and forth between his legs without even looking down.

As Psycho started to guard him, Roy backed up and banked a twenty-footer.

"That's one," said Roy.

A minute later a reverse dunk and then a twenty-foot fader by Roy tied it.

"Three-three."

Five minutes later, and despite Psycho fouling him brutally at every opportunity, Roy was up by six and his opponent was bent over clutching a stitch in his side while Roy wasn't even sweating.

With a perfectly executed crossover dribble that had Psycho frantically backpedaling and then falling on his ass, Roy drove past him and slammed the shot home.

"That's ten," announced Roy. "One more to go."

He took the ball and bounced it back and forth between his legs while he studied his staggered opponent. Psycho was humiliated, tired, and pissed. Roy could at least let the guy make it respectable.

Screw that.

He dribbled backward and stopped, set up, and nailed a twenty-five-footer. The ball didn't even touch the metal rim as it dropped through.

The ball bounced on the asphalt and came to a stop against the post.

"That's eleven. You lose. We walk." He headed over to Mace.

Psycho lunged forward and grabbed a gun from one of his men. Breathing hard, he pointed it at Roy's back.

Roy turned around. "Is there an issue?"

Wiping the sweat from his eyes Psycho said, "Where'd you learn to play ball like that?"

"On a court just like this."

"You lied to me. You said you knew how to play just a little."

"Everything's relative. You might not be as good as you think you are."

Psycho cocked the pistol's hammer back.

Mace pulled free from the two men holding her and moved between Roy and the gun. "Everybody here heard you set the rules. He wins, we walk. *Your* words."

Psycho eyed his crew and then looked back at Mace. The gun came down one inch at a time.

"Get your asses outta here. Now!"

"Just so we're clear, this is not a cop thing. We're with Social. We just came here to help Alisha get a better life, for her and her *son*. Don't make her a part of this, because she's not."

Psycho said nothing. He strode off. His crew followed quickly.

When they were alone Mace turned to Roy. "That was unbelievably kickass."

"Would it be really unmanly if I wet my pants right now?"

"I wouldn't think any less of you."

"So what about Alisha and Tyler? Do you think he'll leave them alone?"

"Call me stupid, but I don't trust anyone whose name is Psycho. I'm going to have Beth get her and the kid out of here."

"And her brother?"

"Yeah, I guess so."

"I suppose we can do some more interviews today," he said doubtfully.

"I think they can wait. Let's go back to Abe's."

"Is he home?"

Mace used her sleeve to wipe the blood off Roy's face. "I don't care if he is or not. I need to get my little hero cleaned up."

She took his hand and led him back to the Honda.

No one bothered them on the way out.

62

Mace put the pack of ice over Roy's nose as he sat in the spa in Altman's guesthouse. "How's it feel?"

"Broken. But then so does my leg, my ankle, and my ribs."

"At least the swelling around your eye's gone down. You want to go to the hospital?"

"No, I'll be okay so long as I stop interacting with guys named Psycho."

"I was going to order out for Chinese, but when I called the main house to see if they had a take-out menu, Herbert seemed indignant. So he's preparing a Chinese dinner just for us."

"Very nice of Herbert. Where's Altman?"

"The Bentley's gone, so maybe he ran out to do something."

Roy sat up straighter, positioning the ice pack under his eye. "Did you get through to your sister?"

"She had Alisha and Tyler picked up and brought to Social Services."

"And her brother?"

"He wasn't there. That guy worries me."

"That he'll go after Psycho, you mean?"

"Yep. And that means he'll be dead."

She sat on the edge of the spa. "You know why I brought you along with me today?"

"For the comedic potential?"

"No, to keep an eye on you."

He took off the ice pack and swiveled around to look at her. "To protect *me*?"

"After those guys came after me I knew they'd run your license plate and find out who you were. I was worried. But the only thing I did was set you up in a death match with an asshole named Psycho. What a genius I am."

He gripped her hand. "Hey, you had no idea that was going to happen. And we did okay. Right?"

"You did great, not just okay."

"You must be rubbing off on me."

They stared at each other. She stroked his hair and he rubbed her arm.

"You up for getting wet, Mace?" he said quietly, his gaze melding into hers.

They heard a sound from downstairs. Mace jumped to her feet. "That must be Herbert. Do you want me to bring the food up here or do you want to eat outside overlooking the stunning gardens?"

He let go of her hand. "Stunning gardens sound good."

"Take your time, I'll keep the food warm."

As she fled down the stairs Roy slowly sank back into the water.

Beth had just come back to her office after attending a meeting in Four D when her phone rang. She picked it up. "Chief," she said.

"Please hold for Interim U.S. Attorney Mona Danforth," a woman's voice said in an overly formal manner.

Beth tapped her fingers on her desk as she waited for Mona to pick up. This was a stunt the lady pulled all the time. She'd probably been standing there watching her secretary make the call and then sauntered back to her office, just to make Beth wait.

Thirty seconds passed and Beth was just about to slam the phone down when the woman's voice came on the line. "Mona Danforth."

"Yeah, that part I got since *you* called *me*. What's up?"

"Something strange on the Meldon case."

"You have specifics?"

"The CIA is disavowing any knowledge of the matter."

"And you're surprised why?"

"Hey, you asked me to make some calls and get back to you."

Beth stared down at her desk as she tried to compartmentalize the one million things she still had to do today after already changing gears a dozen times. But mostly she was thinking of Mona's little plan to ruin both her and Mace. "Go ahead."

"I checked Jamie's caseload. He was not working on anything that would've caused anyone to kill him and throw him in a Dumpster."

"But he was a defense lawyer in NYC, right?"

"More specifically he was a mob lawyer. But the people he represented are either dead, in prison, or no longer in the business. The one guy who might've had a grudge against him is in Witness Protection. And U.S. Marshals don't ordinarily let their protectees run off to commit murders."

"So the CIA claims they're not behind the investigation into Jamie's murder. Let's say they're telling the truth for once. Who else could it be? I heard the order to stand down might've come from the White House. But then I talked to someone I trust who told me that probably wasn't true."

"Who'd you talk to?"

"Sorry, Mona, I start giving away my sources, I won't have any left."

"Fine!"

"Look, the mayor was the one to actually call me off, but when I asked him where the order had come from he clammed up."

"You think the Bureau is playing straight with us on this?"

"I know the director and his top guys, just like you do. They've usually played straight in the past. Why do you ask?"

"Because I got a message from a Fibbie asking to meet with me to go over the Meldon case."

"Why you?"

"I am the interim U.S. attorney, Beth. Jamie worked for me."

"But the last time I checked, a homicide committed in D.C. fell within my purview. I have to catch the damn bandits before you can prosecute them, Mona."

"Well, if you want to meet with him, feel free. I'm swamped as it is. And when I put it up as an option, he said he had no problem with that. In fact, I think he was planning on talking to you anyway."

Beth pulled a piece of scratch paper toward her. "Fine, what's his name."

"Special Agent Karl Reiger."

63

THE SUN was setting as they finished their meal. Herbert had served the dinner in a Roman ruin–style pavilion next to an elaborate water garden with a pond, waterfall, and hundreds of thirsty flowers.

"I wonder if Herbert rents out for parties," said Roy, as he used chopsticks to push a last bit of spicy pork into his mouth.

"If you had a full-time gig here would you ever want to leave?" said Mace as she sipped on a glass of Chinese beer.

Roy glanced at her. "So about me asking you to join me in the hot tub—"

"What about it?" Mace cut in.

"Uh, nothing."

Her tone softened. "Look, it's just been awhile. The last few years did a number on me. Made it hard to have a normal relationship. Hell, if I ever could in my line of work."

"I understand that."

"But I like hanging with you. And you put a lot on the line for me. I won't forget that."

Mace leaned forward and made marks on a cloth napkin with her sticks. "Diane Tolliver's office."

"You want to go back to there? Why?"

"*Something* happened, Roy. Those guys came after me right after I was there."

"How would they have even known you were there? I was the only one up there with you and I didn't tell anybody."

"We also need to get into Diane's house."

"Won't the police have it taped off?"

"It's just tape."

"No, it's *just* a felony. More than one, actually. You could go back to prison."

Her face eased into a hard mask. "I'm already in prison, Roy, but I'm apparently the only one who can see the damn bars."

"What do you hope to find at her house?"

"She wanted us to talk to Andre Watkins. The bandits beat us to it. So we have to get that information from another angle."

"Come on, shouldn't we leave this to the police?"

"Some jerks tried to kill me. I'm not walking away from that."

"You have no idea if that's connected to what happened to Diane."

"My gut is telling me different. And I listen to my gut."

"It's never wrong?"

"Not on the important issues, no."

Roy eyed the immense gymnasium facility Altman had shown them across from the guesthouse.

"You up for a little B-ball?"

"What? You didn't have enough with Psycho?"

"I would assume it would be a little friendlier than that."

"Never assume. Remember how you described my play? I can hard-foul with the best of them. But I didn't bring my uniform."

"I bet a guy like Altman has all that stuff."

"What do you have in mind?"

"One-on-one?"

"I saw what you did to Psycho. You're out of my league."

"Come on, I'll take it easy on you."

"Gee, just what I wanted to hear." She paused. "How about a game of HORSE instead?"

"HORSE?"

"Yeah, you know the game, right."

"I think I played it once or twice."

"Well, in the interest of full disclosure, I spent the last two years of my life playing it every day. Still game?"

"No problem."

"Don't sound so confident. What are we playing for?"

"Playing for?"

"I'm not getting all hot and sweaty for nothing."

"You up for anything?"

"Not if the loser has to give the winner a full-body massage while naked, or some crap like that."

"No nakedness or bodily touching. I promise."

She looked at him warily.

"Come on, Mace, trust your gut."

"Okay, my gut says whatever you propose I accept."

"Okay. You win, we *both* keep investigating this thing without the cops. I win, we go to the cops and tell them everything and let them handle it."

Mace looked at him with a stony expression.

"You're not going to back off your gut, are you?" he said.

"I guess I expected a little more from you, Roy."

"I think you'll thank me at some point. You ready?"

Mace stood. "Better bring your A-game, Kingman."

64

I FEEL LIKE I'm back in college," said Roy as they gazed in awe at the facility Abe Altman had built with Warren Buffett–fueled riches.

"You were on a major college team. I only played girls' high school ball in a Catholic league, meaning we had no money. This is like hoops heaven to me."

Roy pointed to the rafters. "He even has a facsimile of the NCAA championship banners the men's and women's teams won at Maryland."

They spent a few minutes checking out the pool, full-size locker room with showers, sauna, steam room, and exercise room equipped with the latest machines. There was one room with workout clothing neatly laid out that looked like it had never been worn. Rows of athletic shoes lined one wall.

"This is like some sports fantasy," he said.

"Let's get down to business, because I'm really looking forward to kicking your ass," said Mace.

"Now who's overconfident?"

"You must really want out of this." Her tone was flat and hard.

"How about wanting to keep both of us alive? Doesn't that count for something?"

She bumped him with her shoulder. "If you want to call it living."

"What?"

"Being a chickenshit."

"So why'd you go along with the bet?"

"Like I said, because I really want to kick your ass."

They found a large room filled with all the athletic gear one could want, from baseball mitts to boxing gloves. There were at least fifty basketballs placed neatly on racks, many with college logos on them.

Mace pulled out one. "For old times' sake."

He looked down to see the familiar UVA Cavaliers logo painted on it.

They walked out to the court, where Roy did a mock cheer from the invisible crowd. She threw the ball hard at his gut. He easily caught it before impact. "So what was it like to play in front of thousands, Mr. Superstar?" she asked.

"Greatest time of my life."

"Glory days?"

"Being a lawyer pays the bills. It's not like I get out of bed every day thanking the Lord Almighty for the opportunity to make rich people even richer. It's not like what you used to do as a cop."

"Then get out of it. Go back to being a CJA, or join the public defender's office."

"Easier said than done."

"It's only hard if you make it."

"I'll keep that in mind. Ladies first." He bounced the ball to her.

"Shall we just dispense with the layup portion of the program?"

"Whatever you want."

She marched off fifteen feet at a hard right angle from the hoop. She set up and fired. Nothing but net.

Roy clapped. "I'm impressed. Not even warmed up."

"Oh, au contraire. I had the hot sauce on my noodles. And your loser bet made me even hotter. I'm like fire inside."

"Mace, I really think you'll thank me later for—"

"Just shoot!"

Roy took his place and swished it.

Twenty feet out at a forty-five degree angle Mace banked it in.

"About the limit of your range?" he asked.

"Guess you'll find out."

He made a swish.

Mace said, "Okay, that's H for you."

"What the hell are you talking about? I made the shot."

"I *banked* my shot, Roy. You swished it. You got an H." He stared at her openmouthed. "What?" she said. "You thought I banked it because I couldn't do it clean from twenty?"

She grabbed the ball from him, set up at twenty, and hit nothing but the bottom of the net.

"Okay, I've got an H," he said sullenly.

"Yes, you do."

After nearly an hour, over eighty shots and very few misses, each stood at H-O-R-S.

Mace set up her shot and banked in an arced twenty-five-footer.

"So just to be clear, do I need to bank or can I swish?" he asked.

"I'll take it easy on you, wimpy boy. You can choose."

Roy bounced the ball twice, took aim, and released. His shot missed not only the net but the rim as well.

Mace bent down, picked up the ball, and looked over, open-mouthed.

"That's E," said Roy. "I lose. We keep working the case without the cops."

"So did you intend to lose on purpose all the time?"

"I guess that's something you'll never know. So what's our next move?"

"Are you sure about this?" She bounced the ball to him.

He bounced the ball back to her. "Don't ask me again. And don't get all mushy on me—not that that's likely to happen."

"Okay, Tolliver left the office on Friday around seven. The garage record told us that. And then she returned a little before ten."

"But she lived in the south end of Old Town. Why drive all the way out, turn around, and come back?"

"I called in a favor and found out that the cops pulled a credit card receipt. Diane ate at a place in Georgetown on Friday night called Simpsons. Do you know it?"

"Little hole-in-the-wall a block off M Street toward the river. I've been there. Good food. Was she alone?"

"No. The bill showed there were two meals served."

"Who was she with?"

"Don't know."

"Aren't the cops going to check with the people at the restaurant?"

"I don't know. They have the Captain in custody."

"But when the Captain turns out to be innocent?"

"Then we'll be ahead of the curve. But I've got to make one stop first."

"Where?"

"To see an old friend."

65

BETH WAS PILOTING Cruiser One alone tonight, although she had a couple of uniforms in an unmarked car behind her as she sat in the deserted parking lot of a school. She was in uniform and still had her Glock 26 in its holster. Her policy was, when she wore the stars she carried the firepower too. Her radio hung from a clip on her shirt.

Most days the four stars on each shoulder felt like they weighed a ton apiece, and this day was no exception. This meeting tonight might add immeasurably to her professional pain. Yet she sat calmly and idly tapped a tune on her steering wheel as she listened to the police radio. By force of habit she was still monitoring the dispatches and responses from her officers. There'd been a shooting about six blocks from her location. Normally she would've gone to the scene. But tonight she was waiting. And not liking it.

She stopped tapping when the black sedan pulled into the parking lot. It just screamed FBI Bucar. She knew the shouts of "Five-oh" and "whoop-whoop" had started up the second the sedan had entered Five D. All Bucars looked the same, sounded the same, and even smelled the same. She knew that drugs, guns, gangs, and whores had silently pulled back into the shadows to let the Fibbies pass before they took up their illegal business once more. The sedan pulled to a stop next to her ride, hood to trunk. The driver's-side window slid down.

She saw the creds and badge first, the face second.

"Special Agent Karl Reiger." A second face appeared behind his. "My partner, Don Hope."

Beth said, "Your creds are Homeland Security. Danforth said you were Bureau."

"Misunderstanding. Happens sometimes. We actually were with the FBI up until a few years ago. Now we're assigned to a specialized division of DHS tasked to counterterrorism measures."

"Specialized division?"

"Yep. After 9/11 there're lots of them."

"Okay, let's talk."

"Our office or yours?"

Beth popped open her door, nodded to her men in the tail cruiser, and slipped into the backseat of the Town Car. Closing the door, she said, "Mona didn't really fill me in, so I'd appreciate a briefing."

Reiger and Hope turned sideways to look at her. Reiger said, "Up front, you have to know it's going to be limited."

"Not what I wanted to hear. When I get read into something I like all the pages."

"We've got orders just like everybody else."

"Specialized, you said?"

"Joint task force with a limited circle of need to know."

"That's just another name for 'you can't tell me.'"

"National security."

"That excuse I hate even more. The guys who pulled the crime scene plug on me, who where they?"

"Part of the task force."

"I've been doing this nearly twenty years. I have never seen someone waltz past the police tape simply by showing their damn driver's license."

"We don't like it any better than you."

"I doubt that. Did this all really come from the White House?"

"Who told you that?" Reiger said sharply.

"Sorry, can't read you in on that. I'm not sure you're cleared for it."

"Look, Chief, I know you're pissed. And I would be too, but national security—"

Beth cut him off. "I've played the national-security-trumps-everything game with the best of them. What I don't appreciate is being completely cut out of the loop on a homicide committed in my own backyard. I earned my badge and my creds, and I don't like getting blindsided by assholes with shields from DMV."

Reiger said, "We think Meldon was killed by domestic terrorists."

Beth leaned forward. "Domestic terrorists? What's the connection to him?"

"Case he was working. Remember the guy who tried to blow up the Air and Space Museum almost a year ago using four pounds of Semtex and a cell phone detonator?"

"Roman Naylor? How could I forget? It was one of my officers on K-9 duty that nailed the son of a bitch before he could kill a thousand kids from the Midwest who were there on a summer tour."

"Meldon was prosecuting the case. Naylor has groups of supporters in various states. United Sons of the American Patriot was one of them. They've been linked to three bombings of federal property in the last two years. We think that was just the warm-up act for something that will rival 9/11. A bunch of these homegrown whack jobs went underground after we and ATF came after them on a joint op. We suspect that three of Naylor's cronies were in D.C. last week to participate in a protest in front of the federal courthouse where he's being tried, and now they've disappeared."

"Wait a minute, Mona told me she'd reviewed Meldon's caseload and there was nothing he was working on that would account for his murder."

"And you trust Danforth?"

"Not really."

"Good, because that lady would lie to her grandmother on the woman's deathbed if she thought it would help her career. The fact is, we put Danforth on a short leash and *suggested* that she pass off the baton to you. She really didn't seem to mind. Lady doesn't like getting her nails dirty."

"Understood, but why did you suggest it?"

"Because we'd much rather deal with you than her."

"So you really think Naylor's cronies killed Meldon?"

"Doesn't take a big stretch."

"How did he die?'

Hope passed across a single sheet of paper. "This is a summary of the autopsy results. Contact gunshot wound to the back of the head, execution style. We got the slug. It was a .40-caliber round. But we'll never find a gun to match it to. His ride was found in western Maryland with only Meldon's prints on it. No trace at the crime scene. Neat and clean and the killers long gone."

"But if these guys were in D.C. how come I didn't get notice? How come Meldon didn't get protection?"

"We said *suspected*, not confirmed. And if it's the three we think it is, we didn't have anything to hold them on anyway except speculation and gut instincts, and the courts don't look too favorably on that. But we believe that they've been tasked to do the next Oklahoma City."

"If so, why risk it all by killing Meldon?"

"They were tight with Naylor. So it could simply be personal revenge. Now that the guy's dead the trial will be delayed."

"Any leads on these three?"

"Not yet. But we're running it down."

"And will I be in the loop when you do?"

"We can ask, Chief, that's all we can do."

"So by not really telling me anything, why did you call the meeting?"

"We told you our theory on who killed Meldon. And we gave you as much hard info as we could. Let me tell you, it was hell even getting that autopsy summary released."

"If you give me pictures of the three suspects, four thousand police officers can start looking for them."

"I highly doubt they hung around town after doing Meldon."

"Surprise, I also know police chiefs in other cities. And I even have some Feds I call friends."

"We have all that covered."

"So, again, why did you want to see me?"

"Professional courtesy," said Reiger. He paused. "And a high-up buddy of yours asked us to fill you in."

It didn't take Beth long to come up with the answer. "Sam Donnelly?"

"He's not the kind of guy who likes to take credit for stuff, but I won't deny it."

"I owe him."

"I'm sure he'll call in a favor from you one day. And I know this sounds unfair as hell, but if you get any leads we'd appreciate a heads-up."

Beth opened the door. "You'll get it."

"That easy?" said Reiger.

"Unlike you guys, I just want to catch the bandits. I don't really give a damn what agency gets the credit. Why don't you try to pass along that philosophy in your *specialized division*?"

A few seconds later Cruiser One was rolling with the tail car right behind.

As she drove out of sight Reiger looked at Hope, who said, "What do you think?"

"I think we did what we were told and now we report back."

"And the sister and the lawyer?"

"I'm not calling the plays on this thing, Don. I just execute them. But let me tell you, the further we go on this thing, the less I like it. I didn't sign on for this shit and I know you didn't either."

"They're paying us four times what we normally earn."

"Yeah, to kill our fellow Americans?"

"During the vetting Burns told us that we might have to go all the way. But it's to keep the country safe. Sometimes the enemies come from within. Hell, you know that."

"I still wanted to puke when I put that round in Meldon's head."

"Burns told us he was a traitor, showed us the proof. But if the truth came out, it would ruin years of intelligence work. He had to be taken out. This is black ops stuff, Karl, the old rules don't apply."

"Keep telling yourself that, you might start believing it."

Reiger steered the sedan out of the parking lot.

An unmarked car pulled slowly out of an alley opposite the lot and followed Reiger's sedan. The guy riding in the passenger seat said into the radio, "Mobile Two rolling and on their six."

Beth Perry's voice crackled into the car. "Where they go, you go. I don't care if it's hell and back. Chief out."

66

"Remember me, Doc?"

Mace stood in the front lobby of the police forensic facility. Roy was waiting out in the car. Lowell Cassell, the chief medical examiner, smiled.

"I was both surprised and thrilled when they told me you were here."

"I see you're still in the habit of working late."

"Your sister has cut down considerably on the homicide rate, but unfortunately my backlog is still full."

They shook hands and then did a quick hug.

"It's so good to see you, Mace."

She smiled. "I missed you too, Doc."

Mace looked around. "They were just about to finish this place when I . . . went away."

Cassell nodded. "Yes. I hope Beth communicated my sentiments on that subject to you?"

"Loud and clear."

"So tell me, what can I do for you?"

"Well, I wanted to come by, see you, see this place."

"And?"

"I *was* wondering about a certain investigation."

"Diane Tolliver?"

"How'd you guess?"

"Let's discuss this in private."

A minute later they were seated in his office.

"Diane Tolliver?" Mace prompted.

"It's an ongoing investigation."

"That I know."

"Then you also know it's not something I can really talk about."

"Look, Doc, I know I'm not with the blues anymore."

"If it were up to me I'd show you the entire file, but it's not up to me."

"Beth told me some things already."

"She's the chief, I'm simply a worker bee."

"Anyway, hypothetically speaking, if I *were* working the case I'd like to see the autopsy report, list of trace found at the site, tox report, rape kit results, you know, the usual."

"*If* you were working the case."

Mace stood and paced. "Thing is, I can't work the case because I can't be a blue. At least with a felony conviction hanging over my head."

"That's right."

"Unless circumstances change."

He looked intrigued. "How would they change?"

"I prove I was innocent. Or else."

"Or else what?"

"I solve a case. A big case."

"I see. Wasn't there an FBI agent years ago who did something like that?"

"He actually came to visit me in prison."

"Then I can see your motivation."

"Doc, being a cop is all I know. Beth could be anything. She could be running some Fortune 100 company if she put her mind to it, or else be president of the United States. I'm a blue, that's all I can be."

"Don't short-change yourself, Mace."

"Let me rephrase that. It's all I've ever *wanted* to be."

"I can understand that. Especially considering what happened to your father."

"You knew him, didn't you?"

"I had that privilege. And it makes it doubly hard to accept that Mona Danforth is right this moment occupying his old office."

"When I was in prison all I thought about was getting out and seeing Beth. And then proving my innocence and getting back on the force. It seemed so possible in there."

"But now?"

"Not so possible," Mace said resignedly.

"But you have to try? Even if it means you might go back to prison?"

"I don't want to go back. God knows I don't. But living free outside the uniform?" She paused, searching for the right words. "It feels like I'm right back in the box with bars even though I'm free. I guess that's hard to understand."

"No, it's actually not."

"So I'm here asking for your help. Because I can't solve this case without some forensic information."

She sat down, her gaze squarely on him.

He stared back at her for a moment before rising. "I don't have the tox report or the DNA match results back yet."

"Okay."

He opened a file cabinet, took out some documents, and put them on his desk. "I need to use the restroom. Damn prostate. Be grateful you don't have one. I'll be back in a bit." Before he left, he lifted the cover on the tabletop copier on a credenza behind his desk. "Just replaced the toner and loaded in a full supply of paper."

He closed the door behind him. A second later Mace was copying as fast as she could.

67

"Y OU LOOK HAPPY," said Roy as Mace climbed in the car and he pulled off.

"I am. And you're right," she said. "This Marquis really is huge. You could fill it with water and use it for a pool."

He glanced at the papers she had in an expandable file. "What's that?"

"That is the result of a good friend taking a huge risk for me."

"What do you want to do now?"

"You drive us to your office and I'll read."

Twenty minutes later Roy pulled into the parking garage of his office building and Mace turned over the last page of the file she'd copied.

"And?" Roy asked.

"She was raped, but Beth already told me that. The DNA results from the sample taken from your buddy the Captain aren't back yet and neither is the tox report."

"How did she die?"

"Someone crushed her brain stem." She looked up. "Back of the neck. It would've taken a really strong person probably with some special skills to do that."

"Like a former Army Ranger who weighs about three hundred pounds?"

"You said it, I didn't."

"What else?"

"Trace and soiling on her clothes matched samples they took from the Captain."

"So that's why there's been no court appearance scheduled yet for him. They're waiting to see if they hit a home run on the DNA. Normally there's a presentment hearing within twenty-four hours of arrest."

"When they do charge him what are you going to plead?"

"Regardless of whether it's burglary or murder, we scream 'not guilty' and go from there. The prosecutor doesn't need any help from me." He glanced at the file. "Anything that doesn't point to the Captain?"

"Not really."

"But the DNA sample is going to come back as not a match. They can get the Captain on the burglary, but I'll take that over murder in the first."

"Who wouldn't?" Mace said.

"But Diane had dinner with someone on Friday night and it sure wasn't the Captain."

"Maybe it was this guy Watkins. The real Watkins, I mean."

"Hopefully, we'll find out."

They rode the elevator up to Shilling & Murdoch and Roy swiped his card across the contact pad, releasing the doors.

A minute later they were looking through the dead woman's space. Mace sat down at Diane's desk and stared into the large Apple computer screen. "Nice system."

"I'm surprised the cops didn't take her computer."

"They don't have to anymore. They just download everything to a flash drive. It would be nice to see what's on here." She glanced at him. "Any thoughts on that?"

"It's password-protected, but let me give it a shot."

Roy sat down, powered up the Mac, and stared at the password line that appeared.

"What do you use for your password?" Mace asked.

"AVU2778861."

"Okay, the letters I get. UVA spelled backwards. But what about the numbers?"

"Twenty-seven and seven was the record we finished with my senior year."

"And the eight-eight-six-one?"

"Eighty-eight to sixty-one was the score of my last game when we lost to Kansas in the NCAAs."

She gave him a sympathetic look. "Ever thought about just letting it go, Roy?"

"I've *thought* about it."

He refocused on the screen. "Okay, Diane, what would your password be?"

"She's not married, no children. Pets?" Roy shook his head. Mace glanced at the file she'd carried up with her. "Try her date of birth." She read it off to Roy and he hit the keys but the password box shook it off. They tried other combinations of the numbers. They tried her mother's maiden name that Roy just happened to know.

"It's going to lock us out with one more attempt," he said.

"We're not going to break it. Stupid idea." Mace stared at the top edge of the computer screen. "What's that thing?"

Roy looked where she was pointing. "A webcam. You can use it for videoconferencing and stuff."

Mace slowly moved out of the line of sight of the camera and motioned frantically to Roy to get up. But she said in a calm voice, "Well, that's all we can do here tonight. Might as well get going."

When Roy was out of the camera's view, Mace grabbed his arm and hissed in his ear, "Let's get the hell out of here."

She pulled him out the door and closed it behind them.

Roy snapped, "What's wrong?"

"That's why they came after me. They saw me searching Diane's office."

"Who saw you?"

"Whoever's on the other end of that camera. Come on, before they get here."

"Before *who* gets here?"

They both turned as they heard the sound at the same time. The front door to the offices of Shilling & Murdoch had just beeped open.

"Them!"

68

Tнıs way." Roy grabbed Mace's hand and they raced down the hall away from the front doors. They reached the end of the corridor and turned left and the short hallway ended at a door. Roy threw it open and they were staring into a darkened room.

"What is this place?"

"The mail room."

"Great, Roy, now we can check out some cool travel magazines while we count down the last minutes of our freaking lives."

"I actually had another idea. Come on."

He led her to the back of the room where there was a small metal door flush with the wall and about four feet off the floor.

"The firm has some offices on the fifth floor and we also keep an archival space there." He smacked a red button next to the metal and the door slid up, revealing a three-by-three-foot space that barely looked big enough to hold one person.

"A dumbwaiter?" said Mace.

"This shaft feeds right into the storage space on the fifth."

They both turned when they heard the footsteps running down the hall.

"Get in, Mace."

"What about you?"

"There's not enough room for both of us."

She looked inside the space. "If you don't get in this box with me, the next box you will get in will be a coffin."

He boosted her in and then crawled in behind her. As the door to the mail room was kicked open, Roy reached out with a long arm and slapped the green send button. The metal door closed and a moment later the dumbwaiter lurched into action. The space was so tight that Mace's knees were touching her nose and the much taller Roy was curved around her body like a moat around a castle.

Mace squirmed. "Is that a flashlight in your pocket or are you just happy to see me?"

"It *is* a flashlight. I snagged it off a shelf before I jumped in."

The dumbwaiter stopped and the metal door slid open. Roy fell out and pulled Mace along with him. He clicked on the flashlight and a few moments later they were running down the hall.

"The elevators are no good. And they've probably got the stairs covered."

She said, "The stairs at the *bottom,* but not the others. Come on!"

As they raced along, Mace stopped for a moment, covered her hand with her shirtsleeve to eliminate the possibility of prints, reached out and pulled the fire alarm. As the loud clanging and swirling red lights chased them down the corridor she said, "There's a fire engine company not too far from here, but we still have a few minutes to survive on our own."

"So where do we go?"

"Fourth floor."

She led him to the fire stairs and they skipped down one flight. A moment later they were back in the place where Mace had subdued the Captain.

"Now we hide."

"Shouldn't we call the cops? I've got my cell."

She hesitated for an instant. "Yeah, do it."

Roy hit 911. "I've got no bars. What the hell!"

They sprinted to the back of the space.

"Quick, look around for a weapon," she said.

"They've probably got guns and you want to hold them off with what, a screwdriver?"

Mace scanned the floor and spotted it. A long length of chain. She snagged it and wrapped it around her arm. "We can use this."

"Wait a minute. When the fire truck gets here they'll find us and your sister will know you were here."

"I don't plan to be here when the fire trucks get here."

"But I thought—"

"If the bad guys don't come through that door in the next minute, then that means they were scared off by the alarm. Then you and I are going to get the hell out of here before the fire guys show."

"Not exactly the way I would've done it."

"Roy, I'm holding a ten-pound chain. Do not piss me off!"

Sixty seconds later they heard the sirens coming. Mace dropped the chain and they raced to the door and bolted down the stairs. They cleared the lobby and stepped into the elevator to the garage right as the firemen were coming in the front doors. They didn't bother with the Marquis parked in the garage, but fled out the exit and turned away from the building.

"Now what?" said a breathless Roy as they slowed to a fast walk.

She checked her watch. "You up for some coffee?"

"What? Some people were just trying to kill us and you want a stimulant?"

"Yeah, at Simpsons in Georgetown, where Tolliver ate on Friday."

"Oh, okay."

"Then after that we can break into Tolliver's house."

"Oh for the love of God."

CHAPTER

69

Later that night Don Hope and Karl Reiger walked down the long hallway. They were several stories underground and the walls were lined with materials that prevented any form of electronic surveillance. It was a good thing since there were few buildings in the country that housed more secrets than this one, and that included the CIA's command center in Virginia and the NSA headquarters in Maryland.

Both men looked anxious as they came to a stop in front of a metal door. There was a long hiss from hydraulic-powered equipment and the portal slid open. They stepped in and the door automatically closed behind them.

There were two chairs in front of the desk. They sat. Jarvis Burns was seated across from them. He perused his computer screen for another minute before turning to them. He slid off a pair of glasses and set them on the desktop. His hand ventured automatically to his right leg and started rubbing it. When Reiger started to speak, Burns held up his hand and shook his head. This was followed by a deep sigh. Reiger and Hope exchanged a nervous glance. Long sighs, apparently, were not a particularly good sign.

Burns said, "Interesting developments. Not pleased at all. Overly complicated now." Each short sentence came out like an MP5 set on two-shot bursts.

Hope said, "Permission to speak candidly?"

"Of course."

"The chief is covered. We fed her the info like you said and made it clear Director Donnelly was the source. As far as she's concerned it's domestic terrorists and she owes you. The sister and the lawyer are not really an issue, at least in my mind."

Burns sat back, made a temple with his fingers, and settled his gaze on the two men. "Your assessment based on what? Your failures?"

"We haven't failed."

"Really? 'Focus in on A-'? We had spyware on Tolliver's computer. You knew about that e-mail and left it there. You could have erased it from Kingman's computer before he even read it."

Reiger said, "We didn't do that because it sounded innocuous. We thought she'd just hit the send key by mistake. The message wasn't even finished."

"It was finished enough, because they figured out what it meant before you did. They got Watkins's name and went to his apartment just in time to catch one of my people searching it. He had to tap-dance pretty fast."

Reiger spoke up. "We didn't know she had a box there. She's never been to that mailbox place the whole time we've had her under surveillance."

"Well, either she went before you had her under the glass or she had someone else to do it for her."

"But your guy didn't have to answer the damn door at Watkins's apartment," Hope pointed out.

"Trust me, if he hadn't, Mace Perry would've broken in. And the police know about Watkins, too, of course. We could have removed the message after Perry and her friend found it, but then we would've risked her telling her sister and the paper being gone from the box would only have aroused the chief's suspicions. The damage, in any case, was already done. But on the bright side, they have the old soldier in custody and he will no doubt be charged with murder very soon."

"So maybe our work is done, then."

"No, your work is not done. But we cannot afford any more screwups."

Hope placed one large, muscular hand on the desktop. "We've been reactionary from almost the get-go. That's not how successful ops are done, black or otherwise. That's not why you brought us on board."

"You are only technically assigned to DHS, which does not engage in black ops. You and Reiger are actually sterilized weapons, cocked and locked at all times. And we brought you on board to do a job, whatever job you were told to do. There is nothing nice or neat about our line of work. It is invariably messy, dirty, and everchanging. You do deals with one devil because he's slightly better than the next devil. If it were otherwise we wouldn't need you. But we do need you to clean up *your* mess."

"Look, they found nothing in the office, and the spyware surveillance established through Tolliver's computer has already been severed. I don't see what the problem is."

"Then let me show you." Burns clicked a button on his keyboard and spun the screen around to reveal a photo of Mace Perry. "*This* is the problem."

Reiger threw up his hands in frustration. "Come on, she's not even a cop anymore. She's on probation. Her options are limited. She's operating completely outside her sister's authority. I see her as a total non-issue."

"Really? Have you by chance read Perry's psych evaluation?"

"Her psych evaluation?" Reiger said curiously.

Burns rose from behind his desk and limped toward them. "The psych evaluation they did on the woman when she wanted to move to undercover. It's very interesting reading. She never gives up, Reiger. She never walks away. Her father was the U.S. attorney for D.C. I actually knew the man. He was murdered when she was twelve. She has never gotten over that. It burns in her belly with the potential explosive power of a mountain of C-4. She would rather die than be told she was wrong."

"If you're going to worry about someone, I think it should be the police chief. She's a block of granite with a very big brain."

Burns perched on the edge of his desk. "I've known Beth Perry for years. She *is* a formidable adversary. But she tends to operate within strict parameters. However, her sister does not and never will. Quite frankly, Mace Perry scares the crap out of me. And if she is allowed to screw this entire thing up, then none of us are safe." He eyed each man with studied deliberation. "None of us. What we are doing here is right and good for the country but not something the public would approve of once they became aware of it."

Hope said, "But she can't even legally carry a weapon."

Burns smacked his palm against the top of the desk. "Which begs the question of why it is so hard for us to eliminate her. Tonight at the law firm was a golden opportunity missed. I sent in a hand-picked team to get it done while you were occupied with Beth Perry, and it turned out like the Keystone Cops."

"But if she goes down you know her sister will move heaven and earth to find out who did it," Reiger pointed out.

Burns nodded. "It's clear the two sisters would each die for the other."

"See, that's my point."

"But I only need *one* of them to die. And we will help Beth Perry conclude quite clearly that it was the result of one of the many enemies her sister accumulated when she was a cop. A bullet to the head is a damn bullet to the head."

"This is stupid whack-a-mole," barked Reiger. "We pop one person but he or she talked to another person. Then we do that person, but turns out they sent a damn letter to someone else and we have to go after them. Where the hell does it stop, Burns?"

"Hopefully, with the intelligence sources and safety of this country still intact," Burns said as his gaze bore into Reiger. "And watch your tone. Or did you forget the concept of chain of command?"

Reiger let his own stare burn into the man for another moment and then he looked away.

Hope sat back in his chair. "Fine. Then let's do it the right way. We stop chasing her. We lead her down the path right to the target zone. Then we do it. Clean and quick."

"To add some urgency to your mission, we all feel the layers of the onion being peeled away."

"Resources?"

"You have preauthorization for the max push. You don't have to pull the trigger. We have others who will do it. People who will fit the right description, if you get my drift."

Reiger said, "We need to see these new orders in writing, with the proper chain of signatures before we do anything."

Burns didn't look pleased by this. "The elimination order was a standing one. You know that."

Don Hope spoke up. "But it's not guys with turbans we're killing here. It's Americans. It's different. We've already killed three of them and we want new orders."

"Where is it written that Americans can't be terrorists?" asked Burns pointedly. "Are you telling me that Timothy McVeigh wasn't a terrorist? I don't give a damn if he's wearing a turban or looks like my son. I don't give a shit if he's from Iraq or Indiana. If his goal is to harm Americans it's my job to stop him. And I will do so with every means at my disposal."

"All I'm saying is after this is over Karl and I need the get-out-of-jail-free piece of paper. So if you want it done, we need docs for each one with their names spelled out. We're not taking the fall for this. No Abu Ghraib low-level-grunts-run-amuck bullshit. Top down. We all go down. That's just how it's going to be or your sterilized weapons remain in the holster. That's just how it's going to be," he said again firmly.

"You are being compensated at four times your original salaries. You both will be wealthy by the time this is over."

"The paper or it doesn't get done. Period!"

Burns pursed his lips. "All right. You'll have it as soon as possible by secure courier." He returned to his computer screen.

Reiger eyed Hope and then cleared his throat.

Burns looked up, obviously irritated. "Something else?"

"How many people in *this* building know about the op?"

"Counting you, me, and your partner there?"

"Yeah."

"Three."

The tail car on Hope and Reiger had radioed in the results of their surveillance. Beth Perry was there within ten minutes. She slid out of her car and into the backseat of theirs. She was dressed not in stars and bars but in jeans and her FBI Academy hoodie. She trained her binoculars on the building.

"You're absolutely sure they went in there?"

"Chief, it's pretty damn hard to miss."

What she was looking at through her optics was the biggest office building in the world, with a footprint like no other, five-sided, in fact. She slumped back.

What the hell is the connection to the Pentagon?

Yᴇᴀʜ, I remember Ms. Tolliver. Used to come in here all the time."

Mace and Roy were seated at a table at Simpsons. The man speaking to them was a waiter. They'd made inquiries, and by luck this same fellow had waited on Diane Tolliver on Friday night.

"She wasn't alone, right?" asked Mace.

"No, a guy was with her. Damn shame what happened to her."

"Can you describe the guy?" asked Roy.

The waiter turned to him. "You think he had something to do with her death?"

"Haven't ruled out anything yet."

"Are you with the cops?"

"Private eyes," said Mace. "Hired by her family. Have the cops been by yet?"

The man nodded. "Yep."

"So you were going to describe this guy?" prompted Mace.

"White guy. Around fifty, salt-and-pepper hair, cut short and thinning. Not as tall as you," he said, indicating Roy. "About five-ten. Dressed in a suit."

"Glasses? Beard?"

"No."

Mace showed him Watkins's DMV photo.

He shook his head. "Wasn't that guy."

"You didn't get a name?" she asked.

"No, Ms. Tolliver paid the bill."

"See him with her before?"

"Nope."

"How were their appetites?"

"Real good. Ms. Tolliver had the filet mignon, mashed potatoes, and a side of veggies. Coffee but no dessert. The guy had the salmon with a salad and a cup of clam chowder beforehand."

"Wine, cocktails?"

"She had a glass of the house merlot. He had two glasses of chardonnay."

"Good memory."

"Not really. When the police came, I went back and looked at the ticket."

"You remember the times Tolliver and the guy came in and left?" asked Roy.

"In about seven-thirty, left over two hours later. I remember looking at the clock when they sat down because my cousin said he was going to stop by around quarter till and have a drink at the bar, and I knew it was getting close to that time."

"And you're pretty sure on when they left?"

"It was Friday night, but we've only got fifteen tables and traffic was slow. In fact, there were only two other tables occupied, so I did notice. And the bill has a time and date stamp when it comes out of the computer. They didn't hang out after she paid the bill. Bussed their table myself."

"Did either of them appear nervous or anything?" asked Mace.

"Well, they didn't come in together. She was here first and then he came in. They sat at that table over there." He pointed to an eating space in a small niche. "Pretty private because of the wall there."

"Did they leave together?" Roy asked.

"No. She went first, then he did. And he was kind of looking down the whole time, like he didn't want anyone to get a good look at him."

They asked him a few more questions, and Roy left his business card in case the waiter remembered anything else. As they walked along outside Mace pulled the reports she'd gotten from the ME from her pocket and glanced through them.

"What?" asked Roy.

"I don't know. Nothing, I guess."

"So it wasn't Watkins she had dinner with. There's another guy out there."

"Seems to be. And they obviously didn't want folks to see them together. Out-of-the-way place, secluded table, came and left separately."

"We left my car at the garage. What now? We can't walk to Alexandria."

"We can cab it to Altman's house, grab my bike, and then go from there."

"Do you think whoever's after us knows you're staying at Altman's?"

"It's possible."

"But what if they go after Altman for some reason? You know, leverage against you somehow?"

"Herbert told me there are three full-time security guards who live on the premises. I guess after the run-in with the HF-12 drug crew, Abe decided some of his own muscle wasn't a bad thing. One's a former Navy SEAL, another used to be a sniper with the FBI's Hostage Rescue Team, and the other one is former Secret Service with five years in Iraq under his belt in counterterrorism."

"Damn. I never noticed those guys when I was there."

"That's sort of the point, Roy."

The cab dropped them at Altman's. She took a few minutes at the guesthouse to slip some items into her knapsack. As they walked outside to where her bike was parked Roy said, "What's in the goodie bag?"

"Stuff."

"Stuff for breaking and entering?"

"Get on."

Roy barely made it on the Ducati before Mace punched the clutch with her boot and the back wheel gripped the asphalt for a single moment before its energy was released and they shot down the road. The automatic gates parted and Mace worked the clutch to top gear. Minutes later they blew down the windy, tree-bracketed GW Parkway, whipping past cars so fast Roy could barely see the drivers.

He finally yelled into her ear, "Why so damn fast?"

"I have a fetish for speed."

"You ever crash this thing?"

"Not yet," she screamed back over the whine of the Ducati's engine.

Roy clutched her waist with both hands and muttered a brief but heartfelt prayer.

71

"WHY AM I not surprised that you can pick a deadbolt?" Roy was staring over Mace's shoulder while she worked on the lock. They were at the fence-enclosed basement entrance to Diane Tolliver's waterfront luxury town home at Fords Landing. It was an upscale community a little south of the main strip in historic Old Town Alexandria.

Mace had her pick and tension tool inserted in the lock and was manipulating both instruments with ease. "Amazing what you learn in prison," she said.

"You didn't learn that in prison," he said in a scoffing tone.

"How do you know that?"

"Trust me, I just know."

"Are you insinuating that I bent the rules while I was a cop?"

"No."

"Good."

"I mean, I'm not insinuating it, I'm stating it as a fact."

"Go to hell, Roy."

"Wait a minute, how do you know the security system's not on?"

"I already snuck a peek through the glass sidelights on the front door. Green glow coming from the security touchpad means security off. Cops probably had the alarm company shut it down when they came to bag and tag. They almost always forget to tell them to turn it back on."

There was an audible click and Mace turned her tension tool like a key. "And we're in." They closed the door behind them and Mace clicked on a small flashlight with an adjustable beam. She widened the focus and looked around.

"This is a rec room with a full bar over there," Roy said as he pointed up ahead and to the right. "And there's a media room through that door over there."

"Nice."

"If the cops already bagged and tagged, what can we hope to find?"

"Stuff they missed."

They went room by room. One space had been outfitted as a home office. There was a large desk, wooden file cabinets, and built-in bookshelves but no computer.

"I think she had a laptop in here," said Roy. "The cops might've taken it instead of using the flash drive you talked about."

Mace was eyeing a pile of documents she'd pulled from a file cabinet. "Do all lawyers at Shilling bring this much work home?"

Roy ran the light over the papers. "Looks to be some docs from a private stock acquisition we did last month. We repped an oil exploration company in the U.A.E. that was buying a preferred minority interest in a Canadian shale oil field. It was done through a specialized broker in London and there were several other piggyback purchasers with packaged financing securitized over a number of debt platforms in about ten countries that had also had some sovereign fund participation and a buy-sell playing-chicken option."

"I have no idea what you said, but I think it just made me horny."

"If I'd only known that's all it took."

"So how much are we talking dollar-wise?"

"A little over a billion dollars. Paid in cash."

"A billion in cash!"

"That's how Diane could afford this place. She probably paid for *it* in cash."

Mace's brow creased.

"What are you thinking now?"

"I'm thinking I should have gone to law school," she growled.

While Roy went over Tolliver's office, Mace methodically covered the bedroom, guest rooms, bathrooms, and the garage. She finally arrived in the kitchen, which had a small brick fireplace with a wooden mantel and extended into the well-appointed dining area that had as its centerpiece a ten-foot-long table constructed from reclaimed wood. There were views of the Potomac through several large windows.

Mace checked the cupboards, the refrigerator, the stove, and the dishwasher. She opened jars and cookbooks, and dug into flowerpots in case Tolliver had bought one of those mini security boxes that look like something mundane. She examined piece by piece the trash that had obviously *not* been bagged, tagged, and taken by the cops. Roy joined her while she was seated in a chair still going through the garbage.

"Find any banana peels with secret writing?"

"No, but I did find a meat wrapper, veggie peelings, and a moldy piece of bread. Along with an empty bottle of red wine."

"So that was Diane's last meal."

"We'll all have one someday."

Mace rinsed off her hands in the sink. "Anything suspicious in her files?"

"Not really."

Mace started walking up and down the room, hitting the walls, floor, and ceiling with her light. "See all the shiny surfaces?"

"Fingerprint powder."

"That's right."

She reached the wall at the far end of the room, turned, and started back. When her light flicked to the ceiling she stopped. "Roy, grab a chair for me."

He brought it to her and she stood on it on her tiptoes, shining the light around the smoke detector mounted on the ceiling. She handed him the light. "Get up here and tell me what you see."

He stood on the chair. "Scratches on the paint and what looks to be dirt smudges."

"Somebody moved the smoke detector."

"Well, you'd do that to change the battery."

"How about this?"

Roy stepped off the chair and angled the light to where Mace was pointing at the carpet. He got down on his knees for a better look. "Paint flakes?"

"You'd think they would've been vacuumed up. Unless it happened after she was dead. Let me see that detector."

Roy got back on the chair, unhooked the wires, and handed it to her.

She turned it over. "Smoke detectors are popular items to substitute with surveillance pin cameras."

"Surveillance? Of Diane?"

"They tapped her computer, why not her home?"

"So why didn't the police find it?"

"They probably removed it before the cops searched the place. I think you need to go to your office tomorrow and do some real digging."

"You really believe it's tied to Shilling?" he said skeptically.

"Billion-dollar contracts? Companies in the Middle East? Uh, yeah."

"It's actually pretty boring stuff. Just business."

"One man's business is another man's apocalypse."

"What the hell does that mean?"

"Just humor me and check around. Come on, I'll drop you off at your condo."

Outside, they climbed on the Ducati. Before Mace started the engine, she turned and looked at him. "So why did you tank the HORSE game?"

"Why do you think?" Roy said quietly.

Mace found she couldn't meet his gaze. She slowly turned back around, engaged the engine, and they sped off.

CHAPTER

72

H<small>EY</small>, Ned."

Roy walked through the lobby on the way to the office elevators. He'd had pretty much a sleepless night listening for any sound of killers coming for him. He'd taken the bus to work and planned to drive the Marquis home. Ned was behind the marble desk looking excited.

"Roy, did you hear about the fire here last night?"

Roy tried his best to seem surprised. "There was a fire? Where?"

"Well, actually there wasn't a fire. Somebody pulled the fire alarm. That's a crime!"

"Yeah, I know. Who would've done that?" he said impassively.

"The fire department guys were pissed. I heard they traced it to the alarm pull on the fifth floor. I guess they'll run the key card access records to see who was here last night."

At this comment Roy's ass clenched like a boxer's fist. He'd used his key card to get in the building with Mace. That would be on the database. If no one else was in the building last night, how was he going to explain that? What was the penalty for falsely pulling a fire alarm?

This day could not get any worse, he thought.

He was wrong about that.

"Roy?"

He looked up as he entered the firm's lobby. Chester Ackerman was staring at him.

"Yeah, Chester?"

"What the hell happened to your face?"

Roy touched his still swollen eye and bruised cheek. "Ran into a door."

"I need to talk to you. *Now*." Ackerman turned and marched off.

Roy eyed Jill, the young receptionist, who'd been watching the two men closely. "Any idea what's going on, Jill?"

"You're in trouble, Roy."

"That one I'd figured out. Any idea why?"

"You'll find out soon enough."

Roy dropped off his briefcase in his office and headed to Ackerman's. He closed the door behind him and sat down across from the man.

"You're looking less stressed out, Chester," Roy began amiably.

"I have no idea how that's possible," Ackerman shot back. "Because I feel like my damn head is going to explode."

Roy crossed his legs and tried to look mildly curious. "So what's up?" *Please, God, don't let it be about the damn fire alarm.*

"What the hell is this I hear about you representing the man the police have arrested for Diane's murder? Please tell me that is complete and total horseshit."

"Hold on, I can explain that—"

Ackerman rose, looking even more agitated. "So it's true?"

"I met with the guy. He wants me to rep him. I haven't—"

"You *know* Diane's killer? You actually know the bastard?"

"Wait a minute, it hasn't been proved that he is Diane's killer, Chester."

"Oh for God's sakes. He was in the building that morning. No, he was *trespassing*. And I understand some of the evidence the police found ties him to the murder."

"Who told you that?"

"What I want to know is how you could possibly think of defending this person?"

"I guess it's that whole innocent-until-proven-guilty thing they taught us in law school."

"Don't give me that crap. And besides, you work for this firm. We do not do criminal defense work. You cannot accept an assignment like that without the firm's approval, specifically my approval as managing partner." Ackerman added in a snarl, "And you don't have a chance in hell of getting it."

"I only met with the guy once, okay? I defended him on an assault charge when I was with CJA. But I don't think the guy did it, Chester."

"I don't give a damn what you think. You are not representing him. Period."

Roy stood. "I'm not really liking your whole tone here."

"Trust me, you'll like it a lot less if you go down that road."

"I can quit."

"Yes, you can. But why in the hell would you? Give up the golden egg for some homicidal homeless freak?"

Roy felt his face growing hot. "He's *not* a freak. He's a veteran. He fought and bled for this country. He's still got North Vietnamese shrapnel a few millimeters from his spine."

"Right, right. And he killed Diane. So make your choice."

Roy turned to the door. "I'll let you know."

"Kingman!"

"I *said* I'll let you know."

Roy slammed the door behind him.

CHAPTER

73

Mace had barely slept at all. This time, though, it wasn't nightmares about Juanita and the throat-slicing Rose coming for her. It was the recurring image of her father in his coffin. She'd just turned twelve, Beth was eighteen and getting ready to head off to college at Georgetown on full scholarship. The day of the funeral the casket had been closed because of the disfiguring nature of Benjamin Perry's fatal wounds.

Yet Mace had seen her father that final day. She'd snuck away. Her mother was mush, collapsing on any shoulder she could find, while Beth was handling everything that their mom should have been dealing with. They had gotten to the church early, before the coffin had been brought into the chapel.

It was just Mace and the coffin in a small room next to where the memorial service would be held. She remembered every smell, every sound, and every breath she'd drawn in the few minutes she stood there, staring at the big wooden box with the metal handles on the sides containing her dad. To this day she wasn't sure why she'd done it, but she'd gathered her courage, walked up to the casket, held her breath, and pushed the top open.

As soon as she saw him, she wished someone had stopped her. She stared at the body lying there for a few terrible seconds.

That face.

Or what was left of it.

Then she'd turned and run from the room, leaving the top still up. That wasn't her father. Her father didn't look like that.

Mace rushed to the bathroom, and ran cold water over her head and splashed some on her face. She looked at herself in the darkened reflection of the mirror. She could never shake the feeling that she had let him down somehow. If she had just reacted in a different way, seen or heard something, she believed that her father would still be alive. If she only had done something! Anything!

My fault. Age twelve. My fault.

Beth had found her hiding in a closet at the church after closing the casket. She too had seen her father dead. And neither sister had ever talked about it since. Beth had held Mace for what seemed like forever that day, letting her cry, letting her shake, but telling her that everything was going to be okay. That the body in the coffin was just a body, their dad had already gone on to a much better place. And he would watch over them forever. She'd promised. And Mace had believed her. Her sister would never lie to her.

Beth being next to her was the only reason she had made it through the service. It certainly hadn't been her mother, who'd blubbered through the whole event, including when the soldier had handed her the U.S. flag in recognition of her father's service in Vietnam. When the honor guard had started shooting their rifle salute everyone covered their ears. Everyone except the two Perry sisters. Mace remembered quite vividly what she had been thinking when those rifles fired a total of twenty-one rounds.

I wanted a gun. I wanted a gun to kill whoever had killed my dad.

And though she'd never asked, Mace felt certain that Beth had been thinking the very same thing.

Her mother had refused the shell casings offered by the honor guard. Beth had taken them and given eleven to Mace and kept ten for herself. Mace knew that Beth kept her bag of casings in her desk drawer at her office. Once when she'd been with the force and met with her sister to go over some work, she'd seen a pensive Beth open the drawer, take out the casings, and hold them tightly in her hand, as though channeling her father's wisdom.

Mace drank some water from her cupped hand, walked back into her bedroom, opened her knapsack, and pulled out her bag of eleven shell casings. Beth had of course kept them for her when she went to prison. She held them against her chest, the tears staining her cheeks as she desperately tried to absorb some wisdom of her own from the best man she'd ever known. But nothing came.

The aftermath of her father's murder and her mother's withdrawal from the lives of her daughters had made Mace increasingly vulnerable. It was a feeling she hated. She'd become a cop, in part, to allow the weight of the badge and the threat of her gun to override that vulnerability. She desperately wanted to belong to something. And the MPD served that desire.

Did she also want to follow her sister? Even show she might be better than her in certain respects? Mace couldn't, in all honesty, deny that.

A half hour later she changed into her workout clothes and did some stretching and push-ups. The blood rush to her muscles was very welcome, after the weary night and the early morning soul searching.

The sun was well up now and the air outside was warm, which was good because Mace couldn't seem to get rid of the chills. She stepped outside and started her run. The estate was big, with a well-marked trail that wound in and out of trees and head-high bushes. She'd been running for half an hour when she stopped, turned, and her hand flashed to her waist. To pull the gun that wasn't there.

"You *are* good," said the voice. "Lucky for me you're not packing."

The man stepped clear of the tree line. He was a shade below six feet and wore an Army green muscle shirt that showed off his ripped physique and jeans that were very tight around his bulging thighs. Lace-up combat boots were on his feet. A pistol rode in a clip holster on his belt; an extra mag for the weapon sat in a compartment next to the gun. His hair was shaved military short, his face tanned and weathered.

"I've been standing there for ten minutes waiting for you to come by. I didn't move a muscle. Heartbeat's at fifty-two and mellow, so you didn't hear that. Never made a sound. What gave me away?"

Mace walked over to him and lightly smacked him on the face. "Either cut down on the Old Spice or stay upwind of me."

He laughed and put out his hand. "Rick Cassidy."

"You're the former SEAL?"

He cocked his head and gave her a lopsided smile. "Okay, how do you figure? I'm wearing Army green."

"Most SEALS I know like to wear the Army green because they know they look better in it than the trench boys do. Your face has seen a lot of sun, salt, and ocean wind. You've also got on standard-issue Navy-class stomp boots. And a SEAL I dated said you guys swore by the H&K P9S that's riding in your belt holster." As he stared down at his gun she added, "Its silhouette and grip are pretty distinctive."

"You live up to your rep, Ms. Perry, I'll give you that."

"Already got a dossier on me? And the name's Mace."

"Everyone who comes here gets the same intel treatment. Mace."

"I've got no problem with that. How did you end up here?'

"Mr. Altman is a great guy. He made me a great offer." Cassidy paused. "And he helped take care of my little sister. Leukemia. My parents had no health insurance."

"Did she make it?"

"Graduating from college this year."

"That's very cool, Rick."

"Mr. Altman wants to see you up at the main house when you get a chance. I smelled croissants baking in the kitchen. Herbert's on a roll. And the coffee is always fresh. I understand there's a seat waiting for you. No rush. Whenever."

"Thanks, Rick. Any idea what he wants me for?"

"Something about a mom and her kid and a dude named Psycho. Ring any bells?"

"More than one, actually."

"Keep running hard, Mace."

"One more thing, Rick."

"Yeah?"

"This stuff I'm doing for Abe, it might lead to some unsavory characters taking a special interest in me. They might follow me back here. Just a heads-up."

"Forewarned is always a good thing, Mace. Thanks."

She turned to start up her run again. When she looked back, Cassidy had disappeared back into the trees. For a number of reasons, that gave her a great sense of comfort. She ran back to the guesthouse, sat in the hot tub for a while, showered, changed, and killed some more time as images of her dead father finally faded away. Then she trudged over to the main house. To talk about moms, babies, and bandits named Psycho.

CHAPTER

74

The phone buzzed on Beth Perry's desk.

"Chief."

"Got a letter here for you," said her aide.

"Who from, Donna?"

"Mona Danforth."

"Bring it in."

Donna Pierce punched in the numbers on Beth's secure office door, brought the letter in, handed it to her, and then turned to leave.

"Who delivered it?" Beth asked.

"It wasn't Ms. Danforth, of course," Pierce said, barely hiding a smile. "Hard for her to walk all this way in those four-inch heels. Some wimpy guy in a suit who nearly ran out of here when I asked him if he wanted to speak to you directly."

"Thanks."

After Pierce left, Beth slit open the envelope and unfolded the heavy bond paper. The contents of the letter were short and the rise in Beth's blood pressure was swift. She clicked some keys on her computer and read down several screen pages. After that she called the courthouse to check on something. Then she hit her speakerphone. "Pierce, get the wicked witch on the line for me. Now!"

Beth heard her aide struggle to suppress a laugh. "Yes, Chief, right away."

Pierce came back on a minute later. "Her assistant says she's not available for your call."

"Put it through."

Beth picked up the phone. "Chief Perry."

"Yes, I'm sorry, Chief, but Ms. Danforth is—"

"Standing right over your shoulder."

"No, she has court—"

"I just checked with the docket clerk. She's not in court." Beth shouted into the phone, "Mona, if you won't talk to me, then I'll just take this letter you sent me up to Capitol Hill and see what the folks on the Judiciary Committee will make of you abdicating your role as protector of the people. The ensuing sound you'll be hearing is your fading chances of being the AG, much less getting a seat on the Supreme Court."

Beth waited, envisioning Mona walking to her office, slamming the door, and—

Mona's voice barked out, "Listen, Perry, I don't appreciate you talking like that in front of my people!"

"You can either address me as Beth or Chief. You use surnames for underlings. I am *not* your underling."

"What do you want?"

"I read your letter."

"Well? I thought it was pretty self-explanatory."

"Yeah, you caved. In record time. And I want to know why."

"I don't have to explain my actions to you."

"You wrote me a CYA letter that basically says you've washed your hands of Jamie Meldon's murder investigation. What, did somebody threaten that you wouldn't get the USA nod if you didn't go quietly into the night? So much for him being one of *your* people."

"If you were smart you'd back off too, *Chief.*"

"It has nothing to do with self-preservation, Mona. It has to do with right and wrong. And something called integrity."

"Oh please. I don't need you to read me an ethics lesson."

"So what are you going to tell Meldon's wife and kids? 'Sorry, my career's too important. Just get over Jamie's murder and move on'?"

"I'm running the largest U.S. Attorney's Office in the country. I don't have time to run down every little—"

"This isn't little, Mona. Homicide is as big as it gets. Someone is out there who took Jamie's life."

"Then you tackle it if you care so much."

"A little tough to do when I was barred from the crime scene."

"Can't help you there."

"So that's your last word on it?"

"You bet it is!"

"Okay, here's mine. I *will* tackle this. And if I find the least bit of evidence that you or anyone in your office impeded our investigation, I will personally see to it that your Armani-covered *ass* lands right in prison."

Beth slammed down the phone, sat back, and took a deep breath. Her BlackBerry had been buzzing nonstop during her entire conversation. She checked it. Ninety-three e-mails all marked urgent. She had six meetings stacked back-to-back, the first of which was scheduled to begin in twenty minutes. Then she had two hours patrolling in Cruiser One and a roll call in the Second District, followed by her headlining two community events that evening. She also had to oversee the posting of nearly two hundred intersection cops because the president wanted to go to lunch at his favorite dive in Arlington, the Secret Service had informed her at six-thirty this morning.

A murder in Ward Nine last night had interrupted what little sleep she usually got. She'd finally made it to her couch at four a.m., catnapped for two hours, and was in the office at seven. Typical day in the neighborhood. And then there was the information she'd just received thirty minutes ago that had to do with Roy Kingman and her sister. Her phone buzzed again.

"Chief."

It was Pierce. "Guys in Social Services want to know what you want to do with Alisha Rogers and her son. They don't have room for them past this morning. Records show she has her own place so they say their hands are tied unless you really insist."

And if I do insist, someone will leak it to the press and tomorrow's breaking story will be about the police chief abusing her authority to get personal favors unavailable to other needy citizens—

"Donna, reschedule my first three meetings until this afternoon. Just cram them in somehow. I've got somewhere I have to go. Tell Social they can release Alisha and her son into my personal custody."

Beth pulled out her cell phone and punched in a number. "It's Beth. We need to deal with this. Now."

"I know," answered Abe Altman. "I know."

75

MACE HAD JUST finished breakfast and was pouring a second cup of coffee when Altman came into the eating area right off the kitchen.

"Hope you slept well," he said.

"Not bad. Met Rick Cassidy on my run this morning."

"A wonderful young man. He was planning on leaving the Navy to be closer to his sister, so I thought a job here would fit into that. She goes to George Washington and has accepted a full-time position with the World Bank in D.C."

"That was really nice what you did for her."

"When a poor man gives something, that is a sacrifice indeed. When a rich man gives something, it hardly rises to the same level."

"Well, I know some rich people who never give anything."

Altman was dressed in his usual manner, jeans and a long-sleeved shirt. He poured a cup of tea from a pot on the sideboard, bit into a biscuit, and sat down next to her.

"Herbert is a genius in the kitchen," he said. "I have two master's degrees and a Ph.D. and I can't even crack an egg properly."

"I know, I'm a klutz in the kitchen too. I had two croissants and a plate of eggs and had to stop myself from going back for more."

Altman took a sip of tea, set the cup down, and said, "Psycho?"

Mace wiped her mouth. "Look, it was no big deal."

"It was a very big deal. I heard from Carmela, who talked to Non at the apartment building. Non watched the entire confrontation from her window. You and Roy could have been killed. I feel terrible. Terrible, Mace. I had these people vetted with great depth but I had no idea of this man's involvement with Alisha."

"That's probably because everyone's scared of the guy. But we got out okay, and we also removed Alisha and Tyler from the situation. Beth helped me with that."

"I know."

"So you talked to her?"

"Yes. If anything had happened to you, I would never have forgiven myself."

She put a hand on his arm. "Abe, I'm assuming you recruited me for this job because I know my way around those places. That also included knowing how to survive there. My big mistake was taking Roy with me. That was stupid on my part. That won't happen again."

"I don't believe there should be a next time."

"What do you mean?"

"I can't justify sending you into dangerous places, Mace. I can't risk that. No study is worth that."

"Well, I think this study is. Look at Alisha. She's a good kid. She just needs a chance. And Tyler, we can't leave him in that place. He needs some special help. And there are thousands just like them in this town."

"It's too risky."

"I'm willing to take that risk. You offered me the job and I accepted. Now let me do my thing. Abe, you knew these areas were potentially dangerous. What's the big deal now?"

"It all looked good on paper. But paper is not real life. All my calculations aren't worth anything, it seems, when you have people like this Psycho around."

"I can take care of that."

"I thought when they learned you were trying to help folks in those situations, that it would protect you."

"And it will. But for those few who think otherwise, I'll deal with it. I don't think you'll win this one, Abe."

They both looked up to see Beth standing by the door holding pudgy Tyler Rogers. Behind her was Alisha clutching a small bag.

Mace rose. "Alisha? Are you and Tyler okay?"

The young mother came forward, her eyes wide as she took in

the interior of the mansion. "We're fine. Chief Perry took real good care of us."

Mace looked at her sister. "I really appreciated the assist, Beth. I didn't know who else to call when Psycho showed up."

"He's not a guy you mess around with. Although from what I heard you pretty much held your own." She paused. "Did Kingman really play him in one-on-one basketball?"

"And kicked his butt," said Alisha with ill-concealed delight. "I was watching with Non at the window. Kicked his butt," she repeated, tacking on a big smile.

"Where's Darren?" Mace asked.

"Who's that?" asked Beth sharply.

"My brother. He didn't come with us. Don't know where he is."

"So what are you all doing here?" said Mace.

Altman rose and came forward. "Beth and I spoke this morning and Alisha and Tyler are coming to stay with us. I was hoping that they could be in the west wing of the guesthouse if it's not an inconvenience to you."

Mace blurted out, "Inconvenience? That place is so big I'd need a map to find them."

"We staying here?" said Alisha looking around. "I don't have no money for a place like this."

"There is no charge," said Altman, taking her arm lightly after receiving a high sign from Beth. "And I'd be honored to take you and your son to your new quarters and help you get settled in."

Beth handed off Tyler to Alisha and the three left together. Beth turned to her sister and eyed her empty coffee cup. "You might need another jolt of caffeine, because we need to talk. Now."

CHAPTER

76

I HAD my police scanner on last night. Heard about the homicide in Nine. Knew you'd be there. You look beat."

Beth took off her hat and sat down. "You look spent, too. Can't be the accommodations. Having nightmares again?"

"I *don't* have nightmares anymore."

"You sure about that?"

"You held me when I was twelve, Beth. You don't need to hold me anymore." Mace handed her a full cup of black coffee and sat down with her own. Beth took a swallow and spent a moment admiring the room.

"I can see why you split from me to come here."

"I've actually found the concierge service to be pretty average."

"I guess I can leave it to you to find trouble even as a research assistant."

"It's a gift."

"So you're going back in?"

"See no reason not to. So what do we need to talk about?"

Beth hunched forward. "Andre Watkins?"

Mace barely reacted, but it was enough.

Beth said, "I thought so. A-1? Since we're the police we had to resort to a search warrant, but the kid there said a woman and a tall man had come in previously with some story about a diseased aunt."

"You been by Watkins's place?"

"It's empty."

"It wasn't empty when we got there."

Mace told her about the man who'd been there pretending to be Watkins, including his description and her suspicions that the apartment had been searched.

"Nice to have known that before."

"And it wasn't Watkins having dinner with Tolliver on Friday night."

"I know. The description was pretty general. We have a BOLO out on Watkins," Beth added, referring to a "be on the lookout" order.

"The imposter said he was an escort. *Was* Watkins an escort?"

"Yes, worked for an agency in town. No one's seen him since Friday."

"Maybe Tolliver sensed that something bad was going to happen to her and she wanted some cover."

"So presumably they got on to him, either eliminated him or he took off running scared and they sent some goon to roll his place looking for answers."

"And he was doing just that when we knocked."

"Pretty ballsy of the guy to open the door to you."

Mace shrugged. "He peeped us, could tell we weren't the cops, or maybe recognized us and decided to play actor and pump us for info. Unfortunately, we were pretty accommodating." Mace eyed Beth. "Anything else?"

"Just a couple more questions. What were you and Kingman doing at the law firm last night? And which one of you pulled the fire alarm?"

Mace looked blankly at her.

Beth tapped the tabletop. "His key card access was the only one last night."

"That can't be right. The other guys—"

Beth snapped, "What other guys?"

"We had some visitors last night. I pulled the alarm so we could get away. I assumed they used Diane Tolliver's key card to get in."

"They didn't. And again, what guys?"

"I don't know for sure. Maybe the same ones who took a shot at me."

"How did they know you were in the building?"

Mace explained about the webcam on Tolliver's computer.

"We'll check it out." Beth leaned forward. "Remember when you asked me what I would do in your position? Would I risk everything to work the case and get back on the force?"

"You didn't answer me."

"No, because I didn't have a ready answer. But now I've had time to think."

"And?"

"And nothing is worth going back to that hellhole."

"That's you. But you're not me."

"Why are you really doing this?"

"We already covered this, okay? Mona torpedoed your plan, so proving my innocence won't work. And I told you I was going to work the case. If I go down, so be it."

"If you do, the odds are very good that you will go back to prison and you won't walk out alive this time. Where did you even get the idea to solve a case and use that as a way back on?"

"I had a lot of time to think over the last two years."

"Would it have anything to do with a visit you got from an FBI agent who resurrected his career after being convicted of a felony?"

"If you knew, why bother asking me?" she said angrily.

"What did Special Agent Frank Kelly tell you?"

"I'm surprised you didn't already track him down and ask him."

"I did. He said it was between you and him."

"And it is, Beth. Between him and me."

"I didn't think we kept secrets from each other."

"You're the police chief. I am not going to put you in a compromising situation."

"What happened to Kelly was a one-in-a-million shot."

"I'll take those odds."

"This is ridiculous."

"No, Beth, what's ridiculous is me spending over a decade laying it all on the line to protect people, only to have it all crater when someone framed me for shit I don't even remember. I lost two years of my life in prison where every day seemed like it would be my last one. Now I'm out but can't do the one thing that I was born to do. What, did you think I was just going to forget it? Say, 'Oh, well, shit happens'?"

The two women stared at each other, neither one seemingly willing to give in.

Beth's phone buzzed. She didn't move to answer it.

Mace said, "Better grab it. The law waits for no one, not even two pissed-off sisters."

Beth finally broke off eye contact and snatched up her phone. "Chief." She listened and then clicked off. "That was Lowell Cassell."

"I already know. Dockery's DNA didn't match."

"No, it was a perfect match. It was, without a doubt, his sperm inside Diane Tolliver."

77

Roy sat at his desk vigorously squeezing his miniature basketball in his right hand. His anxiety was justified. His secretary Janice had popped in to tell him that the entire firm had been sent an e-mail from Chester Ackerman about his connection with Diane's alleged murderer. She'd gone on to say that right now Roy was about as popular with his coworkers as Osama bin Laden would be.

He'd tried to defend himself. "Janice, will you hear me out. I—"

The slamming door had cut him off.

He clicked on his computer and started checking his e-mails. Work still had to be done and he and Diane had been in the middle of shepherding several large acquisitions through to closure. Ackerman had not yet assigned anyone to take over Diane's work permanently, so Roy was carrying the laboring oar on the legal end. He didn't mind that, but he missed being able to kick ideas around with her, or go to her when something didn't make sense. He wished he could go to her right now, because he was perplexed.

Your death makes no sense to me, Diane. Can't you tell me what happened? Who killed you?

That line of thought was clearly not going to get him anywhere. He returned some calls, opened some files, pulled up some half-finished contracts on his computer, and pored over laborious notes he'd taken at a recent client meeting. He worked for a couple more hours and then checked his e-mails again. There were lots of new ones, some from clients, some from friends, and a few from coworkers telling him to basically get his head out of his butt over defending Diane's killer.

For some reason, he scrolled far down the list and checked one old e-mail.

It was the last one he would ever get from Diane Tolliver.

We need to focus in on A-

Okay, they'd gotten that piece and run it down for naught. Roy's gaze next ran over the initials at the bottom of the e-mail.

DLT.

It was her initials, for Diane Louise Tolliver. He'd seen her full name on several diplomas she had hanging in her office. As he thought about it, her initials being there made sense, but it also didn't make sense. Roy quickly checked a dozen other e-mails that Diane had sent him over the last few months. None of them had her initials at the bottom. She invariably signed her e-mails, when she bothered to do so at all, by simply typing "Diane."

DLT?

For some reason those initials seemed familiar apart from Tolliver's name. Was there another reason she had put those letters in the e-mail? A backup in case the A-1 reference yielded nothing? Thinking back to the highly organized and intelligent lawyer that Diane had been, Roy had to admit that the woman's employing a second clue hidden in the same e-mail was entirely plausible.

But why direct all these clues at him? He worked with her, sure, but they weren't really close friends. Then again, maybe she didn't have any close friends. The woman used a paid escort, after all, when she wanted to go out. But why not go to the police? If she had learned of some criminal activity or even suspected something illegal was going on, why not just go to the cops? As far as Roy knew, Diane had never done any criminal work, but she was still a lawyer. She knew her way around the legal system better than most.

But I was *a criminal defense attorney. Was that why she was sending me the clues?*

A sudden fear gripped him. He stared at the tiny webcam mounted at the top of his computer monitor. What if they were watching him right now? But then his fears receded. Mace had been in here on the night she'd found out about the A-1 clue. They'd talked about her discovery here. If someone had been watching and listening, they would've gotten to the mailbox before Roy and Mace had.

Still.

He slid open his desk drawer, pulled out a Post-it note, and hastily stuck it over the webcam, pulling his fingers quickly back as though the damn thing might bite him.

His cell phone rang.

"Kingman."

It was Mace. Her few words hit Roy harder than Psycho had.

"I'll meet you there in twenty minutes," he said. He grabbed his jacket and sprinted out of the office. The Captain most definitely needed a lawyer now.

He'd just been formally charged with first-degree murder.

CHAPTER

78

"Gᴏᴛ sᴏᴍᴇ damn good news today, Roy."

Roy and Mace were sitting across from the Captain. He'd showered and his wet hair was now slicked back, his revealed widow's peak solid gray. With part of the street grime gone, Roy could actually see some pink skin on the man's face. The Captain was also now wearing a prison jumpsuit. A shackle belt was around his large waist, though his hands and legs were free for the time being.

Roy could see that the Captain had once been a very handsome fellow. His features were sharply defined, there were remnants of a square jaw, and a pair of green eyes was now visible with the shaggy hair out of his face. The only time he got cleaned up was to be charged with murder. The irony was not lost on Roy.

He and Mace exchanged glances. He said, "What's that, Captain?"

"They found my cart."

"Who, the police?"

The Captain nodded. "They came and told me. Seemed happy about it."

"I'm sure. Look, Captain, do you understand what's going on here?"

The Captain sighed heavily. "Damn Twinkies. Always the damn Twinkies."

Mace said, "They don't shackle Twinkie thieves, Captain."

He looked at her with benign curiosity. "Do I know you, hon?"

"We met once. It was a pretty electrifying moment for you."

"Okay, hon. If you say so."

Roy hunched forward. "The photo of the woman I showed you

yesterday? They're charging you with raping and killing her in her office."

Strangely enough, the Captain laughed. "I know. They told me that. The cops just kidding, Roy."

"So you didn't do it?"

"No, sir. They got me on the Twinkies, though. And the tools, don't forget the tools, Roy. I took 'em. For the money." He glanced at Mace and added woefully, "Three dollars, hon. Guy in a turban ripped me off."

"Right, the tools, you told me," said Roy wearily.

"So you my lawyer?"

Mace looked expectantly at Roy. "*Are* you his lawyer?'

Roy hesitated, but only for a moment. "Yeah, I am."

"Then I got money to pay you," said the Captain.

"Okay, fine."

"I got two hundred dollars. Cops took it, but they said they'd give it back."

"Where'd you get two hundred bucks?" asked Mace quickly.

The Captain looked embarrassed. He said in a faltering tone, "I can't say. No, wouldn't be right, hon. Not in front of you."

Roy stood and paced. "Do you know what DNA is?"

The Captain squinted. "I think so, yeah," he said unconvincingly.

"Well, they found your DNA on the dead woman."

The Captain's face brightened. "Are they going to give it back?" He shot a glance at Mace. "It's mine, right? So I'll get my cart, my money, and my DNA. And I won't never take no more Twinkies, swear to God."

Roy let out a small groan and leaned against the wall. Mace walked over to him and whispered, "Has he always been this out of it?"

In a low voice he said, "He can carry on a basic conversation, gets simple concepts okay, but the abstract stuff is way beyond him. When I repped him on the assault three years ago, he was starting to show some early signs of dementia. He got a suspended sentence mainly because the prosecutor was a Vietnam vet too. But that was a simple assault. He's not going to get cut any slack for murder in the first. The problem is, he can carry on a conversation and he understands some things, so no one is going to buy that he didn't know what he was doing."

"I guess the moral is, if you're going to go nuts, go all the way."

"And they have his sperm in Diane's body. And he's admitted to being in the building at the time in question. How the hell do I defend that?"

"You can't. We just have to find the truth. It's the only way."

"Yeah, well, what if the truth is he did rape and kill Diane? What then?"

"I don't know. But my gut is howling that this whole thing stinks."

"Well, when you can get a jury to listen to your gut, let me know." Roy turned back to the Captain and pulled out a legal pad and pen from his briefcase. "Captain, I need you to focus for me. We need to go through some timelines. Can you do that?"

The man looked worried. "I don't know. They took my watch, Roy. I ain't no good with time without my watch."

"It's okay, you can use mine." He slipped it off and handed it to his client.

Mace said, "While you go over the case with him I'm going to have a chat with my sister."

WHEN MACE ARRIVED at Beth's office her sister was hastily shoving files in a briefcase. "Got two minutes, Mace. Late for a bunch of meetings."

"I'll walk with you. Thanks for your help with Alisha and Tyler, by the way."

"I'm assuming you're here for some more help." When Mace didn't say anything, Beth added, "They called me when you two showed up to see Dockery. So is Kingman going to rep him?"

"Looks to be the case. Dockery said you found his cart?"

"That's right. And would Kingman like to know what we found in it?"

"You have to tell him that anyway, Beth."

"He'll get all the proper evidentiary disclosures from the prosecutor's office. Well, at least I assume he will."

"What do you mean you assume he will?"

Beth gave her a knowing look. "Take a guess on who's trying the case?"

"Oh hell, not Mona? She's got an office full of homicide hounds to do that kind of work."

"Did you really think she was going to pass up a case like this? Fine upstanding female law partner in G-town struck down by a homeless nutcase and then stuck in a fridge? She'll get tons of ink on this. She's probably getting her hair and nails done as we speak. She won't do the heavy lifting, but rest assured she will be the voice of the U.S. Attorney's Office at all press conferences and other media opportunities. She'll probably do the closing argument too. If the case gets that far."

"Why wouldn't it?"

"Ever heard of a plea bargain? Although Mona won't plead this out unless your guy takes the max. She's not going to pass up her chance to get on Larry King for anything less than that."

"So what did they find in the cart?"

"Tolliver's missing panties and her purse. Credit cards and cell phone and office key card were inside but there was no cash."

Mace's mind flashed to what the Captain had said.

I got two hundred dollars.

"Two hundred dollars found on Dockery," said Beth, seemingly reading her sister's mind. "It does not look good, Mace."

"I still don't think the guy did it. I mean, look at all the other stuff going on here. The key Diane sent Roy. This Andre Watkins character. The guy rolling his apartment. The people after me. How do they all tie into Tolliver being murdered?"

"Did you ever stop to think that they don't? I agree that there is something strange going on with Tolliver and the stuff with you. But her being killed by Dockery might have been a simple crime of opportunity that has no connection to the other things."

"I just knew you were going to say that."

"Why?"

'Because it's so . . . freaking logical!"

"My apologies for being so freaking logical."

"But look, Dockery said the police found his cart, so it was missing. Anybody could've planted that stuff in there. And the other trace found at the crime scene too."

"Let's not forget the sperm in the woman's vagina. Does Kingman want to make the argument that was planted too?"

"Believe me, I get the point."

"How is his firm going to feel about Kingman defending the guy accused of murdering one of its partners?"

"Probably not too good."

"So why is Kingman doing it?"

Mace gave her an exasperated look. "Why don't you ever just call him Roy?"

"I only call my *friends* by their first names, with the exception of Mona. And I only do that because I found out she hates her name."

"He's doing it because he believes Dockery is innocent. Same as me."

As they walked down the hall, Beth said, "Did you ever wonder how a guy like Dockery is able to sneak into the building like that and no one ever sees him? Sounds to me like he had some inside help."

"What are you saying?"

"Maybe your lawyer friend is repping Dockery because he has a guilty conscience? He helps the guy get in the building, Dockery ends up going berserk and killing Tolliver, and Kingman comes in to help clean up the mess."

"So you think Roy actually believes Dockery is guilty?"

"Most people accused of a crime *are* guilty, Mace, you know that."

"Well, you know something, big sister?"

"What?"

"*I* wasn't guilty."

80

C AN I SMOKE in here?" asked the Captain.

"No, nonsmoking building," said Roy as he wrote some notes down.

"Hey, is it time to eat?"

"Soon."

"I'm hungry."

"I know. Okay, so you got in on Friday a little after six. Hid in the closet by the stairs on the main floor. Then around eight you went up to the fourth floor and settled in for the weekend. What time did you leave on Monday morning?"

"Can't remember."

"You have to try, Lou."

The Captain seemed confused by the use of his real name. Roy noted this and said, "Lawyer-client thing, I need to start using your real name."

"But I tell you what, those damn Twinkies were stale anyway. What's the fuss?"

Roy ran a hand through his hair and wondered why it wasn't falling out with all the stress he was under. "The fuss is they're not charging you with stealing Twinkies, they're charging you with *murder*." He pointed his pen at the Captain. "If you get no other concept down, Lou, please get that one."

"I didn't kill nobody. I would've remembered something like *that*."

"Please don't make that sort of statement to anyone ever again.

And the evidence says otherwise, namely that you did rape and kill her."

"Why I got you. Two hundred bucks. You send me a bill."

I will, to whatever prison you'll be spending the rest of your life in.

"Them cheapskates anyway."

"Who?"

"Twinkie people. Only time I heard church bells."

Roy put his pen down and stared helplessly at the man opposite him. It seemed like the Captain was finally really losing all touch with reality. "Church bells?"

"Yep. Why'd they have to lock up that refrigerator anyway?"

"Lock what refrigerator?"

"The one where I was staying. They didn't lock up the toilet. Or the Twinkies. And they ain't never had much in there anyway so why lock it up?"

"Lock it up how?"

The Captain made a circling motion with his hands. "Big old chain."

Roy had a momentary vision of Mace holding a "big old chain" as a weapon on the fourth floor the previous night when unknown people were coming after them.

"Did they wrap it around the fridge to keep it closed?"

"Why else? Big old padlock. Tried to pick it with my knife. No way, no how. Bet they had Pepsi in there. I like Pepsi better'n Coke."

"Was the chain on there when you got to the fourth floor?"

The Captain thought about this. "Don't know. I think I went to sleep. But it was on there when I woke up."

"Well, that makes sense, Lou, if they thought someone was stealing the food from inside it. They'd lock it up after hours."

"Oh, right. Didn't think of that. You smart, Roy. Glad you're my lawyer."

"Okay, what about the church bells?"

"Yeah, nothing to eat. Ain't staying there. So's I left to look for some food."

"Church bells? You mean you left on Sunday?"

"You sure I can't get me a smoke?"

"I'm sure. You were talking church bells?"

With a vacuous expression the Captain said, "Don't they still have church on Sunday or did they pick another day?"

"No, it's still on Sunday." Roy thought quickly. There were several churches whose bells could be heard at his building. He'd experienced their pealing himself when he'd worked weekends. "So you didn't actually stay in the building all weekend. You left on Sunday?"

"Well, yeah, didn't I already tell you that?"

"No, you didn't!" Roy snapped. "Before you said you left on Monday morning." He drew a calming breath and reminded himself that while his client was nearly sixty, his mental ability was closer to that of a young child. He said in a regular tone, "We've been going through the timeline for an hour now and you never mentioned that, Lou."

The Captain held up Roy's watch. "'Cause this ain't my watch, Roy. I can't tell no good time with yours."

Under different circumstances Roy might've laughed. "Okay, but once you left, did you come back?"

"No, sir. For what? No food is no food. I got me some grub."

"Did you buy it or find it?"

"I got two hundred dollars. I bought it."

"Where?"

"Little grocery store. Man I fought in 'Nam against, he runs it. Only he likes me now. Ain't never once run me off like some other folks."

Roy had a sudden inspiration. "The little shop next to the Starbucks on Wisconsin?" He'd bought some food for lunch there on occasion and had met the owner.

"Yeah, that's right. Starbucks? Sure could use me a cup of java about now."

"And this happened on Sunday when exactly?"

"They have bananas and apples right outside the door like when I was a kid. Bought me some. He likes me now, but back in 'Nam we were trying to kill each other. I sure remember him all right. He shot me and I shot him. Name's Yum-Yum or something."

Roy knew that the Captain hadn't fought against Yum-Yum, whose name was actually Kim Sung. He'd emigrated not from Vietnam but from South Korea into the United States and was only in his early forties. But it didn't matter anyway. Even if the man could place the Captain outside the building on Sunday he could still have sneaked back in to the fourth floor later and attacked Diane on Monday morning. Yet at least it was something. "Did you still hear the church bells when you bought the bananas?'

"Oh yeah."

"Sun was high up in the sky?"

"Yep."

"Okay, how about Sunday night and Monday morning?"

The Captain gave him an alarmed look. "What about 'em? They happened, right?"

Roy took a moment to press against the throbbing pain he had in his left temple. "Yes, they happened. Right on schedule. But, see, if we can find some people who saw you on Sunday night and Monday morning then we can tell the police that you didn't kill . . . that you didn't steal any more Twinkies on Sunday or Monday."

A light finally seemed to dawn in the Captain's emerald eyes. "Oh, right. That's the truth, I didn't. No more damn Twinkies. They were stale anyway. And stale Twinks? Not even Pepsi can make that taste good."

"Okay, I'll check with Kim, I mean with Yum-Yum, and get his statement. So was there anyone else who you saw?"

"Nope. Just went down by the river and got inside the runoff pipe. Slept there."

"And you saw no one? How about somebody in a boat? Early morning rower? Run into anyone when you climbed out of the pipe?"

"I'd have to do me some thinking on that, Roy. And I'm tired."

The Captain put his head down on the table and within a minute he was asleep.

Roy watched him while thinking it would be so easy to just get up and leave. Go back to his cushy job making his big bucks in fancy Georgetown. He didn't need this hassle, taking all the hits for defending some homicidal homeless lost cause. It was like Ackerman had said. Give up the golden egg for *this*?

But he didn't get up. He just continued to stare down at a man who'd pretty much sacrificed his life so Americans could keep on being fat and happy. He said in a tired but clear voice, "I'm going to do my best for you, Captain. And even if we don't win, we'll both go down fighting."

The Captain grunted and then sat up. He looked around groggily. "Is hon gone?"

"Hon? Oh yeah, she's still gone."

"Two hundred dollars, Roy."

"Captain, you don't have to pay me. I'm doing this pro bono, I mean I'm doing this on my dime."

"How I got it." The Captain looked embarrassed. "Peed in a cup."

"Excuse me?"

The Captain gazed at the tabletop and said in a hushed voice, "Peed in a cup."

Roy sat forward, still looking confused. "Someone paid you two hundred dollars to pee in a cup?"

"Not pee, the other thing." Now Roy could really see pink in the man's cheeks because he was blushing.

"The other thing?"

"They gave me a magazine to look at. Couldn't say this in front of hon."

"A magazine?"

"Girlie magazine. Not pee. You know. The other thing."

"You mean?"

The Captain eyeballed Roy with a knowing look. "Two hundred dollars to look at a girlie magazine."

Roy leaned forward and gripped the Captain's arm. "Where did you do this?"

"G-town. Not too far."

"Was it a fertility clinic, a sperm bank?"

The Captain just looked at him with a blank expression.

"Forget that, can you remember *when* you did it?"

"It was daylight."

"Okay, can you remember exactly where this place was?"

"Uh . . . It was white."

"Can you describe the person who asked you to, uh, pee in the cup?"

"Some guy."

"Never mind, I'll find it!" Roy banged his briefcase closed and raced out of the room.

CHAPTER

81

Mace left the mansion and walked over to the guesthouse. Alisha and Tyler were sitting at the dining room table eating a meal that Herbert had prepared. Mace sat down next to Tyler, who alternated between carefully forking mashed potatoes into his mouth and taking large gulps of milk.

"I know, the food here is pretty terrific," said Mace, as she watched the little boy.

"Do you live here?" Alisha asked her.

"For now. You all settled in?"

Alisha nodded. "I can't believe it. I mean just yesterday I was in my little apartment and then at Social. And now. It's like a dream. It's like a movie." She gazed around the expansive room in wonder. She looked over at her son. "I think Ty likes it here too."

"Wait'll I show you the gym. It's got an indoor basketball court."

Ty's eyes widened.

"You hear that, Ty?" said his mother. "A basketball court."

"He likes basketball?"

"Oh, yeah. Don't get a chance to play much. But he likes watching. He was watching from the window when your friend kicked Psycho's butt. Shoulda seen Ty clapping and jumping."

Mace said, "I can show you some cool moves if you want, Ty."

The little boy took another mouthful of food and looked at his mother.

"That'd be good, right, Ty?"

He nodded quickly.

Afterwards they walked over to the gym. Mace got a ball and

took Ty onto the court while Alisha watched. Mace bounced the ball between her legs, turned, and shot. The ball swished through the hoop, barely grazing the net.

Ty's face lit up and he looked over at his mother. Alisha clapped and Ty clapped too, his little arms pumping away. Mace took his hand and they moved closer to the basket. "Hang on one sec, Ty." She hustled over to a switch on the wall that raised and lowered the basket. She cranked it down to about five feet high and rejoined Ty. She instructed him how to hold the ball and then helped him with the first few shots. Three missed, but the fourth one found the bottom of the net.

Ty opened his mouth, and though no sound came out it was clear that he was shouting for joy. Mace showed him to how to bank a shot in. Every time he made a basket he would open his mouth, raise his arms in triumph, and then look at his mother. A few minutes later Alisha and Mace chased Ty all over the court as he bounced the ball and played keep-away. Thirty minutes later the two women sat down on a section of pullout bleachers while Ty kept bouncing the ball and hustling around the court.

"Okay, I'm officially worn out," said Mace as she watched the little boy run.

"He wears me out too. That little apartment ain't big enough to keep him tired. But it better than some alley."

"You should feel good you got out of that, Alisha. Real good."

"That man, Mr. Altman, he say we can stay here long as we want to. And he say he got some folks to look at Ty."

"He's a very kind man. If anyone can help Ty, he can."

Alisha looked around the immense building. "But we can't be staying here too long. I need to get me a real job. Take care of Ty good. Get going on my own."

"That will all come, Alisha. It's all part of the program. Mr. Altman will explain it in more detail."

"Yeah, that what he said. He wants me to get my GED and then he talking maybe college."

"That's great."

She looked worried. "I don't know. Folks in college they real smart. And the way I talk and all."

"The way you talk is fine. And I wonder how many of them could have survived what you did. You can do this. You're smart too."

Alisha smiled. "Sound like my granny. Be anything you want to be."

"You can."

Alisha stretched out her hand and placed it over the top of Mace's. "Thank you."

"Have you talked to Darren?"

"Unh-uh. Thought he call me, but he ain't."

"And he knows what Psycho did to you?"

"I know I shouldn't told him. He in prison when it happened."

"What was he in for?"

"Carjacking and stuff. Stupid. He got in with some real bad dudes. But he's smart. He done real good in school. He got a job to help me and our granny. But then she got sick and ain't had no health insurance. He had to make more money."

"So drug dealing? Carjacking?"

Alisha nodded. "He got arrested on my birthday. Just turned twelve and he bought me a dress and we were having ice cream in the food court over at the train station. And the blues bust in and then he gone. Didn't really see him again till he got outta prison. They sent him all the way to Ohio. Ain't no way I can get there with Ty."

"You think he might try to go after Psycho?"

Alisha's lips trembled. "I pray to God he ain't do something that dumb. Psycho kill him."

"We'll do everything we can to make sure that won't happen." Mace looked over at Ty as the little boy lined up a shot and made it. "I think Ty needs an uncle in his life. And from what I saw at your apartment Darren is really good with him."

"Oh, he loves Ty and Ty loves him. Funny because they ain't been around each other all that long. But it like they know each other a long time, you know what I mean?"

Mace nodded and then her attention turned to the door of the gym as it shot open.

"Darren!" Alisha cried out and jumped to her feet.

Ty stopped bouncing his ball and looked around at his uncle.

Right behind Darren was Rick Cassidy, his arm on Darren's shoulder.

"You know this guy?" said Cassidy.

"We do," said Mace. "What's going on?"

"Caught him climbing the south wall," said Cassidy.

As she drew closer Mace could see that Cassidy had placed a gun against the small of Darren's back.

"It ain't like I gonna just walk up to the door of a place like this and knock," said Darren sullenly.

"You should've given it a try," said Mace in a scolding tone. "We would have let you in."

"Yeah, right."

"Rick, you can lose the gun," said Mace quietly as she saw Ty running toward them.

"Okay, but I confiscated two pistols from him."

"Keep 'em for now."

"You sure, Mace?"

"I'm sure."

Rick holstered his gun and patted Darren on the shoulder. "You were actually pretty stealthy coming over the wall and you sure can run. Might make a good Navy SEAL."

"Yeah? Well, I don't see that in my career future, okay?"

"Never know." Cassidy turned and left.

Alisha put her arms around her brother while Ty gripped his legs.

"Okay, okay, don't knock me over, little guy," Darren said in a mock angry tone. He reached down and lifted Ty up.

"I was worried 'bout you," said Alisha. "Tried calling, but you never answered."

"Got tied up doing stuff."

"How'd you know she was here?" asked Mace.

Darren smiled. "That lady at Social, Carmela? Think she likes me. And the Razor got him some moves." He glanced at the door. "Was that dude really a SEAL?"

"Yep. You're lucky he took it easy on you."

"When he grabbed my arm I couldn't break his grip. Man, it was like steel."

"Welcome to the world of special forces."

He looked around. "Damn, what is this place anyway?"

Ty jumped down, picked up his ball, and bounced it back to Darren. Darren caught it, did a couple of dribbles between his legs, and passed it back. Ty bounced the ball down the court and made a layup.

Darren shot his sister a glance. "Who taught him how to do that?"

Alisha pointed at Mace. "She did."

"Hey, Razor, why don't you go play with your nephew for a while," said Mace. "And keep all thoughts of Psycho from your head."

"Ain't nothing gonna do that, woman. Playing with Ty or not."

"See, that's the very reason you should. Ty and Alisha need you, Darren. Not in prison. And not dead. You let me worry about Psycho."

"What you gonna do about Psycho? You can't do shit about him."

"All I'm asking is that you let me try. That's all."

"Please, Darren," said Alisha. "Please." She gripped his arm tightly.

Darren looked back and forth between the two women. Then he pulled free from Alisha. "Gotta go teach my little man some street moves."

He jogged down the court to join Ty.

Mace's phone rang. It was Roy. His message was brief, blunt, and yet stunning.

"Alisha, I've got to go out for a while. Just chill and I'll be back, okay?"

"Okay. Sure."

Mace ran to her Ducati.

82

Potomac Cryobank, LLP. You sure this is the place?" Mace asked Roy as she looked up at the sign over the door.

They were standing outside of a white brick building just off M Street in Georgetown. They'd driven over on her Ducati. The place was less than a ten-minute walk from Shilling & Murdoch.

"It's not like there are fertility clinics and sperm banks on every corner. Based on what the Captain told me, this is it. It's the only one within walking distance. And it's white."

They went inside and spent five minutes getting nowhere with the receptionist. Finally, a thin woman dressed in white pants, a blue smock, and rubber-soled shoes came out, steered them to a room off the foyer, and seated them at a small table.

"So what exactly is this about?" she asked sternly.

Roy explained as much of the situation as he could.

"That's ridiculous," said the woman.

"Why?" asked Roy.

"This person claims he just walked in off the street and was paid two hundred dollars for a semen donation?"

"That's right. Why is that ridiculous?"

"You don't know much about sperm banks, do you, Mr. Kingman?"

"No, actually, I've never had the need to come to one before. I've been pretty happy with my own product."

"That's why we're here," said Mace. "To become educated."

The woman excused herself and returned a minute later with a large stack of papers that she plopped in front of Mace and Roy.

"Let me give you the run-through of what it takes to become a semen donor," she said, with the irritating air of a person who knows lots of things others don't. She indicated the pages. "These are the forms one must fill out to even be considered as a donor. They're all available online from our website as well." She held up one form. "This is the initial donor app, which as you can see is lengthy and requires extensive medical, physical, and educational backgrounds and other pertinent information. If they pass that stage—and many do not—they are sent a second application covering three generations of family medical history." She picked up another set of pages. "I'm referring to this one. After that comes a specimen screening. This involves a personal interview conducted on these premises and a semen evaluation. They are asked to produce three to four specimens over a two-week period. Those specimens are evaluated for quality and testing of freezing survivability."

"Freezing survivability?" said Mace.

"I'll get to that. Potential donors must be screened for infectious diseases of course, like HIV, syphilis, gonorrhea, hepatitis B and C, and also genetic diseases, as well as blood typing, rhesus factor, and so on. And they must undergo a general physical exam either by their own physician or ours. We expect a six-month commitment from our accepted donors and they must produce one donation per week over that period."

"And they're paid?" said Roy.

"Of course. People do not go through this out of the goodness of their hearts. Our compensation rates range from one to four hundred dollars per acceptable specimen. Precise individual compensation depends on semen quality and the donor's commitment to the program."

"How is it collected?" asked Roy.

"Almost all on-site. Usually via masturbation into leakproof containers. Semen can also be removed surgically, but we don't do that here."

"Almost all, you said?" noted Mace.

"We sometimes do off-site collections in an emergency, but only if the collection is done at a hospital, clinic, or, in very rare cases, the person's home. With that method we provide donors with special condoms for collection purposes. And the specimen must be transported to us within one to two hours without being exposed to extreme temperatures. Otherwise it's not acceptable. But in the seven years I've been here we've only had two cases of off-site collection. We like to control all phases, you see."

"And if it's off-site, then you have no way of knowing if it's actually the person's sperm or not," pointed out Roy.

"That's right. We can of course do a DNA analysis to ensure it was from our donor. And it will still be subjected to the same rigorous checks, so, for example, no infectious diseases get through."

"And the freezing?" prompted Mace.

"The sperm has to be stored under specific and exacting conditions to fully preserve it. We have a cryo-storage room here with cryogenic vats. We use liquid nitrogen among other protocols to maintain the specimens."

"Can we see the room?" asked Mace.

"No. It's an environmentally controlled space and you need special equipment to work in there. I can tell you that each vat holds over seventy thousand semen specimens."

"How do you differ from a fertility clinic?" Mace wanted to know.

"Fertility clinics don't typically store sperm. They get it from us. We match their client's request as to race, height, physical appearance, for example, and provide them the sperm which they will then use for artificial insemination purposes."

"Is there any way to determine if the sperm found at the crime scene I described came from your clinic?" Roy asked.

"I can assure you it didn't," she said flatly.

"Just humor me. Please. A man's freedom is at stake."

She sighed heavily. "From our specific clinic? No, I don't believe so. But you can easily determine if it was a donation to a sperm bank like ours."

"How?" Mace asked quickly.

"As soon as the specimen is provided you have to inject buffers as a preservative into the semen. If done promptly and then frozen, semen can really be stored indefinitely. However, the maximum allowable time by current law is ten years unless the donor was under the age of forty-five when the specimen was given. And even then the sperm can only be used by the donor and his partner, and not given to anyone else."

"Ten years, wow," said Mace. "Long time to keep the little fellows swimming around."

"Without a preservative and proper storage the sperm contained in the semen will have diminished motility after two or three days and the sample will be no good to us after, say, five days. And our clients would not be very happy with that, would they?"

"So, shooting blanks, in other words?" said Mace.

The nurse sniffed. "Crudely put, but accurate. When we send semen out to our clients the specimens are cryopreserved in screw-top vials. The vials come inside a refrigerated tank or dry shipper since it is actually a metal vacuum bottle refrigerated with liquid nitrogen. The semen is sent with detailed instructions on thawing and utilization."

Sort of takes all the romance out of it, thought Mace.

"So to answer your question directly, we use a TEST yolk buffer solution as a preservative. Many other sperm banks do the same."

"Yolk? As in egg?" said Mace with a trace of disgust.

"Not exactly, no, and it's a perfectly accepted method of preservation."

Roy said, "So if it's not a semen donation?"

"Then there will be no preservative. And I can assure you that there won't be with the person you described. He would never have gotten past the initial round of medical forms. And if he's a Vietnam veteran as you mentioned he would've been disqualified right away."

"You disqualify Vietnam vets?" said Roy sharply.

"No, of course not, it's based on *age*. We, along with most sperm banks, don't accept specimens from anyone over the age of forty. Indeed, most of our donors are under the age of thirty, many of them college students."

"Looking for beer money," commented Mace.

"I wouldn't know about that."

"Are you open every day?" asked Mace.

"We're closed on Wednesdays and Sundays."

"So the building is empty then?"

The woman looked at her and said in a contemptuous tone, "That would usually be the case when we're *closed*. Now if you'll excuse me, I have to get back to work."

"Lots of eggs to crack today?" said Mace.

The woman led them out without saying another word.

When they were outside Roy said, "Wow, I really dig your interrogation technique. First, piss the person off, and then see what she won't tell us."

"That woman was not going to knowingly help us from the get-go, but she did tell us at least one thing of importance other than the yolk thing."

"What?"

"That they're closed on Wednesdays and Sundays. Now we need to get the sperm sample they found in Tolliver checked out. Lowell Cassell can do it."

"And if there's no yolk?"

"Then maybe the Captain is lying."

"I don't think he's mentally capable of coming up with something like this."

"I don't think so either, but nothing would surprise me anymore. If it does come back without the preservative, the Captain is probably going down for this."

"But what if he came here and they took sperm from him but didn't inject the preservative in it?"

"And why would they do that, Roy? Because they were planning to kill Diane Tolliver and blame it on the Captain? You think the petite sperm expert back there crushed your partner's brain stem and then injected her with sperm taken under false pretenses?"

"No, but maybe one of the doctors? The Captain said a white building. And he said some guy helped him. He obviously came here."

Mace considered this. "We'll have to get a roster of who works here and check out any viable suspects."

"In the meantime can you call Cassell to run the test?"

"No, but I'll phone my sister. I'll do it tomorrow morning."

"Why not now?"

"Because I have to work up the nerve, that's why!"

"Why not just bypass her?"

"How? I can't exactly order the ME to run the damn test."

Roy's phone buzzed.

"Hello?"

"Mr. Kingman? It's Gary, the waiter from Simpsons."

"Oh, right. Gary from Simpsons," he said so Mace would know. Roy hit the speakerphone button and held the phone up.

"Did you remember something else, Gary?"

"Well, it wasn't what I remembered. It's what I just saw."

"What you just saw? I don't understand."

"The guy Ms. Tolliver was having dinner with? I just saw him."

"What? Where? We're close to the restaurant. Is that where you saw him? We can be there in a few minutes. Can you stall him?"

"No, I'm not at work. I'm at my apartment near Adams Morgan. I meant I just saw his photo in the newspaper."

"Saw him in the newspaper."

"Yeah. He's dead."

"What? Who was he?"

"That attorney guy they found in a Dumpster? Jamie Meldon? He was the guy with Ms. Tolliver Friday night."

H ELLO, Beth."

Beth looked up to see Sam Donnelly and Jarvis Burns coming toward her. It was the next morning and they were in an auditorium at the FBI's Washington Field Office where Beth was to give out some awards to local teenagers enrolled in the Bureau's Junior Agent Program.

"Sam, Jarvis, I didn't expect to see you two here."

Burns's eyes crinkled. "Why not? Some of these young people will be the intelligence operatives of the future."

Donnelly added, "And one can never start too early looking for talent and molding personalities."

"By the way, I spoke with your guys. I appreciate the effort you made."

"Well, they're not technically *my guys*," Donnelly said quickly. "But I value your professional friendship highly. Indeed, Beth, if you hadn't pursued a career in law enforcement you would've made a hell of an intelligence agent."

"High praise coming from you. So Reiger and Hope don't report to you?"

Donnelly and Burns exchanged a quick glance. Donnelly said, "Not even the same intelligence platform. Quite frankly, I made a few phone calls, did the Potomac two-step, and ended up with that pair. They seem quite capable. And their superiors obviously gave the okay to brief you."

"Well, it wasn't much of a briefing. National security tagline basically."

"That, unfortunately, is often the case. You know how these things work. No one wants to read anybody else into anything. The old cold war adage still applies as much today: Don't trust anyone."

"Do Reiger and Hope have any military connections?"

Burns shot her a penetrating stare. "Not that we know of. Why do you ask?"

"Just an observation. They had DHS creds but told me they'd once worked at the Bureau. And I checked into their backgrounds and quickly found that my security clearances weren't high enough to even have a peek into where they really came from."

Donnelly said, "With DHS, the FBI, and sixteen intelligence agencies floating around, it's nearly impossible keeping any of it straight. I know the goal when creating the Director of National Intelligence position was to orchestrate better oversight and coordination among all these unwieldy alliances, but—and you didn't hear this from me—it is a herculean task. Some might say impossible."

"I'm sure. I just have one city and four thousand cops to keep track of. You have the entire world."

"Don't sell yourself short. That one city is the nation's capital. And one of your constituents just happens to be the president."

"Who went for a pizza run yesterday, which cost me two hundred officers off the street for the motorcade deployment."

"The world's most powerful man can do what he wants when he wants." Burns drew closer. "As an aside, I heard you made an arrest in the murder of that female lawyer in Georgetown. Congratulations. The director actually mentioned it at our morning briefing."

Donnelly said, "That's right, Beth. Good work."

"Well, let's hope the case sticks."

"A homeless vet I understand?" said Burns.

"Louis Dockery. A homeless vet with a chest full of medals, including a pair of Purple Hearts and a Combat Bronze."

Burns wagged his head, his silvery hair tipping onto his broad forehead. "So very sad. I can certainly relate to the Purple Heart, I have a pair of those myself."

Donnelly said, "I have one of my own. But unfortunately the two ongoing wars are adding enormously to both the military and the VA's burdens. There's simply not enough funding to cover all the problems."

Beth said, "Well, Washington better rework its priorities. I can't think of a more important goal than taking care of the people who've defended this country with their blood."

Burns patted his bad leg. "When I got out I sought psychiatric counseling, although there was a certain stigma attached to that. Hopefully it's less so now."

"Well, you turned out all right, so there's hope."

"Some would argue with that."

"That there's hope?"

Burns smiled. "No. That I turned out all right."

Donnelly pointed to the teenagers set to receive their awards. "Now, go give them a great pep talk, Chief. In ten years they'll be the first line of defense for this country."

"Preventing attacks instead of responding to them, you mean?"

"Much better to crush the enemy before he can act instead of pulling the bodies of his victims out of the rubble. We save lives, Beth, you and I. We just do it a little differently in my part of the spectrum. But the goals are the same. Always remember that."

The men walked off and a moment later Beth's phone buzzed. She looked at the caller and her brow wrinkled. She almost didn't answer.

"Mace, I'm right in the middle of something. Can this wait? What?" She listened intently for sixty seconds. "I'll take care of it." She clicked off, glanced at the FBI agent emceeing the program, and held up one finger. He nodded.

She rushed to a corner of the auditorium and made a call.

Lowell Cassell seemed surprised. "All right, Beth, if you say so. It's easy enough to check for that. But if it's true that certainly will complicate things."

"Yes, it will."

"How did you come by this theory?"

"Take one guess."

"Your sister is keeping busy."

Beth clicked off and rushed up to the stage to personally greet the teenagers and then settled at the lectern to begin her remarks.

From a far corner, Donnelly and Burns, who'd been watching her intently while she'd been on the calls, turned and left the room.

CHAPTER

84

"THIS WAS a nice surprise." Karl Reiger's wife, Wendy, kissed him on the cheek as her husband flipped another burger on the grill.

"Kids had the day off so I thought what the hell. Nice, sunny day, summer around the corner."

"Well, I'm glad you did. You've been working such long hours lately, sweetie."

Reiger looked at his wife. She was in her mid-thirties, four years younger than him. She still possessed the classic beauty she had when they'd met in college. She wore jean shorts, a white sleeveless blouse, and a Washington Nationals ball cap over her shoulder-length light brown hair.

"Yeah, work is a real bitch right now."

"Oh look, Don and Sally are here."

Reiger glanced over at the driveway of his two-story brick house in Centreville, Virginia. Lots of federal agents lived out this way because everything inside the Beltway was far too expensive if your job was to merely risk your life in serving your country. Don Hope, his wife, and three kids were climbing out of a Dodge minivan, hauling platters of food along with a baseball and several gloves. Hope's two sons put down the food on a wooden picnic table set up in the backyard and joined Reiger's two boys in throwing the ball around. The Hopes' daughter, a ten-year-old, went into the house with Tammy Reiger, who'd just turned eleven. Sally gave Reiger a hug and then she and Wendy busied themselves getting the meal ready.

Don Hope shut the doors of the van, grabbed two beers from a cooler he'd brought, popped the tops, walked over to Reiger at the grill, and handed him one.

Reiger took a long pull of the drink, finishing half of it.

"Cookout?" said Hope. "Little surprised to get the call."

"Why not? Normalcy. It's been a while."

"Guess you're right about that. No orders yet?"

"Why I'm flipping burgers instead of the other thing."

"You think Burns is setting us up to take the fall?"

"Every op I've gone into I'm prepared to be killed by the guys on the other side and screwed by the guys signing my paychecks."

"Hell of a way to make a living, Karl."

"I thought I'd be career military. See the world, good pension when you pull your time. Even do some good."

"Me too. Then—"

"We were too good at what we did, Don. That's why they came calling. They don't pick the dregs, they go for the cream."

"Feeling more like soured milk now."

Reiger slid a burger onto a platter and slapped another piece of raw meat on the grill. "Why, because we keep missing Perry?"

"Dumb luck."

"I'm not so sure about that. I've read up on her after Burns gave us the 'Rome is burning' lecture. Lady is good at what she does. No question. Hell, I'm surprised Burns didn't try to recruit her at some point."

Hope took a swallow of beer and watched the boys throwing the ball. "Sterilized weapons, cocked and locked. What bullshit. I'm a dad. I got a mortgage. I've been married fourteen years and I still have the hots big-time for my wife. I'm not some damn machine."

"To them we are. That's all we are. Fungible. Use up some shells, they got more where we came from. We're just rounds in a magazine."

"How many more do you figure?"

"Never really thought about it, because I could never verify my guess."

"But why meet at the Pentagon? Especially since no one else there knows what we're up to."

Reiger prodded a burger with a long fork. "DNI isn't like the spider at the center of the web. It's more like the snake slithering through the backyard. A mandate to go everywhere, see everything. Pentagon is as big an intelligence player as they come. Used to going its own way, sucking down dollars and data. We saw that when we were in uniform, Don."

"For sure we did."

"But even it has to kowtow to DNI. And so Burns makes the rounds, has offices everywhere, Langley, NSA, National Geospatial."

"And the Pentagon?"

"I know two- and three-star generals who hate the DNI's guts for all the good it'll do them. Sam Donnelly does the daily presidential intelligence briefings now instead of the DCI. Locked tight. You got the man's ear and trust, you can't lose. You're golden."

"Yeah, but Burns is a piece of work. Half of me wishes he'd drop from a stroke."

"And the other half?" Reiger said grinning.

"Nothing you haven't thought about."

Reiger put some cheese on top of an almost done burger. "Read up on him too when we were recruited for this. Vietnam vet. One hard-ass guy. Medals out the ying-yang. Guy was as brave as they come, did his thing, laid it all out there for the Stars and Stripes. Flipped to the intelligence side soon as Saigon fell. Wounds made him unfit for active duty."

"The leg."

"Right. He's in his sixties. Could have got out before now, but apparently he's got nothing else in his life."

"Wife? Kids?"

"Wife left him, apparently his two kids did too."

Hope looked impressed. "Where'd you get that scuttlebutt?"

Reiger cracked a smile. "Your security clearance isn't high enough."

Hope finished his beer. "The hell you say."

"A hardass," Reiger said again. "Loves his country, though. Do anything to protect it. And he expects us to do anything to protect it too. And anything covers a lot."

"Piece of paper, Karl. That's what we need. Our get-out-of-jail-free card."

The ball flew toward them, landing a couple feet from the grill. Reiger snagged it and threw it back to his oldest son.

"Thanks, Pop."

Reiger pointed at the black sedan that had just pulled into the driveway next to the minivan. The man who got out wore a plain suit that did not stand out in any way. It was the sort that Reiger and Hope wore while on duty, allowing them to just blend in. In the man's hand was an equally plain white envelope.

"Well, here it comes right now, Don. I guess we're back to killing Americans."

"I don't like this any better than you, but don't get cold on me now, Karl."

"I've been cold ever since I put a round in Jamie Meldon's brain."

He slapped another piece of raw meat on the grill and watched it sizzle.

85

AFTER PHONING her sister that morning, Mace picked up Roy and drove him in to work. When they arrived she told Roy about the call.

"So you didn't tell her about Meldon having dinner with Diane, but just about the DNA testing?" he said as he climbed off the bike.

"That's right."

"Mind telling me why?"

"It could be the key to breaking this case. If I'm going to use this sucker to get back on the force *I* have to solve it. And I don't want Beth to get in trouble for pulling strings for me."

"I can understand that. You really do care about her."

"She's pretty much all I have left."

"Hey, haven't I gotten a little bit in the loop?"

She smiled. "You're sweet, Roy. And yes you have." Her expression hardened. "So what's the connection between Meldon and Tolliver?"

"It has to predate her coming to Shilling & Murdoch. She never once mentioned him, and I never saw him come to the firm."

"Wouldn't have been some legal dealings?"

"We don't do criminal work. What other legal dealings would they have?"

"Okay, like you said, it must predate her time at Shilling. Where was she before?"

Roy thought for a moment. "She mentioned New Jersey."

"I read that Meldon used to practice law in Manhattan. If she was in Newark or thereabouts, that's practically the same place.

They could have had dealings then. She was in private practice up there too?"

"I think so."

"It's funny."

"What?"

"The D.C. cops got pulled off Meldon's murder."

"You mentioned that but didn't tell me why."

"Beth didn't know why but she was pissed about it. She and Mona Danforth had *words* about it while we were at Café Milano. But the thing is, whoever's investigating Meldon's death should have retraced his steps too. They could've found something or knew that he was meeting with Tolliver. And let me tell you, if their deaths aren't connected it's like the mother of all coincidences. And I don't believe in coincidences anyway."

"So we find Diane's killer, we get Meldon's murderer too."

"That's sort of the plan."

"Any way to find out who *is* investigating Meldon's homicide?"

"If I ask Beth she'll want to know why. I can try a couple other sources. Meantime we need to follow up our own leads."

"But that waiter could call the cops and tell them what he just told us."

"He could but I doubt he will."

"Why?"

"He's probably forgotten about it. It just comes with the chronic ADD mentality of that generation that believes that twittering actually constitutes personal interaction."

"Hey, that waiter was about the same age as me."

"Sorry. So can you find out where Diane worked before Shilling?"

"Yeah. But let me write it down. Otherwise I'll probably forget we even had this conversation because of my generational ADD."

"Oh, Roy, at least you make me laugh."

"Well, while you're laughing I also just remembered where I saw the initials DLT."

"DLT?"

"It was at the bottom of the last e-mail Diane sent me."

"I saw that. Just figured it was her initials."

"That's what I thought too, but she never signed any other e-mails that way."

"Okay. So what else could it mean?"

"I'm betting DLT stands for Daniels, Langford and Taylor."

"And they are?"

"The escrow agent that Shilling & Murdoch uses for all of its closing transactions. Their offices are up on K Street, right in the middle of Lobbyist Alley."

"And they're significant why?"

"They do the money wire transfers for our deals. Billions of dollars go through their office, at least electronically. Billions."

"Okay, billions of anything always gets my attention. What do you think you can find out?"

"I can check the firm archives for a start. I can look through closing docs for the deals that Diane and I worked on, check escrow letters, electronic funds transfer confirmations, that sort of thing."

Before he walked inside she said, "Call me with whatever info you can get on Diane. I'll follow it up from there. But you need to focus on repping the Captain. With Mona on the other side waiting with fangs bared, you're going to really need to bring your A-game."

She roared off, leaving Roy to trudge into the building, his briefcase smacking against his leg.

Ned nodded to him from the security desk.

"You okay, Mr. Kingman?" he asked.

"Never better."

CHAPTER

86

Mace drove back to Abe Altman's place and checked on Alisha and Tyler. She found the pair in Altman's study going over specifics of the program Altman had designed. They looked up when she poked her head in. Ty still had the basketball and was bouncing it in a corner.

"Where's Darren?" Mace asked.

"He left," said Alisha. "Didn't say where he was going and didn't say when he be back. I'm worried about him."

"Hey, Razor can take care of himself." This was a lie, Mace knew. When it came to people like Psycho you'd need an Army battalion to take care of yourself. She walked back to the guesthouse, went up to her bedroom, and pulled something out of her closet. It was the baggie of shell casings the honor guard had given her at her father's funeral. She sat back on the bed and held the bag on her chest, staring at the ceiling. It was so stupid of her to have opened the coffin. Every time she thought of her father, it began with that horrifying image before she could manage to push it aside.

She rattled the metal in the bag.

Okay, Dad, what do you think I should do? Let Beth run with this or keep chugging on? I want to be a blue again, Dad. I have to be a blue again.

She rattled the casings some more, as though trying to get better reception. There was no answer. There would never be an answer. She wasn't a little girl anymore who could run to Daddy for help. These were her problems to solve. Only there was no right or wrong answer. There were only choices. Her choices.

She put the precious bag of used ordnance away, slipped over to the window, and looked over the grounds. Her gaze, by habit, sought out all places of potential danger. Entry points, the shadowy spaces under trees, a secluded corner. She thought for a second that she had seen Rick Cassidy flit by, but it happened so fast she couldn't be sure.

Feeling suddenly lethargic, she scooted down to the kitchen and made some coffee. She brought it back up to the bedroom with a peanut butter and jelly sandwich with sliced bananas on toasted wheat that she'd made with her own two hands. It undoubtedly would not have met Herbert's high culinary standards, but it tasted damn good. Finished, she lay back on the bed with the thought of just resting her eyes. She hadn't really slept in a long time. It was finally catching up to her. Just a few minutes . . .

The vibration woke her. She sat up groggily and looked around for a moment, disoriented. A moment later she snatched her phone from her pocket. As she hit the answer button she noted the time.

Damn, I've been asleep for hours.

"Hello?" She glanced out the window where a gentle rain was starting to fall.

"It's Roy."

"I didn't recognize the number. Where are you calling from?"

"My health club. Just call me paranoid. If they can tap computer cameras, you know?"

"I know. So what's up?"

"Got something to write with?"

She grabbed paper and pen off the nightstand. "Shoot."

"Okay, just so you know, everyone in the firm hates my guts."

"And how magnanimous you'll be when you turn out to be right."

"No, I won't. I'll tell them to eat shit and die. Anyway, I checked out some stuff and talked to some people. I've got Diane's ex-husband's name and number. He lives in Hawaii so you can call him today if you want. It's morning there now."

"Okay. What else?"

"Apparently the divorce was not all that amicable. I'm hoping that the ex can give you some more info on that. Maybe the name of the lawyer who represented Diane."

"And the connection to Meldon?"

"No clue at this point, but at least it's a start."

"What about DLT?"

"I'm planning to sneak down to the archives tonight and poke around."

"Listen, Roy, you staying there after hours alone is not a good thing."

"I'm not sure if anyone here is involved, so I can't exactly waltz down to archives and start going through boxes. I'll find what I can and take the stuff home."

"Why not come to Abe's instead? We've got real security here."

"You think he'll mind?"

"I think the place is so big you could roll in with a tank brigade and he'd have no clue you were even here."

"Okay, maybe that's smarter."

"And that way we can both go over the docs you found. It'll be faster. Are you going back to see the Captain?"

"As soon as I'm done here. They just notified me that the presentment is tomorrow morning at Superior Court. I need to go over some details with him to the extent he can remember any."

"The presentment's pretty perfunctory, right?"

"Nothing's perfunctory when Mona Danforth is in the picture. They'll have to get a grand jury to issue an indictment since it's a first-degree felony."

"Or they can just return a No Bill."

"What, did you enroll in law school this afternoon?"

Mace said, "I was a cop. I've been in court more than most lawyers."

"But there's no way she's not going to get an indictment returned on these facts. They might as well just dispense with the preliminary hearing. They've got more than enough to show cause for the prosecution to go forward. The Captain will be arraigned on murder in the first and a trial date set. Any word from your sister on the semen sample?"

"Uh, hold on a sec."

Mace quickly checked to see if she had any phone messages on the off chance that she had slept through a call from Beth. "No, nothing yet."

"Well, let me know the minute you do. I don't want to be blindsided by that when I walk into court tomorrow."

"And when you do your firm will know for sure where you stand."

"I know. And they'll fire me. That's why I'm going through the archives today. I probably won't get another chance."

"Good luck."

"You too."

Mace clicked off and punched in the number for Joe Cushman, Diane Tolliver's ex-husband who was now living in the Hawaiian paradise.

Must be nice.

CHAPTER

87

THE COOKOUT was over, the sunshine was long gone, replaced with light rain, and Reiger and Hope were back in their plain suits and riding in their new Town Car.

"Orders all in order?" joked Hope.

"Yep, and locked away in my safety deposit box. I dropped by the bank as soon as you and your family left."

"Getting paranoid on me? Good." Hope rolled down the window and breathed in the moist air. "So who signed?"

"Everybody we need. Including Burns *and* Donnelly."

"Guess the guy finally took us seriously." Hope nodded at his partner. "Cookout was nice, Karl. Good idea."

"Yeah, I'd rather be flipping dogs and burgers right now instead of driving to this place."

Hope looked at the address that had come with the signed orders. "Warehouse in Arlington?"

"A front. They're all fronts. We'll see a 'For Sale' or 'For Lease' sign on the wall. A couple cars parked out of sight. A guy with a face you'll never remember will answer our knock, we'll flash our IDs, and the meeting will begin."

"What are we hoping to get out of this tonight?"

"What I want are some recruits to do the trigger pulls while we coordinate from the sidelines. At least that way I can hate myself a little less."

"But that's another set of testimonies in court if this goes wrong. Geez, I can't believe I'm saying this stuff."

"We need to think about it, Don. But I'm not worried about

these guys. I'm guessing Burns made sure they are not from this hemisphere. So we get the executioners in place and then the plan gets knocked together."

"I know Perry has to go down. What about the punk lawyer?"

"If he hadn't gotten in the way that night Perry would already have ceased to be a pain in our ass. But I'm not holding grudges. The order says Perry and anybody else deemed necessary. If we deem him not necessary he can go on being a lawyer after mourning the loss of his friend. I'm not looking to add to my bag of kills here. I've smoked my share of dirtbags, but none of them looked like me."

Reiger looked up ahead. "There it is. What did I tell you?"

As they drove into the parking lot the "For Sale" sign was prominently mounted on one wall of the place that was actually three separate buildings on an acre of land in a section of Arlington that had seen far better days.

"Looks to be 1950s construction," said Hope. "Surprised they haven't knocked it down and put up condos. Land in Arlington is damn hard to come by."

"Yeah, but if it's secretly owned by an intelligence agency that doesn't give a crap about cash flow, that is not your definition of a motivated seller."

Reiger drove through a narrow opening between two of the brick buildings and stopped in the middle of the small interior courtyard.

"Like I said, couple of cars parked here. Now all we need is the faceless guy answering the door and I'm a perfect three for three."

Reiger did not go three for three.

The woman who answered the door was petite with short brown hair angled around an oval face, and dressed in dark slacks, a tan windbreaker, and a pair of black-rimmed glasses. She flicked her badge and ID card at them. They did the same.

"Follow me," she said.

They fell into line behind her as she led them through the darkened hall.

"Didn't catch the name on the ID card," said Reiger.

"Mary Bard."

"Okay, Agent Bard. Karl Reiger and Don Hope."

"Call me Mary. And I know who you are. I've been tasked to help with this assignment," she said over her shoulder.

"Well, we can use the help," said Reiger. "I assume you've been read in?"

"Yes. I can see why you two are frustrated. It seems to me they've been running you around like bulls in a china shop and expecting the impossible."

"Exactly. We need to set the hit up our way instead of chasing them."

She said, "Burns told me we're to go over the logistics, call in resources as needed, and then lay the trap."

"Now that sounds like a strategy."

"Watch your step. I'll turn the lights on once we get to the interior room. Cops sometimes patrol by here."

"Understood. So where are you really from?"

"You saw my creds."

"Right, I've got several sets myself and they all say something different."

"Okay. Justice Department. That do it for you?"

Reiger grinned. "That's what they all say."

Bard smiled too. "I know."

Don Hope was looking down. He lifted up one of his feet. "Plastic on the floors?"

Reiger reached out and touched one of the walls. "And on the walls?"

Mary Bard moved with the grace of a ballerina, but also with the speed of a tiger. The kick caught Reiger in the sternum, driving him back into the wall with such force that it threw his heart out of sinus rhythm. Since there was no light, the shine of the twin six-inch blades was never seen by either man as she whirled them in a blur of synchronized motion. One knife ripped across Reiger's throat first. He didn't even have time to scream. He fell to the floor clutching his severed jugular.

Don Hope managed to pull his weapon. Before his finger could close on the trigger, she drove her foot into his knee, ripping it backwards; supporting bones snapped and tendons tore away like sprung rubber bands. He screamed in agony, at least until she gave a backhanded slash with the second knife. The jagged blade ripped his throat apart; arterial blood erupted from the wounds, spraying the narrow hall.

Hope sank next to his dead partner, his last few breaths jerky, gurgling, and then his chest ceased to heave. As if on cue the lights came on and several people moved forward. As Bard stepped out of the way, hands rolled up the plastic with the men inside it. A truck was parked in the rear of the building. Reiger and Hope were placed inside and the truck sped off.

Bard had the blood of each man on her clothes. She stepped out of them and stood there in her bra and panties until she was handed a jumpsuit by one of her colleagues. Her physique was lean, with ropy muscles in her arms, shoulders, and thighs. The heightened definition of her body and absence of fat threw the scars on her torso into sharpened relief. She zipped up the jumpsuit, turned, and entered a bathroom where she scrubbed the evidence of the twin kills off her face, hands, and hair. She took off the eyeglasses and slid them into her pocket. They were actually night optics, allowing her to see her victims in the dark far better than they could see her. A few minutes later she left by another rear door. Her Smart car started up and she drove out of the parking lot, headed west, and entered Interstate 66. She placed the call.

"Done," she said and then clicked off.

Jarvis Burns put his phone down and allowed himself a rare smile. "Now *that*, Agent Reiger, is chain of command."

As he turned back to his work, he glanced at his watch. Two minutes later, in the safety deposit box where Reiger had placed his precious orders that would enable him and Hope to walk free after the job was done, the time-released chemicals built into the document's threads did their work. In ten seconds there was nothing left except vapor.

CHAPTER

88

INCREDIBLY ENOUGH, Joe Cushman, Diane Tolliver's ex-husband, had just found out that his former wife had been murdered. It seemed news took a while to travel that far west. But then again, Mace thought, it wasn't like the death of an ordinary citizen would make the national news other than as a one-time blip, and only then because of the rather bizarre circumstances. Joe Cushman did not sound all that upset and was not planning to attend the funeral. Yet that was understandable, Mace concluded. His divorce had been final over a decade ago and he told her that he'd remarried. And as Roy had informed her, it had not been an amicable separation. Cushman had bellowed out the reason for that early on in their long-distance conversation.

"She cheated on me!"

"Who with?"

"Don't know. I never was able to find out, and then I just stopped caring."

Every few seconds he would pause and Mace could hear him dragging on a cigarette. He had the smoker's gravelly voice too, his throat and lungs probably already full of nicotine-induced lumps.

"So how do you know she was having an affair?" Mace had asked.

"All the telltale signs. She bought fancy lingerie that she sure as hell never wore for me. She started working out, lost weight, new cosmetics, weekend 'business' trips, the whole shebang. We had no kids so it was basically split up the property and go our separate ways. Still, her law firm played hardball. Hell, I even had to fork up some cash for her attorney's fees, if you can believe that."

"Why?"

"She made good money, but I made a lot more. Commercial real estate developer in New Jersey when you could print money doing it."

"Good for you."

"Yeah? Well, I don't have as much money now, but I like the beaches and the trade winds a lot better than the ice and muck in Jersey."

"You don't by chance remember the name of the firm that represented her?"

"Are you kidding? I sure as hell wrote them enough checks. Hamilton, Petrocelli & Sprissler. In Newark. Three ladies. Three hellcats more like it. Even my lawyer was afraid of them. They were so good I used them later in some of my deals."

"Thanks a lot. I appreciate the info."

"Hope it helps with whatever you're doing. Diane and I didn't get along, obviously, but nobody deserves to die like that. I'm thinking of sending some flowers."

"I'm sure that would be very nice."

Mace clicked off and looked down at her notes. She called information and got the number for Hamilton, Petrocelli & Sprissler, LLP, in Newark.

She got the receptionist and then the call was put through to Julie Hamilton.

"Yes?"

Mace briefly explained why she was calling.

"Diane Tolliver?"

"You probably would have known her as Diane Cushman. She took her maiden name back after the divorce. I spoke with her ex, Joe Cushman. He gave me your name."

"I do remember hearing something about the killing. The refrigerator, right?"

"Yes, the refrigerator."

"But I never associated Tolliver with Cushman. I mean, I knew her maiden name was Tolliver, but it just never occurred to me it was her. It's been over a decade. Murdered. My God!"

"Yes. That's why I'm calling."

"And who are you with?" This was the cautious lawyer's voice now that Mace knew so well.

"I'm in D.C. I'm helping to investigate the matter on behalf of a man charged with the murder."

"Like I said, it's been at least ten years. I can't think of any way I would have relevant information for you."

"Do you know a man named Jamie Meldon?"

"Why do you ask?"

"Because he was murdered too, right after he met with Diane."

Caution had just transformed to ice. "I'm afraid I can't help you."

"I just need to ask some questions about—"

The next sound Mace heard was the line going dead.

She immediately called back.

This time the receptionist would not put the call through.

"Please, it will only take two minutes and it's—"

The receptionist hung up on her.

Mace slowly put the phone down.

CHAPTER

89

AFTER TALKING to Mace, Roy decided to speed up his search of the firm's records. He took the stairs down to the fifth floor. However, the archives room was locked and he didn't have a key. He trudged back to the sixth floor and headed to the mail room. Dave was there sorting letters and packages for the last delivery of the day. "Where's Gene?" Roy asked about the person who manned the archives room.

"Left early. Doctor's appointment. You need anything from down there?"

"It can keep. I'll let you get on with your deliveries."

"Is it true you're going to be the lawyer for that guy they arrested?'

"Why? You want to bust my chops too?"

"No, I thought that's what lawyers were supposed to do. I mean, you can't not represent somebody just because he's not popular, right?"

"Dave, that's the first intelligent thing I've heard today."

Dave headed out with his cart while Roy pretended to follow him out, then he circled back and closed the door to the mail room. He jogged to the very back, lifted the door to the dumbwaiter, climbed in, hit the green button, and pulled his arm back. The door closed, the machine gave a little jolt, and Roy was on his way.

On the brief ride down he thought about the other time he'd been inside here. Wrapped around Mace's body. It *had* been a flashlight in his pocket, though he couldn't say he hadn't been a little aroused, what with her proximity to him and the adrenaline rush that came with knowing your life might soon end violently.

Maybe they should try that technique at the sperm bank.

The dumbwaiter stopped and the doors slid open.

Roy climbed out and looked around. The room was dark but he had to make sure. He did a slow circuit of the large room with its rows of shelves and stacked boxes. He slipped his small flashlight out and shone the beam around. He knew generally how the filing system was set up here and made a beeline to one section. This was where most of his and Diane's client files were kept. He started opening boxes. Securely attached to the inside top of each box was a small hard plastic case. Inside the case was a flash drive containing an electronic record of everything in that box.

The firm had been in the process of scanning all these documents onto their computer system, but it had gotten complicated, because not all lawyers at the firm were authorized to see everything. And certain clients only wanted the attorneys who worked on their matters to be able to access the documents. The problem could be partially solved by requiring passwords to access certain files, but lawyers were notorious for losing such information or even letting colleagues who were not authorized use the passwords. The firm's solution had been to keep the paper archives along with the flash drive in this room. An attorney had to be authorized to look through or take boxes out, and the flash drive was password-protected.

Even though Roy was authorized to look at the boxes he needed, he felt sure that Ackerman would put the kibosh on him looking at anything. He quickly went through a dozen boxes and pulled the flash drives from each and pocketed them. This, he told himself, was only a minor crime compared to the felonies he and Mace had been committing lately. He decided against climbing back in the dumbwaiter and riding it back up just in case someone was in the mail room.

He edged open the door to the archives and looked around. No one was within view. He slipped out and walked quickly through the suite, out the door, and up the stairs back to the sixth floor. He was about to put the first flash drive in his computer when he noted the Post-it he'd stuck over the camera port.

What if they've hacked into my computer? I put the flash in and they'll know what I'm looking at.

He slipped the device back in his pocket, grabbed his briefcase and jacket, and headed to the door. When he opened it he came face-to-face with Chester Ackerman and two security guards.

Ackerman held out his hand. "I would like your key card right now."

"What's going on, Chester?" Roy looked at the two beefy uniforms. "Who are these guys? Did you finally replace Ned like I suggested?"

"They're here to ensure that everything goes smoothly."

"Smoothly? I told you I'd let you know about my representing Dockery."

"And I just called the courthouse and found out that you are his attorney of record and will be representing the killer at a present-ment hearing tomorrow morning."

"Why'd you call the clerk's office?"

"Because I don't trust you. And it seems my instincts were spot-on. Your card?"

Roy handed it over. "Can I at least get my personal things?"

"We'll send them to you. And I think a search of your person is in order."

Roy drew closer to Ackerman. "You lay one hand on me I own your houses, your cars, your retirement plan, and this firm." He glanced at both guards. "You rentals want a piece of that?"

Each guard looked nervously at the other and took small steps back.

Ackerman snapped, "Fine, just leave the premises now, before I have you charged with trespass."

"And you have a great day too."

Roy walked out of the firm while lawyers and staff watched from every nook and cranny. He half expected them to start cheering when the door closed behind him. He passed Ned in the lobby. The man was slurping down a giant Coke.

"Hey, Mr. Kingman, did you see those two security guards who came in?"

"Oh yeah."

"Everything okay?"

Roy jingled the flash drives in his pocket. "Oh yeah."

90

ROY STOPPED at his condo, grabbed some things, and called Mace on the way over to Altman's. He filled her in on what had happened, and she did the same on her conversation with Joe Cushman.

"Herbert is making like a seven-course meal," she said. "But to tell the truth, I'm dying for a greasy burger and fries."

"I'll pick up some on the way. We'll probably have to work through dinner anyway."

He got there an hour later. They ate in the guesthouse in case Herbert happened by and saw them with charbroiled meat and salty fries dangling from their mouths. Mace finished off the last bite, took a long slurp of her Dr. Pepper, and sat back.

"Where are Alisha and Tyler?" Roy asked.

"Up at the main house being fed, among other things, couscous, pork tenderloin with a reduction sauce, and tempura green beans with a nice crème brûlée done in the classic style for dessert."

"Did Herbert tell you that?"

"No, he actually prints menus every day. He dropped one off at the guesthouse. He was not happy to hear we were going to be missing his latest masterpiece."

"I'm not sure a three-year-old is going to be into couscous and classic crème brûlée."

"Oh, for Tyler he prepared his extra-special spaghetti with hand-formed meatballs and Rocky Road for dessert. I think Herbert likes having kids around."

Mace had borrowed a laptop computer from Altman and during

dinner Roy had been scrolling page after page of the content on the flash drives.

"Got anything yet?" asked Mace as she settled next to him.

"Nothing pops out."

"Coffee?"

"Yeah, by the gallon, please."

She made the coffee and carried a tray back in with the pot and two cups along with cream and sugar containers, and set it down on the coffee table. She poured out the beverages.

"Cream and sugar?"

"Yeah, thanks."

She made it up and passed it to him.

Roy took a sip. "Good coffee." He glanced up at her and smiled.

"What?" said Mace suspiciously as she held her cup.

"I don't know, I guess I never pegged you as the domestic type."

"I'm not, so don't hold your breath waiting for the apron and string of pearls."

"Still nice."

Mace was about to shoot off another stinger but paused. "Yeah, maybe it is."

"So you really think you need to go to Newark?"

"The lady lawyer freaked on me when I mentioned that Jamie Meldon had been murdered too after meeting with Diane. She knew him; that was clear."

"But if you go there's no guarantee they'll see you."

"And if I don't go it's a hundred percent that they won't see me. At least if I make the trip I'll have a shot."

"Do you want me to go too?"

"No, you've got your hands full."

"What about your work for Altman?"

"He has no problem with me chilling for a bit. He feels really guilty about Psycho. And he's been spending a lot of time with Alisha. At least he can get his project off the ground with her."

"What about the brother?"

"He was here and now he's not."

Roy was looking at the screen as he was talking to her. "Wait a minute." He clicked a function key and split the screen with one document residing in each half.

Mace leaned forward next to him. "What is it?"

"On the left is a set of wire transfer instructions that Diane and I did for a deal in the Middle East. Well, the buyer was in the Middle East, but the seller was in Ohio."

"What were they selling?"

"Manufacturing facilities tied to the automotive industry. They made things like windshield wipers, radiators, and stuff. It was part of a string of plants that were bought in five different states in a cluster sale. Happened after all the turmoil in Detroit. Total price was nearly a billion dollars."

"There's that billion number again. So what's the problem?"

"Well, the closing instructions we wrote out show where, when, and how the money was supposed to be paid. There were lots of contingencies, recording of deeds for the land, requisite corporate filings with the various state commissions, that sort of thing. It also includes the ABA routing number, bank account, and other required money transfer information."

"Roy, you're putting me to sleep."

"Okay, our instruction letter is on this side of the screen. Now, over here is the confirmation we got back from DLT."

Mace scanned the page. "I'm no math whiz, but the numbers seem to add up."

"Yeah, the dollar figures do, but look at that." He pointed near the bottom of the page at a long number comprised of many digits.

"But isn't that the ABA routing number you mentioned?"

"It is a routing number, but it's different than the one on our instruction sheet, and I don't know what it's doing here. Now, I know the money for this deal was received by the seller, or else I can assure you we would have heard about it."

"So what is that number? A mistake?"

"I guess it could be."

"Okay, how does that help us?"

"I don't know, I'm just sort of guessing here. It would be helpful to see the corresponding file or other supporting docs that DLT has."

"So do we just go in and ask them for it?" Mace said sarcastically.

"Maybe there's another way."

"I'm listening."

"It's possible they don't know I've been canned from Shilling. I just talked to someone from DLT yesterday to go over some details of a deal Diane and I were working on. If I call them and set up an appointment to go over there and meet, I might be able to sneak a peek at their records."

"But if they are involved in something that got your partner killed, you could be in danger."

"I've been shot at, chased, threatened, done the two-step with a guy named Psycho, and gotten thrown in jail. All since meeting you," he added.

Mace looked uncomfortable.

"What's the matter?" he asked.

"But I was with you when all that happened. You'd be going into DLT solo."

"I'm a lawyer, which means I can talk my way out of just about anything."

"The thing is, Roy, these people don't talk. They kill."

CHAPTER

91

THANK YOU for seeing me at such a late hour, Beth."

Jarvis Burns was seated opposite the chief in her office. He glanced around the room. "May you spend many productive years here."

"I'm trying, Jarvis, I'm trying. What's up? Your call was . . . "

"Uninformative?" Burns said. "I don't like communicating over the phone."

"NSA isn't supposed to spy on Americans' phone calls, and certainly not on American intelligence agents."

"But still, one can never be too safe." He sat back, lifted his bad leg up, and crossed it over the other. "I won't waste your time, but I believe I owed you a heads-up." He paused and then added quietly, "Agents Reiger and Hope are dead."

Beth sat forward, her stare piercing. "What the hell happened?"

"Ambush, apparently. They were beaten—looks like torture, actually—and then their throats were slashed."

"Where did it happen?"

"We're not sure. The preliminary indicates they were not killed where they were found. Lack of blood and such." He tapped her desk with his index finger. "They were found in a Dumpster in South Alexandria."

"A Dumpster? Same as Jamie Meldon."

"Precisely, but not the same method of murder. Knife versus bullet."

"You said torture?"

"Bones broken, sternum cracked. Yes, torture."

"It could be Naylor's cronies. His butt is sitting in jail waiting for trial on domestic terrorism charges."

"I'm fully aware of Roman Naylor's atrocities."

"The point is, I told Reiger and Hope that we should have been in on this. We could have worked with them and maybe nailed those assholes."

"It wasn't my call, Beth. Hell, it's not even my case. I was sent here because we'd previously arranged for Reiger and Hope to fill you in, at least in a limited way. In fact, Director Donnelly insisted on my coming to tell you. I guess he felt obligated in a way. I didn't really know the two men, but they were still agents of this government. And we're going to do everything in our power to get the bastards who did this."

"Is there anything I can do?"

"We're working with the FBI, but I'm going to see if there's a role you can play."

"I'll be ready and willing to do whatever I can, Jarvis."

"I know, and believe me, I won't forget it."

He rose to leave. "Beth, a personal question?"

"Yes?"

"Is it true that your sister was arrested?"

She eyed him impassively. "How did you hear about that?"

"Beth, please. If we can't keep track of what's going on in our own backyard what chance do we have with the Iranians and North Koreans?"

"It was a misunderstanding. She was never charged. She said that some people in a car were, uh, shooting at her."

"Shooting at her. Where was she?"

"In D.C. Trinidad."

"Trinidad? When?"

"Middle of the night."

"Okay," Burns said slowly, shaking his head in amazement. "People shoot at each other with some frequency there, particularly at that time of night."

"She should've known better."

"But what in the world was she down there for?"

"She went back to the place where she was kidnapped. She said she just wanted to see it."

"Why would she want to do that?"

Beth sighed. "I think she has it in her head that if she finds who set her up, she can have her record expunged and can rejoin the force. That's all she wants, Jarvis. To be a cop again."

"Well, I wish her every success with that of course, but it is, well, it is—"

"A long shot? Yeah, she knows."

"And the Tolliver case?"

"What about it?"

"There was a false fire alarm there the other night. At the law firm."

Beth looked puzzled. "I didn't think you worried about things like that."

"Normally, I wouldn't. But we have data triggers, Beth. For example, a surge in hospital admissions with folks complaining of symptoms that resemble anthrax exposure coupled with suspicious air quality feed from our sensors in the Metro. So a murder in a Georgetown law firm followed by a false alarm at the same building soon thereafter that wasted a great deal of emergency resources gives me some concern. Flight lessons in Florida where beginner pilots didn't want to learn how to take off and land? In hindsight perfectly clear, but before 9/11 it seemed trivial, insignificant. Thus I can't afford to take anything, no matter how small, for granted. So the law firm activity could have been a diversion of some kind."

"A diversion for what purpose?"

"We may not know until it's too late. I get paid to worry about the entire jigsaw puzzle, Beth. That's why my gut is full of holes and I'm losing my hair at a rapid pace. Any clue on who pulled the alarm?"

Beth's face was unreadable. "Not yet. We're working on it."

"Well, let me know if you have anything."

"Will do."

"Oh, and tell your sister to just chill, Beth. You lost her for a couple of years already. You don't want to lose her permanently."

As Burns left the building he felt good about himself. He had just given Mace Perry an out. If Mace stood down on this, she got to live. It was her choice. And if she didn't stand down, it became *his* choice.

Using a credit card Altman had provided, Mace bought an on-line train ticket to Newark for the next morning. Then she drove over with Roy to interview the Captain. When they got to the jail, the two received a shock. Mona Danforth and two homicide detectives were talking to the Captain in a small interrogation room. Mona had her legal pad out and was scribbling notes fast.

Roy nearly kicked the door open after he'd spotted them through the glass and chicken wire window cut in the door.

"What in the hell are you doing?" he yelled.

Mona and the cops looked up while the Captain stuffed a whole Twinkie in his mouth.

"Hey, Roy," he said between gooey bites.

"You just blew your whole case!" Roy said to Mona, who just sat there smiling.

"And you are?" she said smoothly.

"His lawyer, lady! That's who I am."

Mona's smile faded. "The name is Mona Danforth, not 'lady.' I'm the United States attorney for the District of Columbia. So show some respect."

Mace stepped in behind Roy. "*Interim* attorney, Mona," she pointed out. "Don't get ahead of yourself."

"What the hell are you doing here?" Mona exclaimed.

"She's here with me, meaning she's allowed. But you are not. And like I said, you just blew up your whole damn case."

"Really? And how exactly did I do that, Mr. . . . ?"

"Kingman. My client has been charged. He has counsel of record.

His Sixth Amendment rights have attached. You are not allowed to have any contact with him unless I am present."

"Well, you must be a little rusty, Mr. Kingman."

"Excuse me?"

"That *was* the law. But it's not anymore. The Supreme Court overturned that requirement. Now if the defendant asks to meet with the police he can do so without his attorney present and no prejudice attaches unless you can prove coercion. I can get you a copy of the opinion if you'd like so you can come up to speed on *basic* criminal law."

"And you're trying to tell me that he just *asked* to talk with you?"

"Why don't you *ask* him yourself?" Mona turned to the Captain and patted his hand gently. "Go on, Lou, you can talk to them."

"Lou? He's my client!" shouted Roy. "Not yours!"

Mace noticed that the poor Captain's gaze was locked on the lovely prosecutor's body. Mona's skirt was short and her blouse open just enough to show some cleavage.

"Now don't be mean to hon, Roy," said the Captain. He gave Mona's hand a squeeze before she quickly removed it from his reach.

"She's not *hon*," explained Roy. "She's the lady who's trying to put you in prison for the rest of your life, Lou."

"She brought me Twinkies."

"He asked for them," Mona said quickly. "And then told my people that he wanted to talk to us."

"Did you, Captain?" Mace asked him.

"I think so, yeah. Twinkie's damn good. These ain't stale, Roy, not like them others."

Mona stood, as did the two detectives. She said, "Well, I think that wraps it up for now. I'll give you some alone time with him."

"I'm entitled to it by the law, so don't pretend you're doing me any favors." He eyed her full legal pad. "And I'm still filing a motion to suppress anything he might've told you. And I'm going to demand a full investigation on this whole damn thing 'cause it stinks, Supreme Court decision or not."

"I am curious about one thing," Mona said imperturbably.

"What's that?"

"Since I'm listing you as a material witness in this case—you did find the body after all and may still be considered a person of interest—how is it that you're going to represent Mr. Dockery in this matter with such a blatant conflict?"

Roy looked like someone had just gutted him with a hatchet.

Mona's smile deepened. "I can see from your *poker face* that you really hadn't thought about that. I tell you what, *Roy*, I'll waive any objection I might have to this little point of legal ethics, and if the judge agrees, you can be Mr. Dockery's lawyer."

"And why would you do that?" said Roy cautiously.

"Oh, you mean the quid pro quo? Well, let's put it this way, I hate defense counsel's motions to suppress. And I also hate demands for investigations. I think what we need here is a blank slate." She stared up at him expectantly, her look about as condescending and triumphant as one face could achieve.

"So in other words I forget the stunt you just pulled and you'll let me represent my client?"

"I didn't pull any stunt. I'm perfectly within my rights."

"I can seek a waiver from the court."

"Not over my objections you can't."

"So let me try to understand this. If you're maintaining you did nothing wrong here, why offer me a deal that lets me rep my client?"

"Because I want you to stay on as Lou's attorney."

"Why?"

Mona leaned forward and spoke in a low voice so that only Roy and Mace could hear her. "Because if you get disqualified, then they might appoint a *real* attorney, and that just makes my job harder. There're a ton of highly qualified public defenders just salivating to take this case, and they all know what they're doing. Why play against the varsity when the j.v. is available?" She picked up her briefcase and stuffed her legal pad in it. "See you in court tomorrow." She turned to the Captain. "Oh, Lou, before I forget." She pulled another Twinkie out of her jacket pocket and tossed it to him, like throwing a bone to a dog. The next moment she and the detectives were gone, leaving the Captain to eagerly devour the fresh offering of creamy cake.

93

Roy HUDDLED in a corner of the room with Mace while the Captain sat staring vacantly at the wall and wiping goo off his mouth.

Roy said, "Maybe she's right. Maybe I am j.v."

Mace punched him in the arm. "Let's get one rule down, Mona is never right."

"The Captain deserves the best representation, Mace. I didn't even focus on the material witness issue. And it was big enough to drive a truck through. I would've gone in tomorrow and gotten my head handed to me. By Mona *and* the judge."

"The Captain wants *you*."

"Come on, he doesn't know what he wants. Other than Twinkies."

"You can do this, Roy. You might be a little rusty on some of the case law, and you didn't focus on the material witness angle because you knew you were innocent and you wanted to help the Captain."

"You can't rep a defendant charged with murder in the first with any rust, Mace. There's no room for error. Especially against Mona. I know you hate the woman and I do too, but she's sharp."

"And she's totally unethical. She basically bribed the Captain with junk food and cleavage."

"But that makes her even more dangerous."

"The point is, Roy, you made the decision to rep him. Your firm canned your ass over it. So do you want to go crawling to them begging for your big-dollar job back? And let a homeless vet be assigned some Perry Mason wannabe who could give a shit if the guy spends the rest of his life in the can? Is that what you want?"

"Of course not," Roy said hotly.

"Then what's the problem? Mona just laid down the challenge. She's gonna kick your ass. Okay, fine. But I don't see a guy who's so competitive that he has as his computer password the last score of his college basketball career just turning the other cheek on this. But this time it's not just a game. And the Captain needs you. He needs *you*, Roy."

Roy looked at Mace, then at the Captain, then back at Mace. "Okay, but I'll need help to dig up some useful stuff."

"Consider it done."

"You? But you're going to Newark tomorrow to run down this Meldon lead."

"This Meldon lead may point us to whoever killed Diane."

"Do you really believe that?"

"I don't know what to believe right now. But I can't afford to cut corners on this."

"Fair enough."

"So you're good to go on this?"

"I am."

"Then I guess I can tell you."

"Tell me what?"

"Beth had Lowell Cassell call me on my way over here."

"And?"

"And there was no yolk buffer in the sperm found in Diane. It didn't come from Potomac Cryobank."

He glanced over at the Captain, who was picking something out of his teeth.

"Okay, gut check time. Do you think he did it?"

Mace looked over at the old soldier too. "I talked to Beth about that. She said she agreed there was some strange stuff going on with Diane and your law firm. But she also said her murder could be entirely unrelated to all of it. That it could have just been a crime of opportunity."

"So you think he did it?"

"No, Roy, I don't."

"Then how the hell does all this make sense?"

"It makes perfect sense. We just have to figure out how."

CHAPTER

94

THEY SPENT another hour trying get some answers from the Captain. The conversation was often one-sided, however, as the vet lost interest, snoozed, went off on multiple and irrelevant tangents, or asked for more Twinkies. He couldn't adequately describe the man who'd met him on the street and asked if he wanted to make a quick two hundred bucks. He was variously big, short, fat, thin, bald but with hair. He hadn't gone in the front door of the place; he didn't recall the sign. He did say that he'd rummaged in big green trash cans while the man got things ready. Mace made a note to check the back of Potomac Cryobank for those types of receptacles. He did remember going inside a dark, small room. He'd been given a cup, and a "girlie" magazine. It had taken him a long while, but he'd delivered the requested sample and then gotten his money.

"Anything you can remember about the place, Lou, anything?" Roy asked.

"The smell."

"What did it smell like?" said Roy.

"Hard to say." He stroked the wattles on his neck. "Not like me. Real clean."

Roy looked at Mace. "It did smell really antiseptic in there. Like a hospital."

"Well, it is like a clinic."

"Yeah, but that's hardly concrete evidence for a court."

"Like you were expecting that from him?" Mace said in a low voice.

They left the Captain and returned to Altman's guesthouse,

where Roy began formulating his strategy for the next morning's hearing.

"It'll be quick and perfunctory," he said. "I'll plead him not guilty. Mona will ask for detainment and then get an indictment probably pretty fast. Then the real work begins. When do you leave for Newark?"

"Seven o'clock Acela train. Gets into Newark around 9:30. The law office is about twenty minutes by cab from the station. I can talk to them, hopefully get somewhere, grab the train back, and be here tomorrow afternoon."

"I can call you with the details of the hearing."

"You going to ask for him to be released on personal recog?"

"No. He has a roof and three squares a day in jail."

"And if somebody is setting him up, he's safer in there."

"Yeah, maybe we should get arrested too."

They both looked up when a ball bounced down the stairs and rolled to a stop next to Roy's foot. He palmed it. The next moment Tyler came running down the stairs looking frantically around. When he saw the ball in Roy's hand he darted over, his arms spread wide.

"Ty, what you doing up this late?"

Alisha had appeared at the top of the stairs as soon as Roy handed the ball to her son. She said, "I'm sorry 'bout that. The boy just won't go to sleep. He was bouncing the ball and it got away from him."

Mace tapped Roy on the thigh. "This kid was making layups and dribbling the ball like a real pro, weren't you, Ty?"

The little boy looked at her and his mouth opened, his eyes blinking rapidly.

Mace patted Roy on the shoulder. "This guy here played college basketball. He could've played in the NBA if he could've jumped a little higher."

"Among other things," Roy added.

"You know, you've been doing the legal thing all day, how about taking this big guy over to the gym and let him show you what he can do. Give you a chance to clear your head." She added, "Ty, you want to show Mr. Roy here some of your moves?"

Roy said, "I really should finish—"

But when Ty reached out and gripped Roy's hand tightly, his little mouth still wide open, Roy quickly stood. "Okay, Ty, I'm a little rusty, so take it easy on me, all right?"

"Can I watch?" asked Alisha.

"I was going to suggest it," said Mace.

Roy glanced back at her. "You want to come? Maybe we can do our HORSE tricks for him."

"You go on. I'm gonna hit the sack. I'll have to leave here early to get the train."

When the three of them disappeared out the door, Mace gave them a couple of minutes to get to the gym and then she punched 411, got the number, and made the call.

"Doc, it's Mace Perry. I know it's late, but you got time to meet?"

Lowell Cassell was at his row house in southeast D.C., but he agreed to meet Mace at a coffee shop near Union Station. Mace thanked him, clicked off, grabbed her leather jacket, and ran for the Ducati.

Iᴛ ʀᴇᴀʟʟʏ ɪꜱ ᴄʀᴀᴢʏ for me to be meeting you like this, Mace," said Lowell Cassell.

"Why? I'm just an ordinary citizen."

"An ordinary citizen who I believe is assisting in the defense of an alleged murderer who is right now cooling his heels in a D.C. lockup." When she looked surprised that he knew this, Cassell added, "The water-cooler gossip does reach the morgue, you know."

"Well, I wouldn't really call what I'm doing assisting. And I really did want a nice cup of coffee. I used to come here a lot when I was a cop. Open twenty-four hours. We'd pop in here after hoodling for a bit if the radio was quiet."

Cassell leaned forward and spoke in a low voice even though there wasn't another customer in the place. "I really went out on a limb by allowing you access to my files. In fact, if that comes out, my career is over."

"It will never come out, Lowell. I will die before that comes out."

He sat back, apparently satisfied. "I think you would."

"So why did you do it then?"

"The files?" He spooned more sugar into his cup. "Because I like you."

"Not a good enough answer for a possible career-ender."

"Blunt, just like your sister."

"I like to think I'm more diplomatic."

"I understand that Mona Danforth is personally trying this case?"

"That's right. I'm sure it's only for altruistic reasons."

Cassell took a sip of his coffee and picked at a pastry on his plate.

"Come on, Doc. I know the sperm was pure, no yolk stuff."

"That's right. I assumed you were the reason Beth had me check that."

"The guy said someone paid him two hundred bucks to do it in a cup."

"The homeless vet?"

"Yep," answered Mace.

"You think he just made that up? I mean, sperm in a dead woman is pretty convincing evidence."

"I agree, and no, I don't think he made it up. The guy spends most of his time thinking about Twinkies."

"Circumstantial is also pretty strong."

"Right again. Our work is cut out for us."

"So you *are* working this one?" said Cassell.

"If I can't be a cop, you know."

"I know. Solve a big one."

"Only thing keeping me going."

"What happened to you was an injustice, Mace."

"Thirty percent."

"What?"

"That's roughly the percentage of cops at MPD who think I was bad."

"That means seventy percent think you were railroaded. A politician would love to have those approval ratings."

"Well, for me anything less than a hundred sucks."

"You can't live your life trying to make people understand something they don't want to understand."

"I'm not doing it for them. I'm doing it for me."

"I guess I can see that."

She tapped his hand with her finger. "So why did you agree to meet with me tonight?"

"To tell the truth, I'm not sure."

"Something's bugging you, isn't it?"

"The sperm."

"But it wasn't yolked."

"Planted sperm."

"Okay."

"It's happened before, but not very often. In fact, it's about as rare a forensic misdirection as there is, but not impossible. But the thing is, if you do it and do it well, a conviction is almost inevitable."

"So you think it *was* planted?"

"The cervix."

"Come again?"

"The semen was high up on the cervix. I mean really high. I've read Dockery's arrest file. Nearly sixty. Living on the streets for years. I actually saw him in the jail. I haven't examined him, of course, but to my doctor's eye he has many serious health problems. Arteriosclerosis almost certainly, high blood pressure, probable diabetes, basal cell carcinomas on his face. He's at high risk for stroke, aneurysm, and various cancers. And I would bet a thousand dollars that he has an enlarged prostate and possibly even cancer there."

"Meaning?"

"Meaning that for him to be able to even get it up is a miracle, much less rape the woman and shoot his semen that far up in her cervix."

"Well, he said he did it in a cup."

"A cup is not a woman's vagina. Did he say how long it took him to do it in the cup?"

"He said it took some time. He also told us they gave him a girlie magazine."

"I would bet it took him a long time even with the girlie magazine."

"That could be important, because Tolliver wasn't at the office more than two hours before she was killed. And chances are it was a lot less than that. Maybe thirty minutes to an hour."

"No problem for an eighteen-year-old. But if a guy in Dockery's condition can get an erection in less than four hours, if at all, you can give me what he's taking. Do you know why the pharmaceutical companies make billions of dollars off stuff like Viagra and Cialis?"

"Because older guys can't get it up without help?"

"Exactly, especially for guys Dockery's age. And keep in mind this is just between you and me. I won't repeat this on the witness stand. You can get your own expert. Under the law my findings are an open book for the defendant's counsel to use. But he has to draw his own conclusions and what I've said is just speculation. I really can't form an opinion about it."

"Understood. But speculate on one more thing. Do you think they might have given Dockery a pill to help him do it in the cup?"

"I wouldn't bet against it."

"Hopefully, he'll remember when we ask him. He's not that stellar on details. And they could've stuck it in a Twinkie. But how long would the sperm last in her? If Dockery is telling the truth, they had to get it from him, store it, transport it to the crime scene, and shoot it into her. Someone I talked to said the stuff breaks down after a while. That's why they have to yolk it."

"It does. The motility and other elements do degrade. The sample I examined hadn't been there longer than seventy-two hours."

Mace sat back. "How about less than twenty-four? Say he gave the sample on Sunday and she was killed on Monday?"

"No. Longer than that. At least three days."

"You're sure?"

"I'd stake my reputation on it."

"That's good enough for me." She stood. "Thanks, Doc."

"For what? I'm not sure I was very helpful."

"No, I think you cleared up a lot. The only problem is, if what I'm thinking is right, I've got a ton of new questions that need answers."

"I hope you get them."

"Me too."

A few minutes later Mace burned down the road. She wasn't heading back to Abe Altman's manse. She was heading to Georgetown. If she was right then there was a force behind all of this that scared her. In fact, it might just scare her right to death.

CHAPTER

96

Jarvis Burns left his office building late and hailed a cab. When he was with Sam Donnelly he traveled by motorcade. On his own, public transportation was deemed good enough. He didn't mind. In fact, it was the perfect opportunity to take in another meeting.

He settled back against his seat in the taxi. The cabbie eyed him in the mirror. He wore a white loose-fitting cotton shirt, and in his own country would have also had a black-and-white kaffiyeh on his head, which symbolized the man's Palestinian heritage. This man, Burns knew, had just flown in from the Middle East. He typically lived at thirty-five thousand feet for extended periods of time, passing over oceans and also arid geography where men killed each other with great frequency over issues of religion, land, natural resources, and simple, intractable hate.

"Mahmud," Burns began. "How are you, my friend?"

Mahmud studied Burns closely and then pulled the cab from the curb. He had spent most of his life in constant conflict with others, had lost both parents and two siblings to violent deaths. His parents had been betrayed by those they thought were friends. Therefore their son trusted no one. He had known desperate poverty and didn't care for it. He had known what it was like to be powerless and cared for that even less. He carried bullet holes and bomb shrapnel in his body. He had been a fierce warrior for his cause. Yet he had come to realize that there were other ways to play the game that did not involve the risk of imminent death. And that there were other rewards to be had while one was still living.

In crisp English he said, "I am here. I never take that for granted."

"I share that philosophy."

"Keep your friends close but your enemies closer, Jarvis," he said. "I think your country is finally learning the value of this. Isolation emboldens those who hate you. It allows them to paint a picture of your country to their fellow citizens, and it is never a pretty picture when they do."

"Agreed, agreed," Burns said hastily.

"But that is not what we need to discuss?"

"I wanted to make clear that the situation that has arisen is truly under control."

Mahmud gave him a piercing look in the mirror. "That is good to hear. It was unfortunate, very unfortunate. How exactly did it happen?"

"We believe we've pieced together the sequence of events. It was a chain that should have been broken at numerous points along the line, but unfortunately was not. An inadvertent glimpse at a laptop screen on a flight back from Dubai started Diane Tolliver down the road that would eventually lead to her termination. From there she became ever more curious, comparing documents, making inquiries, and gathering information. Fortunately, she made the mistake of trusting someone. That's how we became aware of the issue."

"A close call, then."

"The blame lies entirely on our side. But I didn't want you to think that it would linger. Or that it will disrupt what we are trying to do. It will not. I give you my word."

"Your word means a great deal. You too have sacrificed much for your country."

"It was my honor and privilege."

"I have stopped thinking about such things."

"That saddens me."

"It is actually uplifting to *me*."

"The money, yes. I can see that. But we are doing the right thing too. It's what we all want. My country in particular."

"If it was what your leaders wanted, my friend, you and the director would not be doing all of this on your own."

"We're not alone, I can assure you. However, sometimes the leadership is unwilling on the record to take the steps necessary to achieve essential goals. But they would not begrudge us the opportunity to employ sufficient if unpopular methods."

"Right. The less they know the better."

"I would not put it exactly that way."

"You talk of course about violent death; the execution of your own people if it jeopardizes those goals. Americans have always been reluctant in that regard. Frankly, I have always seen that as a weakness."

"We are a civilized people, Mahmud."

"Well, perhaps one day my people will be as unfamiliar with violent death as your people are, Jarvis. What a great thing that will be."

"I hope to live to see that day."

"I would have to say that your chances of doing so are far better than mine."

"I hope you are wrong there."

"Even if I'm not, so what? There will be others to take my place. For a people so certain that there will be an afterlife of paradise, you Americans value life too much. None of us are irreplaceable. Even if bin Laden dies, there will be others. That is the way the world works. That is what keeps you gainfully employed, correct?"

"I would happily retire if there would be no more bin Ladens, Mahmud."

"Then you will never retire, my friend. If you require us to assist in 'cleaning up' this problem you will let me know?"

"I think I have the right people for the job."

"So many have said and yet been wrong." There was an edge to the Palestinian's words that caused Burns to draw his gaze from the mirror where he'd been watching the man's eyes and instead look out the window.

"I understand that your people have to survive. By any means possible."

"They have nothing. This way they have something. The money cannot stop now. They have grown used to it. If you don't pay, others will. Your leaders are very shortsighted in that regard. That is why we've had to go this route. Cash trumps all."

"It won't stop. I guarantee it."

"That is good, because they do not love your country. But they can be bought. Anyone can be bought, it seems." He paused and added bluntly, "Even me."

"Enemies closer."

"Allow no one to ever convince you otherwise."

A few minutes later Burns left the cab and climbed into the back-seat of a waiting Town Car and turned to the woman sitting next to him. Mary Bard had discarded the jumpsuit and was dressed in much the same way as she had been when disposing of Karl Reiger and Don Hope.

"I appreciate your professionalism," Burns said. "In a difficult assignment."

Bard shrugged. "One assignment is much like another assignment. They vary only in degrees of complexity."

"Moral as well as logistical?"

"I leave the moral debate to others. The logistical side is quite enough for me."

"I can provide fresh orders for you if you require them," Burns said, testing her.

"I have my orders. Your director has told me to assist you and only you in any way you require."

"I must make a note to ask to have more people like you sent my way."

"For that you will have to talk to my superiors in Moscow," she said.

"I will."

"So what do you wish me to do?"

"I need you to be on the watch for two people." He showed her pictures of Roy Kingman and Mace Perry. She stared at them for a full minute.

"You can keep the photos," he said.

"I don't need them. They are now in my mind."

"All right. We're setting up perimeter defensive positions. But together with that I need to locate some bait, just in case."

"I'm very good at finding bait."

"I know that you are."

MACE PARKED her bike behind the building and got off. Her gaze scanned the rear parking area, which had space for ten slots. As she stepped forward she could see the names of two doctors stenciled in yellow on the asphalt in side-by-side parking slots. The big shots always got their own space, she thought. A short stack of steps led up to the back door, which was solid wood. There were two windows in the back, both barred and curtained.

And there were the green trash cans that the Captain had mentioned. Not that that helped very much since there were only a million of them in the area and they all looked the same. She heard the clink of boots against the pavement before she heard the voice.

"Can I help you?"

She turned to see the rental cop walking toward her, his hand resting lightly on the top of his sidearm. He looked to be in his fifties and was probably a retired cop making some extra money. To her, he had the ease but also the awareness of a guy who'd walked a beat and talked the talk for a lot of years.

"Just checking the place out."

He looked at the rear of Potomac Cryobank. "Just checking it out? Or casing it?"

"I'm not really in the market for sperm right now."

"Lot of people are. It's a hot commodity."

"I bet. You guarding the place?"

"Not out for my health."

"You former MPD?"

"You a cop?"

"Used to be."

"I'm retired now. Do security full-time. What was your beat?"

"Mostly Six and Seven Ds."

"Okay, you earned your stripes."

"I'm doing some PI work now."

"Involving this place?"

"I was hired by a lawyer to check out an alibi that has to do with the sperm bank. Don't think it's going to fly, but you have to go through the motions."

"What sort of alibi?"

"Guy says he was around here going through trash cans when something else was happening at another place."

"And at this other place the something happening was a crime and your guy was arrested for it?"

"You're a fast learner."

"Not really. Story's always the same."

"I've actually been in the sperm bank. I thought it had a security system."

"It does."

"So why you too? Is sperm really *that* hot a commodity?"

"I asked that very same question myself. I'm not some college kid wanting to make some extra bucks or some cop wannabe who doesn't give a crap. I go into a situation I want to know what's what. They told me that the security system had been acting screwy here and so they needed feet on the pavement."

"Acting screwy?"

"Yeah. Energy spikes maybe, or a freak wire or software glitch. But they came in one day and found the alarm not even on. And the nurse said she remembered setting it. She was the last to leave."

"Did you talk to the nurse?" He nodded. Mace described the woman that she and Roy had spoken with.

"Yeah, that's the gal."

"She's pretty efficient. If she said she set it, I bet she did."

"Anyway, they had the alarm company come over but they couldn't figure out what had happened. And there was no record of any break-in or anything, or the alarm going off or any sensors being tripped. It was like the system just went to sleep for no reason. I don't think anything turned up missing and there was no evidence that anyone actually broke in. But the folks still got worried and they're in the process of changing the whole system over. Until they get it done, I'm here."

"Do you remember when all this went down?"

"Why are you interested? Think it has to do with your alibi?"

"Never know. And I'm just naturally curious."

"Most cops are." He stroked his chin. "I got the call to come here on Thursday. So I guess Wednesday of last week."

"I thought you might say that."

He looked surprised. "Why?"

She fired up her bike. "It's a real long story. You might read about it in the papers one day."

98

Mace had learned from her sister that as soon as the Captain had been arrested, the office elevators had been reprogrammed so they would not stop at the fourth floor. The construction workers had not been happy about having to haul their stuff up the stairs, but that was just the way it was. Public safety trumped aching backs.

Mace slowed her Ducati as she drew close to the area. She figured that no one had worked late in the building or come in too early ever since Roy had discovered Diane Tolliver's body in a refrigerator. But still she scanned the building façade looking for signs of anyone being on-site. Her other concern was the possibility of a cop car posted somewhere close by.

Satisfied that the area was clean of surveillance, she parked her bike a block over from the building and made it the rest of the way on foot. She entered the garage. There were no cars parked there. The garage elevators were dead ahead.

Seconds later she entered the lobby, scooted behind the security console, and reached the entrance to the stairs. She paused for a moment, studying the door to the broom closet. She reached for the knob, her other hand in her pocket, and then ripped it open. The only thing that flopped out was a mop.

She made her way up the stairs and reached the fourth floor. Mace crab-walked across the room so as to keep below the window line and reached the small cubby area where the toilet and refrigerator were located. The length of chain was right where she had dropped it when she and Roy had been chased through the building.

She picked it up and eased over to the refrigerator. It was a big, older Amana model with the refrigerator part up top and a smaller freezer unit with its own little door down below. Using her penlight she could see several small rust stains on the white enamel skin of the appliance. She looped the chain around the fridge and held it tight. The stains were right where the chain touched it. She opened the fridge door. There were some plastic containers of food, a few cans of soda, and a battered gray lunch pail.

Roy had told her what the Captain had said about the chain. Roy had dismissed it as the construction guys protecting their food. Mace had initially thought that too. But not now. Now the chain made sense for a far different reason. They couldn't have the Captain stumble on the body over the weekend while he was looking for some chow. So they'd locked him out and Diane Tolliver's body in.

She hadn't been murdered on Monday morning. She'd been killed on Friday night, probably right after she sent Roy that e-mail when she returned from her dinner with Meldon. And the fridge wasn't the only reason Mace thought this. Now the autopsy results started to make sense. She gazed at the microwave next to the fridge. The microwave. She remembered Roy telling her . . .

She slipped back down to the lobby and from there into the little room behind the security console. She saw the microwave perched on one shelf. She tried to turn it on. Nothing happened. It was broken. She hurried back up to the fourth floor, pulled out her phone, and called Roy.

"Hey," he said. "That Tyler is something else. We've been playing ball all this time and the kid is still running circles around me." He paused. "Wait a minute, I thought you went to bed? Where are you calling from?"

"Diane wasn't killed on Monday morning. She was killed on Friday night."

All she got after that was silence.

"Roy, did you hear me?"

"Mace, where are you!"

"On the fourth floor of your office building."

"What! Are you crazy?"

"Did you hear what I said?"

"Yes, I did, and I feel like somebody just hit me with a two-by-four. Why do you think she was killed on Friday night?"

"Think about what was in her stomach."

"The autopsy report said steak, veggies, potatoes, stuff like that."

"Exactly."

"But you found all that food in her town house garbage can."

"It's also the exact food she had on Friday night at Simpsons when she had dinner with Meldon. And Lowell Cassell's report said that there was a strong smell of garlic in the gastric contents. I knew something was bugging me about that. I searched her kitchen and found not a trace of garlic anywhere, not even in the trash. But I recalled from looking at the menu at Simpsons that they serve garlic mashed potatoes. I think whoever killed her knew what she'd eaten at the restaurant and planted all that stuff at her house to make it look like her last meal had been *there*, on Sunday night instead of on Friday night at Simpsons. Only they either didn't know about the garlic or screwed up. And according to the autopsy report her stomach lining was really green from the spinach. I don't think it got that way from it sitting in her gut overnight. More like over two days."

"Then the body?"

"They killed her in your office on Friday night. Then she was put in the fridge on the fourth floor, probably while the Captain was asleep in another part of the construction space. You told me that he said he went to sleep when he got there and didn't know if the chain was on there when he arrived. I'm sure it wasn't because Diane didn't get back to the office until after ten and the Captain was already on the fourth floor by then. So they threw her in and chained the fridge shut. The nail and hammer crew doesn't work weekends. And the Captain left on Sunday like he said, because he probably ate what was lying around the fourth floor on Saturday, found he couldn't open the fridge, and decided to bag it. They moved her body to the fridge in your office early on Monday morning. Then you found her."

"Why not just leave her in our fridge for the weekend?"

"They couldn't be sure some lawyer might not come in to work and pop open the fridge. And they couldn't wrap a chain around *your* refrigerator. And most importantly, I think they did all this to set up the Captain for the fall."

"I guess they could have found out he was sneaking in the building."

"I've got a theory about that too. And I discovered that the sperm bank had an alarm system failure on Wednesday of last week."

"You think that's when they got the sample from the Captain?"

"The place is closed on Wednesdays and Sundays. Sperm only lasts so long. Cassell told me that the sperm in Tolliver clearly had been there longer than a day but not longer than three days. They probably put it in a freezer after they got it from the Captain on Wednesday to preserve it temporarily. Then after they killed Tolliver, they injected it into her vagina on Friday night. Cassell told me that a guy with the probable health problems of the Captain couldn't have had an erection in just an hour or so on Monday morning. And he couldn't have ejaculated to the degree required to place the sperm that high up in her cervix. But I bet a syringe would've done the trick."

"This is incredible, Mace."

"But it fits. The temp in the fridge keeps the body from decomposing. Two hours or two days in an icebox, it's almost impossible to tell the difference, particularly when she was lying on the floor for all that time while the police were investigating. And then the body was taken to the morgue and stuck in a chiller bed. All the normal forensic indicators got messed up big-time."

"But I thought she sent e-mails and made phone calls over the weekend from her house."

"E-mails prove nothing. Anyone could have sent those. And it seems all the calls she made over the weekend were to people she didn't know. So they couldn't recognize her voice. I learned there was one neighbor who saw her but only really observed her drive off. He couldn't make a positive ID. And the lady apparently didn't have many social friends; she used an escort, after all. The imposter probably stayed at her house all weekend playing the role of Diane. She drives her car to the office early Monday morning so no one else would be around to see, goes up in the elevator, and enters the office suite, which leaves an electronic trail of her movements. Then she turns around and walks back out."

"But Ned swears he heard her come in on Monday morning."

"Yeah, Ned. Remember he was in the back microwaving his breakfast?"

"Yeah, that's why he said he heard her but didn't see her."

"But you told me the day porter was on the fourth floor heating up his soup in a microwave. Why not use the one in the room behind the security console? The one Ned said he was using that morning?"

"I don't know."

"Then I'll tell you. Because the microwave in the lobby is broken. I bet if we ask the day porter he'll tell us the same thing. That it's been broken for a while."

"So are you saying fat, stupid Ned planned all this and killed Diane?"

"He's fat, but I'm not sure how stupid he is. And I don't think he did any of this alone. I think he looked the other way when the Captain sneaked in the building, because he was told to."

"Mace, we need to go to your sister and tell her all of this. I'll meet you there."

"And tell her what? A bunch of speculation? Because that's all it is. We don't have solid proof of anything."

"So what do we do?"

"You prepare for your hearing tomorrow. I'm going to Newark. We say nothing. But we keep an eye on old Ned and he might just lead us to where we need to go."

"I don't want you getting your neck crushed by that guy."

"I'd hear him coming from a mile away just by the fat sloshing."

"Okay, but will you get back here please? At least then I'll know you're safe."

"Oh, Roy, you really do care," she said sarcastically.

"If anything happens to you, your sister will blame me. And I'd rather be dead."

She clicked off and walked quickly over to the exit door. She closed it behind her and was turning to walk down the stairs when something hard slammed into her head.

As she hit the floor already unconscious, Ned stood over her. While he was still heavyset, he didn't appear to be as fat as before. He was dressed all in black, was wearing gloves, and moved nimbly as he picked the woman up and slung her over his shoulder. He reentered the construction site and punched in a number on his cell phone.

The voice answered.

Ned said, "Got the bird. On the fourth."

Jarvis Burns sat back in his armchair and put aside the file he was reading.

"Acknowledged," he said.

"Orders?"

"Unchanged. Proceed. Copycat."

"Roger that."

Ned clicked off and carried Mace over to the refrigerator. He searched her and found her phone, which he tossed to the side. He cleared out all the food and shelves, wedged her inside, closed the door, and wrapped the chain around it. Then he inserted a padlock in the chain links and smacked it closed. He tried to pull the door open, but it barely budged a centimeter. A moment later he was hustling down the stairs to the lobby.

In his home on Capitol Hill, Burns picked up the file once more. "I gave you another chance, Mace. Too bad you didn't take it."

As he turned the pages he put Mace Perry completely out of his mind.

CHAPTER

99

WHEN MACE came to she felt like she was going to throw up. As she fought the nausea she wondered why she was having trouble breathing. She reached a hand up and touched the large knot on her head. She could feel the clotted blood there. Someone had really whacked her. She started to shiver. It was cold.

Where the hell am I?

She started to get up and then quickly realized she was in a confined space. A very cold confined space.

"Oh shit!"

She felt around in the total darkness, her hands bumping into the smooth frigid surfaces. She scrambled in her pocket, found her penlight, and turned it on. As soon as the illumination confirmed where she was, Mace groaned. She pushed hard against the door with her shoulder. It barely budged. She knew why. The chain. Just like Diane. Only she was already dead.

And I will be very soon unless I get the hell out of here.

She reached down and unbuckled the belt that she'd gotten from Binder's weapons shop. It had a very special clasp to it. A few seconds later she'd pulled the four-inch knife free from its holder hidden in the elongated metal buckle. She angled her body around and slipped the blade in the slit where the door met the frame of the appliance. There was a molded plastic shelf unit built into the door and the supporting frame for this was right in her way. Yet she managed to work around it and finally reached the flex strip that created a vacuum seal when the door was closed. She inserted the blade in the slit between the two strips and maneuvered it around. If she levered hard enough, she could feel a trace of air. She pushed very hard once and with a sucking sound the vacuum seal broke slightly. Now she could see a sliver of semidarkness, which represented the more illuminated space outside of the death trap she was in.

But a sliver wouldn't cut it. It didn't let in nearly enough air. She was already shaking with the effort of maintaining the break in the seal. A second later her strength failed and the opening resealed itself. Okay, if she didn't suffocate to death the cold would do her in. Would Roy come looking for her when she didn't show? He knew where she was. But it would take time. Perhaps hours, when she had air maybe for another few minutes. Her chest started heaving as her lungs sought out every precious molecule of oxygen. Her mind started to fog up, signaling the lungs that these molecules were far from enough to keep everything going.

The insulation strip!

Holding the penlight between her teeth, she began hacking at it with her knife. The blade struck through it easily and it came away in long strips. Very soon she could feel the air start to flow in more steadily. And if she wedged her head against the door, she could actually see outside. She poked the blade through this new opening and lifted it up and down. On the downward stroke it hit the chain. There was no way she could saw through the chain with the knife in less than a day if at all. But at least she could breathe. Now the issue was the cold; she was still freezing to death. She looked up and saw it built into the top of the fridge's interior: the temperature dial. It was set on four. Seven was the coldest, she quickly discovered. She reached up and dialed it back to one, the warmest. She had no idea in refrigerator technology how "warm" the number one setting would be, but she didn't want to find out it was still in hypothermia range.

Mace started rocking her body front to back. The Amana was a tall appliance, and she was betting there wasn't much in the lower freezer section to anchor it. As much as the confined space would allow her, she kept rocking. She'd hit one side with her legs and then slam against the other side with her back. Very quickly her entire body felt like she'd been hit by a car, but she kept going. She could feel the Amana start to lean a bit, to the right and then to the left. As it kept going, the appliance started to walk, like a washing machine out of control. Encouraged by this, she started flinging herself back and forth with renewed energy.

One last smash against the molded plastic with her combat boots and the Amana finally toppled over sideways. Mace braced herself for the impact, which was easy enough to do since she was wedged in. Still, when the fridge hit the concrete floor, her head banged against the hard interior wall right where the bump on her noggin was and she felt herself black out for an instant.

But she'd accomplished her goal. She could no longer hear the slight hum of the Amana's motor. The power cord had come out of the socket. Now she had air. And she would soon have warmth. But she was still trapped. She had hoped that the collision with the floor might have caused the chain to slip off, but no such luck. One push against the door told her that. She looked down at the molded plastic floor. Below that was the freezer compartment. The chain couldn't be around that door too. She started stomping her feet. The floor was hard, but she could feel it give just a bit.

She worked her body around so that she was nearly upside down. Taking the knife, she started hacking at the plastic but couldn't find traction as the blade just skidded off the smooth surface. She turned back around so that she was sitting up in the box and looked around. She grabbed a portable shelf off the doorframe and pointed the knife into the floor, then put her foot on top of the handle and pushed down with as much force as she could, lifting her butt off the interior floor and pressing her back against the top of the box to provide more leverage. Twice the knife slipped out, but the third time she felt it bite into the plastic and stick there. She took the shelf and started whacking the butt of the knife with it. She didn't have much room to operate, so the swings were shortened, but after a few minutes she could see that the blade was now two inches deep in the plastic floor. She raised herself up, put her foot on top of the handle, and steadily pushed down, her back flat against the ceiling of the fridge to give her additional downward force. The knife slowly pushed through the floor. When it hit the hilt of the blade it stopped.

Mace moved her foot away and with much effort she flipped over and started to saw away at the floor, the blade moving centimeters as it cut into the hard plastic. She withdrew the blade and, using the same stick and pound method, made similar cuts in four other spots. When that was done she slipped the knife back in the belt clasp, rose up again, and started stomping in the middle of all the cuts, her back so tight against the ceiling of the fridge that she felt her spine would snap.

She wasn't sure how long it took, but she felt the floor finally give. A few seconds later the plastic cracked in one spot and then another. A minute later a whole section of it tilted upward. She threw her weight at the spot opposite this and the entire floor broke away and heaved up like a sheet of ice. She fell through this opening and gasped as a jagged edge of hard plastic ripped into her thigh; now warm blood flowed into the cool interior.

She carefully worked her body downward, keeping as far away from the torn edges of the plastic as she could. Her feet hit the freezer door and she kicked it open. She kept sliding downward until she cleared the floor of the fridge unit and her head and torso were in the freezer compartment. Then her feet were out on the concrete floor and soon the rest of her was too.

She sat there for a minute, her head and lungs pounding and her stomach churning. Then she rose on shaky legs and looked around. She slipped out her precious knife and held it in a defensive position. She doubted whoever had stuck her in the death box was waiting around for the finale, because she'd made so much noise he would've come running to finish her off. Yet after her narrow escape she was leaving nothing to chance. After she saw the blood pooling on the floor she found a rag and made a crude bandage for her leg wound. Then she found her phone where it had been tossed, and called Roy. He was already on his way downtown because she'd never shown up at Altman's.

"I'll be there in ten minutes," he said after listening to her woozy account. "Call the cops right now."

This time Mace did exactly what he told her to. Within three minutes two patrol officers had kicked open the door to the fourth floor calling out her name. Three more cops joined them a few seconds

later. Two minutes after that Beth Perry came flying up the stairs. She
walked directly over to her sister and wrapped her arms around her.

Mace felt the tears slide down her cheeks as she hugged her sister
back, as hard as she could. It was like she was twelve years old again.
She had been wrong. She still needed to be held sometimes. Not often,
but sometimes. Just like everybody else.

Beth called out to her officers, "Is this floor secure?"

"Yes, Chief."

"Then search the rest of the building. Leave a man posted to this
door. I'll stay with her. And call an ambulance."

The men headed out.

Mace felt her legs start to give out. Beth seemed to sense this too
and half carried her over to a plastic crate turned upside down and sat
her down. She knelt in front of her, her gaze switching to the remains
of the fridge and then back at Mace. The tears started trickling down
Beth's face as she gripped her sister's hand.

"Damn it, Mace," she said, her voice cracking.

"I know. I know. I'm sorry."

"You didn't see who did it?"

She shook her head. "Happened too fast."

"We need to get you to a hospital."

"I'm okay, Beth."

"You're *getting* checked out. You've got a knot the size of a golf
ball on your head. And your right leg is covered in blood."

"Okay, okay. I'll go."

"And on the ride over you're going to tell me exactly what is
going on."

Moments later Roy came bursting through the door, the officer
posted at the door tightly gripping his shoulder.

"Mace!" yelled Roy. He tried to rush to her but the cop held
him back.

"It's okay," said Beth. "I know him."

The man let Roy go and he sprinted across the room and put his
arm around Mace. "Are you okay? Tell me you're okay."

Beth rose and took a step back.

"I'm all right, Roy," said Mace.

"But we're still taking her to the hospital," said Beth. "And you can ride with us, Kingman. I know you're up to your wingtips in this too. And I want to hear everything."

She grabbed his shoulder and spun him around to stare at the trashed Amana.

"Too close, Kingman. Way too damn close."

CHAPTER

100

An hour later it was determined that Mace did not have a cracked skull.

"Your head must be extremely hard," said the emergency room doctor.

"It is," Beth and Roy said simultaneously.

Her leg stitched up, a bandage on her head, and a prescription for pain meds written, they left the hospital in the early morning hours. Roy and Mace had told Beth some of what had been going on during the ride over, but now she insisted on driving them back to Abe Altman's so they could tell her the rest. Mace's Ducati had been picked up by a police flatbed and also driven over to Altman's.

In the guesthouse, they spent another hour bringing the police chief up to speed on their findings.

"We'll get a BOLO out on Ned Armstrong right now," said Beth, and she took a moment to make this call. After she'd relayed the order, she said, "He may have been the one who attacked you."

"If so, I look forward to returning the favor," said Mace as she lay on couch with a baggie of ice on her head.

Roy said, "He's probably long gone by now."

"How do you figure?" asked Beth.

"If he did put Mace in that fridge he probably hung around for a while to watch the building. He would have seen the police and Mace walking out alive."

Beth shook her head. "We can't take that chance. Ned is obviously not working this alone. So you two are getting round-the-clock protection."

"I've got a case to try," said Roy.

Mace sat up. "And I've got a fat asshole to catch, among lots of others."

"You can leave that to the police now. You should've left it to us from the get-go."

"Hey, I've done a lot of the heavy lifting already," objected Mace.

"And what, you think I'm going to do an end run and take all the credit if we do break this thing?"

"Damn it, Beth, we had this talk. I'm going to keep working this."

"Why don't you start learning that the rules *do* apply to you?"

"I would, except they always seem to be stacked against me!"

"That's just a pitiful excuse."

"I need to do this, Beth," Mace yelled, jumping off the couch. The baggie of ice slid to the floor. For a moment it looked like blows might be launched.

Roy stepped in between them, one hand on each of their shoulders.

At the same time both women cried out, "Stay out of this!"

"No!" he shouted and pushed each of them back. Mace landed on the couch and Beth in a chair. Both sisters stared up at him in shock.

"You just assaulted a police officer, Kingman," snapped Beth.

"Oh, right, throw that in his face!" retorted Mace.

Roy barked, "Will both of you just shut up and listen for one damn minute!"

The women glanced at each other and then back at him.

"Okay," said Roy. "Okay. These people have done things that take enormous resources and manpower."

"And your point?" said Beth.

"That we work together," Roy answered simply. "Like Mace said, she's done a lot of the heavy lifting. I've got a way into DLT to see what that brings. Chief, you've got resources that neither of us have. All I'm saying is that it makes a lot more sense for us to work together. I think we all want the same thing here, even if it is for different reasons."

Beth pulled her gaze from Roy and looked down. "Maybe we can work together."

"Then we need to tell you one more thing," said Roy. He looked nervously at Mace.

She said, "The guy Tolliver was having dinner with Friday was Jamie Meldon."

"How the hell do you know that?"

"Waiter at the restaurant recognized him," said Roy.

Beth looked puzzled. "I've got a contact who thinks Meldon was killed by domestic terrorists."

Roy shook his head. "We think he was killed because someone saw him having dinner with Diane. The lady knew something and they were afraid she'd told Meldon. The guy was a federal prosecutor after all."

Mace added, "And they didn't wait long. Dinner on Friday night and Diane killed right after. Meldon never made it past the weekend. Watkins is probably dead too. That's why I need to clean myself up and head to Newark in a few hours."

"What's in Newark?"

Mace explained about the law firm that had represented Tolliver in her divorce.

"And I've got the presentment this morning," added Roy. "But after that I'm going over to DLT and see what I can find out."

"And what would you have me do?" asked Beth.

Mace said, "Hopefully, you'll find Ned."

"His prints are probably all over the front lobby. We can run them through the databases." She stood. "If I let you do this," she began, staring dead at her sister, "you are to report in regularly and you are not to go into any dangerous situation without backup. No more fourth floors, you got that?"

"Loud and clear. I don't think I can ever even own a refrigerator again."

Roy said anxiously, "So are we good to go?"

Beth glared at him. "Yes, but we go by *my* playbook, not yours."

CHAPTER

101

JARVIS BURNS sat in his cluttered row house in southeast Washington near the Capitol rubbing his forehead. Three Advils had not done the trick, but he had a bottle of Dewar's in his drawer that might. He looked up at the man who sat across from him. Ned Armstrong. Real name Daniel Tyson. He'd worked for Burns for ten years and had never failed him. And yet the only reason he had not sent Mary Bard for a final meeting with Tyson was the fact that the man had followed Burns's order to the letter.

Put her in the fridge alive.

"A bullet to the head would be better," Tyson had told him at the time.

And he'd been right, of course. But Burns wanted the woman to suffer. He wanted her to wake up and see the hopelessness of her situation with warmth and air only a few inches away. It had been a mistake, a rare occurrence for him, but still a mistake.

"You said she went to the microwave and saw that it was broken?" Burns asked.

"She never said anything, but that seemed to be what she was thinking. So she might know I was lying about that. And if they know Tolliver was dead on Friday, they'd know I lied about that too."

"And you didn't hear who Perry was talking to or what she said while on the fourth floor?"

"I was waiting on the other side of the door. I just heard mumbles."

"We can check her cell phone records. Probably either her sister or Roy Kingman. If the former, the concern is vast. If the latter, it might be manageable."

"But they took her to the hospital, sir. And Beth Perry was there. She might've talked about what she knows."

"She may know about the subterfuge regarding Tolliver's death. And the fact that you might be involved somehow. If you disappear then they might think you did it acting alone, and then tried to cover it up."

"Perhaps," said Tyson, as he shifted his bulk in the chair. "But they went to the restaurant where Tolliver ate on Friday. If they put two and two together?"

"I am fully aware of the ramifications of that potential development, Tyson. No solution is perfect. We are clearly in damage control territory. We knew something like this might happen. That was why we had you stationed there as the security guard. Gave us eyes and ears on the ground and complete access to the building. It also allowed us the intelligence about the old soldier sneaking in."

"He makes the perfect patsy."

"Maybe not so perfect now. They must've figured out that the sperm was planted, and that he is not nearly smart enough to pull this off. That was always a risk."

"But unfortunately my own cover is probably blown."

"You're on the next agency flight to Riyadh. You'll spend two years there to let things quiet down before reassignment. I strongly suggest you lose about eighty pounds and have facial reconstructive surgery by approved agency surgical personnel. I'll provide full paper coverage for you. We may be able to convince them that you are indeed one of the great serial killers of all time."

"I'm sorry the mission wasn't successful, sir."

"It was my call, my fault. You were following orders. That is what you're supposed to do. I will never blame you for that."

"Will you require a close-out report?"

"No. Enjoy Saudi Arabia." Burns nodded at the door. A few seconds later he was alone once more.

He spent most of his time alone, thinking through the next doomsday scenario. He was tasked to keep America safe by any means

possible. He thought about nothing else 24/7. He had used his muscle, training, and wits in uniform for his country. And now in a suit
and tie he used what he had left to serve America.

He spent twenty minutes on three different calls. As he set the
phone down for the last time, his mind went back to Mace Perry.

He didn't like losing. Never had since he was a small boy running
through the cornfields of Kansas chasing dreams. She was good, but
she was still just a street cop.

He picked up his phone and made another call. "It's time for the
contingency plan," he said into the receiver.

It was very late but Chester Ackerman was awake and sitting in
the living room of his lavish apartment in the Watergate Building.
The managing partner of Shilling & Murdoch had traded his suit,
wingtips, and braces for khaki pants, an orange cashmere sweater,
and Docksiders. As soon as he heard Burns's voice his thoughts
about taking a ride the next day in his forty-foot cabin cruiser
vanished.

Ackerman put his tumbler of scotch and soda down, sat up straight,
and gathered his courage to say it. "I really think I should maintain a
low profile with all this. I already told you about Diane when she
came to me asking questions. I fired Kingman. I've kept the money
flowing. I think I've done enough."

Burns's retort was like a cannonball fired right into his belly.
"You've also made a bloody fortune for basically sitting on your fat
ass because of business deals that I got for you! Now here's where
you repay the kindness of your beneficent government. So just shut
up and listen. You should already have the legal documents prepared
like I told you to do."

"I do," he said in a shaky voice, his meager courage gone.

"Now you will act exactly in accordance with my instructions.
And if you don't . . ."

Burns spoke uninterrupted for nearly ten minutes. When he'd
finished he hung up and leaned back in his chair.

*That sonofabitch has made more in one year than I've made in
my entire life. A draft dodger who pays his first-year know-nothings*

more than I'll ever make. And he wants to lay low. He wants to take
a time-out after making millions! He's done enough!

Part of Burns wished that Ackerman would fail to follow his orders just so he could order the man's execution. Mary Bard could
probably kill him with simply a stare.

Don't tempt me, you parasite. Don't you dare tempt me.

CHAPTER

102

EARLY in the morning the Ducati roared through the gates at Altman's estate. The female police officer driving it would take any followers on a two-hour ride around the Virginia countryside. A few minutes later the Bentley pulled past the gates, Herbert at the wheel. He was on his way to the market. But he had one delivery to make before then and it would take him into the heart of D.C.

Mace Perry lay in the backseat of the car.

Thirty-five minutes later she was walking through the cavernous Union Station. She got her ticket from the self-serve machine and boarded the Acela train a few minutes before it was to leave. She snagged a window seat and for the next two hours or so watched the scenery of the Northeast go by as she thought about her upcoming encounter with the law firm of Hamilton, Petrocelli & Sprissler. She grabbed a cab at the station and walked into the law firm's suite in a twenty-story building in downtown Newark fifteen minutes later.

The place was all polished wood and marble with tasteful paintings on the wall. It looked very old money, yet Roy had looked up the law firm on an online legal directory for her and told her that it had only been in existence for fifteen years. The firm specialized in divorce and other civil litigation, and had three female partners, Julie Hamilton, Mandy Petrocelli, and Kelly Sprissler. They were all from New Jersey, had graduated from the same law school in the same year, and had returned to their roots to open the firm. From what Roy had been able to find, the practice had been a success from nearly day one and each of the name partners had stellar reputations in the Newark legal community. The firm currently employed a total of fourteen attorneys, and they were known in the area as a go-to legal shop for high-profile divorces, many of which came from nearby Manhattan.

The receptionist, a polished-looking woman in her early thirties, made a face when Mace told her who she was and why she was there.

"They don't want to talk to you," she said bluntly.

"I know. That's why I came all this way. It's really very important. Can you at least let them know I'm here?"

She made the call, spoke briefly with someone, and then put the receiver down.

"That was Ms. Hamilton."

"And?" said Mace hopefully.

"She wishes you a safe trip back home."

"Can I talk to her on the phone?'

"That would not be possible."

"I can wait here until they come out."

"Ms. Hamilton anticipated you might say that, so she told me to tell you that the building has excellent security and that spending several months in jail for trespass was probably not a good use of your time."

"Wow, I haven't even met this woman and already I like her. Okay, I'll just have to turn it over to the FBI. I know some of the agents in the field office up here. They're good people, and very thorough. Since this is a murder investigation with possible national security implications, I hope the firm can do without its computers for a while."

"What do you mean?" the receptionist said in a stunned tone.

"Well, it's standard operating procedure for the Feds to confiscate all computers during an investigation like this."

"You said national security?"

"Jamie Meldon was a U.S. attorney. His murder may be tied to a terrorist organization."

"Oh my God. We don't know anything about that."

"Well, the FBI likes to find that out for itself." Mace pulled out her phone, hit a speed dial button, and said, "FBI Special Agent Morelli, please. It's Mace Perry."

"Wait a minute!"

Mace eyed the woman standing in the doorway. She was about forty, Mace's height, a little heavier, and dressed in a jacket and skirt with black hose and heels. Her brown hair was cut short and precisely traced the outline of her head. Mace clicked off the phone. She'd only dialed 411 after all. "Are you Julie Hamilton? I recognize your voice from the phone call."

"I can give you five minutes."

"Great."

She walked down the hall with Mace scurrying after her. On the way Hamilton leaned into two other offices and gave the people inside a nod of the head. When Mace and Hamilton entered a small conference room, two other women joined them.

Hamilton indicated with her hand, "My partners, Mandy Petrocelli and Kelly Sprissler."

Petrocelli was tall and big-boned with dyed blond hair, while Sprissler was short and wiry and her reddish hair was clipped back in a tight braid. All three women looked tough, professional, and were probably excellent at their work, Mace assumed. If she ever did manage to marry someone and things turned ugly, she'd probably call one of these women to rep her.

"I'm Mace Perry, a private investigator from Washington."

"Get to the point," interjected Sprissler in a harsh tone.

"The point is Diane Tolliver was brutally murdered at her law office on Friday of last week and her body stuffed in a fridge. A few days later Jamie Meldon was found inside a Dumpster. On the night Diane was killed, she and Meldon had dinner together. We think she knew of some illegal activity and might have been trying to get Meldon's help. What we don't know is why she picked him. From what we've been able to determine so far, they never had any connection."

The three lawyers glanced at one another. Hamilton said, "You mentioned out in the lobby that this case had national security implications?"

Mace nodded. "Terrorism potential."

Petrocelli said in a booming voice, "If so, why are you here and not the FBI?"

"I wish I had a good answer to that, but I don't. All I want to know is how Meldon and Tolliver knew each other."

"How did you even find out about us?" Sprissler interjected.

"Joe Cushman. Diane's ex. He spoke highly of your firm."

"That's because we took him to the cleaners during the divorce," said Petrocelli.

"Now we're on retainer to his company," added Sprissler. "That's the mark of good legal work, turning adversaries into clients."

"But getting back to why you're here," said Hamilton.

"Right. How did Meldon and Tolliver know each other?"

"I guess it's all right to tell you. It's public record anyway. Before we were retained to represent her, Jamie was Diane's counsel of record in her divorce proceedings from Joe."

"While he was in private practice in New York?"

"That's right."

"But I was told he was primarily a mob lawyer."

Hamilton said sternly, "Jamie represented many companies and individuals that were involved in myriad civil and criminal matters. I would not describe him as a mob lawyer."

"Okay, but did he also handle divorce cases in New Jersey?"

"Diane lived in New Jersey, although she practiced law in Manhattan," said Sprissler.

"A very common occurrence," added Petrocelli.

"But did Meldon handle divorce cases as a 'very common occurrence'?"

Hamilton cleared her throat. "No, he didn't."

"Is that why he passed the baton to you?"

"We'd worked with Jamie before. He knew we specialized in marital law cases."

"So why not just get you on board from the get-go?"

"There was a matter of timing," explained Hamilton.

"Timing? I know divorce cases can last years. What was the hurry?"

"Jamie got a restraining order against Joe Cushman. He was making threats apparently against Diane. The order had to be obtained quickly for obvious reasons, although having gotten to know Joe over the years I don't believe he meant any of it."

"But that still doesn't explain why Meldon was involved in the first place. *How* did he know Tolliver?"

"I'm not sure that is relevant to anything," barked Sprissler, who looked like she wanted to leap over the table and take a bite out of Mace's leg.

"Well, I think it's relevant. And I damn sure know the FBI would think it was."

"They were friends," said Hamilton after a few tense moments of silence.

Mace arched her eyebrows.

"*Very* good friends," amended Hamilton.

"I see. Did Joe Cushman know they were having an affair?"

"While neither confirming nor denying the accuracy of your words, from a purely hypothetical basis, I would assume not."

"But they didn't end up together," said Mace.

"Jamie's wife developed breast cancer," said Petrocelli. "Let's just say he did the right thing by her."

"We were surprised when he moved to D.C. and became a U.S. attorney," added Hamilton. "But in a way we understood. He wanted to make a clean break of it."

"We were stunned to hear about his death," said Sprissler.

"So were a lot of people," said Mace.

She asked a few more questions, got nothing else helpful, and headed back to the train station. It was good to finally know of the connection between Tolliver and Meldon, but it didn't really advance the investigation as far as Mace could see. As she sat down to wait for her train, it seemed like they were right back at square one and running out of time.

CHAPTER

103

Roy stepped into C-10 for the first time in two years. C-10 was the courtroom where presentments were held in D.C. Superior Court, which was where the Captain was being tried for murder. The place was crammed because C-10 heard all presentments, from relatively minor crimes all the way to the most serious felonies. The defendants who were not in custody sat with their attorneys in the courtroom waiting for their case to be called. Those defendants who were already in jail were held in another room until it was their turn before the judge.

Roy took a seat on one of the crowded benches. As he looked around he could see various defendants gabbing while they were waiting. C-10 was a good place for the criminal classes to catch up with each other, he'd found. When he'd been a CJA he'd more than once had to pull his guy away from another street punk because they were plotting out some future crime right in front of the judge.

Roy suspected that his presentment would be called first, for one reason only. And that reason walked in at one minute to ten, sixty seconds ahead of the opening bell for this C-10 cattle call. Mona Danforth was dressed for battle in navy blue Chanel with a white pocket kerchief, three-inch heels, and lips set in a perfectly horizontal line. Her golden tresses oozed the scent of hairspray like blood from a finger cut.

One minute later the judge entered, everyone rose, and the bailiff called the case. The Captain appeared from behind a door with a police officer on either side of him. He joined Roy at the defense counsel table while Mona stood ready at the prosecutor's table. The judge smiled down at Mona and rested his glasses near the end of his nose as he read over the papers. At this juncture, no evidence was presented by the two lawyers. It was strictly done on the record thus far. And that record completely favored Mona.

The judge said, "Ms. Danforth, I haven't seen you in C-10 in a while."

"Good to be back, Your Honor."

The judge riffled through some notes and then glanced over at Roy. "Plea?"

"Not guilty, Your Honor," said Roy while the Captain stood beside him idly gazing around the room.

"Duly noted. Ms. Danforth?"

"The people request a 1325-A hold. The defendant has no job, no home, and no family locally. We consider him to be a flight risk, and that, coupled with the serious nature of the charges, warrants continued confinement."

"Defense objections?" the judge asked, peering at Roy.

"No, Your Honor."

"I understand that we might have a conflict with defense counsel?"

"It's been resolved, Your Honor," said Mona quickly.

The judge looked from her to Roy. "Is that correct?"

Roy glanced once at Mona and then said, "That's correct."

"Mr. Kingman, the record says your client is homeless and presumably not in a position to hire an attorney. And yet you're not a public defender."

"I'm doing the case pro bono."

"How generous of you."

"I used to be CJA."

"Used to be?"

"I left to go into corporate private practice."

"How long did you practice criminal law in this court?"

"Two years."

The judge laid his glasses down on the bench. "This is a rape and murder-one charge. It doesn't get more serious than that."

"I understand that, Your Honor. I've handled murder cases before."

"How many?"

"At least ten."

"How many of those went to trial?"

Roy licked his lips. "Three."

"And your record in those trials?"

"Unfortunately, I lost all of them."

"I see." He turned his attention to the Captain. "Mr. Dockery, do you want to have Mr. Kingman as your counsel? If not, there are many experienced public defenders that will represent you at no cost."

Roy held his breath, praying that the Captain didn't start asking for Twinkies.

The Captain merely said, "Yes sir. Roy's my lawyer."

"Ms. Danforth?"

She smiled and said coolly, "The people feel that Mr. Kingman is up to the task of *adequately* defending Mr. Dockery's interests in this case. We have no objection to his continued representation."

The judge looked skeptical of this but said, "Okay. The court finds the people have met its burden and the defendant will be detained until further notice." The judge rapped his gavel and the next case was called.

Roy turned to the Captain. "You doing all right?"

"You think I can keep staying there? Three squares and a bed."

"I think I can pretty much guarantee that for the foreseeable future. But look, Captain, we're going to get you out of this, okay? You're not going to prison over this."

"If you say so, Roy. I just want to get back in time for lunch."

He was led off by the police officers and Roy headed out of the courtroom.

"I'm impressed, Kingman. I would've bet your pants would be wet by now."

He turned to see Mona behind him.

"I hope your legal work is as bad as your quips."

"I guess you'll find out sooner rather than later."

"What's that supposed to mean?"

Mona pushed open the courtroom door and motioned Roy out.

She followed. Halfway down the hall Roy flinched as a column of media folks charged toward them. They started shoving mikes, recorders, and notepads in Roy's face while firing off questions at him. "What the hell—" He darted a glance at Mona, who didn't seem surprised by all this attention.

She said, "If you want to play in the big leagues this comes with the territory."

Roy shoved through the crowd as Mona started making prepared remarks. Even as he pushed through the wall he was at risk of being hurled right back into the pit by the sheer weight of the media. That is, until a long arm came out of nowhere and snagged him, pulling him through a side door that slammed shut in the faces of the trailing reporters.

Beth let go of his arm and stepped back.

"Thanks, Chief."

"I figured Mona would pull her usual crap. How'd it go in there?"

"No surprises."

"You can leave through that hallway," she said, pointing to her left.

"I know this is awkward for you, Chief."

"What is?"

"I mean, technically you're on Mona's side. If we prove our case, she loses. In fact, she might look like an idiot in the process."

Beth punched him lightly on the side of the arm. "Keep talking like that, Kingman, I might just grow to tolerate you."

Roy thought he caught a glimpse of a smile as she strode off down the hall. Outside he was heading for his car when a lanky young man in a tweed blazer approached.

"Roy Kingman?"

"Yeah?"

The man thrust a set of rolled documents into Roy's hands. "Consider yourself served." As the guy hurried off, Roy examined the papers.

Shilling & Murdoch was suing him.

CHAPTER

104

SAM DONNELLY did not look particularly pleased as he left the White House in a small motorcade. He was a former Army two-star turned congressman who'd been elevated to the top spy slot based on political payback and his years of military duty, and also because of his membership on the House Intelligence Committee. He'd grown gray in service to his country and had a reputation as a no-nonsense administrator with a hands-on approach.

Jarvis Burns sat across from him in the limo, which had a sound-proof wall separating the driver and a bodyguard from the rear seats. Burns had fought with Donnelly in the swamps of Vietnam before each had gone his own way in life after the military. Once they hooked back up, Donnelly's faith in Burns had allowed him pretty much free rein to run one of the most important top-secret programs in America's counterterrorism operations.

"Tough meeting?" Burns said.

"You can say that."

"Wish I could have been there."

"The DCI gets a burr up his butt from time to time. Just wants what he calls the big boys in the room. I'll throw him the bone. It's not like I can risk making him into an enemy. The DNI is only first among equals."

"It's an unwieldy structure we have. Most countries are far more streamlined on the intelligence side."

"With so many 'intelligence' agencies all jockeying for turf and budget dollars it is pretty much guaranteed that nothing will ever be streamlined on this side of the Atlantic."

"But the results speak for themselves."

"Absolutely they do. There hasn't been a terrorist attack on American soil since 9/11. That is not by happenstance. What we're doing is working. The president understands that. That is the most important thing."

"And so does the public."

"Well, if they knew some of the folks we were bankrolling it would not go over well."

Burns nodded. "But a bag full of rials or dinars doesn't cut it anymore. It's a big business keeping this country safe. We have money and/or financial distribution channels and they don't. They have things we need. It's a simple business transaction."

"It's a deal with the devil, plain and simple."

"But less of a devil than the ones we're fighting."

"How do you keep them straight, Jarv? They keep changing on us. We're paying off the same bastards that just last year were shooting at us and blowing us up."

"We're fighting the good fight with the tools we have, sir. What's the alternative?"

Donnelly gazed out the window as the famous monuments whirled by outside. "There's no alternative, at least for now," he groused.

"We all do what we have to do, sir. You're a political appointee. I'm just a working man."

Donnelly didn't look pleased by this statement. "They can subpoena *anybody*, Jarv. Including you. Don't ever forget that."

"I'm sorry if I conveyed a different impression."

"And everyone is expendable, including you."

"I never thought otherwise," said Burns in a deferential tone.

"We did what we needed to do to survive in Southeast Asia. I'm not proud of all of it, and maybe I'd do things differently today, but I'm not second-guessing anything with my country's security at risk."

"We'll get through this, Director."

"Will we? Well, just remember this, in my agency sacrifice starts from the bottom and works up. Don't ever lose sight of that, Jarv. Don't ever." Donnelly gave the other man a prolonged stare and then looked away. "Money is as tight as I've ever seen it. And if we don't keep paying the sons of bitches, we're going to have a suitcase nuke go off somewhere where we don't want it to. The ends do justify the means. When I was in Congress I would've launched an investigation of any agency head who uttered those words. Now that I'm in the hot seat I can definitely relate."

"The money will continue. The stakes are too high."

"What's being done with Reiger's and Hope's families?"

"As far as they're concerned the two died while serving their country. They'll be taken care of financially, of course."

"I was deeply disappointed it came to this."

"As was I."

"You've got to have the stomach for this sort of thing. We had to deal with this shit in 'Nam. We worked with whoever we had to, to get the damn job done."

"The younger generation just doesn't seem to get it."

"But Mary Bard is a hell of an asset to have."

"Quite accommodating of our Russian friends."

"Even Moscow is scared of the terrorism beast. They've got money now, and an economy worth protecting. They know they're a target. So I snagged her from the FBI as soon as I heard she was in town. I've worked with her before actually. Steve Lanier, the AD, was not pleased, I can tell you that."

"I'm sure. I'm looking forward to deploying her again."

"Don't overuse her. There are enough damn bodies floating around as it is."

"Absolutely, sir."

But one or two more won't really matter, thought Burns.

105

"I APPRECIATE you meeting with me, Cassie."

Roy was walking along K Street with Cassie Benoit, who worked at DLT, the escrow agent Shilling & Murdoch used for its business transactions.

"No problem. I was heading out for a sandwich anyway. What's up?"

"Just a document snafu, at least I think. You remember the Dixie Group purchase we closed two months ago?"

"A bunch of shopping malls in Alabama and Texas. Purchaser was a partnership in the U.A.E."

"Good memory. That's the one."

"What's the snafu? Money got there, I know that."

"Seven hundred and seventy-five million plus assumption of debt."

"I remember it was something like that. I can't keep all the figures straight after a while. Too many deals."

"Tell me about it."

"But anyway, we only dealt with the cash, not the debt assumption, of course," she said, biting into her tuna fish sandwich as they walked along.

"The cash got there, but two of the contingencies may not have been met."

"Which ones?'

"One deed recordation might've had a problem. And there's an outstanding issue with the anchor tenant in the Dallas–Fort Worth mall that was supposed to be resolved prior to the funds going out. There was supposed to be a release in the file but there's not."

"Shit, did we screw up?"

"I don't know. I'm not sure if we screwed up either. I wanted to come by your office and take a look at the records you have."

"I'm swamped today, Roy. That's why I'm eating my sandwich on the run."

"How about after office hours?"

Cassie looked doubtful. "I had concert tickets at Constitution Hall."

"I haven't mentioned anything to the client. I was hoping to clean up the issue before anyone had to make those calls. And you know the U.A.E. guys. If there was a foul-up you and I might have to jump on a jet and go and apologize to the sheiks."

The blood drained from Cassie's face. "But I hate to fly."

"Better we get it resolved on this side of the world, then."

Cassie sighed and threw the rest of her sandwich into a trash bin. "How about seven tonight? Everybody will be gone but I can let you in."

"That sounds perfect, Cassie, I really appreciate it."

Roy left her, checked his watch, and called Mace. She filled him in on her meeting in Newark. She also told him she'd tried to catch an earlier train, but it was full. And the train she had just gotten on was delayed because a piece of equipment on a train in front of them had fallen off, been run over by the engine, and part of the power grid for the Northeast corridor might have been damaged.

"It's going to be a while," she'd said glumly. "Maybe tonight. Hell, I could probably walk there faster."

"Let me know when you get in. By the way, I'm being sued by my old firm."

"What? Why?"

"I looked at the complaint. It's all bullshit."

"Well, if I hear of a good lawyer I'll let you know."

A minute before seven, Roy appeared at the office of DLT. The firm shut down at six-thirty, which seemed early but DLT opened at six a.m. because of all its international work. After long days of crunching numbers, meeting strict deadlines, and authorizing the catapulting of electronic currency around the globe, most of the firm's employees stampeded to the door right at closing.

Cassie answered his knock and let him in. She had taken her hair out of its usual bun and it swept around her shoulders. Her heels had been replaced with socks and tennis shoes.

"I pulled the docs that we have," she said. "Come on back."

"Great. Thanks."

"I went through everything but I couldn't find what you were talking about. But then I'm not a lawyer."

"That's okay, I'm sure I'll be able to figure it out."

He went over the records slowly, looking for an opening while Cassie hovered behind him in her small office. He noted the pack of cigarettes sticking out of her purse where it lay on her desk. He looked up and smiled. "This may take a while. You want to smoke 'em while you got 'em?" He tapped the protruding pack of cigarettes.

"I've been dying for one since lunch. But it's a no-smoking building and I've had no time to sneak out."

"The sidewalk is an option right now."

Cassie's fingers curled and uncurled slowly as she eyed her pack of Winstons. "Okay, I give. I won't be gone that long. I might actually need two cigs."

"And isn't there an Au Bon Pain across the street?"

"Yeah, I love their stuff. Our coffee sucks."

"Then go smoke and when you're done go get us some java." He gave her some money. "Take your time. Looks like we're going to be here a while. No room for error with the Middle East guys," he added ominously.

As soon as she was gone, Roy started clicking keys on her computer. Luckily he didn't need her password as he was already in the database. He wasn't familiar with their electronic filing system, but he figured searching the names of clients would be sufficient. And he was right. He quickly skimmed half a dozen transactions that he and Diane had worked on over the last eighteen months. Now he understood why Cassie had been confused about the dollar amount earlier.

The escrow instruction letters that Diane and Roy had prepared for these deals, which basically told DLT how much money would be sent and on what conditions it could released, did not match up with the DLT records in one critical respect.

The cash.

From his own records Roy had jotted down various facts for each of the six transactions he wanted to compare with DLT's records. The Dixie Group shopping center deal had been for $775 million plus debt assumption. That's what Roy had written down from the Shilling & Murdoch instruction letter they'd sent DLT. DLT had scanned all the instruction letters into their computer system. But the instruction letter Roy was looking at, which appeared to be on Shilling letterhead, had the cash purchase price at $795 million, a $20 million discrepancy. At her level, Cassie would not have caught this because she just followed the instruction letter. And if the funds coming in matched the amount stated in the letter, there would be no red flag. And apparently the incoming funds *had* matched.

Roy sat back. Why would his client in the U.A.E. have sent extra money? No purchaser paid more than the contract price. Or had the client even sent the extra money? He clicked a few computer keys and looked at the confirmation slips on the wire transfers for some of the deals. Money wires coming in from overseas were dealt with a bit differently from wires between U.S. banks, particularly after 9/11. Roy knew there was a list of sensitive countries and American authorities kept a close watch on monies flowing from these places into the United States in case they were being used to fund terrorist activities.

All bank wires, whether domestic or foreign, still ended up moving through the Federal Reserve System in some fashion and with varying levels of scrutiny. But it was still an arena that was fraught with the potential for abuse. Roy glanced at the date of the instruction letter he was looking at on the screen and then looked at the cheat sheet he'd prepared from his own records. The date on the screen was two days after the one from Roy's records. He knew that instruction letters were updated all the time as conditions changed. But conditions hadn't changed in this instance. Roy's date was for the absolute final instruction letter. Someone else had later changed it, and had added $20 million in the process.

He remembered the string of extra numbers that he'd seen on the computerized records he and Mace had looked at over dinner at Altman's guest house. He inputted the name of that client and looked at the instruction letter for that deal. Roy knew that the purchase amount had been $990 million for the manufacturing facilities. But on the instruction sheet another $25 million had been tacked on and the date on the letter again was after the latest date Roy had. And on a confirmation sheet it showed the $990 million going to the seller's bank in New York. But where did the other monies go? To another bank? And who'd sent it? Again, Roy didn't think his client had thrown in an extra $25 million out of the goodness of their heart.

Roy sat straight up as the answer hit him.

This was a classic piggyback scheme.

You open the financial tunnel with a legitimate transaction coming from a country in the Middle East *not* on the sensitive list. The purchase price goes out, but added to it are funds from another source. The legit dollars run interference for the illegitimate dollars and, when they reach the U.S. pipeline, the purchase-price dollars go to where they're supposed to, and the other dollars go somewhere else. But if the instruction letter has the overall correct amount and delivery accounts for the monies, no one would be the wiser. And if an audit was done later the facts might be so muddled that no one could figure it out. There was so much electronic money flying around the world that it was like trying to track down a particular molecule of air.

Roy knew what this was. This was a way around the Patriot Act, which obviously was very concerned about suspicious transfers of money. The extra funds could have come from anywhere, including enemies of the United States.

These could be drug dealers laundering money. Or operating funds for terrorists. Or spies.

And they might have someone at DLT on the inside. And then it struck Roy. DLT was just following instructions. It was far more likely they had someone at *Shilling* in their pocket. He looked at the revised instruction letter. It had Diane's electronic signature on it. But that was easy to get. Especially for someone in management at the firm.

Chester Ackerman. The biggest rainmaker at the firm.

He doubted Ackerman was the driving force behind this. But he felt sure the man knew who was. Roy inserted a flash drive in the USB slot and made copies of as many pages as he could and slipped it in his briefcase. He was walking to the office foyer when he heard Cassie open the door.

"I'm all done, Cassie," he called out. "Found the problem."

The door closed and he stopped.

It wasn't Cassie. It was a petite woman with brown hair, but her gun looked awfully big.

CHAPTER

106

MACE NEARLY LEAPT off the train when it finally pulled to a stop in Union Station. A short trip had turned into an all-day affair. It was already dark outside. She would wait until she got outside to call Roy. Hopefully he had struck pay dirt at the escrow firm.

So intent was she on her thoughts that she never saw the man visibly react as she walked by him in the station and headed for the cab stands. She never saw him pull his cell phone and make a quick call. Never saw him walk up behind her. She did notice when the pistol was wedged against the small of her back.

"Keep your mouth shut or you're dead."

She tried to look back but he pushed the gun deeper. "Eyes straight ahead."

"This place is packed with cops," she said. "How about I start screaming instead?"

"See them kids over there?"

Mace's gaze darted to the left where a group of kids in school uniforms were standing with two older women.

"I see 'em."

"Then you see the dude right behind 'em?"

Mace saw the dude. Big and angry-looking. "Yeah."

"Well he's got a grenade in his pocket. You give me any shit, he's gonna pull the pin, drop it in that trash can, and walk away. Then the kiddies go boom."

"Why the hell are you doing this?"

"Shut up and walk!"

He maneuvered her up the escalators, out to the parking garage, and then far down to a remote corner of the place where no else was around and only one vehicle was parked, a black Escalade. Four men got out as they approached.

Mace flinched when she saw him.

Psycho was not smiling this time. No sparkle in the eye, no levity at all in his features. The man looked all business.

"Dead bitch walking," he said grimly.

"I thought we had a deal," said Mace. "No harm, no foul."

All that got was a backhanded punch from Psycho that dropped Mace on her butt. She sat there wiping the blood off her cheek before one of the boys ripped her back to a standing position just in time for Psycho to knock her on her ass again with an uppercut to her gut.

Mace was tough, but one more hit like that and she wasn't going to be doing much else other than lie in a nursing home bed and dribble into a cup. She turned to the side and threw up right before she was jerked back to her feet. She stood there tottering.

Blood flowing from her nose and cracked mouth she managed to say, "One request."

"Do you understand that I'm about to kill you?"

"That's why I figure I better ask now."

"What?"

"You're a big tough guy. You just knocked me on my ass twice. You're gonna kill me."

"So?"

"So, let me have one punch. Right to *your* gut. You can even harden up the six-pack before I do it."

"What are you, one-ten?"

"About. And you're over two, I know."

"So where's that gonna get you?"

"Satisfaction before I die."

"How do I know you're not some kind of kung fu princess?"

"If I were, you think I'd be letting you kick my ass?" She spit blood out of her mouth and ran her tongue over a loosened tooth. "Hey, but if you're afraid of a girl."

Psycho reared back his fist to hit her again, but stopped when she flinched. He grinned. "You ain't no kung fu nothing. I know, because I am. Double black belt."

"Figures," said Mace wearily, wiping blood off her chin with her jacket sleeve. "So it's a yes?"

Psycho looked around at his guys, who all looked back at him with amused expressions. Mace also glanced around. There wasn't anyone to help her. They were in a dark, deserted corner in the pits of the parking garage. She could scream her lungs out and it wouldn't matter. But she suddenly did see one thing that might help matters. If she lived long enough.

"Okay. But soon as your little love tap connects, we're putting your butt in that SUV, taking you to a favorite place of mine, putting a bullet in your brain, and dropping you in Rock Creek Park."

"Tense the six-pack, Psych. I'm gonna give it all I got."

Psycho zipped open his jacket and exposed a flat belly that Mace knew was probably hard as iron. She was actually surprised no one had noticed, but it was dark out here and so they apparently hadn't seen what she'd done. Her blow was efficiently delivered, driven right into the man's diaphragm. Mace had been right, it was hard as rock. But it didn't matter. The 900,000 volts in her zap knuckles didn't really care how hard someone's gut was. Psycho dropped to the concrete shaking like he was holding a live wire, his mouth making little burps of sound, his eyes popping and fluttering.

His stunned crew just stood there watching him.

Mace sprinted off.

The guy who'd originally grabbed her in the station shouted, "Hey!"

Mace knew she'd never make it. Even as she ran she tensed for the shots that would be hitting her any moment now. The squeal of wheels made her look to her left. The Nissan was coming right at her. She threw herself to the side, only to watch it miss her by design and whip around and come to a stop between her and Psycho's guys.

"Get in!"

Mace jumped to her feet.

"Get in!"

"Darren?"

Alisha's brother had his gun out and pointed it at Psycho's on-rushing crew. He placed two shots right over their heads, and the two lead guys hit the concrete, making draw pulls of their own on the way down.

Mace ripped open the Nissan's passenger door and threw herself in. There was another squeal of wheels and the Nissan shot forward. Mace ducked as bullets pinged off the metal and one round cracked the rear window glass. They rounded a corner and Darren floored it. Two more curves and they zipped out of the garage. Five minutes later they were two miles away and Mace finally sat up in her seat.

"Where the hell did you come from?" she exclaimed. "How'd you know I was even there?"

"Didn't. I was tailing Psycho. Saw what was going down. Figured you needed a little help."

Mace strapped on her seat belt. "Now I know why they call you Razor."

"Got some napkins in the glove box. Don't want you bleeding all over my seat," he added in a surly tone.

"Thanks." She pulled some out and wiped off her face. "Why were you tailing that guy?"

"Why you think?"

"There are several endings to that sort of plan, and none of them are good."

"What you want me to do, let him walk?"

"He's not going to walk."

"That's right, you gonna handle him. That's what you said. Well, you handling him all right. But for me, your ass is dead tonight."

"Hey, don't forget my zap knuckles."

Darren grinned, probably in spite of himself. "That was cool seeing him on his ass like that shaking like a dude coming off meth."

Mace palmed her phone. "Okay, we have kidnapping, assault—"

He glanced at her. "What you talking 'bout?"

"The crimes Psycho and his guys committed tonight."

"Right. He'll have ten people say he was twenty miles away."

"You didn't see it, then?"

"See what?"

"The security camera in the corner of the garage." She punched in a number. "Beth, Mace. Yeah, I'm cool. Just got into D.C. I brought you a present. A guy named Psycho, tied up in a nice little bow."

CHAPTER

107

It was amazing to Roy how quickly and efficiently he was bundled out of the building. The truck had driven for an indeterminate amount of time. He was tied up, gagged and blindfolded, and they'd put something in his ear that buzzed constantly so he couldn't even listen for helpful sounds that might aid in telling him where they were headed. Now he was seated at a table in a room that he sensed was part of a bigger facility. He tensed when the door opened and the woman walked in.

Mary Bard sat down across from him, her hands clasped in front of her and resting on the table. Roy was no longer tied up and the gag and blindfold had been removed. They obviously didn't care if he could identify any of them. They clearly didn't anticipate him sitting in a witness box.

"Who are you? What do you want?"

"You watch too much TV," said Bard with a bemused expression.

"And what exactly did you expect me to ask?"

"Do you want to live?" she said simply.

"Yes. But why do I think it highly unlikely?"

"It is *very* unlikely," she conceded. "But not impossible. And in your situation, it is the impossible you must strive for."

"Like this?" He leapt across the table and attempted to grab her. He outweighed her by at least a hundred pounds and was nearly a foot taller. When he woke, he was lying on the cold floor on his stomach. His right shoulder felt like it was out of its socket. He slowly sat up, holding his damaged wing.

Mary Bard was once more seated at the table and staring at him with the same inscrutable expression. "Are you finished playing John Wayne?"

John Wayne? She either doesn't watch much current TV or isn't from America and subsists on a steady diet of decades-old movies.

"How did you do that?" he asked, grimacing with pain.

"I could tell you, but you wouldn't understand, so what would be the point?"

He got to his feet and slumped down in the chair, holding his injured shoulder. "I think it's popped out of joint," he said. He felt sick to his stomach.

"It is. Would you like me to put it back for you?"

"How about some morphine instead?"

"No. You need to be completely focused for what is coming."

She walked around the table and stood next to him. "Turn toward me."

"I swear if this is some kind of trick, ninja chick or not, I will—"

She moved so fast he had no time to react. There was a pop, an instant of gut-wrenching pain, and then his shoulder was back in place.

She sat back down while he gingerly moved his arm around, testing her work. "Thank you."

"Pleasure," she said as she stared at him.

"You're not American, are you?"

She shrugged. "What does it matter what I am?"

"Okay, I'm focused. What do you want?"

"We want you to text Mace Perry. We want to meet with her too."

Roy sat back. "I don't think so. You've got me, you're not getting her too."

"Mr. Kingman, you really should reconsider."

"Okay, I will. You want me to text Mace. Ask her to meet me in some out-of-the-way place so when you grab and kill her no one will even know. And then you'll just kill me too. I'm thinking about it, thinking about it." He paused and said, "Go to hell, lady."

"We can of course text her ourselves using your phone."

"Then why even ask me?"

"As a test, of course."

"Did I pass or fail?"

"I don't know yet."

"So where does that leave us? If you let me call her, I'll warn her it's a trap. And since I've never sent her a text before, she'll be instantly suspicious if she gets one. She's sort of paranoid by nature. And she'll call me. And when I don't answer. . . ."

"Yes, we thought the same thing."

"I figured it out, you know. The money thing. The piggyback ride. Dialing for terrorists? Is that what you are? You don't look Middle Eastern but are you one of bin Laden's babes?"

"I am not anyone's babe," she said, her voice rising slightly.

"Okay, but maybe you should consider this. Mace doesn't know any of what I found out. And neither does anyone else. I never had a chance to tell anybody."

"Your point?"

"You don't need Mace. You've got me. You kill me, it's over."

"I doubt it would be over."

"What do you mean?"

"My briefing on Mace Perry leads me to conclude that if you are in danger she will stop at nothing to try and help you."

"Your *briefing*? Okay, what government do you work for?"

For the first time Mary Bard exhibited a touch of chagrin. Her lips compressed slightly and there was a certain irritated look to her eyes.

When she didn't answer him, he said, "I'd say the impossible just got *wildly* impossible. I'm never walking out of here, so what incentive do I have to help you?"

There was a buzzing sound. Roy looked around for a moment until he realized it was the woman's phone vibrating. She rose, went to a far corner, and answered. She barely spoke, mostly listened. It dawned on Roy that the room was probably wired for both sound and video. Who was out there?

Bard put the phone back in her pocket and retook her seat. "No incentive at all. But the fact is she will come to try and save you once we tell her we have you. You see, you're the bait."

"Her sister is the D.C. police chief. If she comes it will be with an army."

"No she won't. Because we will tell her that will ensure your death."

"But her coming alone she knows will ensure *both* our deaths."

"And yet she will do so."

"How the hell are you so sure?"

"Because if it were me, I would do the same thing."

108

MACE WAS SITTING in the living room of the guesthouse with a bag of ice on her swollen cheek. She'd tried to call Roy numerous times and hadn't received an answer. The phone call she'd just gotten, however, had stripped the mystery out of this. They had Roy. They wanted her too. If she didn't come, he was dead. The deadline was twenty-four hours from now.

She just sat there, icy water dripping down her face. For one of the few times in her life she didn't know what to do. Then, as if her hand were being guided by some invisible force, she picked up the phone and made the call. Beth arrived in twenty-seven minutes, the roof lights of Cruiser One still whirling as she leapt from the ride and sprinted to the guesthouse. A quick discussion with Mace filled her in.

"Where do they want you to meet them?" Beth asked.

"They will kill him if I don't go alone."

"And if you do they'll kill both of you. Kingman may already be dead, Mace."

"No, he's not dead."

"How do you know?"

"I just know, okay?"

The two stared at each other. Finally, Beth said, "You know, Kingman made some sense when he said you and I should be working together instead of against each other."

"We used to make a pretty good team."

"We've been reactive this whole time. Chasing phantoms down alleys."

"Or getting shot at by them."

"What do we know? I mean, what do we really know about all this?"

"Beth, we don't have time to sit and noodle this."

"If we don't sit and figure this out, Kingman *will* be dead. We've got nearly twenty-three hours. If we use it properly that's a lifetime."

Mace drew a deep breath and calmed. "Okay, I'll start. Diane Tolliver had dinner with Jamie Meldon and then was murdered. Soon thereafter Meldon was killed too."

Beth said, "Meldon's investigation was taken over by people I don't know, and even the FBI was called off the case. I've made inquiries and it seems Meldon might have been the target of a group of domestic terrorists."

"But that would mean that Tolliver was killed because of her connection to Meldon and not the other way around."

Beth looked puzzled. "But according to what we've found out about the two refrigerators, Tolliver was killed on Friday night, before Meldon, and Dockery was supposed to take the fall."

Mace picked it up. "I found out in Newark that Meldon and Tolliver had an affair years ago. If Tolliver had found out something and needed help, she might've gone to him, especially since he was a U.S. attorney."

"But that suggests *Meldon* was killed because of his ties to Tolliver, not the other way around."

"Roy and I were chased through the law firm. And I'm convinced there was spyware on Tolliver's computer. That again supports the theory that she was the key, not Meldon."

"And you ran into an impersonator tossing Andre Watkins's apartment." She glanced sharply at Mace. "The imposter, he strike you as being one of Roman Naylor's cohorts?"

"No, way too slick and sophisticated for that. And Meldon had no connection to Watkins. Only Tolliver. And they manipulated the time of her death to throw us off. I don't see Naylor's 'bubbas' running around putting steak and veggie residue in the lady's trash, planting sperm in her, and installing spyware on the woman's computer."

"And the movement of money at this DLT escrow agency?"

"Tolliver again. And Roy said billions passed through that agency in connection with Shilling & Murdoch clients. And he said the managing partner, Chester Ackerman, was sweating bullets."

"Kingman mentioned he has clients in Dubai."

"I gather a lot of their clients are based in that region."

"So presumably some of these billions were coming from the Middle East?"

"Guess so." Mace grew rigid. "Are you thinking what I'm thinking?"

Beth pulled out her phone.

"Who you calling? Your buddy the DNI?"

"Sam Donnelly? Not yet."

She spoke into the phone. "Steve Lanier please, it's Chief Perry."

"Steve Lanier? Isn't he—"

"FBI AD, yeah."

"Hey, Steve, Beth. I really need to talk to you. Yeah, it's very important."

Two hours later they were seated across from Lanier at the FBI's Washington Field Office and had just finished, in alternating bursts, telling the man their findings.

Lanier leaned back in his chair. "Beth, I've seen some serious crap in my time, but this just blows my mind."

A man entered the room and handed him a file before leaving.

He opened it and scanned the contents. "We got nothing back on the Meldon investigation. Hell, I don't even think there was one. That should've been a red flag. But we did manage, with a lot of finagling, to get autopsy reports back on Agents Hope and Reiger."

"Jarvis Burns told me about that."

"I'm sure. Their throats were surgically sliced. A real professional job."

"Okay, what does that tell us?" asked Beth.

Lanier closed the file. "That tells us we've got a major problem."

"We knew that already," said Mace.

"Not what I meant." He spent the next five minutes filling the sisters in on what he did mean.

"Then it seems pretty clear," said Beth. "What we have to do."

Mace nodded. "I'm with you."

Lanier looked between them. "Did I miss something?"

"It's a sisterly thing," explained Beth as she leaned forward and started talking fast. When she stopped, Mace jumped in and took up the line of thought.

"We'll need Sam Donnelly for this," said Lanier.

"Absolutely," said Beth.

Thirty minutes later, all three rose to implement the plan they'd just hatched.

CHAPTER

109

IT WAS the next night and Mace was in western Maryland pushing the Ducati as hard as it would go. The deep rows of trees on either side of the road flicked by, like the black-and-white frames from an old film projector. She reached the crossroads and turned left, traveled another mile, and hung a right. Five hundred yards later she saw the old farm up ahead. She slowed the Ducati and then came to a stop, her boots hitting the dirt. Her eyes were tearing up a bit. Not from emotion. She was wearing a very special pair of contact lenses.

The falling-down house was to her right, listing like a ship in high rolling swells. To her left was an old silo rising into the sky. She could see that farther down a dirt road was the place she'd been told to go to: the barn. She saw no lights on, which didn't surprise her. She twisted the bike's throttle and headed toward it. Five feet from the barn she cut the engine, slipped off her helmet, and moved forward. Car lights immediately shot on to her left. She held up her hand to shield her eyes. The three men came forward. When they reached her she stumbled and grabbed one of the men for support. The tiny device in her hand with a special adhesive backing was transferred to the inner side of the man's sleeve.

"Stand still," one of them barked.

Mace stood rigidly as another man gave her an expert patdown and then ran a scanner up and down her body. He took his time and ran it several times over her head.

"No follicle implants with tracking devices," she volunteered helpfully.

"Shut up," said the first man.

They herded her to the waiting Range Rover and pushed her in. On the ride they chattered away in a language she'd never heard before. They looked hard and tough; their gaunt faces and lean, athletic physiques evidenced an existence far removed from the typical comforts enjoyed by folks in the West. The Range Rover slowed after driving for what Mace had calculated was eight miles, all on back roads. The silhouette of a large structure suddenly appeared out of the darkness. As the vehicle approached, a stark break in the darkness suddenly appeared as two large double doors were opened. The Rover drove through this gap and stopped. The wide doors closed and the men climbed out of the Rover, pulling Mace with them.

She stood there and looked around. They were in what seemed to be an old manufacturing facility. There was a large open area where rusted tables were situated along with a wrecked conveyor belt. Piles of junked tools lay around the littered floor. A catwalk ran around the perimeter of the second level and a lift chain was suspended from the center of the A-frame ceiling and descended straight down until it stopped about eight feet from the floor. A row of metal support posts ran down the middle of the building, bisecting it. The only light came from a single bank of fluorescents hung overhead controlled by a power box on the wall next to the double doors.

"Roy!"

Roy was sitting on his butt and tied to one of the support poles. He called out furiously, "Why the hell did you come?"

"I told you it was what I would do," said a voice.

Mace turned to see Mary Bard walking toward her from the other end of the building. She was dressed in tight black pants, a short-waisted jean jacket, and thick-soled boots.

"I'm here," said Mace. "So why don't we get this done."

"You are too impatient," said Bard.

Mace glanced over at Roy. "What do I need to do so he goes free?"

"I'm not going anywhere," shouted Roy as he struggled to stand.

"What do I need to do?" Mace said again.

"I'm afraid there is nothing you can do."

"So you just kill us both? Others know about this. They won't let it drop."

"But we won't have to worry about the two of you anymore."

Bard slipped the pair of knives that she had used to kill Reiger and Hope from a holder riding on the back of her belt.

Roy looked helplessly at Mace as Bard advanced. "Mace, she's some kind of hand-to-hand combat freak. She laid me out in like a second."

"Well, Roy, and don't take this the hard way, but you're just not that tough."

Bard stopped her advance and eyed Mace, the dual knives motionless in her hands. "And you think you are?"

"I'm still here, aren't I? I mean, Reiger and Hope tried to kill me but didn't get the job done."

"They were incompetent."

"And that's why you were ordered to kill them, right?"

Bard's eyes glittered at this comment. "It doesn't matter, does it?"

"You're from Russia. Federal Security Service."

"I am impressed. I thought my accent was gone."

"It wasn't a guess on my part. I hear you guys are like the best assassins out there, except for maybe the Israelis."

"I will try not to disappoint you tonight."

"I've got a knife in my belt clasp. How about you let me use it to defend myself? It's still two blades against one, but it'll be a little fairer. I'm clearly not in your league, but I've got a few moves. Let you practice your stuff for the next time."

Bard looked around at the heavily armed men surrounding Mace. "All right."

"But—" began one of the men.

She barked something in the man's tongue and he fell silent.

While the other men pointed their guns at Mace, she undid her clasp and slid out the knife. She examined the slightly dulled blade. "This baby got me out of a very tough situation."

"I don't think it will work again."

Bard started moving in a circle, the blades twirling in front of her.

Mace stood flat-footed, studying the other woman's tactics.

Bard said, "No tears? No begging for mercy?"

"Everybody has to die one day."

"And this is your day."

"Or yours," said Mace.

110

WHAT THE HELL happened, Jarvis?"

Beth was standing in her office in front of a large-screen TV with a remote feed that Jarvis Burns's techs had set up. After leaving the WFO the previous night, Beth had immediately called Sam Donnelly and told him what had happened with Roy Kingman. Donnelly had sent Jarvis Burns to help oversee a rescue operation. Things had been going well until they'd lost track of Mace. A guy in a suit and wearing a headset was frantically typing on a portable keyboard while barking instructions into his headset.

Burns remained focused on the screen where they could see the live feed from the camera mounted on the chopper's skids. The countryside below looked dark and vast. "The plan was the best we had under the circumstances, Beth. We had two stealth units on the ground following her. The tracker was on her Ducati. They will have moved her in another vehicle, but our units should have been able to follow."

He turned to the tech. "Get the ground commander on the horn ASAP."

Seconds later the tech handed the headset to Burns, who listened for a bit and then tossed the headset back to the man before turning to Beth. "They were ambushed. Took heavy fire and casualties. They're out of the hunt. We've got a mole somewhere, Beth. That's the only way they could have found out."

Beth slapped her desktop. "Now we have no idea where she is."

"We have *some* idea," replied Burns calmly. "We had a clear signal out to the abandoned farmhouse and we've got two stealth choppers as backup in the vicinity." He tapped his tech on the shoulder. "Phillips, tell the air support commander to perform a ten-mile grid perimeter sweep. We need to all watch the feed and see if anything pops."

"That will take too long!" snapped an exasperated Beth.

"Not in the choppers it won't. It makes sense that they didn't transport her too far for a number of tactical reasons. With a little bit of luck we'll pick up the trail again."

"And if we're not lucky?"

"I'm doing the best I can, Beth. Remember, you called Director Donnelly in at the last minute. I'm good, but I'm *not* a magician."

Beth calmed. "I know. I'm sorry. It's just that—"

"She's your sister." He laid a hand on Beth's shoulder. "I know, Beth. I swear we'll do everything in our power to bring her back safe."

"Thank you, Jarvis."

"In the spirit of fair play, I propose to allow you the first move," said Bard, who had edged closer to Mace with each move.

"And in the spirit of fair play, I propose to kill you any way I can."

"So you don't want the first move?"

"No, actually I do. But I want them out of the way." Mace pointed to the gunmen arrayed around her. "No bullets in the back if I get the upper hand with you."

Bard hesitated and then motioned to the armed men to clear the area. Mace backed away until she reached the far wall, her knife held in front of her.

"I'm waiting," said Bard. "For the first move."

"And I'm still thinking of what that first move should be."

"This is ridiculous. If you—"

Mace lunged and her hand slammed down on the lever connected to the power box on the wall. The building instantly went dark. With a flick of her wrist, Mace tossed her knife. It flashed across the space and lodged in the chest of the gunman closest to her. He collapsed to the floor, the blade tip resting in the left chamber of his heart.

Mace had no trouble seeing in the pitch dark because she was wearing a pair of latest-generation contact lenses that were actually advanced optics that instantly adapted to all levels of light or darkness. They'd been a gift from the FBI for a situation just like this. From her earlier observations she knew there were four gunmen on this level and three more on the catwalk. They had Heckler and Koch UMPs and MP5s. And she desperately needed some firepower before the bandits figured out a way to light up the place again. She slid across the floor to the dead man and snagged his submachine gun and two extra mags.

Mace opened fire. One of the guys shooting in her vicinity jerked around as two of her rounds impacted his neck and torso. He managed to squeeze off a few more wild rounds before he went down and stayed there. Mace immediately rolled six feet to her left as bullets pounded her last firing position, the bandits taking aim at her previous muzzle flashes. She caught another guy in both knees with another burst. He dropped screaming, but kept firing. Her next round slammed into his face and his UMP went silent.

Lines of fire started coming from the catwalk. Forty-caliber rounds ricocheted off the concrete floor as Mace threw herself behind the guts of a retooling machine and fired off the rest of her mag, dropped it, and slapped in a new one as return fire pinged all around her. A chunk of wood got blown off the end of the table she was behind and she felt the tailing rip into her shoulder and slice across her cheek. Warm blood flowed down her face. Another round cut a groove across her left thigh, searing through her pants and tattooing her skin black.

She sprayed rounds at the catwalk, but even through her optics she couldn't see much because of the smoke from all the weapons discharge. The remaining shooters had taken cover as well. And they had the high ground and superior firepower. Mace was pinned down. The logistics were depressingly simple. Without help it was only a matter of time before they were dead.

"Mace!'

She looked behind her to see Roy slumped over, his face twisted in pain. Even from this distance and with her field of vision a ghostly green Mace could see what she knew was his blood seeping across his shirt. Mary Bard was stooping over him, her knife pulling back for the final stroke while he frantically kicked at her.

"Roy!"

The explosion catapulted both front sliding doors a good ten feet across the floor. Out of the smoke came a sight Mace would never forget.

Twenty FBI Hostage Rescue Team armored assaulters loaded for war emerged from the smoke. Just the sight of these guys was enough to scare the hell out of anyone no matter how battle-tested. Knowing what was coming, Mace instantly dropped down and pulled the plugs from out of her boots and stuffed them in her ears. A second later an array of flash-bangs detonated.

As the HRT laid down precise walls of fire at the enemy positions exposed to their night optics, Mace turned and raced toward Roy. Mary Bard was on her side, dazed by the flash-bangs, blood trickling out of one ear. When she tried to rise up and finish off Roy, Mace leapt, the butt of her UMP catching the woman flush on the temple. She crumpled to the floor.

The all-clear sounded a minute later. Someone hit the wall lever and the interior of the building exploded with light.

"Man down," screamed Mace. In the darkness she'd ripped open Roy's shirt and used the cloth to stop the bleeding. As the medical support personnel that came on every HRT operation rushed forward, Mace told Roy, "You're going to be okay."

"I don't feel like I'm going to be okay."

"You can't die, Roy."

"Why?"

"I've got a pretty good feeling I'm going to need one kick-ass lawyer, and you're the only one I know."

He managed a weak smile before the medics took over. A few minutes later the chopper lifted off with them on their way to the nearest hospital.

CHAPTER

111

FORTY MINUTES later the tech with the headset jerked upright in his seat. On the screen an explosion had just rocked the camera. Beth put down the call she was on and joined them. They all stared dumbfounded at the sight on the screen as a fireball lit the sky.

"My God," said an obviously shaken Burns. "They detonated a bomb." He turned to the tech. "Get that chopper on the ground ASAP."

The tech relayed these instructions and they watched as the chopper headed downward. A moment later the camera feed went dead. A tense minute went by and then the tech jerked again as a stream of words came over his headset. He nodded blankly, his face pale. He turned to the others. "The building was destroyed. There does not appear to be any survivors."

"Are they sure it's the right spot?" said Beth.

"They just pulled a body from the site," said the tech as he glanced nervously at Beth. "A female body with a positive ID."

"My God, Beth," said Burns. "I'm so sorry."

"I am too, Jarvis. I am too. Very sorry."

Something in her tone made him look sharply at her.

"Beth? Are you all right?"

"Okay," Beth called out loudly in the direction of the door.

It opened and in walked Sam Donnelly, along with a half dozen security officers. Behind him came Steve Lanier, the FBI AD, who was wearing a broad smile.

Burns looked from his boss to Beth and then back to his boss. "Sir, what the hell is going on here?"

"I'm sorry, Jarv. It's all over," said Donnelly sadly.

"What is all over?"

"Your secret op. With the FBI's help we set this trap for you. I'd long suspected that something was going on I wasn't aware of. I'm sorry it turned out to be you."

"But—" began Burns.

"Sacrifices, Jarvis. We talked about this before. The national security of this country comes before all."

Burns and Donnelly shared a pronounced stare.

"You will of course have the full support of the DNI if it turns out we were wrong," added Donnelly.

"I see. Thank you, sir. I'm sure everything will be worked out."

Donnelly turned to Lanier. "I think we can handle it from here, Steve. The FBI isn't cleared for this. But I appreciate the assist. I'll have my people—"

Beth approached Burns. "Were you really going to do it, Jarv?'

"Do what?'

"Fall on the sword for Sam?"

"What?" said Donnelly sharply.

She turned to him. "Sacrifices? The full support of the DNI? We'll take over now? We'll never see Jarv again. You'll just move him to Jordan or Iraq to continue doing what he's doing."

"Which is of course what you ordered him to do," added Lanier.

"I have no idea what you people are talking about," said Donnelly furiously.

"If I were you," Lanier said to Donnelly, "I'd save any comments for your defense." He motioned to his men. They moved forward and cuffed Donnelly, Burns, and his tech.

"How dare you!" said Donnelly angrily.

Lanier sat down in a leather chair across from Beth's desk. "Chief, would you like to do the honors?" he said. "I'm a little sick to my stomach, personally."

Beth leaned against the edge of her desk. "Jarvis, do you know when you told me that you were aware of the death of Diane Tolliver, the fire alarm pull, and the rest?"

"What of it?" said Burns with a wary expression.

"When I seemed amazed that you knew this, you remarked that if you couldn't keep track of things going on in your own city how could you be expected to know what was going on in the rest of the world."

"I'm afraid I'm not seeing your—"

"I took you at your word, Jarvis. I accepted that if anything big were going on in D.C., you and Sam would know about it. And if you two weren't doing anything to stop it, it occurred to me that that might be because you were *behind* it. I also tracked Hope and Reiger to the Pentagon one night. I knew they had no military connection, but I was aware that DNI had a satellite office there. And when we learned of the connection between Diane Tolliver and Jamie Meldon, and the fact that she'd been killed on Friday instead of Monday, I knew there was something more here than an old vet raping and killing. We had no proof of anything, so I went to Steve and we hatched a plan to see if we could get that evidence."

"A plan?"

Beth pointed to the screen. "This plan."

Donnelly said, "My God, Beth, I have no idea what you're talking about. But am I to believe that you sacrificed your sister to see if some nonsensical idea was valid or not?"

Lanier said, "Mace is fine. We sent in HRT. We were able to track them when Mace slipped a bug on one of the bandits before they scanned her. The chopper took her and Kingman to the nearest hospital."

Burns glanced nervously at the screen. "Well, apparently the report we received was erroneous. I am very glad that she's all right."

Beth said coldly, "The hell you are, Jarv. You and Sam did your best to kill her. This whole thing tonight was an elaborate charade by you. The camera feed was bogus. You didn't have any choppers out there. No stealth units. All smoke and mirrors."

"You are utterly mistaken," said Burns.

"Don't say anything else, Jarvis," cautioned Donnelly. "We'll get this all straightened out."

"The hell you will," exclaimed Beth.

"You have nothing!" retorted Donnelly. "No proof. And once I speak to the president, heads will roll."

"Oh, the proof's not a problem," she said. "The evidence is overwhelming."

Lanier said, "HRT has several of your goons that you imported to do your dirty work."

"You'll accept the word of 'goons' over ours?" Donnelly said. "Do you realize how ridiculous that will look in court? I strongly suggest that you save yourself the embarrassment, release us immediately, and we'll just drop it here and now."

She said, "What really bugged me was the fact that you disrespected me."

"How exactly did I do that?"

"By assuming I wouldn't be smart enough to figure it all out."

"You still have nothing."

Lanier looked at Beth and then nodded at one of his men. "Bring her in."

A cuffed Mary Bard, her head bandaged, walked in with an armed escort.

"Mary Bard," said Lanier. "Recruited to this country to work with the FBI until you stole her from us, Sam. When I learned how Reiger and Hope died, the surgically precise cuts in the throat, it got me remembering about a little joint op she did with CIA last year."

Bard said bitterly, "The director told me the people tonight were traitors and had killed innocent people. That their terminations had been authorized by your government."

"Shut the hell up!" screamed Donnelly.

"She killed them. *She* killed them," cried Burns. "Not us."

Beth glanced at Lanier. "Can you please get them out of my sight before I shoot all three of them?"

Later that night Beth Perry strode into the hospital and saw her sister standing at the end of the hall. When Mace looked up and spied Beth she walked toward her. The two sisters met in the middle, flinging their arms around each other.

"God, you were great tonight, Mace."

"We both came up with the plan, sis."

"Yeah, but you were in the line of fire executing it, not me. You could have died."

"You're the chief. I'm expendable."

The two women stepped apart and Beth looked at the bandage on Mace's face and the bulge under her thigh. "Are you okay?"

"I got hurt worse than this falling out of bed."

"Liar. How's Kingman?"

"Out of surgery. They said I could see him for a couple of minutes. Do you want to come?"

Roy was still heavily sedated but his eyes opened when he heard Mace's voice. She wrapped her hand around his.

He said weakly, "Everything okay?"

"Everything is great," said Mace. "Beth is here."

Roy slowly turned his head to look at the chief. She reached down and touched his face gently.

"Hey, Roy, I need to tell you something."

"What's that?" he mouthed.

Beth glanced over at Mace before answering. "If you want to keep hanging around Mace, it's okay with me." She leaned down and kissed him on the cheek.

As the sisters walked down the hall to the waiting room Mace said, "You know, you finally called him Roy."

"Yeah. That's because he earned it."

112

So as I said, I'm thrilled to be here today to announce that all charges against my client, Louis Dockery, have been dropped. He has been released from custody and the Veterans Administration has taken it upon itself to see that such a decorated soldier will no longer be living on the streets."

This time Roy was having no problem handling the siege of reporters in front of the steps to D.C. Superior Court. His shoulder and side bandaged, he had just finished his remarks. Standing a few feet from him, a look of absolute revulsion on her face, was Mona Danforth. The only reason she was here was because the mayor and the head of the Justice Department had "requested" that she be present.

One reporter called out, "Mr. Kingman, how did you injure yourself?"

Roy smiled. "During the course of the litigation I accidentally impaled myself on one of Ms. Danforth's legendary stilettos."

The roar of laughter lasted so long that Mona finally stalked off, her face nearly as red as her lipstick. As she made her way inside the court building she bumped into someone.

"Hey, Mona," said Mace. "Isn't it a great day when justice finally triumphs?"

"Go to hell!"

"Nah, it'll be way too crowded with both of us there."

"I'm still going to press assault charges against you for attacking me in the ladies' room. You chipped one of my teeth."

"God, I'm really sorry, Mona. But there's somebody here who wants to give you something."

They turned to see Beth walking up to them with an envelope in hand.

"Here you go, Ms. Interim." She thrust the envelope in Mona's hands.

"What the hell is this?"

"Affidavits from my two detectives you coerced into working with you. They are prepared to testify that you initiated contact with Lou Dockery without benefit of his counsel being there, breaking numerous ethical canons and also the law. Since the U.S. Attorney's Office will be conflicted out over this one, the Justice Department will be prosecuting you."

Now Mona's face turned as white as the envelope she was holding. "Prosecuting me?"

"Yeah," said Mace. "You know, that whole court thing that ends in the bars being slammed behind your ass? If you want I can give you some tips on prison etiquette."

After the press conference was over, Mace, Beth, and Roy climbed into a government sedan and headed to a meeting that they really would rather have avoided. On the way over, they discussed what had happened.

"So the Captain is really going to be taken care of?" asked Mace.

Roy nodded. "The VA guy said he would take it as his personal mission to get him the care he needs. And I'm going to be checking. But I did tell them to order a truckload of Twinkies."

"God, Mona was pissed," said Mace. "You really think they'll nail her this time?"

Beth replied, "All I know is when I showed the affidavits to the DOJ lawyer he screamed out, 'Thank you, Jesus.'"

"And Psycho?" asked Roy.

"Signed, sealed, and delivered. When his gang saw the surveillance video from the security camera in the train station parking lot they rolled on him. They should be able to put him away for a long time."

"And Alisha, Tyler, and Darren?"

Mace answered. "Alisha's enrolled in a GED program. Tyler's being seen by a specialist from Johns Hopkins, and Mr. Razor is going back to school too. He apparently graduated from high school but never bothered to pick up his diploma. He's going the community college route for now. He'll probably be running the world in about ten years."

"So are you still going to be working for Altman?" Roy asked.

"Hey, I made a deal. I'm not going back on it. What about you? You could go back to Shilling."

"Haven't made up my mind yet. But they did drop the lawsuit against me."

"How's the wound?"

"Won't be playing ball anytime soon."

"I know, I'll take you on in HORSE, one-handed style."

"You're on."

The smiles faded from both their faces as the car slowed. They looked out the window as they stopped at the armed gate. The driver flashed his creds and they headed on.

"So what do you think is going to happen in there," Roy said, indicating the two-story building they were heading to. It was set on a multi-acre college-style campus.

Beth spoke up. "I always expect the worst. And today I think I'll be justified."

CHAPTER

113

BETH'S GLOCK had been confiscated at the door. Mace could tell that her sister was not happy about that just by the way her right fingers continued to flick at the empty space there. An armed escort led them down a long hallway where every single door was closed and also had a security lock. No open-style cubicle system here, thought Mace.

They were led into a spacious office with the typical wall of photos and shelves of awards and memorabilia that a high-rising public servant invariably collected. The Director of Central Intelligence, or DCI, was there along with a gent in uniform from the Defense Intelligence Agency, or DIA, someone from NSA, and a fourth gentleman that Mace had seen on TV recently and knew was very high up at the White House. There was no one else present.

"I thought Steve Lanier from the FBI would be here," commented Beth.

"No, he won't," said the DCI bluntly. "But I want to thank each of you for agreeing to come today," he added in a more gracious tone.

"We really didn't have a choice. And we're all here for the same reason," said Beth. "We want information."

"Well, I'm here to provide it, as much as I can."

Beth sighed and sat back, her face showing her displeasure at this disclaimer.

"Under normal circumstances your sister and Mr. Kingman would not even be allowed to know the location of this building, much less be here. Even you, as police chief, would not be allowed in."

"These are not normal circumstances," said Mace.

"Truly not," agreed the DCI while the NSA rep nodded.

"Well then, what can you tell us?" asked Beth. "What happened to Donnelly and Burns?"

"Removed from their posts, of course."

"Removed from their posts?" said Mace, half coming out of her chair. "What, do they get early retirement and a gold watch too?"

"It doesn't quite work that way in the intelligence field, Ms. Perry."

"Will they be prosecuted?" asked Roy.

"That is not possible," said the fellow from the White House.

"The hell it isn't," snapped Beth. "They masterminded the murder of at least five American citizens and did their best to make it seven."

"And in the process let a military veteran take the fall for it," added Roy heatedly.

The DCI put up his hands in mock surrender. "Their acts *were* heinous. I am in total agreement with that."

"But I sense a *but* coming," said Beth.

"But to prosecute them would mean the truth would come out."

"They were rogues, doing their own op. The higher-ups might have to officially take responsibility for that, but the blame still lies with them," argued Beth. "Hell, the FBI prosecuted Hanssen. The CIA did the same with Ames. It's not exactly new territory."

"You are not in possession of all the facts."

"Then enlighten me."

The fellow from the White House interjected. "Their actions were not authorized by anyone higher up on the chain of command; I give you my word on that."

"But other things they did *were* authorized?" said Mace.

"Illegal things?" added Roy.

The CIA director looked at him. "You ventured to the escrow firm, DLT?"

"I did. And I found a pretty slick piggyback scheme using legitimate business transactions to cover other movements of money."

"But no hard proof of same?"

"No."

"What are you getting at?" asked Beth.

"We're at war, Chief. It is not a conventional war. Most Americans realize that by now. We fight fire with fire. And we also fight dirt with dirt."

"Meaning?"

"Meaning that intelligence is king and who gets the most accurate intelligence wins. And the people who possess that intelligence are often folks that, well, that we would not ordinarily choose to associate with."

"Meaning, at least in the eyes of the American public, our enemies."

"Our usual allies are virtually powerless to help us in this fight. We combat the devil by working with the devil. And since they obviously aren't helping us out of the goodness of their hearts . . ."

"The piggyback scheme was a way of paying off people for intelligence?" said Roy.

"Again, I can't answer that."

Beth spoke up. "But if so, and Diane Tolliver found out and then told Meldon, why kill them? Couldn't you have appealed to their patriotism? Jamie certainly wouldn't have done anything to jeopardize this country's interests."

The DCI said, "The real truth is that Donnelly and Burns went way past all orthodoxy in getting the monies needed to pay off these folks. And while these sums started off relatively small, they have, over the years, become enormous."

"And Congress wouldn't appropriate the needed funds?" said Beth.

"You know the deficits we have now."

"So how did they manage the money part?"

"They have not been particularly cooperative. But we have been able, with a little digging, to gain a fairly clear picture of what happened."

"And so what does that picture tell us?" asked Beth."

Something, unfortunately, that none of you are cleared for."

"That is bullshit," barked the chief. "After all this, you're telling me that you won't read us into what happened?"

"Suffice it to say that a lot of the money coming through those piggyback pipelines Mr. Kingman mentioned was very, very dirty. And in order to launder it, Donnelly and Burns were charging a substantial fee. Those monies were used to purchase support."

"Drug dealers, weapon runners, slavery rings?" said Beth.

"Neither confirm nor deny."

"Now that you've basically told us nothing, why did you really ask us here?"

"If any of this comes out it will do this country great harm. I daresay it would destroy any hopes we have of winning the war on terror."

The White House representative added, "It would embolden our enemies. It would weaken our position around the globe. Nothing good will come out of this."

"You mean other than two bastards being punished for their *heinous* crimes?" shot back Mace.

"It's not that simple," murmured the DCI.

"Yeah, it's never that simple for people in high places. But the little guy does something like this he gets squashed like a bug."

Beth shook her head in frustration. "And what exactly do I tell Jamie Meldon's family? And Diane Tolliver's friends?"

"I don't have a good answer for you. In Meldon's case I can tell you that his family will never want for money. Uncle Sam is picking up the tab there."

"Gee, all it cost them was their husband and father," said Mace bitterly.

"If you think I like this any better than you do, you're mistaken. But that's just the way it has to be."

"And Mary Bard?" asked Beth. "Funny name for a Russian, by the way."

"Her father was an American, a defector unfortunately. She's been returned to her country. She really was only following orders. And she's an excellent field agent. We may very well use her again."

Mace looked ready to burst. "I don't believe this crap. That lady was going to kill me and Roy. She *did* kill two American agents. And I thought the Russians weren't exactly our best friends."

The DCI looked at her curiously. "Frankly, Ms. Perry, you obviously don't understand the intelligence business. Enemies and allies are often interchangeable."

"*Frankly* I consider the term 'intelligence business' not only a misnomer but a freaking oxymoron."

Beth spoke up. "Mace cracked this case. She should be reinstated to the police force."

The DCI shook his head. "I'm sorry. That won't be happening. That would entail the truth coming out."

"So she gets zip," said Beth.

The uniform from DIA cleared his throat. "Sacrifice for the greater good."

Mace glared at him. "I'll be sure to tell that to my probation officer, thanks."

The White House rep stood, signaling that the meeting was over. "We very much appreciate all your help in this matter. As does the president himself, which he wishes he could make public but of course cannot for national security reasons."

"Big shit," said Mace as she turned and walked out of the office, Beth and Roy trailing her.

CHAPTER

114

BETH DROVE THEM back to Altman's house. Before she left to return to work she told Mace, "I know you've got the job with Altman, and it doesn't take a rocket scientist to see that Roy will be taking up some of your time too. But don't forget your big sister."

"How could I? Every time I need her, she's right there."

"I can say the same about you."

"No, you really can't, Beth. I wish you could, but I've fallen down on the job."

"It's just a firstborn's fate in life," she said, attempting a smile.

"Was it my imagination or did the DCI seem really pleased about the turn of events?"

"Oh, no, he was. Now that Donnelly went down, guess who's back in charge of the intelligence world and doing the presidential daily briefing?"

"Right."

They shared a brief hug before Beth Perry turned back into Chief Perry, climbed into Cruiser One, and headed back to town to fight crime.

Roy said, "I don't have any plans today. How about going out to lunch with a former college basketball player turned one-armed paper hanger? I'm buying."

"Sounds great. I can help you cut up your food and wipe your mouth for you."

"Yeah, that'll be great practice for down the road."

"Down *what* road?" Mace said sharply as she gave him a piercing stare.

He took a step back, his face turning red. "Uh, the road where I left my mouth with my size thirteen feet in it."

"Oh, Roy, you're so cute."

"Seriously, do you want to go?"

"I'd love to."

Late that night Mace climbed on her Ducati and fired it up. Two minutes later she was ripping down the highway into D.C. She hit the Sixth District and wound her way to the spot where her life had changed forever. Now the sight made her gut clench and her cheeks flame. But there would come a day she told herself when this spot would fill her with supreme satisfaction instead of heartbreak. And when that day came—and it would—Mace Perry would really be back.

The wink of a car's lights made her turn around. She started when she saw the person climb out of the police cruiser.

Beth was still in uniform as she walked over to her and stood beside her sister.

"I thought you might come down here tonight."

"It's scary sometimes how well you know me."

"We are sisters. And . . ." Beth fell silent.

"You were going to say *and cops,* right?"

"We're not giving up on it, Mace."

"I know." After a few moments of silence, Mace said, "Why do I think Donnelly and Burns are sitting in an office somewhere doing business as usual?"

"Because they probably are."

"Some justice."

Beth stared up at the old apartment building. "It doesn't look so bad anymore."

"What are you talking about? It's a dump."

"A little elbow grease, some paint."

"What?"

"It's being turned into a rec center for the community."

"Since when?"

"Since I got the mayor to approve it yesterday."

"Why?" Mace asked.

"Why not? It's an old building that serves no useful purpose. We could leave it here until it falls down. Or we can change it into something that's useful. A way of moving forward. Applies to buildings. And people."

Mace gazed at the place for a long moment. "You and Dad were always much better with symbolism than me."

"I always thought you and Dad were a lot more alike."

"Really?" said a surprised Mace. Beth nodded.

Mace glanced over at Cruiser One where the driver sat patiently. "You done for the night, sis?"

Beth stretched out her back. "Yeah, I was thinking of actually heading home and reading a book in the bathtub."

"You want a ride?" Mace eyed her Ducati.

"What? On the bike?"

"Problem with that?"

"No, it's just that, well, the liability factor if the chief of police—"

"Oh shut up and get on. You can use Roy's helmet."

On the way home, with Beth holding on to her tightly, Mace popped a wheelie and held it as she streaked down the GW Parkway, freaking out motorists as she flew past.

Beth started to scream something in her ear but then stopped. And then the by-the-book chief of police did the unthinkable. She held out her arms straight from her sides, leaned into her sister, and started making whooping sounds.

The sisters were headed back to the safe area of D.C., where people didn't shoot each other over five-dollar crack scratches or to gain elusive respect. But they knew their hearts and their professional lives would always be on that unpredictable side of the line where you ran toward the fight and not away from it. That was where they really belonged.

The front wheel hit asphalt. Mace gunned the throttle and the Perry sisters disappeared down the road.

ACKNOWLEDGMENTS

To MICHELLE, the primary reason I write about strong, independent women.

To Mitch Hoffman, for good counsel, excellent critiques, and well-placed cheers.

To David Young, Jamie Raab, Emi Battaglia, Jennifer Romanello, Tom Maciag, Martha Otis, Anthony Goff, Kim Hoffman, and all at Grand Central Publishing, for helping me every step of the way.

To Aaron and Arlene Priest, Lucy Childs, Lisa Erbach Vance, Nicole Kenealy, Frances Jalet-Miller, and John Richmond, for being so supportive.

To Maria Rejt and Katie James at Pan Macmillan, for all your great work.

To Grace McQuade and Lynn Goldberg, for keeping my name out there.

To D.C. Police Chief Cathy Lanier, for allowing me to see a terrific slice of the job.

To Lt. Morgan Kane, for coordinating everything and being patient and professional.

To Officer Rob Calligaro, thanks for the education and the boat ride.

To Officer Raymond Hawkins, thanks for the ride and the great insight.

To United States Attorneys Jeffrey Taylor and Glenn Kirschner, for your courtroom knowledge and expertise of how the D.C. criminal system works.

To Tom and Bob, for financial brainstorming.

To Dr. Monica Smiddy, who makes my forensics look so good.

To Dr. Alli Guleria, as always, for your help.

To Bob Schule, for your advice and political expertise.

To Tanmoy Mukherjee, M.D., for your medical expertise.

To the charity auction "name" winners. Don, I "hope" I did the name justice. To Julie, Mandy, and Kelly of Hamilton, Petrocelli & Sprissler, I hope you liked your page time.

To Lynette and Deborah, for doing what you do so damn well.